www.wadsworth.com

wadsworth.com is the World Wide Web site for Wadsworth Publishing Company and is your direct source to dozens of online resources.

At *wadsworth.com* you can find out about supplements, demonstration software, and student resources. You can also send e-mail to many of our authors and preview new publications and exciting new technologies.

wadsworth.com
Changing the way the world learns®

SOURCES OF WORLD HISTORY
Readings for World Civilization
Volume I

Second Edition

Mark A. Kishlansky, Editor
Harvard University

with the assistance of
Susan Lindsey Lively
Harvard University

West / Wadsworth

 An International Thomson Publishing Company

Belmont, CA • Albany, NY • Boston • Cincinnati • Johannesburg • London • Madrid • Melbourne
Mexico City • New York • Pacific Grove, CA • Scottsdale, AZ • Singapore • Tokyo • Toronto

History Editor: Clark Baxter
Senior Developmental Editor: Sharon Adams Poore
Print Buyer: Barbara Britton
Production: Aksen Associates
Composition: Aksen Associates
Marketing Manager: Jay Hu
Cover Design: Diane Beasley
Cover: Illustration from the epic poem *The Book of Kings* by Ferdowzi (Persia, 940–1020).
      © Giraudon/Art Resource, NY. National Library, Cairo, Egypt.
Printer: Malloy Lithographing, Inc.

Printed in the United States of America
1 2 3 4 5 6 7 8 9 10

For more information, contact Wadsworth Publishing Company, 10 Davis Drive, Belmont, CA 94002,
or electronically at http://www.wadsworth.com

International Thomson Publishing Europe
Berkshire House
168-173 High Holborn
London, WC1V 7AA, United Kingdom

Nelson ITP, Australia
102 Dodds Street
South Melbourne
Victoria 3205 Australia

Nelson Canada
1120 Birchmount Road
Scarborough, Ontario
Canada M1K 5G4

International Thomson Publishing Southern Africa
Building 18, Constantia Park
138 Sixteenth Road, P.O. Box 2459
Halfway House, 1685 South Africa

International Thomson Editores
Seneca, 53
Colonia Polanco
11560 México D.F. México

International Thomson Publishing
Asia
60 Albert Street
#15-01 Albert Complex
Singapore 189969

International Thomson Publishing
Japan
Hirakawa-cho Kyowa Building, 3F
2-2-1 Hirakawa-cho, Chiyoda-ku
Tokyo 102, Japan

Library of Congress Cataloging-in-Publication Data
Sources of World History : readings for world civilization / Mark A. Kishlansky, editor.
        p.   cm.
    ISBN 0–534–56034–2(vol. 1 : pbk.) —ISBN 0–534–56034–0 (vol. 2 : pbk.)
    1. Civilization—History—Sources.   I. Kishlansky, Mark A.
CB69.S69 1998
909—dc21   98–28253
                                                        CIP

 This book is printed on acid-free recycled paper.

Contents

Part II *Traditional Societies* 119

Preface

Sources of World History is a collection of documents designed to supplement text-book and lectures in the teaching of world civilization. The use of primary materials is an essential component of the study of history. By hearing the voices of the past, students come to realize both the similarities and differences between their society and previous ones. In witnessing others ponder the same questions that rouse their own curiosity, students feel a connection between the past and the present. Moreover, by observing the ways in which such questions and experiences are worked out and described, they come to an understanding and respect for the integrity of other cultures. In confronting the materials of the past, students exercise an historical imagination that is at the heart of the teaching and learning of history.

Historical sources are the building blocks from which instructor and textbook writer have ultimately constructed their accounts and their explanations of world historical development. It is essential that even beginning students learn that the past does not come to us prepackaged, but is formed by historians who exercise their own imaginations on primary materials. Historical thinking involves examining the ideas of others, understanding past experiences on others' terms, and recognizing other points of view. This is a process that makes everyone, student and instructor alike, an historian.

I have observed a number of principles in selecting the materials for this collection, which is designed for beginning-level college students. I believe strongly in the value of primary materials and feel that they should be made as accessible to contemporary students as possible. Thus, I have preferred to use up-to-date translations of many texts despite the costliness of acquiring their rights. Many of the late nineteenth-century translations that are commonly used in source books present texts that are syntactically too complex for modern students to comprehend easily. I have also chosen to present longer selections than is usual in books of this type. Unlike works that contain snippets of hundreds of documents, *Sources of the World History* presents a sizable amount of a small number of sources. It therefore allows students to gain a deeper feeling for authors and texts and to concentrate their energies and resources. No selection is so long that it cannot be easily read at a sitting and none so short as to defy recall. Each selection raises a significant issue around which classroom discussion can take place or to which lectures can refer. Some may even stimulate students to seek out the complete original works.

Two other principles lie behind the selections I have made. The first is that a steady diet of even the world's greatest thinkers is unpalatable without other varieties of social and cultural materials. For this reason, I have tried to leaven the mass of intellectual history with materials that draw on social conditions or common experiences in past eras. These should not only aid students in making connections between past and present, but should also introduce them to the varieties of materials from which history is recreated. Secondly, I have been especially concerned to recover the voices or highlight the experiences of those who are not always adequately represented in surveys of world civilization. The explosion of work in social history, in the history of the family, and in the history of women have made possible the inclusion of materials here that were barely discovered a decade ago. Although this effort can be clearly seen in the materials chosen for the modern sections, it is also apparent in the selections made from more traditional older documents.

By providing longer selections and by expanding the scope of the materials to be incorporated, I have necessarily been compelled to make some hard choices. There exists a superabundance of materials that demand inclusion in a collection such as this. I have tried to find representative examples of the works of each of the major civilization complexes, Asia, Africa, Latin America, and the Islamic world as well as the central works of Western Civilization. This poses very difficult problems of balance, equity, and accessibility. Since early African and Latin American civilizations were oral cultures, they have necessarily left fewer documentary artifacts, despite the richness of their cultures. Much of what is known comes to us through the eyes of travelers or through the memory of later representatives of these cultures. I have included many such documents along with cautions about how to use them. I have also included Western views of Asia in an effort to raise questions of a comparative and cross-cultural nature. Having so few documents for so many civilizations necessarily raises questions of selection. It is my conviction that it is the experience of using primary materials—rather than the primary materials that are used—that is vital. Thus, I have tried to provide a balance among constitutional documents, political theory, philosophy, imaginative literature, and social description. In all cases,L I have made the pedagogical value of the specific texts the prime consideration, selecting for significance, readability, and variety.

The feature, How to Read a Document, is designed to introduce students to a disciplined approach of working with primary sources and to encourage them to use their imaginations in their historical studies. No brief introduction pretends to be authoritative, and there are many other strategies and questions that can be adopted in training students to become critical readers. It is hoped that this introduction will remove some of the barriers that usually exist between student and source by walking them through a single exercise with a document in front of them. Any disciplined approach to source materials will sensitize students to the construction of historical documents, their content and meaning, and the ways in which they relate to modern experience. Individual instructors will easily be able to improve upon the example offered here.

A number of individuals helped to stimulate my thinking about the selection of sources. I would especially like to thank Eric McGeer, R. Bin Wong, Ann Waltner, Leroy Vail, and Mark Wasserman. My greatest debt is to Susan Lindsey Lively for her assistance in compiling these texts. Her discipline helped keep me going as we sifted through hundreds of possible selections and her common sense tempered our final choices.

In this second edition to *Sources of World History,* I have attempted to expand the coverage of non-Western societies as well as to offer more in the way of comparative perspectives by including sections of cultural encounters, particularly in the earlier periods. Two new sections on South Asia attempt to make up for a shortage of materials in the first edition, and I have added an additional set of documents on Japan and the coming of Westernization. In this edition, my thanks are due to the many users of *Sources of World History* who have taken the time to send me suggestions, corrections, and encouragement. At Wadsworth, my thanks go to Clark Baxter, Sharon Adams Poore, and Kathleen Broderick, as well as Howard and Jo Aksen of Aksen Associates, for their editorial and production expertise. My greatest debt is to Tom Cogswell of the University of Kentucky for his guidance and assistance without which this new edition would not have been possible.

Mark A. Kishlansky
Cambridge, MA, 1998

How to Read a Document

Do you remember the first time you ever used a road map? After struggling to unfold it and get the right side up and the right way around you were then confronted by an astonishing amount of information. You could calculate the distance between places, from towns to cities, or cities to cities, even the distance between exits on the toll roads. You could observe relative population density and categorize large and small places. You could even judge the quality of roads. But most likely, you used that map to help you figure out how to get from one place to another, how to find the best route for the trip you were taking.

To make the map tell you that, you had to know how to ask the right questions. It all seems so obvious now—you put one finger on the place where you were and another on the place to which you wanted to go and then you found the best and most direct route between them. In order to do something as simple as this, there are a lot of assumptions that you made about the map. First, you assumed that the map is directionally oriented, north at the top, east to the right, south and west opposite. Second, you assumed that the map is to scale, that the distances between places on the map are proportional to their distances in reality. Third, you assumed that intersections on the map were intersections on the ground, that the two roads that appear to cross on paper actually do cross in reality. These assumptions make possible the answer to your initial question. Of course, if any of them were not true you would have found out soon enough.

Learning to read an historical document is much like learning to read a map. It is important to ask the right questions and to make the right assumptions. But unlike the real voyage that the map makes possible, the voyage made with an historical document is one of the imagination. You will have to learn to test your assumptions and to sharpen your ability to ask questions before you can have any confidence that you are on the right road. Like anything else, this is a matter of concentration and practice. You will have to discipline yourself to ask and answer questions about the document on the first level before you pose questions on higher levels. At the beginning you will be asking questions that you can answer directly; by the end you will be asking questions that will give full play to your imagination and your skills as an historian. Let us consider an example.

Read the following selection slowly and carefully.

1   Ye emperors, kings, dukes, marquises, earls, and knights, and all other people
2   desirous of knowing the diversities of the races of mankind, as well as the
3   diversities of kingdoms, provinces, and regions of all parts of the East, read
4   through this book, and ye will find in it the greatest and most marvellous char-
5   acteristics of the peoples especially of Armenia, Persia, India, and Tartary, as
6   they are severally related in the present work by Marco Polo, a wise and
7   learned citizen of Venice, who states distinctly what things he saw and what
8   things he heard from others. For this book will be a truthful one.

9   Kublai, who is styled grand khan, or lord of lords, is of the middle stature, that
10 is, neither tall nor short; his limbs are well formed, and in his whole figure
11 there is a just proportion. His complexion is fair, and occasionally suffused
12 with red, like the bright tint of the rose, which adds much grace to his coun-
13 tenance. His eyes are black and handsome, his nose is well shaped and promi-
14 nent. He has four wives of the first rank, who are esteemed legitimate, and the
15 eldest born son of any one of these succeeds to the empire, upon the decease
16 of the grand khan. They bear equally the title of empress, and have their sep-
17 arate courts. None of them have fewer than three hundred young female
18 attendants of great beauty, together with a multitude of youths as pages, and
19 other eunuchs, as well as ladies of the bedchamber; so that the number of per-
20 sons belonging to each of their respective courts amounts to ten thousand.
21 Besides these, he has many concubines provided for his use, from a province
22 of Tartary named Ungut, having a city of the same name, the inhabitants of
23 which are distinguished for beauty of features and fairness of complexion.
24 Thither the grand khan sends his officers every second year, or oftener, as it
25 may happen to be his pleasure, who collect for him, to the number of four or
26 five hundred, or more, of the handsomest of the young women, according to
27 the estimation of beauty communicated to them in their instructions....
28 Upon their arrival in his presence, he causes a new examination to be made by
29 a different set of inspectors, and from amongst them a further selection takes
30 place, when thirty or forty are retained for his own chamber.... These, in the
31 first instance, are committed separately to the care of the wives of certain of
32 the nobles, whose duty it is to observe them attentively during the course of
33 the night, in order to ascertain that they have not any concealed imperfec-
34 tions, that they sleep tranquilly, do not snore, have sweet breath, and are free
35 from unpleasant scent in any part of the body. Having undergone this rigor-
36 ous scrutiny, they are divided into parties of five, one of which parties attends
37 during three days and three nights, in his majesty's interior apartment, where
38 they are to perform every service that is required of them, and he does with
39 them as he likes. The remainder of them, whose value had been estimated at
40 an inferior rate, are assigned to the different lords of the household.... in this
41 manner he provides for them all amongst his nobility. It may be asked whether

42   the people of the province do not feel themselves aggrieved in having their
43   daughters thus forcibly taken from them by the sovereign? Certainly not; but,
44   on the contrary, they regard it as a favour and an honour done to them; and
45   those who are the fathers of handsome children feel highly gratified by his
46   condescending to make choice of their daughters.
47   The grand khan usually resides during three months of the year, namely,
48   December, January, and February, in the great city of Kanbalu, situated towards
49   the north-eastern extremity of the province of Cathay; and here, on the south-
50   ern side of the new city, is the site of his vast palace, the form and dimensions
51   of which are as follows. In the first place is a square enclosed with a wall and
52   deep ditch; each side of the square being eight miles in length, and having at
53   an equal distance from each extremity an entrance-gate, for the concourse of
54   people resorting thither from all quarters. Within this enclosure there is, on
55   the four sides, an open space one mile in breadth, where the troops are sta-
56   tioned; and this is bounded by a second wall, enclosing a square of six miles,
57   having three gates on the south side, and three on the north, the middle por-
58   tal of each being larger than the other two, and always kept shut, excepting on
59   the occasions of the emperor's entrance or departure.... Within these walls,
60   which constitute the boundary of four miles, stands the palace of the grand
61   khan, the most extensive that has ever yet been known. It reaches from the
62   northern to the southern wall, leaving only a vacant space (or court), where
63   persons of rank and the military guards pass and repass. It has no upper floor,
64   but the roof is very lofty. The paved foundation or platform on which it stands
65   is raised ten spans above the level of the ground, and a wall of marble, two paces
66   wide, is built on all sides, to the level of this pavement, within the line of which
67   the palace is erected; so that the wall, extending beyond the ground plan of the
68   building, and encompassing the whole, serves as a terrace, where those who
69   walk on it are visible from without. Along the exterior edge of the wall is a hand-
70   some balustrade, with pillars, which the people are allowed to approach. The
71   sides of the great halls and the apartments are ornamented with dragons in
72   carved work and gilt, figures of warriors, of birds, and of beasts, with represen-
73   tations of battles. The inside of the roof is contrived in such a manner that
74   nothing besides gilding and painting presents itself to the eye. On each of the
75   four sides of the palace there is a grand flight of marble steps, by which you
76   ascend from the level of the ground to the wall of marble which surrounds the
77   building, and which constitute the approach to the palace itself. The grand hall
78   is extremely long and wide, and admits of dinners being there served to great
79   multitudes of people. The palace contains a number of separate chambers, all
80   highly beautiful, and so admirably disposed that it seems impossible to suggest
81   any improvement to the system of their arrangement. The exterior of the roof
82   is adorned with a variety of colours, red, green, azure, and violet, and the sort
83   of covering is so strong as to last for many years. The glazing of the windows is
84   so well wrought and so delicate as to have the transparency of crystal. In the
85   rear of the body of the palace there are large buildings containing several

86   apartments, where is deposited the private property of the monarch, or his trea-
87   sure in gold and silver bullion, precious stones, and pearls, and also his vessels
88   of gold and silver plate. Here are likewise the apartments of his wives and con-
89   cubines; and in this retired situation he despatches business with convenience,
90   being free from every kind of interruption.

Now what sense can we make out of all of that? You have just read a historical document, a selection from *The Travels of Marco Polo, The Venetian*. It was written in 1298, while Marco Polo was in prison, and was based on his own observations during 17 years of travel in Asia. Marco Polo was born into a Venetian merchant family. His father and elder brothers had made an earlier trip into Asia where they had met the Grand Khan. Marco accompanied his brothers on their return trip. During his stay he was favored with free passage throughout the khan's dominions and on his return to Venice he was required to tell and retell the stories of his journey. After commanding a ship in an unsuccessful war against Genoa, Marco Polo was captured and imprisoned. It was during this time that he sorted through the many notations that he had made in Asia and composed the tale of his travels.

In order to understand this document we are going to need to ask and answer a series of questions about it. Let us start at the beginning with a number of questions that we might designate Level One questions.

Level One

The first set of questions that need to be addressed are those for which you should be able to find concrete answers. The answers to these questions will give you the basic information you need to begin the process of interpretation. Although Level One questions are seemingly straightforward, they contain important implications for deeper interpretation. If you do not consciously ask these questions, you will deprive yourself of some of the most important evidence there is for understanding documents. Train yourself to underline or highlight the information that will allow you to answer the following questions.

1. Who wrote this document?

In the first place, we need to know how this document came to be created. In the case of *The Travels of Marco Polo, The Venetian* we know that the document was written by Marco Polo (**line 6**), who was an Italian merchant. This document is thus the work of a single author written from his own point of view. What is especially important to remember is that Marco Polo was an outsider, describing a society that was not his own. His account of China in the thirteenth century was an account of a European's impressions of China. We will need to learn as much as we can about the "author" of a document to help us answer more complicated questions.

2. Who is the intended audience?

The audience of a document will tell us much about the document's language, about the amount of knowledge that the writer is assuming, even sometimes about the best form for the document to take. There can be more than one audience in-tended by the writer. *The Travels of Marco Polo, The Venetian* was written in the thirteenth century, and therefore was not written for "publication" in the conventional sense of the word. In fact, *The Travels* was not published for centuries after composition. But Marco Polo obviously intended his work to be read by others, and it was circulated in manuscript and repeated orally. His preface was addressed to "emperors, kings, dukes, marquises, earls, and knights" (**line 1**), a rather distinguished audience. But his real audience was his own countrymen to whom he was describing a foreign place in terms they would understand. Notice, for example, how he describes the khan's complexion, "like the bright tint of the rose" (**line 12**).

3. What is the story line?

The final Level One question has to do with the content of the document. We now know enough about it in a general way to pay attention to what it actually says. To answer this question you might want to take some notes while you are reading or underline the important parts in your text. The story here seems to be simple. Marco Polo is impressed with the splendor of the court of the grand khan and especially with the way in which he finds his wives and concubines. Polygamy is interesting to a European viewing a non-Western society and Marco Polo describes it in a way that will titillate his anticipated audience. He also makes it believable, explaining why parents would volunteer their daughters (**lines 44–45**). He is also impressed with the size of everything that surrounds the Grand Khan. If each of his wives had a retinue of 10,000 (**line 20**) their courts alone would be more populous than the entire city of Venice.

Level Two

If Level One questions allow you to identify the nature of the document and its author, Level Two questions allow you to probe behind the essential facts. Now that you know who wrote the document, to whom it is addressed, and what it is about, you can begin to try to understand it. Since your goal is to learn what this document means, first in its historical context and then in your current context, you now want to study it from a more detached point of view, to be less accepting of "facts" and more critical in the questions you pose. At the first level, the document controlled you; at the second level, you will begin to control the document.

1. Why was this document written?

Understanding the purpose of an historical document is critical to analyzing the strategies that the author employs within it. A document intended to convince will employ logic; a document intended to entertain will employ fancy; a document attempting to motivate will employ emotional appeals. In order to find these strategies we must first know what purpose the document was intended to serve. Travelers' tales generally have two interrelated purposes, first, to impress upon one culture the differences to be found in another, and second to show people their own culture in a new light. Marco Polo is genuinely impressed with the opulence and power of the khan but he is also impressed by the way that the khan provides for his nobles, how he rewards those who have been faithful to him (**lines 40–41**). As the member of an elite merchant family, Marco Polo was concerned that the Venetian doge reward those faithful to him, especially those who might be temporarily imprisoned.

2. What type of document is this?

The form of a document is vital to its purpose. We would expect a telephone book to be alphabetized, a poem to be in meter, and a work of philosophy to be in prose. Here we have a traveler's account and its style and language is employed to create wonder and admiration in its readers. To do this the author needs to provide detailed description that is visually arresting yet sufficiently concrete to be persuasive. This is especially difficult when describing customs as alien to Venetians as those practiced at the court of the grand khan. In order to be believed, the traveler has to overcome the natural skepticism of his audience. During his lifetime, Marco Polo was nicknamed "Marco Millione" (Marco Millions) because people thought he exaggerated the numbers of the Chinese population and the extent of the khan's wealth.

3. What are the basic assumptions made in this document?

All documents make assumptions that are bound up with their intended audience, with the form in which they are written, and with their purpose. Some of the assumptions that are at work in this selection from *The Travels of Marco Polo, The Venetian* relate to the way in which a state is ruled. Marco Polo describes the khan and his court as if government in China were organized in the same way that government in Italy was. Thus the khan can be understood as a sort of pope or doge. Similarly, Marco Polo assumes that his readers will admire great wealth and large quantities of things. He takes pains to describe things as beautiful, great, wide, and large (**lines 52–81**).

Level Three

So far, you have been asking questions of your document that the document itself can answer. Sometimes it is more difficult to know who composed a document or who was the intended audience than it has been with *The Travels of Marco Polo, The Venetian*. Sometimes you have to guess at the purpose of the document, but essentially Level One and Level Two questions have direct answers. Once you have learned to ask them, you will have a great deal of information about the historical document at your disposal. You will then be able to think historically, that is, to pose your own questions about the past and to use the material the document presents you to find answers. In Level Three you will exercise your critical imagination, probing the material and developing your own assessment of its value. Level Three questions will not always have definite answers; in fact, they are the kind of questions that arouse disagreement and debate and that make for lively classroom discussion.

1. Can I believe this document?

If they are successful, documents designed to persuade, to recount events, or to motivate people to act must be believable to their audience. But for the critical historical reader, it is that very believability that must be in question. Every author has a point of view and exposing the assumptions of the document is an essential task for the reader. We must treat all claims skeptically (even while admiring audacity, rhetorical tricks, and clever comparisons). One question we certainly want to ask is, "Is this a likely story?" Do the parents of daughters destined for concubinage at court really believe that it is a sign of good fortune? Do all officers sent by the khan really perform their duties speedily and efficiently? Is there really a wall 8 miles square around the city that contains the khan's palace (**line 52**)? Testing the credibility of a document means looking at it from the other side. What would most impress a subject of the khan about his own society? What would most impress him about Venice?

2. What can I learn about the society that produced this document?

All documents unintentionally reveal things about their authors and about their age. It is the things that are embedded in the very language, structure, and assumptions of the document that can tell us the most about the historical period or event that we are studying. This is centrally important in studying a travel account. We must ask ourselves both what we can learn about China in the late thirteenth century and what we can learn about Venice. Marco Polo is acting as a double filter, running Chinese customs through his own European expectations and then explaining them to Europeans through his expectation of what they will believe and what they will reject. He is also telling us, indirectly, about the things that Venetians would find unusual and wonderful and therefore by contrast what they would find commonplace. We can learn many things about both Chinese and Venetian society by reading into this document rather than by simply reading it.

3. What does this document mean to me?

So what? What does *The Travels of Marco Polo, The Venetian,* written almost 700 years ago, have to do with you? Other than the practical problem of passing your exams and getting your degree, why should you be concerned with historical documents and what can you learn from them? Only you can answer that question. But you will not be able to answer it until you have asked it. You should demand the meaning of each document you read. What it meant to the historical actors—authors, audience, and society—and what it means to our own society. In light of *The Travels of Marco Polo,* how would you go about describing an alien society to your generation? How would you go about appreciating an alien culture? Look around your classroom and ask yourself how often you represent yourself to members of other cultures and how often you have to understand the assumptions of other cultures to understand your classmates.

Now that you have seen how to unfold the map of a historical document, you must get used to asking these questions by yourself. The temptation will be great to jump from Level One to Level Three, to start in the middle, or to pose the questions in no sequence at all. After all, you probably have a ready-made answer to the question, "What does this document mean to me?" If you develop the discipline of asking all your questions in the proper order, however, you will soon find that you are able to gain command of a document on a single reading and that the complicated names and facts that ordinarily would confuse you will easily settle into a pattern around one or another of your questions. After a few weeks, reread these pages and ask yourself how careful you have been to maintain the discipline of posing historical questions. Think also about how much more comfortable you now feel about reading and discussing historical documents.

PART I

The Origins of Civilization

Stories of Creation

Mesopotamian cylinder of the Shar-Kali Sham.

Popol Vuh (n.d.)   **1**

The Popol Vuh, or Sacred Book, of the Quiché Indians is a creation myth that has been handed down for millennia in an unbroken oral tradition. The Quiché Indians were one of the most powerful tribes in the area that came to be known as Guatemala in Central America. They were descended from the Mayans, founders of an advanced civilization, and there is reason to believe that Quiché and Mayan cultures held to the same beliefs about the nature of creation. The Quiché were one of the tribes encountered by Cortés during his conquest of New Spain. Utatlan, the Quiché capital, was razed, and a new Spanish community, Santo Thomas, was built in its place. It remains the cultural center of the present-day Quiché community.

Popol Vuh is an account of the mythology, history, and traditions of the Quiché and Mayan peoples. Since it existed as part of oral tradition, it was not until the arrival of the Spaniards in the sixteenth century that a Quiché Indian first recorded Popol Vuh in the Quiché language but in Latin script. It was not until the nineteenth century that it was translated into French and Spanish and became known

Chapter 1

This is the account of how all was in suspense, all calm, in silence; all motionless, still, and the expanse of the sky was empty.

This is the first account, the first narrative. There was neither man, nor animal, birds, fishes, crabs, trees, stones, caves, ravines, grasses, nor forests; there was only the sky.

The surface of the earth had not appeared. There was only the calm sea and the great expanse of the sky.

There was nothing brought together, nothing which could make a noise, nor anything which might move, or tremble, or could make noise in the sky.

There was nothing standing; only the calm water, the placid sea, alone and tranquil. Nothing existed.

There was only immobility and silence in the darkness, in the night. Only the Creator, the Maker, Tepeu, Gucumatz, the Forefathers, were in the water surrounded with light. They were hidden under green and blue feathers, and were therefore called Gucumatz. By nature they were great sages and great thinkers. In this manner the sky existed and also the Heart of Heaven, which is the name of God and thus He is called.

Then came the word. Tepeu and Gucumatz came together in the darkness, in the night, and Tepeu and Gucumatz talked together. They talked then, discussing and deliberating; they agreed, they united their words and their thoughts.

Then while they mediated, it became clear to them that when dawn would break, man must appear. Then they planned the creation, and the growth of the trees and the thickets and the birth of life and the creation of man. Thus it was arranged in the darkness and in the night by the Heart of Heaven who is called Huracain.

Then Tepeu and Gucumatz came together; then they conferred about life and light, what they would do so that there would be light and dawn, who it would be who would provide food and sustenance.

Thus let it be done! Let the emptiness be filled! Let the water recede and make a void, let the earth appear and become solid; let it be done. Thus they spoke. Let there be light, let there be dawn in the sky and on the earth! There shall be neither glory nor grandeur in our creation and formation until the human being is made, man is formed. So they spoke.

Then the earth was created by them. So it was, in truth, that they created the earth. Earth! they said, and instantly it was made.

Like the mist, like a cloud, and like a cloud of dust was the creation, when the mountains appeared from the water; and instantly the mountains grew.

Only by a miracle, only by magic art were the mountains and valleys formed; and instantly the groves of cypresses and pines put forth shoots together on the surface of the earth.

And thus Gucumatz was filled with joy, and exclaimed: "Your coming has been fruitful, Heart of Heaven; and you, Huracán, and you, Chipi-Caculhá, Raxa-Caculhá!"

"Our work, our creation shall be finished," they answered.

First the earth was formed, the mountains and the valleys; the currents of water were divided, the rivulets were running freely between the hills, and the water was separated when the high mountains appeared.

Thus was the earth created, when it was formed by the Heart of Heaven, the Heart of Earth, as they are called who first made it fruitful, when the sky was in suspense, and the earth was submerged in the water.

So it was that they made perfect the work, when they did it after thinking and meditating upon it.

Chapter 2

Then they made the small wild animals, the guardians of the woods, the spirits of the mountains, the deer, the birds, pumas, jaguars, serpents, snakes, vipers, guardians of the thickets.

And the Forefathers asked: "Shall there be only silence and calm under the trees, under the vines? It is well that hereafter there be someone to guard them."

So they said when they meditated and talked. Promptly the deer and the birds were created. Immediately they gave homes to the deer and the birds. "You, deer, shall sleep in the fields by the river bank and in the ravines. Here you shall be amongst the thicket, amongst the pasture; in the woods you shall multiply, you shall walk on four feet and they will support you. Thus be it done!" So it was they spoke.

Then they also assigned homes to the birds big and small. "You shall live in the trees and in the vines. There you shall make your nests; there you shall multiply; there you shall increase in the branches of the trees and in the vines." Thus the deer and the birds were told; they did their duty at once, and all sought their homes and their nests.

And the creation of all the four-footed animals and the birds being finished, they were told by the Creator and the Maker and the Forefathers: "Speak, cry, warble, call, speak each one according to your variety, each, according to your kind." So was it said to the deer, the birds, pumas, jaguars, and serpents.

"Speak, then, our names, praise us, your mother, your father. Invoke then, Huracán, Chipi-Caculhá, Raxa-Caculhá, the Heart of Heaven, the Heart of Earth, the Creator, the Maker, the Forefathers; speak, invoke us, adore us," they were told.

But they could not make them speak like men; they only hissed and screamed and cackled; they were unable to make words, and each screamed in a different way.

When the Creator and the Maker saw that it was impossible for them to talk to each other, they said: "It is impossible for them to say our names, the names of us, their Creators and Makers. This is not well," said the Forefathers to each other.

Then they said to them: "Because it has not been possible for you to talk, you shall be changed. We have changed our minds: Your food, your pasture, your homes, and your nests you shall have; they shall be the ravines and the woods, because it has not been possible for you to adore us or invoke us. There shall be those who adore us, we shall make other [beings] who shall be obedient. Accept your destiny: your flesh shall be torn to pieces. So shall it be. This shall be your lot." So they said, when they made known their will to the large and small animals which are on the face of the earth.

They wished to give them another trial; they wished to make another attempt; they wished to make [all living things] adore them.

But they could not understand each other's speech; they could succeed in nothing, and could do nothing. For this reason they were sacrificed, and the animals which were on earth were condemned to be killed and eaten.

For thin. reason another attempt had to be made to create and make men by the Creator, the Maker, and the Forefathers.

"Let us try again! Already dawn draws near: Let us make him who shall nourish and sustain us! What shall we do to be invoked, in order to be remembered on earth? We have already tried with our first creations, our first creatures; but we could not make them praise and venerate us. So, then, let us try to make obedient, respectful beings who will nourish and sustain us." Thus they spoke.

Then was the creation and the formation. Of earth, of mud, they made [man's] flesh. But they saw that it was not good. It melted away, it was soft, did not move, had no strength, it fell down, it was limp, it could not move its head, its face fell to one side, its sight was blurred, it could not look behind. At first it spoke, but had no mind. Quickly it soaked in the water and could not stand.

And the Creator and the Maker said: "Let us try again because our creatures will not be able to walk nor multiply. Let us consider this," they said.

Then they broke up and destroyed their work and their creation. And they said: "What shall we do to perfect it, in order that our worshipers, our invokers, will be successful?'

Thus they spoke when they conferred again: "Let us say again to Xpiyacoc, Xmucané, Hunahpú-Vuch, Hunahpú-Utiú: 'Cast your lot again. Try to create again." ' In this manner the Creator and the Maker spoke to Xpiyacoc and Xmucané.

Then they spoke to those soothsayers, the Grandmother of the day, the Grandmother of the Dawn, as they were called by the Creator and the Maker, and whose names were Xpiyacoc and Xmucané.

And said Huracán, Tepeu, and Gucumatz when they spoke to the soothsayer, to the Maker, who are the diviners: "You must work together and find the means so that man, whom we shall make, man, whom we are going to make, will nourish and sustain us, invoke and remember us."

"Enter, then, into council, grandmother, grandfather, our grandmother, our grandfather, Xpiyacoc, Xmucané, make light, make dawn, have us invoked, have us adored, have us remembered by created man, by made man, by mortal man. Thus be it done.

"Let your nature be known, Hunahpú-Vuch, Hunahpú-Utiú, twice mother, twice father, NimAc, Nima-Tziís, the master of emeralds, the worker in jewels, the sculptor, the carver, the maker of beautiful plates, the maker of green gourds, the master of resin, the master Toltecat, grandmother of the sun, grandmother of dawn, as you will be called by our works and our creatures.

"Cast the lot with your grains of corn and the *tzité*. Do it thus, and we shall know if we are to make, or carve his mouth and eyes out of wood." Thus the diviners were told.

They went down at once to make their divination, and cast their lots with the corn and the *tzité*. "Fate! Creature!" said an old woman and an old man. And this old man was the one who cast the lots with *Tzité*, the one called Xpiyacoc. And the old woman was the diviner, the maker, called Chiracán Xmucané.

Beginning the divination, they said: "Get together, grasp each other! Speak, that we may hear." They said, "Say if it is well that the wood be got together and that it be carved by the Creator and the Maker, and if this [man of wood] is he who must nourish and sustain us when there is light when it is day!

"Thou, corn; thou, *tzité*; thou, fate; thou, creature; get together, take each other," they said to the corn, to the *tzité*, to fate, to the creature. "Come to sacrifice here, Heart of Heaven; do not punish Tepeu and Gucumatz!"

Then they talked and spoke the truth: "Your figures of wood shall come out well; they shall speak and talk on earth."

"So may it be," they answered when they spoke.

And instantly the figures were made of wood. They looked like men, talked like men, and populated the surface of the earth.

They existed and multiplied; they had daughters, they had sons, these wooden figures; but they did not have souls, nor minds, they did not remember their Creator, their Maker; they walked on all fours, aimlessly.

They no longer remembered the Heart of Heaven and therefore they fell out of favor. It was merely a trial, an attempt at man. At first they spoke, but their face was without expression; their feet and hands had no strength; they had no blood, nor substance, nor moisture, nor flesh; their cheeks were dry, their feet and hands were dry, and their flesh was yellow.

Therefore, they no longer thought of their Creator nor their Maker, nor of those who made them and cared for them.

These were the first men who existed in great numbers on the face of the earth.

Study Questions

1. What existed before the earth was created?

2. Why were the animals punished?

3. Did the creator and the maker achieve their goal when they created humans?

4. What does this creation story tell us about Mayan conceptions of human nature?

5. Can you compare this creation story to the one found in the Old Testament?

The Creation Epic (ca. 2000 B.C.E.)   2

Mesopotamian civilization emerged in a land that knew little continuity or order. Both climate and geography made life hazardous and unpredictable. In contrast to life in ancient Egypt, where the seasonal flooding of the Nile and the relative isolation of the country fostered a sense of regularity, Mesopotamians lived with uncertainty. The religion of the people reflects these environmental conditions. Faced by a world in which change was often rapid and violent, Mesopotamians sought an explanation for their social reality through a belief in the capriciousness of the gods.

The Creation Epic describes a bitter conflict between the gods Marduk and Tiamat that led to the creation of the world that the Mesopotamians knew. Tiamat was the oldest of the gods, but she was also the patron of the primeval chaos. Marduk was the warrior god whose purpose was to institute order. The world that emerged from this battle maintained precarious stability—subject always to the whims of inexplicable divinity.

Tablet I

When on high, heaven was not named;
Below, dry land was not named.
Apsu, their first begetter,
Mummu (and) Tiamat, the mother of all of them.
Their waters combined together.
Field was not marked off, sprout had not come forth.
When none of the gods had yet come forth
Had not borne a name,
No destinies had been fixed;
Then gods were created in the midst of heaven.
Lakhmu and Lakhamu came forth
Ages increased ...
Anshar and Kishar were created.
After many days had passed by there came forth...
Anu, their son...
Anshar and Anu...
Anu ...
Nudimmud whom his father, his mother,...
Of large intelligence, knowing (wise),
Exceeding strong ...
Without a rival ...
Then were established....
Then Apsu, the begetter of the great gods,
Cried out, to Mummu, to his messenger, he spoke:
"Oh Mummu, joy of my liver,
Come, unto Tiamat let us go."
They went, and before Tiamat they crouched,

Hatching a plan with regard to the gods ...
Apsu opened his mouth and spoke,
Unto Tiamat, the splendid one addressed a word:
"... their course against me
By day I have no rest, at night I cannot lie down, I wish to destroy their course,
So that clamor cease and we may again lie down to sleep."
When Tiamat (heard) this,
She raged and shrieked for (revenge?),
She herself became furiously enraged.
Evil she conceived in her heart.
"All that we have made let us destroy,
That their course may be full of misery so that we may have release."
Mummu answered and counselled Apsu,
Hostile was the counsel of Mummu.
"Come, their course is strong, destroy it!
Then by day thou wilt have rest,
At night thou wilt lie down."
Apsu (hearkened), and his face shone;
Evil he planned against the gods, his sons....
They uttered curses and at the side of Tiamat advanced.
In fury and rage they devised plans ceaselessly night and day.
They rushed to the conflict, raging and furious.
They grouped themselves and ranged the battle array.
Ummu-Khubar, creator of all things,
Gathering invincible weapons, she brought forth huge monsters,

Sharp of tooth and merciless of fang.
With poison instead of blood she filled their
  bodies.
She clothed with terror the terrible dragons,
Decking them with brilliancy, giving them a
  lofty stature,
So that whoever beheld them would be over-
  come with terror.
With their bodies reared up, none could with-
  stand their attack.
She brought forth great serpents, dragons and
  the Lakhami,
Hurricanes, raging dogs and scorpion men,
Mighty tempests, fish men, and rams,
Bearing cruel weapons, fearless in combat,
Mighty in command, irresistible.
In all eleven monsters of this kind she made.
Among the gods, the first born who formed
  the assembly,
She exalted Kingu, giving him high rank in
  their midst;
To march in advance and to direct the host;
To be foremost in arming for the attack,
To direct the fight in supreme control,
To his hand she confided. She decked him out
  in costly garments:
"I have uttered thy magic formula, in the
  assembly of the gods I have exalted thee."
The dominion over all the gods was entrusted
  unto his hands:
"Be thou exalted, my one and only husband;
May the Anunnaki exalt thy name above all
  the gods!"
She gave him the tablets of fate, to his breast
  she attached them.
"Oh, thou, thy command will be irresistible!
Firmly established be the utterance of thy
  mouth!
Now Kingu is exalted, endowed with the
  power of Anu;
Among the gods, his children, he fixes des-
  tinies.
By the word of thy mouth fire will quenched;
The strong in battle will be increased in
  strength."

Tablet II

Tiamat finished her work.
(The evil that) she contrived against the gods
  her offspring,
To avenge Apsu, Tiamat planned evil.
When she had equipped her army, it was
  revealed to Ea;
Ea heard the words,
And was grievously afflicted, and over-
  whelmed with grief.
Days passed by and his anger was appeased.
To Anshar, his father, he took the way.
To Father Anshar who begot him he went.
All that Tiamat had planned he repeated to
  him.
"Tiamat our mother has taken a dislike for us,
She has assembled a host, she rages furiously.
All the gods are gathered to her,
Aye, even those whom thou hast created,
  march at her side."
[Anshar asks his son Marduk to fight Tiamat]
"Thou art my son of strong courage,...draw
  nigh to the battle!
... at sight of thee there shall be peace."
The Lord rejoiced at the word of his father.
He drew nigh and stood in front of Anshar;
Anshar saw him and his heart was full of joy.
He kissed him on the mouth, and fear
  departed from him.
"(Oh my father), may the words of thy lips
  not be taken back,
May I go and accomplish the desire of thy
  heart"
"Oh, my son, full of all knowledge,
Quiet Tiamat with thy supreme incantation;
Quickly proceed (on thy way)!
Thy blood will not be poured out, thou shalt
  surely return."
The lord rejoiced at the word of his father,
His heart exulted and he spoke to his father.
"Oh Lord of the gods, (who fixes) the fate of
  the great gods,
If I become thy avenger,
Conquering Tiamat, and giving life to thee,

Call an assembly and proclaim the preeminence of my lot!

That when in Upshukkinaku thou joyfully seatest thyself,

My command in place of thine should fix fates.

What I do should be unaltered,

The word of my lips be never changed or annulled."

Tablet III

Then they gathered and went,

The great gods, all of them, who fix fates,

Came into the presence of Anshar, they filled (the assembly hall),

Embracing one another in the assembly (hall),

They prepared themselves to feast at the banquet.

They ate bread, they mixed the wine,

The sweet mead confused (their senses).

Drunk, their bodies filled with drink,

They shouted aloud, with their spirits exalted,

For Marduk, their avenger, they fixed the destiny.

Tablet IV

They prepared for him a royal chamber,

In the presence of his fathers as ruler he stood

"Thou art the weightiest among the great gods.

Thy (power of decreeing) fate is unrivalled, thy command is (like that of) Anu.

Oh Marduk, thou art mightiest among the great gods!

Thy power of decreeing fate unrivalled, thy word is like that of Anu!

From now on thy decree will not be altered,

Thine it shall be to raise up and to bring low,

Thy utterance be established, against they command no rebellion!

None among the gods will transgress the limit (set by thee).

Abundance is pleasing to the shrines of the gods,

The place of their worship will be established as thy place.

Oh Marduk, thou art our avenger!

We give thee kingship over the entire universe,

Take they seat in the assembly, thy word be exalted;

Thy weapon be not overcome, may it crush thy enemies.

Oh lord, the life of him who trusts in thee will be spared,

But pour out the life of the god who has planned evil." ...

He sent forth the winds which he had created, the seven of them;

To trouble the spirit of Tiamat, they followed behind him.

Then the lord raised on high the Deluge, his mighty weapon.

He mounted the storm chariot, unequalled in power.

He harnessed and attached to it four horses,

Merciless, overwhelming, swiftly flying.

(Sharp of) teeth, bearing poison....

Then the lord drew nigh, piercing Tiamat with his glance;

He saw the purpose of Kingu, her spouse,

As he (i.e., Marduk) gazed, he (i.e., Kingu) tottered in his gait. His mind was destroyed, his action upset,

And the gods, his helpers, marching at his side,

Saw (the terror of) the hero and leader.

But Tiamat (uttered a cry) and did not turn her back

From her lips there gushed forth rebellious words

... "coming to thee as lord of the gods,

As in their own sanctuaries they are gathered in thy sanctuary."

Then the lord raised on high the Deluge, the great weapon

And against Tiamat, who was foaming with wrath, thus sent forth (his answer).

"Great art thou! Thou has exalted thyself greatly.

Thy heart hath prompted thee to arrange for
 battle....
Thou hast (exalted) Kingu to be thy husband,
(Thou hast given him power to issue) the
 decrees of Anu.
(Against the gods, my fathers), thou hast
 planned evil;
Against the gods, my fathers, thou hast
 planned evil.
Let thy army be equipped, thy weapons be
 girded on;
Stand; I and thou, let us join in battle."
When Tiamat heard this,
She was beside herself, she lost her reason.
Tiamat shouted in a paroxysm of fury,
Trembling to the root, shaking in her founda-
 tions.
She uttered an incantation, she pronounced a
 magic formula.
The gods of battle, appeal to their weapons.
Then stepped forth Tiamat and the leader of
 the gods, Marduk.
To the fight they advanced, to the battle they
 drew nigh.
The lord spread his net and encompassed her,
The evil wind stationed behind him he drove
 into her face.
Tiamat opened her mouth to its full extent.
He drove in the evil wind before she could
 close her lips.
The terrible winds filled her belly,
Her heart was seized, and she held her mouth
 wide open.
He drove in the spear and burst open her
 belly,
Cutting into her entrails, he slit her heart.
He overcame her and destroyed her life;
He cast down her carcass and stood upon it.
When he had thus subjected Tiamat, the
 leader,
Her host was scattered, her assembly was dis-
 solved;
And the gods, her helpers, who marched
 beside her,
In fear and trembling turned about,
Taking to flight to save their lives.

But they were surrounded and could not
 escape.
He captured them and smashed their weapons,
They were cast into the net, and brought into
 the snare; ...
After he (i.e., Marduk) had bound and cast
 down his enemies,
Had battered down the arrogant foe,
Had completely gained the victory of Anshar
 over the enemy,
The hero Marduk had attained the aim of
 Nudimmud,
He strengthened his hold over the captive
 gods.
To Tiamat, whom he had bound, he came
 back,
And the lord trampled under foot the founda-
 tion of Tiamat.
With his merciless weapon he smashed her
 skull,
He cut the channels of her blood,
And made the north wind carry them to
 secret places.
His fathers beheld and rejoiced exceeding glad,
Presents and gifts they brought to him.
Then the lord rested and looked at the carcass.
He divided the flesh of the monster, and cre-
 ated marvellous things.
He split her like a fish flattened into two
 halves;
One half he took and made it a covering for
 heaven.
He drew a bolt, he stationed a watchman,
.Enjoining that the waters be not permitted to
 flow out.
He passed over the heavens, inspecting the
 regions (thereof),
And over against the Apsu, he set the dwelling
 of Nudimmud.
The lord measured the structure of the Deep.
He established E-sharra as a palace corrspond-
 ing to it.
The palace E-sharra which he created as
 heaven,
He caused Anu, Enlil and Ea to inhabit their
 districts.

Tablet V

He made stations for the great gods,
The stars, their counterparts, the twin stars he
    fixed.
He fixed the year and divided it into divisions.
For the twelve months he fixed three stars.
Also for the days of the year (he had fash-
    ioned) pictures....

Tablet VI

Upon (Marduk's) hearing the word of the
    gods,

His heart led him to create (marvellous things)
He opened his mouth and (spoke) to Ea
(What) he had conceived in his heart he
    imparted to him;
"My blood I will take and bone I will (form).
I will set up man that man ...
I will create man to inhabit (the earth),
That the worship of the gods be fixed, that
    they may have shrines.
But I will alter the ways of the gods, I will
    change...
They shall be joined in concert, unto evil shall
    they" ...
Ea answered him and spoke.

Study Questions

1. Conflict seems to be a major theme of this creation epic. What, in practical terms, does
   war among gods mean for mere mortals?

2. Mortals play little part in the struggles of the gods. Why? What assumptions about
   humanity and its relations to the gods are revealed in the epic?

3. Who won the battle between Marduk and Tiamat? What followed the end of that war?

4. Extreme violence marks much of the creation epic. What lessons might you draw from
   this about the nature of Mesopotamian society?

The Book of Genesis (ca. 10th–6th century B.C.E.)   3

The Book of Genesis is the first book of the Old Testament as well as the first
book of the Hebrew Torah. It was probably composed between the tenth and sixth
century B.C.E. Genesis tells the Judeo-Christian story of creation and the early history of the Hebrew people. The Judeo-Christian creation was the work of a single
God who formed the environment for the life of humans. The story is anthro-
pocentric, that is, it revolves around the deeds of men and women from their
creation through the expulsion from the Garden of Eden to their corruption of the
earth. God cleanses this corruption with a mighty flood of water that eliminates all
but one human family, that of Noah.

The story told in Genesis is so well known that it is difficult to attempt to read it critically as an historical document. Because it is the best known of all the creation epics, there is a temptation to regard it as the unique story of the origins of humanity and the universe. It is most fruitfully read in comparison with other stories of creation.

Chapter 1

In the beginning God created the heaven and the earth.

And the earth was without form, and void; and darkness *was* upon the face of the deep. And the Spirit of God moved upon the face of the waters.

And God said, Let there be light: and there was light.

And God saw the light, that it *was* good: and God divided the light from the darkness.

And God called the light Day, and the darkness he called Night.

And the evening and the morning were the first day.

And God said, Let there be a firmament in the midst of the waters, and let it divide the waters from the waters.

And God made the firmament, and divided the waters which *were* under the firmament from the waters which *were* above the firmament: and it was so.

And God called the firmament Heaven. And the evening and the morning were the second day.

And God said, Let the waters under the heaven be gathered together unto one place, and let the dry *land* appear: and it was so.

And God called the dry *land* Earth; and the gathering together of the waters called he Seas: and God saw that *it was* good.

And God said, Let the earth bring forth grass, the herb yielding seed, *and* the fruit tree yielding fruit after his kind, whose seed *is* in itself, upon the earth: and it was so.

And the earth brought forth grass, and herb yielding seed after his kind, and the tree yielding fruit, whose seed *was* in itself, after his kind: and God saw that *it was* good.

And the. evening and the morning were the third day.

And God said, Let there be lights in the firmament of the heaven to divide the day from the night; and let them be for signs, and for seasons, and for days, and years:

And let them be for lights in the firmament of the heaven to give light upon the earth: and it was so.

And God made two great lights; the greater light to rule the day, and the lesser light to rule the night: *he made* the stars also.

And God set them in the firmament of the heaven to give light upon the earth,

And to rule over the day and over the night, and to divide the light from the darkness: and God saw that *it was* good.

And the evening and the morning were the fourth day.

And God said, Let the waters bring forth abundantly the moving creature that hath life, and fowl *that* may fly above the earth in the open firmament of heaven.

And God created great whales, and every living creature that moveth, which the waters brought forth abundantly, after their kind, and every winged fowl after his kind: and God saw that *it was* good.

And God blessed them, saying, Be fruitful, and multiply, and fill the waters in the seas, and let fowl multiply in the earth.

And the evening and the morning were the fifth day.

Michelangelo, Creation of Adam. In 1508, Pope Julius II recalled Michelangelo to Rome and commissioned him to decorate the ceiling of the Sistine Chapel. This colossal project was not completed until 1512. Michelangelo attempted to tell the story of the Fall of Man by depicting nine scenes from the biblical book of Genesis. In this scene, the well-proportioned figure of Adam, meant by Michelangelo to be a reflection of divine beauty, awaits the divine spark.

And God said, Let the earth bring forth the living creature after his kind, cattle, and creeping thing, and beast of the earth after his kind: and it was so.

And God made the beast of the earth after his kind, and cattle after their kind, and every thing that creepeth upon the earth, after his kind: and God saw that *it was* good.

And God said, Let us make man in our image, after our likeness: and let them have dominion over the fish of the sea, and over the fowl of the air, and over the cattle, and over all the earth, and over every creeping thing that creepeth upon the earth.

So God created man in his *own* image, in the image of God created he him; male and female created he them.

And God blessed them, and God said unto them, Be fruitful, and multiply, and replenish the earth, and subdue it: and have dominion over the fish of the sea, and over the fowl of the air, and over every living thing that moveth upon the earth.

And God said, Behold, I have given you every herb bearing seed, which *is* upon the face of all the earth, and every tree, in the which *is* the fruit of a tree yielding seed; to you it shall be for meat.

And to every beast of the earth, and to every fowl of the air, and to every thing that creepeth upon the earth, wherein *there* is life, *I have given* every green herb for meat: and it was so.

And God saw every thing that he had made, and, behold, *it was* very good. And the evening and the morning were the sixth day.

Chapter 2

Thus the heavens and the earth were finished, and all the host of them.

And on the seventh day God ended his work which he had made; and he rested on the seventh day from all his work which he had made.

And God blessed the seventh day, and sanctified it: because that in it he had rested from all his work which God created and made.

These *are* the generations of the heavens and of the earth when they were created, in the day that the LORD God made the earth and the heavens,

And every plant of the field before it was in the earth, and every herb of the field before it grew: for the LORD God had not caused it to rain upon the earth, and *there was* not a man to till the ground.

But there went up a mist from the earth, and watered the whole face of the ground.

And the LORD God formed man *of* the dust of the ground, and breathed into his nostrils the breath of life; and man became a living soul.

And the LORD God planted a garden eastward in Eden; and there he put the man whom he had formed.

And out of the ground made the LORD God to grow every tree that is pleasant to the sight, and good for food; the tree of life also in the midst of the garden, and the tree of knowledge of good and evil.

And a river went out of Eden to water the garden; and from thence it was parted, and became into four heads.

The name of the first *is* Pi'son: that *is* it which compasseth the whole land of Hav'i-lah, where *there is* gold;

And the gold of that land *is* good: there *is* bdellium and the onyx stone.

And the name of the second river *is* Gi'hon: the same *is* it that compasseth the whole land of E-thi-o'pi-a.

And the name of the third river *is* Hid'-dekel: that *is* it which goeth toward the east of Ass-yr'i-a. And the fourth river *is* Eu-phra'tes.

And the LORD God took the man, and put him into the garden of Eden to dress it and to keep it.

And the LORD God commanded the man, saying, Of every tree of the garden thou mayest freely eat:

But of the tree of the knowledge of good and evil, thou shalt not eat of it: for in the day that thou eatest thereof thou shalt surely die.

And the LORD God said, *It is* not good that the man should be alone; I will make him an help meet for him.

And out of the ground the LORD God formed every beast of the field, and every fowl of the air; would call *them* unto Adam to see what he would call them; and whatsoever Adam called every living creature, that *was* the name thereof. And Adam gave names to all cattle, and to the fowl of the air, and to every beast of the field; but for Adam there was not found an help meet for him.

And the LORD God caused a deep sleep to fall upon Adam, and he slept: and he took one of his ribs, and closed up the flesh instead thereof;

And the rib, which the LORD God had taken from man, made he a woman, and brought her unto the man.

And Adam said, This *is* now bone of my bones, and flesh of my flesh: she shall be called Woman, because she was taken out of Man.

Therefore shall a man leave his father and his mother, and shall cleave unto his wife: and they shall be one flesh.

And they were both naked, the man and his wife, and were not ashamed.

Chapter 3

Now the serpent was more subtil than any beast of the field which the LORD God had made. And he said unto the woman, Yea, hath God said, Ye shall not eat of every tree of the garden?

And the woman said unto the serpent, We may eat of the fruit of the trees of the garden:

But of the fruit of the tree which *is* in the midst of the garden, God hath said, Ye shall not eat of it, neither shall ye touch it, lest ye die.

And the serpent said unto the woman, Ye shall not surely die:

For God doth know that in the day ye eat thereof, then your eyes shall be opened, and ye shall be as gods, knowing good and evil.

And when the woman saw that the tree *was* good for food, and that it *was* pleasant to the eyes, and a tree to be desired to make *one* wise, she took of the fruit thereof, and did eat, and gave also unto her husband with her; and he did eat.

And the eyes of them both were opened, and they knew that they *were* naked; and they sewed fig leaves together, and made themselves aprons.

And they heard the voice of the LORD God walking in the garden in the cool of the day: and Adam and his wife hid themselves from the presence of the LORD God amongst the trees of the garden.

And the LORD God called unto Adam, and said unto him, Where *art* thou?

And he said, I heard thy voice in the garden, and I was afraid, because I *was* naked; and I hid myself.

And he said, Who told thee that thou *wast* naked? Hast thou eaten of the tree, whereof I commanded thee that thou shouldest not eat?

And the man said, The woman whom thou gavest *to be* with me, she gave me of the tree, and I did eat.

And the LORD God said unto the woman, What *is* this *that* thou hast done? And the woman said, The serpent beguiled me, and I did eat.

And the LORD God said unto the serpent, Because thou hast done this, thou *art* cursed above all cattle, and above every beast of the field; upon thy belly shalt thou go, and dust shalt thou eat all the days of thy life:

And I will put enmity between thee and the woman, and between thy seed and her seed; it shall bruise thy head, and thou shalt bruise his heel.

Unto the woman he said, I will greatly multiply thy sorrow and thy conception; in sorrow thou shalt bring forth children; and thy desire *shall be* to thy husband, and he shall rule over thee.

And unto Adam he said, Because thou hast hearkened unto the voice of thy wife, and hast eaten of the tree, of which I commanded thee, saying, Thou shalt not eat of it: cursed *is* the ground for thy sake; in sorrow shalt thou eat *of* it all the days of thy life;

Thorns also and thistles shall it bring forth to thee; and thou shalt eat the herb of the field;

In the sweat of thy face shalt thou eat bread, till thou return unto the ground; for out of it wast thou taken: for dust thou *art,* and unto dust shalt thou return.

And Adam called his wife's name Eve; because she was the mother of all living.

Unto Adam also and to his wife did the LORD God make coats of skins, and clothed them.

And the LORD God said, Behold, the man is become as one of us, to know good and evil: and now, lest he put forth his hand, and take also of the tree of life, and eat, and live for ever:

Therefore the LORD God sent him forth from the garden of Eden, to till the ground from whence he was taken.

So he drove out the man; and he placed at the east of the garden of Eden Cher'u-bims, and a flaming sword which turned every way, to keep the way of the tree of life.

Chapter 4

And Adam knew Eve his wife; and she conceived, and bare Cain, and said, I have gotten a man from the Lord.

And she again bare his brother Abel. And Abel was a keeper of sheep, and Cain was a tiller of the ground.

And in process of time it came to pass, that Cain brought of the fruit of the ground an offering unto the LORD

And Abel, he also brought of the firstlings of his flock and of the fat thereof And the LORD had respect unto Abel and to his offering:

But unto Cain and to his offering he had not respect. And Cain was very wroth, and his countenance fell.

And the LORD said unto Cain, Why art thou wroth? and why is thy countenance fallen?

If thou doest well, shalt thou not be accepted? and if thou doest not well, sin lieth at the door. And unto thee *shall be* his desire, and thou shalt rule over him.

And Cain talked with Abel his brother: and it came to pass, when they were in the field, that Cain rose up against Abel his brother, and slew him.

And the LORD said unto Cain, Where *is* Abel thy brother? And he said, I know not: *Am* I my brother's keeper?

And he said, What hast thou done? the voice of thy brother's blood crieth unto me from the ground.

And now *art* thou cursed from the earth, which hath opened her mouth to receive thy brother's blood from thy hand;

When thou tillest the ground, it shall not henceforth yield unto thee her strength; a fugitive and a vagabond shalt thou be in the earth.

And Cain said unto the LORD, My punishment *is* greater than I can bear.

Behold, thou hast driven me out this day from the face of the earth; and from thy face shall I be hid; and I shall be a fugitive and a vagabond in the earth; and it shall come to pass, *that* every one that findeth me shall slay me.

And the LORD said unto him, Therefore whosoever slayeth Cain, vengeance shall be taken on him sevenfold. And the LORD set a mark upon Cain, lest any finding him should kill him.

And Cain went out from the presence of the LORD, and dwelt in the land of Nod, on the east of Eden.

And Cain knew his wife; and she conceived, and bare E'noch: and he builded a city, and called the name of the city, after the name of his son, E'noch.

And unto E'noch was born I'rad: and I'rad begat Me-hu'ja-el: and Me-hu'ja-el begat Me-thu'-sa-el: and Me-thu'sa-el begat La'mech.

And La'mech took unto him two wives: the name of the one *was* Adah, and the name of the other Zil'lah.

And Adah bare Ja'bal: he was the father of such as dwell in tents, and *of such as have* cattle.

And his brother's name *was* Ju'bal: he was the father of all such as handle the harp and organ.

And Zil'lah, she also bare Tu'bal-cain, an instructer of every artificer in brass and iron: and the sister of Tu'bal-cain *was* Na'a-mah.

And La'mech said unto his wives, Adah and Zil'lah, Hear my voice; ye wives of La'mech, hearken unto my speech: for I have slain a man to my wounding, and a young man to my hurt.

If Cain shall be avenged sevenfold, truly La'mech seventy and sevenfold.

And Adam knew his wife again; and she bare a son, and called his name Seth: For God, *said she*, hath appointed me another seed instead of Abel, whom Cain slew.

And to Seth, to him also there was bore a son; and he called his name E'nos: then began men to call upon the name of the LORD.

Chapter 6

And it came to pass, when men began to multiply on the face of the earth, and daughters were born unto them,

That the sons of God saw the daughters of men that they *were* fair; and they took them wives of all which they chose.

And the LORD said, My spirit shall not always strive with man, for that he also *is* flesh: yet his days shall be an hundred and twenty years.

There were giants in the earth in those days; and also after that, when the sons of God came in unto the daughters of men, and they bare *children* to them, the same *became* mighty men which *were* of old, men of renown.

And GOD saw that the wickedness of man was great in the earth, and *that* every imagination of the thoughts of his heart *was* only evil continually.

And it repented the LORD that he had made man on the earth, and it grieved him at his heart.

And the LORD said, I will destroy man whom I have created from the face of the earth; both man, and beast, and the creeping thing, and the fowls of the air; for it repenteth me that I have made them.

But Noah found grace in the eyes of the LORD.

These *are* the generations of Noah: Noah was a just man *and* perfect in his generations, *and* Noah walked with God.

And Noah begat three sons, Shem, Ham, and Ja'pheth.

The earth also was corrupt before God, and the earth was filled with violence.

And God looked upon the earth, and, behold, it was corrupt; for all flesh had corrupted his way upon the earth.

And God said unto Noah, The end of all flesh is come before me; for the earth is filled with violence through them; and behold, I will destroy them with the earth.

Make thee an ark of gopher wood; rooms shalt thou make in the ark, and shalt pitch it within and without with pitch.

And this *is the fashion* which thou shalt make it *of.* The length of the ark *shall be* three hundred cubits, the breadth of it fifty cubits, and the height of it thirty cubits.

A window shalt thou make to the ark, and in a cubit shalt thou finish it above; and the door of the ark shalt thou set in the side thereof; *with* lower, second, and third *stories* shalt thou make it.

And, behold, I, even I, do bring a flood of waters upon the earth, to destroy all flesh, wherein *is* the breath of life, from under heaven; *and* every thing that *is* in the earth shall die.

But with thee will I establish my covenant; and thou shalt come into the ark, thou, and thy sons, and thy wife, and thy sons' wives with thee.

And of every living thing of all flesh, two of every *sort* shalt thou bring into the ark, to keep *them* alive with thee; they shall be male and female.

Of fowls after their kind, and of cattle after their kind, of every creeping thing of the earth after his kind, two of every *sort* shall come unto thee, to keep *them* alive.

And take thou unto thee of all food that is eaten, and thou shalt gather *it* to thee; and it shall be for food for thee, and for them.

Thus did Noah; according to all that God commanded him, so did he.

Chapter 7

And the LORD said unto Noah, Come thou and all thy house into the ark; for thee have I seen righteous before me in this generation.

Of every clean beast thou shalt take to thee by sevens, the male and his female: and of beasts that *are* not clean by two, the male and his female.

Of fowls also of the air by sevens, the male and female; to keep seed alive upon the face of all the earth.

For yet seven days, and I will cause it to rain upon the earth forty days and forty nights; and every living substance that I have made will I destroy from off the face of the earth.

And Noah did according unto all that the LORD commanded him.

And Noah *was* six hundred years old when the flood of waters was upon the earth.

And Noah went in, and his sons, and his wife, and his sons' wives with him, into the ark, because of the waters of the flood.

Of clean beasts, and of beasts that *are* not clean, and of fowls, and of every thing that creepeth upon the earth,

They went in two and two unto Noah into the ark, the male and the female, as God had commanded Noah.

And it came to pass after seven days, that the waters of the flood were upon the earth.

In the six hundredth year of Noah's life, in the second month, the seven-teenth day of the month, the same day were all the fountains of the great deep broken up, and the windows of heaven were opened.

And the rain was upon the earth forty days and forty nights.

In the selfsame day entered Noah, and Shem, and Ham, and Ja'pheth, the sons of Noah, and Noah's wife, and the three wives of his sons with them, into the ark;

They, and every beast after his kind, and all the cattle after their kind, and every creeping thing that creepeth upon the earth after his kind, and every fowl after his kind, every bird of every sort.

And they went in unto Noah into the ark, two and two of all flesh, wherein *is* the breath of life.

And they that went in, went in male and female of all flesh, as God had commanded him: and the LORD shut him in.

And the flood was forty days upon the earth; and the waters increased, and bare up the ark, and it was lift up above the earth.

And the waters prevailed, and were increased greatly upon the earth; and the ark went upon the face of the waters.

And the waters prevailed exceedingly upon the earth; and all the high hills, that *were* under the whole heaven, were covered.

Fifteen cubits upward did the waters prevail; and the mountains were covered.

And all flesh died that moved upon the earth, both of fowl, and of cattle, and of beast, and of every creeping thing that creepeth upon the earth, and every man:

All in whose nostrils *was* the breath of life, of all that *was* in the dry *land*, died.

And every living substance was destroyed which was upon the face of the ground, both man, and cattle, and the creeping things, and the fowl of the heaven; and they were destroyed from the earth: and Noah only remained *alive*, and they that *were* with him in the ark.

And the waters prevailed upon the earth an hundred and fifty days.

Study Questions

1. Why is it significant that God created man in his own image?

2. What is the relationship between humans and animals?

3. What is the position of women in Genesis?

4. What is the significance of the story of the flood?

The Cradle of Civilization

The Great Pyramid of Giza

The Epic of Gilgamesh (ca. 2000 B.C.E)   **4**

The Epic of Gilgamesh, the best known of the Mesopotamian myths, is one of The world's oldest surviving pieces of literature. Only incomplete versions have come down to us, the longest of which is a copy written on 12 tablets found in the Royal Library of Nineveh. The epic tells the story of the wanderings of Gilgamesh, the part-human, part-divine king of Uruk. Around 2000 B.C.E., Uruk, one of the most important of the Mesopotamian city-states, was ruled by a King Gilgamesh' but it is impossible to be certain that the events recounted in the epic derive from his reign.

The peoples of the ancient Near East lived precariously, always at the mercy of nature. Flood and drought were the most common natural disasters, and *The Epic of Gilgamesh* contains echoes of the great flood narrated in the Bible. Gilgamesh's travels are motivated by a search for the survivors of this great flood, who supposedly know the secret of everlasting life. The twin themes of the unpredictability of the gods and the inevitability of death dominate the epic.

Siduri, she the divine cup-bearer,
Sits there by the rim of the sea.
Sits there and looks afar off ...
She is wrapped in a shawl ...
Gilgamesh ran thither and drew nigh unto her.
He is clad in skins,
His shape is awesome,
His body godlike,
Woe is in his heart.
He is like a wanderer of far ways.
The face of her, the cup-bearer, looks afar off,
She talks to herself and says the word,
Takes counsel in her heart:
"Is he yonder one who deviseth ill?
Whither is he going in the wrath of his heart?"
As Siduri saw him, she locked her gate,
Locked her portal, locked her chamber....

Gilgamesh says to her, to the cup-bearer:
"Cup-bearer, what ails thee,
That thou lockest thy gate,
Lockest thy portal,
Lockest thy chamber?
I will crash the door, I will break the lock." ...
The cup-bearer says to him, to Gilgamesh:

"Why are thy cheeks so wasted,
Thy visage so sunken,
Thy heart so sad,
Thy shape so undone?
Why is woe in thy heart?
Why art thou like a wanderer of far ways?
Why is thy countenance
So destroyed with grief and pain?
Why hast thou from wide-away
Made haste over the steppes?"

Gilgamesh says to her, to the cup-bearer:
"Why should my cheeks not be so wasted,
My visage so sunken,
My heart so sad,
My shape so undone?
How should woe not be in my heart?
Why should I not be like
A wanderer of far ways?
Why should not my countenance
Be destroyed with grief and pain?
Why should I not to the far-away
Make haste over the steppes?
My beloved friend, the panther of the steppes,
Engidu, my beloved friend,

The panther of the steppes who could do all
   things,
So that we climbed the mountain,
Overthrew Khumbaba,
Who housed in the cedar-forest,
So that we seized and slew the bull-of-heaven,
So that we laid lions low
In the ravines of the mountain,
My friend,
Who with me ranged through all hardships,
Engidu, my friend, who killed lions with me,
Who with me ranged through all hardships,
Him hath the fate of mankind overtaken.
Six days and six nights have I wept over him,
Until the seventh day
Would I not have him buried.
Then I began to be afraid ...
Fear of death seized upon me.
Therefore I make away over the steppes.
The fate of my friend weighs me down.
Therefore I make haste
On a far way over the steppes.
The fate of Engidu, my friend,
Weigheth me down.
Therefore I make haste on a long road over the
   steppes.
Why should I be silent thereon?
Why should I not cry it forth?
My friend, whom I love,
Hath turned into earth.
Must not I too, as he,
Lay me down
And rise not up again
For ever and for ever?—
Ever since he is gone, I cannot find Life,
And rove, like a hunter, round over the fields.
Cup-bearer, now I behold thy face;
But Death, whom I fear, I would not behold

"The cup-bearer, she says to him, to Gilgamesh:
"Gilgamesh, whither runnest thou?
Life, which thou seekest, thou wilt not find.
When the gods created mankind,
They allotted to mankind Death,
But Life they withheld in their hands.
So, Gilgamesh, fill thy body,

Make merry by day and night,
Keep each day a feast of rejoicing!
Day and night leap and have thy delight!
Put on clean raiment,
Wash thy head and bathe thee in water,
Look cheerily at the child who holdeth thy
   hand,
And may thy wife have joy in thy arms!'

Gilgamesh says again to her, to the cup-bearer:
"Go to, cup-bearer!
Where is the way to Utnapishtim?
What is his sign? Give it to me!
If it can be done,
I will pass over the sea;
If it cannot be done,
I will make away over the steppes."
Ur-Shanabi says to him, to Gilgamesh:
"What is thy name? Say forth!
I am Ur-Shanabi,
Man-servant of Utnapishtim, the far one."

Gilgamesh speaks to him, to Ur-Shanabi:
"My name is Gilgamesh,
I have come from long away ...
At last, Ur-Shanabi, I behold thy face.
Let me look on Utnapishtim, the far one."

Ur-Shanabi says to him, to Gilgamesh:
"Why are thy cheeks so wasted,
Thy visage so sunken,
Thy heart so sad,
Thy shape so undone?
Why is woe in thy heart?
Why art thou like a wanderer of far ways?
Why is thy countenance
So destroyed with grief and pain?
Why hast thou from long away
Come ahaste over the steppes?"

Gilgamesh says to him,
To Ur-Shanabi, the shipman:
"Why should my cheeks not be so wasted,
My visage so sunken,
My heart so sad,
My shape so undone?

Gilgamesh and Ur-Shanabi boarded the ship,
They headed the ship into the flood
And sailed forth,
A way of one month and fifteen days.
As he took his bearings on the third day,
Ur-Shanabi had reached the water of death.
Ur-Shanabi says to him, to Gilgamesh:
"Quick, Gilgamesh, take a pole!
For thy hands must not touch
The waters of death."

Utnapishtim descrieth his face afar;
Talks to himself and saith the word,
Takes counsel in his heart:
"Why are the stone-coffers
Of the ship all to-broken?
And one who belongs not to me
Sails in the ship!
He who comes yonder, he cannot be man! ...
I gaze thither, but I understand it not.
I gaze thither, but I grasp it not." ...

Utnapishtim says to him, to Gilgamesh:
"What is thy name? Say forth!
I am Utnapishtim who hath found Life."
Gilgamesh says to him, to Utnapishtim:
"My name is Gilgamesh.
I have come from wide-away ...
Now I behold thee, Utnapishtim, thou far one."
Gilgamesh says again to him, to Utnapishtim:
"Methought, I will go and see
Utnapishtim, of whom men tell.
So I betook me through all lands to and fro,
So I betook me over the mountains
That are hard to cross over,
So I fared over all seas.
With good have I not been glutted ...
I filled my body with pain;
Ere ever I got to Siduri, the cup-bearer,
Was my clothing gone ...
I had to hunt all the wild of the fields,
Lions and panthers,
Hyenas, and deer, and ibex.
Their flesh do I eat,
With their skins do I clothe me."...

And whilst Gilgamesh sits there in a posture of
     rest,
Sleep bloweth upon him like a stormwind.
Utnapishtim says to her, to his wife:
"Look at the strong one
Who longed after Life
Like a stormwind, sleep bloweth against him!"
His wife speaks to him, to Utnapishtim,
To the far one:
"Touch him, that the man may wake up!
Let him, on the way whence he came,
Safe and sound return home.
Through the gate, through which he went,
May he return back to his land!"
Utnapishtim says to her, to his wife:
"Oh, thou hast pity upon the man!
Go to, bake loaves for him,
And lay them at his head!
And the days which he sleeps

Do thou mark on the house-wall."
She baked loaves for him and laid them at his
     head.
And the days which he slept she marked on the
     wall.
Utnapishtim announced to him:
"One is dry, a loaf for him,
A second is kneaded, a third damp,
A fourth is become white, a roasted loaf for
     him,
A fifth is become old,
A sixth is baked, a seventh—"
Then of a sudden he touched him,
And the man awoke.
Gilgamesh says to him,
To Utnapishtim, the far one:
I was benumbed by the sleep that fell on me.
Then didst thou touch me quick and awaken
     me."
Utnapishtim says to him, to Gilgamesh:
"Go to, Gilgamesh, thy loaves are counted ...
One was dry, a loaf for thee,
A second was kneaded, a third damp,
A fourth was become white, a roasted loaf for
     thee,

A fifth was become old,
A sixth was baked, a seventh—
Then of a sudden I touched thee,
And thou awokest!"
Gilgamesh says to him,
To Utnapishtim, the far one:
"What shall I do, Utnapishtim?
Whither shall I go,
Now that the Snatcher hath laid hold on my
    body?
In my sleeping-chamber dwells Death,
And whithersoever I flee, is he, is Death,
    there."

Utnapishtim says to him,
To Ur-Shanabi, the shipman:.
"Ur-Shanabi, the landing-place
Shall no more desire thee;
The crossing-spot shall hate thee ...
The man whom thou leddest hither,
Whose body filth covers,
From whom beast-skins have taken
The beauty of the body,
Escort him, Ur-Shanabi,
And bring him to the bathing-place;
Let him wash clean as snow
His filth in the water!
Let him cast off his skins
That the sea bear them away!
His body shall again show beautiful!
Be the band round his head made new!
Let him be clad in a robe,
In a shirt for his nakedness!
Until he comes again to his city,
Until he gets to his journey's end,
The robe shall not grow old,
Shall always be made new."

Gilgamesh and Ur-Shanabi boarded the ship,
They headed the ship into the flood,
And sailed away.
Then said his wife to him,
To Utnapishtim, the far one:
"Gilgamesh hath set forth;
He hath worn himself out, and suffered tor-
    ments.

What wilt thou give him,
That with it he may reach his homeland?"

And Gilgamesh has already lifted the pole,
And brings the ship again near the shore:
Utnapishtim says to him, to Gilgamesh:
"Gilgamesh, thou hast set forth;
Thou hast worn thyself out, and suffered tor-
    ments.
What shall I give thee
That with it thou reachest thy homeland?
I will lay open before thee
Knowledge deep-hidden;
About a plant of life will I tell thee.
The plant looks like the prick-thorn ...
Its thorn like the thorn of the rose
Can prick the hand hard.
When thou gettest this plant in thy hands,
Eat thereof and thou wilt live."

When Gilgamesh learned of this ...
He bound heavy stones on his feet;
These drew him down deep in the sea. He him-
    self took the plant,
And it pricked his hand hard.
He cut off the heavy stones ...
And laid the plant beside him.
Gilgamesh says to him,
To Ur-Shanabi, the shipman:
"Ur-Shanabi, this plant
Is a plant-of-promise,
Whereby a man obtains his desire.
I will bring it to ramparted Uruk;
I will make the warriors eat thereof ...
Its name is: 'The-old-man-becomes-young-
    again.'
I myself will eat thereof,
And return back to my youth."

After twenty miles they took a little food,
After thirty miles they rested for the night.
Then Gilgamesh saw a pit with cool water;
He stepped into it and bathed in the water.
Then a serpent savoured the smell of the plant;
She crept along and took the plant ...

When he returned, he shrieked out a curse.

Gilgamesh sat himself down and weeps,
His tears run over his face.
He speaks and says to Ur-Shanabi, the shipman:
"For whom, Ur-Shanabi,
Have my arms worn themselves out?
For whom hath been spent the blood of my heart?
I worked good not for myself—
For the worm of the earth have I wrought good...."

After twenty miles they took a little food,
After thirty miles they rested for the night.
At last they reached ramparted Uruk.
Gilgamesh says to him,
To Ur-Shanabi, the shipman:
"Mount up, Ur-Shanabi,
Go up along the walls of ramparted Uruk,
Observe the bricks, behold the ground-work,
If the bricks are not firm and lasting,
And if the foundations were not
Laid by the seven wise-men...."

Study Questions

1. What does Gilgamesh run from and what is he searching for?

2. Life in Mesopotamia was very hazardous. Describe some of the dangers Gilgamesh faced.

3. How do gods such as Siduni and Utnapishtim intervene in the lives of mortals?

4. What can you say about the Mesopotamian view of life as illustrated by the epic? What answers to the problems of survival does it offer?

Code of Hammurabi (early 18th century B.C.E.)   5

Hammurabi (d. 1750 B.C.E.) was a ruler of the Old Babylonian or Amorite dynasty fsrom 1792 to 1750 B.C.E. His principle achievement was unifying his Mesopotamian kingdom by controlling the Euphrates River. Though little is known about either his family life or the events of his reign, Hammurabi's military achievements are undoubted.

Discovered in the early twentieth century, the *Code of Hammurabi* was hailed as the first law code in Western history. Its severe punishments for criminal offenses and its explicit statement of the doctrine of "an eye for an eye" also led to its connection with the Mosaic code. It is now clear that Hammurabi's *Code* is a compendium of earlier laws rather than an innovation of this Babylonian ruler. Its influence on Hebrew law is also less direct than was once thought. What remains significant about Hammurabi's *Code*, however, is what it tells us about the importance of writing and literacy among the elites of Babylonian society and about their well developed notions of law and justice.

The Laws

If a seignior accused a(nother) seignior and brought a charge of murder against him, but has not proved it, his accuser shall be put to death.

If a seignior brought a charge of sorcery against a(nother) seignior, but has not proved it, the one against whom the charge of sorcery was brought, upon going to the river, shall throw himself into the river, and if the river has then overpowered him, his accuser shall take over his estate; if the river has shown that seignior to be innocent and he has accordingly come forth safe, the one who brought the charge of sorcery against him shall be put to death, while the one who threw himself into the river shall take over the estate of his accuser.

If a seignior came forward with false testimony in a case, and has not proved the word which he spoke, if that case was a case involving life, that seignior shall be put to death.

If he came forward with (false) testimony concerning grain or money, he shall bear the penalty of that case.

If a seignior stole the property of church or state, that seignior shall be put to death; also the one who received the stolen goods from his hand shall be put to death.

If a seignior has purchased or has received for safekeeping either silver or gold or a male slave or a female slave or an ox or a sheep or an ass or any sort of thing from the hand of a seignior's son or a seignior's slave without witnesses and contracts, since that seignior is a thief, he shall be put to death.

If a seignior stole either an ox or a sheep or an ass or a pig or a boat, if it belonged to the church (or) if it belonged to the state, he shall make thirtyfold restitution; if it belonged to a private citizen, he shall make good tenfold. If the thief does not have sufficient to make restitution, he shall be put to death.

If a seignior has stolen the young son of a(nother) seignior, he shall be put to death.

If a seignior has helped either a male slave of the state or a female slave of the state or a male slave of a private citizen or a female slave of a private citizen to escape through the city-gate, he shall be put to death.

If a seignior has harbored in his house either a fugitive male or female slave belonging to the state or to a private citizen and has not brought him forth at the summons of the police, that householder shall be put to death.

If a seignior committed robbery and has been caught, that seignior shall be put to death.

If the robber has not been caught, the robbed seignior shall set forth the particulars regarding his lost property in the presence of god, and the city and governor, in whose territory and district the robbery was committed, shall make good to him his lost property.

If either a sergeant or a captain has obtained a soldier by conscription or he accepted and has sent a hired substitute for a campaign of the king, that sergeant or captain shall be put to death.

If either a sergeant or a captain has appropriated the household goods of a soldier, has wronged a soldier, has let a soldier for hire, has abandoned a soldier to a superior in a lawsuit, has appropriated the grant which the king gave to a soldier, that sergeant or captain shall be put to death.

If a seignior has bought from the hand of a soldier the cattle or sheep which the king gave to the soldier, he shall forfeit his money.

When a seignior borrowed money from a merchant and pledged to the merchant a field prepared for grain or sesame, if he said to him, "Cultivate the field, then harvest (and) take the grain or sesame that is produced," if the tenant has produced grain or sesame in the field, the owner of the field at harvest-time shall himself take the grain or sesame that was produced in the field and he shall give to the merchant grain for his money, which he borrowed from the merchant, together with its interest, and also for the cost of cultivation.

If he pledged a field planted with (grain) or a field planted with sesame, the owner of the field shall himself take the grain or sesame that was produced in the field and he shall pay back the money with its interest to the merchant.

If he does not have the money to pay back, (grain or) sesame at their market value in accordance with the ratio fixed by the king he shall give to the merchant for his money, which he borrowed from the merchant, together with its interest.

If the tenant has not produced grain or sesame in the field, he may not change his contract.

If a seignior was too lazy to make [the dike of] his field strong and did not make his dike strong and a break has opened up in his dike and he has accordingly let the water ravage the farmland, the seignior in whose dike the break was opened shall make good the grain that he let get destroyed.

If he is not able to make good the grain, they shall sell him and his goods, and the farmers whose grain the water carried off shall divide (the proceeds).

If a seignior, upon opening his canal for irrigation, became so lazy that he has let the water ravage a field adjoining his, he shall measure out grain on the basis of those adjoining his.

If a seignior pointed the finger at a nun or the wife of a(nother) seignior, but has proved nothing, they shall drag that seignior into the presence of the judges and also cut off half his (hair).

If a seignior acquired a wife, but did not draw up the contracts for her, that woman is no wife.

If the wife of a seignior has been caught while lying with another man, they shall bind them and throw them into the water. If the husband of the woman wishes to spare his wife, then the king in turn may spare his subject.

If a seignior bound the (betrothed) wife of a(nother) seignior, who had had no intercourse with a male and was still living in her father's house, and he has lain in her bosom and they have caught him, that seignior shall be put to death, while that woman shall go free.

If a seignior's wife was accused by her husband, but she was not caught while lying with another man, she shall make affirmation by god and return to her house.

If the finger was pointed at the wife of a seignior because of another man, but she has not been caught while lying with the other man, she shall throw herself into the river for the sake of her husband.

If a seignior was taken captive, but there was sufficient to live on in his house, his wife [shall not leave her house, but she shall take care of her person by not] entering [the house of another].

If that woman did not take care of her person, but has entered the house of another, they shall prove it against that woman and throw her into the water.

If the seignior was taken captive and there was not sufficient to live on in his house, his wife may enter the house of another, with that woman incurring no blame at all.

If, when a seignior was taken captive and there was not sufficient to live on in his house, his wife has then entered the house of another before his (return) and has borne children, (and) later her husband has returned and has reached his city, that woman shall return to her first husband, while the children shall go with their father.

If, when a seignior deserted his city and then ran away, his wife has entered the house of another after his (departure), if that seignior has returned and wishes to take back his wife, the wife of the fugitive shall not return to her husband because he scorned his city and ran away.

If a seignior wishes to divorce his wife who did not bear him children, he shall give her money to the full amount of her marriage-price and he shall also make good to her the dowry which she brought from her father's house and then he may divorce her.

If there was no marriage-price, he shall give her one mina of silver as the divorce-settlement.

If he is a peasant, he shall give her one-third mina of silver.

If a seignior's wife, who was living in the house of the seignior, has made up her mind to leave in order that she may engage in business, thus neglecting her house (and) humiliating her husband, they shall prove it against her; and if her husband has then decided on her divorce, he may divorce her, with nothing to be given her as her divorce-settlement upon her departure. If her husband has not decided on her divorce, her husband may marry another woman, with the former woman living in the house of her husband like a maidservant.

If a woman so hated her husband that she has declared, 'You may not have me," her record shall be investigated at her city council, and if she was careful and was not at fault, even though her husband has been going out and disparaging her greatly, that woman, without incurring any blame at all, may take her dowry and go off to her father's house.

If she was not careful, but was a gadabout, thus neglecting her house (and) humiliating her husband, they shall throw that woman into the water.

If a seignior's wife has brought about the death of her husband because of another man, they shall impale that woman on stakes.

If a seignior has had intercourse with his daughter, they shall make that seignior leave the city.

If a seignior chose a bride for his son and his son had intercourse with her, but later he himself has lain in her bosom and they have caught him, they shall bind that seignior and throw him into the water.

If a seignior chose a bride for his son and his son did not have intercourse with her, but he himself has lain in her bosom, he shall pay to her one-half mina of silver and he shall also make good to her whatever she brought from her father's house in order that the man of her choice may marry her.

If a seignior has lain in the bosom of his mother after (the death of) his father, they shall bum both of them.

If a son has struck his father, they shall cut off his hand.

If a seignior has destroyed the eye of a member of the aristocracy, they shall destroy his eye.

If he has broken a(nother) seignior's bone, they shall break his bone.

If he has destroyed the eye of a commoner or broken the bone of a commoner, he shall pay one mina of silver.

If he has destroyed the eye of a seignior's slave or broken the bone of a seignior's slave, he shall pay one-half his value.

Study Questions

1. Many ancient law codes were transmitted orally, through memorization. What are some advantages of a written legal code? Can you think of some disadvantages?

2. The areas of society that are regulated often indicate something about what is important to those who make the laws. What seem to be the main concerns of this law code?

3. Does the code make distinctions among people? Are some more important than others? How are people of different status dealt with under the law?

4. The penalties for breaking the law in Babylon were often very harsh. Why do you think the code was so severe?

The Book of the Dead (ca. 16th century B.C.E.)   6

The Book of the Dead is a collection of spells and prayers that the Egyptians believed were crucial to well-being in the afterlife. Composed of some two hundred chapters, it contains charms from as early as 2400 B.C.E. as well as more recent incantations. Sometime in the sixteenth century B.C.E. anonymous priests and scribes collected the chapters into a single volume. Many copies of the book have been found in tombs and burial chambers where they were presumably placed for the use of the dead. They were copied on papyrus rolls and some of the surviving ones are elaborately illustrated.

The following selection is an incantation meant to prepare the deceased for the judgment of the gods. The chant provides much direct evidence of the manners and values of everyday life in ancient Egypt.

The Protestation of Guiltlessness

What is said on reaching the Broad-Hall of the Two Justices, absolving *X* of every sin which he has committed, and seeing the faces of the gods:

Hail to thee, O great god, lord of the Two Justices! I have come to thee, my lord, I have been brought that I might see thy beauty. I know thee; I know thy name and the names of the forty-two gods who are with thee in the Broad-Hall of the Two Justices, who live on them who preserve evil and who drink their blood on that day of reckoning up character in the presence of Wenofer. Behold, "Sati-mertifi, Lord of Justice," is thy name. I have come to thee; I have brought thee justice; I have expelled deceit for thee.

I have not committed evil against men.

I have not mistreated cattle.

I have not blasphemed a god.

I have not done violence to a poor man.

I have not done that which the gods abominate.

I have not defamed a slave to his superior.

I have not made (anyone) sick.

I have not made (anyone) weep.

I have not killed.

I have given no order to a killer.

I have not caused anyone suffering.

I have not cut down on the food-(income) in the temples.

I have not damaged the bread of the gods.

I have not taken the loaves of the blessed (dead).

Egyptian Female Musicians. This New Kingdom tomb painting shows a group of musicians in graceful poses. The three women are carefully individualized and supple in rendition. Their hand gestures and head positions lend a distinct expressiveness to the whole composition.

I have not had sexual relations with a boy.

I have not defiled myself.

I have neither increased or diminished the grain-measure.

I have not taken milk from the mouths of children.

I have not driven cattle away from their pasturage.

I have not snared the birds of the gods.

I have not caught fish in their marshes.

I have not held up the water in its season.

I have not built a dam against running water.

I have not driven away the cattle of the god's property.

I have not stopped a god on his procession.

I am pure! My purity is the purity of the great benu-bird which is in Herakleopolis, because I am really that nose of the Lord of Breath, who makes all men to live, on that day of filling out the Eye (of Horus) in Heliopolis, in the second month of the second season, the last day, in the presence of the lord of this land. I am the one who has seen the filling out of the Eye in Heliopolis. Evil will never happen to me in this land or in this Broad-Hall of the Two justices, because I know the names of these gods who are in it, the followers of the great god.

O Wide-of-Stride, who comes forth from Heliopolis. I have not committed evil.

O Embracer-of-Fire, who comes forth from Babylon, I have not stolen.

O Nosey, who comes forth from Hermopolis, I have not been covetous.

O Swallower-of-Shadows, who comes forth from the pit, I have not robbed.

O Dangerous-of-Face, who came forth from Rostau, I have not killed men.

O Ruti, who comes forth from heaven, I have not damaged the grain-measure.

O Flamer, who comes forth backward, I have not stolen the property of a god.

O Breaker-of-Bones, who comes forth from Herakleopolis, I have not told lies.

O Commander-of-Fire, who comes forth from Memphis, I have not taken away food.

O Dweller-in-the-Pit, who comes forth from the west, I have not been contentious.

O White-of-Teeth, who comes forth from the Faiyum, I have not trespassed.

O Eater-of-Blood, who comes forth from the execution-block, I have not slain the cattle of the god.

O Eater-of-Entrails, who comes forth from the Thirty, I have not practised usury.

O Lord-of-Justice, who comes forth from Ma'ati, I have not stolen the bread-ration.

O Wanderer, who comes forth from Bubastis, I have not gossiped.

O Djudju-serpent, who comes forth from Busiris, I have not argued with some one summoned because of his property.

O Wamemti-serpent, who comes forth from the place of judgment, I have not committed adultery.

O Superior-of-the-Nobles, who comes forth from Imau, I have not caused terror.

O Wrecker, who comes forth from the Saite Nome, I have not trespassed.

O Mischief-Maker, who comes forth from the sanctuary, I have not been (over)heated.

O Child, who comes forth from the Heliopolitan Nome, I have not been unresponsive to a matter of justice.

O Ser-kheru, who comes forth from Wensi, I have not been quarrelsome.

O Dark-One, who comes forth from the darkness, I have not been abusive.

O Bringer-of-His-Peace, who comes forth from Sais, I have not been (over)-energetic.

O Lord-of-Faces, who comes forth from the Heroonpolite Nome, my heart has not been hasty.

O Tern-sep, who comes forth from Busiris, I have not been abusive against a king.

O Acting-with-His-Heart, who comes forth from Tjebu, I have not waded in water.

O Flowing-One, who comes forth from Nun, my voice has not been loud.

O Commander-of-the-People, who comes forth from his shrine, I have not been abusive against a god.

O In-af serpent, who comes forth from the cemetery, I have not blasphemed against my local god.

Words to be spoken by X:

Hail to you, ye gods who are in this Broad-Hall of the Two Justices! I know you; I know your names. I shall not fall for dread of you. Ye have not reported guilt of mine up to this god in whose retinue ye are; no deed of mine has come from you. Ye have spoken truth about me in the presence of the All-Lord, because I acted justly in Egypt.

Hail to you who are in the Broad-Hall of the Two Justices, who have no deceit in your bodies, who live on truth and who eat of truth in the presence of Horus, who is in his sun disc. May ye rescue me from Babi, who lives on the entrails of elders on that day of the great reckoning. Behold me—I have come to you without sin, without guilt, without evil, without a witness (against me), without one against whom I have taken action. I live on truth, and I eat of truth. I have done that which men said and that with which gods are content. I have satisfied a god with that which he desires. I have given bread to the hungry, water to the thirsty, clothing to the naked, and a ferry-boat to him who was marooned. I have provided divine offerings for the gods and mortuary offerings for the dead. (So) rescue me, you; protect me, you. Ye will not make report against me in the presence [of the great god.] I am one pure of mouth and pure of hands, one to whom "Welcome, welcome, in peace!" is said by those who see him. I am one who has a concern for the gods, who knows the nature of their bodies. I have come here to testify to justice and to bring the scales to their (proper) position in the cemetery.

O thou who art high upon his standard, Lord of the Atef-Crown, whose name has been made "Lord of Breath," mayest thou rescue me from thy messengers who give forth uncleanliness and create destruction, who have no covering up of their faces, because I have effected justice for the Lord of Justice, being pure—my front is pure, my rear is clean, my middle is in the flowing water of justice; there is no part of me free of justice....

Instructions for the Use of the Spell

To be done in conformance with what takes place in this Broad-Hall of the Two Justices. This spell is to be recited when one is clean and pure, clothed in (fresh) garments, shod with white sandals, painted with stibium, and anointed with myrrh, to whom cattle, fowl, incense, bread, beer, vegetables have been offered. Then make thou this text in writing on a clean pavement with ochre smeared with earth upon which pigs and (other) small cattle have not trodden. As for him on whose behalf this book is made, he shall be prosperous and his children shall be prosperous, without greed, because he shall be a trusted man of the king and his courtiers. Loaves, jars, bread, and joints of meat shall be given to him from the altar of the great god. He cannot be held back at any door of the west, (but) he shall be ushered in with the Kings of Upper and Lower Egypt, and he shall be in the retinue of Osiris.

Right and true a million times.

Study Questions

1. Passing into the afterlife was not easy. What hurdles did the dead face before reaching safety?

2. Egyptian society obviously had a very well-developed sense of right and wrong. What kinds of things should a righteous person do? What are some of the sins a person might commit?

3. In what ways do Egyptian ideas of right and wrong resemble our own? How are they different?

4. *The Book of the Dead* was clearly thought to be a very important means to everlasting life by contemporary Egyptians, who often brought it with them to the tomb. How could it also have been useful for the living?

Instructions in Letter Writing by an Egyptian Scribe (c. 1200 B.C.E.)

7

ANONYMOUS

We now know so much about ancient Egypt because the Egyptians developed a system of writing, which they used for personal and public business as well as for religious purposes. They also discovered an ideal medium for recording their thoughts, for the marsh grass that surrounded them could be processed into papyrus, a relatively inexpensive and quite durable form of paper. These developments made the Egyptians place particular emphasis on scribes.

Gaining the necessary skills and education for this profession, however, was not easy, since it required years of assiduous training. In the following selection from a surviving papyri, a teacher rebukes a promising student for his failure to take his studies seriously. In addition to outlining the inherent merits of being a scribe, the teacher also reviews the other possible professions that the failing student might be forced to adopt if he is not fortunate enough to enjoy the lifestyle of a scribe.

Young fellow, how conceited you are! You do not listen when I speak. Your heart is denser than a great obelisk, a hundred cubits high, ten cubits thick.

But though I beat you with every kind of stick, you do not listen. If I knew another way of doing it, I would do it for you, that you might listen. You are a person fit for writing, though you have not yet known a woman. Your heart discerns, your fingers are skilled, your mouth is apt for reciting

You are worse than the goose of the shore, that is busy with mischief. It spends the summer destroying the dates, the winter destroying the seed-grain. It spends the balance of the year in pursuit of the cultivators.

You are worse than the desert antelope that lives by running. It spends no day in plowing. Never at all does it tread on the threshing-floor. It lives on the oxen's labor, without entering among them. But though I spend the day telling you "Write," it seems like a plague to you. Writing is very pleasant!

See for yourself with your own eye. The occupations lie before you.

The washerman's day is going up, going down. All his limbs are weak, <from > whitening his neighbors' clothes every day, from washing their linen.

The maker of pots is smeared with soil, like one whose relations have died. His hands, his feet are full of clay; he is like one who lives in the bog.

The cobbler mingles with vats. His odor is penetrating. His hands are red with madder, like one who is smeared with blood. He looks behind him for the kite, like one whose flesh is exposed.

The watchman prepares garlands and polishes vase-stands. He spends a night of toil just as one on whom the sun shines.

The merchants travel downstream and upstream. They are as busy as can be, carrying goods from one town to another. They supply him who has wants. But the tax collectors carry off the gold, that most precious of metals.

The ships' crews from every house (of commerce), they receive their loads. They depart from Egypt for Syria, and each man's god is with him. (But) not one of them says: "We shall see Egypt again!"

The carpenter who is in the shipyard carries the timber and stacks it. If he gives today the output of yesterday, woe to his limbs! The shipwright stands behind him to tell him evil things.

His outworker who is in the fields, his is the toughest of all the jobs. He spends the day loaded with his tools, tied to his tool-box. When he returns home at night, he is loaded with the tool-box and the timbers, his drinking mug, and his whetstones.

The scribe, he alone, records the output of all of them. Take note of it!

Let me also expound to you the situation of the peasant, that other tough occupation. [Comes] the inundation and soaks him—, he attends to his equipment. By day he cuts his farming tools; by night he twists rope. Even his midday hour he spends on farm labor. He equips himself to go to the field as if he were a warrior. The dried field lies before him; he goes out to get his team. When he has been after the herdsman for many days, he gets his team and comes back with it. He makes for it a place in the field. Comes dawn, he goes to make a start and does not find it in its place. He spends three days searching for it; he finds it in the bog. He finds no hides on them; the jackals have chewed them. He comes out, his garment in his hand, to beg for himself a team.

When he reaches his field he finds <it> 'broken up'. He spends time cultivating, and the snake is after him. It finishes off the seed as it is cast to the ground. He does not see a green blade. He does three plowings with borrowed grain. His wife has gone down to the merchants and found nothing for 'barter'. Now the scribe lands on the shore. He surveys the harvest. Attendants are behind him with staffs, Nubians with clubs. One says (to him): "Give grain." "There is none." He is beaten savagely. He is bound, thrown in the well, submerged head down. His wife is bound in his presence. His children are in fetters. His neighbors abandon them and flee. When it's over, there's no grain.

If you have any sense, be a scribe. if you have learned about the peasant, you will not be able to be one. Take note of it!

The scribe of the army and commander of the cattle of the house of Amun, Nebmare-nakht, speaks to the scribe Wenemdiamun, as follows. Be a scribe! Your body will be sleek; your hand will be soft. You will not flicker like a flame, like one whose body is feeble. For there is not the bone of a man in you. You are tall and thin. If you lifted a load to carry it, you would stagger, your legs would tremble. You are lacking in strength; you are weak in all your limbs; you are poor in body.

Set your sight on being a scribe; a fine profession that suits you. You call for one; a thousand answer you. You stride freely on the road.

You will not be like a hired ox. You are in front of others.

I spend the day instructing you. You do not listen! Your heart is like an <empty > room. My teachings are not in it. Take their ('meaning') to yourself!

The marsh thicket is before you each day, as a nestling is after its mother. You follow the path of pleasure; you make friends with revellers. You have made your home in the brewery, as one who thirsts for beer. You sit in the parlor with an idler. You hold the writings in contempt. You visit the whore. Do not do these things! What are they for? They are of no use. Take note of it!

Furthermore. Look, I instruct you to make you sound; to make you hold the palette freely. To make you become one whom the king trusts; to make you gain entrance to treasury and granary. To make you receive the ship-load at the gate of the granary. To make you issue the offerings on feast days. You are dressed in fine clothes; you own horses. Your boat is on the river; you are supplied with attendants. You stride about inspecting. A mansion is built in your town. You have a powerful office, given you by the king. Male and female slaves are about you. Those who are in the fields grasp your hand, on plots that you have made. Look, I make you into a staff of life! Put the writings in your heart, and you will be protected from all kinds of toil. You will become a worthy official.

Do you not recall the (fate of) the unskilled man? His name is not known. He is ever burdened < like an ass carrying > in front of the scribe who knows what he is about.

Come, <let me tell you> the woes of the soldier, and how many are his superiors: the general, the troop-commander, the officer who leads, the standard-bearer, the lieutenant, the scribe, the commander of fifty, and the garrison-captain. They go in and out in the halls of the palace, saying: "Get laborers!" He is awakened at any hour. One is after him as (after) a donkey. He toils until the Aten sets in his darkness of night. He is hungry, his belly hurts; he is dead while yet alive. When he receives the grain-ration, having been released from duty, it is not good for grinding.

He is called up for Syria. He may not rest. There are no clothes, no sandals. The weapons of war are assembled at the fortress of Sile. His march is uphill through mountains. He drinks water every third day; it is smelly and tastes of salt. His body is ravaged by illness. The enemy comes, surrounds him with missiles, and life recedes from him. He is told: "Quick, forward, valiant soldier! Win for yourself a good name!" He does not know what he is about. His body is weak, his legs fail him. When victory is won, the captives are handed over to his majesty, to be taken to Egypt. The foreign woman faints on the march; she hangs herself <on> the soldier's neck. His knapsack drops, another grabs it while he is burdened with the woman. His wife and children are in their village; he dies and does not reach it. If he comes out alive, he is worn out from marching. Be he at large, be he detained, the soldier suffers. If he leaps and joins the deserters, all his people are imprisoned. He dies on the edge of the dcsert, and there is none to perpetuate his name. He suffers in death as in life. A big sack is brought for him; he does not know his resting place.

Be a scribe, and be spared from soldiering! You call and one says: "Here I am." You are safe from torments. Every man seeks to raise himself up. Take note of it!

Study Questions

1. What were the material rewards of an ancient Egyptian scribe?

2. What are the drawbacks of attempting to win fame and fortune on the battle-field?

3. Use this discussion of different professions to describe the ancient Egyptian economy and its social structure.

4. Compose a modem version of this teacher's exhortation.

The Book of Exodus (ca. 10th–6th century B.C.E.)   8

The Book of Exodus is the second book of the Old Testament as well as the second book of the Hebrew Torah. It was probably composed between the tenth and sixth centuries B.C.E. Exodus tells the story of the enslavement of the Hebrew people at the hands of the Egyptians, of their liberation under the leadership of Moses, and of their journey into the promised land. The central actions are the confrontation between Moses and the pharaoh and God's deliverance of the Hebrews across the Red Sea. Much of the story takes place during the 40 years when the Hebrews wandered in the desert and when a nation was forged through tribulation. On Mount Sinai, Moses received the Ten Commandments, the foundation of Judeo-Christian ethics.

On the third new moon after the people of Israel had gone forth out of the land of Egypt, on that day they came into the wilderness of Sinai.

And when they set out from Rephidim and came into the wilderness of Sinai, they encamped in the wilderness; and there Israel encamped before the mountain. And Moses went up to God, and the Lord called to him out of the mountain, saying, "Thus you shall say to the house of Jacob, and tell the people of Israel; You have seen what I did to the Egyptians, and how I bore you on eagles' wings and brought you to myself. Now therefore, if you will obey my voice and keep my covenant, you shall be my own possession among all peoples; for all the earth is mine, and you shall be to me a kingdom of priests and a holy nation. These are the words which you shall speak to the children of Israel."

So Moses came and called the elders of the people, and set before them all these words which the Lord had commanded him. And all the people answered together and said, "All that the Lord has spoken we will do." And Moses reported the words of the people to the Lord. And the Lord said to Moses, "Lo, I am coming to you in a thick cloud, that the people may hear when I speak with you, and may also believe you for ever."

On the morning of the third day there were thunders and lightnings, and a thick cloud upon the mountain, and a very loud trumpet blast, so that all the people who were in the camp trembled. Then Moses brought the people out of the camp to meet God; and they took their stand at the foot of the mountain. And Mount Sinai was wrapped in smoke, because the Lord descended upon it in fire; and the smoke of it went up like the smoke of a kiln, and the whole mountain quaked greatly. And as the sound of the trumpet grew louder and louder, Moses spoke, and God answered him in thunder. And the Lord came down upon Mount Sinai, to the top of the mountain;

and the Lord called Moses to the top of the mountain, and Moses went up. And the Lord said to Moses, "Go down and warn the people, lest they break through to the Lord to gaze and many of them perish. And also let the priests who come near to the Lord consecrate themselves, lest the Lord break out upon them."

And Moses said to the Lord, "The people cannot come up to Mount Sinai; for thou thyself didst charge us, saying, 'Set bounds about the mountain, and consecrate it.' "And the Lord said to him, "Go down, and come up bringing Aaron with you; but do not let the priests and the people break through to come up to the Lord, lest he break out against them." So Moses went down to the people and told them.

And God spoke all these words, saying,

"I am the Lord your God, who brought you out of the land of Egypt, out of the house of bondage.

"You shall have no other gods before me.

"You shall not make for yourself a graven image, or any likeness of anything that is in heaven above, or that is in the earth beneath, or that is in the water under the earth; you shall not bow down to them or serve them; for I the Lord your God am a jealous God, visiting the iniquity of the fathers upon the children to the third and the fourth generation of those who hate me, but showing steadfast love to thousands of those who love me and keep my commandments.

"You shall not take the name of the Lord your God in vain; for the Lord will not hold him guiltless who takes his name in vain.

"Remember the sabbath day, to keep it holy. Six days you shall labor, and do all your work; but the seventh day is a sabbath to the Lord your God; in it you shall not do any work, you, or your son, or your daughter, your manservant, or your maidservant, or your cattle, or the sojourner who is within your gates; for in six days the Lord made heaven and earth, the sea, and all that is in them, and rested the seventh day; therefore the Lord blessed the sabbath day and hallowed it.

"Honor your father and your mother, that your days may be long in the land which the Lord your God gives you.

"You shall not kill.

"You shall not commit adultery.

'You shall not steal.

"You shall not bear false witness against your neighbor.

"You shall not covet your neighbor's house; you shall not covet your neighbor's wife, or his manservant, or his maidservant, or his ox, or his ass, or anything that is your neighbor's."

Now when all the people perceived the thunderings and the lightnings and the sound of the trumpet and the mountain smoking, the people were afraid and trembled; and they stood afar off, and said to Moses, "You speak to us, and we will hear; but let not God speak to us, lest we die." And Moses said to the people, "Do not fear; for God has come to prove you, and that the fear of him may be before your eyes, that you may not sin."

And the people stood afar off, while Moses drew near to the thick darkness where God was. And the Lord said to Moses, "Thus you shall say to the people of Israel: 'You have seen for yourselves that I have talked with you from heaven. You shall not make gods of silver to be with me, nor shall you make for yourselves gods of gold. "

When the people saw that Moses delayed to come down from the mountain, the people gathered themselves together to Aaron, and said to him, 'Up, make us gods, who shall go before us; as for this Moses, the man who brought us up out of the land of Egypt, we do not know what has become of him." And Aaron said to them, "Take off the rings of gold which are in the ears of your wives, your sons, and your daughters, and bring them to me." So all the people took off the rings of gold which were in their ears, and brought them to Aaron. And he received the gold at their hand, and

fashioned it with a graving tool, and made a molten calf; and they said, "These are your gods, O Israel, who brought you up out of the land of Egypt!" When Aaron saw this, he built an altar before it; and Aaron made proclamation and said, "Tomorrow shall be a feast to the Lord."

And they rose up early on the morrow, and offered burnt offerings and brought peace offerings; and the people sat down to eat and drink, and rose up to play.

And the Lord said to Moses, "Go down; for your people, whom you brought up out of the land of Egypt, have corrupted themselves; they have turned aside quickly out of the way which I commanded them; they have made for themselves a molten calf, and have worshiped it and sacrificed to it, and said, 'These are your gods, O Israel, who brought you up out of the land of Egypt!' " And the Lord said to Moses, "I have seen this people, and behold, it is a stiffnecked people; now therefore let me alone, that my wrath may burn hot against them and I may consume them; but of you I will make a great nation."

But Moses besought the Lord his God, and said, "O Lord, why does thy wrath burn hot against thy people, whom thou has brought forth out of the land of Egypt with great power and with a mighty hand? Why should the Egyptians say, 'With evil intent did he bring them forth, to slay them in the mountains, and to consume them from the face of the earth'? Turn from thy fierce wrath, and repent of this evil against thy people. Remember Abraham, Isaac, and Israel, thy servants, to whom thou didst swear by thine own self, and didst say to them, 'I will multiply your descendants as the stars of heaven, and all this land that I have promised I will give to your descendants, and they shall inherit it for ever.' "d the Lord repented of the evil which he thought to do to his people.

And Moses turned, and went down from the mountain with the two tables of the testimony in his hands, tables that were written on both sides; on the one side and on the other were they written. And the tables were the work of God, and the writing was the writing of God, graven upon the tables.

When Joshua heard the noise of the people as they shouted, he said to Moses, "There is a noise of war in the camp." But he said, "It is not the sound of shouting for victory, or the sound of the cry of defeat, but the sound of singing that I hear." And as soon as he came near the camp and saw the calf and the dancing, Moses' anger burned hot, and he threw the tables out of his hands and broke them at the foot of the mountain. And he took the calf which they had made, and burnt it with fire, and ground it to powder, and scattered it upon the water, and made the people of Israel drink it.

On the morrow Moses said to the people, "You have sinned a great sin. And now I will go up to the Lord; perhaps I can make atonement for your sin." So Moses returned to the Lord and said, "Alas, this people have sinned a great sin; they have made for themselves gods of gold. But now, if thou wilt forgive their sin— and if not, blot me, I pray thee, out of thy book which thou hast written." But the Lord said to Moses, "Whoever has sinned against me, him will I blot out of my book. But now go, lead the people to the place of which I have spoken to you; behold, my angel shall go before you. Nevertheless, in the day when I visit, I will visit their sin upon them."

And the Lord sent a plague upon the people, because they made the calf which Aaron made.

The Lord said to Moses, "Depart, go up hence, you and the people whom you have brought up out of the land of Egypt, to the land of which I swore to Abraham, Isaac, and Jacob, saying, 'To your descendants I will give it.' And I will send an angel before you, and I will drive out the Canaanites, the Amorites, the Hittites, the Per'izzites, the Hivites, and the Jeb'usites. Go up to a land flowing with milk and honey; but I will not go up among you, lest I consume you in the way, for you are a stiff-necked people."

When the people heard these evil tidings, they mourned; and no man put on his ornaments. For the Lord had said to Moses, "Say to the people of Israel, 'You are a stiff-necked people; if for a single moment I should go up among you, I would consume you. So now put off your ornaments from you, that I may know what to do with you.' " Therefore the people of Israel stripped themselves of their ornaments, from Mount Horeb onward.

Now Moses used to take the tent and pitch it outside the camp, far off from the camp; and he called it the tent of meeting. And every one who sought the Lord would go out to the tent of meeting, which was outside the camp. Whenever Moses went out to the tent, all the people rose up, and every man stood at his tent door, and looked after Moses, until he had gone into the tent. When Moses entered the tent, the pillar of cloud would descend and stand at the door of the tent, and the Lord would speak with Moses. And when all the people saw the pillar of cloud standing at the door of the tent, all the people would rise up and worship, every man at his tent door. Thus the Lord used to speak to Moses face to face, as a man speaks to his friend.

Study Questions

1. In the Book of Exodus, Moses is the main intermediary between God and the Hebrew people. How does he manage his task? What problems does he face?

2. What is the relationship between God and the Hebrews like? Is it a smooth one?

3. The Ten Commandments were the basis of Hebrew law and later were incorporated into Christian thought. They also had contemporary utility. In what ways could they be useful to a tribe of nomads?

4. How does the story told in Exodus create a sense of identity and purpose for the Hebrews?

5. How different is the Hebrews' view of their God from those of other Near Eastern cultures, such as the Mesopotamians or Egyptians? Do you see any similarities?

Archaic and Classical Greece

The Parthenon, Athens

The Iliad (9th–8th century B.C.E.)   **9**

HOMER

Homer is the name given to the composer of the two greatest epic poems in the Western tradition, *The Iliad* and *The Odyssey*. It appears that Homer lived in either the ninth or eighth century B.C.E., if evidence from the epics can be used to date the life of their author. The Homeric poems formed part of an oral tradition, sung by troubadours and passed from generation to generation, changed in the process of retelling. The characteristic meter of the verses undoubtedly aided memory. Homer, reputed to have been a blind poet, is credited with the composition of *The Iliad* and with being the inspiration behind *The Odyssey,* the story of the travels of the Greek warrior Odysseus. Both works were committed to written form and codified during the Hellenistic period of Greek history.

    The Iliad tells the story of the Greek siege of Troy (Ilion in Greek) after the abduction of Helen, wife of Menelaus, the king of Sparta. The central actors in the story are Achilles and Hector, the greatest Greek and Trojan warriors, respectively. The war serves as a backdrop for their personal confrontation, and the story ends with the resolution of their conflict. The values of Greek and Trojan society are readily identifiable in the final meeting between the two warriors, which the following excerpt describes.

The aged monarch Priam was the first
To see him as he scoured the plain, and shone
Like to the star which in the autumn time
Rises and glows among the lights of heaven
With eminent lustre at the dead of night—
Orion's Hound they call it—bright indeed,
And yet of baleful omen, for it brings
Distressing heat to miserable men.
So shone the brass upon the warrior's breast
As on he flew. The aged Priam groaned,
And smote his head with lifted hands, and called
    called
Aloud, imploring his beloved son,
Who eagerly before the city gate
Waited his foe Achilles. Priam thus,
With outstretched hands, besought him
    piteously:

"O wait not, Hector, my beloved son,
To combat with Pelides thus alone
And far from succor, lest thou meet thy death,
Slain by his hand, for he is mightier far
Than thou art. Would that he, the cruel one,
Were but as much the favorite of the gods
As he is mine! then should the birds of prey
And dogs devour his carcass, and the grief
That weighs upon my spirit would depart.
Come within the walls,
My son, that thou mayst still be the defence
Of Ilium's sons and daughters, nor increase
The glory of Pelides with the loss
Of thine own life. Have pity upon me,
Who only live to suffer—whom the son
Of Saturn, on the threshold of my age,
Hath destined to endure a thousand griefs,

And then to be destroyed—to see my sons
Slain by the sword, my daughters dragged away
Into captivity, their chambers made
A spoil, our infants dashed against the ground
By cruel hands, the consorts of my sons
Borne off by the ferocious Greeks....
So the old monarch spake, and with his hands
Tore his gray hair, but moved not Hector thus.
Then came, with lamentations and in tears,
The warrior's mother forward. One hand laid
Her bosom bare; she pressed the other hand
Beneath it, sobbed, and spake these winged
    words—
    "Revere this bosom, Hector, and on me
Have pity. If when thou wert but a babe
I ever on this bosom stilled thy cries,
Think of it now, beloved child; avoid
That dreadful chief; withdraw within the walls,
Nor madly think to encounter him alone,
Son of my love and of my womb! If he
Should slay thee, I shall not lament thy death
Above thy bier—I, nor thy noble wife—
But far from us the greedy dogs will throng
To mangle thee beside the Grecian fleet."
    Thus weeping bitterly, the aged pair
Entreated their dear son, yet moved him not.
He stood and waited for his mighty foe
Achilles, as a serpent at his den,
Fed on the poisons of the wild, awaits
The traveller, and, fierce with hate of man,
And glaring fearfully, lies coiled within.
So waited Hector with a resolute heart,
And kept his ground, and, leaning his bright
    shield
Against a tower that jutted from the walls,
Conferred with his great soul impatiently:
    "Ah me! if I should pass within the walls,
Then will Polydamas be first to cast
Reproach upon me; for he counselled me
To lead the Trojans back into the town
That fatal night which saw Achilles rise
To join the war again. I yielded not
To his advice; far better if I had.
Now, since my fatal stubbornness has brought
This ruin on my people, I most dread

The censure of the men and long-robed dames
Of Ilium. Men less brave than I will say,
'Foolhardy Hector in his pride has thrown
His people's lives away'. So they will speak,
And better were it for me to return,
Achilles slain, or, slain myself by him,
To perish for my country gloriously.
But should I lay aside this bossy shield
And this stout helm, and lean against the wall
This spear, and go to meet the gallant son
Of Peleus, with a promise to restore
Helen and all the treasure brought with her
To Troy by Paris, in his roomy ships—
All that the war was waged for—that the sons
Of Atreus may convey it hence, besides
Wealth drawn from all the hoards within the
    town,
And to be shared among the Greeks; for I
Would bind the Trojans by a solemn oath
To keep back nothing, but divide the whole—
Whate'er of riches this fair town contains
Into two parts. But why should I waste
    thought
On plans like these? I must not act the part
Of suppliant to a man who may not show
Regard or mercy, but may hew me down
Defenceless, with my armor laid aside
As if I were a woman. Not with him
May I hold parley from a tree or rock,
As youths and maidens with each other hold
Light converse. Better 't were to rush at once
To combat, and the sooner learn to whom
Olympian Jove decrees the victory."
    Such were his thoughts. Achilles now drew
    near.
Like crested Mars, the warrior-god, he came.
On his right shoulder quivered fearfully
The Pelian ash, and from his burnished mail
There streamed a light as of a blazing fire,
Or of the rising sun. When Hector saw,
He trembled, nor could venture to remain,
But left the gates and fled away in fear.
Pelides, trusting to his rapid feet,
Pursued him. As, among the mountain wilds,
A falcon, fleetest of the birds of air,

Darts toward a timid dove that wheels away
To shun him by a sidelong flight, while he
Springs after her again and yet again,
And screaming follows, certain of his prey,
Thus onward flew Achilles, while as fast
Fled Hector in dismay, with hurrying feet,
Beside the wall; ... one fled, and one pursued,
A brave man fled, a braver followed close,
And swiftly both. Not for a common prize,
A victim from the herd, a bullock's hide,
Such as reward the fleet of foot, they ran—
The race was for the knightly Hector's life.
As firm-paced coursers, that are wont to win,
Fly toward the goal, when some magnificent
    prize,
A tripod or a damsel, is proposed
In honor of some hero's obsequies.
So these flew thrice on rapid feet around
The city of Priam. All the gods of heaven
Looked on, and thus the Almighty Father
spake:
    "Alas! I see a hero dear to me
Pursued around the wall. My heart is grieved
For Hector, who has brought so many thighs
Of bullocks to my altar on the side
Of Ida ploughed with glens, or on the heights
Of Ilium. The renowned Achilles now
Is chasing him with rapid feet around
The city of Priam. Now bethink yourselves,
And answer. Shall we rescue him from death?
Or shall we doom him, valiant as he is,
To perish by the hand of Peleus' son?"
When the twain had come
For the fourth time beside Scamander's
    springs,
The All-Father raised the golden balance high,
And, placing in the scales two lots which bring
Death's long dark sleep—one lot for Peleus'
    son,
And one for knightly Hector—by the midst
He poised the balance. Hector's fate sank down
To Hades, and Apollo left the field.
And when the advancing-chiefs stood face to
    face,
The crested hero, Hector, thus began:
"No longer I avoid thee as of late,

O son of Peleus! Thrice around the walls
Of Priam's mighty city have I fled,
Nor dared to wait thy coming. Now my heart
Bids me encounter thee; my time is come
To slay or be slain. Now let us call
The gods to witness, who attest and guard
The covenants of men. Should Jove bestow
On me the victory, and I take thy life,
Thou shalt meet no dishonor at my hands;
But, stripping off the armor, I will send
The Greeks thy body. Do the like by me."
    The swift Achilles answered with a frown:
"Accursed Hector, never talk to me
Of covenants. Men and lions plight no faith,
Nor wolves agree with lambs, but each must
    plan
Evil against the other. So between
Thyself and me no compact can exist,
Or understood intent. First, one of us
Must fall and yield his life-blood to the god
Of battles. Summon all thy valor now.
A skilful spearman thou hast need to be,
And a bold warrior. There is no escape,
For now doth Pallas doom thee to be slain
By my good spear. Thou shalt repay to me
The evil thou hast done my countrymen,
My friends whom thou hast slaughtered in thy
    rage."
    He spake, and, brandishing his massive
        spear,
Hurled it at Hector, who beheld its aim
From where he stood. He stooped, and over
    him
The brazen weapon passed, and plunged to
    earth.
Unseen by royal Hector, Pallas went
And plucked it from the ground, and brought
    it back
And gave it to the hands of Peleus' son,
While Hector said to his illustrious foe:
    "Godlike Achilles, thou hast missed thy
        mark;
Nor hast thou learned my doom from Jupiter,
As thou pretendest. Thou art glib of tongue,
And cunningly thou orderest thy speech.
In hope that I who hear thee may forget

My might and valor. Think not I shall flee,
That thou mayst pierce my back; for thou shalt
     send
Thy spear, if God permit thee, through my
     breast
As I rush on thee. Now avoid in turn
My brazen weapon. Would that it might pass
Clean through thee, all its length! The tasks of
     war
For us of Troy were lighter for thy death,
Thou pest and deadly foe of all our race!"
     He spake, and brandishing his massive spear,
Hurled it, nor missed, but in the centre smote
The buckler of Pelides. Far away
It bounded from the brass, and he was vexed
To see that the swift weapon from his hand
Had flown in vain. He stood perplexed and sad;
No second spear had he. He called aloud
On the white-bucklered chief, Deiphobus,
To bring another: but that chief was far,
And Hector saw that it was so, and said:—
     "Ah me! the gods have summoned me to
          die.
My hour at last is come;
Yet not ingloriously or passively
I die, but first will do some valiant deed,
Of which mankind shall hear in after time."
     He spake, and drew the keen-edged sword
          that hung,
Massive and finely tempered, at his side,
And sprang—as when an eagle high in heaven,
Through the thick cloud, darts downward to
     the plain
To clutch some tender lamb or timid hare,
So Hector, brandishing that keen-edged sword,
Sprang forward, while Achilles opposite
Leaped toward him, all on fire with savage
     hate,
And holding his bright buckler, nobly wrought,
Before him. On his shining helmet waved
The fourfold crest; there tossed the golden
     tufts
With which the hand of Vulcan lavishly
Had decked it. As in the still hours of night
Hesper goes forth among the host of stars,
The fairest light of heaven, so brightly shone,

Brandished in the right hand of Peleus' son,
The spear's keen blade, as, confident to slay
The noble Hector, o'er his glorious form
His quick eye ran, exploring where to plant
The surest wound. The glittering mail of brass
Won from the slain Patroclus, guarded well
Each part, save only where the collar-bones
Divide the shoulder from the neck, and there
Appeared the throat, the spot where life is most
In peril. Through that part the noble son
Of Peleus drave his spear; it went quite through
The tender neck, and yet the brazen blade
Cleft not the windpipe, and the power to speak
Remained. The Trojan fell amid the dust,
And thus Achilles boasted o'er his fall:
     "Hector, when from the slain Patroclus thou
Didst strip his armor, little didst thou think
Of danger. Thou hadst then no fear of me,
Who was not near thee to avenge his death.
Fool! there was left within the roomy ships
A mightier one than he, who should come
     forth,
The avenger of his blood, to take thy life.
Foul dogs and birds of prey shall tear thy flesh;
The Greeks shall honor him with funeral rites."
     And then the crested Hector faintly said:
"I pray thee by thy life, and by thy knees,
And by thy parents, suffer not the dogs
To tear me at the galleys of the Greeks.
Accept abundant store of brass and gold,
Which gladly will my father and the queen,
My mother, give in ransom. Send to them
My body, that the warriors and the dames
Of Troy may light for me the funeral pile."
     The swift Achilles answered with a frown:
"Nay, by my knees entreat me not, thou cur,
Nor by my parents. I could even wish
My fury prompted me to cut thy flesh
In fragments, and devour it, such the wrong
That I have had from thee. There will be
     none
To drive away the dogs about thy head,
Not though thy Trojan friends should bring to
     me
Tenfold and twenty-fold the offered gifts,
And promise others, not though Priam, sprung

From Dardanus, should send thy weight in
    gold.
Thy mother shall not lay thee on thy bier,
To sorrow over thee whom she brought forth;
But dogs and birds of prey shall mangle thee."
And then the crested Hector, dying, said:
"I know thee, and too clearly I foresaw
I should not move thee, for thou hast a heart
Of iron. Yet reflect that for my sake

The anger of the gods may fall on thee,
When Paris and Apollo strike thee down,
Strong as thou art, before the Scaean gates."
Thus Hector spake, and straightway o'er him
    closed
The night of death; the soul forsook his limbs,
And flew to Hades, grieving for its fate—
So soon divorced from youth and youthful
    might.

Study Questions

1. What does *The Iliad* tell us about the Greek style of warfare?

2. What does *The Iliad* suggest to be the nature of the relations between city-states in Homer's time?

3. What role do the gods play in the lives of mortals? How closely involved are they in the outcome of the struggle between Hector and Achilles?

4. Judging from the story Horner tells, what might you say about the ideals of the Greek warrior? How do warriors behave?

Antigone (441 B.C.E.)   10

SOPHOCLES

Sophocles (ca. 496–406 B.C.E), the greatest of the ancient dramatists, lived an extraordinarily full life during the height of Athenian civilization. The son of a prosperous armor manufacturer, Sophocles was endowed with all the qualities most admired by the Greeks: good birth, wealth, a pleasing appearance, and creative skills, especially as a musician. Even as a teenager he was singled out by his peers, and he soon entered the service of the state. Ultimately he held high elective office as a treasurer, a military administrator, and a diplomat; but his fame rested upon his ability as a dramatist. In 468 B.C.E. he won the coveted award for the best playwright of the year, defeating Aeschylus, then the leading dramatist of the day. Sophocles won the award an astonishing 24 times, composing over 120 plays in the process. Only seven have come down to us, including the Oedipus trilogy.

Antigone displays Sophocles' remarkable talent for presenting drama through conflict. Antigone's dilemma clearly portrays the competing interests between family and state. The battle of wits between Antigone and King Creon gives us insight into the role of women in Greek society.

ANTIGONE. MESSENGERS.
ISMENE HAEMON.
CHORUS TIRESIAS.
CREON EURYDICE.

ANTIGONE. O kindred form of my own sister Ismene, knowest thou what of the ills which spring from Oedipus—what not—doth Jove yet accomplish to us in life? for there is nothing, either wretched or ruinous, or base and degrading which I have not beheld in your evils and mine. And now again, what is this proclamation which they say the ruler has just propounded to all the people of the city? Knowest thou? and hast thou heard aught? or do the injuries of enemies advancing against friends escape thee?

ISMENE. To me indeed, Antigone, no tidings of friends, either sweet or sorrowful, have come from the time that we two were bereft of two brothers, dying on the same day by a twin slaughter: and since the army of the Argives has disappeared during this night, I know nothing farther, whether I fare better or am more afflicted.

ANTIGONE. I knew it well; and therefore have I brought thee without the gates of the courts, that you might hear alone.

ISMENE. But what is it? for you appear stirred at some tidings.

ANTIGONE. For has not Creon distinguished one of our brothers with burial rites, but deprived the other of this honor? Eteocles, indeed, as they say, acting upon the rights of justice and law, he has intombed beneath the earth, honorable to the gods below; but the corpse of Polynices, which wretchedly fell, they say it has been proclaimed to the citizens that no one shall inclose in the tomb, nor wail over, but leave it unlamented and unburied, a sweet store for birds greedily eyeing the delight of the banquet. Such things they say that the good Creon has proclaimed to you and me, for I say even me, and that he is coming hither to herald them clearly forth to those who do not know them, and to bid them consider the matter not as a thing of nought, but whosoever shall do one of those things, that a death by the stoning of the people is decreed him in the city. Thus rests this case to you, and you will quickly show whether you have been born of generous spirit, or degenerate from the good.

ISMENE. But what, oh wretched woman! if these things are in this state, what could I avail, loosing or binding?

ANTIGONE. Consider if thou wilt labor along with me, and assist me in the work.

ISMENE. In what sort of hazard? Where possibly are you in thought?

ANTIGONE. If you will raise up along with this hand the dead body.

ISMENE. For do you design to bury him, a thing forbidden by the state?

ANTIGONE. Yes, him who is at all events my brother; and yours, though you wish it not; for I will not be caught betraying him.

ISMENE. Oh daring woman! when Creon has forbidden?

ANTIGONE. But he has no business to put a barrier betwixt me and mine.

ISMENE. Ah me! consider, oh sister! how our father perished in odium and infamy, having, upon his self-detected guilt, himself torn out both his eyes with self-destroying hand; then his mother and wife, a double title, mars her life by the suspended cords; and third, the two wretched brothers, slaying themselves on the same day, wrought their mutual death each by a brother's hand. And now we two, being left alone, consider by how much the worst of all we shall perish, if, in violation of the law, we transgress the decree or power of superiors. But it behooves us, indeed, to reflect, in the first place, that we are by nature women, so as not able to contend against men; and then, since we are ruled by those most powerful, to submit to these things, and things still more painful than these. I then, indeed, asking those below the earth to forgive me, since I am constrained to this, will obey those who walk in office; for to attempt those things beyond our power implies no wisdom.

ANTIGONE. Neither will I request you, nor though you now wish to do it, should you act along with me, at least with my goodwill. But be of such a character as seems good to you; but I will bury him: it were glorious to me, doing this,—to die. I beloved will lie with him with him I love, having audaciously done what is holy; since the time is longer which it behooves me to please those below than those here; for there I shall ever lie. But if it seems good to you, do you hold in dishonor those things which are honored of the gods.

CREON. You, you bending your head to the ground, do you confess or do you deny having done this?

ANTIGONE. I both confess I did it, and I do not deny that I did not.

CREON. You may take yourself off where you please, free from the heavy charge. But do you tell me not at length, but briefly, did you know the proclamation forbidding this?

ANTIGONE. I knew it. And why should I not? for it was plain.

CREON. And have you dared then to transgress these laws?

ANTIGONE. For it was not Jove who heralded these commands, nor Justice, that dwells with the gods below the earth, who established these laws among men; nor did I think your proclamations had so much power so as being a mortal to transgress the unwritten and immovable laws of the gods. For not now, at least, or of yesterday, but eternally they live, and no one knows from what time they had their being. I was not going through fear of the spirit of any man to pay the penalty of their violation to the gods. For I knew I must die (and why not?), even though you had not proclaimed it, and if I die before my day I account it gain; for whosoever lives like me in many sorrows, how does not he by death obtain advantage? Thus to me, at least, to meet with this fate, the sorrow is nothing; but if I had suffered him who was born of my mother to lie in death an unburied corpse, in that case I would have sorrowed: in this I sorrow not. But if I seem to you now to happen to do what is foolish, I merely incur the imputation of folly from a fool.

CHORUS. The spirit of the daughter shows itself stern from a stern father, and she knows not to yield to misfortune.

CREON. But know in truth that too stem spirits bend the most; and you will most frequently see the hardest steel, forged in the fire till brittle, shivered and broken; and I have known high-mettled horses discipline by a small bit; for it is not right for him to have proud thoughts whosoever is the slave of others. She indeed then first learned to be guilty if insolence, transgressing the ordained laws; and this, when she had done it, is the second insult, to glory in such deeds, and to laugh having done them. In sooth, then, I am no man, but she a man, if this victory shall accrue to her without hurt. But whether she be sprung from my sister, or one more near of blood than all beneath the protection of our household god, she and her sister shall not escape the most wretched fate; for I charge her equally with having planned the measures respecting this burial. And summon her; for just now I saw her within raving, not possessed of her senses; and the mind of those who unjustly devise any thing in the dark, is wont to be prematurely detected in its fraud. I indeed at least hate when any one, discovered in guilt, may then wish to gloss it over.

ANTIGONE. Do you wish any thing more than taking me to put me to death?

CREON. I indeed wish nothing more. Having this I have all.

ANTIGONE. Why in truth do you delay? since to me none of your words are pleasing, nor may they ever be pleasing; and in like manner also, to you mine are naturally displeasing.

And yet whence could I have gained a glory of higher renown than by laying my own brother in the tomb? It would be said that this was approved of by all these, did not fear seal their tongues. But regal power is fortunate in many other things, and in this, that it is allowed to say and to do what it pleases.

CHORUS. Having advanced to the extreme of audacity, thou hast violently dashed, my child, against the lofty throne of justice. Thou payest some penalty of thy father.

ANTIGONE. Thou hast touched on a thought most painful to me, the thrice-renowned griefs of my father, and the fate of all our race, the illustrious children of Labdacus. Woe! for the curses that attended my mother's bed, the incestuous connection of my wretched mother with my father, from which I, unhappy, formerly sprung! and now accurst, unblessed by nuptials, I go to sojourn with my parents. O my brother! having met with an ill-fated marriage, dying, thou hast destroyed me, yet in life.

CHORUS. To act reverently is an act of piety; but power, to whomsoever power is intrusted, must not in any way be transgressed. Thy self-willed temper has destroyed thee.

ANTIGONE. Unwept, and friendless, and unwedded, I, wretched, am conducted on this destined way. It is no longer allowed me, unhappy, to look on this luminary's sacred eye; and no friend mourns mine unwept doom.

CREON. Know ye not that no one would cease from dirges and wailings before death, if it were of avail to utter them? Will ye not lead her as quickly as possible, having inclosed her, as I directed, in the caverned tomb, leave her by herself alone, whether it is fated she shall die or lead a life entombed in such a dwelling. For we are free from pollution as respects this virgin, but, at all events, she shall be deprived of abode above.

ANTIGONE. O tomb! O bridal chamber! O excavated, ever-guarded dwelling! where I go to mine own, of whom now perished Proserpine has received the greatest number among the dead, and of whom I descend the last, and by a fate far the most wretched, before having fulfilled my term of life! Departing, however, I strongly cherish in my hope that I shall come dear to my father, and dear to thee, my mother, and dear to thee, O brother dear; since I, with my own hand, washed you when dead, and decked you out, and poured the libations over your tomb; and now, Polynices, having buried your body, I gain such a reward. And yet, in opinion of those who have just sentiments, I honored you aright. For neither, though I had been the mother of children, nor though my husband dying, had mouldered away, would I have undertaken this toil against the will of the citizens. On account of what law do I say this? There would have been another husband for me if the first died, and if I lost my child there would have been another from another man! but my father and my mother being laid in the grave, it is impossible a brother should ever be born to me. On the principle of such a law, having preferred you, my brother, to all other considerations, I seemed to Creon to commit a sin, and to dare what was dreadful. And now, seizing me by force, he thus leads me away, having never enjoyed the nuptial bed, nor heard the nuptial lay, nor having gained the lot of marriage, nor of rearing my children; but, thus I, an unhappy woman, deserted by my friends, go, while alive, to the cavern of the dead. Having transgressed what justice of the gods? what need is there for me, a miserable wretch, to look any longer to the gods? What ally can I invoke, since at least by observing piety I have obtained the reward of impiety? But if these things are good among the gods, suffering, we may be made conscious of our error; but if my enemies be guilty, may they not suffer more evils than they unjustly inflict on me.

Study Questions

1. How do the interests of the state and the family clash in *Antigone?* Which is vindicated in the end?

2. Antigone and Ismene, though sisters, have different views of their duties as women and subjects of Creon. How do they differ?

3. *Antigone* is about kingship and politics as much as about family; what does the drama reveal about the nature of kings and governments?

4. What might you say about the position of women in ancient Greece from your reading of *Antigone?*

5. Using Antigone herself as a model, what would you say are the qualities most valued in women by the Greeks?

The Apology (399 B.C.E.)   11

PLATO

The Apology recounts Socrates' trial for heresy and corrupting the morals of the youth of Athens. Socrates (469–399 B.C.E.) lived his entire life as an Athenian. He served as an armored soldier in the Peloponnesian Wars but did not enter state service as might have been expected of one of his intellectual skills. Rather he took to walking throughout Athens, questioning those who followed him about the things they saw and delving for the underlying principles of human life. He took particular delight in showing that individuals reputed to be wise or honorable were nothing of the sort. Although Socrates was not officially a teacher—that is, he received no fees and worked in no fixed school—he instructed hundreds of Athenians in the technique of critical questioning that we now call the Socratic method. Among his pupils was Plato, a devoted follower who was present at the trial and who went into self-imposed exile after Socrates' death.

   The Apology, which means defense rather than retraction, relates to the speech that Socrates made to the jury at his trial, both before and after a verdict was reached by the 501 Athenian citizens who heard the evidence against him. Socrates was 70 at the time, and the imposition of the death penalty came as a shock to many of his admirers. The death of Socrates is narrated in another work of Plato's, *The Phaedo.*

How you have felt, O men of Athens, at hearing the speeches of my accusers, I cannot tell; but I know that their persuasive words almost made me forget who I was—such was the effect of them; and yet they have hardly spoken a word of truth. But many as their falsehoods were, there was one of them which quite amazed me—I mean when they told you to be upon your guard, and not to let yourselves be deceived by the force of my eloquence. They ought to have been ashamed of saying this, because they were sure to be detected as soon as I opened my lips and displayed my deficiency: they certainly did appear to be most shameless in saying this, unless by the force of eloquence they mean the force of truth; for then I do indeed admit that I am eloquent. But in how different a way from theirs! I must beg of you to grant me one favor, which is this—If you hear me using the same words in my defence which I have been in the habit of using, and which most of you may have heard in the agora, and at the tables of the money-changers, or anywhere else, I would ask you not to be surprised at this, and not to interrupt me. For I am more than seventy years of age, and this is the first time that I have ever appeared in a court of law, and I am quite a stranger to the ways of the place; and therefore I would have you regard me as if I were really a stranger, whom you would excuse if he spoke in his native tongue, and after the fashion of his country; that I think is not an unfair request. Never mind the manner, which may or may not be good; but think only of the justice of my cause, and give heed to that: let the judge decide justly and the speaker speak truly.

And first, I have to reply to the older charges and to my first accusers, and then I will go on to the later ones. For I have had many accusers, who accused me of old, and their false charges have continued during many years; and I am more afraid of them than of Anytus and his associates, who are dangerous, too, in their own way. But far more dangerous are these, who began when you were children, and took possession of your minds with their falsehoods, telling of one Socrates, a wise man, who speculated about the heaven above, and searched into the earth beneath, and made the worse appear the better cause. These are the accusers whom I dread; for they are the circulators of this rumor, and their hearers are too apt to fancy that speculators of this sort do not believe in the gods.

There is another thing: young men of the richer classes, who have not much to do, come about me of their own accord; they like to hear the pretenders examined, and they often imitate me, and examine others themselves; there are plenty of persons, as they soon enough discover, who think that they know something, but really know little or nothing; and then those who are examined by them instead of being angry with themselves are angry with me: This confounded Socrates, they say; this villainous misleader of youth!—and then if somebody asks them, Why, what evil does he practice or teach? they do not know, and cannot tell; but in order that they may not appear to be at a loss, they repeat the ready-made charges which are used against all philosophers about teaching things up in the clouds and under the earth, and having no gods, and making the worse appear the better cause; for they do not like to confess that their pretence of knowledge has been detected—which is the truth; and as they are numerous and ambitious and energetic, and are all in battle array and have persuasive tongues, they have filled your ears with their loud and inveterate calumnies.

Some one will say: And are you not ashamed, Socrates, of a course of life which is likely to bring you to an untimely end? To him I may fairly answer: There you are mistaken: a man who is good for anything ought not to calculate the chance of living or dying; he

The School of Athens. In this painting the Rennaissance master Raphael presented his version of the humanist ideal of classical antiquity. Many Greek and Roman cultural heroes are depicted in the dress of 16th-century Italiens in a setting of Rennaiscence architecture and sculpture. At the center of the composition, framed by the arch, Plato and Aristotle are deep in discussion.

ought only to consider whether in doing anything he is doing right or wrong—acting the part of a good man or of a bad. For this fear of death is indeed the pretence of wisdom, and not real wisdom, being the appearance of knowing the unknown; since no one knows whether death, which they in their fear apprehend to be the greatest evil, may not be the greatest good. Is there not here conceit of knowledge, which is a disgraceful sort of ignorance? And this is the point in which, as I think, I am superior to men in general, and in which

I might perhaps fancy myself wiser than other men,—that whereas I know but little of the world below, I do not suppose that I know; but I do know that injustice and disobedience to a better, whether God or man, is evil and dishonorable, and I will never fear or avoid a possible good rather than a certain evil. If you say to me, Socrates, this time we will let you off, but upon one condition, that you are not to inquire and speculate in this way anymore, and that if you are caught doing this again you shall die—if this was the condition on which you let me go, I should reply: Men of Athens, I honor and love you; but I shall obey God rather than you, and while I have life and strength I shall never cease from the practice and teaching of philosophy, exhorting any one whom I meet after my manner, and convincing him, saying: O my friend, why do you, who are a citizen of the great and mighty and wise city of Athens, care so much about laying up the greatest amount of money and honor and reputation, and so little about wisdom and truth and the greatest improvement of the soul, which you never regard or heed at all? Are you not ashamed of this? And if the person with whom I am arguing, says: Yes, but I do care; I do not depart or let him go at once; I interrogate and examine and cross-examine him, and if I think that he has no virtue, but only says that he has, I reproach him with undervaluing the greater, and overvaluing the less. And this I should say to every one whom I meet, young and old, citizen and alien, but especially to the citizens, inasmuch as they are my brethren. For this is the command to God, as I would have you know; and I believe that to this day no greater good has ever happened in the state than my service to the God. For I do nothing but go about persuading you all, old and young alike, not to take thought for your persons of your properties, but first and chiefly to care about the greatest improvement of the soul. I tell you that virtue is not given by money, but that from virtue come money and every other good of man, public as well as private. This is my teaching, and if this is the doctrine which corrupts the youth, my influence is ruinous indeed. But if any one says that this is not my teaching, he is speaking an untruth. Wherefore, O men of Athens, I say to you, do as Anytus bids or not as Anytus bids, and either acquit me or not; but whatever you do, know that I shall never alter my ways, not even if I have to die many times.

And now, Athenians, I am not going to argue for my own sake, as you may think, but for yours, that you may not sin against the God, or lightly reject his boon by condemning me. For if you kill me you will not easily find another like me, who, if I may use such a ludicrous figure of speech, am a sort of gadfly, given to the state by the God; and the state is like a great and noble steed who is tardy in his motions owing to his every size, and requires to be stirred into life. I am that gadfly which God has given the state, and all day long and in all places am always fastening upon you, arousing and persuading and reproaching you. And as you will not easily find another like me, I would advise you to spare me. I dare say that you may feel irritated at being suddenly awakened when you are caught napping; and you may think that if you were to strike me dead, which you easily might, then you would sleep on for the remainder of your lives, unless God in his care of you gives you another gadfly. And that I am given to you by God is proved by this: that if I had been like other men, I should not have neglected all my own concerns or patiently seen the neglect of them during all these years, and have been doing yours, coming to you individually like a father or elder brother, exhorting you to regard virtue; this, I say, would not be like human nature. And had I gained anything, or if my exhortations had been paid, there would have been some sense in that; but now, as you will perceive, not even the impudence of my accusers dares to say that I have ever exacted or sought pay of any one; they have no witness of that. And I have a witness of the truth of what I say; my poverty is a sufficient witness.

There are many reasons why I am not grieved, O men of Athens, at the vote of condemnation. I expected this, and am only surprised that the votes are so nearly equal; for I had thought that the majority against me would have been far larger; but now, had thirty votes gone over to the other side, I should have been acquitted.

And so [the death penalty is proposed]. And what shall I propose on my part, O men of

Athens? Clearly that which is my due. And what is that which I ought to pay or to receive? What shall be done to the man who has never had the wit to be idle during his whole life; but has been careless of what the many care about—wealth, and family interests, and military offices, and speaking in the assembly, and magistracies, and plots, and parties. Reflecting that I was really too honest a man to follow in this way and live, I did not go where I could do no good to you or to myself; but where I could do the greatest good privately to every one of you, thither I went, and sought to persuade every man among you, that he must look to himself, and seek virtue and wisdom before he looks to his private interests, and look to the state before he looks to the interests of the state; and that this should be the order which he observes in all his actions. What shall be done to such an one? Doubtless some good thing, O men of Athens, if he has his reward; and the good should be of a kind suitable to him. What would be a reward suitable to a poor man who is your benefactor, who desires leisure that he may instruct you? There can be no more fitting reward than maintenance in the Prytaneum, O men of Athens, a reward which he deserves far more than the citizen who has won the prize at Olympia in the horse or chariot race, whether the chariots were drawn by two horses or by many. For I am in want, and he has enough; and he only gives you the appearance of happiness, and I give you the reality. And if I am to estimate the penalty justly, I say that maintenance in the Prytaneum is the just return.

Not much time will be gained, O Athenians, in return for the evil name which you will get from the detractors of the city, who will say that you killed Socrates, a wise man; for they will call me wise even although I am not wise when they want to reproach you. If you had waited a little while, your desire would have been fulfilled in the course of nature. For I am far advanced in years, as you may perceive, and not far from death. I am speaking now only to those of you who have condemned me to death. And I have another thing to say to them: You think that I was convicted through deficiency of words—I mean, that if I had thought fit to leave nothing undone, nothing unsaid, I might have gained an acquittal. Not so: the deficiency which led to my conviction was not of words—certainly not. But I had not the boldness or impudence or inclination to address you as you would have liked me to address you, weeping and wailing and lamenting, and saying and doing many things which you have been accustomed to hear from others, and which, as I say, are unworthy of me. But I thought that I ought not to do anything common or mean in the hour of danger: nor do I now repent of the manner of my defence, and I would rather die having spoken after my manner, than speak in your manner and live. For neither in war nor yet at law ought any man to use every way of escaping death. For often in battle there is no doubt that if a man will throw away his arms, and fall on his knees before his pursuers, he may escape death; and in other dangers there are other ways of escaping death, if a man is willing to say and do anything. The difficulty, my friends, is not in avoiding death, but in avoiding unrighteousness; for that runs faster than death. I am old and move slowly, and the slower runner has overtaken me, and my accusers are keen and quick, and the faster runner, who is unrighteousness, has overtaken them. And now I depart hence condemned by you to, suffer the penalty of death, and they too go their ways condemned by the truth to suffer the penalty of villainy and wrong; and I must abide by my award—let them abide by theirs. I suppose that these things may be regarded as fated,—and I think that they are well.

And now, O men who have condemned me, I would fain prophesy to you; for I am about to die, and that is the hour in which men are gifted with prophetic power. And I prophesy to you who are my murderers, that immediately after my death punishment far heavier than you have inflicted on me will surely await you. Me you have killed because you wanted to escape the accuser, and not to give an account of your lives. But that will not be as you suppose: far otherwise. For I say that there will be more accusers of you than there are now; accusers whom hitherto I have restrained: and as they are younger they will be more severe with you, and you will be more offended at them. For if you think that by killing men you can avoid the accuser censuring your lives, you are mistaken; that is not a way of escape which is either possible or honorable; the easiest and the noblest way is not to be crushing others but to be improving yourselves. This is the prophecy which I utter before my departure to the judges who have condemned me.

Wherefore, O judges, be of good cheer about death, and know this of a truth—that no evil can happen to a good man, either in life or after death. He and his are not neglected by the gods; nor has my own approaching end happened by mere chance. But I see clearly that to die and be released was better for me; and therefore the oracle gave no sign. For which reason, also, I am not angry with my accusers or my condemners; they have done me no harm, although neither of them meant to do me any good; and for this I may gently blame them.

Still I have a favor to ask of them. When my sons are grown up, I would ask you, O my friends, to punish them; and I would have you trouble them, as I have troubled you, if they seem to care about riches, or anything, more than about virtue; or if they pretend to be something when they are really nothing, then reprove them, as I have reproved you, for not caring about that for which they ought to care, and thinking that they are something when they are really nothing. And if you do this, I and my sons will have received justice at your hands.

The hour of departure has arrived, and we go our ways—I to die, and you to live. Which is better God only knows.

Study Questions

1. What impressions do you get of Socrates from *The Apology*?

2. Socrates considers himself to be a philosopher. What does that mean? What does a philosopher do?

3. What, according to Socrates, was Athens losing by condemning him to death? What will be the consequences for the city?

4. Why did many Athenians think Socrates was such a dangerous man?

5. What fate did Socrates predict for those who condemned him?

6. *The Apology* presents a very sympathetic view of Socrates. If you were one of his accusers, how might you have put your case?

The Republic (ca. 327 B.C.E.)   **12**

PLATO

Plato (428–347 B.C.E.), a member of an aristocratic Athenian family, studied under Socrates, whose ideas and methods of teaching he was later to immortalize. Plato trained for a career in politics, but the turbulent events of the late fifth century B.C.E. turned him against the ruling regime. After the death of Socrates in 399 B.C.E. Plato began to travel and remained away from Athens for over a decade. He returned as a teacher and philosopher, spreading the views that had been taught to him by his master. In keeping with his idea that the state should be ruled by philosopher-kings, Plato founded his Academy for philosophical and political study. During this time he wrote extensively, producing his famous *Dialogues*. His philosophy centered on the belief that a fixed reality existed beyond the experience of the senses. Although a polytheist, Plato believed in a single, universal Good.

The Republic, one of the most important philosophical tracts in Western history, takes the form of a dialogue about the composition of a perfect society ruled by a philosopher-king who always strives to achieve the Good. In the selection reprinted here the dialogue between Socrates and Glaucon presents Plato's ideas about the proper education of women in the republic.

I suppose that I must retrace my steps and say what I perhaps ought to have said before in the proper place. The part of the men has been played out, and now properly enough comes the turn of the women. Of them I will proceed to speak, and the more readily since I am invited by you.

For men born and educated like our citizens, the only way, in my opinion, of arriving at a right conclusion about the possession and use of women and children is to follow the path on which we originally started, when we said that the men were to be the guardians and watchdogs of the herd.

True.

Let us further suppose the birth and education of our women to be subject to similar or nearly similar regulations; then we shall see whether the result accords with our design.

What do you mean?

What I mean may be put into the form of a question, I said: Are dogs divided into hes and shes, or do they both share equally in hunting and in keeping watch and in the other duties of dogs? or do we entrust to the males the entire and exclusive care of the flocks, while we leave the females at home, under the idea that the bearing and suckling their puppies is labour enough for them?

No, he said, they share alike; the only difference between them is that the males are stronger and the females weaker.

But can you use different animals for the same purpose, unless they are bred and fed in the same way?

You cannot.

Then, if women are to have the same duties as men, they must have the same nuture and education?

Yes.

The education which was assigned to the men and music and gymnastic.

Yes.

Then women must be taught music and gymnastic and also the art of war, which they must practise like the men?

That is the inference, I suppose.

I should rather expect, I said, that several of our proposals, if they are carried out, being unusual, may appear ridiculous.

No doubt of it.

Yes, and the most ridiculous thing of all will be the sight of women naked in the palaestra, exercising with the men, especially when they are no longer young; they certainly will not be a vision of beauty, any more than the enthusiastic old men who in spite of wrinkles and ugliness continue to frequent the gymnasia.

Yes, indeed, he said: according to present notions the proposal would be thought ridiculous.

But then, I said, as we have determined to speak our minds, we must not fear the jests of the wits which will be directed against this sort of innovation; how they will talk of women's attainments both in music and gymnastic, and above all about their wearing armour and riding upon horseback!

Very true, he replied.

First, then, whether the question is to be put in jest or in earnest, let us come to an understanding about the nature of woman: Is she capable of sharing either wholly or partially in the actions of men, or not at all? And is the art of war one of those arts in which she can or cannot share? That will be the best way of commencing the enquiry, and will probably lead to the fairest conclusion.

That will be much the best way.

Shall we take the other side first and begin by arguing against ourselves; in this manner the adversary's position will not be undefended.

Why not? he said.

Then let us put a speech into the mouths of our opponents. They will say: "Socrates and Glaucon, no adversary need convict you, for you yourselves, at the first foundation of the State, admitted the principle that everybody was to do the one work suited to his own nature." And certainly, if I am not mistaken, such an admission was made by us. "And do not the natures of men and women differ very much indeed?" And we shall reply: Of course they do. Then we shall be asked, "Whether the tasks assigned to men and to women should not be different, and such as are agreeable to their different natures?" Certainly they should. "But if so, have you not fallen into a serious inconsistency in saying that men and women, whose natures are so entirely different, ought to perform the same actions?"—What defence will you make for. us my good Sir, against any one who offers these objections?

That is not an easy question to answer when asked suddenly; and I shall and I do beg of you to draw out the case on our side.

These are the objections, Glaucon, and there are many others of a like kind, which I foresaw long ago; they made me afraid and reluctant to take in hand any law about the possession and nurture of women and children.

By Zeus, he said, the problem to be solved is anything but easy.

Why yes, I said, but the fact is that when a man is out of his depth, whether he has fallen into a little swimming bath or into mid ocean, he has to swim all the same.

Very true.

And must not we swim and try to reach the shore: we will hope that Arion's dolphin or some other miraculous help may save us?

I suppose so, he said.

Well then, let us see if any way of escape can be found. We acknowledged—did we not? that different natures ought to have different pursuits, and that men's and women's natures are different. And now what are we saying?—that different natures ought to have the same pursuits, this is the inconsistency which is charged upon us.

Precisely.

Verily, Glaucon, I said, glorious is the power of the art of contradiction!

Why do you say so?

Because I think that many a man falls into the practice against his will. When he thinks that he is reasoning he is really disputing, just because he cannot define and divide, and so know that of which he is speaking; and he will pursue a merely verbal opposition in the spirit of contention and not of fair discussion.

Yes, he replied, such is very often the case; but what has that to do with us and our argument?

A great deal; for there is certainly a danger of our getting unintentionally into a verbal opposition.

In what way?

Why we valiantly and pugnaciously insist upon the verbal truth, that different natures ought to have different pursuits, but we never considered at all what was the meaning of sameness or difference of nature, or why we distinguished them when we assigned different pursuits to different natures and the same to the same natures.

Why, no, he said, that was never considered by us.

I said: Suppose that by way of illustration we were to ask the question whether there is not an opposition in nature between bald men and hairy men; and if this is admitted by us, then, if bald men are cobblers, we should forbid the hairy men to be cobblers, and conversely?

That would be a jest, he said.

Yes, I said, a jest; and why? because we never meant when we constructed the State, that the opposition of natures should extend to every difference, but only to those differences which affected the pursuit in which the individual is engaged; we should have argued, for example, that a physician and one who is in mind a physician may be said to have the same nature.

True.

Whereas the physician and the carpenter have different natures?

Certainly.

And if, I said, the male and female sex appear to differ in their fitness for any art or pursuit, we should say that such pursuit or art should be assigned to one or the other of them; but if the difference consists only in women bearing and men begetting children, this does not amount to a proof that a woman differs from a man in respect of the sort of education she should receive; and we shall therefore continue to maintain that our guardians and their wives ought to have the same pursuits.

Very true, he said.

Next, we shall ask our opponent how, in reference to any of the pursuits or arts of civic live, the nature of a woman differs from that of a man?

That will be quite fair.

And perhaps he, like yourself, will reply that to give a sufficient answer on the instant is most easy; but after a little reflection there is no difficulty.

Yes, perhaps.

Suppose then that we invite him to accompany us in the argument, and than we may hope to show him that there is nothing peculiar in the constitution of women which would affect them in the administration of the State.

By all means.

Let us say to him: Come now, and we will ask you a question—when you spoke of a nature gifted or not gifted in any respect, did you mean to say that one man will acquire a thing easily, another with difficulty; a little learning will lead the one to discover a great deal; whereas the other, after much study and application, no sooner learns than he forgets; or again, did you mean, that the one has a body which is a good servant to his mind, while the body of the other is a hindrance to him? Would not these be the sort of differences which distinguish the man gifted by nature from the one who is ungifted?

No one will deny that.

And can you mention any pursuit of man-kind in which the male sex has not all these gifts and qualities in a higher degree than the female? Need I waste time in speaking of the art of weaving, and the management of pan-cakes and preserves, in which womankind does really appear to be great, and in which for her to be beaten by a man is of all things the most absurd?

You are quite right, he replied, in maintain-ing the general inferiority of the female sex: although many women are in many things sup-erior to men, yet on the whole what you say is true.

And if so, my friend, I said, there is no special faculty of administration in a state which a woman has because she is a woman, or which a man has by virtue of his sex, but the gifts of nature are alike diffused in both; all the pursuits of men are the pursuits of women also, but in all of them a woman is inferior to a man.

Very true.

Then are we to impose all our enactments on men and none of them on women?

That will never do.

One woman has a gift of healing, another not; one is a musician, and another has no music in her nature?

Very true.

And one woman has a turn for gymnastic and military exercises, and another is unwarlike and hates gymnastics?

Certainly.

And one woman is a philosopher, and anoth-er is an enemy of philosophy; one has spirit, and another is without spirit?

That is also true.

Then one woman will have the temper of a guardian, and another not. Was not the selection of the male guardians determined by differences of this sort?

Yes.

Men and women alike possess the qualities which make a guardian; they differ only in their comparative strength or weakness.

Obviously.

And those women who have such qualities are to be selected as the companions and col-leagues of men who have similar qualities and whom they resemble in capacity and in charac-ter?

Very true.

And ought not the same natures to have the same pursuits?

They ought.

Then, as we were saying before, there is nothing unnatural in assigning music and gym-nastic to the wives of the guardians—to that point we come round again.

Certainly not.

The law which we then enacted was agree-able to nature, and therefore not an impossibil-ity or mere aspiration; and the contrary prac-tice, which prevails at present, is in reality a vio-lation of nature.

That appears to be true.

We had to consider, first, whether our pro-posals were possible, and secondly whether they were the most beneficial?

Yes.

And the possibility has been acknowledged?

Yes.

The very great benefit has next to be estab-lished?

Quite so.

You will admit that the same education which makes a man a good guardian will make a woman a good guardian; for their original nature is the same?

Yes.

I should like to ask you a question.

What is it?

Would you say that all men are equal in excellence, or is one man better than another?

The latter.

And in the commonwealth which we were founding do you conceive the guardians who have been brought up on our model system to be more perfect men, or the cobblers whose education has been cobbling?

What a ridiculous question!

You have answered me, I replied: Well, and may we not further say that our guardians are the best of our citizens?

By far the best.

And will not their wives be the best women?

Yes, by far the best.

And can there be anything better for the interests of the State than that of the men and women of a State should be as good as possible?

There can be nothing better.

And this is what the art of music and gymnastic, when present in such manner as we have described, will accomplish?

Certainly.

Then we have made an enactment not only possible but in the highest degree beneficial to the State?

True.

Then let the wives of our guardians strip, for their virtue will be their robe, and let them share in the toils of war and the defence of their country; only in the distribution of labours the lighter are to be assigned to the women, who are the weaker natures, but in other respects their duties are to be the same. And as for the man who laughs at naked women exercising their bodies from the best of motives, in his laughter he is plucking "A fruit of unripe wisdom," and he himself is ignorant of what he is laughing at, or what he is about; for that is, and ever will be, the best of sayings, *That the useful is the noble and the hurtful is the base.*

Study Questions

1. Does Plato believe that the perfect society should be bound by tradition or convention?

2. Why, according to the conventional argument, should women be kept to their own "separate sphere"? Does Plato seem to agree?

3. Are men and women equal in Plato's *Republic?* What are the differences between them?

4. How should the state educate women? How does Plato's plan differ from the Greek reality?

5. What do you think Plato means when he says "the useful is the noble and the hurtful is the base"?

Politics (4th century B.C.E.)   13

ARISTOTLE

Aristotle (384–322 B.C.E.) was the third of the great Greek philosophers and was arguably the most influential of all. The son of a physician, Aristotle was taught medicine and biology from an early age. He was sent to Athens specifically to be educated at Plato's Academy and there he imbibed the wisdom of Socrates as well.

Aristotle's original philosophical achievements are nearly beyond comprehension. His scientific works include major treatises on astronomy, botany, physics, and zoology. His philosophical works include discourses on cosmology, ethics, logic, poetry, and politics. Like Plato, Aristotle founded a school in Athens, the Lyceum, but he taught by lecture rather than by Socratic cross-questioning. Aristotle's works were neither written nor published during his lifetime. They consisted mostly of lecture notes taken by his students and brought together into treatises. Thirty such works survive today, although it is believed that there were nearly two hundred in existence in ancient times.

Politics was an attempt to establish principles of government along scientific lines. Aristotle was the first philosopher to explore the basic forms of government and to discuss their inherent strengths and weaknesses.

As what has already been said finishes the preface of this subject, and as we have considered at large the nature of all other states, it now remains that I should first say what ought to be the form laid down as that of the state which is in accordance with our idea; for no good state can exist without a proportionate supply of what is necessary. Many things therefore ought to be previously laid down as objects desirable, but none of them such as are impossible; I mean, relative to the number of citizens, and the extent of the territory. For as other artificers, such as the weaver and the shipwright, ought to have such materials as are fit for their work, so also ought the legislator and politician to endeavour to procure proper materials for the business they have in hand. Now the first and principal instrument of the politician is the number of people; he should therefore know how many and what they naturally ought to be; in like manner as to the country, how large and of what kind it ought to be. Most persons think that it is necessary for a city to be large in order to be happy; but even should this be true, still they cannot tell what is a large one and what a small one. For they estimate its greatness according to the multitude of its inhabitants, but they ought rather to look to its strengths than to its numbers. But even if it were proper to determine the strength of the city from the number of its inhabitants, it should never be inferred from the multitude in general who may happen to be in it—(for in a city there must necessarily be many slaves, sojourners, and foreigners)—but from those who are really part of the state, and properly constitute the members of it. A multitude of these is indeed a proof that the city is large, but where a large number of mechanics dwell, and but few soldiers, such a state cannot be great; for a great city and a populous one are not the same thing. This too is evident from the fact that it is very difficult, if not impossible, properly to govern a very numerous body of men; for of all the states which appear well governed, we find not one where the rights of a citizen are laid open to the entire multitude. And this is also made evident by proof from the nature of the thing; for as law is a certain order, so good law is of course a certain good order; but too large a multitude is incapable of this. For this is in very truth the prerogative of that Divine Power which comprehends the universe. Not but that, as quantity and greatness are usually essential to beauty, the perfection of a city consists in its being large, if only consistent with that order already mentioned. But still there is a determinate size to all cities, as well as everything else, whether animals, plants, or machines; for each of these have their proper powers, if they are neither too little nor too large; but when they have not their due growth, or are badly constructed, so it is with a city. One that is too small has not in itself the power of self-defence, but this power is essential to a city; one that is too large is capable of self-defence in what is necessary, in the same way as a nation, but then it is not a city; for it will be difficult to find a form of government for it. The first thing therefore necessary is, that a city should consist of the lowest numbers which will be sufficient to enable the inhabitants to live happily in their political community. And it follows, that the more the inhabitants exceed that necessary number, the greater will the city be. But, as we have already said, this must not be without bounds; but what is the proper limit of the excess, experience will easily show, and this experience is to be collected from the actions both of the governors and the governed. Now, as it belongs to the first to direct the inferior magistrates and to act as judges, it follows that they can neither determine causes with justice, nor issue their orders with propriety, without they know the characters of their fellow-citizens: so that whenever this happens to be impossible in these two particulars, the state must of necessity be badly managed; for in both of them it is unjust to determine too hastily, and without proper knowledge, which must evidently be the case where the number of the citizens is too many. Besides, it is more easy for strangers and sojourners to assume the rights of citizens, as they will easily escape detection owing to the greatness of the multitude. It is evident then, that the best boundary for a city is that wherein the numbers are the greatest possible, that they may be the better able to be sufficient in themselves, while they are not too large to be under the eye of the magistrates. And thus let us determine the extent of a city.

As to the extent of a country, it should be such as may enable the inhabitants to live at their ease with freedom and temperance. What the situation of the country should be, is not difficult to determine; but in some particulars respecting this point, we ought to be advised by those who are skilful in military affairs. It should be difficult of access to an enemy, but easy of egress to the inhabitants; and, as we said that the number of inhabitants ought to be such as can come under the eye of the magistrate, so should it be with the country; for by that means the country is easily defended. As to the position of the city, if one could place it to one's wish, it ought to lie well both for sea and land. One situation which it ought to have has been already mentioned; for it should be so placed as easily to give assistance to all parts, and also to receive the necessaries of life from every quarter; as also it should be accessible for the carriage of wood, or any other materials of the like kind which may happen to be in the country.

We now proceed to a point out of what natural disposition the citizens ought to be: but this surely any one would easily perceive who casts his eye over those states of Greece which bear a high repute, and indeed over all the habitable world, as it is divided among the nations. Those who live in cold countries, as the north of Europe, are full of courage, but wanting in understanding and in art; therefore they remain free for a long time; but, not being versed in the political science, they cannot reduce their neighbours under their power. But the Asiatics, whose understandings are quick, and who are conversant in the arts, are deficient in courage; and therefore they continue to be always conquered, and the slaves of others. But the Greeks, placed as it were between these two parts, partake of the nature of both, so as to be at the same time both courageous and intellectual; for which reason Greece continues free, and governed in the best manner possible, and capable of commanding the whole world, could it be combined into one system of policy. The races of the Greeks have the very same difference among themselves: for part of them possess but one of these qualities, whereas in the other they are both happily blended together. Hence it is evident, that those persons ought to be both intelligent and courageous who will be readily obedient to a legislator, whose object is virtue.

We are now to consider what those things are without which a city cannot possibly exist; for what we call parts of the city must of necessity be inherent in it. And this we shall more plainly understand, if we know the number of things necessary to a city. First, the inhabitants must have food: secondly, arts, for many instruments are necessary in life: thirdly, arms, for it is necessary that the community should have an armed force within themselves, both to support their government against the disaffected of themselves, and also to defend it from those who seek to attack it from without: fourthly, a certain revenue, as well for the internal necessities of the state, as for the business of war: fifthly, and indeed chief of all, the care of the service of gods: sixthly in order, but most necessary of all, a court to determine both civil and criminal causes. These things are matters which are absolutely required, so to speak, in every state: for a city is a number of people, not accidentally met together, but with a purpose of insuring to themselves sufficient independency and self-protection; and if anything necessary for these purposes is wanting, it is impossible that in such a situation these ends can be obtained. It is necessary therefore that a city should be composed with reference to these various trades; for this purpose a proper number of husbandmen are necessary to procure food; as also artificers and soldiers, and rich men, and priests, and judges, to determine what is necessary and beneficial.

Since we are inquiring what is the best government possible, and as it is admitted to be that in which the citizens are happy, and that, as we have already said, it is impossible to obtain happiness without virtue; it follows, that in the best governed states, where the citizens are really men of intrinsic and not relative goodness, none of them should be permitted to exercise any low mechanical employment or traffic, as being ignoble and destructive to virtue: neither should they who are destined for office be husbandmen; for leisure is necessary in order to improve in virtue, and to perform the duty which they owe to the state.

It is necessary that the citizens should be rich, and these are the men proper for citizens; for no low mechanic ought to be admitted to the rights of a citizen, nor any other sort of people, whose employment is not productive of virtue.

Study Questions

1. Why is size an important consideration in the construction of a state? What are the advantages and disadvantages of large and small cities? What is the best size?

2. By using *Politics* as a guide, what seems to be the ideal physical setting for a city-state? Could you make some broader generalization about Greek city-states with this knowledge?

3. Why does Aristotle feel that the Greeks are more successful than other peoples in the ancient world?

4. What does a city-state require to survive?

5. Who is excluded from citizenship in the state? Why?

The Religions of the East

Buddha and Worshipers. This third-century relief from northwestern India shows the influence of the art of Greece and Rome. The development of devotional Buddhism led to the large-scale production of Buddha images.

The Upanishads (ca. 600–500 B.C.E.)   **14**

The Upanishads are compilations from the teachings of late Vedic philosophers. They were composed during the seventh and sixth centuries B.C.E., although the Sanskrit texts that have survived are from later periods. They take the form of dialogues between teachers and pupils, in which a single great question is pondered, frequently through the use of allegory and paradox. Unlike earlier Vedic writings, they are introspective and seek to illuminate an inner spirit. The texts, over a hundred of which survive, are regarded as the crowning intellectual achievement of the Vedic age, introducing the concepts of karma and reincarnation into Indian thought.

Upanishad can be translated roughly as meaning "at the feet of a teacher"; or in the case of the selection chosen here from the *Kaushîtake-Upanishad*, "at the couch of the Brahman." The Upanishads center upon the most basic of all philosophical questions: the nature of divinity and humanity and the relationships among sense, reason, and faith. They show elements of spiritualism and mysticism and are meant to be contemplated deeply.

The Couch of Brahman

And Kitra said: "All who depart from this world go to the moon. In the former, the bright half, the moon delights in their spirits; in the other, the dark half, the moon sends them on to be born again. Verily, the moon is the door of the Svarga, i.e., the heavenly world. Now, if a man objects to the moon and is not satisfied with life there, the moon sets him free. But if a man does not object, then the moon sends him down as rain upon this earth. And according to his deeds and according to his knowledge he is born again here as a worm, or as an insect, or as a fish, or as a bird, or as a lion, or as a boar, or as a serpent, or as a tiger, or as a man, or as something else in different places. When he has thus returned to the earth, someone, a sage, asks: 'Who art thou?' And he should answer: 'From the wise moon, who orders the seasons, when it is born consisting of fifteen parts, from the moon who is the home of our ancestors,

the seed was brought. This seed, even me, they, the gods, mentioned in the Pañkâgnividyâ, gathered up in an active man, and through an active man they brought me to a mother. Then I, growing up to be born, a being living by months, whether twelve or thirteen, was together with my father, who also lived by years of twelve or thirteen months, that I might either know the true Brahman or not know it. Therefore, O ye seasons, grant that I may attain immortality, i.e., knowledge of Brahman. By this my true saying, by this my toil, beginning with the dwelling in the moon and ending with my birth on earth, I am like a season, and the child of the seasons.' 'Who art thou?' the sage asks again. 'I am thou,' he replies. Then he sets him free to proceed onward.

"He, at the time of death ...approaches the couch Amitaugas. That is Prâna, i.e., speech. The past and the future are its eastern feet; prosperity and earth its western feet.... On this couch sits Brahman, and he who knows himself one with Brahman, sitting on the couch, mounts it first with one foot only. Then Brahman says to him: 'Who art thou?' and he shall answer: 'I am like a season, and the child of the seasons, sprung from the womb of endless space, from the light, from the luminous Brahman. The light, the origin of the year, which is the past, which is the present, which is all living things, and all elements, is the Self. Thou art the Self. What thou art, that am I.' Brahman says to him: 'Who am I?' He shall answer: 'That which is, the true.' Brahman asks: 'What is the true?' He says to him: 'What is different from the gods and from the senses that is Sat, but the gods and the senses are Tyam. Therefore, by that name Sattya, or true, is called all this whatever there is. All this thou art.' This is also declared by a verse: 'This great Rishi, whose belly is the Yagus, the head the Sâman, the form the Rik, is to be known as being imperishable, as being Brahman.'

"Brahman says to him: 'How dost thou obtain my male names?' He should answer: 'By breath.' Brahman asks: 'How my female names?' He should answer: 'By speech.' Brahman asks: 'How my neuter names?' He should answer: 'By mind.' 'How smells?' 'By the nose.' 'How forms?' 'By the eye.' 'How sounds?' 'By the ear.' 'How flavors of food?' 'By the tongue.' 'How actions?' 'By the hands.' 'How pleasures and pain?' 'By the body.' 'How joy, delight, and offspring?' 'By the organ.' 'How journeyings?' 'By the feet.' 'How thoughts, and what is to be known and desired?' 'By knowledge alone.'

"Brahman says to him: 'Water indeed is this my world, the whole Brahman world, and it is thine.'

'Whatever victory, whatever might belongs to Brahman, that victory and that might he obtains who knows this, yea, who knows this.'"

Knowledge of the Living Spirit

"Prâna, or breath, is Brahman," thus says Kaushitaki. "Of this prâna, which is Brahman, the mind is the messenger, speech the housekeeper, the eye the guard, the ear the informant. He who knows mind as the messenger of prâna, which is Brahman, becomes possessed of the messenger. He who knows speech as the housekeeper, becomes possessed of the housekeeper. He who knows the eye as the guard, becomes possessed of the guard. He who knows the ear as the informant, becomes possessed of the informant.

"Now to that prâna, which is Brahman, all these deities, mind, speech, eye, ear, bring an offering, though he asks not for it, and thus to him who knows this all creatures bring an offering, though he asks not for it. For him who knows this, there is this Upanishad, or secret vow, 'Beg not!' As a man who has begged through a village and got nothing sits down and says, 'I shall never eat anything given by those people,' and as then those who formerly refused him press him to accept their alms, thus is the rule for him who begs not, but the charitable will press him and say, 'Let us give to thee.' "

Life and Consciousness

Pratardana, the son of Divodâsa, King of Kâsî, came by means of fighting and strength to the beloved abode of Indra. Indra said to him: "Pratardana, let me give you a boon to choose." And Pratardana answered: "Do you yourself choose that boon for me which you deem most beneficial for a man." Indra said to him: "No one who chooses, chooses for another; choose thyself." Then Pratardana replied: "Then that boon to choose is no boon for me."

Then, however, Indra did not swerve from the truth, for Indra is truth. Indra said to him: "Know me only; that is what I deem most beneficial for man, that he should know me. I slew the three-headed son of Tvashtri; I delivered the Arunmukhas, the devotees, to the wolves; breaking many treaties, I killed the people of Prahlâda in heaven, the people of Puloma in the sky, the people of Kâlakañga on earth. And not one hair of me was harmed there. And he who knows me thus, by no deed of his is his life harmed: not by the murder of his mother, not by the murder of his father, not by theft, not by the killing of a Brahman. If he is going to commit a sin, the bloom does not depart from his face. I am prâna, meditate on me as the conscious self, as life, as immortality. Life is prâna, prâna is life. Immortality is prâna, prâna is immortality. As long as prâna dwells in this body, so long surely there is life. By prâna he obtains immortality in the other world, by knowledge true conception. He who meditates on me as life and immortality, gains his full life in this world, and obtains in the Svarga world immortality and indestructibility."

Pratardana said: "Some maintain here, that the prânas become one, for otherwise no one could at the same time make known a name by speech, see a form with the eye, hear a sound with the ear, think a thought with the mind. After having become one, the prânas perceive all these together, one by one. While speech speaks, all prânas speak after it. While the eye sees, all prânas see after it. While the ear hears, all prânas hear after it. While the mind thinks, all prânas think after it. While the prâna breathes, all prânas breathe after it."

"Thus it is indeed," said Indra, "but nevertheless there is a preeminence among the prânas. Man lives deprived of speech, for we see dumb people. Man lives deprived of sight, for we see blind people. Man lives deprived of hearing, for we see deaf people. Man lives deprived of mind, for we see infants. Man lives deprived of his arms, deprived of his legs, for we see it thus. But prâna alone is the conscious self, and having laid hold of this body, it makes it rise up. Therefore it is said, 'Let man worship it alone as uktha.' What is prâna, that is pragñâ, or self-consciousness; what is pragñâ (self-consciousness), that is prâna, for together they live in this body, and together they go out of it. Of that, this is the evidence, this is the understanding. When a man, being thus asleep, sees no dream whatever, he becomes one with that prâna alone. Then speech goes to him, when he is absorbed in prâna, with all names, the eye with all forms, the ear with all sounds, the mind with all thoughts. And when he awakes, then, as from a burning fire sparks proceed in all directions; thus from that self the prânas, proceed, each towards its place: from the prânas the gods, from the gods the worlds.

"Of this, this is the proof, this is the understanding. When a man is thus sick, going to die, falling into weakness and faintness, they say: 'His thought has departed, he hears not, he sees not, he speaks not, he thinks not.' Then he becomes one with that prâna alone. Then speech goes to him who is absorbed in prâna, with all names, the eye with all forms, the ear with all sounds, the mind with all thoughts. And when he departs from this body, he departs together with all these.

"Let no man try to find out what speech is, let him know the speaker. Let no man try to find out what odor is, let him know him who smells. Let no man try to find out what form is, let him know the seer. Let no man try to find out what sound is, let him know the hearer. Let no man try to find out the tastes of food, let him know the knower of tastes. Let no man try to find out what action is, let him know the agent. Let no man try to find out what pleasure and pain are, let him know the knower of pleasure and pain. Let no man try to find out what happiness, joy, and offspring are, let him know the knower of happiness, joy, and offspring. Let no man try to find out what movement is, let him know the mover. Let no man try to find out what mind is, let him know the thinker. These ten objects (what is spoken, smelled, seen, felt) have reference to self-consciousness; the ten subjects (speech, the senses, mind) have reference to objects. If there were no objects, there would be no subjects; and if there were no subjects, there would be no objects. For on either side alone nothing could be achieved. But the self of pragñâ, consciousness, and prâna, life, is not many, but one. For as in a car the circumference of a wheel is placed on the spokes, and the spokes on the nave, thus are these objects, as a circumference, placed on the subjects as spokes, and the subjects on the prâna. And that prâna, the living and breathing power, indeed is the self of pragñâ, the self-conscious self: blessed, imperishable, immortal. He does not increase by a good action, nor decrease by a bad action. For the self of prâna and pragñâ makes him, whom he wishes to lead up from these worlds, do a good deed; and the same makes him, whom he wishes to lead down from these worlds, do a bad deed. And he is the guardian of the world, he is the king of the world, he is the lord of the universe—and he is my (Indra's) self: thus let it be known, yea, thus let it be known!

Study Questions

1. What is prâna?

2. What role do the five senses (taste, hearing, sight, smell, and touch) play in the Upanishads?

3. What is the worldview embraced in the Upanishads? How does its vision of immortality differ from the older Vedic Aryan idea of life after death in either heaven or hell?

4. Numerous people, including many warrior-nobles, abandoned their class distinctions and ritualistic religious practices in order to seek Upanishadic truth. These people became hermits or wanderers seeking an ascetic existence. What effect, potentially, would this have on their society?

Sermons and Teachings (6th century B.C.E.)   15

THE BUDDHA

Siddhartha Gautama (ca. 563–483 B.C.E.) was the son of the king of a small Indian state. Legend holds that it was foretold at his birth that he would either be a great monarch or a great Buddha (literally, "an enlightened one"). His father, hoping for the former, raised Siddhartha in luxury. But at the age of 29 Siddhartha experienced a vision of human suffering that led him to renounce his worldly status and goods and take to the road as a wandering ascetic. He joined at least two ascetic sects, whose philosophies he quickly mastered; but neither allowed him to achieve the highest truth. He finally attained this goal when one night while he was meditating he was able to comprehend his past and future lives. Siddhartha determined to teach the truths he had realized; he gathered disciples and preached a middle way between worldliness and asceticism. His teachings swept throughout east Asia, becoming the foundation for one of the world's great religions. Buddhist traditions flourished in both India and China, although they developed separately.

The teachings of the Buddha were recorded by his students and then codified over the next 500 years. The Buddha's sermons are regarded by scholars as largely authentic, and part of his first sermon, the Sermon at Benares, is reproduced here. The Selection following that is a disquisition on the concept of Nirvana.

The Sermon at Benares

On seeing their old teacher approach, the five bhikkhus agreed among themselves not to salute him, nor to address him as a master, but by his name only. "For," so they said, "he has broken his vow and has abandoned holiness. He is no bhikkhu but Gotama, and Gotama has become a man who lives in abundance and indulges in the pleasures of worldliness."

But when the Blessed One approached in a dignified manner, they involuntarily rose from their seats and greeted him in spite of their resolution. Still they called him by his name and addressed him as "friend Gotama."

When they had thus received the Blessed One, he said: "Do not call the Tathagata. by his name nor address him as 'friend,' for he is the Buddha, the Holy One. The Buddha looks with a kind heart equally on all living beings, and they therefore call him 'Father.' To disrespect a father is wrong; to despise him, is wicked.

"The Tathagata," the Buddha continued, "does not seek salvation in austerities, but neither does he for that reason indulge in worldly pleasures, nor live in abundance. The Tathagata has found the middle path.

"There are two extremes, O bhikkhus, which the man who has given up the world ought not to follow—the habitual practice, on the one hand, of self-indulgence which is unworthy, vain and fit only for the worldly-minded—and the habitual practice, on the other hand, of self-mortification, which is painful, useless and unprofitable.

"Neither abstinence from fish or flesh, nor going naked, nor shaving the head, nor wearing matted hair, nor dressing in a rough garment, nor covering oneself with dirt, nor sacrificing to Agni, will cleanse a man who is not free from delusions.

"Reading the Vedas, making offerings to priests, or sacrifices to the gods, self-mortification by heat or cold, and many such penances performed for the sake of immortality, these do not cleanse the man who is not free from delusions.

"Anger, drunkenness, obstinacy, bigotry, deception, envy, self-praise, disparaging others, superciliousness and evil intentions constitute uncleanness; not verily the eating of flesh.

"A middle path, O bhikkhus, avoiding the two extremes, has been discovered by the Tathagata—a path which opens the eyes, and bestows understanding, which leads to peace of mind, to the higher wisdom, to full enlightenment, to Nirvana!

"What is that middle path, O bhikkhus, avoiding these two extremes, discovered by the Tathagata—a that path which opens the eyes, and bestows understanding, which leads to peace of mind, to the higher wisdom, to full enlightenment, to Nirvana?

"Let me teach you, O bhikkhus, the middle path, which keeps aloof from both extremes. By suffering, the emaciated devotee produces confusion and sickly thoughts in his mind. Mortification is not conducive even to worldly knowledge; how much less to a triumph over the senses!

"He who fills his lamp with water will not dispel the darkness, and he who tries to light a fire with rotten wood will fail. And how can anyone be free from self by leading a wretched life, if he does not succeed in quenching the fires of lust, if he still hankers after either worldly or heavenly pleasures. But he in whom self has become extinct is free from lust; he will desire neither worldly nor heavenly pleasures, and the satisfaction of his natural wants will not defile him. However, let him be moderate, let him eat and drink according to the needs of the body.

"Sensuality is enervating; the self-indulgent man is a slave to his passions, and pleasure-seeking is degrading and vulgar.

"But to satisfy the necessities of life is not evil. To keep the body in good health is a duty, for otherwise we shall not be able to trim the lamp of wisdom, and keep our mind strong and clear. Water surrounds the lotus-flower, but does not wet its petals.

"This is the middle path, O bhikkhus, that keeps aloof from both extremes."

And the Blessed One spoke kindly to his disciples, pitying them for their errors, and pointing out the uselessness of their endeavors, and the ice of ill-will that chilled their hearts melted away under the gentle warmth of the Master's persuasion.

Now the Blessed One set the wheel of the most excellent law rolling, and he began to preach to the five bhikkhus, opening to them the gate of immortality, and showing them the bliss of Nirvana.

The Buddha said:

"The spokes of the wheel are the rules of pure conduct: justice is the uniformity of their length; wisdom is the tire; modesty and thoughtfulness are the hub in which the immovable axle of truth is fixed.

"He who recognizes the existence of suffering, its cause, its remedy, and its cessation has fathomed the four noble truths. He will walk in the right path.

"Right views will be the torch to light his way. Right aspirations will be his guide. Right speech will be his dwelling-place on the road. His gait will be straight, for it is right behavior. His refreshments will be the right way of earning his livelihood. Right efforts will be his steps: right thoughts his breath; and right contemplation will give him the peace that follows in his footprints.

"Now, this, O bhikkhus, is the noble truth concerning suffering:

"Birth is attended with pain, decay is painful, disease is painful, death is painful. Union with the unpleasant is painful, painful is separation from the pleasant; and any craving that is unsatisfied, that too is painful. In brief, bodily conditions which spring from attachment are painful.

"This, then, O bhikkhus, is the noble truth concerning suffering.

'Now this, O bhikkhus, is the noble truth concerning the origin of suffering:

"Verily, it is that craving which causes the renewal of existence, accompanied by sensual delight, seeking satisfaction now here, now there, the craving for the gratification of the passions, the craving for a future life, and the craving for happiness in this life.

"This, then, O bhikkhus, is the noble truth concerning the origin of suffering.

"Now this, O bhikkhus, is the noble truth concerning the destruction of suffering:

"Verily, it is the destruction, in which no passion remains, of this very thirst; it, is the laying aside of, the being free from, the dwelling no longer upon this thirst.

"This, then, O bhikkhus, is the noble truth concerning the destruction of suffering.

"Now this, O bhikkhus, is the noble truth concerning the way which leads to the destruction of sorrow. Verily! it is this noble eightfold path; that is to say:

"Right views; right aspirations; right speech; right behavior; right livelihood; right effort; right thoughts; and right contemplation.

"This, then, O bhikkhus, is the noble truth concerning the destruction of sorrow.

"By the practice of lovingkindness I have attained liberation of heart, and thus I am assured that I shall never return in renewed births. I have even now attained Nirvana."

And when the Blessed One had thus set the royal chariot wheel of truth rolling onward, a rapture thrilled through all the universes.

The devas left their heavenly abodes to listen to the sweetness of the truth; the saints that had parted from life crowded around the great teacher to receive the glad tidings; even the animals of the earth felt the bliss that rested upon the words of the Tathagata: and all the creatures of the host of sentient beings, gods, men, and beasts, hearing the message of deliverance, received and understood it in their own language.

And when the doctrine was propounded, the venerable Kondanna, the oldest one among the five bhikkhus, discerned the truth with his mental eye, and he said: "Truly, O Buddha, our Lord, thou hast found the truth!" Then the other bhikkhus too, joined him and exclaimed: "Truly, thou art the Buddha, thou has found the truth."

And the devas and saints and all the good spirits of the departed generations that had listened to the sermon of the Tathagata, joyfully received the doctrine and shouted: "Truly, the Blessed One has founded the kingdom of righteousness. The Blessed One has moved the earth; he has set the wheel of Truth rolling, which by no one in the universe, be he god or man, can ever be turned back. The kingdom of Truth will be preached upon earth; it will spread; and righteousness, good-will, and peace will reign among mankind."

What Is Nirvana?

"Revered Nagasena, things produced of karma are seen in the world, things produced of cause are seen, things produced of nature are seen. Tell me what in the world is born not of karma, not of cause, not of nature."

"These two, sire, in the world are born not of karma, not of cause, not of nature. Which two? Ether, sire, and Nirvana."

"Do not, revered Nagasena, corrupt the Conqueror's words and answer the question ignorantly."

"What did I say, sire, that you speak thus to me?"

"Revered Nagasena, what you said about ether—that it is born not of karma nor of cause nor of nature—is right. But with many a hundred reasons did the Lord, revered Nagasena, point out to disciples the Way to the realization of Nirvana—and then *you* speak thus: 'Nirvana is born of no cause.'"

"It is true, sire, that with many a hundred reasons did the Lord point out to disciples the Way to the realization of Nirvana; but he did not point out a cause for the production of Nirvana."

"Well then, sire, attend carefully, listen closely, and I will tell the reason as to this. Would a man, sire, with his natural strength be able to go from here up a high Himalayan mountain?"

"Yes, revered Nagasena."

"But would that man, sire, with his natural strength be able to bring a high Himalayan mountain here?"

"Certainly not, revered sir."

"Even so, sire, it is possible to point out the Way for the realization of Nirvana, but impossible to show a cause for the production of Nirvana. Would it be possible, sire, for a man who, with his natural strength, has crossed over the great sea in a boat to reach the farther shore?"

"Yes, revered sir."

"But would it be possible, sire, for that man, with his natural strength, to bring the farther shore of the great sea here?"

"Certainly not, revered sir."

"Even so, sire, it is possible to point out the Way to the realization of Nirvana, but impossible to show a cause for the production of Nirvana. For what reason? It is because of the uncompounded nature of the thing."

"Revered Nagasena, is Nirvana uncompounded?"

"Yes, sire, Nirvana is uncompounded; it is made by nothing at all. Sire, one cannot say of Nirvana that it arises or that it does not arise or that it is to be produced or that it is past or future or present, or that it is cognizable by the eye, ear, nose, tongue or body."

"If, revered Nagasena, Nirvana neither arises nor does not arise and so on, as you say, well then, revered Nagasena, you indicate Nirvana as a thing that is not: Nirvana is not."

"Sire, Nirvana is; Nirvana is cognizable by mind; an ariyan-disciple, faring along rightly with a mind that is purified, lofty, straight, without obstructions, without temporal desires, sees Nirvana."

"But what, revered sir, is that Nirvana like that can be illustrated by similes? Convince me with reasons according to which a thing that is can be illustrated by similes."

"Is there, sire, what is called wind?"

"Yes, revered sir."

"Please, sire, show the wind by its colour or configuration or as thin or thick or long or short."

"But it is not possible, revered Nagasena, for the wind to be shown; for the wind cannot be grasped in the hand or touched; but yet there is the wind."

"If, sire, it is not possible for the wind to be shown, well then, there is no wind."

"I, revered Nagasena, know that there is wind, I am convinced of it, but I am not able to show the wind."

"Even so, sire, there is Nirvana; but it is not possible to show Nirvana by colour or configuration."

"Very good, revered Nagasena, well shown is the simile, well seen the reason; thus it is and I accept it as you say: There is Nirvana."

Study Questions

1. What were some of the personal characteristics of the Buddha?

2. Why, when the five bhikkhus in The Sermon at Benares saw the Buddha, did they decide to ignore him? What made them change their minds?

3. In The Sermon at Benares, the Buddha laid out the basic tenets of Buddhism. What are the four noble truths? What is the worldview espoused by these beliefs?

4. According to the Buddha, what is Nirvana? What role does Nirvana play in Buddhism?

5. The Buddhist movement fostered participation at different levels. Many followers sought the "ordinary" norm; one of their duties was to support those who sought the "extraordinary" norm and became monks and nuns. What effect would this dual community of believers have on their society?

Bhagavad-Gita (ca. 200 B.C.E.)   16

The Bhagavad-Gita (*The Lord's Song*) is the most famous work of the Hindu tradition. Like many other epics, it was transmitted orally for centuries before being put in writing around 200 B.C.E. The *Bhagavad-Gita* is only one part of a larger epic known as the *Mahabharata,* the story of two branches of the same family who struggle for worldly power against each other. In it, the Hindu Gods mix with humans to provide strategy and advice. The *Bhagavad-Gita* is a long interlude during which Arjuna, the warrior chieftain of one branch of the family, searches his soul for the ethical foundations of the battle he is about to fight. He cannot reconcile his worldly ambitions with the slaughter of his own kin. He is answered by Krishna, the highest Hindu deity, who reveals himself as Arjuna's charioteer and offers him a foundation for his actions. The *Bhagavad-Gita* remains a tract of philosophical power and literary beauty and continues to be the most influential work of Hinduism.

Arjuna spake:—

"As I look, O Krishna, upon these kinsfolk meeting for battle,

my limbs fail and my face withers.

Trembling comes upon my body, and upstanding of the hair;

Gandiva falls from my hand, and my skin burns. I cannot stand in my place; my mind is as if awhirl.

Contrary are the omens that I behold, O Long-Haired One. I see no blessing from slaying of kinsfolk in strife;

I desire not victory, O Krishna, nor kingship, nor delights. What shall avail me kingship, O Lord of the Herds, or pleasures, or life?

They for whose sake I desired kingship, pleasures, and delights stand here in battle array, offering up their lives and substance—

teachers, fathers, sons, likewise grandsires, uncles, fathers-in-law, grandsons, brothers-in-law, kinsmen also.

These though they smite me I would not smite, O Madhu-Slayer, even for the sake of empire over the Three Worlds, much less for the sake of the earth.

What pleasure can there be to us, O Troubler of the Folk, from slaughter of Dhritarashtra's folk? Guilt in sooth will lodge with us for doing these to death with armed hand.

Therefore it is not meet that we slay Dhritarashtra's folk, our kinsmen; for if we do to death our own kith how can we walk in joy, O Lord of Madhu?

Albeit they, whose wits are stopped by greed, mark not the guilt of destroying a stock and the sin of treason to friends,

yet how, O Troubler of the Folk, shall not we with clear sight see the sin of destroying a stock, so that we be stayed from this guilt?

In the destruction of a stock perish the ancient Laws of the stock; when Law perishes, Lawlessness falls upon the whole stock.

When Lawlessness comes upon it, O Krishna, the women of the stock fall to sin; and from the women's sinning, O thou of Vrishni's race, castes become confounded.

Confounding of caste brings to hell alike the stock's slayers and the stock; for their Fathers fall when the offerings of the cake and the water to them fail.

By this guilt of the destroyers of a stock, which makes castes to be confounded, the everlasting Laws of race and Laws of stock are overthrown.

For men the Laws of whose stock are overthrown, O Troubler of the Folk, a dwelling is ordained in hell; thus have we heard.

Ah me! a heavy sin have we resolved to do, that we strive to slay our kin from lust after the sweets of kingship!

It were more comfortable to me if Dhritarashtra's folk with armed hand should slay me in the strife unresisting and weaponless." Sanjaya spake:—

So spake Arjuna, and sate down on the seat of his chariot in the field of war; and he let fall his bow and arrows, for his heart was heavy with sorrow.

Sanjaya spake:—

So was he stricken by compassion and despair, with clouded eyes full of tears; and the Slayer of Madhu spake to him this word.

The Lord spake:—

"Wherefore, O Arjuna, hath come upon thee in thy straits this defilement, such as is felt by the ignoble, making not for heaven, begetting dishonour?

Fall not into unmanliness, O Pritha's son; it is unmeet for thee. Cease from this base faintness of heart and rise up, O affrighter of the foe!"

Arjuna spake:—

"O Madhu's Slayer, how shall I contend in the strife with my arrows against Bhishma and Drona, who are meet for honour, O smiter of foes?

Verily it were more blest to eat even the food of beggary in this world, without slaughter of noble masters; were I to slay my masters, I should enjoy here but wealth and loves—delights sullied with blood.

We know not which is the better for us, whether we should overcome them or they overcome us; before us stand arrayed Dhritarashtra's folk, whom if we slay we shall have no wish for life.

My soul stricken with the stain of unmanliness, my mind all unsure of the Law, I ask thee—tell me clearly what will be the more blest way. I am thy disciple; teach me, who am come to thee for refuge.

I behold naught that can cast out the sorrow that makes my limbs to wither, though I win to wide lordship without rival on earth and even to empire over the gods."

So spake to the High-Haired One the Wearer of the Hair-Knot, affrighter of foes; "I will not war," he said to the Lord of the Herds, and made an end of speaking.

And as he sat despairing between the two hosts, O thou of Bharata's race, the High-Haired One with seeming smile spake to him this word.

The Lord spake:—

"Thou hast grieved over them for whom grief is unmeet, though thou speakest words of understanding. The learned grieve not for them whose lives are fled nor for them whose lives are not fled.

Never have I not been, never hast thou and never have these princes of men not been; and never shall time yet come when we shall not all be.

As the Body's Tenant goes through childhood and manhood and old age in this body, so does it pass to other bodies; the wise man is not confounded therein.

It is the touchings of the senses' instruments, O Kunti's son, that beget cold and heat, pleasure and pain; it is they that come and go, that abide not; bear with them, O thou of Bharata's race.

Verily the man whom these disturb not, indifferent alike to pain and to pleasure, and wise, is meet for immortality, O chief of men.

Of what is not there cannot be being; of what is there cannot be aught but being. The bounds of these twain have been beheld by them that behold the Verity.

But know that That which pervades this universe is imperishable; there is none can make to perish that changeless being.

It is these bodies of the everlasting, unperishing, incomprehensible Body-Dweller that have an end, as it is said. Therefore fight, O thou of Bharata's race.

He who deems This to be a slayer, and he who thinks This to be slain, are alike without discernment; This slays not, neither is it slain.

This never is born, and never dies, nor may it after being come again to be not; this unborn, everlasting, abiding Ancient is not slain when the body is slain.

Knowing This to be imperishable, everlasting, unborn, changeless, O son of Pritha, how and whom can a man make to be slain, or slay?

As a man lays aside outworn garments and takes others that are new, s o the Body-Dweller puts away outworn bodies and goes to others that are new.

Weapons cleave not This, fire bums not This, waters wet not This, wind dries it not.

Not to be cleft is This, not to be burned, nor to be wetted, nor likewise to be dried; everlasting is This, dwelling in all things, firm, motionless, ancient of days.

Unshown is This called, unthinkable This, unalterable This; therefore, knowing it in this wise, thou dost not well to grieve.

So though thou deemest it everlastingly to pass through births and everlastingly through deaths, nevertheless, O strong of arm, thou shouldst not grieve thus.

For to the born sure is death, to the dead sure is birth; so for an issue that may not be escaped thou dost not well to sorrow.

Born beings have for their beginning the unshown state, for their midway the shown, O thou of Bharata's race, and for their ending the unshown; what lament is there for this?

As a marvel one looks upon This; as a marvel another tells thereof; and as a marvel another hears of it; but though he hear of This none knows it.

This Body's Tenant for all time may not be wounded, O thou of Bharata's stock, in the bodies of any beings. Therefore thou dost not well to sorrow for any born beings.

Looking likewise on thine own Law, thou shouldst not be dismayed; for to a knight there is no thing more blest than a lawful strife.

Happy the knights, O son of Pritha, who find such a strife coming unsought to them as an open door to Paradise.

But if thou wilt not wage this lawful battle, then wilt thou fail thine own Law and thine honour, and get sin.

Also born beings will tell of thee a tale of unchanging dishonour; and to a man of repute dishonour is more than death.

The lords of great chariots will deem thee to have held back from the strife through fear; and thou wilt come to be lightly esteemed of those by whom thou wert erstwhile deemed of much worth.

They that seek thy hurt will say many words of ill speech, crying out upon thee for thy faintness; now what is more grievous than this?

If thou be slain, thou wilt win Paradise; if thou conquer, thou wilt have the joys of the earth; therefore rise up resolute for the fray, O son of Kunti.

Holding in indifference alike pleasure and pain, gain and loss, conquest and defeat, so make thyself ready for the fight; thus shalt thou get no sin....

Into a godlike nature, O son of Pritha, enter great-hearted men who worship Me with undivided mind, knowing Me to be the Beginning of born beings, the unchanging;

Ever singing My praises, labouring firm in their vows, devoutly doing homage, everlastingly under the Rule, men wait on Me.

Others again there are that wait on Me, offering the Sacrifice of Knowledge, according to My unity, or My severalty, or My manifold aspects that face all ways.

The sacrifice am I, the offering am I, the Fathers' oblation am I, the herb am I, the spell am I, the butter-libation am I, the fire am I, the rite of oblation am I;

father of this universe am I, mother, ordainer, grandsire, the thing that is known and the being that makes clean, the word *Om*, the Rik, the Sama, and the Yajus;

the way, the supporter, the lord, the witness, the dwelling, the refuge, the friend, the origin, the dissolution, the abiding-place, the house of ward, the changeless seed.

I give heat; I arrest and let loose the rain; I am likewise power of immortality and death, Being and No-Being, O Arjuna.

Men of the Threefold Lore that drink the *soma* and are cleansed of sin, worshipping me with sacrifices, pray for the way to paradise; winning as meed of righteousness the world of the Lord of Gods, they taste in heaven the heavenly delights of the gods.

When they have enjoyed that wide world of paradise and their wage of righteousness is spent, they enter into the world of mortals; thus the lovers of loves who follow the Law of the Three Books win but a going and a coming.

But to the men everlastingly under the Rule, who in undivided service think and wait on Me, I bring power to win and to maintain.

They also who worship other gods and make offering to them with faith, O son of Kunti, do verily make offering to Me, though not according to ordinance.

For I am He that has enjoyment and lordship of all sacrifices; but they recognise Me not in verity, and therefore they fall.

They whose vows are to the gods go to the gods, they whose vows are to the Fathers go to the Fathers; they who offer to ghosts go to ghosts; but they that offer to Me go to Me.

If one of earnest spirit set before Me with devotion a leaf, a flower, fruit, or water, I enjoy this offering of devotion.

Whatever be thy work, thine eating, thy sacrifice, thy gift, thy mortification, make thou of it an offering to Me, O son of Kunti.

Thus shalt thou be released from the bonds of Works, fair or foul of fruit; thy spirit inspired by casting-off of Works and following the Rule, thou shalt be delivered and come unto Me.

I am indifferent to all born beings; there is none whom I hate, none whom I love. But they that worship Me with devotion dwell in Me, and I in them.

Even though he should be a doer of exceeding evil that worships Me with undivided worship, he shall be deemed good; for he is of right purpose.

Speedily he becomes righteous of soul, and comes to lasting peace. O son of Kunti, be assured that none who is devoted to Me is lost.

For even they that be born of sin, O son of Pritha,—women, traffickers, and serfs,—if they turn to Me, come to the supreme path;

how much more then shall righteous Brahmans and devout kingly sages? As thou has come into this unstable and joyless world, worship Me.

Have thy mind on Me, thy devotion toward Me, thy sacrifice to Me, do homage to Me. Thus guiding thyself, given over to Me, so to Me shalt thou come."

The Lord spake:—

"Again, O strong-armed one, hearken to My sublime tale, which in desire for thy weal I will recite to thy delighted ear.

The ranks of the gods and the saints know not My origin; for I am altogether the Beginning of gods and saints.

He who unbewildered knows Me to be the unborn, the one without beginning, great lord of worlds, is released from all sins amidst mortals.

Understanding, knowledge, unconfounded vision, patience, truth, restraint of sense and spirit, joy and sorrow, origination and not-being, fear and fearlessness,

harmlessness, indifference, delight, mortification, almsgiving, fame, and infamy—these

are the forms of born beings' existence severally dispensed by Me.

The seven Great Saints, the four Ancients,
and the Manus had their spirit of Me, and were
born of My mind; of them are these living creatures in the world.

He that knows in verity My power and rule
is assuredly ruled by unwavering Rule.

I am the origin of the All; from Me
the All proceeds; with this belief the enlightened, possessed of the spirit, pay worship to
Me.

Study Questions

1. What is Arjuna's dilemma?

2. What is Krishna's answer?

3. How does the philosophy espoused by Krishna complement India's caste system?

4. What does this passage tell us about Hindu beliefs regarding the soul?

Analects (ca. 500 B.C.E.)   17

CONFUCIUS

Confucius (Master K'ung in Chinese) (ca. 551–479 B.C.E.) was born in Shantung
province; his family was probably of the knightly class, just below that of the aristocracy. He made his living teaching the sons of the nobility. Along with traditional
subjects, Confucius taught his students his own philosophy of principled service to
the state; many of his pupils went on to distinguished careers in government.
Despite his teachings and ambition, however, Confucius himself was never called to
serve in government.

Little is known for certain about his life and none of his own writings survived.
He seems to have been a head of a family and also to have migrated within several
regions of China. Wherever he went he attracted a following. After his death
he was elevated to the status of Divine Sage, which made his pronouncements
infallible.

The *Analects* (which comes from the Greek word for the original Chinese,
meaning roughly "selected sayings," the origin of the phrase, "Confucius says")
were preserved and handed down by his followers. They are therefore cast in the
form of pithy sayings rather than treatises and have a strongly didactic flavor. Their
underpinning is a moral rather than a religious philosophy that emphasizes education and self-sacrifice. Confucianism has been the most influential philosophy in
world history.

Book II

The Master said, He who rules by moral force is like the pole-star, which remains in its place while all the lesser stars do homage to it.

The Master said, If out of the three hundred *Songs* I had to take one phrase to cover all my teaching, I would say 'Let there be no evil in your thoughts.'

The Master said, Govern the people by regulations, keep order among them by chastisements, and they will flee from you, and lose all self-respect. Govern them by moral force, keep order among them by ritual and they will keep their self-respect and come to you of their own accord.

The Master said, At fifteen I set my heart upon learning. At thirty, I had planted my feet firm upon the ground. At forty, I no longer suffered from perplexities. At fifty, I knew what were the biddings of Heaven. At sixty, I heard them with docile ear. At seventy, I could follow the dictates of my own heart; for what I desired no longer overstepped the boundaries of right.

Mêng I Tzu asked about the treatment of parents. The Master said, Never disobey! When Fan Ch'ih was driving his carriage for him, the Master said, Mêng asked me about the treatment of parents and I said, Never disobey! Fan Ch'ih said, In what sense did you mean it? The Master said, While they are alive, serve them according to ritual. When they die, bury them according to ritual and sacrifice to them according to ritual.

Mêng Wu Po asked about the treatment of parents. The Master said, Behave in such a way that your father and mother have no anxiety about you, except concerning your health.

Tzu-yu asked about the treatment of parents. The Master said, 'Filial sons' nowadays are people who see to it that their parents get enough to eat. But even dogs and horses are cared for to that extent. If there is no feeling of respect, wherein lies the difference?

Tzu-hsia asked about the treatment of parents. The Master said, It is the demeanour that is difficult. Filial piety does not consist merely in young people undertaking the hard work, when anything has to be done, or serving their elders first with wine and food. It is something much more than that.

The Master said, Look closely into his aims, observe the means by which he pursues them, discover what brings him content—and can the man's real worth remain hidden from you, can it remain hidden from you?

The Master said, He who by reanimating the Old can gain knowledge of the New is fit to be a teacher.

The Master said, A gentleman is not an implement.

Tzu-kung asked about the true gentleman. The Master said, He does not preach what he practises till he has practised what he preaches.

The Master said, A gentleman can see a question from all sides without bias. The small man is biased and can see a question only from one side.

The Master said, 'He who learns but does not think, is lost.' He who thinks but does not learn is in great danger.

The Master said, He who sets to work upon a different strand destroys the whole fabric.

The Master said, Yu, shall I teach you what knowledge is? When you know a thing, to recognize that you know it, and when you do not know a thing, to recognize that you do not know it. That is knowledge.

The Master said, Hear much, but maintain silence as regards doubtful points and be cautious in speaking of the rest; then you will seldom get into trouble. See much, but ignore what it is dangerous to have seen, and be cautious in acting upon the rest; then you will seldom want to undo your acts. He who seldom gets into trouble about what he has said and seldom does anything that he afterwards

Portrait of Confucius. This tradtitional portrait of Confucius is by an unknown artist. It shows a serene old teacher.

dignity, and they will respect you. Show piety towards your parents and kindness towards your children, and they will be loyal to you. Promote those who are worthy, train those who are incompetent; that is the best form of encouragement.

Someone, when talking to Master K'ung, said, How is it that you are not in the public service? The Master said, The Book says: 'Be filial, only be filial and friendly towards your brothers, and you will be contributing to government.' There are other sorts of service quite different from what you mean by 'service.'

The Master said, Just as to sacrifice to ancestors other than one's own is presumption, so to see what is right and not do it is cowardice.

Book IV

The Master said, It is Goodness that gives to a neighbourhood its beauty. One who is free to choose, yet does not prefer to dwell among the Good—how can he be accorded the name of wise?

The Master said, Without Goodness a man

Cannot for long endure adversity,
Cannot for long enjoy prosperity.

The Good Man rests content with Goodness; he that is merely wise pursues Goodness in the belief that it pays to do so.

Of the adage 'Only a Good Man knows how to like people, knows how to dislike them,' the Master said, He whose heart is in the smallest degree set upon Goodness will dislike no one.

Wealth and rank are what every man desires; but if they can only be retained to the detriment of the Way he professes, he must relinquish them. Poverty and obscurity are what every man detests; but if they can only be avoided to the detriment of the Way he professes, he must accept them. The gentleman

wishes he had not done, will be sure incidentally to get his reward.

Duke Ai asked, What can I do in order to get the support of the common people? Master Kung replied, If you 'raise up the straight and set them on top of the crooked,' the commoners will support you. But if you raise the crooked and set them on top of the straight, the commoners will not support you.

Chi K'ang-tzu asked whether there were any form of encouragement by which he could induce the common people to be respectful and loyal. The Master said, Approach them with who ever parts company with Goodness does not fulfil that name. Never for a moment does a gentleman quit the way of Goodness. He is never so harried but that he cleaves to this; never so tottering but that he cleaves to this.

The Master said, I for my part have never yet seen one who really cared for Goodness, nor one who really abhorred wickedness. One who really cared for Goodness would never let any other consideration come first. One who abhorred wickedness would be so constantly doing Good that wickedness would never have a chance to get at him. Has anyone ever managed to do Good with his whole might even as long as the space of a single day? I think not. Yet I for my part have never seen anyone give up such an attempt because he had not the *strength* to go on. It may well have happened, but I for my part have never seen it.

The Master said, In the morning, hear the Way; in the evening, die content!

The Master said, If it is really possible to govern countries by ritual and yielding, there is no more to be said. But if it is not really possible, of what use is ritual?

The Master said, In the presence of a good man, think all the time how you may learn to equal him. In the presence of a bad man, turn your gaze within!

The Master said, In serving his father and mother a man may gently remonstrate with them. But if he sees that he has failed to change their opinion, he should resume an attitude of deference and not thwart them; may feel discouraged, but not resentful.

The Master said, In old days a man kept a hold on his words, fearing the disgrace that would ensue should he himself fail to keep pace with them.

The Master said, Those who err on the side of strictness are few indeed!

The Master said, A gentleman covets the reputation of being slow in word but prompt in deed.

The Master said, Moral force never dwells in solitude; it will always bring neighbours.

Study Questions

1. Who are the people in the text who ask the Master questions?

2. Why do the *Analects* take the form of short, pithy sayings? How would their form affect their reception by the general population?

3. What are some of the personal characteristics Confucius values most?

4. The five Confucian relationships are husband-wife, older brother–younger brother, friend–friend, ruler–subject, and father–son. How are some of these relationships illustrated in the text? Why was having such a well-ordered, hierarchical society important to Confucius?

Te-Tao Ching (ca. 500 B.C.E.)   18

LAO-TZU

There remains considerable doubt about whether the *Te-Tao Ching* was written by a single person known as Lao-tzu. Tradition has it that Lao-tzu (ca. 570–490 B.C.E.) was a scholar at the Chou court entrusted with the keeping of sacred texts. He is said to have met Confucius and chided him for his vanity and to have disappeared while traveling in the west. Both stories are probably fictitious although they are found in a biography of Lao-tzu written in 100 B.C.E.

What is not in doubt is the importance of Taoism in Chinese philosophical thinking. The *Te-Tao Ching* is composed in two parts, the *Tao*, which means "the way," and the *Te*, which means "virtue." Its 81 chapters are written in few characters, a form that is best rendered into verse. Taoism is a wholistic philosophy, fundamentally materialistic, which nevertheless provides a practical guide to morality and government. The various texts of the *Te-Tao Ching* show changes made as late as the first century, C.E. The oldest surviving text was discovered in 1973 and dates from before 168 B.C.E.

1

As for the Way, the Way that can be spoken of
    is not the constant Way;
As for names, the name that can be named is
    not the constant name.
The nameless is the beginning of the ten thousand things;
The named is the mother of the ten thousand
    things.

Therefore, those constantly without desires, by
    this means will perceive its subtlety.
Those constantly with desires, by this means
    will see only that which they yearn for and
    seek.

These two together emerge;
They have different names yet they're called the
    same;
That which is even more profound than the
    profound—
The gateway of all subtleties.

6

The valley spirit never dies;
We call it the mysterious female.
The gates of the mysterious female—
These we call the roots of Heaven and Earth.
Subtle yet everlasting! It seems to exist.
In being used, it is not exhausted.

14

We look at it but do not see it;
We name this "the minute."
We listen to it but do not hear it;
We name this "the rarefied."
We touch it but do not hold it;
We name this "the level and smooth."

These three cannot be examined to the limit.
Thus they merge together as one.
"One"—there is nothing more encompassing
    above it,

And nothing smaller below it.
Boundless, formless! It cannot be named,
And returns to the state of no-thing.

This is called the formless form,
The substanceless image.
This is called the subtle and indistinct.
Follow it and you won't see its back;
Greet it and you won't see its head.
Hold on to the Way of the present—
To manage the things of the present,
And to know the ancient beginning.
This is called the beginning of the thread of the
    Way.

16

Take emptiness to the limit;
Maintain tranquility in the center.

The ten thousand things—side-by-side they
    arise;
And by this I see their return.
Things come forth in great numbers;
Each one returns to its root.
This is called tranquility.
"Tranquility"—This means to return to your
    fate.
To return to your fate is to be constant;
To know the constant is to be wise.
Not to know the constant is to be reckless and
    wild;
If you're reckless and wild, your actions will
    lead to misfortune.

To know the constant is to be all-embracing;
To be all-embracing is to be impartial;
To be impartial is to be kingly;
To be kingly is to be like Heaven;
To be like Heaven is to be one with the Tao;
If you're one with the Tao, to the end of your
    days you'll suffer no harm.

25

There was something formed out of chaos,
That was born before Heaven and Earth.

Quiet and still! Pure and deep!
It stands on its own and doesn't change.
It can be regarded as the mother of Heaven
    and Earth.
I do not yet know its name:
I "style" it "the Way."
Were I forced to give it a name, I would call it
    "the Great."

"Great" means "to depart";
"To depart" means "to be far away";
And "to be far away" means "to return."

The Way is great;
Heaven is great;
Earth is great;
And the king is also great.
In the country there are four greats, and the
    king occupies one place among them.

Man models himself on the Earth;
The Earth models itself on Heaven;
Heaven models itself on the Way;
And the Way models itself on that which is so
    on its own.

34

The Way floats and drifts;
It can go left or right.
It accomplishes its tasks and completes its
    affairs, and yet for this it is not given a name.
The ten thousand things entrust their lives to
    it, and yet it does not act as their master.
Thus it is constantly without desires.
It can be named with the things that are small.
The ten thousand things entrust their lives to
    it, and yet it does not act as their master.
It can be named with the things that are great.

Therefore the Sage's ability to accomplish the
    great
Comes from his not playing the role of the
    great.
Therefore he is able to accomplish the great.

52

The world had a beginning,
Which can be considered the mother of the
world.
Having attained the mother, in order to understand her children,
If you return and hold on to the mother, till
the end of your life you'll suffer no harm.

Block up the holes;

Close the doors;
And till the end of your life you'll not labor.
Open the holes;
Meddle in affairs;
And till the end of your life you'll not be saved.

To perceive the small is called "discernment."
To hold on to the pliant is called "strength."
If you use the rays to return to the bright light,
You'll not abandon your life to peril.
This is called Following the Constant.

Study Questions

1. What is "the Way"?

2. What is the role of the sage in Taoism?

3. The basis for Taoist political philosophy is *wu wei*, or "not doing." How is this illustrated
   in the text? What, according to Lao-tzu, is the consequence of *wu wei*?

4. It has been asserted that the Chinese were Confucian while in public office but Taoist in
   their private lives because Taoism allowed them to escape the burden of their social
   responsibilities. What characteristics of Taoism allowed them to think this?

China: War and Politics

The Great Wall of China.

The Art of War (ca. 500 B.C.E.)   **19**

SUN-TZU

Although almost nothing is known of the life of Sun-tzu, his tract, *The Art of War* has been one of the most influential military handbooks in world history. Legend has it that he served the Wu dynasty after being challenged by the emperor to make an effective army out of his concubines. Sun-tzu placed the emperor's two favorites at the head of two different files of concubines and when they failed to discipline their charges he cut their heads off despite the protests of the emperor. After that the concubines drilled effectively. He became known as Sun the Warrior and is reputed never to have lost a battle.

The Art of War is notable for its realistic assessment of the political constraints on warfare. It is part drill book, part tactical survey, and part political treatise. Its advice has been followed for centuries and it continues to be consulted by modern Chinese leaders.

Laying Plans

Sun-tzu said:

The art of war is of vital importance to the state. It is a matter of life and death, a road either to safety or to ruin. Hence under no circumstances can it be neglected.

The art of war is governed by five constant factors, all of which need to be taken into account. They are: the Moral Law; Heaven; Earth; the Commander; Method and discipline.

The Moral Law causes the people to be in complete accord with their ruler, so that they will follow him regardless of their lives, undismayed by any danger.

Heaven signifies night and day, cold and heat, times and seasons.

Earth comprises distances, great and small; danger and security; open ground and narrow passes; the chances of life and death.

The Commander stands for the virtues of wisdom, sincerity, benevolence, courage, and strictness.

By *Method and discipline* are to be understood the marshaling of the army in its proper subdivisions, the gradations of rank among the officers, the maintenance of roads by which supplies may reach the army, and the control of military expenditure.

These five factors should be familiar to every general. He who knows them will be victorious; he who knows them not will fail.

Therefore, when seeking to determine your military conditions, make your decisions on the basis of a comparison in this wise:

Which of the two sovereigns is imbued with the Moral Law?

Which of the two generals has the most ability?

With whom lie the advantages derived from Heaven and Earth?

On which side is discipline most rigorously enforced?

Which army is the stronger?

On which side are officers and men more highly trained?

A Terracotta Army. Ranks of life-size infantrymen, horses, and chariots made of pottery are drawn up in battle formation in underground pits that flank the tomb of the first emperor of the Ch'in. They were intended to protect him in death.

In which army is there the most absolute certainty that merit will be properly rewarded and misdeeds summarily punished?

By means of these seven considerations I can forecast victory or defeat.... But remember: While heeding the profit of my counsel, avail yourself also of any helpful circumstances over and beyond the ordinary rules and modify your plans accordingly.

All warfare is based on deception. Hence, when able to attack, we must seem unable; when using our forces, we must seem inactive; when we are near, we must make the enemy believe we are far away; when far away, we must make him believe we are near. Hold out baits to entice the enemy. Feign disorder, and crush him. If he is secure at all points, be prepared for him. If he is in superior strength, evade him. If your opponent is of choleric temper, seek to irritate him. Pretend to be weak, that he may grow arrogant. If he is taking his ease, give him no rest. If his forces are united, separate them. Attack him where he is unprepared, appear where you are not expected.

On Waging War

When you engage in actual fighting, if victory is long in coming, the men's weapons will grow dull and their ardor will be dampened. If you lay siege to a town, you will exhaust your strength, and if the campaign is protracted, the resources of the state will not be equal to the strain. Never forget: When your weapons are dulled, your ardor dampened, your strength exhausted, and your treasure spent, other chieftains will spring up to take advantage of your extremity. Then no man, however wise, will be able to avert the consequences that must ensue.

Thus, though we have heard of stupid haste in war, cleverness has never been seen associated with long delays. In all history, there is no instance of a country having benefited from prolonged warfare. Only one who knows the disastrous effects of a long war can realize the supreme importance of rapidity in bringing it to a close. It is only one who is thoroughly acquainted with the evils of war who can thoroughly understand the profitable way of carrying it on.

The skillful general does not raise a second levy, neither are his supply wagons loaded more than twice. Once war is declared, he. will not waste precious time in waiting for reinforcements, nor will he turn his army back for fresh supplies, but crosses the enemy's frontier without delay. The value of time—that is, being a little ahead of your opponent—has counted for more than either numerical superiority or the nicest calculations with regard to commissariat.

In war, then, let your great object be victory, not lengthy campaigns. Thus it may be known that the leader of armies is the arbiter of the people's fate, the man on whom it depends whether the nation shall be in peace or in peril.

The Sheathed Sword

To fight and conquer in all your battles is not supreme excellence; supreme excellence consists in breaking the enemy's resistance without fighting. In the practical art of war, the best thing of all is to take the enemy's country whole and intact; to shatter and destroy it is not so good. So, too, it is better to capture an army entire than to destroy it, to capture a regiment, a detachment, or a company entire than to destroy them.

Thus the highest form of generalship is to balk the enemy's plans; the next best is to prevent the junction of the enemy's forces; the next in order is to attack the enemy's army in the field; and the worst policy of all is to besiege walled cities, because the preparation of mantlets, movable shelters, and various implements of war will take up three whole months: and the piling up of mounds over against the walls will take three months more. The general, unable to control his irritation, will launch his men to the assault like swarming ants, with the result that one third of his men are slain, while the town still remains untaken. Such are the disastrous effects of a siege.

The skillful leader subdues the enemy's troops without any fighting; he captures their cities without laying siege to them; he overthrows their kingdom without lengthy operations in the field. With his forces intact he disputes the mastery of the empire, and thus, without losing a man, his triumph is complete.

This is the method of attacking by stratagem of using the sheathed sword.

It is the rule in war: If our forces are ten to the enemy's one, to surround him; if five to one, to attack him; if twice as numerous, to divide our army into two, one to meet the enemy in front, and one to fall upon his rear; if he replies to the frontal attack, he may be crushed from behind; if to the rearward attack, he may be crushed in front.

If equally matched, we can offer battle; if slightly inferior in numbers, we can avoid the enemy; if quite unequal in every way, we can flee from him. Though an obstinate fight may be made by a small force, in the end it must be captured by the larger force.

The general is the bulwark of the state: if the bulwark is strong at all points, the state will be strong; if the bulwark is defective, the state will be weak.

There are three ways in which a sovereign can bring misfortune upon his army:

By commanding the army to advance or to retreat, being ignorant of the fact that it cannot obey. This is called hobbling the army.

By attempting to govern an army in the same way as he administers a kingdom, being ignorant of the conditions that obtain in an army. This causes restlessness in the soldiers' minds. Humanity and justice are the principles on which to govern a state, but not an army; opportunism and flexibility, on the other hand, are military rather than civic virtues.

He will win who knows when to fight and when not to fight.

He will win who knows how to handle both superior and inferior forces.

He will win whose army is animated by the same spirit throughout all its ranks.

He will win who, prepared himself, waits to take the enemy unprepared.

He will win who has military capacity and is not interfered with by the sovereign.

If you know the enemy and know yourself, you need not fear the result of a hundred battles. If you know yourself but not the enemy, for every victory gained you will also suffer a defeat. If you know neither the enemy nor yourself, you will succumb in every battle.

Tactics

The good fighters of old first put themselves beyond the possibility of defeat, and then waited for an opportunity of defeating the enemy.

To secure ourselves against defeat lies in our own hands, but the opportunity of defeating the enemy is provided by the enemy himself. Hence the saying: One may *know* how to conquer without being able to *do* it.

Security against defeat implies defensive tactics; ability to defeat the enemy means taking the offensive. Standing on the defensive indicates insufficient strength; attacking, a superabundance of strength.

The general who is skilled in defense hides in the most secret recesses of the earth; he who is skilled in attack flashes forth from the topmost heights of heaven. Thus, on the one hand, we have ability to protect ourselves; on the other, to gain a victory that is complete.

To see victory only when it is within the ken of the common herd is not the acme of excellence. Nor is it the acme of excellence if you fight and conquer and the whole empire says, "Well done!" True excellence is to plan secretly, to move surreptitiously, to foil the enemy's intentions and balk his schemes, so that at last the day may be won without shedding a drop of blood....

What the ancients called a clever fighter is one who not only wins, but excels in winning with ease. But his victories bring him neither reputation for wisdom nor credit for courage. For inasmuch as they are gained over circumstances that have not come to light, the world at large knows nothing of them, and he therefore wins no reputation for wisdom; and inasmuch as the hostile state submits before there has been any bloodshed, he receives no credit for courage.

He wins his battles by making no mistakes. Making no mistakes is what establishes the certainty of victory, for it means conquering an enemy that is already defeated.

Hence the skillful fighter puts himself into a position that makes defeat impossible and does not miss the moment for defeating the enemy. Thus it is that in war the victorious strategist only seeks battle after the victory has been won, whereas he who is destined to defeat first fights and afterward looks for victory. A victorious army opposed to a routed one is as a pound's weight placed in the scale against a single grain. The onrush of a conquering force is like the bursting of pent-up waters into a chasm a thousand fathoms deep.

The consummate leader cultivates the Moral Law and strictly adheres to method and discipline; thus it is in his power to control success.

Study Questions

1. What is Sun-tzu's attitude toward war?

2. What does Sun-tzu see as the highest form of victory in a war? What does he think it takes in order to achieve victory?

3. *The Art of War* has been used to illustrate the creativity of Chou thought. Why?

4. What does *The Art of War* tell us about the society for which it was written? What were its values and view of human nature?

The Book of Songs (ca. 1200–1100 B.C.E.) 20

ANONYMOUS

One of the oldest collections of poems in any language, the *Book of Songs* has long held a central place in Chinese culture. Indeed, thanks to Confucius's fondness for citing these verses, they became one of the Five Classics in Confucian literature, and they long served as a set text in the Chinese examination system. Equally important as their role in Confucian thought is their subject matter, which makes the *Book of Songs* as delightful and as accessible now as it was three thousand years ago. Although most of the early texts in world literature chronicled the deeds of gods and monarchs, the *Book of Songs* offers a poignant look at the daily routine of ordinary people in north China.

The following poems illustrate the central themes of the collection. The first three underscore individuals' often difficult relationships with the state; two lament the rigors of military service (122 and 127], and the last one voices a local official's frustration (272). The next two deal with the common problems of a rural community: the first evokes the rhythm of agricultural life (159), and the second stresses the importance of clan unity (194). Finally the last two, recording a wife's longing for an absent husband (100) and a lover's impatience (46), might have been written yesterday.

122 How few of us are left, how few!
    Why do we not go back?
    Were it not for our prince and his concern,
    What should we be doing here in the dew?

    How few of us are left, how few!
    Why do we not go back?
    Were it not for our prince own concerns,
    What should we be doing here in the mud?

127 Minister of War,
    We are the king's claws and fangs.
    Why should you roll us on from misery to misery,
    Giving us no place to stop in or take rest?

    Minister of War,
    We are the king's claws and teeth.
    Why should you roll us from misery to misery,
    Giving us no place to come to and stay?

    Minister of War,
    Truly you are not wise.
    Why should you roll us from misery to misery?
    We have Mothers who lack food.

272 I go out at the northern gate;
    Deep is my grief
    I am utterly poverty-stricken and destitute;
    Yet no one heeds my misfortunes.
    Well, all is over now.
    No doubt it was Heaven's doing,

So what's the good of talking about it?

The king's business came my way;
Government business of every sort was put upon me.
When I came in from outside
The people of the house all turned on me and scolded me.
Well, it's over now.
No doubt it was Heaven's doing.
So what's the good of talking about it?

The king's business was all piled upon me;
Government business of every sort was put upon me.
When I came in from outside
The people of the house all turned upon me and abused me.
Well, it's over now
No doubt it was Heaven's doing,
So what's the good of talking about it?

159 In the seventh month the Fire ebbs;
    In the ninth month I hand out the coats.
    In the days of the First, sharp frosts;
    In the days of the Second, keen winds.
    Without coats, without serge,
    How should they finish the year?
    In the days of the Third they plough;
    In the days of the Fourth out I step
    With my wife and children,
    Bringing hampers to the southern acre
    Were the field-hands come to take good cheer.

In the seventh month the Fire ebbs;
    In the ninth month I hand out the coats.
    But when the spring days grow warm
    And the oriole sings
    The girls take their deep baskets
    And follow the path under the wall
    To gather the soft mulberry-leaves:
    'The spring days are drawing out;
    They gather the white aster in crowds.
    A girls heart is sick and sad
    Till with her lord she can go home.'

    In the seventh month the Fire ebbs;
    In the eighth month they pluck the
      rushes,
    In the silk-worm month they gather the
      mulberry-leaves,
    Take that chopper and bill
    To lop the far boughs and high,
    Pull towards them the tender leaves.
    In the seventh month the shrike cries;
    In the eighth month they twist thread,
    The black thread and the yellow:
    'With my red dye so bright
    I make a robe for my lord.'

    In the fourth month the milkwort is in
      spike,
    In the fifth month the cicada cries.
    In the eighth month the harvest is
      gathered,
    In the tenth month the boughs fall.
    In the days of the First we hunt the
      racoon,
    And take those foxes and wild-cats
    To make furs for our Lord.
    In the days of the Second is the great
      Meet;
    Practice for deeds of war.
    The one-year-old [boar] we keep;
    The three-year we offer to our Lord.
In the fifth month the locust moves its leg,
    In the sixth month the grasshopper shakes
      its wing,
    In the seventh month, out in the wilds:

In the eighth month, in the farm,
In the ninth month, at the door.
In the tenth month the cricket goes under
    my bed.
I stop up every hole to smoke out the rats,
Plugging the windows, burying the
    doors:
'Come, wife and children,
The change of the year is at hand.
Come and live in this house.'

In the sixth month we eat wild plums and
    cherries,
In the seventh month we boil mallows
    and beans.
In the eighth month we dry the dates,
In the tenth month we take the rice
To make with it the spring wine,
So that we may be granted long life.
In the seventh month we eat melons,
In the eighth month we cut the gourds,
In the ninth month we take the seeding
    hemp,
We gather bitter herbs, we cut the ailanto
    for firewood,
That our husbandmen may eat.

In the ninth month we make ready the
    stackyards,
In the tenth month we bring in the har-
    vest,
Millet for wine, millet for cooking, the
    early and the late,
Paddy and hemp, beans and wheat.
Come, my husbandmen,
My harvesting is over,
Go up and begin your work in the house,
In the morning gather thatch-reds,
In the evening twist rope;
 Go quickly on to the roofs.
 Soon you will be beginning to sow your
    many grains.
 In the days of the Second they cut the ice
    with tingling blows;

In the days of the Third they bring it into
    the cold shed.
In the days of the Fourth very early
They offer lambs and garlic.
In the ninth month are shrewd frosts;
In the tenth month they clear the stack-
    grounds.
With twin pitchers they hold the village
    feast,
Killing for it a young lamb
Up they go into their lord's hall,
Raise the drinking-cup of buffalo-horn:
'Hurray for our lord; may he live for ever
    and ever!'

194   The flowers of the cherry-tree,
    Are they not truly splendid?
    Of men that now are,
    None equals a brother.

When death and mourning affright us
Brothers are very dear;
As 'upland' and 'lowland' form a pair,
So 'elder brother' and 'younger brother'
    go together.

There are wagtails on the plain;
When brothers are hard pressed
Even good friends
At the most do but heave a sigh.

Brothers may quarrel within the walls,
But outside they defend one another
    from insult;
Whereas even good friends
Pay but short heed.

But when the times of mourning or
    violence are over,
When all is calm and still,
Even brothers
Are not the equal of friends.

Set out your dishes and meat-stands,
Drink wine to your fill;

All you brothers are here together,
Peaceful, happy, and mild.

Your wives and children chime as well
As little zithern with big zithern.
You brothers are in concord,
Peaceful, merry, in great glee.

Thus you bring good to house and home,
Joy to wife and child.
I have deeply studied, I have pondered,
And truly it is so.

100   My lord is on service;
    He did not know for how long.
    Oh, when will he come?
    The fowls are roosting in their holes,
    Another day is ending,
    The sheep and cows are coming down.
    My lord is on service;
    How can I not be sad?

My lord is on service;
Not a matter of days, nor months.
Oh, when will he be here again?
The fowls are roosting on their perches,
Another day is ending,
The sheep and cows have all come down.
My lord is on service;
Were I but sure that he gets drink and
    food!

46   Oh you with the blue collar,
    On and on I think of you.
    Even though I do not go to you,
    You might surely send me news?

Oh, you with the blue collar,
Always and ever I long for you.
Even though I do not go to you,
You might surely sometimes come?

Here by the wall-gate
I pace to and fro.
One day when I do not see you
Is like three months.

Study Questions

1. Using evidence from the poems, discuss the crops and farming techniques of an ancient Chinese village.

2. What picture do you form of the social hierarchy in these villages?

3. To what extent is the royal government able to intrude into the lives of ordinary people?

4. If these poems were applied to the rural society of late twentieth-century America, which themes would still apply? Which would not?

The Records of the Grand Historian of China (110–85 B.C.E.) 21

SSU-MA CH'IEN

Ssu-ma Ch'ien (ca. 145–85 B.C.E.) was an official at the Han court during its greatest era. His father had served in the office of Grand Historian and Ssu-ma Ch'ien succeeded to it after his father's death in 110 B.C.E. The Grand Historian was responsible both for establishing and maintaining the royal calendar (the method of numbering the years of the dynasty) and for composing a record of the principal events of the reign. Thus Ssu-ma Ch'ien had trained as an astronomer as well as an historian and he was responsible for an important reorganization of the Chinese calendar.

His *Records of the Grand Historian* went far beyond the conventional listing of court appointments and events in the life of the imperial family. Ssu-ma Ch'ien believed that with the accession of the Emperor Wu Ti, the Han dynasty had reached its apex and he decided to write a history of the dynasty as a whole. He divided his work into a chronology, a description of Han government, and a long biographical section in which the lives and deeds of great men were recorded. Ssu-ma Ch'ien believed that history was a moral and didactic subject, that it should teach lessons and reveal the values of the society being remembered. This method is clearly seen in his biographical sketches, like those of Pu Shih and Chi An, which follow.

Pu Shih

The emperor, impressed by the words of a man named Pu Shih, summoned him to court and made him a palace attendant, giving him the honorary rank of *tso-shu-ch'ang* and presenting him with ten *ch'ing* of land. These rewards were announced throughout the empire so that everyone might know of Pu Shih's example.

Pu Shih was a native of Ho-nan, where his family made a living by farming and animal raising. When his parents died, Pu Shih left home, handing over the house, the lands, and all the family wealth to his younger brother, who by this time was full grown. For his own share he took only a hundred or so of the sheep they had been raising, which he led off into the mountains to pasture. In the course of ten years or so, Pu Shih's sheep had increased to over a thousand and he had bought his own house and fields. His younger brother in the meantime had failed completely in the management of the farm, but Pu Shih promptly handed over to him a share of his own wealth. This happened several times. Just at that time the Han was sending its generals at frequent intervals to attack the Hsiung-nu. Pu Shih journeyed to the capital and submitted a letter to the throne, offering to turn over half of his wealth to the district officials to help in the defense of the border. The emperor dispatched an envoy to ask if Pu Shih wanted a post in the government.

"From the time I was a child," Pu Shih replied, "I have been an animal raiser. I have had no experience at government service and would certainly not want such a position."

"Perhaps then your family has suffered some injustice that you would like to report?" inquired the envoy.

But Pu Shih answered, "I have never in my life had a quarrel with anyone. If there are poor men in my village, I lend them what they need, and if there are men who do not behave properly, I guide and counsel them. Where I live, everyone does as I say. Why should I suffer any injustice from others? There is nothing I want to report!"

"If that is the case," said the envoy, "then what is your objective in making this offer?"

Pu Shih replied, "The Son of Heaven has set out to punish the Hsiung-nu. In my humble opinion, every worthy man should be willing to fight to the death to defend the borders, and every person with wealth ought to contribute to the expense. If this were done, then the Hsiungnu could be wiped out!"

The envoy made a complete record of Pu Shih's words and reported them to the emperor. The emperor discussed the matter with the chancellor Kung-sun Hung, but the latter said, "The proposal is simply not in accord with human nature! Such eccentric people are of no use in guiding the populace, but only throw the laws into confusion. I beg Your Majesty not to accept his offer!"

For this reason the emperor put off answering Pu Shih for a long time, and finally, after several years had passed, turned down the offer, whereupon Pu Shih went back to his fields and pastures.

A year or so later the armies marched off on several more expeditions, and the Hun-yeh king and his people surrendered to the Han. As a result the expenditures of the district officials increased greatly and the granaries and treasuries were soon empty. The following year a number of poor people were transferred to other regions, all of them depending upon the district officials for their support, and there were not enough supplies to go around. At this point Pu Shih took two hundred thousand cash of his own and turned the sum over to the governor of Ho-nan to assist the people who were emigrating to other regions. A list of the wealthy men of Honan who had contributed to the aid of the poor was sent to the emperor and he recognized Pu Shih's name. "This is the same man who once offered half his wealth to aid in the defense of the border!" he exclaimed, and presented Pu Shih with a sum of money equivalent to the amount necessary to buy off four hundred men from military duty. Pu Shih once more turned the entire sum over to the district officials. At this time the rich families were all scrambling to hide their wealth; only Pu Shih, unlike the others, had offered to contribute to the expenses of the government. The emperor decided that Pu Shih was really a man of exceptional worth after all, and therefore bestowed upon him the honors mentioned above in order to hint to the people that they might well follow his example.

At first Pu Shih was unwilling to become a palace attendant, but the emperor told him, "I have some sheep in the Shang-lin Park which I would like you to take care of."Pu Shih then accepted the post of palace attendant and, wearing a coarse robe and straw sandals, went off to tend the sheep. After a year or so, the sheep had grown fat and were reproducing at a fine rate. The emperor, when he visited the park and saw the flocks, commended Pu Shih on his work. "It is not only with sheep," Pu Shih commented. "Governing people is the same way. Get them up at the right time, let them rest at the right time, and if there are any bad ones, pull them out at once before they have a chance to spoil the flock!"

The emperor, struck by his words, decided to give him a trial as magistrate of the district of Kou-shih. When his administration proved beneficial to the people of Kou-shih, the emperor transferred him to the post of magistrate of Ch'eng-kao and put him in charge of the transportation of supplies, where his record was also outstanding. Because of his simple, unspoiled ways and his deep loyalty, the emperor finally appointed him grand tutor to his son Liu Hung, the king of Ch'i.

Chi An

Chi An, whose polite name was Chi Ch'ang-ju, was a native of P'u-yang. His ancestors won favor with the rulers of the state of Wei and for seven generations, down to the time of Chi An, served without break as high officials.

During the reign of Emperor Ching, Chi An, on the recommendation of his father, was appointed as a mounted guard to the heir apparent. Because of his stern bearing he was treated with deference. Later, when Emperor Ching passed away and the heir apparent ascended the throne, Chi An was appointed master of guests.

When the tribes of Eastern and Southern Yüeh began to attack each other, the emperor dispatched Chi An to go to the area and observe the situation. He did not journey all the way, however, but went only as far as Wu and then turned around and came back to the capital to make his report. "The Yüeh people have always been in the habit of attacking each other," he said. "There is no reason for the Son of Heaven's envoy to trouble himself about such matters!"

When a great fire broke out in Ho-nei and destroyed over a thousand houses, the emperor once more sent Chi An to observe the situation. On his return he reported, "The roofs of the houses were so close together that the fire spread from one to another; that is why so many homes were burned. It is nothing to worry about. As I passed through Ho-nan on my way, however, I noted that the inhabitants were very poor, and over ten thousand families had suffered so greatly from floods and droughts that fathers and sons were reduced to eating each other. I therefore took it upon myself to use the imperial seals to open the granaries of Ho-nan and relieve the distress of the people. I herewith return the seals and await punishment for overstepping my authority in this fashion."

The emperor, impressed with the wisdom he had shown, overlooked the irregularity of his action and transferred him to the post of governor of Ying-yang. Chi An, however, felt that he was unworthy of a governorship and, pleading illness, retired to his home in the country. When the emperor heard of this, he summoned him to court again and appointed him a palace counselor. But because he sharply criticized the emperor on several occasions, it proved impossible to keep him around the palace for long. The emperor therefore transferred him to the post of governor of Tung-hai.

Chi An studied the doctrines of the Yellow Emperor and Lao Tzu. In executing his duties and governing the people he valued honesty and serenity, selecting worthy assistants and secretaries and leaving them to do as they saw fit. In his administration he demanded only that the general spirit of his directives be carried out and never made a fuss over minor details. He was sick a great deal of the time, confined to his bed and unable to go out, and yet after only a year or so as governor of Tunghai he had succeeded in setting the affairs of the province in perfect order and winning the acclaim of the people.

The emperor, hearing of his success, summoned him to court and appointed him master of titles chief commandant, promoting him to one of the nine highest offices in the government. In this post, as well, Chi An emphasized a policy of laissez-faire, interpreting his duties very broadly and not bothering with the letter of the law.

Chi An was by nature very haughty and ill-mannered. He could not tolerate the faults of others and would denounce people to their faces. Those who took his fancy he treated very well, but those who didn't he could not even bear to see. For this reason most men gave him a wide berth. On the other hand he was fond of learning and liked to travel about doing daring and generous things for others, and his conduct was always above reproach. He was also fond of outspoken criticism and his words frequently brought scowls to the emperor's face. His constant ambition was to be as direct and outspoken as the Liang general Fu Po and Emperor Ching's minister Yuan Ang.

The emperor at the time was busy summoning scholars and Confucians to court and telling them, "I want to do thus-and-so, I want to do thus-and-so." Commenting on this, Chi An said to the emperor, "On the surface Your Majesty is practicing benevolence and righteousness, but in your heart you have too many desires. How do you ever expect to imitate the rule of the sage emperors Yao and Shun in this way?"

The emperor sat in silence, his face flushed with anger, and then dismissed the court. The other high officials were all terrified of what would happen to Chi An. After the emperor had left the room, he turned to his attendants and said, "Incredible—the stupidity of that Chi An!"

Later, some of the officials reproached Chi An for his behavior, but he replied, "Since the Son of Heaven has gone to the trouble of appointing us as his officials and aides, what business have we in simply flattering his whims and agreeing with whatever he says, deliberately leading him on to unrighteous deeds? Now that we occupy these posts, no matter how much we may value our own safety, we cannot allow the court to suffer disgrace, can we?"

"What sort of man is Chi An anyway?" the emperor asked, to which Chuang Chu replied, "As long as he is employed in some ordinary post as an official, he will do no better than the average person. But if he were called upon to assist a young ruler or to guard a city against attack, then no temptation could sway him from his duty, no amount of entreaty could make him abandon his post. Even the bravest men of antiquity, Meng Pen and Hsia Yu, could not shake his determination!"

"Yes," said the emperor. "In ancient times there were ministers who were deemed worthy to be called the guardians of the altars of the nation. And men like Chi An come near to deserving the same appellation."

Study Questions

1. Why did the emperor's counselors think that Pu Shih was eccentric? What behavior did they think reasonable?

2. What were the values that make the shepherd Pu Shih suited to serve as grand tutor to the emperor's son?

3. Why did Chi An not bother to investigate the civil war in Yüeh but did bother to distribute grain in Ho-nan?

4. What did Chi An think was the role of a counselor to the emperor of China?

Memorials (ca. 230 B.C.E.)   22

HAN FEI TZU

In the turbulent period in Chinese history known as the Era of Warring States, the Han kingdom, both smaller and poorer than its chief rivals, struggled for survival. At the end of this chaotic era, one of the Han princes, Han Fei Tzu, wrote a series of memorials, advising the Han king about how to check the state's decline. Although the Han king refused to acknowledge the wisdom of Han Fei Tzu's counsel, a neighboring ruler did, and he attempted to secure the prince's services. Unfortunately for Han Fei Tzu this led to charges of disloyalty and ultimately to his execution in 233 B.C.E.

Han Fei Tzu's *Memorials* have remained one of the classics of ancient Chinese law and statecraft. In contrast to the more philosophical approaches to the problems of government, common to Buddhist and Confucian writers, Han Fei Tzu analyzes the problems of government in a practical and realistic manner. What follows is his discussion of how ruler and subjects alike could detect the warning signs of imminent disaster, what he called the "Portents of Ruin."

1. As a rule, if the state of the lord of men is small but the fiefs of private families are big, or if the ruler's sceptre is insignificant but the ministers are powerful, then ruin is possible.

2. If the ruler neglects laws and prohibitions, indulges in plans and ideas, disregards the defence works within the boundaries and relies on foreign friendship and support, then ruin is possible.

3. If all officials indulge in studies, sons of the family are fond of debate, peddlars and shopkeepers hide money in foreign countries, and poor people suffer miseries at home, then ruin is possible.

4. If the ruler is fond of palatial decorations, raised kiosks, and embanked pools, is immersed in pleasures of having chariots, clothes, and curios, and thereby tires out the hundred surnames and exhausts public wealth, then ruin is possible.

5. If the ruler believes in date-selecting, worships devils and deities, believes in divination and lot-casting, and likes fêtes and celebrations, then ruin is possible.

6. If the ruler takes advice only from ministers of high rank, refrains from comparing different opinions and testifying to the truth, and uses only one man as a channel of information, then ruin is possible.

7. If posts and offices can be sought through influential personages and rank and bounties can be obtained by means of bribes, then ruin is possible.

8. If the ruler, being easy-going, accomplishes nothing, being tender-hearted, lacking in decision, and, wavering between acceptance and rejection, has no settled opinion, then ruin is possible.

9. If the ruler is greedy, insatiable, attracted to profit, and fond of gain, then ruin is possible.

10. If the ruler enjoys inflicting unjust punishment and does not uphold the law, likes debate and persuasion but never sees to their practicability, and indulges in style and wordiness but never considers their effect, then ruin is possible.

11. If the ruler is shallow-brained and easily penetrated, reveals everything but conceals nothing, and cannot keep any secret but communicates the words of one minister to another, then ruin is possible.

12. If the ruler is stubborn-minded, uncompromising, and apt to dispute every remonstrance and fond of surpassing everybody else, and never thinks of the welfare of the Altar of the Spirits of Land and Grain but sticks to self-confidence without due consideration, then ruin is possible.

13. The ruler who relies on friendship and support from distant countries, makes light of his relations with close neighbours, counts on the aid from big powers, and provokes surrounding countries, is liable to ruin.

14. If foreign travellers and residents, whose property and families are abroad, take seats in the state council and interfere in civil affairs, then ruin is possible.

15. If the people have no confidence in the premier and the inferiors do not obey the superiors while the sovereign loves and trusts the premier and cannot depose him, then ruin is possible.

16. If the ruler does not take able men of the country into service but searches after foreign gentlemen, and if he does not make tests according to meritorious services but would appoint and dismiss officials according to their mere reputations till foreign residents are exalted and ennobled to surpass his old acquaintances, then ruin is possible.

17. If tile ruler disregards the matter of legitimacy and lets bastards rival legitimate sons, or if the sovereign dies before he inaugurates the crown prince, then ruin is possible.

18. If the ruler is boastful but never regretful, makes much of himself despite the disorder prevailing in his country, and insults the neighbouring enemies without estimating the resources within the boundaries, then ruin is possible.

19. If the state is small but the ruler will not acquiesce in a humble status; if his forces are scanty but he never fears strongfoes; if he has no manners and insults big neighbours; or if he is greedy and obstinate but unskilful in diplomacy; then ruin is possible.

20. If, after the inauguration of the crown prince, the ruler take in a woman from a strong enemy state, the crown prince will be endangered and the ministers will be worried. Then ruin is possible.

21. If the ruler is timid and weak in self-defence and his mind is paralysed by the signs of future events; or if he knows what to decide on but dare not take any drastic measure; then ruin is possible.

22. If the exiled ruler is abroad but the country sets up a new ruler, or if before the heir apparent taken abroad as hostage returns, the ruler changes his successor, then the state will divide. And the state divided against itself is liable to ruin.

23. If the ruler keeps near and dear to the chief vassals whom he has disheartened and disgraced or stands close by the petty men whom he has punished, then he will make them bear

anger and feel shame. If he goes on doing this, rebels are bound to appear. When rebels appear, ruin is possible.

24. If chief vassals rival each other in power and uncles and brothers are many and powerful, and if they form juntas inside and receive support from abroad and thereby dispute state affairs and struggle for supreme influence, then ruin is possible.

25. If words of maids and concubines are followed and the wisdom of favourites is used, and the ruler repeats committing unlawful acts regardless of the grievances and resentments inside and outside the court, then ruin is possible.

26. If the ruler is contemptuous to chief vassals and impolite to uncles and brothers, overworks the hundred surnames, and slaughters innocent people, then ruin is possible.

27. If the ruler is fond of twisting laws by virtue of his wisdom, mixes public with private affairs from time to time, alters laws and prohibitions at random, and issues commands and orders frequently, then ruin is possible.

28. If the terrain has no stronghold, the city-walls are in bad repair, the state has no savings and hoardings, resources and provisions are scarce, and no preparations are made for defence and attack, but the ruler dares to attack and invade other countries imprudently, then ruin is possible.

29. If the royal seed is short-lived, new sovereigns succeed to each other continuously, babies become rulers, and chief vassals have all the ruling authority to themselves and recruit partisans from among foreign residents and maintain inter-state friendship by frequently ceding territories, then ruin is possible.

30. If the crown prince is esteemed and celebrated, has numerous dependents and protégés, develops friendships with big powers, and exercises his authority and influence from his early years, then ruin is possible.

31. If the ruler is narrow-minded, quick-tempered, imprudent, easily affected, and, when provoked, becomes blind with rage, then ruin is possible.

32. If the sovereign is easily provoked and fond of resorting to arms and neglects agricultural and military training but ventures warfare and invasion heedlessly, then ruin is possible.

33. If nobles are jealous of one another, chief vassals are prosperous, seeking support from enemy states and harassing the hundred surnames at home so as to attack their wrongdoers, but the lord of men never censures them, then ruin is possible.

34. If the ruler is unworthy but his half-brothers are worthy; if the heir apparent is powerless and the bastard surpasses him; or if the magistrates are weak and the people are fierce; then the state will be seized with a panic. And a panic-stricken state is liable to ruin.

35. If the ruler conceals his anger, which he would never reveal, suspends a criminal case, which he never would censure, and thereby makes the officials hate him in secret and increases their worries and fears, and if he never comes to know the situation even after a long time, then ruin is possible.

36. If the commander in the front line has too much power, the governor on the frontier has too much nobility, and if they have the ruling authority to themselves, issue orders at their own will and do just as they wish without asking permission of the ruler, then ruin is possible.

37. If the queen is adulterous, the sovereign's mother is corrupt, attendants inside and outside the court intercommunicate, and male and female have no distinction, such a régime is called "bi-regal." Any country having two rulers is liable to ruin.

38. If the queen is humble but the concubine is noble, the heir apparent is low but the bastard is high, the prime minister is despised but the court usher is esteemed, then disobedience will appear in and out of the court. If

disobedience appears in and out of the court, the state is liable to ruin.

39. If chief vassals are very powerful, have many strong partisans, obstruct the sovereign's decisions, and administer all state affairs on their own authority, then ruin is possible.

40. If vassals of private families are employed but descendants of military officers are rejected, men who do good to their village communities are promoted but those who render distinguished services to their official posts are discarded, self-seeking deeds are esteemed but public-spirited works are scorned, then ruin is possible.

41. If the state treasury is empty but the chief vassals have plenty of money, native subjects are poor but foreign residents are rich, farmers and warriors have hard times but people engaged in secondary professions are benefited, then ruin is possible.

42. The ruler who sees a great advantage but does not advance towards it, hears the outset of a calamity but does not provide against it, thus neglecting preparations for attack and defence and striving to embellish himself with the practice of benevolence and righteousness, is liable to ruin.

43. If the ruler does not practise the filial piety of the lord of men but yearns after the filial piety of the commoner, does not regard the welfare of the Altar of the Spirits of Land and Grain but obeys the orders of the dowager queen, and if he allows women to administer the state affairs and eunuchs to meddle with politics, then ruin is possible.

44. If words are eloquent but not legal, the mind is sagacious but not, tactful, the sovereign is versatile but performs his duties not in accordance with laws and regulations, then ruin is possible.

45. If new ministers advance when old officials withdraw, the unworthy meddle with politics when the virtuous pass out of the limelight, and men of no merit are esteemed when hard-working people are disdained, then the people left behind will resent it. If the people left behind resent it, ruin is possible.

46. If the bounties and allowances of uncles and brothers exceed their merits, their badges and uniforms override their grades, and their residences and provisions are too extravagant, and if the lord of men never restrains them, then ministers will become insatiable. If ministers are insatiable, then ruin is possible.

47. If the ruler's sons-in-law and grandsons live behind the same hamlet gate with the commoners and behave unruly and arrogantly towards their neighbours, then ruin is possible.

Thus, portents of ruin do not imply certainty of ruin but liability to ruin.

Study Questions

1. According to Han Fei Tzu, what is the ideal relationship between king and people?

2. Discuss the role of the nobility in Han Fei Tzu's *Memorials*.

3. What is the importance of the royal family to Han Fei Tzu?

4. Would a Buddhist or Confucian writer have approved of Han Fei Tzu's advice?

Ancient Rome

Interior of the Colosseum of Rome. The Colosseum was a large amphitheater constructed under the emperor Vespasian and his son Titus. The amphitheaters in which the gladiatorial contests were held varied in size throughout the empire. The Roman emperors understood that gladiatorial shows and other forms of entertainment helped to divert the poor and destitute from any political unrest.

On the Laws (ca. 52 B.C.E.)   23

CICERO

Marcus Tullius Cicero (106–43 B.C.E.) is remembered as the greatest orator and rhetorician of the ancient world. He was born in the Italian countryside to a well-off family, although not one of the highest social ranking. Cicero's family moved to Rome where he received an exceptional education, especially in law. In 80 B.C.E. he spoke on his first legal case and was an immediate sensation. He embarked upon a political career which was helped at every step by his remarkable rhetorical skills. Most unusually, given his class background, Cicero was elected consul in 63 B.C.E. He served with honor and achieved much before he fell victim to the factious politics surrounding Julius Caesar's rise to power. Although he took no part in Caesar's assassination, Cicero was condemned by Mark Antony and murdered.

Cicero claimed no originality in his writings and was important chiefly for transmitting Greek philosophy throughout the Roman world. Nevertheless his treatise on oratory was among the most important of the ancient texts, and his reflections upon political life were of central importance to the classical revival of the Renaissance. *On the Laws* was begun in 52 B.C.E. but was not published until after its author's death. Written in dialogue form, it espouses a view of natural law.

MARCUS.   But the whole subject of universal law and jurisprudence must be comprehended in this discussion, in order that this which we call civil law, may be confined in some one small and narrow space of nature. For we shall have to explain the true nature of moral justice, which must be traced back from the nature of man. And laws will have to be considered by which all political states should be governed. And last of all, shall we have to speak of those laws and customs of nations, which are framed for the use and convenience of particular countries, (in which even our own people will not be omitted,) which are known by the title of civil laws.

QUINTUS.   You take a noble view of the subject, my brother, and go to the fountainhead, in order to throw light on the subject of our consideration: and those who treat civil law in any other manner, are not so much pointing out the paths of justice as those of litigation.

MARCUS.   That is not quite the case, my Quintus. It is not so much the science of law that produces litigation, as the ignorance of it. But more of this by and by. At present let us examine the first principles of Right.

Now, many learned men have maintained that it springs from law. I hardly know if their opinion be not correct, at least according to their own definition; for "law," say they, "is the highest reason implanted in nature, which prescribes those things which ought to be done, and forbids the contrary." And when this same reason is confirmed and established in men's minds, it is then law.

They therefore conceive that prudence is a law, whose operation is to urge us to good actions, and restrain us from evil ones. And they think, too, that the Greek name for law which is derived from "to distribute," implies the very nature of the thing, that is, to give every man his due. The Latin name, *lex,* conveys the idea of selection, a *legendo.* According to the Greeks, therefore, the name of law implies an equitable distribution: according to the Romans, an equitable selection. And, indeed, both characteristics belong peculiarly to law.

And if this be a correct statement, which it seems to me for the most part to be, then the origin of right is to be sought in the law. For this is the true energy of nature—this is the very soul and reason of a wise man, and the test of virtue and vice. But since all this discussion of ours relates to a subject, the terms of which are of frequent occurrence in the popular language of the citizens, we shall be sometimes obliged to use the same terms as the vulgar, and to call that law, which in its written enactments sanctions what it thinks fit by special commands or prohibitions.

Let us begin, then, to establish the principles of justice on that supreme law, which has existed from all ages before any legislative enactments were drawn up in writing, or any political governments constituted.

Do you then grant that the entire universe is regulated by the power of the immortal Gods, that by their nature, reason, energy, mind, divinity, or some other word of clearer signification, if there be such, all things are governed and directed? For if you will not grant me this, that is what I must begin by establishing.

This animal—prescient, sagacious, complex, acute, full of memory, reason, and counsel, which we call man—has been generated by the supreme God in a most transcendent condition. For he is the only creature among all the races and descriptions of animated beings who is indued with superior reasons and thought, in which the rest are deficient. And what is there, I do not say in man alone, but in all heaven and earth, more divine than reason, which, when it becomes right and perfect, is justly termed wisdom?

There exists, therefore, since nothing is better than reason, and since this is the common property of God and man, a certain aboriginal rational intercourse between divine and human natures. But where reason is common, there right reason must also be common to the same parties; and since this right reason is what we call law, God and men must be considered as associated by law. Again, there must also be a communion of right where there is a communion of law. And those who have law and right thus in common, must be considered members of the same commonwealth.

And if they are obedient to the same rule and the same authority, they are even much more so to this one celestial regency, this divine mind and omnipotent deity. So that the entire universe may be looked upon as forming one vast commonwealth of gods and men. And, as in earthly states certain ranks are distinguished with reference to the relationships of families, according to a certain principle which will be discussed in its proper place, that principle, in the nature of things, is far more magnificent and splendid by which men are connected with the Gods, as belonging to their kindred and nation.

Now, the law of virtue is the same in God and man, and in no other disposition besides them. This virtue is nothing else than a nature perfect in itself, and wrought up to the most consummate excellence. There exists, therefore, a similitude between God and man. And as this is the case, what connection can there be which concerns us more nearly, and is more certain?

Since, then, the Deity has been pleased to create and adorn man to be the chief and president of all terrestrial creatures, so it is evident, without further argument, that human nature has also made very great advances by its own intrinsic energy: that nature, which without any other instruction than her own, has developed the first rude principles of the understanding, and strengthened and perfected reason to all the appliances of science and art.

ATTICUS.   Oh ye immortal Gods! to what a distance back are you tracing the principles of justice! However, you are discoursing in such a style that I will not show any impatience to hear what I expect you to say on the Civil Law. But I will listen patiently, even if you spend the whole day in this kind of discourse: for assuredly these, which perhaps you are embracing in your argument for the sake of others, are grander topics than even the subject for which they prepare the way.

MARCUS.   You may well describe these topics as grand, which we are now briefly discussing. But of all the questions which are ever the subject of discussion among learned men, there is none which it is more important thoroughly to understand than this, that man is born for justice, and that law and equity have not been established by opinion, but by nature. This truth will become still more apparent if we investigate the nature of human association and society.

For there is no one thing so like or so equal to another, as in every instance man is to man. And if the corruption of customs, and the variation of opinions, did not induce an imbecility of minds, and turn them aside from the course of nature, no one would more nearly resemble himself than all men would resemble all men. Therefore, whatever definition we give of man, will be applicable to the whole human race. And this is a good argument that there is no dissimilarity of kind among men; because if this were the case, one definition could not include all men.

It follows, then, that nature made us just that we might share our goods with each other, and supply each other's wants. You observe in this discussion, whenever I speak of nature, I mean nature in its genuine purity, but that there is, in fact, such corruption engendered by evil customs, that the sparks, as it were, of virtue which have been given by nature are extinguished, and that antagonist vices arise around it and become strengthened.

But if, as nature prompts them to, men would with deliberate judgment, in the words of the poet, "being men, think nothing that concerns mankind indifferent to them," then would justice be cultivated equally by all. For to those to whom nature has given reason, she has also given right reason, and therefore also law, which is nothing else than right reason enjoining what is good, and forbidding what is evil. And if nature has given us law, she hath also given us right. But she has bestowed reason on all, therefore right has been bestowed on all.

It is therefore an absurd extravagance in some philosophers to assert, that all things are necessarily just which are established by the civil laws and the institutions of nations. Are then the laws of tyrants just, simply because they are laws? Suppose the thirty tyrants of Athens had imposed certain laws on the Athenians? or, suppose again that these Athenians were delighted with these tyrannical laws, would these laws on that account have been considered just? For my own part, I do not think such laws deserve any greater estimation than that passed during our own interregnum, which ordained that the dictator should be empowered to put to death with impunity whatever citizens he pleased, without hearing them in their own defence.

For there is but one essential justice which cements society, and one law which establishes this justice. This law is right reason, which is the true rule of all commandments and prohibitions. Whoever neglects this law, whether written or unwritten, is necessarily unjust and wicked.

But if justice consists in submission to written laws and national customs, and if, as the same school affirms, everything must be measured by utility alone, he who thinks that such conduct will be advantageous to him will neglect the laws, and break them if it is in his power. And the consequence is, that real justice has really no existence if it have not one by nature, and if that which is established as such on account of utility is overturned by some other utility.

But if nature does not ratify law, then all the virtues may lose their sway. For what becomes of generosity, patriotism, or friendship? Where will the desire of benefitting our neighbours, or the gratitude that acknowledges kindness, be able to exist at all? For all these virtues proceed from our natural inclination to love mankind. And this is the true basis of justice, and without this not only the mutual charities of men, but the religious services of the Gods, would be at an end; for these are preserved as I imagine, rather by the natural sympathy which subsists between divine and human beings, than by mere fear and timidity.

It follows that I may now sum up the whole of this argument by asserting, as is plain to every one from these positions which have been already laid down, that all right and all that is honourable is to be sought for its own sake. In truth, all virtuous men love justice and equity for what they are in themselves; nor is it like a good man to make a mistake, and love that which does not deserve their affection. Right, therefore, is desirable and deserving to be cultivated for its own sake; and if this be true of right, it must be true also of justice. What then shall we say of liberality? Is it exercised gratuitously, or does it covet some reward and recompense? If a man does good without expecting any recompense for his kindness, then it is gratuitous: if he does expect compensation, it is a mere matter of traffic. Nor is there any doubt that he who truly deserves the reputation of a generous and kindhearted man, is thinking of his duty, not of his interest. In the same way the virtue of justice demands neither emolument nor salary, and therefore we desire it for its own sake. And the case of all the moral virtues is the same, and so is the opinion formed of them.

Study Questions

1. What are these laws? Are they the work of legislators, or do they have less definite roots?

2. Cicero is remembered especially for transmitting the ideas of Greek philosophers and shaping those ideas for a Roman audience. Can you identify any Greek influence in *On the Laws*?

3. *On the Laws* dwells upon human nature. What is the Roman vision of the individual? With what qualities are individuals endowed?

4. What is the difference between natural law and the civil law made by mortals?

5. *On the Laws* was very widely read by generations of Romans. What do you think the popularity of *On the Laws* reveals about Roman society?

The Aeneid (30–19 B.C.E.)   **24**

VIRGIL

Publius Virgilius Maro, known as Virgil (70–19 B.C.E.), was born near Mantua to a peasant family. Remarkably, given his family background, he was able to receive an education, first at local schools and then in Rome. He was especially skilled in rhetoric and philosophy, the two central subjects of the time. Unlike most other distinguished Romans, Virgil never aspired to public life but devoted himself entirely to writing poetry. His early works were merely preparation for the creation of an epic, regarded as the highest form of poetic expression.

This work was *The Aeneid*, Virgil's story of the founding of Rome and the fulfillment of its great destiny. Initially, the poem was meant to honor the emperor; in it, Augustus was compared favorably to the mythical founder of Rome, Aeneas, after whom the poem was named. Virgil worked on *The Aeneid* for over a decade and it remained unfinished at his death. The following selection comes from the opening stanzas of the poem.

Arms and the man I sing, who first made way,
Predestined exile, from the Trojan shore
To Italy, the blest Lavinian strand.
Smitten of storms he was on land and sea
By violence of Heaven, to satisfy
Stern Juno's sleepless wrath; and much in war
He suffered, seeking at the last to found
The city, and bring o'er his fathers' gods
To safe abode in Latium; whence arose
The Latin race, old Alba's reverend lords.
And from her hills wide-walled, imperial Rome.

O Muse, the causes tell! What sacrilege,
Or vengeful sorrow, moved the heavenly
    Queen
To thrust on dangers dark and endless toil
A man whose largest honor in men's eyes
Was serving Heaven? Can gods such anger feel?

In ages gone an ancient city stood—
Carthage, a Tyrian seat, which from afar
Made front on Italy and on the mouths

Of Tiber's stream: its wealth and revenues
Were vast, and ruthless was its quest of war.
'T'is said that Juno, of all lands she loved,
Most cherished this—not Samos' self so dear.
Here were her arms, her chariot; even then
A throne of power o'er nations near and far,
If Fate opposed not, 't was her darling hope
To 'stablish here; but anxiously she heard
That of the Trojan blood there was a breed
Then rising, which upon the destined day
Should utterly o'erwhelm her Tyrian towers;
A people of wide sway and conquest proud
Should compass Libya's doom; such was the
    web
The Fatal Sisters spun.

Aeneas' wave-worn crew now landward
    made,
And took the nearest passage, whither lay
The coast of Libya. A haven there
Walled in by bold sides of a rocky isle,
Offers a spacious and secure retreat,

Where every billow from the distant main
Breaks, and in many a rippling curve retires.
Huge crags and two confronted promontories
Frown heaven-high, beneath whose brows out-
    spread
The silent, sheltered waters; on the heights
The bright and glimmering foliage seems to
    show
A woodland amphitheatre: and yet higher
Rises a straight-stemmed grove of dense, dark
    shade.
Fronting on these a grotto may be seen.
O'erhung by steep cliffs; from its inmost wall
Clear springs gush out; and shelving seats it has
Of unhewn stone, a place the wood-nymphs
    love.
In such a port, a weary ship rides free
Of weight of firm-fluked anchor or strong
    chain.
Hither Aeneas, of his scattered fleet
Saving but seven, into harbor sailed:
With passionate longing for the touch of land,
Forth leap the Trojans to the welcome shore,
And fling their dripping limbs along the
    ground.
Then good Achates smote a flinty stone.
Secured a flashing spark, heaped on light
    leaves,
And with dry branches nursed the mounting
    flame
Then Ceres' gift from the corrupting sea
They bring away; and wearied utterly
Ply Ceres' cunning on the rescued corn.
And parch in flames, and mill 'twixt two
    smooth stones.

"Companions mine, we have not failed to feel
Calamity till now. O, ye have borne
Far heavier sorrow: Jove will make an end
Also of this. Ye sailed a course hard by
Infuriate Scylla's howling cliffs and caves.
Ye knew the Cyclops' crags. Lift up your
    hearts!
No more complaint and fear! It well may be
Some happier hour will find this memory fair.

Through chance and change and hazard with-
    out end.
Our goal is Latium: where our destinies
Beckon to blest abodes, and have ordained
That Troy shall rise new-born! Have patience
    all!
And bide expectantly that golden day."
Such was his word, but vexed with grief and
    care.
Feigned hopes upon his forehead firm he wore,
And locked within his heart a hero's pain.

After these things were past, exalted Jove,
From his ethereal sky surveying clear
The seas all winged with sails, lands widely
    spread.
And nations populous from shore to shore,
Paused on the peak of heaven, and fixed his
    gaze
On Libya. But while he anxious mused,
Near him, her radiant eyes all dim with tears,
Nor smiling any more, Venus approached,
And thus complained: "O thou who dost con-
    trol
Things human and divine by changeless laws,
Enthroned in awful thunder! What huge wrong
Could my Aeneas and his Trojans few
Achieve against thy power? For they have borne
Unnumbered deaths, and, failing Italy,
The gates of all the world again them close.
Hast thou not give us thy convenant
That hence the Romans when the rolling
    years
Have come full cycle, shall arise to power
From Troy's regenerate seed, and rule supreme
The unresisted lords of land and sea?
O sire, what swerves thy will? How oft have I
In Troy's most lamentable wreck and woe.
Consoled my heart with this, and balanced oft
Our destined good against our destined ill!
But the same storinful fortune still pursues
My band of heroes on their perilous way.
When shall these labors cease, O glorious King?
Antenor, though th' Achoeans pressed him
    sore,

Found his way forth, and entered unassailed
Illyria's haven, and the guarded land
Of the Liburni. Straight up stream he sailed
Where like a swollen sea Timavus pours
A nine-fold flood from roaring mountain
    gorge,
And whelms with voiceful wave the fields below.
He built Patavium there, and fixed abodes
For Troy's far-exiled sons; he gave a name
To a new land and race; the Trojan arms
Were hung on temple walls; and, to this day,
Lying in perfect peace, the hero sleeps.
But we of thine own seed, to whom thou dost
A station in the arch of heaven assign,
Behold our navy vilely wrecked, because
A single god is angry; we endure
This treachery and violence, whereby
Wide seas divide us from th' Hesperian shore.
Is this what piety receives? Or thus
Doth Heaven's decree restore our fallen
    thrones?"
Smiling reply, the Sire of gods and men,
With such a look as clears the skies of storm,
Chastely his daughter kissed, and thus spake on:
"Let Cythera cast her fears away!
Irrevocably blest the fortunes be
Of thee and thine. Nor shalt thou fail to see
That City, and the proud predestined wall
Encompassing Lavinium. Thyself
Shall starward to the heights of heaven bear
Aeneas the great-hearted. Nothing swerves
My will once uttered. Since such carking cares
Consume thee, I this hour speak freely forth,
And leaf by leaf the book of fate unfold.
Thy son in Italy shall wage vast war
And quell its nations wild; his city-wall
And sacred laws shall be a mighty bond
About his gathered people. Summers three
Shall Latium call him king; and three times
    pass
The winter o'er Rutulia's vanquished hills.
His heir, Ascanius, now Iulus called
(Ilus it was while Ilium's kingdom stood),
Full thirty months shall reign, then move the
    throne

From the Lavinian citadel, and build
For Alba Longa its well-bastioned wall.
Here three full centuries shall Hector's race
Have kingly power; till a priestess queen,
By Mars conceiving, her twin offspring bear;
Then Romulus, wolf-nursed and proudly
    clad
In tawny wolf-skin mantle, shall receive
The sceptre of his race. He shall uprear
The war-god's citadel and lofty wall,
And on his Romans his own name bestow.
To these I give no bounded times or power,
But empire without end. Yea, even my Queen,
Juno, who now chastiseth land and sea
With her dread frown, will find a wiser way,
And at my sovereign side protect and bless
The Romans, masters of the whole round
    world,
Who, clad in peaceful toga, judge mankind.
Such my decree! In lapse of seasons due,
The heirs of Ilium's kings shall bind in chains
Mycenae's glory and Achilles' towers,
And over prostrate Argos sit supreme.
Of Trojan stock illustriously sprung,
Lo, Caesar comes! whose power the ocean
    bounds,
Whose fame, the skies. He shall receive the
    name
Iulus nobly bore, great Julius, he.
Him to the skies, in Orient trophies dight,
Thou shalt with smiles receive; and he, like us,
Shall hear at his own shrines the suppliant vow.
Then will the world grow mild; the battle-
    sound
Will be forgot; for olden Honor then,
With spotless Vesta, and the brothers twain,
Remus and Romulus, at strife no more,
Will publish sacred laws. The dreadful gates
Whence issueth war, shall with close-jointed
    steel
Be barred impregnably; and prisoned there
The heaven-offending Fury, throned on
    swords,
And fettered by a hundred brazen chains,
Shall belch vain curses from his lips of gore."

Study Questions

1. *The Aeneid* offered Romans an explanation of their origins. Why would such a myth have been useful? What purpose might it have served?

2. What is Rome's destiny as foretold in *The Aeneid?* What stands in the way of success?

3. Virgil gives us a glimpse of what the Romans thought they were like. What sort of people do the founders of Rome appear to be?

4. Why do you think Virgil chose to tell his story in the form of an epic poem?

5. The links between *The Aeneid* and the works of Homer seem very clear. Why did the Romans want to connect themselves so closely with Homeric legends?

The Life of Cato the Elder (ca. 52–116 C.E.)   25

PLUTARCH

Plutarch (46–124 C.E.) was a Greek philosopher and biographer and is one of the best-known sources for information about ancient personalities. Though educated in Athens, Plutarch traveled extensively in the Roman Empire and may even have achieved high office within it. Little is known of his life until he returned to Greece where he was a teacher and a priest at the oracle of Apollo at Delphi. Plutarch wrote extensively on ethical and philosophical issues, but his most popular work was his *Lives*, which he began in middle age.

Plutarch considered himself a biographer rather than an historian. He paired the life of a Greek with that of a Roman and then wrote an explicit comparison of the two. Twenty-two such pairs survive, each using narrative, description, and anecdote to provide a portrait. Plutarch's *Lives* was enormously popular in the Roman world and became a vital source of knowledge about the ancients after they were rediscovered in the sixteenth century. Shakespeare relied upon the *Lives* heavily for his Roman plays.

Marcus Cato, we are told, was born at Tusculum, though (till he betook himself to civil and military affairs) he lived and was bred up in the country of the Sabines, where his father's estate lay. His ancestors seeming almost entirely unknown, he himself praises his father Marcus, as a worthy man and a brave soldier, and Cato, his great grandfather too, as one who had often obtained military prizes, and who, having lost five horses under him, received, on the account of his valor, the worth of them out of the public exchequer.

He gained, in early life, a good habit of body by working with his own hands, and living temperately, and serving in war; and seemed to have an equal proportion both of health and strength. And he exerted and practised his eloquence through all the neighborhood and little villages; thinking it as requisite as a second body, and an all but necessary organ to one who looks forward to something above a mere humble and inactive life. He would never refuse to be counsel for those who needed him, and was, indeed, early reckoned a good lawyer, and, ere long, a capable orator.

Hence his solidity and depth of character showed itself gradually, more and more to those with whom he was concerned, and claimed, as it were, employment in great affairs, and places of public command. Nor did he merely abstain from taking fees for his counsel and pleading but did not even seem to put any high price on the honor which proceeded from such kind of combats, seeming much more desirous to signalize himself in the camp and in real fights; and while yet but a youth, had his breast covered with scars he had received from the enemy; being (as he himself says) but seventeen years old, when he made his first campaign; in the time when Hannibal, in the height of his success, was burning and pillaging all Italy. In engagements he would strike boldly, without flinching, stand firm to his ground, fix a bold countenance upon his enemies, and with a harsh threatening voice accost them, justly thinking himself and telling others, that such a rugged kind of behavior sometimes terrifies the enemy more than the sword itself. In his marches, he bore his own arms on foot, whilst one servant only followed, to carry the provisions for his table, with whom he is said never to have been angry or hasty, whilst he made ready his dinner or supper, but would, for the most part, when he was free from military duty, assist and help him himself to dress it. When he was with the army, he used to drink only water; unless, perhaps, when extremely thirsty, he

might mingle it with a little vinegar; or if he found his strength fail him, take a little wine.

There was a man of the highest rank, and very influential among the Romans, called Valerius Flaccus, who was singularly skillful in discerning excellence yet in the bud, and, also, much disposed to nourish and advance it. He, it seems, had lands bordering upon Cato's; nor could he but admire, when he understood from his servants the manner of his living, how he labored with his own hands, went on foot betimes in the morning to the courts to assist those who wanted his counsel; how, returning home again, when it was winter, he would throw a loose frock, over his shoulders, and in the summer time would work without any thing on among his domestics, sit down with them, eat of the same bread, and drink of the same wine. When they spoke, also, of other good qualities, his fair dealing and moderation, mentioning also some of his wise sayings, he ordered, that he should be invited to supper; and thus becoming personally assured of his fine temper and his superior character which, like a plant, seemed only to require culture and a better situation, he urged and persuaded him to apply himself to state affairs at Rome. Thither, therefore, he went, and by his pleading soon gained many friends and admirers; but, Valerius chiefly assisting his promotion, he first of all got appointed tribune in the army, and afterwards was made quaestor, or treasurer. And now becoming eminent and noted, he passed, with Valerius himself, through the greatest commands, being first his colleague as consul, and then censor. But among all the ancient senators, he most attached himself to Fabius Maximus; not so much for the honor of his person, and greatness of his power, as that he might have before him his habit and manner of life, as the best examples to follow: and so he did not hesitate to oppose Scipio the Great, who, being then but a young man, seemed to set himself against the power of Fabius, and to be envied by him. For being sent together with him as treasurer, when he saw him, according to his natural custom, make great expenses, and distribute among the soldiers without sparing, he freely told him that the expense in itself was not the greatest thing to be considered, but that he was corrupting the ancient frugality of the soldiers, by giving them the means to abandon themselves to unnecessary pleasures and luxuries. Scipio answered, that he had no need for so accurate a treasurer, (bearing on as he was, so to say, full sail to the war), and that he owed the people an account of his actions, and not of the money he spent.

Cato grew more and more powerful by his eloquence, so that he was commonly called the Roman Demosthenes, but his manner of life was yet more famous and talked of. For oratorical skill was, as an accomplishment, commonly studied and sought after by all young men; but he was very rare who would cultivate the old habits of bodily labor, or prefer a light supper, and a breakfast which never saw the fire; or be in love with poor clothes and a homely lodging, or could set his ambition rather on doing without luxuries than on possessing them. For now the state, unable to keep its purity by reason of its greatness, and having so many affairs, and people from all parts under its government, was fain to admit many mixed customs, and new examples of living. With reason, therefore, everybody admired Cato, when they saw others sink under labors, and grow effeminate by pleasures; and yet beheld him unconquered by either, and that not only when he was young and desirous of honor, but also when old and greyheaded, after a consulship and triumph; like some famous victor in the games, persevering in his exercise and maintaining his character to the very last.

He gave most general annoyance, by retrenching people's luxury; for though (most of the youth being thereby already corrupted) it seemed almost impossible to take it away with an open hand and directly, yet going, as it were, obliquely around, he caused all dress, carriages, women's ornaments, household furniture, whose price exceeded one thousand five hundred drachmas, to be rated at ten times as much as they were worth; intending by thus making the assessments greater, to increase the taxes paid upon them. And thus, on the one side, not only those were disgusted at Cato, who bore the taxes for the sake of their luxury, but those, too, who on the other side laid by their luxury for fear of the taxes. For people in general reckon, that an order not to display their riches, is equivalent to the taking away their riches; because riches are seen much more in superfluous, than in necessary, things.

Cato, notwithstanding, being little solicitous as to those who exclaimed against him, increased his austerity. He caused the pipes, through which some persons brought the public water into their own houses and gardens, to be cut, and threw down all buildings which jutted out into the common streets. He beat down also the price in contracts for public works to the lowest, and raised it in contracts for farming the taxes to the highest sum; by which proceedings he drew a great deal of hatred on himself. Those who were of Titus Flamininus's party cancelled in the senate all the bargains and contracts made by him for the repairing and carrying on of the sacred and public buildings, as unadvantageous to the commonwealth. They incited also the boldest of the tribunes of the people to accuse him, and to fine him two talents. They likewise much opposed him in building the court or basilica, which he caused to be erected at the common charge, just by the senate-house, in the market-place, and called by his own name, the Porcian. However, the people, it seems, liked his censorship wondrously well; for, setting up a statue for him in the temple of the goddess of Health, they put an inscription under it, not recording his commands in war or his triumph, but to the effect, that this was Cato the Censor, who, by his good discipline and wise and temperate ordinances, reclaimed the

Roman commonwealth when it was declining and sinking down into vice.

He was also a good father, an excellent husband to his wife, and an extraordinary economist; and as he did not manage his affairs of this kind carelessly, and as things of little moment, I think I ought to record a little further whatever was commendable in him in these points. He married a wife more noble than rich; being of opinion, that the rich and the high-born are equally haughty and proud; but that those of noble blood, would be more ashamed of base things, and consequently more obedient to their husbands in all that was fit and right. A man who beat his wife or child, laid violent hands, he said, on what was most sacred; and a good husband he reckoned worthy of more praise than a great senator; and he admired the ancient Socrates for nothing so much, as for having lived a temperate and contented life with a wife who was a scold, and children who were half-witted.

Some will have the overthrow of Carthage to have been one of his last acts of state; when, indeed, Scipio the younger, did by his valor give it the last blow, but the war, chiefly by the counsel and advice of Cato, was undertaken on the following occasion. Cato was sent to the Carthaginians and Masinissa, king of Numidia, who were at war with one another, to know the cause of their difference. He, it seems, had been a friend of the Romans from the beginning; and they, too, since they were conquered by Scipio, were of the Roman confederacy, having been shorn of their power by loss of terri-

tory, and a heavy tax. Finding Carthage, not (as the Romans thought) low and in an ill condition, but well manned, full of riches and all sorts of arms and ammunition, and perceiving the Carthaginians carry it high, he conceived that it was not a time for the Romans to adjust affairs between them and Masinissa; but rather that they themselves would fall into danger, unless they should find means to check this rapid new growth of Rome's ancient irreconcilable enemy. Therefore, returning quickly to Rome, he acquainted the senate, that the former defeats and blows given to the Carthaginians, had not so much diminished their strength, as it had abated their imprudence and folly; that they were not become weaker, but more experienced in war, and did only skirmish with the Numidians, to exercise themselves the better to cope with the Romans; that the peace and league they had made was but a kind of suspension of war which awaited a fairer opportunity to break out again.

Moreover, they say that, shaking his gown, he took occasion to let drop some African figs before the senate. And on their admiring the size and beauty of them, he presently added, that the place that bore them was but three days' sail from Rome. Nay, he never after this gave his opinion, but at the end he would be sure to come out with this sentence, "Also, Carthage, methinks, ought utterly to be destroyed."

Thus Cato, they say, stirred up the third and last war against the Carthaginians: but no sooner was the said war begun, than he died.

Study Questions

1. How might a Roman gentleman like Cato rise in politics?

2. What were the qualities that made Cato the model of the noble Roman?

3. Why did Cato create so many enemies while he held political office?

4. Plutarch clearly meant his biography of Cato to be an inspiration for his readers. Could you argue that Cato was not the best role model Plutarch might have chosen? Does Cato have any flaws?

The Life of Augustus (ca. 122 C.E.)   **26**

SUETONIUS

Gaius Suetonius Tranquillus (ca. 69–122 C.E.) gained fame for his biographies of the first 12 Roman emperors. Born into a knightly family, Suetonius studied but never practiced law. He saw military and diplomatic service before entering the government of the Emperor Hadrian. Suetonius' historical interests shaped his public career and he soon became the imperial archivist, the director of the Roman libraries, and a cultural advisor to the emperor. In 121 Suetonius rose to the key position of imperial secretary but was dismissed from office for failing to abide by court etiquette. He spent the rest of his life writing biographies.

   The Life of Augustus is one of the best known of the *Lives of the Twelve Caesars.* It was Suetonius' purpose to provide both a vivid portrayal of his subject as well as an account of the social environment in which Augustus lived.

In military affairs he made many alterations, introducing some practices entirely new, and reviving others, which had become obsolete. He maintained the strictest discipline among the troops; and would not allow even his lieutenants the liberty to visit their wives, except reluctantly, and in the winter season only. A Roman knight having cut off the thumbs of his two young sons, to render them incapable of serving in the wars, he exposed both him and his estate to public sale. But upon observing the farmers of the revenue very greedy for the purchase, he assigned him to a freedman of his own, that he might send him into the country, and suffer him to retain his freedom. The tenth legion becoming mutinous, he disbanded it with ignominy; and did the same by some others which petulantly demanded their discharge; withholding from them the rewards usually bestowed on those who had served their stated time in the wars. The cohorts which yielded their ground in time of action, he decimated, and fed with barley. Centurions, as well as common sentinels, who deserted their posts when on guard, he punished with death. For other misdemeanors he inflicted upon them various kinds of disgrace; such as obliging them to stand all day before the praetorium, sometimes in their tunics only, and without their belts, sometimes to carry poles ten feet long, or sods of turf.

He was advanced to public offices before the age at which he was legally qualified for them: and to some, also, of a new kind, and for life. He seized the consulship in the twentieth year of his age, quartering his legions in a threatening manner near the city, and sending deputies to demand it for him in the name of the army. When the senate demurred, a centurion, named Cornelius, who was at the head of the chief deputation, throwing back his cloak, and shewing the hilt of his sword, had the presumption to say in the senate-house, "This will make him consul, if ye will not." His second consulship he filled nine years afterwards; his third, after the interval of only one year, and held the same office every year successively until the eleventh. From this period, although the consulship was frequently offered him, he always declined it, until, after a long interval,

Statue depicting Augustus as Emperor.

He twice entertained thoughts of restoring the republic; first, immediately after he had crushed Antony, remembering that he had often charged him with being the obstacle to its restoration. The second time was in consequence of a long illness, when he sent for the magistrates and the senate to his own house, and delivered them a particular account of the state of the empire. But reflecting at the same time that it would be both hazardous to himself to return to the condition of a private person, and might be dangerous to the public to have the government placed again under the control of the people, he resolved to keep it in his own hands, whether with the better event or intention, is hard to say. His good intentions he often affirmed in private discourse, and also published an edict, in which it was declared in the following terms: "May it be permitted me to have the happiness of establishing the commonwealth on a safe and sound basis, and thus enjoy the reward of which I am ambitious, that of being celebrated for moulding it into the form best adapted to present circumstances; so that, on my leaving the world, I may carry with me the hope that the foundations which I have laid for its future government, will stand firm and stable."

The city, which was not built in a manner suitable to the grandeur of the empire, and was liable to inundations of the Tiber, as well as to fires, was so much improved under his administration, that he boasted, not without reason, that he "found it of brick, but left it of marble." He also rendered it secure for the time to come against such disasters, as far as could be effected by human foresight. A great number of public buildings were erected by him, the most considerable of which were a forum, containing the temple of Mars the Avenger, the temple of Apollo on the Palatine hill, and the temple of Jupiter Tonans in the capitol. The reason of his building a new forum was the vast increase in the population, and the number of cases to be tried in the courts, for which, the

not less than seventeen years, he voluntarily stood for the twelfth, and two years after that, for a thirteenth; that he might successively introduce into the forum, on their entering public life, his two sons, Caius and Lucius, while he was invested with the highest office in the state.

He accepted of the tribunitian power for life, but more than once chose a colleague in that office for ten years successively. He also had the supervision of morality and observance of the laws, for life, but without the title of censor; yet he thrice took a census of the people, the first and third time with a colleague, but the second by himself.

two already existing not affording sufficient space, it was thought necessary to have a third. It was therefore opened for public use before the temple of Mars was completely finished; and a law was passed, that cases should be tried, and judges chosen by lot, in that place.

He corrected many ill practices, which, to the detriment of the public, had either survived the licentious habits of the late civil wars, or else originated in the long peace. Bands of robbers showed themselves openly, completely armed, under colour of self-defence; and in different parts of the country, travellers, freemen and slaves without distinction, were forcibly carried off, and kept to work in the houses of correction. Several associations were formed under the specious name of a new college, which banded together for the perpetration of all kinds of villainy. The bandits he quelled by establishing posts of soldiers in suitable stations for the purpose; the houses of correction were subjected to a strict superintendence; all associations, those only excepted which were of ancient standing, and recognised by the laws, were dissolved. He burnt all the notes of those who had been a long time in arrear with the treasury, as being the principal source of vexatious suits and prosecutions. Places in the city claimed by the public, where the right was doubtful, he adjudged to the actual possessors. He struck out of the list of criminals the names of those over whom prosecutions had been long impending, where nothing further was intended by the informers than to gratify their own malice, by seeing their enemies humiliated; laying it down as a rule, that if any one chose to renew a prosecution, he should incur the risk of the punishment which he sought to inflict. And that crimes might not escape punishment, nor business be neglected by delay, he ordered the courts to sit during the thirty days which were spent in celebrating honorary games.

He was desirous that his friends should be great and powerful in the state, but have no exclusive privileges, or be exempt from the laws which governed others. When Asprenas Nonius, an intimate friend of his, was tried upon a charge of administering poison at the instance of Cassius Severus, he consulted the senate for their opinion what was his duty under the circumstances: "For," said he, "I am afraid, lest, if I should stand by him in the cause, I may be supposed to screen a guilty man; and if I do not, to desert and prejudge a friend." With the unanimous concurrence, therefore, of the senate, he took his seat amongst his advocates for several hours, but without giving him the benefit of speaking to character, as was usual. He likewise appeared for his clients; as on behalf of Scutarius, an old soldier of his, who brought an action for slander. He never relieved any one from prosecution but in a single instance, in the case of a man who had given information of the conspiracy of Muraena; and that he did only by prevailing upon the accuser, in open court, to drop his prosecution.

The whole body of the people, upon a sudden impulse, and with unanimous consent, offered him the title of Father of His Country. It was announced to him first at Antium, by a deputation from the people, and upon his declining the honour, they repeated their offer on his return to Rome, in a full theatre, when they were crowned with laurel. The senate soon afterwards adopted the proposal, not in the way of acclamation or decree, but by commissioning M. Messala, in an unanimous vote, to compliment him with it in the following terms: "With hearty wishes for the happiness and prosperity of yourself and your family, Caesar Augustus, (for we think we thus most effectually pray for the lasting welfare of the state), the senate, in agreement with the Roman people, salute you by the title of Father of Your Country." To this compliment Augustus replied, with tears in his eyes, in these words (for I give them exactly as I have done those of Messala): "Having now arrived at the summit of my wishes, O Conscript Fathers, what else have I to beg of the Immortal Gods, but the continuance of this your affection for me to the last moments of my life?"

In person he was handsome and graceful, through every period of his life. But he was negligent in his dress; and so careless about dressing his hair, that he usually had it done in great haste, by several barbers at a time. His beard he sometimes clipped, and sometimes shaved; and either read or wrote during the operation. His countenance, either when discoursing or silent, was so calm and serene, that a Gaul of the first rank declared amongst his friends, that he was so softened by it, as to be restrained from throwing him down a precipice, in his passage over the Alps, when he had been admitted to approach him, under pretence of conferring with him. His eyes were bright and piercing; and he was willing it should be thought that there was something of a divine vigour in them. He was likewise not a little pleased to see people, upon his looking steadfastly at them, lower their countenances, as if the sun shone in their eyes. But in his old age, he saw very imperfectly with his left eye. His teeth were thin set, small and scaly, his hair a little curled, and inclining to a yellow colour. His eyebrows met; his ears were small, and he had an aquiline nose. His complexion was betwixt brown and fair; his stature but low; though Julius Marathus, his freedman, says he was five feet and nine inches in height. This, however, was so much concealed by the just proportion of his limbs, that it was only perceivable upon comparison with some taller person standing by him.

He expired in the same room in which his father Octavius had died, when the two Sextus's, Pompey and Apuleius, were consuls, upon the fourteenth of the calends of September [the 19th August], at the ninth hour of the day, being seventy-six years of age, wanting only thirty-five days. His remains were carried by the magistrates of the municipal towns and colonies, from Nola to Bovillae, and in the night-time, because of the season of the year. During the intervals, the body lay in some basilica, or great temple, of each town. At Bovillae it was met by the Equestrian Order, who carried it to the city, and deposited it in the vestibule of his own house. The senate proceeded with so much zeal in the arrangement of his funeral, and paying honour to his memory, that, amongst several other proposals, some were for having the funeral procession made through the triumphal gate, preceded by the image of Victory which is in the senate-house, and the children of highest rank and of both sexes singing the funeral dirge. Others proposed, that on the day of the funeral, they should lay aside their gold rings, and wear rings of iron; and others, that his bones should be collected by the priests of the principal colleges. One likewise proposed to transfer the name of August to September, because he was born in the latter, but died in the former. Another moved, that the whole period of time, from his birth to his death, should be called the Augustan age, and be inserted in the calendar under that title. But at last it was judged proper to be moderate in the honours paid to his memory. Two funeral orations were pronounced in his praise, one before the temple of Julius, by Tiberius; and the other before the rostra, under the old shops, by Drusus, Tiberius's son. The body was then carried upon the shoulders of senators into the Campus Martius, and there burnt. A man of praetorian rank affirmed upon oath, that he saw his spirit ascend from the funeral pile to heaven. The most distinguished persons of the equestrian order, bare-footed, and with their tunics loose, gathered up his relics, and deposited them in the mausoleum, which had been built in his sixth consulship between the Flaminian Way and the bank of the Tiber; at which time likewise he gave the groves and walks about it for the use of the people.

Study Questions

1. What did Augustus accomplish as emperor?

2. How did Augustus attempt to avoid appearing as a dictator? Can you cite an example from Suetonius' *Life?*

3. Would an author such as Suetonius be limited in his freedom to write a biography of a Roman emperor? What factors might he have considered in assessing Augustus' accomplishments?

4. What skills did Augustus need to manipulate the extremely complex Roman political system? How did he manage?

5. Was Augustus' regime appreciated? How did Rome show its gratitude toward the emperor?

The Sermon on the Mount (ca. 28–35 C.E.)   27

The Sermon on the Mount was delivered by Jesus some time after the beginning of his ministry in 27 C.E., and was recorded by the Apostle Matthew. It is a classic example of Jesus' method of teaching, but more importantly, its message lies at the heart of the religion that he founded. Unlike most teachers and prophets of his day, Jesus did not teach in a synagogue; rather he brought his message directly to the people by traveling to various centers of population where he would preach in the open air. Thus the setting of the Sermon on the Mount, while unusual in the context of his contemporaries, was typical of Jesus' style.

The message in the Sermon is set firmly within the Jewish tradition. Jesus urges his listeners to a commitment to righteousness, which he defines with poignant simplicity.

Then Jesus was led up by the Spirit into the wilderness to be tempted by the devil. And he fasted forty days and forty nights, and afterward he was hungry. And the tempter came and said to him, "If you are the Son of God, command these stones to become loaves of bread." But he answered, "It is written,

'Man shall not live by bread alone, but by every word that proceeds from the mouth of God.' "

Then the devil took him to the holy city, and set him on the pinnacle of the temple, and said to him. "If you are the Son of God, throw yourself down; for it is written,

'He will give his angels charge of you,'

and

On their hands they will bear you up, lest you strike your foot against a stone.' "

Jesus said to him, "Again it is written, 'You shall not tempt the Lord your God.' " Again, the devil took him to a very high mountain, and showed him all the kingdoms of the world and the glory of them; and he said to him, "All these I will give you, if you will fall down and worship me." Then Jesus said to him, "Begone, Satan! for it is written,

'You shall worship the Lord your God
and him only shall you serve.' "

Then the devil left him, and behold, angels came and ministered to him.

From that time Jesus began to preach, saying, "Repent, for the kingdom of heaven is at hand."

As he walked by the Sea of Galilee, he saw two brothers, Simon who is called Peter and Andrew his brother, casting a net into the sea; for they were fishermen. And he said to them, "Follow me, and I will make you fishers of men." Immediately they left their nets and followed him. And going on from there he saw two other brothers, James the son of Zebedee and John his brother, in the boat with Zebedee their father, mending their nets, and he called them. Immediately they left the boat and their father, and followed him.

And he went about all Galilee, teaching in their synagogues and preaching the gospel of the kingdom and healing every disease and every infirmity among the people. So his fame spread throughout all Syria, and they brought him all the sick, those afflicted with various diseases and pains, demoniacs, epileptics, and paralytics, and he healed them. And great crowds followed him from Galilee and the Decapolis and Jerusalem and Judea and from beyond the Jordan.

Seeing the crowds, he went up on the mountain, and when he sat down his disciples came to him. And he opened his mouth and taught them, saying:

"Blessed are the poor in spirit, for theirs is the kingdom of heaven.

"Blessed are those who mourn, for they shall be comforted.

"Blessed are the meek, for they shall inherit the earth.

'Blessed are those who hunger and thirst for righteousness, for they shall be satisfied.

"Blessed are the merciful, for they shall obtain mercy.

"Blessed are the pure in heart, for they shall see God.

"Blessed are the peacemakers, for they shall be called sons of God.

"Blessed are those who are persecuted for righteousness' sake, for theirs is the kingdom of heaven.

"Blessed are you when men revile you and persecute you and utter all kinds of evil against you falsely on my account. Rejoice and be glad, for your reward is great in heaven, for so men persecuted the prophets who were before you.

"You are the salt of the earth; but if salt has lost its taste, how shall its saltness be restored? It is no longer good for anything except to be thrown out and trodden under foot by men.

'You are the light of the world. A city set on a hill cannot be hid. Nor do men light a lamp and put it under a bushel, but on a stand, and it gives light to all in the house. Let your light so shine before men, that they may see your good works and give glory to your Father who is in heaven.

"Think not that I have come to abolish the law and the prophets; I have come not to abolish them but to fulfill them. For truly, I say to you, till heaven and earth pass away, not an iota, not a dot, will pass from the law until all is accomplished. Whoever then relaxes one of the least of these commandments and teaches men so, shall be called least in the kingdom of heaven; but he who does them and teaches them shall be called great in the kingdom of heaven. For I tell you, unless your righteousness exceeds that of the scribes and Pharisees, you will never enter the kingdom of heaven. -

"You have heard that it was said to the men of old, 'You shall not kill; and whoever kills shall be liable to judgment.' But I say to you that every one who is angry with his brother shall be liable to judgment; whoever insults his brother shall be liable to the council, and whoever says, 'You fool!' shall be liable to the hell of fire. So if you are offering your gift at the altar, and there remember that your brother has something against you, leave your gift there before the altar and go; first be reconciled to your brother, and then come and offer your gift. Make friends quickly with your accuser, while you are going with him to court, lest your accuser hand you over to the judge, and the judge to the guard, and you be put in prison; truly, I say to you, you will never get out till you have paid the last penny.

"You have heard that it was said, 'You shall not commit adultery.' But I say to you that every one who looks at a woman lustfully has already committed adultery with her in his heart.

"If your right eye causes you to sin, pluck it out and throw it away; it is better that you lose one of your members than that your whole body be thrown into hell. And if your right hand causes you to sin, cut it off and throw it away; it is better that you lose one of your members than that your whole body go into hell.

"It was also said, 'Whoever divorces his wife, let him give her a certificate of divorce.' But I say to you that every one who divorces his wife, except on the ground of unchastity, makes her an adulteress; and whoever marries a divorced woman commits adultery.

"Again you have heard that it was said to the men of old, 'You shall not swear falsely, but shall perform to the Lord what you have sworn.' But I say to you, Do not swear at all, either by heaven, for it is the throne of God, or by the earth, for it is his footstool, or by Jerusalem, for it is the city of the great King. And do not swear by your head, for you cannot make one hair white or black. Let what you say be simply 'Yes' or 'No'; anything more than this comes from evil.

"You have heard that it was said, 'An eye for an eye and a tooth for a tooth.' But I say to you, Do not resist one who is evil. But if any one strikes you on the right cheek, turn to him the other also; and if any one would sue you and take your coat, let him have your cloak as well; and if any one forces you to go one mile, go with him two miles. Give to him who begs from you, and do not refuse him who would borrow from you.

"You have heard that it was said, 'You shall love your neighbor and hate your enemy.' But I say to you, Love your enemies and pray for those who persecute you, so that you may be sons of your Father who is in heaven; for he makes his sun rise on the evil and on the good, and sends rain on the just and on the unjust. For if you love those who love you, what reward have you? Do not even the tax collectors do the same? And if you salute only your brethren, what more are you doing than others? Do not even the Gentiles do the same? You, therefore, must be perfect, as your heavenly Father is perfect.

Study Questions

1. The Sermon on the Mount was written down and preserved for later generations, but it had originally been delivered orally. How might the transformation of the spoken to the written word affect the impact of the original message?

2. How does the Sermon resemble earlier expressions of the Jewish moral tradition?

3. How does Jesus elaborate on the Hebrew law?

4. To whom Jesus' message principally directed? Is it to the rich and powerful or the humble? What is his advice?

5. Jesus taught his message through sermons, but he also demonstrated special powers. How did he do this?

PART II

Traditional Societies

Africa and the Muslim World

Mansa Musa: Mansa Musa (1312–1337), king of the West African state of Mali, was one of the richest and most powerful rulers of his day. During his famous pilgrimage to Mecca, he arrived in Cairo with a hundred camels laden with gold and gave away so much gold that its value depreciated there for several years. His fame spread to Europe as well, evidenced by this Spanish map of 1375, which depicts Mansa Musa seated on his throne in Mali, holding an impressive gold nugget.

Code (529–565)   **28**

JUSTINIAN

Justinian I (483–565) began life as a peasant, although his uncle Justin, born a swineherd, had already become a Byzantine general. Justin ultimately rose to become emperor in 518, and, as he had no children of his own, he brought his nephew Justinian to Constantinople to be groomed as his successor. Justinian was named emperor in 527 only a few months before his uncle died. Justinian's rule was characterized by his desire to expand the borders of his empire and to reform its civil administration, but he was more successful as a reformer than a conqueror. He undertook a series of governmental reforms, began a public works program, and finally codified Byzantine law.

The Justinian *Code* was compiled at the emperor's command between 529 and 565. The state of Roman and Byzantine law had grown increasingly chaotic over the centuries, with a vast accumulation of contradictory laws and statutes. The *Code* was designed to remove these anomalies by examining every known law to reduce duplication and contradiction. Teams of lawyers worked for decades on the project, and the result surpassed even the most optimistic hopes of the emperor. The *Code* formed the basis of European law for centuries. The section reproduced here relates to family law and covers marriage, divorce, and the responsibilities of parents and children.

Formation of Marriage

Marriage is the union of a man and a woman, a partnership for life involving divine as well as human law.

Marriage cannot take place unless everyone involved consents, that is, those who are being united and those in whose power they are.

According to Pomponius, if I have a grandson by one son and a granddaughter by another who are both in my power, my authority alone will be enough to allow them to marry, and this is correct.

A girl who was less than twelve years old when she married will not be a lawful wife until she reaches that age while living with her husband.

Where a grandson marries, his father must also consent: but if a granddaughter gets married, the consent and authority of the grandfather will suffice. Insanity prevents marriage being contracted, because consent is required; but once validly contracted, it does not invalidate the marriage.

When the relationship of brother and sister arises because of adoption, it is an impediment to marriage while the adoption lasts. So I will be able to marry a girl whom my father adopted and then emancipated. Similarly, if she is kept in his power and I am emancipated, we can be married. It is advisable, then, for someone who wishes to adopt his son-in-law to emancipate his daughter-in-law and for someone who wished to adopt his daughter-in-law to emancipate his son. We are not allowed to marry our paternal or maternal aunts or paternal or maternal great-aunts although paternal and maternal great-aunts are related in the fourth degree. Again, we are not allowed to marry a paternal aunt or great-aunt, even though they are related to us by adoption.

People who wrongfully prevent children in their power from marrying, or who refuse to provide a dowry for them can be forced by proconsuls and provincial governors to arrange marriages and provide dowries for them. Those who do not try to arrange marriages are held to prevent them.

Where he marries someone because his father forces him to do so and he would not have married her if the choice had been his, the marriage will nevertheless be valid, because marriage cannot take place without the consent of the parties; he is held to have chosen this course of action.

The *lex Papia* provides that all freeborn men, apart from senators and their children, can marry freedwomen.

Living with a freewoman implies marriage, not concubinage, as long as she does not make money out of prostitution.

An emancipated son can marry without his father's consent, and any son he has will be his heir.

Women accused of adultery cannot marry during the lifetime of their husbands, even before conviction.

Women who live in a shameful way and make money out of prostitution, even where it is not done openly, are held in disgrace. If a woman lives as a concubine with anyone other than her patron, I would say that she lacks the character of the mother of a household.

As far as marriages are concerned, it is always necessary to consider not just what is lawful but also what is decent. If the daughter, granddaughter, or great-granddaughter of a senator marries a freedman or someone who was an actor, or whose father or mother were actors, the marriage will be void.

Divorces and Repudiations

Marriage is dissolved by the divorce, death, captivity, or other kind of slavery of either of the parties.

The word "divorce" derives from either the diversity of views it involves or because people who dissolve their marriage go in different directions. Where repudiation, that is, renunciation, is involved, these words are used: "Keep your things to yourself": or "Look after your own things." It is agreed that in order to end betrothals a renunciation must be made. Here the established words are: "I do not accept your conditions." It makes no difference whether the repudiation is made in the presence of the other party.

A true divorce does not take place unless an intention to remain apart permanently is present. So things said or done in anger are not effective until the parties show by their persistence that they are an indication of their considered opinion. So where repudiation takes place in anger and the wife returns shortly afterward, she is not held to have divorced her husband.

Julian asks in the eighteenth book of his *Digest* whether an insane woman can repudiate her husband or be repudiated by him. He writes that an insane woman can be repudiated, because she is in the same position as a person who does not know of the repudiation. But she could not repudiate her husband because of her madness, and her curator cannot do this either but her father can repudiate for her. He would not have dealt with repudiation here unless it was established that the marriage was to continue. This opinion seems to me to be correct.

The wives of people who fall into enemy hands can still be considered married women only in that other men cannot marry them hastily. Generally, as long as it is certain that a husband who is in captivity is still alive, his wife does not have the right to contract another marriage, unless she herself has given some ground for repudiation. But if it is not certain whether the husband in captivity is alive or has died, then if five years have passed since his capture, his wife has the right to marry again so that the first marriage will be held to have been dissolved with the consent of the parties and each of the parties will have their rights withdrawn. The same rule applies where a husband stays at home and his wife is captured.

Where someone who has given the other party written notice of divorce regrets having done this and the notice is served in ignorance of the change of mind, the marriage is held to remain valid, unless the person who receives the notice is aware of the change of mind and wants to end the marriage himself. Then the marriage will be dissolved by the person who received the notice.

The Recognition of Children

It is not just a person who smothers a child who is held to kill it but also the person who abandons it, denies it food, or puts it on show in public places to excite pity which he himself does not have.

If anyone asks his children to support him or children seek support from their father, a judge should look into the question. Should a father be forced to support only children in his power or should he also support children who have been emancipated or have become independent in some other way? I think it is better to say that even where children are not in power, they must be supported by their parents and they, on the other hand, must support their parents. Must we support only our fathers, our paternal grandfathers, paternal great-grandfathers, and other relatives of the male sex, or are we compelled to support our mothers and other relatives in the maternal line? It is better to say that in each case the judge should intervene so as to give relief to the necessities of some of them and the infirmity of others. Since this obligation is based on justice and affection between blood relations, the judge should balance the

claims of each person involved. The same is true in the maintenance of children by their parents. So we force a mother to support her illegitimate children and them to support her. The deified Pius also says that a maternal grandfather is compelled to support his grandchildren. He also stated in a rescript that a father must support his daughter, if it is proved in court that he was really her father. But where a son can support himself, judges should decide not to compel the provision of maintenance for him. So the Emperor Pius stated: "The appropriate judges before whom you will appear must order you to be supported by your father according to his means, provided that where you claim you are a tradesman, it is your ill health which makes you incapable of supporting yourself by your own labor." If a father denies that the person seeking support is his son and so maintains that he need not provide it, or where a son denies that the person seeking support is his father, the judges must decide this summarily. If it is established that the person is a son or a father, they must order him to be supported. But if this is not proved, they should not award maintenance. Remember if the judges declare that support must be provided, this does not affect the truth of the matter; for they did not declare that the person was the man's son, but only that he must be supported. If anyone refuses to provide support, the judges must determine the maintenance according to his means. If he fails to provide this, he can be forced to comply with the judgment by the seizing of his property in execution and selling it. The judges must also decide whether a relative or a father has any good reason for not supporting his children.

Concubines

Can a woman living in concubinage leave her patron against his will and either marry someone else or become his concubine? I think that a concubine should not be granted the right to marry if she leaves her patron without his consent, since it is more respectable for a freedwoman to be her patron's concubine rather than the mother of a family. I agree with the view of Atilicinus that it is only women who have not been debauched that can be kept as concubines without fear of committing a crime. Where a man keeps a woman who has been convicted of adultery as a concubine, I do not think the *lex Julia* on adultery will apply, although it will if he marries her. If a woman has been her patron's concubine and then becomes his son's or grandson's or vice versa, I do not think she is behaving properly, since a relationship of this kind is almost criminal. So this sort of bad behavior is prohibited. Clearly, a man can keep a concubine of any age unless she is less than twelve years old.

If a patron who has a freedwoman as his concubine becomes insane, it is more humane to say that she is still his concubine.

Another person's freedwoman can be kept as a concubine as well as a freeborn woman, especially where she is of low birth or has been a prostitute. But if a man would rather have a freeborn woman with respectable background as his concubine, he will not be allowed to do this unless he clearly states the position in front of witnesses. But it will be necessary for him to marry her, or if he refuses, to commit debauchery with her. A person does not commit adultery by having a concubine; for because concubinage exists because of statute law, it is not penalized by statute.

A man can have a concubine in the province where he holds office.

Study Questions

1. What does the *Code* reveal about the status of women in Justinian's time?

2. Upon what grounds could a divorce be procured under the *Code?*

3. The law has a great deal to say about the parent-child relationship. Could you make some generalization about parents and children in Byzantium from the *Code?*

4. The *Code* talks about concubines and wives alike. How were they different? What rights did each have?

5. Judging from the *Code's* discussion of marriage, could you offer any generalizations about the institution in Justinian's time?

Secret History (ca. 560)   29

PROCOPIUS

Procopius was a Byzantine civil servant and historian whose works provide important information about the reign of the emperor Justinian. Procopius was probably born in Palestine sometime between 490 and 510. After his early education he sought a career in civil service and migrated to Constantinople, then the center of the Roman Empire. He served on a general's staff and was thus able to travel to Persia, Italy, and Africa, so his experience of Byzantine administration was extensive and firsthand. He had apparently returned to Constantinople by 540, but there is no trace of him thereafter.

Procopius wrote several official histories during his career, of which the most important is an account of the military campaigns of Justinian's reign, entitled *On the Wars*. He also left a description of Justinian's public works projects called *The Buildings*. His most famous work, however, was published after his death. This was the *Secret History*, a highly personal account of Justinian and the Empress Theodora. Whether Procopius' point of view was unique or common among Byzantine civil servants remains an open question.

I think this is as good a time as any to describe the personal appearance of the man. Now in physique he was neither tall nor short, but of average height; not thin, but moderately plump; his face was round, and not bad looking, for he had good color, even when he fasted for two days. To make a long description short, he much resembled Domitian, Vespasian's son.

Now such was Justinian in appearance; but his character was something I could not fully describe. For he was at once villainous and amenable; as people say colloquially, a moron. He was never truthful with anyone, but always guileful in what he said and did, yet easily hoodwinked by any who wanted to deceive him. His nature was an unnatural mixture of folly and wickedness. What in olden times a peripatetic philosopher said was also true of him, that opposite qualities combine in a man as in the mixing of colors. I will try to portray him, however, insofar as I can fathom his complexity.

This Emperor, then, was deceitful, devious, false, hypocritical, two-faced, cruel, skilled in dissembling his thought, never moved to tears by either joy or pain, though he could summon them artfully at will when the occasion demanded, a liar always, not only offhand, but in writing, and when he swore sacred oaths to his subjects in their very hearing. Then he would immediately break his agreements and pledges, like the vilest of slaves, whom indeed only the fear of torture drives to confess their perjury. A faithless friend, he was a treacherous enemy, insane for murder and plunder, quarrelsome and revolutionary, easily led to anything evil, but never willing to listen to good counsel, quick to plan mischief and carry it out, but finding even the hearing of anything good distasteful to his ears.

How could anyone put Justinian's ways into words? These and many even worse vices were disclosed in him as in no other mortal: nature seemed to have taken the wickedness of all other men combined and planted it in this man's soul. And besides this, he was too prone to listen to accusations; and too quick to punish. For he decided such cases without full examination, naming the punishment when he had heard only the accuser's side of the matter. Without hesitation he wrote decrees for the plundering of countries, sacking of cities, and slavery of whole nations, for no cause whatever. So that if one wished to take all the calamities which had befallen the Romans before this time and weigh them against his crimes, I think it would be found that more men had been murdered by this single man than in all previous history.

He had no scruples about appropriating other people's property, and did not even think any excuse necessary, legal or illegal, for confiscating what did not belong to him. And when it was his, he was more than ready to squander it in insane display, or give it as an unnecessary bribe to the barbarians. In short, he neither held on to any money himself nor let anyone else keep any: as if his reason were not avarice, but jealousy of those who had riches. Driving all wealth from the country of the Romans in this manner, he became the cause of universal poverty.

Now this was the character of Justinian, so far as I can portray it.

As soon as Justinian came into power he turned everything upside down. Whatever had before been forbidden by law he now introduced into the government, while he revoked all established customs: as if he had been given the robes of an Emperor on the condition he would turn everything topsy-turvy. Existing offices he abolished, and invented new ones for the management of public affairs. He did the same thing to the laws and to the regulations of the army; and his reason was not any improvement of justice or any advantage, but simply that everything might be new and named after himself. And whatever was beyond his power to abolish, he renamed after himself anyway.

Of the plundering of property or the murder of men, no weariness ever overtook him. As soon as he had looted all the houses of the wealthy, he looked around for others; meanwhile throwing away the spoils of his previous robberies in subsidies to barbarians or senseless building extravagances. And when he had ruined perhaps myriads in this mad looting, he immediately sat down to plan how he could do likewise to others in even greater number.

As the Romans were now at peace with all the world and he had no other means of satisfying his lust for slaughter, he set the barbarians all to fighting each other. And for no reason at all he sent for the Hun chieftains, and with idiotic magnanimity gave them large sums of money, alleging he did this to secure their friendship. These Huns, as soon as they had got this money, sent it together with their soldiers to others of their chieftains, with the word to make inroads into the land of the Emperor: so that they might collect further tribute from him, to buy them off in a second peace. Thus the Huns enslaved the Roman Empire, and were paid by the Emperor to keep on doing it.

This encouraged still others of them to rob the poor Romans; and after their pillaging, they too were further rewarded by the gracious Emperor. In this way all the Huns, for when it was not one tribe of them it was another, continuously overran and laid waste the Empire. For the barbarians were led by many different chieftains, and the war, thanks to Justinian's senseless generosity, was thus endlessly protracted. Consequently no place, mountain or cave, or any other spot in Roman territory, during this time remained uninjured; and many regions were pillaged more than five times.

These misfortunes, and those that were caused by the Medes, Saracens, Slavs, Antes, and the rest of the barbarians, I described in my previous works. But, as I said in the preface to this narrative, the real cause of these calamities remained to be told here.

Moreover, while he was encouraging civil strife and frontier warfare to confound the Romans, with only one thought in his mind, that the earth should run red with human blood and he might acquire more and more booty, he invented a new means of murdering his subjects. Now among the Christians in the entire Roman Empire, there are many with dissenting doctrines, which are called heresies by the established church: such as those of the Montanists and Sabbatians, and whatever others cause the minds of men to wander from the true path. All of these beliefs he ordered to be abolished, and their place taken by the orthodox dogma: threatening, among the punishments for disobedience, loss of the heretic's right to will property to his children or other relatives.

Now the churches of these so-called heretics, especially those belonging to the Arian dissenters, were almost incredibly wealthy. Neither all the Senate put together nor the greatest other unit of the Roman Empire, had anything in property comparable to that of these churches. For their gold and silver treasures, and stores of precious stones, were beyond telling or numbering: they owned mansions and whole villages, land all over the world, and everything else that is counted as wealth among men.

As none of the previous Emperors had molested these churches, many men, even those of the orthodox faith, got their livelihood by working on their estates. But the Emperor Justinian, in confiscating these properties, at the same time took away what for many people had been their only means of earning a living.

Agents were sent everywhere to force whomever they chanced upon to renounce the faith of their fathers. This, which seemed impious to rustic people, caused them to rebel against those who gave them such an order. Thus many perished at the hands of the persecuting faction, and others did away with themselves, foolishly thinking this the holier course of two evils; but most of them by far quitted the land of their fathers, and fled the country. The Montanists, who dwelt in Phrygia, shut themselves up in their churches, set them on fire, and ascended to glory in the flames. And thenceforth the whole Roman Empire was a scene of massacre and flight.

A similar law was then passed against the Samaritans, which threw Palestine into an indescribable turmoil. Those, indeed, who lived in my own Caesarea and in the other cities, deciding it silly to suffer harsh treatment over a ridiculous trifle of dogma, took the name of Christians in exchange for the one they had borne before, by which precaution they were able to avoid the perils of the new law. The most reputable and better class of these citizens, once they had adopted this religion, decided to remain faithful to it; the majority, however, as if in spite for having not voluntarily, but by the compulsion of law, abandoned the belief of their fathers, soon slipped away into the Manichean sect and what is known as polytheism.

The country people!, however, banded together and determined to take arms against the Emperor: choosing as their candidate for the throne a bandit named Julian, son of Sabarus. And for a time they held their own against the imperial troops; but finally, defeated in battle, were cut down, together with their leader. Ten myriads of men are said to have perished in this engagement, and the most fertile country on earth thus became destitute of farmers. To the Christian owners of these lands, the affair brought great hardship: for while their profits from these properties were annihilated, they had to pay heavy annual taxes on them to the Emperor for the rest of their lives, and secured no remission of this burden.

Next he turned his attention to those called Gentiles, torturing their persons and plundering their lands. Of this group, those who decided to become nominal Christians saved themselves for the time being; but it was not long before these, too, were caught performing libations and sacrifices and other unholy rites. And how he treated the Christians shall be told hereafter.

After this he passed a law prohibiting pederasty: a law pointed not at offenses committed after this decree, but at those who could be convicted of having practised the vice in the past. The conduct of the prosecution was utterly illegal. Sentence was passed when there was no accuser: the word of one man or boy, and that perhaps a slave, compelled against his will to bear witness against his owner, was defined as sufficient evidence. Those who were convicted were castrated and then exhibited in a public parade. At the start, this persecution was directed only at those who were of the Green party, were reputed to be especially wealthy, or had otherwise aroused jealousy.

The Emperor's malice was also directed against the astrologer. Accordingly, magistrates appointed to punish thieves also abused the astrologers, for no other reason than that they belonged to this profession: whipping them on the back and parading them on camels throughout the city, though they were old men, and in every way respectable, with no reproach against them except that they studied the science of the stars while living in such a city.

Consequently there was a constant stream of emigration not only to the land of the barbarians but to places farthest remote from the Romans; and in every country and city one could see crowds of foreigners. For in order to escape persecution, each would lightly exchange his native land for another, as if his own country had been taken by an enemy.

Study Questions

1. What are the emperor's principal failings, according to Procopius?

2. Do Justinian's character flaws affect his ability to rule?

3. Justinian is criticized for his reforms by Procopius, a professional civil servant. If the emperor were to speak in his own defense, how might he answer the charges?

4. Why does Justinian's foreign policy fail? What do you think he was trying to accomplish?

5. Procopius presents us with an extremely biased picture of Justinian. Can such an unfair portrayal teach us anything of value about Justinian?

6. What does Procopius' bias tell us about him? Could you say something about his own views, given the picture he gives us of Justinian?

The Koran (7th century)   30

The Koran is the Holy Book of Islam. Revealed by God to Muhammad (ca. 570–632) over the course of two decades beginning in 610, it is the foundation upon which Islam was built. Believers consider the book to be literally true in all respects and to be the final authority on all moral and legal questions.

Roughly the same length as the New Testament, the Koran contains many references to both the Jewish and Christian traditions. It recognizes the contribution of biblical figures such as Noah and Moses and the importance of Jesus as a prophet. Nevertheless, it contains much that is unique. The Koran emphasizes the singularity of God as well as His divine plan. It also includes a system of ritual laws and ethics. Each man, for example, is allowed to marry no more than four wives. Followers are presented with a strict moral and dietary code and are required to make a pilgrimage to Mecca, the center of Islam. They are also required to treat all persons, believers and infidels, with compassion.

In the name of God, the most merciful and compassionate.

Praise be to God, the Lord of the worlds;

The most merciful, the compassionate;

The king of the day of Judgment.

Thee do we worship, and of Thee do we beg assistance.

Direct us on the right way,

The way of those to whom Thou has been gracious; not of those against whom Thou art angry, nor of those who go astray.

In the name of God, the most merciful and cornpassionate.

Praise the name of thy Lord, the Most High, Who hath created and completely formed His creatures: Who determineth them to various ends, and directeth them to attain the same, Who produceth the pastures for cattle, and afterwards rendereth the same dry stubble of a dusky hue.

God will enable thee to rehearse His revelations, and thou shalt not forget any part thereof, except what God shall please, for He knoweth that which is manifest, and that which is hidden. And God will facilitate unto thee the most easy way. Therefore admonish thy people, if thy admonition shall be profitable unto them.

Whosoever feareth God, he will be admonished: but the most wretched unbeliever will turn away from it; who shall be cast to be broiled in the greater fire of hell, wherein he shall not die, neither shall he live.

Now hath he attained felicity who is purified by faith, and who remembereth the name of his Lord, and prayeth. But ye prefer this present life: yet the life to come is better, and more durable.

Verily this is written in the ancient Books, the Books of Abraham and Moses.

God! There is no god but Him, the Living, the Self-subsisting: He hath sent down unto thee the Book of the Koran with truth, confirming that which was revealed before it; For He had formerly sent down the Law and the Gospel, a guidance unto men; and He had also sent down the Salvation.

Verily those who believe not the signs of God shall suffer a grievous punishment; for God is mighty, able to revenge.

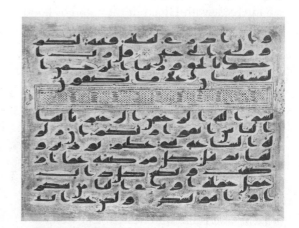

Koran Cover with Decorative Writing. During Muhammed's lifetime, scribes were already collecting and transferring the suras, or chapters, of the Koran onto parchment. The caliph Umar was responsible for codifying these. This gilt Koran cover dates from the thirteenth century and is an outstanding example of the fine Arabic calligraphy for which Islamic artists were renowned.

Surely nothing is hidden from God, of that which is on earth, or in the heavens; it is He who formeth you in the wombs, as He pleaseth; there is no God but Him, the Mighty, the Wise.

It is He who hath sent down unto thee the Book, wherein are some verses clear to be understood: they are the foundation of the Book; and others are parabolical. But they whose hearts are perverse will follow that which is parabolical therein, out of love of schism, and a desire of the interpretation thereof-, yet none knoweth the interpretation thereof, except God. But they who are well grounded in knowledge say, We believe therein, the whole is from our Lord; and none will consider except the prudent.

The Doctrine of One God

God! There is no God but Him; the Living, the Self-subsisting: neither slumber nor sleep seizeth Him; to Him belongeth whatsoever is in the heavens, and on earth. Who is he that can intercede with Him, but through His good pleasure? He knoweth that which is past, and that which is to come unto them, and they shall not comprehend anything of His knowledge, but so far as He pleaseth. His throne is extended over the heavens and the earth; and the preservation of both is no burden unto Him. He is the High, the Mighty.

Let there be no compulsion in religion. Now is right direction manifestly distinguished from deceit: whoever therefore shall deny Tagut [Satan] and believe in God, he shall surely take hold on a strong handle, which shall not be broken; God is He who heareth and seeth.

God is the patron of those who believe; He shall lead them out of darkness into light; but as to those who believe not, their patrons are Tagut; they shall lead them from the light into darkness; they shall be the companions of hell fire, they shall remain therein forever.

Alms to the Poor

Who is he that will lend unto God an acceptable loan? For God will double the same unto him, and he shall receive moreover an honorable reward.

Verily as to those who give alms, both men and women, and those who lend unto God an acceptable loan, He will double the same unto them; and they shall moreover receive an honorable reward.

And they who believe in God and His apostles, these are the men of veracity and the witnesses in the presence of their Lord: they shall have their reward and their light. But as to those who believe not, and lie about God's signs; they shall be the companions of hell.

Know ye that this present life is only a play and a vain amusement; and worldly pomp, and the affectation of glory among you, and the multiplying of riches and children, are as the plants nourished by the rain, the springing up whereof delighteth the husbandman; then they wither, so that thou seest the same turn yellow, and at length they become dry stubble. But in the life to come will be a severe punishment for those who covet worldly grandeur; and pardon from God, and favor for those who renounce it: for this present life is no other than a deceitful provision.

Hasten with emulation to obtain pardon from your Lord, and Paradise, the extent whereof equaleth the extent of heaven and earth, prepared for those who believe in God and His apostles. Such is the bounty of God; He will give the same unto whom He pleaseth: and God is endured with great bounty.

It is not righteousness that ye turn your faces in prayer towards the East and the West, but righteousness is of him who believeth in God and the last day, and the angels and the Scriptures, and the prophets; who giveth money for God's sake unto his kindred, and unto orphans, and the needy, and the wayfarer, and those who ask, and for the redemption of captives; who is constant in prayer, and giveth alms; and of those who perform their promises which they have made, and who behave themselves patiently in adversity, and hardships, and in time of violence: these are they who are true, and these are they who fear God.

The Devil threateneth you with poverty, and commandeth you filthy covetousness; but God promiseth you pardon from Himself and abundance: God is Bounteous and Wise. He giveth wisdom unto whom He pleaseth; and he unto whom wisdom is given, hath received much good: but none will consider it, except the wise of heart.

And whatever alms ye shall give, or whatever vow ye shall vow, verily God knoweth it; but the ungodly shall have none to help them. If ye make your alms to appear, it is well; but if ye conceal them, and give them unto the poor, this will be better for you, and will remove some of your sins: and God is well informed of that which ye do.

The guidance of them belongeth not unto thee [O Apostle]; but God guideth whom He pleaseth. The good that ye shall give in alms shall redound unto yourselves; and ye shall not give unless out of desire of seeing the face of God. And what good thing ye shall give in alms, it shall be repaid you, and ye shall not be treated unjustly.

Alms unto the poor who are wholly employed in fighting for the religion of God, and cannot freely travel in the land; the ignorant man thinketh them rich, because of their modesty: thou shalt know them by this mark, they ask not men with importunity; and what good ye shall give them in alms, verily God knoweth it.

They who distribute alms of their substance night and day, in private and in public, shall have their reward with the Lord; on them shall no fear come, neither shall they be grieved.

Wine and Gambling

O true believers! surely wine, and gambling and images, and divining arrows, are an abomination of the work of Satan; therefore avoid them, that ye may prosper.

Satan seeketh to sow dissension and hatred among you, by means of wine and gambling, and to divert you from remembering God, and from prayer; will ye not therefore abstain from them?

Obey God, and obey the Apostle, and take heed to yourselves; but if ye turn back, know that the duty of God's Apostle is only to preach publicly.

On those who believe and do good works, it is no sin that they have tasted wine or gambled before they were forbidden; if they fear God, and believe, and do good works, and shall for the future fear God, and believe, and shall persevere to fear him, and to do good, for God loveth those who do good.

Paradise

The description of Paradise, which is promised unto the pious: therein are rivers of incorruptible water; and rivers of milk, the taste whereof changeth not; and rivers of wine, pleasant unto those who drink; and rivers of clarified honey. And therein shall they have plenty of all kinds of fruits; and pardon from their Lord. Shall the man for whom these things are prepared, be as they who must dwell forever in hell fire, and will have the boiling water given them to drink, which shall burst their bowels?

They [the righteous] shall repose on couches, the linings thereof shall be of thick silk interwoven with gold: and the fruit of the two gardens shall be near at hand to gather.

Which, therefore, of your Lord's benefits will ye ungratefully deny?

Therein shall be damsels, remaining their eyes from beholding any besides their spouses:

whom no man or Jinni shall have touched before them,

Which, therefore, of your Lord's benefits will ye ungratefully deny?

Having complexions like rubies and pearls.

Which, therefore, of your Lord's benefits will ye ungratefully deny?

Shall the reward of good works be any other than good?

Which, therefore, of your Lord's benefits will ye ungratefully deny?

And besides these there shall be two other gardens.

Which, therefore, of your Lord's benefits will ye ungratefully deny?

Of a dark green color.

Which, therefore, of your Lord's benefits will ye ungratefully deny?

In each of them shall be two fountains pouring forth plenty of water.

Which, therefore, of your Lord's benefits will ye ungratefully deny?

In each of them shall be fruits, and palm trees, and pomegranates.

Which, therefore, of your Lord's benefits will ye ungratefully deny?

Therein shall be agreeable and beauteous damsels.

Which, therefore, of your Lord's benefits will ye ungratefully deny?

Having fine black eyes; and kept in pavilions from public view.

Which, therefore, of your Lord's benefits will ye ungratefully deny?

Whom no man shall have touched before their destined spouses, nor any Jinni.

Which, therefore, of your Lord's benefits will ye ungratefully deny?

Therein shall they delight themselves, lying on green cushions and beautiful carpets.

Which, therefore, of your Lord's benefits will ye ungratefully deny?

Blessed be the name of thy Lord, possessed of Glory and Honor!

Study Questions

1. What are some of the characteristics shared by Islam, Christianity, and Judaism?

2. What is the responsibility of the believer toward the poor?

3. In what way is the Koran a code of conduct for everyday life?

4. What does the Koran teach should be done to the nonbeliever?

5. What does paradise look like? Why do you think the Koran portrays it as it does?

Book of the Maghrib (13th century)   31

IBN SAID

Ibn Said (ca. 1204–1274) was a North African Muslim. Although the events of his life are shrouded in mystery, some of his historical works have survived. The best known is the *Book of the Maghrib*. Said was fascinated by life in Spain, and it is possible that he settled there during the Muslim occupation. The *Book of the Maghrib* tells of the Muslim conquest and occupation of Iberia. Writing from the point of view of the Muslim occupiers, Ibn Said nevertheless uncovers the divisions within Muslim rule, thus foretelling the eventual Christian reconquest of Spain.

The greatest importance of the *Book of the Maghrib* lies in its description of the rich Moorish culture that developed in Muslim Spain. The art and science of the Moors far surpassed the achievements of the Spanish, and Said celebrates the work of Muslim poets and writers. His book leaves an unforgettable impression of a new society in Europe.

Andalus [the Iberian peninsula], which was conquered in the year 92 of the Hijra, continued for many years to be a dependency of the Eastern Khalifate, until it was snatched away from their hands by one of the surviving members of the family of Umeyyah (Umayyad), who, crossing over from Barbary, subdued the country, and formed therein an independent kingdom, which he transmitted to his posterity. During three centuries and a half, Andalus, governed by the princes of this dynasty, reached the utmost degree of power and prosperity, until civil war breaking out among its inhabitants, the Muslims, weakened by internal discord, became every where the prey of the artful Christians, and the territory of Islam was considerably reduced, so much so that at the present moment the worshippers of the crucified hold the greatest part of Andalus in their hands, and their country is divided into various powerful kingdoms, whose rulers assist each other whenever the Muslims attack their territories. This brings to my recollection the words of an eastern geographer who visited Andalus in the fourth century of the Hijra (tenth century A.D.), and during the prosperous times of the Cordovan Khalifate, I mean Ibnu Haukal Annassibi, who, describing Andalus, speaks in very unfavourable terms of its inhabitants. As his words require refutation I shall transcribe here the whole of the passage. "Andalus," he says, "is an extensive island, a little less than a month's march in length, and twenty and odd days in width. It abounds in rivers and springs, is covered with trees and plants of every description, and is amply provided with every article which adds to the comforts of life; slaves are very fine, and may be procured for a small price on account of their abundance; owing, too, to the fertility of the land, which yields all sorts of grain, vegetables, and fruit, as well as to the number and goodness of its pastures in which innumerable flocks of cattle graze, food is exceedingly abundant and cheap, and the inhabitants are thereby plunged into indolence and sloth, letting mechanics and men of the lowest ranks of society overpower them and conduct their affairs. Owing to this it is really astonishing how the Island (i.e., peninsula) of Andalus still remains in the hands of the Muslims, being, as they are, people of vicious habits and low inclinations, narrow-minded, and entirely devoid of fortitude, courage, and the military accomplishments necessary to meet face to face the formidable nations of Christians who surround them on every side, and by whom they are continually assailed."

Such are the words of Ibnu Haukal; but, if truth be told, I am at a loss to guess to whom they are applied. To my countrymen they certainly are not; or, if so, it is a horrible calumny, for if any people on the earth are famous for their courage, their noble qualities, and good habits, it is the Muslims of Andalus; and indeed their readiness to fight the common enemy, their constancy in upholding the holy tenets of their religion, and their endurance of the hardships and privations of war, have become almost proverbial. So, as far as this goes, Ibnu Haukal is decidedly in error, for as the proverb says, "the tongue of stammering is at times more eloquent than the tongue of eloquence." As to the other imputation, namely, their being devoid of all senses, wisdom, and talent, either in the field or in administration, would to God that the author's judgment were correct, for then the ambition of the chiefs would not have been raised, and the Muslims would not have turned against each other's breasts and dipped in each other's blood those very weapons which God Almighty put into their hands for the destruction and annihilation of the infidel Christian. But, as it is, we ask—were those Sultans and Khalifs wanting in prudence and talents who governed this country for upwards of five hundred years, and who administered its affairs in the midst of foreign war and civil discord? Were those fearless warriors deficient in courage and military science who withstood on the frontiers of the Muslim empire the frightful shock of the innumerable infidel nations who dwell within and out of Andalus, whose extensive territories cover a surface of three months' march, and all of whom ran to arms at a moment's notice to defend the religion of the crucified? And if it be true that at the moment I write the Muslims have been visited by the wrath of heaven, and that the Almighty has sent down defeat and shame to their arms, are we to wonder at it at a time when the Christians, proud of their success, have carried their arms as far as Syria and Mesopotamia, have invaded the districts contiguous to the country which is the meeting-place of the Muslims, and the cupola of Islam, committed all sorts of ravages and depredations, and conquered the city of Haleb (Aleppo) and its environs, and done other deeds which are sufficiently declared in the histories of the time? No, it is by no means to be wondered at, especially when proper attention is paid to the manner in which the Andalusian Muslims have come to their present state of weakness and degradation. The process is this: the Christians will rush down from their mountains, or across the plain, and make an incursion into the Muslim territory; there they will pounce upon a castle and seize it: they will ravage the neighbouring country, take the inhabitants captive, and then retire to their country with all the plunder they have collected, leaving, nevertheless, strong garrisons in the castles and towers captured by them. In the meanwhile the Muslim king in whose dominions the inroad has been made, instead of attending to his own interests and stopping the disease by applying cauterization, will be waging war against his neighbours of the Muslims; and these, instead of defending the common cause, the cause of religion and truth,—instead of assisting their brother, will confederate and ally to deprive him of whatever dominions still remain in his hands. So, from a trifling evil at first, it will grow into an irreparable calamity, and the Christians will advance farther and farther until they subdue the whole of that country exposed to their inroads, where, once established and fortified, they will direct their attacks to another part of the Muslim territories, and carry on the same war of havoc and destruction. Nothing of this, however, existed at the time when Ibnu Haukal visited Andalus; for although we are told by Ibnu Hayyan and other writers that the Christians began as early as the reign of 'Abdu-r-rahman II (912–961) to grow powerful, and to annoy the Muslims on the frontiers, yet it is evident that until the breaking out of the civil wars, which raged with uncommon violence throughout Andalus, the encroachments of the barbarians on the extensive and unprotected frontiers of the Muslim empire were but of little consequence.

But to return to our subject. During the first years after the conquest the government of Andalus was vested in the hands of military commanders appointed by the Viceroys of Africa, who were themselves named by the

Khalifs of Damascus. These governors united in their hands the command of the armies and the civil power, but, being either removed as soon as named, or deposed by military insurrections, much confusion and disorder reigned at all times in the state, and the establishment and consolidation of the Muslim power in Andalus were thwarted in their progress at the very onset. It was not until the arrival of the Beni Umeyyah in Andalus that the fabric of Islam may be said to have rested on a solid foundation. When 'Abdu-r-rahman Ibn Mu'awiyeh had conquered the country, when every rebel had submitted to him, when all his opponents had sworn allegiance to him, and his authority had been universally acknowledged, then his importance increased, his ambition spread wider, and both he and his successors displayed the greatest magnificence in their court, and about their persons and retinue, as likewise in the number of officers and great functionaries of the state. At first they contented themselves with the title of *Benú-l-khaláyif* (sons of the Khalifs), but in process of time, when the limits of their empire had been considerably extended by their conquests on the opposite land of Africa, they took the appellation of Khalifs and *Omará-l-múmenín* (Princes of the believers). It is generally known that the strength and solidity of their empire consisted principally in the policy pursued by these princes, the magnificence and splendour with which they surrounded their court, the reverential awe with which they inspired their subjects, the inexorable rigour with which they chastised every aggression on their rights, the impartiality of their judgments, their anxious solicitude in the observance of the civil law, their regard and attention to the learned, whose opinions they respected and followed, calling them to their sittings and admitting them to their councils, and many other brilliant qualities; in proof of which frequent anecdotes occur in the works of Ibnu Hayyan and other writers; as, for instance, that when-ever a judge

summoned the Khalif, his son, or any of his most beloved favourites, to appear in his presence as a witness in a judicial case, whoever was the individual summoned would attend in person—if the Khalif, out of respect for the law—and if a subject, for fear of incurring his master's displeasure.

But when this salutary awe and impartial justice had vanished, the decay of their empire began, and it was followed by a complete ruin. I have already observed that the princes of that dynasty were formerly styled *Omará-bná-l-kholafá* (Amirs, sons of the Khalifs), but that in latter times they assumed the title of *Omará-l-múmenín* (Princes of the believers). This continued until the disastrous times of the civil war, when the surviving members of the royal family hated each other, and when those who had neither the nobility nor the qualities required to honour the Khalifate pretended to it and wished for it; when the governors of provinces and the generals of armies declared themselves independent and rose every where in their governments, taking the title of *Molúku-t-tawáyif* (Kings of small estates), and when confusion and disorder were at their highest pitch. These petty sovereigns, of whom some read the *khotbah* for the Khalifs of the house of Merwan—in whose hands no power whatsoever remained—while others proclaimed the Abbasside Sultans, and acknowledged their Imam, all began to exercise the powers and to use the appendages of royalty, assuming even the titles and names of former Khalifs, and imitating in every thing the bearing and splendour of the most powerful sovereigns,—a thing which they were enabled to accomplish from the great resources of the countries over which they ruled,—for although Andalus was divided into sundry petty kingdoms, yet such was the fertility of the land, and the amount of taxes collected from it, that the chief of a limited state could at times display at his court a greater magnificence than the ruler of extensive dominions. However, the greatest among them did not hesitate to assume, as I. have already observed, the names and tides of the most famous Eastern Khalifs; for instance, Ibnu Rashik Al-kairwání says that 'Abbád Ibn Mohammed Ibn 'Abbád took the surname of Al-mu'atadhed, and imitated in all things the mode of life and bearing of the Abbaseside Khalif Al-mu'atadhed-billah; his son, Mohammed Ibn 'Abbád, was styled Almu'atamed; both reigned in Seville, to which kingdom they in process of time added Cordova and other extensive territories in the southern and western parts of Andalus, as will hereafter be shown.

As long as the dynasty of Umeyyah occupied the throne of Cordova, the successors of 'Abdurrahmán contrived to inspire their subjects with love of their persons, mixed with reverential awe; this they accomplished by surrounding their courts with splendour, by displaying the greatest magnificence whenever they appeared in public, and by employing other means which I have already hinted at, and deem it not necessary to repeat: they continued thus until the times of the civil war, when, having lost the affections of the people, their subjects began to look with an evil eye at their prodigal expense, and the extravagant pomp with which they surrounded their persons. Then came the Bení Hamúd, the descendants of Idrís, of the progeny of 'Ali Ibn Abí Tálib, who, having snatched the Khalifate from the hands of the Bení Merwán, ruled for some time over the greatest part of Andalus. These princes showed also great ostentation, and, assuming the same titles that the Abbasside Khalifs had borne, they followed their steps in every thing concerning the arrangements of their courts and persons; for instance, whenever a *munshid* wanted to extemporize some verses in praise of his sovereign, or any subject wished to address him on particular business, the poet or the petitioner was introduced to the presence of the Khalif, who sat behind a curtain and spoke without showing himself, the *Hájib*

or curtaindrawer standing all the time by his side to communicate to the party the words or intentions of the Khalif. So when Ibnu Mokéná Al-lishbóní (from Lisbon), the poet, appeared in presence of the Hájib of ldrís Ibn Yahya Al-hamúdí, who was proclaimed Khalif of Malaga, to recite the *kassídah* of his which is so well known and rhymes in *min*, when he came to that part which runs thus—

> The countenance of Idrís, son of Yahya, son of Alí, son of Hamúd, prince of the believers, is like a rising sun; it dazzles the eyes of those who look at it—
>
> Let us see it, let us seize the rays of yonder light, for it is the light of the master of the worlds—

The Sultan himself drew the curtain which concealed him, and said to the poet—"Look, then," and showed great affability to Ibn Mokéná, and rewarded him very handsomely.

But when, through the civil war, the country was broken up into sundry petty sovereignties, the new monarchs followed quite a different line of politics; for, wishing to become popular, they treated their subjects with greater familiarity, and had a more frequent intercourse with all classes of society; they often reviewed their troops, and visited their provinces; they invited to their presence the doctors and poets, and wished to be held from the beginning of their reign as the patrons of science and literature: but even this contributed to the depression of the royal authority, which thus became every day less dreaded; besides, the arms of the Muslims being employed during the long civil wars against one another, the inhabitants of the different provinces began to look on each other with an evil eye; the ties by which they were united became loose, and a number of independent states were formed, the government of which passed from father to son in the same manner as the empire of Cordova had been transmitted to the sons and heirs of the Khalifs. Thus separated from each other, the Muslims began to consider themselves as members of different nations, and it became every day more difficult for them to unite in the common cause; and owing to their divisions, and to their mutual enmity, as well as to the sordid interest and extravagant ambition of some of their kings, the Christians were enabled to attack them in detail, and subdue them one after the other. However, by the arrival of the Bení 'Abdu-l-múmen all those little states were again blended into one, and the whole of Andalus acknowledged their sway, and continued for many years to be ruled by their successors, until, civil war breaking out again, Ibn Húd, surnamed Almutawákel, revolted, and finding the people of Andalus ill-disposed against the Almohades, and anxious to shake off their yoke, he easily made himself master of the country. Ibn Húd, however, followed the policy of his predecessors (the kings of the small states); he even surpassed them in folly and ignorance of the rules of good government, for he used to walk about the streets and markets, conversing and laughing with the lowest people, asking them questions, and doing acts unsuitable to his high station, and which no subject ever saw a Sultan do before, so much so that it was said, not without foundation, that he looked more like a performer of legerdemain than a king. Fools, and the ignorant vulgar seemed, it is true, to gaze with astonishment and pleasure at this, familiarity, but as the poet has said—

> These are things to make the fools laugh, but the consequences of which prudent people are taught to fear.

These symptoms went on increasing until populous cities and extensive districts became the prey of the Christians, and whole kingdoms were snatched from the hands of the Muslims. Another very aggravating circumstance added its weight to the general calamity, namely, the facility with which the power changed hands. Whoever has read attentively what we have just said about the mode of attaining and using the royal power in Andalus, must be convinced that nothing was so easy, especially in latter times, as to arrive at it. The process is this: whenever a knight is known to surpass his countrymen in courage, generosity, or any of those qualities which make a man dear to the vulgar, the people cling to him, follow his party, and soon after proclaim him their king, without paying the least regard to his ascendancy, or stopping to consider whether he is of royal blood or not. The new king then transmits the state as an inheritance to his son or nearest relative, and thus a new dynasty is formed. I may, in proof of this, quote a case which has just taken place among us: a certain captain made himself famous by his exploits, and the victories he won over the enemy, as likewise by his generous and liberal disposition towards the citizens and the army; all of a sudden his friends and partisans resolved to raise him to the throne, and regardless of their own safety, as well as that of their families, friends, and clients residing at court, and whose lives were by their imprudence put in great jeopardy, they rose in a castle, and proclaimed him king; and they never ceased toiling, calling people to their ranks, and fighting their opponents, until their object was accomplished, and their friend solidly established on his throne. Now Eastern people are more cautious about altering the succession, and changing the reigning dynasty; they will on the contrary avoid it by all possible means, and do their best to leave the power in the hands of the reigning family, rather than let discord and civil dissensions sap the foundations of the state, and introduce dissolution and corruption into the social body.

Among us the change of dynasty is a thing of frequent occurrence, and the present ruler of Andalus, Ibnu-l-ahmar, is another instance of what I have advanced. He was a good soldier, and had been very successful in some expeditions against the Christians, whose territories he was continually invading, sallying out at the head of his followers from a castle called *Hisn-Arjónah* (Arjona), where he generally resided. Being a shrewd man, and versed in all the stratagems of war, he seldom went out on an expedition without returning victorious, and laden with plunder, owing to which he amassed great riches, and the number of his partisans and followers were considerably increased. At last, being prompted by ambition to aspire to the royal power, he at first caused his troops to proclaim him king; then sallying out of his stronghold he got possession of Cordova, marched against Seville, took it, and killed its king Al-bájí. After this he subdued Jaen, the strongest and most important city in all Andalus, owing to its walls and the position it occupies, conquered likewise Malaga, Granada, and their districts, and assumed the title of *Amíru-l-moslemín* (Prince of the Muslims); and at the moment I write he is obeyed all over Andalus, and every one looks to him for advice and protection.

Study Questions

1. For most Christians, the Muslim world was monolithic. Is this generalization borne out by Ibn Said?

2. What seems to be the Muslim view of Christians?

3. How do political leaders establish themselves in Muslim Spain?

4. How might Muslims defend themselves from Christian aggression? Why have they been unsuccessful?

5. What characterizes warfare between Christians and Muslims?

The Muqaddimah (1377)   32

IBN KHALDÛN

Ibn Khaldûn (1332–1406) was born into an aristocratic family in the Muslim city of Tunis. Both his grandfather and father were prominent intellectuals and political advisors, and Ibn Khaldûn was trained to follow in their footsteps. He was tutored in Arabic, studied the Koran (Qur'ân) with churchmen, and was groomed for political office, which he first achieved at the age of 20. Ibn Khaldûn soon moved to Fez, one of the great intellectual centers of Northern Africa. For the next decade he served as a political advisor to a series of Moorish rulers, traveling to both Granada and Seville on diplomatic missions. In the unstable world of the mid-fourteenth century, his political life propelled him into high offices and low dungeons. After his second period of incarceration, Ibn Khaldûn briefly retired from public life and entered a monastery to concentrate upon scholarly activities.

Ultimately he found the time to compose the *Muqaddimah* (introduction) to what he planned would be a universal history.

The *Muqaddimah* is unique in its period for being both a chronicle of historical events and a presentation of Ibn Khaldûn's view of the process of history. He believed that the historical process displayed a rational pattern, that it was dominated by humans, and that it had both purpose and meaning. Thus he spent much of his "introduction" describing the origin and rationale for institutions. In the excerpted section he recounts the history of the office of the imam.

The position of imam is a necessary one. The consensus of the men around Muhammad and the men of the second generation shows that (the imamate) is necessary according to the religious law. At the death of the Prophet, the men around him proceeded to render the oath of allegiance to Abû Bakr and to entrust him with the supervision of their affairs. And so it was at all subsequent periods. In no period were the people left in a state of anarchy. This was so by general consensus, which proves that the position of imam is a necessary one.

Some people have expressed the opinion that the necessity of the imamate is apparent for rational reasons, and that the consensus which happens to exist merely confirms the authority of the intellect in this respect. As they say, what makes (the imam rationally) necessary is the need of human beings for social organization and the impossibility of their living and existing by themselves. One of the necessary consequences of social organization is disagreement, because of the pressure of cross-purposes. As long as there is no ruler who exercises a restraining influence, this leads to trouble which, in turn, may lead to the destruction and uprooting of mankind. Now, the preservation of the species is one of the necessary intentions of the religious law.

This very idea is the one the philosophers had in mind when they considered prophethood as something (intellectually) necessary for mankind. We have already shown the incorrectness of their reasoning. One of its premises is that the restraining influence comes into being only through a religious law from God, to which the mass submits as a matter of belief and religious creed. This premise is not acceptable. The restraining influence comes into being as the result of the impetus of royal authority and the forcefulness of the mighty, even if there is no religious law. This was the case among heathens and other nations who had no scriptures and had not been reached by a prophetic mission.

Or, we might say: In order to remove disagreement, it is sufficient that every individual should know that injustice is forbidden him by the authority of the intellect. Then, their claim that the removal of disagreement takes place only through the existence of the religious law in one case, and the position of the imam in another case, is not correct. It may (be removed) as well through the existence of powerful leaders, or through the people refraining from disagreement and mutual injustice, as through the position of the imam. Thus, the intellectual proof based upon that premise does not stand up. This shows that the necessity of (an imam) is indicated by the religious law, that is, by the consensus, as we have stated before.

Some people have taken the exceptional position of stating that the position of imam is not necessary at all, neither according to the intellect nor according to the religious law.

People who have held that opinion include the Mu'tazilah al-Asamm and certain Khârijites, among others. They think that it is necessary only to observe the religious laws. When Muslims agree upon (the practice of) justice and observance of the divine laws, no imam is needed, and the imamate is not necessary. Those (who so argue) are refuted by the consensus. They adopted such an opinion because they were (attempting to) escape the royal authority and its overbearing, domineering, and worldly ways. They had seen that the religious law was full of censure and blame for such things and for the people who practised them, and that it encouraged the desire to abolish them.

The religious law does not censure royal authority as such and does not forbid its exercise. It merely censures the evils resulting from it, such as tyranny, injustice, and pleasure-seeking. Here, no doubt, we have forbidden evils. They are the concomitants of royal authority. The religious law praises justice, fairness, the fulfilment of religious duties, and the defence of religion. It states that these things will of necessity find their reward (in the other world). Now, all these things are concomitants of royal authority, too. Thus, censure attaches to royal authority only on account of some of its qualities and conditions, not others. (The religious law) does not censure royal authority as such, nor does it seek to suppress it entirely. It also censures concupiscence and wrathfulness in responsible persons, but it does not want to see either of these qualities relinquished altogether, because necessity calls for their existence. It merely wants to see that proper use is made of them. David and Solomon possessed royal authority such as no one else ever possessed, yet they were divine prophets and belonged, in God's eyes, among the noblest human beings that ever existed.

Furthermore, we say to them: The (attempt to) dispense with royal authority by (assuming) that the institution (of the imamate) is not necessary does not help you at all. You agree that observance of the religious laws is a necessary thing. Now, that is achieved only through group feeling and power, and group feeling, by its very nature, requires royal authority. Thus, there will be royal authority, even if no imam is set up. Now, that is just what you (wanted to) dispense with.

If it has been established that the institution (of the imamate) is necessary by the consensus, (it must be added that this institution) is a community duty and is left to the discretion of all competent Muslims. It is their obligation to see to it that (the imamate) is set up, and everybody has to obey (the imam) in accordance with the verse of the Qur'ân, 'Obey God, and obey the apostle and the people in authority among you.'

It is not possible to appoint two men to the position (of imam) at the same time. Religious scholars generally are of this opinion, on the basis of certain traditions.

Others hold that (the prohibition against two imams) applies only to two imams in one locality, or where they would be close to each other. When there are great distances and the imam is unable to control the farther region, it is permissible to set up another imam there to take care of public interests....

The pre-requisites governing the institution of (the imamate) are four: (1) knowledge, (2) probity, (3) competence, and (4) freedom of the senses and limbs from any defect that might affect judgment and action. There is a difference of opinion concerning a fifth prerequisite, that is, (5) Qurashite descent.

1. The necessity of knowledge as a prerequisite is obvious. The imam can execute the divine laws only if he knows them. Those he does not know, he cannot properly present. His knowledge is satisfactory only if he is able to make independent decisions. Blind acceptance of tradition is a shortcoming, and the imamate requires perfection in all qualities and conditions.

2. Probity is required because (the imamate) is a religious institution and supervises all the other institutions that require (this quality). There is no difference of opinion as to the fact that his probity is nullified by the actual commission of forbidden acts and the like. But there is a difference of opinion on the question of whether it is nullified by innovations in dogma.

3. Competence means that he is willing to carry out the punishments fixed by law and to go to war. He must understand warfare and be able to assume responsibility for getting the people to fight. He also must know about group feeling and the fine points (of diplomacy). He must be strong enough to take care of political duties. All of which is to enable him to fulfil his functions of protecting religion, leading in the holy war against the enemy, maintaining the (religious) laws, and administering the (public) interests.

4. Freedom of the senses and limbs from defects or disabilities such as insanity, blindness, muteness, or deafness, and from any loss of limbs affecting (the imam's) ability to act, such as missing hands, feet, or testicles, is a prerequisite of the imamate, because all such defects affect his full ability to act and to fulfil his duties. Even in the case of a defect that merely disfigures the appearance, as, for instance, loss of one limb, the condition of freedom from defects (remains in force as a condition in the sense that it) aims at his perfection.

Lack of freedom of action is connected with loss of limbs. Such a lack may be of two kinds. One is forced (inaction) and complete inability to act through imprisonment or the like. (Absence of any restriction upon freedom of action) is as necessary a condition (of the imamate) as freedom from bodily defects. The other kind is in a different category. (This lack of freedom of action implies that) some of (the imam's) men may gain power over him, although no disobedience or disagreement may be involved, and keep him in seclusion. Then,

the problem is shifted to the person who has gained power. If he acts in accordance with Islam and justice and praiseworthy policies, it is permissible to acknowledge (him). If not, Muslims must look for help from persons who will restrain him and eliminate the unhealthy situation created by him, until the caliph's power of action is reestablished.

5. The pre-requisite of a Qurashite origin is based upon the consensus on this point that obtained in the men around Muhammad on the day of Abû Bakr's elevation to the caliphate....

Among those who deny that Qurashite descent is a condition of the imamate is judge Abû Bakr al-Bâqillânî. The Qurashite group feeling had come to disappear and dissolve (in his day), and non-Arab rulers controlled the caliphs. Therefore, when he saw what the condition of the caliphs was in his day, he dropped the pre-requisite of a Qurashite origin.

Scholars in general, however, retain Qurashite descent as a condition (of the imamate). (They maintain that) the imamate rightly belongs to a Qurashite, even if he is too weak to handle the affairs of the Muslims. Against them is the fact that this involves dropping the pre-requisite of competence, which requires that he have the power to discharge his duties. If his strength has gone with the disappearance of group feeling, his competence, too, is gone. And if the condition of competence be eliminated, that will reflect further upon knowledge and religion. (In this case, then, all) the conditions governing the institution would no longer be considered, and this would be contrary to the consensus....

When one considers what God meant the caliphate to be, nothing more needs (to be said) about it. God made the caliph his substitute to handle the affairs of His servants. He is to make them do the things that are good for them and forbid them to do those that are harmful. He has been directly told so. A person who lacks the power to do a thing is never told directly to do it. The religious leader, Ibn al-Khatîb, said that most religious laws apply to women as they do to men. However, women are not directly told (to follow the religious laws) by express reference to them in the text, but, in (Ibn al-Khatîb's) opinion, they are included only by way of analogical reasoning. That is because women have no power whatever. Men control their (actions), except in as far as the duties of divine worship are concerned, where everyone controls his own. Therefore, women are directly told (to fulfil the duties of divine worship) by express reference to them in the text, and not (merely) by way of analogical reasoning.

Furthermore, (the world of) existence attests to (the necessity of group feeling for the caliphate). Only he who has gained superiority over a nation or a race is able to handle its affairs. The religious law would hardly ever make a requirement in contradiction to the requirements of existence....

26 The Transformation of the Caliphate into Royal Authority

Royal authority is the natural goal of group feeling. It results from group feeling, not by choice but through (inherent) necessity and the order of existence, as we have stated before. All religious laws and practices and everything that the masses are expected to do requires group feeling. Only with the help of group feeling can a claim be successfully pressed, as we have stated before.

Group feeling is necessary to the Muslim community. Its existence enables (the community) to fulfil what God expects of it. Still, we find that Muhammad censured group feeling and urged us to reject it and to leave it alone. He said: 'God removed from you the arrogance of pre-Islamic times and its pride in ancestry. You are the children of Adam, and Adam was made of dust.' God said: 'Most noble among you in God's eyes is he who fears God most.'

We also find that Muhammad censured royal authority and its representatives. He blamed them because of their enjoyment of good fortune, their senseless waste, and their deviations from the path of God. He enjoined friendship among all Muslims and warned against discord and dissension.

It should be known that in Muhammad's opinion, all of this world is a vehicle for transport to the other world. He who loses the vehicle can go nowhere. When Muhammad forbids or censures certain human activities or urges their omission, he does not want them to be neglected altogether. Nor does he want them to be completely eradicated, or the powers from which they result to remain altogether unused. He wants those powers to be employed as much as possible for the right aims. Every intention should thus eventually become the right one and the direction of all human activities one and the same.

Muhammad did not censure wrathfulness with the intention of eradicating it as a human quality. If the power of wrathfulness were no longer to exist in man, he would lose the ability to help the truth become victorious. There would no longer be holy war or glorification of the word of God. Muhammad censured the wrathfulness that is in the service of Satan and reprehensible purposes, but the wrathfulness that is one in God and in the service of God deserves praise. Such praiseworthy wrathfulness was one of the qualities of Muhammad.

Likewise, when he censures the desires, he does not want them to be abolished altogether, for a complete abolition of concupiscence in a person would make him defective and inferior. He wants the desires to be used for permissible purposes to serve the public interests, so that man becomes an active servant of God who willingly obeys the divine commands.

Likewise, when the religious law censures group feeling and says: 'Neither your blood relatives nor your children will be of use to you (on the Day of Resurrection),' (such a statement) is directed against a group feeling that is used for worthless purposes, as was the case in pre-Islamic times. It is also directed against a group feeling that makes a person proud and superior. For an intelligent person to take such an attitude is considered a gratuitous action, which is of no use for the other world, the world of eternity. On the other hand, a group feeling that is working for the truth and for fulfilment of the divine commands is something desirable. If it were gone, religious laws would no longer be, because they materialize only through group feeling, as we have stated before.

Likewise, when Muhammad censures royal authority, he does not censure it for gaining superiority through truth, for forcing the great mass to accept the faith, nor for looking after the (public) interests. He censures royal authority for achieving superiority through worthless means and for employing human beings for indulgence in (selfish) purposes and desires, as we have stated. If royal authority would sincerely exercise its superiority over men for the sake of God and so as to cause those men to worship God and to wage war against His enemies, there would not be anything reprehensible in it....

When the Messenger of God was about to die, he appointed Abû Bakr as his representative to (lead the) prayers, since (prayer) was the most important religious activity. People were, thus, content to accept him as caliph, that is, as the person who causes the great mass to act according to the religious laws. No mention was made of royal authority, because royal authority was suspected of being worthless, and because at that time it was the prerogative of unbelievers and enemies of Islam. Abû Bakr discharged the duties of his office in a manner pleasing to God, following the traditions of his master. He fought against apostates until all the Arabs were united in Islam. He then appointed 'Umar his successor. 'Umar followed Abû Bakr's example and fought against (foreign) nations. He defeated them and permitted the Arabs to appropriate their worldly possessions and their royal authority, and the Arabs did that.

Al-Ma'ûdî says: 'In the days of 'Uthmân, the men around Muhammad acquired estates and money. On the day 'Uthmân was killed, 150,000 dinars and 1,000,000 dirhams were in the hands of his treasurer. The value of his estates in Wâdi l-Qurâ and Hunayn and other places was 200,000 dinars. He also left many camels and horses. The eighth part of the estate of az-Zubayr after his death amounted to 50,000 dinars. He also left 1,000 horses and 1,000 female servants. Talhah's income from the 'Irâq was 1,000 dinars a day, and his income from the region of ash-Sharâh was more than that. The stable of 'Abd-arRahmân b. 'Awf contained 1,000 horses. He also had 1,000 camels and 10,000 sheep. One-fourth of his estate after his death amounted to 84,000. Zayd b. Thâbit left silver and gold that was broken into pieces with pickaxes, in addition to the (other) property and estates that he left, in the value of 100,000 dinars. Az-Zubayr built himself a residence in al-Basrah and other residences in Egypt and al-Kûfah and Alexandria. Talhah built one in al-Kûfah and had his residence in Medina improved. He used plaster, bricks, and teakwood. Sa'd b. Abî Waqqâs built himself a residence in al-'Aqîq, (a suburb of Medina). He made it high and spacious, and had balustrades put on top of it. Al-Miqdâd built his residence in Medina and had it plastered inside and out. Ya'lâ b. Munyah left 50,000 dinars and estates and other things the value of which amounted to 300,000 dirharms.' End of the quotation from al-Mas'ûdî.

Such were the gains people made. Their religion did not blame them for (amassing so much), because, as booty, it was lawful property. They did not employ their property wastefully but in a planned way in all their conditions, as we have stated. Amassing worldly property is reprehensible, but it did not reflect upon them, because blame attaches only to waste and lack of planning, as we have indicated. Since their expenditure followed a plan and served the truth and its ways, amassing (so much property) helped them along on the path of truth and served the purpose of attaining the other world.

Soon, the desert attitude of the Arabs and their low standard of living approached its ends. The nature of royal authority—which is the necessary consequence of group feeling as we have stated—showed itself, and with it, there came superiority and force. Royal authority, as (the early Muslims) saw it, belonged in the same category as luxury and amassed property. They did not apply their superiority to worthless things, and they did not abandon the intentions of their religion or the ways of truth.

When trouble arose between 'Ali and Mu'âwiyah as a necessary consequence of group feeling, they were guided in (their dissensions by the truth and by independent judgment. They did not fight for any worldly purpose or over preferences of no value, or for reasons of personal enmity. This might be suspected, and heretics might like to think so. However, what caused their difference was their independent judgment as to where the truth lay. It was on this matter that each side opposed the point of view of the other. Even though 'Ali was in the fight, Mu'âwiyah's intentions were not evil. He wanted the truth, but missed it. Each was right in so far as his intentions were concerned. Now, the nature of royal authority requires that one person claim all the glory for himself and appropriate it to himself. It was not for Mu'âwiyah to deny (the natural requirement of royal authority) to himself and his people. (Royal authority) was a natural thing that group feeling, by its very nature, brought in its train. Even the Umayyads and those of their followers who were not after the

truth like Mu'awiyah felt that. They banded together around him and were willing to die for him. Had Mu'âwiyah tried to lead them on another course of action, had he opposed them and not claimed all the power for (himself and them), it would have meant the dissolution of the whole thing that he had consolidated. It was more important to him to keep it together than to bother about a course of action that could not entail much criticism.

When royal authority is obtained and we assume that one person has it all for himself, no objection can be raised if he uses it for the various ways and aspects of the truth. Solomon and his father David had the royal authority of the Israelites for themselves, as the nature of royal authority requires, and it is well known how great a share in prophecy and truth they possessed.

Likewise, Mu'âwiyah appointed Yazîd as his successor, because he was afraid of the dissolution of the whole thing, inasmuch as the Umayyads did not like to see the power handed over to any outsider. Had Mu'âwiyah appointed anyone else his successor, the Umayyads would have been against him. Moreover, they had a good opinion of Yazîd. Mu'âwiyah would not have been the man to appoint Yazîd his successor, had he believed him to be really so wicked. Such an assumption must be absolutely excluded in Mu'âwiyah's case.

The same applies to Marwân b. al-Hakam and his sons. Even though they were kings, their royal ways were not those of worthless men and oppressors. They complied with the intentions of the truth with all their energy, except when necessity caused them to do something (unworthy). Such (a necessity existed) when there was fear that the whole thing might face dissolution. (To avoid that) was more important to them than any (other) intention. That this was (their attitude) is attested by the fact that they followed and imitated (the early Muslims).

Then came the later Umayyads. As far as their worldly purposes and intentions were concerned, they acted as the nature of royal authority required. They forgot the deliberate planning and the reliance upon the truth that had guided the activities of their predecessors. This caused the people to censure their actions and to accept the 'Abbâsid propaganda in the place of the Umayyads'. Thus, the 'Abbâsids took over the government. The probity of the 'Abbâsids was outstanding. They used their royal authority to further, as far as possible, the different aspects and ways of the truth. (The early 'Abbâsids) eventually were succeeded by the descendants of ar-Rashîd. Among them there were good and bad men. Later on, when the power passed to their descendants, they gave royal authority and luxury their due. They became enmeshed in worldly affairs of no value and turned their backs on Islam. Therefore, God permitted them to be ruined, and the Arabs to be completely deprived of their power, which He gave to others. Whoever considers the biographies of these caliphs and their different approaches to truth and worthlessness knows that what we have stated is correct....

It has thus become clear how the caliphate was transformed into royal authority. The form of government in the beginning was a caliphate. Everybody had his restraining influence in himself, that is, (the restraining influence of) Islam. They preferred (Islam) to their worldly affairs, even if (the neglect of worldly affairs) led to their own destruction.

When 'Uthmân was besieged in his house, al-Hasan, al-Husayn, 'Abdallâh b. 'Umar, Ibn Ja'far, and others came and offered to defend him. But he refused and did not permit swords to be drawn among Muslims. He feared a split and wanted to preserve the harmony that would keep the whole thing intact, even if it could be done only at the cost of his own destruction.

At the beginning of his (term of) office, 'Alî himself was advised by al-Mughîrah to leave az-Zubayr, Mu'âwiyah, and Talhah in their positions, until the people had a greed to render the oath of allegiance to him and the whole thing was consolidated. After that, he might do what he wanted. That was good power politics. 'Ali, however, refused. He wanted to avoid deceit, because deceit is forbidden by Islam. Al-Mughîrah came back to him the following morning and said: I gave you that advice yesterday, but then I reconsidered it and realized that it was neither right nor good advice. You were right.' 'Alî replied: 'Indeed, no. I know that the advice you gave me yesterday was good advice and that you are deceiving me today. However, regard for the truth prevented me from following your good advice.' To such a degree were these early Muslims concerned with improving their religion at the expense of their worldly affairs.

It has thus been shown how the form of government came to be royal authority. However, there remained the traits that were characteristic of the caliphate, namely, preference for Islam and its ways, and adherence to the path of truth. A change became apparent only in the restraining influence that had been Islam and now came to be group feeling and the sword. That was the situation in the time of Mu'âwiyah, Marwân, his son 'Abd-al-Malik, and the first 'Abbâsid caliphs down to ar-Rashîd and some of his sons. Then, the characteristic traits of the caliphate disappeared, and only its name remained. The form of government came to be royal authority pure and simple. Superiority attained the limits of its nature and was employed for particular (worthless) purposes, such as the use of force and the arbitrary gratification of desires and for pleasure.

This was the case with the successors of the sons of 'Abd-al-Malik and the 'Abbâsids after al-Mu'tasim and al-Mutawakkil. They remained caliphs in name, because the Arab group feeling continued to exist. In these two stages caliphate and royal authority existed side by side. Then, with the disappearance of Arab group feeling and the annihilation of the race and complete destruction of (Arabism), the caliphate lost its identity. The form of government remained royal authority pure and simple.

This was the case, for instance, with the nonArab rulers in the East. They showed obedience to the caliph in order to enjoy the blessings (involved in that), but royal authority belonged to them with all its titles and attributes. The caliph had no share in it.

It is thus clear that the caliphate at first existed without royal authority. Then, the characteristic traits of the caliphate became mixed up and confused. Finally, when its group feeling had separated from the group feeling of the caliphate, royal authority came to exist alone.

27 The Meaning of the Oath of Allegiance

It should be known that the *bay'ah* (oath of allegiance) is a contract to render obedience. It is as though the person who renders the oath of allegiance made a contract with his amir, to the effect that he surrenders supervision of his own affairs and those of the Muslims to him and that he will not contest his authority and that he will obey him by (executing) all the duties with which he might be charged, whether agreeable or disagreeable.

When people rendered the oath of allegiance to the amir and concluded the contract, they put their hands into his hand to confirm the contract. This was considered to be something like the action of buyer and seller (after concluding a bargain). Therefore, the oath of allegiance was called *bay'ah*, the infinitive of *ba'a* to sell (or buy).' The *bay'ah* was a handshake. Such is its meaning in customary linguistic terminology and the accepted usage of the religious law.

The oath of allegiance that is common at present is the Persian custom of greeting kings by kissing the earth, or their hand, their foot, or the lower hem of their garment. The term *bay'ah*, which means a contract to render obedience, was used metaphorically to denote this, since such an abject form of greeting and politeness is one of the consequences and concomitants of obedience. (The practice) has become so general that it has become customary and has replaced the handshake which was originally used, because shaking hands with everybody meant that the ruler lowered himself and made himself cheap, things that are detrimental to leadership and the dignity of the royal position. However, (the handshake is practised) by a very few rulers who want to show themselves humble and who, therefore, themselves shake hands with their nobles and with famous divines among their subjects.

This customary meaning of the oath of allegiance should be understood. A person must know it, because it imposes upon him certain duties toward his ruler and imam. His actions will thus not be frivolous or gratuitous. This should be taken into consideration in one's dealings with rulers.

Study Questions

1. What is the relationship between religious law and royal authority?

2. Why is the prerequisite that the Imam be of Qurashite origins disputed?

3. How do religious laws affect women?

4. What does Ibn Khaldûn mean by "group feeling"? What effect does group feeling have on Islamic society?

Travels in Africa (1364)   **33**

IBN BATTUTA

Muhammad Ibn Abdullah Ibn Battuta (1304–1377) spent most of his long life traveling in Asia and Africa. He was born in Tangier and made the first of his four pilgrimages to Mecca at the age of 25. After performing his religious obligations Ibn Battuta kept traveling for 24 years. He visited all of the Muslim states of the Middle East as well as Sri Lanka, India, and China. Ibn Battuta remains one of the central sources of knowledge about African and Muslim civilization in this early period.

His journey to the empire of Mali, the subject of these selections, began in 1352. He has left a vivid picture of the desert crossing, describing in detail his adventures as he traveled by camel on a traditional caravan route. Much of the information that he provides is unique, but all of it is shaped by his own background, religion, and sense of cultural superiority.

Then I set off at the beginning of … February 1352 with a caravan whose leader was Abu Muhammad Yandakan al-Masufi, may God have mercy on him. In the caravan was a company of merchants of Sijilmasa and others. After 25 days we arrived at Taghaza. This is a village with nothing good about it. One of its marvels is that its houses and mosque are of rock salt and its roofs of camel skins. It has no trees, but is nothing but sand with a salt mine. They dig in the earth for the salt, which is found in great slabs lying one upon the other as though they have been shaped and placed underground. A camel carries two slabs of it. Nobody lives there except the slaves of the Masufa who dig for the salt. They live on the dates imported to them from Dar'a and Sijilmasa, on camel-meat, and on anli imported from the land of the Sudan. The Sudan come to them from their land and carry the salt away. One load of it is sold at Iwalatan for eight or ten mithqals, and at the city of Mali for 30 or twenty mithqals. It has sometimes fetched 40 mithqals.

The Sudān use salt for currency as gold and silver is used. They cut it into pieces and use it for their transactions. Despite the meanness of the village of Taghaza they deal with *qintar* upon *qintar* of gold there.

We stayed there for ten days, under strain because the water there is brackish. It is the most fly-ridden of places.

Water is taken on there for entering the wilderness which comes after it. This is a distance of ten days without water except rarely. As for us, we found plenty of water there in pools left by the rain. On one day we found a pool between two rocky hillocks with sweet water in it, so we renewed our water supplies and washed our clothes.

There are many truffles in that wilderness and lice are so numerous that people suspend cords round their necks with mercury in them, which kills them.

In those days we used to go on ahead of the caravan and whenever we found a place suitable for grazing we pastured the beasts there. This we continued to do till a man named Ibn Ziri became lost in the desert. After that we neither went on ahead nor lagged behind. Strife and the exchange of insults had taken place between Ibn Ziri and his maternal cousin, named Ibn 'Adi, so that he fell behind the caravan and lost the way, and when the people encamped there was no news of him. I advised his cousin to hire one of the Masufa to follow his track in the hope of finding him, but he refused. Next day one of the Masufa undertook, without pay, to look for him. He found his traces, which sometimes followed the beaten track and sometimes left it, but could get no news of him. We met a caravan on our way, and they told us that some men had become separated from them. We found one of them dead, with his clothes on him and a whip in hand, under a little tree of the kind that grows in the sand. There was water a mile or so away from him.

Takshif is the name for any man of the Masufa who is hired by the people of the caravan to go on ahead to Iwalatan with people's letters to their associates there, so that they may rent houses for them and come out to meet them with water for a distance of four days' travel. Anyone who has no associate at Iwalatan writes to one of the merchants there who is known for his honesty and he acts as his partner in the matter. Sometimes the *takshif* perishes in that wilderness so that the people of Iwalatan do not know about the caravan and all or many of its people perish.

There are many demons in this wilderness. If the *takshif* is alone they play with him and seduce him so that he becomes diverted from his purpose and perishes since there is no clear road or track. There is nothing but sand blown about by the wind so that you see mountains of sand in one place then you see them transported to another. The guide there is the one who has been many times to and fro and is sagacious. I thought it remarkable that our guide was blind in one eye and diseased in the other and yet knew the way better than anyone.

There was in the caravan a merchant of Tlemcen called al-Hajj Zayyan. He had a habit of seizing snakes and playing with them. I used to forbid him but he would not desist. One day he put his hand into the hole of a lizard to pull it out and found in its place a snake, which he took in his hand. He was about to mount when it stung him on the index finger of the right hand. He suffered great pain so his hand was cauterized, but during the evening the pain increased. He therefore slaughtered a camel and put his hand into its stomach and left it like that for the night, whereupon the flesh of his finger fell off piece by piece, so he cut it off at the root. The people of the Masufa told us that the snake had drunk water before stinging him; if it had not drunk it would have killed him.

When those who had come out to meet us with water arrived our horses drank and we entered an exceedingly hot wilderness unlike those we have been accustomed to. We used to set off after the afternoon prayer and travel for the whole night and encamp in the morning. Men of the Masufa and Bardama and others used to come with loads of water for sale.

Then we reached the town of Iwalatan at the beginning of the month of Rabi' al-awwal after a journey from Sijilmasa of two whole months.... When we arrived there the merchants placed their belongings in an open space, where the Sudan took over the guard of them while they went to the *farba*. He was sitting on a carpet under a *saqif* with his assistants in front of him with lances and bows in their hands and the chief men of the Masufa behind him. The merchants stood before him while he addressed them, in spite of their proximity to him, through an interpreter, out of contempt for them. At this I repented at having come to their country because of their ill manners and their contempt for white men. I made for the house of Ibn Badda', a respectable man of Sala to whom I had written to rent a house for me. He had done so. Then the *mushrif* of Iwalatan, invited those who had come with the caravan to receive his reception-gift (*diyafa*). I declined to go but my companions entreated me urgently, so I went with those who went. Then the *diyafa* was brought. It was *anili* meal mixed with a little honey and yoghourt (*laban*) which they had placed in half a gourd made into a kind of bowl. Those present drank and went away. I said to them: "Was it to this that the black man invited us?" They said: "Yes, for them this is a great banquet." Then I knew for certain that no good was to be expected from them and I wished to depart with the pilgrims of Iwalatan. But then I thought it better to go to see the seat of their king.

My stay in Iwalatan lasted about 50 days. Its inhabitants did me honour and made me their guest. Among them was the qadi of the place Muhammad b. 'Abd Allah b. Yanumur and his brother the faqih and teacher Yahya . The town of Iwalatan is extremely hot. There are a few little palm trees there in the shade of which they sow water melons. Their water comes from *ahsa* there. Mutton is abundant there and the people's clothes are of Egyptian cloth, of good quality. Most of the inhabitants there belong to the Masufa, whose women are of surpassing beauty and have a higher status than the men.

These people have remarkable and strange ways. As for their men, they feel no jealousy. None of them traces his descent through his father, but from his maternal uncle, and a man's heirs are the sons of his sister only, to the exclusion of his own sons. This is something that I have seen nowhere in the world except among the Indian infidels in the land of Mulaybar, whereas these are Muslims who observe the prayer and study fiqih and memorize the Koran. As for their women, they have no modesty in the presence of men and do not veil themselves in spite of their assiduity in prayer. If anybody wishes to marry one of them he may do so, but they do not travel with the husband, and if one of them wished to do so her family would prevent her.

The women there have friends and companions among the foreign men, just as the men have companions from among the foreign women. One of them may enter his house and find his wife with her man friend without making any objection.

One day I went into the presence of the qadi of Iwalatan, after asking his permission to enter, and found with him a young and remarkably beautiful woman. When I saw her I hesitated and wished to withdraw, but she laughed at me and experienced no shyness. The qadi said to me: "Why are you turning back? She is my friend." I was amazed at their behaviour, for he was a faqih and a pilgrim. I was informed that he had asked the sultan's permission to make the Pilgrimage that year with his lady friend (I do not know whether it was this one or not) but he had not allowed him.

One day I went into the presence of Abu Muhammad Yandakan al-Masufi in whose company we had come and found him sitting on a carpet. In the courtyard of his house there was a canopied couch with a woman on it conversing with a man seated. I said to him: "Who is this woman?" He said: "She is my wife." I said: "What connection has the man with her?" He replied: "He is her friend." I said to him: "Do you acquiese in this when you have lived in our country and become acquainted with the precepts of the Shar'?" He replied: "The association of women with men is agreeable to us and a part of good conduct, to which no suspicion attaches. They are not like the women of your country." I was astonished at his laxity. I left him, and did not return thereafter. He invited me several times but I did not accept.

What I Approved of and What I Disapproved of among the Acts of the Sudan

One of their good features is their lack of oppression. They are the farthest removed of people from it and their sultan does not permit anyone to practise it. Another is the security embracing the whole country, so that neither traveller there nor dweller has anything to fear from thief or usurper. Another is that they do not interfere with the wealth of any white man who dies among them. They simply leave it in the hands of a trustworthy white man until the one to whom it is due takes it. Another is their assiduity in prayer and their persistence in performing it in congregation and beating their children to make them perform it. If it is a Friday and a man does not go early to the mosque he will not find anywhere to pray because of the press of the people. It is their habit that every man sends his servant with his prayer-mat to spread it for him in a place which he thereby has a right to until he goes to the mosque. Their prayer-carpets are made from the fronds of the tree resembling the palm which has no fruit. Another of their good features is their dressing in fine white clothes on Friday. If any one of them possesses nothing but a ragged shirt he washes it and cleanses it and attends the Friday prayer in it. Another is their eagerness to memorize the great Koran. They place fetters on their children if there appears on their part a failure to memorize it and they are not undone until they memorize it.

I went into the house of the qadi on the day of the festival and his children were fettered so I said to him: "Aren't you going to let them go?" He replied: "I shan't do so until they've got the Koran by heart!" One day I passed by a youth of theirs, of good appearance and dressed in fine clothes, with a heavy fetter on his leg. I said to those who were with me: "What has this boy done? Has he killed somebody?" The lad understood what I had said and laughed, and they said to me: "He's only been fettered so that he'll learn the Koran!"

One of their disapproved acts is that their female servants and slave girls and little girls appear before men naked, with their privy parts uncovered. During Ramadan I saw many of them in this state, for it is the custom of the *farariyya* to break their fast in the house of the sultan, and each one brings his food carried by twenty or more of his slave girls, they all being naked. Another is that their women go into the sultan's presence naked and uncovered, and that his daughters go naked. On the night of 25 Ramadan I saw about 200 slave girls bringing out food from his palace naked, having with them two of his daughters with rounded breasts having no covering upon them. Another is their sprinkling dust and ashes on their heads out of good manners. Another is what I mentioned in connection with the comic anecdote about the poets' recitation. Another is that many of them eat carrion. and dogs, and donkeys.

Study Questions

1. What was it like to travel in western Africa in the fourteenth century?

2. How was Ibn Battuta treated by the people of Mali. How do you think Ibn Battuta treated them?

3. What did Ibn Battuta find unusual about the customs of the people with whom he came into contact? What do his observations tell us about his own culture?

4. What role did religion play in the life of Ibn Battuta? What role did it play in the lives of the people of Mali?

Ethiopia Oriental (1609)   **34**

JOAO DOS SANTOS

Joao dos Santos was a Dominican friar of Portuguese extraction. Little is known about his life before he was sent with a group of priests to east Africa and ultimately India. He spent nearly a decade along the east African coast between 1585 and 1597. There he joined other Portuguese missionaries and soldiers and was eyewitness to a number of ferocious battles between African tribes. He also witnessed several massacres by cannibalistic tribes.

Dos Santos's *Ethiopia Oriental* provides a horrifying account of the brutality of life in Africa. Warring tribes and Portuguese adventurers proved an explosive mixture. Christian missionaries were spared neither the rigors of the environment nor the danger of capture and annihilation.

About Tete are eleven Towns of Cafres which have each their Encosse, or Cafar Captayne, all Vassels, and subject to the jurisdiction of the Captayne of Tete. The Manamotapa having conquered those parts, distributed to diverse divers governments, and these to the Captayne of Tete and his Successors, to whom they are subject as to their King, asking his license when they will sow their rounds; the Encosses comming accompanied with some of his Cafres, and a Present, when they petition him. Before Tete, on the otherside of the River within Land to the East and North-East, are two kinds of Man-eating Cafres, the Mumbos and Zimbas or Muzimbas, who eate those they take in warre, and their slaves also when they are past labour, and sell it as Beefe or Mutton. The Captayne of Tete with his eleven Encosses, and their Companies slue six hundred of the Mumbos in a Battell, not leaving one alive, and carried away their Wives and Children Captives. This was at Chicoronga a Mumbos Towne, in which was a slaughter-house, where every day they butchered their Captives; neere which the Portugals found many Negroes, men and women, bound hand and foot, destined to the slaughter for the next dayes food, whom with many others they freed. They undertooke this Expedition in behalfe of a friend of theirs, against whom these Mumbos led by their Captayne Quizura made warre. All the ground before Quizuras Gate was paved with mens Skuls, which he had killed in that war, upon which they must passe which went in or out; a thing in his conceit of great Majestie. But now he lost himselfe and all his. These Cafres about Tete are prone to warres, saying, If they dye their troubles are ended; if they live, they shall enjoy spoyles. Whiles I was there, the Captayne Pero Fernandez de Chaves, wanting Timber for a Church Doores and Porch, pretended warre, and summoned these eleven Encosses, which came willingly, but were diverted to this Timber businesses

Whiles I was at Sena, the Muzimbas warred on some of the Portugals friends, and did eate many of them, who besought helpe of Andre de Santiago, Captayne of Sena; who went and set upon them in their Fort, which they had fortified round with a wall of

Wood, with wings (revezes) and port-holes, and a deepe wide ditch, insomuch, that he was forced to send to Chaves for his best helpe, who came with above one hundred Portugals and Misticos, and those eleven Encosses. The Muzimbas by their Espials had Intelligence of their comming on the other-side the River without order, and therefore stole out of the Fort by night, and Embuscadoed themselves, and set upon the Portugals (which marched halfe a league before the Cafres) suddenly and furiously; killed them every one, and cut off their armes and legges, which with their armes they carried privily to their Fortresse. The Cafres arriving at the Wood, and seeing the slaughter returned home to Tete, and related the late Tragedie. These Zimbas worship no God, nor Idol, but their King, who (they say) is God of the Earth: and if it rains when hee would not, they shoot their Arrowes at the Skie for not obeying him; and he only eates not mans flesh. These are talle, bigge, strong; and have for Armes, small Hatchets, Arrowes, Azagaies, great Bucklers, with which they cover their whole bodies of light wood, lined with wild beasts skinnes. They eate those which they kill in warre and drink, in their skuls. If any of their own Cafres be sicke or wounded, to save labour of cure they kill and eate them.

They feasted with great jollities that day of their Victorie, and the night following; and the next morning early sallied out of their Fortresse, the Captayne arrayed in a Dominicans Casula, or Massing Vestment (Nicolas de Rosario, whom they had taken with the Portugals, and carried with them, and put to a cruell death) with a gilt Chalice in his left hand, and an Azagay in his right; and all the other Zimbas with the quarters of the Portugals at their backes, and the Captaynes head on the point of a long Lance; and drumming on the Drumme which they had taken, they presented themselves with great cryes to Santiago, and the Portugals, and after this

muster returned to their Fort, saying, they must goe eate their Tete friends, Santiago, and his Portugals (which stayed wayting for Chaves, and knew nothing) now terrified with this Spectacle, resolved (if feare be capable of that word) to haste away as soone as night came, and passing over the River was perceived by the Muzimbas, who issued out upon them with great force and slue many on the banke, and amongst others Santiago. Thus of Tete and Sena were one hundred and thirtie Portugals and Misticos, with their two valiant Captaines slayne, with little losse on their part, comming on them with sudden advantage: this was done An. 1592. Don Pedro de Sousa, Captaine of Mozambique, the next yeere, with two hundred Portugals, and fifteene hundred Cafres passed the River Zambeze, pitched his tents where Santiago had done, battered the walls of their Fort with his Artillery; but to no purpose, because they were of grosse wood, having on the inside much earth of that which was taken out of the ditch. Whereupon he resolved to stop up part of the ditch, which with much labour and perill, and some losse, he effected; some passed with hatchets to the foot of the trench, and began to cut; but the Zimbas from the walls scalded them with hot water and Oyle, specially the naked Cafres, so that none durst approach againe, as well for scalding, as for long Iron hookes which they put out of the portholes, wherewith they wounded the assaylants, and held them fast, pulling them to the holes, and killing them: so that they were forced to retire to their Tents. The next day hee caused rods to be gathered, and great baskets thereof to be made as high as their trenches, which were carried thither, and filled with earth, for the Souldiers to stand and fight upon them, that the Zimbas might not issue with their scalding liquors. Two moneths were spent in this warre, when some of the Inhabitants of that River (which liked their living by wares better than to endanger dying by warres) fained Letters from Sena, written from their wives, pretending great danger from a Cafer, which came to robbe them in the Portugals absence; which Sousa believing to bee true, brake up the siege, and passing the River by night was perceived by the Zimbas; who sallied forth with a great Crie, assayled the Campe, killed some which were behind, tooke the most of the spoiles with the Artillerie. Thus returned the Portugals with disgrace, and the Zimbas grew prouder, and after made peace with them notwithstanding.

One of these Zimbas ambitious of that honour, which they place in killing and eating of men, to get himselfe a name, adjoyned others of his Nation to him, and went Eastward, killing and eating every living thing, Men, Women, Children, Dogs, Cats, Rats, Snakes, Lizards, sparing nothing but such Cafres as adjoyned themselves to their companie in that designer. And thus five thousand of them were assembled, and went before the Ile of Quiloa; where the Sea prohibiting their passage, a traiterous Moore came and offered his service to guide them over at the low ebbes of spring tides, upon condition to spare his kindred, and to divide the spoyles with him. The Zimba accepted it, and effected his cruell purpose, slaying and taking (for future dainties to eate at leasure) three thousand Moores, and tooke the Citie Quiloa, with great riches, the people escaping by hiding themselves in the wildernesse till the Zimbas were gone; then returning to their Citie (antiently the royall Seat of the Kings of that Coast) and to this day are seene the ruines of their sumptuous Mezquites and Houses. Now, for the reward of the Traytor, he sentenced him with all his kindred to be cast into the Sea, bound hand and foot, to bee food for the fishes; saying, it was not meet that one should remayne of so wicked a generation, nor would he eate their flesh, which could not but be venomous.

After this he passed along the Coast, till he came against the Ile of Mombaza; which foure Turkish Galleyes of the Red Sea defended, and slue many of them with their Artillery: but Thome de Sousa arriving with a fleet from India tooke the Turkes, and withall destroyed Mombaza in the sight of the Muzimbas. The Captaine said that the Portugals were the Gods of the Sea, and hee of the Land; and sent an Ambassadour to Sousa, professing friendship to them, and requesting that seeing they had honourably ended their enterprise, he might beginne his, namely, to kill and eate every living thing in the Iland, which by their consent he did accordingly, burning the Palme-trees and Woods where many men were hidden, whom hee tooke and eate with all hee could get.

Thence he returned to the Coast, and went to Melinde, where Mathew Mendez with thirty Portugals ayded the King, and three thousand warlike Cafres, called Mossegueios, came also to his succour, which came suddenly on their backes when they had gotten up the wall, and were almost possessed of the Bulwarke, and chased them with such a furie, that only the Captaine with above one hundred others escaped; having found none in three hundred leagues march, which durst encounter them. And thus much of the Zimbas....

[There follows a brief description of the coast of Mozambique and the islands off it, which were under the jurisdiction of the Captain, or Governor, of Mozambique. He then turns to the part of the coast which was under the jurisdiction of the Captain of Mombasa.]

From this last Cape [Cape Delgado] to the Line [of the Equator] is the Coast of Melinde, which is of the jurisdiction of the Captaine of Mombaça. The firme Land is inhabited by Cafres, differing in Language and Customes, agreeing in barbarousnesse. Along the King-dome of Mongallo runnes to the North the Kingdome of Munimugi, a great Cafte which confines on the South with the

Lands of Mauraca and of Embeoe, and on the North with the Abyssine. The principall Iland of this Coast, Quiloa, hath beene in times past the Seat Royall, the King of the whole Coast residing there, who is now a Pety Prince; and Mombaça is the chiefe Ile and Citie, where the Portugals have a Fort, the residence of the Captaine of the Coast of Melinde. Pemba is an Iland about eight leagues from the Shoare, and ten long, plentifull of Rice and Kine, Fruits and Wood: sometime subject to the Portugalls till the pride and lazinesse of some made the people rebell, and could never after be regayned. In the Ile of Pate are Pate, Sio and Ampaza, three Cities governed by so many Kings, tributarie to Portugal. Ampaza hath been best builded of any Citie in those parts, but destroyed by the Portugals, the Citie sacked and burnt with eight thousand Palme-Trees, which grew about it, cut downe. The Ile of Lamo hath great Asses, but of little service. This Island was chastised when Ampaza was destroyed, and Mombaça also, by Martin Alfonso de Mello. The King of Ampaza was slaine, and his head carried on a Pole at Goa in triumph. When he was gone, Mirale Beque [Amir Ali Bey] the Turks came with foure Galleys out of the Red Sea, and infested that Coast, till the Zimbas and the Portugalls ended the businesse with a new Armada, the Portugals captiving and spoyling, the Zimbas eating the Turkes and Inhabitants. The King of Lamo for betraying the Portugals to the Turkes were beheaded. The Ile and Citie of Mandra [? Manda] which had denyed the Portugals to land, saying, the Sunne onely might enter there, was sacked and two thousand Palme-trees cut down. In the Coast of Melinde they are great Witches. The Mossegueyos live of their Kine, which they oft let blond both to prevent the garget, and to make therewith a kinds of pottage with milke and fresh dung of the same Kine, which mixed together and heat at the fire they drinke, say-

ing, it makes them strong. The Boyes of seven or eight yeeres weare Clay fastened on the hayre of the head, and still renewed with new Clay, weighing sometimes five or six pounds. Nor may they be free hereof till the Warre or lawfull fight hee hath killed a man, and show to the Captaine some tokens of that fact; which only makes them free and Knights of their cast. Hereupon they grow audacious, and prove dreadfull to others.

Brava is a small Citie but strong, inhabited with Moores, Friends and Vassals to the Portugals. It is in one Degree North, and very hot. Magadoxo is in 3° 30°. Within the land are the Maracatos, which have a custome to sew up their Females, specially their Slaves being young to make them unable for conception, which makes these Slaves sell dearer both for their chastitie, and for better confidence which their Masters put in them. They cut also their Boyes and make them Eunuches.

In the Ile of Zanzibar dwelt one Chande a great Sorcerer, which caused his Pangayo [*pangaia*, small dhow], which the Factor had taken against his will, to stand still as it were in defiance of the Winde, till the Factor had satisfied him, and then to flye forth the River after her fellowes at his words. Hee made that a Portugall which had angred him, could never open his mouth to speake, but a Cock crowed in his belly, till he had reconciled himselfe: with other like odious sorceries.

From Magadoxo to Sacotora [Socotra] one hundred and fifty leagues is a desart Coast, and dishabited without Rivers. In which Desarts breed the great birds, called Emas, which breed on the Sands, and have but two young ones, as Pigeons. Their stomacks will consume Iron and Stones, and flye not but touch the ground with their feet, running with their wings spread, as lightly as other Birds flye. They are white, ash-coloured; their egges white, holding almost three pints.

Study Questions

1. What was the attitude of the Mumbos toward life and death? Does it relate to their cannibalism?

2. What is Joao dos Santos's reaction to the cannibalism of the Mumbos? To their slaughter?

3. What were the symbols of the Zimbas' monarchy? How did they sustain the king's power?

4. What was the nature of warfare as practiced by the Portuguese against Ampaza?

Asian Cultures

The Emperor's Favorite. Lady Yang was a favorite concubine of the T'ang ruler Ming-huang and was blamed for luring him from his official duties. This later painting shows several people helping Lady Yang mount a horse.

The Lotus of the Wonderful Law (406)   **35**

In the eighth century, a new form of Buddhism spread from China to Japan. It was known as the Tendai sect and it derived its inspiration from a series of Sanskrit texts that focused on the Lotus Sutra, regarded by the Tendai as the final and most authentic teaching of the Buddha. The Tendai sect was established in Japan by Siacho (767–822) who had made several missions to China and was permitted to remain there in search of Buddhist texts. On his return Siacho was given imperial permission to found a new Buddhist sect on Mt. Hiei based on the teaching of the Lotus Sutra.

The use of parables was one of the favorite methods of Tendai teaching. The Parable of the Burning House, which is a part of the *Lotus of the Wonderful Law*, is designed to show the superiority of the single sutra (that of the Lotus) over traditional Buddhist teaching of the equal power of the three sutras. Tendai Buddhists believed that all humans could be redeemed and reach universal enlightenment.

A Parable of the Burning House

Let us suppose the following case, Sariputra.... There was a certain housekeeper, old, aged, decrepit, very advanced in years, rich, wealthy, opulent; he had a great house, high, spacious, built a long time ago and old, inhabited by some two, three, four, or five hundred living beings. The house had but one door, and a thatch; its terraces were tottering, the bases of its pillars rotten, the coverings and plaster of the walls loose. On a sudden the whole house was from every side put in conflagration by a mass of fire. Let us suppose that the man had many little boys, say five, or ten, or even twenty, and that he himself had come out of the house.

Now, Sariputra, that man, on seeing the house from every side wrapt in a blaze by a great mass of fire, got afraid, and ... calls to the boys: "Come, my children; the house is burning with a mass of fire; come, lest you be burnt in the mass fire, and come to grief and disaster," But the ignorant boys do not heed the words of him who is their well-wisher; they are not afraid ... nor know the purport of the word "burning"; they run hither and thither, walk about, and repeatedly look at their father; all, because they are so ignorant.

... The man has a clear perception of their inclinations. Now these boys happen to have many and manifold toys to play with, pretty, nice, pleasant, dear, amusing, and precious. The man, knowing the disposition of the boys, says to them: "My children, your toys, which you are so loath to miss, which are so various and multifarious, [such as] bullock-carts, goat-carts, deer-carts, which are so pretty, nice, dear, and precious to you, have all been put by me outside the house-door for you to play with. Come, run out, leave the house; to each of you I shall give what he wants. Come soon, come out for the sake of these toys." And the boys, on hearing the names mentioned of such playthings as they like and desire, quickly rush out from the burning house, with eager effort and great alacrity, one having no time to wait for the other, and pushing each other on with the cry of "Who shall arrive first, the very first?"

The man, seeing that his children have safely and happily escaped, goes and sits down in the open air on the square of the village, his heart is filled with joy and delight. The boys go up to the place where their father is sitting, and say: "Father, give us those toys to play with, those bullock-carts, and deer-carts." Then, Sariputra, the man gives to his sons, who run swift as the wind, bullock-carts only, made of seven precious substances, provided with benches, hung with a multitude of small bells, lofty, adorned with rare and wonderful jewels, embellished with jewel wreaths, decorated with garlands of flowers, carpeted with cotton mattresses and woolen coverlets, covered with white cloth and silk, having on both sides rosy cushions, yoked with white, very fair and fleet bullocks, led by a multitude of men. To each of his children he gives several bullock-carts of one appearance and one kind, provided with flags, and swift as wind. That man does so, Sariputra, because being rich, ... he rightly thinks: "Why should I give these boys inferior carts, all these boys being my own children, dear and precious? I have such great vehicles, and ought to treat all the boys equally and without partiality. As I won many treasures and granaries, I could give such great vehicles to all beings, how much more then to my own children." Meanwhile the boys are mounting the vehicles with feelings of astonishment and wonder. Now, Sariputra, what is thy opinion? Has that man made himself guilty of a falsehood by first holding out to his children the prospect of three vehicles and afterwards giving to each of them the greatest vehicles only, the most magnificent vehicle?

Sariputra answered: By no means, Lord. That is not sufficient to qualify the man as a speaker of falsehood, since it only was a skilful device to persuade his children to go out of the burning house and save their lives. Nay, besides recovering their very bodies, O Lord, they have received all those toys. If that man, O Lord, had given no single cart, even then he would not have been a speaker of falsehood, for he had previously been meditating on saving the little boys from a great mass of pain by some able device....

The venerable Sariputra having thus spoken, the Lord said to him: Very well, Sariputra, quite so; it is even as you say. So too, Sariputra, the Tathagata is free from all dangers, wholly exempt from all misfortune, despondency, calamity, pain, grief, the thick enveloping dark mists of ignorance. He, the Tathagata, endowed with Buddha-knowledge, forces, absence of hesitation, uncommon properties, and mighty by magical power, is the father of the world, who has reached the highest perfection in the knowledge of skillful means, who is most merciful, long-suffering, benevolent, compassionate. He appears in this triple world, which is like a house the roof and shelter whereof are decayed, [a house] burning by a mass of misery, ... Once born, he sees how the creatures are burnt, tormented, vexed, distressed by birth, old age, disease, death, grief, wailing, pain, melancholy, despondency; how for the sake of enjoyment, and prompted by sensual desires, they severally suffer various pains. In consequence both of what in this world they are seeking and what they have acquired, they will in a future state suffer various pains, in hell, in the brute creation, in the realm of Yamaraja (king of the dead); suffer such pains as poverty in the world of gods or men, union with hateful persons or things, and separation from the beloved ones. And while incessantly whirling in that mass of evils they are sporting, playing, diverting themselves; they do not fear, nor dread, nor are they seized with terror; they do not know, nor mind; they are not startled, do not try to escape, but are enjoying themselves in that triple world which is like unto a burning house, and run hither and thither. Though overwhelmed by that mass of evil, they do not conceive the idea that they must beware of it.

Under such circumstances, Sariputra, the Tathagata reflects thus: "Verily, I am the father of these beings; I must save them from this mass of evil, and bestow on them the immense, inconceivable bliss of Buddha-knowledge, wherewith they shall sport, play, and divert themselves, wherein they shall find their rest. If, in the conviction of my possessing the power of knowledge and magical faculties, I manifest to these beings the knowledge, forces, and absence of hesitation of the Tathagata, without availing myself of some device, these beings will not escape. For they are attached to the pleasures of the five senses, to worldly pleasures; they will not be freed from birth, old age, disease, death, grief, wailing, pain, melancholy, despondency, by which they are burnt, tormented, vexed, distressed. Unless they are forced to leave the triple world which is like a house the shelter and roof whereof is in a blaze, how are they to get acquainted with Buddha-knowledge?"

Now, Sariputra, even as that man with powerful arms, without using the strength of his arms, attracts his children out of the burning house by an able device, and afterwards gives them magnificent, great carts, so Sariputra, the Tathagata possessed of knowledge and freedom from all hesitation, without using them, in order to attract the creatures out of the triple world which is like a burning house with decayed roof and shelter, shows, by his knowledge of able devices, three vehicles, viz. the vehicle of the disciples, the vehicle of the pratyeka-buddhas, and the vehicle of the bodhisattvas. By means of these three vehicles he attracts the creatures and speaks to them thus: "Do not delight in this triple world, which is like a burning house, in these miserable forms, sounds, odors, flavors, and contacts. For in delighting in this triple world you are burnt, heated, inflamed with the thirst inseparable from the pleasures of the five senses. Fly from this triple world; betake yourselves to the three vehicles.... I give you my pledge for it, that I shall give you these three vehicles, make an effort to run out of this triple world. And to attract them I say: "These vehicles are grand, praised by the Aryas, and provided with most pleasant things; with such you are to sport, play, and divert yourselves in a noble manner. You will feel the great delight of the faculties, powers, constituents of Bodhi, meditations, the eight degrees of emancipation, self-concentration, and the results of self-concentration, and you will become greatly happy and cheerful."

Study Questions

1. Why did Sariputra have to bribe the boys with toys to get them of the burning house?

2. With what dilemma is Sariputra faced once the boys escaped?

3. What is the Lord's answer?

4. How does the parable prove the superiority of the single sutra?

A Record of Buddhistic Kingdoms (394–414)   **36**

FA-HSIEN

Fa-hsien (also Fa-hien), which means "illustrious master of the law," was a Chinese Buddhist monk. Orphaned at an early age, Fa-hsien decided to continue the religious life planned for him by his father rather than to be incorporated into the family of his uncle. Little is known of his novitiate, though one legend tells of how he shamed a band of thieves from stealing the grain of his monastery. At the age of 25 Fa-hsien began a quest to learn about Buddhist traditions in India and to discover authentic Buddhist writings. His travels, in Sumatra, Ceylon, India, and Tibet, coincided with a general curiosity of Chinese Buddhists about the practice of their religion abroad. Fa-hsien recovered a large quantity of Buddhist writings and returned to China where he devoted the rest of his life to translating them from Sanskrit. It is recorded that he died at the age of 88.

A Record of Buddhistic Kingdoms (394–414) is an account of the journey of Fa-hsien and his companions, mostly in India. They visited as many of the Buddhist sacred shrines as they could, especially those associated with the presence of the Buddha. The selections presented here show the reasons for the establishment of these shrines, the legends that surrounded them, and the ways in which they were maintained.

Buddha's alms-bowl is in this country. Formerly, a king of Yüeh-she raised a large force and invaded this country, wishing to carry the bowl away. Having subdued the kingdom, as he and his captains were sincere believers in the Law of Buddha, and wished to carry off the bowl, they proceeded to present their offerings on a great scale. When they had done so to the Three Precious Ones, he made a large elephant be grandly caparisoned, and placed the bowl upon it. But the elephant knelt down on the ground, and was unable to go forward. Again he caused a four-wheeled waggon to be prepared in which the bowl was put to be conveyed away. Eight elephants were then yoked to it, and dragged it with their united strength; but neither were they able to go forward. The king knew that the time for an association between himself and the bowl had not yet arrived, and was sad and deeply ashamed of himself. Forthwith he built a tope at the place and a monastery, and left a guard to watch (the bowl), making all sorts of contributions.

There may be there more than seven hundred monks. When it is near midday, they bring out the bowl, and, along with the common people, make their various offerings to it, after which they take their midday meal. In the evening, at the time of incense, they bring the bowl out again. It may contain rather more than two pecks, and is of various colours, black predominating, with the seams that show its fourfold composition distinctly marked. Its thickness is about the fifth of an inch, and it has a bright and glossy lustre. When poor people throw into it a few flowers, it becomes immediately full, while some very rich people, wishing to make offering of many flowers, might not stop till they had thrown in hundreds, thousands, and myriads of bushels, and yet would not be able to fill it.

Going west for sixteen yojanas, Fa-hsien came to the city He-lo in the borders of the country of Nagâra, where there is the flat-bone of Buddha's skull, deposited in a vihâra adorned all over with gold-leaf and the seven sacred substances. The king of the country, revering and honouring the bone, and anxious lest it should be stolen away, has selected eight individuals, representing the great families in the kingdom, and committed to each a seal, with which he should seal (its shrine) and guard (the relic). At early dawn these eight men come, and after each has inspected his seal, they open the door. This done, they wash their hands with scented water and bring out the bone, which they place outside the vihâra, on a lofty platform, where it is supported on a round pedestal of the seven precious substances, and covered with a bell of lapis lazuli, both adorned with rows of pearls. Its colour is of a yellowish white, and it forms an imperfect circle twelve inches round, curving upwards to the centre. Every day, after it has been brought forth, the keepers of the vihâra ascend a high gallery, where they beat great drums, blow conchs, and clash their copper cymbals. When the king hears them, he goes to the vihâra, and makes his offerings of flowers and incense. When he has done this, he (and his attendants) in order, one after another, (raise the bone), place it (for a moment) on the top of their heads, and then depart, going out by the door on the west as they had entered by that on the east. The king every morning makes his offerings and performs his worship, and afterwards gives audience on the business of his government. The chiefs of the Vaisyas also make their offerings before they attend to

their family affairs. Every day it is so, and there is no remissness in the observance of the custom. When all the offerings are over, they replace the bone in the vihâra, where there is a vimoksha tope, of the seven precious substances, and rather more than five cubits high, sometimes open, sometimes shut, to contain it. In front of the door of the vihâra, there are parties who every morning sell flowers and incense, and those who wish to make offerings buy some of all kinds. The kings of various countries are also constantly sending messengers with offerings. The vihâra stands in a square of thirty paces, and though heaven should shake and earth be rent, this place would not move.

From this place they travelled south-east, passing by a succession of very many monasteries, with a multitude of monks, who might be counted by myriads. After passing all these places, they came to a country named Muttra. They still followed the course of the P'oo-na river, on the banks of which, left and right, there were twenty monasteries, which might contain three thousand monks; and (here) the Law of Buddha was still more flourishing. Everywhere, from the Sandy Desert, in all the countries of India, the kings had been firm believers in that Law. When they make their offerings to a community of monks, they take off their royal caps, and along with their relatives and ministers, supply them with food with their own hands. That done, (the king) has a carpet spread for himself on the ground, and sits down on it in front of the chairman;—they dare not presume to sit on couches in front of the community. The laws and ways, according to which the kings presented their offerings when Buddha was in the world, have been handed down to the present day.

All south from this is named the Middle Kingdom. In it the cold and heat are finely tempered, and there is neither hoarfrost nor snow. The people are numerous and happy; they have not to register their households, or attend to any magistrates and their rules; only those who cultivate the royal land have to pay (a portion of) the gain from it. If they want to go, they go; if they want to stay on, they stay. The king governs without decapitation or (other) corporal punishments. Criminals are simply fined, lightly or heavily, according to the circumstances (of each case). Even in cases of repeated attempts at wicked rebellion, they only have their right hands cut off. The king's body-guards and attendants all have salaries. Throughout the whole country the people do not kill any living creature, nor drink intoxicating liquor, nor eat onions or garlic. The only exception is that of the Chandâlas. That is the name for those who are (held to be) wicked men, and live apart from others. When they enter the gate of a city or a market-place, they strike a piece of wood to make themselves known, so that men know and avoid them, and do not come into contact with them. In that country they do not keep pigs and fowls, and do not sell live cattle; in the markets there are no butchers' shops and no dealers in intoxicating drink.... Only the Chandâlas are fishermen and hunters, and sell flesh meat.

At the places where Buddha, when he was in the world, cut his hair and nails, topes are erected; and where the three Buddhas that preceded Sâkyamuni Buddha and he himself sat; where they walked, and where images of their persons were made. At all these places topes were made, and are still existing. At the place where 'Sakra, Ruler of the Devas, and the king of the Brahmaloka followed Buddha down (from the Trayastrimsas heaven) they have also raised a tope.

At this place the monks and nuns may be a thousand, who all receive their food from the common store, and pursue their studies, some of the mahâyâna and some of the hînayâna. Where they live, there is a white-eared dragon,

which acts the part of patron to the community of these monks, causing abundant harvests in the country, and the enriching rains to come in season, without the occurrence of any calamities, so that the monks enjoy their repose and ease. In gratitude for its kindness, they have made for it a dragon-house, with a carpet for it to sit on, and appointed for it a diet of blessing, which they present for its nourishment. Every day they set apart three of their number to go to its house, and eat there. Whenever the summer retreat is ended, the dragon straightway changes its form, and appears as a small snake, with white spots at the side of its ears. As soon as the monks recognise it, they fill a copper vessel with cream, into which they put the creature, and then carry it round from the one who has the highest seat (at their tables) to him who has the lowest, when it appears as if saluting them. When it has been taken round, immediately it disappears; and every year it thus comes forth once. The country is very productive, and the people are prosperous, and happy beyond comparison. When people of other countries come to it, they are exceedingly attentive to them all, and supply them with what they need.

When Fâ-hsien and Tâo-ching first arrived at the Jetavana monastery, and thought how the World-honoured one had formerly resided there for twenty-five years, painful reflections arose in their minds. Born in a border-land, along with their like-minded friends, they had travelled through so many kingdoms; some of those friends had returned (to their own land), and some had (died), proving the impermanence and uncertainty of life; and to-day they saw the place where Buddha had lived now unoccupied by him. They were melancholy through their pain of heart, and the crowd of monks came out, and asked them from what kingdom they were come. 'We are come,' they replied, 'from the land of Han.' 'Strange,' said the monks with a sigh, 'that men of a border country should be able to come here in search of our Law!' Then they said to one another, 'During all the time that we, preceptors and monks, have succeeded to one another, we have never seen men of Han, followers of our system, arrive here.'

To each of the great residences for the monks at the Jetavana vihâra there were two gates, one facing the east and the other facing the north. The park (containing the whole) was the space of ground which the (Vaisya) head Sudatta purchased by covering it with gold coins. The vihâra was exactly in the centre. Here Buddha lived for a longer time than at any other place, preaching his Law and converting men. At the places where he walked and sat they also (subsequently) reared topes, each having its particular name; and here was the place where Sundari murdered a person and then falsely charged Buddha (with the crime). Outside the east gate of the Jetavana, at a distance of seventy paces to the north, on the west of the road, Buddha held a discussion with the (advocates of the) ninety-six schemes of erroneous doctrine, when the king and his great officers, the householders, and people were all assembled in crowds to hear it. Then a woman belonging to one of the erroneous systems, by name Chañchamana, prompted by the envious hatred in her heart, and having put on (extra) clothes in front of her person, so as to give her the appearance of being with child, falsely accused Buddha before all the assembly of having acted unlawfully (towards her). On this, 'Sakra, Ruler of Devas, changed himself and some devas into white mice, which bit through the strings about her waist; and when this was done, the (extra) clothes which she wore dropt down on the ground. The earth at the same time was rent, and she went (down) alive into hell.

Study Questions

1. Why do Fa-hsien and the monks he meets at Jetavana think of China as a borderland?

2. What is the relationship between the relic of the Buddha's skull and the community in which it is kept?

3. What form of government does Fa-hsien most admire? How is order kept?

4. What is the significance of the dragon/snake to the monks?

5. What conclusions do you draw from the accusations made against the Buddha?

The Examination System During the T'ang Dynasty (8th century C.E.)   37

As the first T'ang emperors had themselves been bureaucrats, it is not surprising that after they seized power they initiated a series of reforms designed to centralize power. A hierarchy of the departments of state was created with power ascending to the emperor's three central councils. T'ang reforms began with a stiffening of the examination system by which government servants were chosen. The tests became harder to pass and more difficult to corrupt. Aspirants, even from noble families, thus had to devote their teenage years to study if they were to rise to high levels of imperial service. Those who passed were honored, and brought honor to their villages and regions. Even those who failed were respected for making the attempt.

The importance of the examination system in identifying the future governors of China inevitably led to snobbery and hypocrisy. Stories of abuses became a part of folk culture and served both as warnings and instruction for succeeding generations. The following is a selection of such tales.

Hsiao Ying-shih passed the imperial examination in 735. Proud of his talent, he was unequaled in conceit and arrogance. He often took a pot of wine and went out to visit rural scenic areas. Once during such an outing, he stayed at an inn, drinking and chanting poetry by himself. Suddenly a storm arose, and an old man dressed in a purple robe came in with a page boy to take shelter. Because of their informality, Hsiao Ying-shih treated them rather insolently. In a short while, the storm was over, the rain stopped, carriages and retinues came, and the old man was escorted away. Flustered, Hsiao Ying-shih inquired about the old man's identity, and the people around him said, "That was the Minister of the Board of Civil Office."

Now, Hsiao Ying-shih had gone to see the Minister many times, yet had not been received. When he heard that the old man was none other than the Minister himself, he was flabbergasted.

The next day, Hsiao brought a long letter with him and went to the Minister's residence to apologize. The Minister had him brought into the hallway and scolded him severely. "I regret that I am not related to you in any way, otherwise I would like to give you some good 'family discipline,' " said the Minister. "You are reputed to be a literary talent, yet your arrogance and poor manners are such that it is perhaps better for you to remain a mere *chin-shih* (presented scholar)."

Hsiao Ying-shih never got anywhere in officialdom, dying as a Chief Clerk in Yang prefecture.

Lu Chao was from I-ch'un of Yüan-chou. He and Huang P'o, also from the same prefecture, were equally famous. When they were young, Huang P'o was wealthy, but Lu Chao was very poor. When they were ready for the imperial examination, the two of them decided to set out on the trip together. The Prefect gave a farewell dinner at the Pavilion of Departure, but Huang P'o alone was invited. When the party was at its peak, with lots of wine and music, Lu Chao passed by the Pavilion, riding on an old, weak horse. He traveled some ten *li* out of the city limits, then stopped to wait for Huang P'o to join him.

The next year, Lu Chao came back to his hometown, having been awarded the tide of *chuang--yüan* [number one]. All the officials from the Regional Commander on down came out to welcome him, and the Prefect of Yüan-chou was greatly embarrassed.

Once when the Prefect invited him to watch the Dragon Boat Race, Lu Chao composed a poem during the banquet which read:

"It is a dragon," I told you.
But you had refused to believe.
Now it returns with the trophy,
Much in the way I predicted.

Lu Hui's mother's brother was Cheng Yü. As his parents died when he was small, Lu Hui was brought up in his mother's family, and Cheng Yü often encouraged him to take the imperial examination and become a *chin-shih*. Lu Hui was recommended for the examinations for the "widely brilliant" in the early part of 870, but in 880, bandits encroached on the capital, forcing him to flee to the south. At that same time Cheng Yü's son Hsü was stationed in Nanhai as a Regional Commander. Lu Hui and Cheng Hsü had gone to school together, but when Hsü was already a county official, Hui was still a commoner. The two of them, however, equally enjoyed the favor of Cheng Yü.

During the ten years in which Cheng Hsü rose to become a Governor-General, Lu Hui remained a destitute scholar. Once again he managed to escape an uprising and came to Cheng Hsü, carrying but one sack of personal belongings. Cheng Hsü still treated him kindly. At this time, the Emperor was on the expedition to Shu, and the whole country was in turmoil. Cheng Hsü encouraged Lu Hui to seize the opportunity to advance himself. "How long can a man live?" he said to Lu Hui. "If there is a shortcut to riches and fame, why insist on going through the examination?"

But Lu Hui was adamant. Cheng Hsü asked his friends and assistants to try to persuade Lu Hui to give up the exams; he even left the seat on his right-hand side vacant for Lu Hui to occupy. Lu Hui therefore said to him, "Our great nation has established the examination system for the outstanding and the talented. I do not have the ability and dare not dream of such honors. However, when he was alive, my uncle again and again encouraged me to take the examinations. Now his study is empty and quiet, but I cannot bring myself to break our agreement. If I have to die as a mere student, it is my fate. But I will not change my mind for the sake of wealth. I would sooner die."

When Cheng Hsü saw Lu Hui's determination, he respected him even more than before.

Another ten years passed before Lu Hui finally passed the examination under the Lord of Hung-nung, and he died as one of the highest officials in the whole empire.

Liu Hsü-po and Lord P'ei of T'ai-ping had once sat close to each other during the imperial examination. When Lord P'ei became the administrator of the imperial examinations, Liu was still only a candidate for the examination. On the day when the examinees were tested on their "miscellaneous essays," Liu presented a poem to the chief examiner, his old classmate:

> I remember evenings like this twenty years
>   ago:
> The candles were the same, so was the
>   breeze.
> How many more years will I have, I wonder,
> To wear this gunny robe,
> And to wait to reach you.

The Chief Minister Wang Ch'i was appointed chief examiner in the imperial examinations during the Ch'ang-ch'ing period (821–824). He had Po Min-chung in mind as the candidate for the *chuang-yüan* [number one] but was displeased with Min-chung's close association with Ho Pa-chi, a talented but eccentric man. Therefore, Wang Ch'i had a confidant reveal his displeasure to Min-chung, hinting to him to break off his friendship.

This messenger went to see Po Min-chung and told him the Chief Minister's intentions. "I will do as you say," Min-chung readily agreed.

In a little while Ho Pa-chi came to visit, as usual, and the servants lied to him, saying that Min-chung was not home. He waited a little, then left without saying a word. A moment later, Po Min-chung rushed out and ordered the servants to send for Ho. When he arrived, Min-Chung told him everything, and then said, "I can be a *chin-shih* under any examiner. I can't, however, wrong my best friend for this reason." The two of them then merrily drank wine and took a nap.

This whole sequence took place right before the eyes of the messenger from the Chief Minister, and he left in a fury. When he returned to the Chief Minister, he told him the story and thought this was the end of Po Min-chung. But Wang Ch'i said instead, "I only thought of taking Po Min-chung; now I should also consider Ho Pa-chi."

Hsü T'ang was from Ching county of Hsüan-chou and had been taking the examinations since he was young. In the same village there was a man named Wang Tsun, who had served as a minor government clerk when young. After Hsü T'ang had taken the examination, Hsü T'ang treated him with contempt, still but a low functionary in the government. Yet Wang Tsun wrote good poetry, although no one knew about it because he kept it a secret.

One day, Wang Tsun resigned from his post and set out for the capital to take the imperial examination. As he was approaching the capital, he met Hsü T'ang, who was seeing some friends off at the outskirts of the city.

"Eh," Hsü T'ang asked him, "what are you doing here in the capital?"

"I have come to take the imperial examination," answered the former functionary.

Upon hearing this, Hsü T'ang angrily declared, "How insolent you are, you lowly clerk!" Although they were now fellow candidates for the imperial examination, Hsü T'ang treated him with contempt. But in the end, Wang Tsun passed the examination and became very famous. Hsü T'ang did not pass until five years later.

P'eng K'an and Chan Pi were both from I-ch'un of Yüan-chou, and their wives were sisters. P'eng K'an passed the imperial examination and became a *chin-shih*, whereas Chan Pi remained a mere functionary in the county.

At the celebration banquet given by P'eng K'an's in-laws, all the guests were either high officials or renowned scholars. P'eng K'an was seated at the head of the table, and the whole company was enchanted by his exuberant character. When Chan Pi arrived at the banquet, he was told to eat his food in the back room.

Seeing that Chan Pi was not even disturbed by this, his wife scolded him severely: "You are a man, yet you cannot push yourself ahead. Now that you are so humiliated where is your sense of shame?" These words stimulated Chan Pi, and he began to study very hard. Within a few years, he also passed the imperial examination.

Previously, P'eng K'an used to insult Chan Pi. On the day when the results of the imperial examination were announced, P'eng K'an was out in the countryside, donkey riding for pleasure. Suddenly a servant boy came running and reported to him the good news about Chan Pi. P'eng K'an was so shocked that he fell off his saddle.

This is the origin of the lampoon that spread throughout Yüan-chou:

When Chan Pi the exams did pass,
P'eng K'an fell off his ass.

Chang Shu and Ts'ui Chao-wei were both sent up from Hsi-ch'uan to take the examination in the early years of Chung-ho [881–884]. While there the two of them went together to have their fortunes told.

At the time, Chang Shu was reputed for his literary talent, and was generally known as the "number-one-to-be." Even Ts'ui Chao-wei was regarded as inferior to him. However, the fortune-teller hardly paid any attention to Chang Shu but looked Ts'ui Chao-wei over and told him, "You will definitely pass the imperial examination and come out on top." Then, seeing that Chang Shu was annoyed, the fortune-teller said to him, "As to you, sir, you will also pass, but not until Mr. Ts'ui here becomes the Minister and you pay homage to him."

When they were taking the examination that year, Chang Shu had a death in the family and had to withdraw while Ts'ui Chao-wei turned out to be the "number one." Frustrated, Chang Shu vented his indignation in writing lines such as "I had followed you a thousand miles but only lost your tail during the morning's storm." Naturally, Ts'ui Chao-wei was very disturbed. At a drinking party, Ts'ui Chao-wei toasted Chang Shu, asking him to drink a huge horn-shaped goblet of wine. When Chang declined, Ts'ui said to him, "Just drink it, and when I become the Chief Minister, I will let you be the number-one." Chang walked out in a fury, and the two of them became foes.

Seven years later, Ts'ui was appointed Chief Minister by the Emperor, and Chang Shu later passed the examination under the chief-examiner Lord P'ei. As predicted, Chang had to pay homage to Ts'ui.

Study Questions

1. What values do these tales hold to be more important than passing the civil service examination?

2. What do the aspirants hope to gain by passing the examinations?

3. What do these passages tell us about the structure of Chinese government in the eighth and ninth centuries?

4. What was the role of status and deference in this society?

The Tale of Genji (ca. 1000)   38

LADY MURASAKI

Lady Murasaki Shikibu (ca. 978–1026) spent most of her life at the Heian court. Her father was a government official and, in keeping with tradition, she was called by his office rather than her own name, which has not survived. Lady Murasaki was a success at court because she had learned Chinese and was able to teach it to one of the imperial princesses. She married a lieutenant in the imperial guard but was soon widowed. It was after her husband's death that she began to compose *The Tale of Genji*, which was written over many years and remained unfinished at her death.

The Tale of Genji is the world's first surviving novel. It is a loosely woven account of the life of Genji ("the shining one"), a fictitious imperial prince who lived in the eighth century. The depiction of courtly love became a model for aristocratic behavior. The tale was immediately popular and remains the best loved of all Japanese novels.

Yugao

He had come in a plain coach with no outriders. No one could possibly guess who he was, and feeling quite at his ease he leant forward and deliberately examined the house. The gate, also made of a kind of trellis-work, stood ajar, and he could see enough of the interior to realize that it was a very humble and poorly furnished dwelling. For a moment he pitied those who lived in such a place, but then he remembered the song 'Seek not in the wide world to find a home; but where you chance to rest, call that your house'; and again, 'Monarchs may keep their palaces of jade, for in a leafy cottage two can sleep.'

There was a wattled fence over which some ivy-like creeper spread its cool green leaves, and among the leaves were white flowers with petals half unfolded like the lips of people smiling at their own thoughts. 'They are called Yugao, "Evening Faces",' one of his servants told him; 'how strange to find so lovely a crowd clustering on this deserted wall!' And indeed it was a most strange and delightful thing to see how on the narrow tenement in a poor quarter of the town they had clambered over rickety eaves and gables and spread wherever there was room for them to grow. He sent one of his servants to pick some. The man entered at the half-opened door, and had begun to pluck the flowers, when a little servant girl in a long yellow tunic came through a quite genteel sliding door, and holding out towards Genji's servant a white fan heavily perfumed with incense, she said to him 'Would you like something to put them on? I am afraid you have chosen a wretched-looking bunch,' and she handed him the fan.... He looked at the fan upon which the white flowers had been laid. He now saw that there was writing on it, a poem carelessly but elegantly scribbled: 'The flower that puzzled you was but the *Yugao*, strange beyond knowing in its dress of shining dew.' It was written with a deliberate negligence which seemed to aim at concealing the writer's status and identity. But for all that the hand showed a breeding and distinction which agreeably surprised him.

He had never ... been interested in anyone of quite the common classes. But now ... he had explored (so it seemed to him) every corner of society, including in his survey even those categories which his friends had passed over as utterly remote and improbable. He thought of the lady who had, so to speak, been thrown into his life as an extra.

Genji never asked her by what name he was to call her, nor did he reveal his own identity. He came very poorly dressed and—what was most unusual for him—on foot. But Koremitsu regarded this as too great a tribute to so unimportant a lady, and insisted upon Genji riding his horse, while he walked by his side. In doing so he sacrificed his own feelings; for he too had reasons for wishing to create a good impression in the house, and he knew that by arriving in this rather undignified way he would sink in the estimation of the inhabitants. Fortunately his discomfiture was almost unwitnessed, for Genji took with him only the one attendant who had on the first occasion plucked the flowers—a boy whom no one was likely to recognize; and lest suspicions should be aroused, he did not even take advantage of his presence in the neighbourhood to call at his foster-nurse's house.

The lady was very much mystified by all these precautions and made great efforts to discover something more about him. She even sent someone after him to see where he went to when he left her at day-break; but he succeeded in throwing his pursuer off the scent and she was no wiser than before. He was now growing far too fond of her. He was miserable if anything interfered with his visits; and though he utterly disapproved of his own conduct and worried a great deal about it, he soon found

Palace Scene. This thirteenth-century painting of the emperor, in flowing robes, playing a game of go is an illustration from *The Tale of Genji*, Japan's most famous novel.

that he was spending most of his time at her house.

He knew that at some time or another in their lives even the soberest people lose their heads in this way; but hitherto he had never really lost his, or done anything which could possibly have been considered very wrong. Now to his astonishment and dismay he discovered that even the few morning hours during which he was separated from her were becoming unendurable. 'What is it in her that makes me behave like a madman?' he kept on asking himself. She was astonishingly gentle and unassuming, to the point even of seeming rather apathetic, rather deficient perhaps in depth of character and emotion; and though she had a certain air of girlish inexperience, it was clear that he was not by any means her first lover; and certainly she was rather plebeian. What was it exactly that so fascinated him? He asked himself the question again and again, but found no answer.

She for her part was very uneasy to see him come to her thus in shabby old hunting-clothes, trying always to hide his face, leaving while it was still dark and everyone was asleep. He seemed like some demon-lover in an old ghost-tale, and she was half-afraid. But his smallest gesture showed that he was someone out of the ordinary, and she began to suspect that he was a person of high rank, who had used Koremitsu as his go-between. But Koremitsu obstinately pretended to know nothing at all about his companion, and continued to amuse himself by frequenting the house on his own account.

What could it mean? She was dismayed at this strange love-making with—she knew not whom. But about her too there was something fugitive, insubstantial. Genji was obsessed by the idea that, just as she had hidden herself in this place, so one day she would once more vanish and hide, and he would never be able to find her again. There was every sign that her residence here was quite temporary. He was sure that when the time came to move she would not tell him where she was going. Of course her running away would be proof that she was not worth bothering about any more, and he ought, thankful for the pleasure they had had together, simply to leave the matter at that. But he knew that this was the last thing he would be likely to do.

'I am going to take you somewhere very nice where no one will disturb us' he said at last. 'No, No' she cried; 'your ways are so strange, I should be frightened to go with you.' She spoke in a tone of childish terror, and Genji answered smiling: 'One or the other of us must be a fox-in-disguise. Here is a chance to find out which it is!' He spoke very kindly, and suddenly, in a tone of absolute submission, she consented to do whatever he thought best. He could not but be touched at her willingness to follow him in what must appear to her to be the most hazardous and bizarre adventure.

Their room was in the front of the house. Genji got up and opened the long, sliding shutters. They stood together looking out. In the courtyard near them was a clump of fine Chinese bamboos; dew lay thick on the borders, glittering here no less brightly than in the great gardens to which Genji was better accustomed. There was a confused buzzing of insects. Crickets were chirping in the wall. He had often listened to them, but always at a distance; now, singing so close to him, they made a music which was unfamiliar and indeed seemed far lovelier than that with which he was acquainted. But then, everything in this place where one thing was so much to his liking, seemed despite all drawbacks to take on a new tinge of interest and beauty. She was wearing a white bodice with a soft, grey cloak over it. It was a poor dress, but she looked charming and almost distinguished; even so, there was nothing very striking in her appearance—only a certain fragile grace and elegance. It was when she was speaking that she looked really beautiful, there was such pathos, such earnestness in her manner. If only she had a little more spirit! But even as she was he found her irresistible and longed to take her to some place where no one could disturb them: 'I am going to take you somewhere not at all far away where we shall be able to pass the rest of the night in peace. We cannot go on like this, parting always at break of day.' 'Why have you suddenly come to that conclusion?' she asked, but she spoke submissively. He vowed to her that she should be his love in this and in all future lives and she answered so passionately that she seemed utterly transformed from the listless creature he had known, and it was hard to believe that such vows were no novelty to her.

They drove to an untenanted mansion which was not far off. While he waited for the steward to come out Genji noticed that the gates were crumbling away; dense shinobu-grass grew around them. So sombre an entrance he had never seen. There was a thick mist and the dew was so heavy that when he raised the carriage-blind his sleeve was drenched. 'Never yet has such an adventure as this befallen me' said Genji; 'so I am, as you may imagine, rather excited,' and he made a poem in which he said that though love's folly had existed since the beginning of the world, never could man have set out more rashly at the break of day into a land unknown. 'But to you this is no great novelty?' She blushed and in her turn made a poem: 'I am as the moon that walks the sky not knowing what menace the cruel hills may hold in store; high though she sweeps, her light may suddenly be blotted out.'

Study Questions

1. Why was it significant to Genji that his lover was of the common class?

2. What were some of the different signs of class in Heian Japan?

3. How are women portrayed in this passage? Is it surprising to realize that a woman wrote *The Tale of Genji?*

4. What does this passage tell us about the importance of manners and appearance in Heian Japan?

5. How does Lady Murasaki portray the relationship between love and nature?

The Comprehensive Mirror for Aid in Government (1071–1085)   39

Ssu-ma Kuang

Ssu-ma Kuang (1019–1086) was the son of a provincial magistrate who spent his life in government service. A child prodigy who could recite Confucian texts at the age of 7, he passed the highest state civil examination by the time he was 20. He served ably in a variety of offices and rose to prominence in the service of successive emperors. He was, however, an outspoken opponent of the reforms known as the New Laws, and when his criticisms went unheeded he resigned his posts in 1071. Fourteen years later he was restored to power and swept away the New Laws. He died the following year.

It was during his 14 years of enforced leisure that Ssu-ma Kuang compiled his vast history of China from 403 B.C.E. to 959 C.E. *The Comprehensive Mirror* was largely a compilation of sources for the study of Chinese history without much interpretive commentary. It preserved vital records from which later histories were written.

A Discussion of Dynastic Legitimacy

Your servant Kuang observes: Heaven gave birth to the multitudes of people. But conditions make it impossible for them to govern themselves, so that they must have a ruler to govern over them. Anyone who is able to prevent violence and remove harm from the people so that their lives are protected, who can reward good and punish evil and thus avoid disaster—such a man may be called a ruler. Thus before the Three Dynasties the feudal lords had a countless number of states, and anyone who had subjects and possessed altars to the soil and grain went by the name of ruler. But he who united all these countless states and who set up laws and issued commands which no one dared to disobey was called a king. When the power of the king declined, there were rulers of strong states who were able to lead the other feudal lords and enforce respect for the Son of Heaven and such were called "overlords." Thus since ancient times there have been instances when the world was in disorder and the feudal lords contended with each other for power, and for a number of generations there was no king at all.

After Ch'in had burned the books and buried the Confucianists alive, the Han arose, and at this time scholars first began to propound the theory of how the five agents produce and overcome each other according to which the Ch'in was an "intercalary" reign coming between those of wood [Chou] and fire [Han], ruled by an "overlord" and not by a true king. Thus began the theory of legitimate and intercalary dynasties.

After the House of Han was overthrown, the Three Kingdoms ruled simultaneously like the legs of a tripod. Then the Chin lost its control of the empire and the five barbarian tribes swarmed in. From the time of the Sung and the Northern Wei, north and south were divided politically. Each had its own dynastic histories which disparaged the other, the south calling the north "slaves with bound hair," the north calling the south "island barbarians." When Chu Ch'üan-chung succeeded to the T'ang the empire was once again rent to pieces, but when the Chu-yeh clan entered Pien and overthrew him they compared him to the ancient usurpers Yi and Wang Mang and discarded completely the chronology of his dynasty. All these are examples of biased phraseology based on personal interest and do not represent enlightened and just opinions.

Your servant, being stupid, is surely not qualified to know anything about the legitimate and intercalary dynasties of former times. But he would be bold enough to consider that unless rulers were able to unite the nine provinces under one government, although

they all bore the name Son of Heaven there was no reality behind it. Although distinctions may be made on the basis of the fact that one dynasty was Chinese and another foreign, one humane and another tyrannical, or that they differed in size and power, yet essentially they were just the same as the various feudal states of ancient times. How can we single out one state for honor and call it the legitimate successor, and consider all the rest as false or usurpers?

Are we to consider those states legitimate which received the throne from the hands of their immediate predecessors? Then from whom did the Ch'en receive the throne, and from whom the Northern Wei? Should we consider as legitimate those who occupied parts of China proper? Then we must recognize the rule of the [barbarian families] Liu, the Shih, the Mu-jung, the Fu, the Yao, and the Ho-lien [of the Five Dynasties period], all of whom ruled territory that had been the domain of the ancient five emperors and three kings. Or are we perhaps to make virtuous ways the criterion of legitimacy? But even the tiniest state must sometimes have its good sovereigns, while in the declining days of the Three Dynasties there were surely unrighteous kings. Thus from ancient times to the present these theories of legitimate dynasties have never possessed the kind of logic sufficient to compel men to accept them without question.

Now your servant in his narrative has sought only to trace the rise and fall of the various states and make clear the people's times of joy and sorrow so that the reader may select for himself what is good and what is bad, what profitable and what unprofitable, for his own encouragement and warning. He has no intention of setting up standards of praise and blame in the manner of the *Spring and Autumn Annals* which could compel a disorderly age to return to just ways.

Your servant does not presume to know anything about the distinctions of legitimate and intercalary, but treats each state only in accordance with its actual accomplishments. Chou, Ch'in, Han, Chin, Sui, and T'ang each in turn unified the nine provinces and transmitted the throne to its descendants. And though their descendants in time grew weak and were forced to move their capitals, they still carried on the undertaking of their ancestors, continued the line of succession, and hoped to bring about a restoration of power. Those with whom rulers contended for power were all their former subjects. Therefore your servant has treated these rulers with all the respect due the Son of Heaven. All other states who were approximately equal in territory and virtue and unable to overcome each other, and who employed the same titles and did not stand in a ruler-subject relationship, have been treated the same as the ancient feudal states, presented equally and without favoritism. This way would seem to avoid doing violence to the facts and accord the fairest treatment.

Nevertheless for times when the empire was split up it is necessary to have some overall chronology in order to distinguish the sequence of events. The Han transmitted rule to the Wei, from whom the Chin received it; Chin passed it on to Sung and thence to Ch'en, whence Sui took it; T'ang passed it to the Latter Liang and so down to the Latter Chou, from whom our Great Sung inherited it. Therefore it has been necessary to adopt the reign titles of these dynasties in chronicling the events that took place in all the various states. This does not mean, however, that one state is being honored and another disparaged, or that any distinction of legitimate or intercalary dynasties is intended.

Study Questions

1. What are kings and from where do they come?

2. According to Ssu-ma, what determines the legitimacy of a dynasty?

3. What are the differences among rulers, kings, and overlords?

4. How does Ssu-ma express the Chinese conception of empire during the Sung period?

The Seventeen Article Constitution (604 A.D.)   **40**

PRINCE SHOTOKU

Developments in Chinese culture have often had a profound impact on neighboring states. Beginning in the sixth century, for example, Japan became interested in all things Chinese. First, Japan adopted the Chinese variety of Buddhism, and this religious change in turn led to a general transformation of traditional Japanese society. Consequently, a culture, long dominated by powerful clans and by customary Shinto rituals, became one with a strong Emperor and central bureaucracy, governing according to Confucian and Buddhist ideals.

This transformation can clearly be seen in *The Seventeen Article Constitution*, which Prince Shotoku instituted in 604 during his regency, which lasted from 593 to 622. Not so much a formal legal document as a string of moral precepts, liberally borrowed from Chinese sources, the *Constitution* guided the Taika reforms later in the century, which greatly enhanced the authority of the central government at the expense of the clans.

The Seventeen Article Constitution, 604 A.D.

Summer, 4th month, 3rd day [12th year of Empress Suiko, 604 A.D.] The Crown Prince personally drafted and promulgated a constitution consisting of seventeen articles, which are as follows:

I. Harmony is to be cherished, and opposition for opposition's sake must be avoided as a matter of principle. Men are often influenced by partisan feelings, except a few sagacious ones. Hence there are some who disobey their lords and fathers, or who dispute with their neighboring villages. If those above are harmonious and those below are cordial, their discussion will be guided by a spirit of conciliation, and reason shall naturally prevail. There will be nothing that cannot be accomplished.

II. With all our heart, revere the three treasures. The three treasures, consisting of Buddha, the Doctrine, and the Monastic Order, are the final refuge of the four generated beings, and are the supreme objects of worship in all countries. Can any man in any age ever fail to respect these teachings? Few men are utterly devoid of goodness, and men can be taught to follow the teachings. Unless they take refuge in the three treasures, there is no way of rectifying their misdeeds.

III. When an imperial command is given, obey it with reverence. The sovereign is likened to heaven, and his subjects are likened to earth. With heaven providing the cover and earth supporting it, the four seasons proceed in orderly fashion, giving sustenance to all that which is in nature. If earth attempts to overtake the functions of heaven, it destroys everything Therefore when the sovereign speaks, his subjects must listen; when the superior acts, the inferior must follow his examples. Mien an imperial command is given, carry it out with diligence. If there is no reverence shown to the imperial command ruin will automatically result.

IV. The ministers and functionaries must act on the basis of decorum, for the basis of governing the people consists in decorum. If the superiors do not behave with decorum, offenses will ensue. If the ministers behave with decorum, there will be no confusion about ranks. If the people behave with decorum, the nation will be governed well of its own.

V. Cast away your ravenous desire for food and abandon your covetousness for material possessions. If a suit is brought before you, render a clear-cut judgment.... Nowadays, those who are in the position of pronouncing judgment are motivated by making private gains, and as a rule, receive bribes. Thus the plaints of the rich are like a stone flung into water, while those of the poor are like water poured over a stone. Under these circumstances, the poor will be denied recourses to justice, which constitutes a dereliction of duty of the minister.

VI. Punish that which is evil and encourage that which is good. This is an excellent rule from antiquity. Do not conceal the good qualities of others, and always correct that which is evil which comes to your attention. Consider those flatterers and tricksters as constituting a superb weapon for the overthrow of the state, and a sharp sword for the destruction of people. Smooth-tongued adulators love to report to their superiors the errors of their inferiors; and to their inferiors, castigate the errors of their superiors. Men of this type lack loyalty to the sovereign and have no compassion for the people. They are the ones who can cause great civil disorders.

VII. Every man must be given his clearly delineated responsibility. If a wise man is entrusted with office, the sound of praise arises. If a wicked man holds office, disturbances become frequent.... In all things, great or small, find the right man, and the country will be well governed. On all occasions, in an emergency or otherwise, seek out a wise man, which in itself is an enriching experience. In this manner, the state will be lasting and its sacerdotal functions will be free from danger. Therefore did the sage kings of old seek the man to fill the office, not the office for the sake of the man.

VIII. The ministers and functionaries must attend the court early in the morning and retire late. The business of the state must not be taken lightly. A full day is hardly enough to complete work, and if the attendance is late, emergencies cannot be met. If the officials retire early, the work cannot be completed.

IX. Good faith is the foundation of righteousness, and everything must be guided by faith. The key to the success of the good and the failure of the bad can also be found in good faith. If the officials observe good faith with one another, everything can be accomplished. If they do not observe good faith, everything is bound to fail.

X. Discard wrath and anger from your heart and from your looks. Do not be offended when others differ with you. Everyone has his own mind, and each mind has its own leanings. Thus what is right with him is wrong with us, and what is right with us is wrong with him. We are not necessarily sages, and he is not

necessarily a fool. We are all simply ordinary men, and none of us can set up a rule to determine the right from wrong.... Therefore, instead of giving way to anger as others do, let us fear our own mistakes. Even though we may have a point, let us follow the multitude and act like them.

XI. Observe clearly merit and demerit and assign reward and punishment accordingly. Nowadays, rewards are given in the absence of meritorious work, punishments without corresponding crimes. The ministers, who are in charge of public affairs, must therefore take upon themselves the task of administering a clear-cut system of rewards and punishments.

XII Provincial authorities or local nobles are not permitted to levy exactions on the people. A country cannot have two sovereigns, nor the people two masters. The people of the whole country must have the sovereign as their only master. The officials who are given certain functions are all his subjects. Being the subjects of the sovereign, these officials have no more right than others to levy exactions on the people.

XIII. All persons entrusted with office must attend equally to their functions. If absent from work due to illness or being sent on missions, and work for that period is neglected, on their return, they must perform their duties conscientiously by taking into account that which transpired before and during their absence. Do not permit lack of knowledge of the intervening period as an excuse to hinder effective performance of public affairs.

XIV. Ministers and functionaries are asked not to be envious of others. If we envy others, they in turn will envy us, and there is no limit to the evil that envy can cause us. We resent others when their intelligence is superior to ours, and we envy those who surpass us in talent. This is the reason why it takes five hundred years before we can meet a wise man, and in a thousand years it is still difficult to find one sage. If we cannot find wise men and sages, how can the country be governed?

XV. The way of a minister is to turn away from private motives and to uphold public good. Private motives breed resentment, and resentful feelings cause a man to act discordantly. If he fails to act in accord with others, he sacrifices the public interests for the sake of his private feelings. When resentment arises, it goes counter to the existing order and breaks the law. Therefore it is said in the first article that superiors and inferiors must act in harmony. The purport is the same.

XVI. The people may be employed in forced labor only at seasonable times. This is an excellent rule from antiquity. Employ the people in the winter months when they are at leisure. However, from spring to autumn, when they are engaged in agriculture or sericulture, do not employ them. Without their agricultural endeavor, there is no food, and without their sericulture, there is no clothing.

XVII. Major decisions must not be made by one person alone, but must be deliberated with many. On the other hand, it is not necessary to consult many people on minor questions. If important matters are not discussed fully, there may always be a fear of committing mistakes. A thorough discussion with many can prevent it and bring about a reasonable solution.

Study Questions

1. What is the role that Shotoku assigns to the Emperor?

2. From the evidence of the *Constitution,* what kind of economy did Japan have in the seventh century?

3. How does Shotoku incorporate Buddhist ideals into the *Constitution?*

4. What do you think of the *Constitution* as a practical document for governance?

Precepts for Social Life (1178)   41

YÜAN TS'AI

Though we know few actual details of his early life, we do know that Yüan Ts'ai (ca. 1140–1195) came from a family of educated property holders. He attended Hangchow University in order to prepare for the rigorous civil service examinations, which he passed in 1163. He served as a provincial magistrate in four different jurisdictions before finally gaining a high office in the capital toward the end of his life. He wrote a number of political treatises but showed little interest in the more characteristic intellectual pursuits of philosophy or poetry.

Precepts for Social Life was written as a conduct book. As such it is difficult to tell how much of Yüan Ts'ai's observations are descriptive, showing how things were, and how much prescriptive, showing how things ought to be. The sections excerpted here focus on the role of women during the Sung Dynasty.

The Problems of Women

WOMEN SHOULD NOT TAKE PART IN AFFAIRS OUTSIDE THE HOME

Women do not take part in extra-familial affairs. The reason is that worthy husbands and sons take care of everything for them, while unworthy ones can always find ways to hide their deeds from the women.

Many men today indulge in pleasure and gambling; some end up mortgaging their lands, and even go so far as to mortgage their houses without their wives' knowledge. Therefore, when husbands are bad, even if wives try to handle outside matters, it is of no use. Sons must have their mothers' signatures to mortgage their family properties, but there are sons who falsify papers and forge signatures, sometimes borrowing money at high interest from people who would not hesitate to bring their claim to court. Other sons sell illicit tea and salt to get money, which, if discovered by the authorities, results in fines. Mothers have no control in such matters. Therefore, when sons are bad, it is useless for mothers to try to handle matters relating to the outside world.

For women, these are grave misfortunes, but what can they do? If husbands and sons could only remember that their wives and mothers are helpless and suddenly repent, would that not be best?

WOMEN'S SYMPATHIES SHOULD BE INDULGED

Without going overboard, people should marry their daughters with dowries appropriate to their family's wealth. Rich families should not consider their daughters outsiders but should give them a share of the property. Sometimes people have incapable sons and so have to entrust their affairs to their daughters' families; even after their deaths, their burials and sacrifices are performed by their daughters. So how can people say that daughters are not as good as sons?

Generally speaking, a woman's heart is very sympathetic. If her parents' family is wealthy and her husband's family is poor, she wants to take her parents' wealth to help her husband's family prosper. If her husband's family is wealthy but her parents' family is poor, then she wants to take from her husband's family to enable her parents to prosper. Her parents and husband should be sympathetic toward her feelings and indulge some of her wishes. When her own sons and daughters are grown and married, if either her son's family or her daughter's family is wealthy while the other is poor, she wishes to take from the wealthy one to give to the poor one. Her sons and daughters should understand her feelings and be somewhat indulgent. But taking from the poor to make the rich richer is unacceptable, and no one should ever go along with it.

ORPHANED GIRLS SHOULD HAVE THEIR MARRIAGES ARRANGED EARLY

When a widow remarries she sometimes has an orphaned daughter not yet engaged. In such cases she should try to get a respectable relative to arrange a marriage for her daughter. She should also seek to have her daughter reared in the house of her future in-laws, with the marriage to take place after the girl has grown up. If the girl were to go along with the mother to her step-father's house, she would not be able to clear herself if she were subjected to any humiliations.

FOR WOMEN OLD AGE IS PARTICULARLY HARD TO BEAR

People say that, though there may be a hundred years allotted to a person's life, only a few reach seventy, for time quickly runs out. But for those destined to be poor, old age is hard to endure. For them, until about the age of fifty, the passage of twenty years seems like only ten; but after that age, ten years can feel as long as twenty. For women who live a long life, old age is especially hard to bear, because most women must rely on others for their existence. Before a woman's marriage, a good father is even more important than a good grandfather; a good brother is even more important than a good father; a good nephew is even more important than a good brother. After her marriage, a good husband is even more important than a good father-in-law; a good son is even more important than a good husband; and a good grandson is even more important than a good son. For this reason women often enjoy comfort in their youth but find their old age difficult to endure. It would be well for their relatives to keep this in mind..

IT IS DIFFICULT FOR WIDOWS TO ENTRUST THEIR FINANCIAL AFFAIRS TO OTHERS

Some wives with stupid husbands are able to manage the family's finances, calculating the outlays and receipts of money and grain, without being cheated by anyone. Of those with degenerate husbands, there are also some who are able to manage the finances with the help of their sons without ending in bankruptcy. Even among those whose husbands have died and whose sons are young, there are occasionally women able to raise and educate their sons, keep the affection of all their relatives, manage the family business, and even prosper. All of these are wise and worthy women. But the most remarkable are the women who manage a household after their husbands have died leaving them with young children. Such women could entrust their finances to their husbands' kinsmen or their own kinsmen, but not all relatives are honorable, and the honorable ones are not necessarily willing to look after other people's business.

When wives themselves can read and do arithmetic, and those they entrust with their affairs have some sense of fairness and duty with regard to food, clothing, and support, then things will usually work out all right. But in most of the rest of the cases, bankruptcy is what happens.

BEWARE OF FUTURE DIFFICULTIES IN TAKING IN FEMALE RELATIVES

You should take into your own house old aunts, sisters, or other female relatives whose children and grandchildren are unfilial and do not support them. However, take precautions. After a woman dies, her unfilial sons or grandsons might make outrageous accusations to the authorities, claiming that the woman died from hunger or cold or left valuables in trunks. When the authorities receive such complaints, they have to investigate and trouble is unavoidable. Thus, while the woman is alive, make it clear to the public and to the government that the woman is bringing nothing with her but herself. Generally, in performing charitable acts, it is best to make certain that they will entail no subsequent difficulties.

BEFORE BUYING A SERVANT GIRL OR CONCUBINE, MAKE SURE OF THE LEGALITY

When buying a female servant or concubine, inquire whether it is legal for her to be indentured or sold before closing the deal. If the girl is impoverished and has no one to rely on, then she should be brought before the authorities to give an account of her past. After guarantors have been secured and an investigation conducted, the transaction can be completed. But if she is not able to give an account of her past, then the agent who offered her for sale should be questioned. Temporarily she may be hired on a salaried basis. If she is ever recognized by her relatives, she should be returned to them.

HIRED WOMEN SHOULD BE SENT BACK WHEN THEIR PERIOD OF SERVICE IS OVER

If you hire a man's wife or daughter as a servant, you should return her to her husband or father on completion of her period of service. If she comes from another district, you should send her back to it after her term is over. These practices are the most humane and are widely carried out by the gentry in the Southeast. Yet there are people who do not return their hired women to their husbands but wed them to others instead; others do not return them to their parents but marry them off themselves. Such actions are the source of many lawsuits.

How can one not have sympathy for those separated from their relatives, removed from their hometowns, who stay in service for their entire lives with neither husbands nor sons? Even in death these women's spirits are left to wander all alone. How pitiful they are!

Study Questions

1. What was the status of women in twelfth-century China?

2. What were the most important functions of women in this society? Could they step outside of their traditional roles?

3. What was the role of men in the lives of women?

4. How did the concept of honor regulate women's lives?

Europe After the Fall of Rome

The Coronation of Charlemagne. This manuscript illustration shows Leo III placing a crown on Charlemagne's head.

The Germania (98)   **42**

TACITUS

Cornelius Tacitus (ca. 56–120) was the greatest of the Roman historians. Little is known of his early life, but he must have come from comfortable surroundings, for he was trained for a public career. He practiced law and moved up the ranks of public service, benefiting from his marriage to the daughter of Julius Agricola, governor of Britain. Elected consul in 97, Tacitus, distinguished himself by his oratory. It appears that soon after his election he retired from public life to devote himself to writing, although he served as proconsul of Asia in 112. Both a biographer and a scholar of recent Roman history, Tacitus prepared a life of his father-in-law as well as his *History,* which ended just before his consulship.

The Germania (98) was one of Tacitus' earliest works, describing firsthand the customs and characteristics of the Germanic tribes living on the Roman frontier. It remains a principal source for understanding Roman attitudes toward other peoples and for recreating early Germanic life.

The people of Germany appear to me indigenous, and free from intermixture with foreigners, either as settlers or casual visitants. For the emigrants of former ages performed their expeditions not by land, but by water; and that immense, and, if I may so call it, hostile ocean, is rarely navigated by ships from our world. Then, besides the dangers of a boisterous and unknown sea, who would relinquish Asia, Africa, or Italy, for Germany, a land rude in its surface, rigorous in its climate, cheerless to every beholder and cultivator, except a native?

In the election of kings they have regard to birth; in that of generals, to valor. Their kings have not an absolute or unlimited power; and their generals command less through the force of authority than of example. If they are daring, adventurous, and conspicuous in action, they procure obedience from the admiration they inspire. None, however, but the priests are permitted to judge offenders, to inflict bonds or stripes; so that chastisement appears not as an act of military discipline, but as the instigation of the god whom they suppose present with warriors. They also carry with them to battle certain images and standards taken from the sacred groves.

Tradition relates that armies beginning to give way have been rallied by the females, through the earnestness of their supplications, the interposition of their bodies, and the pictures they have drawn of impending slavery, a calamity which these people bear with more impatience for their women than themselves; so that those states who have been obliged to give among their hostages the daughters of noble families, are the most effectually bound to fidelity. They even suppose somewhat of sanctity and prescience to be inherent in the female sex; and therefore neither despise their counsels, nor disregard their responses. We have beheld, in the reign of Vespasian, Veleda, long reverenced by many as a deity. Aurima, moreover, and several others, were formerly held in equal veneration, but not with a servile flattery, nor as though they made them goddesses.

No people are more addicted to divination by omens and lots. The latter is performed in the following simple manner. They cut a twig from a fruit-tree, and divide it into small pieces, which, distinguished by certain marks, are thrown promiscuously upon a white garment. Then, the priest of the canton, if the occasion be public; if private, the master of the family; after an invocation of the gods, with his eyes lifted up to heaven, thrice takes out each piece, and, as they come up, interprets their signification according to the marks fixed upon them. If the result prove unfavorable, there is no more consultation on the same affair that day; if propitious, a confirmation by omens is still required. In common with other nations, the Germans are acquainted with the practice of auguring from the notes and flight of birds; but it is peculiar to them to derive admonitions and presages from horses also. Certain of these animals, milk-white, and untouched by earthly labor, are pastured at the public expense in the sacred woods and groves. These, yoked to a consecrated chariot, are accompanied by the priest, and king, or chief person of the community, who attentively observe their manner of neighing and snorting; and no kind of augury is more credited, not only among the populace, but among the nobles and priests. For the latter consider themselves as the ministers of the gods, and the horses, as privy to the divine will. Another kind of divination, by which they explore the event of momentous wars, is to oblige a prisoner, taken by any means whatsoever from the nation with whom they are at variance, to fight with a picked man of their own, each with his own country's arms; and, according as the victory falls, they presage success to the one or to the other party.

The Germans transact no business, public or private, without being armed: but it is not customary for any person to assume arms till the state has approved his ability to use them.

Then, in the midst of the assembly, either one of the chiefs, or the father, or a relation, equips the youth with a shield and javelin. These are to them the manly gown; this is the first honor conferred on youth; before this they are considered as part of a household: afterward, of the state. The dignity of chieftain is bestowed even on mere lads, whose descent is eminently illustrious, or whose fathers have performed signal services to the public; they are associated, however, with those of mature strength, who have already been declared capable of service; nor do they blush to be seen in the rank of companions. For the state of companionship itself has its several degrees, determined by the judgment of him whom they follow; and there is a great emulation among the companions, which shall possess the highest place in the favor of their chief; and among the chiefs, which shall excel in the number and valor of his companions. It is their dignity, their strength, to be always surrounded with a large body of select youth, an ornament in peace, a bulwark in war. And not in his own country alone, but among the neighboring states, the fame and glory of each chief consists in being distinguished for the number and bravery of his companions. Such chiefs are courted by embassies; distinguished by presents; and often by their reputation alone decide a war.

In the field of battle, it is disgraceful for the chief to be surpassed in valor; it is disgraceful for the companions not to equal their chief, but it is reproach and infamy during a whole succeeding life to retreat from the field surviving him. To aid, to protect him; to place their own gallant actions to the account of his glory, is their first and most sacred engagement. The chiefs fight for victory; the companions for their chief. If their native country be long sunk in peace and inaction, many of the young nobles repair to some other state then engaged in war. For, besides that repose is unwelcome to their race, and toils and perils afford them a better opportunity of distinguishing themselves; they are unable, without war and violence, to maintain a large train of followers. The companion requires from the liberality of his chief, the warlike steed, the bloody and conquering spear; and in place of pay he expects to be supplied with a table, homely indeed, but plentiful. The funds for this munificence must be found in war and rapine; nor are they so easily persuaded to cultivate the earth, and await the produce of the seasons, as to challenge the foe, and expose themselves to wounds; nay, they even think it base and spiritless to earn by sweat what they might purchase with blood.

During the intervals of war, they pass their time less in hunting than in a sluggish repose, divided between sleep and the table. All the bravest of the warriors, committing the care of the house, the family affairs, and the lands, to the women, old men, and weaker part of the domestics, stupefy themselves in inaction: so wonderful is the contrast presented by nature, that the same persons love indolence, and hate tranquility! It is customary for the several states to present, by voluntary and individual contributions, cattle or grain to their chiefs; which are accepted as honorary gifts, while they serve as necessary supplies. They are peculiarly pleased with presents from neighboring nations, offered not only by individuals, but by the community at large; such as fine horses, heavy armor, rich housing, and gold chains. We have now taught them also to accept of money.

It is well known that none of the German nations inhabit cities, or even admit of contiguous settlements. They dwell scattered and separate, as a spring, a meadow, or a grove may chance to invite them. Their villages are laid out, not like ours in rows of adjoining buildings; but every one surrounds his house with a vacant space, either by way of security against fire, or through ignorance of the art of building. For, indeed, they are unacquainted with the use of mortar and tiles; and for every purpose employ rude unshapen timber, fashioned with no regard to pleasing the eye. They

bestow more than ordinary pains in coating certain parts of their buildings with a kind of earth, so pure and shining that it gives the appearance of painting.

The dress of the women does not differ from that of the men; except that they more frequently wear linen, which they stain with purple, and do not lengthen their upper garment into sleeves, but leave exposed the whole arm, and part of the breast.

The matrimonial bond is, nevertheless, strict and severe among them; nor is there any thing in their manners more commendable than this. Almost singly among the barbarians, they content themselves with one wife.; a very few of them excepted, who, not through incontinence, but because their alliance is solicited on account of their rank, practice polygamy. The wife does not bring a dowry to her husband, but receives one from him. The parents and relations assemble, and pass their approbation on the presents—presents not adapted to please a female taste, or decorate the bride; but oxen, a caparisoned steed, a shield, a spear, and sword. By virtue of these, the wife is espoused; and she in her turn makes a present of some arms to her husband. This they consider as the firmest bond of union; these, the sacred mysteries, the conjugal deities. That the woman may not think herself excused from exertions of fortitude, or exempt from the casualties of war, she is admonished by the very ceremonial of her marriage, that she comes to her husband as a partner in toils and dangers; to suffer and to dare equally with him, in peace and in war; this is indicated by the yoked oxen, the harnessed steed, the offered arms. Thus she is to live; thus to die. She receives what she is to return inviolate and honored to her children; what her daughters-in-law are to receive, and again transmit to her grandchildren.

They live, therefore, fenced around with chastity, corrupted by no seductive spectacles, no convivial incitements. Men and women are alike unacquainted with Clandestine correspondence. Adultery is extremely rare among so numerous a people. Its punishment is instant, and at the pleasure of the husband. He cuts off the hair of the offender, strips her, and in presence of her relations expels her from his house, and pursues her with stripes through the whole village. Nor is any indulgence shown to a prostitute. Neither beauty, youth, nor riches can procure her a husband; for none there looks on vice with a smile, or calls mutual seduction the way of the world. Still more exemplary is the practice of those states in which none but virgins marry, and the expectations and wishes of a wife are at once brought to a period. Thus, they take one husband as one body and one life; that no thought, no desire, may extend beyond him; and he may be loved not only as their husband, but as their marriage. To limit the increase of children, or put to death any of the later progeny, is accounted infamous: and good habits have there more influence than good laws elsewhere.

Study Questions

1. Tacitus' view of the Germans is that of an outsider looking in. How might his background affect his description?

2. How is German society organized? Who bear authority within it, and how do they achieve power?

3. Why is German society so warlike? What purpose does warfare serve among the Germanic tribes?

4. What is the family life of the Germans like?

5. Implicit in Tacitus' account of the morals of the Germans is a comment upon the Romans of his own time. What do you think he is trying to say?

The Burgundian Code (ca. 474)   43

The Burgundians were a Germanic tribe that moved westward across the Rhine River until stopped by the Roman army. In the fourth century they were incorporated into the Roman Empire and settled north of Lake Geneva. During the reign of Gundobad (474–516), one of the greatest Burgundian kings, the tribe occupied the largest amount of territory in its history and became a major power in northwestern Europe, even defeating the Franks. After his death, the kingdom contracted and was soon absorbed into the Frankish empire.

Gundobad's codification, known as *The Burgundian Code*, was undoubtedly a combination of older laws and those current in the late fifth century. As Romans and Burgundians had been neighbors for over a century, procedures such as those outlined here must have developed slowly.

1. In the name of God in the second year of the reign of our lord the most glorious king Gundobad, this book concerning laws past and present, and to be preserved throughout all future time, has been issued on the fourth day before the Kalends of April (March 29) at Lyons.

2. For the love of justice, through which God is pleased and the power of earthly kingdoms acquired, we have obtained the consent of our counts and leaders, and have desired to establish such laws that the integrity and equity of those judging may exclude all rewards and corruptions from themselves.

3. Therefore all administrators and judges must judge from the present time on between Burgundians and Romans according to our laws which have been set forth and corrected by a common method, to the end that no one may hope or presume to receive anything by way of reward or emolument from any party as the result of the suits or decisions: but let him whose case is deserving obtain justice and let the integrity of the judge alone suffice to accomplish this.

4. We believe the condition of this law should be imposed on us that no one may presume to tempt our integrity in any kind of case with favors or rewards; first, since our zeal for equity repudiates from ourselves those things which we forbid to all judges under our rule, let our treasury accept nothing more than has been established in the laws concerning the payment of fines.

5. Therefore let all nobles, counsellors, bailiffs, mayors of our palace, chancellors, counts of the cities or villages, Burgundian as well as Roman, and all appointed judges and military judges know that nothing can be accepted in connection with those suits which have been acted upon or decided, and that nothing can be sought in the name of promise or reward from those litigating: nor can the parties (to the suit) be compelled by the judge to make a payment in order that they may receive anything (from their suit).

Of Murders

1. If anyone presumes with boldness or rashness bent on injury to kill a native freeman of our people of any nation or a servant of the king, in any case a man of barbarian tribe, let him make restitution for the committed crime not otherwise than by the shedding of his own blood.

2. We decree that this rule be added to the law by a reasonable provision, that if violence shall have been done by anyone to any person, so that he is injured by blows of lashes or by wounds, and if he pursues his persecutor and overcome by grief and indignation kills him, proof of the deed shall be afforded by the act itself or by suitable witnesses who can be believed. Then the guilty party shall be compelled to pay to the relatives of the person killed half his wergeld according to the status of the person: that is, if he shall have killed a noble of the highest class, we decree that the payment be set at one hundred fifty solidi, i.e., half his wergeld; if a person of middle class, one hundred solidi; if a person of the lowest class, seventy-five solidi.

3. If a slave unknown to his master presumes to kill a native freeman, let the slave be handed over to death, and let the master not be made liable for damages.

4. If the master knows of the deed, let both be handed over to death.

5. If the slave himself flees after the deed, let his master be compelled to pay thirty solidi to the relatives of the man killed for the value (wergeld) of the slave.

Of the Commission of Crimes Which Are Charged Against Native Freeman

1. If a native freeman, either barbarian or Roman, is accused of a crime through suspicion, let him render oath, and let him swear with his wife and sons and twelve relatives: if indeed he does not have wife and sons and

he has mother or father, let him complete the designated number with father and mother. But if he has neither father nor mother, let him complete the oath with twelve relatives.

2. But if he who must take oath wishes to take it with raised hand, and if those who are ordered to hear the oath—those three whom we always command to be delegated by the judges for hearing an oath—before they enter the church declare they do not wish to receive the oath, then he who was about to take oath is not permitted to do so after this statement, but they (the judges) are hereby directed by us to commit the matter to the judgment of God (i.e., to ordeal).

3. If however, having received permission, he has taken the oath, and if he has been convicted after the oath, let him know that he must make restitution by a ninefold payment to those in whose presence the judge ordered him to give his oath.

4. But if they (those appointed to hear the oath) fail to come to the place on the appointed day, and, if they shall not have been detained by any illness or public duty, let them pay a fine of six solidi. But if they were detained by any illness or duty, let them make this known to the judge or send other persons in their place whom they can trust to receive the oath for them.

5. If moreover he who is about to take the oath does not come to the place, let the other party wait until the sixth hour of the day; but if he has not come by the sixth hour, let the case be dismissed without delay.

6. But if the other (the accusing party) does not come, let him who was about to take the oath depart without loss.

Let Burgundians and Romans Be Held Under the Same Conditions in the Matter of Killing Slaves

1. If anyone kills a slave, barbarian by birth, a trained (select) house servant or messenger, let him compound sixty solidi; moreover, let the amount of the fine be twelve solidi. If anyone kills another's slave, Roman or barbarian, either ploughman or swine-herd, let him pay thirty solidi.

2. Whoever kills a skilled goldsmith, let him pay two hundred solidi.

3. Whoever kills a silversmith, let him pay one hundred solidi.

4. Whoever kills a blacksmith, let him pay fifty solidi.

5. Whoever kills a carpenter, let him pay forty solidi.

Of the Stealing of Girls

1. If anyone shall steal a girl, let him be compelled to pay the price set for such a girl ninefold, and let him pay a fine to the amount of twelve solidi.

2. If a girl who has been seized returns uncorrupted to her parents, let the abductor compound six times the wergeld of the girl; moreover, let the fine be set at twelve solidi.

3. But if the abductor does not have the means to make the above-mentioned payment, let him be given over to the parents of the girl that they may have the power of doing to him whatever they choose.

4. If indeed, the girl seeks the man of her own will and comes to his house, and he has intercourse with her, let him pay her marriage price threefold; if moreover, she returns uncorrupted to her home, let her return with all blame removed from him.

5. If indeed a Roman girl, without the consent or knowledge of her parents, unites in marriage with a Burgundian, let her know she will have none of the property of her parents.

Of Succession

1. Among Burgundians we wish it to be observed that if anyone does not leave a son, let a daughter succeed to the inheritance of the father and mother in place of the son.

2. If by chance the dead leave neither a son or daughter, let the inheritance go to the sisters or nearest relatives.

3. It is pleasing that it be contained in the present law that if a woman having a husband dies without children, the husband of the dead wife may not demand back the marriage price which had been given for her.

4. Likewise, let neither the woman nor the relatives of the woman seek back that which a woman pays when she comes to her husband if the husband dies without children.

5. Concerning those women who are vowed to God and remain in chastity, we order that if they have two brothers they receive a third portion of the inheritance of the father, that is, of that land which the father, possessing by the right of sors (allotment), left at the time of his death. Likewise, if she has four or five brothers, let her receive the portion due to her.

6. If moreover she has but one brother, let not a half, but a third part go to her on the condition that, after the death of her who is a woman and a nun, whatever she possesses in usufruct from her father's property shall go to the nearest relatives, and she will have no power of transferring anything therefrom, unless perhaps from her mother's goods, that is, from her clothing or things of the cell, or what she has acquired by her own labor.

7. We decree that this should be observed only by those whose fathers have not given them portions; but if they shall have received from their father a place where they can live, let them have full freedom of disposing of it at their will.

Of Those Things Which Happen by Chance

1. If any animal by chance, or if any dog by bite, causes death to a man, we order that among Burgundians the ancient rule of blame be removed henceforth: because what happens by chance ought not to conduce to the loss or discomfiture of man. So that if among animals, a horse kills a horse unexpectedly, or an ox gores an ox, or a dog gnaws a dog, so that it is crippled, let the owner hand over the animal or dog through which the loss is seen to have been committed to him who suffers the loss.

2. In truth, if a lance or any kind of weapon shall have been thrown upon the ground or set there without intent to do harm, and if by accident a man or animal impales himself thereupon, we order that he to whom the weapon belongs shall pay nothing unless by chance he held the weapon in his own hands in such a manner that it could cause harm to a man.

Of Burgundian Women Entering a Second or Third Marriage

1. If any Burgundian woman, as is the custom, enters a second or third marriage after the death of her husband, and she has children by each husband, let her possess the marriage gift in usufruct while she lives; after her death, let what his father gave her be given to each son, with the further provision that the mother has the power neither of giving, selling, or transferring any of the things which she received in the marriage gift.

2. If by chance the woman has no children, after her death let her relatives receive half of whatever has come to her by way of marriage gift, and let the relatives of the dead husband who was the donor receive half.

3. But if perchance children shall have been born and they shall have died after the death of their father, we command that the inheritance of the husband or children belong wholly to the mother. Moreover, after the death of the mother, we decree that what she holds in usufruct by inheritance from her children shall belong to the legal heirs of her children. Also we command that she protect the property of her children dying intestate.

4. If any son has given his mother something by will or by gift, let the mother have the power of doing whatever she wishes therewith; if she dies intestate, let the relatives of the

woman claim the inheritance as their possession.

5. If any Burgundian has sons (children?) to whom he has given their portions, let him have the power of giving or selling that which he has reserved for himself to whomever he wishes.

Of Injuries Which Are Suffered by Women

1. If any native freewoman has her hair cut off and is humiliated without cause (when innocent) by any native freeman in her home or on the road, and this can be proved with witnesses, let the doer of the deed pay her twelve solidi, and let the amount of the fine be twelve solidi.

2. If this was done to a freedwoman, let him pay her six solidi.

3. If this was done to a maidservant, let him pay her three solidi, and let the amount of the fine be three solidi.

4. If this injury (shame, disgrace) is inflicted by a slave on a native freewoman, let him receive two hundred blows; if a freedwoman, let him receive a hundred blows; if a maidservant, let him receive seventy-five blows.

5. If indeed the woman whose injury we have ordered to be punished in this manner commits fornication voluntarily (i.e., if she yields), let nothing be sought for the injury suffered.

Of Divorces

1. If any woman leaves (puts aside) her husband to whom she is legally married, let her be smothered in mire.

2. If anyone wishes to put away his wife without cause, let him give her another payment such as he gave for her marriage price, and let the amount of the fine be twelve solidi.

3. If by chance a man wishes to put away his wife, and is able to prove one of these three crimes against her, that is, adultery, witchcraft, or violation of graves, let him have full right to put her away: and let the judge pronounce the sentence of the law against her, just as should be done against criminals.

4. But if she admits none of these three crimes, let no man be permitted to put away his wife for any other crime. But if he chooses, he may go away from the home, leaving all household property behind, and his wife with their children may possess the property of her husband.

Of the Punishment of Slaves Who Commit a Criminal Assault on Freeborn Women

1. If any slave does violence to a native freewoman, and if she complains and is clearly able to prove this, let the slave be killed for the crime committed.

2. If indeed a native free girl unites voluntarily with a slave, we order both to be killed.

3. But if the relatives of the girl do not wish to punish their own relative, let the girl be deprived of her free status and delivered into servitude to the king.

Of Incestuous Adultery

If anyone has been taken in adultery with his relative or with his wife's sister, let him be compelled to pay her wergeld, according to her status, to him who is the nearest relative of the woman with whom he committed adultery; and let the amount of the fine be twelve solidi. Further, we order the adulteress to be placed in servitude to the king.

Of the Inheritance of Those Who Die Without Children

1. Although we have ordered many things in former laws concerning the inheritance of those who die without children, nevertheless after considering the matter thoroughly, we

perceive it to be just that some of those things which were ordered before should be corrected. Therefore we decree in the present constitution that if a woman whose husband has died without children has not taken her vows a second time, let her possess securely a third of all the property of her husband to the day of her death; with the further provision that after her death, all will revert to the legitimate heirs of her husband.

2. Let that remain in effect which has been stated previously concerning the mourning gift. For if she wishes to marry within a year from the time of the death of her first husband, let her have full right to do so, but let her give up that third part of the property which she had been permitted to possess. However, if she wishes to take a husband after a year or two have passed, let her give up all as has been stated above which she received from her first husband, and let the heirs in whose portion the inheritance of her former husband belongs receive the price which must be paid for her (second) marriage.

Study Questions

1. How free is Gundobad to make laws? What limits are there upon his authority as king?

2. How does the code distinguish between classes of peoples? Does social status matter?

3. What principles underlie the Burgundian view of crime and punishment? How do the Burgundians ppunish criminals, and how do they determine guilt?

4. The code says a great deal about women and family matters. What is the status of women in Burgundian society?

5. You have read several excerpts from legal codes in earlier parts of this book. What are the sorts of things that seem common to these codes in general? Can you think of ways in which *The Burgundian Code* is quite different?

The Life of Charlemagne (ca. 829-836)   **44**

EINHARD

Einhard (ca. 770–840) was a prominent scholar and historian of the reign of Charlemagne. Little has been preserved concerning Einhard's youth, although it is supposed that he was born in Germany near the monastery of Fulda where he was educated. While at Fulda, he developed a reputation as a brilliant scholar, and he soon entered Charlemagne's court in the city of Aachen, which was renowned for its intellectual sophistication—despite the fact that the emperor himself was illiterate—and where many promising young scholars came to serve. Einhard took a position as a teacher in the school that trained the children of the nobility. Einhard grew to become one of the emperor's most trusted advisors.

The Life of Charlemagne was written during Einhard's retirement, between 829 and 836. It was produced as a token of gratitude to the emperor as well as to teach Charlemagne's children about the achievements of their father. Though it is based on classical models, *The Life* was the first medieval biography of a layman. It became one of the most frequently copied works of the Middle Ages.

Private Life and Character of Charlemagne

I have shown, then, how Charles protected and expanded his kingdom and also what splendour he gave to it. I shall now go on to speak of his mental endowments, of his steadiness of purpose under whatever circumstances of prosperity or adversity, and of all that concerns his private and domestic life.

In educating his children he determined to train them, both sons and daughters, in those liberal studies to which he himself paid great attention. Further, he made his sons, as soon as their age permitted it, learn to ride like true Franks, and practise the use of arms and hunting. He ordered his daughters to learn wool work and devote attention to the spindle and distaff, for the avoidance of idleness and lethargy, and to be trained to the adoption of high principles.

He bore the deaths of his two sons and of his daughters with less patience than might have been expected from his usual stoutness of heart, for his domestic affection, a quality for which he was as remarkable as for courage, forced him to shed tears. Moreover, when the death of Hadrian, the Roman Pontiff, whom he reckoned as the chief of his friends, was announced to him, he wept for him as though he had lost a brother or a very dear son. For he showed a very fine disposition in his friendships: he embraced them readily and maintained them faithfully, and he treated with the utmost respect all whom he had admitted into the circle of his friends.

He had such care of the upbringing of his sons and daughters that he never dined without them when he was at home, and never travelled without them. His sons rode along with him, and his daughters followed in the rear. Some of his guards, chosen for this very purpose, watched the end of the line of march where his daughters travelled. They were very beautiful, and much beloved by their father, and, therefore, it is strange that he would give them in marriage to no one, either among his own people or of a foreign state. But up to his death he kept them all at home, saying that he could not forego their society. And hence the good fortune that followed him in all other respects was here broken by the touch of scandal and failure. He shut his eyes, however, to everything, and acted as though no suspicion of anything amiss had reached him, or as if the rumour of it had been discredited.

He had a great love for foreigners, and took such pains to entertain them that their numbers were justly reckoned to be a burden not only to the palace but to the kingdom at large. But, with his usual loftiness of spirit, he took little note of such charges, for he found in the reputation of generosity and in the good fame that followed such actions a compensation even for grave inconveniences.

He paid the greatest attention to the liberal arts, and showed the greatest respect and bestowed high honours upon those who taught them. For his lessons in grammar he listened to the instruction of Deacon Peter of Pisa, an old man; but for all other subjects Albinus, called Alcuin, also a deacon, was his teacher—a man from Britain, of the Saxon race, and the most learned man of his time. Charles spent much time and labour in learning rhetoric and dialectic, and especially astronomy, from Alcuin. He learnt, too, the art of reckoning, and with close application scrutinised most carefully the course of the stars. He tried also to learn to write, and for this purpose used to carry with him and keep under the pillow of his couch tablets and writing-sheets that he might in his spare moments accustom himself to the formation of letters. But he made little advance in this strange task, which was begun too late in life.

He paid the most devout and pious regard to the Christian religion, in which he had been brought up from infancy. And, therefore, he built the great and most beautiful church at Aix, and decorated it with gold and silver and candelabras and with wicket-gates and doors of solid brass. And, since he could not procure marble columns elsewhere for the building of it, he had them brought from Rome and Ravenna. As long as his health permitted it he used diligently to attend the church both in the morning and evening, and during the night, and at the time of the Sacrifice. He took the greatest care to have all the services of the church performed with the utmost dignity, and constantly warned the keepers of the building not to allow anything improper or dirty either to be brought into or to remain in the building. He provided so great a quantity of gold and silver vessels, and so large a supply of priestly vestments, that at the relgious services not even the doorkeepers, who form the lowest ecclesiastical order, had to officiate in their ordinary dress. He carefully reformed the manner of reading and singing; for he was thoroughly instructed in both, though he never read publicly himself, nor sang except in a low voice, and with the rest of the congregation.

He was most devout in relieving the poor and in those free gifts which the Greeks call alms. For he gave it his attention not only in his own country and in his own kingdom, but he also used to send money across the sea to Syria, to Egypt, to Africa—to Jerusalem, Alexandria, and Carthage—in compassion for the poverty of any Christians whose miserable condition in those countries came to his ears. It was for this reason chiefly that he cultivated the friendship of kings beyond the sea, hoping thereby to win for the Christians living beneath their sway some succour and relief.

Beyond all other sacred and venerable places, he loved the church of the holy Apostle Peter at Rome, and he poured into its treasury great wealth in silver and gold and precious stones. He sent innumerable gifts to the Pope; and during the whole course of his reign he strove with all his might (and, indeed, no object was nearer to his heart than this) to restore to the city of Rome her ancient authority, and not merely to defend the church of Saint Peter but to decorate and enrich it out of his resources above all other churches. But although he valued Rome so much, still during all the forty-seven years that he reigned, he only went there four times to pay his vows and offer up his prayers.

When he had taken the imperial tide he noticed many defects in the legal systems of his people; for the Franks have two legal systems, differing in many points very widely from one another, and he, therefore, determined to add what was lacking, to reconcile the differences, and to amend anything that was wrong or wrongly expressed. He completed nothing of all his designs beyond adding a few capitularies, and those unfinished. But he gave orders that the laws and rules of all nations comprised within his dominions which were not already written out should be collected and committed to writing.

He also wrote out the barbarous and ancient songs, in which the acts of the kings and their wars were sung, and committed them to memory. He also began a grammar of his native language.

Study Questions

1. What does Einhard's biography tell us about the education and upbringing of royal children? How does Charlemagne treat his children, and is he, by the standards of the time, a successful father?

2. Although Charlemagne was never literate, Einhard still counted him a learned man. How did the emperor qualify for this distinction?

3. In what ways was Charlemagne a model king?

4. Einhard based his work on the biographies of ancient rulers, such as Suetonius' *Life of Augustus.* Can you detect any similarities with such classical biographies?

5. What would you say is the message that Einhard is trying to put across with his work? How does he do it?

Feudal Documents (11th–12th century)   45

The feudal system, the name usually given to medieval social organization, developed as a result of the need for security in a violent and disorderly world. Based upon deeply felt concepts of obligation and justice, the heart of the system lay in the relationship between lord and vassal, as well as in an implicit belief in the active presence of God in everyday life.

A letter from the Bishop of Chartres, written in 1020, offers a brief account of the mutual duties of lords and vassals to serve and protect one another. Both lord and vassal benefited from the system. As the charter of homage between the monastery of Saint Mary of Grasse and Bernard Atton (1110) illustrates, promises of service were rewarded with a *fief*—that is, lands the vassal could use to support himself and his family.

The contract between lord and vassal was a sacred one and was enforced by appeals to God. The importance of God to all human endeavors, especially in the creation of feudal bonds and in the execution of justice, was never questioned. This belief in divine intervention in everyday life justified the use of the ordeal in criminal trials. During the ordeal, called the Judgment of God, authorities relied upon heavenly signs to determine guilt or innocence. Reprinted here is a tract written in either the eleventh or the twelfth century that describes the procedure to be followed in the ordeal of boiling water.

Duties of Vassals and Lords

To William most glorious duke of the Aquitanians, bishop Fulbert the favor of his prayers.

Asked to write something concerning the form of fealty, I have noted briefly for you on the authority of the books the things which follow. He who swears fealty to his lord ought always to have these six things in memory; what is harmless, safe, honorable, useful, easy, practicable. Harmless, that is to say that he should not be injurious to him in his secrets or in the defences through which he is able to be secure; honorable, that he should not be injurious to him in his justice or in other matters that pertain to his honor; useful that he should not be injurious to him in his possessions; easy or practicable, that that good which his lord is able to do easily, he make not difficult, nor that which is practicable he make impossible to him.

However, that the faithful vassal should avoid these injuries is proper, but not for this does he deserve his holding; for it is not sufficient to abstain from evil, unless what is good is done also. It remains, therefore, that in the same six things mentioned above he should faithfully counsel and aid his lord, if he wishes to be looked upon as worthy of his benefice and to be safe concerning the fealty which he has sworn.

The lord also ought to act toward his faithful vassal reciprocally in all these things. And if he does not do this he will be justly considered guilty of bad faith, just as the former, if he should be detected in the avoidance of or the doing of or the consenting to them, would be perfidious and perjured.

I would have written to you at greater length, if I had not been occupied with many other things, including the rebuilding of our city and church which was lately entirely consumed in a great fire; from which loss though we could not for a while be diverted, yet by the hope of the comfort of God and of you we breathe again.

Charter of Homage and Fealty, A.D. 1110

In the name of the Lord, I, Bernard Atton, Viscount of Carcassonne, in the presence of my sons, Roger and Trencavel, and of Peter Roger of Barbazan, and William Hugo, and Raymond Mantellini, and Peter de Vietry, nobles, and of many other honorable men, who have come to the monastery of St. Mary of Grasse, to the honor of the festival of the august St. Mary: since lord Leo, abbot of the said monastery, has asked me, in the presence of all those above mentioned, to acknowledge to him the fealty and homage for the castles, manors, and places which the patrons, my ancestors, held from him and his predecessors and from the said monastery as a fief, and which I ought to hold as they held, I have made to the lord abbot Leo acknowledgment and homage as I ought to do.

Therefore, let all present and to come know that I the said Bernard Atton, lord and viscount of Carcassonne, acknowledge verily to thee my lord Leo, by the grace of God, abbot of St. Mary of Grasse, and to thy successors that I hold and ought to hold as a fief in Carcassonne the following: that is to say, the castles of Confoles, of Leocque, of Capendes (which is otherwise known as St. Martin of Sussagues); and the manors of Mairac, of Albars and of Musso; also, in the valley of Aquitaine, Rieux, Traverina, Hérault, Archas, Servians, Villatritoes, Tansiraus, Presler, Cornelles. Moreover, I acknowledge that I hold from thee and from the said monastery as a fief the castle of Termes in Narbonne; and in Minerve the castle of Ventaion, and the manors of Cassanolles, and of Ferral and Aiohars; and in Le Rogés, the little village of Longville; for each and all of which I make homage and fealty with hands and with mouth to thee my said lord abbot Leo and to thy successors, and I swear upon these four gospels of God that I will always be a faithful vassal to thee and to thy successors and to St. Mary of Grasse in all things in which a vassal is required to be faithful to his lord, and I will defend thee, my lord, and all thy successors, and the said monastery and the monks present and to come and the castles and manors and all your men and their possessions against all malefactors and invaders, at my request and that of my successors at my own cost; and I will give to thee power over all the castles and manors above described, in peace and in war, whenever they shall be claimed by thee or by thy successors.

Moreover I acknowledge that, as a recognition of the above fiefs, I and my successors ought to come to the said monastery, at our own expense, as often as a new abbot shall have been made, and there do homage and return to him the power over all the fiefs described above. And when the abbot shall mount his horse I and my heirs, viscounts of Carcassonne, and our successors ought to hold the stirrup for the honor of the dominion of St. Mary of Grasse; and to him and all who come with him, to as many as two hundred beasts, we should make the abbot's purveyance in the borough of St. Michael of Carcassonne, the first time he enters Carcassonne, with the best fish and meat and with eggs and cheese, honorably according to his will, and pay the expense of shoeing of the horses, and for straw and fodder as the season shall require.

And if I or my sons or their successors do not observe to thee or to thy successors each and all the things declared above, and should come against these things, we wish that all the aforesaid fiefs should by that very fact be handed over to thee and to the said monastery of St. Mary of Grasse and to thy successors.

I, therefore, the aforesaid lord Leo, by the grace of God abbot of St. Mary of Grasse, receive the homage and fealty for all the fiefs of castles and manors and places which are described above: in the way and with the agreements and understandings written above; and likewise I concede to thee and thy heirs and their successors, the viscounts of Carcassonne, all the castles and manors and places aforesaid, as a fief, along with this present charter, divided through the alphabet. And I promise to thee and thy heirs and successors, viscounts of Carcassonne, under the religion of my order, that I will be good and faithful lord concerning all those things described above.

Moreover, I, the aforesaid viscount, acknowledge that the little villages of Cannetis,

Maironis, Villamagna, Aiglino, Villadasas, Villafrancos, Villadenz, Villaudriz, St. Genese, Conguste and Mata, with the farm-house of Mathus and the chateaux of Villalauro and Claromont, with the little villages of St. Stephen of Surlac, and of Upper and Lower Agrifolio, ought to belong to the said monastery, and whoever holds anything there holds from the same monastery, as we have seen and have heard read in the privileges and charters of the monastery, and as was there written.

Made in the year of the Incarnation of the Lord 1110, in the reign of Louis. Seal of Bernard Atton, viscount of Carcassonne, seal of Raymond Mantellini, seal of Peter Roger of Barbazon, seal of Roger, son of the said viscount of Carcassonne, seal of Peter de Vitry, seal of Trencavel, son of the said viscount of Carcassonne, seal of William Hugo, seal of lord abbot Leo, who has accepted this acknowledgment of the homage of the said viscount.

And I, the monk John, have written this charter at the command of the said lord Bernard Atton, viscount of Carcassonne and of his sons, on the day and year given above, in the presence and witness of all those named above.

Formula for Conducting the Ordeal of Boiling Water

Let the priest go to the church with the prosecutors and with him who is about to be tried. And while the rest wait in the vestibule of the church let the priest enter and put on the sacred garments except the chasuble and, taking the Gospel and the chrismarium and the relics of the saints and the chalice, let him go to the altar and speak thus to all the people standing near: Behold, brethren, the offices of the Christian religion. Behold the law in which is hope and remission of sins, the holy oil of the chrisma, the consecration of the body and blood of our Lord. Look that ye be not deprived of the heritage of such great blessing and of participation in it by implicating yourselves in the crime of another, for it is written, not only are they worthy of death who do these things, but they that have pleasure in them that do them.

Then let him thus address the one who is to undertake the ordeal: I command thee, N., in the presence of all, by the Father, the Son, and the Holy Ghost, by the tremendous day of judgment, by the ministry of baptism, by thy veneration for the saints, that, if thou art guilty of this matter charged against thee, if thou hast done it, or consented to it, or hast knowingly seen the perpetrators of this crime, thou enter not into the church nor mingle in the company of Christians unless thou wilt confess and admit thy guilt before thou are examined in public judgment.

Then he shall designate a spot in the vestibule where the fire is to be made for the water, and shall first sprinkle the place with holy water, and shall also sprinkle the kettle when it is ready to be hung and the water in it, to guard against the illusions of the devil. Then, entering the church with the others, he shall celebrate the ordeal mass. After the celebration let the priest go with the people to the place of the ordeal, the Gospel in his left hand, the cross, censer and relics of the saints being carried ahead, and let him chant seven penitential psalms with a litany.

Prayer over the boiling water: O God, just judge, firm and patient, who art the Author of peace, and judgest truly, determine what is right, O Lord, and make known Thy righteous judgment. O Omnipotent God, Thou that lookest upon the earth and makest it to tremble, Thou that by the gift of Thy Son, our Lord Jesus Christ, didst save the world and by His most holy passion didst redeem the human race, sanctify, O Lord, this water being heated by fire. Thou that didst save the three youths, Sidrac, Misac, and Abednago, cast into the fiery furnace at the command of Nebuchadnezzar, and didst lead them forth unharmed by the hand of Thy angle, do Thou O clement and most holy Ruler, give aid if he shall plunge his hand into the boiling water, being innocent, and, as Thou didst liberate the three youths from the fiery furnace and didst free Susanna from the false charge, so, O Lord, bring forth his hand safe and unharmed from this water. But if he be guilty and presume to plunge in his hand, the devil hardening his heart, let Thy holy justice deign to declare it, that Thy virtue may be manifest in his body and his soul be saved by penitence and confession. And if the guilty man shall try to hide his sins by the use of herbs or any magic, let Thy right hand deign to bring it to no account. Through Thy only begotten Son, our Lord Jesus Christ, who dwelleth with Thee.

Benediction of the water: I bless thee, O creature of water, boiling above the fire, in the name of the Father, and of the Son, and of the Holy Ghost, from whom all things proceed; I adjure thee by Him who ordered thee to water the whole earth from the four rivers, and who summoned thee forth from the rock, and who changed thee into wine, that no wiles of the devil or magic of men be able to separate thee from thy virtues as a medium of judgment; but mayest thou punish the vile and the wicked, and purify the innocent. Through Him whom hidden things do not escape and who sent thee in the flood over the whole earth to destroy the wicked and who will yet come to judge the quick and the dead and the world by fire. Amen.

Prayer: Omnipotent, Eternal God, we humbly beseech Thee in behalf of this investigation which we are about to undertake here amongst us that iniquity may not overcome justice but that falsehood may be subjected to truth. And if any one seek to hinder or obscure this examination by any magic or by herbs of the earth, deign to ring it to naught by Thy right hand, O upright Judge.

Then let the man who is to be tried, as well as the kettle or pot in which is the boiling water, be fumed with the incense of myrrh, and let this prayer be spoken: O God, Thou who within this substance of water hast hidden Thy most solemn sacraments, be graciously present with us who invoke Thee, and upon this element made ready by much purification pour down the virtue of Thy benediction that this creature, obedient to Thy mysteries, may be endued with Thy grace to detect diabolical and human fallacies, to confute their inventions and arguments, and to overcome their multiform arts. May all the wiles of the hidden enemy be brought to naught that we may clearly perceive the truth regarding those things which we with finite senses and simple hearts are seeking from Thy judgment through invocation of Thy holy name. Let not the innocent, we beseech Thee, be unjustly condemned, or the guilty be able to delude with safety those who seek the truth from Thee, who art the true Light, who seest in the shadowy darkness, and who makest our darkness light. O Thou who perceivest hidden things and knowest what is secret, show and declare this by Thy grace and make the knowledge of the truth manifest to us who believe in Thee.

Then let the hand that is to be placed in the water be washed with soap and let it be carefully examined whether it be sound; and before it is thrust in let the priest say: I adjure thee, O vessel, by the Father, and the Son, and the Holy Ghost, and by the holy resurrection, and by the tremendous day of judgment, and by the four Evangelists, that if this man be guilty of this crime either by deed or by consent, let the water boil violently, and do thou, O vessel, turn and swing.

After this let the man who is to be tried plunge in his hand, and afterwards let it be immediately sealed up. After the ordeal let him take a drink of holy water. Up to the time of the decision regarding the ordeal it is a good thing to mix salt and holy water with all his food and drink.

Study Questions

1. Bishop Fulbert describes the ideal relationship between a lord and his vassal. What should each expect from the other?

2. What might you deduce from these documents about the position of the Church in feudal society?

3. Feudal relationships often involved some kind of symbolic gesture of submission on the part of a vassal. How does Bernard, viscount of Carcassonne, demonstrate his vassalage?

4. How do these documents demonstrate the medieval belief of the presence of God in everyday life?

5. Why do you think people relied upon the ordeal as a method of justice?

Magna Carta (1215)   46

Magna Carta (the Great Charter) was a series of concessions made by King John of England to his rebellious barons in 1215. English participation in the Third Crusade had disastrous consequences for England's internal stability. Not only had the great barons of the realm been forced to pay for the army led by King Richard I, they were also faced with the expense of ransoming him back from Germany. Failures of English policy in France and a dispute between John and the Catholic Church added to the problems of this unpopular ruler. Finally, under the leadership of the Archbishop of Canterbury, a segment of the aristocracy rebelled and asserted the nobles' traditional rights against the monarchy. These were conceded in *Magna Carta*.

Magna Carta was not a bill of rights, nor did it institute any major reforms in the relationship between kings and their subjects. Its original purpose was to bind the king to respect the privileges of the barons, especially in matters of taxation. But its significance in constitutional history was that it formally defined these rights for posterity. Over the centuries, *Magna Carta* has been seen as the bedrock for the protection of the rights of subjects against arbitrary rule by the crown.

John, by the Grace of God, King of England, Lord of Ireland, Duke of Normandy and Acquitaine, and Earl of Anjou, to his Archbishops, Bishops, Abbots, Earls, Barons, Justiciaries, Foresters, Sheriffs, Governors, Officers, and to all Bailiffs, and his faithful subjects—Greeting. Know ye, that We, in the presence of God, and for the salvation of our own soul, and of the souls of all our ancestors, and of our heirs, to the honour of God, and the exaltation of the Holy Church and amendment of our Kingdom, by this our present Charter, have confirmed, for us and our heirs forever:

1. That the English Church shall be free, and shall have her whole rights and her liberties inviolable; and we will this to be observed in such a manner, that it may appear from thence, that the freedom of elections, which was reputed most requisite to the English Church, which we granted, and by our Charter confirmed, and obtained the Confirmation of the same, from our Lord Pope Innocent the Third, before the rupture between us and our Barons, was of our own free will; which Charter we shall observe, and we will it to be observed with good faith, by our heirs forever.

We have also granted to all the freemen of our Kingdom, for us and our heirs forever, all the underwritten Liberties, to be enjoyed and held by them and by their heirs, from us and from our heirs.

2. If any of our Earls or Barons, or others who hold of us in chief by military service, shall die, and at his death his heir shall be of full age, and shall owe a relief; he shall have his inheritance by the ancient relief; that is to say, the heir or heirs of an Earl, a whole Earl's Baron, for one hundred pounds; the heir or heirs of a Baron, for a whole Barony, by one hundred pounds; the heir or heirs of a Knight, for a whole Knight's fee, by one hundred shillings at most; and he who owes less, shall give less, according to the ancient custom of fees.

3. But if the heir of any such be under age, and in wardship, when he comes to age he shall have his inheritance without relief and without fine.

4. The warden of the land of such heir who shall be under age, shall not take from the lands of the heir any but reasonable issues, and reasonable customs, and reasonable services, and that without destruction and waste of the men or goods....

The Vikings Attack England. This illustration from an eleventh-century English manuscript depicts a band of armed Vikings invading England. Two ships have already reached the shore, and a few Vikings are shown walking down a long gangplank onto English soil.

6. Heirs shall be married without disparagement, so that before the marriage be contracted it shall be notified to the relations of the heir by consanguinity.

7. A widow after the death of her husband shall immediately, and without difficulty, have her marriage and her inheritance; nor shall she give anything for her dower, or for her marriage, or for her inheritance, which her husband and she held at the day of his death; and she may remain in her husband's house forty days after his death, within which time her dower shall be assigned.

8. No widow shall be distrained to marry herself, while she is willing to live without a husband; but yet she shall give security that she will not marry herself without our consent, if she hold of us, or without the consent of the lord of whom she does hold, if she hold of another....

12. No scutage nor aid shall be imposed in our kingdom, unless by the common council of our kingdom; excepting to redeem our person, to make our eldest son a knight, and once to many our eldest daughter, and not for these, unless a reasonable aid shall be demanded.

13. In like manner let it be concerning the aids of the City of London. And the City of London shall have all its ancient liberties, and its free customs, as well by land as by water. Furthermore, we will and grant that all other Cities, Burghs, and Towns, and Ports, should have all their liberties and free customs.

14. And also to have the common council of the kingdom, to assess and aid, otherwise than in the three cases aforesaid: and for the assessing of scutages, we will cause to be summoned the Archbishops, Bishops, Abbots, Earls, and great Barons, individually by our letters. And besides, we will cause to be summoned in general by our Sheriffs and Bailiffs, all those who hold of us in chief, at a certain day, that is to say at the distance of forty days

(before their meeting), at the least, and to a certain place; and in all the letters of summons, we will express the cause of the summons; and the summons being thus made, the business shall proceed on the day appointed, according to the counsel of those who shall be present, although all who have been summoned have not come....

27. If any free-man shall die intestate, his chattels shall be distributed by the hands of his nearest relations and friends, by the view of the Church, saving to every one the debts which the defunct owed.

28. No Constable nor other Bailiff of ours shall take the corn or other goods of any one without instantly paying money for them, unless he can obtain respite from the free-will of the seller.

29. No Constable (Governor of a Castle) shall distrain any Knight to give money for castle-guard, if he be willing to perform it in his own person, or by another able man, if he cannot perform it himself, for a reasonable cause; and if we have carried or sent him into the army he shall be excused from castle-guard, according to the time that he shall be in the army by our command.

30. No Sheriff nor Bailiff of ours, nor any other person shall take the horses or carts of any free-man for the purpose of carriage, without the consent of the said free-man.

31. Neither we, nor our Bailiffs, will take another man's wood, for our castles or other uses, unless by the consent of him to whom the wood belongs....

35. There shall be one measure of wine throughout all our kingdom, and one measure of ale, and one measure of corn, namely, the quarter of London; and one breadth of dyed cloth, and of russets, and of halberjects, namely, two ells within the lists. Also it shall be the same with weights as with measures....

39. No free-man shall be seized, or imprisoned, or dispossessed, or outlawed, or in any way destroyed; nor will we condemn him, nor will we commit him to prison, excepting by the legal judgment of his peers, or by the laws of the land.

40. To none will we sell, to none will we deny, to none will we delay right or justice.

41. All Merchants shall have safety and security in coming into England, and going out of England, and in staying and in traveling through England, as well by land as by water, to buy and sell, without any unjust exactions, according to ancient and right customs, excepting in the time of war....

54. No man shall be apprehended or imprisoned on the appeal of a woman for the death of any other man than her husband....

61. But since we have granted all these things aforesaid, for God and for the amendment of our kingdom, and for the better extinguishing the discord which has arisen between us and our Barons, we being desirous that these things should possess entire and unshaken stability forever, give and grant to them the security underwritten, namely, that the Barons may elect twenty-five Barons of the kingdom, whom they please, who shall with their whole power, observe, keep, and cause to be observed, the peace and liberties which we have granted to them, and have confirmed by this, our present charter, in this manner; that is to say, if we, or our Justiciary, or our bailiffs or any of our officers, shall have injured any one in anything, or shall have violated any article of the peace or security, and the injury shall have been shown to four of the aforesaid twenty-five Barons, the said four Barons shall come to us, or to our Justiciary if we be out of the kingdom, and making known to us the excess committed, petition that we cause that excess to be redressed without delay. And if we shall not have redressed the excess, or, if we have been out of the kingdom, our Justiciary shall not have redressed it within the term of forty days, computing from the time when it shall have been made known to us, or to our Justiciary, if we have been out of the kingdom, the aforesaid four Barons shall lay that cause before the residue of the twenty-five Barons; and they, the twenty-five Barons, with the community of the whole land, shall distress and harass us by all the ways in which they are able; that is to say, by the taking of our castles, lands and possessions, and by any other means in their power, until the excess shall have been redressed, according to their verdict, saving harmless our person and the persons of our Queen and children, and when it hath been redressed they shall behave to us as they have done before....

62. And we have fully remitted and pardoned to all men all the ill-will, rancour and resentments which have arisen between us and our subjects, both clergy and laity, from the commencement of the discord.

63. Wherefore our will is, and we firmly command that the Church of England be free, and that the men in our kingdom have and hold the aforesaid liberties, rights and concessions, well in peace, freely and quietly, fully and entirely, to them and their heirs, of us and our heirs, in all things and places for ever, as is aforesaid. It is also sworn, both on our part and on that of the Barons, that all the aforesaid shall be observed in good faith and without any evil intention. Witnessed by the above and many others. Given by our hand in the Meadow which is called Runningmead, between Windsor and Staines, this 15th day of June, in the 17th year of our reign.

Study Questions

1. Who do you think the chief beneficiaries of the charter were?

2. What are the general issues that seem to concern the barons most? How has the king infringed upon the rights of the barons?

3. Some historians have said that the real importance of the charter is that it made the king subject to the laws. How does the charter do that, and why is this important?

4. There are several important clauses in *Magna Carta* that deal with the king's powers over the family lives of his nobility. What was the king's interest in these matters?

5. Do you think that the barons thought the king was trustworthy? How were the provisions of the charter to be enforced?

6. In what areas can you see *Magna Carta* as an ancestor of later views about individual freedom?

The Battle of Maldon (991 C.E.)   47

In 991, a Viking force landed on an island off the English coast, from which it planned to raid the neighboring countryside, either for *danegeld* (tribute money) from King Aethelred II or for plunder. But it was opposed by Earl Bryhtnoth, the king's local commander, who blocked the way with a shield wall of the local Saxon *fyrd* (militia). In order to cross to the mainland and give battle, the Vikings taunted their English opponents until Bryhtroth offered to fight them. In the ensuing fray, a Viking arrow killed Bryhtnoth and most of the Saxons fled.

The story of the battle of Maldon became one of the great epic poems of Anglo-Saxon England, and although only a fragment of the complete poem has survived, it is more than enough to let us see why contemporaries ranked it with *Beowulf*. Not only does the fragment convey a stirring tale, but the anonymous poet has captured the values of the Germanic tribes like the Saxons that had overrun the Roman Empire in the West. These values would survive for centuries and become the basis for feudalism.

The Battle of Maldon

... would be broken.

Then he bade each man let go bridles
drive far the horses and fare forward,
fit thought to hand-work and heart to
    fighting.

Whereat one of Offa's kin, knowing the Earl
would not suffer slack-heartedness,
loosed from his wrist his loved hawk;
over the wood it stooped, he stepped to
    battle.
By that a man might know this young man's
    will
to weaken not at the war-play: he had taken
    up weapons.

Eadric also would serve the Earl,
his lord, in the fight. He went forth
with spear to battle, his spirit failed not
while he with hand might yet hold
board and broadsword: he made good his boast
to stand fast in fight before his lord.

Then Bryhtnoth dressed his band of warriors,
from horseback taught each man his task,
where he should stand, how keep his station.
He bade them brace their linden-boards aright,
fast in finger-grip, and to fear not.
Then when his folk was fairly ranked
Bryhtnoth alighted where be loved best to be
and was held most at heart—among hearth-
    companions.

Then stood on strand and called out sternly
a Viking spokesman. He made speech—
threat in his throat, threw across the seamen's
errand to the Earl where he stood on our shore.

    'The swift-striking seafarers send me to
        thee,
    bid me say that thou send for thy safety
    rings, bracelets. Better for you
    that you stay straightaway our onslaught
        with tribute
    than that we should share bitter strife.
    We need not meet if you can meet our
        needs:
    or a gold tribute a truce is struck.

    Art captain here: if thou tak'st this course,
    art willing to pay thy people's ransom,
    wilt render to Vikings what they think
        right,
    buying our peace at our price,
    we shall with that tribute turn back to ship,
    fare out on the flood, and hold you as
        friends,

Bryhtnoth spoke. He raised shield-board,
shook the slim ash-spear, shaped his words.
Stiff with anger, he gave him answer:

'Hearest 'our, seaman, what this folk sayeth?
Spears shall be all the tribute they send you,
viper-stained spears and the swords of
    forebears,
such a haul of harness as shall hardly profit
    you.

Spokesman for scavengers, go speak this
    back again,
bear your tribe a bitterer tale:
that there stands here 'mid his men not the
    meanest of Earls,
pledged to fight in this land's defence,
the land of Aethelred, my liege lord,
its soil, its folk. In this fight the heathen
shall fall. It would be a shame for your
    trouble
if you should with our silver away to ship
without fight offered. It is a far step hither:
you have come a long way into our land.

But English silver is not so softly won:
first iron & edge shall make arbitrement,
harsh war-trial, ere we yield tribute.

He bade his brave ,men bear their shields
    forward
until they all stood at the streams edge,
though they might not clash yet for the
    cleaving waters.
After the ebb the flood came flowing in;
the sea's arms locked. Overlong it seemed
before they might bear spear-shafts in shock
    together.

So they stood by Panta's stream in proud array,
the ranks of the East Saxons and the host from
    the ash-ships,
nor might any of them harm another
save who through arrow-flight fell dead.

The flood went out. Eager the fleet-men stood,
the crowding raiders, ravening for battle;
then the heroes' Helm bade hold the causeway
a war-hard warrior—Wulfstan was his name—

come of brave kin. It was this Ceola's son
who with his Frankish spear struck down the
   first man there
as he so boldly stepped onto tile bridge's
   stonework.

There stood with Wulfstan staunch warriors,
Aelfhere & Maccus, men of spirit
who would not take flight from the ford's
   neck
but fast defence make against the foemen
the while that may wield their weapons.
When the hated strangers saw and understood
what bitter bridge-warders were brought
   against them there,
they began to plead with craft, craving leave
to fare over tile ford and lead across their
   footmen.

Then the Earl was overswayed by his heart's
   arrogance
to allow overmuch land to that loath nation:
the men stood silent as Brighthelm's son
called out over the cold water.

   'The ground is cleared for you: come
      quickly to us,
   gather to battle. God one knows
   who shall carry the wielding of this waste
      grounds'

The war-wolves waded across, mourned not
   for the water,
the Viking warrior-band; came West over
   Pant,
bearing shield-boards over sheer water
and up onto land, lindenwood braced.

Against their wrath there stood in readiness
Bryhtnoth amid his band. He bade them work
the war-hedge with their targes, and the troop
   to stand
fast against foe. Then neared the fight,
the glory-trial. The time grew on
when there the fated men must fall;

the war-cry was raised up. Ravens wound
   higher.
the eagle, carrion-eager; on earth—the cry!

Out flashed file-hard point from fist,
sharp-ground spears sprang forth,
bows were busy, bucklers flinched,
it was a bitter battle-clash. On both halves
brave men fell, boys lay still.

It was then that Wulfmaer was wounded,
   war-rest chose,
'Bryhtnoth's kinsman; he was beaten down,
his sister's son, under the swords' flailing.
But straight wreaking requital on the Vikings,
Edward (as I heard) so struck one man
—the sword-arm stiff, not stinting the blow—
that the fated warrior fell at his feet:
deed for which Bryhtnoth, when a breathing
   space came,
spoke his thanks to his bower-thane.

So they stood fast, these stout-hearted
warriors at the war-play, watching fiercely
who there with spear might first dispatch
a doomed man's life. The dying fell to earth;
others stood steadfast. Bryhtnoth stirred
   them,
bade every man there turn mood to deeds
who would that day's doom wrest from out
   the Danish ranks.

Bryhtnoth war-hard braced shield-board,
shook out his sword, strode firmly
toward his enemy, earl to churl,
in either's heart harm to the other.

The sea-man sped his southern spear
so that it wounded the warriors' lord
who with his shield checked, so that the shaft
   burst,
shivered the spear-head; it sprang away.
Stung then to anger he stabbed with ash-point
the proud sea-warrior that wrought him his
   wound,

old in war-skills let die weapon drive
through the man's throat, his thrust steered
so as to reach right to the reaver's life-breath.
And afresh he struck him, stabbed so swiftly
that the ring-braid burst apart; breast pierced
through the locked hauberk, in his heart
    stood
the embittered ash-point. The Earl was the
    blither,
his brave mood laughed, loud thanks he made
for the day's work the Lord had dealt him.

Flashed a dart from Danish hand,
fist-driven, and flew too truly,
bit the Earl, Aethelred's thane.
There stood at his side a stripling warrior,
young Wulfmaer, Wulfstan's son,
fresh to the field. In a flash he
plucked from its place the blood-black point,
flung back the filed spear; again it flew.
Home sank the steel, stretched on the plain
him who so late had pierced the Prince so
    grievously.

A mailed man then moved toward the Earl
thinking to strip him of his steel harness,
war-dress, armbands and ornate sword.
Bryhtnoth broke out brand from sheath,
broad, bright-bladed, and on the breastplate
    struck;
but one of the spoilers cut short the blow,
his swing unstringing the Earl's sword-arm.

He yielded to the ground the yeflow-hilted
    sword,
strengthless to hold the hard blade longer up
or wield weapon. One word more,
the hoar-headed warrior, heartening his men:
he bade them go forward, good companions.
Fast on his feet he might not further stand;
he looked to heaven....

'I give Thee thanks, Lord God of hosts,
    for I have known in this world a wealth of
        gladness,

but now, mild Maker, I have most need
    that Thou grant my ghost grace for this
        journey so that my soul may unscathed
            cross
    into Thy keeping, King of angels,
    pass through in peace: my prayer is this,
    that the hates of hell may not harm her.'

Then they hewed him, down, the heathen
    churls,
and with him those warriors, Wulfmaer and
    Aelfnoth,
who had stood at his side: stretched on the
    field,
the two followers fellowed in death.

Then did the lack-willed leave the battlefield;
Odda's kin came first away:
Godric turned, betrayed the lord
who had made him a gift of many good
    horses.
He leapt onto the harness that had been
    Bryhtnoth's,
unrightfully rode in his place,
and with him his brothers both ran,
Godwine and Godwiy, who had no gust for
    fighting;
they wheeled from the war to the wood's
    fastness,
sought shelter and saved their lives;
and more went with them than were it all
    meet
had they called to mind the many heart-claims
Bryhtnoth had wrought them, worthying
    them.

This Offa had told him on an earlier day
at the council-place when he had called a
    meeting,
that many gathered there who were making
    brave speeches
would not hold in the hour of need.
And now the folk's father had fallen lifeless,
Aethelred's Earl. All the hearthsharers
might see their lord lying dead.

Proudly the thanes pressed forward,
uncowed the warriors crowded eager
for one of two things: each man wanted
either to requite that death or to quit life.
Aelfric's son sped them on,
a warrior young in winters; his words rang
keen in the air. Aelfwine called out:

> 'Remember the speeches spoken over mead,
> battle-vows on the bench, the boasts we
>   vaunted,
> heroes in hall, against the harsh war-trial!
> *Now* shall be proven the prowess of the man.
>
> I would that you all hear my high
>   descendance:
> know that in Mercia I am of mighty kin,
> that my grandfather was the great Ealhelm,
> wise Earl, world-blessed man.
> Shall the princes of that people reproach
>   Aelfwine
> that he broke from the banded bulwark of
>   the Angles
> to seek his own land, with his lord lying
> felled on the field? Fiercest of griefs!
> Beside that he was my lord he was allied to
>   me in blood.

Then he advanced on the Vikings intent on
    vengeance.
Straight his spearpoint sprang at a man
among the press of pirates, pitched him to the
    ground,
killed outright. Then he called to his compan-
    ions
friends and fellow-thanes to come forth to
    battle.

Offa spoke, shook his ash-spear:

> 'In right good time dost thou recall us to
> our allegiance, Aelfwine. Now that the Earl
>   who led us
> lies on the earth, we all need
> each and every thane to urge forth the other

warriors to the war while weapon lives
quick in a hand, hardened blade,
spear or good sword. Godric the coward,
the coward son of Odda, has undone us all:
too many in our ranks, when he rode away
on Bryhtnoth's big horse, believed it was
    the Earl,
and we are scattered over the field. The folk
    is split,
shield-wall shattered. Shame on that defec-
    tion
that has betrayed into retreat the better half
    of the army!'

Linden-board high-lifted, Leofsunu stood;
from the shadow of his shield shouted out this
    answer:

> 'I swear that from this spot not one foot's
>   space
> of ground shall I give up. I shall go onwards,
> in the fight avenge my friend and lord.
> My deeds shall give no warrant for words of
>   blame
> to steadfast men on Stour, now he is
>   stretched lifeless,
>
> —that I left the battlefield a lordless man,
> turned for home. The irons shall take me,
> point or edge.'
>   Angrily he strode forth

and fought very fiercely; flight was beneath
him.

Dart brandished, Dunnere spoke,
bidding his brothers avenge Bryhtnoth.
The humble churl called out over all:

> 'A man cannot linger when his lord lies
> unavenged among Vikings, cannot value
>   breath.'

So the household companions, careless of life,
bore spears to battle and set to bitter fighting:
they went out into the press, praying God

that among their enemies they might so acquit
    themselves
as to redress the death of their dear lord.

The hostage lent them help willingly;
he was a Northumbrian of a hard-fighting
    clan,
the son of Edgeleave, Ashferth his name;
wavered not at the war-play, but, while he
    might,
shot steadily from his sheaf of arrows,
striking a shield there, or shearing into a man,
and every once in a while wounding wryly.

At that time Long Edward still led the attack,
breathing his readniness, rolling out boasts,
that nothing would budge him now that the
    best man lay,
nothing force him to flee one foot of ground.
He broke the board-wall, burst in among
    them,
wrought on the sea-wreckers a revenge worthy
his goldgiving lord before the ground claimed
    him.

So did the noble Aetheric, another of our
    company,
he too fought fixedly, furious to get on,
Sibyrht's brother; and so did many another,
cleaving in halves the hollow shields.
Board's border burst asunder,
corselet sang its chilling song.
How they beat off the blows!
                    At the battle's turn
Offa sent a seafarer stumbling to the ground;
but crippling strokes crashed down
and Gadd's kinsman was grounded also.

Yet Offa had made good his given word,
the oath undertaken to his open-handed lord,
that either they should both ride back to the
    burg's stockade,
come home whole, or harry the Danes
till life leaked from them and left them on the
    field.
Thane-like he lay at his lord's hand.

Then was a splintering of shields, the sea-
    wolves coming on
in war-whetted anger. Again the spears
burst breast-lock, breached life-wall
of Wierd-singled men. Wistan went forth,
that Wurstan fathered, fought with the
    warriors
where they thronged thickest. Three he slew
before the breath was out of Offa's body.

It was a stark encounter, but they stood their
    ground—
the warriors in that fight, fought till wounds
dragged them down. The dead fell.
All the while Eadwold and Oswold his brother
cried on their kinsmen, encouraging them
to stand up under the stress, strike out the
    hour,
weaving unwavering the web of steel

Then Byrhtwold spoke, shook ash-spear,
raised shield-board. In the bravest words
this hoar companion handed on the charge:

'Courage shall grow keener, clearer the will,
the heart fiercer, as our force faileth.
Here our lord lies levelled in the dust,
    the man all marred: he shall mourn to the
        end
who thinks to wend off from this war-play
    now.
Though I am white with winters I will not
    away,
for I think to lodge me alongside my dear
    one,
lay me down by my lord's right hand.'

Godric likewise gave them all heart,
Aethelgar's son, sending spears,
death-darts, driving on the Danish ranks;
likewise he forged foremost among them,
scattering blows, bowing at last.

That was not the Godric who galloped away....

Study Questions

1. Why didn't all of the Saxons attempt to save themselves once they believed they had lost the battle?

2. Why does the poet depict the final speeches of the Saxon stalwarts so lovingly?

3. Discuss the role of honor and reputation among the Saxons.

4. Would modem soldiers display such devotion for the body of a slain commander?

The Development of Christianity

A Prospect of Carcassonne. The best preserved walled medieval town in France, Carcassonne shows how important protection from enemy armies and marauders was in the Middle Ages. Most West European towns once possessed such walls but demolished them later in order to expand.

The City of God (413–426) **48**

AUGUSTINE OF HIPPO

Augustine of Hippo (354–430) was the most important Christian philosopher and theologian of late antiquity. Born in Roman North Africa, the son of a pagan father and a devoutly Christian mother, Augustine himself remained pagan until adulthood. Although his family was not rich, he was sent for schooling at Carthage, where he developed a taste and aptitude for philosophy. At the age of 32 he converted to Christianity and became a priest in 391. He recounted the story of his inner struggles in *The Confessions* (ca. 400), one of the most famous of all Christian autobiographies. In 396 Augustine was consecrated Bishop of Hippo, a position he held until his death. There he combined pastoral duties with the writing of major theological and philosophical works. His great achievement was a synthesis of classical and Christian traditions. He died when Hippo was besieged by the Vandals in 430.

The City of God (413–426) was Augustine's major work. It provides a summary of Christian thought at the moment when the Roman empire was under seige. Augustine contrasts the world of corruption and sin inhabited by humans with God's world of blissful perfection.

Of that Part of the Work Wherein the Demonstration of the Beginnings and Ends of the Two Cities, the Heavenly and the Earthly, Are Declared

We give the name of the city of God unto that society whereof that scripture bears witness, which has gained the most exalted authority and pre-eminence over all other works whatsoever, by the disposing of the divine providence, not the chance decisions of men's judgments. For there it is said: 'Glorious things are spoken of thee, thou city of God': and in another place: 'Great is the Lord, and greatly to be praised in the city of our God, even upon His holy mountain, increasing the joy of all the earth.' And by and by in the same psalm: 'As we have heard, so have we seen in the city of the Lord of Hosts, in the city of our God: God has established it for ever.' And in another:

'The rivers' streams shall make glad the city of God, the most High sanctified His tabernacle, God is in the midst of it unmoved.' These testimonies, and thousands more, teach us that there is a city of God, whereof His inspired love makes us desire to be members. The earthly citizens prefer their gods before this heavenly city's holy Founder, knowing not that He is the God of gods, not of those false, wicked, and proud ones, (which lacking His light so universal and unchangeable, and being thereby reduced to a state of extreme need, each one follows his own state, as it were, and begs divine honours of his deluded servants), but of the godly and holy ones, who select their own submission to Him, rather than the world's to them, and love rather to worship Him their God, than to be worshipped for gods themselves. And now, knowing what is next expected of me, as my promise—viz. to dispute (as far as my poor talent allows) of the origin, progress, and consummation of the two cities that in this world lie confusedly together, by the assistance of the same God and King of ours, I set pen to paper, intending first to show the beginning of these two, arising from the difference between the angelical powers.

The State of the Two Cities, the Heavenly and the Earthly

Two loves therefore have given origin to these two cities, self-love in contempt of God unto the earthly, love of God in contempt of one's self to the heavenly. The first seeks the glory of men, and the latter desires God only as the testimony of the conscience, the greatest glory. That glories in itself, and this in God. That exalts itself in self-glory: this says to God: 'My glory and the lifter up of my head.' That boasts of the ambitious conquerors led by the lust of sovereignty: in this all serve each other in charity, both the rulers in counselling and the subjects in obeying. That loves worldly virtue in the potentates: this says unto God: 'I will love thee, O Lord, my strength.' And the wise men of that follow either the good things of the body, or mind, or both: living according to the flesh; and such as might know God; 'honoured Him not as God, nor were thankful, but became vain in their own imaginations, and their foolish heart was darkened; for professing themselves to be wise, that is, extolling themselves proudly in their wisdom, they became fools; changing the glory of the incorruptible God to the likeness of the image of a corruptible man, and of birds and four-footed beasts and serpents': for they were the people's guides or followers unto all those idolatries, and served the creature more than the Creator who is blessed for ever. But in this other, this heavenly city, there is no wisdom of man, but only the piety that serves the true God and expects a reward in the society of the holy angels, and men, that God may be all in all.

Of the Two Contrary Courses Taken by the Human Race from the Beginning

Of the place and felicity of the local paradise, together with man's life and fall therein, there are many opinions, many assertions, and many books, as several men thought, spoke, and wrote. What we held hereof, or could gather out of holy scriptures, correspondent unto their truth and authority, we related in some of the foregoing books. If they be farther looked into, they will give birth to more questions and longer disputations than we have now room for. Our time is not so large as to permit us to argue scrupulously upon every question that may be asked by busy heads that are more curious of inquiry than capable of understanding. I think we have sufficiently discussed the doubts concerning the beginning of the world, the soul, and mankind; which last is divided into two sorts, such as live according to man, and such as live according to God. These we mystically call two cities or societies, the one predestined to being eternally with God, the other condemned in perpetual torment with the devil. This is their end, of which hereafter. Now seeing we have said sufficient concerning their origin, both in the angels whose number we know not, and in the two first parents of mankind. I think it fit to pass on to their progression from man's first offspring until he cease to beget anymore. All the time included between these two points, wherein the livers ever succeed the diers, is the progression of these two cities. Cain therefore was the first begotten of those two that were mankind's parents, and he belongs to the city of man; Abel was the later, and he belongs to the city of God. For as we see that in an individual man (as the apostle says) that which is spiritual is not first, but that which is natural first, and then the spiritual (whereupon all that comes from Adam's corrupted nature must needs be evil and carnal at first, and then if a man be regenerate by Christ, becomes good and spiritual afterward): so in the first propagation of man, and progression of the two cities of which we dispute, the carnal citizen was born first, and the pilgrim on earth or heavenly citizen afterwards, being by grace predestined, and by grace elected, by grace a pilgrim upon earth, and by grace a citizen in heaven. For as for his birth; it was out of the same corrupted mass that was condemned from the beginning; but God like a potter (for this simile the apostle himself uses) out of the same lump, made 'one vessel to honour and another to reproach.' The vessel of reproach was made first, and the vessel of honour afterwards. For in each individual, as I said, there is first reprobation, whence we must needs begin (and wherein we need not remain), and afterwards goodness, to which we come by profiting, and coming thither therein make our abode. Whereupon it follows that no one can be good that has not first been evil, though all that be evil become not good; but the sooner a man betters himself the quicker does this name follow him, abolishing the memory of the other. Therefore, it is recorded of Cain that he built a city, but Abel was a pilgrim, and built none. For the city of the saints is above, though it have citizens here upon earth, wherein it lives as a pilgrim until the time of the kingdom come; and then it gathers all the citizens together in the resurrection of the body, and gives them a kingdom to reign in with their King for ever and ever.

Of the Sons of the Flesh and the Sons of Promise

The shadow and prophetical image of this city (not making it present but signifying it) served here upon earth, at the time when such a foreshadowing was needed; and was called the holy city, because it was a symbol of the city that was to be, though not the reality. Of this city serving as an image, and the free city herein prefigured, the apostle speaks thus unto the Galatians: 'Tell me, ye that desire to be under the law, do ye not hear the law? For it is written that Abraham had two sons, one by a bondwoman, and the other by a free: but the son of the bondwoman was born of the flesh, and the son of the freewoman by promise. Which things are an allegory: for these are the two Testaments, the one given from Mount Sinai, begetting man in servitude, which is Hagar; for Sinai is a mountain in Arabia, joined to the Jerusalem on earth, for it serves with her children. But our mother the celestial Jerusalem is free, for it is written: "Rejoice, thou barren that bearest not: break forth into joy, and cry out, thou that travailest not with child, for the desolate hath many more children than the married wife." But we, brethren, are the sons of promise to Isaac. But as then he that was born of the flesh persecuted him that was born after the spirit, even so it is now. But what says the scripture? "Cast out the bondwoman and her son, for the bondwoman's son shall not be heir with the freewoman's." Then, brethren, we are not children of the bondwoman, but of the free.' Thus the apostle authorizes us to conceive of the Old and New Testaments. For a part of the earthly city was made an image of the heavenly, not signifying itself but another, and therefore serving: for it was not ordained to signify itself but another, and itself was signified by another precedent type; for Hagar, Sarah's servant, and her son, were an image hereof. And because, when the light comes, the shadows must flee away, Sarah the freewoman signifying the free city (which that shadow of the earthly Jerusalem signified in another manner) said: 'Cast out the bondwoman and her son: for the bondwoman's son shall not be heir with my son Isaac': whom the apostle calls the freewoman's son. Thus then we find this earthly city in two forms; the one presenting itself, and the other prefiguring the celestial city, and serving it. Our nature corrupted by sin produces citizens of earth; and grace freeing us from the sin of nature makes us citizens of heaven: the first are called the vessels of wrath, the last of mercy. And this was signified in the two sons of Abraham, the one of whom being born of the bondwoman was called Ishmael, being the son of the flesh; the other, the free-woman's, Isaac, the son of promise. Both were Abraham's sons; but natural custom begot the first, and gracious promise the latter. In the first was a demonstration of man's use, in the second was a revelation of God's goodness.

Of the Eternal Felicity of the City of God, and the Perpetual Sabbath

How great shall that felicity be, where there shall be no evil thing, where no good thing shall lie hidden, where we shall have leisure to utter forth the praises of God, which shall be all things in all! There shall be true glory, where no man shall be praised for error or flattery. True honour, which shall be denied unto none which is worthy, shall be given unto none unworthy. But neither shall any unworthy person covet after it, where none is permitted to be but he who is worthy. There is true peace, where no man suffers anything which may molest him, either from himself or from any other. He Himself shall be reward of virtue, who has given virtue, and has promised Himself unto him, than whom nothing can be better and greater. For what other thing is that which He has said by the prophet: 'I will be their God, and they shall be My people; but 'I will be whereby they shall be satisfied: I will be whatsoever is lawfully desired of men, life, health, food, abundance, glory, honour, peace, and all good things'? For so also is that rightly understood, which the apostle says: 'That God may be all in all.' He shall be the end of our desires, who shall be seen without end, who shall be loved without any disgust, and praised without any tediousness. This function, this affection, this action verily shall be unto all, as the eternal life shall be common to all. But who is sufficient to think, much less to utter, what degrees there shall also be of the rewards for merits, of the honours and glories? But we must not doubt but that there shall be degrees. And also that blessed city shall see this in itself—that no inferior shall envy his superior, even as now the other angels do not envy the archangels; as every one will not wish to be what he has not received, although he be bound in a most peaceable bond of concord with him who has received, even as the finger does not wish to be the eye in the body, since a peaceable conjunction and knitting together of the whole flesh contains both members. Therefore one shall so have a gift less than another has, that he also has this further gift that he does not wish to have any more. By Him being restored and perfected with a greater grace we shall rest for ever, seeing that He is God, with whom we shall be replenished, when He shall be all in all.

Study Questions

1. How do you think that Augustine's background as an urban Roman affected his thought?

2. What is the difference between the city of God and the earthly city?

3. How, according to Augustine, do people become "residents" of the city of God?

4. Augustine does not envisage a community of social equals in the city of God. Would this, in Augustine's view, lead to conflict? Why or why not?

5. There are several clues in *The City of God* about the nature of society in late classical cities: Augustine makes assumptions about social status, for example. Judging from his work, what might you say about the real cities that Augustine knew?

The Rule (ca. 535–540)   **49**

BENEDICT OF NURSIA

Benedict of Nursia (ca. 480–547), the patron saint of Europe, played a key role in the foundation of Christian monasteries throughout the continent. Benedict came from a prosperous Italian family and was sent to Rome for his education. He grew up during a period of social and political disorder as the Roman world was fast vanishing. Benedict was shocked by the immorality and corruption that he witnessed in Rome, and in reaction he retreated to a cave outside of the city where he lived as a hermit for three years. During this time his reputation as a holy man spread, and he was persuaded to take charge of a local monastery. His attempts to reform this institution were not altogether successful and Benedict narrowly escaped being poisoned there. He subsequently founded his own monastery at Monte Cassino, which became the model for the Benedictine order.

Benedict's *Rule* was a system of regulations for a monastic order. It is a guide to life in a religious community and enjoins the residents to prayer, hard work, obedience, and hospitality. *The Rule* became the constitution of countless monasteries and nunneries in succeeding centuries.

What are the Instruments of Good Works.—

1. First Instrument: in the first place to love the Lord God with all one's heart, all one's soul, and all one's strength.
2. Then, one's neighbour as oneself.
3. Then not to kill.
4. Not to commit adultery.
5. Not to steal.
6. Not to covet.
7. Not to bear false witness.
8. To honour all men.
9. Not to do to another what one would not have done to oneself.
10. To deny oneself, in order to follow Christ.
11. To chastise the body.
12. Not to seek after delicate living.
13. To love fasting.
14. To relieve the poor.
15. To clothe the naked.
16. To visit the sick.
17. To bury the dead.
18. To help in affliction.
19. To console the sorrowing.
20. To keep aloof from worldly actions.
21. To prefer nothing to the love of Christ.
22. Not to gratify anger.
23. Not to harbour a desire of revenge.
24. Not to foster guile in one's heart.
25. Not to make a feigned peace.
26. Not to forsake charity.
27. Not to swear, lest perchance, one forswear oneself.
28. To utter truth from heart and mouth.
29. Not to render evil for evil.
30. To do no wrong to anyone, yea, to bear, patiently wrong done to oneself

31. To love one's enemies.
32. Not to render cursing for cursing, but rather blessing.
33. To bear persecution for justice's sake.
34. Not to be proud.
35. Not given to wine,
36. Not a glutton.
37. Not drowsy.
38. Not slothful.
39. Not a murmurer.
40. Not a detractor.
41. To put one's hope in God.
42. To attribute any good that one sees in oneself to God and not to oneself.
43. But to recognize and always impute to oneself the evil that one does.
44. To fear the Day of Judgement.
45. To be in dread of hell.
46. To desire with all spiritual longing everlasting fife.
47. To keep death daily before one's eyes.
48. To keep guard at all times over the actions of one's life.
49. To know for certain that God sees one everywhere.
50. To dash down at the feet of Christ one's evil thoughts, the instant that they come into the heart.
51. And to lay them open to one's spiritual father.
52. To keep one's mouth from evil and wicked words.
53. Not to love much speaking.
54. Not to speak vain words or such as move to laughter.
55. Not to love much or excessive laughter.
56. To listen willingly to holy reading.
57. To apply oneself frequently to prayer.
58. Daily to confess in prayer one's past sins with tears and sighs to God, and to amend them for the time to come.
59. Not to fulfill the desires of the flesh: to hate one's own will.
60. To obey in all things the commands of the Abbot, even though he himself (which God forbid) should act otherwise; being mindful of that precept of the Lord: "What they say, do ye; but what they do, do ye not."
61. Not to wish to be called holy before one is so: but first to be holy, that one may be truly so called.
62. Daily to fulfill by one's deeds the commandments of God.
63. To love chastity.
64. To hate no man.
65. Not to be jealous, nor to give way to envy.
66. Not to love strife.
67. To fly from vainglory.
68. To reverence seniors.
69. To love juniors.
70. To pray for one's enemies in the love of Christ.
71. To make peace with an adversary before the setting of the sun.
72. And never to despair of God's mercy.

Behold, these are the tools of the spiritual craft, which, if they be constantly employed day and night, and duly given back on the Day of Judgment, will gain for us from the Lord that reward which He Himself has promised— "which eye hath not seen, nor ear heard; nor hath it entered into the heart of man to conceive what God hath prepared for them that love him." And the workshop where we are to labour diligently at all these things is the cloister of the monastery, and stability in the community.

Of Obedience

The first degree of humility is obedience without delay. This becomes those who hold nothing dearer to them than Christ, and who on account of the holy servitude which they have taken upon them, and for fear of hell, and for the glory of life everlasting, as soon as anything is ordered by the superior, just as if it had been commanded by God Himself, are unable to bear delay in doing it. It is of these that the Lord says: "At the hearing of the ear he hath obeyed me." And again, to teachers he saith: "He that heareth you heareth me."

The Spirit of Silence

Let us do as says the prophet: "I said, I will take heed to my ways, that I sin not with my tongue: I have placed a watch over my mouth; I became dumb, and was silent, and held my peace even from good things." Here the prophet shows that if we ought to refrain even from good words for the sake of silence, how much more ought we to abstain from evil words, on account of the punishment due to sin!

Therefore, on account of the importance of silence, let leave to speak be seldom granted even to perfect disciples, although their conversation be good and holy and tending to edification; because it is written: "In much speaking thou shalt not avoid sin"; and elsewhere: "Death and life are in the power of the tongue." For it becomes the master to speak and to teach, but it beseems the disciple to be silent and to listen.

And, therefore, if anything has to be asked of a superior, let it be done with all humility and subjection of reverence, lest he seem to say more than is expedient.

But as for buffoonery or silly words, such as move to laughter, we utterly condemn them in every place, nor do we allow the disciple to open his mouth in such discourse.

Of Humility

The Holy Scripture cries out to us, brethren, saying: "Everyone that exalteth himself shall be humbled, and he that humbleth himself shall be exalted." In saying this, it teaches us that all exaltation is a kind of pride, against which the prophet shows himself to be on his guard when he says: "Lord, my heart is not exalted nor mine eyes lifted up: nor have I walked in great things, nor in wonders above me." And why? "If I did not think humbly, but exalted my soul: like a child that is weaned from his mother, so wilt thou requite my soul."

Whence, brethren, if we wish to arrive at the highest point of humility and speedily to reach that heavenly exaltation to which we can only ascend by the humility of this present life, we must by our ever-ascending actions erect such a ladder as that which Jacob beheld his dream, by which the angels appeared to him descending and ascending. This descent and ascent signify nothing else than that we descend by exaltation and ascend by humility. And the ladder thus erected is our life in the world, which, if the heart be humbled, is lifted up by the Lord to heaven. The sides of the same ladder we understand to be our body and soul, in which the call of God has placed various degrees of humility or discipline, which we must ascend.

How the Monks Are to Sleep

Let them sleep each one in a separate bed, receiving bedding suitable to their manner of life, as the Abbot shall appoint.

If it be possible, let all sleep in one place; but if the number do not permit of this, let them repose by tens or twenties with the seniors who have charge of them. Let a candle burn constantly in the cell until morning.

Let them sleep clothed, and girded with belts or cords—but not with knives at their sides, lest perchance they wound themselves in their sleep—and thus be always ready, so that when the signal is given they rise without delay, and hasten each to forestall the other in going to the Work of God, yet with all gravity and modesty.

Let not the younger brethren have their beds by themselves, but among those of the seniors. And when they rise for the Work of

God, let them gently encourage one another, because of the excuses of the drowsy.

Of the Daily Manual Labour

Idleness is the enemy of the soul. Therefore should the brethren be occupied at stated times in manual labour, and at other fixed hours in sacred reading.

We think, therefore, that the times for each may be disposed as follow: from Easter to the Calends of October, on coming out in the morning let them labour at whatever is necessary from the first until about the fourth hour. From the fourth hour until close upon the sixth let them apply themselves to reading. After the sixth hour, when they rise from table, let them rest on their beds in all silence; or if anyone chance to wish to read to himself, let him so read as not to disturb anyone else. Let None be said rather soon, at the middle of the eighth hour; and then let them again work at whatever has to be done until Vespers.

If, however, the needs of the place or poverty require them to labour themselves in gathering in the harvest, let them not grieve at that; for then are they truly monks when they live by the labour of their hands, as our Fathers and the Apostles did. But let all things be done in moderation for the sake of the faint-hearted.

From the Calends of October until the beginning of Lent let the brethren devote themselves to reading till the end of the second hour. At the second hour let Terce be said, after which they shall all labour at their appointed work until None. At the first signal for the hour of None all shall cease from their work, and be ready as soon as the second signal is sounded. After their meal let them occupy themselves in their reading or with the psalms.

Of the Reception of Guests

Let all guests that come be received like Christ Himself, for He will say: "I was a stranger and ye took me in." And let fitting honour be shown to all, especially, however, to such as are of the household of the faith and to pilgrims.

Study Questions

1. The creation of *The Rule* is a comment upon Benedict's view of the nature of humanity. What are people like, and what good is *The Rule*?

2. Benedict has taken great care to order the lives of his monks in great detail. What is their daily life like?

3. Why does Benedict have such a high regard for silence? Why is talk dangerous?

4. Monasteries that kept to Benedict's *Rule* could be very useful institutions. How?

5. Every monastery reflected something about the society of which it was a part. What does *The Rule* tell us about the social and economic structure of the time?

Admonitions (ca. 1220) **50**

FRANCIS OF ASSISI

Francis of Assisi (1181 or 1182–1226) was one of the best-loved and most influential saints of the medieval Church. The son of an Italian cloth merchant, Francis was a typical youth. He was taught to read and write Latin as a boy, and as he grew up he became a popular figure in his hometown. Not especially religious in his youth, he was briefly a soldier, and a prisoner of war in 1202. In 1205 a vision turned his thoughts to religion and he renounced all of his material possessions, donned a hair shirt, and set out to preach to the unconverted. Francis's charm and magnetic personality quickly drew a large following. After receiving the pope's blessing, Francis became the leader of a new order of monks, the Franciscans. Unlike other monastic orders, the friars, as they were known, had no abbeys or property of any kind. They traveled the highways, first of Italy and later of all of Europe, preaching the gospel and living from the alms of the people. In his later years, Francis received the stigmata, or the imprint of the wounds of Christ, and suffered from a series of painful illnesses. His fame grew, as did his order. He was canonized only two years after his death, a measure of his popularity and holiness.

The *Admonitions* were probably written around the time of the foundation of the Franciscan order. They are a simple prescription for a Christian life, meant for his fellow Franciscans. In these instructions Francis emphasizes the virtues of humility, obedience, and poverty.

The Blessed Sacrament

Our Lord Jesus told his disciples, *I am the way, and the truth, and the life. No one comes to the Father but through me. If you had known me, you would also have known my Father.*

Sacred Scripture tells us that the Father dwells in *light inaccessible* and that *God is spirit*, and St. John adds, *No one at any time has seen God.* Because God is a spirit, he can be seen only in spirit; *It is the spirit that gives life; the flesh profits nothing.* But God the Son is equal to the Father and so he too can be seen only in the same way as the Father and the Holy Spirit. That is why all those were condemned who saw our Lord Jesus Christ in his humanity but did not see or believe in spirit in his divinity, that he was the true Son of God. In the same way now, all those are damned who see the sacrament of the Body of Christ which is consecrated on the altar in the form of bread and wine by the words of our Lord in the hands of the priest, and do not see or believe in spirit and in God that this is really the most holy Body and Blood of our Lord Jesus Christ. It is the Most High himself who has told us, This is my Body and Blood *of the new covenant*, and, *He who eats my flesh and drinks my blood has life everlasting.*

And so it is really the Spirit of God who dwells in his faithful who receive the most holy Body and Blood of our Lord. Anyone who does not have this Spirit and presumes to receive him *eats and drinks judgement to himself.* And so we may ask in the words of

Scripture, *Men of rank, how long will you be dull of heart?* Why do you refuse to recognize the truth *and believe in the Son of God?* Every day he humbles himself just as he did when he came from his *heavenly throne* into the Virgin's womb; every day he comes to us and lets us see him in abjection, when he descends from the bosom of the Father into the hands of the priest at the altar. He shows himself to us in this sacred bread just as he once appeared to his apostles in real flesh. With their own eyes they saw only his flesh, but they believed that he was God, because they contemplated him with the eyes of the spirit. We, too, with our own eyes, see only bread and wine, but we must see further and firmly believe that this is his most holy Body and Blood, living and true. In this way our Lord remains continually with his followers, as he promised, *Behold, I am with you all days, even unto the consummation of the world.*

Perfect and Imperfect Obedience

Our Lord tells us in the Gospel, *Everyone of you who does not renounce all that he possesses cannot be my disciple*, and, *He who would save his life will lose it.* A man takes leave of all that he possesses and loses both his body and his life when he gives himself up completely to obedience in the hands of his superior. Any good that he says or does which he knows is not against the will of his superior is true obedience. A subject may realize that there are many courses of action that would be better and more profitable to his soul than what his superior commands. In that case he should make an offering of his own will to God, and do his best to carry out what the superior has enjoined. This is true and loving obedience which is pleasing to God and one's neighbour.

If a superior commands his subject anything that is against his conscience, the subject should not spurn his authority, even though he cannot obey him. If anyone persecutes him because of this, he should love him all the more, for God's sake. A religious who prefers to suffer persecution rather than be separated from his confrères certainly perseveres in true obedience, because he lays down his life for his brethren. There are many religious who under the pretext of doing something more perfect than what their superior commands look behind and go back to their own will that they have given up. People like that are murderers, and by their bad example they cause the loss of many souls.

No One Should Claim the Office of Superior as His Own

I did *not come to be served but to serve*, our Lord tells us. Those who are put in charge of others should be no prouder of their office than if they had been appointed to wash the feet of their confrères. They should be no more upset at the loss of their authority than they would be if they were deprived of the task of washing feet. The more they are upset, the greater the risk they incur to their souls.

No One Should Give Way to Pride but Boast Only in the Cross of the Lord

Try to realize the dignity God has conferred on you. He created and formed your body in the image of his beloved Son, and your soul in his own likeness. And yet every creature under heaven serves and acknowledges and obeys its Creator in its own way better than you do. Even the devils were not solely responsible for crucifying him; it was you who crucified him with them and you continue to crucify him by taking pleasure in your vices and sins.

What have you to be proud of? If you were so clever and learned that you knew everything and could speak every language, so that the things of heaven were an open book to you, still you could not boast of that. Any of the devils knew more about the things of heaven, and knows more about the things of earth, than any human being, even one who might have received from God a special revelation of the highest wisdom. If you were the most handsome and the richest man in the world, and could work wonders and drive out devils, all that would be something extrinsic to you; it would not belong to you and you could not boast of it. But there is one thing of which we can all boast; we can boast of our humiliations and in taking up daily the holy cross of our Lord Jesus Christ.

The Imitation of Christ

Look at the Good Shepherd, my brothers. To save his sheep he endured the agony of the cross. They followed him in trials and persecutions, in ignominy, hunger, and thirst, in humiliations and temptations, and so on. And for this God rewarded them with eternal life. We ought to be ashamed of ourselves; the saints endured all that, but we who are servants of God try to win honour and glory by recounting and making known what they have done.

Good Works Must Follow Knowledge

St. Paul tells us, *The letter kills, but the spirit gives life*. A man has been killed by the letter when he wants to know quotation only so that people will think he is very learned and he can make money to give to his relatives and friends. A religious has been killed by the letter when he has no desire to follow the spirit of Sacred Scripture, but wants to know what it says only so that he can explain it to others. On the other hand, those have received life from the spirit of Sacred Scripture who, by their words and example, refer to the most high God, to whom belongs all good, all that they know or wish to know, and do not allow their knowledge to become a source of self-complacency.

Beware the Sin of Envy

St. Paul tells us, *No one can say Jesus is Lord, except in the Holy Spirit* and, *There is none who does good, no, not even one*. And so when a man envies his brother the good God says or does through him, it is like committing a sin of blasphemy, because he is really envying God, who is the only source of every good.

Charity

Our Lord says in the Gospel, *Love your enemies*. A man really loves his enemy when he is not offended by the injury done to himself, but for love of God feels burning sorrow for the sin his enemy has brought on his own soul, and proves his love in a practical way.

No One Should Be Scandalized at Another's Fall

Nothing should upset a religious except sin. And even then, no matter what kind of sin has been committed, if he is upset or angry for any other reason except charity, he is only drawing blame upon himself. A religious lives a good life and avoids sin when he is never angry or disturbed at anything. Blessed the man who keeps nothing for himself, but renders *to Caesar the things that are Caesar's, and to God the things that are God's*.

How to Know the Spirit of God

We can be sure that a man is a true religious and has the spirit of God if his lower nature does not give way to pride when God accomplishes some god through him, and if he seems all the more worthless and inferior to others in his own eyes. Our lower nature is opposed to every good.

Patience

We can never tell how patient or humble a person is when everything is going well with him. But when those who should co-operate with him do the exact opposite, then we can tell. A man has as much patience and humility as he has then, and no more.

Poverty of Spirit

Blessed are the poor in spirit, for theirs is the kingdom of heaven. There are many people who spend all their time at their prayers and other religious exercises and mortify themselves by long fasts and so on. But if anyone says as much as a word that implies a reflection on their self-esteem or takes something from them, they are immediately up in arms and annoyed. These people are not really poor in spirit. A person is really poor in spirit when he hates himself and loves those who strike him in the face.

The Humble Religious

Blessed the religious who takes no more pride in the good that God says and does through him, than in that which he says and does through someone else. It is wrong for anyone to be anxious to receive more from his neighbour than he himself is willing to give to God.

Compassion for One's Neighbour

Blessed the man who is patient with his neighbour's shortcomings as he would like him to be if he were in a similar position himself.

The Virtuous and Humble Religious

Blessed the religious who has no more regard for himself when people praise him and make much of him than when they despise and revile him and say that he is ignorant. What a man is before God, that he is and no more. Woe to that religious who, after he has been put in a position of authority by others, is not anxious to leave it of his own free will. On the other hand, blessed is that religious who is elected to office against his will but always wants to be subject to others.

The Happy and the Silly Religious

Blessed that religious who finds all his joy and happiness in the words and deeds of our Lord and uses them to make people love God gladly. Woe to the religious who amuses himself with silly gossip, trying to make people laugh.

The Talkative Religious

Blessed that religious who never says anything just for what he can get out of it. He should never be *hasty in his words* or open his heart to everyone, but he should think hard before he speaks. Woe to that religious who does not keep the favours God has given him to himself; people should see them only through his good works, but he wants to tell everybody about them, hoping he will get something out of it. In this way he has received his reward, and it does not do his listeners any good.

True Correction

Blessed that religious who takes blame, accusation, or punishment from another as patiently as if it were coming from himself. Blessed the religious who obeys quietly when he is corrected, confesses his fault humbly and makes atonement cheerfully. Blessed the religious who is in no hurry to make excuses, but accepts the embarrassment and blame for some fault he did not commit.

True Love

Blessed that friar who loves his brother as much when he is sick and can be of no use to him as when he is well and can be of use to him.

Blessed that friar who loves and respects his brother as much when he is absent as when he is present and who would not say anything behind his back that he could not say charitably to his face.

Religious Should be Respectful Towards the Clergy

Blessed is that servant of God who has confidence in priests who live according to the laws of the holy Roman Church. Woe to those who despise them. Even if they fall into sin, no one should pass judgement on them, for God has reserved judgement on them to himself. They are in a privileged position because they have charge of the Body and Blood of our Lord Jesus Christ, which they receive and which they alone administer to others, and so anyone who sins against them commits a greater crime than if he sinned against anyone else in the whole world.

Virtue and Vice

Where there is Love and Wisdom,
there is neither Fear nor Ignorance.
Where there is Patience and Humility,
there is neither Anger nor Annoyance.
Where there is Poverty and joy,
there is neither Cupidity nor Avarice.
Where there is Peace and Contemplation,
there is neither Care nor Restlessness.
Where there is the Fear of God to guard the
    dwelling,
there no enemy can enter.
Where there is Mercy and Prudence
there is neither Excess nor Harshness.

Study Questions

1. Whom do you think St. Francis was addressing in his *Admonitions*? How might his message differ if it were meant for a different audience?

2. What qualities does Francis seem to admire most?

3. What seems to be Francis's opinion about material things?

4. Several of the sections of *Admonitions* deal with relationships between superiors and subordinates. What should these relationships be like?

5. Does Francis give clergymen and monks a special place in society? Are his expectations different for them?

Summa Theologica (1266–1273)   51

THOMAS AQUINAS

Thomas Aquinas (1225–1274) was born in Italy near the town of Aquino from which he took his name. His family was minor nobility, but Thomas was destined for a career in the Church from an early age. He was sent to a monastery to be

trained as a monk, but his outstanding intellectual abilities led to further education. Aquinas studied first at the University of Naples and then, after he joined the
newly formed Dominican order, at the University of Paris, where he studied philosophy and theology. His special interest was in ancient Greek thought, especially
that of Aristotle, which he did much to popularize at the university. His reputation,
however, was derived from his theological knowledge, which was unsurpassed within his generation. He was summoned to Rome in 1259 to become a theological
advisor to the pope. He died in 1274 on his way to a Church council called to heal
the split between the Roman and Eastern churches. Canonized in 1323, he is
widely regarded as the most important philosopher of Catholicism.

Summa Theologica is a massive compilation of Aquinas' learning. It treats the
entire range of subjects with which the Church dealt, from the existence of God to
the definition of a just war. The Summa takes the form of questions and answers.
The answer sections provide pros and cons of the views expressed by the Church
and clarified by Aquinas. As its importance grew over the next four hundred years,
it became the central work of Catholicism.

Whether It Can Be Demonstrated That God Exists?

Objection 1. It seems that the existence of
God cannot be demonstrated. For it is an article of faith that God exists. But what is of faith
cannot be demonstrated, because a demonstration produces scientific knowledge; whereas
faith is of the unseen. Therefore it cannot be
demonstrated that God exists....

Obj. 3. Further, if the existence of God were
demonstrated, this could only be from His
effects. But His effects are not proportionate to
Him, since He is infinite and His effects are
finite; and between the finite and infinite there
is no proportion. Therefore, since a cause cannot be demonstrated by an effect not proportionate to it, it seems that the existence of God
cannot be demonstrated.

On the contrary, The Apostle says: The invisible things of Him are clearly seen, being understood by the things that are made. But this would
not be unless the existence of God could be
demonstrated through the things that are

made; for the first thing we must know of anything is, whether it exists.

I answer that, Demonstration can be made
in two ways: One is through the cause, and is
called a priori, and this is to argue from what is
prior absolutely. The other is through the
effect, and is called a demonstration a posteriori; this is to argue from what is prior relatively
only to us. When an effect is better known to
us than its cause, from the effect we proceed to
the knowledge of the cause. And from every
effect the existence of its proper cause can be
demonstrated, so long as its effects are better
known to us; because since every effect
depends upon its cause, if the effect exists, the
cause must preexist. Hence the existence of
God, in so far as it is not self-evident to us, can
be demonstrated from those of His effects
which are known to us.

Reply Obj. 1. The existence of God and
other like truths about God, which can be
known by natural reason, are not articles of
faith, but are preambles to the articles; for faith
presupposes natural knowledge, even as grace
presupposes nature, and perfection supposes

something that can be perfected. Nevertheless, there is nothing to prevent a man, who cannot grasp a proof, accepting, as a matter of faith, something which in itself is capable of being scientifically known and demonstrated....

Reply Obj. 3. From effects not proportionate to the cause no perfect knowledge of that cause can be obtained. Yet from every effect the existence of the cause can be clearly demonstrated, and so we can demonstrate the existence of God from His effects: though from them we cannot perfectly know God as He is in His essence.

We must now consider war, under which head there are four points of inquiry: Whether some kind of war is lawful? Whether it is lawful for clerics to fight? Whether it is lawful to fight on holy days?

Whether It Is Always Sinful to Wage War?

Objection 1. It would seem that it is always sinful to wage war. Because punishment is not inflicted except for sin. Now those who wage war are threatened by Our Lord with punishment, according to Matth. xxvi. 52: *All that take the sword shall perish with the sword.* Therefore all wars are unlawful.

Obj. 2. Further, whatever is contrary to a Divine precept is a sin. But war is contrary to a Divine precept, for it is written: *But I say to you not to resist evil; and: Not revenging yourselves, my dearly beloved, but give place unto wrath.* Therefore war is always sinful.

Obj. 3. Further, nothing, except sin, is contrary to an act of virtue. But war is contrary to peace. Therefore war is always a sin.

Obj. 4. Further, the exercise of a lawful thing is itself lawful, as is evident in scientific exercises. But warlike exercises which take place in tournaments are forbidden by the Church, since those who are slain in these trials are deprived of ecclesiastical burial. Therefore it seems that war is a sin in itself.

On the contrary, Augustine says in a sermon on the son of the centurion: *If the Christian Religion forbade war altogether, those who sought salutary advice in the Gospel would rather have been counselled to cast aside their arms, and to give up soldiering altogether. On the contrary, they were told: "Do violence to no man; ... and be content with your pay." If he commanded them to be content with their pay, he did not forbid soldiering.*

I answer that, In order for a war to be just, three things are necessary. First, the authority of the sovereign by whose command the war is to be waged. For it is not the business of a private individual to declare war, because he can seek for redress of his rights from the tribunal of his superior. Moreover it is not the business of a private individual to summon together the people, which has to be done in wartime. And as the care of the common weal is committed to those who are in authority, it is their business to watch over the common weal of the city, kingdom or province subject to them. And just as it is lawful for them to have recourse to the sword in defending that common weal against internal disturbances, when they punish evildoers, according to the words of the Apostle: *He beareth not the sword in vain: for he is God's minister, an avenger to execute wrath upon him that doth evil;* so too, it is their business to have recourse to the sword of war in defending the common weal against external enemies. Hence it is said to those who are in authority: *Rescue the poor. and deliver the needy out of the hand, of the sinner;* and for this reason Augustine says: *The natural order conducive to peace among mortals demands that the power to declare and counsel war should be in the hands of those who hold the supreme authority.*

Secondly, a just cause is required, namely that those who are attacked, should be attacked because they deserve in on account of some fault. Wherefore Augustine says: *A just war is wont to be described as one that avenges wrongs, when a nation or state has to be punished, for refusing to make amends for the wrongs inflicted by its subjects, or to restore what it has seized unjustly.*

Thirdly, it is necessary that the belligerents should have a rightful intention, so that they intend the advancement of good, or the avoidance of evil. Hence Augustine says: *True religion looks upon as peaceful those wars that are waged not for motives of aggrandizement, or cruelty, but with the object of securing peace, of punishing evil-doers, and of uplifting the good.* For it may happen that the war is declared by the legitimate authority, and for a just cause, and yet be rendered unlawful through a wicked intention. Hence Augustine says: *The passion for inflicting harm, the cruel thirst for vengeance, an unpacific and relentless spirit, the fever of revolt,* the lust of power, and such like things, all these are rightly condemned in war.

Reply Obj. 1. As Augustine says: *To take the sword is to arm oneself in order to take the life of anyone, without the command or permission of superior or lawful authority.* On the other hand, to have recourse to the sword (as a private person) by the authority of the sovereign or judge, or (as a public person) through zeal for justice, and by the authority, so to speak, of God, is not to *take the sword,* but to use it as commissioned by another, wherefore it does not deserve punishment. And yet even those who make sinful use of the sword are not always slain with the sword, yet they always perish with their own sword, because, unless they repent, they are punished eternally for their sinful use of the sword.

Reply Obj. 2. Such like precepts, as Augustine observes should always be borne in readiness of mind, so that we be ready to obey them, and, if necessary, to refrain from resistance or self-defence. Nevertheless it is necessary sometimes for a man to act otherwise for the common good, or for the good of those with whom he is fighting. Hence Augustine says: *Those whom we have to punish with a kindly*

severity, it is necessary to handle in many ways against their will. For when we are stripping a man of the lawlessness of sin, it is good for him to be vanquished, since nothing is more hopeless than the happiness of sinners, whence arises a guilty impunity, and an evil will, like an internal enemy.

Reply Obj. 3. Those who wage war justly aim at peace, and so they are not opposed to peace, except to the evil peace, which Our Lord came not to send upon earth. Hence Augustine says: *We do not seek peace in order to be at war, but we go to war that we may have peace. Be peaceful, therefore, in warring, so that you may vanquish those whom you war against, and bring them to the prosperity of peace.*

Reply Obj. 4. Manly exercises in warlike feats of arms are not all forbidden, but those which are inordinate and perilous, and end in slaying or plundering. In olden times warlike exercises presented no such danger, and hence they were called *exercises of arms* or *bloodless wars,* as Jerome states in an epistle.

Whether It Is Lawful for Clerics and Bishops to Fight?

Objection 1. It would seem lawful for clerics and bishops to fight. For, as stated above, wars are lawful and just in so far as they protect the poor and the entire common weal from suffering at the hands of the foe. Now this seems to be above all the duty of prelates, for Gregory says: *The wolf comes upon the sheep, when any unjust and rapacious man oppresses those who are faithful and humble. But he who was thought to be the shepherd, and was not, leaveth the sheep, and flieth, for he fears lest the wolf hurt him, and dares not stand up against his injustice.* Therefore it is lawful for prelates and clerics to fight.

Obj. 2. Further, Pope Leo IV writes: *As untoward tidings had frequently come from the Saracen side, some said that the Saracens would come to the port of Rome secretly and covertly; for which reason we commanded our people to gather together, and ordered them to go down to the seashore.* Therefore it is lawful for bishops to fight.

Obj. 3. Further, apparently, it comes to the same whether a man does a thing himself, or consents to its being done by another, according to Rom. i. 32: *They who do such things, are worthy of death, and not only they that do them, but they also that consent to them that do them.* Now those, above all, seem to consent to a thing, who induce others to do it. But it is lawful for bishops and clerics to induce others to fight: for it is written that Charles went to war with the Lombards at the instance and entreaty of Adrian, bishop of Rome. Therefore they also are allowed to fight.

Obj. 4. Further, whatever is right and meritorious in itself, is lawful for prelates and clerics. Now it is sometimes right and meritorious to make war, for it is written that if *a man die for the true faith, or to save his country, or in defense of Christians, God will give him a heavenly reward.* Therefore it is lawful for bishops and clerics to fight.

On the contrary, It was said to Peter as representing bishops and clerics: *Put up again thy sword into the scabbard.* Therefore it is not lawful for them to fight.

I answer that, Several things are requisite for the good of a human society: and a number of things are done better and quicker by a number of persons than by one, as the Philosopher observes, while certain occupations are so inconsistent with one another, that they cannot be fittingly exercised at the same time; wherefore those who are deputed to important duties are forbidden to occupy themselves with things of small importance. Thus according to human laws, soldiers who are deputed to warlike pursuits are forbidden to engage in commerce.

Now warlike pursuits are altogether incompatible with the duties of a bishop and a cleric, for two reasons. The first reason is a general one, because, to wit, warlike pursuits are full of unrest, so that they hinder the mind very much

from the contemplation of Divine things, the praise of God, and prayers for the people, which belong to the duties of a cleric. Wherefore just as commercial enterprises are forbidden to clerics, because they unsettle the mind too much, so too are warlike pursuits, according to 2 Tim. ii. 4: *No man being a soldier to God, entangleth himself with secular business.* The second reason is a special one, because, to wit, all the clerical Orders are directed to the ministry of the altar, on which the Passion of Christ is represented sacramentally, according to 1 Cor. xi. 26: *As often as you shall eat this bread, and drink the chalice, you shall show the death of the Lord, until He come.* Wherefore it is unbecoming for them to slay or shed blood, and it is more fitting that they should be ready to shed their own blood for Christ, so as to imitate in deed what they portray in their ministry. For this reason it has been decreed that those who shed blood, even without sin, become irregular. Now no man who has a certain duty to perform, can lawfully do that which renders him unfit for that duty. Wherefore it is altogether unlawful for clerics to fight, because war is directed to the shedding of blood.

Reply Obj. 1. Prelates ought to withstand not only the wolf who brings spiritual death upon the flock, but also the pillager and the oppressor who work bodily harm; not, however, by having recourse themselves to material arms, but by means of spiritual weapons, according to the saying of the Apostle: *The weapons of our warfare are not carnal, but mighty through God.* Such are salutary warnings, devout prayers, and, for those who are obstinate, the sentence of excommunication.

Reply Obj. 2. Prelates and clerics may, by the authority of their superiors, take part in wars, not indeed by taking up arms themselves, but by affording spiritual help to those who fight justly, by exhorting and absolving them, and by other like spiritual helps. Thus in the Old Testament the priests were commanded to sound the sacred trumpets in the battle. It was for this purpose that bishops or clerics were first allowed to go to the front: and it is an abuse of this permission, if any of them take up arms themselves.

Reply Obj. 3. As stated above every power, art or virtue that regards the end, has to dispose that which is directed to the end. Now, among the faithful, carnal wars should be considered as having for their end the Divine spiritual good to which clerics are deputed. Wherefore it is the duty of clerics to dispose and counsel other men to engage in just wars. For they are forbidden to take up arms, not as though it were a sin, but because such an occupation is unbecoming their personality.

Reply Obj. 4. Although it is meritorious to wage a just war, nevertheless it is rendered unlawful for clerics, by reason of their being deputed to works more meritorious still. Thus the marriage act may be meritorious; and yet it becomes reprehensible in those who have vowed virginity, because they are bound to a yet greater good.

Whether It Is Lawful to Fight on Holy Days?

Objection 1. It would seem unlawful to fight oil holy days. For holy days are instituted that we may have our time to the things of God. Hence they are included in the keeping of the Sabbath prescribed in Exod. xx. 8: for *sabbath* is interpreted *rest*. But wars are full of unrest. Therefore by no means is it lawful to fight on holy days.

Obj. 2. Further, certain persons are reproached because on fast-days they exacted what was owing to them, were guilty of strife, and of smiting with the fist. Much more, therefore, is it unlawful to fight on holy days.

Obj. 3. Further, no ill deed should be done to avoid temporal harm. But fighting on a holy day seems in itself to be an ill deed. Therefore no one should fight on a holy day even through the need of avoiding temporal harm.

On the contrary, It is written: The Jews rightly determined ... saying: *Whosoever shall come up against us to fight on the Sabbath-day, we will fight against him.*

I answer that, The observance of holy days is no hindrance to those things which are ordained to man's safety, even that of his body. Hence Our Lord argued with the Jews, saying: *Are you angry at Me because I have healed the whole man on the Sabbath-day?* Hence physicians may lawfully attend to their patients on holy days. Now there is much more reason for safeguarding the common weal (whereby many are saved from being slain, and innumerable evils both temporal and spiritual prevented), than the bodily safety of an individual. Therefore, for the purpose of safeguarding the common weal of the faithful, it is lawful to carry on a war on holy days, provided there be need for doing so: because it would be to tempt God, if notwithstanding such a need, one were to choose to refrain from fighting.

However, as soon as the need ceases, it is no longer lawful to fight on a holy day, for the reasons given: wherefore this suffices for the *Replies* to the *Objections*.

Study Questions

1. How does Aquinas prove the existence of God?

2. What are Aquinas' views about war? What is a just war?

3. War is, of course, a political act. What are the political assumptions Aquinas makes in his discussion of war?

4. How does Christianity limit war?

5. Who do you think Aquinas was trying to persuade with his book? What kind of audience would have been best suited for this method of argument?

Witchcraft Documents (15th century)   **52**

Evidence of the supernatural world abounded for the people of premodern Europe. The birth of monsters—two-headed calves and deformed babies—a sudden attack of paralysis, the onset of an epileptic seizure: all of these phenomena required explanation. Many found the answer in the work of the devil and his disciples, witches. Accusations of witchcraft tended to multiply in communities under severe stress. Natural disasters such as plague or human-created disasters such as war promoted fear of witchcraft. When the world seemed out of balance and the forces of good retreated before the forces of evil, people sought someone to blame for their troubles. Witches were an obvious choice.

Accused witches were most commonly women on the margins of society. Elderly spinsters, widows, or antisocial women in the village were the usual suspects. Once brought before the authorities, many admitted their traffic with Satan; indeed, some were convinced of their command of the magic arts. There was a long tradition in European society of white magic, and the line between magic for good and magic for evil was a thin one.

Both the medieval Church and state believed they had a solemn duty to stamp out witchcraft. "Thou shalt not suffer a witch to live" was a biblical injunction. The documents reproduced here include a papal bull of 1484 ordering the persecution of witches in Germany. The inquisitors charged with tracking witches down composed a handbook for their job, *The Witch Hammer,* which included instructions on methods of torture. This book became the standard guide for inquisitors for several centuries and was reprinted in many editions.

1. The Papal Bull of 1484

Desiring with supreme ardor, as pastoral solicitude requires, that the catholic faith in our days everywhere grow and flourish as much as possible, and that all heretical pravity be put far from the territories of the faithful, we freely declare and anew decree this by which our pious desire may be fulfilled, and, all errors being rooted out by our toil as with the hoe of a wise laborer, zeal and devotion to this faith may take deeper hold on the hearts of the faithful themselves.

The Persecution of Witches. Hysteria over witchcraft affected the daily lives of many Europeans in the sixteenth and seventeenth centuries. This picture by Frans Francken the Young, painted in 1607, shows a number of witches. In the center, several witches are casting spells with their magic books and instruments, and at the the top, a witch on a post prepares to fly off on her broomstick.

It has recently come to our ears, not without great pain to us, that in some parts of upper Germany, as well as in the provinces, cities, territories, regions, and dioceses of Mainz, Köln, Trier, Salzburg, and Bremen, many persons of both sexes, heedless of their own salvation and forsaking the catholic faith, give themselves over to devils male and female, and by their incantations, charms, and conjurings, and by other abominable superstitions and sortileges, offences, crimes, and misdeeds, ruin and cause to perish the offspring of women, the foal of animals, the products of the earth, the grapes of vines, and the fruits of trees, as well as men and women, cattle and flocks and herds and animals of every kind, vineyards also and orchards, meadows, pastures, harvests, grains and other fruits of the earth; that they afflict and torture with dire pains and anguish, both internal and external, these men, women, cattle, flocks, herds, and animals, and hinder men from begetting and women from conceiving, and prevent all consummation of marriage; that, moreover, they deny with sacrilegious lips the faith they received in holy baptism; and that, at the instigation of the enemy of mankind, they do not fear to commit and perpetrate many other abominable offences and crimes, at the risk of their own souls, to the insult of the divine majesty and to the pernicious example and scandal of multitudes. And, although our beloved sons Henricus Institoris and Jacobus Sprenger, of the order of Friars Preachers, professors of theology, have been and still are deputed by our apostolic letters as inquisitors of heretical pravity, the former in the aforesaid parts of upper Germany, including the provinces, cities, territories, dioceses, and other places as above, and the latter throughout certain parts of the course of the Rhine; nevertheless certain of the clergy and of the laity of those parts, seeking to be wise above what is fitting, because in the said letter of deputation the aforesaid provinces, cities, dioceses, territories, and other places, and the persons and offences in question were not individually and specifically named, do not blush obstinately to assert that these are not at all included in the said parts and that therefore it is illicit for the aforesaid inquisitors to exercise their office of inquisition in the provinces, cities, dioceses, territories, and other places aforesaid, and that they ought not to be permitted to proceed to the punishment, imprisonment, and correction of the aforesaid persons for the offences and crimes above named. Wherefore in the provinces, cities, dioceses, territories, and places aforesaid such offences and crimes, not without evident damage to their souls and risk of eternal salvation, go unpunished.

We therefore, desiring, as is our duty, to remove all impediments by which in any way the said inquisitors are hindered in the exercise of their office, and to prevent the taint of heretical pravity and of other like evils from spreading their infection to the ruin of others who are innocent, the zeal of religion especially impelling us, in order that the provinces, cities, dioceses, territories, and places aforesaid in the said parts of upper Germany may not be deprived of the office of inquisition which is their due, do hereby decree, by virtue of our apostolic authority, that it shall be permitted to the said inquisitors in these regions to exercise their office of inquisition and to proceed to the correction, imprisonment, and punishment of the aforesaid persons for their said offences and

crimes, in all respects and altogether precisely as if the provinces, cities, territories, places, persons, and offences aforesaid were expressly named in the said letter. And, for the greater sureness, extending the said letter and deputation to the provinces, cities, dioceses, territories, places, persons, and crimes aforesaid, we grant to the said inquisitors that they or either of them, joining with them our beloved son Johannes Gremper, cleric of the diocese of Constance, master of arts, their present notary, or any other notary public who by them or by either of them shall have been temporarily delegated in the provinces, cities, dioceses, territories, and places aforesaid, may exercise against all persons, of whatsoever condition and rank, the said office of inquisition, correcting, imprisoning, punishing, and chastising, according to their deserts, those persons whom they shall find guilty as aforesaid.

And they shall also have full and entire liberty to propound and preach to the faithful the word of God, as often as it shall seem to them fitting and proper, in each and all of the parish churches in the said provinces, and to do all things necessary and suitable under the aforesaid circumstances, and likewise freely and fully to carry them out.

2. *Johannes Nider, the Ant Hill*

I will relate to you some examples, which I have gained in part from the teachers of our faculty, in part from the experience of a certain upright secular judge, worthy of all faith, who from the torture and confession of witches and from his experiences in public and private has learned many things of this sort—a man with whom I have often discussed this subject broadly and deeply—to wit, Peter, a citizen of Bern, in the diocese of Lausanne, who has burned many witches of both sexes, and has driven others out of the territory of the Bernese. I have moreover conferred with one Benedict, a monk of the Benedictine order, who, although now a very devout cleric in a reformed monastery at Vienna, was a decade ago, while still in the world, a necromancer, juggler, buffoon, and strolling player, well-known as an expert among the secular nobility. I have likewise heard certain of the following things from the Inquisitor of Heretical Pravity at Autun, who was a devoted reformer of our order in the convent at Lyons, and has convicted many of witchcraft in the diocese of Autun.

The same procedure was more clearly described by another young man, arrested and burned as a witch, although as I believe, truly, penitent, who had earlier, together with his wife, a witch invincible to persuasion, escaped the clutches of the aforesaid judge, Peter. The aforesaid youth, being again indicted at Bern, with his wife, and placed in a different prison from hers, declared: "If I can obtain absolution for my sins, I will freely lay bare all I know about witchcraft, for I see that I have death to expect." And when he had been assured by the scholars that, if he should truly repent, he would certainly be able to gain absolution for his sins, then he gladly offered himself to death, and disclosed the methods of the primeval infection.

The ceremony, he said, of my seduction was as follows: First, on a Sunday, before the holy water is consecrated, the future disciple with his masters must go into the church, and there in their presence must renounce Christ and his faith, baptism, and the church universal. Then he must do homage to the *magisterulus,* that is, to the little master (for so, and not otherwise, they call the Devil). Afterward he drinks from the aforesaid flask: and, this done, he forthwith feels himself to conceive and hold within himself an image of our art and the chief rites of this sect. After this fashion was I seduced; and my wife also, whom I believe of so great pertinacity that she will endure the flames rather than confess the least whit of the truth; but, alas, we are both guilty. What the young man

had said was found in all respects the truth. For, after confession, the young man was seen to die in great contrition. His wife, however, though convicted by the testimony of witnesses, would not confess the truth even under the torture or in death; but, when the fire was prepared for her by the executioner, uttered in most evil words a curse upon him, and so was burned.

3. The Witch Hammer

The method of beginning an examination by torture is as follows: First, the jailers prepare the implements of torture, then they strip the prisoner (if it be a woman, she has already been stripped by other women, upright and of good report). This stripping is lest some means of witchcraft may have been sewed into the clothing—such as often, taught by the Devil, they prepare from the bodies of unbaptized infants, [murdered] that they may forfeit salvation. And when the implements of torture have been prepared, the judge, both in person and through other good men zealous in the faith, tries to persuade the prisoner to confess the truth freely; but, if he will not confess, he bids attendants make the prisoner fast to the strappado or some other implement of torture. The attendants obey forthwith, yet with feigned agitation. Then, at the prayer of some of those present, the prisoner is loosed again and is taken aside and once more persuaded to confess, being led to believe that he will in that case not be put to death.

Here it may be asked whether the judge, in the case of a prisoner much defamed, convicted both by witnesses and by proofs, nothing being lacking but his own confession, can properly lead him to hope that his life will be spared—when, even if he confess his crime, he will be punished with death.

It must be answered that opinions vary. Some hold that even a witch of ill repute, against whom the evidence justifies violent suspicion, and who, as a ringleader of the witches, is accounted very dangerous, may be assured her life, and condemned instead to perpetual imprisonment on bread and water, in case she will give sure and convincing testimony against other witches; yet this penalty of perpetual imprisonment must not be announced to her, but only that her life will be spared, and that she will be punished in some other fashion, perhaps by exile. And doubtless such notorious witches, especially those who prepare witch-potions or who by magical methods cure those bewitched, would be peculiarly suited to be thus preserved, in order to aid the bewitched or to accuse other witches, were it not that their accusations cannot be trusted, since the Devil is a liar, unless confirmed by proofs and witnesses.

Others hold, as to this point, that for a time the promise made to the witch sentenced to imprisonment is to be kept, but that after a time she should be burned.

A third view is, that the judge may safely promise witches to spare their lives, if only he will later excuse himself from pronouncing the sentence and will let another do this in his place....

But if, neither by threats nor by promises such as these, the witch can be induced to speak the truth, then the jailers must carry out the sentence, and torture the prisoner according to the accepted methods, with more or less of severity as the delinquent's crime may demand. And, while he is being tortured, he must be questioned on the articles of accusation, and this frequently and persistently, beginning with the lighter charges—for he will more readily confess the lighter than the heavier. And, while this is being done, the notary must write down everything in his record of the trial—how the prisoner is tortured, on what points he is questioned, and how he answers.

And note that, if he confesses under the torture, he must afterward be conducted to another place, that he may confirm it and certify that it was not due alone to the force of the torture.

But, if the prisoner will not confess the truth satisfactorily, other sorts of tortures must be placed before him, with the statement that, unless he will confess the truth, he must endure these also. But, if not even thus he can be brought into terror and to the truth, then the next day or the next but one is to be set for a *continuation* of the tortures—not a *repetition*, for they must not be repeated unless new evidences be produced.

The judge must then address to the prisoners the following sentence: We, the judge, etc., do assign to you, such and such a day for the continuation of the tortures, that from your own mouth the truth may be heard, and that the whole may be recorded by the notary.

And during the interval, before the day assigned, the judge, in person or through approved men, must in the manner above described try to persuade the prisoner to confess, promising her (if there is aught to be gained by this promise) that her life shall be spared.

The judge shall see to it, moreover, that throughout this interval guards are constantly with the prisoner, so that she may not be left alone; because she will be visited by the Devil and tempted into suicide.

Study Questions

1. Why did the Church devote such energy to the destruction of witches? Why were witches considered so dangerous?

2. The pope complains of people who obstruct the work of the inquisitors. Why might such obstruction occur?

3. Why might a person, as the young man described in *The Ant Hill,* make such a full confession of his witchcraft?

4. Why did authorities employ torture in cases of witchcraft? What does the use of torture reveal about the nature of the crime and medieval society's view of it?

5. What was the procedure followed by the inquisitor when torturing a suspect?

6. Inquisitors recommended lying to suspected witches in order to secure a confession. What does *The Witch Hammer* suggest about such cases? Why did inquisitors feel such tactics were justified?

PART III

Dynasties and Empires

The Italian Renaissance

A modern view of St. Peter's in Rome.

On the Family (1435–1444)   **53**

LEON BATTISTA ALBERTI

Leon Battista Alberti (1404–1472) was one of the great virtuosi of the Renaissance. The illegitimate son of one of the wealthiest Florentine merchants, Alberti was an outstanding athlete and man of action as well as an influential writer. After having studied law and entering the service of the church, he achieved his greatest fame as an architect, designing a number of exquisite private mansions. His writings include classic works on the principles of painting and architecture.

On the Family is an exploration of the duties, obligations, and benefits of family life. Alberti uses the popular dialogue form to elaborate on the themes of parental responsibility, love, marriage, and the management of the household. He views the family from a variety of perspectives: as a kinship group, an economic unit, and a political body.

In our discussion we may establish four general precepts as sound and firm foundation for all the other points to be developed or added. I shall name them. In the family the number of men must not diminish but augment; possessions must not grow less, but more; all forms of disgrace are to be shunned—a good name and fine reputation is precious and worth pursuing; hatreds, enmities, rancor must be carefully avoided, while good will, numerous acquaintances, and friendships are something to look for, augment, and cultivate.

We shall take up these four points of wisdom in order to see how men become rich, good, and well-beloved. First we must begin by seeing how a family becomes, as we may say, populous. We shall give some thought to the reasons for a decline in numbers. Then we shall turn to the second point. I am delighted to find that by some providential chance we happened to begin our talk with a kind of prelude to all this, in which I urged you to avoid all lust and lascivious greed. Did I not intend to be brief in this matter, as before so in what is to come?

Perhaps I would show you more clearly how in all four things that remain to our consideration, sensual pleasure and lascivious love are the most destructive cause of total ruin. Another time and place for this discussion may arise, while you, I know, I need no persuasion to make you keep to your education, your noble pursuits, and your studies, and avoid idleness and less than honorable desires. So let us return to our subject. There we shall speak as lucidly and simply as we can, without any elegant and very polished rhetoric. I think among ourselves good thoughts are far more important than a pretty style. Listen to me.

Families increase in population no differently than do countries, regions, and the whole world. As anyone who uses his imagination will quickly realize, the number of mortal men has grown from a small number to the present almost infinite multitude through the procreation and rearing of children. And, for the procreation of children, no one can deny that man requires woman. Since a child comes into the world as a tender and delicate creature, he needs someone to whose care and devotion he comes as a cherished trust. This person must nourish him with diligence and love and must defend him from harm. Too much cold or too much sun, rain, and the wild blowing of a storm are harmful to children. Woman, therefore, did first find a roof under which to nourish and protect herself and her offspring. There she remained, busy in the shadow, nourishing and caring for her children. And since woman was busy guarding and taking care of the heir, she was not in a position to go out and find what she and her children required for the maintenance of their life. Man, however, was by nature more energetic and industrious, and he went out to find things and bring what seemed to him necessary. Sometimes the man remained away from home and did not return as soon as his family expected. Because of this, when he came back laden, the woman learned to save things up in order to make sure that if in the future her husband stayed away for a time, neither she nor her children would suffer. In this way it seems clear to me that nature and human reason taught mankind the necessity of having a spouse, both to increase and continue generations and to nourish and preserve those already born. It also became clear that careful gathering and diligent preserving were essential to the maintenance of human life in the married state.

Nature showed, further, that this relationship could not be permitted with more than one wife at a time, since man was by no means able to provide and bring home more than was needed for himself and one wife and children. Had he wished to find food and to gather goods for more wives and families, one or another of them would certainly sometimes have lacked some of the necessities. And the woman who found herself lacking what are or ought to be the necessities of life, would she not have had sufficient reason even to abandon her offspring in order to preserve her own life? Perhaps under pressure of such need she would

even have had the right to seek out another companion. Marriage, therefore, was instituted by nature, our most excellent and divine teacher of all things, with the provision that there should be one constant life's companion for a man, and one only. With her he should dwell under one roof, her he should not forget or leave all alone, but to her return, bearing things with him and ordering matters so that his family might have all that was necessary and sufficient. The wife was to preserve in the house the things he brought to her. To satisfy nature, then, a man need only choose a woman with whom he can dwell in tranquillity under one roof all his life.

Young people, however, very often do not cherish the good of the family enough to do this. Marriage, perhaps, seems to them to take away their present liberty and freedom. It may be, as the comic poets like to tell us, that they are held back and dissuaded by some mistress. Sometimes, too, young men find it hard enough to manage one life, and fear as an excessive and undesirable burden the task of supporting a wife and children besides. They may doubt their capacity to maintain in honorable estate a family which grows in needs from day to day. Viewing the conjugal bed as a troublesome responsibility, they then avoid the legitimate and honorable path to the increase of a family.

If a family is not to fall for these reasons into what we have described as the most unfortunate condition of decline, but is to grow, instead, in fame and in the prosperous multitude of its youth, we must persuade our young men to take wives. We must use every argument for this purpose, offer incentive, promise reward, employ all our wit, persistence, and cunning. A most appropriate reason for taking a wife may be found in what we were saying before, about the evil of sensual indulgence, for the condemnation of such things may lead young men to desire honorable satisfactions. As other incentives, we may also speak to them of the delights of this primary and natural companionship of marriage. Children act as pledges and securities of marital love and kindness. At the same time they offer a focus for all a man's hopes and desires. Sad, indeed, is the man who has labored to get wealth and power and lands, and then has no true heir and perpetuator of his memory. No one can be more suited than a man's true and legitimate sons to gain advantages by virtue of his character, position, and authority, and to enjoy the fruits and rewards of his labor. If a man leaves such heirs, furthermore, he need not consider himself wholly dead and gone. His children keep his own position and his true image in the family.

It will serve our purpose, also, to remind the young of the dignity conferred on the father in the ancient world. Fathers of families wore precious jewels and were given other tokens of dignity forbidden to any who had not added by his progeny to the population of the republic. It may also help to recall to young men how often profligates and hopeless prodigals have been restored to a better life by the presence of a wife in the house. Add to this what a great help sons can be as hands to get work done—how they give zealous and loyal aid and support when fortune is hard and men unkind—and how your sons more than anyone spring to your defense and are ready to avenge the injury and harm inflicted upon you by evil and outrageous men. Likewise, our children are our comfort and are apt at every age to make us happy and give us great joys and satisfactions. These things it is good to tell them. It also helps to point out how much children come to mean in old age, when we live under the pressure of various needs.

Let it be the responsibility of the whole house to see that once they have the desire they have also the ability honorably to establish a family. Let the entire family contribute, as if to purchase its own growth, and let them all join by gathering something from each member to put up a sufficient sum for a fund which will support those who shall be born. In this way an expense which would have been disastrously heavy for one alone shall be shared among many and become merely a light obligatory payment. It seems to me that in a family where good customs prevail, no one would be unwilling to pay any amount to ransom back from slavery a humble member, not even of his own family but of his country and language. No attempt should be made, therefore, to evade the light expense which might restore a greater number to one's own blood and to one's family. Year after year you give wages to strangers, to various outsiders. You feed and clothe both foreigners and slaves, not so much to enjoy the fruit of their labor as to have a large company in your household. To contribute to a single charity which would support your own kinsmen would cost you far less. The company of your own relatives will yield you more honor and more pleasure than that of strangers. Cherished and faithful kinsmen will do more useful work and suit your household better than the workers you have taken into your service, whose loyalty you have merely bought. One should show such kindness and charity toward one's family, then, so that a father may be sure his children need never want for the necessities of life.

Perhaps it will help to put our young people under some compulsion like this: fathers could say in their wills, "If you do not marry when you reach the appropriate age, you are no heir of mine." As to what is the appropriate time of life to take a wife, to relate all the ancient opinions on this matter would take a long time. Hesiod would have a man marry at thirty; Lycurgus wanted fatherhood to begin at thirty-seven; to our modern minds it seems to be practical for a man to marry at twenty-five. Everyone at least agrees that to give this kind of responsibility to the willful and ardent youth under twenty-five is dangerous. A man of that age spends his fire and force better in establishing and strengthening his own position than in procreating. The youthful seed, moreover, seems faulty and frail and less full of vigor than that which is ripened. Let men wait for solid maturity.

When, by the urging and counsel of their elders and of the whole family, young men have arrived at the point of marriage, their mothers and other female relatives and friends, who have known the virgins of the neighborhood from earliest childhood and know the way their upbringing has formed them, should select all the well-born and well-brought-up girls and present that list to the new groom-to-be. He can then choose the one who suits him best. The elders of the house and all of the family shall reject no daughter-in-law unless she is tainted with the breath of scandal or bad reputation. Aside from that, let the man who will have to satisfy her satisfy himself. He should act as do wise heads of families before they acquire some property—they like to look it over several times before they actually sign a contract. It is good in the case of any purchase and contract to inform oneself fully and to take counsel. One should consult a good number of persons and be very careful in order to avoid belated regrets. The man who has decided to marry must be still more cautious. I recommend that he examine and anticipate in every way, and consider for many days, what sort of person it is he is to live with for all his years as husband and companion. Let him be minded to marry for two purposes: first to perpetuate himself in his children, and second to have a steady and constant companion all his life. A woman is needed, therefore, who is likely to bear children and who is desirable as a perpetual mate.

They say that in choosing a wife one looks for beauty, parentage, and riches. The beauty of a man accustomed to arms, it seems to me, lies in his having a presence betokening pride, limbs full of strength, and the gestures of one who is skilled and adept in all forms of exercise. The beauty of an old man, I think, lies in his prudence, his amiability, and the reasoned judgment which permeates all his words and his counsel. Whatever else may be thought beautiful in an old man, certainly it differs sharply from what constitutes beauty in a young cavalier. I think that beauty in a woman, likewise, must be judged not only by the charm and refinement of her face, but still more by the grace of her person and her aptitude for bearing and giving birth to many fine children.

Among the most essential criteria of beauty in a woman is an honorable manner. Even a wild, prodigal, greasy, drunken woman may be beautiful of feature, but no one would call her a beautiful wife. A woman worthy of praise must show first of all in her conduct, modesty, and purity. Marius, the illustrious Roman, said in that first speech of his to the Roman people: "Of women we require purity, of men labor." And I certainly agree. There is nothing more disgusting than a coarse and dirty woman. Who is stupid enough not to see clearly that a woman who does not care for neatness and cleanliness in her appearance, not only in her dress and body but in all her behavior and language, is by no means well mannered? How can it be anything but obvious that a bad mannered woman is also rarely virtuous? We shall consider elsewhere the harm that comes to a family from women who lack virtue, for I myself do not know which is the worse fate for a family, total celibacy or a single dishonored woman. In a bride, therefore, a man must first seek beauty of mind, that is, good conduct and virtue.

In her body he must seek not only loveliness, grace, and charm but must also choose a woman who is well made for bearing children, with the kind of constitution that promises to make them strong and big. There's an old proverb, "When you pick your wife, you choose your children." All her virtues will in fact shine brighter still in beautiful children. It is a well-known saying among poets: "Beautiful character dwells in a beautiful body." The natural philosophers require that a woman be neither thin nor very fat. Those laden with fat are subject to coldness and constipation and slow to conceive. They say that a woman should have a joyful nature, fresh and lively in her blood and her whole being. They have no objections to a dark girl. They do reject girls with a frowning black visage, however. They have no liking for either the undersized or the overlarge and lean. They find that a woman is most suited to bear children if she is fairly big and has limbs of ample length. They always have a preference for youth, based on a number of arguments which I need not expound here, but particularly on the point that a young girl has a more adaptable mind. Young girls are pure by virtue of their age and have not developed any spitefulness. They are by nature modest and free of vice. They quickly learn to accept affectionately and unresistingly the habits and wishes of their husbands.

Now we have spoken of beauty. Let us next consider parentage, and what are the qualities to look for there. I think the first problem in choosing a family is to investigate closely the customs and habits of one's new relatives. Many marriages have ruined the family, as one may hear and read every day, because they involved union with a litigious, quarrelsome, arrogant, and malevolent set of men. For brevity's sake I cite no examples here. I think that no one is so great a fool that he would not rather remain unmarried than burden himself with terrible relatives. Sometimes the links of family have proved a trouble and disaster to the man, who has had to support both his own family and that of the girl he married. Not infrequently it happens that the new family, because they feel unable to manage their own affairs or because they really are so unfortunate, all settle down in the house of their new kinsman. As the new husband you cannot keep them without harm to yourself, nor can you send them away without incurring censure.

To sum up this whole subject in a few words, for I want above all to be brief on this point, let a man get himself new kinsmen of better than

plebeian blood, of a fortune more than diminutive of a decent occupation, and of modest and respectable habits. Let them not be too far above himself, lest their greatness overshadow his own honor and position. Too high a family may disturb his own and his family's peace and tranquillity, and also, if one of them falls, you cannot help to support him without collapsing or wearing yourself out as you stagger under a weight too great for your arms and your strength. I also do not want the new relatives to rank too low, for while the first error puts you in a position of servitude, the second causes expense. Let them be equals, then, and, to repeat, modest and respectable people.

The matter of dowry is next, which I would like to see middling in size, certain and prompt rather than large, vague, or promised for an indefinite future. I know not why everyone, as if corrupted by a common vice, takes advantage of delay to grow lazy in paying debts. Sometimes, in cases of marriage, people are further tempted because they hope to evade payment altogether. As your wife spends her first year in your house, it seems impossible not to reinforce the new bonds of kinship by frequent visiting and parties. But it will be thought rude if, in the middle of a gathering of kinsmen, you put yourself forward to insist and complain. If, as new husbands usually do, you don't want to lose their still precarious favor, you may ask your in-laws in restrained and casual words. Then you are forced to accept any little excuse they may offer. If you make a more forthright demand for what is your own, they will explain to you their many obligations, will complain of fortune, blame the conditions of the time, complain of other men, and say that they hope to be able to ask much of you in greater difficulties. As long as they can, in fact, they will promise you bounteous repayment at an ever-receding date. They will beg you, and overwhelm you, nor will it seem possible for you to spurn the prayers of people you have accepted as your own family. Finally, you will be put in a position where you must either suffer the loss in silence or enter upon expensive litigation and create enmity.

What is more, it will seem that you can never put an end to the pressure from your wife on this point. She will weep many tears, and the pleadings and insistent prayers of a new love that has just begun are apt to have a certain force. However hard and twisted your temperament you can hardly impose silence on someone who pleads with an outsider, thus softly and tear-fully, for the sake of her own father and brothers. Then imagine how impossible for you to turn a deaf ear on your own wife doing so in your own house, in your own room. You are bound, in the end, to suffer either financial loss or loss of affection. This is why the dowry should be precisely set, promptly paid, and not too high. The larger the payments are to be and the longer they are to be carried, the more discussion you will be forced into, the more reluctantly you will be paid, and the more obliged you will feel to spend inordinate sums for all sorts of things. There will be indescribable bitterness and often totally ruinous results in setting dowries very high. We have said now how a wife is to be selected from outside and how she is to be received into the house. It remains to be seen how she is to be treated once she is within.

Study Questions

1. Many historians view the Renaissance as a period of increasing secularization. How does Alberti's work reflect this trend?

2. How did Alberti define the role of the father in a family? Where does he get his examples?

3. In what ways is the family like a state?

4. How, according to Alberti, does nature shape the role of women in the family?

5. What are the qualities of a good wife? Why do you think Alberti has nothing to say about the qualifications of a good husband?

The Life of Leonardo da Vinci (1550)   54

GIORGIO VASARI

Giorgio Vasari (1511–1574) celebrated the achievements of hundreds of artists in his *Lives of the Most Eminent Italian Architects, Painters, and Sculptors*, which he published first in 1550 and then in an enlarged edition 18 years later. Vasari undertook his project not as a historian or biographer, but as an artist. He believed that only a creative artist could understand the momentous accomplishments of the Renaissance.

Vasari's father was a potter; his uncle, with whom he lived as a teenager, was a painter. Apprenticed at an early age, Giorgio studied for a time in Michelangelo's studio. He secured the backing of powerful patrons and was soon in demand throughout the Italian peninsula. As he traveled, he collected materials for his *Lives*. His biography of Leonardo is one of the best known and shows Vasari's concern for detail, anecdote, and instruction.

Life of Leonardo Da Vinci

PAINTER AND SCULPTOR OF FLORENCE

The greatest gifts are often seen, in the course of nature, rained by celestial influences on human creatures; and sometimes, in supernatural fashion, beauty, grace, and talent are united beyond measure in one single person, in a manner that to whatever such an one turns his attention, his every action is so divine, that, surpassing all other men, it makes itself clearly known as a thing bestowed by God (as it is), and not acquired by human art. This was seen by all mankind in Leonardo da Vinci, in whom, besides a beauty of body never sufficiently extolled, there was an infinite grace in all his actions; and so great was his genius, and such its growth, that to whatever difficulties he turned his mind, he solved them with ease. In him was great bodily strength, joined to dexterity, with a spirit and courage ever royal and magnanimous; and the fame of his name so increased, that not only in his lifetime was he held in esteem, but his reputation became even greater among posterity after his death.

Truly marvellous and celestial was Leonardo, the son of Ser Piero da Vinci; and in learning and in the rudiments of letters he would have made great proficience, if he had not been so variable and unstable, for he set himself to learn many things, and then, after having begun them, abandoned them. Thus, in arithmetic, during the few months that he studied it, he made so much progress, that, by continually suggesting doubts and difficulties to the master who was teaching him, he would very often bewilder him. He gave some little attention to music, and quickly resolved to learn to play the lyre, as one who had by nature a spirit most lofty and full of refinement: wherefore he sang divinely to that instrument, improvising upon it. Nevertheless, although he occupied himself with such a variety of things, he never ceased drawing and working in relief, pursuits which suited his fancy more than any other. Ser Piero, having observed this, and having considered the loftiness of his intellect, one day took some of his drawings and carried them to Andrea del Verrocchio, who was much his friend, and besought him straitly [sic] to tell him whether Leonardo, by devoting himself to drawing, would make any proficience. Andrea was astonished to see the extraordinary beginnings of Leonardo, and urged Ser Piero that he should make him study it; wherefore he arranged with Leonardo that he should enter the workshop of Andrea, which Leonardo did with the greatest willingness in the world. And he practised not one branch of art only, but all those in which drawing played a part; and having an intellect so divine and marvellous that he was also an excellent geometrician, he not only worked in sculpture, making in his youth, in clay, some heads of women that are smiling, of which plaster casts are still taken, and likewise some heads of boys which appeared to have issued from the hand of a master; but in architecture, also, he made many drawings both of ground-plans and of other designs of buildings; and he was the first, although but a youth, who suggested the plan of reducing the river Arno to a navigable canal from Pisa to Florence. He made designs of flour-mills, fulling-mills, and engines, which might be driven by the force of water; and since he wished that his profession should be painting, he studied much in drawing after nature, and sometimes in making models of figures in clay, over which he would lay soft pieces of cloth dipped in clay, and then set himself patiently to draw them on a certain kind of very fine Rheims cloth, or prepared linen; and he executed them in black and white with the point of his brush, so that it was a marvel, as some of them by his hand, which I have in our book of drawings, still bear witness; besides which, he drew on paper with such diligence and so well, that there is no one who has ever equalled him in perfection of finish; and I have one, a head drawn with the style in chiaroscuro, which is divine.

Leonardo da Vinci, *The Last Supper.* Leonardo da Vince was the impetus behind the High Renaissance concern for the idealization of nature, moving from a realistic portrayal of the human figure to an idealized form. Evident in Leonardo's *Last Supper* is his effort to depict a person's character and inner nature by the use of gesture and movement. Unfortunately, Leonardo used an experimental technique in this fresco, which soon led to its physical deterioration.

And there was infused in that brain such grace from God, and a power of expression in such sublime accord with the intellect and memory that served it, and he knew so well how to express his conceptions by draughtmanship, that he vanquished with his discourse, and confuted with his reasoning, every valiant wit. And he was continually making models and designs to show men how to remove mountains with ease, and how to bore them in order to pass from one level to another; and by means of levers, windlasses, and screws, he showed the way to raise and draw great weights, together with methods for emptying harbours, and pumps for removing water from low places, things which his brain never ceased from devising.

It is clear that Leonardo, through his comprehension of art, began many things and never finished one of them, since it seemed to him that the hand was not able to attain to the perfection of art in carrying out the things which he imagined; for the reason that he conceived in idea difficulties so subtle and so marvellous, that they could never be expressed by the hands, be they ever so excellent. And so many were his caprices, that, philosophizing of natural things, he set himself to seek out the properties of herbs, going on even to observe the motions of the heavens, the path of the moon, and the courses of the sun....

He also painted in Milan, for the Friars of S. Dominic, at S. Maria dell Grazie, a Last Supper, a most beautiful and marvellous thing; and to the heads of the Apostles he gave such majesty and beauty, that he left the head of Christ unfinished, not believing that he was able to give it that divine air which is essential to the image of Christ. This work, remaining thus all but finished, has ever been held by the Milanese in the greatest veneration, and also by strangers as well; for Leonardo imagined and succeeded in expressing that anxiety which had seized the Apostles in wishing to know who should betray their Master. For which reason in all their faces are seen love, fear, and wrath, or rather, sorrow, at not being able to understand the meaning of Christ; which thing excites no less marvel than the sight, in contrast to it, of obstinacy, hatred, and treachery in Judas; not to mention that every least part of the work displays an incredible diligence, seeing that even in the tablecloth the texture of the stuff is counterfeited in such a manner that linen itself could not seem more real.

It is said that the Prior of that place kept pressing Leonardo, in a most importunate manner, to finish the work; for it seemed strange to him to see Leonardo sometimes stand half a day at a time, lost in contemplation, and he would have like him to go on like the labourers hoeing in his garden, without ever stopping his brush. And not content with this, he complained of it to the Duke, and that so warmly, that he was constrained to send for Leonardo and delicately urged him to work, contriving nevertheless to show him that he was doing all this because of the importunity of the Prior. Leonardo, knowing that the intellect of that Prince was acute and discerning, was pleased to discourse at large with the Duke on the subject, a thing which he had never done with the Prior: and he reasoned much with him about art, and made him understand that men of lofty genius sometimes accomplish the most when they work the least, seeking out inventions with the mind, and forming those perfect ideas which the hands afterwards express and reproduce from the images already conceived in the brain. And he added that two heads were still wanting for him to paint; that of Christ, which he did not wish to seek on earth; and he could not think that it was possible to conceive in the imagination that beauty and heavenly grace which should be the mark of God incarnate. Next, there was wanting that of Judas,

which was also troubling him, not thinking himself capable of imagining features that should represent the countenance of him who, after so many benefits received, had a mind so cruel as to resolve to betray his Lord, the Creator of the world. However, he would seek out a model for the latter; but if in the end he could not find a better, he should not want that of the importunate and tactless Prior. This thing moved the Duke wondrously to laughter, and he said that Leonardo had a thousand reasons on his side. And so the poor Prior, in confusion, confined himself to urging on the work in the garden, and left Leonardo in peace, who finished only the head of Judas, which seems the very embodiment of treachery and inhumanity; but that of Christ, as has been said, remained unfinished.

Leonardo undertook to execute, for Francesco del Giocondo, the portrait of Mona Lisa, his wife; and after toiling over it for four years, he left it unfinished; and the work is now in the collection of King Frances of France, at Fontainebleau. In this head, whoever wished to see how closely art could imitate nature, was able to comprehend it with ease; for in it were counterfeited all the minutenesses that with subtlety are able to be painted, seeing that the eyes had that lustre and watery sheen which are always seen in life, and around them were all those rosy and pearly tints, as well as the lashes, which cannot be represented without the greatest subtlety. The eyebrows, through his having shown the manner in which the hairs spring from the flesh, here more close and here more scanty, and curve according to the pores of the skin, could not be more natural. The nose, with its beautiful nostrils, rosy and tender, appeared to be alive. The mouth, with its opening, and with its ends united by the red of the lips to the flesh-tints of the face, seemed, in truth, to be not colours but flesh. In the pit of the throat, if one gazed upon it intently, could be seen the beating of the pulse. And, indeed, it may be said that it was painted in such a manner as to, make every valiant crafts-man, be he who he may, tremble and lose heart. He made use, also, of this device: Mona Lisa being very beautiful, he always employed, while he was painting her portrait, persons to play or sing, and jesters, who might make her remain merry, in order to take away that melancholy which painters are often wont to give to the portraits that they paint. And in this work of Leonardo's there was a smile so pleas-ing, that it was a thing more divine than human to behold; and it was held to be something marvellous, since the reality was not more alive....

There was very great disdain between Michelangelo Buonarroti and him, on account of which Michelangelo departed from Flor-ence, with the excuse of Duke Giuliano, having been summoned by the Pope to the competi-tion for the façade of S. Lorenzo. Leonardo, understanding this, departed and went into France, where the King, having had works by his hand, bore him great affection; and he desired that he should colour the cartoon of S. Anne, but Leonardo, according to his custom, put him off for a long time with words.

Finally, having grown old, he remained ill many months, and, feeling himself near to death, asked to have himself diligently informed of the teaching of the Catholic faith, and of the good way and holy Christian reli-gion; and then, with many moans, he confessed and was penitent; and although he could not raise himself well on his feet, support-ing himself on the arms of his friends and servants, he was pleased to take devoutly the most holy Sacrament, out of his bed. The King, who was wont often and lovingly to visit him, then came into the room; wherefore he, out of reverence, having raised himself to sit upon the bed, giving him an account of his sick-ness and the circumstances of it, showed withal how much he had offended God and mankind in not having worked at his art as he should have done. Thereupon he was seized by a paroxysm, the messenger of death; for which reason the King hav-ing risen and having taken his head, in order to assist him and show him favour, to the end that he might alleviate his pain, his spirit, which was divine, knowing that it could not have any greater honour, expired in the arms of the King, in the seventy-fifth year of his age.

Study Questions

1. If Leonardo is the classic example of the "Renaissance Man," how would you define the term?

2. What flaws does Vasari identify in Leonardo?

3. What might you deduce from the Vasari's *Life* about the social position of the artist in Renaissance Italy?

4. Why was Leonardo such a successful painter?

5. How did the famous artists of Leonardo's time get along with one another?

The Prince (1513)   **55**

NICCOLÒ MACHIAVELLI

Niccolò Machiavelli (1469–1527) was born in Florence, the son of a struggling lawyer. Marked from his youth as a brilliant student, he received a sound humanist education, which he put to use in the service of the state. At the age of 25, Machiavelli entered the service of the Republic of Florence as a diplomat and political advisor. His career brought him into contact with many of the most powerful figures of his age, but it was abruptly cut short in 1512 when the Republic was overthrown. Machiavelli was jailed and tortured before being sent into exile.

Forced into retirement, Machiavelli studied ancient history and began to write. In 1513 he finished *The Prince*, which remains one of the classics of Western political theory. A distillation of his experience in government and colored by his own cynical view of human nature, *The Prince* is a treatise on the art of governing successfully. Machiavelli wrote it in hopes of being allowed to return to government service, and it reflects his passionate desire for the restoration of political stability in Florence.

Niccolò Machiavelli to the Magnificent Loremzo de' Medici

It is a frequent custom for those who seek the favor of a prince to make him presents of those things they value most highly or which they know are most pleasing to him. Hence one often sees gifts consisting of horses, weapons, cloth of gold, precious stones, and similar ornaments suitable for men of noble rank. I too would like to commend myself to Your Magnificence with some token of my readiness to serve you; and I have not found among my belongings anything I prize so much or value so highly as my knowledge of the actions of men, acquired through long experience of contemporary affairs and extended reading in those of antiquity. For a long time I have thought carefully about these matters and examined them minutely; now I have condensed my thoughts into a little volume, and send it to Your Magnificence. My book is not stuffed with pompous phrases or elaborate, magnificent words, neither is it decorated with any form of extrinsic rhetorical embroidery, such as many authors use to present or adorn their materials. I wanted my book to be absolutely plain, or at least distinguished only by the variety of the examples and the importance of the subject.

I hope it will not be thought presumptuous if a man of low social rank undertakes to discuss the rule of princes and lay down principles for them. When painters want to represent landscapes, they stand on low ground to get a true view of the mountains and hills; they climb to the tops of the mountains to get a panorama over the valleys. Similarly, to know the people well one must be a prince, and to know princes well one must be, oneself, of the people.

On Different Kinds of Troops, Especially Mercenaries

I said before that a prince must lay strong foundations, otherwise he is bound to come to grief The chief foundations on which all states rest, whether they are new, old, or mixed, are good laws and good arms. And since there cannot be good laws where there are not good arms, and where there are good arms there are bound to be good laws, I shall set aside the topic of laws and talk about arms.

Let me say, then, that the armies with which a prince defends his state are either his own or are mercenaries, auxiliaries, or mixed. Mercenaries and auxiliaries are useless and dangerous. Any man who founds his state on mercenaries can never be safe or secure. The reason is that they have no other passions or incentives to hold the field, except their desire for a bit of money, and that is not enough to make them die for you.

Military Duties of the Prince

A prince, therefore, should have no other object, no other thought, no other subject of study, than war, its rules and disciplines; this is the only art for a man who commands, and it is of such value [*virtù*] that it not only keeps born princes in place, but often raises men from private citizens to princely fortune. On the other hand, it is clear that when princes have thought more about the refinements of life than about war, they have lost their positions. The quickest way to lose a state is to neglect this art; the quickest way to get one is to study it. Because he was a soldier, Francesco Sforza raised himself from private citizen to duke of Milan; his successors, who tried to avoid the hardships of warfare, became private citizens after being dukes. Apart from the other evils it brings with it, being defenseless makes you contemptible. This is one of the disgraces from which a prince must guard himself, as we shall

see later. Between a man with arms and a man without them there is no proportion at all. It is not reasonable to expect an armed man to obey one who is unarmed, nor an unarmed man to be safe among armed servants; because, what with the contempt of the former and the mistrust of the latter, there's no living together. Thus a prince who knows nothing of warfare, apart from his other troubles already described, can't hope for respect from his soldiers or put any trust in them.

On the Reasons Why Men Are Praised or Blamed—Especially Princes

It remains now to be seen what style and principles a prince ought to adopt in dealing with his subjects and friends. I know the subject has been treated frequently before, and I'm afraid people will think me rash for trying to do so again, especially since I intend to differ in this discussion from what others have said. But since I intend to write something useful to an understanding reader, it seemed better to go after the real truth of the matter than to repeat what people have imagined. A great many men have imagined states and princedoms such as nobody ever saw or knew in the real world, for there's such a difference between the way we really live and the way we ought to live that the man who neglects the real to study the ideal will learn how to accomplish his ruin, not his salvation. Any man who tries to be good all the time is bound to come to ruin among the great number who are not good. Hence a prince who wants to keep his post must learn how not to be good, and use that knowledge, or refrain from using it, as necessity requires.

Putting aside, then, all the imaginary things that are said about princes, and getting down to the truth, let me say that whenever men are discussed (and especially princes because they are prominent), there are certain qualities that bring them either praise or blame. Thus some are considered generous, others stingy; some are givers, others grabbers; some cruel, others merciful; one man is treacherous, another faithful; one is feeble and effeminate, another fierce and spirited; one humane, another proud; one lustful, another chaste; one straightforward, another sly; one harsh, another gentle; one serious, another playful; one religious, another skeptical, and so on. I know everyone will agree that among these many qualities a prince certainly ought to have all those that are considered good. But since it is impossible to have and exercise them all, because the conditions of human life simply do not allow it, a prince must be shrewd enough to avoid the public disgrace of those vices that would lose him his state. If he possibly can, he should also guard against vices that will not lose him his state; but if he cannot prevent them, he should not be too worried about indulging them. And furthermore, he should not be too worried about incurring blame for any vice without which he would find it hard to save his state. For if you look at matters carefully, you will see that something resembling virtue, if you follow it, may be your ruin, while something else resembling vice will lead, if you follow it, to your security and well-being.

On Cruelty and Clemency Whether It Is Better to Be Loved or Feared

The question arises: is it better to be loved than feared, or vice versa? I don't doubt that every prince would like to be both; but since it is hard to accommodate these qualities, if you have to make a choice, to be feared is much safer than to be loved. For it is a good general rule about men, that they are ungrateful, fickle, liars and deceivers, fearful of danger and greedy for gain. While you serve their welfare, they are all yours, but when the danger is close at hand, they turn against you. People are less concerned with offending a man who makes himself loved than one who makes himself feared: the reason is that love is a link of obligation

which men, because they are rotten, will break any time they think doing so serves their advantage; but fear involves dread of punishment, from which they can never escape.

Still, a prince should make himself feared in such a way that, even if he gets no love, he gets no hate either; because it is perfectly possible to be feared and not hated, and this will be the result if only the prince will keep his hands off the property of his subjects or citizens, and off their women. When he does have to shed blood, he should be sure to have a strong justification and manifest cause; but above all, he should not confiscate people's property, because men are quicker to forget the death of a father than the loss of a patrimony.

Returning to the question of being feared or loved, I conclude that since men love at their own inclination but can be made to fear at the inclination of the prince, a shrewd prince will lay his foundations on what is under his own control, not on what is controlled by others. He should simply take pains not to be hated, as I said.

The Way Princes Should Keep Their Word

How praiseworthy it is for a prince to keep his word and live with integrity rather than by craftiness, everyone understands; yet we see from recent experience that those princes have accomplished most who paid little heed to keeping their promises, but who knew how craftily to manipulate the minds of men. In the end, they won out over those who tried to act honestly.

You should consider then, that there are two ways of fighting, one with laws and the other with force. The first is properly a human method, the second belongs to beasts. But as the first method does not always suffice, you sometimes have to turn to the second. Thus a prince must know how to make good use of both the beast and the man. Ancient writers made subtle note of this fact when they wrote that Achilles and many other princes of antiquity were sent to be reared by Chiron the centaur, who trained them in his discipline. Having a teacher who is half man and half beast can only mean that a prince must know how to use both these two natures, and that one without the other has no lasting effect.

Since a prince must know how to use the character of beasts, he should pick for imitation the fox and the lion. As the lion cannot protect himself from traps, and the fox cannot defend himself from wolves, you have to be a fox in order to be wary of traps, and a lion to overawe the wolves. Those who try to live by the lion alone are badly mistaken. Thus a prudent prince cannot and should not keep his word when to do so would go against his interest, or when the reasons that made him pledge it no longer apply. Doubtless if all men were good, this rule would be bad; but since they are a sad lot, and keep no faith with you, you in your turn are under no obligation to keep it with them.

How a Prince Should Act to Acquire Reputation

Nothing gives a prince more prestige than undertaking great enterprises and setting a splendid example for his people.

A prince ought to show himself an admirer of talent, giving recognition to men of ability and honoring those who excel in a particular art. Moreover, he should encourage his citizens to ply their callings in peace, whether in commerce, agriculture, or in any other business. The man who improves his holdings should not be made to fear that they will be taken away from him; the man who opens up a branch of trade should not have to fear that he will be taxed out of existence. Instead, the prince should bestow prizes on the men who do these things, and on anyone else who takes the pains to enrich the city or state in some special way. He should also, at fitting times of the year, entertain his people with festivals and spectacles.

The Influence of Luck on Human Affairs and the Ways to Counter It

I realize that many people have thought, and still do think, that events are so governed in this world that the wisdom of men cannot possibly avail against them, indeed is altogether useless. On this basis, you might say that there is no point in sweating over anything, we should simply leave all matters to fate. This opinion has been the more popular in our own times because of the tremendous change in things during our lifetime, that actually is still going on today, beyond what anyone could have imagined. Indeed, sometimes when I think of it, I incline toward this opinion myself. Still, rather than give up on our free will altogether, I think it may be true that Fortune governs half of our actions, but that even so she leaves the other half more or less, in our power to control.

I conclude, then, that so long as Fortune varies and men stand still, they will prosper while they suit the times, and fail when they do not. But I do feel this: that it is better to be rash than timid, for Fortune is a woman, and the man who wants to hold her down must beat and bully her. We see that she yields more often to men of this stripe than to those who come coldly toward her. Like a woman, too, she is always a friend of the young, because they are less timid, more brutal, and take charge of her more recklessly.

Study Questions

1. Why does Machiavelli think that he is fit to offer advice to princes?

2. How important is force in the rule of states?

3. What seems to be Machiavelli's view of human nature?

4. Machiavelli addressed his book to a prince. How do you think this fact shaped the book?

5. Many people believed *The Prince* was immoral, and yet it was very widely read. How do you think it might have been useful?

6. Contemporaries saw Machiavelli as a dangerous man. Does *The Prince* offer any ground for this opinion?

Cultures in Collision

The Doge of Venice This painting shows Enrico Dandolo and his crusaders storming the city of Zara in 1202.

The Alexiad (1097)   **56**

ANNA COMNENA

After the great Moslem victory at Manzikert in 1071, which enabled them to over-run central Asia Minor, the Byzantine Emperor appealed to the Christian West for assistance. Only in 1095, after many delays, did Pope Urban II finally respond to this plea by launching the First Crusade with the exhortation, "God wills it!" Two years later, the "Frankish" leaders of the Crusade—Godfrey of Bouillon, Robert of Normandy, Baldwin of Flanders, Raymond of Toulouse, and Bohemund of Otranto—finally stood before Emperor Alexius I in his palace in Byzantium. Their audience was as awkward as it was momentous. The crusaders needed the Emperor's assistance in ferrying their troops to Asia Minor, and Alexius first sought an oath of homage and fealty from these counts. Both sides were curious about each other.

Attending this audience was the Emperor's learned daughter, Anna, who recorded the Byzantines' first reactions to the approach of the crusaders and then her impressions of the meetings in her later history of Alexius I's reign.

He [Alexius] heard a report of the approach of innumerable Frankish armies. Now he dreaded their arrival for he knew their irresistible manner of attack, their unstable and mobile character and all the peculiar natural and concomitant characteristics which the Frank retains throughout; and he also knew that they were always agape for money, and seemed to disregard their truces readily for any reason that cropped up. For he had always heard this reported of them, and found it very true. However, he did not lose heart, but prepared himself in every way so that, when the occasion called, he would be ready for battle. And indeed the actual facts were far greater and more terrible than rumour made them. For the whole of the West and all the barbarian tribes which dwell between the further side of the Adriatic and the pillars of Heracles, had all migrated in a body and were marching into Asia through the intervening Europe, and were making the journey with all their household.

After him [Count Raymond] came another innumerable, heterogeneous crowd collected from nearly all the Frankish countries, together with their leaders, kings, dukes, counts and even bishops. The Emperor sent men to receive them kindly and to convey promises of reasonable help, for he was always clever at providing for the future, and in grasping at a glance what was expedient for the moment. He also gave orders to men specially appointed for this purpose to supply them with victuals on their journey, so that they might not for any reason whatsoever have a handle for a quarrel against him. And they (the Crusaders) hastened on to the capital. One might have likened them to the stars of heaven or the sand poured out along the edge of the sea. For these men that hurried on to approach Constantinople were 'as many as there are leaves and flowers in the spring time,' as Homer says. Though I much desire to do so, I cannot detail the names of the leaders. For my speech is paralysed partly because I cannot articulate these strange names which are so unpronounceable, and partly because of the number of them. And, why indeed should we endeavour to recount the names of such a multitude, when even the men who were present were soon filled with in dif-ference at the sight? When they finally reached the capital they disposed their armies at the Emperor's bidding close to the Monastery of Cosmidium and they extended right up to the Hieron. It was not nine heralds, as formerly in Greece, who controlled this army by their shouts, but a large number of brave hoplites who accompanied them and persuaded them to yield to the Emperor's orders. Now the Emperor was anxious to force them all to take the same oath as Godfrey had taken, so he invited them separately and conversed with them privately about his wishes, and made use of the more reasonable ones as intermediaries with the more recalcitrant. As they would not obey, for they were expecting Bohemund to arrive, but found various means of evasion by continually making some fresh demands, the Emperor very easily saw through their pre-tences and by harassing them in every possible way, he forced them to take Godfrey's oath, and sent for Godfrey from over the sea at Pelecanus that he might be present during the taking of the oath. Thus they all assembled, Godfrey amongst them, and after the oath had been taken by all the Counts, a certain ven-turesome noble sat down on the Emperor's seat. The Emperor put up with him and said not a word, knowing of old the Latins' haughty nature. But Count Baldwin stepped forward and taking him by the hand raised him up, rebuked him severely, and said, " It was wrong of you to do such a thing here, and that

too when you have promised fealty to the Emperor; for it is not customary for the Roman Emperors to allow their subjects to sit beside them on the throne, and those who become his Majesty's sworn bondmen must observe the customs of the country." He made no reply to Baldwin, but darted a fierce glance at the Emperor and muttered some words to himself in his own language, saying , "Look at this rus-tic that keeps his seat, while such valiant cap-tains are standing round him." The movement of the Latin's lips did not escape the Emperor, who called one of the interpreters of the Latin tongue and asked the purport of his words. When he heard what the remark was, he said nothing to the Latin for some time, but kept the saying in his heart. As they were all taking leave of the Emperor, he called that haughty-minded, audacious Latin, and enquired who he was and of what country and lineage. "I am a Frank of the purest nobility," he replied, "all that I know is that at the cross-roads in the country whence I come there stands an old sanctuary, to which everyone who desires to fight in single combat goes ready accoutred for single combat, and there prays to God for help while he waits in expectation of the man who will dare to fight him. At those cross-roads I too have often tarried, waiting and longing for an antagonist; but never has one appeared who dared to fight me." In reply to this the Emperor said, "If you did not find a fight when you sought for it then, now the time has come which will give you your fill of fighting. But I strongly advise you not to place yourself in the rear nor in the front of your line, but to stand in the centre for I have had a long expe-rience of the Turkish method of fighting." It was not to this man only that he gave this advice, but to all the others he foretold the accidents likely to happen on their journey, and counselled them never to pursue the barbarians very far when God granted them a victory over them, for fear of being killed by falling into ambushes.

The Emperor sent for Bohemund and requested him to take the customary oath of the Latins. And he, mindful of his own position, namely, that he was not descended from illustrious ancestors, nor had a great supply of money, and for this reason not even many troops, but only a very limited number of Frankish retainers, and being moreover by nature ready to swear falsely, yielded readily to the Emperor's wish. Then the Emperor selected a room in the palace and had the floor strewn with every kind of riches, … and so filled the chamber with garments and stamped gold and silver, and other materials of lesser value, that one could not even walk because of their quantity. And he told the man who was to show Bohemund these things, to throw open the doors suddenly. Bohemund was amazed at the sight and exclaimed "If all these treasures were mine, I should have made myself master of many countries long ere this!" and the attendant replied, "The Emperor makes you a present of all these riches to-day." Bohemund was overjoyed and after thanking for the present he went away to rest in the house where he lodged. But when these treasures were brought to him, he who had admired them before had changed his mind and said, "Never did I imagine that the Emperor would inflict such dishonour on me. Take them away and give them back to him who sent them." But the Emperor, knowing the Latins' characteristic fickleness, quoted the popular proverb, 'Let bad things return to their own master.' When Bohemund heard of this and saw the porters carefully packing the presents up again, he changed his mind—he, who a minute before was sending them away and was annoyed at them, now gave the porters pleasant looks, just like a polypus that changes its form in an instant. For by nature the man was a rogue and ready for any eventualities; in roguery and courage he was far superior to all the Latins who came through then, as he was inferior to them in forces and money. But in spite of

his surpassing all in superabundant activity in mischief, yet fickleness like some natural Latin appendage attended him too. So he who first rejected the presents, afterwards accepted them with great pleasure. For he was sad in mind as he had left his country a landless man, ostensibly to worship at the Holy Sepulchre, but in reality with the intent of gaining a kingdom for himself, or rather, if it were possible, to follow his father's advice and seize the Roman Empire itself, and as he wanted to let out every reef, as the proverb has it, he required a great deal of money. But the Emperor, who understood his melancholy and ill-natured disposition, did his best cleverly to remove anything that would assist him in his secret plans. Therefore when Bohemund demanded the office of Great Domestic of the East, he did not gain his request, for he was trying to 'out-Cretan a Cretan.' For the Emperor feared that if he gained power he would make the other Counts his captives and bring them round afterwards to doing whatever he wished. Further, he did not want Bohemund to have the slightest suspicion that he was already detected, so he flattered him with fair hopes by saying, "The time for that has not come yet; but by your energy and reputation and above all by your fidelity it will come ere long." After this conversation and after bestowing gifts and honours of many kinds on them, the next day he took his seat on the imperial throne and summoned Bohemund and all the Counts. To them he discoursed of the things likely to befall them on their journey, and gave them useful advice; he also instructed them in the Turks' usual methods of warfare, and suggested the manner in which they should dispose the army and arrange their ranks, and advised them not to go far in pursuit of the Turks when they fled. And after he had in this way somewhat softened their savage behaviour by dint of money and advice, and had given them good counsel, he suggested their crossing into Asia.

Study Questions

1. Considering that the crusaders had come to help battle the Moslems, why were the Byzantines so reserved about the arrival of the Franks?

2. What did the Byzantines think of the crusaders? What did they see as their strengths and weaknesses?

3. Emperor Alexius plainly treated Prince Bohemund differently from the rest of the crusading lords. What lay behind the Emperor's attitude?

4. What did Anna mean when she said that Bohemund was trying to "out-Cretan a Cretan"? From this comment, can you deduce what the crusaders thought of the Byzantines?

The Journey of Louis VII to the East (1147 C.E.)   57

ODO OF DEUIL

Fifty years after the leaders of the First Crusade had appeared before Alexius I and Anna Comnena, those of the Second Crusade stood before Alexius's grandson, Emperor Manuel in the same audience chamber. This time, the crusaders were led by Emperor Conrad III and Louis VII of France. Again they requested Byzantine assistance in crossing into Asia, for which Emperor Manuel attempted to secure concessions. Because he had recently concluded a treaty with his Moslem neighbor, though which the crusaders would also have to pass, negotiations were difficult and ultimately the Europeans were denied safe passage. Without Byzantine military support, the Second Crusade was unable to march overland to the Holy Land, and the crusaders suffered heavy losses in their attempt to pass through Asia Minor.

One of Louis VII's bishops, Odo of Deuil (d. 1162), recorded his impressions of the visit to Byzantium in his later history of Louis's involvement in the Second Crusade. In spite of the bishop's repeated protestations of impartiality, his recollections were inevitably colored by the disasters, which were soon to overwhelm the expedition, all of which the French blamed on the Byzantines. The following passage begins just after Emperor Maneul has provided the crusaders with food and lodging.

This outcome would have satisfied the messengers if they had not judged one crime in the light of another; for they learned that the emperor had an agreement with the Turks and that the very man who had written to our king that he was going to accompany him in fighting the infidels and had won a recent and renowned victory over them had actually confirmed a twelve-year armistice with them. Also, his treachery was increased and made manifest by the fact that only a great number could get through his realm in safety; for the bishop of Langres and the count of Warenne and certain others, who had sent a few men ahead to Constantinople to provide arms and food for the journey, had suffered a considerable loss of possessions and were mourning their wounded and dead. And this did not happen just once; for from the time when we entered his territory we endured the robberies which his people perpetrated on us because our strength did not equal theirs. Perhaps this condition would have been bearable, and it could have been said that we deserved the evils which we suffered on account of the evils which we had committed, if blasphemy had not been added. For instance, if our priests celebrated mass on Greek altars, the Greeks afterwards purified them with propitiatory offerings and ablutions, as if they had been defiled. All the wealthy people have their own chapels, so adorned with paintings, marble and lamps that each magnate might justly say, "O Lord, I have cherished the beauty of Thy house," if the light of the true faith shone therein. But, O dreadful thing! we heard of an ill usage of theirs which should be expiated by death; namely, that every time they celebrate the marriage of one of our men, if he has been baptized in the Roman way, they rebaptize him before they make the pact. We now other heresies of theirs, both concerning their treatment of the Eucharist and concerning the procession of the Holy Ghost, but none of these matters would mar our page if not pertinent to our subject. Actually, it was for these reasons that the Greeks had incurred the hatred of our men, for their error had become known even among the lay people. Because of this they were judged not to be Christians, and the Franks considered killing them a matter of no importance and hence could with the more difficulty be restrained from pillage and plundering.

But let us return to the king, who, although he received new messengers from the emperor nearly every day, nevertheless complained about the delay of his own ambassadors, because he did not know what had happened to them. The Greeks always reported good news, but they never showed any proof of it, and they were the less believed because on every occasion all used the same prefatory flattery. The king accepted, but considered of slight, value their *polychroniae* [lavish flattery] (for that is the name of the gestures of honor which they exhibit, not only toward kings, but even toward certain of their nobles, lowering the head and body humbly or kneeling on the ground or even prostrating themselves). Occasionally the empress wrote to the queen. And then the Greeks degenerated entirely into women; putting aside all manly vigor, both of words and of spirit, they lightly swore whatever they thought would please us, but they neither kept faith with us nor maintained respect for themselves. In general they really have the opinion that anything which is done for the holy empire cannot be considered perjury. Let no one think that I am taking vengeance on a race of men hateful to me and that because of my hatred I am inviting a Greek whom I have not seen. Whoever has known the Greeks will, if asked, say that when they are afraid they become despicable in their excessive debasement and when they have the upper hand they are arrogant in their severe violence to those subjected to them. However, they toiled most zealously in advising the king to turn his route from Adrianople to St. George of Sestos and there to cross the sea the more swiftly and advantageously. But the king did not wish to undertake something which he had heard that the Franks had done. Thus, by the same paths, but not with the same omens, he followed the Germans who had preceded us, and when a day's journey from Constantinople met his own messengers, who told him the stories concerning the emperor which we have already related in part.

There were those who then advised the king to retreat and to seize the exceedingly rich land with its castles and cities and meanwhile to write to King Roger [of Sicily], who was then vigorously attacking the emperor, and, aided by his fleet, to attack Connstantinople itself. But, alas for us, nay, for all St. Peter's subjects, their words did not prevail! Therefore, we proceeded, and when we approached the city, lo, all its nobles and wealthy men, clerics as well as lay people, trooped out to meet the king and received him with due honor, humbly asking him to appear before the emperor and to fulfil the emperor's desire to see and talk with him. Now the king, taking pity on the emperor's fear and obeying his request, entered with a few of his men and received an imperial welcome in the portico of the palace. The two sovereigns were almost identical in age and stature, unlike only in dress and manners. After they had exchanged embraces and kisses, they went inside, where, when two chairs had been arranged, they both sat down. Surrounded by a circle of their men, they conversed with the help of an interpreter. The emperor asked about the king's present state and his wishes for the future, wishing for him the things which are God's to give and promising him those within his own power. Would it had been done as sincerely as it was gracefully! If his gestures, his liveliness of expression, and his words had been a true indication of his inner thoughts, those who stood nearby would have attested that he cherished the king with great affection; but such evidence is only plausible, not conclusive. Afterwards they parted as if they were brothers, and the imperial nobles took the the king away to the palace which had been designated as his lodging.

Conducted by the emperor, the king also visited the shrines and, after returning, when won over by the urgency of his host's requests, dined with him. That banquet afforded pleasure to ear, mouth, and eye with pomp as marvelous, viands as delicate, and pastimes as pleasant as the guests were illustrious. There

many of the king's men feared for him; but he, who had entrusted the care of himself to God, feared nothing at all, since he had faith and courage; for one who is not inclined to do harm does not easily believe that anyone will harm him.

Although the Greeks furnished us no proof that they were treacherous, I believe that they would not have exhibited such unremitting servitude if they had had good intentions. Actually, they were concealing the wrongs which were to be avenged after we crossed the Arm. However, it was not held against the Greeks that they closed the city gates to the throng, since it had burned many of their houses and olive trees, either for want of wood or by reason of arrogance and the drunkenness of fools. The king frequently punished offenders by cutting off their ears, hands, and feet, yet he could not thus check the folly of the whole group. Indeed, one of two things was necessary, either to kill many thousands at one time or to put up with their numerous evil deeds. As I was saying, a ship supplied us an ample market, and in front of the palace and even in the tents we had a rate of exchange which would have been adequate if it had lasted; namely, less than two denarii for one staminae and a mark for thirty stamina (three solidi). But after we had traveled three days beyond the city we paid five or six denarii for one stamina and lost a mark on twelve soldi.

Now while the king was awaiting the forces coming from Apulia, when they were crossing between Brindisi and Durazzo, the feast of St. Denis [patron saint of France] occurred, and he celebrated it with proper veneration. Since the Greeks celebrate this feast, the emperor knew of it, and he sent over to the king a carefully selected group of his clergy, each of whom he had equipped with a large taper decorated elaborately with gold and a great variety of colors; and thus he increased the glory of the ceremony. These clergy certainly differed from ours as to words and order of service, but they made a favorable impression because of their sweet chanting; for the mingling of voices, the heavier with the light, the eunuch's, namely, with the manly voice (for many of them were eunuchs), softened the hearts of the Franks. Also, they gave the onlookers pleasure by their graceful bearing and gentle clapping of hands and genuflexions. We recall these favors on the part of the emperor so that there may be manifest the treachery of him who simulated the friendship which we are accustomed to show only to our most intimate friends, while he harbored a feeling which we could not have appeased save by our very death. Surely no one could understand the Greeks without having had experience of them or without being endowed with prophetic inspiration.

Study Questions

1. Why were the Franks so suspicious of the Byzantines even after they had received their hospitality?

2. What accounts for the religious tensions between the Byzantines and the Franks, both of whom were Christian?

3. Was there anything about Byzantium and the Byzantines that Odo admired?

4. Do you think that there was anything that the Emperor could have done to remedy the situation, or was hostility between the Greeks and the Franks culturally inevitable?

Memoirs (after 1175 c.e.)   58

USAMA IBN MUNQIDH

Following their capture of Antioch in 1098 and Jerusalem in 1099, the crusaders established several Christian states in Palestine and Syria. Although the new crusading rulers encouraged immigration from western Europe, the bulk of their new subjects remained native Moslems. Fortunately, we can see something of how these Moslems viewed the Franks thanks to the memoirs of Usama ibn Manqidh. (1095–1188). Usama, a prominent Syrian nobleman, frequently fought against the crusaders, but he also had extensive commercial and personal dealings with them. Though the Franks alternatively angered and amused him, they also fascinated him.

Near the end of his long life, Usama recorded a series of short vignettes about his recollections of the Franks, and the following selections from his memoirs reveal the clash of cultures that resounded throughout the Middle East in the twelfth century. One deals with Usama's experience traveling on a safe-conduct pass from Baldwin III, the Christian King of Jerusalem; another records his astonishment of the lack of common sense displayed by a Frankish knight; and the last group illustrates the difference between new and old Christian residents of the Holy Land and between Christian monks and Moslem sufis.

I entered the, service of the just King Nur ad Din—God have mercy on him!—and he wrote to al-Malik as-Salih asking him to send my household and my sons out to me; they were in Egypt, under his patronage. Al-Malik as-Salih wrote back that he was unable to comply because he feared that they might fall into Frankish hands. He invited me instead to return to Egypt myself: 'You know,' he wrote, 'how strong the friendship is between us. If you have reason to mistrust the Palace, you could go to Mecca, and I would send you the appointment to the governorship of Aswan and the means to combat the Abyssinians. Aswan is on the frontier of the Islamic empire. I would send your household and your sons to you there.' I spoke to Nur ad-Din about this, and asked his advice, which was that he would certainly not choose to return to Egypt once he had extricated himself. 'Life is too short!' he said. 'It would be better if I sent to the Frankish King for a safe-conduct for your family, and gave them an escort to bring them here safely.' This he did—God have mercy on him!—and the Frankish King gave him his cross, which ensures the bearer's safety by land and sea. I sent it by a young slave of mine, together with letters to al-Malik as-Salih from Nur ad-Din and myself. My family were dispatched for Damietta on a ship of the vizier's private fleet, under his protection and provided with everything they might need.

At Damietta they transferred to a Frankish ship and set sail, but when they neared Acre, where the Frankish King was—God punish him for his sins—he sent out a boatload of men to break up the ship with hatchets before the eyes of my family, while he rode down to the beach and claimed everything that came ashore as booty. My young slave swam ashore with the safe-conduct, and said: 'My Lord King, is not this your safe-conduct?' 'Indeed it is,' he replied, 'But surely it is a Muslim custom that when a ship is wrecked close to land the local people pillage it?' 'So you are going to make us

your captives?' 'Certainly not.' He had my family escorted to a house, and the women searched. Everything they had was taken; the ship had been loaded with women's trinkets, clothes, jewels, swords and other arms, and gold and silver to the value of about 30,000 *dinar*. The King took it all, and then handed five hundred *dinar* back to them and said: 'Make your arrangements to continue your journey with this money.' And there were fifty of them altogether! At the time I was with Nur ad-Din in the realm of Kin Mas 'ud, at Ru'ban and Kaisun; compared with the safety of my sons, my brother and our women, the loss of the rest meant little to me, except for my books. There had been 4,000 fine volumes on board, and their destruction has been a cruel loss to me for the rest of my life.

Among the Franks—God damn them!—no quality is more highly esteemed in a man than military prowess. The knights have a monopoly of the positions of honour and importance among them, and no one else has any prestige in their eyes. They are the men who give counsel, pass judgment and command the armies. On one occasion I went to law with one of them about some herds that the Prince of Baniyas seized in a wood; this was at a time when there was a truce between us, and I was living in Damascus. I said to King Fulk, the son of Fulk. 'This man attacked and seized my herd. This is the season when the cows are in calf; their young died at birth, and he has returned the herd to me completely ruined.' The King turned to six or seven of his knights and said: 'Come, give a judgment on this man's case.' They retired from the audience chamber and discussed the matter until they all agreed. Then they returned to the King's presence and said: 'We have decided that the Prince of Baniyas should indemnify this man for the cattle that he has ruined.' The King ordered that the indemnity should be paid, but such was the pressure put on me and the courtesy shown me that in the end I accepted four hundred *dinar* from the Prince. Once the knights have given their judgment neither the King nor any other commander can alter or annul it, so great an influence do their knights have in their society. On this occasion the King swore to me that he had been made very happy the day before. When I asked him what had made him happy he said: 'They told me that you were a great knight, but I did not believe that you would be chivalrous.' 'Your Majesty,' I replied, 'I am a knight of my race and my people.' When a knight is tall and well-built they admire him all the more.

A very important Frankish knight was staying in the camp of King Fulk, the son of Fulk. He had come on a pilgrimage and was going home again. We got to know one another, and became firm friends. He called me 'brother' and an affectionate friendship grew up between us. When he was due to embark for the return journey he said to me: 'My brother, as I am about to return home, I should be happy if you would send your son with me,' (the boy, who was about fourteen years old, was beside me at the time), 'so that he could meet the noblemen of the realm and learn the arts of politics and chivalry. On his return home he would be a truly cultivated man.' A truly cultivated man would never be guilty of such a suggestion; my son might as well be taken prisoner as go off into the land of the Franks. I turned to my friend and said: 'I assure you that I could desire nothing better for my son, but unfortunately the boy's grandmother, my mother, is very attached to him, and she would not even let him come away with me without extracting a promise from me that I would bring him back to her.' 'Your mother is still alive?' 'Yes.' 'Then she must have her way.'

This is an example of Frankish barbarism, God damn them! When I was in Jerusalem I used, to go to the Masjid al-Aqsa, beside which is a small oratory which the Franks have made into a church. Whenever I went into the Mossque, which was in the hands of Templars who were friends of mine, they would put the little oratory at my disposal, so that I could say my prayers there. One day I had gone in, said the *Allah akhbar* and risen to begin my prayers, when a Frank threw himself on me from behind, lifted me up and turned me so that I was facing east. 'That is the way to pray!' he said. Some Templars at once intervened, seized the man and took him out of my way while I resumed my prayer. But the moment they stopped watching him he seized me again and forced me to face east, repeating that this was the way to pray. Again the Templars intervened and took him away. They apologized to me and said: 'He is a foreigner who has just arrived today from his homeland in the north, and he has never seen anyone pray facing any other direction than east.' I have finished my prayers,' I said, and left, stupefied by the fanatic who had been so perturbed and upset to see someone praying facing Mecca.

I paid a visit to the tomb of John the son of Zechariah—God's blessing on both of them— in the village of Sebastea in the province of Nablus. After saying my prayers, I came out into the square that was bounded on one side by the Holy Precinct. I found a half-closed gate, opened it and entered a church. Inside were about ten old men, their bare heads as white as combed cotton. They were facing the east, and wore (embroidered?) on their breasts staves ending in crossbars turned up like the rear of a saddle. They took their oath on this sign, and gave hospitality to those who needed it. The sight of their piety touched my heart, but at the same time it displeased and saddened me, for I had never seen such zeal and devotion among the Muslims. For some time I brooded on this experience, until one day, as Mu'in ad-Din and I were passing the Peacock House, he said to me: 'I want to dismount here and visit the Old Men (the ascetics).' 'Certainly,' I replied, and we dismounted and went into a long building set at an angle to the road. For the moment I thought there was no one there. Then I saw about a hundred prayer-mats, and on each a sufi, his face expressing peaceful serenity, and his body humble devotion. This was a reassuring sight, and I gave thanks to Almighty God that there were among the Muslims men of even more zealous devotion than those Christian priests. Before I had never seen sufis in their monastery, and was ignorant of the way they lived.

Study Questions

1. Quite plainly, Usama's views of Christian knights were mixed. What did he admire about the crusaders and what baffled him about them?

2. Many Moslem kings particularly despised the Templars, a Christian order of fighting monks, whom they often executed immediately on their capture. Why was Usama friendly with them?

3. Discuss the differences in the notions of honor among Christian knights and Usama's Moslem warriors.

4. Was there anything Usama admired in the Christian practice of their religion?

The Dissipator of Anxieties (1250)   59

JAMAL AD-DIN IBN WASIL

By the middle of the thirteenth century, the Moslems had driven the Franks out of almost all of their former possessions in Palestine. Desperate to reverse these losses, King Louis IX of France launched the West's last major crusade in 1250. Marshaling a formidable army and fleet, he attempted to capture a series of Egyptian towns, which he hoped to ransom in exchange for Jerusalem. The crusaders managed to seize Damietta, the Egyptian Delta, before their plans went awry when the Moslems cut off Louis's army from its base in Damietta and forced the king of the Franks to surrender.

In a later history of thirteenth-century Egypt, Ibn Wasil (1233–1293), a prominent Moslem diplomat and administrator, presented an eyewitness account of this great victory and of Louis's negotiations for his own ransom. The verses that Jamal ad-Din ibn Yahya ibn Matruh composed on this occasion, taunting Louis for his humiliation, stand as an epitaph for the first attempt by a Western power to exert its influence outside of Europe.

While the Franks stabilized their positions, reinforcements were reaching them from further up the Nile, from Damietta. The Muslims took some ships on camel-back up to the Bahr al-Mahalla,[1] and there launched them and embarked troops. There was water at that time from the flooding of the Nile, stagnant, but communicating with the Nile itself. When the Frankish vessels coming upstream from Damietta passed close to the Bahr al-Mahalla the Muslims, who were lying in wait, fell on them and gave battle. The Muslim squadron from al-Mansura came downstream to join the fight and they surrounded the Franks and captured them and their ships. Fifty-two Frankish men-of-war were taken, with about a thousand men on board and all the provisions they were carrying. The prisoners were taken on camels to the Muslim camp. For the Franks the defeat broke their supply-line and seriously weakened their position. They found themselves very short of provisions and blockaded without the means either of staying put or of leaving their position. The Muslims had the upper hand, and now nourished plans to attack.

On 1 dhu l-hijja/7 March 1250 the Franks took seven Muslim fire-ships on the Bahr al-Mahalla, but the Muslims escaped with their gear. On the second, al-Malik al-Mu'azzam ordered the amir Husam ad-Din to enter Cairo and take up residence in the vizier's palace and to perform all the usual functions of the Sultan's viceroy. The Qadi Jamal ad-Din ibn Wasil, the author, says: The Sultan gave robes of honour to me and also to a group of lawyers who presented themselves to do him homage. Al-Malik al-Mu'azzam's liberality extended in this way to anyone who presented himself at his gate. So I entered Cairo with the amir Husam ad-Din. On Monday 9 dhu l-hijja, the day of 'Arafa,[2] Muslim galleys attacked the Frankish

supply-ships. The encounter took place near the Mosque of Victory and the Muslims took thirty-two vessels from the Franks, of which seven were galleys. This weakened the Franks even more, and supplies in the camp were even scarcer. Then the Franks opened negotiations for a truce with the Muslims. Their ambassadors arrived and went into consultation with the amir Zain ad-Din, a *jamdar* amir, and the Grand Qadi Badr ad-Din. The Franks wanted to exchange Damietta for Jerusalem and a part of the Syrian coast, but this was not acceptable. On Friday 26 dhu l-hijja the Franks burnt all their encampments, sparing only the ships, and decided to take refuge in Damietta. At the end of the year (647) they were still in the same position, facing the Muslims.

On the night before Wednesday 3 muharram 648/7 April 1250, the resplendent night that disclosed a great victory and a stupendous triumph, the Franks marched out with all their forces towards Damietta, which they counted on to defend them, and their ships began to move downstream in convoy.

When the Muslims heard the news they set out after them, crossed to the Frankish bank of the river and were soon at their heels. As Wednesday dawned the Muslims had surrounded the Franks and were slaughtering them, dealing out death and captivity. Not one escaped. It is said that the dead numbered 30,000. In the battle the Bahrite mamluks of al-Malik as-Salih distinguished themselves by their courage and audacity: they caused the Franks terrible losses and played the major part in the victory. They fought furiously: it was they who flung themselves into the pursuit of the enemy: they were Islam's Templars. The accursed King of France and the great Frankish princes retreated to the hill of Munya, where they surrendered and begged for their lives.

---

[1] A backwater of the Nile, mentioned in operations in the Fifth Crusade.

[2] A solemn festival during the Muslim Pilgrimage.

They were given assurances by the eunuch Jamal ad-Din Muhsin as-Salihi, on the strength of which they surrendered. They were all taken to Mansura, where chains were put on the feet of the King of France and his companions, They were imprisoned in the house where the secretary Fakhr ad-Din ibn Luqman was living, and the eunuch Sabih al-Mu'azzami, a servant of al-Malik al-Mu'azzam Turanshah, son of al-Malik as-Salih Najm ad-Din Ayyub, was set to guard them; he had come with his master from Hisn Kaifa and had been promoted and shown great honour.

> The amir Husam ad-Din told me: 'The King of France was an extremely wise and intelligent man. In one of our conversations I said to him: "How did Your Majesty ever conceive the idea, a man of your character and wisdom and good sense, of going on board ship and riding the back of this sea and coming to a land so full of Muslims and soldiers, thinking that you could conquer it and become it's ruler? This undertaking is the greatest risk to which you could possibly expose yourself and your subjects." The King laughed but did not reply. "In our land," I added, "when a man travels by sea on several occasions, exposing himself and his possessions to such a risk, his testimony is not accepted as evidence by a Court of Law." "Why not?" "Because such behaviour suggests to us that he lacks sense, and a man who lacks sense is not fit to give evidence." The King laughed and said: "By God, whoever said that was right, and whoever made that ruling did not err."

Referring to this episode, the imprisonment of the King of France in Fakhr ad-Din ibn Luqman's house, and the appointment of the eunuch Sabih to look after him, Jamal ad-Din ibn Yahya ibn Matrub wrote:

> Speak to the Frenchman, if you visit him, a true word from a good counsellor:
> 'God requite you for what has happened, the slaughter of the Messiah's adorers!
> You came to the East boasting of conquest, believing our martial drum-roll to be a mere breath of wind.
> And your stupidity has brought you to a place where your eyes can no longer see in the broad plain any way of escape.
> And of all your company, whom you commanded so well that you led them into the tomb's embrace,
> Of fifty thousand not one can be seen that is not dead, or wounded and a prisoner.
> God help you to other similar adventures: who knows that in the end Jesus will not breathe freely (of your impious worship)!'
> If your Pope is content with this, how often is a statesman guilty of deceit!
> And say to them, if they ever think of returning to take their revenge, or for any other reason:
> 'The house of Ibn Luqman is always ready here, and the chain and the eunuch Sabih are still here.'

Study Questions

1. Why did Louis have to surrender?

2. In the negotiations for his release, why did King Louis agree that his testimony should not be accepted in a court of law?

3. Use Jamal ad-Din's poem to discuss the Moslem attitude to Christianity.

4. What did the poet mean when he concluded, "the house of Ibn Luqam is always ready"?

China and Japan in the Middle Ages

Samurai. During the Kamakura period, painters began to depict the adventures of the new warrior class. Here is an imposing mounted samurai warrior, the Japanese equivalent of the medieval knight in feudal Europe. Like his European counterpart, the samurai was supposed to live by a strict moral code and was expected to maintain an unquestioning loyalty to his liege lord. Above all, a samurai's life was one of simplicity and self-sacrifice.

The Hojo Code (1232)

60

Feudalism in thirteenth-century Japan resulted from the breakup of central authority and the rise of military commanders, known as Shoguns. The head of the Hojo family attained this office at the beginning of the thirteenth century and wrote a code to establish relations between lords and vassals as well as to define civil and criminal laws. Like other feudal systems, the crucial relationships were hierarchical, with lords owning and vassals serving. *The Hojo Code* covers all forms of public conduct from religious observances to personal behavior. One striking difference between feudalism in the West and in Japan involves the property rights of women.

Institutes of Judicature

1.—The Shrines of the gods must be kept in repair; and their worship performed with the greatest attention.

The majesty of the gods is augmented by the veneration of men, and the fortunes of men are fulfilled by the virtue of the gods. Therefore the established sacrifices to them must not be allowed to deteriorate; and there must be no remissness in paying ceremonial honours to them as if they were present. Accordingly throughout the provinces of the Kwanto Dominion and likewise in the Manors, the Land Reeves, the *Kannushi* (Shinto) priests and others concerned must each bear this in mind, and carefully carry out this duty. Moreover, in the case of shrines which have been enfeoffed (endowed with benefices) the deed of grant must be confirmed each generation, and minor repairs executed from time to time as prescribed therein. If serious damage should happen to a shrine a full report of the circumstances is to be made, and such directions will be given (from Kamakura) as the exigencies of the case may require.

2.—(Buddhist) Temples and pagodas must be kept in repair and the Buddhist services diligently celebrated.

Although (Buddhist) temples are different from (Shinto) shrines, both are alike as regards worship and veneration. Therefore the merit of maintaining them both in good order and the duty of keeping up the established services, as provided in the foregoing article is the same in both cases. Let no one bring trouble on himself through negligence herein.

In case the incumbent does what he pleases with the income of the temple benefice or covetously misappropriates it, or if the duties of the clergy be not diligently fulfilled by him, the offender shall be promptly dismissed, and another incumbent appointed.

3.—Of the duties devolving on Protectors in the Provinces.

In the time of the august Right General's House it was settled that those duties should be the calling out and despatching of the Grand Guard for service at the capital, the suppression of conspiracies and rebellion and the punishment of murder and violence (which included night attacks on houses, robbery, dacoity and piracy). Of late years, however, Official Substitutes (*Daikwan*) have been taken on and distributed over the countries and townships and these have been imposing public burdens (corvée) on the villages. Not being Governors of the provinces they yet hinder the (Agricultural) work of the province: not being Land-Reeves they are yet greedy of the profits of the land. Such proceedings and schemes are utterly unprincipled.

Be it noted that no person, even if his family were for generations vassals of the August House (of the Minamoto) is competent to impress for military service unless he has an investiture of the present date.

On the other hand again, it is reported that inferior managers and village officials in various places make use of the name of vassals of the August House as a pretext for opposing the orders of the Governor of the provinces or of the lord of the Manor. Such persons, even if they are desirous of being taken into the service of the Protectors, must not under any circumstances be included in the enrolment for service in the Guards. In short, conformably to the precedents of the time of the August General's House, the Protectors must cease altogether from giving directions in matters outside of the hurrying-up of the Grand Guards and the suppression of plots, rebellion, murder and violence.

In the event of a Protector disobeying this article and intermeddling in other affairs than those herein named, if a complaint is instituted against him by the Governor of the Province or the lord of a Manor, or if the Land-Reeve or the folk aggrieved petition for redress, his downright lawlessness being thus brought to light, he shall be divested of his office and a person of gentle character appointed in his stead. Again, as regards Delegates (*Daikwan*) not more than one is to be appointed by a Protector.

4.—Of Protectors omitting to report cases of crime and confiscating the successions to fiefs, on account of offences.

When persons are found committing serious offences, the Protectors should make a detailed report of the case (to Kamakura) and follow such directions as may be given them in relation thereto; yet there are some who, without ascertaining the truth or falsehood of an accusation, or investigating whether the offence committed was serious or trifling, arbitrarily pronounce the escheat of the criminal's heriditaments, and selfishly cause them to be confiscated. Such unjust judgments are a nefarious artifice for the indulgence of license. Let a report be promptly made to us of the circumstances of each case and our decision upon the matter be respectfully asked for, any further persistence in transgressions of this kind will be dealt with criminally.

In the next place, with regard to a culprit's rice-fields and other fields, his dwelling-house, his wife and children, his utensils and other articles of property. In serious cases, the offenders are to be taken in charge by the Protector's office; but it is not necessary to take in charge their farms, houses, wives, children and miscellaneous gear along with them.

Furthermore, even if the criminal should in his statement implicate others as being accomplices or accessories, such are not to be included in the scope of the Protector's judgment, unless they are found in possession of the booty (or other substantial evidence of guilt be forthcoming).

5.—Of Land-Reeves in the provinces detaining a part of the assessed amounts of the rice-tax.

If a plaint is instituted by the lord of the Manor alleging that a Land-Reeve is withholding the land-tax payable to him, a statement of account will be at once taken, and the plaintiff shall receive a certificate of the balance that may be found to be due to him. If the Land-Reeve be adjudged to be in default, and has no valid plea to urge in justification, he will be required to make compensation in full. If the amount is small, judgment will be given for immediate payment. If the amount be greater than he is able to pay at once, he will be allowed three years within which to completely discharge his liability. Any Land-Reeve who, after such delay granted, shall make further delays and difficulties, contrary to the intention of this article, shall be deprived of his post.

6.—Governors of provinces and Manorial Houses may exercise their normal jurisdiction without referring to the Kwanto (authorities).

In cases where jurisdiction has heretofore been exercised by the Governor's Yamens, by lords of Manors, by Shinto Shrines or by Buddhist Temples on the footing of lords of Manors, it will not be necessary for us now to introduce interference. Even if they wish to refer a matter to us for advice, they are not permitted to do so.

In the next place, as regards the bringing of suits before us direct, without producing a letter of recommendation from the local tribunal.

The proper procedure in bringing a suit is for the parties to come provided with letters of recommendation from their own tribunal, whether it be that of a Provincial Governor, a manor, a shrine, or a temple. Hence persons who come unprovided with such letters have already committed a breach of propriety and henceforth their suits will not be received injudicature.

7.—Whether the fiefs which have been granted since the time of Yoritomo by the successive *Shogun*'s and by Her Ladyship the Dowager (Masako) are to be revoked or exchanged in consequence of suits being brought by the original owners.

Such fiefs having been granted as rewards for distinguished merit in the field, or for valuable services in official employment, have not been acquired without just title. And if judgment were to be given in favour of some one who alleged that such was originally the fief of his ancestors, though the one face might beam with joy, the many comrades could assuredly feel no sense of security. A stop must be put to persons bringing such unsettling suits.

In case, however, one of the grantees of the present epoch should commit a crime, and the original owner, watching his opportunity should thereupon bring a suit for recovery of possession, he cannot well be prohibited from doing so.

In the next place, as regards attempts that may be made to disturb tenures by occasion of the *Shogun*'s judicature having through failure of heirs come to an end.

Whereas some persons who, in consequence of not having right on their side, were formerly non-suited are found scheming, after allowing an interval of years to elapse, to bring suit a second time, the mere framing of such an intention is an offence of no light criminality. Henceforward should any persons, disregarding the adjudications of the *Shogun* and his successors, wantonly institute suits of disturbance, in every such case the grounds of the invalidity of the claim are to be endorsed at full length upon the title-deeds in his possession.

8.—Of fiefs which, though deeds of investiture are held, have not been had in possession through a series of years.

With respect to the above, if more than twenty years have elapsed since the present holder was in possession his title is not to be enquired into and no change can be made: following herein the precedent of the time of the Yoritomo house. And if any one falsely alleging himself to be in possession, obtains by deceit a deed of grant, even though he may have the document in his possession it is not to be recognized as having validity.

9.—Of plotters of treason.

The purport of the provision relating to such persons cannot well be settled beforehand. In some cases, precedent is to be followed; in others, such action should be taken as the particular circumstances may require.

10.—Of the crimes of killing, maiming and wounding: furthermore, whether parents and children are to be held mutually responsible for each other's guilt.

A person who is guilty of killing or maiming, unless he acted without premeditation, as in a chance altercation or in the intoxication of a festive party, shall be punished in his own person by death or else by banishment or by confiscation of his investiture; but his father, or his son, unless they have actually been accomplices, shall not be held responsible.

Next, the offence of cutting or wounding must be dealt with in the same way, the culprit alone being responsible.

Next, in case a son or a grandson slays the enemy of his father or grand-father, the father or grand-father, even if they were not privy to the offence, are nevertheless to be punished for it. The reason is that the gratification of the father's or grand-father's rage was the motive prompting to the sudden execution of a cherished purpose.

Next, in case a man's son, without his knowledge, is guilty of killing or maiming another, or attempting to do so, for the pupose of appropriating that other's post or seizing his property or valuables, if the fact of the father's non-connivance is clearly proven by the evidence, he is not to be held responsible.

11.—Whether in consequence of a husband's crime the estate of the wife is to be confiscated or not.

In cases of serious crime, treason, murder and maiming, also dacoity, piracy, night-attacks, robbery and the like, the guilt of the husband extends to the wife also. In cases of murder and maiming, cutting and wounding, arising out of a sudden dispute, however, she is not to be held responsible.

12.—Of abusive language.

Quarrels and murders have their origin in abusive and insulting language. In grave cases the offender shall be sent into banishment, in minor cases, ordered into confinement. If during the course of a judicial hearing one of the parties gives vent to abuse or insults, the matter in dispute shall be decided in favour of the other party. If the other party however has not right on his side, some other

fief of the offender shall be confiscated. If he has no fief he shall be punished by being sent into banishment.

13.—Of the offence of striking (or beating) a person.

In such cases the person who receives the beating is sure to want to kill or maim the other in order to wipe out the insult; so the offence of beating a person is by no means a trivial one. Accordingly, if the offender be a *Samurai*, his fief shall be confiscated; if he has no fief he shall be sent into banishment: persons of lower rank, servants, pages and under, shall be placed in confinement.

14.—When a crime or offence is committed by Deputies, whether the principals are responsible.

When a Deputy is guilty of murder or any lesser one of the serious crimes, if his principal arrests and sends him on for trial, the master shall not be held responsible. But if the master in order to shield the Deputy reports that the latter is not to blame, and the truth is afterwards found out, incriminating him, the former cannot escape responsibility and accordingly his fief shall be confiscated. In such cases the Deputy shall be imprisoned (in order to be tried and dealt with).

Again, if a Deputy either detains the rice-tax payable to the lord of the Manor or contravenes the laws and precedents even though the action is that of the Deputy alone, his principal shall nevertheless be responsible.

Moreover, whenever, either in consequence of a suit instituted by the lord of a Manor, or in connection with matters of fact alleged in a plaintiff's petition, a Deputy receives a summons from the Kwanto or is sent for from Rokuhara, and instead of making up his mind to come at once, shilly-shallies and delays, his principal's investiture shall in like manner be revoked. Extenuating circumstances may, however, be taken into consideration.

15.—Of the crime of forgery.

If a *Samurai* commits the above, his fief shall be confiscated; if he has no investiture he shall be sent into exile. If one of the lower class commits it, he shall be branded in the face by burning. The amanuensis shall receive the same punishment.

Next, in suits if it is persistently alleged that the title-deed in the defendant's possession is a forgery and when the document is opened and inspected, if it is found to be indeed a forgery then the punishment shall be as above provided; but if it be found to be without flaw, then a fine propordonate to his position shall be inflicted on the false accuser, to be paid into the fund for the repairing of Shrines and temples. If he have not means wherewith to pay the fine he shall be deported.

19.—Of kinsmen, whether near or distant, who having been reared and supported, afterwards turn their backs on the descendants of their original masters.

Of persons who were dependent on a kinsman for their upbringing some were treated on a footing of affectionate intimacy as if they were sons; and where that was not so (owing to their belonging to a lower rank in life) they were maintained as if they were vassals. When persons so circumstanced rendered some loyal service to their masters, the latter, in their abounding appreciation of the spirit so displayed have in some cases handed them an allocation-note and in other cases have granted them a deed of enfeoffment. Yet they pretend that those grants were merely free-will gifts and take a view of things opposite to that taken by the sons or grandsons of their first master, with the result that the tenor of the relations to each other becomes very different from what it ought to be. For a time they act coquettishly, and those who were on the footing of sonship keep it up whilst the others observe the etiquette proper to vassalship; and then after a period of shilly-shallying some of them avail themselves of (literally, borrow) the badge of somebody who is not related to them, whilst the others go the length

of taking up the opposite way of thinking. When such persons forge all at once the predecessors benefaction and act in opposition to his son or grandson the fiefs which were so assigned to them are to be taken from them and given back to the descendant of the original holder.

20.—Of the succession to a fief when the child, after getting the deed of assignment, predeceases the parents.

Even when the child is alive, what is to hinder the parents from revoking the assignment? How much more, then, are they free to dispose of the fief after the child has died; the thing must be left entirely to the discretion of the father or grandfather.

21.—Whether when a wife or concubine, after getting an assignment from the husband, has been divorced, she can retain the tenure of the fief or not.

If the wife in question has been repudiated in consequence of having committed some serious transgression. even if she holds a written promise of the by-gone days she may not hold the fief of her former husband. On the other hand, if the wife in question had a virtuous record and was innocent of any fault and was discarded by reason of the husband's preference for novelty, the fief which had been assigned to her cannot be revoked.

22.—Of parents who when making a disposition of their fief pass over a grown up son whose relationship has not been severed.

When parents have brought up their son to man's estate and he has shown himself to be diligent and deserving then, either in consequence of a stepmother's slanders or out of favouritism to the son of a concubine although the son's relationship has not been severed, suddenly to leave him out and without rhyme or reason make no grant to him, would be the very extreme of arbitrariness. Accordingly; for the wife's son who has now arrived at manhood one fifth of the fief must be cut off and assigned as his share to any older brother who is without sufficient means. However this grant should be made to depend upon proofs given, no matter whether the recipient be the son of the wife or the son of a concubine, and however small the amount of the share may be. Even if he be the son of the wife but has no service to show he does not come within the scope of the rule; neither, on the other hand, do persons who have been unfilial (even though they have rendered service).

23.—Of the adoption of heirs by women.

Although the spirit of the (ancient) laws does not allow of adoption by females, yet since the time of the General of the Right (Yoritomo) down to the present day it has been the invariable rule to allow women who had no children of their own to adopt an heir and transmit the fief to him. And not only that, but all over the country, in the capital as well as in the rural districts there are abundant evidences of the existence of the same practice. It is needless to enumerate the cases. Besides, after full consideration and discussion, its validity has been recognized, and it is hereby confirmed.

24.—Whether a widow who has succeeded to her husband's fief and who marries again should continue to hold it.

Widows who have succeeded to the fief of their deceased husband should give up everything else and devote themselves to their husbands' welfare in the after-world and those who disregard that observance cannot be held blameless. Hence if any such, soon forgetting their conjugal constancy marry again, the fief held by their late husband is to be granted to the husband's son. If the deceased husband had no son, the fief should be disposed of in some other way.

33.—Of robbing and theft; also of incendiaries. For the two kinds of stealing the punishment (death) is already established by precedents. Can there be hesitation or reconsideration on that point? Next as regards the man who sets on fire (a house, etc.) he is to be regarded in the same light as a brigand and it is right that he should be outlawed.

34.—Of illicit intercourse with another person's wife.

Whoever embraces another person's wife is to be deprived of half of his fief, and to be inhibited from rendering service any more, regardless of whether it was a case of rape or adultery. If he have no investiture he must be sent into banishment. A woman who commits adultery shall in like manner be deprived of her fief, and if she have none she must also be sent into banishment.

41.—Of Slaves and unclassed persons.

(In cases of dispute respecting the ownership of such persons) the precedent established by the late *Shogun*'s House must be adhered to; that is to say, if more than ten years have elapsed without the former owner having asserted his claim, there shall be no discussion as to the merits of the case and the possession of the present owner is not to be interfered with.

42.—Of inflicting loss and ruin on absconding farmers under the pretext of smashing runaways.

When people living in the provinces run away and escape, the lord of the fief and others, proclaiming that runaways must be smashed up, detain their wives and children, and confiscate their property. Such a mode of procedure is quite the reverse of benevolent government. Henceforth such must be referred (to Kamakura) for adjudication, and if it is found that the farmer is in arrear as regards payment of his land tax and levies, he shall be compelled to make good the deficiency. If he is found not to be so in arrear, the property seized from him shall be forthwith restored to him. And it shall be entirely at the option of the farmer himself whether he shall continue to live in the fief or go elsewhere.

Study Question

1. What is the relationship between lords and vassals in *The Hojo Code?*

2. What is the place of agriculture in medieval Japan? How is it regulated in the *Code?*

3. Do women have the same legal rights as men?

4. Why was kinship so important in Japanese society?

5. Why did it seem important to codify laws in the early thirteenth century?

A Chronicle of Gods and Sovereigns (1339–1343)   61

KITABATAKE CHIKAFUSA

Kitabatake Chikafusa (1292–1354) was descended from a branch of the Japanese imperial family. He became its head at the age of 13 when his father took Buddhist vows. Most of Kitabatake's life was spent at the imperial court where he held important posts as a counselor and as head of the academies that trained the children of other courtiers. He was personally responsible for the education of one of the imperial princes. He lived through a long period of civil war and governmental instability and twice fled the capital. It was during his second period of voluntary exile that he wrote *A Chronicle of Gods and Sovereigns.*

The *Chronicle* is an expression of the divine origins of Japan and a celebration of the imperial dynasty, which Kitabatake claims has descended unbroken from its creation by the goddess of the sun. This succession is what makes Japan the greatest of all nations in Kitabatake's account.

Japan is the divine country. The heavenly ancestor it was who first laid its foundations, and the Sun Goddess left her descendants to reign over it forever and ever. This is true only of our country, and nothing similar may be found in foreign lands. That is why it is called the divine country.

The Names of Japan

In the Age of the Gods, Japan was known as the "ever-fruitful land of reed-covered plains and luxuriant ricefields." This name has existed since the creation of heaven and earth. It appeared in the command given by the heavenly ancestor Kunitokotachi to the Male Deity and the Female Deity. Again, when the Great Goddess Amaterasu bequeathed the land to her grandchild, that name was used; it may thus be considered the primal name of Japan. It is also called the country of the great eight islands. This name was given because eight islands were produced when the Male Deity and the Female Deity begot Japan. It is also called Yamato, which is the name of the central part of the eight islands. The eighth offspring of the deities was the god Heavenly-August-Sky-Luxuriant-Dragon-fly-Lord Youth [and the land he incarnated] was called Oyamato, Luxuriant-Dragon-fly-Island. It is now divided into forty-eight provinces. Besides being the central island, Yamato has been the site of the capital through all the ages since Jimmu's conquest of the east. That must be why the other seven islands are called Yamato. The same is true of China, where All-Under-Heaven was at one time called Chou because the dynasty had its origins in the state of Chou, and where All-Within-the-Seas was called Han when the dynasty arose in the territory of Han.

The word Yamato means "footprints on the mountain." Of old, when heaven and earth were divided, the soil was still muddy and not yet dry, and people passing back and forth over the mountains left many footprints; thus it was called Yama-to—"mountain footprint." Some say that in ancient Japanese *to* meant "dwelling" and that because people dwelt in the mountains, the country was known to Yama-to—"mountain dwelling."

In writing the name of the country, the Chinese characters Dai-Nippon and Dai-Wa have both been used. The reason is that, when Chinese writing was introduced to this country, the characters for Dai-Nippon were chosen to represent the name of the country, but they were pronounced as "Yamato." This choice may have been guided by the fact that Japan is the Land of the Sun Goddess, or it may have thus been called because it is near the place where the sun rises....

The creation of heaven and earth must everywhere have been the same, for it occurred within the same universe, but the Indian, Chinese, and Japanese traditions are each different. According to the Indian version, the beginning of the world is called the "inception of the kalpas." (A kalpa has four stages—growth, set-tlement, decline, and extinction—each with twenty rises and falls. One rise and fall is called a minor kalpa; twenty minor kalpas constitute a middle kalpa, and four middle kalpas constitute a major kalpa.) A heavenly host called "Light-Sound" spread golden clouds in the sky which filled the entire Brahmaloka. Then they caused great rains to fall, which accumulated on the circle of wind to form the circle of water. It expanded and rose to the sky, where a great wind blew from it foam which it cast into the void; this crystallized into the palace of Brahma. The water gradually receding formed the palaces of the realm of desire, Mount Sumeru, the four continents, and the Iron Enclosing Mountain. Thus the countless millions of worlds came into existence at the same time. This was the kalpa of creation. (These countless millions of worlds are called the three-thousand-great-thousand worlds.)

The heavenly host of Light-Sound came down, were born, and lived. This was the kalpa of settlement. During the kalpa of settlement there were twenty rises and falls. In the initial stage, people's bodies shone with a far-reaching effulgence, and they could fly about at will. Joy was their nourishment. No distinction existed between the sexes. Later, sweet water, tasting like cream and honey, sprang from the earth. (It was also called earth-savor.) One sip of it engendered a craving for its taste. Thus were lost the godlike ways, and thus also was the light extinguished, leaving the wide world to darkness. In retribution for the actions of living creatures, black winds blew over the oceans, bearing before them on the waves the sun and the moon, to come to rest half-way up Mount Sumeru, there to shine forth on the four continents under the heavens. From that time on there were the day and the night, the months, and the seasons. Indulgence in the sweet waters caused men's faces to grow pale and thin. Then the sweet waters vanished, and vegetable food (also called earth-rind) appeared, which all creatures ate. Then the vegetable food also vanished, and wild rice of multiple tastes was provided them. Cut in the morning, it ripened by evening. The eating of the rice left dregs in the body, and thus the two orifices were created. Male and female came to differ, and this led to sexual desire. They called each other husband and wife, built houses, and lived together. Beings from the Light-Sound Heaven who were later to be born entered women's wombs, and once born became living creatures.

Later, the wild rice ceased to grow, to the dismay of all creatures. They divided the land and planted cereals, which they made their food. Then there were those who stole other people's crops, and fighting ensued. As there was no one to decide such cases, men got together and established a Judge-King whom they called kshatriya (which means landowner). The first king bore the title of People's Lord [*Minshu*]. He enjoyed the love and respect of the people because he ruled the country with laws which embodied the ten virtues. The realm of Jambu was prosperous and peaceful with no sickness or extremes of cold or heat. Men lived so long that their years were almost without number. Successive descendants of People's Lord ruled the land for many years, but as the good laws gradually fell into abeyance, the life-span decreased until it was only 84,000 years. People were eighty feet tall. During this period there was a king, the wheels of whose chariot rolled everywhere without hindrance. First the precious Golden Wheel came down from heaven and appeared before the king. Whenever the king went abroad, the wheel rolled ahead of him, and the lesser rulers evinced their welcome and homage. No one dared do otherwise. He reigned over the four continents and enjoyed all treasures— elephants, horses, pearls, women, lay-Buddhists, and military heroes. He who is possessed of these Seven Treasures is called a Sovereign of the Golden Wheel. There followed in succession [sovereigns of] Silver, Copper, and Iron Wheels. Because of the

inequality of their merits, the rewards also gradually diminished. The life-span also decreased by one year each century, and human stature was similarly reduced by one foot a century. It was when the life-span had dropped to 120 years that Shakya Buddha appeared. (Some authorities say that it was when the life-span was 100 years. Before him three Buddhas had appeared.)

When the life-span has been reduced to a bare ten years, the so-called Three Disasters will ensue, and the human species will disappear almost entirely, leaving a mere 10,000 people. These people will practice good deeds, and the life-span will then increase and the rewards improve. By the time that a life-span of 20,000 years is reached, a King of the Iron Wheel will appear and rule over the southern continent. When the life-span reaches 40,000 years, a King of the Copper Wheel will appear and rule over the eastern and southern continents. When the life-span reaches 60,000 years, a King of the Silver Wheel will appear and rule over three continents, the eastern, western, and southern. When the life-span reaches 84,000 years, a King of the Golden Wheel will appear and rule over all four continents. The rewards in his reign will be those mentioned above. In his time a decline will again set in, followed by the appearance of Maitreya Buddha. There are then to follow eighteen other rises and falls....

In China, nothing positive is stated concerning the creation of the world even though China is a country which accords special importance to the keeping of records. In the Confucian books nothing antedates King Fu-hsi. In other works they speak of heaven, earth, and man as having begun in an unformed, undivided state, much as in the accounts of our Age of the Gods. There is also the legend of King P'an-ku, whose eyes were said to have turned into the sun and the moon, and whose hair turned into grasses and trees. There were afterwards sovereigns of Heaven, sovereigns of Earth, and sovereigns of Man, and the Five

Dragons, followed by many kings over a period of 10,000 years.

The beginnings of Japan in some ways resemble the Indian descriptions, telling as it does of the world's creation from the seed of the heavenly gods. However, whereas in our country the succession to the throne has followed a single undeviating line since the first divine ancestor, nothing of the kind has existed in India. After their first ruler, King People's Lord, had been chosen and raised to power by the populace, his dynasty succeeded, but in later times most of his descendants perished, and men of inferior genealogy who had powerful forces became the rulers, some of them even controlling the whole of India. China is also a country of notorious disorders. Even in ancient times, when life was simple and conduct was proper, the throne was offered to wise men, and no single lineage was established. Later, in times of disorder, men fought for control of the country. Thus some of the rulers rose from the ranks of the plebeians, and there were even some of barbarian origin who usurped power. Or, some families after generations of service as ministers surpassed their princes and eventually supplanted them. There have already been thirty-six changes of dynasty since Fu-hsi, and unspeakable disorders have occurred.

Only in our country has the succession remained inviolate, from the beginning of heaven and earth to the present. It has been maintained within a single lineage, and even when, as inevitably has happened, the succession has been transmitted collaterally, it has returned to the true line. This is due to the ever-renewed Divine Oath, and makes Japan unlike all other countries.

It is true that the Way of the Gods should not be revealed without circumspection, but it may happen that ignorance of the origins of things may result in disorder. In order to prevent that disaster, I have recorded something of the facts, confining myself to a description of how the succession has legitimately been transmitted from the Age of the Gods. I have not included information known to everyone.

Then the Great Sun Goddess conferred with Takami-musubi and sent her grandchild to the world below. Eighty million deities obeyed the divine decree to accompany and serve him. Among them were thirty-two principal deities, including the gods of the Five Guilds—Amieno Koyane (the first ancestor of the Nakatomi family), Ameno Futodama (the first ancestor of the Imbe family), Ameno Uzume (the first ancestor of the Sarume family), Ishikoridome (the first ancestor of the mirrormakers), and Tamaya (the first ancestor of the jewel-makers). Two of these deities, those of the Nakatomi and the Imbe, received a divine decree specially instructing them to aid and protect the divine grandchild. The Sun Goddess, on bestowing the three divine treasures on her grandchild, uttered these words of command, "The reed-plain-of-one-thousand-five-hundred-autumns-fair-rice-ear land is where my descendants shall reign. Thou, my illustrious grandchild, proceed thither and govern the land. Go, and may prosperity attend thy dynasty, and may it, like Heaven and Earth, endure forever."

Then the Great Goddess, taking in her own hand the precious mirror, gave it to her grandchild, saying, "When thou, my grandchild, lookst on this mirror, it will be as though thou lookst at myself. Keep it with thee, in the same bed, under the same roof, as thy holy mirror." She then added the curved jewel of increasing prosperity and the sword of gathered clouds, thus completing the three regalia. She again spoke, "Illumine all the world with brightness like this mirror. Reign over the world with the wonderful sway of this jewel. Subdue those who will not obey thee by brandishing this divine sword." It may indeed be understood from these commands why Japan is a divine country and has been ruled by a single imperial line following in legitimate succession. The

Imperial Regalia have been transmitted [within Japan] just as the sun, moon, and stars remain in the heavens. The mirror has the form of the sun; the jewel contains the essence of the moon; and the sword has the substance of the stars. There must be a profound significance attached to them.

The precious mirror is the mirror made by Ishikoridome, as is above recorded. The jewel is the curved bead of increasing prosperity made by Tamanoya, and the sword is the sword of gathered clouds, obtained by the god Susa-no-o and offered by him to the Great Goddess. The goddess's commands on the Three Regalia must indicate the proper methods of governing the country. The mirror does not possess anything of its own, but without selfish desires reflects all things, showing their true qualities. Its virtue lies in its response to these qualities, and as such represents the source of all honesty. The virtue of the jewel lies in its gentleness and submissiveness; it is the source of compassion. The virtue of the sword lies in its strength and resolution; it is the source of wisdom. Unless these three virtues are joined in a ruler, he will find it difficult indeed to govern the country. The divine commands are clear; their words are concise, but their import is far-reaching. Is it not an awe-inspiring thing that they are embodied in the imperial regalia?

The mirror stands first in importance among the regalia, and is revered as the true substance of ancestor-worship. The mirror has brightness as its form: the enlightened mind possesses both compassion and decision. As it also gives a true reflection of the Great Goddess, she must have given her profound care to the mirror. There is nothing brighter in heaven than the sun and the moon. That is why, when the Chinese characters were devised, the symbols for sun and for moon were joined to express the idea of brightness. Because our Great Goddess is the spirit of the sun, she illuminates with a bright virtue which is incomprehensible in all its aspects, but dependable alike in the realm of the visible and invisible. All sovereigns and ministers have inherited the bright seeds of the divine light, or they are the descendants of the deities who received personal instruction from the Great Goddess. Who would not stand in reverence before this fact? The highest object of all teachings, Buddhist and Confucian included, consists in realizing this fact and obeying in perfect consonance its principles. It has been the power of the dissemination of the Buddhist and Confucian texts which has spread these principles. It is just the same as the fact that a single mesh of a net suffices to catch a fish, but you cannot catch one unless the net has many meshes. Since the reign of the Emperor Ojin, the Confucian writings have been disseminated, and since Prince Shotoku's time Buddhism has flourished in Japan. Both these men were sages incarnate, and it must have been their intention to spread a knowledge of the way of our country, in accordance with the wishes of the Great Sun Goddess.

Study Questions

1. Why does Kitabatake believe that Japan is a divine country?

2. What is Kitabatake's attitude toward other countries?

3. What is significant about Kitabatake's interpretation of the meaning of the three sacred regalia of the imperial family?

4. Why, in the fourteenth century, does someone feel it is necessary to tell the story of the creation of Japan?

Kadensho (1440–1442)   **62**

ZEAMI MOTOKIYO

Zeami Motokiyo (1363–1443) was -the greatest of the early Japanese dramatists and the cofounder, with his father, Kan'ami, of No drama. He was first an actor who became the favorite of the Shogun, Ashikaga Yoshimitsu. Zeami then became a playwright and composed over a hundred No dramas, many of which are still performed. Father and son both fell out of favor with the accession of a new Shogun, and in 1422 Zeami became a Zen monk.

Along with his literary creations, Zeami wrote a series of instructional manuals for No actors. The *Kadensho* established the underlying philosophy of No as well as prescribing training rituals for the complex singing, dancing, miming, and acting that was required. The following selection presents some of the philosophy and ritual of No drama.

On Attaining the Stage of Yugen

Yugen is considered to be the mark of supreme attainment in all of the arts and accomplishments. In the art of the N6 in particular the manifestation of *yugen* is of the first importance. In general, a display of *yugen* in the No is apparent to the eye, and it is the one thing which audiences most admire, but actors who possess *yugen* are few and far between. This is because they do not in fact know the true meaning of *yugen*. There are thus none who reach that stage.

In what sort of place, then, is the stage of *yugen* actually to be found? Let us begin by examining the various classes of people on the basis of the appearance that they make in society. May we not say of the courtiers, whose behavior is distinguished and whose appearance far surpasses that of other men, that theirs is the stage of *yugen*? From this we may see that the essence of *yugen* lies in a true state of beauty and gentleness. Tranquility and elegance make

for *yugen* in personal appearance. In the same way, the *yugen* of discourse lies in a grace of language and a complete mastery of the speech of the nobility and gentry, so that even the most casual utterance will be graceful. With respect to a musical performance, it may be said to possess *yugen* when the melody flows beautifully and sounds smooth and sensitive. In the dance there will be *yugen* when the discipline has been thoroughly mastered and the audience is delighted by the beauty of the performer's movements and by his serene appearance. In acting, there will be *yugen* when the performance of the Three Roles is beautiful. If the characterization calls for a display of anger or for the representation of a devil, the actions may be somewhat forceful, but as long as the actor never loses sight of the beauty of the effect and bears in mind always the correct balance between his mental and physical actions and between the movements of his body and feet, his appearance will be so beautiful that it may be called "the *yugen* of a devil."

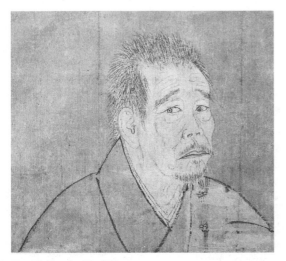

Portrait of a Zen Master. Reflecting the chaos of the fourteenth century, the art of portraiture flourished, and artists produced a full gallery of warriors and holy men in startlingly realistic detail. This painting of a Zen master, complete with crooked mouth, stubble, and worry lines, is an unflattering one. Nevertheless, with economy of line, the artist has managed to convey the master's spiritual and mental intensity.

All these aspects of *yugen* must be kept in mind and made a part of the actor's body, so that whatever part he may be playing *yugen* will never be absent. Whether the character he portrays be of high or low birth, man or woman, priest, peasant, rustic, beggar, or outcast, he should think of each of them as crowned with a wreath of flowers. Although their positions in society differ, the fact that they can all appreciate the beauty of flowers makes flowers of all of them. Their particular flower is shown by their outward appearance. An actor, by the use of his intelligence, makes his presentation seem beautiful. It is through the use of intelligence that the above principles are thoroughly grasped; that poetry is learned so as to impart *yugen* to his discourse; that the most elegant costuming is studied so as to impart *yugen* to his bearing: though the characterization varies according to the different parts, the actor should realize that

the ability to appear beautiful is the seed of *yugen*. It is all too apt to happen that an actor, believing that once he has mastered the characterization of the various parts he has attained the highest stage of excellence, forgets his appearances and therefore is unable to enter the realm of *yugen*. Unless an actor enters the realm of *yugen* he will not attain the highest achievements. If he fails to attain the highest achievements, he will not become a celebrated master. That is why there are so few masters. The actor must consider *yugen* as the most important aspect of his art and study to perfect his understanding of it.

The "highest achievement" of which I have spoken refers to beauty of form and manners. The most careful attention must therefore be given to the appearance presented. Accordingly, when we thoroughly examine the principles of *yugen* we see that when the form is beautiful, whether in dancing, singing, or in any type of characterization, it may properly be called the "highest achievement." When the form is poor, the performance will be inferior. The actor should realize that *yugen* is attained when all of the different forms of visual or aural expression are beautiful. It is when the actor himself has worked out these principles and made himself their master that he may be said to have entered the realm of *yugen*. If he fails to work out these principles for himself, he will not master them, and however much he may aspire to attain *yugen*, he will never in all his life do so.

On the One Mind Linking All Powers

Sometimes spectators of the No say, "The moments of 'no-action' are the most enjoyable." This is an art which the actor keeps secret. Dancing and singing, movements and the different types of miming are all acts performed by the body. Moments of "no-action" occur in between. When we examine why such moments without actions are enjoyable, we find that it is due to the underlying spiritual strength of the actor which unremittingly holds the attention. He does not relax the tension when the dancing or singing come to an end or at intervals between the dialogue and the different types of miming, but maintains an unwavering inner strength. This feeling of inner strength will faintly reveal itself and bring enjoyment. However, it is undesirable for the actor to permit this inner strength to become obvious to the audience. If it is obvious, it becomes an act, and is no longer "no-action." The actions before and after an interval of "no-action" must be linked by entering the state of mindlessness in which one conceals even from oneself one's intent. This, then, is the faculty of moving audiences, by linking all the artistic powers with one mind.

> Life and death, past and present—
> Marionettes on a toy stage.
> When the strings are broken,
> Behold the broken pieces.

This is a metaphor describing human life as it transmigrates between life and death. Marionettes on a stage appear to move in various ways, but in fact it is not they who really move—they are manipulated by strings. When these strings are broken, the marionettes fall and are dashed to pieces. In the art of the No too, the different sorts of miming are artificial things. What holds the parts together is the mind. This mind must not be disclosed to the audience. If it is seen, it is just as if a marionette's strings were visible. The mind must be made the strings which hold together all the powers of the arts. If this is done the actor's talent will endure. This resolution must not be confined to the times when the actor is appearing on the stage. Day or night, wherever he may be, whatever he may be doing, he should not forget this resolution, but should make it his constant guide, uniting all his powers. If he unremittingly works at this his talent will steadily grow. This article is the most secret of the secret teachings.

The Nine Stages of the No in Order

THE HIGHER THREE STAGES

1. The flower of the miraculous
"At midnight in Silla the sun is bright."
The miraculous transcends the power of speech and is where the workings of the mind are defeated. And does "the sun at midnight" lie within the realm of speech? Thus, in the art of the No, before the *yugen* of a master-actor all praise fails, admiration transcends the comprehension of the mind, and all attempts at classification and grading are made impossible. The art which excites such a reaction on the part of the audience may be called the flower of the miraculous.

2. The flower of supreme profundity
"Snow covers the thousand mountains— why does one lonely peak remain unwhitened?"
A man of old once said, "Mount Fuji is so high that the snow never melts." A Chinese disagreed, saying, "Mount Fuji is so deep...." What is extremely high is deep. Height has limits but depth is not to be measured. Thus the profound mystery of a landscape in which a solitary peak stands unwhitened amidst a thousand snow-covered mountains may represent the art of supreme profundity.

3. The flower of stillness
"Snow piled in a silver bowl."
When snow is piled in a silver bowl, the purity of its white light appears lambent indeed. May this not represent the flower of stillness?

THE MIDDLE THREE STAGES

1. The flower of truth
"The sun sinks in the bright mist, the myriad mountains are crimson."
A distant view of hills and mountains bathed in the light of the sun in a cloudless sky represents the flower of truth. It is superior to the art of versatility and exactness, and is already a first step towards the acquisition of the flowers of the art.

2. The art of versatility and exactness

"To tell everything—of the nature of clouds on the mountains, of moonlight on the sea."

To describe completely the nature of clouds on the mountains and of moonlight on the sea, of the whole expanse of green mountains that fills the eyes, this is indeed desirable in acquiring the art of versatility and exactness. Here is the dividing point from which one may go upward or downward.

3. The art of untutored beauty

"The Way of ways is not the usual way."

One may learn the Way of ways by traveling along the usual way. This means that the display of beauty should begin at the stage of the beginner. Thus the art of untutored beauty is considered the introduction to the mastery of the nine stages.

THE LOWER THREE STAGES

1. The art of strength and delicacy

"The metal hammer flashes as it moves, the glint of the precious sword is cold."

The movement of the metal hammer represents the art of strong action. The cold glint of the precious sword suggests the unadorned style of singing and dancing. It will stand up to detailed observation.

2. The art of strength and crudity.

"Three days after its birth the tiger is disposed to devour an ox."

That the tiger cub only three days after its birth has such audacity shows its strength; but to devour an ox is crude.

3. The art of crudity and inexactness

"The squirrel's five talents."

Confucius said, "The squirrel can do five things. He can climb a tree, swim in the water, dig a hole, jump, and run: all of these are within its capacities but it does none well." When art lacks delicacy it becomes crude and inexact.

In the attainment of art through the nine stages, the actor begins with the middle group, follows with the upper group, and finally learns the lower three. When the beginner first enters the art of the Nō, he practices the various elements of dancing and singing. This represents the stage of untutored beauty. As the result of persistent training, his untutored style will develop into greater artistry, constantly improving until, before he is aware of it, it reaches the stage of versatility and exactness. At this stage if the actor's training is comprehensive and he expands his art in versatility and magnitude until he attains full competence, he will be at the stage of the flower of truth. The above are the stages from the learning of the Two Disciplines to the mastery of the Three Roles.

Next the actor progresses to the stage of calm and the flower that arouses admiration. It is the point where it becomes apparent whether or not he has realized the flower of the art. From this height the actor can examine with insight the preceding stages. He occupies a place of high achievement in the art of calm and the realization of the flower. This stage is thus called the flower of stillness.

Rising still higher, the actor achieves the ultimate degree of *yūgen* in his performance, and reveals a degree of artistry which is of that middle ground where being and nonbeing meet. This is the flower of supreme profundity.

Above this stage, words fail before the revelation of the absolute miracle of the actor's interpretation. This is the flower of the miraculous. It is the end of the road to the higher mysteries of the art.

It should be noted that the origin of all these stages of the art may be found in the art of versatility and exactness. It is the foundation of the art of the Nō, for it is the point where are displayed the breadth and detail of performance which are the seeds of the flowers of the highest forms of the art. The stage of versatility and exactness is also the dividing line where is determined the actor's future. If he succeeds here in obtaining the flower of the art he will rise to the flower of truth; otherwise he will sink to the lower three stages.

The lower three stages are the turbulent waters of the No. They are easily understood and it is no special problem to learn them. It may happen, however, that an actor who has gone from the middle three stages to the upper three stages, having mastered the art of calmness and the flower of the miraculous, will purposely descend and indulge in the lower three stages. Then the special qualities of these stages will be blended with his art. However, many of the excellent actors of the past who had mounted to the upper three stages of the art refused to descend to the lower three. They were like the elephant of the story who refused to follow in the tracks of a rabbit. There has been only one instance of an actor who mastered all the stages—the middle, then the upper, and then the lower: this was the art of my late father. Many of the heads of theatres have been trained only up to the art of versatility and exactness and, without having risen to the flower of truth, have descended to the lower three stages, thus failing in the end to achieve success. Nowadays there are even actors who begin their training with the lower three stages and perform with such a background. This is not the proper order. It is therefore no wonder that many actors fail even to enter the nine stages.

There are three ways of entering the lower three stages. In the case of a great master who has entered the art by way of the middle stages, ascended to the upper stages of the art, and then descended to the lower stages, it is quite possible to give a superb performance even within the lower stages. Actors who have dropped to the lower stages from the level of versatility and exactness will be capable only of parts which call for strength with delicacy or crudity. Those actors who have willfully entered the art from the lower three stages have neither art nor fame and cannot be said even to be within the nine stages. Although they have taken the lower three stages as their goal, they fail even in this, to say nothing of reaching the middle three stages.

Study Questions

1. What is *yugen*?

2. What is the role of beauty in No drama?

3. What makes good No actors?

4. How is No drama influenced by religion?

All Men Are Brothers (14th C.E.)   63

SHIH NAI-AN

All Men Are Brothers, one of the classics of Chinese literature, is a loosely connected novel composed of stories that had been part of an oral tradition before it was first written down in the fourteenth century. Very little is known of its supposed author, Shih Nai-an, and scholars continue to dispute whether this obscure bureau-crat did indeed codify the stories. The novel revolves around the activities of a group of bandits whose bravery and daring in the face of a corrupt government gain the support of the common people. The bandits live by their own code, expose official corruption, and deal out a form of rough justice. *All Men Are Brothers*, a very loose translation of its actual title, was so popular that it was banned in the seventeenth century and an imperial decree was made to destroy all existing copies of the work.

The story here involves Wu Sung, "the wounded star," who avenges his broth-er's murder by himself killing his brother's wife and her lover. He throws himself upon the mercy of the local court. The work is graphically and gratuitously violent.

It is said: So—Wu Sung told these four neigh-bors, "I, this humble one, swore I would revenge my brother's death and it was meet that I should commit this crime and although I die I shall not repent. Yet when I killed my sister-in-law I frightened you, Honorable Neighbors. Yet now when I go forth I cannot say whether it is to death or to life and so will I at this moment burn the tablet of my elder brother. As for all these household goods, I pray you to sell them for me that I may have sil-ver wherewith to plead my case at court and to use in my need. Today I will go myself to the court and make report, and you are not to take on yourselves the task of judging whether my sin be light or heavy. Only be true witnesses for me."

Straightway then he burned the spirit tablet and the paper money. There were two boxes upstairs which he brought down and he opened them to see what was there and he gave all to the neighbors to sell for him. Then guarding the old woman Wang he drove her forth before him and taking up the two heads he went straight to the magistrate's court. By now he had aroused the whole city of Yang Ku and the people on the street to see him were beyond counting.

Now the magistrate had heard the report from one who came to tell it and first he was afraid and he went at once to his Hall Of Audience.

Thither did Wu Sung come still guarding that old woman Wang and he came and knelt in that hall before the magistrate and he placed there the dagger with which he had committed the fierce deed and he laid the two heads there. Then Wu Sung knelt at the right side and the old woman knelt in the center and the four neighbors knelt at the left, and Wu Sung drew out of his bosom the paper that the man Hu had written and he read it out from first to last. The magistrate commanded his assistants first to inquire into the old woman Wang's story and they all told the same tale. The witness of the four neighbors was equally clear. Then Ho and Yün Ko told their stories clearly and they also gave clear witness.

After this the magistrate called for those who were this day appointed to examine into wounds and causes of death and the like and he appointed one in charge of all and all these were sent under guard to the Street Of Purple Stone and there they examined carefully the body of the murdered woman, and below the Bridge Of The Lions in front of the wine shop they found also the body of Hsi Men Ch'ing. And they wrote down all they found, who these were who had been so killed and how old they were and all concerning them, and they returned to the court and placed their report there. Then the magistrate commanded long racks to be brought made of wood and these were fastened upon the necks of Wu Sung and the old woman and they were locked into gaol. As for the other common folk, they were put into the gatehouse.

Now the magistrate himself thought that Wu Sung was a very honorable, fearless fellow and he remembered the time when he had sent him to the capital city and he meditated in his heart upon all the goodness of Wu Sung and so he called to his presence the one in control of such matters as these and he said, "We must also remember that Wu Sung is a good fellow and we must change somewhat the stories that have been written down about him, and we will say that the matter came about because Wu Sung was about to sacrifice to his brother Wu The Elder and his sister-in-law would not let him and so because of this they struggled together. The woman pushed over the spirit tablet and Wu Sung because he would protect the box where the tablet stood and the spirit therein, in his anger killed her. Then Hsi Men Ch'ing, because he before this had evil intercourse with this woman, forced his way forward to protect her and so there was a struggle and neither could win over the other and thus struggling they fought their way to the Bridge Of The Lions and there Wu Sung killed him."

When this was written it was read to Wu Sung and he heard it and the magistrate wrote his explanation and sent all to the governor who was above him and he sent messengers to this governor and besought him to manage the affair.

Now although this city of Yang Ku was but a small county seat yet there were honorable and just men there who were of families of noble people, and these were all ready to help Wu Sung with silver and there were those who sent to him gifts of wine and food and money and rice. And Wu Sung went to the rooms where he lived and he took his possessions and gave them to a soldier and he took out some twelve or thirteen ounces of silver and gave these to Yün Ko's old father. Of all the soldiers who were under Wu Sung's command more

than half made haste to send wines and meats and one appointed to it took the report of all these things and the proofs, the silver that Ho had kept, the bones, the confession the neighbor had written down from the murdered woman, and the knife with which Wu Sung had killed the pair. All these various men went also and they all set forth on the road toward the city called Tung P'ing, where the higher governor was.

All these men then gathered in front of this governor's court and all the onlookers crowded about the gates. When the governor, who was named Ch'en Wen Chao, heard what was come about he immediately went into his Hall Of Justice. Now this governor was a wise man and a man clever to examine into matters and he had already heard about this affair. So he commanded that all these persons be brought forward and there in the hall he looked first and read this report from the city of Yang Ku. Then he read all that had been written of what people had witnessed, and when this was done he questioned every man again himself and all the proofs, the silver, the bones, the knife, he took and wrapped up and he set his seal upon the parcel and he entrusted it to the keeper of such things in the court.

After this he took off the heavy rack that Wu Sung wore and put on his neck a light one in its place and put him in the gaol. As for the old woman, he had a heavy rack put upon her neck and cast her in that part of the gaol which was for those condemned to die. Then he called the representative of the magistrate at Yang Ku and he gave him an answering letter and he commanded Ho and Win Ko and the four neighbors, these six, to return first to the county seat and remain in their homes, and if they were summoned, to come quickly.

Among these who had come from the city of Yang Ku was the wife of Hsi Men Ch'ing and this one the governor ordered to remain in his court until later when judgment was come down from above and this matter might be decided.

Then Ho and Yün Ko and the four neighbors led all those who had come thither from the county seat and they returned again. Wu Sung was locked in the gaol and he had but a few soldiers to bring him food.

Now let it be told how the governor Ch'en pitied Wu Sung. He saw that Wu Sung was a righteous, brave man and he sent men to the gaol to see to him and because of this the gaol keepers and those who were in charge of the prisoners did not dare to ask Wu Sung for any money but they gave him wine and food to eat. The governor Ch'en corrected clearly all the reports and accusations that had been sent him of the matter and sent them all to the one who was yet above him and he sent a secret letter by one whom he trusted to go by day and by night to the capital to manage the affair rightly for him there.

Now that one who controlled the laws was a friend of the governor Ch'en's, and he reported this matter to the highest official and the degree of each crime was fixed thus; as for the old woman Wang she was the one who roused the evil desire between Hsi Men Ch'ing and the woman who was Wu The Elder's wife and she had deceived the woman and led her into evil with the man. Nor did the woman plan at first to kill her husband but the old woman bid her do it so that in the end she even poisoned her own husband. Moreover, it was this old hag who led this woman to drive out Wu Sung and prevent him from making sacrifice to his elder brother, and for this murder was done. Thus by enticing the woman and enticing the man she enticed them to violate a sacred relationship. According to the law, therefore, the old woman ought to die by the slicing of her flesh from her bones, bit by bit.

As for Wu Sung, although it was meet that he should revenge his brother's death and although he did quarrel and kill Hsi Men Ch'ing, and although he went himself and reported his deed to the magistrate, yet his crime could not be forgiven and he must be branded on his face and exiled to some place

many hundreds of miles away. As for the two who were adulterers, they were dead and it was not necessary to fix their sentence. As for all these other persons, they were to be released and restored to their homes.

When this judgment came it was to be carried out at once. When the governor Ch'en saw the answer that had come he wrote straightway a special proclamation and he bade Ho and Yün Ko and the four neighbors brought again to him and Hsi Men Ch'ing's wife also, the whole group of them, and they all went before the governor to hear the judgment. And Wu Sung was brought out of the jail and before all these the judgment was read aloud.

Then the rack was taken from Wu Sung's neck and his back was beaten forty strokes. But high and low they all protected Wu Sung and of these forty strokes only five or seven touched his flesh and a new rack was put upon his neck to hold his hands fast also as he went into exile, and upon his face were branded the two lines of gold letters, and after this he was sent step by step to Meng Chou. As for these other persons, all was done to them according to the judgment and each was allowed to go home.

But out of the great gaol the old woman Wang was brought and she stood alone before them all to hear her sentence. When it had been read to her, her crime was written down upon a placard and she set her own mark there. Then this old woman was laid across a rack of wood, a beam set upon four posts, and four long nails were pinned through her and three ropes also bound her fast and a sign was written upon her that she was to be sliced to strips. Then the rack was carried through the city and upon broken drums and gongs a great noise was made. In front of her a banner was held high telling of her crime and behind her came guards with poles who urged them on, and they held aloft two sharp-pointed knives, from which waved bunches of paper flowers. The procession was led to the part of the city that was most crowded and there the old woman was sliced.

Study Questions

1. What does Wu Sung expect will happen to him after he murders his sister-in-law?

2. What is the role of the four neighbors?

3. Why is the old woman made the victim?

4. What is the basis for the way Wu Sung is judged?

5. Why would the story of Wu Sung be popular? What lessons would it teach?

European Encounters

Emperor Qianlong Meets Lord Macartney. In 1793, Lord Macartney was dispatched to China to press for the liberalization of trade restrictions. Although he offered gifts of Western scientific instruments and texts, the Chinese, who believed their nation had been the cultural center of the world for the last two thousand years, were not impressed. Lord Macartney won little Chinese sympathy for his refusal to kowtow to the emperor. Here the two prepare to meet.

The History of the Great and Mightie Kingdom of China (1585)   64

JUAN GONZALEZ DE MENDOZA

Juan Gonzalez de Mendoza was a Spanish missionary who spent most of his early life abroad. He went first to Mexico City where he was involved with the earliest missions from Spanish America to the Philippines. His interest in missionary work in Asia led to his return to Spain and to an audience with King Philip II. Although Mendoza hoped to be appointed to a second mission to the Philippines, instead he remained in Madrid to process the reports sent back from the Asian missions. In 1580 he was appointed one of the heads of a new mission to China, but by the time he reached Spanish America the mission had been postponed. Mendoza returned to Europe, was called to Rome and commissioned by the Pope to collect all of the information that was known about China. The result was *The History of the Great and Mightie Kingdom of China* (1585), one of the most popular books of the sixteenth century, going through 46 editions in 15 years.

Mendoza compiled his history from the few eyewitness accounts of early Portuguese ambassadors and from the dispatches of Christian missionaries. He read everything that had previously been written about China and synthesized it in a lively and direct style. His work is notable for its description of the political structure of Ming rule as well as for its description of social customs. The following selection includes his famous description of the custom of footbinding.

Both men and women of this countrie are of a good disposition of their bodies, well proportioned and gallant men, somewhat tall: they are all for the most part brode faced, little eyes and flat noses, and without bearde save only upon the ball of the chinne: but yet there be some that have great eyes and goodly beardes, and their faces well proportioned, yet of these sorts (in respect of the others) are verie few: and it is to bee beleeved that these kinde of people doo proceede of some strange nation, who in times past when it was lawfull to deale out of that countrie, did joyne one with another.

Those of the province of Canton (which is a hot country) be browne of colour like to the Moores: but those that be farther within the countrie be like unto Almaines, Italians and Spanyardes, white and redde, and somewhat swart. All of them do suffer their nailes of their left hande to grow very long, but the right hand they do cut: they have long haire, and esteeme it very much and maintaine it with curiositie: of both they make a superstition, for that they say thereby they shall be carried into heaven. They do binde their haire up to the crowne of their heade, in calles of golde verie curious, and with pinnes of the same.

The garments which the nobles and principals do use, bee of silke of different colours, of the which they have excellent good and verie perfite: the common and poore people doo apparell themselves with another kinde of silke more courser, and with linnen, serge, and cotton: of all the which there is great abundance. And for that the countrie for the most part is temperate, they may suffer this kinde of apparell, which is the heaviest that they doo use: for in all the whole kingdome they have no cloth, neither doo they suffer it to be made, although they have great aboundance of woolle, and very good cheape: they do use their coates according unto our old use of antiquities with long skirts and full of plaites, and a flappe over the brest to be made fast under the left side, the sleeves verie bigge and wide: upon their coates they doo use cassockes or long garments according unto the possibilitie of either of them, made according as wee doo use, but only their sleeves are more wider. They of royall bloode and such as are constituted unto dignitie, do differ in their apparell from the other ordinarie gentlemen: for that the first have their garments laide on with gold and silver downe to the waste, and the others alonely garnished on the edges, or hem: they do use hose verie well made and stitched, shoes and buskins of velvet, verie curious. In the winter (although it be not very colde,) they have their garments furred with beasts skins, but in especiall with Martas Cevellinas, of the which they have great aboundance (as aforesaid) and generally they do use them at all times about their necks. They that be not married doo differ from them that be married, in that they do kirrle their haire on their foreheade, and wear higher hattes. Their women do apparell themselves verie curiouslie, much after the fashion of Spaine: they use many jewels of gold and precious stones: their gownes have wide sleeves; that wherewith they do apparel themselves is of cloath of gold and silver and divers sortes of silkes, whereof they have great plentie, as aforesaid, and excellent good, and good cheape: and the poore folkes doo apparell themselves with velvet, unshorne velvet and serge. They have verie faire haire,

and doo combe it with great care and diligence, as do the women of Genouay, and do binde it about their heade with a broad silke lace, set full of pearles and precious stones, and they say it doth become them verie well: they doo use to paint themselves, and in some place in excesse.

Amongst them they account it for gentilitie and a gallant thing to have little feete, and therefore from their youth they so swadell and binde them verie straight, and do suffer it with patience: for that she who hath the least feete is accounted the gallantest dame. They say that the men hath induced them unto this custome, for to binde their feete so harde, that almost they doo loose the forme of them, and remaine halfe lame, so that their going is verie ill, and with great travell: which is the occasion that they goe but little abroad, and fewe times doo rise up from their worke that they do; and was invented onely for the same intent. This custome hath indured manie yeares, and will indure many more, for that it is stablished for a law: and that woman which doth break it, and not use it with her children, shalbe counted as evill, yea shalbe punished for the same. They are very secreat and honest, in such sort that you shall not see at any time a woman at her window nor at her doores: and if her husband doo invite any person to dinner, she is never seene nor eateth not at the table, except the gest be a kinsman or a very friende: when they go abroade to visite their father, mother, or any other kinsfolkes, they are carried in a little chaire by foure men, the which is made close, and with lattises rounde about made of golde wyre and with silver, and curteines of silke; that although they doo see them that be in the streete, yet they cannot be seene. They have many servants waiting on them. So that it is a great marvell when that you shall meete a principall woman in the streete, yea you will thinke that there are none in the citie, their keeping in is such: the lameness of their feet is a great helpe thereunto. The women as well as the men be ingenious; they doo use drawne workes and carved works, excellent painters of flowers, birds and beasts, as it is to be seene upon beddes and bords that is brought from thence. I did see my selfe, one that was brought unto Lysborne in the yeare 1582, by Captaine Ribera, chiefe sergant of Manilla, that it was to be wondred at the excellencie thereof: it caused the kings maiestie to have admyration, and he is a person that little wondreth at things. All the people did wonder at it: yea the famous imbroiderers did marvaile at the curiousnesse thereof. They are great inventers of things, that although they have amongst them many coches and wagons that goe with sailes, and made with such industrie and policie that they do governe them with great ease: this is crediblie informed by many that have seen it: besides that, there be many in the Indies, and in Portugall, that have seene them painted upon clothes, and on their earthen vessell that is brought from thence to be solde: so that it is a signe that their painting hath some foundation. In their buying and selling they are verie subtill, in such sort that they will depart a haire. Such merchants as do keepe shoppes (of whom in every citie there is a great number) they have a table or signe hanging at their doore, whereon is written all such merchandise as is within to be sold.

That which is commonly sold in their shops is cloth of golde and silver, cloth of tissue, silkes of divers sorts and excellent colours: others there be of poorer sort that selleth serges, peeces of cotton, linnen and fustian of all colours; yet both the one and the other is verie goode cheape, for that there is great aboundance, and many workemen that do make it. The apothecarie that selleth simples, hath the like table: there be also shops full of earthen vessels of divers making, redde, greene, yellow, and gilt; it is so good cheape that for foure rials of plate they give fiftie peeces: very strong earth, the which they doo breake all to peeces and grinde it, and put it into sesternes with water, made of lime and stone; and after that they have well tumbled and tossed it in the water, of the creame that is upon it they make the finest sort of them, and the lower they go, spending that substance that is the courser: they make them after the forme and fashion as they do here, and afterward they do gild them, and make them of what colour they please, the which will never be lost: then they put them into their killes and burne them. This hath beene seene and is of a truth, as appeareth in a booke set foorth in the Italian toonge, by Duardo Banbosa, that they do make them of periwinkle shelles of the sea: the which they do grinde and put them under the ground to refine them, whereas they lie 100 years: and many other things he doth treat of to this effect. But if that were true, they should not make so great a number of them as is made in that kingdome, and is brought into Portugall, and carried into the Peru, and Nova Espania, and into other parts of the world: which is a sufficient proofe for that which is said. And the Chinos do agree for this to be true. The finest sort of this is never carried out of the countries for that it is spent in the service of the king, and his governours, and is so fine and deere, that it seemeth to be of fine and perfite cristal: that which is made in the province of Saxii is the best and finest. Artificers and mechanicall officers doo dwell in streets appointed, whereas none do dwell amongst them, but such as be of the same occupation or arte: in such sort that if you doo come at the beginning of the street, looke what craft or art they are there, it is to be understood that all that streete are of that occupation. It is ordayned by a law and statute, that the sonne shall inherite his fathers occupation, and shall not use any other without licence of the justice: if one of them bee verie rich and will not worke, yet he cannot let but have in his shop men that must worke of his occupation. Therefore they that do use it, by reason that they are brought up in it from their youth, they are famous and verie curious in that which they do worke, as it is plainelie seene in that which is brought from thence to Manilla, and into the Indies, and unto Portugall. Their currant monie of that kingdome is made of golde and silver, without any signe or print, but goeth by waight: so that all men carrieth a ballances with them, and little peeces of silver and golde, for to buy such things as they have neede of. And for things of a greater quantitie they have bigger ballances in their houses, and waights, that are sealed, for to give to every man that which is theirs: for therein the justices have great care. In the government of Chincheo they have copper monie coyned, but it is nothing woorth out of that province.

Study Questions

1. To whom does Mendoza compare the Chinese people? Why?

2. What does the passage tell us about the position of women in Chinese society?

3. What does he think about the custom of foot-binding?

4. Why do you think Mendoza's *History* was so popular in the sixteenth century?

Journals (1583–1610)   65

MATTEO RICCI

Matteo Ricci (1552–1610) was born into a noble Italian family. At the age of 16 he was sent to Rome to study law but became more interested in the new science that was sweeping Western Europe. He studied mathematics and astronomy and then petitioned to join the Jesuits. He was sent on a Jesuit mission to the Far East and studied for the priesthood in east India. He was assigned the difficult task of organizing a mission to China, a task at which earlier Jesuit missionaries had failed. Ricci learned the Chinese language with such proficiency that he persuaded officials to allow him into the country, where he taught Chinese intellectuals about mathematics and science and published the first six books of Euclid's *Elements* in Chinese. After a long delay, he was finally allowed to enter the closed City of Peking in 1601, where he stayed for the rest of his life teaching science, mathematics, and Christianity to Chinese intellectuals.

Ricci's most important published work was his *History of the Introduction of Christianity into China*. But the journals that he kept and edited for publication allow one of the few glimpses of an outsider's view of Chinese society and government during a period when China was closed to foreign visitors. In this selection Ricci describes Chinese government.

We shall touch upon this subject only insofar as it has to do with the purpose of our narrative. It would require a number of chapters, if not of whole books, to treat this matter in full detail.... Chinese imperial power passes on from father to son, or to other royal kin, as does our own. Two or three of the more ancient kings are known to have bequeathed the throne to successors without royal relationship rather than to their sons, whom they judged to be unfitted to rule. More than once, however, it has happened that the people, growing weary of an inept ruler, have stripped him of his authority and replaced him with someone pre-eminent for character and courage whom they henceforth recognized as their legitimate King. It may be said in praise of the Chinese that ordinarily they would prefer to die an honorable death rather than swear allegiance to a usurping monarch. In fact, there is a proverb extant among their philosophers, which reads: "No woman is moral who has two husbands, nor any vassal faithful to two lords."

There are no ancient laws in China under which the republic is governed in perpetuum, such as our laws of the twelve tables and the Code of Caesar. Whoever succeeds in getting possession of the throne, regardless of his ancestry, makes new laws according to his own way of thinking. His successors on the throne are obliged to enforce the laws which he promulgated as founder of the dynasty, and these laws cannot be changed without good reason....

The extent of their kingdom is so vast, its borders so distant, and their utter lack of knowledge of a transmaritime world is so complete that the Chinese imagine the whole world as included in their kingdom. Even now, as from time beyond recording, they call their Emperor, Thiencu, the Son of Heaven, and because they worship Heaven as the Supreme Being, the Son of Heaven and the Son of God are one and the same. In ordinary speech, he is referred to as Hoamsi, meaning supreme ruler or monarch, while other and subordinate rulers are called by the much inferior title of Guam.

Only such as have earned a doctor's degree or that of licentiate are admitted to take part in the government of the kingdom, and due to the interest of the magistrates and of the King himself there is no lack of such candidates. Every public office is therefore fortified with and dependent upon the attested science, prudence, and diplomacy of the person assigned to it, whether he be taking office for the first time or is already experienced in the conduct of civil life. This integrity of life is prescribed by ... law ... , and for the most part it is lived up to, save in the case of such as are prone to violate the dictates of justice from human weakness and from lack of religious training among the gentiles. All magistrates, whether they belong to the military or to the civil congress, are called Quon-fu, meaning commander or president, though their honorary or unofficial title is Lau-ye or Lau-sie, signifying lord or father. The Portuguese call the Chinese magistrates, mandarins, probably from mandando, mando mandare, to order or command, and they are now generally known by this title in Europe.

Though we have already stated that the Chinese form of government is monarchical, it must be evident from what has been said, and it will be made clearer by what is to come, that it is to some extent an aristocracy. Although all legal statutes inaugurated by magistrates must be confirmed by the King in writing on the written petition presented to him, the King himself makes no final decision in important matters of state without consulting the magistrates or considering their advice....

Tax returns, impost, and other tribute, which undoubtedly exceed a hundred and fifty million a year, as is commonly said, do not go into the Imperial Exchequer, nor can the King dispose of this income as he pleases. The silver, which is the common currency, is placed in the public treasury, and the returns paid in rice are placed in the warehouses belonging to the government. The generous allowance made for the support of the royal family and their relatives, for the palace eunuchs and the royal household, is drawn from this national treasury. In keeping with the regal splendor and dignity of the crown, these annuities are large, but each individual account is determined and regulated by law. Civil and military accounts and the expenses of all government departments are paid out of this national treasury, and the size of the national budget is far in excess of what Europeans might imagine. Public buildings, the palaces of the King and of his relations, the upkeep of city prisons and fortresses, and the renewal of all kinds of war supplies must be met by the national treasury, and in a kingdom of such vast dimensions the program of building and of restoration is continuous. One would scarcely believe that at times even these enormous revenues are not sufficient to meet the expenses. When this happens, new taxes are imposed to balance the national budget.

Relative to the magistrates in general, there are two distinct orders or grades. The first and superior order is made up of the magistrates who govern the various courts of the royal palace, which is considered to be a model for the rule of the entire realm. The second order includes all provincial magistrates or governors who rule a province or a city. For each of these orders of magistrates, there are five or six large books containing the governmental roster of the entire country. These books are for sale throughout the kingdom. They are being continually revised, and the revision, which is dated twice a month in the royal city of Pekin, is not very difficult because of the singular typographical arrangement in which they are printed. The entire contents of these books consist of nothing other than the current lists of the names, addresses, and grades of the court offi-

cers of the entire government, and the frequent revision is necessary if the roster is to be kept up to date. In addition to the daily changes, occasioned by deaths, demotions, and dismissals in such an incredibly long list of names, there are the frequent departures of some to visit their homes at stated periods. We shall say more later on of this last instance, which is occasioned by the custom requiring every magistrate to lay aside his official duties and return to his home for three full years, on the death of his father or his mother. One result of these numerous changes is that there are always a great many in the city of Pekin awaiting the good fortune of being appointed to fill the vacancies thus created.

Besides the classes or orders of the magistrates already described and many others which we shall pass over because they differ but little from our own, there are two special orders never heard of among our people. These are the Choli and the Zauli, each consisting of sixty or more chosen philosophers, all prudent men and tried, who have already given exceptional proof of their fidelity to the King and to the realm. These two orders are reserved by the King for business of greater moment pertaining to the royal court or to the provinces, and by him they are entrusted with great responsibility, carrying with it both respect and authority. They correspond in some manner to what we would call keepers of the public conscience, inasmuch as they inform the King as often as they see fit, of any infraction of the law in any part of the entire kingdom. No one is spared from their scrutiny, even the highest magistrates, as they do not hesitate to speak, even though it concerns the King himself or his household. If they had the power of doing something more than talking, or rather of writing, and if they were not wholly dependent upon the King whom they admonish, their particular office would correspond to that of the Lacedemonian Ephors. And yet they do their duty so thoroughly that they are a source of wonder to outsiders and a good example for imitation. Neither King nor magistrates can escape their courage and frankness, and even when they arouse the royal wrath to such an extent that the King becomes severely angry with them, they will never desist from their admonitions and criticism until some remedy has been applied to the public evil against which they are inveighing. In fact, when the grievance is particularly acute, they are sure to put a sting into their complaints and to show no partiality where the crown or the courts are concerned. This same privilege of offering written criticism is also granted by law to any magistrate and even to a private citizen, but for the most part it is exercised only by those to whose particular office it pertains. Numerous copies are made of all such written documents submitted to the crown and of the answers made to them. In this way, what goes on in the royal headquarters is quickly communicated to every corner of the country. These documents are also compiled in book form, and whatever of their content is deemed worthy of handing down to posterity is transcribed into the annals of the King's regime.

Besides the regular magistrates there are in the royal palace various other organizations, instituted for particular purposes. The most exalted of these is what is known as the Han-lin-yuen, made up of selected doctors of philosophy and chosen by examination. Members of this cabinet have nothing to do with public administration but outrank all public officials in dignity of office. Ambition for a place in this select body means no end of labor and of sacrifice. These are the King's secretaries, who do both his writing and his composing. They edit and compile the royal annals and publish the laws and statutes of the land. The tutors of kings and princes are chosen from their number. They are entirely devoted to study and there are grades within the cabinet which are determined by the publications of its members. Hence, they are honored with the highest dignity within the regal court, but not beyond it....

The Chinese can distinguish between their magistrates by the parasols they use as protection against the sun when they go out in public. Some of these are blue and others yellow. Sometimes for effect they will have two or three of these sunshades, but only one if their rank does not permit of more. They may also be recognized by their mode of transportation in public. The lower ranks ride on horseback, the higher are carried about on the shoulders of their servants in gestatorial chairs. The number of carriers also has a significance of rank; some are allowed only four, others may have eight. There are other ways also of distinguishing the magistracy and the rank of dignity therein; by banners and pennants, chains and censer cups, and by the number of the guards who give orders to make way for the passage of the dignitary. The escort itself is held in such high esteem by the public that no one would question their orders. Even in a crowded city everyone gives way at the sound of their voices with a spontaneity that corresponds to the rank of the approaching celebrity.

Before closing this chapter on Chinese public administration, it would seem to be quite worthwhile recording a few more things in which this people differ from Europeans. To begin with, it seems to be quite remarkable when we stop to consider it, that in a kingdom of almost limitless expanse and innumerable population, and abounding in copious supplies of every description, though they have a well-equipped army and navy that could easily conquer the neighboring nations, neither the King nor his people ever think of waging a war of aggression. They are quite content with what they have and are not ambitious of conquest. In this respect they are much different from the people of Europe, who are frequently discontent with their own governments and covetous of what others enjoy. While the nations of the West seem to be entirely consumed with the idea of supreme domination, they cannot even preserve what their ancestors have bequeathed them, as the Chinese have done through a period of some thousand of years....

Another remarkable fact and quite worthy of note as marking a difference from the West, is that the entire kingdom is administered by the Order of the Learned, commonly known as The Philosophers. The responsibility for orderly management of the entire realm is wholly and completely committed to their charge and care. The army, both officers and soldiers, hold them in high respect and show them the promptest obedience and deference, and not infrequently the military are disciplined by them as a schoolboy might be punished by his master. Policies of war are formulated and military questions are decided by the Philosophers only, and their advice and counsel has more weight with the King than that of the military leaders. In fact very few of these, and only on rare occasions, are admitted to war consultations. Hence it follows that those who aspire to be cultured frown upon war and would prefer the lowest rank in the philosophical order to the highest in the military, realizing that the Philosophers far excel military leaders in the good will and the respect of the people and in opportunities of acquiring wealth.

Study Questions

1. What is the relationship between emperor and magistrate in Ricci's account of Chinese administration?

2. What characteristics of Chinese government does Ricci most admire?

3. What is the role of the Choli and the Zauli?

4. Why did Ricci write the *Journals?* Who was his intended audience?

5. Do you think that Ricci's description of Chinese government is accurate?

The True History of the Conquest of New Spain (1552-1568)   66

BERNAL DÍAZ

Bernal Díaz del Castillo (ca. 1492–1581) was one of the soldiers who accompanied Hernán Cortés on the conquest of the Aztecs. Díaz left Spain for the New World at the age of 18 and had explored both Cuba and the Yucatan peninsula before he joined the Cortés expedition. After the conquest of Mexico, Díaz accompanied Cortés on his unsuccessful expedition into Honduras. He remained in Central America for most of his life, settling in what is now Guatemala, where his papers, including the manuscript copy of his *True History*, remain.

Díaz wrote *The True History of the Conquest of New Spain* to refute what he regarded as inaccurate accounts of the conquest. Although he was an eyewitness and participant, his history was not written until many years later, and was undoubtedly colored by his polemical purpose. Nevertheless, his description of Tenochtitlán, capital of Montezuma's empire, remains compelling.

As we had already been in Mexico for four days and none of us had left our quarters except to go to the houses and gardens, Cortés told us it would be a good idea to go to the main plaza and see the great temple of their Uichilobos....

Many of Montezuma's chiefs were sent to accompany us, and when we arrived at the great square we were struck by the throngs of people and the amount of merchandise they displayed, at the efficiency and administration of everything.

The chiefs who accompanied us showed us how each kind of merchandise was kept separate and had its place marked out. Let us start with the dealers in gold, silver, and precious stones, feathers, cloth, and embroidered goods, and other merchandise in the form of men and women to be sold as slaves. There were as many here as the Negroes brought from Guinea by the Portuguese. Some were tied to long poles with collars around their necks so they couldn't escape, and others were left free. Then there were merchants who sold homespun clothing, cotton, and thread, and others who sold cacao, so that one could see every sort of goods that is to be found in all of New Spain, set out the way it's done where I come from, Medina del Campo, during fair time....

I wonder why I waste all these words in telling what they sold in that great square, for I shall never finish describing everything in detail. But I must mention the paper, which is called *amal,* the little pipes scented with liquidambar and filled with tobacco, and the yellow ointments and other things of the same sort, all sold separately. Cochineal was sold under the arcades, and herbs and many other kinds of goods. There were buildings where three judges sat, and magistrates who inspected the merchandise.... I wish I could get through with telling all the things they sold there, but only to finish looking and inquiring about everything in that great square filled with people would have taken two days, and then you wouldn't have seen everything.

When we climbed to the top of the great *cu* there was a kind of platform, with huge stones where they put the poor Indians to be sacrificed, and an image like a dragon and other evil figures, with a great deal of blood that had been shed that day. Montezuma, accompanied by two priests, came out from an oratory dedicated to the worship of his cursed idols at the top of the *cu,* and said with great deference toward all of us, "You must be tired, Señor Malinche, after climbing up this great temple of ours."

Through our interpreters, who went with us, Cortés replied that neither he nor the rest of us ever got tired from anything. Then Montezuma took him by the hand and bade him look at his great city and at all the other cities rising from the water, and the many towns around the lake; and if he had not seen the market place well, he said, he could see it from here much better.

There we stood looking, for that large and evil temple was so high that it towered over everything. From there we could see all three

Quetzalcoatl. Quetzalcoatl was one of the favorite deities of the Central American peoples. His visage of a plumed serpent, as shown here, was prominent in the royal capital of Teotihuacán. According to legend, Quetzalcoatl, the leader of the Toltecs, was tricked into drunkenness and humiliated by a rival god. In disgrace he left his homeland, but promised to return. In 1519, the Aztec monarch Moctezuma welcomed Hernán Cortés, the leader of the Spanish expedition, believing he was a representative of Quetzalcoatl.

of the causeways that led into Mexico: the road from Iztapalapa, by which we had entered four days earlier; the Tacuba road, by which we fled the night of our great rout; and the road from Tepeaquilla.

We saw the fresh water that came from Chapultepec, which supplied the city, and the bridges on the three causeways, built at certain intervals so the water could go from one part of the lake to another, and a multitude of canoes, some arriving with provisions and others leaving with merchandise. We saw that every house in this great city and in the others built on the water could be reached only by wooden drawbridges or by canoe. We saw temples built like towers and fortresses in these cities, all whitewashed; it was a sight to see. We could look down on the flat-roofed houses and other little towers and temples like fortresses along the causeways.

After taking a good look and considering all that we had seen, we looked again at the great square and the throngs of people, some buying and others selling. The buzzing of their voices could be heard more than a league away. There were soldiers among us who had been in many parts of the world, in Constantinople and Rome and all over Italy, who said that they had never before seen a market place so large and so well laid out. and so filled with people.

Then Cortés said to Montezuma, through Doña Marina, "Your Highness is indeed a great prince, and it has delighted us to see your cities. Now that we are here in your temple, will you show us your gods?"

Montezuma replied that he would first have to consult with his priests. After he had spoken with them, he bade us enter a small tower room, a kind of hall where there were two altars with very richly painted planks on the ceiling. On each altar there were two giant figures, their bodies very tall and stout. The first one, to the right, they said was Uichilobos, their god of war. It had a very broad face with monstrous, horrible eyes, and the whole body was covered with precious stones, gold, and pearls that were stuck on with a paste they make in this country out of roots. The body was circled with great snakes made of gold and precious stones, and in one hand he held a bow and in the other some arrows. A small idol standing by him they said was his page; he held a short lance and a shield rich with gold and precious stones. Around the neck of Uichilobos were silver Indian faces and things that we took to be the hearts of these Indians, made of gold and decorated with many precious blue stones. There were braziers with copal incense, and they were burning in them the hearts of three Indians they had sacrificed that day. All the walls and floor were black with crusted blood, and the whole place stank.

To the left stood another great figure, the height of Uichilobos, with the face of a bear and glittering eyes made of their mirrors, which they call *tezcal*. It was decorated with precious stones the same as Uichilobos, for they said that the two were brothers. This Tezcatepuca was the god of hell and had charge of the souls of the Mexicans. His body was girded with figures like little devils, with snakclikc tails. The walls were so crusted with blood and the floor was so bathed in it that in the slaughterhouses of Castile there was no such stink. They had offered to this idol five hearts from the day's sacrifices.

In the highest part of the *cu* there was another recess, the wood of which was very richly carved, where there was another figure, half man and half lizard, covered with precious stones and with a mantle over half of it. They said that its body was filled with all the seeds there are in all the world. It was the god of sowing and ripening, but I do not remember its name. Everything was covered with blood, the walls as well as the altar, and it stank so much that we couldn't get out fast enough.

Our captain said to Montezuma, half laughingly, "Lord Montezuma, I do not understand how such a great prince and wise man as yourself can have failed to come to the conclusion that these idols of yours are not gods, but evil things—devils is the term for them. So that you and your priests may see it clearly, do me a favor: Let us put a cross on top of this tower, and in one part of these oratories, where your Uichilobos and Tezcatepuca are, we will set up an image of Our Lady [an image that Montezuma had already seen], and you will see how afraid of it these idols that have deceived you are,"

The two priests with Montezuma looked hostile, and Montezuma replied with annoyance, "Señor Malinche, if I had thought that you would so insult my gods, I would not have shown them to you. We think they are very good, for they give us health, water, good seedtimes and weather, and all the victories we desire. We must worship and make sacrifices to them. Please do not say another word to their dishonor."

When our captain heard this and saw how changed Montezuma was, he didn't argue with him any more, but smiled and said, "It is time for Your Highness and ourselves to go."

Montezuma agreed, but he said that before he left he had to pray and make certain offerings to atone for the great sin he had committed in permitting us to climb the great *cu* and see his gods, and for being the cause of the dishonor that we had done them by speaking ill of them.

Study Questions

1. What impressed Díaz most about the city? Is his list of the merchandise he saw for sale random or ordered?

2. Why does Díaz describe the Aztec gods as devils?

3. How does the fact that the Aztecs sacrificed humans color Díaz's account of their religion?

4. Who do you have more sympathy for, Cortés or Montezuma? How does Díaz manipulate your sympathies?

An Aztec Account of the Conquest of Mexico (1528)   67

There are several surviving accounts of the conquest of Mexico written by indigenous tribesmen. They tell the story of the fall of Tenochtitlán and the suffering of the tribesmen who defended it. One of these accounts is cast in a narrative form not unlike that of Bernal Díaz. It relates the experience of the warriors of Tlatelolca in attempting to defend their city and the suffering they experienced during the Spanish siege.

The manuscript of this anonymous account has been preserved in Paris. It was written in 1528 in the Nahuatl language, perhaps by more than one author. Whoever composed it was clearly an eyewitness to the events being described. "The Captain" referred to is Cortés and "The Sun" is Don Pedro de Alvarado, one of Cortés's lieutenants.

Year 1—Canestalk. The Spaniards came to the palace at Tlayacac. When the Captain arrived at the palace, Motecuhzoma sent the Cuetlaxteca to greet him and to bring him two suns as gifts. One of these suns was made of the yellow metal, the other of the white. The Cuetlaxteca also brought him a mirror to be hung on his person, a gold collar, a great gold pitcher, fans and ornaments of quetzal feathers and a shield inlaid with mother-of-pearl.

The envoys made sacrifices in front of the Captain. At this, he grew very angry. When they offered him blood in an "eagle dish," he shouted at the man who offered it and struck him with his sword. The envoys departed at once.

Then the Captain marched to Tenochtitlán. He arrived here during the month called Bird, under the sign of the day 8-Wind. When he entered the city, we gave him chickens, eggs, corn, tortillas and drink. We also gave him firewood, and fodder for his "deer." Some of these gifts were sent by the lord of Tenochtitlán, the rest by the lord of Tlatelolco.

During this time, the people asked Motecuhzoma how they should celebrate their god's fiesta. He said: "Dress him in all his finery, in all his sacred ornaments."

During this same time, The Sun commanded that Motecuhzoma and Itzcohuatzin, the military chief of Tlatelolco, be made prisoners. The Spaniards hanged a chief from Acolhuacan named Nezahualquentzin. They also murdered the king of Nauhtla, Cohualpopocatzin, by wounding him with arrows and then burning him alive.

For this reason, our warriors were on guard at the Eagle Gate. The sentries from Tenochtitlán stood at one side of the gate, and the sentries from Tlatelolco at the other. But messengers came to tell them to dress the figure of Huitzilopochtli. They left their posts and went to dress him in his sacred finery: his ornaments and his paper clothing.

When this had been done, the celebrants began to sing their songs. That is how they celebrated the first day of the fiesta. On the second day they began to sing again, but without warning they were all put to death. The dancers and singers were completely unarmed. They brought only their embroidered cloaks, their turquoises, their lip plugs, their necklaces, their clusters of heron feathers, their trinkets made of deer hooves. Those who played the drums, the old men, had brought their gourds of snuff and their timbrels.

The Spaniards attacked the musicians first, slashing at their hands and faces until they had killed all of them. The singers—and even the spectators—were also killed. This slaughter in the Sacred Patio went on for three hours. Then the Spaniards burst into the rooms of the temple to kill the others: those who were carrying water, or bringing fodder for the horses, or grinding meal, or sweeping, or standing watch over this work.

The king Motecuhzoma, who was accompanied by Itzcohuatzin and by those who had brought food for the Spaniards, protested: "Our lords, that is enough! What are you doing? These people are not carrying shields or *macanas*. Our lords, they are completely unarmed!"

The Sun treacherously murdered our people on the twentieth day after the Captain left for the coast. We allowed the Captain to return to the city in peace. But on the following day we attacked him with all our might, and that was the beginning of the war.

Now the Spaniards began to wage war against us. They attacked us by land for ten days, and then their ships appeared. Twenty days later, they gathered all their ships together near Nonohualco, off the place called Mazatzintamalco. The allies from Tlaxcala and Huexotzinco set up camp on either side of the road.

Our warriors from Tlatelolco immediately leaped into their canoes and set out for Mazatzintamalco and the Nonohualco road. But no one set out from Tenochtitlán to assist us: only the Tlatelolcas were ready when the Spaniards arrived in their ships. On the following day, the ships sailed to Xoloco.

The fighting at Xoloco and Huitzillan lasted for two days. While the battle was under way, the warriors from Tenochtitlán began to mutiny. They said: "Where are our chiefs? They have fired scarcely a single arrow! Do they think they have fought like men?" Then they seized four of their own leaders and put them to death. The victims were two captains, Cuauhnochtli and Cuapan, and the priests of Amantlan and Tlalocan. This was the second time that the people of Tenochtitlán killed their own leaders.

The Flight to Tlatelolco

The Spaniards set up two cannons in the middle of the road and aimed them at the city. When they fired them, one of the shots struck the Eagle Gate. The people of the city were so terrified that they began to flee to Tlatelolco. They brought their idol Huitzilopochtli with them, setting it up in the House of the Young Men. Their king Cuauhtemoc also abandoned Tenochtitlán. Their chiefs said: "Mexicanos! Tlatelolcas! All is not lost! We can still defend our houses. We can prevent them from capturing our storehouses and the produce of our lands. We can save the sustenance of life, our stores of corn. We can also save our weapons and insignia, our clusters of rich feathers, our gold earrings and precious stones. Do not be discouraged; do not lose heart. We are Mexicanos! We are Tlatelolcas!"

During the whole time we were fighting, the warriors of Tenochtitlán: were nowhere to be seen. The battles at Yacacolco, Atezcapan, Coatlan, Nonohualco, Xoxohuitlan, Tepeyacac and elsewhere were all fought by ourselves, by Tlatelolcas. In the same way, the canals were defended solely by Tlatelolcas.

The captains from Tenochtitlán cut their hair short, and so did those of lesser rank. The Otomies and the other ranks that usually wore headdresses did not wear them during all the time we were fighting. The Tlatelolcas surrounded the most important captains and their women taunted them: "Why are you hanging back? Have you no shame? No woman will ever paint her face for you again!" The wives of the men from Tenochtitlán wept and begged for pity.

When the warriors of Tlatelolco heard what was happening, they began to shout, but still the brave captains of Tenochtitlán hung back. As for the Tlatelolcas, their humblest warriors died fighting as bravely as their captains.

The Spaniards made ready to attack us, and the war broke out again. They assembled their forces in Cuepopan and Cozcacuahco. A vast number of our warriors were killed by their metal darts. Their ships sailed to Texopan, and the battle there lasted three days. When they had forced us to retreat, they entered the Sacred Patio, where there was a four-day battle. Then they reached Yacacolco.

The Tlatelolcas set up three racks of heads in three different places. The first rack was in the Sacred Patio of Tlilancalco [Black House], where we strung up the heads of our lords the Spaniards. The second was in Acacolco, where we strung up Spanish heads and the heads of two of their horses. The third was in Zacatla, in front of the temple of the earth-goddess Cihuacoatl, where we strung up the heads of Tlaxcaltecas.

The women of Tlatelolco joined in the fighting. They struck at the enemy and shot arrows at them; they tucked up their skirts and dressed in the regalia of war.

The Spaniards forced us to retreat. Then they occupied the market place. The Tlatelolcas—the Jaguar Knights, the Eagle Knights, the great warriors—were defeated, and this was the end of the battle. It had lasted five days, and two thousand Tlatelolcas were killed in action. During the battle, the Spaniards set up a canopy for the Captain in the market place. They also mounted a catapult on the temple platform.

Epic Description of the Besieged City

And all these misfortunes befell us. We saw them and wondered at them; we suffered this unhappy fate.

Broken spears lie in the roads;
we have torn our hair in our grief.
The houses are roofless now, and their walls are
   red with blood.
Worms are swarming in the streets and plazas,
and the walls are splattered with gore.
The water has turned red, as if it were dyed,
and when we drink it,
it has the taste of brine.

We have pounded our hands in despair against
   the adobe walls,
for our inheritance, our city, is lost and dead.
The shields of our warriors were its defense,
   but they could not save it.

We have chewed dry twigs and salt grasses;
we have filled our mouths with dust and bits of
   adobe;
we have eaten lizards, rats and worms....

When we had meat, we ate it almost raw. It was scarcely on the fire before we snatched it and gobbled it down.

They set a price on all of us: on the young men, the priests, the boys and girls. The price of a poor man was only two handfuls of corn, or ten cakes made from mosses or twenty cakes of salty couch-grass. Gold, jade, rich cloths, quetzal feathers—everything that once was precious was now considered worthless.

Study Questions

1. How were the Spaniards greeted when they first arrived? How was the offering of blood understood by the natives? How was it understood by the Spaniards?

2. How did the war begin? Why does the author believe that it was the natives who started it?

3. What was the nature of Montezuma's army? Did he command a single state?

4. How did the Tlatelolcas taunt their own allies? What values are implicit in their insults?

History of the Inca Empire (1653)   68

BERNABE COBO

Bernabe Cobo (1580–1657), a Jesuit missionary, was one of the great historians of the civilizations of South America. He left his home in southern Spain as a teenager to travel to the New World. He spent most of his life in Peru, where he worked to convert Incas to Western religion and agricultural practices. Little is known of his life, but it is clear that he spent many years diligently collecting materials for his history and, as a result, preserved many oral accounts of the nature of Incan life before the coming of the Spanish.

The portion of the *History of the Inca Empire* that has survived is more a sociological and anthropological account of pre-Columbian South American culture than a conventional history. Cobo collected the legends of the founding of the Incas and recorded the oral traditions surrounding the monarchy, but he was most interested in customs and social organization.

Of the Laws and Punishments with Which the Incas Governed Their Kingdom

Since the Indians lacked writing, they had no written laws, but the ones that their kings had established were preserved by tradition, use, and observance. I will record here the most important laws that were most prominent in their memories.

Where the Inca was present, he alone was the judge, and before him all offenses committed were tried; and where he was not present, his governors and caciques administered justice. They were selected to serve as judges according to the nature of the case.

When someone committed an offense that was deserving of punishment, he was apprehended and put in jail, and in order to bring his case to trial, he was taken out of jail and brought before the Inca or the presiding judge and *curaca*. During the trial, witnesses were brought out and confronted the accused. Each one told what he knew about the case against the accused, and in this way they convinced the judge. After the case was heard, without other proceedings, time limit, or delay, the Inca or judge pronounced the sentence and ordered that the delinquent be punished in accordance with his guilt.

He that killed another in order to rob him received the death penalty, and before it was executed, the guilty person was tortured in jail to increase the punishment, and after being tortured, he was killed.

He that killed by treachery was put to death publicly and insultingly, even though he was a nobleman and the dead man was of much lesser station.

He that killed by casting spells received the death penalty. This punishment was executed with much publicity, bringing together the people of the surrounding towns so that they would be present at the execution, and likewise all of his household and family were killed because it was presumed that they all knew that craft.

If someone was killed in a quarrel, first it was determined who caused it; if the dead man did, the killer was given a light punishment at the discretion of the Inca; if the one who caused the fight was the slayer, he received the death penalty, or at the very best, he was exiled to the provinces of the Andes, a sick and unhealthy land for the Indians of the sierra; there he would serve for his whole life, as on the galleys, in the Inca's *chacaras* of coca.

The cacique that killed one of his subjects without permission from the Inca was punished in public by being given certain blows on the back with a stone (this was called stone punishment, and it was a great insult). It was done even though the Indian may have been guilty of some act of disobedience against the cacique in question. If after the cacique was reprehended and punished, he repeated the same offense, he died for it; and if this punishment was not executed, due to pleas and intercessions, the Inca took the offender's *cacicazgo* away from him and gave it to another.

The husband that killed his wife for adultery was set free without punishment, but if he killed her due to anger and passion, he received the death penalty if he was an ordinary man, but if he was an important gentleman who commanded respect, he did not die, but he was given another punishment.

The woman that killed her husband received the death penalty, and it was executed in this way: she was hung up by the feet in some public place, and she was left like this until she died, without anyone daring to take her down.

The pregnant woman that took potions in order to kill her baby received the death penalty, and the same punishment was given to the person that gave her the potions or maliciously made her abort by striking her or some other mistreatment.

He that forced a single woman was given the stone punishment for the first time, and the second time, the death penalty.

He that forcibly corrupted some maiden received the death penalty if she was a noble woman, and if she was not, the first time, he was given a certain torture that was used, and the second time, he died.

He that committed adultery with another man's wife who was not of the nobility was tortured, but if she was of the nobility, he received the death penalty and she died also.

He that took the daughter from her father against his will got no punishment at all, if the daughter consented and was not forced and both were from the same town; however, the father could punish her if he wished for having taken a husband without his consent, but the Inca would order that they be apprehended and separated because nobody could take a wife without his permission.

When someone was found in the house of another with his daughter, if the father made a complaint, the delinquent was punished at the discretion of the Inca and his governor.

He that scaled the walls of the house or retreat of the *mamaconas* was killed; he was hung by the feet and left that way within the very house where he committed the offense, and if any of the *mamaconas* let him inside and sinned with him, she was given the same punishment.

In certain cases marriage was prohibited, and fornication in the cases in which marriage was prohibited was punishable with the death penalty, and this punishment was executed without remission, if the guilty party was not a noble, because a noble got only a public reprimand.

He that robbed without reason, besides paying for the stolen item if he had the resources, was exiled to the Andes, nor would he dare to return without the Inca's permission.

He that stole things to eat from necessity was reprimanded and given no other punishment than being warned to work and that if he did it again he would be punished by being struck on the back with a stone in public.

He that stole some fruit from the fields or orchards by necessity while traveling was killed for it if the property belonged to the Inca; if the property belonged to someone else, the man was pardoned.

When one of the Indians that served in the *tambos* did not turn over the load that he was carrying to the proprietor, the town that the Indian in question was from had to pay for it because the town was responsible for the service of that *tambo*, and the Indian was punished.

He that stole the water with which the *chacaras* were irrigated and brought it to his *chacara* before it was his turn was punished with an arbitrary penalty.

He that insulted another was given an arbitrary punishment, but he that had provoked the words was given a greater penalty.

He that injured another or caused some similar harm was punished with an arbitrary penalty, and if it was done treacherously, he was tortured.

He that maimed another in a quarrel to such an extent that the injured party could not do ordinary work was obliged to support the injured party from his own property, apart from the punishment that was given to him for the offense, and if he had no property, the Inca fed the injured party from his property, and the delinquent was given a greater punishment.

He that maliciously burned a bridge received the death penalty, and it was executed without fail.

The Indian that was disobedient to his cacique for the first time was given the punishment that the Inca deemed appropriate: the second time he did it, he was given the stone punishment, and the third time, death.

The *mitima* Indian that left the place where he had been put by the Inca to serve as *mitima* was tortured the first time, and the second, he was killed.

He that changed the dress and insignia of the province where he was born committed a great offense against the Inca, against his nation, and against the province whose dress he adopted, and thus he was accused by all of them and punished with rigor.

He that removed the stone boundary markers or entered into the land or property of another was given the stone punishment for the first time, and the second time, he received the death penalty.

He that hunted without permission on any land where trespassing was prohibited was castigated by being struck on the back with a stone and tortured.

If someone's livestock damaged someone else's property, the owner of the property could take as much of the livestock as the damage was worth, and they had established how many feet of maize equaled a certain unit of measurement, by which they assigned a specific penalty that was paid in proportion to the amount of damage done.

When travelers had something stolen from them in a *tambo*, first of all the cacique in charge of the *tambo* was punished, and afterward the latter punished the rest of his subjects for negligence and not having been watchful.

The Indian that did not show the proper respect for the Inca and lords was put in jail, where he was left for a long time, and if, in addition to this, they found him to be guilty of something else, he was killed.

He that was a liar and perjurer was tortured as a punishment, and if he was very addicted to this vice and did not mend his ways with this punishment, he was killed in public.

If a governor failed to administer justice or covered up anything for reasons of bribery or because he was so inclined, the Inca himself punished him, taking his *cacicazgo* and post away from him and denying him the right to have others, and if the injustice involved something serious, the Inca ordered that the offender be killed.

The Incas had two prisons in Cuzco. One of them was half a league away from the city, in front of the parish of San Sebastian, which used to be called Arauaya. and was located in a place named Umpillay; here thieves and other criminals were punished with the death penalty, which was executed by hanging the wrongdoers upside down and leaving them hanging there until they died. The other prison was underground within the city; in it they had enclosed lions [pumas], bears, tigers [jaguars], and serpents; and the people who committed the most atrocious offenses, such as treason against the king and the like, were thrown to these wild beasts and eaten by them. These Indians had many other laws which were very beneficial for governing their republic well. True it is that some of them were too rigorous, such as those that required the death penalty and other exorbitant punishments for light offenses. Also it should be known that justice was not uniform and equal among them; although they prided themselves on being just and punishing all offenses, they always gave different penalties to the nobles and the wealthy than they gave to the humble and poor. This was due to an illusion that they had which was to say that a public reprimand was a far greater punishment for an Inca of noble blood than the death penalty for a plebeian. They justified their follies as well as their lofty positions on the assumption that they were children of the Sun and the first ones to found the religion and

sacrifices of the Sun. Therefore, in the enforcement of their laws, they paid careful attention to these privileges, and thus the punishments were different according to the social status of the person that broke the laws. It turned out that for the same offenses that a common person would get the death penalty, nobles of Inca lineage would get no other punishment than a public reprimand; but this reprimand was so feared that the Indians affirm that it has happened only a few times, and very rarely has a noble been executed.

How the Incas Administered Newly Conquered Lands

Although it was very extensive and composed of many and very different nations, the entire empire of the Incas was a single republic, governed by the same laws, privileges, and customs, and it was observant of the same religion, rites, and ceremonies; however, before being brought under Inca rule, the several nations had their own common law and a different way of living and governing themselves. This union and uniformity was maintained everywhere; and it must be understood that what we say here that the Incas introduced into the nations that they subjugated was the same type of government that they maintained at the Inca court and where they ruled before.

The first thing that these kings did when they won a province was to take out of it six or seven thousand families (more or less, according to what seemed fitting to them, judging by the number and disposition of the people they found) and send them to other parts of the quiet and peaceful provinces, distributing them throughout a number of towns; and in exchange for them they put the same number of other people, who were made to leave the places where the first were settled, or from wherever the Incas wished, and among them were many *orejones* of noble blood. These individuals who settled in new lands were called *mitimaes*, which is the same as to say "newcomers" or "outsiders" in contrast to the natives; this name referred to the new vassals as well as to the old ones who were exchanged for them; in fact, both went from their own lands to strange lands; and even today we use the word in this way, calling all of the newcomers who are settled in all the provinces of this kingdom *mitimaes*. Care was taken in this transmigration that those who were transferred, the recently conquered as well as the others, did not move to just any land, in a haphazard way, but to the places that were of the same climate and qualities or very similar to those they were leaving and in which they were raised. Therefore, those who were native to cold lands were taken to cold lands and those from hot lands to hot lands, so that in this way they would not regret moving from their natural home so much and they would be healthier in the new lands, without falling ill from the change, which would be the case if they were taken to lands of the opposite climate of their homeland. The people who were moved by the Inca in this way were relieved from obedience to their former caciques, and they were ordered to submit to the rule of the caciques of the lands where they were placed; and there it was ordered that both types of *mitimaes* be given places to build homes and lands in which to prepare their *chacaras* and plant their crops, and they were to remain there as perpetual residents of the towns where they were placed; and they were to follow the practices and way of life of the local people, except that they retained the dress, emblems, and symbols of the people from their nation or province; moreover, this custom has been preserved up to the present time, for even now on the basis of the aforementioned things, we can distinguish between the natives of each town and the *mitimaes*.

The Inca introduced this change of residence in order to keep his dominion quiet and safe. The city of Cuzco, capital of the kingdom where the Inca had his court and residence, was far away from the most remote provinces in which there were many nations of barbaric and warlike people; therefore, the Inca felt that he could not maintain peace and obedience in any other way, and since this was the main reason why this measure was taken, the Inca ordered that the majority of the *mitimaes* who were made to go to recently subjugated towns settle in the provincial capitals so that they could serve as a garrison and presidio—not for a salary or for a limited time; rather, the *mitimaes* and their descendants would remain perpetually. And, as would be the case with warriors, they were given some privileges so they would appear to be more noble, and the Inca commanded that they always be very obedient and do whatever their captains and governors might order. With this skillful plan, as long as these *mitimaes* were loyal to the governors, if the natives rebelled, soon they would be reduced to obeying the Inca, and if the *mitimaes* made a disturbance and started an uprising, they would be repressed and punished by the natives; and thus, by means of this resolution to make the majority of their people reestablish themselves by shifting some to the places of others, the king kept his states secure from rebellion. Moreover, trade and commerce between provinces was more frequent and all the land better supplied with what was needed. Furthermore, with this transfer of their vassals from one place to another, the Incas aimed to achieve throughout their kingdom similarity and uniformity in matters pertaining to religion and political government, and they expected all of the nations of the kingdom to learn the language of Cuzco, which in this way came to be the general language of all Peru. With this shuffling of domiciles, the newly conquered, who were transferred within the kingdom, learned all this in a short time and without suffering or compulsion, and the old vassals who settled as *mitimaes* in the newly pacified areas taught the natives; great care was taken in this and the natives were compelled to learn, for the Incas obliged everyone to accept their language, laws, and religion, along with all of the opinions related to these matters that were established in Cuzco. The Incas eliminated, either completely or partially, the practices and rites that the conquered people had before Inca ways were imposed. In order to introduce and establish these things more effectively, besides the aforementioned conversion of the people, upon conquering a province, the Incas had the people's main idol taken away and placed in Cuzco with the same services and cult that it used to have in the province of its origin, and the natives were obliged to take care of all this, exactly as had been done when the aforementioned idol or *guaca* was in their province. For that reason Indians from all the provinces of the kingdom resided in Cuzco. These Indians were occupied in the care and ministry of their idols, and there they learned the practices and customs of the courtiers. Since they took turns by their *mitas* and assigned time for service, after returning to their own province they maintained the practices they had seen and learned in the court, and they taught all this to their people.

In the process of moving the *mitimaes*, no thought was given to the distance that there was from their lands to where they were ordered to go, even though it was very great. On the contrary, not infrequently, it happened that they were transplanted from one end of the kingdom to the other; other times they were moved three or four hundred leagues, more or less, as the prince deemed fitting; for this reason, today in the provinces of Collao there are *mitimaes* who are natives originally from the provinces of Chinchaysuyu, and in the latter provinces there are many Indians from the former. It is a proven fact that the Indians of different provinces were so mixed and thrown together that there is hardly a valley or

town throughout Peru where some *ayllo* and tribal group of *mitimaes* would not be found. Mainly, the Inca took two things into consideration when moving his subjects. The first one was (as has been stated) that they not go to a climate that was contrary to their nature, and the other, that all the provinces of his empire be well populated and well supplied with food and everything necessary for human life. For this reason, he put people from elsewhere in the sparsely populated areas, and from the places that had more people than could be comfortably supported, the Inca took colonies to settle in the less populous ones; and these people who by order of the king left their own land and the jurisdiction of their caciques and settled in strange lands, giving obedience at the same time to the local caciques, are the ones who were actually called *mitimaes* during the time of the Incas. But after the Spaniards occupied this land, this name has been extended to others who were not actually *mitimaes* formerly; in fact, the word was extended to include the Indians who, by order of their caciques and with their permission or that of the Inca, lived away from their towns and provinces of origin in the districts of other caciques, although they were not under the jurisdiction of the latter, but under the caciques of the province from whence they came or where they were born. For an explanation of this, it is necessary to presuppose the existence of an ancient custom of these people, and it is that when some province did not produce certain foods, especially none of their bread, which was *maize*, but was suitable for other uses, special arrangements were made. For example, due to the extreme cold, the provinces of Collao do not produce maize or other seeds or fruits of temperate lands, but they are very abundant in pasture lands and most appropriate for raising livestock and producing *papas* [potatoes], from which *chuño*, their substitute for bread, is made, as well as some other roots. For the inhabitants of these provinces, the Inca had picked out lands which lie in the hot valleys of the seacoast on one side and on the other side of the mountains toward the Andes; in these temperate valleys they plant the crops that they lack in their own lands; and since these valleys were from twenty, thirty, and more leagues away from their land and they could not come to cultivate them as a community group the way they do in the rest of the kingdom, the caciques took care to send, at the appropriate times, people to farm there, and after the crops were harvested, these people returned to their own towns. Apart from this, by order of the Inca, on the outskirts of each town there were a certain number of Indians with their women and houses; they resided permanently with their children and descendants in the aforementioned valleys, in order to care for and cultivate the *chacaras* of their caciques and their communities. These people, although they lived in the land of others, were under the jurisdiction of their own caciques, and not those of the land where they resided; but after the Spaniards entered into this kingdom, at the time that the land was visited for the first time in order to parcel it out and entrust it to the settlers, these Indians who were found in the aforementioned valleys, put there by their caciques for the reason just stated, were counted and assigned in repartimiento along with the natives of the district where they were living. They were also relieved from obedience to their former caciques, and they were put under the control of the caciques in whose jurisdiction and land they were living. Consequently, they were entrusted to the same encomendero to whom the district in question was parceled out and not to the encomendero of the *cacicazgo* of which they were natives. To all of these people who, in the aforementioned manner, had remained in the lands where we find them, we also give now the name of *mitimaes*, without distinguishing them from the first ones, the only people that were *mitimaes* at the time of the Incas.

Study Questions

1. Characterize the Inca nation before the Spanish arrived.

2. How did Cobo's background influence his interpretation of Incan culture?

3. How did Cobo get his information? Why is his work written in the past tense?

4. Why was illicit intercourse with a noble woman punished more harshly than if committed with a common woman?

Journal of the First Voyage of Vasco da Gama (1497–1499)   69

Vasco da Gama (ca. 1460–1524) was the greatest of the Portuguese explorers and sea captains. Little is known about his childhood. His father was also a sea captain, and had been given command of the voyage that da Gama ultimately undertook. He must have studied mathematics and navigation, for his first public employment was in command of a squadron of ships. After his father's death in 1496, da Gama was commissioned to explore further the eastern coast of Africa, which had been opened when the Portuguese sailed around the Cape of Good Hope. Da Gama rounded the continent, discovered Mozambique, and then, with the aid of an African navigator crossed the Indian Ocean. When he returned two years later laden with Eastern spices he was hailed as a hero. Da Gama made two more voyages to India and was ultimately appointed Portuguese viceroy.

The anonymous *Journal of the First Voyage of Vasco da Gama* is an eyewitness account of da Gama's path-breaking journey. The selections here describe what the Portuguese found when they landed in West Africa.

On Wednesday, April 4 [1498], we made sail to the north-west, and before noon we sighted an extensive country, and two islands close to it, surrounded with shoals. And when we were near enough for the pilots to recognize these islands, they told us that we had left three leagues behind us an island inhabited by Christians. We manoeuvred all day in the hope of fetching this island, but in vain, for the wind was too strong for us. After this we thought it best to bear away for a city called Mombasa, reported to be four days ahead of us.

The above island was one of those which we had come to discover, for our pilots said it was inhabited by Christians.

When we bore away for the north it was already late, and the wind was high. At night-fall we perceived a large island, which remained to the north of us. Our pilot told us that there were two towns on this island, one of Christians and the other of Moors.

That night we stood out to sea, and in the morning (5 April) we no longer saw the land. We then steered to the north-west, and in the evening we again beheld the land. During the following night we bore awry to the N. by W., and during the morning-watch we changed our course to the north-north-west. Sailing thus before a favourable wind, the *S. Raphael*, two hours before the break of day (6 April), ran aground on a shoal, about two leagues from the land. Immediately the *Raphael* touched bottom, the vessels following her were warned by shouts, and these were no sooner heard than they cast anchor about the distance of a gunshot from the stranded vessel, and lowered their boats. When the tide fell the *Raphael* lay high and dry. With the help of the boats many anchors were laid out, and when the tide rose again, in the course of the day, the vessel floated and there was much rejoicing.

On the mainland, facing these shoals, there rises a lofty range of mountains, beautiful of aspect. These mountains we called Serras de Sao Raphael, and we gave the same name to the shoals.

When the vessel was high and dry, two *almadias* approached us. One was laden with fine oranges, better than those of Portugal. Two of the Moors remained on board, and accompanied us next day to Mombasa.

On Saturday morning, the 7th of the month, and eve of Palm Sunday, we ran along the coast and saw some of the islands at a distance of fifteen leagues from the mainland, and about six leagues in extent. They supply the vessels of the country with masts. All are inhabited by Moors.

On Saturday (7 April) we cast anchor off Mombasa, but did not enter the port. No sooner had we been perceived than a *zavra* [small boat] manned by Moors came out to us: in front of the city there lay numerous vessels all dressed in flags. And we, anxious not to be outdone, also dressed our ships, and we actually surpassed their show, for we wanted in nothing but men, even a few whom we had being very ill. We anchored here with much pleasure, for we confidently hoped that on the following day we might go on land and hear mass jointly with the Christians reported to live there under their own *alcaide* in a quarter separate from that of the Moors.

The pilots who had come with us told us there resided both Moors and Christians in this city; that these latter lived apart under their own lords, and that on our arrival they would receive us with much honour and take us to their houses. But they said this for a purpose of their own, for it was not true. At midnight there approached us a *zavra* with about 100 men, all armed with cutlasses and bucklers. When they came to the vessel of the captain-major they attempted to board her, armed as they were, but this was not permitted, only four or five of the most distinguished men among them being allowed on board. They remained about a couple of hours, and it seemed to us that they paid us this visit merely to find out whether they might not capture one or the other of our vessels.

On Palm Sunday (8 April) the King of Mombasa sent the captain-major a sheep and large quantities of oranges, lemons and sugar-cane, together with a ring, as a pledge of safety, letting him know that in case of his entering the port he would be supplied with all he stood in need of. This present was conveyed to us by two men, almost white, who said they were Christians, which appeared to be the fact. The captain-major sent the king a string of coral-beads as a return present, and let him know that he purposed entering the port on the following day. On the same day the captain-major's vessel was visited by four Moors of distinction.

Two men were sent by the captain-major to the king, still further to confirm these peaceful assurances. When these landed they were followed by a crowd as far as the gates of the palace. Before reaching the king they passed through four doors, each guarded by a door-keeper with a drawn cutlass. The king received them hospitably, and ordered that they should be shown over the city. They stopped on their way at the house of two Christian merchants, who showed them a paper, an object of their adoration, on which was a sketch of the Holy Ghost. When they had seen all, the king sent them back with samples of cloves, pepper and corn, with which articles he would allow us to load our ships.

On Tuesday (10 April), when weighing anchor to enter the port, the captain-major's vessel would not pay off, and struck the vessel which followed astern. We therefore again cast anchor. When the Moors who were in our ship saw that we did not go on, they scrambled into a *zavra* attached to our stern; whilst the two pilots whom we had brought from Mozambique jumped into the water, and were picked up by the men in the *zavra*. At night the captain-major questioned two Moors (from Mozambique) whom we had on board, by dropping boiling oil upon their skin, so that they might confess any treachery intended against us. They said that orders had been given to capture us as soon as we entered the port, and thus to avenge what we had done at Mozambique. And when the torture was being applied a second time, one of the Moors, although his hands were tied, threw himself into the sea, whilst the other did so during the morning watch.

About midnight two *almadias*, with many men in them, approached. The *almadias* stood off whilst the men entered the water, some swimming in the direction of the *Berrio*, others in that of the *Raphael*. Those who swam to the *Berrio* began to cut the cable. The men on watch thought at first that they were tunny fish, but when they perceived their mistake they shouted to the other vessels. The other swimmers had already got hold of the rigging of the mizzenmast. Seeing themselves discovered, they silently slipped down and fled. These and other wicked tricks were practised upon us by these dogs, but our Lord did not allow them to succeed, because they were unbelievers.

Mombasa is a large city seated upon an eminence washed by the sea. Its port is entered daily by numerous vessels. At its entrance stands a pillar, and by the sea a low-lying fortress. Those who had gone on shore told us that in the town they had seen many men in irons; and it seemed to us that these must be Christians, as the Christians in that country are at war with the Moors.

The Christian merchants in the town are only temporary residents, and are held in much subjection, they not being allowed to do anything except by the order of the Moorish king.

It pleased God in his mercy that on arriving at this city all our sick recovered their health, for the climate of this place is very good.

After the malice and treachery planned by these dogs had been discovered, we still remained on Wednesday and Thursday (11 and 12 April).

We left in the morning (13 April), the wind being light, and anchored about eight leagues from Mombasa, close to the shore. At the break of day (14 April) we saw two boats about three leagues to the leeward, in the open sea, and at once gave chase, with the intention of capturing them, for we wanted to secure a pilot who would guide us to where we wanted to go. At vespertime we came up with one of them, and captured it, the other escaping towards the land. In the one we took we found seventeen men, besides gold, silver, and an abundance of maize and other provisions; as also a young woman, who was the wife of an old Moor of distinction, who was a passenger. When we came up with the boat they all threw themselves into the water, but we picked them up from our boats.

That same day (14 April) at sunset, we cast anchor off a place called Milinde, which is thirty leagues from Mombasa. The following places are between Mombasa and Milinde, viz. Benapa, Toca, and Nuguoquioniete.

On Easter Sunday (15 April) the Moors whom we had taken in the boat told us that there were at this city of Melinde four vessels belonging to Christians from India, and that if it pleased us to take them there, they would provide us, instead of them, Christian pilots and all we stood in need of, including water, wood and other things. The captain-major much desired to have pilots from the country, and having discussed the matter with his Moorish prisoners, he cast anchor off the town, at a distance of about half a league from the mainland. The inhabitants of the town did not venture to come aboard our ships, for they had already learnt that we had captured a vessel and made her occupants prisoners.

On Monday morning (16 April) the captain major had the old Moor taken to a sandbank in front of the town, where he was picked up by an *almadia*. The Moor explained to the king the wishes of the captain-major, and how much he desired to make peace with him. After dinner the Moor came back in a *zavra*, accompanied by one of the king's cavaliers and a Sharif: he also brought three sheep. These messengers told the captain-general that the king would rejoice to make peace with him, and to enter into friendly relations; that he would willingly grant to the captain-major all his country afforded, whether pilots or anything else. The captain-major upon this sent word that he proposed to enter the port on the following day, and forwarded by the king's messengers a present consisting of a *balandrau* [a tunic worn by the Brothers of Mercy in Portugal], two strings of coral, three wash-hand basins, a hat, little bells and two pieces of lambel [striped cotton stuff].

Consequently, on Tuesday (17 April) we approached nearer to the town. The king sent the captain-major six sheep, besides quantities of cloves, cumin, ginger, nutmeg, and pepper, as also a message, telling him that if he desired to have an interview with him he (the king) would come out in his *zavra*, when the captain-major could meet him in a boat.

On Wednesday (18 April), after dinner, when the king came up close to the ships in a *zavra*, the captain-major at once entered one of his boats, which had been well furnished, and many friendly words were exchanged when they lay side by side. The king having invited the captain-major to come to his house to rest, after which he (the king) would visit him on board his ship, the captain-major said that he was not permitted by his master to go on land, and if he were to do so a bad report would be given of him. The king wanted to know what would be said of himself by his people if he were to visit the ships, and what account could he render them? He then asked for the name of our king, which was written down for him, and said that on our return he would send an ambassador with us, or a letter.

When both had said all they desired, the captain-major sent for the Moors whom he had taken prisoner, and surrendered them all. This gave much satisfaction to the king, who said he valued this act more highly than if he had been presented with a town. And the king, much pleased, made the circuit of our ships, the bombards of which fired a salute. About three hours were spent in this way. When the king went away he left in the ship one of his sons and a Sharif, and took two of us away with him, to whom he desired to show his palace. He, moreover, told the captain that as he would not go ashore he would himself return on the following day to the beach, and would order his horsemen to go through some exercises.

The king wore a robe (royal cloak) of damask trimmed with green satin, and a rich *touca* (turban). He was seated on two cushioned chairs of bronze, beneath a round sunshade of crimson satin attached to a pole. An old man, who attended him as a page, carried a short sword in a silver sheath. There were many players on *anafils*, and two trumpets of ivory, richly carved, and of the size of a man, which were blown from a hole in the side, and made sweet harmony with the *anafils*.

On Thursday (19 April) the captain-major and Nicolau Coelho rowed along the front of the town, bombards having been placed in the poops of their long-boats. Many people were along the shore, and among them two horsemen, who appeared to take much delight in a sham fight. The king was carried in a palanquin from the stone steps of his palace to the side of the captain-major's boats. He again begged the captain to come ashore, as he had a helpless father who wanted to see him, and that he and his sons would go on board the ships as hostages. The captain, however, excused himself.

We found here four vessels belonging to Indian Christians. When they came for the first time on board Paulo da Gama's ship, the captain-major being there at the time, they were shown an altar-piece representing Our Lady at the foot of the cross, with Jesus Christ in her arms and the apostles round her. When the Indians saw this picture they prostrated themselves, and as long as we were there they came to say their prayers in front of it, bringing offerings of cloves, pepper, and other things.

These Indians are tawny men; they wear but little clothing and have long beards and long hair, which they braid. They told us that they ate no beef Their language differs from that of the Arabs, but some of them know a little of it, as they hold much intercourse with them.

On the day on which the captain-major went up to the town in the boats, these Christian Indians fired off many bombards from their vessels, and when they saw him pass they raised their hands and shouted lustily, *Christ! Christ!*

That same night they asked the king's permission to give us a night-fête. And when night came they fired off many bombards, sent up rockets, and raised loud shouts.

These Indians warned the captain-major against going on shore, and told him not to trust to their 'fanfares,' as they neither came from their hearts nor from their goodwill.

On the following Sunday, 22 April, the king's *zavra* brought on board one of his confidential servants, and as two days had passed without any visitors, the captain-major had this man seized, and sent word to the king that he required the pilots whom he had promised. The king, when he received this message, sent a Christian pilot, and the captain-major allowed the gentlemen, whom he had retained in his vessel, to go away.

We were much pleased with the Christian pilot whom the king had sent us. We learnt from him that the island of which we heard at Moçambique as being inhabited by Christians was in reality an island subject to this same King of Moçambique; that half of it belonged to the Moors and the other half to the Christians; that many pearls were to be found there, and that it was called Quylee [Kilwa]. This is the island the Moorish pilots wanted to take us to, and we also wished to go there, for we believed that what they said was true.

The town of Malindi lies in a bay and extends along the shore. It may be likened to Alcouchette. Its houses are lofty and well whitewashed, and have many windows; on the land side are palm-groves, and all around it maize and vegetables are being cultivated.

We remained in front of this town during nine days, and all this time we had fêtes, sham fights, and musical performances ('fanfares').

Study Questions

1. Why did da Gama and his crew stop in so many African ports?

2. Why does the king of Mombasa send da Gama sheep, fruit, and a ring?

3. Why does the author compare Malindi to Alcouchette?

4. Why is it important to the author to identify people as Christians when he encounters them in Africa?

Letter from the First Voyage (1493)   70

CHRISTOPHER COLUMBUS

The Italian Christopher Columbus (1451–1506) dreamed of making his fortune in the spice trade. As a young mariner he had worked with a mapmaker and became obsessed with the idea of reaching the Spice Islands via a western route. This was as much a practical as a theoretical idea—Muslim conquests had disrupted the traditional Mediterranean trade, and the Portuguese had to make the long journey around Africa in stages. Columbus lobbied for his plan in both Portugal and Spain before convincing Queen Isabella of Castile to provide limited financial backing in return for a hefty share of any profits from the voyage. In 1492, Columbus sailed west in command of three ships from the Canary Islands and landed in the Caribbean, which he believed was a string of islands off of the China mainland.

This letter is one of Columbus's early communications, though it was written nearly six months after his discovery. It was obviously composed for public consumption and was one of the most widely printed documents from the voyages of discovery.

A Letter addressed to the noble Lord Raphael Sanchez, Treasurer to their most invincible Majesties, Ferdinand and Isabella, King and Queen of Spain, by Christopher Columbus, to whom our age is greatly indebted, treating of the islands of India recently discovered beyond the Ganges, to explore which he had been sent eight months before under the auspices and at the expense of their said Majesties.

Knowing that it will afford you pleasure to learn that I have brought my undertaking to a successful termination, I have decided upon writing you this letter to acquaint you with all the events which have occurred in my voyage, and the discoveries which have resulted from it. Thirty-three days after my departure from Cadiz I reached the Indian sea, where I discovered many islands, thickly peopled, of which I took possession without resistance in the name of our most illustrious Monarch, by public proclamation and with unfurled banners. To the first of these islands, which is called by the Indians Guanahani, I gave the name of the blessed Saviour (San Salvador), relying upon whose protection I had reached this as well as the other islands; to each of these I also gave a name. In the meantime I had learned from some Indians whom I had seized, that that country was certainly an island: and therefore I sailed towards the east, coasting to the distance of three hundred and twenty-two miles, which brought us to the extremity of it; from this point I saw lying eastwards another island, fifty-four miles distant from Juana, to which I gave the name of Española: I went thither, and steered my course eastward as I had done at Juana, even to the distance of five hundred and sixty-four miles along the north coast. This said island of Juana is exceedingly fertile, as indeed are all the others; it is surrounded with many bays, spacious, very secure, and surpassing any that I have ever seen; numerous large and healthful rivers intersect it, and it also contains many very lofty mountains. All these islands are very beautiful, and distinguished by a diversity of scenery; they are filled with a great variety of trees of immense height, and which I believe to retain their foliage in all seasons; for when I saw them they were as verdant and luxuriant as they usually are in Spain in the month of May— some of them were blossoming, some bearing fruit, and all flourishing in the greatest perfection, according to their respective stages of growth, and the nature and quality of each: yet the islands are not so thickly wooded as to be impassable. The nightingale and various birds were singing in countless numbers, and that in November, the month in which I arrived there, There are besides in the same island of Juana seven or eight kinds of palm trees, which, like all the other trees, herbs, and fruits, considerably surpass ours in height and beauty. The pines also are very handsome, and there are very extensive fields and meadows, a variety of birds, different kinds of honey, and many sorts of metals, but no iron. In that island also which I have before said we named Española, there are mountains of very great size and beauty, vast plains, groves, and very fruitful fields, admirably adapted for tillage, pasture, and habitation. The inhabitants of both sexes in this island, and in all the others which I have seen, or of which I have received information, go always naked as they were born, with the exception of some of the women, who use the covering of a leaf, or small bough, or an apron of cotton which they prepare for that purpose. None of them are possessed of any iron, neither have they weapons, being unacquainted with, and indeed incompetent to use them, not from any deformity of body (for they are well-formed), but because they are timid and full of fear.

They carry however in lieu of arms, canes dried in the sun, on the ends of which they fix heads of dried wood sharpened to a point, and even these they dare not use habitually; for it has often occurred when I have sent two or three of my men to any of the villages to speak with the natives, that they have come out in a disorderly troop, and have fled in such haste at the approach of our men, that the fathers forsook their children and the children their fathers. This timidity did not arise from any loss or injury that they had received from us; for, on the contrary, I gave to all I approached whatever articles I had about me, such as cloth and many other things, taking nothing of theirs in return: but they are naturally timid and fearful. As soon however as they see that they are safe, and have laid aside all fear, they are very simple and honest, and exceedingly liberal with all they have; none of them refusing any thing he may possess when he is asked for it, but on the contrary inviting us to ask them. They exhibit great love towards all others in preference to

themselves: they also give objects of great value for trifles, and content themselves with very little or nothing in return.

I however forbad that these trifles and articles of no value (such as pieces of dishes, plates, and glass, keys, and leather straps) should be given to them, although if they could obtain them, they imagined themselves to be possessed of the most beautiful trinkets in the world. It even happened that a sailor received for a leather strap as much gold as was worth three golden nobles, and for things of more trifling value offered by our men, especially-newly coined blancas, or any gold coins, the Indians would give whatever the seller required: as, for instance, an ounce and a half or two ounces of gold, or thirty or forty pounds of cotton, with which commodity they were already acquainted. Thus they bartered, like idiots, cotton and gold for fragments of bows, glasses, bottles, and jars; which I forbade as being unjust, and myself gave them many beautiful and acceptable articles which I had brought with me, taking nothing from them in return; I did this in order that I might the more easily conciliate them, that they might be led to become Christians, and be inclined to entertain a regard for the King and Queen, our Princes and all Spaniards, and that I might induce them to take an interest in seeking out, and collecting, and delivering to us such things as they possessed in abundance, but which we greatly needed.

They practise no kind of idolatry, but have a firm belief that all strength and power, and indeed all good things, are in heaven, and that I had descended from thence with these ships and sailors, and under this impression was I received after they had thrown aside their fears. Nor are they slow or stupid, but of very clear understanding; and those men who have crossed to the neighbouring islands give an admirable description of everything they observed; but they never saw any people clothed, nor any ships like ours.

In all these islands there is no difference of physiognomy, of manners, or of language, but they all clearly understand each other, a circumstance very propitious for the realization of what I conceive to be the principal wish of our most serene King, namely, the conversion of these people to the holy faith of Christ, to which indeed, as far as I can judge, they are very favourable and well-disposed. There was one large town in Española of which especially I took possession, situated in a remarkably favourable spot, and in every way convenient for the purposes of gain and commerce. To this town I gave the name of Navidad del Señor, and ordered a fortress to be built there, which must by this time be completed, in which I left as many men as I thought necessary, with all sorts of arms, and enough provisions for more than a year. I also left them one caravel, and skilful workmen both in ship-building and other arts, and engaged the favor and friendship of the King of the island in their behalf, to a degree that would not be believed, for these people are so amiable and friendly that even the King took a pride in calling me his brother. But supposing their feelings should become changed, and they should wish to injure those who have remained in the fortress, they could not do so, for they have no arms, they go naked, and are moreover too cowardly; so that those who hold the said fortress, can easily keep the whole island in check, without any pressing danger to themselves, provided they do not transgress the directions and regulations which I have given them.

As far as I have learned, every man throughout these islands is united to but one wife, with the exception of the kings and princes, who are allowed to have twenty: the women seem to work more than the men. I could not clearly understand whether the people possess any private property, for I observed that one man had the charge of distributing various things to the rest, but especially meat and provisions and the like. I did not find, as some of us had expected, any cannibals amongst them, but on the contrary men of great deference and kindness. Neither are they black, like the Ethiopians: their hair is smooth and straight: for they do not dwell where the rays of the sun strike most vividly, and the sun has intense power there, the distance from the equinoctial line being, it appears, but six-and-twenty degrees. On the tops of the mountains the cold is very great, but the effect of this upon the Indians is lessened by their being accustomed to the climate, and by their frequently indulging in the use of very hot meats and drinks.

Finally, to compress into few words the entire summary of my voyage and speedy return, and of the advantages derivable therefrom, I promise, that with a little assistance afforded me by our most invincible sovereigns, I will procure them as much gold as they need, as great a quantity of spices, of cotton, and of mastic (which is only found in Chios), and as many men for the service of the navy as their Majesties may require. I promise also rhubarb and other sorts of drugs, which I am persuaded the men whom I have left in the aforesaid fortress have found already and will continue to find; for I myself have tarried no where longer than I was compelled to do by the winds, except in the city of Navidad, while I provided for the building of the fortress, and took the necessary precautions for the perfect security of the men I left there. Although all I have related may appear to be wonderful and unheard of, yet the results of my voyage would have been more astonishing if I had had at my disposal such ships as I required.

But these great and marvellous results are not to be attributed to any merit of mine, but to the holy Christian faith, and to the piety and religion of our Sovereigns; for that which the unaided intellect of man could not compass, the spirit of God has granted to human exertions, for God is wont to hear the prayers of his servants who love his precepts even to the performance of apparent impossibilities. Thus it has happened to me in the present instance, who have accomplished a task to which the powers of mortal men had never hitherto attained; for if there have been those who have anywhere written or spoken of these islands, they have done so with doubts and conjectures, and no one has ever asserted that he has seen them, on which account their writings have been looked upon as little else than fables. Therefore let the king and queen, our princes and their most happy kingdoms, and all the other provinces of Christendom, render thanks to our Lord and Savior Jesus Christ, who has granted us so great a victory and such prosperity. Let processions be made, and sacred feasts be held, and the temples be adorned with festive boughs. Let Christ rejoice on earth, as he rejoices in heaven in the prospect of the salvation of the souls of so many nations hitherto lost. Let us also rejoice, as well on account of the exaltation of our faith, as on account of the increase of our temporal prosperity, of which not only Spain, but all Christendom will be partakers.

Such are the events which I have briefly described. Farewell.

Lisbon, the 14th of March.
CHRISTOPHER COLUMBUS,
Admiral of the Fleet of the Ocean.

Study Questions

1. What was Columbus's purpose when he wrote this letter?

2. Columbus found the islands he explored to be "thickly peopled." What seems to be his attitude toward the inhabitants of the islands?

3. The Europeans engaged in trade with the Indians and prided themselves upon getting a good deal. How did the trade work? Do you think the Indians felt the same way?

4. What appear to be the overall goals of the Spanish explorers?

5. Can you make some generalizations about fifteenth-century European views of alien cultures?

Apologetic History of the Indies (1566)   71

BARTOLOMÉ DE LAS CASAS

Bartolomé de las Casas (1474–1566) was a Dominican friar, a bishop in the New World, and the Spanish government's unofficial "Protector of the Indians." Born in the bustling port of Seville, Las Casas witnessed Columbus's triumphant return from his first voyage. The exotic goods and the exotic tales with which the mariners returned fired the young friar's imagination. In 1498 Las Casas was presented with an Indian for use as a personal servant, and he was entranced by the simplicity and gentle nature of the Native Americans; he thereupon decided to devote his life to their salvation.

Arriving in the New World in 1502, Las Casas set about his mission, preaching among the Indians and baptizing those that he converted. He was appalled by the harsh treatment some Spaniards meted out to these innocent people. He returned to Spain in 1515 and launched a vigorous campaign to ensure the Indians' protection. The *Apologetic History* (1566) was a reflection of Las Casas's belief in the inherent goodness of the Native Americans, and of his conviction that all of humanity were God's children.

Apologetic and Summary History Treating the Qualities, Disposition, Description, Skies and Soil of These Lands; and the Natural Conditions, Governance, Nations, Ways of Life and Customs of the Peoples of These Western and Southern Indies, Whose Sovereign Realm Belongs to the Monarchs of Castile.

Argument of the Work

The ultimate cause for writing this work was to gain knowledge of all the many nations of this vast new world. They had been defamed by persons who feared neither God nor the charge, so grievous before divine judgment, of defaming even a single man and causing him to lose his esteem and honor. From such slander can come great harm and terrible calamity, particularly when large numbers of men are concerned and, even more so, a whole new world. It has been written that these peoples of the Indies, lacking human governance and order nations, did not have the power of reason to govern themselves—which was inferred only from their having been found to be gentle, patient and humble. It has been implied that God became careless in creating so immense a number of rational souls and let human nature, which He so largely determined and provided for, go astray in the almost infinitesimal part of the human lineage which they comprise. From this it follows that they have all proven themselves unsocial and therefore monstrous, contrary to the natural bent of all peoples of the world; and that He did not allow any other species of corruptible creature to err in this way, excepting a strange and occasional case. In order to demonstrate the truth, which is the opposite, this book brings together and compiles certain natural, special and accidental causes which are specified below.... Not only have [the Indians] shown themselves to be very wise peoples and possessed of lively and marked understanding, prudently governing and providing for their nations (as much as they can be nations, without faith in or knowledge of the true God) and making them prosper injustice; but they have equalled many diverse nations of the world, past and present, that have been praised for their governance, politics and customs, and exceed by no small measure the wisest of all these, such as the Greeks and Romans, in adherence to the rules of natural reason. This advantage and superiority, along with everything said above, will appear quite clearly when, if it please God, the peoples are compared one with another. This history has been written with the aforesaid aim in mind by Fray Bartolomé de Las Casas, or Casaus, a monk of the Dominican Order and sometime bishop of Chiapa, who promises before the divine word that everything said and referred to is the truth, and that nothing of an untruthful nature appears to the best of his knowledge.

Chapter CXXVII. The Indians Possessed More Enlightenment and Natural Knowledge of God Than the Greeks and Romans

... These Indian peoples surpassed the Greeks and Romans in selecting for their gods, not sinful and criminal men noted for their great baseness, but virtuous ones—to the extent that virtue exists among people who lack the knowledge of the true God that is gained by faith.... The following argument can be formed for the proof of the above: The Indian nations seem to show themselves to be or to have been of better rational judgment and more prudent and upright in what they considered God to be. For nations which have reached the knowledge that there is a God hold in common the natural concept that God is the best of all things that can be imagined. Therefore the nation which has elected virtuous men as God or gods, though it might have erred in not selecting the true God, has a better concept and estimation of God and more natural purity than one which has selected and accepted for God or gods men known to be sinful and criminal. The latter was the case of the Greek and Roman states, which the former is that of all these Indian nations.... It seems probable that none of these Indian peoples will be more difficult of conversion than the ancient idolaters. First, because, as we have proved and are still proving, all these peoples are of good reason. Second, because they show less duplicity and more simplicity of heart than others. Third, because they are in their natural persons better adjusted, as has been proved above—a quality characteristic of men who may more easily be persuaded of the truth. Fourth, because an infinite number in their midst have already been converted (although some with certain difficulty, namely, those who worshiped many gods; for it is not possible except by a great miracle for a religion so aged, mellowed and time-honored to be abandoned suddenly, in a short time or with ease—as proven by all of the world's past and ancient idolaters)....

Chapter CCLXII. From All That Has Been Said It Is Inferred That the Indian Nations Equalled and Even Surpassed All the Ancient Ones in Good Laws and Customs

... Let us compare [the ancients] with the people of the realms of Peru as concerns women, marriage and chastity. The [Peruvian] kings honored and favored marriages with their presence and performed them themselves or through their proconsuls and delegates. They themselves exhorted the newlyweds to live happily, and in this these people were superior to all nations. They were certainly superior to the Assyrians and Babylonians, ... even to our own Spaniards of Cantabria, ... more especially to the renowned isle of England ... and to many others.... To whom were they not superior in the election and succession of kings and those who were to govern the country? They always chose the wisest, most virtuous and most worthy of ruling, those who had subordinated all natural and sensual affection and were free and clean of repugnant ambition and all private interests

They were likewise more than moderate in exacting tribute of vassals and, so that the people should not be molested, in levying the costs of war. Their industries existed so that nations might communicate among each other and all live in peace. They had a frequent and meticulous census of all deaths and births and of the exact number of people in all estates of the realms. All persons had professions, and each one busied himself and worked to gain his necessary livelihood. They possessed abundant deposits of provisions which met all the necessities of their warriors, reduced the burden and trouble for the subjects and were distributed in the lean years.... Who of the peoples and kings of the world ever kept the men of their armies under such discipline that they would not dare to touch even a single fruit hanging over the road from a tree behind a wall? Not the Greeks, nor Alexander, nor the Romans, nor even our own Christian monarchs. Has anyone read of soldiers who, no matter where they were marching when not in battle, were as well commanded, trained, sober and orderly as good friars in a procession? They established order and laws for the obedience which vassals must show toward their immediate lords and for reverence between each other, the humble to the humble and the mighty to the mighty. The rearing of children, in which parents inculcate the obedience and faithfulness owed to superiors—where is it surpassed? ... Has anyone read of any prince in the world among the ancient unbelievers of the past or subsequently among Christians, excepting St. Louis of France, who so attentively assisted and provided for the poor among his vassals—those not only of his own village or city but of all his large and extensive realms? They issued public edicts and personal commands to all nobles and provincial governors, of whom there were many, that all poor, widows and orphans in each province should be provided for from their own royal rents and riches, and that alms should be given according to the need, poverty and desert of each person. Where and among what people or nation was there a prince endowed with such piety and beneficence that he never dined unless three or four poor people ate from his plate and at his table? ... Then, there is that miracle—such it may be called for being the most remarkable, singular and skilful construction of its kind, I believe, in the world—of the two highways ... across the mountains and along the coast. The finer and more admirable of these extends for at least six and perhaps eight hundred leagues and is said to reach the provinces of Chile.... In Spain and Italy I have seen portions of the highway said to have been built by the Romans from Spain to Italy, but it is quite crude in comparison with the one built by these peoples....

Chapter CCLXIII. The Indians Are as Capable as Any Other Nations to Receive the Gospel

Thus it remains stated, demonstrated and openly concluded ... throughout this book that all these peoples of the Indies possessed—as far as it possible through natural and human means and without the light of faith—nations, towns, villages and cities, most fully and abundantly provided for. With a few exceptions in varying degrees they lacked nothing, and some were endowed in full perfection for political and social life and for attaining and enjoying that civic happiness which in this world any good, rational, well provided and happy republic wishes to have and enjoy; for all are by nature of very subtle, lively, clear and most capable understanding. This they received (after the will of God, Who wished to create them in this way) from the favorable influence of the heavens, the gentle attributes of the regions which God gave them to inhabit, the clement and soft weather; from the composition of their limbs and internal and external sensory organs; from the quality and sobriety of their diet; from the fine disposition and healthfulness of the lands, towns and local winds; from their temperance and moderation in food and drink; from the tranquility, calmness and quiescence of their sensual desires; from their lack of concern and worry over the worldly matters that stir the passions of the soul, these being joy, love, wrath, grief and the rest; and also, *a posteriori*, from the works they accomplished and the effects of these. From all these causes, universal and superior, particular and inferior, natural and accidental, it followed, first by nature and then by their industry and experience, that they were endowed with the three types of prudence: the monastic, by which man knows how to rule himself; the economic, which teaches him to rule his house; and the political, which sets forth and ordains the rule of his cities. As for the divisions of this last type (which presupposes the first two types of prudence to be perfect) into workers, artisans, warriors, rich men, religion (temples, priests and sacrifices), judges and magistrates, governors, customs and into everything which concerns acts of understanding and will, ... they were equal to many nations of the world outstanding and famous for being politic and reasonable.... We have, then, but slight occasion to be surprised at defects and uncouth and immoderate customs which we might find among our Indian peoples and to disparage them for these; for many and perhaps all other peoples of the world have been much more perverse, irrational and corrupted by depravity, and in their governments and in many virtues and moral qualities much less temperate and orderly. Our own forbears were much worse, as revealed in irrationality and confused government and in vices and brutish customs throughout the length and breadth of this our Spain, which has been shown in many places above. Let us, then, finish this book and give immense thanks to God for having given us enough life, strength and help to see it finished.

Study Questions

1. Las Casas wrote at nearly the same time as Columbus. Do their views of Native Americans differ? How? In what ways do they operate from the same assumptions?

2. How did some Europeans justify the mistreatment of Native Americans? How does Las Casas refute those arguments?

3. In his letter, Columbus depicted a simple, almost primitive society. Does Las Casas find this to be the case?

4. Why, according to Las Casas, were the Native Americans a more admirable people than the ancient Greeks and Romans?

The Golden Age of Islam

Two Lovers. Safavid painting continued Persian tradition, but shifted from landscapes to portraits, mostly of young ladies, boys, lovers, or dervishes. This delicate painting of a couple embracing was produced in the early seventeenth century by Riza-i-Abassi, the most famous artist of Isfahan. It conveys passion with refined elegance.

The Ruba'iyat (11th C.E.)   72

OMAR KHAYYÁM

Omar Khayyám (ca. 1048–1131) was a mathematician, astronomer, and philosopher whose fame rests on his poetry. He was born in Nishapour, Iran, one of the greatest cities of the Middle East before its destruction during the thirteenth century. Nishapour was famed for its schools, and Omar Khayyám studied mathematics and philosophy there. He wrote a treatise on algebra that gained him recognition and patronage. He was appointed to head a commission to make astronomical observations and to reform the Eastern calendar. His efforts resulted in the Jalali Calendar, which many regard as more accurate than those used in the West.

The *Ruba'iyat* consists of 1200 individual quatrains, that is, sets of four lines in which the first, second, and fourth rhyme. They are not connected to each other and seem to have been composed over many years. They reveal Omar Khayyám's philosophical and scientific interests as well as his personality. The *Ruba'iyat* went unpublished for 700 years until a chance discovery of a manuscript by an English professor. By the end of the nineteenth century the *Ruba'iyat* had become some of the best loved poetry in the world.

I

Awake! for Morning in the Bowl of Night
Has flung the Stone that puts the Stars to
    Flight:
    And Lo! the Hunter of the East has caught
The Sultán's Turret in a Noose of Light.

VI

And David's Lips are lock't; but in divine
High piping Pehleví, with "Wine! Wine! Wine!
    Red Wine!"—the Nightingale cries to the
    Rose
That yellow Cheek of hers to incarnadine.

VII

Come, fill the Cup, and in the Fire of Spring
The Winter Garment of Repentance fling:
    The Bird of Time has but a little way
To fly—and Lo! the Bird is on the Wing.

IX

But come with old Khayyám, and leave the Lot
Of Kaikobád and Kaikhosrú forgot:
    Let Rustum lay about him as he will,
Or Hátim Tai cry Supper—heed them not.

XVI

Think, in this batter'd Caravanserai
Whose Doorways are alternate Night and Day,
    How Sultán after Sultán with his Pomp
Abode his Hour or two, and went his way.

XVII

They say the Lion and the Lizard keep
The Courts where Jamsh yd gloried and drank
    deep;
    And Bahrám, that great Hunter—the Wild
    Ass
Stamps o'er his Head, and he lies fast asleep.

XVIII

I sometimes think that never blows so red
The Rose as where some buried Caesar bled;
   That every Hyacinth the Garden wears
Dropt in its Lap from some once lovely Head.

XXI

Lo! some we loved, the loveliest and the best
That Time and Fate of all their Vintage prest,
   Have drunk their Cup a Round or two
      before,
And one by one crept silently to Rest.

XXXII

There was a Door to which I found no Key:
There was a Veil past which I could not see:
   Some little Talk awhile of Me and Thee
There seem'd—and then no more of Thee and
   Me.

XLI

For "Is" and "Is-not" though *with* Rule and
   Line
And "Up-and-down" *without*, I could define,
   I yet in all I only cared to know,
Was never deep in anything but—Wine.

XLIX

'Tis all a Chequer-board of Nights and Days
Where Destiny with Men for Pieces plays:
   Hither and thither moves, and mates, and
      slays,
And one by one back in the Closet lays.

LXVIII

That ev'n my buried Ashes such a Snare
Of Perfume shall fling up into the Air,
   As not a True Believer passing by
But shall be overtaken unaware.

LXXII

Alas, that Spring should vanish with the Rose!
That Youth's sweet-scented Manuscript should
      close!
   The Nightingale that in the Branches sang,
Ah, whence, and whither flown again, who
      knows!

LXXVII

For let Philosopher and Doctor preach
Of what they will, and what they will not—each
   Is but one Link in an eternal Chain
That none can slip, nor break, nor overreach.

LXXXV

What! from his helpless Creature be repaid
Pure Gold for what he lent us dross-allay'd
   Such for a Debt we never did contract,
And cannot answer—Oh, the sorry trade!

XCVI

"Well," said another, "Whoso will, let try,
My Clay with long oblivion is gone dry:
   But fill me with the old familiar Juice,
Methinks I might recover by-and-by!"

Study Questions

1. What is Khayyám's attitude toward wine? love? life? death?

2. Does Khayyám's expertise in math and science influence his poems?

3. What do Khayyám's quatrains tell us about the state of religion in eleventh- and twelfth-century Persia?

4. Why is the *Ruba'iyat* so popular in the West? Why do you think that it has been frequently banned in Muslim countries?

The History of Mehmed the Conqueror (1453)   73

KRITOVOULOS

Mehmed II (1432–1481) was one of the great military geniuses of world history. He consolidated the expansion of the Ottoman Empire in Asia Minor, and in 1453 organized the siege of Constantinople. He personally directed the combined land and naval assault and brilliantly improvised the tactics that led to the fall of the city. The fall of Constantinople to the Ottomans was a watershed. No longer could the West assume military superiority over the East. Ottoman dominance of Asia Minor and its threat to the lands of the Holy Roman Empire continued for nearly two centuries.

Kritovoulos was a Greek who entered the service of Mehmed II, probably after the siege. Nothing is known of his personal life. Although he was not an eyewitness of the fall of Constantinople, he gathered numerous accounts together in composing his history. He was a servant and admirer of the Ottoman Sultan; however, he was also a Greek who mourned the collapse of the center of the Greek Orthodox Church and the inheritor of the Eastern Empire.

To the Supreme Emperor, King of Kings, Mehmed, the fortunate, the victor, the winner of trophies, the triumphant, the invincible, Lord of land and sea, by the will of God, Kritovoulos the Islander, servant of thy servants.

Seeing that you are the author of many great deeds, O most mighty Emperor, and in the belief that the many great achievements of generals and kings of old, nor merely of Persians and Greeks, are not worthy to be compared in glory and bravery and martial valor with yours, I do not think it just that they and their deeds and accomplishments, as set forth in the Greek historians and their writings from contemporary times and up to the present, should be celebrated and admired by all, and that these should enjoy everlasting remembrance, while you, so great and powerful a man, possessing almost all the lands under the sun, and glorious in your great and brilliant exploits, should have no witness, for the future, of your valor and the greatest and best of your deeds, like one of the unknown and inglorious ones who are till now unworthy of any memorial or record in Greek; or that the deeds of others, petty as they are in comparison to yours, should be better known and more famed before men because done by Greeks and in Greek history, while your accomplishments, vast as they are, and in no way inferior to those of Alexander the Macedonian, or of the generals and kings of his rank, should not be set forth in Greek to the Greeks, nor passed on to posterity for the undying praise and glory of your deeds.

Sultan Mehmed considered it necessary in preparation for his next move to get possession of

Mehmet II, Conqueror of Constantinople. Identified with the seizure of Constantinople from the Byzantine Empire in 1453, Mehmet II was one of the most illustrious Ottoman sultans. This Turkish miniature portrays Mehmet II with his handkerchief, a symbol of the supreme power of the Ottoman ruler. He is also smelling a rose, representing his cultural interests, especially as patron of the arts.

the harbor and open the Horn for his own ships to sail in. So, since every effort and device of his had failed to force the entrance, he made a wise decision, and one worthy of his intellect and power. It succeeded in accomplishing his purpose and in putting an end to all uncertainties.

He ordered the commanders of the vessels to construct as quickly as possible glideways leading from the outer sea to the inner sea, that is, from the harbor to the Horn, near the place called Diplokion, and to cover them with beams. This road, measured from sea to sea, is just about eight stadia. It is very steep for more than half the way, until you reach the summit of the hill, and from there again it descends to the inner sea of the Horn. And as the glideways were completed sooner than expected, because of the large number of workers, he brought up the ships and placed large cradles under them, with stays against each of their sides to hold them up. And having under-girded them well with ropes, he fastened long cables to the corners and gave them to the soldiers to drag, some of them by hand, and others by certain machines and capstans.

So the ships were dragged along very swiftly. And their crews, as they followed them, rejoiced at the event and boasted of it. Then they manned the ships on the land as if they were on the sea. Some of them hoisted the sails with a shout, as if they were setting sail, and the breeze caught the sails and bellied them out. Others seated themselves on the benches, holding the oars in their hands and moving them as if rowing. And the commanders, running along by the sockets of the masts with whistlings and shouting, and with their whips beating the oarsmen on the benches, ordered them to row. The ships, borne along over the land as if on the sea, were some of them being pulled up the ascent to the top of the hill while others were being hauled down the slope into the harbor, lowering the sails with shouting and great noise.

It was a strange spectacle, and unbelievable in the telling except to those who actually did see it—the sight of ships borne along on the mainland as if sailing on the sea, with their crews and their sails and all their equipment. I believe this was a much greater feat than the cutting of a canal across at Athos by Xerxes, and much stranger to see and to hear about....

Thus, then, there assembled in the bay called Cold Waters, a little beyond Galata, a respectable fleet of some sixty-seven vessels. They were moored there.

The Romans, when they saw such an unheard-of thing actually happen, and warships lying at anchor in the Horn—which they never would have suspected—were astounded at the impossibility of the spectacle, and were overcome by the greatest consternation and perplexity. They did not know what to do now, but were in despair. In fact they had left unguarded the walls along the Horn for a distance of about thirty stadia, and even so they did not have enough men for the rest of the walls, either for defense or for attack, whether citizens or men from elsewhere. Instead, two or even three battlements had but a single defender.

And now, when this sea-wall also became open to attack and had to be guarded, they were compelled to strip the other battlements and bring men there. This constituted a manifest danger, since the defenders were taken away from the rest of the wall while those remaining were not enough to guard it, being so few.

Then, with fine insight, the Sultan summoned the shield-bearers, heavy infantry and other troops and said: "Go to it, friends and children mine! It is time now to show yourselves good fighters!" They immediately crossed the moat, with shouts and fearful yells, and attacked the outer wall. All of it, however, had been demolished by the cannon. There were only

stockades of great beams instead of a wall, and bundles of vine-branches, and jars full of earth. At that point a fierce battle ensued close in and with the weapons of hand-to-hand fighting. The heavy infantry and shield-bearers fought to overcome the defenders and get over the stockade, while the Romans and Italians tried to fight these off and to guard the stockade. At times the infantry did get over the wall and the stockade, pressing forward bravely and unhesitatingly. And at times they were stoutly forced back and driven off.

The Sultan followed them up, as they struggled bravely, and encouraged them. He ordered those in charge of the cannon to put the match to the cannon. And these, being set off, fired their stone balls against the defenders and worked no little destruction on both sides, among those in the near vicinity.

So, then, the two sides struggled and fought bravely and vigorously. Most of the night passed, and the Romans were successful and prevailed not a little. Also, Giustinianni and his men kept their positions stubbornly, and guarded the stockade and defended themselves bravely against the aggressors....

Sultan Mehmed saw that the attacking divisions were very much worn out by the battle and had not made any progress worth mentioning, and that the Romans and Italians were not only fighting stoutly but were prevailing in the battle. He was very indignant at this, considering that it ought not to be endured any longer. Immediately he brought up the divisions which he had been reserving for later on, men who were extremely well armed, daring and brave, and far in advance of the rest in experience and valor. They were the elite of the army: heavy infantry, bowmen, and lancers, and his own bodyguard, and along with them those of the division called Janissaries.

Calling to them and urging them to prove themselves now as heroes, he led the attack against the wall, himself at the head until they reached the moat. There he ordered the bowmen, stingers, and musketeers to stand at a distance and fire to the right, against the defenders on the palisade and on the battered wall. They were to keep up so heavy a fire that those defenders would be unable to fight, or to expose themselves because of the cloud of arrows and other projectiles falling like snowflakes.

To all the rest, the heavy infantry and the shieldbearers, the Sultan gave orders to cross the moat swiftly and attack the palisade. With a loud and terrifying war-cry and with fierce impetuosity and wrath, they advanced as if mad. Being young and strong and full of daring, and especially because they were fighting in the Sultan's presence, their valor exceeded every expectation. They attacked the palisade and fought bravely without any hesitation.

Needing no further orders, they knocked down the turrets which had been built out in front, broke the yardarms, scattered the materials that had been gathered, and forced the defenders back inside the palisade.

… The Romans in that section fought bravely with lances, axes, pikes, javelins, and other weapons of offense. It was a hand-to-hand encounter, and they stopped the attackers and prevented them from getting inside the palisade. There was much shouting on both sides—the mingled sounds of blasphemy, insults, threats, attackers, defenders, shooters, those shot at, killers and dying, of those who in anger and wrath did all sorts of terrible things. And it was a sight to see there: a hard fight going on hand-to-hand with great determination and for the greatest rewards, heroes fighting valiantly, the one party struggling with all their might to force back the defenders, get possession of the wall, enter the City, and fall upon the children and women and the treasures, the other party bravely agonizing to drive them off and guard their possessions, even if

they were not to succeed in prevailing and in keeping them.

Instead, the hapless Romans were destined finally to be brought under the yoke of servitude and to suffer its horrors. For although they battled bravely.... They abandoned the palisade and wall where they had been fighting, and thought of only one thing—how they could get away safe themselves.

But the Emperor Constantine besought them earnestly, and made promises to them if they would wait a little while, till the fighting should subside. They would not consent, however, but taking up their leader and all their armor, they boarded the galleons in haste and with all speed, giving no consideration to the other defenders.

The Emperor Constantine forbade the others to follow. Then, though he had no idea what to do next—for he had no other reserves to fill the places thus left vacant, the ranks of those who had so suddenly deserted, and meantime the battle raged fiercely and all had to see to their own ranks and places and fight there—still, with his remaining Romans and his bodyguard, which was so few as to be easily counted, he took his stand in front of the palisade and fought bravely.

Sultan Mehmed, who happened to be fighting quite nearby, saw that the palisade and the other part of the wall that had been destroyed were now empty of men and deserted by the defenders. He noted that men were slipping away secretly and that those who remained were fighting feebly because they were so few. Realizing from this that the defenders had fled and that the wall was deserted, he shouted out: "Friends, we have the City! We have it! They are already fleeing from us! They can't stand it any longer! The wall is bare of defenders! It needs just a little more effort and the City is taken! Don't weaken, but on with the work with all your might, and be men and I am with you!"

So saying, he led them himself. And they, with a shout on the run and with a fearsome yell, went on ahead of the Sultan, pressing on up to the palisade. After a long and bitter struggle they hurled back the Romans from there and climbed by force up the palisade. They dashed some of their foe down into the ditch between the great wall and the palisade, which was deep and hard to get out of, and they killed them there. The rest they drove back to the gate.

He had opened this gate in the great wall, so as to go easily over to the palisade. Now there was a great struggle there and great slaughter among those stationed there, for they were attacked by the heavy infantry and not a few others in irregular formation, who had been attracted from many points by the shouting. There the Emperor Constantine, with all who were with him, fell in gallant combat.

The heavy infantry were already streaming through the little gate into the City, and others had rushed in through the breach in the great wall. Then all the rest of the army, with a rush and a roar, poured in brilliantly and scattered all over the City. And the Sultan stood before the great wall, where the standard also was and the ensigns, and watched the proceedings. The day was already breaking.

Then a great slaughter occurred of those who happened to be there: some of them were on the streets, for they had already left the houses and were running toward the tumult when they fell unexpectedly on the swords of the soldiers; others were in their own homes and fell victims to the violence of the Janissaries and other soldiers, without any rhyme or reason; others were resisting, relying on their own courage; still others were fleeing to the churches and making supplication—men, women, and children, everyone, for there was no quarter given.

The soldiers fell on them with anger and great wrath. For one thing, they were actuated by the hardships of the siege. For another, some foolish people had hurled taunts and curses at them from the battlements all through the siege. Now, in general they killed so as to frighten all the City, and to terrorize and enslave all by the slaughter.

When they had had enough of murder, and the City was reduced to slavery, some of the troops turned to the mansions of the mighty, by bands and companies and divisions, for plunder and spoil. Others went to the robbing of churches, and others dispersed to the simple homes of the common people, stealing, robbing, plundering, killing, insulting, taking and enslaving men, women, and children, old and young, priests, monks—in short, every age and class.

And the desecrating and plundering and robbing of the churches—how can one describe it in words? Some things they threw in dishonor on the ground—ikons and reliquaries and other objects from the churches. The crowd snatched some of these, and some were given over to the fire while others were torn to shreds and scattered at the crossroads. The last resting places of the blessed men of old were opened, and their remains were taken out and disgracefully torn to pieces, even to shreds, and made the sport of the wind while others were thrown on the streets.

Chalices and goblets and vessels to hold the holy sacrifice, some of them were used for drinking and carousing, and others were broken up or melted down and sold. Holy vessels and costly robes richly embroidered with much gold or brilliant with precious stones and pearls were some of them given to the most wicked men for no good use, while others were consigned to the fire and melted down for gold.

After this the Sultan entered the City and looked about to see its great size, its situation, its grandeur and beatuy, its teeming population, its loveliness, and the costliness of its churches and public buildings and of the private houses and community houses and of those of the officials. He also saw the setting of the harbor and of the arsenals, and how skilfully and ingeniously they had everything arranged in the City—in a word, all the construction and adornment of it. When he saw what a large number had been killed, and the ruin of the buildings, and the wholesale ruin and destruction of the City, he was filled with compassion and repented not a little at the destruction and plundering. Tears fell from his eyes as he groaned deeply and passionately:

"What a city we have giaven over to plunder and destruction!"

Thus he suffered in spirit. And indeed this was a great blow to us, in this one city, a disaster the like of which had occurred in no one of the great renowned cities of history, whether one speaks of the size of the captured City or of the bitterness and harshness of the deed. And no less did it astound all others than it did those who went through it and suffered, through the unreasonable and unusual character of the event and through the overwhelming and unheard-of horror of it.

Study Questions

1. What is the author's attitude toward Mehmed?

2. Why should Mehmed be compared to Alexander the Great and other ancients?

3. What was warfare like in the middle of the fifteenth century? Does Kritovoulos glorify it or treat it critically?

4. Why did Kritovoulos write his history? What lessons did he wish to convey?

Letters Between Sultan Selîm I and Shah Ismâ'îl (1514)   74

The Ottoman Empire did not only expand at the expense of the Christian West. By the sixteenth century Ottomans were invading the territory of other Muslim states and taking tribute where they could. In 1502 a conflict began between the Ottomans and the Safavids, a powerful and rival Muslim family that contested the legitimacy of Ottoman rule over their territory. Ismâ'îl, head of the Safavid family, proclaimed himself shah and attempted to drive the Ottomans from his lands. Sultan Selîm I responded with a reign of terror against Safavid communities. Matters came to a head in 1514 when armies of the two Muslim states fought at Chaldirân. The Ottomans won decisively.

In the months before the war, the shah and sultan conducted an unusual form of personal diplomacy by sending each other letters setting out their respective positions. They provide a unique glimpse into the attitudes of sixteenth-century Muslim rulers.

Selîm to Ismâ'îl (undated, ca. 1514)

It is from Solomon and it is: 'In the Name of God, the Merciful, the Compassionate. Rise not up against me, but come to me in surrender.'

[Qur'ân XXVII: 30–31]

God's blessings upon the best of his creatures, Muhammad, his family, and his companions all.

This is a Scripture We have sent down, blessed; so follow it, and be godfearing; haply so you will find mercy.

[Qur'ân VI: 156]

This missive which is stamped with the seal of victory and which is, like inspiration descending from the heavens, witness to the verse "We never chastise until We send forth a Messenger" [Qur'ân XVII:15] has been graciously issued by our most glorious majesty—we who are the Caliph of God Most High in this world, far and wide; the proof of the verse "And what profits men abides in the earth" [Qur'ân XIII:17] the Solomon of Splendor, the Alexander of eminence; haloed in victory, Faridûn[1] triumphant; slayer of the wicked and the infidel, guardian of the noble and the pious; the warrior in the Path, the defender of the Faith; the champion, the conqueror; the lion, son and grandson of the lion; standard-bearer of justice and righteousness, Sultân Selîm Shâh, son of Sultân Bayezîd, son of Sultân Muhammad Khân—and is addressed to the ruler of the kingdom of the Persians, the possessor of the land of tyranny and perversion, the captain of the vicious, the chief of the malicious, the usurping Darius of the time, the malevolent Zahhâk of the age, the peer of Cain, Prince Ismâ'il.

As the Pen of Destiny has drawn up the rescript "Thou givest the kingdom to whom Thou wilt" [Qur'ân III:26] in our sublime name and has signed it with the verse "Whatsoever mercy God opens to men, none can withhold" [Qur'ân XXXV:2], it is manifest in the Court of Glory and the Presence of Deity that we, the instrument of Divine Will, shall hold in force upon the earth both the commandments and prohibitions of Divine Law as well as the provisions of royal proclamations. 'That is the bounty of God; he gives it unto whomsoever He will [Qur'ân LVII:21].

It has been heard repeatedly that you have subjected the upright community of Muhammad (Prayers and salutations upon its founder!) to your devious will, that you have undermined the firm foundation of the Faith, that you have unfurled the banner of oppression in the cause of aggression, that you no longer uphold the commandments and prohibitions of the Divine Law, that you have incited your abominable Shî'î faction to unsanctified sexual union and to the shedding of innocent blood, that like they "Who listen to falsehood and consume the unlawful" [Qur'ân V:42] you have given ear to idle deceitful words and have eaten that which is forbidden:

He has laid waste to mosques, as it is said,
Constructing idol temples in their stead,

that you have rent the noble stuff of Islâm with the hand of tyranny, and that you have called the Glorious Qur'ân the myths of the Ancients. The rumor of these abominations has caused your name to become like that of Hârith deceived by Satan.[2]

---

[1] An ancient and celebrated king of Persia, who began to reign about 750 B.C.E.

[2] *Hârith:* possibly a reference to Hârith ibn Suwayd, who pretended to convert to Islâm in Muhammad's time, apostasized, and was ordered executed by Muhammad when he tried to rejoin the young Muslim community. Selîm is alluding to parallels between Hârith's and Ismâ'il's career.

Indeed, as both the *fatwas* of distinguished *'ulamâ'*[3] who base their opinion on reason and tradition alike and the consensus of the Sunnî[4] community agree that the ancient obligation of extirpation, extermination, and expulsion of evil innovation must be the aim of our exalted aspiration, for "Religious zeal is a victory for the Faith of God the Beneficent"; then, in accordance with the words of the Prophet (Peace upon him!) "Whosoever introduces evil innovation into our order must be expelled" and "Whosoever does aught against our order must be expelled," action has become necessary and exigent. Thus, when the Divine Decree of Eternal Destiny commended the eradication of the infamously wicked infidels into our capable hands, we set out for their lands like ineluctable fate itself to enforce the order "Leave not upon the earth of the Unbelievers even one" [Qur'ân LXXI:26]. If God almighty wills, the lightning of our conquering sword shall uproot the untamed bramble grown to great heights in the path of the refulgent Divine Law and shall cast them down upon the dust of abjectness to be trampled under the hooves of our legions, for "They make the mightiest of its inhabitants abased. Even so they too will do" [Qur'ân XXVII:34]; the thunder of our avenging mace shall dash out the muddled brains of the enemies of the Faith as rations for the lionhearted *ghâzîs*. "And those who do wrong shall surely know by what overthrowing they will be overthrown" [Qur'ân XXVI:227].

When I the sharp-edged sword draw from its sheath,

Then shall I raise up doomsday on the earth.

Then shall I roast the hearts of lion-hearted men,

And toast the morning with a goblet of their blood.

My crow-feathered arrow will fix the eagle in his flight;

My naked blade will make the sun's heart tremble.

Inquire of the sun about the dazzle of my rein;

Seek news of Mars about the brilliance of my arms.

Although a Sûfî[5] crown you wear, I bear a trenchant sword:

The owner of the sword will soon possess the crown.

O Mighty Fortune, pray grant this my single wish:

Pray let me take both crown and power from the foe.

But "Religion is Counsel," and should you turn the countenance of submission to the *qibla* of bliss and the Ka'ba[6] of hope—our angelic threshold, the refuge of the noble moreover, should you lift up the hand of oppression from the heads of your subjects ruined by tyranny and sedition, should you take up a course of repentance, become like one blameless and return to the sublime straight path of the Sunna[7] of Muhammad (Prayers and salutations upon him and God's satisfaction upon his immaculate family and his

---

3 *Fatwas:* legal opinions; *'ulamâ':* learned men.

4 *Sunnî community:* those who follow the practice of Muhammad, i.e., not those like Shî'îtes who followed 'Alî.

5 Allusion to Safavî origins as mystical order. The "crown" was their special headgear.

6 *Qibla:* direction of prayer for Muslims, i.e., the Ka'ba or holy building in Mecca.

7 *Sunna:* practice, example, custom.

rightly-guided companions all!). For "My companions are like the stars: whomever you choose to follow, you will be guided aright" and finally should you consider your lands and their people part of the well-protected Ottoman state, then shall you be granted our royal favor and our imperial patronage.

> He whose face touches the dust of my threshold in submission
> Will be enveloped in the shadow of my favor and my justice.

> How great the happiness of him who complies with this!

On the other hand, if your evil, seditious habits have become a part of your nature, that which has become essential can never again be accidental.

What avail sermons to the black-hearted?

Then, with the support and assistance of God, I will crown the head of every gallows tree with the head of a crown-wearing Sûfî and clear that faction from the face of the earth—"The party of God, they are the victors" [Qur'ân V:56]; I will break the oppressors' grip with the power of the miraculous white hand of Moses, for "God's hand is over their hands" [Qur'ân XLVIII:10]. Let them remove the cotton of negligence from the ears of their intelligence and, with their shrouds on their shoulders, prepare themselves for "Surely that which you are promised will come to pass" [Qur'ân VI:134]. The triumphant troops "As though they were a building well-compacted" [Qur'ân LXI:4] crying out like fate evoked "When their term comes they shall not put it back a single hour nor put it forward" [Qur'ân VII:34] and maneuvering in accordance with "Slay them wherever you find them" [Qur'ân IV:89], will

wreak ruin upon you and drive you from that land. "To God belongs the command before and after, and on that day the believers shall rejoice" [Qur'ân XXX:4]. "So the last roots of the people who did evil were cut off. Praise be to God, the Lord of the Worlds" [Qur'ân VI:45].

Ismâ'îl to Selîm (undated, ca. 1514)

May his godly majesty, the refuge of Islâm, the might of the kingdom, he upon whom God looks with favor, the champion of the sultanate and of the state, the hero of the faith and of the earth, Sultân Selîm Shâh (God grant him immortal state and eternal happiness!) accept this affectionate greeting and this friendly letter, considering it a token of our good will.

Now to begin: Your honored letters have arrived one after another, for "No sooner has a thing doubled than it has tripled." Their contents, although indicative of hostility, are stated with boldness and vigor. The latter gives us much enjoyment and pleasure, but we are ignorant of the reason for the former. In the time of your late blessed father (May God enlighten his proof!) when our royal troops passed through the lands of Rûm to chastise the impudence of Alâ' al-Dawla Dhû'l) Qadr,[8] complete concord and friendship was shown on both sides. Moreover, when your majesty was governor at Trebizond [i.e., before his accession] there existed perfect mutual understanding. Thus, now, the cause of your resentment and displeasure yet remains unknown. If political necessity has compelled you on this course, then may your problems soon be solved.

> Dispute may fire words to such a heat
> That ancient houses be consumed in flames.

---

8 *Alâ' al-Dawla Dhû'l-Qadr:* ruler of partially Shî'ite Dhû'l-Qadr Turkomans in Elbistan and Mar'ash, buffer state between Ottomans and Safavids. Ismâ'îl had attacked them in 1507.

The intention of our inaction in this regard is twofold:

1. Most of the inhabitants of the land of Rûm are followers of our forefathers (May God the All-Forgiving King have mercy upon them!).

2. We have always loved the *ghâzî*-titled[9] Ottoman house and we do not wish the outbreak of sedition and turmoil once again as in the time of Tîmûr.

Why should we then take umbrage at these provocations? We shall not.

> The mutual hostility of kings is verily an ancient rite.
> Should one hold the bride of worldly rule too close,
> His lips those of the radiant sword will kiss.

Nevertheless, there is no cause for improper words: indeed, those vain, heretical imputations are the mere fabrications of the opium-clouded minds of certain secretaries and scribes. We therefore think that our delayed reply was not completely without cause for we have now dispatched our honored personal companion and servant Shâh Qulî Aghâ (May he be sustained!) with a golden casket stamped with the royal seal and filled with a special preparation for their use should they deem it necessary. May he soon arrive so that with assistance from above the mysteries concealed behind the veil of fate might be disclosed. But one should always exercise free judgment not bound solely by the words of others and always keep in view that in the end regrets avail him naught.

At this writing we were engaged upon the hunt near Isfahân; we now prepare provisions and our troops for the coming campaign. In all friendship we say do what you will.

> Bitter experience has taught that in this world of trial
> He who falls upon the house of 'Alî[10] always falls.

Kindly give our ambassador leave to travel unmolested. "No soul laden bears the load of another" [Qur'ân VI:164; LIII:38].

When war becomes inevitable, hesitation and delay must be set aside, and one must think on that which is to come. Farewell.

Study Questions

1. Why does Selîm quote the Koran (Qur'ân) so often in his letter?

2. What is Selîm's self-conception?

3. What is Ismâ'îl's attitude toward Selîm? What does he mean when he says, "In all friendship we say do what you will do"?

4. What purpose do you think these letters served?

---

[9] An allusion to the Ottoman origin as frontier warriors for the faith.

[10] House of 'Alî, i.e., the Shî'îtes.

The History and Description of Africa (1550)   75

LEO AFRICANUS

Leo Africanus (ca. 1485–1554), whose Arabic name was al-Hassan ibn-Mohammed al-Wazzan, was born in Granada to a prominent Moorish family. After the expulsion of the Moors from Spain in 1492, his family left Granada, and Leo was raised in Morocco, where he studied under the tutelage of Arabic scholars. Ultimately, Leo Africanus became a merchant and traveled throughout northern Africa and the Arabian Middle East. In 1517, during a voyage to Constantinople, he was captured by pirates. Because he was obviously an educated man, Leo Africanus was taken to Rome and presented to Pope Leo X, who personally instructed him in both Latin letters and Christianity. He was baptized John Leo, in honor of the Pope, and spent the next decade living in Rome.

Leo Africanus wrote a number of works that introduced Europeans to the achievements of Arabic science and philosophy as well as composing an Arabic–Spanish dictionary. He was chiefly known for his *History and Description of Africa,* which was written first in Arabic and then rewritten in Italian by Leo himself. *The History and Description of Africa* was first published in 1550 and was the principal source of European knowledge about the peoples of northern Africa.

Abassia, or the Empire of Prete Ianni

The Abassins are a people subject to *Prete Ianni.* whose empire (if we consider the stile which he useth in his letters) hath most ample confines. For he intituleth himselfe emperour of the great and higher Ethiopia, king of Goiame, which (as *Botera* supposeth) is situate betweene Nilus and Zaire; of Vangue a kingdome beyond Zaire; of Damut which confineth with the land of the Anzichi; and towards the south he is called king of Cafate and Bagamidri, two provinces bordering upon the first great lake, which is the originall fountains of Nilus; as likewise of the kingdomes of Xoa, Fatigar, Angote, Baru, Baaliganze, Adea, Amara, Ambea, Vague, Tigremahon, Sabaim, where the Queene of Saba governed, and lastly of Barnagaes, and lorde as farre as Nubia, which bordereth upon Egypt. But at this present the center or midst of his Empire (as *John Barros* writeth) is the lake of Barcena. For it extendeth eastward towarde the Red sea, as farre as Suaquen, the space of two hundred twentie and two leagues. Howbeit betweene the sea and his dominions runneth a ridge of mountaines inhabited by Moores, who are masters of al the seacoast along, except the porte of Ercoco, which belongeth to the *Prete.* And likewise on the west, his empire is restrained by another mountainous ridge stretching along the river of Nilus, where are founde most rich mines of golde; amongst which are the mines of Damut and of Sinassij, wholie in the possession of Gentiles which pay tribute unto the *Prete.* Northward it is bounded by an imaginarie line supposed to be drawn from Suachen to the beginning of the isle Meroe above mentioned;

which line extendeth an hundred and five and twentie leagues. From thence the Abassin borders trend south somewhat crookedly in manner of abowe, as farre as the kingdome of Adea (from the mountaines whereof springeth a riuer called by *Ptolemey* Raptus which falleth into the sea about Melinde) for the space of two hundred and fiftie nine leagues; next unto the which borders, inhabite certaine Gentiles of blacke colour, with curled haire. And heere the saide empire is limited by the kingdome of Adel, the head citie whereof called Arar, standeth in the latitude nine degrees. So that all this great empire may containe in compasse sixe hundred threescore and two leagues, little more or lesse. It is refreshed and watered by two mightie rivers which convey their streames into Nilus, called by *Ptolemey* Astaboras and Astapus, and by the naturall inhabitants Abagni and Tagassi; the first whereof taketh his originall from the lake of Barcena, and the second from the lake of Colve. Barcena lieth in seven degrees of north latitude; & Colve under the verie Equinoctiall. The first (besides Abagni) ingendereth also the river of Zeila: and the second (besides Tagassi) giveth effence to the river of Quilimanci Between Abagni and the Red sea lieth the province of Barnagasso: betweene Abagni and Tagassi are the kingdomes of Angote and Fatigar; and more towards the bay of Barbarians, the provinces of Adea and of Baru: and somewhat lower, that of Amara. In briefe, beyond the river of Tagassi ly the regions of Bileguanzi, and of Tigremahon.

The Abassins have no great knowledge of Nilus by reason of the mountaines which devide them from it; for which cause they call Abagni, the father of rivers. Howbeit they say that upon Nilus do inhabite two great and populous nations; one of Iewes towards the west, under the government of a mightie king; the other more southerly, consisting of Amazones or warlike women; whereof wee will speake more at large in our relation of Monomotapa.

Throughout all the dominion of the *Prete* there is not any one city of importance, either for multitude of inhabitantes, for magnificent buildings, or for any other respect. For the greatest townes there, containe not above two thousand housholds; the houses being (cottage-like) reared up with clay and covered with straw, or such like base matter. Also *Ptolemey* entreating of these partes, maketh mention but of three or foure cities onely, which he appointeth to the south of the Isle Meroe. Howbeit in some places upon the frontiers of Abassia there are certaine townes verie fairely built, and much frequented for traffique. The Portugales in their travailes throughout the empire have often declared unto the Abassins, how much better it were, for avoiding of the outrageous injuries and losses daily inflicted by the Moores and Mahumetans both upon their goods and persons, if the emperour would build cities and castles stronglie walled and fortified. Whereunto they made answere, that the power of their Neguz, or emperour, consisted not in stone-walles, but in the armes of his people. They use not ordinarily any lime or stone, but onely for the building of churches (saying, that so it becommeth us to make a difference between the houses of men, and churches dedicated to God) and of their Beteneguz or houses of the emperour, wherein the governours of provinces are placed to execute justice. These Beteneguz stand continually open, and yet in the governours, absence no man dare enter into them, under paine of being punished as a traytour. Moreover in the city of Axuma (esteemed by them to have beene the seate of the Queene of *Saba*) stand certaine ruinous buildings like unto pyramides; which by reason of their greatness, remaine even til this present, notwithstanding their many yeeres antiquitie. Likewise there are in this countrie divers churches and oratories hewen out of the hard rocke, consisting but of one onely stone, some sixtie, some fortie, and some thirtie fathomes long, being full of windowes, and engraven with strange and unknowne characters. Three such churches there are of twelve fathomes broade and eightie in length.

The Abassins which are subject to the *Prete,* hold opinion, that their prince deriveth his petigree from *Melich* the sonne of *Salomon,* which (as they say) he begot of the Queene of *Saba;* and that themselves are descended from the officers and attendants which *Salomon* appointed unto this his sonne when he sent him home unto his mother: which seemeth not altogether unlikely, if you consider the Jewish ceremonies of circumcision, observing of the sabaoth, & such like, which they use untill this present: likewise they abhorre swines flesh and certaine other meates, which they call uncleane. The *Prete* absolutely governeth in all matters, except it be in administring of the sacraments, and ordaining of priests. Hee giveth and taketh away benefices at his pleasure; and in punishing offenders, maketh no difference betweene his clergie and laitie. The administration of their sacraments is wholie referred to the Abuna or Patriarke. The *Prete* is lorde and owner of all the lands and possessions in his empire, except those of the church; which are in number infinite; for the monasteries of saint *Antonie* (besides which there are none of any other order) and the colleges of the Canons and of the Hermites, togither with the parishes, are innumerable. They are all provided by the king, both of revenewes and of ornaments.

They have two winters and two summers; which they discerne not by colde and heate, but by rainie and faire weather. They begin their yeere upon the 26 of August, and divide it into twelve moneths, each moneth containing thirtie daies, whereunto they adde every common yeere five daies, and in the leape yeere sixe, which odde daies they call Pagomen, that is, The end of the yeere. Their ordinaire journeies in travelling are twelve miles a day. The common harlots dwell without their townes, and have wages allowed them out of the common purse: neither may they enter into any cities, nor apparell themselves, but only in yellow.

The soil of Abassia aboundeth generally with graine, and in especiall with barly and all kindes of Pulse, but not so much with wheate; they have sugar likewise (not knowing how to refine it) and hony, and cotton-wooll, orenges, cedars, and limons, grow naturally there. They have neither melons, citrons, nor rape-roots: but many plants & herbes different from ours. Their drinke is made of barley and millet: neither have they any wine made of grapes, but onely in the houses of the emperour, and the Abuna. They are not destitute of Elephants, mules, lions, tygres, ounces, and deere. Their owne countrey horses are but of a small size: howbeit they have also of the Arabian and the Egyptian breed, the coltes whereof within fower daies after they be foled, they use to suckle with kine. They have great and terrible apes; and infinite sorts of birds; but neither cuckowes nor Pies, so farre as ever could bee learned. Heere are likewise great store of mines of gold, silver, iron, and copper; but they know not how to digge and refine the same: for the people of this countrey are so rude and ignorant, that they have no knowledge nor use of any arte or occupation. Insomuch as they esteeme the carpenters or smithes craft for an unlawful and diabolicall kinde of science; and such as exercise the same, live among them like infamous persons; neither are they permitted to enter into any of their churches. In the kingdome of Bagamidri are founde most excellent mines of silver, which they knowe none other way how to take from the ore, but onely by melting it with fire into thinne plates. Goiame aboundeth with base gold. In the kingdome of Damut they digge and refine it somewhat better. They have neither the arte of making cloth (for which cause the greater part of them go clad in beasts skins) nor yet the manner of hauking, fowling, or hunting; so that their countries swarme with partridges, quailes, fesants, cranes, geese, hens, hares, deere, and other like creatures: neither knowe they how to make any full use nor benefite of the fruitefulness of their countrey, or of the commoditie of rivers. They sowe mill for the most parte, sometimes in one place, and sometimes in another, according as the raine giveth them opportunitie. In summe, they shew no wit nor dexterity in any thing so much as in robbery and warre; unto both which they have a kind of naturall inclination. Which is occasioned (as I suppose) by the continuall voyages made by the *Prete*, and by their usuall living in the wide fields, and that in divers and sundry places. For to travaile continually, and remaine in the fields without any stable or firme habitation, compelleth men as it were, of necessitie, to lay holde on all that comes next to hande, be it their owne, or belonging to others.

They are much subject to tempests; but to an inconvenience far more intollerable, namely to innumerable swarmes of locusts, which bring such desolation upon them, as is most dreadfull to consider: for they consume whole provinces, leaving them quite destitute of succour both for man and beast. They use no stamped coine in all this empire, but insteede thereof certaine rude pieces of golde, and little balls of iron, especially in Angote; as likewise salt and pepper, which are the greatest riches that they can enjoy.

Hence it is, that the tributes which are payed to the prince, consist onely of such things as his owne dominions do naturally afforde; as namely of salt, gold, silver, corne, hides, elephants teeth, the horne of the Rhinoceros, with slaves, and such like. Which forme of tribute (being most agreeable to nature) is used also in other parts of Africa. Their salt is taken out of a certaine great mountaines in the province of Balgada, and is made into square pieces.

The most populous place in all Abassia is the court of the *Prete*, wheresoever it resideth; and there are erected five or sixe thousand tents of cotton of divers colours, with so notable a distinction of streetes, lanes, market-places, and Tribunals; that even in a moment every man knoweth his owne station and the place where he is to doe his business. A man may conjecture the greatnes of this courte, if he doe but consider, that (according to the report of some who have there bin personally present) besides the camels which carry the tents, the mules of carriage exceede the number of fiftie thousand. Their mules serve them to carry burthens, and to ride upon: but their horses are onely for the warres. The Mahumetans have now brought this prince to great extremity: but heretofore while he was in his flourishing estate, he lived so majestically, that he never spake but by an interpreter; nor would be seene to his subjects, but onely upon solemne dayes. At other times it was held as a great favour, if he did shew but the halfe part of his feete to ambassadours, and to his favorites. And no marvel: for amongst the Ethiopians it hath beene an ancient custome (as *Strabo* writeth) To adore their kinges like gods, who for the most part live enclosed at home. This so strange and stately kinde of government, did exceedingly abase his subjects, whom the *Prete* used like slaves; so that upon the smallest occasions that might be, he would deprive them of all honour and dignity, were they never so great. Abassia containeth many large plaines, and very high mountaines, all fruitfull. In some places you shall have most extreame coulde and frostie weather: but not any snowe throughout the whole empire, no not in the mountaines.

The *Prete* hath many moores in his dominions, and upon his borders; but the most populous of all others are the Moores called Dobas, who are bound by a law never to marry, till they can bring most evident testimony, that each of them hath slaine twelve Christians. Wherefore the Abassin merchants passe not by their country, but with most strong guardes.

Study Questions

1. What do the Ethiopians believe to be the source of their emperor's power?

2. What were the symbols of the prince's greatness?

3. What threatened the well-being of the Ethiopians?

4. What aspects of Ethiopia does Leo Africanus think are important to describe? What does he leave out?

Travels in the Mughal Empire (1656–1668)   76

FRANÇOIS BERNIER

François Bernier (1620–1688) was a Frenchman who spent most of his life traveling in the East. He came from humble origins, his father leased a farm, but was successful academically. Bernier studied medicine and for a time was a companion to Gassendi, one of the great French philosophers. In 1656 he began a long journey to the East that brought him first to Egypt and then to the Indian subcontinent. During a ten-year exploration of India and Persia, he kept a journal and wrote a number of books. The most important of these, *The History of the Late Rebellion in the States of the Great Mogol*, was an instant success throughout Europe, where it was translated into English, Dutch, German, and Italian. The exotic civilizations described in Bernier's work captured the imagination of Europeans.

Bernier's descriptive accounts of the cities he visited in the East are remarkable for their detail. They are the best surviving records of everyday life in the Mughal Empire, even though they are unabashedly Eurocentric in outlook.

It is about forty years ago that *Chah-Jehan,* father of the present *Great Mogol, Aureng-Zebe,* conceived the design of immortalising his name by the erection of a city near the site of the ancient *Dehli....* Here he resolved to fix his court, alleging as the reason for its removal from *Agra,* that the excessive heat to which that city is exposed during summer rendered it unfit for the residence of a monarch....

Dehli, then, is an entirely new city, situated in a flat country, on the banks of the *Gemna,* a river which may be compared to the *Loire,* and built on one bank only in such a manner that it terminates in this place very much in the form of a crescent, having but one bridge of boats to cross to the country. Excepting the side where it is defended by the river, the city is encompassed by walls of brick.

... The walls of the citadel, as to their antique and round towers, resemble those of the city, but being partly of brick, and partly of a red stone which resembles marble, they have a better appearance. The walls of the fortress likewise excel those of the town in height, strength, and thickness, being capable of admitting small field-pieces, which are pointed toward the city. Except on the side of the river, the citadel is defended by a deep ditch faced with hewn stone, filled with water, and stocked with fish....

Adjoining the ditch is a large garden, filled at all times with flowers and green shrubs, which, contrasted with the stupendous red walls, produce a beautiful effect.

Next to the garden is the great royal square, faced on one side by the gates of the fortress, and on the opposite side of which terminate the two most considerable streets of the city.

The tents of such *Rajas* as are in the King's pay, and whose weekly turn it is to mount guard, are pitched in this square; those petty sovereigns having an insuperable objection to be enclosed within walls. The guard within the fortress is mounted by the *Omrahs* and *Mansebdars*.

In this place also at break of day they exercise the royal horses, which are kept in a spacious stable not far distant....

Here too is held a *bazar* or market for an endless variety of things; which like the *Pont-neuf* at *Paris*, is the rendezvous for all sorts of mountebanks and jugglers. Hither, likewise, the astrologers resort, both *Mahometan* and *Gentile*. These wise doctors remain seated in the sun, on a dusty piece of carpet, handling some old mathematical instruments, and having open before them a large book which represents the signs of the zodiac. In this way they attract the attention of the passengers, and impose upon the people, by whom they are considered as so many infallible oracles. They tell a poor person his fortune for a *payssa* (which is worth about one sol); and after examining the hand and face of the applicant, turning over the leaves of the large book, and pretending to make certain calculations, these impostors decide upon the *Sahet* or propitious moment of commencing the business he may have in hand. Silly women, wrapping themselves in a white cloth from head to foot, flock to the astrologers, whisper to them all the transactions of their lives, and disclose every secret with no more reserve than is practised by a scrupulous penitent in the presence of her confessor. The ignorant and infatuated people really believe that the stars have an influence which the astrologers can control.

I am speaking only of the poor *bazar-astrologers*. Those who frequent the court of the grandees are considered by them eminent doctors, and become wealthy. The whole of *Asia* is degraded by the same superstition. Kings and nobles grant large salaries to these crafty diviners, and never engage in the most trifling transaction without consulting them. They read whatever is written in heaven; fix upon the *Sahet*, and solve every doubt by opening the *Koran*.

Of the numberless streets which cross each other, many have arcades....

Amid these streets are dispersed the habitations of *Mansebdars*, or petty *Omrahs*, officers of justice, rich merchants, and others; many of which have a tolerable appearance. Very few are built entirely of brick or stone, and several are made only of clay and straw, yet they are airy and pleasant, most of them having courts and gardens, being commodious inside and containing good furniture. The thatched roof is supported by a layer of long, handsome, and strong canes, and the clay walls are covered with a fine white lime.

Intermixed with these different houses is an immense number of small ones, built of mud and thatched with straw, in which lodge the common troopers, and all that vast multitude of servants and camp-followers who follow the court and the army.

It is owing to these thatched cottages that *Dehli* is subject to such frequent conflagrations. More than sixty thousand roofs were consumed this last year by three fires, during the prevalence of certain impetuous winds which blow generally in summer. So rapid were the flames that several camels and horses were burnt. Many of the inmates of the seraglio also fell victims to the devouring element; for these poor women are so bashful and helpless that they can do nothing but hide their faces at the sight of strangers, and those who perished possessed not sufficient energy to fly from the danger.

That which so much contributes to the beauty of European towns, the brilliant appearance of the shops, is wanting in *Dehli*. For though this city be the seat of a powerful and magnificent court, where an infinite quantity of the richest commodities is necessarily collected, yet there are no streets like ours of *S. Denis*, which has not perhaps its equal in any part of *Asia*. Here the costly merchandise is generally kept in warehouses, and the shops are seldom decked with rich or showy articles. For one that makes a display of beautiful and fine cloths, silk, and other stuffs striped with gold and silver, turbans embroidered with gold, and brocades, there are at least five-and-twenty where nothing is seen but pots of oil or butter, piles of baskets filled with rice, barley, chick-peas, wheat, and an endless variety of other grain and pulse, the ordinary aliment not only of the *Gentiles*, who never eat meat, but of the lower class of

Mahometans, and a considerable portion of the military.

There is, indeed, a fruit-market that makes some show....

There are many confectioners' shops in the town, but the sweetmeats are badly made, and full of dust and flies....

Bakers also are numerous, but the ovens are unlike our own, and very defective....

In the *bazars* there are shops where meat is sold roasted and dressed in a variety of ways. But there is no trusting to their dishes, composed, for aught I know, of the flesh of camels, horses, or perhaps oxen which have died of disease. Indeed no food can be considered wholesome which is not dressed at home.

Meat is sold in every part of the city; but instead of goats' flesh that of mutton is often palmed upon the buyer; an imposition which ought to be guarded against, because mutton and beef, but particularly the former, though not unpleasant to the taste, are heating, flatulent, and difficult of digestion. Kid is the best food, but being rarely sold in quarters, it must be purchased alive, which is very inconvenient, as the meat will not keep from morning to night, and is generally lean and without flavour. The goats' flesh found in quarters at the butchers' shops is frequently that of the she-goat, which is lean and tough.

But it would be unreasonable in me to complain; because since I have been familiarised with the manners of the people, it seldom happens that I find fault either with my meat or my bread.

Study Questions

1. What is Bernier's attitude toward Dehli and its inhabitants?

2. Why was a new Dehli built in the seventeenth century?

3. What was life like for a merchant in seventeenth-century Dehli? What was it life for a peasant?

4. What role did astrologers play in the Mughal Empire?

The Reform of Christianity

Martin Luther and the Wittenberg Reformers. In this painting by Cranach the Younger in 1543, Luther is at the far left. The large figure in the center foreground is Elector John Frederick of Saxony, who gave Luther crucial protection and support against the church.

In Praise of Folly (1509)   77

DESIDERIUS ERASMUS

Desiderius Erasmus (ca. 1466–1536) was the leading intellectual light of the early sixteenth century. An orphan, Erasmus was educated in a monastery and became a monk. His intellectual gifts were so great that he was allowed to travel throughout the continent searching for ancient manuscripts and perfecting his skills as a linguist, philologist, and writer. His principal scholarly achievements, an edition of the Greek New Testament and of the Writings of Saint Jerome, were both published in 1516. But Erasmus was better known for his popular writings, especially his *Adages* and the satirical *In Praise of Folly*.

In Praise of Folly was written for Sir Thomas More with whom Erasmus had made friends on his first trip to England. It is a spoof, in which Folly demands praise for all of the ways of the world. It is under Folly's influence that people behave as they do and that institutions are organized with an upside-down logic. Erasmus was particularly scathing in his description of the state of religion and of the Catholic Church. Historians are fond of saying that Erasmus laid the egg that Luther hatched.

The next to be placed among the regiment of fools are such as make a trade of telling or inquiring after incredible stories of miracles and prodigies: never doubting that a lie will choke them, they will muster up a thousand several strange relations of spirits, ghosts, apparitions, raising of the devil, and such like bugbears of superstition, which the farther they are from being probably true, the more greedily they are swallowed, and the more devoutly believed. And these absurdities do not only bring an empty pleasure, and cheap divertisement, but they are a good trade, and procure a comfortable income to such priests and friars as by this craft get their gain. To these again are nearly related such others as attribute strange virtues to the shrines and images of saints and martyrs, and so would make their credulous proselytes believe, that if they pay their devotion to St. Christopher in the morning, they shall be guarded and secured the day following from all dangers and misfortunes: if soldiers, when they first take arms, shall come and mumble over such a set prayer before the picture of St. Barbara, they shall return safe from all engagements: or if any pray to Erasmus on such particular holidays, with the ceremony of wax candles, and other fopperies, he shall in a short time be rewarded with a plentiful increase of wealth and riches.

The next to these are another sort of brain-sick fools, who style themselves monks and of religious orders, though they assume both tides very unjustly: for as to the last, they have very little religion in them; and as to the former, the etymology of the word monk implies a solitariness, or being alone; whereas they are so thick abroad that we cannot pass any street or alley without meeting them. Now I cannot imagine what one degree of men would be more hopelessly wretched, if I did not stand their friend, and buoy them up in that lake of misery, which by the engagements of a holy vow they have voluntarily immerged themselves in. But when this sort of men are so unwelcome to others, as that the very sight of them is thought ominous, I yet make them highly in love with themselves, and fond admirers of their own happiness. The first step whereunto they esteem a profound ignorance, thinking carnal knowledge a great enemy to their spiritual welfare, and seem confident of becoming greater proficients in divine mysteries the less they are poisoned with any human learning. They imagine that they bear a sweet consort with the heavenly choir, when they tone out their daily tally of psalms, which they rehearse only by rote, without permitting their understanding or affections to go along with their voice.

Among these some make a good profitable trade of beggary, going about from house to house, not like the apostles, to break, but to beg, their bread; nay, thrust into all public-houses, come aboard the passage-boats, get into the travelling waggons, and omit no opportunity of time or place for the craving people's charity; doing a great deal of injury to common highway beggars by interloping in their traffic of alms. And when they are thus voluntarily poor, destitute, not provided with two coats, nor with any money in their purse, they have the impudence to pretend that they imitate the first disciples, whom their master expressly sent out in such an equipage.

It is pretty to observe how they regulate all their actions as it were by weight and measure to so exact a proportion, as if the whole loss of their religion depended upon the omission of the least punctilio. Thus they must be very critical in the precise number of knots to the tying on of their sandals: what distinct colours their respective habits, and what stuff made of, how broad and long their girdles: how big, and in what fashion, their hoods; whether their bald crowns be to a hair's-breadth of the right cut; how many hours they must sleep, at what minute rise to prayers, and so on. And these several customs are altered according to the humours of different persons and places. While they are sworn to the superstitious observance of these trifles, they do not only despise all others, but are very inclinable to fall out among themselves; for though they make profession of an apostolic charity, yet they will pick a quarrel, and be implacably passionate for such poor provocations, as the girting on a coat the wrong way, for the wearing of clothes a little too darkish coloured or any such nicety not worth the speaking of.

Some are so obstinately superstitious that they will wear their upper garment of some coarse dog's hair stuff, and that next their skin as soft as silk: but others on the contrary will have linen frocks outermost, and their shirts of wool, or hair. Some again will not touch a piece of money, though they make no scruple of the sin of drunkenness, and the lust of the flesh. All their several orders are mindful of nothing more than of their being distinguished from each other by their different customs and habits. They seem indeed not so careful of becoming like Christ, and of being known to be his disciples, as the being unlike to one another, and distinguishable for followers of their several founders.

Most of them place their greatest stress for salvation on a strict conformity to their foppish ceremonies, and a belief of their legendary traditions; wherein they fancy to have acquitted themselves with so much of supererogation, that one heaven can never be a condign reward for their meritorious life; little thinking that the Judge of all the earth at the last day shall put them off, with a who hath required these things at your hands; and call them to account only for the stewardship of his legacy, which was the precept of love and charity. It will be pretty to hear their pleas before the great tribunal: one will brag how he mortified his carnal appetite by feeding only upon fish: another will urge that he spent most of his time on earth in the divine exercise of singing psalms: a third will tell how many days he fasted, and what severe penance he imposed on himself for the bringing his body into subjection: another shall produce in his own behalf as many ceremonies as would load a fleet of merchant-men: a fifth shall plead that in threescore years he never so much as touched a piece of money, except he fingered it through a thick pair of gloves: a sixth, to testify his former humility, shall bring along with him his sacred hood, so old and nasty, that any seaman had rather stand bare headed on the deck, than put it on to defend his ears in the sharpest storms: the next that comes to answer for himself shall plead, that for fifty years together, he had lived like a sponge upon the same place, and was content never to change his homely habitation: another shall whisper softly, and tell the judge he has lost his voice by a continual singing of holy hymns and anthems: the next shall confess how he fell into a lethargy by a strict, reserved, and sedentary life: and the last shall intimate that he has forgot to speak, by having always kept silence, in obedience to the injunction of taking heed lest he should have offended with his tongue.

Now as to the popes of Rome, who pretend themselves Christ's vicars, if they would but imitate his exemplary life, in the being employed in an unintermitted course of preaching; in the being attended with poverty, nakedness, hunger, and a contempt of this world; if they did but consider the import of the word pope, which signifies a father; or if they did but practice their surname of most holy, what order or degrees of men would be in a worse condition? There would be then no such vigorous making of parties, and buying of votes, in the conclave upon a vacancy of that see: and those who by bribery, or other indirect courses, should get themselves elected, would never secure their sitting firm in the chair by pistol, poison, force, and violence.

How much of their pleasure would be abated if they were but endowed with one dram of wisdom? Wisdom, did I say? Nay, with one grain of that salt which our Saviour bid them not lose the savour of. All their riches, all their honour, their jurisdictions, their Peter's patrimony, their offices, their dispensations, their licenses, their indulgences, their long train and attendants (see in how short a compass I have abbreviated all their marketing of religion); in a word, all their perquisites would be forfeited and lost; and in their room would succeed watchings, fastings, tears, prayers, sermons, hard studies, repenting sighs, and a thousand such like severe penalties: may, what's yet more deplorable, it would then follow, that all their clerks, amanuenses, notaries, advocates, proctors, secretaries, the offices of grooms, ostlers, serving-men, pimps (and somewhat else, which for modesty's sake I shall not mention); in short, all these troops of attendants, which depend on his holiness, would all lose their several employments. This indeed would be hard, but what yet remains would be more dreadful: the very Head of the Church, the spiritual prince, would then be brought from all his splendour to the poor equipage of a scrip and staff.

But all this is upon the supposition only that they understood what circumstances they are placed in; whereas now, by a wholesome neglect of thinking, they live as well as heart can wish: whatever of toil and drudgery belongs to their office that they assign over to St. Peter, or St. Paul, who have time enough to mind it; but if there be any thing of pleasure and grandeur, that they assume to themselves, as being hereunto called: so that by my influence no sort of people live more to their own ease and content. They think to satisfy that Master they pretend to serve, our Lord and Saviour, with their great state and magnificence, with the ceremonies of instalments, with the titles of reverence and holiness, and with exercising their episcopal function only in blessing and cursing. The working of miracles is old and out-dated; to teach the people is too laborious; to interpret scripture is to invade the prerogative of the schoolmen; to pray is too idle; to shed tears is cowardly and unmanly; to fast is too mean and sordid; to be easy and familiar is beneath the grandeur of him, who, without being sued to and entreated, will scarce give princes the honour of kissing his toe; finally, to die for religion is too self-denying; and to be crucified as their Lord of Life, is base and ignominious.

Their only weapons ought to be those of the Spirit; and of these indeed they are mighty liberal, as of their interdicts, their suspensions, their denunciations, their aggravations, their greater and lesser excommunications, and their roaring bulls, that fright whomever they are thundered against; and these most holy fathers never issue them out more frequently than against those, who, at the instigation of the devil, and not having the fear of God before their eyes, do feloniously and maliciously attempt to lessen and impair St. Peter's patrimony: and though that apostle tells our Saviour in the gospel, in the name of all the other disciples, we have left all, and followed you, yet they challenge as his inheritance, fields, towns, treasures, and large dominions; for the defending whereof, inflamed with a holy zeal, they fight with fire and sword, to the great loss and effusion of Christian blood, thinking they are apostolical maintainers of Christ's spouse, the church, when they have murdered all such as they call her enemies; though indeed the church has no enemies more bloody and tyrannical than such impious popes, who give dispensations for the not preaching of Christ; evacuate the main effect and design of our redemption by their pecuniary bribes and sales; adulterate the gospel by their forced interpretations, and undermining traditions; and lastly, by their lusts and wickedness grieve the Holy Spirit, and make their Saviour's wounds to bleed anew.

Study Questions

1. How has superstition affected the message of the Church, according to Erasmus?

2. What is wrong with most members of religious orders?

3. The papacy, Erasmus says, is also corrupt. How? How might it be reformed?

4. Erasmus identifies many serious failings in the Church. Why do you think people allowed them to continue? What purpose was the Church serving?

5. The Church comes in for a great deal of criticism from Erasmus. Do you think he contributed to the origins of the Reformation? How might the scope of his criticism have been limited by his choice of forum?

The Freedom of a Christian (1520) and On Marriage (1566)

78

MARTIN LUTHER

Martin Luther (1483–1546) was undoubtedly the central figure of the sixteenth century. Trained for the law, he underwent a spiritual crisis that led him to enter an Augustinian monastery. There his extraordinary gifts were recognized, and he quickly distinguished himself as a scholar, teacher, and pastor. In 1517 he protested against the sale of indulgences and found himself at the center of a political and religious controversy. Luther refused to recant his views and was condemned by both the pope and the Holy Roman emperor. He broke from the Roman Catholic church and founded his own religious movement, first called Protestantism and later Lutheranism.

Throughout his political struggles, Luther wrote incessantly. The spread of his message and his movement was aided by the invention of printing and by the increase of literacy. He translated parts of the Bible into German, prepared a new church service, and even wrote hymns. But his most important works were the explanations of his faith. *The Freedom of a Christian* is one of the central statements of Luther's theology.

Among the many church reforms that Luther undertook was permitting clergy to marry. In his later years, he took a wife, a former nun from a dissolved monastery. Luther's views on marriage, however, were not part of his systematic theology. They were collected in *The Table Talk*, a work complied by his followers after his death.

The Freedom of a Christian

Many people have considered Christian faith an easy thing, and not a few have given it a place among the virtues. They do this because they have not experienced it and have never tasted the great strength there is in faith. It is impossible to write well about it or to understand what has been written about it unless one has at one time or another experienced the courage which faith gives a man when trials oppress him. But he who has had even a faint taste of it can never write, speak, meditate, or hear enough concerning it. It is a living "spring of water welling up to eternal life," as Christ calls it in John 4 [:14].

As for me, although I have no wealth of faith to boast of and know how scant my supply is, I nevertheless hope that I have attained to a little faith, even though I have been assailed by great and various temptations; and I hope that I can discuss it, if not more elegantly, certainly more to the point, than those literalists and subtile disputants have previously done, who have not even understood what they have written.

To make the way smoother for the unlearned—for only them do I serve—I shall set down the following two propositions concerning the freedom and the bondage of the spirit:

A Christian is a perfectly free lord of all, subject to none.

A Christian is a perfectly dutiful servant of all, subject to all.

These two theses seem to contradict each other. If, however, they should be found to fit together they would serve our purpose beautifully. Both are Paul's own statements, who says in I Cor. 9 [:19], "For though I am free from all men, I have made myself a slave to all," and in Rom. 13 [:8], "Owe no one anything, except to love one another." Love by its very nature is ready to serve and be subject to him who is loved. So Christ, although he was Lord of all, was "born of woman, born under the law" [Gal. 4:4], and therefore was at the same time a free man and a servant, "in the form of God" and "of a servant" [Phil. 2:6–7].

Let us start, however, with something more remote from our subject, but more obvious. Man has a twofold nature, a spiritual and a bodily one. According to the spiritual nature, which men refer to as the soul, he is called a spiritual, inner, or new man. According to the bodily nature, which men refer to as flesh, he is called a carnal, outward, or old man. Because of this diversity of nature the Scriptures assert contradictory things concerning the same man, since these two men in the same man contradict each other, "for the desires of the flesh are against the Spirit, and the desires of the Spirit are against the flesh," according to Gal. 5 [:17].

First, let us consider the inner man to see how a righteous, free, and pious Christian, that is, a spiritual, new, and inner man becomes what he is. It is evident that no external thing has any influence in producing Christian righteousness or freedom, or in producing unrighteousness or servitude. A simple argument will furnish the proof of this statement. What can it profit the soul if the body is well, free, and active, and eats, drinks, and does as it pleases? For in these respects even the most godless slaves of vice may prosper. On the other hand, how will poor health or imprisonment or hunger or thirst or any other external misfortune harm the soul?

One thing, and only one thing, is necessary for Christian life, righteousness, and freedom. That one thing is the most holy Word of God, the gospel of Christ, as Christ says, John 11 [:25], "I am the resurrection and the life; he who believes in me, though he die, yet shall he live"; and John 8 [:36], "So if the Son makes you free, you will be free indeed"; and Matt. 4 [:4], "Man shall not live by bread alone, but by every word that proceeds from the mouth of God." Let us then consider it certain and firmly established that the soul can do without anything except the Word of God and that where the Word of God is missing there is no help at all for the soul. If it has the Word of God it is rich and lacks nothing since it is the Word of life, truth, light, peace, righteousness, salvation, joy, liberty, wisdom, power, grace, glory, and of every incalculable blessing.

You may ask, "What then is the Word of God, and how shall it be used, since there are so many words of God?" I answer: The Apostle explains this in Romans 1. The Word is the gospel of God concerning his Son, who was made flesh, suffered, rose from the dead, and was glorified through the Spirit who sanctifies. Faith alone is the saving and efficacious use of the Word of God, according to Rom. 10 [:9]: "If you confess with your lips that Jesus is Lord and believe in your heart that God raised him from the dead, you will be saved." Furthermore, "Christ is the end of the law, that every one who has faith may be justified" [Rom. 10:4]. Again, in Rom. 1 [:17], "He who through faith is righteous shall live." The Word of God cannot be received and cherished by any works whatever but only by faith.

Therefore it is clear that, as the soul needs only the Word of God for its life and righteousness, so it is justified by faith alone and not any works; for if it could be justified by anything else, it would not need the Word, and consequently it would not need faith.

Should you ask how it happens that faith alone justifies and offers us such a treasure of great benefits without works in view of the fact that so many works, ceremonies, and laws are prescribed in the Scriptures, I answer: First of all, remember what has been said, namely, that faith alone, without works, justifies, frees, and saves; we shall make this clearer later on. Here we must point out that the entire Scripture of God is divided into two parts: commandments and promises. Although the commandments teach things that are good, the things taught are not done as soon as they are taught, for the commandments show us what we ought to do but do not give us the power to do it. They are intended to teach man to know himself, that through them he may recognize his inability to do good and may despair of his own ability. That is why they are called the Old Testament and constitute the Old Testament. For example, the commandment, "You shall not covet" [Exod. 20:17], is a command which proves us all to be sinners, for no one can avoid coveting no matter how much he may struggle against it. Therefore, in order not to covet and to fulfil the commandment, man is compelled to despair of himself, to seek the help which he does not find in himself elsewhere and from someone else, as stated in Hosea [13:9]: "Destruction is your own, O Israel: your help is only in me." As we fare with respect to one commandment, so we fare with all, for it is equally impossible for us to keep any one of them.

Now when a man has learned through the commandments to recognize his helplessness and is distressed about how he might satisfy the law—since the law must be fulfilled so that not a jot or tittle shall be lost, otherwise man will be condemned without hope—then, being truly humbled and reduced to nothing in his own eyes, he finds in himself nothing whereby he may be justified and saved. Here the second part of Scripture comes to our aid, namely, the promises of God which declare the glory of God, saying, "If you wish to fulfil the law and not covet, as the law demands, come, believe in Christ in whom grace, righteousness, peace, liberty, and all things are promised you. If you believe, you shall have all things; if you do not believe, you shall lack all things."

The following statements are therefore true: "Good works do not make a good man, but a good man does good works: evil works do not make a wicked man, but a wicked man does evil works." Consequently it is always necessary that the substance or person himself be good before there can be any good works, and that good works follow and proceed from the good person, as Christ also says, "A good tree cannot bear evil fruit, nor can a bad tree bear good fruit" [Matt. 7:18]. It is clear that the fruits do not bear the tree and that the tree does not grow the fruits, also that, on the contrary, the trees bear the fruits and the fruits grow on the trees. As it is necessary, therefore, that the trees exist before their fruits and the fruits do not make trees either good or bad, but rather as the trees are, so are the fruits they bear; so a man must first be good or wicked before he does a good or wicked work, and his works do not make him good or wicked, but he himself makes his works either good or wicked.

Illustrations of the same truth can be seen in all trades. A good or bad house does not make a good or a bad builder; but a good or a bad builder makes a good or a bad house. And in general, the work never makes the workman like itself, but the workman makes the work like himself. So it is with the works of man. As the man is, whether believer or unbeliever, so also is his work—good if it was done in faith, wicked if it was done in unbelief. But the converse is not true, that the work makes the man either a believer or an unbeliever. As works do not make a man a believer, so also they do not make him righteous. But as faith makes a man a believer and righteous, so faith does good works. Since, then, works justify no one, and a man must be righteous before he does a good work, it is very evident that it is faith alone which, because of the pure mercy of God through Christ and in his Word, worthily and sufficiently justifies and saves the person. A Christian has no need of any work or law in order to be saved since through faith he is free from every law and does everything out of pure liberty and freely. He seeks neither benefit nor salvation since he already abounds in all things and is saved through the grace of God because in his faith he now seeks only to please God.

So a Christian, like Christ his head, is filled and made rich by faith and should be content with this form of God which he has obtained by faith; only, as I have said, he should increase this faith until it is made perfect. For this faith is his life, his righteousness, and his salvation: it saves him and makes him acceptable, and bestows upon him all things that are Christ's, as has been said above, and as Paul asserts in Gal. 2 [:20] when he says, "And the life I now live in the flesh I live by faith in the Son of God." Although the Christian is thus free from all works, he ought in this liberty to empty himself, take upon himself the form of a servant, be made in the likeness of men, be found in human form, and to serve, help, and in every way deal with his neighbor as he sees that God through Christ has dealt and still deals with him. This he should do freely, having regard for nothing but divine approval.

He ought to think: "Although I am an unworthy and condemned man, my God has given me in Christ all the riches of righteousness and salvation without any merit on my part, out of pure, free mercy, so that from now on I need nothing except faith which believes that this is true. Why should I not therefore freely, joyfully, with all my heart, and with an eager will do all things which I know are pleasing and acceptable to such a Father who has overwhelmed me with his inestimable riches? I will therefore give myself as a Christ to my neighbor, just as Christ offered himself to me; I will do nothing in this life except what I see is necessary, profitable, and salutary to my neighbor, since through faith I have an abundance of all good things in Christ."

Behold, from faith thus flow forth love and joy in the Lord, and from love a joyful, willing, and free mind that serves one's neighbor willingly and takes no account of gratitude or ingratitude, of praise or blame, of gain or loss. For a man does not serve that he may put men under obligations. He does not distinguish between friends and enemies or anticipate their thankfulness or unthankfulness, but he most freely and most willingly spends himself and all that he has, whether he wastes all on the thankless or whether he gains a reward. As his Father does, distributing all things to all men richly and freely, making "his sun rise on the evil and on the good" [Matt. 5:45], so also the son does all things and suffers all things with that freely bestowing joy which is his delight when through Christ he sees it in God, the dispenser of such great benefits.

Therefore, if we recognize the great and precious things which are given us, as Paul says [Rom. 5:5], our hearts will be filled by the Holy Spirit with the love which makes us free, joyful, almighty workers and conquerors over all tribulations, servants of our neighbors, and yet lords of all. For those who do not recognize the gifts bestowed upon them through Christ, however, Christ has been born in vain; they go their way with their works and shall never come to taste or feel those things. Just as our neighbor is in need and lacks that in which we abound, so we were in need before God and lacked his mercy. Hence, as our heavenly Father has in Christ freely come to our aid, we also ought freely to help our neighbor through our body and it works, each one should become as it were a Christ to the other that we may be Christs to one another and Christ may be the same in all, that is, that we may be truly Christians.

Of Marriage and Celibacy

DCCXV

A preacher of the gospel, being regularly called, ought, above all things, first, to purify himself before he teaches others. Is he able, with a good conscience, to remain unmarried? let him so remain; but if he cannot abstain living chastely, then let him take a wife; God has made that plaster for that sore.

DCCXVI

It is written in the first book of Moses, concerning matrimony: God created a man and woman and blessed them. Now, although this sentence was chiefly spoken of human creatures, yet we may apply it to all the creatures of the world—to the fowls of the air, the fish in the waters, and the beasts of the field, wherein we find a male and a female consorting together, engendering and increasing. In all these, God has placed before our eyes the state of matrimony. We have its image, also, even in the trees and earth.

DCCXVII

Between husband and wife there should be no question as to *meum* and *tuum*. All things should be in common between them, without any distinction or means of distinguishing.

DCCXVIII

St. Augustine said, finely: A marriage without children is the world without the sun.

DCCXIX

Maternity is a glorious thing, since all mankind have been conceived, born, and nourished of women. All human laws should encourage the multiplication of families.

DCCXX

The world regards not, nor comprehends the works of God. Who can sufficiently admire the state of conjugal union, which God has instituted and founded, and whence all human creatures, yea, all states proceed. Where were we, if it existed not? But neither God's ordinance, nor the gracious presence of children, the fruit of matrimony, moves the ungodly world, which beholds only the temporal difficulties and troubles of matrimony, but sees not the great treasure that is hid therein. We were all born of women—emperors, kings, princes, yea, Christ himself, the Son of God, did not disdain to be born of a virgin. Let the contemners and rejecters of matrimony go hang, the Anabaptists and Adamites, who recognise not marriage, but live all together like animals, and the papists, who reject married life, and yet have strumpets; if they must needs contemn matrimony, let them be consistent and keep no concubines.

DCCXXI

The state of matrimony is the chief in the world after religion: but people shun it because of its inconveniences, like one who, running out of the rain, falls into the river. We ought herein to have more regard to God's command and ordinance, for the sake of the generation, and the bringing up of children, than to our untoward humours and cogitations; and further, we should consider that it is a physic against sin and unchastity. None indeed, should be compelled to marry; the matter should be left to each man's conscience, for bride-love may not be forced. God has said, "It is not good that the man should be alone;" and St. Paul compares the church to a spouse, or bride and a bridegroom. But let us ever take heed that, in marrying, we esteem neither money nor wealth, great descent, nobility, nor lasciviousness.

DCCXXII

The Lord has never changed the rules he imposed on marriage, but in the case of the conception of his Son Jesus Christ. The Turks, however, are of opinion that 'tis no uncommon thing for a virgin to bear a child. I would by no means introduce this belief into my family.

DCCXXV

Men have broad and large chests, and small narrow hips, and more understanding than the women, who have but small and narrow breasts, and broad hips, to the end they should remain at home, sit still, keep house, and bear and bring up children.

DCCXXVI

Marrying cannot be without women, nor can the world subsist without them. To marry is physic against incontinence. A woman is, or at least should be, a friendly, courteous, and merry companion in life, whence they are named, by the Holy Ghost, house-honours, the honour and ornament of the house, and inclined to tenderness, for thereunto are they chiefly created, to bear children, and be the pleasure, joy, and solace of their husbands.

DCCXXVII

Dr. Luther said one day to his wife: You make me do what you will; you have full sovereignty here, and I award you, with all my heart, the command in all household matters, reserving my rights in other points. Never any good came out of female domination. God created Adam master and lord of living creatures, but Eve spoilt all, when she persuaded him to set himself above God's will. 'Tis you women, with your tricks and artifices, that lead men into error.

Study Questions

1. What role does faith play in Luther's thought?

2. How important is the "Word of God?" What is it, according to Luther?

3. Luther believes that faith offers more hope for salvation than good works. Why is this?

4. *On Marriage* is composed of words spoken by Luther, taken down by his followers. How does this make it different from *The Freedom of a Christian*?

5. Why does Luther think clergy should be allowed to marry?

6. Why is matrimony important?

7. What is Luther's view of women? What does he see as their role in marriage, and how does he think they should be treated?

8. Luther spent most of his early adulthood as a celibate monk. How do you think this might have affected his views of marriage?

Institutes of the Christian Religion (1534)   **79**

JOHN CALVIN

John Calvin (1509–1564) was the seminal thinker among the post-Luther generation of religious reformers. French by birth and a lawyer by training, Calvin found
himself the leader of the Reformation in the Swiss city of Geneva. There he helped
establish a new form of church government that depended not upon a hierarchy of
priests and bishops as in the Catholic church but instead gave power to individual
congregations of believers. Calvin's principal theological contribution was to
emphasize the doctrine of predestination as the foundation of individual salvation.

The *Institutes of the Christian Religion* was first written for the purpose of gaining acceptance for Protestantism in France. Through successive editions, Calvin
expanded and refined his theology.

Knowledge of God Involves Trust and Reverence

What is God? Men who pose this question are
merely toying with idle speculations. It is far
better for us to inquire, "What is his nature?"
and to know what is consistent with his nature.
What good is it to profess with Epicurus some
sort of God who has cast aside the care of the
world only to amuse himself in idleness? What
help is it, in short, to know a God with whom
we have nothing to do? Rather, our knowledge
should serve first to teach us fear and reverence; secondly, with it as our guide and teacher,
we should learn to seek every good from him,
and having received it, to credit it to his
account. For how can the thought of God penetrate your mind without your realizing immediately that, since you are his handiwork, you
have been made over and bound to his command by right of creation, that you owe your
life to him?—that whatever you undertake,
whatever you do, ought to be ascribed to him?
If this be so, it now assuredly follows that your
life is wickedly corrupt unless it be disposed to

his service, seeing that his will ought for us to
be the law by which we live. Again, you cannot
behold him clearly unless you acknowledge him
to be the fountainhead and source of every
good. From this too would arise the desire to
cleave to him and trust in him, but for the fact
that man's depravity seduces his mind from
rightly seeking him.

Because it acknowledges him as Lord and
Father, the pious mind also deems it meet and
right to observe his authority in all things, reverence his majesty, take care to advance his
glory, and obey his commandments. Because it
sees him to be a righteous judge, armed with
severity to punish wickedness, it ever holds his
judgment seat before its gaze, and through fear
of him restrains itself from provoking his anger.
And yet it is not so terrified by the awareness of
his judgment as to wish to withdraw, even if
some way of escape were open. But it embraces
him no less as punisher of the wicked than as
benefactor of the pious. For the pious mind
realizes that the punishment of the impious
and wicked and the reward of life eternal for
the righteous equally pertain to God's glory.

John Calvin. After a conversion experience, John Calvin abandoned his life as a humanist and became a reformer. In 1536, Calvin began working to reform the city of Geneva, where he remained until his death in 1564. This sixteenth-century portrait of Calvin pictures him near the end of his life.

veneration for God, but very few really reverence him; and wherever there is great ostentation in ceremonies, sincerity of heart is rare indeed.

Superstition

Experience teaches that the seed of religion has been divinely planted in all men. But barely one man in a hundred can be found who nourishes in his own heart what he has conceived; and not even one in whom it matures, much less bears fruit in its season (cf. Ps. 1:3). Now some lose themselves in their own superstition, while others of their own evil intention revolt from God, yet all fall away from true knowledge of him. As a result, no real piety remains in the world. But as to my statement that some erroneously slip into superstition, I do not mean by this that their ingenuousness should free them from blame. For the blindness under which they labor is almost always mixed with proud vanity and obstinacy. Indeed, vanity joined with pride can be detected in the fact that, in seeking God, miserable men do not rise above themselves as they should, but measure him by the yardstick of their own carnel stupidity, and neglect sound investigation; thus out of curiosity they fly off into empty speculations. They do not therefore apprehend God as he offers himself, but imagine him as they have fashioned him in their own presumption. When this gulf opens, in whatever direction they move their feet, they cannot but plunge headlong into ruin. Indeed, whatever they afterward attempt by way of worship or service of God, they cannot bring as tribute to him, for they are worshiping not God but a figment and a dream of their own heart. Paul eloquently notes this wickedness: "Striving to be wise, they make fools of themselves" (Rom. 1:22f.). He had said before that "they became futile in their thinking" (Rom. 1:21). In order, however, that no one might excuse their guilt, he

Besides, this mind restrains itself from sinning, not out of dread of punishment alone; but, because it loves and reveres God as Father, it worships and adores him as Lord. Even if there were no hell, it would still shudder at offending him alone.

Here indeed is pure and real religion; faith so joined with an earnest fear of God that this fear also embraces willing reverence, and carries with it such legitimate worship as is prescribed in the law. And we ought to note this fact even more diligently: all men have a vague general adds that they are justly blinded. For not content with sobriety but claiming for themselves more than is right, they wantonly bring darkness upon themselves—in fact, they become fools in their empty and perverse haughtiness. From this it follows that their stupidity is not excusable, since it is caused not only by vain curiosity but by an inordinate desire to know more than is fitting, joined with a false confidence.

The Divine Wisdom Displayed for all to See

There are innumerable evidences both in heaven and on earth that declare his wonderful wisdom; not only those more recondite matters for the closer observation of which astronomy, medicine, and all natural science are intended, but also those which thrust themselves upon the sight of even the most untutored and ignorant persons, so that they cannot open their eyes without being compelled to witness them. Indeed, men who have either quaffed or even tasted the liberal arts penetrate with their aid far more deeply into the secrets of the divine wisdom. Yet ignorance of them prevents no one from seeing more than enough of God's workmanship in his creation to lead him to break forth in admiration of the Artificer. To be sure, there is need of art and of more exacting toil in order to investigate the motion of the stars, to determine their assigned stations, to measure their intervals, to note their properties. As God's providence shows itself more explicitly when one observes these, so the mind must rise to a somewhat higher level to look upon his glory. Even the common folk and the most untutored, who have been taught only by the aid of the eyes, cannot be unaware of the excellence of divine art, for it reveals itself in this innumerable and yet distinct and well-ordered variety of the heavenly host. It is, accordingly, clear that there is no one to whom the Lord does not abundantly show

his wisdom. Likewise, in regard to the structure of the human body one must have the greatest keenness in order to weigh, with Galen's skill, its articulation, symmetry, beauty, and use. But yet, as all acknowledge, the human body shows itself to be a composition so ingenious that its Artificer is rightly judged a wonder-worker.

Man as the Loftiest Proof of Divine Wisdom

Certain philosophers, accordingly, long ago not ineptly called a man a microcosm because he is a rare example of God's power, goodness, and wisdom, and contains within himself enough miracles to occupy our minds, if only we are not irked at paying attention to them. Paul, having stated that the blind can find God by feeling after him, immediately adds that he ought not to be sought afar off (Acts 17:27). For each one undoubtedly feels within the heavenly grace that quickens him. Indeed, if there is no need to go outside ourselves to comprehend God, what pardon will the indolence of that man deserve who is loath to descend within himself to find God? For the same reason, David, when he has briefly praised the admirable name and glory of God, which shine everywhere, immediately exclaims: "What is man that thou art mindful of him?" (Ps. 8:4). Likewise, "Out of the mouths of babes and sucklings thou hast established strength" (Ps. 8:2). Indeed, he not only declares that a clear mirror of God's works is in humankind, but that infants, while they nurse at their mother's breasts, have tongues so eloquent to preach his glory that there is no need at all of other orators. Consequently, also, he does not hesitate to bring their infant speech into the debate, as if they were thoroughly instructed, to refute the madness of those who might desire to extinguish God's name in favor of their own devilish pride. Consequently, too, there comes in that which Paul quotes from Aratus, that we are God's offspring (Acts 17:28), because by adorning us with such great excellence he testifies that he is our Father. In the same way the secular poets, out of a common feeling and, as it were, at the dictation of experience, called him "the Father of men." Indeed, no one gives himself freely and willingly to God's service unless, having tasted his fatherly love, he is drawn to love and worship him in return.

God Bestows the Actual Knowledge of Himself Upon Us Only in the Scriptures

That brightness which is borne in upon the eyes of all men both in heaven and on earth is more than enough to withdraw all support from men's ingratitude—just as God, to involve the human race in the same guilt, sets forth to all without exception his presence portrayed in his creatures. Despite this, it is needful that another and better help be added to direct us aright to the very Creator of the universe. It was not in vain, then, that he added the light of his Word by which to become known unto salvation; and he regarded as worthy of this privilege those whom he pleased to gather more closely and intimately to himself. For because he saw the minds of all men tossed and agitated, after he chose the Jews as his very own flock, he fenced them about that they might not sink into oblivion as others had. With good reason he holds us by the same means in the pure knowledge of himself, since otherwise even those who seem to stand firm before all others would soon melt away. Just as old or bleary-eyed men and those with weak vision, if you thrust before them a most beautiful volume, even if they recognize it to be some sort of writing, yet can scarcely construe two words, but with the aid of spectacles will begin to read distinctly; so Scripture, gathering up the otherwise confused knowledge of God in our minds, having dispersed our dullness, clearly shows us the true God.

The Word of God as Holy Scripture

But whether God became known to the patriarchs through oracles and visions or by the work and ministry of men, he put into their minds what they should then hand down to their posterity. At any rate, there is no doubt that firm certainty of doctrine was engraved in their hearts, so that they were convinced and understood that what they had learned proceeded from God. For by his Word, God rendered faith unambiguous forever, a faith that should be superior to all opinion. Finally, in order that truth might abide forever in the world with a continuing succession of teaching and survive through all ages, the same oracles he had given to the patriarchs it was his pleasure to have recorded, as it were, on public tablets. With this intent the law was published, and the prophets afterward added as its interpreters. For even though the use of the law was manifold, as will be seen more clearly in its place, it was especially committed to Moses and all the prophets to teach the way of reconcilation between God and men, whence also Paul calls "Christ the end of the law" (Rom. 10:4). Yet I repeat once more: besides the specific doctrine of faith and repentance that sets forth Christ as Mediator, Scripture adorns with unmistakable marks and tokens the one true God, in that he has created and governs the universe, in order that he may not be mixed up with the throng of false gods. Therefore, however fitting it may be for man seriously to turn his eyes to contemplate God's works, since he has been placed in this most glorious theater to be a spectator of them, it is fitting that he prick up his ears to the Word, the better to profit. And it is therefore no wonder that those who were born in darkness become more and more hardened in their insensibility; for there are very few who, to contain themselves within bounds, apply themselves teachably to God's Word, but they rather exult in their own vanity. Now, in order that true religion may shine upon us, we ought to hold that it must take its beginning from heavenly doctrine and that no one can get even the slightest taste of right and sound doctrine unless he be a pupil of Scripture. Hence, there also emerges the beginning of true understanding when we reverently embrace what it pleases God there to witness of himself. But not only faith, perfect and in every way complete, but all right knowledge of God is born of obedience. And surely in this respect God has, by his singular providence, taken thought for mortals through all ages.

Faith Rests Upon God's Word

This, then, is the true knowledge of Christ, if we receive him as he is offered by the Father: namely, clothed with his gospel. For just as he has been appointed as the goal of our faith, so we cannot take the right road to him unless the gospel goes before us. And there, surely, the treasures of grace are opened to us; for if they had been closed, Christ would have benefited us little. Thus Paul yokes faith to teaching, as an inseparable companion, with these words: "You did not so learn Christ if indeed you were taught what is the truth in Christ" (Eph. 4:20–21 p.)

Yet I do not so restrict faith to the gospel without confessing that what sufficed for building it up had been handed down by Moses and the prophets. But because a fuller manifestation of Christ has been revealed in the gospel, Paul justly calls it the "doctrine of faith" (cf. I Tim. 4:6). For this reason, he says in another passage that by the coming of faith the law was abolished (Rom. 10:4; cf. Gal. 3:25). He understands by this term the new and extraordinary kind of teaching by which Christ, after he became our teacher, has more clearly set forth the mercy of the Father, and has more surely testified to our salvation.

Yet it will be an easier and more suitable method if we descend by degrees from general to particular. First, we must be reminded that there is a permanent relationship between faith and the Word. He could not separate one from the other any more than we could separate the rays from the sun from which they come. For this reason, God exclaims in The Book of Isaiah: "Hear me and your soul shall live" (ch 55:3). And John shows this same wellspring of faith in these words: "These things have been written that you may believe" (John 20:31). The prophet, also, desiring to exhort the people to faith, says: "Today if you will hear his voice" (Ps. 95:7; 94:8, Vg.). "To hear" is generally understood as meaning to believe. In short, it is not without reason that in The Book of Isaiah, God distinguishes the children of the church from outsiders by this mark: he will teach all his children (Isa. 54:13; John 6:45) that they may learn of him (cf. John 6:45). For if benefits were indiscriminately given, why would he have directed his Word to a few? To this corresponds the fact that the Evangelists commonly use the words "believers" and "disciples" as synonyms. This is especially Luke's usage in The Acts of the Apostles: indeed he extends this title even to a woman in Acts 9:36.

Therefore if faith turns away even in the slightest degree from this goal toward which it should aim, it does not keep its own nature, but becomes uncertain credulity and vague error of mind. The same Word is the basis whereby faith is supported and sustained; if it turns away from the Word, it falls. Therefore, take away the Word and no faith will then remain.

We are not here discussing whether a human ministry is necessary for the sowing of God's Word, from which faith may be conceived. This we shall discuss in another place. But we say that the Word itself, however it be imparted to us, is like a mirror in which faith may contemplate God. Whether, therefore, God makes use of man's help in this or works by his own power alone, he always represents himself through his Word to those whom he wills to draw to himself. And for this reason, Paul defines faith as that obedience which is given to the gospel (Rom. 1:5), and elsewhere praises allegiance to faith in Philippians (Phil. 1:3–5; cf. I Thess. 2:13). In understanding faith it is not merely a question of knowing that God exists, but also—and this especially— of knowing what is his will toward us. For it is not so much our concern to know who he is in himself, as what he wills to be toward us.

Now, therefore, we hold faith to be a knowledge of God's will toward us, perceived from his Word. But the foundation of this is a preconceived conviction of God's truth. As for its certainty, so long as your mind is at war with itself, the Word will be of doubtful and weak authority, or rather of none. And it is not even enough to believe that God is trustworthy (cf. Rom. 3:3), who can neither deceive nor lie (cf. Titus 1:2), unless you hold to be beyond doubt that whatever proceeds from him is sacred and inviolable truth.

Study Questions

1. What seems to be Calvin's view of human nature?

2. How, according to Calvin, does God reveal himself?

3. Historians have often noted the importance of Scripture in Protestant thought. What is Calvin's view? What do you think the practical effect of this might have been for society?

4. How does Calvin's background as a lawyer and literate member of the professional class affect his work?

5. Both Calvin and Luther are Protestants, but they have very different theological views. Can you detect some of these differences in their writings?

The Life of St. Teresa (1611)   80

TERESA OF AVILA

One of the most remarkable women of her age, Teresa de Cepeda (1515–1582) was born at Avila into a prosperous Spanish family. From childhood she was extremely pious and believed that she had been singled out for some special service to the Lord. Over the objections of her father, she entered a Carmelite convent at the age of 21. There she undertook a rigorous spiritual regimen that ultimately broke her health. During this period she had visions that convinced her that her mission was to travel throughout Spain founding new monasteries and convents. Against the objections of leaders of her order, Teresa followed this spiritual guidance. A prolific author of devotional works, she was widely revered during her lifetime, and canonized as Saint Teresa of Avila in 1622.

In her autobiography, which was published after her death, Teresa describes her intensely personal and mystical relationship with God. Her writings had a profound impact upon ordinary men and women who identified with the new spiritual rebirth of Spanish Catholicism.

I was one day in prayer, when I found myself in a moment, without knowing how, plunged apparently into hell. I understood that it was our Lord's will I should see the place which the devils kept in readiness for me, and which I had deserved by my sins. It was but a moment, but it seems to me impossible I should ever forget it even if I were to live many years.

The entrance seemed to be by a long and narrow pass, like a furnace, very low, dark, and close. The ground seemed to be saturated with water, mere mud, exceedingly foul, sending forth pestilential odours, and covered with loathsome vermin. At the end was a hollow place in the wall, like a closet, and in that I saw myself confined. All this was even pleasant to behold in comparison with what I felt there. There is no exaggeration in what I am saying.

But as to what I then felt, I do not know where to begin, if I were to describe it; it is utterly inexplicable. I felt a fire in my soul. I cannot see how it is possible to describe it. My bodily sufferings were unendurable. I have undergone most painful sufferings in this life, and, as the physicians say, the greatest that can be borne, such as the contraction of my sinews when I was paralysed, without speaking of others of different kinds, yea, even those of which I have also spoken, inflicted on me by Satan; yet all these were as nothing in comparison with what I felt then, especially when I saw that there would be no intermission, nor any end to them.

These sufferings were nothing in comparison with the anguish of my soul, a sense of oppression, of stifling, and of pain so keen, accompanied by so hopeless and cruel an inflic-tion, that I know not how to speak of it. If I said that the soul is continually being torn from the body, it would be nothing, for that implies the destruction of life by the hands of another; but here it is the soul itself that is tearing itself in pieces. I cannot describe that inward fire or that despair, surpassing all torments and all pain. I did not see who it was that tormented me, but I felt myself on fire, and torn to pieces, as it seemed to me; and, I repeat it, this inward fire and despair are the greatest torments of all.

Left in that pestilential place, and utterly without the power to hope for comfort, I could neither sit nor lie down; there was no room. I was placed as it were in a hole in the wall; and those walls, terrible to look on of themselves, hemmed me in on every side. I could not breathe. There was no light, but all was thick darkness. I do not understand how it is; though there was no light, yet everything that can give pain by being seen was visible.

I know not how it was, but I understood dis-tinctly that it was a great mercy that our Lord would have me see with mine own eyes the very place from which His compassion saved me. I have listened to people speaking of these things, and I have at other times dwelt on the various torments of hell, though not often, because my soul made no progress by the way of fear; and I have read of the divers tortures, and how the devils tear the flesh with red-hot pincers. But all is as nothing before this; it is a wholly different matter. In short, the one is a reality, the other a picture; and all burning here in this life is as nothing in comparison with the fire that is there.

Ever since that time, as I was saying, everything seems endurable in comparison with one instant of sufferings such as those I had then to bear in hell. I am filled with fear when I see that, after frequently reading books which describe in some manner the pains of hell, I was not afraid of them, nor made any account of them. Where was I? How could I possibly take any pleasure in those things which led me directly to so dreadful a place? Blessed forever be Thou, O my God! and oh, how manifest is it that Thou didst love me much more than I did love Thee! How, often, O Lord, didst Thou save me from that fearful prison! and how I used to get back to it contrary to Thy will!

It was that vision that filled me with the very great distress which I feel at the sight of so many lost souls, especially of the Lutherans—for they were once members of the Church by baptism—and also gave me the most vehement desires for the salvation of souls; for certainly I believe that, to save even one from those overwhelming torments, I would most willingly endure many deaths. If here on earth we see one whom we specially love in great trouble or pain, our very nature seems to bid us compassionate him; and if those pains be great, we are troubled ourselves. What, then, must it be to see a soul in danger of pain, the most grievous of all pains, forever? Who can endure it? It is a thought no heart can bear without great anguish. Here we know that pain ends with life at last, and that there are limits to it; yet the sight of it moves our compassion so greatly. That other pain has no ending; and I know not how we can be calm, when we see Satan carry so many souls daily away.

The Effects of the Divine Graces in the Soul—The Inestimable Greatness of One Degree of Glory

It is painful to me to recount more of the graces which our Lord gave me than these already spoken of; and they are so many, that nobody can believe they were ever given to one so wicked: but in obedience to our Lord, who has commanded me to do it, and you, my fathers, I will speak of some of them to His glory. May it please His Majesty it may be to the profit of some soul! For if our Lord has been thus gracious to so miserable a thing as myself, what will He be to those who shall serve Him truly? Let all people resolve to please His Majesty, seeing that He gives such pledges as these even in this life.

My love of, and trust in, our Lord, after I had seen Him in a vision, began to grow, for my converse with Him was so continual. I saw that, though He was God, He was man also; that He is not surprised at the frailties of men; that He understands our miserable nature, liable to fall continually, because of the first sin, for the reparation of which He had come. I could speak to Him as a friend, though He is my Lord, because I do not consider Him as one of our earthly lords, who affect a power they do not possess, who give audience at fixed hours, and to whom only certain persons may speak. If a poor man have any business with these, it will cost him many goings and comings, and currying favour with others, together with much pain and labour before he can speak to them. Ah, if such a one has business with a king! Poor people, not of gentle blood, cannot approach him, for they must apply to those who are his friends; and certainly these are not persons who tread the world under their feet; for they who do this speak the truth, fear nothing, and ought to fear nothing; they are not courtiers, because it is not the custom of a court, where they must be silent about those things they dislike, must not even dare to think about them, lest they should fall into disgrace.

O my Lord! O my King! who can describe Thy Majesty? It is impossible not to see that Thou art Thyself the great Ruler of all, that the beholding of Thy Majesty fills men with awe.

But I am filled with greater awe, O my Lord, when I consider Thy humility, and the love Thou hast for such as I am. We can converse and speak with Thee about everything whenever we will; and when we lose our first fear and awe at the vision of Thy Majesty, we have a greater dread of offending Thee—not arising out of the fear of punishment, O my Lord, for that is as nothing in comparison with the loss of Thee!

I am not yet fifty, and yet I have seen so many changes during my life, that I do not know how to live. What will they do who are only just born, and who may live many years? Certainly I am sorry for those spiritual people who, for certain holy purposes, are obliged to live in the world; the cross they have to carry is a dreadful one.

Certain Heavenly Secrets, Visions, and Revelations

One night I was so unwell that I thought I might be excused making my prayer; so I took my rosary, that I might employ myself in vocal prayer, trying not to be recollected in my understanding, though outwardly I was recollected, being in my oratory. These little precautions are of no use when our Lord will have it otherwise. I remained there but a few moments thus, when I was rapt in spirit with such violence that I could make no resistance whatever. It seemed to me that I was taken up to heaven; and the first persons I saw there were my father and my mother. I saw other things also; but the time was no longer than that in which the *Ave Maria* might be said, and I was amazed at it, looking on it all as too great a grace for me. But as to the shortness of the time, it might have been longer, only it was all done in a very short space.

It happened, also, as time went on, and it happens now from time to time, that our Lord showed me still greater secrets. The soul, even if it would, has neither the means nor the power to see more than what He shows it; and so, each time, I saw nothing more than what our Lord was pleased to let me see. But such was the vision, that the least part of it was enough to make my soul amazed, and to raise it so high that it esteems and counts as nothing all the things of this life. I wish I could describe in some measure, the smallest portion of what I saw; but when I think of doing it, I find it impossible; for the mere difference alone between the light we have here below, and that which is seen in a vision—both being light—is so great, that there is no comparison between them; the brightness of the sun itself seems to be something exceedingly loathsome. In a word, the imagination, however strong it may be, can neither conceive nor picture to itself this light, nor any one of the things which our Lord showed me in a joy so supreme that it cannot be described; for then all the senses exult so deeply and so sweetly, that no description is possible.

I was in this state once for more than an hour, our Lord showing me wonderful things. He seemed as if He would not leave me. He said to me: "See, My daughter, what they lose who are against Me; do not fail to tell them of it." Ah, my Lord, how little good my words will do them, who are made blind by their own conduct, if Thy Majesty will not give them light! Some, to whom Thou hast given it, there are, who have profited by the knowledge of Thy greatness; but as they see it revealed to one so wicked and base as I am, I look upon it as a great thing if there should be any found to believe me. Blessed be Thy name, and blessed be Thy compassion; for I can trace, at least in my own soul, a visible improvement. Afterwards I wished I had continued in that trance for ever, and that I had not returned to consciousness.

Study Questions

1. How does Teresa's gender affect her account of her life? Can you note any differences from male religious writers of the period?

2. What, according to Teresa's vision, was hell like?

3. What sort of relationship did Teresa have with God?

4. Judging from Teresa's work, what sort of generalizations might you make about contemporary views of heaven and hell?

5. Why do you think Teresa wrote about her experiences? How do you think society responded to her?

European Politics and War

Palace of Versailles. Louis XIV spent untold sums of money in the construction of a new royal residence at Versailles. The enormous palace of Versailles also housed the members of the king's government and served as home for thousands of French nobles. As the largest royal residence in Europe, Versailles impressed foreigners and became a source of envy for other rulers.

The Edict of Nantes (1598)   **81**

HENRY IV

Henry IV was the Protestant king of Navarre (1589–1610) who led the Huguenot cause during the French wars of religion. His grandmother was Marguerite de Navarre and his mother Jeanne d'Albret, both educated and remarkably talented women. Henry achieved the French throne through a series of accidents, the last of which was the assassination of Henry III in 1589. It was clear that no Protestant could ever command the allegiance of the mass of French people or peacefully rule in the Catholic capital of Paris. Henry converted to Catholicism, defeated his enemies, and ended the long years of religious warfare.

The Edict of Nantes was the compromise settlement that granted limited toleration for the Huguenots. It was a landmark in the history of religious toleration, although its main features were watered down under Louis XIII. The *Edict* was finally rescinded under Louis XIV in 1685.

Henry, by the grace of God king of France and of Navarre, to all to whom these presents come, greeting: Among the infinite benefits which it has pleased God to heap upon us, the most signal and precious is his granting us the strength and ability to withstand the fearful disorders and troubles which prevailed on our advent in this kingdom. The realm was so torn by innumerable factions and sects that the most legitimate of all the parties was fewest in numbers. God has given us strength to stand out against this storm; we have finally surmounted the waves and made our port of safety—peace for our state. For which his be the glory all in all, and ours a free recognition of his grace in making use of our instrumentality in the good work.... We explore and await from the Divine Goodness the same protection and favor which he has ever granted to this kingdom from the beginning....

We have, by this perpetual and irrevocable edict, established and proclaimed and do establish and proclaim:

First, that the recollection of everything done by one party or the other between March, 1585, and our accession to the crown, and during all the preceding period of troubles, remain obliterated and forgotten, as if no such things had ever happened.

We ordain that the Catholic Apostolic and Roman religion shall be restored and reestablished in all places and localities of this our kingdom and countries subject to our sway, where the exercise of the same has been interrupted, in order that it may be peaceably and freely exercised, without any trouble or hindrance; for bidding very expressly all persons, of whatsoever estate, quality, or condition, from troubling, molesting, or disturbing ecclesiastics in the celebration of divine service, in the enjoyment or collection of tithes, fruits, or revenues of their benefices, and all other rights and dues belonging to them; and that all those who during the troubles have taken possession of churches, houses, goods or revenues, belonging to the said ecclesiastics, shall surrender to them entire possession and peaceable enjoyment of such rights, liberties, and sureties as they had before they were deprived of them.

And in order to leave no occasion for troubles or differences between our subjects, we have permitted, and herewith permit, those of the said religion called Reformed to live and abide in all the cities and places of this our kingdom and countries of our sway, without being annoyed, molested, or completed to do anything in the matter of religion contrary to their consciences ... upon condition that they comport themselves in other respects according to that which is contained in this our present edict.

It is permitted to all lords, gentlemen, and other persons making profession of the said religion called Reformed, holding the right of high justice [or a certain feudal tenure], to exercise the said religion in their houses.

We also permit those of the said religion to make and continue the exercise of the same in all villages and places of our dominion where it was established by them and publicly enjoyed several and divers times in the year 1597, up to the end of the month of August, notwithstanding all decrees and judgments to the contrary.

We very expressly forbid to all those of the said religion its exercise, either in respect to ministry, regulation, discipline, or the public instruction of children, or otherwise, in this our kingdom and lands of our dominion, otherwise then in the places permitted and granted by the present edict.

It is forbidden as well to perform any function of the said religion in our court or retinue, or in our lands and territories beyond the mountains, or in our city of Paris, or within five leagues of the said city.

We also forbid all our subjects, of whatever quality and condition, from carrying off by force of persuasion, against the will of their parents, the children of the said religion, in order to cause them to be baptized or confirmed in the Catholic Apostolic and Roman Church; and the same is forbidden to those of the said religion called Reformed, upon penalty of being punished with especial severity.

Books concerning the said religion called Reformed may not be printed and publicly sold, except in cities and places where the public exercise of the said religion is permitted.

We ordain that there shall be no difference or distinction made in respect to the said religion, in receiving pupils to be instructed in universities, colleges, and schools; nor in receiving the sick and poor into hospitals, retreats and public charities.

Those of the said religion called Reformed shall be obliged to respect the laws of the Catholic Apostolic and Roman Church, recognized in this our kingdom, for the consummation of marriages contracted, or to be contracted, as regards the degrees of consanguinity and kinship.

Study Questions

1. Does Henry IV grant complete liberty of conscience in his edict? If not, how is freedom of religion restricted?

2. What is the position of the Catholic Church under the edict?

3. *The Edict of Nantes* is often seen as a step toward religious toleration. How tolerant is it?

4. Although the edict helped restore order to France, many people argued that it created more problems than it solved. Can you think what some of these might have been?

5. The edict was a declaration made by the king alone, without the advice or assistance of any other governmental institution. What does it reveal about the power of the monarch? About the king's role in religious affairs?

The Political Testament (1638)   **82**

CARDINAL RICHELIEU

Armand-Jean du Plessis, Cardinal and Duke Richelieu (1585–1642), was the son of a minor official of the French court. He was trained for church service and made his mark as a delegate to the Estates-General of 1614. He was brought into the service of Louis XIII by the Queen Regent, Marie de Medici, and eventually became the king's favorite and chief advisor. An able diplomat and a master politician, Richelieu played an important role in the consolidation of the royal state. His principal goal was to centralize administration and to harness the power of the nobility and localities. He was chiefly responsible for French foreign policy, including France's participation in the Thirty Years' War.

Written for the instruction of Louis XIII, Richelieu's *Political Testament* contains the cardinal's assessment of his own achievements. It was composed over the course of several years, with the last events mentioned dating from 1638. It was not published for another half-century, and then only in a pirated Dutch edition.

When Your Majesty resolved to admit me both to your council and to an important place in your confidence for the direction of your affairs, I may say that the Huguenots shared the state with you; that the nobles conducted themselves as if they were not your subjects, and the most powerful governors of the provinces as if they were sovereign in their offices.

I may say that the bad example of all of these was so prejudicial to the welfare of this realm that even the best courts were affected by it, and endeavored, in certain cases, to diminish your legitimate authority as far as it was possible in order to carry their own powers beyond the limits of reason.

I may say that everyone measured his own merit by his audacity; that in place of esteeming the benefits which they received from Your Majesty at their proper worth, they all valued them only as they satisfied the demands of their imaginations; that the most scheming were held to be the wisest, and often found themselves the most prosperous.

In broadest outline, Sire, these have been the matters with which Your Majesty's reign has thus far been concerned. I would consider them most happily concluded if they were followed by an era of repose during which you could introduce into your realm a wealth of benefits of all types. In order to present the problem to you, it is necessary to look into the nature of the various classes in your realm and the state which it comprises, together with your own role, both as a private and a public person. In sum, what will be indicated is the need for a competent and faithful council, whose advice should be listened to and followed in governing the state. It is to the detailed explanation and urging of this that the remainder of my testament will be devoted.

While the nobility merits to be generously treated if it does well, it is necessary at the same time to be severe with it if it ever fails in what its status demands of it. I do not hesitate to say that those nobles who, degenerating from the virtuous conduct of their forebears, fail to serve the crown constantly and courageously with both their swords and their lives, as the laws of the state require, deserve the loss of the privileges of their birth and should be reduced to sharing the burdens of the common people. Since honor should be more dear to them than life itself, it would be much more of a punishment to them to be deprived of the former than the latter.

All students of politics agree that when the common people are too well off it is impossible to keep them peaceable. The explanation for this is that they are less well informed than the members of the other orders in the state, who are much more cultivated and enlightened, and so if not preoccupied with the search for the necessities of existence, find it difficult to remain within the limits imposed by both common sense and the law.

It would not be sound to relieve them of all taxation and similar charges, since in such a case they would lose the mark of their subjection and consequently the awareness of their station. Thus being free from paying tribute, they would consider themselves exempted from obedience. One should compare them with mules, which being accustomed to work, suffer more when long idle than when kept busy. But just as this work should be reasonable, with the burdens placed upon these animals proportionate to their strength, so it is likewise with the burdens placed upon the people. If they are not moderate, even when put to good public use, they are certainly unjust. I realize that when a king undertakes a program of public works it is correct to say that what the people gain from it is returned by paying the taille. In the same fashion it can be maintained that what a king takes from the people returns to them, and that

they advance it to him only to draw upon it for the enjoyment of their leisure and their investments, which would be impossible if they did not contribute to the support of the state.

I also know that many princes have lost their countries and ruined their subjects by failing to maintain sufficient military forces for their protection, fearing to tax them too heavily. Some people have even fallen into slavery under their enemies because they have wanted too much liberty under their natural sovereign. There is, however, a certain level which one cannot exceed without injustice, common sense indicating in each instance the proportion which should prevail between the burden and the ability of those who sustain it. This consideration ought always to be religiously observed, although a prince cannot be esteemed good just because he taxes his subjects no more than necessary, nor considered evil because occasionally he takes more.

Also, just as when a man is wounded, his heart, weakened by the loss of blood, draws upon the reserves of the lower parts of the body only after the upper parts are exhausted, so in moments of great public need the king should, in so far as he is able, make use of the abundance of the rich before bleeding the poor heavily. This is the best advice Your Majesty can follow, and it is easy to put into practice since in the future you will draw the principal income for your state from the general tax farms, which are much closer to the interests of the rich than of the poor, since the latter, spending less, contribute less to the total.

The public interest ought to be the sole objective of the prince and his councillors, or, at the least, both are obliged to have it foremost in mind, and preferred to all private gain. It is impossible to overestimate the good which a prince and those serving him in government can do if they religiously follow this principle, and one can hardly imagine the evils which befall a state if private interest is preferred to the public good and actually gains the ascendancy. True philosophy, as well as the precepts of both Christianity and sound politics, teach this truth so clearly that a prince's councillors can hardly too often remind him of so necessary a principle, nor the prince punish too severely those members of his council despicable enough not to practice it.

Princes ordinarily easily consent to the overall plans proposed for their states because in so doing they have nothing in mind save reason and justice, which they easily accept when they meet no obstacle which turns them off the path. When the occasion arises, however, of putting into practical action the wise programs they have adopted, they do not always show the same firmness. Distracting interests, pity and compassion, favoritism and importunities of all sorts obstruct their best intentions to a degree they often cannot overcome sufficiently to ignore private consideration, which ought never influence public affairs. It is in such matters that they should summon up all their strength against inclinations toward weakness, keeping before their eyes the fact that those whom God has destined to protect others should have no characteristics but those advantageous to the public interest, and to which they should adhere inflexibly.

Power being one of the things most necessary to the grandeur of kings and the success of their governments, those who have the principal management of states are particularly obliged to omit nothing which could contribute to making their masters fully and universally respected. As goodness is the object of love, so power is the cause of fear. It is certain that of all the forces capable of producing results in public affairs, fear, if based on both esteem and reverence, is the most effective, since it can drive everyone to do his duty. If this principle is of great efficacy with regard to internal affairs, it is of no less value externally, since both foreigners and subjects take the same view of redoubtable power and both refrain from offending a prince whom they recognize as being able to hurt them if he so wishes. I have said already that this power of which I speak should be based on esteem and respect. I hasten to add that this is so necessary that if it is based on anything else there is the grave danger that instead of producing a reasonable fear the result will be a hatred of princes, for whom the worst possible fate is to incur public disapprobation.

There are several kinds of power which can make princes respected and feared—it is a tree with various branches, all nourished by the same root. The prince ought to be powerful because of his good reputation, because of a reasonable number of soldiers kept continuously under arms, because of a sufficient revenue to meet his ordinary expenses, plus a special sum of money in his treasury to cover frequent but unexpected contingencies, and, finally, because of the possession of the hearts of his subjects, as we will clearly demonstrate.

A good reputation is especially necessary to a prince, for if we hold him in high regard he can accomplish more with his name alone than a less well esteemed ruler can with great armies at his command. It is imperative that he guard it above life itself, and it is better to risk fortune and grandeur than to allow the slightest blemish to fall upon it, since it is certain that the first lessening of his reputation, no matter how slight, is a step in the most dangerous of directions and can lead to his ruin.

Those who guide themselves by the rules and precepts contained in this testament will without doubt acquire names of no little weight in the minds of both their subjects and their foreign neighbors. This is particularly so if, being devoted to God, they are also devoted to themselves; that is, if they keep their word and are faithful to their promises. These are indispensable conditions to the maintenance of the reputation of a prince, for just as he who is destitute of them is esteemed by no one, so he who possesses them is revered and trusted by all.

Study Questions

1. What problems did Richelieu face when he took power?

2. Richelieu is in a delicate position because he is totally dependent upon the king's good will for his success. How is his weakness reflected in his testament?

3. Richelieu compares the common people with mules. Why? What does this analogy reflect about his view of society and social relations?

4. What, according to Richelieu, is the most important prop of a king's power?

5. Does the cardinal's advice resemble Machiavelli's program in any way? How do the two programs differ?

Simplicissimus (1669) 83

HANS VON GRIMMELSHAUSEN

Hans von Grimmelshausen (ca. 1622–1676) was the son of a German innkeeper. Orphaned as a youth, he was carried away by soldiers during the Thirty Years' War. He was soon pressed into service as a musketeer in the imperial army. His literary skills, however, gained him a job as a secretary to a general and then as a clerk to a noble family. A charge of embezzlement brought his career full circle, for he ended his life as an innkeeper.

Grimmelshausen began his writings while still a soldier. He specialized in satires and in picaresque stories, of which *Simplicissimus* was the most famous. The title is translated as "The Simplest of the Simple." Much of the early part of the work (which includes the section excerpted here) is thought to be autobiographical. No other work of the period so vividly depicts the horror of the Thirty Years' War.

Although it was not my intention to lead these riders to my dad's farm, truth demands that I leave to posterity the cruelties committed in this our German war, to prove these evils were done to our advantage. Who else would have told me there was a God in Heaven if the warriors had not destroyed my father's house and forced me, through my captivity, to meet other people, for till this moment I had imagined my dad, mum and the rest of our household to be the sole inhabitants of this earth as no other man nor human dwelling were known to me but the one where I daily went in and out. Soon I had to learn man's origin in this world. I was merely a human in shape and a Christian only in name, otherwise just an animal. Our gracious God looked upon my innocence with pity and wished to bring me both to his and my awareness, and although there were a thousand ways of doing this, he used the one by which my dad and mum were punished as an example to others for their careless education of me.

The first thing that the riders did was to stable their horses. After that each one started his own business which indicated nothing but ruin and destruction. While some started to slaughter, cook and fry, so that it looked as though they wished to prepare a gay feast, others stormed through the house from top to bottom as if the golden fleece of Colchis were hidden there. Others again took linen, clothing and other goods, making them into bundles as if they intended going to market; what they did not want was broken up and destroyed. Some stabbed their swords through hay and straw as if they had not enough pigs to stab. Some shook the feathers out of the beds and filled the ticks with ham and dried meat as if they could sleep more comfortably on these. Others smashed the ovens and windows as if to announce an eternal summer. They beat copper and pewter vessels into lumps and packed the mangled pieces away. Bedsteads, tables, chairs and benches were burned although many stacks of dried wood stood in the yard. Earthenware pots and pans were all broken, perhaps because our guests preferred roasted meats, or perhaps they intended to eat only one meal with us. Our maid had been treated in the stable in such a way that she could not leave it any more—a shameful thing to tell! They bound the farmhand and laid him on the earth, put a clamp of wood in his mouth, and emptied a milking churn full of horrid dung water into his belly. This they called the Swedish drink, and they forced him to lead a party of soldiers to another place, where they looted men and cattle and brought them back to our yard. Among them were my dad, my mum and Ursula.

The soldiers now started to take the flints out of their pistols and in their stead screwed the thumbs of the peasants, and they tortured the poor wretches as if they were burning witches. They put one of the captive peasants into the baking-oven and put fire on him, although he had confessed nothing. Then they tied a rope round the head of another one, and twisted it with the help of a stick so tightly that blood gushed out through his mouth, nose and ears. In short everybody had his own invention to torture the peasants and each peasant suffered his own martyrdom. My dad alone appeared to me the most fortunate for he confessed with laughter what others were forced to say under pains and miserable lament, and such honour was done to him without doubt because he was the master of the house. They put him next to a fire, tied him so that he could move neither hands nor feet, and rubbed the soles of his feet with wet salt, which our old goat had to lick off. This tickled him so much that he almost wanted to burst with laughter, and it seemed to me so gentle and pleasant— for I had never seen nor heard my dad making such long-lasting laughter—that I half in companionship and half in ignorance joined heartily with him. In such merriment he confessed his guilt and revealed the hidden treasure, which was richer in gold, pearls and jewels than might have been expected of a peasant. What happened to the captive women, maids and daughters I do not know as the soldiers would not let me watch how they dealt with them. I only very well remember that I heard them miserably crying in comers here and there, and I believe my mum and Ursula had no better fate then the others.

In the midst of this misery I turned the spit and did not worry as I hardly understood what all this meant. In the afternoon I helped to water the horses and so found our maid in the stable looking amazingly dishevelled. I did not recognise her but she spoke to me with pitiful voice:

'Oh, run away, boy, or the soldiers will take you with them. Look out, escape! Can't you see how evil.....'

More she could not say.

So I made my way to a village but when I arrived found it in full flame; a troop of horsemen had just looted it and put it on fire. They had killed some of the peasants, driven away many and captured a few amongst whom was the vicar. Oh, God, how human life is full of pain and misery! Scarcely one misfortune has ended when we are overcome by another. The riders were ready to go and were leading the vicar on a rope. Some shouted: 'Shoot the rascal down!,' and others demanded money from him. He raised his hands and asked for the sake of the Last Judgment for pardon and Christian charity. But in vain. One of them rode toward him giving him a blow over the head so that he fell to the ground and recommended his soul to God. Nor had the other captive peasants any better fate.

The day following the burning of the village, as I was sitting in my hut saying my prayers and cooking carrots for sustenance, about forty to fifty musketeers surrounded me. These, although astonished at my unusual appearance, stormed through my hut seeking that which was not to be found; for I had nothing but books which they threw about as they were of no value to them. Finally, looking at me more carefully and seeing what a poor bird they had trapped, they realised that there was no good booty to be gained from me. My hard life amazed them and they had great pity for my tender youth, especially the officer who was in command. Indeed he honoured me and politely requested me to show him and his men the way out of the wood in which they had been lost for a long time. I did not refuse but led them by the nearest path toward the village where the vicar had been so badly treated, as I knew no other way. Before we left the wood we saw about ten peasants partly armed with blunderbusses and others occupied in burying something. The musketeers went up to them shouting: 'Halt! Halt!' The peasants answered with their guns but when they saw they were overpowered by the soldiers, they dispersed so

that the tired musketeers could not follow them.

When I arrived back I discovered that my flintbox and all my belongings, including my whole store of miserable victuals, which I had grown all through the summer in my garden and saved up for the winter, had disappeared. Whither now, I thought. Need taught me to pray the more. I exercised all my poor wit to find out what to do and what not to do-but with my small experience I could not come to any real decision. The best was to recommend myself to God and put all my trust in him, otherwise I would have despaired and perished. My mind was still full of that which I had seen and heard that very day. I did not think so much about food and my own preservation as about the hatred between soldiers and peasants, and in my foolishness there seemed no other explanation than that there must undoubtedly be two kinds of men in the world, not one single stock derived from Adam, but as different as wild and tame animals, for they persecute each other so cruelly.

Once at the end of May when I again in my usual although forbidden way crept into a farmyard to fetch my food, I found myself in the kitchen, but soon realised that the folk were still awake (where dogs hung about I wisely never went). I kept the kitchen door leading into the courtyard wide open so that if danger came I should be able to run away, and there I remained quiet as a mouse, waiting until the people would go to bed. In the meantime I noticed a slit in the kitchen-hatch leading to the living room. There I stealthily crept to see whether the peasants would not soon go to sleep. But my hopes came to nothing, as they had just dressed themselves, and instead of a candle a sulphurous blue flame stood on a bench, near which they smeared grease on sticks, brooms, forks, stools and benches, and rode out on these through the windows. At this I was terribly amazed and felt great horror, but as I had been accustomed to still more horrible things and had all my life neither read nor heard of witches, I did not take it too seriously, mostly because everything happened so quietly.

After all had flown away, I went into the room and here I considered what I could take with me and where to look for it. With such thoughts I sat down astride on a bench but as soon as I did so, I flew with the bench out through the window, leaving behind knapsack and blunderbuss, which I had put down almost as a reward for witches' ointment. My sitting down, flying off and descent happened in one moment, for I arrived as it seemed to me instantly amongst a great mass of people; possibly because of fear I did not realise the length of my journey. These people were dancing a remarkable dance such as I had never seen in my life. They held hands and turned their backs inwards as one has seen the Three Graces painted, so that their faces turned outwards, forming many rings one within the other. The innermost ring consisted of seven or eight persons; the next one of double this number; the third more than both, and so on, so that in the outer circle were more than two hundred. And as always one circle danced to the left and the other to the right, I could not see how many rings they had formed nor what stood in the middle around which they danced. It looked strange and horrid as all bobbed their heads ludicrously, and just as strange was the music. Everyone, it appeared to me, sang as he danced which gave an amazing harmony. My bench which carried me there came to rest near the musicians who stood about outside the rings of the dancers. Some of the musicians had instead of flutes, bagpipes and shawms, nothing but

adders, vipers and blindworms, on which they whistled merrily. Some had cats into whose behinds they blew and fingered on the tail, which sounded similar to bagpipes. Others bowed on the skulls of horses as on the best fiddles, and others played the harp upon cow skeletons like those which lie in the flayer's pit. One held a bitch under his arm whose tail he turned and fingered her teats. In between devils trumpeted through their noses that the whole forest echoed, and when the dance came to an end, the whole hellish crowd started to rage, shriek, rustle, roar, howl and storm as if they were all mad and senseless. And so one can imagine how I was struck by horror and fear.

In this turmoil a fellow approached me with a gigantic toad under his arm, easily as big as a kettledrum. Its guts had been pulled out through the arse and pushed into its mouth, which looked so revolting that I had to vomit.

'Look here, Simplicius,' he said, 'I know that you are a good lute player. Let's hear a fine tune!'

I was so terrified that I almost fell down on hearing the fellow call me by name; out of fear I became completely speechless and imagined I lay in a deep dream and prayed fervently in my heart that I might wake up. The fellow with the toad however, at whom I stared, pushed his nose forwards and backwards like a Calcutta cock, and at last he knocked me with it on the breast so that I nearly choked. At this I started to cry loudly to God and thereupon the whole host disappeared, and in a flash it was pitch dark and my heart felt so fearful that I fell to the ground, making the sign of the cross well nigh a hundred times.

Study Questions

1. What is the nature of war in the seventeenth century? Who appears to suffer most?

2. Why were soldiers so brutal toward the common people who crossed their paths?

3. *Simplicissimus* speculates that peasants and soldiers must have been different species; yet in fact most soldiers were of peasant stock themselves. What might this fact indicate about the peasantry and about the military?

4. How might Grimmelshausen's status as a village innkeeper have biased his views of peasants?

5. Grimmelshausen's description of a witches' coven is typical of many such accounts. What is it like? How does it demonstrate the taboos and dark fears of the age?

Literary Credits

How to Read a Document

Thomas Wright, editor. *The Travels of Marco Polo, The Venetian*. (London: George Bell & Sons, 1880), pp. B, 171–179.

Part I The Origins of Civilization

Stories of Creation

1. From Popol Vuh: *The Sacred Book of the Ancient Quiché Maya*, from the translation of Adrian Recinos. Copyright © 1950 by the University of Oklahoma Press. Reprinted by permission.

2. *The Creation Epic*. Morris Jastrow. *The Civilization of Babylonia and Assyria*. (Philadelphia: J.B. Lippincott, 1915), pp. 428–441 passim.

3. From the Book of Genesis from The Holy Bible, King James Version.

The Cradle of Civilization

4. From *Gilgamesh* by William Ellery Leonard, translated by William Ellery Leonard. Translation copyright 1934 by William Ellery Leonard, renewed © 1962 by Barbara A. Hayward. Used by permission of Viking Penguin, a division of Penguin Books USA Inc.

5. "The Code of Hammurabi" from Pritchard, James B., *Ancient Near Eastern Texts Relating to the Old Testament, 2E*. Copyright 1950,1955, © renewed 1969 by Princeton University Press. Reprinted by permission of Princeton University Press.

6. Pritchard, James B., *Ancient Near Eastern Texts Relating to the Old Testament, 2E*. Copyright 1950, 1955, © renewed 1969 by Princeton University Press. Reprinted by permission of Princeton University Press.

7. From Mirlam Lichthelm, *Ancient Egyptian Literature*, Three Volumes., Anonymous, "Instructions in Letter Writing by an Egyptian Scribe," Copyright © 1973–1980 by the Regents of the University of California. Reprinted by permission of the publisher.

8. Excerpts from the Book of Exodus from the Revised Standard Version of the Bible, Copyright 1946, 1952, 1971 by the Division of Christian Education of the National Council of the Churches of Christ in the USA.

Archaic and Classical Greece

9.   Homer, *The Iliad,* translated by William Cullen Bryant. (Boston: Houghton Mifflin, 1898),pp. 259–267,269–274.

10.   Sophocles, *Antigone.* In *The Tragedies of Sophocles.* The Oxford Translation. (New York: Harper & Brothers, 1859), pp. 163–165, 177–179, 190–19 1.

11.   Plato, *The Apology. The Best Known Works of Plato,* translated into English by B. Jowett, M.A. Garden City, NY: Blue Ribbon Books, 1942.

12.   Plato, *The Republic.* In *The Dialogues of Plato, Volume 3,* translated by B. Jowett. (Oxford: Clarendon Press, 1892), pp. 42–50.

13.   Aristotle, *The Politics.* In *The Politics and Economics of Aristotle,* translated by Edward Walford. (London: Bell & Daldy, 1866), pp. 239–243, 245–250.

The Religions of the East

14.   Epiphanius Wilson, *Sacred Books of the East,* Revised Edition. (London: The Colonial Press, 1900), pp. 158, 160–161, 168–169, 171–172.

15.   Edward Conze, editor, *Buddhist Texts Through the Ages.* (Oxford: Bruno Cassirer (Publishers) Ltd., 1954.)

16.   Lionel D. Barnett, translator, *The Bhagavad Gita.* (London: J.M. Dent & Sons, Ltd., 1905), pp. 84–91, 127–131 passim. Reprinted by permission.

17.   From *The Analects of Confucius,* translated and annotated by Arthur Waley. Reprinted by permission of Unwin Hyman, an imprint of HarperCollins Publishers Limited.

18.   From *Lao-Tzu, Te-Tao Ching* by Robert G. Henricks, translator. Copyright © 1989 by Robert G. Henricks. Reprinted by permission of Ballantine Books, a Division of Random House, Inc.

China: War and Politics

19.   Sun Tzu, *The Art of War,* edited and with a Foreword by James Clavell. (New York: Delacorte Press, 1983), pp. 9–20.

20.   Selected songs from *The Book of Songs,* edited and translated by Arthur Waley. Copyright © 1937 by Arthur Waley. Used by permission of Grove/Atlantic, Inc.

21.   From *Records of The Grand Historian of China,* translated from the Shih chi of Ssu-Ma Ch'ien by Burton Watson, Volume II. Copyright © 1961 Columbia University Press, New York. Reprinted with the permission of the publisher.

22.   From Han Fei Tzu, "Memorials," In *The Complete Works of Han Fei Tzu, A Classic of Chinese Legalism.* Reprinted by permission of Arthur Probsthain, London, England.

Ancient Rome

23.   Cicero, *On the Laws.* In *The Treatises of M. T. Cicero,* translated by C.D. Yonge. (London: Henry G. Bohn, 1853), pp. 406–413, 416–417, 419.

24.   Virgil, *The Aeneid,* translated by Theodore C. Williams. (Boston: Houghton Mifflin, 1910), pp. 1–2, 8–14.

25..   Plutarch, *Life of Cato*. In *Plutarch's Lives. Volume 2*, revised translation by Arthur Hugh Clough. (Philadelphia: The John C. Winston Co., 1908), pp. 658–663,679, 682,689–690.

26.   Suetonius, *Life of Augustus*. In *The Lives of the Twelve Caesars*, translated by Alexander Thomson, revised by T. Forester: (London: George Bell & Sons, 1909), pp. 87–92,96–97,115–116,129–130,145–146.

27.   The Sermon on the Mount from the Revised Standard Version of the Bible, copyright 1946, 1952, 1971 by the Division of Christian Education of the National Council of the Churches of Christ in the USA.

Part II Traditional Societies

Africa and the Muslim World

28.   From *The Digest of Justinian*, Latin text edited by Theodor Mommsen with the aid of Paul Krueger, English translation edited by Alan Watson, Vol. IL Copyright © 1985 by The University of Pennsylvania Press. Reprinted by permission.

29.   From *Secret History* by Procopius, translated by Richard Atwater. Reprinted by permission of The University of Michigan Press.

30.   Reprinted by permission from The Short Koran, edited by George M. Lamsa. Copyright © 1949, Ziff-Davis Publishing Company.

31.   Ibn Said, *Book of the Maghrib*. Ahmed ibn Mohammed al-Makkari, *The History of the Mohammedan Dynasties in Spain*, translated by Pascual de Gayangos (London: Oriental Translation Fund, 1840), 1, 95–102.

32.   Ibn Khaldfin, translated from the Arabic by Franz Rosenthal; *The Muqaddimah: An Introduction to History*. Copyright © 1967 by Princeton University Press, Bollingen Series XLIII. Reprinted by permission of Princeton University Press.

33.   From *Corpus of Early Arabic Sources for West African History*, translated by J.F.P. Hopkins, edited and annotated by N. Levtzion & J.F.P. Hopkins. Copyright © University of Ghana, International Academic Union, Cambridge University Press 1981. Reprinted with the permission of Cambridge University Press.

34.   Hakluytus Posthumus or Purchas His Pilgrimes (Vol. IX, J. Maclehose, Glasgow, 1905), pp. 241–245,253–255.

Asian Cultures

35.   David J. Lu, editor. *Sources of Japanese History Volume One*. (New York: McGraw-Hill Book Company, 1974), pp. 52–54.

36.   Fa-hsien, *A Record of Buddhistic Kingdoms*, translated and annotated by James Legge., (Oxford: Clarendon Press, 1886), pp. 34–38, 42–43, 51–52, 57–60.

37.   Reprinted with the permission of The Free Press, a Division of Macmillan, Inc., from *Chinese Civilization and Society: A Sourcebook* by Patricia Buckley Ebrey. Copyright © 1981 by The Free Press.

38.   From *The Tale of Genji* by Lady Murasaki, translated from the Japanese by Arthur Waley, 1926. Reprinted by permission of Houghton Mifflin Company.

39.   From *Sources of Chinese Tradition*, compiled by Wm. Theodore de Bary, Wing-tsit Chan and Burton Watson. Copyright © 1960 Columbia University Press, New York. Reprinted with the permission of the publisher.

40.   From Prince Shotoku, "The Seventeen Article Constitution," In *Sources of Japanese History, Volume 1*, by David John Lu, 1974. Reprinted by permission of M. E. Sharpe, Inc.

41.   Reprinted with the permission of The Free Press, a Division of Macmillan, Inc., from *Chinese Civilization and Society: A Sourcebook* by Patricia Buckley Ebrey. Copyright © 1981 by The Free Press.

Europe After the Fall of Rome

42.   Tacitus, *The Germania*, The Oxford Translation, Revised. (New York: Arthur Hinds & Co., n.d.), pp. 3,11–13,15–16,19–26.

43.   From *The Burgundian Code*, translated by Katherine Fischer. Copyright 1949 by The University of Pennsylvania Press. Reprinted by permission.

44.   From *Early Lives of Charlemagne* by Einhard & The Monk of St. Gall: Translated and edited by Professor A. J. Grant. Cooper Square Publishers, Inc., New York, 1966.

45.   From *Translations and Reprints from. the Original Sources of European History, Volume IV*. Reprinted by permission of The University of Pennsylvania Press.

46.   Boyd C. Barrington, ed. *Magna Carta*. (Philadelphia: William J. Campbell, 1900), pp. 228–234,237–240,244,246–250.

47.   From "The Battle of Malden," pp. 9–111, from *The Earliest English Poems*, translated by Michael Alexander, [Penguin Classics 1966, 3rd edition 1991]. Copyright © Michael Alexander, 1977, 1991. Reproduced by permission of Penguin Books.

The Development of Christianity

48.   From *The City of God* by St. Augustine, 1945 Edition. Reprinted by permission of Everyman's Library J.M. Dent & Sons, Ltd.).

49.   Saint Benedict of Nursia, *The Rule*, translated by Dom Justin McCann. (Latrobe, Penn.: The Archabbey Press, 1950), pp. 63ff. Reprinted by permission.

50.   From *The Admonitians of St. Francis of Assisi* by Lothar Hardick O.F.M., translated by David Smith. Reprinted by permission of the Franciscan Press of Quincy College.

51.   From *Summa Theologica* by St. Thomas Aquinas, translated by Fathers of the English Dominican Province. Copyright 1948 by Benziger Brothers, Inc. Reprinted by permission of Glencoe Publishing Co., Inc.

52.   From "Medieval Witchcraft" in *Translations and Reprints from the Original Sources of European History, Volume III*. Reprinted by permission of The University of Pennsylvania Press.

Part III Dynasties and Empires

The Italian Renaissance

53.   From *The Family in Renaissance Florence*, a translation by Renee Neu Watkins of I Libra Della Famiglia by Leon Battista Alberti. Copyright © 1969 by Renee Watkins. Reprinted by permission.

54.   Giorgio Vasari, "Life of Leonardo da Vinci" in *Lives of the Most Eminent Painters, Sculptors, and Architects*, translated by Gaston DeC. De Vere. (London: Philip Lee Warner, Publishers, 1912–1914), pp. 89–92, 95–101, 104–105.

55.   Niccolò Machiavelli, *The Prince*, translated and edited by Robert M. Adams. (New York: Norton, 1977), pp. 3ff.

Cultures in Collision

56.   From *The Alexiad of the Princess Anna Comnena*, translated by Elizabeth A. S. Dawes, 1967 edition published by Routledge & Kegan Paul Ltd. Reprinted by permisssion of Routledge Ltd., UK.

57.   From *De Profectione Ludovici VII in Orientem,* (by Odo of Deuil) with an English translation by Virginia Ginerick Berry. Copyright © 1948, Columbia University Press. Reprinted with permission of the publisher.

58.   From *Arab Historians of the Crusades*, selected and translated from the Arabic sources by Francesco Gabrieli, translated from the Italian by E. J. Costello. Copyright © 1957 by Giulio Einaudi Editore S. P. A., Turin. This translation © 1969 by Routledge & Kegan Paul Limited. Reprinted by permission of the Regents of the University of California.

59.   From *Arab Historians of the Crusades*, selected and translated from the Arabic sources by Francesco Gabrieli, translated from the Italian by E. J. Costello. Copyright © 1957 by Giulio Einaudi Editore S.P.A., Turin. This translation © 1969 by Routledge & Kegan Paul Limited. Reprinted by permission of the Regents of the University of California.

China and Japan in the Middle Ages

60.   From "Japanese Feudal Law" by John Carey Hall in *Transactions of the Asiatic Society of Japan*, 1906.

61.   From *Sources of Japanese Tradition, Volume I*, compiled by Ryusaku Tsunoda, Wm. Theodore de Bary, and Donald Keene. Copyright © 1958 Columbia University Press, New York. Reprinted with the permission of the publisher.

62.   From *Sources of Japanese Tradition, Volume 1*, compiled by Ryusaku Tsunoda, Wm. Theodore de Bary, and Donald Keene. Copyright © 1958 Columbia University Press, New York. Reprinted with the permission of the publisher.

63.   From *All Men Are Brothers* by Shui Hu Chuan, translated by Pearl S. Buck. Reprinted by permission of Harold Ober Associates Incorporated. Copyright 1933, 1937, by Pearl S. Buck.

European Encounters

64.   Juan Gonzalez de Mendoza, *The History of the Great and Mighty Kingdom of China and the Situation Thereof*, edited by Sir George T. Staunton, Bart. (London: The Hakluyt Society, 1853), pp. 29–35.

65.   From *China in the Sixteenth Century: The Journals of Matthew Ricci* by Matthew Ricci, translated by Louis J. Gallagher, SJ. Copyright 1942 and renewed 1970 by Louis J. Gallagher, SJ. Reprinted by permission of Random House, Inc.

66.   From *The Bernard Diaz Chronicles*, translated by Albert Idell, Translation copyright 1956 by Albert Idell. Used by permission of Doubleday, a division of Bantam Doubleday Dell Publishing Group, Inc.

67.   From *The Broken Spears* by Miguel Leon Portilla. Copyright © 1962, 1990 by Beacon Press. Reprinted by permission of Beacon Press.

68.   Reprinted from *History of the Inca Empire* by Father Bernabe Cobo, translated and edited by Roland Hamilton. Copyright © 1979. Reprinted by permission of the translator and The University of Texas Press.

69.   E.G. Ravenstein, translator, *Journal of the First Voyage of Vasco da Gama, 1497–1499*. (London: Hakluyt Society, 1898), pp. 32–46.

70.   Christopher Columbus, *Letters*, translated and edited by R. H. Major. (London: Hakluyt Society, 1847), pp. 1–17.

71.   Bartolomé de las Casas, *Apologetic History of the Indies*. From *Introduction to Contemporary Civilization in the West*, a source book prepared by the Contemporary Civilization Staff of Columbia College, Columbia University, Volume I, Third Edition. Copyright 1946, 1954,(D 1960, Columbia University Press. Reprinted by permission.

The Golden Age of Islam

72.   *Rubaiyat of Omar Khayyam*, translated by Edward Fitzgerald. (Garden City, NY: Doubleday & Company, Inc., 1952.)

73.   Kritovoulos, translated by Charles T. Riggs, *History of Mehmed the Conqueror*. Copyright 1954, © renewed 1982 by Princeton University Press. Reprinted by permission of Princeton University Press.

74.   From "Letters from Selim and Ismail,' translated by John E. Woods in *The Islamic World*, edited by William H. McNeill and Marilyn Robinson Waldman. Reprinted by permission of John E. Woods.

75.   Leo Africanus, *The History and Description of Africa and of the Notable Things Therein Contained*, edited by Dr. Robert Brown. (London: Hakluyt Society, 1896), pp. 30–37.

76.   Francois Bernier, *Travels in the Mogul Empire*, A.D. 1656–1668. (London: Archibald Constable & Co., 1891.)

The Reform of Christianity

77.   Erasmus, *In Praise of Folly*. (London: Reeves & Turner, 1876), pp. 81–82, 134–138, 139, 156–160.

78.   Adapted and reprinted from *Luther's Works, Volume 31*. Copyright © 1957 Fortress Press. Used by permission of Augsburg Vortress. Martin Luther, Table Talk translated and edited by William Hazlitt. (London: George Bell and Sons, 1895). pp. 297–300.

79.   From *John Calvin, Selections from His Writings*, edited and with an introduction by John Dillenberger. Copyright © 1975 by American Academy of Religion. Anchor Books Edition: 1971. Copyright © 1971 by John Dillenberger. All Rights Reserved. Reprinted by permission of Scholars Press.

80.   From *The Life of St. Teresa of Avila*, written by herself, translated from the Spanish by David Lewis. Reprinted by permission of Burnes & Oates Ltd.

European Politics and War

81.   Henry IV, The Edict of Nantes. In *Readings in European History. Volume II. From the Opening of the Protestant Revolt to the Present Day*, translated by James Harvey Robinson. (Boston: Ginn & Company, 1906), pp. 183–185. Reprinted by permission.

82.   From *The Political Testament of Cardinal Richelieu*, translated by Henry Bertram Hill. Copyright © 1961, by the Regents of the University of Wisconsin. Reprinted by permission of The University of Wisconsin Press.

83.   From *Simplicius Simplicissimus* by Hans Jacob Christoffel von Grimmelshausen, translated from the original German edition of 1669 by Hellmuth Weissenborn and Lesley Macdonald. Copyright © The Translators 1964. Reprinted by permission of The Calder Educational Trust, London.

Photo
Acknowledgments

Unless otherwise acknowledged, all photographs are the property of Wadsworth Publishing Company.

Part I The Origins of Civilization

Part II Traditional Socities

Part III Dynasties and Empires

234   © Robert Frerck/Odyssey/Chicago

242   Scala/Art Resource, N.Y.

250   Erich Lessing/Art Resource, N.Y.

263   Michael Holford, London

276   Courtesy of the Tokyo National Museum

284   © British Museum

294   Courtesy of William J. Duiker, The Pennsylvania State University

319   Rezza-ye Abbasi, *Two Lovers*, 1630, The Metropolitan Museum of Art, Francis M. Weld Fund 1950 (50, 164)

323   Courtesy of the Topkapi Sarayi Muszei

339   Lucas Cranach the Younger, German, 1515-1586 *Martin Luther and the Wittenberg Reformers* about 1543, oil on panel, The Toledo Museum of Art, Toledo, OH. Purchased with funds from the Libbey Endowment, gift of Edward Drummond Libbey

351   Bibliotheque Publique et Universitaire, Geneva

360   Giraudon/Art Resource, N.Y.

Introduction to
Language Development

Sandra Levey

PLURAL
PUBLISHING
INC.

SAN DIEGO
OXFORD
MELBOURNE

PLURAL PUBLISHING
INC.

5521 Ruffin Road
San Diego, CA 92123

e-mail: info@pluralpublishing.com
Web site: http://www.pluralpublishing.com

FSC
www.fsc.org
MIX
Paper from
responsible sources
FSC® C011935

Library of Congress Cataloging-in-Publication Data

Levey, Sandra.
  Introduction to language development / Sandra Levey.
      p. ; cm.
  Includes bibliographical references and index.
  ISBN-13: 978-1-59756-489-2 (alk. paper)
  ISBN-10: 1-59756-489-3 (alk. paper)
  I. Title.
  [DNLM: 1. Language Development. 2. Adolescent. 3. Child. 4. Infant.
WS 105.5.C8]
  LC Classification not assigned
  616.85'5—dc23
                    2013000765

side of" or "beside" and *para + linguistic* is connection between paralinguistic (emotional and attitudinal) and linguistic information.

These paralinguistic cues include intonation (voice or vocal pitch), stress (emphasis), speech rate (fast, moderate, or slow), and pause (hesitation). We use intonation to signal a question (*Are you GOing?*), whereas we use stress to signal emphasis (*I AM going!*). In other words, we can change the meaning of an utterance through the use of paralinguistic cues (spoken emphasis shown in bolded words). **Prosody** is a communicative tool that uses duration (length), intensity (loudness), and frequency (pitch). Prosody allows us to communicate different attitudes, such as sarcasm or sympathy, by changing the duration, intensity, and frequency of our spoken language. For example, notice that you can express sarcasm by making the first syllable in the word *really* longer than the second syllable (i.e., **REA**lly?).

Communication begins in infancy, when 3-month-olds produce speech-like sounds in response to adults' vocalizations (Gleason & Ratner, 2009). Children focus on a speaker's eye region as early as 2 months of age, showing recognition that the eyes convey social information connected with verbal and nonverbal communication (Carter, Davis, Klin, & Volkmar, 2005). Communication becomes more sophisticated as children's language skills develop over time.

Speech

Speech is defined as the verbal means of communicating through articulation (the production of speech sounds), voice (the use of the vocal folds and breath support to produce sounds), and fluency (the rhythm of speech). At times, the rhythm of speech is broken by hesitations as a speaker tries to think of a word.

Speech production begins with impulses or signals in the brain (Cavallo, 2011). These neural impulses result in muscle contractions that move structures called the articulators (e.g., tongue, lips, and jaw). Articulation is the movement of the articulators that lead to the production of speech sounds that form words. For example, notice that you bring your lips together to form the sounds "p" and "b" when producing the first sounds in the words *pat* and *bat*. Chapter 3 presents a detailed introduction to speech sounds and articulation.

The sounds "p" and "b," along with many other sounds in English, are termed **phonemes**, the smallest unit of sounds that create a difference in meaning. There are English consonant phonemes (Table 1–1) and vowel phonemes (Table 1–2) that, when combined, form words. Phonemes are the abstract representation of speech sounds (phones), with phonemes indicated by slashes (e.g., /p/ and /b/), as found in the words *pat* /pæt/ and *bat* /bæt/. Note in the following examples that the change of the initial phoneme in a word results in a change in word meaning.

Sue-two	/su/-/tu/
tip-dip	/tɪp/-/dɪp/
bat-cat	/bæt/-/kæt/

Orthography describes the symbols or alphabet letters (**graphemes**) of written language. Note that there is not a one-to-one correlation between graphemes and phonemes. For example, the phoneme /f/ is the last sound in the word *laugh* /læf/ but is spelled with the graphemes -*gh*.

Table 1–1. Consonant Phonemes of English

Phoneme	Word		
	Initial	Medial	Final
/p/	pie	apple	lap
/b/	boy	table	cab
/t/	tip	attic	pot
/d/	do	ladder	bad
/k/	cap	actor	pick
/g/	go	tiger	peg
/m/	mop	summer	sum
/n/	note	tunnel	sun
/ŋ/		hanger	sang
/f/	fact	taffy	calf
/v/	vest	silver	leave
/s/	sit	passing	bus
/z/	zoo	buzzard	buzz
/θ/	throw	bathtub	path
/ð/	they	bother	bathe
/ʃ/	shop	pressure	bush
/ʒ/		treasure	beige
/l/	leaf	balloon	call
/r/	rope	farmer	bar
/j/	you	tri( )al	
/w/	we		
/tʃ/	chain	teacher	beach
/dʒ/	jam	badger	lodge

Note: The consonant phonemes /ŋ/ and /ʒ/ occur only in medial and final position in words, whereas the phoneme /w/ occurs only in initial position in words. The consonant phoneme /j/ is the sound produced in the word trial (i.e., tri /j/al).

Source: From *Language Development: Understanding Language Diversity in the Classroom* (p. 40), by S. Levey & S. Polirstok (Eds.), 2011, Los Angeles, CA: Sage. Reprinted with permission.

Table 1–2. *Vowel Phonemes of English*

Phoneme	Word	Phonetic Transcription
/i/	feet, eat, ski	/fit/, /it/, /ski/
/ɛ/	pet, meant, friend	/pɛt/, /mɛnt/, /frɛnd/
/e/	late, main, beige	/let/, /men/, /beʒ/
/ɪ/	sit, pit, hit	/sɪt/, /pɪt/, /hɪt/
/æ/	cat, ladder, bad	/kæt/, /lædɚ/, /bæd/
/u/	you, soon, tune	/ju/, /sun/, /tun/
/ʊ/	book, should, foot	/bʊk/, /ʃʊd/, /fʊt/
/o/	go, shoulder, load	/go/, /ʃoldɚ/, /lod/
/ɑ/	on, cot, father	/ɑn/, /kɑt/, fɑðɚ/
/ɔ/	law, bought, caught	/lɔ/, /bɔt/, /kɔt/
/ʌ/	sun, love, uncle	/sʌn/, /lʌv/, /ʌnkl/
/ə/	about, banana, undo	/əbaʊt/, /bənænə/, /əndu/
/ɝ/	fur, her, sir, learn	/fɝ/, /hɝ/, /sɝ/, /lɝn/
/ɚ/	father, bother, burner	/fɑðɚ/, /bɑðɚ/, /bɝnɚ/

Source: From *Language Development: Understanding Language Diversity in the Classroom* (p. 41), by S. Levey & S. Polirstok (Eds.), 2011, Los Angeles, CA: Sage. Reprinted with permission.

It is also the first sound in the word *physician* /fɪzɪʃən/ but is spelled with the two graphemes *ph-*. Children must learn to recognize these variations between written and spoken language to develop basic reading skills.

Keep in mind that written language is also a method of communication with a strong connection between writing skills and literacy (the ability to read and understand written text). Children begin their writing with scribbles and drawing, advance to writing letters, and progress to writing their names. These early writing skills are associated with the development of literacy (Graham, Harris, & Fink, 2000), whereas name-writing and shape-copying skills are predictors of word reading skills, reading comprehension, and spelling in early grades (Badian, 1998). Engaging children in writing games prepares them for later reading tasks in early grades.

Language

Language is a shared code that represents concepts through the use of arbitrary symbols and rules that govern those symbols. The term *arbitrary* is used because there is no direct relationship between a particular symbol or word and its meaning. For example, English speakers label the entity *apple* as "apple," whereas this entity has a different name across many other languages: *pomme* (French), *manzana*

(Spanish), and *æble* (Danish). The term **generative** is also used to describe the nature of language. This describes a speaker's ability to generate many types of sentences, including novel sentences produced by children (*I'm crackering my soup*).

Grammar is the set of structural rules that apply to sentence construction, such as the following rules that apply to phonology, morphology, semantics, and syntax.

Phonology: How sounds are combined to form words (*c + a + t = cat*)

Morphology: How words and smaller units can be combined to form other words with a different meaning (*go + ing = going*)

Semantics: How words (e.g., It's raining outside) correspond to things and events in the world (e.g., a rainy day) and how language reflects a speaker's intent or meaning (*I'm feeling good today*)

Syntax: How words are combined to form sentences (*I + see + a + bird*)

The components of language consist of **Form**, **Content**, and **Use** (Table 1–3). We begin with a discussion of the component Form, which includes **syntax**, **morphology**, and **phonology**.

FORM

Syntax

Syntax is the component of language that involves the rules for combining words to form meaningful sentences. Basic sentences are composed of Subject + Verb (e.g., *Tania ran*). The subject of a sentence contains nouns. Common nouns label a person, place, or thing.

mother, dog, home, book

Proper nouns label particular persons, places, or things and are usually marked with a capital letter.

Sue, New York, Sesame Street

Verbs label an action.

run, cry, eat, sleep

A basic syntactic structure consists of a *noun phrase* (which must contain a noun) and a *verb phrase* (which must contain a verb). Syntactic structure can be expanded by adding articles (*the, a, an*), adjectives (*big, pretty, dirty*), adverbs (*slowly, quietly, loudly*), prepositional phrases (*on the table, in the bowl, next to the chair*), or a direct or an indirect object noun (*home* and *to the park*). The sentence *The boy threw a ball* is represented in a syntactic tree (Figure 1–1).

Children begin to produce single words at about 12 months of age. Syntax emerges with the combination of two

Table 1–3. The Components of Language

Form	Content	Use
Syntax	Semantics	Pragmatics
Morphology		
Phonology		

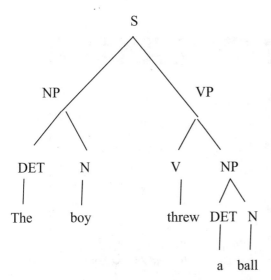

Figure 1–1. *This sample syntactic tree consists of the sentence (S), a noun phrase (NP), and a verb phrase (VP). The noun phrase contains a determiner (DET), such as the, a, and an, and a noun (N). The verb phrase (VP) contains a verb (V) and another noun phrase (NP). This noun phrase contains another determiner (D) and a noun (N). There are many kinds of sentences and this is only one example of a tree diagram.*

Table 1–4. *Children's Early Sentence Production*

Sentence	Example
Declaratives	*I'm sleepy.*
Interrogatives	*Where mommy?*
Imperatives	*Gimme cookie.*
Negatives	*No more milk.*
Quantity use	*I have **two** cars.*
Adjective use	*Give me the **big** ball.*
Adverb use	*Run **fast**.*

words at about 18 months of age. Syntactic development begins with sentences that express requests (*More cookie*), notification (*That doggy*), and negation (*No bed*). Syntactic development continues with increased length and complexity of sentences over time. This development occurs with the inclusion of grammatical morphemes (e.g., *going* and *toys*) and children's development of vocabulary skills. Children's early sentence production, at about 3 years of age (Table 1–4), shows the development of a variety of different structures (Bernstein, 2011).

It is also important to understand that children's language skills consist of *receptive language* (the ability to understand others) and *expressive language* (the ability to express and share thoughts, ideas, and feelings). Receptive and expressive skills are complementary aspects of language. For example, a child with a receptive language disorder may have difficulty understanding directions or spoken words. This receptive language disorder impacts this child's expressive language abilities because the child will have difficulty using words to communicate needs or requests.

Morphology

Morphology is concerned with the structure or organization of words. **Morphemes** are the minimal distinctive units of meaning or the meaningful parts of words. For example, the word *dog* cannot be broken down into smaller units (*d* or *og*) while maintaining the meaning of the word *dog*. Free morphemes are those that have meaning by themselves (*nouns, verbs, adjectives, adverbs*, and *prepositions*), and morphemes that occur in combination with free morphemes are called bound morphemes (e.g., *-ed, -s, -ing*) (Table 1–5).

Table 1–5. Free and Bound Morphemes

Morpheme	Example
Free	
Nouns	*car, boy, tree, book, girl*
Verbs	*run, walk, eat, drink*
Adverbs	*slowly, quickly, faster, fastest, late*
Adjectives	*good, better, best; rich/richer; dirty*
Bound	
Derivational	
Prefix: *un-, non-, in-, pre-, trans-*	*unlucky, nonstick, inappropriate, preview, insufficient, transatlantic*
Suffix: *-ly, -ist, -er, -ness, -ment*	*slowly, bicyclist, farmer, happiness, contentment*
Inflectional	
Plural	*cats, dogs, horses,*
Possessive	*cat's, mommy's*
Third person singular	*eats, drinks*
Past tense	*walked* (regular) and *ate* (irregular)
Past participle	*eaten*
Present participle (present progressive)	*eating*
Comparative	*bigger*
Superlative	*biggest*

Bound morphemes can be divided into two types: inflectional morphemes (e.g., *-s, -est, -ing*) and derivational morphemes (e.g., *-ful, -like, -ly, un-, dis-*).

Inflectional morphemes modify verb tense (*walk + **ed***) or noun number (*dog + **s***) with no change in the meaning of a word. Inflectional morphemes include the plural *-s* attached to nouns to indicate plurality, the possessive *'s* to indicate possession (*mommy's*), the present progressive *-ing* attached to verb stems to indicate pres-

ent and ongoing action (**running**), and the past tense marker *-ed* to indicate prior activity (*walked*).

> *cats*, **biggest**, and *running*

Derivational morphemes involve a prefix or suffix.

> Prefix: *un-, non-, in-, pre-, trans-*
> *unlucky, nonstick, inappropriate, preview, transatlantic*

Suffix: *-ly, -ist, -er, -ness, -ment*

slowly, bicyclist, farmer, happiness, contentment

Derivational morphemes can change a word's meaning (*kind* becoming *un + kind*) and can also change a verb to a noun (e.g., *farm* becomes *farm + er*). Derivational morphemes can change the meaning of a word, along with the part of speech (or both meaning and part of speech). In the examples that follow, meaning changes, part of speech changes, and both meaning and part of speech change.

Meaning (positive → negative)

lucky → **un**lucky

appropriate → **in**appropriate

Part of speech (verb *farm* → noun *farmer*)

He farms → He is a farm**er**

Meaning and part of speech (adjective → noun)

happy → happ**iness**

Grammatical morphemes also consist of conjunctions (*and, but*), articles (*the, and*), and prepositions (*in, under*) that play a role in expanding children's sentence productions (Table 1–6). We can also combine morphemes (*house, boat, out,* and *law*) to form compound words (e.g., *houseboat and outlaw*).

The following examples demonstrate the role of morphemes in sentences. Note that the sentence with six morphemes consists of four *free* morphemes (*I, got, mommy,* and *shoe*) and two *bound* morphemes (possessive *'s* and plural *-s*).

No bed	Two morphemes
Daddy go bye-bye	Three morphemes
Baby gotta go night-night now	Five morphemes
I got mommy's shoes	Six morphemes

To form the past tense of certain verbs, we can add the morpheme *-ed* (e.g., *walked* and *talked*), whereas other verbs require changes in consonants and vowels (*eat/ate; throw/threw;* and *catch/caught*). Young children often **overgeneralize** the regular past tense *-ed* (e.g., *walk + ed*) to form the past tense of irregular verbs, as shown in the following examples.

I eated the cookie

I throwed the ball

I catched the ball

Asked if he had *left* during a hiding game, 3½-year-old Micah said, *Yes, I leaved.* Told that the word was *left*, he continued to argue, saying, *No, I leaved!* Over time, children learn the irregular verbs and can say, *I ate, threw, and caught.*

Phonology

Phonology is the part of language that is concerned with the combination of speech sounds for word formation. For example, we can combine the sounds associated with "c" /k/, "a" /æ/ and "t" /t/ to form the word *cat* /kæt/. A different combination would result in *act* /ækt/. Over time, children understand sound contrasts, such as the difference between the speech sounds "p" /p/ and "b" /b/, and learn that these sound contrasts signal differences in meaning (e.g., *pin* and *bin*). The understanding of these sound contrasts plays an essential role in children's reading development.

Table 1–6. *The Role of Grammatical Morphemes*

Morphemes	Grammatical Function	Example
Plural	Marks more than one of a noun	
Regular		dogs, chairs
Irregular		child/**children**
Possessive	Marks possession or ownership	mommy's
Comparative	Marks a comparison	big**ger**, clos**er**
Superlative	Marks something as exceptional	big**gest**, quick**est**
Third person singular	Marks agreement with singular third person (i.e., *he, she, it*)	eats, walks, barks
Past tense	Marks past action	
Regular		walk**ed**, bark**ed**
Irregular		ate, threw, swam
Past participle	Verb form used as an action; follows *be* or *have*	
Regular		chosen, proven
Irregular		drunk, sung
Present progressive	Marks present action	eat**ing**, sing**ing**, bark**ing**
Uncontractible auxiliary	The *be* verb preceding other verbs; examples are *am, is, are, was, were, been*	The dog **is** barking
Contractible copula	The main copular verb is the verb *to be*	I**'m** happy, he**'s** big (from *I **am** happy* and *he **is** big*)
Contractible auxiliary	The *be* verb contracted	Baby**'s** crying (*baby **is** crying*)

Phonological rules govern the distribution and sequencing of sounds in words (Owens, 2008). Distributional rules govern the position of sounds in words. For instance, the sequence *ng* can occur in word final position (*sing*) in English but cannot occur in initial position in this language. However, this sound does appear in initial position in some other languages.

Sequencing rules not only govern the order of sounds in a word, but also the effect of one sound on another. For instance, note that the past tense morpheme *-ed* in the word *plugged* is produced as the phoneme /d/ but is produced as the phoneme /t/ in the word *walked*. This reflects the interaction between phonology and morphemes (**morphophonology**).

Children's **perception** of words may affect their production of words (Levey & Schwartz, 2002). For example, some sounds have greater emphasis, such as the second syllable in the word *banana* (e.g., ba**NA**na). Consequently, young children often produce this word as *nana*, omitting the first unstressed syllable in the word. This production results from their bias toward a strong-weak pattern in words (e.g., **NA**na).

Young children's productions of words that differ from the target are termed **phonological processes** (Table 1–7). Many of these phonological processes disappear by 3 years of age.

CONTENT

Semantics

Semantics is the component of language that describes the *meaning* that is conveyed by words, sentences, narratives, and conversations. Meaning is based on entities (e.g., things and people) and events (walking, throwing, rain falling) that children encounter in the world. Semantics also refers to the relationship between entities and events, as shown in the following example, which illustrates the semantic relationship between *children, ball,* and *dog* (entities) and *throwing* (action).

*The **children** are **throwing** a **ball** to the dog.*

Semantic knowledge combines knowledge of *words* with *knowledge of the world*. Word knowledge involves learning that there are names for entities, such as people, animals, and things (*boy, dog, tree*), actions and events (*throw, drive, birthday party*), and concepts that label feelings (*happy, sad, surprised*), space (*in, on, under*), and time (*soon, late, next*). Young children's observations and interaction within the environment results in their development of concepts (ideas or theories) about the things they see, hear, and experience.

Table 1–7. Selected Phonological Processes in Early Learning

Child Production	Adult Target	Phonological Process
"nana"	*banana*	Unstressed syllable deletion
"top"	*stop*	Consonant cluster reduction
"gogi"	*doggie*	Assimilation (final sound *g* produced in place of *d*)
"bu"	*bus*	Final sound deletion (final *s* deleted)
"dada"	*daddy*	Reduplication (first syllable duplicated)

Source: From Language Development: Understanding Language Diversity in the Classroom (p. 44), by S. Levey & S. Polirstok (Eds.), 2011, Los Angeles, CA: Sage. Reprinted with permission.

There is a relationship between word meaning and **semantic features** and **selection restrictions**. Semantic features are those that distinguish one entity (*person, animal,* or *thing*) from another. For example, the semantic features of a dog include *animal* and *four-legged*. For a mother, the semantic features include *female* and *parent*. Selection restrictions draw on the semantic features of a word and prohibit redundancy (e.g., *female woman*). When children are developing their semantic knowledge, they may identify entities with similar semantic features as having the same label. For example, it is not uncommon to hear very young children call all four-legged animals *doggie*. Over time, children acquire a more refined set of features and word meanings. They are later able to understand the concept of synonyms, or words with shared semantic features (e.g., *big, large,* and *enormous*), and antonyms, or words with differing semantic features (e.g., *big-little*).

Over time, children learn that words can have multiple meanings. For example, the word *block* is first learned as the label for a toy (*toy block*), then as a place (*going around the block*), then as a verb (*blocking the door*), and later as a metaphor (*mental block*). Children first have a very restricted idea of a word's meaning. For example, Daniel, age 4, was amazed when he was told that the picture of a dog on the front cover of a dog-training book was his dog's "grandfather." He asked, *Shanti's grandfather was a dog?* This represents a restricted meaning, given that Daniel believed that the word *grandfather* could only refer to a person (not an animal).

Children's early semantic development consists of semantic roles, used to convey meaning at the one-word stage of development. Some examples of the semantic roles are agent, action, and affected.

> Agent: active initiator of the action — *daddy, mommy, doggie*
>
> Action: event — *throw, kiss, drink*
>
> Affected: entity or thing influenced by act — *ball, baby, water*

At around 2 to 3 years of age, children begin to combine words to form **semantic relations** (Bloom, Lahey, Hood, Lifter, & Fiess, 1980), such as a child's production of *Mommy pigtail* when her mother was combing her hair. Given the context (*hair being combed*), we might interpret the semantic relationship as agent + action (i.e., *mommy combing*). Additional examples of semantic relations follow.

Agent + Action: initiator + event
Daddy throw

Action + Affected: thing influenced by act
Drink water

USE

Pragmatics

Use refers to **pragmatics**, which involves rules for the use of language in social interaction. Pragmatic rules include the appropriate behaviors involved in communication, such as *eye contact*, when someone is talking to you and *turn taking* as sender and receiver when involved in a conversation. Children learn these pragmatic rules over time through observation of behaviors in their environment and through insight into others' feelings and needs. Halliday (1975) described children's early attempts to communicate their intentions (meanings) as pragmatic functions (Table 1–8). These early productions convey meanings, such as obtaining a goal or communicating the request for interaction.

Speech Acts

Speech acts label a speaker's intent or meaning when he or she produces a sentence in social interaction (Searle, 1983). Toddlers produce certain types of speech acts, with some examples produced by Sara at age 3½.

Greeting: *Hi.*

Promise: *I promise I eat my beans.*

Request: *I need chocolate ice cream.*

Indirect request: *Can I have a snack?*

Complaint: *Why I can't have snack?*

Invitation: *Come play with me?*

Refusal: *Don't need lunch.*

The speech act *request* occurs when a child asks for *milk* or an adult says, *Can you close the window?* Note that the request to close the window takes the syntactic form of a question, but it would not be pragmatically appropriate for the listener to treat it as a question and say, *Yes, I can close the window* while remaining seated in a chair.

There are two types of speech acts: speech acts that take a direct form (e.g., *Close the window*) and speech acts that take an indirect form (e.g., *Can you close the window?*). The more indirect method of requesting an action is a speech act that requests action in a more subtle or roundabout manner. Over time, when language skills develop and the use of more polite forms have been observed, children learn to make requests in even more pragmatic

Table 1–8. Early Pragmatic Functions

Pragmatic Function	Example
Instrumental used to obtain a goal, to have wants and needs met	child holds out a cup and says, *more*
Regulatory used to control others' behaviors	child gives a ball to an adult to request play and says, *ball*
Interactional used to obtain joint attention	child calls *mama*
Personal used to express feelings or attitudes	child says, *yum* while eating a cookie
Heuristic used to obtain information	child says, *What's that*
Imaginative used in creative language	child says, *Let's pretend*
Informative used to tell	child says, *Doggie*

Source: From *Learning How to Mean* (p. 33), by M. A. K. Halliday, 1975, New York: Elsevier. Reprinted with permission.

or appropriate manners. Children's pragmatic skills become more appropriate over time through observation and through better understanding of others' minds.

2-year-old	*COOKIE!*
3-year-old	*Gimme cookie.*
5-year-old	*Can I have a cookie?*
7-year-old	*Those cookies sure smell good.*

Children are also able to make requests in a more appropriate manner when their language skills develop to include **modal auxiliaries** (e.g., *can, could, shall, should, may,* and *might*). Modal auxiliaries allow children to form polite requests beyond the use of *please.* Thus, there is a relationship between children's language and pragmatic skills as the acquisition of modal auxiliaries leads to more adult-like and polite requests.

COGNITION

Cognition involves knowledge and intellectual capacity (Levey, 2011b). Cognition is the mental ability to adapt to the environment, draw abstractions, generalize experiences, think about objects and events at various times, compare and contrast objects and events, infer conclusions, use symbols (words) to represent objects and events, learn language, and store information for later retrieval (Gentner, 2003). There is a connection between language and cognition that appears with the development of object permanence and word acquisition. Children's exposure to language, and how language is used in the environment, stimulates children's cognitive development.

Social cognition appears between 9 and 12 months of age with interaction between child and adults or older peers. Social cognition—essential for language development—involves the ability to learn by observing what others do and say. As children are able to read (interpret) others' minds and intentions, they develop a better understanding of language. They also begin to play a more active role in directing attention to things that interest them. In social interactive contexts, children develop an understanding of others' actions and internal intent (speaker meaning). Language develops within these joint interaction contexts with adult and child sharing attention on a particular topic and experience (Carpenter, Nagell, & Tomasello, 1998). Within these interactive contexts, children learn new words and new ways of expressing ideas.

There are two important factors associated with cognition: attention and working memory (Levey, 2011b). Attention consists of the ability to focus on the essential factors in a particular context or task, along with the ability to ignore distractions and irrelevant information. Working memory, also sometimes termed *short-term memory,* provides the ability to store information, such as when one must remember a series of spoken directions. A child with difficulty following directions may have auditory working memory problems (Gathercole & Baddeley, 1990). Consequently, this child may forget books at home and not be able to generalize information learned from an earlier time. These are essential skills for a child to store, internalize, and establish information to retrieve or remember information.

Executive Function

Executive function labels the cognitive processes that involve initiation, planning, working memory, attention, discrimination, problem solving, and verbal reasoning (Table 1–9). These processes play a major role in children's academic success for understanding, remembering, and attending within an academic context. Children who lack intact executive functions are frequently misidentified as being unmotivated, confused, and disorganized (Geffner, 2007), whereas problems may result from issues associated with executive functions.

Theory of Mind

One of the most interesting aspects of cognition is the **theory of mind**. Theory of mind describes the understanding of other individuals' mental states (Baron-Cohen, 1993, 1996). This ability marks a difference between typical language development and atypical language development. A child with typical development is able to step into another's shoes to see things from this person's point of view. Failure to develop a theory of mind is a factor in certain disorders, such as autism (Baron-Cohen, 1996).

Children's theory of mind develops through exposure to conversations about these mental state concepts (Astington, 1990), such as mental state verbs (e.g., *thinks*, *knows*, and *believes*), which correspond to another person's thoughts, knowledge, desires, and beliefs (Miller, 2006).

> *He thinks he will get a new bike.*
>
> *He knows where I put the car.*
>
> *He believes that I will share my candy.*

Table 1–9. *Cognitive Abilities*

Cognitive Function	Examples
Executive Functions	
Initiation	Beginning an activity or thought process
Planning	Ability to list steps needed to attain a goal or complete a task
Working memory	Capacity to hold and process information
Attention	Sustained focus on a task and the ability to disregard distractions
Discrimination	Recognition of differences
Problem solving	Defining and solving a problem in an efficient manner
Verbal reasoning	Ability to understand facts and concepts or ideas expressed in words and to manipulate this information to solve a problem
Theory of mind	Ability to understand others' thoughts, feelings, and ideas

Theory of mind also allows a child to understand and predict how someone else will act, explain why this person acted in a certain manner, and describe these actions with mental state verbs (de Villiers & de Villiers, 2003).

A theory of mind plays a role in understanding narratives (Guajardo & Watson, 2002), such as the early stories read to children (e.g., *The Three Bears*). Narratives introduce children to characters' feelings, beliefs, and thoughts, along with the language associated with these concepts. Narrative knowledge also helps children understand the motivation and behaviors of characters, along with the ability to predict what might happen next in a story. Children may also use this knowledge to understand the feelings and behaviors of peers and adults in the child's environment.

A theory of mind appears around the ages of 28 to 32 months, when toddlers first begin to use (but do not truly understand) the mental state terms *know, think, mean, forget,* and *guess* in pretend play (Shatz, Wellman, & Silber, 1983). A true understanding of the mental state terms *think* and *know* appears around 31 months (Bartsch &Wellman, 1995), whereas the ability to understand someone else's mind does not emerge until around 4 years of age (Feinfeld, Lee, Flavell, Green, & Flavell, 1999; Hale & Tager-Flusberg, 2003; Miller, 2006; Schult, 2002; Wellman, 1990). At this stage of development, children are able to understand and use mental terms, as shown in the following example, when Maxi heard his newborn baby brother crying while being examined by the doctor (with mental state terms underlined).

I think his feelings are hurt. I know what to do. I can fix it.

Through language and **metacognition** (a child's self-knowledge of his or her own language and thought processes), children learn to self-monitor to determine what they need to do to complete a goal and how successful they are at completing this goal. This skill provides children with the skills needed for successful academic progress (e.g., preparing for class and completing assignments).

Verbal Reasoning

Verbal reasoning is another essential cognitive ability, reflected in understanding the relationship between things in analogies (Masterson, Evans, & Aloia, 1993). For example, the analogy *Books go with read* as *toys go with* _____, requires that a child understand the relationship between *book* and *read* to draw an analogy between *toys* and *play*. Analogy means similarity, and a child must determine what similarity exists in the first relationship that can be drawn in the second while also possessing the words that label this relationship.

Cookie goes with eat as *juice goes with drink.*

There is a connection between language development and the ability to draw analogies. Children's language develops as they are able to draw analogies and find patterns in sentence productions by adults (Tomasello, 2003). For example, the frequent use of *want* by adults appears in early productions, such as *wa* and *wanna*. As children later learn new vocabulary items (e.g., *cookie, shoe, juice*), they attach these vocabulary items to previously learned words with a production such as, *Wanna cookie!* The ability to draw analogies allows children to notice how language patterns are used in a meaningful manner in different contexts (e.g., *I want a new battery, I want more potatoes,* and *I want to take a nap*).

In summary, cognitive and language abilities are closely related in the following skills: drawing analogies, understanding and describing feelings and thoughts, and understanding and expressing meaning.

A SURVEY OF COMMUNICATION DISORDERS

The ability to engage in communication depends on intact hearing, speech, expressive language, and receptive language abilities. Speech is the articulation and the production of sounds, expressive language is the communication of intent (meaning), and receptive language is the processing and understanding of the meaning of language. Processing allows children to understand language and their experiences in the world. Auditory processing skills include the ability to listen, analyze sounds and words, discriminate sounds, attach meaning to input, and to integrate all of this information into a significant whole to provide a meaningful response, as shown in the following example.

> Paul, a 5-year-old child, has difficulty in his kindergarten classroom. He frequently has difficulty with long directions (e.g., put away your toys, go to your cubby, and find your blanket). He is also easily distracted during the book-reading task. When asked questions, he does not always provide meaningful responses.

Along with verbal language skills, nonverbal processing skills include the ability to comprehend what a speaker is communicating through gestures, facial cues, eye contact, and voice quality (happiness, anger, and other internal emotions). Keep in mind that we can also communicate through drawing and writing. Cognitive abilities are also factors in communication, such as the ability to attend to the topic at hand and to store or remember spoken language and events. All of these factors are essential for communication, but they also play a role in academic skills and successful learning in the classroom.

Speech and Language Disorders

Speech and language disorders may involve (a) form (phonology, morphology, and syntax), (b) content (semantics), and/or (c) use (pragmatics). The American Speech-Language-Hearing Association (ASHA, 1993) describes a communication disorder as the impaired ability to receive, send, process, or comprehend concepts presented by verbal, nonverbal, and graphic symbol systems. A language disorder is reflected in impaired comprehension (understanding) and/or production of spoken, written, and/or other symbol systems. ASHA (1993, 2012) provides a definition of disorders that encompass language, articulation, fluency, voice, hearing, and central auditory processing (CAPD), presented next. Paul (2007) provides a review of Specific Language Impairment (SLI).

An articulation disorder is the impaired production of speech sounds that may interfere with intelligibility. This is only a disorder if difficulty continues beyond the age that most sounds should be acquired (by 4 years of age).

A phonological disorder is the use of phonological processes, such as unstressed syllable deletion (e.g., *nana/banana*), final consonant deletion (e.g., *ca/cat*), and consonant cluster reduction (e.g., *top/stop*). These processes are typical of younger children whereas absent in the productions of children over the 3 years of age.

A fluency disorder is an interruption in the flow of speaking characterized by deficits in rate, rhythm, and repetitions in sounds, syllables, words, and phrases. Fluency disorders are generally accompanied by excessive tension, struggle behavior, and secondary mannerisms.

A voice disorder is characterized by the abnormal production and/or absence of vocal quality, pitch, loudness, resonance, and/or duration that is inappropriate for an individual's age and/or sex.

A hearing impairment is the result of impaired sensitivity of the physiological auditory system that limits the development, comprehension, production, and/or maintenance of speech and/or language. Hearing disorders are described in terms of difficulties in detection, recognition, discrimination, comprehension, and perception of auditory information. ASHA defines *deafness* as a hearing disorder that limits an individual's aural/oral communication performance to the extent that the primary sensory input for communication may be other than the auditory channel. Reduced hearing acuity, whether fluctuating or permanent, adversely affects an individual's ability to communicate using the auditory channel as the primary sensory input for communication.

Central auditory processing disorders (CAPD) are deficits in the information processing of audible signals (signals that can be heard and are understood) that are not credited to impaired peripheral hearing sensitivity or intellectual impairment (ASHA, 1993). According to

ASHA, information processing is based on the following abilities.

- To attend, discriminate, and identify acoustic signals
- To store and retrieve information efficiently with the ability to restore, organize, and use retrieved information
- To segment and decode acoustic stimuli using phonological, semantic, syntactic, and pragmatic knowledge; and attach meaning to a stream of acoustic signals through use of linguistic and nonlinguistic contexts

Specific Language Impairment (SLI)

- General language acquisition is at a slower pace
- Children communicate less often than peers
- Repertoires of consonant sounds are smaller
- Delayed acquisition of CVC syllables and multisyllabic productions
- Vocabulary deficits, such as the delayed acquisition of words, are the first sign of language delay
- Word combinations do not appear at age 18 to 24 months as expected
- Difficulty learning inflectional morphemes, auxiliary verbs, and articles
- At risk for attention difficulties
- Difficulties with symbolic play, classification, figurative thought
- A possible correlation between SLI and learning problems

Language disorders can encompass receptive language:

Understanding gestures

Following directions

Answering questions

Identifying objects and picture

Language disorders appear in expressive language:

Asking questions

Naming objects

Putting words together to form sentences

Learning to produce songs and rhymes

Using correct pronouns, such as *he, she, they*

Engaging in and maintaining a conversation

Language difficulties can also appear in early reading and writing skills:

Holding a book right side up

Looking at pictures and turning pages of a book

Telling a story with a clear beginning, middle, and end

Naming letters and numbers

Learning the alphabet

Autism

Autism —
impaired social
interaction
and communic-
ation, delayed
language
development,
avoidance of
eye contact,
interaction
difficulties
with peers,
restricted/
repetative
behavior

l *Statistical Manual of*
(DSM-IV-TR) (Ameri-
sociation [APA], 2000)
r features of autism to
social interaction and
elayed language devel-
e of eye contact, inter-
with peers, as well as
etitive behavior, such
ing the same sound or
sing on a particular toy.
must be manifested by

delays and abnormal function in at least one or several of the following behaviors before 3 years of age (APA, 2000).

Social interaction

Language as used in social communication

Symbolic or imaginative play

In some cases, parents report that children younger than 3 years old exhibit typical development, such as the acquisition of a few words. However, if autism is present, these children lose these words and development stagnates or does not progress. In summary, if there is a typical period of development, it cannot extend beyond age 3 for the diagnosis of autism. In many cases, there may be an associated diagnosis of mental retardation, ranging from mild to profound.

Autism spectrum disorders represent a range of disorders that affect socialization, communication, and behavior. Impairments exist in the following areas (APA, 2000, p. 69): reciprocal social interaction, communication, or stereotyped behavior, interests, or activities. Stereotyped behaviors are those that are restricted and repetitive, such as spinning or repeated actions with an object. Previously called pervasive developmental disorders (PDDs), autism was designated as the most severe of the PDDs. The classification of pervasive developmental delay not otherwise specified (PDD-NOS) was assigned to a child who exhibited impaired social interaction, verbal and nonverbal communication, or stereotyped behavior or actions but did meet the criteria of any specific pervasive developmental disorder.

Table 1–10 presents the description of the Autistic, Rett's, and Childhood Disintegrative Disorders found in DSM-IV-TR (2000).

Table 1–10. *Autism Spectrum Disorders*

Diagnostic Criteria for 299.00 Autistic Disorder

A. A total of six or more items from (1), (2), and (3), with at least two from (1), and one each from (2) , and (3):

  (1) qualitative impairment in social interaction, as manifested by at least two of the following:

   (a) marked impairment in the use of multiple nonverbal behaviors such as eye-to-eye gaze, facial expression, body postures, and gestures to regulate social interaction

   (b) failure to develop peer relationships appropriate to developmental level

   (c) a lack of spontaneous seeking to share enjoyment, interests, or achievements with other people (e.g., by a lack of showing, bringing, or pointing out objects of interest)

   (d) Lack of social or emotional reciprocity

  (2) Qualitative impairments in communication as manifested by at least one of the following:

   (a) delay in, or total lack of, the development of spoken language (not accompanied by an attempt to compensate through alternative modes of communication such as gesture or mime)

   (b) in individuals with adequate speech, marked impairment in the ability to initiate or sustain a conversation with others

   (c) stereotyped and repetitive use of language or idiosyncratic language

   (d) lack of varied, spontaneous, make-believe play or social imitative play appropriate to developmental level

  (3) restricted repetitive and stereotyped patterns of behavior, interests, and activities, as manifested by at least one of the following:

   (a) encompassing preoccupation with one or more stereotyped and restricted patterns of interest that is abnormal either in intensity or focus

   (b) apparently inflexible adherence to specific, nonfunctional routines or rituals

   (c) stereotyped and repetitive motor mannerisms (e.g., hand or finger flapping or twisting, or complex whole–body movements)

   (d) persistent preoccupation with parts of objects

B. Delays or abnormal functioning in at least one of the following areas, with onset prior to age 3 years: (1) social interaction, (2) language as used in social communication, or (3) symbolic, or imaginative play.

C. The disturbance is not better accounted for by Rett's Disorder or Childhood Disintegrative Disorder.

Diagnostic Criteria for 299.80 Rett's Disorder

A. All of the following:

  (1) apparently normal prenatal and perinatal development

  (2) apparently normal psychomotor development through the first 5 months after birth

  (3) normal head circumference at birth

Table 1–10. continued

B. Onset of all the following after the period of normal development:

(1) deceleration of head growth between ages 5 and 48 months

(2) loss of previously acquired purposeful hand skills between ages 5 and 30 months, with the subsequent development of stereotyped hand movements (e.g., hand- wringing or hand-washing)

(3) loss of social engagement early in the course (although often social interaction develops later)

(4) appearance of poorly coordinated gait or trunk movements

(5) severely impaired expressive and receptive language development, with severe psychomotor retardation

Diagnostic Criteria for 299.10 Childhood Disintegrative Disorder

A. Apparently normal development for at least the first two years after birth as manifested by the presence of age–appropriate verbal and nonverbal communication, social relationships, play, and adaptive behavior

B. Clinically sufficient loss of previously acquired skills (before age 10 years) in at least two of the following areas:

(1) expressive or receptive language

(2) social skills or adaptive behavior

(3) bowel or bladder control

(4) play

(5) motor skills

C. Abnormalities of functioning in at least two of the following areas:

(1) qualitative impairment in social interaction (e.g., impairment in nonverbal behaviors, failure to develop peer relationships, lack of social or emotional reciprocity)

(2) qualitative impairments in communication (e.g., delay or lack of spoken language, inability to initiate or sustain a conversation, stereotyped and repetitive use of language, lack of varied make-believe play)

(3) restricted, repetitive, and stereotyped patterns of behavior, interests, and activities, including motor stereotypes and mannerisms

D. The disturbance is not better accounted for by another specific pervasive developmental disorder or by schizophrenia.

Diagnostic Criteria for Attention-Deficit/Hyperactivity Disorder

A. Either (1) or (2):

(1) Six (or more) of the following symptoms of **inattention** have persisted for at least 6 months to a degree that is maladaptive and inconsistent with developmental level:

Inattention

(a) often fails to give close attention to details or makes careless mistakes in schoolwork, work, or other activities

(b) often has difficulty sustaining attention in tasks or play activities

continues

Table 1–10. *continued*

(c) often does not seem to listen when spoken to directly

(d) often does not follow through on instructions and fails to finish schoolwork, chores, or duties in the workplace (not due to oppositional behavior or failure to understand instructions)

(e) often has difficulty organizing tasks and activities

(f) often avoids, dislikes, or is reluctant to engage in tasks that require sustained mental effort (such as schoolwork or homework)

(g) often loses things necessary for tasks or activities (e.g., toys, school assignments, pencils, books, or tools)

(h) is often easily distracted by extraneous stimuli

(i) is often forgetful in daily activities

(2) Six (or more) of the following symptoms of **hyperactivity-impulsivity** have persisted for at least 6 months to a degree that is maladaptive and inconsistent with developmental level:

Hyperactivity

(a) often fidgets with hands or feet or squirms in seat

(b) often leaves seat in classroom or in other situations in which remaining seated is expected

(c) often runs about or climbs excessively in situations in which it is inappropriate (in adolescents or adults, may be limited to subjective feelings of restlessness)

(d) often has difficulty playing or engaging in leisure activities quietly

(e) is often "on the go" or often acts as if "driven by a motor"

(f) often talks excessively

Impulsivity

(g) often blurts out answers before questions have been completed

(h) often has difficulty awaiting turn

(i) often interrupts or intrudes on others (e.g., butts into conversations or games)

B. Some hyperactive–impulsive or inattentive symptoms that caused impairments were present before age 7 years.

C. Some impairment from the symptoms is present in two or more settings (e.g., at school [or work] and at home).

D. There must be clear evidence of clinically sufficient impairment in social, academic, or occupational functioning.

E. The symptoms do not occur exclusively during the course of a pervasive developmental disorder, schizophrenia, or other psychotic disorder and are not better accounted for by another mental disorder (e.g., Mood Disorder, Anxiety Disorder, Dissociative Disorder, or a Personality Disorder).

Source: From the *Diagnostic and Statistical Manual of Mental Disorders, Fourth Edition,* Text Revision (pp. 75–79; 92–93), 2000, American Psychiatric Association. Reprinted with permission.

In the DSM-IV-TR (2000), the American Psychiatric Association (APA) defined Asperger's syndrome as falling within the autism spectrum while characterized by fluent language, intact intellectual skills, and full inclusion in school. The fifth edition of the *Diagnostic and Statistical Manual of Mental Disorders* (DSM-V) (APA, 2013) includes Asperger's disorder into the category of Autism Spectrum Disorder. Thus, it no longer exists as a separate diagnostic category.

COMMUNICATION DISORDERS AND SPEECH AND LANGUAGE DIFFERENCES

There has been a growing awareness of bilingual cultural and linguistic differences over the last decade (Beverly-Ducker & Polovoy, 2009) with efforts to improve the quality of speech, language, and hearing services, research, and knowledge for diverse language speakers. Children from bilingual homes who become proficient in both their native and second languages have improved educational outcomes in terms of school completion rates, grades, achievement test scores, educational aspiration, and personal adjustment (Bedore, 2010). There is also evidence that the promotion of bilingualism and biliteracy has intellectual, economic, and social benefits (Snow, Burns, & Griffin, 1998).

Research shows that first-language literacy development is strongly related to both second-language learning and academic progress, given that literacy skills in a child's native language transfer to their second language (Thomas & Collier, 1998). The goal of these studies is to ensure that practitioners are aware that "differences" (i.e., dialect or language differences from a speaker's dialect or language) do not imply "disorders" or "deficiencies." There may be negative outcomes in regard to therapy when a clinician does not take into account a family's cultural or linguistic characteristics because the family may feel that the clinician does not respect differences. Practitioners should obtain the education, training, and experience necessary for providing services to a diverse population. The appropriate approach to assessment is to gather information from multiple sources, such as interviews with parents and teachers. Standardized tests may often show depressed test performance but not reveal true abilities or learning potential (Gutierrez-Clellen and Peña, 2001, p. 212). Informal assessment, such as language samples, may reveal true abilities (Roseberry-McKibbin & O'Hanlon, 2005). Chapter 9 presents a comprehensive explanation of assessment and intervention when working with children learning English as a second language.

It is essential to recognize the differences between the different disorders to provide children with evidence-based intervention. Evidence-based practice is defined as the use of the most current and best research to provide quality intervention. Evidence-based practice also involves adapting practice to the child's cultural background. To provide evidence-based practice, the speech-language pathologist must integrate three factors: clinical expertise/expert opinion; external scientific evidence; and client/patient/caregiver values. The goals of evidence-based practice follow (ASHA, 2005).

◆ Recognize the needs, abilities, values, preferences, and interests of individuals and families to whom they provide clinical services, and integrate those factors along with best current research evidence and their clinical expertise in making clinical decisions

◆ Acquire and maintain the knowledge and skills that are necessary to provide high-quality professional services, including knowledge and skills related to evidence-based practice

◆ Evaluate prevention, screening, and diagnostic procedures, protocols, and measures to identify maximally informative and cost-effective diagnostic and screening tools using recognized appraisal criteria described in the evidence-based practice literature

◆ Evaluate the efficacy, effectiveness, and efficiency of clinical protocols for prevention, treatment, and enhancement using criteria recognized in the evidence-based practice literature

◆ Evaluate the quality of evidence appearing in any source or format, including journal articles, textbooks, continuing education offerings, newsletters, advertising, and Web-based products, prior to incorporating such evidence into clinical decision making

◆ Monitor and incorporate new and high-quality research evidence having implications for clinical practice

In summary, evidence-based practice involves integrating clinical practice with current research appropriate to an individual's difficulties (Sackett, Rosenberg, Gray, Haynes, & Richardson, 1996).

It is also essential that speech-language pathologists recognize the difference between speech and/or language disorders and linguistic or cultural differences so that they may determine if a communicative disorder actually exists. For second-language learners of English, there are variations of proficiencies in English (ASHA, 1985): (a) bilingual English proficient, (b) limited English proficient, and (c) limited in both English and the minority language. A bilingual English *proficient* speaker is fluent in speaking English, whereas some *limited* English proficient speakers may be proficient in their native language but not for communicating in English. In any case, assessment should be based on the speaker's native language, along with assessment of English language skills. Assessment should also determine what language (English or the native language) is dominant.

To assess an individual's native language, a speech-language pathologist must also be able to distinguish a communication disorder from a language or a dialectal difference. Speakers of a dialect may have difficulties in linguistic factors: form (phonology, morphology, and syntax), content (semantics), or function (pragmatics). According to ASHA (1993), a dialect difference is a variation of a symbol system determined by regional, social, or cultural/ethnic factors. These differences do not constitute a speech or language disorder (ASHA, 1983).

If a speech-language pathologist is unfamiliar with a child's language or dialect background, he or she may follow these guidelines to provide appropriate cultural intervention.

Sample peers or adult speakers in the child's linguistic community

Obtain information from interpreters/support personnel

Become thoroughly familiar with features of the dialect and language

There may be professional interpreters available or the speech-language pathologist may ask a family member or friend for assistance. Interpreters and family members must be trained so that they do not use cues (e.g., gestures or vocal intonations) during the assessment of the child's speech and language. In this way, with the help of others, the speech-language pathologist can determine if there is a disorder.

The American Speech-Language-Hearing Association (2011) states that speech-language pathologists should possess cultural competence.

Value diversity

Conduct cultural assessment

Possess cultural knowledge

It is also important to understand that intervention approaches may differ among children and that the same intervention approach may not be appropriate for all children. For example, some areas of language may be intact whereas other areas may need intervention. As described in Chapter 9, it is important to consider each of the areas of language to determine what areas present difficulty (i.e., phonology, morphology, syntax, or semantics). In summary, speech-language pathologists should possess cultural competence with knowledge, understanding, and appreciation for cultural and linguistic factors. Speech-language pathologists must acquire knowledge of bilingual differences, given so many children whose primary language is not English are currently enrolled in kindergarten to 12th-grade programs in the United States (U.S. Department of Education's Office of English Language Acquisition, 2002).

STRATEGIES TO IDENTIFY CHILDREN WITH COMMUNICATION DISORDERS

There are criteria that can be used to create a checklist of behaviors for determining the possible existence of a communication disorder, taking into account the parameters established for the cultural and language background of a child. The following behaviors may be observed by a speech-language pathologist to identify a child's difficulties (Levey, 2011a).

Expressive Language

◆ Rarely initiates verbal interactions or activities with peers or family members
◆ Does not respond verbally to questions or comments from peers or family members
◆ Language observed to be lower than the level used by peers
◆ Smaller vocabulary than expected for age, in first language or second (if second-language learner)
◆ Shorter, less complex sentences than expected for age
◆ Difficulty communicating verbally with peers or family members
◆ Relies heavily on gestures and nonverbal means to communicate
◆ Peers rarely initiate verbal exchanges
◆ Does not attempt to repair communication failures
◆ Does not verbally request help or clarification when needed
◆ Makes frequent use of empty, meaningless words: *it, thing, this,* or *that*
◆ Peers have difficulty understanding the child's speech or language efforts

Receptive Language

◆ Instructions need to be repeated
◆ Slow in responding to questions or instructions
◆ Does not learn new concepts or vocabulary
◆ Forgets material assumed to be learned
◆ Has difficulty understanding words

PRAGMATICS

- Does not take turns or maintain conversations with peers
- Eye contact may be absent or inconsistent
- Does not engage peers in an appropriate manner

It is also important to observe the child in the classroom (or in various classrooms for older children) and to consult with the family to determine if there are any additional areas of difficulty. In summary, speech-language pathologists must understand the full range of disorders so that the children can be given appropriate support.

SUMMARY

In this chapter, we have reviewed the following factors, which introduce the components of language:

- We reviewed the components of speech and language and the relationship between language and cognition.
- We learned that there is a close relationship between the components of language: A speaker's meaning (semantics) is conveyed in the appropriate sentence form (syntax), with the correct morphemes assigned to indicate past tense (morphology), with the correct phonetic patterns assigned (phonology), and the appropriate manner of interaction between the speaker and listener (pragmatics).
- We also learned that children form hypotheses or theories of how language works, as when children produce the word *eated*. This shows that children have acquired grammar but have not yet learned the correct application of the rules that govern language.
- We reviewed the factors that characterize children's atypical development, along with signs of difficulty in expressive, receptive, and pragmatic development.
- We discussed the difference between a disorder and cultural and linguistic differences.

Chapter 2 explores the theories that account for children's language acquisition and development to help you understand how children acquire and develop language.

KEY WORDS

Cognition

Communication

Communicative competence

Content

Decode

Encode

Executive function

Form

Generative

Grammar

Graphemes

Language

Metacognition

Modal auxiliaries

Morphemes

Morphology

Morphophonology

Orthography

Overgeneralize

Paralinguistic

Perception

Phonemes

Phonological processes

Phonology

Pragmatics

Prosody

Proximity

Selection restrictions

Semantic features

Semantic relations

Semantics

Speech

Speech act

Syntax

Theory of mind

Use

STUDY QUESTIONS

1. What is the difference between communication, speech, and language?

2. Describe some of the differences between typical and atypical language development.

3. Explain why morphology is an important part of sentence development.

4. Describe and give some examples of the connection between morphology and phonology.

5. Explain why a child may say, *I eated a cookie.*

REFERENCES

American Psychiatric Association. (2000). *Diagnostic and statistical manual of mental disorders* (4th ed., text rev.). Arlington, VA: Author.

American Psychiatric Association. (2013). *Diagnostic and statistical manual of mental disorders* (5th ed.). Arlington, VA: Author.

American Speech-Language-Hearing Association. (1983). *Social dialects* [Position statement]. Retrieved from http://www.asha.org/policy

American Speech-Language-Hearing Association. (1985). *Clinical management of communicatively handicapped minority language populations* [Position statement]. Retrieved from http://www.asha.org/policy

American Speech-Language-Hearing Association. (1993). *Definitions of communication disorders and variations* [Relevant paper]. Retrieved from http://www.asha.org/policy

American Speech-Language-Hearing Association. (2005). *Evidence-based practice in communication disorders* [Position statement]. Retrieved from http://www.asha/policy

American Speech-Language-Hearing Association. (2011). *Cultural competence in professional service delivery* [Position statement]. Retrieved from http://www.asha.org/policy

American Speech-Language-Hearing Association. (2012). *Preschool language disorders.* Retrieved from http://www.asha.org/public/speech/disorders/Preschool-Language-Disorders/

Astington, J. W. (1990). Narrative and the child's theory of mind. In B. K. Britton & A. D. Pellegrini (Eds.), *Narrative thought and narrative language* (pp. 151–171). Hillsdale, NJ: Erlbaum.

Badian, N. A. (1998). A validation of the role of preschool phonological and orthographic skills in the prediction of reading. *Journal of Learning Disabilities, 31,* 472–482.

Baron-Cohen, S. (1993). From attention-goal psychology to belief-desire psychology: The development of a theory of mind, and its dysfunction. In S. Baron-Cohen, H.

Tager-Flusberg, & D. J. Cohen (Eds.), *Understanding other minds: Perspectives from autism* (pp. 59–82). New York, NY: Oxford University Press.

Baron-Cohen, S. (1996). *Mind blindness: An essay on autism and theory of mind.* Cambridge, MA: MIT Press.

Bartsch, K., & Wellman, H. M. (1995). *Children talk about the mind.* Oxford, UK: Oxford University Press.

Bedore, L. M. (2010). Choosing the language of intervention for Spanish-English bilingual preschoolers with language impairment. *Evidence-Based Practice Briefs, 5*(1), 1–13.

Bernstein, D. K. (2011). Language development form age 3 to 5. In S. Levey & S. Polirstok (Eds.), *Language development: Understanding language diversity in the classroom* (pp. 139–160). Los Angeles, CA: Sage.

Beverly-Ducker, K., & Polovoy, C. (2009, June 16). *ASHA multiculturalism expands as 20th century closes. The ASHA Leader.*

Bloom, L., Lahey, M., Hood, L., Lifter, K., & Fiess, K. (1980). Complex sentences: Acquisition of syntactic connectives and the semantic relations they encode. *Journal of Child Language, 7,* 235–261.

Carpenter, M., Nagell, K., & Tomasello, M. (1998). Social cognition, joint attention, and communicative competence from 9 to 15 months of age. *Monographs of the Society for Research in Child Development, 63*(4), 1–176.

Carter, A. S., Davis, N. O., Klin, A., & Volkmar, F. R. (2005). Social development in autism. In F. R. Volkmar, R. Paul, A. Klin, & D. Cohen (Eds.), *Handbook of autism and pervasive developmental disorders: Vol. 1. Diagnosis, development, neurobiology, and behavior.* Hoboken, NJ: John Wiley & Sons.

Cavallo, S. A. (2011). The production of speech sounds. In S. Levey & S. Polirstok (Eds.), *Language development: Understanding language diversity in the classroom* (pp. 79–100). Los Angeles, CA: Sage.

De Villiers, J. G., & de Villiers, P. A. (2003). Language for thought: Coming to understand false beliefs. In D. Gentner &. S. Goldin-Meadow (Eds.), *Language in mind; advances in the study of language and thought* (pp. 335–384). Cambridge, MA: MIT Press.

Feinfeld, K. A., Lee, P. P., Flavell, E. R., Green, F. L., & Flavell, J. H. (1999). Young children's understanding of intention. *Cognitive Development, 14,* 463–486.

Gathercole, S. E., & Baddeley, A. D. (1990). Phonological memory deficits in language disordered children: Is there a causal connection? *Journal of Memory and Language, 29,* 336–360.

Geffner, D. (2007, November). *Managing executive function disorders.* Paper presented at a meeting of the American Speech-Language-Hearing Association, Boston, MA.

Gentner, D. (2003). Why we're so smart. In D. Gentner & S. Goldin-Meadow (Eds.), *Language in mind: Advances in the study of language and thought* (pp. 195–235). Cambridge, MA: MIT Press.

Gleason, J. B., & Ratner, N. B. (2009). *The development of language* (7th ed.). Boston: MA: Allyn & Bacon.

Gopnik, M. (1997). *The inheritance and innateness of grammars.* Oxford, UK: Oxford University Press.

Graham, S., Harris, K. R., & Fink, B. (2000). Extra handwriting instruction: Prevent writing difficulties right from the start. *Teaching Exceptional Children, 33,* 88–92.

Guajardo, N. R., & Watson, A. C. (2002). Narrative discourse and theory of mind development. *The Journal of Genetic Psychology, 163,* 305–325.

Gutierrez-Clellen, V. F., & Peña, E. (2001). Dynamic assessment of diverse children with low school achievement: A tutorial. *Language, Speech, and Hearing Services in Schools, 32,* 212–224.

Hale, C. M., & Tager-Flusberg, H. (2003). The influence of language on theory of mind: A training study. *Developmental Science, 6*(3), 346–359.

Halliday, M. A. K. (1975). *Learning how to mean: Explorations in the development of language.* London, England: Edward Arnold. (New York, NY: Elsevier, 1977)

Levey, S. (2011a). Typical and atypical language development. In S. Levey & S. Polirstok (Eds.), *Language development: Understanding language diversity in the classroom* (pp. 37–58). Los Angeles, CA: Sage.

Levey, S. (2011b). Theories and explanations of language development. In S. Levey & S. Polirstok (Eds.), *Language development: Understanding language diversity in the classroom* (pp. 17–36). Los Angeles, CA: Sage.

Levey, S., & Schwartz, R. G. (2002). Syllable omission by two-year-old children. *Communication Disorders Quarterly, 23*(4), 169–177.

Masterson, J. J., Evans, L. H., & Aloia, M. (1993). Verbal analogy reasoning in children with language-learning disabilities. *Journal of Speech and Hearing Research, 36,* 76–82.

Miller, C. A. (2006). Developmental relationships between language and theory of mind. *American Journal of Speech-Language Pathology, 15,* 142–154.

Office of English Language Acquisition. (2002, October). *Survey of the states' limited English proficient students and available educational programs and services 2000–2001* (Summary report). Washington, DC: Author.

Owens, R. E., Jr. (2008). *Language development: An introduction* (7th ed.). Boston, MA: Pearson.

Paul, R. (2007). *Language disorders from infancy through adolescence*. St. Louis, MO: Mosby Elsevier.

Roseberry-McKibbin, C., & O'Hanlon, L. (2005). Nonbiased assessment of English language learners: A tutorial. *Communication Disorders Quarterly, 26*(3), 178–185.

Sackett, D., Rosenberg, W. M. C., Gray, J. A. M., Haynes, R. B., & Richardson, W. S. (1996). *Evidence-based medicine: What it is and what it isn't. It's about integrating individual clinical expertise and the best external evidence.* Retrieved from http://www.ncbi.nlm.nih.gov/pmc/articles/PMC2349778/pdf/bmj00524-0009.pdf

Schult, C. A. (2002). Children's understanding of the distinction between intentions and desires. *Child Development, 73*(6), 1727–1747.

Searle, J. (1983). *Intentionality: An essay in the philosophy of mind.* New York, NY: Cambridge University Press.

Shatz, M., Wellman, H. M., & Silber, S. (1983). The acquisition of mental verbs: A systematic investigation of the first reference to mental state. *Cognition, 14,* 301–321.

Snow, C. E., Burns, M. S., & Griffin, P. (Eds.). (1998). *Preventing reading difficulties in young children.* Committee on the Prevention of Reading Difficulties in Young Children. Commission on Behavioral and Social Sciences and Education: National Research Council. Washington, DC: National Academy Press.

Thomas, W. P., & Collier, V. P. (1998). Two languages are better than one. *Educational Leadership, 23–26.*

Tomasello, M. (2000). First steps toward a usage-based theory of language acquisition. *Cognitive Linguistics, 11*(1/2), 61–82.

Tomasello, M. (2003). *Constructing a language: A usage-based theory of language acquisition.* Cambridge, MA: Harvard University Press.

Wellman, H. M. (1990). *The child's theory of mind.* Cambridge, MA: MIT Press.

CHAPTER 2

An Introduction to Theories of Language Development

Sandra Levey

Micah was asked if he ate his dinner. He said, "Yes, I eated it." Over time, with greater exposure to language used in the environment, he produced the word "ate" when asked if he had finished his meal. After reading the theories presented in this chapter, you will come to understand the processes that support children's learning language in the absence of direct instruction in how to produce irregular past tense verbs (e.g., eat/ate).

Understanding how children acquire language information is important to speech-language pathologists. Much of the information in theories of language development has been taken from investigations that provide us with the factors that play a role in the development of language. One of the things that we have learned is that children learn best when given greater exposure to certain language items. For example, there are items that occur more frequently in spoken language, such as past tense verbs that end in -ed. Because these items occur more frequently than verbs with irregular past tense forms (e.g., *eat/ate*, *throw/threw*, and

fly/flew), children use the more frequent past tense verb ending -ed to form the past tense (e.g., *eated*, *throwed*, and *flyed*). Children have been called *scientists in the crib* (Gopnik, Meltzoff, & Kuhl, 2001), given that they begin to investigate and form hypotheses or theories about how language works at a very early age. Based on experience with exposure to spoken language over time, they revise their ideas about how language works. The theories we review in this chapter attempt to explain children's language development. These theories also include insights on how we might provide support for language development to children with language disorders.

CHAPTER OBJECTIVES

Theories of language development attempt to explain how children learn the complex system of communication. The theories presented in this chapter can be placed into three main categories: nurture, nature, and those that argue for the role of both nature and nurture in language development.

Nurture theories hold that language develops primarily from experience and interaction within the external **environment**, where children gain information about how to use language to label things, actions, events, and another person's state of mind (e.g., feelings, belief, and knowledge). This view, expressed by Skinner (1957), is covered in this chapter.

Nature theories, sometimes called nativist or psycholinguistic theories, hold that there is a biological basis to language. In this theory, the human brain is viewed as prewired (inborn) to provide children with the syntactic rules for the language spoken in their environment. Within this chapter, this view is represented by the psycholinguistic or nativist theory of language development held by Chomsky (1957, 1965).

There are also theories that view both nature and nurture as playing a similarly important role in language development. This is a more coherent view of language development. In this view, the faculty of *language* is not **innate**, but general *cognitive* processes of the human brain (human thought, attention, memory, and problem solving) provide the mechanisms for language development. Language emerges from an interaction between (a) cognitive mechanisms in the human brain and (b) experience with language in the external environment. These views are expressed by the cognitive theory (Piaget, 1954); the social interaction theory (Vygotsky, 1935); the pragmatic theory (Bates, 1976) that emerged from the ideas developed by Vygotsky's social interaction theory; the semantic-cognitive theory (Bloom, 1970); the usage-based theory of language (Tomasello, 2003, 2009); and the emergentism theory (Bates & MacWhinney, 1988; Seidenberg & Elman, 1999).

To understand these theories better, it is important to be aware of the main arguments associated with each before reading this chapter.

◆ Behavioral theory (Skinner, 1957): Language emerges from reinforcement and imitation and develops as children learn a behavior that provides a cue to the next related behavior, such as a noun signaling the following verb (e.g., *dogs bark*).

◆ Nativist or psycholinguistic theory (Chomsky, 1957, 1965): Language emerges from a biological or innate language acquisition device (LAD) that contains the principles of universal grammar rules for sentence organization, with the external environment providing only information for developing rules and about the syntactic structures of language.

◆ Social interaction theory (Vygotsky, 1935): Language emerges from social purposes in social interaction and adults and children with greater knowledge provide guidance to support children's language development and learning.

◆ Cognitive theory (Piaget, 1954): Language emerges from a connection between language and cognition, and certain cognitive abilities must be present for language to develop; children solve problems on their own with less emphasis on **environmental** input for guidance.

◆ Pragmatic theory (Bates, 1976, 2004): Language emerges from children's desire to interact in a social manner with a connection between children's preverbal behaviors (e.g., gestures, eye contact, and prelinguistic vocalizations) and later language skills; the pragmatic theory emerged from the social interaction theory (Vygotsky, 1935) and led to the development of the theory of emergentism (Bates & MacWhinney, 1982, 1988).

◆ Semantic-cognitive theory (Bloom, 1970): Language emerges from children's expression of the meaning of things and activities in the environment; children's early productions reflect their experience with things and actions in the environment; this theory developed to describe the semantic content (meaning) expressed by children's early language productions.

◆ Usage-based theory (Tomasello, 2003, 2009): Language emerges from an initial concrete understanding of language and children must apply their general cognitive abilities (e.g., observation and interaction) to learn the association between spoken language and the meaning associated with spoken language.

◆ Emergentism/guided distributional learning theory (Bates & MacWhinney, 1982,1988; Seidenberg & Elman, 1999): Language emerges from an interaction between innate cognitive abilities and the ability to connect words with objects and actions that occur in the external environment (e.g., the word *fall* as things fall) and the ability to note more frequent patterns in spoken language (e.g., nouns are followed by verbs in sentences).

This chapter ends with a summary of the most important factors found in each of these theories that play a role in children's language development. After reading this chapter, you should understand the following concepts:

◆ The role of the environment in language acquisition

◆ The role of innate skills in language acquisition

◆ The role of the interaction between innate skills and the environment in language development

◆ The factors that best support children's language development

AN INTRODUCTION TO THE THEORIES OF LANGUAGE ACQUISITION AND DEVELOPMENT

The Role of the Environment in Language Development

The external environment provides the essential information to support children's language development (Bates, 1976; Bates & MacWhinney, 1982; Piaget, 1954; Skinner, 1957; Vygotsky, 1935). The external environment includes entities (e.g., people and animals), objects (e.g., balls, vases, and cars), actions (e.g., running, eating, and drinking), and events (e.g., birthday parties, weddings, and parades). Exposure to these entities, objects, and actions contribute to children's early language development as children learn the names that label them.

Entities	*mommy, doggy, baby*
Objects	*ball, car, milk*
Actions	*walk, run, play*

The Role of Cognition in Language Development

Children also learn **concepts** about the meaning of things (objects or animals), actions or events (crying, falling, birth-day parties), and qualities and feelings of things and people (tall, dirty, shiny, happy, scared) in the environment. Their cognitive skills allow them to learn how language acts to label these things, events, and qualities, providing them with the ability to draw a connection between words and things or events in the environment. The process of concept formation occurs when a child develops an idea about the properties or meanings of things, events, or qualities of things by observing the features or characteristics of these things and events (Owens, 2008). In the case of developing a concept of *dog,* a child may combine the concept of four legs, tail, and hair.

Concept learning also appears when children learn how an object may be used in relation to another thing, such as a *brush* used to brush a person's hair, clothing, or a dog. Other basic concepts consist of locations (e.g., up/down), quality descriptions (e.g., big/little), times (e.g., today/yesterday), and thoughts or feelings (e.g., happy/sad). Children learn these concepts and others from those around them (Gelman, 2009).

According to Gelman, concept development begins in infancy. For example, an infant may learn the concept of *happy* when seeing an adult smiling while pointing to a cat and saying "kitty." Children's concepts of things change over time as they gain experience with things and events (Owens, 2008). For example, the initial concept of *brushing* may apply only to the child's hair but expand to include a number of other examples of *brush* (e.g., brush off an insult or a brush with danger). The external environment provides the information for language development through the cognitive process of concept formation.

We begin our exploration of the theories of language development with an example of the nurture explanation: the behavioral theory of language development.

THE NURTURE THEORY OF LANGUAGE DEVELOPMENT

Behavioral Theory

Skinner (1957) offers a behavioral view of language development. In this view, children are provided with cues from the environment that set the conditions for a behavior to occur. The environment plays a role in language development through **operant conditioning**. Operant conditioning consists of reinforcement (positive or negative response) and imitation (modeling). Reinforcement occurs when a child says "mama" and the adult responds with a positive response, such as a smile or verbal response. Initially, adults may reinforce younger children's utterances that are not fully adultlike. Later, adults may reinforce only more adultlike utterances as children's language develops over time.

Reinforcement frequently consists of scaffolds (shown in Table 2–1) that provide an example of the adult target (e.g., *banana* in place of *nana*). Consequently, lack of reinforcement may occur if the productions vary greatly from an expected form, such as a child producing *Muma* instead of *Mama*. In this way, children learn language through the association between the stimulus (something that causes a response) and the response (reinforcement or lack of reinforcement). Adults also provide children with imitative **models** that provide a more adultlike example.

Table 2–1. *Scaffolds*

Modeling a target	Adult: Why won't the elephant fit through the door? Child: No response. Adult: He won't fit *because he's too big*! (emphasizing the answer *because he's too big*).
Recasts	
Simple expansion	Child: He eat Adult: He *is* eat*ing*
Structural or modality recasts	Child: He is coming? Adult: *Is* he coming?
Buildup recasts	Child: I ate a cookie. It yummy. Adult: Yes, you ate a *yummy cookie*.
Breakdown	Child: I want peas, not carrots. Adult: Ok, you want *the* peas—not *the* ... I'll get *the* peas.
Eliciting atte...	
False asse...	...dog! ...g!
Feigned...	...! ...belong to me? ...ant it. ...*I* want it (placing hand on ...dicate the correct pronoun
For...	...want a cookie or a carrot?
WH qu...	...o you like cookies? *Who* ate the ...is the cookie? *What* is that?
Environmental manipulation	Adult... forgot something! (deliberately leaving out an important element for a game) Child: We no got monkeys. Adult: We need to get the monkeys.
Violation of object function	Adult: I'll cut the paper with this ruler. Child: No, not with a ruler! Need scissors. Adult: That's right. We need scissors to cut paper.

[Handwritten note overlaid on table:]

Behavioral Theory – (SKINNER)
Operant conditioning –
immitation and reinforcement
When The child says
Mama you smile which
makes child aware They
are good and They
will continue behavior
Also, modeling by
adults

35

Syntax (sentence formation and production) develops when children learn to produce longer sentences through **chaining**. Initially, children produce single words (e.g., *me, cup, cookie*). Chaining occurs when a behavior provides a cue to the next related behavior, such as the sequence of the alphabet letter "A" followed by the alphabet letter "B" and so on. In a similar way, syntax develops when children learn that the pronoun "I" is followed by a verb (e.g., *I + want + cookie*). Over time, children learn that the word *cookie* might be preceded by an adjective, such as *big* (e.g., *I + want + big + cookie*). Through chaining, syntax develops. Although syntax begins when children produce two-word utterances (e.g., *Wanna cookie*), there are earlier stages of development, beginning with single words.

In summary, children learn language through reinforcement, imitation, and chaining. Imitation provides a model for learning these forms, and positive reinforcement leads to the repeated production of these, along with more advanced language forms. Syntax develops when children learn that one word precedes another (e.g., pronouns are followed by verbs). The environment plays a major role in shaping children's behaviors, such as the development of language.

THE NATURE THEORY OF LANGUAGE DEVELOPMENT

The Psycholinguistic or Nativist Theory

Proponents of the innateness theory (sometimes termed the *nativist* or *psycholinguistic theory*) argue that children possess preprogrammed, innate (inborn/native) abilities that are specialized for syntactic language acquisition (Chomsky, 1957, 1959, 1964, 1965; Pinker, 1994). Language development occurs as the result of an interaction between children's innate skills and linguistic data (McLeish & Martin, 1975).

> Children's innate linguistic competence: knowledge that enables a language learner or user to produce and comprehend language that provides him or her with knowledge of the principles of universal grammar (i.e., rules allowing for the production of sentences in any and all languages of the world)
>
> Linguistic data: information that children use to develop the language consistent with the language spoken in their environment

hypotheses or ideas about the regularities or consistent patterns found in language, such as the order of words that occur in sentences (e.g., nouns followed by verbs).

[Handwritten margin note: The Psycholinguistic or Nativist Theory (chomsky) children are born with an innate ability for grammar and syntax. The innate ability allows children allows children to know the patterns in sentences (LAD) language acquisition device analyze, hypothesis, patterns]

In this theory, the environment provides the data needed for the language learner to derive the rules for sentence structure from the language spoken in the child's environment.

In this theory of language development infants are born with an innate mental capacity, the **language acquisition device (LAD)** (Chomsky (1957, 1965). The LAD allows children to develop language in the following manner:

The LAD allows children to form hypotheses (ideas and theories) about how language works based on regular patterns found in language.

The LAD contains universal information (applicable to all languages) that allows children to form hypotheses regarding language output and form rules, such as rules for the correct order of words in sentences (e.g., *the boy is eating bread* versus *is eating the boy bread*).

The LAD allows children to analyze the sentences spoken in the surrounding environment and to use their analyses to produce grammatical sentences.

The LAD provides children with innate or inborn universal linguistic rules for generating sentences.

According to Chomsky (1965), there are two sets of rules learned for producing sentences. The first rules are the **phrase structure rules** that use the basic sentence structure (N + V = *Dogs bark*) to develop more complex sentences, such as *The big mean dog barked loudly last night*. The second rules are **transformational rules.** The transformational rules provide a connection between **deep structure** (a structure

in the brain that determines the meaning of the sentence) and **surface structure** (the spoken sentence). The deep structure accounts for meanings and provides the basis for turning the deep structure into surface structure, or the sentence we actually hear. Transformational rules allow a basic sentence structure (*Mommy eats cookies*) to be transformed into various other syntactic forms, such as questions, negatives, passives, imperatives, and complex sentence structures.

Questions	*Does mommy eat cookies?*
Negatives	*Mommy doesn't eat cookie.*
Passives	*The cookies were eaten by Mommy.*
Imperatives	*Eat cookies.*
Complex structures	*Mommy eats cookies and drinks milk.*

Note that the passive construction involves a transformation from subject + verb + object (*Mommy eats cookies*) to object + verb + subject (*The cookies were eaten by Mommy*).

In summary, this theory posits that children acquire language based on a genetically innate capacity. Children are able to acquire language through the analysis of spoken language and derive rules through exposure to spoken language in the environment. Note that the environment provides the data necessary to extract rules for language development, whereas innate skills are the primary vehicle for language development. The LAD contains all of the grammatical rules for any language spoken in the world.

THE NATURE AND NURTURE THEORIES OF LANGUAGE DEVELOPMENT

The Social Interaction Theory

Vygotsky (1935) focused on the social aspects of learning, believing that language develops from communication within social interaction. Vygotsky used the term **zone of proximal development** to describe the distance between a child's actual developmental level (determined by independent problem solving) and his or her level of potential development.

The zone of proximal development is the distance between what children can do by themselves (**retrospective mental development**) and the concepts or skills that they learn with assistance from adults or children with greater knowledge of language skills (**prospective mental development**). **Social interaction** is the vehicle that facilitates development of the skills that have not yet matured to help children reach prospective mental development.

Language development is determined by the cognitive process of problem solving under adult guidance or in collaboration with more advanced peers to achieve prospective mental development. Communicative interaction between children and individuals in a social context within the environment activates children's internal developmental processes based on tasks that demand conscious reflection or problem solving (Vygotsky, 1962, 1988). In other words, tasks that involve problem solving (working above the child's current level of skills) are those that support learning abilities.

In one example, we may present a task that is above the child's current knowledge level (e.g., how to understand categorization, such as separating animals and clothing). The adult may use **scaffolds** to help the child to understand this task, shown in Table 2–1 (Cleave & Fey, 1997). Scaffolds are environmental cues that provide the information to increase children's understanding of language while playing a significant role in learning grammatical structure (Proctor-Williams, Fey, & Loeb, 2001). The goal of scaffolds is to highlight the correct use of a linguistic form in a particular relevant context, as shown in Table 2–1. Language development is facilitated by the use of scaffolds, such as models that teach a word or a grammatical form, **expansions** to extend the length and meaning content of an utterance, and **recasts** to correct a grammatical error. An adult may use the following types of scaffolds to help the child understand the categorization task.

> Look at this (pointing to a *horse*). Can you wear it? If not, what box should we put it in? Look at this (pointing to a *hat*). Does it have legs? If not, where should we put it?

Once the child puts the objects in the correct place (i.e., animals in one box and clothing in the other), the adult may say, "Tell me how you did this." This will help the child develop the language to explain this task.

Children's early language development is based on **egocentrism** or **private speech** (Vygotsky, 1986), used to talk aloud as they work through a task. Younger children focus on themselves, their own experiences with objects and events, and their own needs and wants. External speech is used for social communicative interaction with other speakers. After age 2, the external speech used in social interaction becomes internal language that is used for mental reasoning. At this point in development, thought and language merge.

Children no longer need to use private speech to talk aloud because they now work to use inner speech to mentally solve problems. As cognitive skills develop, children consider others' points of view and inner speech functions to organize children's thought processes in terms of conscious understanding people's actions, objects, and events.

In summary, Vygotsky (1935) posits that children learn through social interaction. Social interaction is the vehicle that facilitates development of the skills that have not yet matured to help children reach prospective mental development. Children learn concepts and skills with help from adults or older peers. This assistance helps a child move from his or her actual developmental level to a higher level of knowledge. Language is the means of transmitting information to children to help them reach the higher level of mental development. Thus, language develops within these social interactive contexts and is the key to the growth of cognition as a whole.

The Pragmatic Theory

The social interaction theory (Vygotsky, 1935) provided the foundation to the pragmatic theory developed by Bates (1976). Bates introduced the term **pragmatics** to define the connection between language development and communicative interaction with language developing within the framework of social interaction. In this theory, word learning is completely social (Bruner, 1983; Tomasello, 1992a, 2000) and language develops because children desire to interact in a social manner.

Pragmatic theorists share the belief that children first use expressions in a social manner with more advanced language use related to more advanced cognitive development (Dore, 1978; Gopnik & Meltzoff, 1988). Bates (1976) attributes language development to children's understanding the association between language and events. When a child sees that a parent is putting on a coat, followed by the parent leaving, the child makes an association between *coat* and *leaving*. The act of putting on a coat is an index (predictor) of a parent's departing, and the word *coat* is a symbol for this object and event.

A pragmatic theory of language development holds that language depends on social interaction with others, especially those with advanced language skills. Communicative intentions are social in that they are oriented and directed toward another person's understanding. Eye gaze is an essential part of communicative development, reflected in the following eye gaze patterns found at 3 months of age (Owens, 2008).

Mutual gaze: shared eye gaze between infant and adult

Gaze coupling: turn-taking eye gaze pattern

Gaze coupling mirrors the turn-taking gaze patterns of adult conversation, with speakers breaking eye contact from time to time in a conversation. An infant will engage in mutual eye gaze with an adult and follow the same patterns found in adult conversation: making and breaking eye contact within an interaction (such as diaper changing or feeding). Around 9 to 12 months of age, children follow adults' gaze and eye direction, imitate actions, and gesture to obtain and direct adults' attention to certain objects or events (Tomasello, 2000). This period of development coincides with children's understanding of spoken language, followed by the production of first words. One of the predictors of children's word comprehension and production is the amount of time spent in joint attention contexts with adults (Carpenter, Nagell, & Tomasello, 1998) because children's vocabulary develops within these contexts.

Bates viewed a path of **continuity** between children's preverbal behaviors (e.g., gestures, eye contact, and prelinguistic vocalizations) and later language skills. The vehicle for social interaction is **communication**, both through verbal acts (e.g., words, sentences, **narratives**, and conversations) and nonverbal acts (e.g., eye gaze, gesture, turn taking in conversation, and facial expressions) (Prutting, 1982). These nonverbal acts provide continuity between children's early skills and later language development. For example, children's first words are frequently produced in joint attention and joint action contexts, with the infant and adult focused on the same object and task at hand. Following are examples:

> Joint attention: "Look at the ball!" (adult directs the child's attention toward the ball)

> Joint action: "Let's play!" (the ball is rolled back and forth between the adult and toddler)

Evidence for the importance of joint attention in word learning was found in a study that presented 24-month-old children with a novel word (*modi*) that labeled a novel object (not familiar to the children). This novel word was presented with a distraction to determine if chil-

dren would look at and learn the name of the object the adult was naming (Moore, Angelopoulos, & Bennett, 1999) or would be distracted by the light (and not learn the novel word *modi*).

- ◆ Learning target (*modi*): The adult looked at and pointed to an object, saying, "Look! A modi!"
- ◆ Distraction: A second object lit up at the same time that the adult pointed to the first object and said, "Look! A modi!"

At a later time, a comprehension test was used to see if the children had learned the word *modi* in spite of the distraction by the object that lit up. Which one do you think the children picked when asked to "Find the *modi?*" If you guessed that children identified the object that lit up, you would be wrong. In fact, children identified the object that the adult labeled and pointed to as the *modi*. This showed that children attached more importance to the adult's **intention** (meaning and goal) than to the distraction object. This study suggests that children most likely learn new words by relying on eye gaze (where the adult is looking and what the adult is looking at) as a signal of the adult's intention or intent.

The meaning of a speaker's intent is the reference to a thing, event, or quality of something in the world that underlies the speaker's utterance (e.g., *I am wet*). In this utterance, the speaker *intends* that a listener recognize the *meaning* of what has been said (Grice, 1957). **Intention reading** occurs when the listener comprehends the speaker's intent (e.g., that the listener knows that the speaker is not dry). Intention reading plays an essential role in successful communication (Mazzone, 2009), as in the following examples:

◆ The ability to share attention with persons, objects, and events of mutual interest (Bakeman & Adamson, 1984)
◆ The ability to follow the attention of gestures of another person (Corkum & Moore, 1995)
◆ The ability to direct others' attention to persons, objects, and/or events by pointing, showing, and using other gestures to gain their attention (Bates, 1979)
◆ The ability to learn, through imitation, the intentional actions and communicative intentions of others (Tomasello, Kruger, & Ratner, 1993)

Intention reading begins when children develop joint attention skills, such as sharing an experience, following another person's direction of gaze, and following the direction of someone's pointing, between 9 and 12 months of age (Figure 2–1).

Bates (2004) proposed an infrastructure in the infant brain (the underlying foundation or basic framework) that are the initial skills that correlate with, and are necessary for, the emergence of language development (p. 251):

Object orientation (gaze directed at object) → joint reference

Social orientation (gaze directed at human) → joint reference (gaze shared with adult) and imitation

Cross modal perception (e.g., the interaction between vision and hearing) → imitation and sound-meaning mapping

Figure 2–1. *Joint Attention and Eye-Gaze.*

Sensorimotor precision → sound-meaning mapping and rapid induction (generalization based on observation)

Computational power → rapid induction

As these elements show, infants possess an interest in tracking objects; in human faces and voices; in detecting similarities in sounds, visual, and tactile experiences; in analysis of sensory (e.g., the sensation of hearing, seeing, touching, and tasting) and motor experiences (e.g., movements associated with actions); and learning, based on the computational powers of the human brain (Bates, 2004).

> Imitation allows an infant to learn the actions, gestures, and sounds that comprise language (p. 251), whereas the infrastructure of the human brain (the underlying structure or basic framework of the brain) provides the infant with language learning skills.

In summary, the pragmatic theory posits a role of cognition in language development, shown when children learn to use the symbols (words) for things and events. Children learn language through adult models in pragmatic (social) contexts of joint attention and joint focus. Language skills further develop when

> *[handwritten note, on a sticky note:]*
> **Cognitive Theory**
> language comes from connection between language and thoughts
> children problem solving & theory of mind (understanding someone elses behavior)

Cognition is defined as a child's mental ability to adapt to the environment, to draw abstractions, to generalize experiences, to think about objects and events at various times, to compare and contrast objects and events, and to infer conclusions. Within the environment, children learn to use symbols (words) to represent objects and events. In this way, they learn language (Gentner, 2003). Experiential contact consists of **input** from adults, animals, objects, activities, and experiences. These experiences also provide children with labels or names for these events and experiences (e.g., hearing the word *fix* when a toy is broken).

Piaget (1954) developed a theory of children's cognitive development that depends on experiences gained within the environment. Events that occur in children's external environment chal-

lenge their cognitive problem-solving skills. For example, when a child has to reach something that is outside of his or her grasp, problem-solving skills have to be applied. One of the solutions is to ask for help and another is to climb on a chair. Children store their understanding of their experiences (and the words that are used to label these experiences) for later retrieval in the production of words and longer utterances. For example, learning that the word *leak* refers to water dripping out of the faucet can be used to label other similar experiences (liquids that leak from other objects or places).

Piaget focused on the concepts that children develop that support their language learning. A *concept* is defined as the mental representation that can serve as the meaning of a linguistic expression (Jackendoff, 1991, p. 11). For example, when children develop a concept of an object (e.g., *ball*), they can identify the object when it is named (e.g., *Where is the ball?*) and later label it themselves (e.g., *Wanna ball*). Children develop their understanding of entities, objects, and actions without the active intervention of adults or peers.

> Certain cognitive abilities have a close relationship with language development. For example, **object permanence** is the ability to produce words for entities or events that are *out of sight*. Once children achieve this cognitive ability, at around 10 months, they understand that entities (e.g., *mommy*) and objects (e.g., *ball*) exist even when they cannot be seen or heard. Object permanence also leads to the production of meaningful utterances to refer to the disappearance of entities, such

as *Doggy go*. Before a child can produce certain utterances (e.g., *I want the big cookie*), the child must develop the cognitive concept of dimensions (e.g., big/little). Children's cognitive abilities allow them to (a) understand the consistencies that represent shared meanings (e.g., *big cookie* versus *little cookie*) and (b) how words relate to these shared meanings (e.g., *big* versus *little*). In other words, cognitive development precedes language development.

Piaget also emphasized the role of play as an essential part of learning language (Mooney, 2000). Play represents imitation of activities and experiences in a child's environment (e.g., taking care of a baby, shopping, cooking, going to school, or going to the doctor) as children learn the language used to label these experiences (e.g., *diapering*, paying at *checkout*, put your coat in the *cubby*, and *open* your mouth and say "ahh"). Play schemes frequently involve activities and language that are more advanced than a child's independent skills. The connection between play and language is found in the use of language to reconstruct these play events (e.g., *First, you can be the mommy; next, the baby has to go to the doctor*).

Children possess psychological structures (**schemas** or schemata) that help them construct a representation of spoken language and nonverbal events, such as the actions that occur in their external environment (Witt, 1998). It is important to understand that schemas are present in everyday life. For example, when a child learns to play a game by a set of rules, a schema for this game is formed (e.g., base-ball or a board game). In this way, the child understands that games have rules that must be learned and followed so that the child can enter the game and be successful in his or her interaction with peers. Schemas for visual, auditory, and nonlinguistic factors (e.g., eye gaze and gesture) act to establish language (Tomasello, 1999). For example, the visual characteristics of entities teach children the difference between animate and inanimate entities, such as *vases do not move* but *dogs do*.

Schemas develop with experience, as when a child is first introduced to a dog. The child uses the visual characteristics of this experience to establish a schema of *dog* (hairy, tail, four legs, and movement). This schema changes with exposure to new information or events in the environment. When the child visits the zoo and sees a *cow*, the child uses the existing schema established for *dog* to label this animal, based on the perceived similarities between the characteristics of the two animals (e.g., number of legs, tail, and hairy). **Assimilation** occurs when children are exposed to some new information or event that fits into a preexisting schema. **Accommodation** occurs when children are exposed to new information or an event that does not easily fit into a preexisting schema. **Equilibrium** (cognitive balance) is the goal of assimilation and accommodation. When the child hears the cow produce the sound "moo," this may lead to the distinguishing the dog (who barks) from the cow (who moos).

Piaget's (1929) theory of schemas also reflects the development of a **theory of mind** (TOM). A theory of mind allows a child to understand another individual's mental state: what this individual knows, thinks, and believes; what action this individual is likely to take; and how this individual feels. Children are able to develop theories about how things work and are able to change these theories rapidly within the space of a few months (Gopnik & Meltzoff, 1997; Meltzoff, 2007).

A theory of mind helps a child to understand another's behavior and to predict his or her actions. Children's psychological schemas allow them to process this information and develop theories based on their observations. To develop a TOM, children must first understand others' perceptions of the world (e.g., what they can see, smell, touch, taste, and hear). This understanding leads to the acquisition of **mental state verbs** (e.g., *think* and *know*), the verbs that mark the benchmark of human cognition (Shatz, Wellman, & Silber, 1983). The order of acquisition of these mental state verbs can be found in Table 2–2 (Shatz et al., 1983, p. 312).

Table 2–2. *The Relationship Between Language and the Development of a Theory of Mind (TOM): Order of Development of Mental State Verbs*

Age 2;4	*know, forget*
Age 2;6	*figure*
Age 2;7	*hope*
Age 2;8	*think, guess, believe, mean*

Source: From "The acquisition of mental verbs: a systematic investigation of the first reference to mental state," by M. Schatz, H. M. Wellman, and S. Silber, 1983, *Cognition*, 14, p. 312. Reprinted with permission.

An example of the development of an early theory of mind is shown when an object is hidden under a cover. Next, the object is moved from the first cover to a second cover. Children observing these actions will look under the first cover (where the object was first hidden before being moved to the second cover). However, by 8 to 10 months of age, children understand that the object has been displaced to the second cover and they search for it there. By this age, children understand that the adult has intentionally moved the object from one place to another. This shows an understanding of the adult's intention. This achievement reflects a new and sophisticated theory of actions and consequences that contributes to their theory of mind.

In summary, the cognitive theory posits that language development depends on cognitive skills. Schemas allow children to process information, along with the ability to connect external contextual information with the language to describe their experiences. Play schemes are important in the development of language because these activities frequently involve language that is more advanced than a child's independent language skills. Children use this language to reconstruct these play events that mirror the events in their environment (e.g., shopping for groceries).

The Semantic-Cognitive Theory

In this theory, early language development is based on the semantics (meaning) that develop before children develop syntax (sentence production). It is important to understand that the language learner cannot acquire the syntax (sentence structure) of a language without an understanding of the underlying meaning of a spoken utterance (Jackendoff, 1983, p. 13), along with the meaning that associates the words in that utterance with things, actions, or qualities. Syntax, or the ability to produce sentences, is unlearnable without the understanding of the underlying meaning. Once the meaning of an utterance is learned, syntax will follow. For example, the early meanings produced by children reflect the mental knowledge that is drawn from their experience with things and actions in the environment (e.g., *All gone!*).

The relationship between semantic and cognitive skills is found in children's understanding of (a) relationships perceived in the environment (e.g., the word *kiss* associated with animate entities, such as people) and (b) rules that govern language (e.g., the word *kiss* must be associated with an animate noun, such as *Daddy*, and not with an inanimate noun, such as a rock). The information of the meaning between words and things in the environment is internalized (stored in children's memory) and later appears in their productions.

In children's early productions, single words express their understanding of events (e.g., *kiss* to label the act of kissing). In later language development, they use syntactic forms (sentences) to express these and more complex meanings (e.g., *Daddy kissing mommy*). In other words, children learn words and connect words

with their meanings. An example of the development of children's semantic development is learning the word *block* while interacting in play with this object. The child then hears a word used in other contexts and, in that way, learns the meanings associated with difference contexts (e.g., *toy block, going around the block to see a friend*, and *blocking a movement*). In essence, cognitive semantics theories posit that meaning is not fixed but that it depends on different contexts.

Children also create semantic categories that draw associations among the concepts that they have learned. For example, children may acquire a prototype for a concept, consisting of the first object or activity that was encountered (Bowerman, 1978). For example, a child may first learn that the term *bird* applies to pigeons in the park. Next, the child encounters robins, wrens, and other similar birds. The comparison of the prototype (pigeon) to similar birds presents no problems because there are no extreme differences in the characteristics of these birds compared with the pigeon. When visiting the zoo, the child is told that a penguin is a bird. Difficulty appears because the penguin does not share many of the characteristics of the birds that were encountered earlier. Note that this process of creating semantic categories is similar to the cognitive process of assimilation and accommodation. The child must now change the concept of *bird* to include penguins.

Case grammar describes the role of semantics in language acquisition (Fillmore, 1968). In this view, there are universal semantic concepts that specify the relationship between words. For example, the word *rock* cannot play the semantic role of a noun in the sentence *Noun + kissed the boy*. In this case, the noun can only play the semantic role of agentive (an active do-er of some action). Case grammar consists of the following semantic roles: agentive, dative, experiencer, instrumental, locative, and objective (Table 2–3).

At about 10 months of age, children acquire these semantic roles in their early acquisition of language, shown in children's early vocabulary production (e.g., *shoe, cup, ball*). Early learned words are quickly attached to meanings (Yu, Ballard, & Aslin, 2005). These semantic roles develop into semantic relations at around 2 to 3 years of age, as described in Chapter 1 (Bloom, Lahey, Hood, Lifter, & Fiess, 1980), with productions of the semantic

relationships that involve the semantic roles of *agent + action* (e.g., *Daddy throw*).

Semantic-cognitive theories hold that there should always be a full account of *semantics* or meaning when describing children's language development. The interpretation of a child's intended meaning can be found by examining the connection between the context and the child's production. For example, Bloom (1970) found that there was a difference in the meaning of a child's production of the syntactic form *noun + verb* (i.e., *Mommy sock*) when (a) the child found her mother's sock and (b) the child watched her mother putting on her socks. Even though the syntactic structure of the sentence was the same in both productions (i.e., *Mommy sock*), this utterance represented two different meanings that could

Table 2–3. *Semantic Roles*

Semantic Role	Definition	Example
Agentive	Doer of an action	*Mommy* put on her sock
Dative	Expresses an indirect object relationship	She gave the book *to the girl*
Experiencer	Receives, accepts, experiences, or undergoes the effect of an action	The explosion was heard by *everyone*
Instrumental	An inanimate thing that an agent uses to do something	He cut the bread with a *knife*
Locative	Identifies the location or spatial orientation of a state or action	The book is *on the table*
Objective	Identifies the object of a transitive verb and the thing that is having something done to it	The cat drank the *milk*
Patient	The entity or thing undergoing the action	*Mary* fell down

only be found in a semantic analysis of the child's utterance within the context that it was produced.

Semantic analysis	Meaning
Possessor + possession	sock belonging to ~~mom~~
Action + ~~object~~	

In summ~~ary~~ involves kno~~wledge~~ about the wo~~rld~~ activities tha~~t~~ dren create ~~meaning~~ on associatio~~ns~~ they have lea~~rned~~ ture *bark* is as~~sociated~~ this feature di~~fferentiates~~ animals (i.e., ~~the~~ use semantic ~~relations like~~ experiencer, i~~nstrument,~~ objective) to d~~escribe~~ things and activities that they have learned (as shown in Table 2–3).

[Handwritten note overlaid:]

The Usage-Based Theory TOMSELLO

Children learn language through their observation and imitation of language used in actual contexts.

THEORIES THAT COMBINE INNATE SKILLS AND THE ENVIRONMENT IN LANGUAGE DEVELOPMENT

The following theories have common foundations in factors that support children's language learning:

◆ Innate cognitive abilities allow children to acquire language (e.g., thought processing and the ability to learn through observation).

◆ Cognitive abilities allow children to understand or *read* a speaker's inten-

tion or meaning (e.g., when a speaker points to something and says its name, such as *wet, dirty, gone, apple,* or *parade*).

◆ Cognitive abilities allow children to find patterns in the language they hear (e.g., verbs follow nouns in sentences, ~~leading to~~ syntactic development).

◆ ~~Cognitive~~ abilities allow children to ~~analyze the~~ frequency of words and ~~that the~~y hear in the environment ~~(e.g., the inf~~lectional morpheme *-ed* is ~~the most fre~~quent way of marking the ~~past tense o~~f a verb, such as *walked*, ~~but ther~~e are less frequent irregular ~~forms su~~ch as *eat/ate, throw/threw,* ~~catch/cau~~ght).

◆ ~~Social~~ interaction provides children ~~with e~~xposure to language use ~~(e.g., lan~~guage is used to refer to ~~the ac~~tions in the environment).

~~The Usage-Ba~~sed Theory

The **usage-based theory** of language acquisition posits that innate cognitive abilities provide children with the skills to acquire language (Tomasello, 2003, 2009). Human cognition is reflected in the human species' unique motivation to share emotions, experiences, and activities with others (Tomasello, Carpenter, Call, Behne, & Moll, 2005). This theory posits that language develops over a more extended time. During this period of language learning, children apply their general cognitive skills (thought processing), learn through observation and interaction (social-cognitive), and are able to make sense out of what they hear (vocal-auditory processing) (Tomasello, 2000, p. 163). In this theory, children learn language through their observation and imitation of language used in actual contexts.

Mother: points to a wet dog and says, "That dog is all wet."

Child: observes the mother's utterance and the dog that is wet. The child says, "Wet doggie."

At a later time, the child is able to use the word *wet* to other objects or situations (e.g., hands wet, hair wet, and floor wet). Children are motivated to understand spoken language while interacting socially and linguistically with more advanced language users. Children's joint attention skills play an important role in this process because they must learn the connection between an utterance, the speaker's intention (meaning) while using this utterance, and the connection between the spoken utterance and the context (how word meaning connects to context). Initially, children gain information about the meaning of a new word or concept after limited exposure through **fast mapping**. Fast mapping allows children to quickly form a hypothesis about the meaning of a word from how it is used (Heibeck & Markman, 1987).

> Micah was walking with his mother through the park. A big dog approached and Micah looked back and forth between his mother and the dog, evidencing some anxiety. His mother smiled and said, "That's a nice doggie." Following her smile and words, Micah relaxed. He had understood her meaning based on both the words and her positive expression.

In the usage-based theory of language development, children begin with imitation. Children attempt to imitate expressions spoken by more advanced language users, such as *What's this? What are you doing?* and *What is that?* Unanalyzed productions are utterances that children do not identify as consisting of separate words. Examples are children's productions of adult forms as *Whassis, Watchadoing,* and *whatsthat?* (Tomasello, 2003).

The cognitive skills responsible for language learning consist of *intention reading* (discerning a speaker's goals and meaning associated with a specific linguistic form, such as *wet dog*) and *pattern finding* (discerning the same phonological form and the use of a particular form across different events, such as *Hello* when greeting someone). Using intention reading, children learn to understand the speaker's intention (meaning) when observing the use of these utterances in different contexts. At 12 months, children begin to understand communicative intentions. They also begin to direct others' attention to certain objects and events (e.g., pointing and gesturing to things of interest), showing their own development of intentions.

Pattern finding consists of creating analogies (finding similarities) in the patterns of spoken utterances. Pattern finding occurs when children are able to find patterns in the way language is used across different utterances and across different situations. For example, children learn the phonological pattern for the word *for* as it is used in different contexts and in different relationships (e.g., *for you; for him; for swimming; for lunch; for the dog*). Learning is also supported by repeated patterns, such as *I want to go, I want to nap,* and *I want to eat.* In this way, children learn grammar or the rules that govern language.

Over time, children's earlier productions are divided into separate words, as shown in the progress over time.

Whasss	*Wha dis*	*What's this*
Whatchagoing	*Whatya doin?*	*What are you doing?*

Children's early productions show the use of specific verbs to construct sentences, based on the specific patterns of productions (Tomasello, 1992b).

Find-it funny	*Block get-it*	*Peter Pan gone*
Find-it bird	*Bottle get-it*	*Raisins gone*
Find-it chess	*Towel get-it*	*Hammer gone*
Find-it bricks	*Coffee get-it*	*Fox gone*
Find-it ball	*Mama get-it*	*French fries gone*

Tomasello (1992b) termed these productions *construction islands,* showing that children acquire language in frames of specific combinations (e.g., *Find it + noun, noun + get it,* and *noun + gone*). Children's early grammatical knowledge is limited to these constructional islands, giving them a limited use of expressions. Over time, their productions are used across several constructions as they learn to use syntactic patterns productively and move from the earlier forms.

The usage-based theory explains children's early language productions. Children are seen as producing utterance schemas (e.g., *Where X, wanna X,* and *more X*). Children will add to these schemas by adding new words, as shown in these examples that show progress over time:

Where mama	*Where mama go*
Wanna tissue	*Wanna tissue now*
More More juice	*More juice cup*

In the usage-based view of language development, children produce utterances from their stored language experience as they cut and paste together what is necessary for the communicative needs at any time (Tomasello, 2000, p. 77).

Another factor in acquisition is the frequency of exposure to certain linguistic structures in spoken language (Tomasello, 2003). For example, English-speaking children acquire passive constructions late, at about 4 to 5 years of age, given that passives are spoken less frequently in English than declarative structures. Examples of the difference between declarative and passive sentences follow.

Declarative: *Micah threw the ball*
Subject + Verb + Object

Passive: *The ball was thrown by Micah*
Object + Verb + Subject

Passives are infrequently produced in English, estimated to be produced in every 1 out of 1,000 spoken utterances (Gordon & Chafetz, 1990). However, passive forms are acquired early by children in languages with more frequent production of these syntax structures, such as Inuktitut (Eskimo-Aleut language family), K'iche' (Mayan language family), Mayan (divided into the Huastec, Yucatec, Western Maya, and Eastern Maya groups), Sesotho (spoken in South Africa), and Zulu (a Bantu language spoken in South Africa). The more frequent production of passives in a language leads to earlier acquisition because these sentence types are more salient to children.

In summary, language development begins with imitation. Over time, pattern

[handwritten notes:]

The Emergentism Theory
Guided Distributional
Learning Theory

~ based on children's active
participation in learning

~ language emerges from
an interaction between
words with objects and
actions

~ the ability to note
patterns in language.

- ◆ The cognitive basis for language learning consists of the child's innate learning skills.
- ◆ The social-pragmatic factors consist of sensitivity to pointing and eye gaze, which play a significant role in early word learning.
- ◆ Attentional factors consist of the child's ability to connect sight and sound, leading to the ability to connect words with objects and events in the environment.

The Emergentism Theory/ Guided Distributional Learning Theory

In this theory, we review the guided distributional learning theory, the competition model, and the parallel distributed processing theory. The **emergentism/ guided distributional learning theory** presents the hypothesis that interaction between innate skills and the environment explains language learning (Hirsh-Pasek, Golinkoff, & Hollich, 1999; Karmiloff-Smith, 1992). Social interaction and cognitive skills are seen to account for a child's language development with children playing an active role in acquiring language. Emergentism ascribes language learning to the "emergent" effect of cognitive, social, pragmatic, and attentional factors. Language input plays the most essential role in language learning with cues to learning based on the rhythm, stress, and intonational patterns of spoken language.

Emergentists argue that language develops from an interaction between a child's cognitive structures and the environment. Investigators argue that it is only reasonable to conclude that genes (innate skills) and the environment interact to determine outcomes in children's language and cognitive development (Bates et al., 1998). Cognitive skills (e.g., attention and working memory) are essential for processing environmental activities and language input (Bates & Elman, 1996; Seidenberg & Elman, 1999).

The guided distributional learning theory posits that children's language learning is guided by their bias to attend to certain environmental cues. Children attend to particular environmental inputs or information at different stages of development (Hirsh-Pasek & Golinkoff, 1997). For example, children are able to distinguish sounds in their own language from sounds in another language as early as 9 months of age (Jusczyk, Friederici, Wessels, Svenkerud, & Jusczyk, 1993), based on their ability to attend to certain aspects of language (e.g., intonation, rhythm, and the duration of sounds). Environmental cues, such as the sound patterns of words, may contribute to language development in two different ways: (a) as a trigger to children's innate skills or (b) as an influence on the structure of the brain that supports language development (Karmiloff-Smith, 1992).

Infants are sensitive to the prosodic aspects of language (e.g., intonation, rhythm, and the duration of sounds). The prosodic and melodic organization of language is among the first aspects of speech that infants are sensitive to or produce themselves (Lieberman, 1986). We produce **intonation** through pitch changes by moving our voices upward or downward. We use **rhythm** to provide a melodic pattern to words in sentences, along with equal intervals for word emphasis (e.g., "I *KNOW* you *LOVE* cookies") (Borden, Harris, & Raphael, 2003). We use **duration** to lengthen certain syllables in words to give these syllables more emphasis (e.g., baNANa). A child's sensitivity to these prosodic cues in speech allows them to notice repeated sequences of sounds, such as the sounds in his or her own name.

There are two other theories that are part of an emergentism theory of language development: the **competition model** (Bates & MacWhinney, 1982) and the theory of **parallel distributed processing** (Hulit & Howard, 1997). In the competition model, children become aware that there are more consistent language cues spoken in the environment. For example, children become aware of word order forms (syntax) and note that nouns are most frequently followed by verbs in sentences. Word order is a strong and consistent cue for children to connect syntactic forms (syntax) with meanings (semantics), shown in the following example.

Syntax	Noun + verb
Semantics	Agent + action
Spoken sentence	Daddy runs

In terms of the competition between cues, language learners become aware that certain cues are more consistently present and more reliable in spoken language. For example, animate entities are more frequently found to occur before verbs (e.g., *The boy kicked the rock*) than inanimate objects (e.g., *The rock kicked the boy*). In this way, the first example is a more reliable cue to language processing because it is more consistent in speakers' productions (e.g., animate entity followed by a verb).

The competition model includes a theory of parallel distributed processing. In this theory, the more frequently produced language forms activate and strengthen connections in children's cognitive processing of language (Hulit & Howard, 1997), as shown in the following consistently used language forms.

Words: *Hi* when meeting someone

Syntax: Adjectives preceding nouns, such as *big + apple*

Phonological patterns: The sequence of sounds that occur in a language, such as *Zb* to begin a name in Polish but not in English

Another example is the regular past tense verb form *-ed* (e.g., *walked*) that is more frequently spoken in English than irregular past tense forms (e.g., *run/ran*). This explains why children may produce words such as *eated* due to the higher frequency of regular past morpheme forms (i.e., *-ed*) than irregular past verb forms (e.g., *ate, threw, fell,* and *caught*). Over time, children's active language processing leads to their productions of correct irregular past tense forms (Poll, 2011).

In summary, the emergentism theory of language learning is based on children's active participation in learning. For example, they are able to take advantage of what they hear most frequently spoken around them. These more frequently occurring productions activate and strengthen language learning. In various stages, children attend to different cues that guide their language development. For example, very young children take advantage of intonation, whereas older children observe and become aware of word order forms and patterns (syntax), noting that nouns are most frequently followed by verbs in sentences (e.g., *dogs bark*).

SUMMARY

Recent research has expanded our view of language acquisition. Piaget and Vygotsky have provided current research with observations and ideas about the connections among language, cognition, and social interaction (Tomasello, 1996). Given the evidence from language development studies, general cognitive mental faculties and systems (e.g., working memory, attention, and general intelligence) are essential for the process of language acquisition and language use (Jackendoff, 2011). With the exception of the psycholinguistic or nativist theory of language development, all other theories involve an interaction between these following innate abilities and the external environment.

Auditory system: the sensory system for hearing

Motor system: the central nervous system involved in movement

Vocal tract control: the ability to make finer and varied adjustments of the vocal tract to produce meaningful sound units

Working memory: the temporary storage of information required for long-term memory

Attention: focus on the essential factors of a task while ignoring distractions

General intelligence: the ability to think about ideas, analyze situations, and solve problems

A theory of mind: the ability to understand someone else's mind in terms of mental states, such as desires, beliefs, and knowledge; the ability to predict how someone will act, to explain why a person acted in a certain manner, and to describe actions in psychological terms with mental state verbs such as *thinks* and *knows*

Joint attention: the process of sharing an experience of observing an object or event and following gaze or gestures

Vocal imitation: the ability to imitate sounds and words

Many investigators consider it only reasonable to conclude that genes (innate skills) and the environment interact to determine outcomes in children's language and cognitive development (Bates et al., 1998). Cognitive skills allow a child to take advantage of language input (Bates & Elman, 1996; Seidenberg & Elman, 1999).

The review of the theories presented in this chapter suggests the following factors that may support children's language development. We know that:

◆ Language develops within joint attention contexts, based on the finding that children with early emergence of nonlinguistic joint attention acquire language skills at an earlier age.

◆ *Play* is a vehicle for language development and play schemes can develop language through the incorporation of the language that describes these schemes.

◆ More frequent input and multiple examples of language meaning and use are essential factors in learning with evidence that children learn syntactic structures (i.e., passives and regular past tense verb forms) when languages contain more examples of these structures.

◆ Language emerges within social purposes in communicative interaction so that these types of interaction contexts may support children's language development through games and interaction with peers and older language learners.

◆ It is important for adults and children with greater language and cognitive knowledge to provide guidance, through scaffolds, to children who require support for language development and learning within the classroom and play contexts. These scaffolds are found to play a significant role in language learning.

◆ Children benefit from contexts that show how language is used, what words "mean," and how words can be generalized across different contexts; it is important to provide rich examples of the use of language in varied contexts, along with examples of how a word may be used in different contexts (e.g., *block*).

◆ Children must learn the underlying rules that govern language use; to achieve this goal, it is important to model the correct use of the language form for the context target, such as how to request, reject, or describe a thing or activity.

◆ Children better learn when exposed to how language connects with the world: what words mean; how words are used; how words relate to similar words; and how words can be used in functional ways for a child to request, describe, and express ideas.

◆ Children form schemas or schemata about things and events, including the rules and patterns associated with games (e.g., turn taking and how to play the game) and everyday events (e.g., shopping and going to the doctor). The schemes associated with games and different play scenarios can help develop understanding rules and the language associated with these events.

◆ Children have the desire to engage in social interaction, so contexts that engage the child in turn-taking and verbal guessing games can facilitate the use of language in social situations.

◆ Children with language disorders can benefit from imitative models, especially when language skills are not functional. In this case, examples of the appropriate target words or sentences may aid the child in learning language.

◆ A theory of mind (TOM) is important for children to understand others' thoughts and feelings and to predict how and why a person acted the way he or she did. TOM is essential for understanding characters' motivations and behaviors in stories and to engage in meaningful conversations with others that fits the topic at hand. It is important for children to learn mental state verbs to develop a TOM (e.g., *see, hear, smell, taste, feel, want, need, say, tell, ask, know, think,* and *believe*).

The goal of this chapter was to provide an understanding of the theories that explain language acquisition, along with the current consensus view on the factors that play a major role in children's learning. Chapter 3 will introduce you to children's speech production, an essential factor in communication.

KEY WORDS

Accommodation

Assimilation

Cognition

Communication

Competition model

Concepts

Continuity

Deep structure

Duration

Egocentrism

Emergentism

Environment

Environmental

Equilibrium

Expansions

Fast mapping

Guided distributional learning theory

Innate

Innateness theory

Input

Intention

Intention reading

Intonation

Language acquisition device (LAD)

Mental state verbs

Models

Narrative

Object permanence

Parallel distributed processing

Phrase structure rules

Pragmatics

Private speech

Prospective mental development

Recasts

Retrospective mental development

Rhythm

Scaffolds

Schema

Social interaction

Surface structure

Theory of mind

Transformational rules

Usage-based theory

Zone of proximal development

STUDY QUESTIONS

1. Explain the connection between mental state verbs and language development.

2. What are the main differences between the usage-based theory and the nativist theory of language acquisition?

3. How would you explain why a child might use the word *eated* instead of the correct irregular past tense form *ate*?

4. Explain why more frequent input leads to changes in children's language production.

5. Explain social cognition. What is the connection between social cognition and a theory of mind?

REFERENCES

Bakeman, R., & Adamson, L. B. (1984). Coordinating attention to people and objects in mother-infant and peer-infant interaction. *Child Development, 55,* 1278–1289.

Bates, E. (1976). *Language and context: The acquisition of pragmatics.* San Diego, CA: Academic Press.

Bates, E. (1979). Intentions, conventions, and symbols: Cognition and communication in infancy. New York, NY: Academic Press.

Bates, E. (2004). Explaining and interpreting deficits in language development across clinical groups: Where do we go from here? *Brain and Language, 88,* 248–253.

Bates, E., & Elman, J. (1996). Learning rediscovered: A perspective on Saffran, Aslin, & Newport. *Science, 274,* 1849–1850.

Bates, E., Elman, J., Johnson, M., Karmiloff-Smith, A., Parisi, D., & Plunkett, K. (1998). In W. Bechtel & G. Graham (Eds.), *A companion to cognitive sciences* (pp. 590–601). Oxford, UK: Basil Blackwell.

Bates, E., & MacWhinney, B. (1982). Functionalist approaches to grammar. In E. Wanner & L. R. Gleitman (Eds.), *Language acquisition: The state of the art.* Cambridge, UK: Cambridge University Press.

Bates, E., & MacWhinney, B. (1988). "What is functionalism?" *Papers and Reports on Child Language Development, 27,* 137–152.

Bloom, L. (1970). *Language development: Form and function in emerging grammars.* Cambridge, MA: MIT Press.

Bloom, L., Lahey, M., Hood, L., Lifter, K., & Fiess, K. (1980). Complex sentences: Acquisition of syntactic connectives and the semantic relations they encode. *Journal of Child Language, 7,* 235–261.

Borden, G. J., Harris, K. S., & Raphael, L. J. (2003). *Speech science primer: Physiology, acoustic, and perception of speech.* Philadelphia, PA: Lippincott Williams & Wilkins.

Bowerman, M. (1978). Systematizing semantic knowledge: Changes over time in the child's organization of word meaning. *Child Development, 49*(4), 977–987.

Bruner, J. (1983). *Child's talk.* New York, NY: Norton.

Carpenter, M., Nagell, K., & Tomasello, M. (1998). Social cognition, joint attention, and communicative competence from 9 to 15 months of age. *Monographs of the Society for Research in Child Development, 63*(4), 1–176.

Chomsky, N. (1957). *Syntactic structures.* The Hague, Netherlands: Mouton.

Chomsky, N. (1959). Review of Skinner's verbal behavior. *Language, 35,* 26–58.

Chomsky, N. (1964). *Current issues in linguistic theory.* The Hague, Netherlands: Mouton.

Chomsky, N. (1965). *Aspects of the theory of syntax.* Cambridge, MA: MIT Press.

Cleave, P. L., & Fey, M. E. (1997). Two approaches to the facilitation of grammar in children with language impairments: Rationale and description. *American Journal of Speech-Language Pathology, 6*(1), 22–32.

Corkum, V., & Moore, C. (1995). Development of joint visual attention in infants. In C. Moore & P. Dunham (Eds.), *Joint attention: Its origin and role in development.* Hillsdale, NJ: Erlbaum.

Dore, J. (1978). Requestive systems in nursery school conversations: Analysis of talk in its social context. In R. Campbell & P. Smith (Eds.), *Recent advances in the psychology of language: Language development and mother-child interaction* (pp. 271–292). New York, NY: Plenum.

Fillmore, C. J. (1968). The case for case. In E. Bach & R. Harmas (Eds.), *Universals in Linguistic Theory* (pp. 1–88). New York, NY: Holt, Rinehart, and Winston.

Gelman, S. A. (2009). Learning from others: Children's construction of concepts. *Annual Review of Psychology, 60,* 115–140.

Gentner, D. (2003). Why we're so smart. In D. Gentner & S. Goldin-Meadow (Eds.), *Language in mind: Advances in the study of language and thought* (pp. 195–235). Cambridge, MA: MIT Press.

Gopnik, A., & Meltzoff, A. N. (1988). From people, to plans, to object: Changes in the meaning of early words and their relation to cognitive development. In M. B. Franklin & S. S. Barten (Eds.), *Child language: A reader* (pp. 60–69). New York, NY: Oxford University Press. (Reprinted from *Journal of Pragmatics, 9,* 496–512).

Gopnik, A., & Meltzoff, A. N. (1997). *Words, thoughts, and theories.* Cambridge, MA: MIT Press.

Gopnik, A., Meltzoff, A. N., & Kuhl, P. K. (2001). *Scientist in the crib: What early learning tells us about the mind.* New York, NY: Harper Collins.

Gordon, P., &. Chafetz, J. (1990). Verb-based versus class-based accounts of actionality effects in children's comprehension of passives. *Cognition, 36,* 227–254.

Grice, P. (1957). Meaning. *The Philosophical Review, 66,* 147–177.

Heibeck, T. H., & Markman, E. M. (1987). Word learning in children: An examination of fast mapping. *Child Development, 58*(4), 1021–1034.

Hirsh-Pasek, K., & Golinkoff, R. M. (1997). *The origins of grammar: Evidence from early language comprehension.* Cambridge, MA: MIT Press.

Hirsh-Pasek, K., Golinkoff, R., & Hollich, G. (1999) .Trends, and transitions in language development: Looking for the missing piece. *Developmental Neuropsychology, 16*(2), 139–162.

Hulit, L. M., & Howard, M. R. (1997). *Born to talk: An introduction to speech and language development.* Boston, MA: Allyn & Bacon.

Jackendoff, R. (1983). *Semantics and cognition.* Cambridge, MA: MIT Press.

Jackendoff, R. (1991). *Semantic structures.* Cambridge, MA: MIT Press.

Jackendoff, R. (2011). What is the human language faculty? Two views. *Language, 87*(3), 586–624.

Jusczyk, P. W., Friederici, A. D., Wessels, J., Svenkerud, V. Y., & Jusczyk, A. M. (1993). Infants' sensitivity to the sound patterns of native language words. *Journal of Memory and Language, 32,* 402–420.

Karmiloff-Smith, A. (1992). *Beyond modularity: A developmental perspective on cognitive science.* Cambridge, MA: MIT Press.

Kuhl, P. K., & Meltzoff, A. N. (2001). *The scientist in the crib: What early learning tells us about the mind.* Hammersmith, UK: Harper-Perennial.

Lieberman, P. (1986). The acquisition of intonation by infants: Physiology and neural control. In C. John-Lewis (Ed.), *Intonation in discourse* (pp. 239– 257). London, England: Croom-Helm.

Mazzone, M. (2009). Pragmatics and cognition: Intentions and pattern recognition in context. *International Review of Pragmatics, 1,* 321–347.

McLeish, J., & Martin, J. (1975). Verbal behavior: A review and experimental analysis. *Journal of General Psychology, 93,* 3–66.

Meltzoff, A. N. (2007). Infants' causal learning: Intervention, observation, imitation. In A. Gopnik & L. Schulz (Eds.), *Causal learning: Psychology, philosophy, and computation* (pp. 37–47). Oxford, UK: Oxford University Press.

Mooney, C. G. (2000). *An introduction to Dewey, Montessori, Erikson, Piaget, & Vygotsky.* St. Paul, MN: Redleaf Press.

Moore, C., Angelopoulos, M., & Bennett, P. (1999). Word learning in the context of referential and salience cues. *Developmental Psychology, 35*(1), 60–68.

CHAPTER 3

Speech Production

Stephen A. Cavallo and Sandra Levey

*There are differences between the way sounds are written and the way sounds are produced. For example, the written letters "gh" can sometimes sound like "f" (e.g., enou**gh**). After reading this chapter, you will have a greater appreciation of the difference between written and spoken language. You will also understand how speech sounds are produced. This knowledge is essential so that speech-language pathologists can provide evidence-based (effective) assessment and intervention for children with speech difficulties. You will also learn that sounds can differ across languages, an understanding that will help you provide appropriate assessment and intervention to second-language English learners.*

Throughout the first year of life, infants demonstrate the precursors to speech, beginning with reflexive (automatic) vocalizations and ending with the production of first words by 12 months of age. The young child's preverbal vocalizations will ultimately emerge as an expression of language when he or she begins to attach meaning to sounds. It is important to understand how sounds are produced because the production of speech sounds is the basis of forming words and longer utterances. Knowledge of the processes that underlie typical speech production is essential so that a speech-language pathologist can identify atypical speech processes and effectively assist children in achieving standard speech sound production. It is also important that speech-language pathologists understand that a child's ability to identify sounds, and to associate spoken sounds with written letters, is an essential to developing literacy skills (i.e., the ability to read). For example, a child must understand the connection between sounds and letters to identify written words. Without this ability, the development of literacy will be impaired. Finally, it is also important for speech-language pathologists to understand that sounds differ across languages. In particular, some English sounds may not be present in a speaker's first language, and some sounds from the speaker's first language may not be present in English. It is important for the speech-language pathologist to understand these differences and to have an understanding of **phonetics** and the **phonemes** that represent sounds in words as well as how these sounds are produced. This knowledge prepares practitioners with the ability to provide appropriate assessment and intervention.

CHAPTER OBJECTIVES

This chapter introduces the process of speech production, a motor act that is the primary mode of human communication. After reading this chapter, you should have a basic understanding and appreciation of the:

◆ Major components of the speech mechanism
◆ Anatomy and physiology relevant to speech production
◆ The phonemes of English: consonants and vowels

SPEECH PRODUCTION: A COMPLEX, MOTOR ACT

Speech is produced through the combined efforts of three systems: the respiratory system, the **laryngeal system**, and the supralaryngeal system (the air-filled cavities above the larynx).

◆ The respiratory system consists of the lungs, rib cage, abdomen, and associated muscles. Air from the lungs is pressurized to provide the power for speech sound production (Figure 3–1).
◆ The laryngeal mechanism houses the vocal folds. The vocal folds are energized by air from the lungs and vibrate to produce phonation (sound produced by the vibration of the vocal folds). The space between the vocal folds is known as the **glottis** (Figure 3–2).
◆ **The supralaryngeal vocal tract** consists of the oral, pharyngeal, and nasal cavities. Found within the pharyngeal and oral cavities are the speech **articulators**: the tongue, pharynx, palate, lips, and jaw (Figure 3–3). Articulation involves the movement of the articulators against one another (or another structure) to produce speech.
◆ Speech sounds are produced as a result of carefully timed movements of

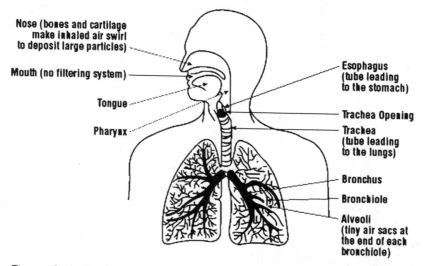

Figure 3–1. *The Respiratory System. Reproduced with permission from the Canadian Lung Association.*

the articulators, and different speech sounds are created through particular configurations of the articulators. For example, we use the lips to produce the sound /p/ in the word *pea*. We use the lips and vocal fold vibration to produce the sound /b/ in the word **may***be*.

In Figure 3–1, we see three major components of the lungs: the **bronchus**, **bronchiole**, and **alveoli**. Their functions are described next.

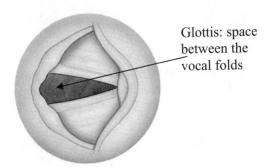

Glottis: space between the vocal folds

Figure 3–2. *Vocal Folds. Reproduced with permission from Getty Images.*

Bronchus: A large air tube that begins at the end of the trachea and branches into the lungs

Bronchiole: A tiny branch of air tubes within the lungs that is a continuation of the bronchus. The bronchioles connect to the alveoli (air sacs)

Alveoli: Tiny air sacs within the lungs where the exchange of oxygen and carbon dioxide takes place (this is where respiration occurs)

Prior to speech production, air is drawn into the lungs and pressurized. Speech is generated as pressurized air from the lungs is released into the larynx and the supralaryngeal vocal tract. The lungs, diaphragm, and related muscles provide the necessary power to initiate the airflow that is necessary for phonation (voicing) and speech production. The supralaryngeal vocal tract consists of a series of interconnected, air-filled cavities above the larynx: the **pharyngeal**, **oral**, and **nasal cavities** (Figure 3–4).

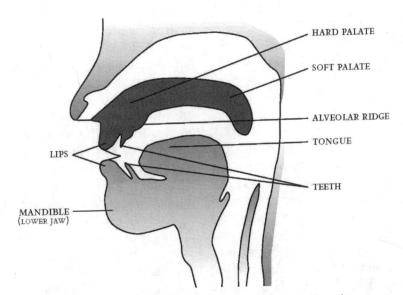

Figure 3–3. *Speech Articulators. From* Language Development: Understanding Language Diversity in the Classroom *(p. 85), by S. Levey & S. Polirstok (Eds.), 2011, Los Angeles, CA: Sage. Reprinted with permission..*

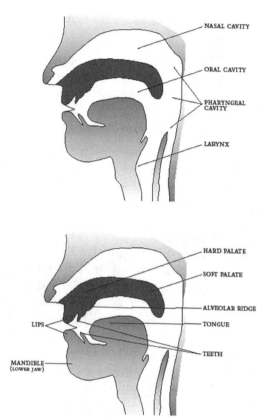

Figure 3–4. *The Air-Filled Cavities of the ocal Tract. From* Language Development: Understanding Language Diversity in the Classroom *(p. 83), by S. Levey & S. Polirstok (Eds.), 2011, Los Angeles, CA: Sage. Reprinted with permission.*

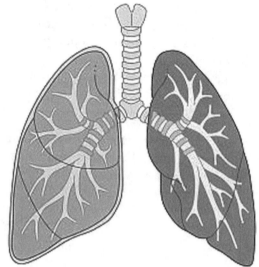

Figure 3–5. *The Respiratory System. Reproduced with permission from Getty Images.*

PHONATION

The **vocal folds**, sometimes called the vocal cords, convert the pressurized air in the lungs into audible sound (sound that can be heard). **Phonation** is the term for the sound produced by vocal fold vibration. The vocal folds, when positioned close to midline, can be set into rapid vibration by the airstream from the lungs (Figure 3–5). The articulators create sounds in the oral cavity and transform sounds generated in the larynx phonation into intelligible speech (speech that can be understood by a listener).

After inspiration, phonation (voice) is produced when the vocal folds are brought together (**adduct**), and set into rapid vibration, interrupting the flow of air from the lungs after inspiration (Figure 3–6). Phonation requires an increase in pressure below the vocal folds. When the pressure below the folds becomes greater than the resistance offered by the adducted vocal folds, they are forced open (**abduct**). The vocal folds then close rapidly due to their elasticity, laryngeal muscle tension, and other effects. As the vocal folds continue to open and close, puffs of air are released from the glottis (space between the folds). The vibration of the vocal folds results in a buzzing sound that we call phonation or voice. Voice is the result of the release of successive pulses of air from the vibrating vocal folds. These pulses of air correspond to the vibrations of the vocal folds.

CLOSED   OPEN

NORMAL VOCAL CORDS

Figure 3–6. *Vocal Folds in Adducted (Closed) and Abducted (Open) Position. From* Language Development: Understanding Language Diversity in the Classroom *(p. 83), by S. Levey & S. Polirstok (Eds.), 2011, Los Angeles, CA: Sage. Reprinted with permission.*

The frequency of a sound is determined by the mass and tension of the vocal folds and the air pressure generated below the vocal folds. The frequency of the produced sound corresponds closely to perceived pitch and carries important linguistic and emotional information. For example, a rising pitch at the end of a sentence signals question, whereas a lowered pitch signals a statement. For example, if the sentence *John is coming* is produced with a rising intonation, this signals a question form (i.e., *John is COMING?*), whereas a falling intonation would represent a statement (i.e., *JOHN is coming*).

The vocal folds act as a valve for air passing into and out the lungs. The skeletal framework of the **larynx**, colloquially known as "voice box," is composed of car-

tilage and contains the vibrators essential to voice production: the vocal folds (or vocal cords). The position, tension, and mass of the vocal folds are controlled by a number of muscles within the larynx. The pharynx is the passageway leading from the cavities of the nose and mouth to the larynx and esophagus (see Figure 3–1). Upon inhalation, air travels through the pharynx to the lungs. The trachea, also known as the windpipe, is a tube descending from the larynx through which air is carried to the lungs.

Sounds produced in the larynx and vocal tract are modified (altered or changed) by the **resonances** of the vocal tract. As stated earlier, the vocal tract consists of the cavities above the vocal folds: the oral, nasal, and pharyngeal cavities (see Figure 3–1). The effect of different vocal tract configurations (shapes) on the production of speech sounds is known as **acoustic resonance**. It is the resonance characteristics of the vocal tract that transform vocal fold vibration, a crude buzzing sound, into a variety of speech sounds that leave the mouth (e.g., "ah," "mm," and "r").

To understand the resonance characteristics of the vocal tract, produce the vowel sound "ah." While producing the "ah" sound, round your lips. You will note that the "ah" sound is transformed into a different sound with the lips rounded (i.e., "oo"). In this example, you have altered the vocal tract configuration (size and shape of the vocal tract), which has acoustically filtered the sound produced in the larynx into two distinct sounds. In short, you have changed the resonance characteristics of the vocal tract. The resonances of the vocal tract are what give the speech sounds their unique character or quality. When an individual experiences difficulty moving the articulators, speech sounds will not be clearly produced or resonated.

PHONEMES

Phonemes are a group or "family" of sounds that can signal a difference in meaning. We use special symbols of the International Phonetic Alphabet (IPA) when transcribing or recording these sounds. IPA symbols are placed between slash marks (or virgules).

Phonemes function to distinguish meaning, as shown in the examples that follow.

bat, cat, fat, hat, mat, pat, rat, sat

Note that the difference in meaning among these words is signaled by a change in the initial sound (or phoneme).

/bæt/, /kæt/, /fæt/, /mæt/, /pæt/, /ræt/, /sæt/

In English, there is often a considerable difference between the way a sound is produced and the way it is written. A classic example is the word *enough*. The final sound in this word is "f" /f/, which is written as -*gh*. Thus, because of the difference between written and spoken sounds (and because speakers may produce sounds in different manners), we use phonetic transcription to describe the way words are actually produced. See Chapter 1 for a complete inventory of English consonants (see Table 1–1) and vowels (see Table 1–2).

ENGLISH VOWELS

When we describe the production of **vowels**, we refer to the degree of tongue height (high, mid, or low), the degree of tongue advancement (tongue position along the length of the oral cavity (front, central, or back), and the lip configuration (degree to which the lips are rounded or spread). All English vowels are produced with voice or vocal fold vibration, except for whispered speech (produced without vocal fold vibration). The discussion that follows assumes normal speech production with appropriate phonation. We begin with a description of front vowels, shown in Figure 3–7.

Front Vowels

Front vowels consist of sounds that are produced with the tongue positioned in the anterior portion (front) of the oral cavity with varying degrees of tongue height (indicated next as high, mid, or low). Note that lip position is spread or retracted (not rounded) for all English front vowels.

/i/ kn**ee**, **eat**, sh**e**
High, front, lips retracted

/ɪ/ **it**, pr**i**nt, f**i**t
Mid-high, front, lips retracted

/e/ **ate**, tr**ai**n, b**ei**ge
Mid, front, lips retracted

/ɛ/ l**e**t, m**ea**nt, fr**ie**nd
Mid-low, front, lips retracted

/æ/ h**a**t, c**a**ttle, f**a**t
Low, front, lips retracted

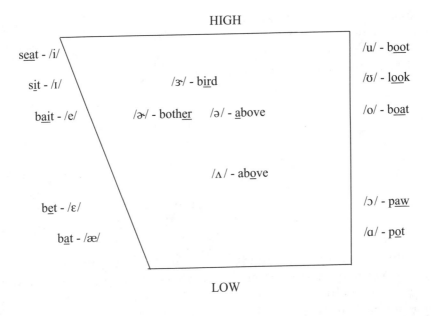

HIGH

seat - /i/   /u/ - boot

sit - /ɪ/   /ɜ˞/ - bird   /ʊ/ - look

bait - /e/   /ɚ/ - bother   /ə/ - above   /o/ - boat

/ʌ/ - above

bet - /ɛ/   /ɔ/ - paw

bat - /æ/   /ɑ/ - pot

LOW

FRONT---BACK

Figure 3–7. *The Vowel Quadrilateral. From* Language Development: Understanding Language Diversity in the Classroom *(p. 86), by S. Levey & S. Polirstok (Eds.), 2011, Los Angeles, CA: Sage. Reprinted with permission.*

Back Vowels

Back vowels are produced with the tongue positioned in the posterior portion (back) of the oral cavity. Lips are rounded to varying degrees for the production of back vowels. The degree of lip rounding decreases as you move from the production of the high back vowel /u/ to the production of the low back vowel /ɑ/. The back vowels of English are:

/u/ **you**, fl**u**te, t**oo**
High, back vowel, lips rounded

/ʊ/ b**oo**k, c**ou**ld, f**oo**t
Mid-high, back vowel, lips rounded

/o/ g**o**, sh**ou**lder, l**oa**d
Mid, back vowel, lips rounded

/ɔ/ j**aw**, c**au**ght, f**ou**ght
Mid-low, back vowel, lips rounded

/ɑ/ c**o**t, b**o**ttle, f**a**ther
Low, back vowel, lips rounded

> To illustrate the difference in lip position between the front and back vowels, contrast your production of the front vowel /i/, found in the word *he*, with your production of the back vowel /u/, found in the word *too*. Notice that your lips are retracted or spread during the production of the vowel /i/ and are rounded during production of the vowel /u/.

It is important to remember that vowels differ across languages. For example, Spanish lacks certain vowels that are present in English, as shown in the following examples:

/ɪ/ hit

/æ/ cat

/ɛ/ pet

/ɔ/ paw

/ʊ/ book

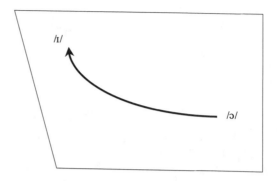

Figure 3–8. *The Diphthong /ɔɪ/.*

It is important for speech-language pathologists to consider these differences when working with individuals from different language backgrounds.

Diphthongs

Diphthongs are vowel-like sounds that are produced with a gradually changing articulation (Shriberg & Kent, 2003). The following diphthongs are recognized in English:

/aʊ/ cow, mountain, found

/aɪ/ high, tie, sigh

/ɔɪ/ boy, foil, coin

A diphthong is a vowel with a slowly changing quality, as shown in the production of the diphthong /ɔɪ/ (Figure 3–8). Although often described as a combination of two vowel sounds, a diphthong is considered a single speech sound (phoneme).

CONSONANTS

When we describe the production of consonants, we refer to place, manner, and the presence or absence of voicing. Place refers to *where* in the vocal tract a sound is produced, manner refers to *how* a sound is produced (and how the airflow is passing through the oral or nasal cavity), and voice or voicing refers to the presence/absence of vocal fold vibration (phonation). Consonant sounds are produced at or near the following landmarks in the oral cavity (see Figure 3–4):

- ◆ **Hard palate**: the bony roof of the mouth
- ◆ **Alveolar ridge**: the prominent, bony ridge behind the upper teeth
- ◆ **Velum** (soft palate): the fleshy structure that hangs from the hard palate in the posterior (back) portion of the mouth

When the velum is raised, sound energy will pass through the oral cavity and not the nasal cavity (Figure 3–9). **Velopharyngeal closure** is the closing off of the nasal cavity by raising the velum against the pharynx (throat). When the velum is lowered and a complete closure is formed in the oral cavity, sound energy will pass through the nasal cavity. The only sounds of English that are produced with the velum lowered are the nasal sounds: /m/, /n/, /ŋ/. For all other

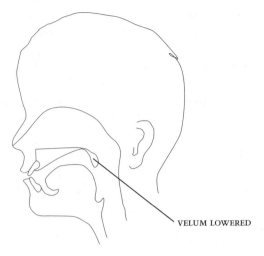

VELUM LOWERED

VELOPHARYNGEAL VALVE "OPEN"

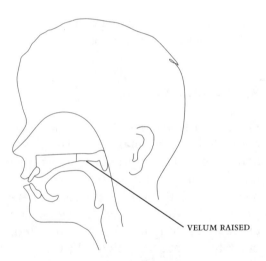

VELUM RAISED

VELOPHARYNGEAL VALVE "CLOSED"

Figure 3–9. *Velopharyngeal "Valve" in the Open and Closed Positions. From* Language Development: Understanding Language Diversity in the Classroom *(p. 88), by S. Levey & S. Polirstok (Eds.), 2011, Los Angeles, CA: Sage. Reprinted with permission.*

Bilabial (two lips): /p, b, m, w/

Labio-dental (lip-teeth): /f, v/

Lingua-dental (tongue-teeth): /θ, ð/

Lingua-alveolar (tongue-alveolar ridge): /t, d, s, z, n, l/

Lingua-palatal: /tʃ, dʒ/

Velar (tongue-velum): /k, g, ŋ/

Glottal (produced at the glottis): /h/

Consonants are produced with a significant constriction (complete or partial closure) in the oral and/or pharyngeal cavity, whereas vowels are produced with little or no constriction. Note the relative open vocal tract when you produce a vowel sound, /a/, for example. Note the difference between the production of the consonant /b/ found in the word *bee* and the vowel /i/ that follows in this word (i.e., **bee**). Notice that your lips are closed (forming a complete vocal tract closure) for the production of the consonant /b/ but that your mouth opens rapidly to create a relatively unconstricted vocal tract for the production of the vowel /i/.

VOICING

To appreciate the difference between voiced and unvoiced consonant sounds, produce the words *bus* (the final consonant /s/ is unvoiced) and *buzz* (the final consonant /z/ is voiced). When you produce these words, prolong or extend the final sounds, and place your hand gently on either side of your larynx (voice box). You should feel the vibration associated with vocal fold vibration at the end of the word *buzz*, but no vibration will be perceived at the end of the word *bus* (the unvoiced /s/ sound is produced with the vocal folds open, not vibrating).

consonant sounds (non-nasal consonants) the velopharyngeal mechanism is closed (velum raised). English consonant sounds are produced in the region of the following articulatory contacts:

Nasal Sounds

Nasal consonants are produced when sound generated in the larynx (vocal fold vibration) is passed through the nasal cavity. The presence of sound passing through the nasal cavity can be observed by placing your fingers gently on the side of your nose while producing the nasal consonant /m/, as in the word *me*. Note the vibration that takes place when this sound passes through and is resonated within the nasal cavity. Examples of nasal sounds follow.

/m/   **m**e, ca**m**el, la**mb**,

/n/   **n**o, can**n**on, fa**n**

/ŋ/   ha**ng**, da**ng**le, ha**ng**er

The production of nasal sounds requires two articulatory processes:

Closure at one of three places of articulation within the oral cavity so that air does not escape from the mouth

Lowering of the velum (soft palate) so that air passes through the nasal cavity and out the **nares** (the nostrils)

> Note that the nasal phoneme /ŋ/ does not occur in the initial position in English words. It only occurs in final or in medial (middle) position. In addition, note that this sound differs from the phoneme /g/, found in the words *go*, *flag*, and *magazine*.

The manner of production of these consonants is *nasal* because of the resonance characteristics (i.e., sound resonated in the nasal cavity). There are three places of production for the nasal consonants: lips (/m/), alveolar ridge (/n/), and velum /ŋ/). The unique quality of these three sounds is determined by the different places of closure for these three sounds. All **nasals** are voiced, which means that the sound energy for nasal sounds originates in the larynx (vocal fold vibration). The places of articulation of the nasal sounds follow.

Bilabial: Closure at the lips; /m/, **m**e

Lingua-alveolar: Tongue tip contacts the alveolar ridge; /n/, **n**eed

Lingua-velar: Tongue dorsum contacts the velum; /ŋ/, ha**ng**

Approximants

There are two classes of consonants that are called **approximants**. These consonants are called approximants because the articulators only *approximate* (come near one another) as these sounds are produced (MacKay, 1987). Thus, the articulators (tongue and/or lips) do not meet to form a complete closure or a significant constriction to produce a sound. Rather, articulators are approximated to form a unique resonator for sounds produced in the larynx. To experience the difference, produce the sound /p/, as in the word *pea*. Notice that your lips make contact to produce the /p/. To produce the sound /w/, as in the word *we*, note that your lips only *approximate* one another and do not completely close as in the production of /p/. The two classes of approximants are **glides** and **liquids**. Examples follow.

/j/ yellow, you, young
Voiced, lingua-palatal

/w/ we, twinkle, window
Voiced, labio-velar

Glides are resonated by a gliding movement from a narrow (constricted) vocal tract to a wider (less constricted) vocal tract. Notice the gliding motion when you produce the phoneme /j/, the initial sound in the word *yes*. The place of production for the glides are lingua-palatal (tongue contact with the hard palate) for /j/ and labio-velar (lips and tongue-velum approximate for /w/.

Liquids are very similar to glides, but a major difference is that the liquids /l/ and /r/ are not produced with the gliding movement for their unique auditory identification (Shriberg & Kent, 2003).

/l/ lion, balloon, boil

/r/ red

There is a group of sounds that should not be confused with the liquid /r/. These sounds are called rhotic diphthongs. Examples follow.

/iɚ/ **ear**

/eɚ/ **air**

/kɑɚ/ c**ar**

Rhotic diphthongs are phonemes that combine a vowel (e.g., /i, e, a/) with the phoneme /ɚ/, found in words such as *brother* and *bother*. As the articulators move from a vowel to an /r/ sound in a word, a rhotic diphthong (sometimes referred to as "r-coloring) is produced.

Stop Consonants

Stop consonants are produced with a sequence of events that describe the manner of production (i.e., *how* a sound is produced). Because the sequence of events begins with complete closure (stopped) and ends with a sudden release of this trapped air (a type of explosion), these sounds are also sometimes called **stop-plosives**. Stops are produced in the following manner:

◆ Forming a complete closure at one of three places of articulation in the oral cavity. Closure in the oral cavity is accompanied by the elevation of the velum (soft palate), which seals off the oral cavity from the nasal cavity
◆ Building up pressure in the oral cavity behind the point of closure
◆ And, finally, releasing the closure

Like the nasal consonants discussed earlier in this chapter, the stop consonant phonemes have three places of articulation: lips (/p/ and /b), alveolar ridge (/t/ and /d/), and velum (/k/ and /g/).

Bilabial: Two lips; /p/-/b/, **pea-bee**

Lingua-alveolar: Tongue contact with alveolar ridge; /t/-/d/, **to-d**o

Lingua-palatal: Tongue contact with velum; /k/-/g/, **K**ate-**g**ate

The stops /p, t, k/ are considered "unvoiced" sounds (**voiceless stops**), whereas the stops /b, d, g/ are typically classified as "voiced" (**voiced stops**). Examples follow.

/p/ **p**ie Unvoiced, bilabial stop

/b/ **b**uy Voiced, bilabial stop

/t/	two	Unvoiced, lingua-alveolar stop
/d/	do	Voiced, lingua-alveolar stop
/k/	Kate	Unvoiced, lingua-velar stop
/g/	gate	Voiced, lingua-velar stop

Fricative Sounds

Fricative consonants are produced by bringing the articulators close together, forming a significant constriction but not complete closure (close to one another but not forming a total closure). Next, pressure is built behind this partial closure and air is forced through the constriction. The result is noise production. As air is forced through the constriction, turbulent airflow results, which is perceived as a "hissing" sound. The five places of articulation for the *fricative sounds* are:

/f/ and /v/: Labio-dental (lower lip–upper teeth constriction)

/θ/ and /ð/: Lingua-dental (tongue–teeth constriction)

/s/ and /z/: Lingua-alveolar (tongue–alveolar ridge constriction)

/ʃ/ and /ʒ/: Lingua-palatal (tongue–hard palate constriction), and

/h/: Glottal (constriction at glottis)

The sounds /f/, /θ/, /s/, /ʃ/, and /h/ are classified as "voiceless" fricatives and the /v/, /ð/, /z/, and /ʒ/ sounds are classified as "voiced" fricatives. **Voiced fricatives** are produced by creating noise in the oral cavity while the vocal folds are set into vibration. **Voiceless fricatives** are produced by creating noise created in the

oral cavity (or the glottis in the case of /h/). Examples follow:

/f/	five	Voiceless, labial-dental
/v/	vase	Voiced, labial-dental
/θ/	thumb	Voiceless, lingua-dental
/ð/	these	Voiced, lingua-dental
/s/	sun	Voiceless, lingua-alveolar
/z/	zoo	Voiced, lingua-alveolar
/ʃ/	shoe	Voiceless, lingua-palatal
/ʒ/	pleasure	Voiced, lingua-palatal

Affricate Sounds

An affricate phoneme is produced as a combination of a stop with a fricative release (Kent, 1997; Shriberg & Kent, 2003). The affricated /tʃ/ is unvoiced and /dʒ/ is voiced. Examples follow.

| /tʃ/ | **ch**ew, **ch**ur**ch**, cat**ch** Unvoiced affricatives |
| /dʒ/ | **j**aw, **j**u**dge**, bad**ge** Voiced affricates |

An affricate is a consonant that begins as a stop (i.e., /d/ or /t/), with a complete obstruction of the outgoing airstream by the articulators (i.e., front of tongue and alveolar ridge), and is released as a fricative (a sound produced by forcing air through a smaller opening). There is a requirement for the affricates that the stop closure (e.g., /t/) to be **homorganic** (formed in the same place in the vocal tract) with the fricative release (e.g., /ʃ/) (Hardcastle, Gibbon, & Scobbie, 1995). Note that your tongue does not move from the alveolar ridge when you produce the final sound in the word *itch*.

SUMMARY

Speech production is a complex motor skill that requires precise coordination and carefully timed adjustments of the vocal tract articulators. Good speech communication skills lead to successful communication with others. The ability to identify sounds in words is an essential component of successful literacy development, as discussed in Chapter 8. Understanding children's speech development is essential. For example, toddlers and preschool-aged children may have difficulty with certain speech sounds, but we expect children to approximate or roughly achieve adult-like speech skills by 4 years of age. It is important that speech-language pathologists understand how sounds are produced so that they can provide appropriate intervention to children with delayed or abnormal articulation development. For example, knowledge of the correct place and manner of speech sound production is essential to help children with articulation disorders achieve age-appropriate speech skills. It is also important to understand that sounds differ across languages. Thus, practitioners must be aware of these differences to provide appropriate assessment and intervention to children or adult English-language learners.

KEY WORDS

Abduct
Acoustic resonance
Adduct
Alveolar ridge
Alveolar stop
Alveoli
Approximants
Articulators
Bilabial stop
Bronchiole
Bronchus
Diphthongs
Glides
Glottis
Homorganic
Labio-dental
Laryngeal system
Larynx
Lingua-alveolar
Lingua-dental
Lingua-palatal
Lingua-velar
Liquids
Nares
Nasal cavity
Nasals
Oral cavity
Pharyngeal cavity
Phonation
Phoneme
Phonetics
Resonance
Stop-plosive
Supralaryngeal vocal tract
Velar stop
Velopharyngeal closure
Velum
Vocal folds
Voiced fricatives
Voiced stops
Voiceless fricatives
Voiceless stops
Vowels

STUDY QUESTIONS

1. A child produced the sound /t/ in place of the target sound /θ/ (e.g., "bat" in place of *bath*). Describe the differences between these sounds in terms of place and manner.

2. Explain why phonetic transcription is necessary.

3. Describe the production differences between fricative and stops.

4. What articulators are involved in the production of the following speech sounds: /p/, /t/, /f/, /v/, and /θ/?

5. Describe the differences between vowels in English and Spanish by comparing the examples presented in this chapter.

REFERENCES

Cavallo, S. A. (2011). The production of speech sounds. In S. Levey & S. Polirstok (Eds.), *Language development* (pp. 79–99). Los Angeles, CA: Sage.

Hardcastle, W. J., Gibbon, F., & Scobbie, J. M. (1995). Phonetic and phonological aspects of English affricate production in children with speech disorders. *Phonetica, 52*(3), 242–250.

Kent, R. D. (1997). *The speech sciences.* San Diego, CA: Singular.

Mackay, I. R. A. (1987). *Phonetics: The science of speech production.* Boston, MA: Allyn & Bacon.

Shriberg, L. D., & Kent, R. D. (2003). *Clinical phonetics.* Boston, MA: Allyn and Bacon.

CHAPTER 4

The Brain and Speech and Language Development

Sandra Levey and Stephen A. Cavallo

Sammy is a 3-year-old child who has difficulty producing words, especially when these words contain more than two or three syllables (e.g., gorilla, banana, and television). After reading this chapter, you will be able to understand and explain these difficulties. You will also develop an understanding of how the brain plays a role in language development and the function of the brain in certain disorders.

The development of the brain begins in utero and continues through adolescence and early adulthood. Early language development is influenced by a child's environmental experiences and the stimulation that comes from interaction with language and events in the environment (Levey & West, 2011). Based on the child's life experiences, specific neural pathways develop. Neural pathways associated with behaviors that are repeated frequently will be strengthened and reinforced, whereas neurons that are not used are discarded. By 5 years of age, the structure of the child's brain approximates that of an adult (Mildner, 2008). Brain imaging studies have found that the brain continues to develop beyond early childhood with specific changes in neural architecture occurring during adolescence. The changes that occur during puberty and adolescence support the essential skills for executive functions (e.g., attention, memory, reasoning, logic, and problem solving) and social cognition (Blakemore & Choudhury, 2006). Social cognition consists of the mental operations that govern the theory of mind (e.g., the ability to understand and relate to another person's thoughts and feelings), allowing an individual to interact appropriately with others. It is important to understand the role of the brain in language development and why some children and adolescents may have difficulty with the executive functions that play an essential role in learning. It is also important to be aware of the disorders associated with neurological deficits.

CHAPTER OBJECTIVES

This chapter introduces the human nervous system. After reading this chapter, you should have a basic understanding and appreciation of:

◆ The components and divisions of the **central nervous system** (CNS) and **peripheral nervous system** (PNS)
◆ The role of the brain in speech and language development and abilities
◆ The role of the brain in cognition
◆ The role of the brain in executive functions
◆ The role of the brain in neurological disorders

SKILLS ASSOCIATED WITH THE BRAIN

The brain makes it possible for an individual to plan, organize, and learn. Sensitivity to learning new information is termed **neuroplasticity** (Kleim & Jones, 2008).

Neuroplasticity is the lifelong ability of the brain to reorganize neural pathways based on novel or new experiences, along with anatomical or physiological changes caused by injury. This means that the brain is able to change as learning occurs through experience or instruction. For speech-language pathologists (SLPs), the brain represents the vehicle for the acquisition and development of speech and language. Knowledge of the brain also helps the SLP to understand language deficits. For example, a sudden inability to speak can be a consequence of damage to the brain, such as a stroke or traumatic brain injury (TBI). In 1861, Broca found that loss of the ability to produce words was associated with damage to the left front side of the brain (Berker, Berker, & Smith, 1986). This area became known as **Broca's area**, found in the left frontal lobe of the brain (Figure 4–1). In 1876, Karl Wernicke found that damage to the temporal lobe of the brain also resulted in language problems that affect language comprehension or understanding spoken language,

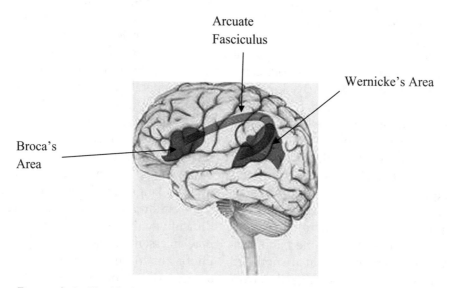

Figure 4–1. *The Human Brain. Reproduced with permission from Getty Images.*

along with the production of meaningful language. This area became known as **Wernicke's area**, found in the temporal lobe of the brain. The **arcuate fasciculus** is a bundle of nerve fibers that connect Broca's and Wernicke's areas, linking the speech and language areas in the brain (see Figure 4–1). The arcuate fasciculus connects Wernicke's area (phonological recognition) to Broca's area (phonological production). In other words, there is a connection between the recognition of words and the production of words.

THE HUMAN NERVOUS SYSTEM

The human **nervous system** consists of the central nervous system (CNS) and the peripheral nervous system (PNS) (Figure 4–2). The areas of the human nervous system associated with speech and language abilities follow (LaPointe, 2012).

Central nervous system: Brain, spinal cord

Peripheral nervous system: **Nerves**, ganglia (nerve tissue external to the brain or spinal cord found in the PNS)

We begin the exploration of the human nervous system with a review of the CNS.

The Central Nervous System

The CNS consists of the brain and spinal cord (Figure 4–3). The CNS controls our **motor** activities (e.g., walking, sitting, and speech) and movements that are connected to essential body functions (e.g.,

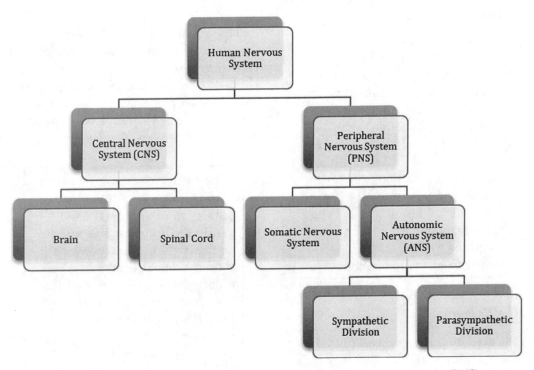

Figure 4–2. *The Central Nervous System (CNS) and Peripheral Nervous System (PNS).*

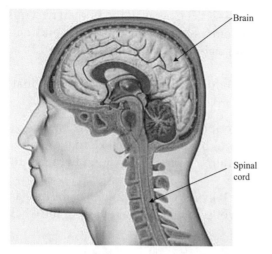

Figure 4–3. *The Brain and Spinal Cord. Reproduced with permission from Getty Images.*

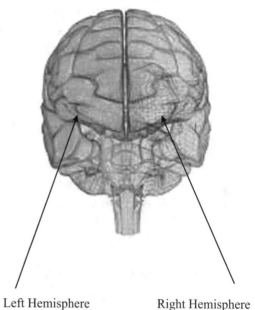

Left Hemisphere   Right Hemisphere

Posterior (back) view of the human brain

Figure 4–4. *The Cerebrum. Reproduced with permission from Getty Images.*

breathing). The CNS is also responsible for our thought processes that emerge from our interaction with the environment. The spinal cord is the main pathway for information connecting the brain and the PNS.

> The PNS enables the human body to interact with the environment through sensations sent to the CNS through the skin, muscles, and internal organs. The brain and spinal cord comprise the CNS. The spinal cord conducts sensory information (e.g., touch, smell, and taste) from the PNS to the brain and conducts motor information (e.g., movements required to achieve a goal) throughout the human body.

The Cerebrum

The **cerebrum** is the largest portion of the brain (Figure 4–4). Note that the cerebrum is divided into two hemispheres: the right

and the left hemispheres. The two cerebral hemispheres are connected by the **corpus callosum** (Figure 4–5) that connects the right and left cerebral hemispheres. The role of the corpus callosum is to allow the transfer of sensory, motor, and cognitive information between hemispheres.

> The corpus callosum is involved in the transfer of both motor and sensory information. The right side of the brain controls muscles on the left side of the body and the left side of the brain controls muscles on the right side of the body. Sensory information from the left side of the body crosses over to the right side of the brain and information from the right side of the body crosses over to

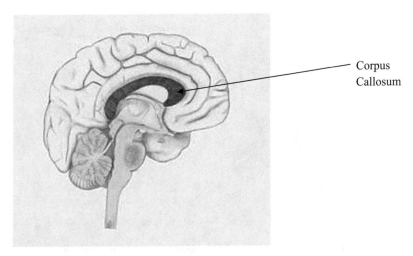

Corpus
Callosum

Figure 4–5. *The Corpus Callosum. Reproduced with permission from Getty Images.*

the left side of the brain. For example, auditory information from the left ear is first transferred to the right brain hemisphere and then to the left brain hemisphere, via the corpus callosum (McLaughlin et al., 1992).

On the surface of the cerebrum are a series of elevations or ridges (**gyri**) and valleys or depressions (**fissures** or **sulci**), as shown in Figure 4–1. This convoluted cerebral covering markedly increases the surface area of the brain, which is confined to a relatively small space within the cranium. The cerebral cortex is the outer surface of the brain but there are other major areas of the brain below the surface. These areas below the surface of the cerebral cortex are called subcortical structures.

Subcortical Structures and Functions

The **thalamus** and **hypothalamus** (Figure 4–6), **basal ganglia** (Figure 4–7), and **limbic system** (Figure 4–8) play a role in

motor control, memory, and basic functions of the human body, as shown in the following descriptions of the functions of these subcortical structures.

Basal ganglia: Motor control of muscle tone and posture; organization and guidance of complex motor functions

Limbic system: Self-preservation, emotions, memory, **olfaction** (the sensory function associated with smell or scents)

Thalamus: The chief sensory integrator in the brain and can be considered a relay station, conveying sensory and motor information to and from the cerebral cortex. All afferent information (information traveling to the brain), with the exception of olfaction (sense of smell), is routed through the thalamus. The thalamus also regulates sleep, emotion, and arousal

Hypothalamus: Associated with basic functions, such as eating and temperature

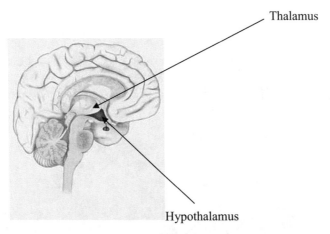

Figure 4–6. *The Subcortical Structures of the Human Brain. Reproduced with permission from Getty Images.*

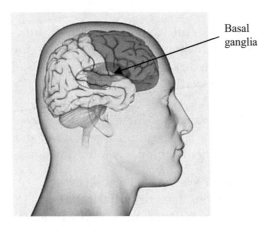

Figure 4–7. *The Basal Ganglia. Reproduced with permission from Getty Images.*

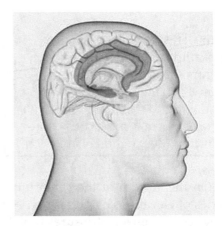

Figure 4–8. *The Limbic System. Reproduced with permission from Getty Images.*

The Basal Ganglia and Cerebellum

Speech production requires coordination of the articulators (e.g., lips, tongue, and velum/soft palate), larynx (e.g., vocal folds), lungs, and respiratory muscles. The coordination of these motor activities is controlled by the basal ganglia (shown in Figure 4–7) and the **cerebellum** (Figure 4–9). Lesions or injuries to these areas may lead to speech production difficulties

(Wildgruber, Ackermann, & Grodd, 2001). The following examples show the relationship between speech difficulties that are associated with motor functions (i.e., reduced loudness in relation to difficulties associated with respiration):

Reduced loudness: Respiration

Slowed speaking rate: Articulators

Voice tremor: Larynx

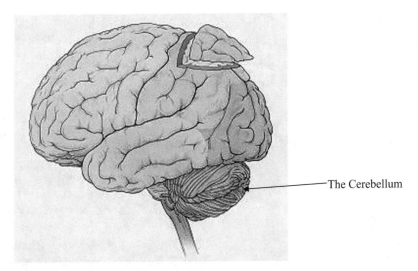

The Cerebellum

Figure 4–9. *The Cerebellum. Reproduced with permission from Getty Images.*

Irregular pitch shifts: Larynx

Hypernasality: Insufficient or poorly controlled elevation of the soft palate/velum

> Although the role of the basal ganglia in speech production is well known, the basal ganglia may also play a role in language abilities (Fabbro, Clarici, & Bava, 1996) with basal ganglia damage leading to difficulty in sentence production (e.g., the choice of the correct word or words to compose sentences when communicating with others). Thus, both speech production and language abilities may require the joint activity of cortical (i.e., Broca's area) and subcortical areas (i.e., basal ganglia and cerebellum).

The cerebellum sits beneath the occipital lobe, inferior to the cerebrum and posterior to the brainstem. The cerebellum is critical to the coordination and facilitation of fine and gross motor movement, body movement, and balance. Investigators have found that the cerebellum also may play a role in language abilities (De Smet, Baillieux, De Deyn, Mariën, & Paquier, 2007), as shown in the following examples:

Impaired phonological fluency: Difficulty producing sounds to form words

Impaired semantic fluency: Difficulty finding the correct word when communicating with others

Aphasia: Loss of the ability to use or understand language

Reading difficulties: Difficulty understanding written language

Writing problems: Difficulty composing written language

Disturbed listening comprehension: Difficulty understanding spoken language

The Four Lobes of the Cerebrum

Each hemisphere of the cerebrum is divided into four lobes: frontal, temporal, parietal, and occipital (Figure 4–10).

The Frontal Lobes. The frontal lobes are involved in the following functions:

> Motor functions
>
> > Movement
>
> Cognitive functions
>
> > Planning
> >
> > Reasoning
> >
> > Judgment
> >
> > Memory

The frontal lobe has three divisions:

> Prefrontal cortex: Responsible for the planning of cognitive behaviors, such as problem solving, emotion, and complex thought

Premotor: Uses information from other cortical regions to select appropriate movements and imitation (Gallese, Fadiga, Fogassi, & Rizzolatti, 1996).

Motor areas: Responsible for the planning and the execution of movements

> There is an elevated area of the frontal lobe known as the motor strip. This motor strip is believed to be responsible for voluntary control of striated muscle on the contralateral side of the body. Striated muscle is also called skeletal muscle because it is attached to bones in the human body. Striated muscle produces movement and is under voluntary control. In contrast, muscles that are not under voluntary control are smooth muscle, found in the walls of blood vessels, and cardiac muscle, found in the heart.

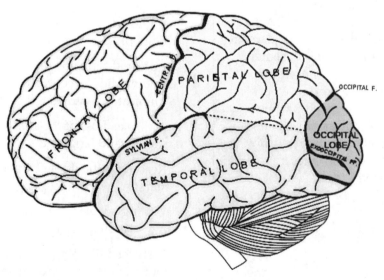

Figure 4–10. *The Four Lobes of the Brain.*

Also located in the frontal lobe of the left hemisphere is an area called Broca's area. Broca's area is critical to motor planning for speech. Broca's area activates the articulators for speech production (e.g., lips and tongue). Information related to the external environment and internal states is managed in the frontal lobes (Hécaen & Albert, 1975).

The prefrontal cortex is essential to the cognitive functions of working memory and decision making. Sousa (2006) demonstrated high levels of activity in the frontal lobes of the brain associated with working memory, the brain system that provides temporary storage and manipulation of information for language comprehension, learning, and reasoning. Executive functions, such as generating and carrying out action plans, along with the modification of plans when considering potential outcomes and past experiences, are located in the prefrontal cortex.

The Parietal Lobe. Within the parietal lobe is an elevation of the cerebral cortex known as the postcentral gyrus, or the sensory strip. **Sensory information** (e.g., pain, touch, temperature sense, and limb proprioception or limb position) from the contralateral side of the body is integrated in the postcentral gyrus of the parietal lobe. Damage to a specific area of the parietal lobe, the **angular gyrus**, may result in anomia (word finding difficulty) and writing problems. Left parietal damage may affect verbal memory (memory for spoken language) (Warrington & Weiskrantz, 1973).

Temporal Lobe. The temporal lobe is often described as the primary auditory area. It is important for processing auditory information. Wernicke's area, located in the temporal lobe, is the auditory association area that is important to language comprehension and language development. Speech sounds activate the primary auditory cortex (Hirano et al., 1997) with interpretation of these sounds in Wernicke's area. Heschl's gyrus, the primary auditory area (shown in Figure 4–15), is an area in the temporal lobe in which linguistic information is processed (Owens, 2008). The temporal lobe also contains the hippocampus, located in the medial or middle portion of the temporal lobe. The hippocampus plays an important role in long-term memory (i.e., the storage of information).

The Occipital Lobe. The occipital lobe is critical to the interpretation of visual sensory information. The primary visual cortex is located here. Visual stimuli (visual-spatial processing, discrimination of movement and color) are interpreted in the occipital lobe. Damage to the occipital lobe can also result in visual hallucinations (visual images of things not actually present) and illusions, such as objects appearing larger or smaller than they are, lacking color, or possessing abnormal color (Westmoreland & Eduardo, 1994).

The Brainstem

The **brainstem** consists of the medulla oblongata (also called the myelencephalon), the pons, and the midbrain (called the mesencephalon) (Figure 4–11).

Medulla oblongata: Respiration (breathing), heart rate, and blood pressure

Pons: Sleep, respiration, swallowing, bladder control, hearing, equilibrium, taste, eye movement, facial expressions, facial sensation, and posture

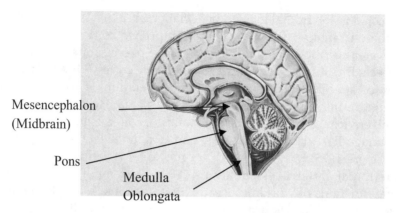

Mesencephalon
(Midbrain)

Pons

Medulla
Oblongata

Figure 4–11. *The Brainstem. Reproduced with permission from Getty Images.*

Midbrain: The region of the brain that acts as a relay station for auditory and visual information. The midbrain controls the visual and auditory systems as well as eye movement. The midbrain is also involved in controlling respiratory muscles, the vocal folds, and oral and nasal passages associated with resonance (discussed in Chapter 3). The midbrain is also involved in control of the palate, tongue, lips, and mandible, which are involved in articulation

The Peripheral Nervous System

The PNS consists of two parts: the **somatic** nervous system and the **autonomic** nervous system (shown in Figure 4–2).

Somatic nervous system: Carries motor (movement) and sensory (e.g., hearing, touch, and sight) information to and from the CNS. Responsible for voluntary muscle movements. Responsible for processing sensory information

Autonomic nervous system: Innervates muscles and glands for involuntary actions (e.g., gland secretions). Responsible for the control of visceral functions (e.g., heart, digestion, respiration)

The autonomic nervous system has two divisions: **sympathetic** and **parasympathetic**. The sympathetic nervous system plays an excitatory role in the nervous system, such as preparing the body for a fight or flight response. In contrast, the parasympathetic nervous system plays an opposite role in the processes of the body (LaPointe, 2012, p. 137). These differences are illustrated in these examples.

Sympathetic nervous system: Increases the heart rate and dilates the pupils

Parasympathetic nervous system: Slows the heart rate and contracts the pupils

Sensory, Motor, Cranial, and Somatic Nerves

In the PNS, we find sensory, motor, cranial, and somatic nerves. Their functions are described next.

Sensory (afferent) nerves: Carry information into the CNS about the sensations of touch, pain, temperature, and vibration

Motor (efferent) nerves: Carry information away from the CNS for muscle control

Cranial nerves: Exit the brain to reach the sense organs and/or muscles of the head and neck

Somatic nerves: Enable the body to interact with the environment. Connect skin, muscle, and internal organs with the CNS

Nerve fibers that carry information to the CNS are called **afferent** fibers. Nerve fibers that carry information away from the CNS are called **efferent** fibers. These afferent and efferent fibers control motor functions (movement) and the processing of sensory information for touch (tactile perception), vision (visual perception), taste (gustatory perception), hearing (auditory perception), and smell (olfactory perception), as shown in the following neurophysiological pathways:

Tactile perception: Sensory cell receptors send information to sensory nerves that pass through the spinal cord into the parietal lobe of the cerebral cortex

Visual perception: The retina is a light-sensitive membrane in the back of the eye, a part of the brain that transfers patterns of light into neural impulses that are processed by the brain

Auditory perception: Sound travels through the ear to sensory cells in the inner ear, where it is relayed to the auditory cortex in the temporal lobe of the brain

Gustatory perception: The sensation of taste occurs when a substance in the mouth interacts with taste bud receptors (these receptors send information to the gustatory cortex in the frontal lobes)

Olfactory perception: Olfactory sensory cells of the nasal cavity detect smells (and send information to the olfactory bulb location above the nasal cavity)

THE NEURON

The neuron (nerve cell) is the anatomical and functional unit of the nervous system (Webb & Adler, 2008), underlying all neural behavior (Figure 4–12). These neural behaviors include speech, language, and hearing. There are three types of neurons: sensory neurons, motor neurons, and interneurons. Interneurons connect nearby neurons, or neurons within the same region, in the neural system. Sensory neurons are nerve cells that transmit information to the CNS (spinal cord or brain). This information includes sensations, such as touch and taste. A motor neuron transmits "directions" to muscles for movement.

The Structure of the Neuron

Most neurons have three structural components: a cell body (**soma**), an **axon**, and a branching complex of **dendrites** (see Figure 4–12). The soma is the main part of the neuron and contains the **nucleus** of the cell. Dendrites are projections of the

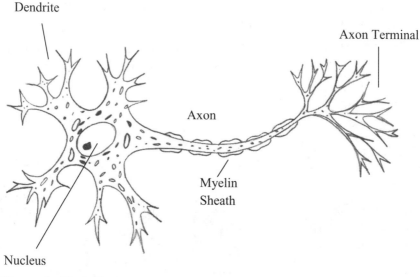

Dendrite

Axon Terminal

Axon

Myelin
Sheath

Nucleus

Figure 4–12. *A Neuron.*

neuron that conduct stimulation received from other neurons to the cell body (soma) of a neuron. An axon is the projection of a nerve cell that conducts impulses from the neuron. The dendrites are projections of the cell body that gather information (electrical energy) from other neurons and direct that information toward the cell body. Axons transmit information (electrochemical information) to other cells. The process of nerve transmission continues from neuron to neuron, leading to the contraction of a muscle fiber, the secretion of a gland, or the response of specialized structures in the brain designed to perceive pain, pressure, or temperature. In the nervous system, the **synapse** is the structure that allows a neuron to pass a signal to another neuron using chemical neurotransmitters (Figure 4–13). Connections between nerve cells are an essential factor in both sensory and motor abilities with synapses providing the mechanism of this connection.

Some of the nerve fibers are covered with a white sheath or cover called **myelin**. Myelin sheaths, which cover many axons in the CNS, are critical to neural transmission and normal muscle function. These myelin sheaths allow the rapid transmission of an electrical impulse along the myelinated nerve fiber. For example, transmission of the electrical impulse along a myelinated fiber is 50 times faster than along an unmyelinated fiber (Webb & Adler, 2008). As the nervous system matures during the first 2 years of life, there is a rapid increase in the myelination of nerve fibers. The development of speech and language may be correlated with the development of myelin in the nervous system (Webb & Adler, 2008).

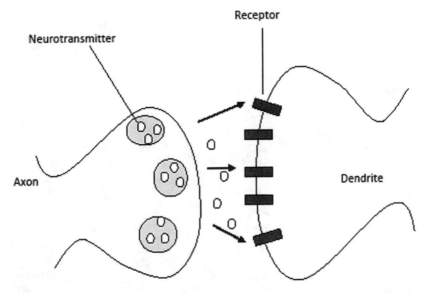

Figure 4–13. *A Synapse.*

THE CRANIAL NERVES

Cranial nerves play an important role in speech, language, and hearing processes. Consequently, SLPs' knowledge of the functions of the cranial nerves is essential. Some of the cranial nerves have motor functions, some have sensory functions, and others have both functions. Figure 4–14 presents a schema of the functions of the cranial nerves, whereas Table 4–1 presents the functional organization of the cranial nerves. The cranial nerves involved in speech, language, hearing, and swallowing functions are presented in Table 4–2 (LaPointe, 2012, pp. 94–109).

Cranial nerves III through XII enter or emerge from the brainstem (LaPointe, 2012). The origin of cranial nerve I is the olfactory epithelium found in the nose (specialized tissue in the nasal cavity that detects odors). The origin of cranial nerve II is the retina (the light-sensitive membrane in the back of the eye that receives an image and sends it through the optic nerve).

LANGUAGE AND THE BRAIN

Changes in regional cerebral blood flow, accessed by real-time functional magnetic resonance imaging (rtfMRI), are used to measure oxygen levels in the brain. In this way, we are able to determine which areas of the brain are active in which conditions. For example, there is increased activity and blood flow to the front regions of the brain when children are asked to think about someone else's state of mind (Baron-Cohen et al., 1994). This response occurs when children are asked questions about what a story character *thinks, feels, wants,* or *believes.* Through scientific research, certain regions of the brain have been determined to be actively involved

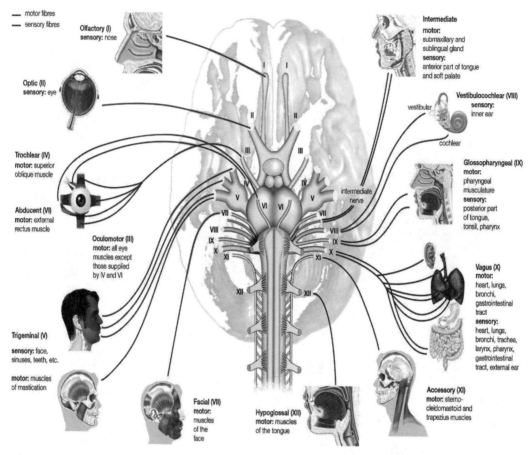

Figure 4–14. *The Cranial Nerves. Reproduced with permission from Getty Images.*

in language processing (Friederici, 2002), shown in the following examples:

Left temporal region: Semantic processing (determining the meaning of spoken language)

Left frontal cortex: Sequencing and the formation of structural (syntax) and semantic relations

Right temporal region: Identification of prosodic information

Right frontal cortex: Processing of sentence melody

Prosodic information and melodic information involve the rhythm, stress, and intonation that characterize spoken language. For example, word stress helps you distinguish between the meanings of the words *SUBject* (noun) versus *subJECT* (verb). Sentence melody involves the intonation patterns that differentiate a question (*Is he COMing?*) from a statement (*He IS coming!*).

In addition, cognitive abilities allow a listener to interpret unspoken cues that are communicated only through intonation. For example, the sentence *There*

WAS a cookie here (often accompanied by an accusatory tone of voice) implies that the listener may be responsible for the missing cookie.

Table 4–1. *Cranial Nerves*

Sensory Cranial Nerves	
I. Olfactory nerve	Smell
II. Optic nerve	Vision
III. Oculomotor nerve	Eye movement; pupil constriction; lens adjustment
IV. Trochlear nerve	Eye movement
V. Trigeminal nerve	Sensory function for the face, mouth, teeth, nasal cavity, and surface of the eye Motor function for innervation of the muscles of mastication (chewing or grinding food)
VI. Abducens nerve	Eye movement
VII. Facial nerve	Sensory function for taste (anterior two thirds of tongue) and information from ear Motor function for innervation of muscles for facial expression
VIII. Vestibulocochlear nerve	Hearing and balance
IX. Glossopharyngeal nerve	Sensory information for taste (posterior one third of tongue) and tongue, tonsil, and pharynx (the passage that leads from nose and mouth to the larynx or voice box and esophagus) Motor control for swallowing
X. Vagus nerve	Sensory, motor, and autonomic (automatic and unconscious) functions of viscera (glands, digestion, and heart rate)
XI. Spinal Accessory nerve	Motor control muscles for head movement, shoulder shrugging, and head rotation
XII. Hypoglossal nerve	Controls muscles of the tongue

Table 4–2. *Cranial Nerves Associated With Speech, Language, Hearing, and Swallowing Functions*

V.	Trigeminal nerve	
	Damage results in dysarthria	
	Speech sounds affected	
	Bilabials	/p, b, m, w/
	Labio-dentals	/f, v/
	Lingua-dentals	/θ, ð/
	Lingua-alveolars	/t, d, n, s, z, l/
	Glides	/j, w/
	Liquids	/l, r/
VII.	Facial nerve	
	Speech sounds affected	
	Bilabial closure poor	/p, b, m, w/
	Bilabial articulation slow	
	Bilabials distorted	
	Labio-dentals distorted	/f, v/
VIII.	Vestibulocochlear nerve	
	Damage results in hearing loss	
IX.	Glossopharyngeal nerve	
	Damage results in a swallowing disorder	
	Resonance affected (as shaping the pharynx into different shapes and positions is affected to produce phonemes correctly)	
X.	Vagus nerve	
	Damage results in hypernasality (excessive air emission from the nose)	
	Speech production characteristics	
	Breathy and hoarse vocal quality	
	Low vocal intensity	
	Diplophonia (the production of two tones)	
	Reduced pitch	
	Pitch breaks	
	Stridor (noisy inhalation)	
	Speech sounds affected: sounds that require oral pressure	
	Stops	/p, b, t, d, k, g/
	Fricatives	/f, v, θ, ð, s, z, ʃ, ʒ, h/
	Affricates	/tʃ, dʒ/

Table 4–2. *continued*

XI.   Spinal accessory nerve
Damage results in paralytic dysphonia (vocal cord paralysis)
Speech production characteristics
Air wastage
Hoarse and harsh voice quality
XII. Hypoglossal nerve
Imprecise articulation
Reduced range of lingual movement (tongue movement limited)
Speech sounds affected   /s, ʃ, tʃ, r, l/
Vowels

Language Processing and the Brain

Language comprehension involves cognitive processing (deriving meaning from spoken language) and decoding (analyzing and interpreting) language symbols (words). Auditory information is received by the part of the midbrain known as the thalamus (shown in Figure 4–6) and relayed to **Heschl's gyrus** in the auditory cortex (labeled as the primary motor area in Figure 4–15). Here linguistic information is filtered from nonessential sounds and sent to Wernicke's area in the left temporal lobe, where linguistic analysis of auditory information takes place (linguistic analysis of the spoken language that is heard). Language production involves the formation of linguistic structure in Wernicke's area that is then sent to Broca's area in the frontal lobes (Figure 4–16). Here the verbal form of the message is programmed. Next, information is sent to areas of the brain responsible for respiratory support for speech production (the lungs and muscles that control respira-

tion), phonation (the vocal folds that create voicing through vibration), and articulation (the articulators that create different speeech sounds through movement).

Neural studies have shown that the areas responsible for speech and language functions are more widely distributed within the brain than previously thought (LaPointe, 2012). For example, there are connections between the primary language areas (i.e., Broca and Wernicke areas) and other areas of the brain. We have also learned that the basal ganglia and the cerebellum play important roles in speech production (Wildgruber et al., 2001).

Cognition and the Brain

Cognition includes the cognitive skills that distinguish humans from other living entities (Gentner, 2003, p. 195), including:

◆ The ability to create abstractions (e.g., inner language used to create thoughts about experiences) and to generalize experiences and to store common

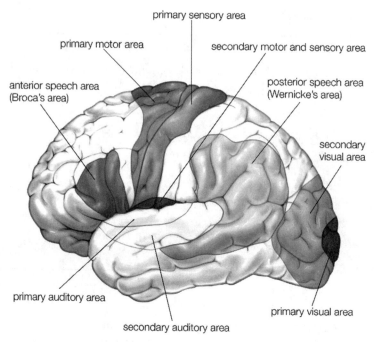

primary sensory area

primary motor area

secondary motor and sensory area

anterior speech area
(Broca's area)

posterior speech area
(Wernicke's area)

secondary
visual area

primary auditory area

primary visual area

secondary auditory area

Figure 4–15. *The Connection Between Broca's and Wernicke's Areas. Reproduced with permission from Getty Images.*

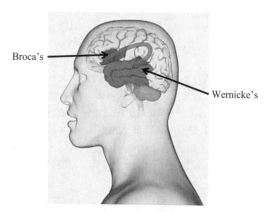

Broca's

Wernicke's

Figure 4–16. *Heschl's Area (the Primary Auditory Area) and other Motor and Sensory Areas of the Human Brain. Reproduced with permission from Getty Images.*

thoughts about your pet dog, dogs in general, and other living things)

◆ The ability to arrive at a conclusion, given certain facts or pieces of information

◆ The ability to compare and contrast things for similarities and differences

◆ The ability to learn that symbols represent numerical, spatial, and conceptual information (e.g., numbers, locations in space, and concepts about time and other abstract ideas)

Traditional views of cognitive development have focused on changes in infants' minds. In **embodied cognition**, cognition is believed to develop through an important relationship between an infant's mind and physical body (Wilson, 2002). In this model, cognitive development depends on the following interactions (Varela, Thompson, & Rosch, 1991; Wilson & Foglia, 2011):

experiences and results across varied outcomes (e.g., use past experience to predict consequences)

◆ The ability to maintain hierarchies of abstraction to store information (e.g.,

- Sensory input from the environment from objects, interactions with living entities, and events
- An infant's visual and physical action within the natural and social environment

According to the embodied cognitive theory, infants' innate sensorimotor skills (perceptual and physical skills) prepare them for their cognitive development. Infants' neurological development shows that the sensorimotor cortex (responsible for sensory skills) and motor skills develop before the temporal and parietal cortices (responsible for language and spatial skills) (Goswami, 2008). Thus, the underlying skills for language development (e.g., perceptual skills, such as vision and hearing, and physical skills, such as movement) develop before children's language skills. Visual perception allows infants to perceive objects and events in the environment. Physical capabilities allow the infant to explore these objects and interact with objects and entities. This is a dynamic and active process in which infants organize and develop their cognitive skills over time, given greater experience with adults, peers, objects, and events in the environment.

Mirror Neurons

At 1 to 3 days after birth, infants' innate or inborn sensorimotor skills are demonstrated by their perception and physical imitation of adults' tongue protrusion and mouth opening (Meltzoff & Moore, 1983). What is most interesting is that imitation of the adult's movements occurs even though infants are totally unaware of their own facial structure or physical movement. Cognitive neuroscience is able to explain these early behaviors through the role of **mirror neurons** (Jackson, Brunet, Meltzoff, & Decety, 2006; Rizolatti & Craighero, 2004).

You will recall that neurons are nerve cells that are specialized to transmit information. Mirror neurons are a type of neuron in the brain that fire when we undertake an action or perceive the actions of others. They provide an inner simulation or mirror of the actions that we observe, allowing the viewer's brain to symbolize and understand the actions of others (Rizzolatti & Craighero, 2004).

By creating a copy of the target action, mirror neurons provide an explanation of the imitation skills of infants, such as imitating adults' facial gestures, while lacking knowledge of their own facial structure (Meltzoff & Moore, 1983). Mirror neurons may also play a role in interpreting another person's emotions or feelings, laying the foundation for such higher-order social processes as empathy (sympathy, compassion, and understanding) and theory of mind. Theory of mind describes the ability to understand someone else's mind and mental state (e.g., happy, sad, or worried). Theory of mind is expressed in language, as shown in mental verbs that describe the human mind (e.g., *what someone thinks, knows,* or *believes*). The ability to understand someone else's mind marks the difference between typical language development and atypical language development.

> Children with typical cognitive and language development develop an understanding of others' mental states. Although traditional explanations of human thought looked at the processes of the mind to explain cognition, neuroscience has helped us understand the connection between the mind and body to provide an explanation of these early skills through the study of the function of the human brain.

NEUROLOGICAL DISORDERS AND SPEECH AND LANGUAGE FUNCTIONS

Executive Functions

Executive functions consist of attention and memory, along with the ability to plan, organize, and learn from prior experiences. For example, children with intact executive functions can learn from prior errors and can correct these errors when reviewing their work or when given new assignments within the classroom. Executive functions are involved in the development of academic skills, such as **abstract thought** (drawing conclusions from written text), the ability to revise plans (to correct errors), to initiate action (to prepare for exams and assignments), to reject inappropriate actions (to interact appropriately with peers), and to learn from past mistakes (to learn from prior errors). Children who have executive function difficulties may be disorganized, forgetful, and have poor critical thinking skills. Children with executive function difficulties may also be **disinhibited** (lacking the ability to restrain from impulsive actions), resulting in inappropriate social behaviors. Critical thinking skills include attention, discrimination, reasoning, logic, organization, memory, transfer, metacognition, problem solving, planning, mental flexibility, response inhibition, and self-monitoring. Examples of executive functions are described next.

Attention: Active and alert processing of a situation

Discrimination: Identification of differences based on some feature or features

Reasoning: Forming conclusions, inferences, or judgments

Logic: Reasoning or the process of drawing conclusions from facts or evidence

Organization: Mentally classifying and categorizing thoughts, tasks, or objects

Memory: Recall of information

Transfer: Generalization of knowledge to apply to new situations

Metacognition: Knowledge and awareness of language and thought

Problem solving: The thought processes involved in finding a way to resolve a problem

Planning: Monitoring, evaluating, and updating actions

Mental flexibility: The ability to shift to a different thought or action in response to situational changes

Response inhibition: The ability to suppress irrelevant (not relevant to the situation or learning context) or interfering information or impulses

Generativity: The ability to generate novel ideas and behaviors

Self-monitoring: The ability to monitor one's thoughts and actions

Deficient executive functions have been found in children with autism and in attention-deficit hyperactivity disorder (ADHD) (Ozonoff & Jensen, 1999). The symptoms of ADHD include (a) lack of sustained attention or (b) hyperactivity/impulsivity (a tendency to act on sudden urges), or (c) a combination of (a) and (b). These behaviors negatively affect learning because a child must be able to attend to spoken language, control excessive activity or movement, and take the time to consider actions or responses before acting. The executive functions affected in children diagnosed with autism and ADHD are planning, mental flexibility, response inhibition, and self-monitoring (Robinson, Goddard, Dritschel, Wisley, & Howlin, 2009).

Autism

There are several theories associated with **autism**. One theory is that autism is associated with brain overgrowth that results in the lack of neural connectivity with *connectivity* defined as communication between neural locations in the brain (Santangelo & Tsatsanis, 2005). Functional brain imaging (fMRI) studies have found that autism is characterized by early brain overgrowth, at 9 to 12 months of age, followed by growth stabilization. The frontal lobes of the brain show the greatest degree of overgrowth (Carper, Moses, Tigue, & Courchesne, 2002; Piven, 2004), resulting in excessive or extreme connectivity *within* the frontal lobes and limited connectivity *between* the frontal lobes and other parts of the brain. There is lower than normal connectivity between the frontal lobes and other regions of the brain for autistic children (Cohen, 2007). This limits the connection between the region of the brain that controls the cognitive functions of attention, social behavior, and language and other parts of the brain.

The second theory of autism is that there is a disturbance in the function of the transmission of information within the brain. The brain processes information by the transmission of signals at synapses, responsible for the processing of information in the brain. **Neurotransmitters** are chemicals that allow the transmission of signals from one neuron to the next across synapses. There are also certain genes that facilitate the transmission of signals across synapses (Luscher & Issac, 2009) with synapses shown in Figure 4–13. Alterations in the presence or the function of these genes can lead to significant changes in the neural network, affecting neural networks that process signals. These alterations in the genes that facilitate the transmission of signals have been implicated in cognitive disorders, such as autism (Südhof, 2008).

In summary, two theories of autism have been presented. The first posits that brain overgrowth during early development limits the connectivity between the cognitive functions of the frontal lobe with other areas of the brain. The second posits that alterations in the genes that facilitate the transmission of information across synapses play a role in the cognitive deficits associated with autism. Research continues in the investigation of autism and methods of intervention to address the cognitive deficits found in this disorder.

apraxia. The inability to produce longer words is due to difficulties with initiation of producing words, selecting the correct sounds to produce this word, and sequencing the syllables of the word.

Apraxia

Apraxia is a neurological disorder that results in difficulty initiating (beginning), planning, and/or programming the production of speech sequences (ASHA, 2007). Apraxia of speech is characterized by the following speech patterns (Webb & Adler, 2008):

Inconsistent initiation: Initiating or attempting to produce an utterance

Selection: Selecting or choosing the correct sound or sounds

Sequencing: Producing the sequence of sounds and syllables required for more complex or lengthier words

Apraxia of speech reflects a disturbance of the motor program that provides input to the motor (movement) system of speech production (Ackermann & Riecker, 2010). Demands on motor planning increase as the child attempts to produce longer utterances.

An example of apraxia was given in the vignette that appears at the beginning of the chapter. In this vignette, Sammy has difficulty with producing words that contain multiple syllables, such as the three-syllable word *banana*, consistent with the presence of

Childhood apraxia of speech (CAS) is a neurological childhood speech disorder that appears with impaired precision and consistency of speech movement with the absence of neuromuscular deficits (Aziz, Shohdi, Osman, & Habib, 2010). Motor sequencing is impaired (Ayres, 1985), which affects the order of elements in speech production (the order of syllables in words) and motor planning to move from one element to another (from one syllable to the next).

Motor planning is controlled by Broca's area, although motor production may also be affected if there is a lesion in the basal ganglia (Wildgruber et al., 2001). Because of the impairment in sequencing and forming speech sounds, the resulting productions are inconsistent, as shown in the following example of attempts to produce a sequence of sounds to form the word *banana*:

nanaba, babana, nana, banana

The productions of children with CAS are marked by inconsistent accuracy because difficulties are shown in timing, sequencing, and the transitions between articulatory movements. This means that children will have difficulty combining smaller units into larger wholes (Velleman, 2006), such as the sequence of syllables that form longer words. CAS appears in early speech development with the absence of cooing or babbling. These problems are not caused by muscle weakness or paralysis. Instead, the brain has difficulty planning to move the articulators (lips, tongue, and jaw) required for speech.

The complexity of speech is described in Chapter 3. Even the simple two-syllable sequence required to produce the word *mama* requires a number of transitions and sequenced speech efforts by a child. To appreciate the complexity of speech as a learned motor behavior, consider a young child producing the simple consonant-vowel-consonant-vowel (CVCV) combination /mɑmə/ ("mama").

First, a child must draw air into the lungs. This is accomplished by contracting muscles of inhalation

Following the pre-speech inspiration, a child must bring together the vocal folds to generate the necessary subglottal pressure to set the vocal folds into rapid vibration for the initial consonant sound (/m/)

As the vocal folds are set into vibration, the child must position the articulators to create the specific vocal tract size and shape required to produce the /m/ sound. This is accomplished by lip closure and lowering the velum so that the sound produced in the larynx is directed through the pharyngeal and nasal cavities for the nasal phoneme /m/

To produce the next sound (i.e., /ɑ/), the child must simultaneously coordinate the movements of a number of speech articulators in the following manner: the mouth opens, the tongue,

lips, and lower jaw assume specific positions while the velum is raised, sealing off the nasal cavity. If these carefully timed articulatory adjustments are accomplished properly, sound will pass through the oral cavity and an intelligible /a/ will be produced. Similar articulatory adjustments will occur to produce the final two phonemes in /mɑmə/

Given the complex articulatory adjustments required to produce a simple CVCV combination such as /mɑmə/, it is not difficult to imagine the neuromuscular challenges confronting a child when producing more complex speech utterances.

The American Speech-Language-Hearing Association (2007) defines childhood apraxia of speech (CAS) in the following manner:

Childhood apraxia of speech (CAS) is a neurological childhood (pediatric) speech sound disorder in which the precision and consistency of movements underlying speech are impaired in the absence of neuromuscular deficits (e.g., abnormal reflexes, abnormal tone). CAS may occur as a result of known neurological impairment, in association with complex neurobehavioral disorders of known or unknown origin, or as an idiopathic neurogenic speech sound disorder. The core impairment in planning and/or programming spatiotemporal parameters of movement sequences results in errors in speech sound production and prosody.

Children with CAS may also have impaired prosody. **Prosody** refers to the use of inappropriate loudness patterns, inconsistent hypernasality (air inappropriately exhaled from nasal cavity for non-nasal sounds), hyponasality (air inappropriately not exhaled for sounds that are nasals), and the absence of typical pitch patterns (no pitch variation or excessive pitch variation). Prosody also refers to multisyllabic words (e.g., words with two or more syllables) produced with incorrect stress or lack of stress (Velleman & Shriberg, 1999). For example, the stress pattern in the word *baNAna* (primary stress on the second syllable "na") might be produced as "BAnana" (incorrect position of stress on the first syllable "ba") or "banana" (with no syllable given greater stress). In summary, apraxia is characterized by difficulty in the voluntary execution of the movements for articulation with the absence of paralysis, weakness, or incoordination of the speech musculature (Webb & Adler, 2008).

Dysarthria

Dysarthria is a collective name for a group of speech disorders associated with damage to the central or peripheral nervous system (Darley, Aronson, & Brown, 1975). These problems are reflected in oral communication problems due to paralysis, weakness, or incoordination of the speech musculature. Dysarthria is a motor speech disorder that affects the muscles of the mouth, face, pharynx, larynx, and respiratory system. Muscles may become weak, move slowly, or not move at all after a stroke or other brain injury. Some causes of dysarthria include stroke, accidents or falls, cerebral palsy, and muscular dystrophy.

> Dysarthria can affect all systems required for speech: respiration (breath support for speech efforts), phonation (voicing), articulation, and prosody. Speech characteristics show impaired pitch levels (too low, too high, or absent variation with monopitch); loudness (too loud; too quiet; or decreased loudness as utterances become longer); voice (breathy, harsh, strained, or stoppages); nasality (hyper- or hyponasal); rate (slow or variable rate); and sound production (imprecise consonants, phonemes prolonged, phonemes repeated, vowels distorted, and irregular articulatory breakdown). Overall, intelligibility or the precision of speech is impaired. The movements of the velum (soft palate), lips, tongue, and jaw may be impaired not only during speech, but also in the context of vegetative functions. Thus, there may be problems with chewing and swallowing.

Both children and adults can have dysarthria. Speech efforts are slurred and slowed because of limited tongue, lip, and jaw movement. Because the articulators that are used to produce speech are affected, speech productions are characterized by nasality (excessive nasal air emission) and vocal quality may be impaired. The role of the SLP is to evaluate a person with speech difficulties and determine the nature and severity of the problem. The SLP will examine movement of the lips, tongue, velum, and face, as well as breath support for speech and voice quality.

A Comparison of Childhood Apraxia of Speech (CAS) and Dysarthria

There are differences between CAS and childhood dysarthria (Velleman, 2006, p. 7). In contrast to childhood dysarthria, children with CAS have the following characteristics:

◆ Children with CAS have little or no muscle weakness
◆ Difficulty appears more frequently when trying to produce complex or sequential elements (i.e., producing sequenced syllables to form words, such as *banana*)
◆ Errors are inconsistent
◆ Errors are greater with purposeful speech attempts (e.g., asked to imitate or produce), rather than more automatic
◆ Speech production errors consist of substitutions, additions, omissions, and repetitions of phonemes or syllables with the production of later occurring phonemes (out of developmental sequence)

In contrast, childhood dysarthria is characterized by the following:

◆ Children with childhood dysarthria have muscle weakness: difficulty with sucking, chewing, and swallowing
◆ Difficulty is more likely to appear in connected speech efforts (sentences) than in single words
◆ Errors are consistent
◆ Errors are consistent in voluntary or automatic contexts
◆ Errors consist of phoneme distortions (imprecise productions)

SUMMARY

We have gained a better understanding of the brain through recent technological advances, such as transcranial magnetic stimulation (TMS), electromyography (EMG) (Watkins, Strafella, & Paus, 2003), positron emission tomography (PET), magnetic resonance imaging (MRI) (Watkins & Paus, 2004), fMRI (Buccino et al., 2001), and magnetoencephalography (MEG) (Mottonen, Jarvelainen, Sams, & Hari, 2004). These technologies have permitted imaging studies of the brain that have revealed new insights into the organization and functioning of the nervous system. Through these methods, we have learned that both speech production and language abilities may require the joint activity of cortical (i.e., Broca's area) and subcortical areas (i.e., basal ganglia and cerebellum). A summary of the anatomy and the functions of the human brain are presented in Figure 4–17.

The SLP must have a good understanding of the brain for various reasons. First, there is frequent interaction between the SLP and other practitioners, such as neurologists, psychologists, physicians, occupational therapists, and physical therapists. Knowledge of the nervous system allows for intelligent communication between the SLP and these professionals, some of whom have expert knowledge of the connection of the brain with cognitive and physical disorders. With this knowledge comes a better understanding and use of the terminology associated with neurological disorders. The SLP must also have a good understanding of the systems that relate to speech, language, and cognitive disorders for both assessment and intervention. With this knowledge, the SLP has a better understanding of the nervous

Anatomy and Functional Areas of the Brain

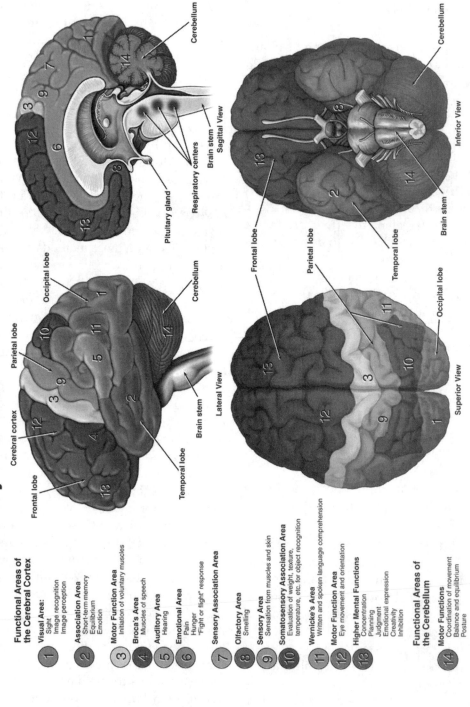

Figure 4–17. A Summary of the Anatomy and Functional Areas of the Human Brain. Reproduced with permission from Getty Images.

system and can engage in evidence-based practice, based on clinical expertise, experience, and education.

KEY WORDS

Abstract thought

Afferent

Angular gyrus

Apraxia

Arcuate fasciculus

Autism

Autonomic

Axon

Basal ganglia

Brainstem

Broca's area

Central nervous system (CNS)

Cerebellum

Cerebrum

Cognition

Corpus callosum

Dendrites

Disinhibited

Dysarthria

Efferent

Embodied cognition

Fissures

Gyri

Heschl's gyrus

Hypothalamus

Limbic system

Mirror neurons

Motor

Myelin

Nerves

Nervous system

Neuroplasticity

Neurotransmitters

Nucleus

Olfaction

Parasympathetic

Peripheral nervous system (PNS)

Prosody

Sensory information

Soma

Somatic

Sulci

Sympathetic

Synapse

Thalamus

Wernicke's area

STUDY QUESTIONS

1. Describe the role of the brain in speech production.

2. Describe the differences between apraxia and dysarthria.

3. Explain the importance of the knowledge of the human neurological system when working with individuals with speech or language difficulties.

4. Describe the role of executive functions that may affect children's progress in learning.

5. Explain the role of social cognition in communication.

REFERENCES

Ackermann, H., & Riecker, A. (2010). The contribution(s) of the insula to speech production: A review of the clinical and functional imaging literature. *Brain Structure and Function, 214*(5–6), 419–433.

American Speech-Language-Hearing Association. (2007). *Childhood apraxia of speech* [Position statement]. Retrieved from http://www.asha.org/policy

Ayres, A. J. (1985). *Developmental dyspraxia and adult-onset apraxia*. Torrance, CA: Sensory Integration International.

Aziz, A. A., Shohdi, S., Osman, D. M., & Habib, E. (2010). Childhood apraxia of speech and multiple phonological disorders in Cairo-Egyptian Arabic speaking children: Language, speech, and oro-motor differences. *International Journal of Pediatric Otorhinolaryngology, 74* (6), 578–585.

Baron-Cohen, S., Ring, H., Moriarty, J., Schmitz, B., Costa, D., & Ell, P. (1994). Recognition of mental state terms. Clinical findings in children with autism and a functional neuroimaging study of normal adults. *British Journal of Psychiatry, 165*(5), 640–649.

Berker, E. A., Berker, A. H., & Smith, A. (1986). Translation of Broca's 1865 report. Localization of speech in the third left frontal convolution. *Archives of Neurology, 43*(10), 1065–1072.

Blakemore, S., & Choudhury, S. (2006). Development of the adolescent brain: Implications for executive function and social cognition. *Journal of Child Psychology and Psychiatry, 47*(3), 296–312.

Buccino, G., Binkofski, F., Fink, G. R., Fadiga, L., Fogassi, L., Gallese, V., Seitz, R. J., . . . Freund, H. J. (2001). Action observation activates premotor and parietal areas in a somatotopic manner: An fMRI study. *European Journal of Neuroscience, 13*, 400–404.

Carper, R. A., Moses, P., Tigue, Z. D., & Courchesne, E. (2002). Cerebral lobes in autism: Early hyperplasia and abnormal age effects. *NeuroImage, 16*, 1038–1051.

Cohen, R. (2007). Connectivity-guided neurofeedback for autistic spectrum disorder. *Biofeedback, 35*(4), 131–135.

Darley, F. L., Aronson, A. E., & Brown, J. R. (1975). *Motor speech disorders*. Philadelphia, PA: W. B. Saunders.

De Smet, H. J., Baillieux, H., De Deyn, P. P., Mariën, P, & Paquier, P. (2007). The cerebellum and language: The story so far. *Folia Phoniatrica et Logopaedica, 59*(4), 165–170.

Fabbro, F., Clarici, A., & Bava, A. (1996). Effects of left basal ganglia lesions on language production. *Perceptual and Motor Skills, 82*(3), 1291–1298.

Friederici, A. D. (2002). Towards a neural basis of auditory sentence processing. *Trends in Cognitive Sciences, 6*(2), 78–84.

Gallese, V., Fadiga, L., Fogassi, L, & Rizzolatti, G. (1996). Action recognition in the premotor cortex. *Brain, 119*, 593–609.

Gentner, D. (2003). Why we're so smart. In D. Gentner & S. Goldin-Meadow (Eds.), *Language in mind: Advances in the study of language and thought* (pp. 195–235). Cambridge, MA: MIT Press.

Goswami, U. (2008). *Cognitive development: The learning brain*. New York, NY: Psychology Press.

Hécaen, H., & Albert, M. L. (1975). *Human neuropsychology*. New York, NY: John Wiley.

Hirano, S., Naito Y., Okazawa, H., Kojima, H., Honjo, I., Ishizu, K., . . . Konishi, J. (1997). Cortical activation by monaural speech sound stimulation demonstrated by positron emission tomography. *Experimental Brain Research, 113*, 75–80.

Jackson, P. L., Brunet, E., Meltzoff, A. N., & Decety, J. (2006). Empathy examined through the neural mechanisms involved in how I feel versus how you feel pain. *Neuropsychologia, 44*, 752–761.

Kleim, J. A., & Jones, T .A. (2008). Principles of experience-dependent neural plasticity: Implications for rehabilitation after brain damage. *Journal of Speech, Language, and Hearing Research, 51,* S226–S239.

LaPointe, L. L. (2012). *Atlas of neuroanatomy for communication science and disorders.* New York, NY: Thieme.

Levey, S., & West, J. F. (2011). The role of the brain in speech and language. In S. Levey & S. Polirstok (Eds.), *Language development: Understanding language diversity in the classroom* (pp. 101–114). Los Angeles, CA: Sage.

Luscher, C., & Issac, J. T. (2009). The synapse: Center stage for many brain diseases. *Journal of Physiology, 587*(4), 727–729.

McLaughlin, T., Steinberg, B., Christensen, B., Law, L., Parving, A., & Friberg, L. (1992). Potential language and attentional networks revealed through factor analysis of rCBF data measured with SPECT. *Journal of Cerebral Blood Flow Metabolism, 12*(4), 535–545.

Meltzoff, A. N., & Moore, K. (1983). Newborn infants imitate adult facial gestures. *Child Development, 54*(3), 702–709.

Mildner, V. (2008). *The cognitive neuroscience of human communication.* New York, NY: Erlbaum.

Mottonen, R., Jarvelainen, J., Sams, M., & Hari, R. (2004). Viewing speech modulates activity in the left SI mouth cortex. *NeuroImage, 24,* 731–737.

Owens, R. O. (2008). *Language development: An introduction.* Boston, MA: Allyn & Bacon.

Ozonoff, S., & Jensen, J. (1999). Brief report: Specific executive disorders in three developmental disorders. *Journal of Autism and Developmental Disorders, 29*(2), 171– 177.

Piven, J. (2004, May). *Longitudinal MRI study of 18–35 month olds with autism.* Abstract presented at the International Meeting for Autism Research, Sacramento, CA.

Rizzolatti, G., & Craighero, L. (2004). The mirror-neuron system. *Annual Review of Neuroscience, 27,* 169–192.

Robinson, S., Goddard, L., Dritschel, B., Wisley, M., & Howlin, P. (2009). Executive functions in children with autism spectrum disorders. *Brain and Cognition, 71,* 362–368.

Santangelo, S., & Tsatsanis, K. (2005). What is known about autism: Genes, brain, and behavior. *American Journal of Pharmaco-Genomics, 5*(2), 71–92.

Sousa, D. A. (2006). *How the brain learns* (3rd ed.). Thousand Oaks, CA: Corwin.

Südhof, T. C. (2008). Review article: Neuroligins and neurexins link synaptic function to cognitive disease. *Nature, 455,* 903–911.

Varela, F. J., Thompson, E., & Rosch, E. (1991). *The embodied mind: Cognitive science and human experience.* Cambridge, MA: MIT Press.

Velleman, S. L. (2006, November 16). *Childhood apraxia of speech: Assessment/treatment for the school-aged child.* Presentation at the Meeting of the American Speech-Language-Hearing Convention, Miami, FL.

Velleman, S. L., & Shriberg, L. D. (1999). Metrical analysis of the speech of children with suspected developmental apraxia of speech. *Journal of Speech, Language, and Hearing Research, 42,* 1444–1460.

Warrington, E., & Weiskrantz, L. (1973). *An analysis of short-term and long-term memory defects in man.* New York, NY: Academic Press.

Watkins, K. E., & Paus, T. (2004). Modulation of motor excitability during speech perception: The role of Broca's area. *Journal of Cognitive Neuroscience, 16*(6), 978–987.

Watkins, K. E., Strafella, A. P., & Paus, T. (2003). Seeing and hearing speech excites the motor system involved in speech production. *Neuropsychologia, 41,* 989–994.

Webb, W. G., & Adler, R. K. (2008). *Neurology for the speech-language pathologist.* St. Louis, MO: Mosby.

Westmoreland, B. F., & Eduardo, E. (1994). *Medical neurosciences: An approach to anatomy, pathology, and physiology by systems and levels.* Boston, MA: Little Brown & Co.

Wildgruber, D., Ackermann, H., & Grodd, W. (2001). Differential contributions of motor cortex, basal ganglia, and cerebellum to speech motor control: Effects of syllable repetition rate evaluated by fMRI. *NeuroImage, 13,* 101–109.

Wilson, M. (2002). Six views of embodied cognition. *Psychonomic Bulletin and Review, 9*(4), 625–636.

Wilson, R. A., & Foglia, L. (2011). Embodied cognition. *Stanford Encyclopedia of Philosophy.* Retrieved from http://philosophysother.blogspot.com/2011/08/wilson-robert-and-lucia-foglia-embodied.html

CHAPTER 5

Infant and Toddler Language Development

Sandra Levey

Everyone in Denise's family noticed how quickly the 2-year-old picked up new words when engaged in play with her older siblings and cousins. She seemed to enjoy repeating the words they used, along with the activities in their play schemes (e.g., playing house or going shopping for groceries). After reading this chapter, you will understand how language develops between birth and 3 years of age, along with the contexts that play a major role in learning language (e.g., pretend play and interaction with others).

2005). Soon after birth, infants show a preference for animate (living) entities. For example, they prefer to gaze at human faces rather than nonhuman, inanimate objects (Nelson, 1987). At 2 months of age, they imitate the facial gestures made by humans but not those made by objects imitating human movement (Legerstee, 2000). Although cognitive mechanisms for learning language are present in the newborn, language develops only through experience and interaction with people, things, and actions in the environment.

AN OVERVIEW OF INFANT AND TODDLER LANGUAGE DEVELOPMENT

Newborn infants possess a powerful **innate** learning mechanism that equips them for language acquisition (Gopnik, Meltzoff, & Kuhl, 1999). Infants possess **perceptual** preferences that prepare them for interaction with people and the task of learning language (Barna & Legerstee,

CHAPTER OBJECTIVES

This chapter describes children's language development from birth to 3 years of age. After reading this chapter, you should understand:

◆ Language development from birth to 3 years of age
◆ The relationship between cognition and language development

◆ The role of play in language development
◆ Differences associated with second-language learners of English

INFANT PERCEPTION AND PRODUCTION

Infant Perception

The examination of infants' **perception** tells us a great deal about the human mind. The duration of infants' eye gaze or auditory perception shows us what stimuli (objects, pictures, videos, faces, or movement patterns) elicit a stronger response and engage their interest. In one study, 4-day-old infants looked longer at their mothers' faces than at less familiar faces (Bushnell, Sai, & Mullin, 1989), indicating a preference for familiar visual stimuli. Between 6 and 12 months, infants choose an object based on an adult's positive or negative facial expression (Moses, Baldwin, Rosicky, & Tidball, 2002), choosing the object that matches the adult's positive facial expression. As mentioned in Chapter 1, a **theory of mind (TOM)** provides us with the ability to interpret facial expressions. Thus, infants are able to *read* another person's feelings and thoughts, a sign of a developing but still primitive TOM.

As early as 3 months of age, infants engage in vocal turn taking in response to sounds produced by adults (Masataka, 1995). At 1 to 4 months, infants can detect intonational changes in speech patterns (Jusczyk, 1992). By 5 months, infants begin to imitate some sounds (Owens, 2008). Although infants respond to their names by 5 months of age (Mandel, Jusczyk, & Pisoni, 1995), they often confuse their names with words that have the same number of syllables (e.g., *Missa* and *monkey*). Between 5 and 8 months, infants recognize that their own voices differ from other nonsocial stimuli (e.g., whistles and horns) (Legerstee, Anderson, & Schaffer, 1998). At about 6 months of age, infants become more sensitive to changes between sounds. For example, they react to the change when a series of stop-plosive sounds, /b, d, g/ (e.g., *stop-stop-stop*), is followed by a series of nasal sounds, /m, n, ŋ/ (e.g., *nasal-nasal-nasal*) (Hillenbrand, 1983). Their reaction to these sound differences shows that language-relevant abilities are present at an early age, providing support for understanding differences between words (e.g., *bud* vs. *mud*).

One study found that 7-month-old infants had a preference for sentences that contained a word that they previously had heard in isolation. In other words, if presented with the word *dog*, they showed a greater response to the sentence that contained this word rather than a sentence that contained a word *not* previously heard in isolation (Jusczyk & Aslin, 1995). This suggests an innate ability for learning words (van Heugten & Johnson, 2011).

By 18 to 20 months, infants recognize the connection between mouth movements and sounds connected with these movements (Kuhl & Meltzoff, 1997). Infants are also able to perceive sound differences that are absent from their own native language (Werker & Tees, 1984). This sensitivity to nonnative sound differences is lost at about 8 to 10 months of age, following longer exposure to the language spoken in the infant's environment (Jusczyk, 1992). By the end of the first year, infants understand many words. For example, between 7 and 12 months, children listen when spoken to, recognize words for common objects present in their environment, and respond to simple requests.

In summary, infants possess innate abilities that prepare them for the acquisition of language. We examine infants' sound production next.

Infant Production

Newborn infants' productions move through several stages of development, beginning with reflexive sounds, followed by attempts to imitate sounds produced by caregivers.

At about 2 months, **reflexive** sounds appear (e.g., burping and crying), along with laughter. Infants engage in turn taking at about 3 months, producing syllables (e.g., *bah*) in interaction with adults. Imitation appears at 5 months for the production of sounds, such as *ah* and *oh*. Although crying is the earliest form of infant vocalization, infants begin to coo at about 1 month of age (Shaffer, 1999). Cooing consists of vowel-like sounds, such as *aaaah*, appearing most often in interaction with caregivers. At around 3 to 4 months, infants add consonants to their cooing with consonant-vowel combinations marking the onset of reduplicated babble (e.g., *mamama*).

Reduplicated babbling is defined as the production of duplicated syllable sequences (e.g., *babababbaba*). Reduplicated babbling should appear at 6 to 7 months.

Variegated babbling appears at about 8 to 9 months, characterized by varied consonants and/or vowels in syllable sequences (e.g., *babibuga*).

Phonetically consistent forms (PCFs), also known as **vocables** or **performatives** (Dore, Franklin, Miller, & Ramer, 1976), appear in infants' early productions before the production of first words. PCFs refer to a consistent relation between an infant's production and a particular thing. For example, a PCF is meaningful when a child produces *ah* to mean *Pick me up* and produces *oh* to mean *I want a bottle*. This marks the beginning of meaningful communication.

Jargon appears at 9 to 12 months, when children produce syllables that appear to mirror real words (e.g., *Wada ja noba ga?*). Jargon is composed of nonsense syllables that have the intonational patterns of adult language (e.g., the intonational pattern of questions or statements).

Words appear at 12 months, starting with the production of words that identify familiar entities (e.g., *mommy, doggie,* and *birdie*) and objects (e.g., *cookie, car,* and *shoe*) in the child's environment. Jargon may also appear in children's productions when they begin to produce real words (e.g., *Dawa go?*).

PARENT AND CHILD INTERACTION

Parent-to-child interaction plays a role in children's language development. This interaction is characterized by the adult's production of shorter sentences, simplified syntactic structure, slowed speech rate, pauses between separate utterances, and a greater number of prompts (questions and commands) (Bernstein & Levey, 2009; James, 1990). This type of interaction ensures that children are able to better comprehend spoken language.

In Chapter 2, we presented the type of scaffolds used by adults when interacting with children (see Table 2–1). Examples consist of *recasts* (e.g., *ate*) used when children produce the incorrect form of a word (e.g., *eated*) and models to provide a child with a word when it is absent from his or her vocabulary.

The amount of talk that children hear from caregivers and those outside of their home environment is a predictor of vocabulary size (Shneidman, Arroyo, Levine, & Goldin-Meadow, 2012). Children acquire many new words through **incidental learning** (Akhtar, Jipson, & Callanan, 2001; Senechal, LeFevre, Hudson, & Lawson, 1996), such as overhearing conversations or listening to stories. In incidental learning, children are not taught new words directly and purposefully. Instead, children learn new words through exposure to communicative events, such as conversations and television shows. Children rely on contextual information to learn the meaning and use of these new words independently. For example, a child may listen to a conversation about a broken piece of furniture and the methods required for repair. In this encounter, the child may learn the vocabulary items *broken*, *fix*, and *glue* as they apply to this particular context. Later, the child will use these words to apply to new contexts, such as describing how to fix a broken toy.

Although incidental learning plays a role in learning new words, speech directed at children in interactive contexts also plays a significant role in vocabulary development (Shneidman et al., 2012). A study of Spanish-speaking children's vocabulary development found that children with mothers who provided more spoken language input at 18 months had larger receptive and expressive vocabularies at 24 months (Hurtado, Marchman, & Fernald, 2008). These findings show that more frequent spoken language input plays a significant role in children's vocabulary development. An example is the interaction that occurs during play with more advanced language users (Beals & Tabors, 1995).

Although the number and frequency of words produced by caregivers may play a role in children's vocabulary growth (Hart & Risley, 1995), evidence shows that a child's vocabulary growth is also related to the diversity of words produced by a caregiver (Pan, Rowe, Singer, & Snow, 2005). In other words, the greater variety of words used in interaction (not the total number of words) is an additional factor in children's vocabulary development (Ruston & Schwanenflugel, 2010).

The review of children's language development reveals the presence of innate cognitive skills that prepare children for learning language, such as their early sensitivity to sound differences. We also know that the frequency of spoken language input and the diversity of words play a role in their language development. As we examine children's early language development, we see that the environment plays a significant role in language acquisition.

EARLY LANGUAGE DEVELOPMENT

At about 12 months, children begin to produce words that represent objects (e.g., *ball*), living entities (e.g., *mommy* and *doggie*), and actions (e.g., *go* and *throw*). One of the characteristics of vocabulary development is that early words are remarkably similar for children across all languages (e.g., the words for *book, cookie, ball, dog, cat, eye, nose, bed, mommy,* and *shoes*) (Rescorla, Alley, Christine, 2001, p. 605). These early productions take the form of consonant-vowel (CV) and vowel-consonant (VC) productions with later production of consonant-vowel-consonant (CVC) forms.

CV   go /go/

VC   up /ʌp/

CVC   cup /kʌp/

> Children's early words are not always accurate **phonemic representations** (words produced in a manner consistent with adult targets). For example, one young child attempted to produce the target word *baby* with attempts consisting of *bih* and *bihbi*, along with the correct phonemic representation of the target word *baby* (Sosa & Stoel-Gammon, 2006). Phonemic representation is also variable when children combine words to produce two-word utterances.
>
> I wa ai ai for *I want ice cream*
>
> Children's production accuracy increases when they have acquired 150 to 200 words (Maekawa & Storkel, 2006).

Two-word utterances, such as *push it* and *more cookie*, appear at about 18 months. By 24 to 36 months, children are able to produce longer utterances as their vocabulary increases (e.g., *I want more cookies and milk*). By age 3, children use language to communicate their feelings, observations, and needs with greater phonemic accuracy.

A summary of the stages of language development for infants and toddlers can be found in the Appendix to this chapter.

JOINT ATTENTION AND JOINT ACTION

Joint attention (the infant and another person sharing the direction of eye gaze) and **joint action** (shared action on the same object or task) are essential components of early word learning (Tomasello, 1998). The most significant feature of joint attention and action is that children's first word productions appear in these contexts. There is also a high correlation (connection) between the amount of time spent in joint attention tasks and the infant's vocabulary development (Tomasello & Todd, 1983) because joint attention events supply the infant with information on the adult's actions and the language associated with these actions. The following is an example of an infant's joint interaction with an adult or an older peer:

> The adult or older peer is demonstrating how to manipulate a toy by saying *Look* to draw the infants' attention and visual gaze toward the toy
>
> The adult or older peer says *Push* to demonstrate how to open a slot
>
> The adult or older peer says *It's your turn* to engage the infant in turn taking

Between 9 and 12 months, children begin to notice where adults are looking (gaze following), use adults as social reference points (social referencing), and model adults' actions (imitation) (Tomasello, 2003, p. 21). Gaze following occurs when an infant follows the direction and focus of the adult's eye gaze. Social referencing occurs when an infant identifies the feelings of the adult toward an object and later uses this information for his or her own feelings toward the object. As mentioned earlier in this chapter, 9-month-old infants are able to interpret an adult's choice of an object, given a field of two objects, by viewing the adult's facial expressions of pleasure or displeasure while gazing at each object (Barna & Legerstee, 2005). Imitation occurs when an infant uses an adult's actions toward an object or objects as a model for his or her own actions. These skills mark an important change in infants' understanding of the social environment.

Sciafe and Bruner (1975) examined infants' eye gaze to determine the stages of joint attention and concluded that joint attention increases steadily with age. Infants achieved joint visual attention 33% of the time at 2 to 4 months, 66% of the time at 8 to 10 months, and 100% of the time at 11 to 14 months. Sciafe and Bruner found that infants are able to understand an adult's perspective (visual focus) by 11 to 14 months of age, an essential component in language development.

COGNITIVE DEVELOPMENT

Cognition includes the mental ability to draw abstractions; generalize experiences; think about objects, entities, actions, and events; compare and contrast objects and entities; make inferences or assumptions; draw conclusions; and use words (symbols) to represent these things (Gentner, 2003). In children's early cognitive devel-

opment, **schemas** (psychological structures) allow them to process information and organize knowledge about the world (Piaget, 1954). Schemas also provide them with the ability to construct a representation of the entities and events that appear around them (Witt, 1998).

Schemas

Schemas develop when children first encounter a thing or event. For example, when children first encounter a bird (e.g., *pigeon*), they form a schema that represents this entity. Children create schemas from their perceptions of the structural attributes of an entity (e.g., *two legs, feathers, wings,* and *flying*). Children also create schema from the functional attributes of an entity (e.g., the word *hat* associated with anything related to *hair*). When children encounter something that does not fit into an existing schema for *bird* (such as a penguin, a decidedly un-bird-like entity), the schema must change. **Adaptation** is the process for changing a schema in response to a new entity. **Assimilation** is a cognitive process that involves fitting this new entity into an existing schema, and **accommodation** involves changing an existing schema to make the new entity fit. **Equilibrium** (cognitive balance) is the goal that is achieved through assimilation or accommodation. Children's cognitive abilities are present at birth. Piaget's (1954) view of cognitive development is presented in Table 5–1. Piaget's stages were part of an influential theory that contributed to our current understanding of children's development. Piaget provided us with the understanding that cognition and social interaction are significantly associated with the acquisition of language (Tomasello, 1996).

Table 5–1. *Piaget's Stages of Cognitive Development*

Stage	Age (years)	Characteristics
Sensorimotor stage	0–2	Children become aware of words and use words to refer to entities, actions, and attributes
Preoperational thought	2–7	Children become aware of time, space, and quantity concepts and relations
Concrete operations	7–11	Children develop logical thought processes
Formal operations	11–15	Children develop abstract thought

Source: From *The Construction of Reality in the Child*, by J. Piaget, 1954, New York, NY: Basic Books, Inc. Adapted with permission.

The Stages of Cognitive Development

The sensorimotor stage is the first stage of cognitive development. In this stage, infants discover the environment and learn through sensory perception and motor activity. The sensorimotor stage consists of the following six substages:

In substage 1 (birth to 1 month), children operate through innate reflexes, such as sucking and looking at things in the environment that catch their attention. Children demonstrate accommodation or modification of a schema in response to environmental stimuli. For example, infants become more efficient at locating a nipple when offered milk, given greater experience.

In substage 2 (1 to 4 months), there is increased eye–hand coordination. Children's perceptual abilities show the ability to visually track moving objects, and auditory perceptual abilities show the ability to localize sounds. Primitive anticipation

appears as the infant identifies signals associated with an event. For instance, infants perform sucking-like movements prior to presentation of the nipple. This is an advance over the earlier stage, when sucking began only when the nipple entered the infant's mouth.

At substage 3 (4 to 8 months), children are able to anticipate the path of a moving object, to reach for an object even if partially hidden, and to manipulate this object. Children are also able to purposefully reach for and pick up an object to put it in their mouths.

At substage 4 (8 to 12 months), children are able to anticipate events; establish a goal; establish a method to obtain that goal (**means-end behavior**); imitate others' behaviors; understand that an object remains the same, even when it is viewed from a different perspective, such as upside-down or empty (**object constancy**); understand that actions have a cause (**causality**); and possess the memory that an object exists when it is absent from their sight (**object permanence**).

Egocentrism decreases during this stage. Egocentrism refers to the inability of a child to step into another person's shoes or to see things from another's point of view. Egocentrism appears when a child is unable to know or care about the interest or topic of another child. For example, young children who are asked to buy a present for their mother may choose a toy car or a doll rather than a gift that is more appropriate for an adult.

At substage 5 (12 to 18 months), children draw on earlier established problem-based schemes to solve new problems. They also use trial and error experimentation when confronted by new problems. For example, children are able to produce new behaviors to obtain attention, such as using words to convey requests. **Deferred imitation** appears between 12 and 18 months of age. This occurs when children observe an activity, establish this action in their memory, and imitate the action at a later time. **Symbolic functions** appear with the production of first words, when words are used to represent an entity or activity (e.g., *dog* to represent the thing that is furry, has four legs, and barks).

Children produce their first words when the entity *dog* is present in the environment (**referent present**) but achieve genuine symbolic knowledge when using the word when the entity is not present (**referent absent**). In this case, children have established an internal representation of this entity and use a word to represent the entity.

At substage 6 (18 to 24 months), **representational thought** appears when children understand the world through mental operations rather than actions. Now, they are able to solve problems through thought rather than physical means. For example, a child may look at a problem and consider various solutions rather than using a trial and error approach to solve the problem.

In the **preoperational stage** (2 to 6 years of age), children's language continues to develop as they acquire new sentence forms. Vocabulary soars and children's play and pretend skills reach more advanced levels when they use objects symbolically (e.g., a block becomes a phone, a train, or a car). They also engage in role-play, relying on familiar entities in play routines (e.g., *mommy, daddy,* and *teacher*).

The preoperational stage culminates in the mental representation of entities and events in play schemes, such as pretending to be a teacher and constructing a nursery school out of boxes. Symbolic play becomes more complex over time as children represent real events, such as using a spoon to stir an imaginary substance in an empty cup (Bates, Benigni, Bretherton, Camaioni, & Volterra (1979).

Children develop more advanced and complex play schemes by ages 3 to 5. At this stage, they combine isolated play schemes to form more complex schemes (e.g., feed the baby, dress the baby, take the baby to day care, and so on). The relationship between play and representational thought appears in children's language used to construct the play scheme with the development of more complex language with more complex play schemes. This marks the connection between cognitive and language development.

Cognition and Language

There are three theories of the relationship between cognition and language development: the strong theory, the weak theory, and the correlational theory. The strong cognitive theory argues for parallel development between cognition and language (Piaget, 1962). In this theory, a specific cognitive accomplishment is sufficient for acquisition of a corresponding language milestone. For example, children who have achieved object permanence are able to represent things that are not present (e.g., referent absent), using words to label the referent.

The weak cognitive theory argues that cognitive accomplishment is not sufficient or necessary to account for language milestones. For example, children with the diagnosis of Williams syndrome may not function in Piaget's preoperational period as adolescents, but they possess excellent language skills (Mervis & Becerra, 2007).

The correlational theory predicts that language and cognition are temporally and loosely associated in development. At any given time, a greater level of attainment or development is seen in either language or cognition (Bates, 1979). For example, some children with advanced language skills lack advanced cognitive skills, and some children with advanced cognitive skills lack more advanced language skills (Kelly & Dale,

1989). This points to individual differences among children and to no strong association between cognition and language.

We next examine children's play, along with the connection between play and children's language development.

PLAY

There is a close relationship between pretend play and language development (Patterson & Westby, 1998). For example, the appearance of first words co-occurs with the emergence of children's pretend play. In addition, pretend (symbolic) play demonstrates the ability to decontextualize (to separate an object from its immediate context). This occurs when a child uses a block to represent a train or telephone and uses *words* to represent a thing, even when the thing (*block*) is not the thing itself (e.g., *train* or *telephone*).

Children first engage in pretend play by using their own daily activities (e.g., preschool or home activities). Next, they engage in pretend play for others' activities, using dolls and stuffed animals (e.g., playing house, feeding the baby, or going to work). This stage reflects **decentration**, which is the ability to take into account several aspects of a situation and to consider others' roles in the play scheme.

Early pretend play depends on real objects as props to support the play scheme. Late in the second year, children are less dependent on props. This reflects increased cognitive skills as children mentally construct a play scheme (without props) and use language to construct the play scheme. For example, a child can now symbolically create a play scheme using one object to represent another (e.g., *cardboard box* for *stove*) and use words to create the pretend play scheme (e.g., . . . *now you are the daddy and you just came home from work* . . .).

The Stages of Play Development

There are stages that characterize children's play development (Westby, 1980). Children's play schemes begin to include events that they have observed in their own environments.

Stage I (9 to 12 months): Children develop object permanence (awareness that an object exists even when not in sight) and are able to search for and discover hidden toys. **Means-end** skills appear, characterized by pulling a string or a blanket to bring a toy closer. Mouthing toys begins to disappear, marking the emergence of more advanced play skills.

Stage II (13 to 17 months): Children explore toys, manipulating their parts to create movement, and operate mechanical toys.

Stage III (17 to 19 months): Representational thought appears as children exhibit autosymbolic play. This consists of play involving activities that represent their own daily activities (e.g., pretending to sleep and drinking from a cup).

Stage IV (19 to 22 months): Symbolic play expands to include receivers

of action (e.g., feeding a doll). At this stage, dolls and stuffed toys are included in the pretend play scheme. Note that in the earlier stage, the play scheme consisted of the children's own activities. Now, children's play extends to include another actor or receiver.

Stage V (24 months): Children represent daily experiences (e.g., feeding dolls). Now, it is clear that children have observed activities within their environment and have internalized these activities to create a play scheme.

Stage VI (2½ years): Less frequently experienced events are represented in play (e.g., visits to the doctor and going to school). Realistic props remain a part of play (e.g., the use of books and papers for pretending to be in school).

Stage VII (3 years of age): Play schemas become connected (e.g., cooking dinner, serving dinner, cleaning up the dinner plates). These schemas are unplanned and evolve as the activity develops over time. Realistic props remain a necessary part of play.

Stage VIII (3 to 3½ years of age): Objects are used to represent other things (e.g., blocks for houses or fences and a row of chairs for a bus or train). At this stage, realistic props are no longer required for the play scheme. Children are able to use their imagination to create the scheme.

Stage IX (4 years of age): Hypothetical events (those not yet experienced and problems that need to be solved) are incorporated into play schemes to solve problems or to complete a project (e.g., building an enclosure for animals and looking around for materials to create a roof).

Stage X (5 years of age): Multiple events are incorporated into the play scheme (e.g., the child pretends to go to the store to buy food for dinner, sends another child out to take the baby to school, and plans for a party upon their return). Play is cooperative and imagination takes the place of using realistic props.

> Children's play develops over time as they involve more activities in their environment and move away from the use of more realistic props for play schemes. As language develops, children are also able to use these skills to enhance a play scheme and to explain this scheme to other children to engage their participation.

Multicultural Differences and Play

There are also multicultural differences that factor into play. For example, children in New Guinea play games that all players win (Cliff, 1990), rather than more competitive play that requires only one winner. Farver, Kim, and Lee (1995) found that Korean American preschools focused on academic skills, task perseverance, and involvement in learning and that play was limited to outdoor activity. Korean American children were also found to engage less often in pretend play than were Anglo-American children. However, Farver et al. also found that these children's play contexts had few materials available for them

to engage in pretend play, in comparison to the contexts of Anglo-American children. Investigators found that Chinese preschool-age children were offered free play in limited periods, involving play in outdoor gross motor activities (Tobin, Wu, & Davidson, 1989). In summary, it is important to consider that cultural differences are an important factor when assessing children's play, given the variability in the attitudes toward play across cultures.

We next examine children's phonological development. Much like an increased awareness of events in the environment, children develop greater awareness of the sounds in words over time.

PHONOLOGICAL DEVELOPMENT

Between ages 1 and 1½, children produce their first words with recognizable meaning, but these early productions do not exactly match adult productions. For example, at 2 years of age, Daniel produced "dus" [dus] for the word *juice* and Micah produced "nana" [nænə] for the word *banana* /bənænə/. At 3 years of age, Carla, exposed to Russian and English, produced "hankerbush" when she perceived the words *handkerchief* and *babushka* (word for *scarf* in Slavic languages).

Children must learn to perceive differences among sounds to establish differences in meaning. Over time, they learn that there is a subtle difference between sounds, such as /p-b, t-d, k-g/, that distinguish the words *pie-buy, toe-doe,* and *Kate-gate.* Because of difficulty perceiving or producing certain sounds, children's early productions frequently differ from those produced by adults. Children's early word productions are shaped by **phonological processes**, as shown in Table 5–2.

Table 5–2. *Phonological Processes*

Phonological Process	Adult Target	Child's Production
Unstressed syllable deletion	banana	"nanuh"
Reduplication	daddy	"dada"
Consonant cluster reduction	stop	"top"
Final consonant deletion	bus	"bu"
Initial consonant deletion	cup	"up"
Syllable repetition	daddy	"dada"
Fronting	top	"cop"
Backing	cop	"top"
Assimilation	dog	"gog"
	cat	"cac"
Vocalization	car	"cah"
Prevocalic voicing	top	"dop"
Depalatization	chew	"too"
Gliding	run	"wun"
	lip	"wip"
Epenthesis	cup	"cupuh"

Note: Most phonological processes disappear by age 3, except for consonant cluster reduction, which generally disappears later.

Source: From *Language Development: Understanding Language Diversity in the Classroom* (p. 44), by S. Levey & S. Polirstok (Eds.), 2011, Los Angeles, CA: Sage. Reprinted with permission..

Phonological Processes

Most phonological processes generally disappear by 3 years of age with syllable omission (e.g., *nana* for banana), reduplication (*dada* for *daddy*), and consonant deletion (e.g., *bu* for *bus*) most common for younger children. Phonological processes that persist beyond age 3 or 3½ may require intervention. It is also important that all children receive audiological assessment to rule out hearing loss, which may affect their perception of sounds in words.

Unstressed syllable omission or deletion (e.g., *nana* produced for the target word *banana*) reflects children's bias toward a strong or stressed syllable in the initial position of words (e.g., MONkey, MAma, and BUnny) (Gerken, 1996; Levey & Schwartz, 2002). Notice that the word *banana* is produced with stronger emphasis on the second syllable (e.g., baNANa), as is the word *giraffe*. In both cases, the first syllable is weak (receives no stress) and the second syllable is strong (receives main or primary stress). Consequently, a child's bias toward a strong syllable in the initial position results in the following productions:

Target word	Child's production
Banana /bənænə/	nana [nænə]
Giraffe /dʒəræf/	*raf* [ræf]

Children's bias toward a strong first syllable in words is found in other languages with similar stress patterns to English, such as Dutch (Wijnen, Krikhaar, & den Os, 1994), Czech, Slovenian, Estonian (Vihman, 1980), and Spanish (Macken, 1992). This suggests that a perceptual bias toward a strong syllable in the initial position in words may extend to children learning other languages.

Consonant cluster reduction can occur in words that contain a consonant cluster (e.g., *stop* and *street*). When cluster reduction occurs, children produce these words as *top* and *treet*. One theory that explains this phonological process posits that certain consonants have greater sonority (strength) (Hayes, 2009). This theory argues that children will produce the consonant clusters that have greater sonority differences. Table 5–3 shows the sonority scale for speech sounds.

Note that there is a greater difference between the sonority of the consonants /p/ and /l/ on the hierarchy scale (9 – 3 = **6**) than between the consonants *t* and *s* (5 – 7 = **2**). Because of the greater sonority differences between the consonants /p/ and /l/, children are more likely to produce both consonants in the cluster *pl* (*please, play,* and *plum*). Because of the smaller sonority difference between the consonants /t/ and /s/ on the sonority hierarchy, children are likely to produce only one of the consonants in the cluster *st* (*stop, stamp,* and *stay*). Examples of these productions follow.

Table 5–3. *Sonority Hierarchy*

Phoneme	Examples
1. Vowel	i, ɪ, e, ɛ, æ, u, ʊ, o, ɔ, ɑ
2. Glide	j, w
3. Liquid	l, r
4. Nasal	m, n, ŋ
5. Voiced fricative	v, ð, z, ʒ
6. Voiceless fricative	f, θ, s, ʃ, h
7. Affricate	tʃ, dʒ
8. Voiced stop	b, d, g
9. Voiceless stop	p, t, k

Greater difference between /p/ and /l/	Child's production
Please	*please*
Play	*play*
Plum	*plum*

Less difference between /s/ and /t/	Child's production
Stop	*top*
Stamp	*tamp*
Stay	*tay*

Assimilation is a process whereby a consonant becomes more similar to another consonant in a word. The examples in Table 5–3 show that the initial consonant /d/ in the word *dog* /dɔg/ becomes more similar to the final consonant /g/. Another example of assimilation occurs when the final consonant in the word *cat* /t/ becomes more similar to the initial consonant /k/.

Target word		Child's production	
Dog	/dɔg/	*gog*	[gɔg]
Cat	/kæt/	*cac*	[kæk]

Vocalization occurs when children produce a vowel instead of a rhotic diphthong in a word. Unlike the single phoneme /r/, rhotic diphthongs always contain the phoneme /ɚ/ and are preceded by a vowel (e.g., car /ɑɚ/, b**ear** /ɛɚ/, and *ear* /iɚ/).

Target word		Child's production	
Car	/ɑɚ/	*cah*	[kɑ]
Bear	/ɛɚ/	*beh*	[bɛ]
Ear	/iɚ/	*ih*	[i]

In these productions, children produce only the consonant and the vowel in the target words. They may also sometimes produce a different vowel in words that contain a rhotic diphthong, such as the schwa /ə/.

Car	/kɑɚ/	*cuh*	[kə]

Gliding occurs when a glide consonant (e.g., /w/) replaces a liquid consonant (/l/ and /r/).

Target word		Child's production	
Red	/rɛd/	*wed*	[wɛd]
Ride	/raɪd]	*wide*	[waɪd]
Lip	/lɪp/	*wip*	[wɪp]

Phonological processes disappear as children become more aware of sounds in words and are able to produce longer utterances.

We now explore children's morphological development. We will see that children's utterances increase in length when they become more aware of the construction of words and add morphemes to their productions.

MORPHOLOGICAL DEVELOPMENT

Morphology is concerned with the structure or organization of words, and **morphemes** are the minimal distinctive meaningful units of words. For example, the lexical morpheme *hat* /hæt/ cannot be broken down into smaller parts (e.g., *ha* or *at*) without the meaning of the word *hat* being lost.

Morphosyntactic development describes the relationship between morphemes and sentences. Children's sentences expand when they begin to attach morphemes to words. For example, the lexical morpheme *walk* has its own meaning. The addition of the inflectional morphemes *-ed* and *-ing* to the word *walk* adds meaning by indicating an action that occurred in the past (past tense *-ed*) and an action that is present and ongoing (present progressive *-ing*).

Walk + *ed* (regular past tense inflectional morpheme) *walk**ed***

Walk + *ing* (present progressive inflectional morpheme) *walk**ing***

Sentences are also expanded by the inclusion of articles (e.g., *a, an, the*), prepositions (e.g., *in, on, under*), pronouns (e.g., *I, me, he*), and auxiliary verbs (e.g., *am, is, are*).

Morphosyntactic Development

Children's morphosyntactic development goes through the following stages (Bernstein, 2011; Bernstein & Levey, 2009; Owens, 2008).

Stage I begins with single-word utterances (e.g., *cookie, milk,* and *juice*) and expands to include two-word utterances (e.g., *more cookie, drink milk,* and *gimme juice*).

Stage II is characterized by the appearance of grammatical morphemes (e.g., *-ing,* plural *-s*), and prepositions (*in* and *on*). Utterances, such as *I eating, put shoe on,* and *see cats,* are characteristic of this stage. At Stage II, children begin to produce additional grammatical morphemes. These 14 morphemes are **obligatory,** meaning that the use of these morphemes is required for meaning. For example, without morphemes, a listener may not understand what you mean when you say *I go.* However, if you say *I am going,* the listener will understand you will be going now. Examples of these 14 morphemes can be found in Table 5–4.

Table 5–4. *Order of Development of 14 Grammatical Morphemes**

Grammatical Morpheme	Example	Age of Mastery (months)
Present progressive verb ending *-ing*	go*ing,* play*ing*	19–28
Preposition *in*	Put *in* cup	27–30
Preposition *on*	Put *on* shoes	27–30
Regular plural *-s*	Want block*s*	24–33
Past irregular verbs *came, fell, went, broke*	He *broke* it	25–46
Possessive noun *'s*	Mommy*'s* shoe	26–40
Uncontractible copula (*be* as main verb) *am, is, are, was, were, be, been*	He *was* nice	27–39
Articles *a, an, the*	*The* boy ran home	28–46
Past regular *-ed*	He walk*ed* home	26–48
Third person singular regular *-s*	He walk*s*	26–46
Third person singular irregular *has, does*	He *does* walk	28–50
Uncontractible auxiliary (*be* verbs preceding another verb)	The boy *is walking*	29–48
Contractible copula	I*'m* happy	29–49
Contractible auxiliary	I*'m* jumping	30–50

*Used correctly 90% of the time in obligatory or required contexts.

Source: From *A First Language: The Early Stages,* by R. Brown (p. 358), Cambridge, MA: Harvard University Press, Copyright 1973 by the President and Fellows of Harvard College. Reprinted with permission.

In Stage III, utterance length continues to grow as children produce simple declarative sentences (*That's my ball*), imperatives (*Don't take my ball*), *Wh-* questions (*Where's my toy?*), and simple negative sentences (*No wanna go*).

In Stage IV, children's language expands to contain complex constructions. In this stage, children produce **compound** (*Daddy is working **and** Mommy is reading*) and **complex sentences** (*That boy, **who is in my school**, is my friend*). Examples of additional utterances produced in Stage IV and beyond include the following: *The first boy is nice, Jill wants to buy the dress with the green band, She likes to eat chocolate ice cream*, and *I want to push the red truck*.

Mean Length of Utterance (MLU)

Mean length of utterance (MLU) is the average number of morphemes in children's utterances. For example, the word *walk* is a single morpheme, whereas *walked* (*walk + ed*) and *walking* (*walk + ing*) are each composed of two morphemes. Brown (1973) described five stages of children's language development based on MLU, shown in Table 5–5.

There are rules for the calculation of morphemes, as described in the following examples (Lund & Duchan, 1993, pp. 205–206). The productions that are not used in calculation of MLU are the following:

◆ Imitation that follows a model
◆ Elliptical answers, such as *Yes* in response to a question
◆ Partial utterances: *That's a . . .*

Table 5–5. *Brown's Stages of MLU Development*

Linguistic Stage	MLU	Approximate Age Chronological Age (Months)	Characteristics
Stage I	1.0–2.0	12–26	Semantic rules
Stage II	2.0–2.5	27–30	Morphological development
Stage III	2.5–3.0	31–34	Sentence variety development: negatives, imperatives, and interrogatives
Stage IV	3.0–3.75	35–40	Complex constructions emerge: coordination, complementation, and relativization
Stage V	3.75–4.5	41–46	
Stage VI	4.5+	47+	

Source: From *A First Language: The Early Stages,* by R. Brown (p. 56), Cambridge, MA: Harvard University Press, Copyright 1973 by the President and Fellows of Harvard College. Reprinted with permission.

◆ Rote passages: nursery rhymes, songs, and other memorized material
◆ Repetitions or disfluencies: *I . . . uh . . . uh . . .*
◆ Social phrases, such as *Hi, Thank you,* and *Know what?*

Count the following productions as *one morpheme* when calculating MLU.

◆ Lexical morphemes: nouns (e.g., *dog, man, car*), verbs (e.g., *walk, jump, eat*), adjectives (e.g., *big, pretty, dirty*), and adverbs (e.g., *slowly, quickly, abruptly*)
◆ Grammatical morphemes: articles (e.g., *the, a, an*), auxiliary verbs (e.g., *am, is, are, was*), and prepositions (e.g., *above, across, under*)
◆ Catenative verbs (verbs that can be followed by another verb): *wanna, gonna,* and *hafta* (each of which can be followed by the verbs *go* or *make*)
◆ Plurals that do not have a singular form: *pants, clothes, scissors, binoculars*
◆ Count these two- and three-word phrases as only a single word: *Big Bird, Cookie Monster,* and *New York City*

When calculating MLU, we are able to count the following as two morphemes.

◆ Inflected verb forms: *walked, walking*
◆ Regular plural forms: *cats, dogs, hats*
◆ Irregular plural forms (the plural follows the singular form): *foot/feet, goose/geese, tooth/teeth*
◆ Possessive nouns: *mommy's, cat's, baby's*
◆ Third-person singular: *eats, sits, hits*
◆ Reflexive pronouns: *himself, herself, ourselves*
◆ Comparative adjectives: *bigger, higher, brighter*
◆ Superlative adjectives: *biggest, highest, brightest*

We calculate MLU by counting the number of morphemes in each utterance produced, usually assessing at least 50 to 100 separate utterances. After counting all morphemes, we divide the number of morphemes by the number of utterances. For example, if a child produces 150 morphemes in 50 utterances, the MLU would be 3.0.

$$\text{MLU} = \frac{150 \text{ morphemes}}{50 \text{ utterances}} = 3.0 \text{ MLU}$$

Morphological Differences

It is important to understand that languages and dialects differ in morphemes, so it is only appropriate to use these examples of MLU to assess English-speaking children. For example, one of the rules found in African American English (AAE) is to omit redundant (unnecessary) elements, such as omitting the plural when the adjective (*three*) already signals plurality (e.g., three boy). When we omit the redundant elements, note the differences in MLU between the first and second example below. It is important to understand that morphological and other language differences do not signal a disorder.

I saw three boys = 5 morphemes
(*I, saw, three, boy, -s*)

I saw three boy = 4 morphemes
(*I, saw, three, boy*)

There are also differences between the morphological patterns found in native Spanish-speaking children learning English and native mainstream American English (MAE) speakers (Table 5–6).

Table 5–6. *Morphological Differences Between Mainstream American English (MAE) and Spanish-English Speakers*

	Native English Speakers	Spanish-English Speakers
Past Tense (ed) (Regular)	Yesterday, I paint**ed**.	Yesterday I paint.
Plurals (s)	The flower**s** are pretty.	The flower are pretty.
Possessive ('s)	My friend**'s** coat.	My friend coat.
Negative	She does **not** walk.	She no walk.
Interrogative (question inversion)	**Is** Juan coming?	Juan is coming?

Source: From *Language Development: Understanding Language Diversity in the Classroom* (p. 157), by S. Levey & S. Polirstok (Eds.), 2011, Los Angeles, CA: Sage. Reprinted with permission.

The morphological and syntactic differences between MAE and AAE speakers shown in Table 5–7 derive from a large number of contributions to AAE from West African languages (e.g., Bambara, Ewe, Fanta, Twi, Mende, Wolof, and Yoruba), along with contributions from native American languages, French, and English. Again, it is important to understand that the differences found in language dialects and English-learning children signal *differences* and not *disorders*.

Given that morphological differences exist among languages, there are alternative means to assess children's language skills. Nonword or novel word repetition has been found to correlate with language impairment in children who are learning English as their second language (Atkins & Baddeley, 1998; Gottardo, Stanovich, & Siegel, 1996; Laing & Kamhi, 2003). For example, one nonword repetition test measures children's ability to repeat 18 nonwords that ranged from 3 (i.e., *meb*) to 15 sounds (e.g., *shaburiehuvoimush*) (Wagner, Torgesen, & Rashotte, 1999). Intact working memory allows children to store these nonword or novel items for comparison and analysis (Polka, Jusczyk, & Rvachew, 1995). There is considerable evidence that children with language impairments have difficulties with nonword repetition tasks (Thal, Miller, Carlson, & Moreno Vega, 2005), for both English- and Spanish/English-speaking children (Gutiérrez-Clellen & Simon-Cereijido, 2010; Windsor, Kohnert, Lobitz, & Pham, 2010). Thus, this is a valid approach to identifying language disorders.

Morphophonology

Morphophonology describes the connection between morphemes and phonology. Morphological rules apply to changes in phonemes due to their environment. For example, note that the production of the final plural sound -*s* varies, depending on the sound that it follows.

Cat + s = cats /kæts/

Dog + s = dogs /dɔgz/

Table 5–7. *Characteristics of African American English Morphology and Syntax*

AAE Feature/ Characteristic	Mainstream American English	Sample AAE Utterance
Omission of noun possessive	That's the woman's car. It's John's pencil.	That **the woman** car. It **John** pencil.
Omission of noun plural	He has 2 boxes of apples. She gives me 5 cents.	He got 2 **box** of **apple**. She give me 5 **cent**.
Omission of third person singular present tense marker	She walks to school. The man works in his yard.	She **walk** to school. The man **work** in his yard.
Omission of "to be" forms, such as "is, are"	She is a nice lady. They are going to a movie.	**She a** nice lady. **They going** to a movie.
Present tense "is" may be used regardless of person/ number	They are having fun. You are a smart man.	**They is** having fun. **You is** a smart man.
Utterances with "to be" may not show person number agreement with past and present forms	You are playing ball. They are having a picnic.	You **is** playing ball. They **is** having a picnic.
Present tense forms of auxiliary "have" are omitted	I have been here for 2 hours. He has done it again.	I been here for 2 hours. He done it again.
Past tense endings may be omitted	He lived in California. She cracked the nut.	He **live** in California. She **crack** the nut.
Past "was" may be used regardless of number and person	They were shopping. You were helping me.	They **was** shopping. You **was** helping me.
Multiple negatives (each additional negative form adds emphasis to the negative meaning)	We don't have any more. I don't want any cake. I don't like broccoli.	We **don't** have **no** more. I **don't never** want **no** cake. I **don't never** like broccoli.
"None" may be substituted for "any"	She doesn't want any.	She don't want **none**.
Perfective construction; "been" may be used to indicate that an action took place in the distant past	I had the mumps last year. I have known her for years.	I **been had** the mumps last year. I **been known** her.

continues

Table 5–7. *continued*

AAE Feature/ Characteristic	Mainstream American English	Sample AAE Utterance
"Done" may be combined with a past tense form to indicate that an action was started and completed	He fixed the stove. She tried to paint it.	He **done fixed** the stove. She **done tried** to paint it.
The form "be" may be used as the main verb	Today she is working. We are singing.	Today **she be** working. **We be** singing.
Distributive "be" may be used to indicate actions and events over time	He is often cheerful. She's kind sometimes.	**He be** cheerful. **She be** kind.
A pronoun may be used to restate the subject	My brother surprised me. My dog has fleas.	My brother, **he** surprise me. My dog, **he** got fleas.
"Them" may be substituted for "those"	Those cars are antiques. Where'd you get those books?	**Them cars**, they be antique. Where you got **them books**?
Future tense "is, are" may be replaced by "gonna"	She is going to help us. They are going to be there.	She **gonna** help us. They **gonna** be there.
"At" is used at the end of "where" questions	Where is the house? Where is the store?	Where is the house **at**? Where is the store **at**?
Additional auxiliaries are often used	I might have done it.	I **might could have** done it.
"Does" replaced by "do"	She does funny things. It does make sense.	**She do** funny things. **It do** make sense.

Source: From *Multicultural Students with Special Language Needs: Practical Strategies for Assessment and Intervention* (pp. 75–76), by C. Roseberry-McKibbin, 2008, Oceanside, CA: Academic Communication Associates. Reprinted by permission.

The plural *-s* remains intact as the unvoiced fricative /s/ when following the unvoiced stop-plosive /t/ in the word *cat*. However, the plural *-s* changes to the voiced fricative /z/ when it follows the voiced stop-plosive /g/ in the word *dog*. This is an example of the interaction between morphemes and phonology.

We next review children's syntactic development, beginning with the production of two-words utterances to form simple sentences (e.g., *Want cookie*). By the end of the stages described in this chapter, children begin to produce longer utterances with a wider set of meanings.

SYNTACTIC DEVELOPMENT

Syntax describes rules for producing sentences through the combination of words (e.g., The + apple + is + on + the + table). Syntax emerges when children begin to produce two-word utterances at about 18 months of age. At this stage of syntactic development, children produce utterances that indicate requests and observations of the world (e.g., *pick up, see doggy, push ball, allgone doggy, wanna snack, sock off, and daddy go*). These early sentences are composed of the basic components of noun phrases (*dogs*) and verb phrases (*bark*).

Noun phrase	*boy*
Verb phrase	*running*

Nouns label entities (*people, animals,* and *things*) and verbs label actions (e.g., *run, eat, sleep*). There is also a class of verbs termed **mental verbs** (e.g., *frighten, like, disappoint*) that refer to a person's mental state.

In a sentence, syntactic rules state that the noun phrase must contain a noun and the verb phrase must contain a verb, as shown in the following example.

Mommy go

> Initially, children omit the subject in the noun phrase, producing sentences such as *Want cookie.* Subject drop, as this is termed, starts to occur less frequently at around age 2½, when children's utterances increase in length (MacWhinney & Snow, 1985).

Pronoun Acquisition

Pronouns first appear in Brown's Stage III at 31 to 34 months of age. There is an association between children's **perspective taking** and correct pronoun use (Ricard, Girouard, & Decarie, 1999). Perspective taking involves understanding that the point of view of others differ from the child's own. Thus, the correct use of *you* and *I* requires recognizing that perspective changes, depending on who is speaking. An example of a pronoun error is found in Micah's production *I want **me** to pick **you** up,* when requesting to be picked up at age 2½. Children must be able to be shift roles and see another's perspective or point of view to acquire the difference between these pronouns (Perner, 1991).

The pronouns that refer to self (*I, mine, my,* and *me*) emerge early, whereas those that refer to others (*he, she,* and *they*) emerge later. Children acquire objective pronouns (*him, her,* and *them*) before they acquire possessive pronouns (*his, hers,* and *theirs*). The reflexive pronouns (*himself, herself, ourselves,* and *themselves*) are generally not mastered until 5 years of age. Table 5–8 presents the general order of pronoun acquisition (Moorehead & Ingram, 1973; Owens, 2008).

The Development of Nouns and Verbs

Nouns

Nouns comprise the largest category of words in a child's early vocabulary. When children acquire words, almost half are nouns, one-quarter are verbs and adjectives, and one-quarter are function words (e.g., *prepositions, pronouns, determiners, conjunctions,* and *auxiliary verbs*) (Bates et al., 1994). Gleason and Ratner (2009, p. 114) provide a list of children's earliest words, showing the prevalence of nouns in their acquisition.

Table 5–8. Pronouns

Stage	Pronoun
Level I	*I*
Level II	*my, it, me, mine*
Level III	*you, your, she, them*
Level IV	*we, he, they, us, you, him, his, theirs*
Level V	*her, its, our, herself, himself, ourselves, yourselves, themselves*

Sources: From *Language Development: An Introduction* (7th ed.), by R. E. Owens, 2008, Upper Saddle River, NJ: Pearson Education, Inc. Reprinted by permission. From "The Development of Base Syntax in Normal and Linguistically Deviant Children," by D. Moorehead and D. Ingram, 1973, *Journal of Speech and Hearing Research, Volume 16*, pp. 330–352. Republished with permission from the American Speech-Language-Hearing Association.

Food and drink: *Apple, banana, cookie, cheese, juice, milk, water*

Body parts and clothing: *Diaper, ear, eye, foot, hair, hand, hat, mouth, nose, shoe*

Household/outdoor objects: *Blanket, chair, cup, door, flower, keys, spoon, tree, TV*

People: *Baby, daddy, grandma, grandpa, mommy, child's name*

Toys and vehicles: *Ball, balloon, bike, boat, book, bubbles, plane, truck, toy*

Children's early acquisition of nouns is associated with their semantic properties and concrete object reference (e.g., *cookie*). In terms of semantic properties, nouns refer to people, animals, and objects in the child's environment, such as the entities that gain the child's interest.

In terms of their concrete references, nouns offer less conceptual complexity than verbs (Gentner, 1982). Nouns are mapped onto cohesive perceptual qualities (e.g., *shape* and *use*), allowing children to internalize these entities in their cognitive schemes. Verbs are more complex because they convey the meaning of events (e.g., *Dogs bark*) and are harder to remember and identify (Gentner, 1981). Consider the verbs *walk, jog,* and *run*. It may be difficult for children to distinguish between these actions, whereas *apple* is relatively easy to identify and remember.

There is variation across languages for the prevalence of nouns in children's first word productions. For example, Korean-speaking children's first words consist of a greater number of verbs (Choi & Gopnik, 1995). Levey and Cruz (2003) found that bilingual English/Mandarin Chinese-speaking children produced a greater number of nouns than verbs in their first words. Although nouns were produced in both English and Chinese, verbs were produced only in Mandarin Chinese. This suggests that parental input plays a role in children's first word learning because parents may have produced verbs only in Mandarin Chinese.

> Children's word learning has been explained by various factors. One of the explanations of learning new words is the **mutual exclusivity bias**. When children are presented with a new word and a new object (e.g., *bunny*), they gaze at the only object for which they lack a name. For example, picture a scene that contains several objects that the child is familiar with: *car, ball, teddy bear,* and *doll*. An adult places a new object within this array of toys (a *bunny*). When told, "Look at the bunny," *the* child looks at the novel object (i.e., *bunny*) instead of those for which he or she already has a name. Children use this strategy until about 17 to 22 months of age (Markman, 1989), holding to the principle that each referent can only have one name.

Verbs

The first verbs produced by young children describe simple actions (Bloom, Lightbown, & Hood, 1978), such as *eat, read, do,* and *fix*. These verbs are followed by *put, go,* and *sit*. Later acquired verbs include the mental verbs *want, have,* and *know*. When children first learn verbs, they use them in the context where they were initially acquired (Tomasello, 1992, 2003). For example, if children learn *cut* when watching someone cut paper, they use the verb only for cutting paper. They do not extend the meaning of this verb beyond the learning context to apply to another type of cutting, such as fingernails or bread.

There is a connection between verb learning and children's awareness of syntactic structure (Gleitman & Gleitman, 1992). For example, certain verbs, such as *hit,* are two-argument verbs (expressing a relationship between two things) and require a transitive clause with a direct object (e.g., *Daddy hit the ball*). In contrast, the verb *cry* is a one-argument verb (e.g., *Mary cries*). As an intransitive verb, it does not require an object. The following examples demonstrate the differences between intransitive and transitive clauses:

Transitive: Subject + Verb + Object; *She wanted an apple*

Intransitive: Subject + Verb; *She cried*

There is more complexity involved in constructing a sentence that requires a direct object (*He hit the ball*) versus a sentence that does not require a direct object (*She sneezed*). Consequently, intransitive forms first appear in children's productions (e.g., *cry, smile,* and *frown*), followed later by transitive forms (e.g., *want, kick,* and *like*).

There is also an interaction between phonology and verb production. The regular past tense of a verb is formed by adding *-ed* (e.g., *walked, talked, voted*). Children often **overgeneralize** the regular verb form (add *-ed*) to produce an irregular verb (e.g., *eated, goed,* and *doed*).

I eated it

I throwed the ball

I goed there

Difficulty with the past tense of certain irregular verbs is associated with the phonological changes shown in certain verbs (Shipley, Maddox, & Driver, 1991, p. 118). For example, note that some irregular past tense verbs do not change (e.g., *cut/cut*), whereas others undergo greater change (e.g., *catch/caught*).

No change: *cut/cut*

Internal vowel change: *come/came*

Internal vowel change with unchanged final dental consonant: *stand/stood*

Internal vowel change with final change: *sweep/swept*

Final consonant change from /d/ to /t/: *build/built*

Children have no difficulty at all in the production of the *no change* category (e.g., *cut/cut* and *hit/hit*), given that these verbs do not require the acquisition of morphology. This is because no phoneme changes occur from present to past tense.

*Watch me **cut** the paper*

*Yesterday, I **cut** the paper*

Overgeneralization occurs most often with irregular past tense verbs with internal vowel change (e.g., *take/took*) and final change from /d/ to /t/ (e.g., *build/built*). In this case, children produce the past tense forms as *taked* and *builded*.

> Advances in cognitive neuroscience have provided information on children's cognitive skills. Real-time functional MRI (rtfMRI) measures oxygen levels in the brain to determine what areas of the brain are active in certain conditions. Cognitive processing of irregular verbs (verbs that require a change in vowel and/or consonant in the change from present to past tense, such as *sleep/slept* and *catch/caught*) results in greater activation than regular verbs (verbs that add *-ed* to form the past tense with no change in vowel and/or consonant, such as *walk/walked* and *wait/waited*) (Campbell et al., 2001). Thus, greater processing is required for irregular verbs than regular verbs.

In summary, children's accuracy is greater for *no change* verbs (e.g., *hit/hit*). The greatest difficulty appears with change from /d/ to /t/ (e.g., *bend/bent, build/built*, and *send/sent*) because children may not perceive the subtle change from /d/ to /t/ for the final sounds in these words. Children may not master the irregular verbs that change from /d/ to /t/ until 9 years of age. The irregular past tense verbs *go/went* may be produced correctly at 3½ to 4 years of age, *see/saw* at 4 to 4½, and *eat/ate* by 4½ to 5.

There are also certain verb contrasts that present children with difficulty. The verbs *ask* and *tell* may present difficulty until children reach school age (Chomsky, 1969). Warden (1981) found that there was a higher frequency of correct responses to the verb *ask* than *tell* with acquisition of this contrast by 5 years of age. At age 3½, Micah said that he was going to *ask* his mother that he had hurt his arm.

Auxiliary verbs (e.g., *am, is, are, was, were, be,* and *been*) are also termed *helping verbs* because they are used in conjunction with main verbs to express time or tense. For example, the verb *walk* is not marked for tense or time. When we add the auxiliary verb *is*, we can mark it as present (i.e., *He **is** walking*).

The auxiliary modal verbs *will, shall, may, might, can, could, must, ought to, should, would, used to,* and *need to* are used to express certain attitudes, such as disapproval (*You might have asked before taking a cookie*), possibility (*I may give you a cookie tomorrow*), or ability (*I can give you a cookie*). The acquisition of auxiliary verbs for the majority of children follows the following pattern of development (Wells, 1979).

Early acquisition: *do, can, will, going to*

Preschool-age acquisition: *have to, shall, could*

Next we examine the components that constitute the basic sentence form: the noun phrase and the verb phrase.

THE COMPONENTS OF THE BASIC SENTENCE FORM

The Noun Phrase

There are five optional components in the noun phrase. The noun is the obligatory (required) component and the optional components are *initiator, determiner, adjectival, object noun,* and *postmodifier*. Note that, in sentences, there are subject nouns (e.g., **Daddy** *went to work*) and object nouns (e.g., *She ate a big **cookie**)*.

Initiators limit or quantify nouns and must precede a determiner (e.g., *just, only, even, at least*), express quantity relations (e.g., *half, both, all, just*), or function as an intensifier for emphasis (e.g., *quite, such*).

All the girls are going

Just one of the girls is going

Both of the girls are going

Determiners are function words that include articles (*the, a, an*), possessive pronouns (e.g., *my, your, his, her, its*), and demonstrative pronouns (*this, that, these, those*).

That girl . . .

Adjectivals are adjectives (*little, big*), ordinals (*first, last*), and quantifiers (*two, few*).

*The **big** girl . . .*

Postmodifiers are modifiers that follow the main noun and may include prepositional phrases (the toy is *on the floor*) and relative clauses (the boy, *who came to my house,* is nice).

The following sentence contains all of these components:

Initiator	Determiner	Adjective
All	*the*	*big*
Noun	Postmodifier	
kids	*in the class*	(are going)

The developmental order for noun phrase production consists of the following (Miller, 1981):

Nouns emerge in the one-word stage

Adjectivals and determiners emerge in the two-word stage

Initiators and postmodifiers emerge in the three- or more word stage

Sentences are composed of phrases and clauses. A phrase is smaller and less complete than a clause, shown next with the phrases that are bolded.

*I ate **in the morning***

*I ran **down the hill***

A clause is a group of words that forms a part of a compound or complex sentence and consists of a subject and predicate. Only the main or independent clause can stand alone as a complete sentence.

Main or independent clause: subject + verb; *doggie bark*

Subordinate or dependent clause: subordinate conjunction + subject + verb; *because doggie likes*

Adjective or relative clause: relative pronoun + subject + verb; *that he spilled*

An example of an early phrase produced is the prepositional phrase. This phrase consists of a *preposition* (e.g., *in, on, around, about, across, between*), an article (e.g., *the*), and the object of the preposition (e.g., *a place*). Early forms develop in Brown's Stage II with the production of *on* and *in*.

*I put the cookie **on the dish***

Children have difficulty producing prepositional phrases in more complex sentence structures (Goodluck, 1986; Tomasello, 1992). For example, older preschool-age children may say *He's pushing over it* (rather than *He's pushing it over*). Embedded prepositional phrases appear in Stage IV. An example of the correct production of an embedded prepositional

phrase *on the wall* describes the location of the noun *boy*.

*The boy **on the wall** took my bike*

A subordinate or dependent clause begins with such words as *after, although, as, as if, because, before, even if, even though, if, in order to, though, unless, when,* and *while.*

*I want my cookie **before I go to bed***

A relative clause begins with a relative pronoun, such as *who, whom, whose, which,* or *that.* A relative clause can also begin with a relative adverb, such as *when, where,* or *why.*

*I know **who took my bike***

*I don't know **where he is***

The Verb Phrase

The verb phrase contains a verb (obligatory) and the following examples of optional elements.

Auxiliary verbs: *am, is, are, was, were, be, been*

Adverbs: *quickly, easily, fast*

Object noun phrase: *the children ate **cookies***

Prepositional phrase: *in the yard, on the table, over the fence*

The verb phrase contains a main verb that can be produced with the inflectional morphemes that indicate present and ongoing action. Examples include the present progressive (is eat + *ing*), modals (e.g., *can eat, could eat, may eat,* and *must eat*), and the perfective used to specify a single occurring, nonhabitual action (i.e., *has eaten*).

*The dog is eat**ing***

*I **can** see the moon*

*The dog **has eaten** our cookies*

The order of acquisition for verb phrase elaboration consists of the following stages of development with the ages in months (Garrard, 1991; Kahmi & Nelson, 1988; Miller, 1981).

Stage I   16–31
  Unmarked main verbs
  -ing inflection emerges

Stage II   21–35
  -ing present progressive
  Gonna, wanna,
  Copula *be*

Stage III   24–42
  Overgeneralizes regular past *-ed*
  Present tense auxiliary
  Modal present *can, may, will*

Stage IV   28–48
  Regular past tense *-ed*
  Auxiliary verb + *-ing*
  Modal auxiliaries past *could, would, should, might*

Stage V   35–52
  Irregular past
  Regular third person singular
  Contractible copula *be*

Stage V+   41+
  Uncontractible auxiliary
  Past tense *were, was, have*

By the end of Brown's Stage II (27 to 30 months of age) or early Stage III (31 to 34 months of age), children have mastered the rules for basic sentence formation and are able to understand and produce simple, active declarative sentences (e.g., *Doggie ate cookie*). Negative, interrogative, and imperative sentence forms emerge next.

THE DEVELOPMENT OF NEGATIVE, INTERROGATIVE, AND IMPERATIVE SENTENCE FORMS

Negative Sentence Forms

Children at the one- and two-word utterance stage express three types of negation.

Nonexistence to indicate disappearance: *Allgone juice*

Rejection to indicate not wanting something: *No milk*

Denial to indicate an untruth: *Not book*

Three phases of negative construction development have been described (Bellugi, 1967; Bloom, 1991; Klima & Bellugi, 1966). Table 5–9 presents the development of negative sentence forms.

In Phase I, children produce the negative element outside the sentence (*No bed*), most likely repeating the order of the words produced in the adult's utterance (*Do you want to go to bed?*) (Drozd, 1995).

In Phase II, children embed the negative element *no* (*I no want milk*) while also producing the negative form *not* (*That not cookie*).

In Phase III, the negative contractible forms *can't* and *don't* emerge (*I don't have a cookie*) when MLU reaches 4.0.

Table 5–9. *Negative Sentences*

Stage	Description	Example
I	Negative + noun or verb	*No cry, no hat, wear no*
II	Internal negative; no auxiliary verb	*I no want*
III	Auxiliary appears	*I don't cry* *You can't touch* *I'm not sad*

Source: From *Language Development: Form and Function in Emerging Grammars* (pp. 163, 170, 220), by L. Bloom, Copyright 1970 Massachusetts Institute of Technology, by permission of the MIT Press. Reprinted with permission.

Indefinite negative words such as *nobody*, *no one*, and *nothing* present young language learners with difficulty. Younger children often say *I want anything* when they mean *I want nothing* (Seymour & Roeper, 1999). Older school-aged children might say *I don't got no books*, and even adults might say *I don't see nobody*.

In some languages and dialects, speakers consider double negatives as grammatically correct (Peccei, 1999). For example, double negatives are a feature of AAE (Seymour & Roeper, 1999) with an origin in languages that use double negatives to intensify the negative meaning (e.g., Spanish and French). Double negation also appeared in Old and Middle English. Thus, it is important for practitioners to understand that double negation does not reflect a language disorder, as shown in the following example:

Nobody don't *like me*

Interrogative Sentence Forms

Yes/no questions (*Do you want a cookie?*) require that the listener simply answer the question with either a *yes* or a *no* word. To form yes/no questions, children must learn to invert the subject and the auxiliary verb, as shown in the following example.

Declarative sentence: *The boy is eating*

Inversion: *Is the boy eating?*

Wh- questions (beginning with *who, what, when, where, why,* or *how*) require more information than a *yes/no* response. For example, *where* questions demand information about location, *when* questions demand temporal information, and *who* questions demand information about people.

There is a correlation between the acquisition of *Wh-* questions and the acquisition of *Wh-* words. *What, where,* and *who* are acquired early because this information is available in a context (e.g., what are we looking at, where is it, and who did it). *Why, how,* and *when* require information that is not found in the immediate context (Bloom, Lightbown, & Hood, 1978). *Why* requires an understanding of the reason for an action, which may also require that a child possess a theory of mind to explain an action (e.g., *He was smiling at me because I brushed my own teeth*). *How* requires understanding in what way something happened (e.g., *He must have stood on that chair to get the cookie jar off the shelf*). *When* requires a child to possess the concept of time, such as the difference between today, tomorrow, and yesterday. Children learn these concepts of time between 2 and 5 years of age (Nelson, 2001).

> Learning *Wh- words* occurs when children are able to engage in conversations with adults or more advanced language users about past and future events, which will help children to think about themselves at different points in time (Hudson, 2006).

The production of *Wh-* questions involves some complexity. For example, it is necessary to perform two operations to produce a *Wh-* question: (a) transpose the subject and the auxiliary verb and (b) add the *Wh-* form at the beginning of the sentence. The following sequence demonstrates the changes that occur from the declarative form to form a question: inversion and addition of the *Wh-* word, beginning with an example of a declarative sentence.

Declarative sentence: *The boy is eating*

Inversion: *Is the boy eating?*

Add the *Wh-* form: *What is the boy eating?*

Four phases of development characterize question development (Bloom, 1991; Klima & Bellugi, 1966).

Phase 1: Rising intonation and some *Wh-* forms (MLU 1.75 to 2.25) occur between 27 to 30 months of age. In this phase, children typically ask yes/no questions by adding a rising intonation to the end of their utterances.

Cookie now?

Go car?

To formulate *Wh-* questions, young children simply attach a *Wh-* word to an assertion. At this stage of development, children mainly ask for names of objects, actions, or locations.

Where daddy?

What dat?

Where and *what* questions are the more prominent *Wh-* questions used during this phase with children often not understanding *why* questions. For example, when asked **Why do you eat breakfast,** children may respond as though asked **What do you eat for breakfast?**

Question asked: *Why do you eat breakfast?*

Child's response: *Cereal*

Phase 2: Between 27 and about 34 months, children produce a greater variety of *Wh-* questions (MLU 2.25 to 2.75) and can understand and respond to *what, who,* and *where* questions. Children continue to ask yes/no questions by using rising intonation. They ask *Wh-* questions by adding the *Wh-* form at the beginning of the question and using an auxiliary verb (e.g., *is, are, was, were*). However, younger children do not always include auxiliary verbs when producing sentences, as shown in the following examples:

Where my car?

What you doing?

Phase 3: Between 31 and 40 months, there is limited use of inversion (e.g., *Where are you?)* at this phase of development (MLU 2.75 to 3.5). Auxiliary use and verb inversion do not appear until children reach 3.5 MLU (O'Grady, 1997). An example of the stages of a child's question formation follows, ending with inversion:

Where you?

Where you are?

Where are you?

At this stage, children are able to invert the subject and verb to produce yes/no questions.

We are going?   Inversion absent

Are we going?   Inversion present

However, inversion does not appear in the production of *Wh-* questions in the early stages of development.

What the man is doing?

Phase 4: Inversion in positive *Wh-* questions appears at about 35 months (MLU 3.5+). Children now invert the

subject and the auxiliary verb when asking positive *Wh-* questions.

What is the man doing?

Difficulty appears with inversion when producing negative *Wh-* questions.

Why I can't have cookie?

> *What, where,* and *who* questions are learned before questions using the words *why, how,* and *when* (Bloom, 1991; Ervin-Tripp, 1970) for the reasons explained in the acquisition of *Wh-* words. There is greater difficulty in the cognitive processing of questions that involve the abstract concepts for *why, how,* and *when*. For example, if someone says *The doggie was bad,* the child can ask *What did the doggie do?* The information for the questions that involve answering *why, how,* and *when* require additional information (e.g., *Why was the doggie bad?*). Children must look for this information from another context or previous **discourse** (e.g., *why, how,* and *when did something happen*).

Table 5–10 presents a summary of the development of question forms (Bloom, Merkin, & Wootten, 1982).

Imperative Sentence Forms

Imperative sentences consist of requests, demands, and commands for a listener to perform an action to satisfy a speaker's intent (meaning). At the prelinguis-

Table 5–10. *The Acquisition of Wh- Questions*

Order of Acquisition
Where
What
Who
How
Why
Which
When
Whose

Source: From "Wh- Questions: Factors That Contribute to the Sequence of Acquisition," by L. Bloom, S. Merkin, and J. Wootten, 1982, *Child Development, 53,* pp. 1084–1092. Copyright 1982 John Wiley & Sons. Reprinted with permission.

tic level, children express imperatives by pointing and gesturing. When children produce two-word utterances, they produce imperatives shown in these examples:

Eat cookie!

No bed!

Imperatives have the following syntactic structure: uninflected verbs (no morphemes attached, such as *-ing*) and the subject *you* omitted (e.g., *Come here!*). More complex imperative sentence forms appear in Brown's Stage III.

Throw the ball to me

SEMANTIC DEVELOPMENT

Semantics is the component of language concerned with meaning conveyed through words, sentences, and discourse (a continuous stretch of speech, such as conversation). Vocabulary development begins at about 12 months when children produce words that label familiar entities, actions, and objects in the environment. This demonstrates the connection between children's vocabulary development and environmental experiences.

Vocabulary Development

Children have an expressive vocabulary of one or more words at 12 months, 4 to 6 words at 15 months, 20 words at 18 months, and 200 to 300 words at 24 months. Children acquire about five new words daily between 1½ and 6 years of age (Carey, 1978). By age 6, a child's vocabulary consists of 10,000 words (Anglin, 1993). Some children's vocabulary shows a *vocabulary burst, vocabulary spurt,* or *naming explosion* when they acquire a 50-word vocabulary during the second year of life. However, not all children show this pattern of rapid vocabulary growth (Ganger & Brent, 2004).

Children's receptive vocabulary generally exceeds their expressive vocabulary, and they are able to understand at least 50 words when their expressive vocabulary consists of 10 words. As noted, English-speaking children's first words consist of nouns such as *doggie* and *ball* (65%), action words such as *go* and *up* (13%), modifiers such as *hot* and *mine* (9%), personal-social words such as *bye-bye* and *no* (8%), and function words such as *what* (4%) (Nelson, 1973).

Young children frequently use the perceptual characteristics of entities to extend the meaning beyond that entity (**overextension**), such as labeling all four-legged animals *doggie*. Overextensions derive from the perceptual or functional characteristics of the target word (Peccei, 1999), such as the number of legs on the animal. Functional characteristics form the basis for a child using the word *hat* to label a hat, scarf, ribbon, and hairbrush, given the similar function of putting something on your head.

Frequently, children produce over-extensions when they lack the appropriate word. In this case, they produce a word as a way of asking *what's that?* Children also sometimes make up words when they lack a word to describe things, such as the phrase *I'm crackering my soup* (Clark, 1981) to describe putting crackers in their soup. Overextension occurs until about 3 years of age, when children's vocabulary skills increase and they have a better understanding of meaning (Bernstein & Levey, 2009).

Underextension can also appear in children's word productions when they have a restricted definition of a word. For example, Daniel was horrified when told that the picture of his dog's grandfather was on the cover of a dog manual, asking *Is Shanti's grandfather a dog?* Children may also deny that their mother's high heels are *shoes*, pointing to their own and saying *No, dis shoe.* These examples highlight the difference between the meaning of words for children and adults. Peccei (1999) provides examples of children's perception of the meaning of words.

A restricted or limited definition of a word is shown when a child learns the word *white* to describe snow and is bewildered when this word is used to refer to a white piece of paper.

The perception of the characteristics of an object can also influence the understanding of a meaning of a word. This occurs when a child uses the word *ball* to refer to balls, marbles, wheels, and cement mixers.

Children's understanding of the meaning of words develops over time as conceptual and vocabulary skills develop.

There are other factors that may affect children's vocabulary development. For example, **phonological awareness** is a factor that may play a role in learning new words (Gathercole & Baddeley, 1990, 1993). Phonological awareness describes children's awareness of the sound structure of words, beginning with whole words (e.g., *banana*), followed by syllables (*ba - na - na*) and the recognition of segments in words (*c-a-t*). At the early stages of language development, word awareness appears. Learning new words requires that children possess phonological awareness so that they can establish the sounds used to form words, such as the sounds that form the word *banana* (e.g., /b, ə, n, æ, n, ə/).

The relationship between vocabulary and phonological awareness was found in children with vocabulary deficits who had difficulty learning novel words (Bishop, North, & Donlan, 1996; Gathercole & Baddeley, 1990). Novel words (e.g., *biguhduh*) are frequently used to assess children's phonological awareness instead of real words (e.g., *banana*) because children may be familiar with real words that they have learned. In this way, novel words are a more realistic test of the ability to develop vocabulary. In addition to phonological awareness, children must be able to establish the meaning of a word through semantic/conceptual analysis (i.e., understanding the meaning of a word based on its use in communication and in social interaction). In summary, children require both phonological awareness and the ability to establish meaning for learning new words (Nash & Donaldson, 2005).

Relational Terms

Semantic development includes the acquisition of **relational terms**. Relationship concepts are listed next (McCune-Nicolich, 1981).

Time (sequence): *first, next, last*

Objects (presence or absence): *allgone, more*

Location: *in, on*

Space (movement): *back, up, down, open*

Relational terms, such as the terms *more, allgone,* and *up,* appear at the single-word stage(McCune-Nicholich, 1980). When children are aware that something is absent, they will code the meaning of **recurrence** (Bloom, 1973), which may be produced when they have finished all of the juice in their cups and ask for *more.*

Learning relational terms is fundamental to language development (Göksun, Hirsh-Pasek, & Golinkoff, 2009) because prepositions allow children to describe relations between objects, such as *the cup is on the table.* The spatial or locational terms that children learn by 3 years of age are *in, on,* and *under* (Johnston, 1988). Children who have acquired relational terms are also better at noticing, using, and maintaining memories of similar relationships in the environment (Lowenstein & Gentner, 1998).

Location relational terms refer to place (e.g., *in* or *on*), whereas physical relational terms denote qualities that characterize a thing (e.g., *hot* or *cold*). There are two classes of temporal relations: temporal order (*after, before*) and temporal duration (*since* and *until*). Examples of these relational terms follow.

Temporal order
He came into the class after John
She went into the room before John

Temporal duration
He has been here since the room opened
She will stay until it gets dark outside

Children understand the temporal order sentence structures *before* and *after* earlier than duration terms (e.g., *since*) (Feagans, 1980). They do not understand the duration relations *since* and *until* before 7 years of age. The developmental order for the acquisition of relational terms is shown in Table 5–11.

Preschool-age children apply their knowledge of syntactic structure to understand certain relational terms (Goodz, 1982). For example, younger children rely on the *order of mention* for understanding the terms *before* and *after* (Bever, 1970). This means that children interpret the first thing mentioned in a sentence as the first thing to receive some sort of action and will misinterpret the following direction:

*Before you put the **ball** in the box, put the **toy** in the box*

Given that *ball* was mentioned first, children interpret this sentence to mean *put the ball in the box* first and *put the toy in the box* second. Children begin to better understand syntactic structure in the later preschool stages (Owens, 2012) with less reliance on the order of mention.

Table 5–11. *Relational Terms*

Relational Relation	Examples	Age (approximate in years)
Locational relations	*in, on, under*	24–36 months
	next to	3½ years
	behind, in front, in back	4 years
Temporal relations	*before, after*	5 years
	since, until	7 years

Source: From "Children's Understanding of Some Temporal Terms Denoting Order, Duration, and Simultaneity," by L. Feagans, 1980, *Journal of Psycholinguistic Research, 9*(1), pp. 41–57. Copyright Springer Publications (2008). Reprinted with permission.

Kinship Relationship Terms

Another category of relationship terms refers to *kinship* or a child's relationship to family members. Piaget's early study (1928) was replicated 34 years later (Elkind, 1962) with similar results for children's understanding of kinship relationships.

Stage I. Primitive definitions
   A brother is a boy and a sister a girl (but adults could not be brothers or sisters)

Stage II. Relational definitions
   Lack of reciprocity; for example, the term *brother* applied only to one's sibling (e.g., Jack can be my brother but I am not Jack's brother)

Stage III. Relational and reciprocal definitions
   Children understand that *to have a brother* means that *you are a brother too*

The first kinship terms to develop refer to immediate family members: *mother, father, brother,* and *sister.* The next to be acquired are *daughter, son, uncle,* and *aunt.*

The last to be acquired are *grandmother, grandfather, grandson, granddaughter,* and *cousin* (Haviland & Clark, 1974). Most kinship terms are established by age 10.

> The sequence of acquisition of kinship terms is based on semantic complexity (Clark, 1973) with children acquiring semantically simpler terms before the more complex. For instance, the semantic features associated with *mother* are [+female] and [+parent], whereas those for *uncle* are [+male] and [+brother], along with [+parent] (as he is the brother of the child's parent). Thus, *mother* is acquired before *uncle,* given less complex semantic features. Another semantic complexity factor is the reciprocal relation found with *brother,* associated with the factors of *male, sibling,* and *sharing parents.* Thus, *brother* has the semantic features of [+child], [+parent], [+male], and [+sibling]. This reciprocal

relation presents difficulty because a child can identify his own brother as *brother* but has difficulty identifying himself as *brother* of the other. Another factor is the presence or absence of kin in the child's family. If there are no relatives to fill certain roles, children will not be exposed to these terms, and these terms will be absent from their vocabulary.

Semantic Roles

Another area of development is children's production of **semantic roles** (Bernstein & Levey, 2009). These semantic roles include *agent, action, object, location, possession, rejection, disappearance, nonexistence,* and *denial*. At 12 to 18 months, semantic roles are expressed in children's one-word speech productions, as presented in Table 5–12.

At about 18 months, children begin to produce two-word utterances. When they acquire at least 20 words, they combine semantic roles (e.g., *mommy* and *go*) to create **semantic relations**: agent (*mommy*) + action (*go*). Examples of these semantic relations are presented in Table 5–13 (Levey, 2011).

The production of semantic relations marks children's productions of new meanings and expanded ways to express meaning. Brown (1973) investigated a variety of languages, including English, Finnish, Samoan, and Spanish, and found that 70% of their utterances could be classified as semantic relations that describe actions and who performed them (agent + action), characteristics of things (attribute + entity), locations of things (entity + location), and other semantic features of the environment.

Table 5–12. *Semantic Roles*

Semantic Role	Definition	Example
Agent	doer of an action	*Daddy* (pointing to daddy kicking a ball)
Action	event	*kick* (pointing to daddy who had just kicked the ball)
Affected	entity influenced by the action	*Ball* (pointing to ball that was kicked)
Location	place	*Bed* (indicating that the dog is *in* his bed)
Possessor	owner	*Mommy's* (while pointing to her shoe)
Possession	entity owned	*shoe* (while bringing mommy's shoe to her)
Attribute	characteristic	*hot* (while pointing to stove)
Recurrence	repetition	*more* (while pointing to cookie plate)
Negation	rejection	*no* (bed rejected)

Source: From *Language Development: Understanding Language Diversity in the Classroom* (p. 127), by S. Levey & S. Polirstok (Eds.), 2011, Los Angeles, CA: Sage. Reprinted with permission.

Table 5–13. *Semantic Relations*

Semantic Relations	Examples
Agent + action	*Mommy kiss*
Action + affected	*Kick ball*
Action + location	*Sleep bed*
Entity + location	*Baby bed*
Possessor + possession	*Mommy shoe*
Entity + attribute	*Doggy big*
Nomination	*That car*
Recurrence	*More juice*
Negation	*No bed*

Source: From *Language Development: Understanding Language Diversity in the Classroom* (p. 46), by S. Levey & S. Polirstok (Eds.), 2011, Los Angeles, CA: Sage. Reprinted with permission.

PRAGMATIC DEVELOPMENT

Pragmatics involves language use, accommodating language to different listeners and situations, and using certain rules to achieve successful communication. Examples of these three pragmatic factors follow.

Language use

Greetings: *Hello, goodbye, how are you?*

Informing : *I'm going home now*

Demanding: *I want to play with your new doll*

Promising: *I promise to share my new toy with you*

Requesting : *Can I play with your new doll?*

Accommodating to different listeners

Talking differently to a baby than to

an adult and to a teacher than to a friend

Giving enough information so that the listener understands what you are talking about, how or why something happened, or how to play a game

Following rules in conversation

Taking turns in conversation as speaker and listener

Introducing topics of conversation that are relevant to the topic at hand

Staying on topic

Making conversational repairs when communication breakdowns occur

Learning to interpret signals (e.g., when someone is bored with the conversation or anxious to add something to the conversation)

Appropriate distance between speaker and listener

Eye contact

Early Pragmatic Development

Infants are capable of producing **intentional** communication to indicate their wants and needs. Infants communicate intentionality with gesture and/or vocalization coupled with eye contact (James, 1990). Children frequently combine a gesture (e.g., pointing) with verbalization (e.g., *doggy*) with toddlers producing more gestures without verbalization than older children. Capone (2007) points out that gesture and language originate in the same neural regions of the brain, suggesting that gestures are an indication of a child's future language development.

Children at the one-word stage use language to regulate others' behaviors, establish joint attention, and engage in social interaction (James, 1990). Between 1 and 2 years of age, children communicate the following intentions in their pragmatic interactions (McShane, 1980).

Regulation intents to gain attention, make requests, and to call adults; state intents through naming, description, and giving information that is beyond the here and now

Exchange intents for descriptions of activities, to communicate the intent to carry out an action, for refusal, and to communicate protests

Children's early attempts to communicate their intentions consist of (a) the **instrumental** function, used to obtain a goal and to have wants and needs met (the child holds out a cup and says *more*); (b) the **regulatory** function, used to control others' behaviors (the child gives a ball to an adult to request play and says *ball*); (c) the **interaction** function, used to obtain joint attention (the child calls *mama*); and (d) the **personal** function, used to express feelings or attitudes (the child says *yum* while eating a cookie) (Bernstein & Levey, 2009; Halliday, 1975).

Children's pragmatic requests develop over time, as shown in the following examples of children requesting a cookie:

1 year	*Waa* (and reaching)
1½ years	*Cookie*
2 years	*Wanna cookie*
3 years	*Cookie please*
7 years	*That cookie sure looks yummy*

Speech Acts

A speaker's intent or meaning can be categorized as a **speech act** (Searle, 1983). Speech acts are called *acts* because many types are intended to result in action. For example, it is expected that an action (*passing the salt*) will follow when someone is asked *Can you pass the salt?* The following examples are offered to illustrate toddlers' speech acts:

Greeting	*Hi*
Promise	*I promise I eat my peas*
Request	*Gimme cookie*
Indirect request	*Can I have a cookie?*
Complaint	*Why I can't play?*
Invitation	*Come play with me?*
Refusal	*No wanna go to bed*

Young children convey **intention** (meaning) through certain early or primitive speech acts (Dore, 1975), shown in Table 5–14.

Speech acts can be direct (e.g., *Close the window*) or indirect (e.g., *Can you close the window?* or *Don't you think it's getting cold in here?*). The indirect speech act is more polite because it makes a request for action in a more indirect and subtle manner. Indirect speech acts appear with more advanced vocabulary, such as the use of modal auxiliaries (e.g., *can, could, would, should,* and *couldn't*). Modal auxiliaries do not appear until 30 months for *can* with continued development over time for *will, shall,* and *could* (Wells, 1979).

Table 5–14. *Primitive Speech Acts*

Primitive Speech Act	Examples	Context
Labeling	*Eye*	Touches nose and says *eye*
Repeating	*Oh, no*	Repeats adults utterance
Answering	*Here*	Responds when asked *Where are you?*
Requesting action	*Up*	Raises arms to be picked up
Requesting answer	*Baby?*	Points to another child and asks *Baby?*
Calling	*Mama*	Calls his mother from crib
Greeting	*Dada*	Greets father as he enters the room
Protesting	*No*	Says *no* when parents says *It's bed time*
Practicing	*No . . . no . . . no*	Practicing words

Source: From "Holophrases: Speech Acts and Language Universals," by J. Dore, 1975, *Journal of Child Language*, 2(1), p. 33. Reprinted with the permission of Cambridge University Press.

An essential part of learning language is recognizing the connection between what a speaker says and what the truth is about the world. *Assertions* are speech acts that draw a connection between two things: the words a speaker utters and the thing or things in the world referred to by this utterance. For example, if a speaker says, "That's a banana" while pointing to a pear, that is an incorrect assertion or description of reality. Children must learn to grasp the connection between what is said and the truth of a speech act (Rakoczy & Tomasello, 2009). Children as young as 16 months are able to distinguish between a match and a mismatch (Koenig & Echols, 2003), as when a speaker labeled a *cup* with the word "dog."

NARRATIVE DEVELOPMENT

Narrative plays a role in social interaction, effective communication, and the development of literacy skills (Bliss & McCabe, 2011). Children who are able to retell the entire story of *The Three Bears* have greater success with later literacy skills (de Hirsch, Jansky, & Langford, 1966).

Children first produce narratives to talk about past events at about 22 months, given assistance from adults (Eisenberg, 1985). At 24 months, their narratives tend to focus on negative past events (Miller & Sperry, 1988), such as being hit by another child. The sequence of toddlers' narrative development follows these stages (Bernstein & Levey, 2009; McLaughlin, 2006).

Scripts: narratives produced by 2-year-olds that involve everyday routines and events that they have experienced. In this stage, an adult might label objects when the child is getting dressed in the morning: *those are socks, that's a shirt,* and *these are your shoes.* In turn, the child will produce the labels for these objects. There is no sequence in the dressing context (e.g., *first we put on . . . , next . . .*)

Heaps: produced at or about 30 months. There is no relationship between the elements or the information that is produced, and children might merely label objects or actions: *There's a car . . . there a doggie . . . doggie won't hurt you . . . there the slide . . . I climb high*

Chaining: at about 3 years of age, talking about events that relate to a central topic with no particular order of occurrence: *I went to school . . . I was the cleanup monitor . . . the teacher said I had my ears on . . . I ate pasta with meat sauce . . . just the pasta*

Vocabulary development also plays a role in the development of narratives because children can use a variety of words to produce stories and report events. Narrative also becomes more organized as children learn connectives, such as *and then, therefore, however,* and *nevertheless*

The man climbed up the ladder. **And then** he started to paint the star

He wanted to stay and play. **However**, he had to go home to eat dinner

She was full from eating all of the popcorn. **Nevertheless**, she managed to eat some candy

The narrative grammar model, shown in Table 5–15, describes the structure that stories take (Stein & Glenn, 1979). It is

Table 5–15. *Story Grammar Structure*

Story Grammar Element	Description
Setting	Introduction of characters, time, and place
Initiating Event	Problem
Internal Response	Character's feelings about the initiating event
Internal Plan	Statement about fixing the problem
Attempt	Action to solve problem
Consequence	Event or events following the Attempt
Resolution or Reaction	The final state following the Attempt
Ending	A statement ending the story

Intra-category connectors:
    AND
    THEN
    BECAUSE	

Note. Initiating event, attempt, and consequence are the essential parts of the narrative for a complete episode.

Source: From "An Analysis of Story Comprehension in Elementary School Children," by N. Stein and C. Glenn, 1979. In R. D. Freedle (Ed.), *Advances in Discourse Processes: Vol. 2. New Directions in Discourse Processing* (pp. 53–119), Norwood, NJ: Ablex. Reprinted with permission of the author (Stein).

essential that children develop an understanding of this structure because this knowledge helps them better understand and remember stories read to them.

An example of the narrative structure is shown in the following story:

Setting: Introduction of characters, time, and place (*Winnie the Pooh looked into his honey pot*)

Initiating Event: Problem (*His honey pot was empty*)

Internal Response: Character's feelings about the initiating event (*He felt sad*)

Internal Plan: Statement about fixing the problem (*Then, he said, "I should fill my pot again"*)

Attempt: Action to solve problem (*He went out to search for more honey to fill his pot*)

Consequence: Event or events following the attempt (*He found a bee's nest and the friendly bees said, "We'll share our honey with you"*)

Resolution or Reaction: The final state of affairs following the attempt (*Winnie the Pooh said, "Thank you" and went home with a full pot of honey*)

Ending: A statement ending the story (*Winnie the Pooh was happy and he also had made new friends*)

Internal responses (words that describe feelings) are largely absent in younger children (Apel & Masterson, 1998). Children are not able to produce a complete episode, including all elements of the narrative structure, until age 7 or 8.

SUMMARY

We have traced the development of children's language, beginning at birth and continuing to age 3. In this period of development, children produce their first words, establish a theory of mind, understand many types of *Wh-* questions, begin to produce narratives, express requests in a more polite manner, and engage in more complex play schemes. In this chapter, we have learned:

◆ What infant perception tells us about the human mind
◆ The role of the theory of mind in language development
◆ The development of infant's productions, beginning with reflexive sounds
◆ The characteristics of children's first words and early word combinations
◆ The important role of joint attention and joint action in language development
◆ The role of innate cognitive skills in children's language development
◆ Children's phonological, morphological, syntactic, semantic, and pragmatic development from birth to age 3
◆ Multilinguistic differences that are found in other dialects and languages

Chapter 6 traces the development of language from ages 3 through 5.

KEY WORDS

Accommodation

Adaptation

Assimilation

Causality

Chaining

Cognition

Complex sentence

Compound sentence

Decentration

Deferred imitation

Denial

Discourse

Egocentrism

Equilibrium

Heaps

Incidental learning

Innate

Instrumental

Intention

Intentional

Interaction

Jargon

Joint action

Joint attention

Means-end

Means-end behavior

Mean length utterance (MLU)

Mental verbs

Morphemes

Morphology

Morphophonology

Morphosyntactic development

Mutual exclusivity bias

Narrative

Nonexistence

Object constancy

Object permanence

Obligatory

Overextension

Overgeneralize

Overgeneralization

Perception

Perceptual

Performatives

Personal

Perspective taking

Phonemic representations

Phonetically consistent forms

Phonological awareness

Phonological processes

Pragmatics

Preoperational stage

Recurrence

Reduplicated babbling

Referent absent

Referent present

Reflexive

Regulatory

Rejection

Relational terms

Representational thought

Schema

Scripts

Semantic relations

Semantic roles

Speech acts

Symbolic functions

Syntax

Theory of mind (TOM)

Underextension

Variegated babbling

Vocables

Words

STUDY QUESTIONS

1. Discuss the role of a theory of mind and interaction with children's peers.

2. Explain why joint attention and joint interaction play a role in children's language development.

3. Describe the importance of adult-to-child interaction in children's language development.

4. Explain why children may have difficulty with understanding the pronouns *you* and *I*.

5. Describe the connection between play and language in children's development.

REFERENCES

American Speech-Language-Hearing Association. (2009). *How does your child hear and talk.* Retrieved from http://www.asha.org/public/speech/development/chart.htm

Akhtar, N., Jipson, J., & Callanan, M. A. (2001). Learning words through overhearing. *Child Development, 72,* 416–430.

Anglin, J. M. (1993). Vocabulary development: A morphological analysis. *Monographs of the Society for Research in Child Development, 58*(10, Serial No. 238), 1–165.

Apel, K., & Masterson, J. (1998). *Assessment and treatment of narrative skills: What's the story.* Rockville, MD: American Speech-Language-Hearing Association.

Atkins, P., & Baddeley, A. (1998). Working memory and distributed vocabulary learning. *Applied Psycholinguistics, 19,* 537–552.

Barna, J., & Legerstee, M. (2005). Nine- and twelve-month-old infants relate emotions to people's actions. *Cognition and Emotion, 19*(1), 53–67.

Bates, E. (1979). *The emergence of symbols: Cognition and communication in infancy.* New York, NY: Academic Press.

Bates, E., Benigni, L., Bretherton, I., Camaioni, L., & Volterra, V. (1979). *The emergence of symbols: Cognition and communication in infancy.* New York, NY: Academic Press.

Bates, E., Marchman, V., Thal, D., Fenson, L., Dale, P., Reznick, S., Reilly, J., & Hartung, J. (1994). Developmental and stylistic variation in the composition of early vocabulary. *Journal of Child Language, 21*(1), 85–124.

Beals, D. E., & Tabors, P. O. (1995). Arboretum, bureaucratic and carbohydrate: Preschoolers' exposure to rare vocabulary at home. *First Language, 15,* 57–76.

Bellugi, U. (1967). The acquisition of negation (Doctoral dissertation). Cambridge, MA: Harvard University Press.

Bernstein, D. K. (2011). Language development from ages 3 to 5. In S. Levey & S. Polirstok (Eds.), *Language development: Understanding language diversity in the classroom* (pp. 139–160). Los Angeles, CA: Sage.

Bernstein, D. K., & Levey, S. (2009). Language development: A review. In D. K. Bernstein & E. Tiegerman-Farber (Eds.), *Language and communication disorders in children* (pp. 28–100). Boston, MA: Pearson.

Bever, T. G. (1970). The cognitive basis for linguistic structure. In J. R. Hayes (Ed.), *Cognition and the development of language.* New York, NY: John Wiley.

Bishop, D. V. M., North, T., & Donlan, C. (1996). Nonword repetition as a behavioral marker of inherited language impairment: Evidence from a twin study. *Journal of Child Psychology and Psychiatry, 37,* 391–403.

Bliss, L. S., & McCabe, A. (2011). Educational implications of narrative discourse. In S. Levey & S. Polirstok (Eds.), *Language development: Understanding language diversity in the classroom* (pp. 209–226). Los Angeles, CA: Sage.

Bloom, L. (1991). *Language development from two to three.* Cambridge, England: Cambridge University Press.

Bloom, L., Lightbown, P., & Hood, L. (1978). Pronominal-nominal variation in child language. In L. Bloom (Ed.), *Readings in language development* (pp. 231–253). New York, NY: John Wiley & Sons.

Bloom, L, Merkin, S., & Wootten, J. (1982). Wh questions: Linguistic factors that contribute to the sequence of acquisition. *Child Development, 53,* 1084–1092.

Brown, R. (1973). *A first language: The early stages.* Cambridge, MA: Harvard University Press.

Bushnell, I. W. R., Sai F., & Mullen J. T. (1989). Neonatal recognition of mother's face. *British Journal of Developmental Psychology, 7*(1), 3–15.

Campbell, C., Beretta, A., Carr, T., Huang, J., & Cao, Y. (2001). *An fMRI study of regular and irregular inflection.* Retrieved from http://research.rad.msu.edu/Neuro/FSR.html

Capone, N. C. (2007). Tapping toddlers' evolving semantic representation via gesture. *Journal of Speech-Language-Hearing Research, 50*(3), 732–745.

Carey, S. (1978). The child as word learner. In M. Halle, J. Bresman, & G. Miller (Eds.), *Linguistic theory and psychological reality* (pp. 265–293). Cambridge, MA: MIT Press.

Choi, S., & Gopnik, A. (1995). Early acquisition of verbs in Korean: A cross-linguistic study. *Journal of Child Language, 22,* 497–529.

Chomsky, N. (1969). *Aspects of the theory of syntax.* Cambridge, MA: MIT Press.

Clark, E. V. (1981). Lexical innovations: How children learn to create new words. In W. Deutsh (Ed.), *The child's construction of language* (pp. 299–328). London, England: Academic Press.

Clark, H. H. (1973). Space, time, semantics, and the child. In T. Moore (Ed.), *Cognitive development and the acquisition of language* (pp. 27–63). New York, NY: Academic Press.

Cliff, J. M. (1990). Navajo games. *American Indian Culture and Research Journal, 14,* 1–81.

de Hirsch, K., Jansky, J. J., & Langford, W. S. (1966). *Predicting reading failure.* New York, NY: Harper and Row.

Dore, J. (1975). Holophrases: Speech acts and language universals. *Journal of Child Language, 2*(1), 33.

Dore, J., Franklin, M., Miller, R., & Ramer, A. (1976). Transitional phenomena in early language acquisition. *Journal of Child Language, 3,* 13–28.

Drozd, K. F. (1995). Child English pre-sentential negation as a metalinguistic exclamatory sentence negation. *Journal of Child Language, 22*(3), 583–610.

Eisenberg, A. R. (1985). Learning to describe past experiences in conversation. *Discourse Processes, 8,* 177–204.

Elkind, D. (1962). Children's conceptions of brother and sister: Piaget replication study V. *Journal of Child Language, 6,* 313–327.

Ervin-Tripp, S. M. (1970). Discourse agreement: How children answer questions. In R. Hayes (Ed.), *Cognition and language learning* (pp. 79–107). New York, NY: Wiley and Sons.

Farver, J., Kim, Y. K., & Lee, Y. (1995). Cultural differences in Korean- and Anglo-American preschoolers' social interaction and play. *Child Development, 66*(4), 1088–1099.

Feagans, L. (1980). Children's understanding of some temporal terms denoting order, duration, and simultaneity. *Journal of Psycholinguistic Research, 9*(1), 41–57.

Ganger, J., & Brent, M. R. (2004). Reexamining the vocabulary spurt. *Developmental Psychology, 40*(4), 621–632.

Garrard, K. R. (1991). A guide for assessing young children's expressive language skills through language sampling. *National Student Speech Language Hearing Association Journal, 18,* 87–95.

Gathercole, S. E., & Baddeley, A. (1990). Phonological memory deficits in language disordered children: Is there a causal connection. *Journal of Memory and Language, 29,* 336–360.

Gathercole, S. E., & Baddeley, A. (1993). *Working memory and language.* Hillsdale, NJ: Erlbaum.

Gentner, D. (1981). Some interesting differences between nouns and verbs. *Cognition and Brain Theory, 4,* 161–178.

Gentner, D. (1982). Why nouns are learned before verbs: Linguistic relativity versus natural partitioning. In S. A. Kuczaj (Ed.), *Language development: Vol. 2. Language, thought, and culture* (pp. 301–334). Hillsdale, NJ: Erlbaum.

Gentner, D. (2003). Why we're so smart. In D. Gentner & S. Goldin-Meadow (Eds.), *Language in mind: Advances in the study of language and thought* (pp. 195–235). Cambridge, MA: MIT Press.

Gerken, L. A. (1996). Prosodic structure in young children's language production. *Language, 72,* 683–712.

Gleason, J. B., & Ratner, N. B. (2009). *The development of language* (7th ed.). Boston, MA: Pearson.

Gleitman, L. R., & Gleitman, H. (1992). A picture is worth a thousand words, but that's the problem: The role of syntax in vocabulary acquisition. *Current Directions in Psychological Sciences, 1,* 31–35.

Göksun, T., Hirsh-Pasek, K., & Golinkoff, R. M. (2009). Trading spaces: Carving up events for learning language. *Perspectives on Psychological Science, 5,* 33–42.

Goodluck, H. (1986). Language acquisition and linguistic theory. In P. Fletcher & M. Garman (Eds.), *Language acquisition* (2nd ed.). New York, NY: Cambridge University Press.

Goodz, N. S. (1982). Is before easier to understand than after? *Child Development, 53,* 822–825.

Gopnik, A., Meltzoff, A. N., & Kuhl, P. K. (1999). *The scientist in n the crib: What early learning tells us about the mind.* New York, NY: Harper.

Gottardo, A., Stanovich, K. E., & Siegel, L. S. (1996). The relationships between phonological sensitivity, syntactic processing, and verbal working memory in the reading performance of third-grade children. *Journal of Experimental Child Psychology, 63,* 563–582.

Gutiérrez-Clellen, V. F., & Simon-Cereijido, G. (2010). Using nonword repetition tasks for the identification of language impairment in Spanish-English-speaking children: Does the language of assessment matter? *Learning Disabilities Research & Practice, 25,* 48–58.

Halliday, M. A. K. (1975). *Learning how to mean: Explorations in the development of language.* New York, NY: Elsevier.

Hart, B., & Risley, T. R. (1995). *Meaningful differences in the everyday experience of young American children.* Baltimore, MD: Paul H. Brookes.

Haviland, S. E., & Clark, E. V. (1974). "This man's father is my father's son": A study of the acquisition of English kin terms. *Language and Speech, 16,* 34–43.

Hayes, B. (2009). *Introductory phonology.* Malden, MA: Blackwell.

Hillenbrand, J. (1983). Perceptual organization of speech sounds by infants. *Journal of Speech and Hearing Research, 26,* 268–282.

Hudson, J. A. (2006). The development of future time concepts through mother-child conversation. *Merrill-Palmer Quarterly, 52*(1), 70–95.

Hurtado, N., Marchman, V. A., & Fernald, A. (2008). Does input influence uptake? Links between maternal talk, processing speed and vocabulary size in Spanish-learning children. *Developmental Science, 11*(6), 31–39.

James, S. L. (1990). *Normal language acquisition.* Boston, MA: Allyn & Bacon.

Johnston, J. R. (1988). Children's verbal representation of spatial location. In J. Stiles-Davis, M. Kritchevsky, & U. Bellugi (Eds.), *Spatial cognition: Brain bases and development* (pp. 195–206). Hillsdale: NJ: Erlbaum.

Jusczyk, P. W. (1992). Developing phonological categories from the speech signal. In C.

A. Ferguson, L. Menn, & C. Stoel-Gammon (Eds.), *Phonological development: Models, research, implications* (pp. 17–64). Timonium, MD: York Press.

Jusczyk, P. W., & Aslin, R. N. (1995). Infants' detection of the sound patterns of words in fluent speech. *Cognitive Psychology, 29,* 1–23.

Kamhi, A., & Nelson, L. (1988). Early syntactic development: Simple clause types and grammatical morphology. *Topics in Language Disorders, 8,* 26–44.

Kelly, C. A., & Dale, P. S. (1989). Cognitive skills associated with the onset of multi-word utterances. *Journal of Speech and Hearing Research, 32,* 645–656.

Klima, E., & Bellugi, U. (1966). Syntactic regularities in the speech of children. In J. Lyons & R. Wales (Eds.), *Psycholinguistic papers* (pp. 183–208). Edinburgh, UK: Edinburgh University Press.

Koenig, M. A., & Echols, C. H. (2003). Infant's understanding of false labeling events: The referential roles of words and the speakers who use them. *Cognition, 87,* 179–203.

Kuhl, P. K., & Meltzoff, A. N. (1997). Evolution, nativism, and learning in the development of language and speech. In M. Gopnik (Ed.), *The inheritance of innateness of grammars* (pp. 7–44). Oxford, England: Oxford University Press.

Laing, S. P., & Kamhi, A. (2003). Alternative assessment of language and literacy in culturally and linguistically diverse populations. *Language, Speech, and Hearing Services in Schools, 45,* 44–55.

Legerstee, M. (2000). Domain specificity and the epistemic triangle: The development of the concept of animacy in infancy. In F. Lacerda, C. von Hofsten, & M. Heinemann (Eds.), *Emerging cognitive abilities in early infancy* (pp. 193–212). Mahwah, NJ: Lawrence Erlbaum Associates.

Legerstee, M., Anderson, D., & Schaffer, A. (1998). Five-and eight-month-old infants recognize their faces and voices as familiar and social stimuli. *Child Development, 69,* 37–50.

Levey, S. (2011). Typical and atypical language development. In S. Levey & S. Polirstok (Eds.), *Language development: Understanding language diversity in the classroom* (pp. 37–58). Los Angeles, CA: Sage.

Levey, S., & Cruz, D. (2003). The first words produced by children in bilingual English/Mandarin Chinese environments. *Communication Disorders Quarterly, 24*(3), 129–136.

Levey, S., & Schwartz, R. G. (2002). Syllable omission by two-year-old children. *Communication Disorders Quarterly, 23*(4), 169–177.

Loewenstein, G., & Gentner, D. (2001). Spatial mapping in preschoolers: Close comparisons facilitate far mappings. *Journal of Cognition and Development, 2,* 189–219.

Lund, N., & Duchan, J. (1993). *Assessing children's language in naturalistic contexts* (3rd ed.). Englewood Cliffs, NJ: Prentice Hall.

Macken, M. A. (1992). Where's phonology? In C. A. Ferguson, L. Menn, & C. Stoel-Gannon (Eds.), *Phonological development: Models, research, implications* (pp. 249–269). Timonium, MD: York Press.

MacWhinney, B., & Snow, C. (1985). The child language data exchange system. *Journal of Child Language, 12,* 271–295.

Maekawa, J. & Storkel, H. L. (2006). Individual differences in the influence of phonological characteristics on expressive vocabulary development by young children. *Journal of Child Language, 33,* 439–459.

Mandel, D. R., Jusczyk, P. W., & Pisoni, D. B. (1995). Infants' recognition of the sound patterns of their own names. *Psychological Sciences, 6,* 315–318.

Markman, E. M. (1989). *Categorization and naming in children.* Cambridge, MA: MIT Press.

Masataka, N. (1995). Absence of mirror-reversal tendency in cutaneous pattern perception and acquisition of a signed language in deaf children. *British Journal of Developmental Psychology, 13,* 97–106.

McCune-Nicolich, L. (1981). The cognitive bases of relational words in the single word period. *Journal of Child Language, 8*(1), 15–34.

McLaughlin, S. (1998). *Introduction to language development.* San Diego, CA: Singular.

McLaughlin, S. (2006). *Introduction to language development* (2nd ed.). San Diego, CA: Singular.

McShane, J. (1980). *Learning to talk*. Cambridge, England: Cambridge University Press.

Mervis, C. B., & Becerra, A. M. (2007). Language and communicative development in Williams syndrome. *Mental Retardation and Developmental Disabilities, 13*, 3–15.

Miller, J. (1981). *Assessing language production in children: Experimental procedures*. Baltimore, MD: University Park Press.

Miller, P., & Sperry, L. (1988). Early talk about the past: The origins of conversational stories of personal experience. *Journal of Child Language, 15*, 293–315.

Moorehead, D., & Ingram, D. (1973). The development of base syntax in normal and linguistically deviant children. *Journal of Speech and Hearing Research, 16*, 330–352.

Moses, L. J., Baldwin, D. A., Rosicky, J. G., & Tidball, G. (2002). Evidence for referential understanding in the emotions domain at twelve and eighteen months. *Child Development, 3*, 718–735.

Nash, M., & Donaldson, M. L. (2005). Word learning in children with vocabulary deficits. *Journal of Speech, Language, and Hearing Research, 48*, 439–458.

Nelson, K. (1973). Structure and strategy in learning to talk. *Monographs of the Society for Research in Child Development, 38* (1–2 Serial No. 149).

Nelson, K. (1987). The recognition of facial expressions in the first two years of life: Mechanisms of development. *Child Development 58*, 889–909.

Nelson, K. (2001). Language and the self: From "experiencing I" to the "continuing me." In C. Moore & K. Lemmon (Eds.), *The self in time* (pp. 15–34). Hillsdale, NJ: Erlbaum.

O'Grady, W. (1997). *Syntactic development*. Chicago, IL: The University of Chicago Press.

Owens, R. E., Jr. (2008). *Language development: An introduction* (7th ed.). Boston, MA: Pearson.

Owens, R. E. (2012). *Language development: An introduction* (8th ed.). Boston, MA: Pearson.

Pan, B. A., Rowe, M. L., Singer, J. D., & Snow, C. E. (2005). Maternal correlates of growth in toddler vocabulary production in low-income families. *Child Development, 76*(4), 763–782.

Patterson, J. L., & Westby, C. E. (1998). The development of play. In W. O. Haynes & B. B. Shulman (Eds.), *Communication development: Foundations, processes, and clinical applications* (pp. 135–163). Baltimore, MD: Williams and Wilkins.

Peccei, J. S. (1999). *Child language* (2nd ed.). London, England: Routledge.

Perner, J. (1991). *Understanding the representational mind*. Cambridge, MA: Bradford Books/MIT Press.

Piaget, J. (1928). *Judgment and reasoning in the child*. London, England: Routledge and Kegan Paul.

Piaget, J. (1954). *The construction of reality in the child*. New York, NY: Basic Books.

Piaget, J. (1962). *Play, dreams, and imitation in childhood*. New York, NY: Norton.

Polka, L., Jusczyk, P. W., & Rvachew, S. (1995). Methods for studying speech perception in infants and children. In W. Strange (Ed.), *Speech perception and linguistic experience: Theoretical and methodological issues in cross-language speech research* (pp. 49–89). Timonium, MD: York Press.

Rakoczy, H., & Tomasello, M. (2009). Done wrong or said wrong? Young children understand the normative directions of fit of different speech acts. *Cognition, 113*, 205–212.

Rescorla, L., Alley, A., & Christine, J. B. (2001). Word frequencies in toddlers' lexicons. *Journal of Speech, Language, and Hearing Research, 44*, 598–609.

Ricard, M., Girouard, P. C., & Decarie, T. G. (1999). Personal pronouns and perspective taking in toddlers. *Journal of Child Language, 26*(3), 687–697.

Roseberry-McKibbin, C. (2008). *Multicultural students with special language needs: Practical strategies for assessment and intervention* (3rd ed.). Oceanside, CA: Academic Communication Associates.

Ruston, H. P., & Schwanenflugel, P. J. (2010). Effects of a conversation on the expressive vocabulary development of prekindergarten children. *Language, Speech, and Hearing Services in Schools, 41*, 303–313.

Sciafe, M., & Bruner, J. S. (1975). The capacity for joint visual attention in the infant. *Nature, 253*, 265–266.

Searle, J. (1983). *Intentionality: An essay in the philosophy of mind* (Vol. 9). Cambridge, UK: Cambridge University Press.

Senechal, M., LeFevre, J., Hudson, E., & Lawson, E. P. (1996). Knowledge of picture books as a predictor of young child's vocabulary. *Journal of Educational Psychology, 88,* 520–536.

Seymour, H. N., & Roeper, T. (1999). Grammatical acquisition of African American English. In L. B. Leonard & O. L. Taylor (Eds.), *Language acquisition across North America: Cross-cultural and cross-linguistic perspectives* (pp. 109–152). San Diego, CA: Singular.

Shaffer, D. R. (1999). *Developmental psychology: Childhood and adolescence.* Pacific Grove, CA: Brook Cole.

Shipley K. G., Maddox M. A., Driver J. E. (1991). Children's development of irregular past tense forms. *Language, Speech and Hearing Services in Schools, 22,* 115–122.

Shneidman, L. A., Arroyo, M. E., Levine, S. C., & Goldin-Meadow, S. (2012). What counts as effective input for word learning? *Journal of Child Language, 10,* 1–15.

Sosa, A. V., & Stoel-Gammon, C. (2006). Patterns of intraword phonological variability during the second year of life. *Journal of Child Language, 33,* 31–50.

Stein, N., & Glenn, C. (1979). An analysis of story comprehension in elementary school children. In R. D. Freedle (Ed.), *Advances in discourse processes: Vol. 2. New directions in discourse processing* (pp. 53–119). Norwood, NJ: Ablex.

Thal, D. J., Miller, S., Carlson, J., & Moreno Vega, M. (2005). Nonword repetition and language development in 4-year-old children with and without a history of early language delay. *Journal of Speech, Language, and Hearing Research, 48,* 1481–1495.

Tobin, J., Wu, D., & Davidson, D. (1989). *Preschool in three cultures: Japan, China, and the United States.* New Haven, CT: Yale University Press.

Tomasello, M. (1992). *First verbs: A case study of early grammatical development.* Cambridge, UK: Cambridge University Press.

Tomasello, M. (1996). Piagetian and Vygotskyian approaches to language acquisition. *Human Development, 39,* 269–276.

Tomasello, M. (1998). Reference: Intending that others jointly attend. *Pragmatics and Cognition, 6,* 219–243.

Tomasello, M. (2003). *Constructing a language.* Cambridge, MA: Harvard University Press.

Tomasello, M., & Todd, J. (1983). Joint attention and lexical acquisition style. *First Language, 4,* 197–212.

van Heugten, M., & Johnson, E. K. (2011). Infants exposed to fluent natural speech succeed at cross-gender word recognition. *Journal of Speech, Language, and Hearing Research, 55*(2), 554–560.

Vihman, M. M. (1980). Sound change and child language. *Current Issues in Linguistic Theory, 14,* 304–320.

Wagner, R. K., Torgesen, J. K., & Rashotte, C. A. (1999). *Comprehensive test of phonological processing.* Austin, TX: PRO-ED.

Warden, D. (1981). Children's understanding of *ask* and *tell. Journal of Child Language, 8,* 139–149.

Wells, C. (1979). Learning and using the auxiliary verb in English. In V. Lee (Ed.), *Language development.* Beckenham: Croom Helm.

Werker, J., & Tees, R. (1984). Cross-language speech perception: Evidence for perceptual reorganization during the first year of life. *Infant Behavior and Development, 7,* 49–64.

Westby, C. E. (1980). Assessment of cognitive and language abilities through play. *Language, Speech, and Hearing Services in Schools, 11,* 154–168.

Wijnen, F., Krikhaar, E., & den Os, E. (1994). The (non)realization of unstressed elements in children's utterance: Evidence for a rhythmic constraint. *Journal of Child Language, 21,* 59–83.

Windsor, J., Kohnert, K., Lobitz, K. F., & Pham, G. T. (2010). Cross-language nonword repetition by bilingual and monolingual children. *American Journal of Speech-Language Pathology. 19,* 298–310.

Witt, B. (1998). Cognition and the cognitive-language relationship. In W. O. Haynes & B. B. Shulman (Eds.), *Communication development: Foundations, processes, and clinical applications* (pp. 101–133). Baltimore, MD: Williams and Wilkins.

APPENDIX A

Highlights of Children's Language Development

Birth to One Year

Hearing and Understanding	Talking
Birth–3 Months ◆ Startles to loud sounds ◆ Quiets or smiles when spoken to ◆ Seems to recognize your voice and quiets if crying ◆ Increases or decreases sucking behavior in response to sound	**Birth–3 Months** ◆ Makes pleasure sounds (cooing, gooing) ◆ Cries differently for different needs ◆ Smiles when sees you
4–6 Months ◆ Moves eyes in direction of sounds ◆ Responds to changes in tone of your voice ◆ Notices toys that make sounds ◆ Pays attention to music	**4–6 Months** ◆ Babbling sounds more speech-like with many different sounds, including p, b and m ◆ Chuckles and laughs ◆ Vocalizes excitement and displeasure ◆ Makes gurgling sounds when left alone and when playing with you
7 Months–1 Year ◆ Enjoys games like peek-a-boo and pat-a-cake ◆ Turns and looks in direction of sounds ◆ Listens when spoken to ◆ Recognizes words for common items like "cup," "shoe," "book," or "juice" ◆ Begins to respond to requests (e.g. "Come here" or "Want more?")	**7 Months–1 Year** ◆ Babbling has both long and short groups of sounds such as "tata upup bibibibi" ◆ Uses speech or noncrying sounds to get and keep attention ◆ Uses gestures to communication (waving, holding arms to be picked up) ◆ Imitates different speech sounds ◆ Has one or two words (hi, dog, dada, mama) around first birthday, although sounds may not be clear

One to Two Years

Hearing and Understanding	Talking
◆ Points to a few body parts when asked. ◆ Follows simple commands and understands simple questions ("Roll the ball," "Kiss the baby," "Where's your shoe?"). ◆ Listens to simple stories, songs, and rhymes. ◆ Points to pictures in a book when named.	◆ Says more words every month. ◆ Uses some one- or two- word questions ("Where kitty?" "Go bye-bye?" "What's that?"). ◆ Puts two words together ("more cookie," "no juice," "mommy book"). ◆ Uses many different consonant sounds at the beginning of words.

Two to Three Years

Talking	Hearing and Understanding
◆ Has a word for almost everything. ◆ Uses two- or three- words to talk about and ask for things. ◆ Uses *k, g, f, t, d,* and *n* sounds. ◆ Speech is understood by familiar listeners most of the time. ◆ Often asks for or directs attention to objects by naming them.	◆ Understands differences in meaning ("go-stop," "in-on," "big-little," "up-down"). ◆ Follows two requests ("Get the book and put it on the table"). ◆ Listens to and enjoys hearing stories for longer periods of time

From *How Does Your Child Hear and Talk*. Available from the website of the American Speech-Language-Hearing Association: http://www/asha.org/pubic/speech/development/chart.htm. All rights reserved. Reprinted with permission.

CHAPTER 6

Preschool-Age Children's Language Development

Sandra Levey

José was 3 years of age and enrolled in a preschool class. He produced longer sentences and was also able to understand and remember longer directions (e.g., go into the garage, get the broom, and give it to grandpa). He also engaged in more appropriate play with peers, such as asking if he could share a toy rather than crying or grabbing. After reading this chapter, you will understand the changes that occur when children enter the preschool stage of language development. You will also learn how to recognize signs of disorders in children, along with the ability to distinguish "differences," associated with dialects or with learning English as a second language, from "disorders."

AN OVERVIEW OF PRESCHOOL-AGE CHILDREN'S LANGUAGE DEVELOPMENT

In this chapter, we trace the development of children's language during the preschool period, between the ages of 3 and 5. By this stage of language development, children are able to produce sentences with deeper meaning and have a better understanding of spoken language. Through the production of longer and more complex utterances, this period marks major changes in children's expressive language skills. There is also a major change in children's language comprehension because they are able to understand lengthier spoken utterances. Their social interaction skills are more developed and they now engage in more advanced play schemes and communicative interaction with other children. This chapter also shows the interrelation among language form (phonology, morphology, and syntax), content (semantics), and use (pragmatics) in children's language development, in spite of the separate presentation of these components. An overview of the highlights of children's language development between the ages of 3 and 5 can be found in Appendix A, which presents children's developmental milestones for hearing, listening, and talking from the ages of 3 to 5.

CHAPTER OBJECTIVES

After reading this chapter, you should understand:

◆ Language development during the preschool stage

◆ The major changes in vocabulary, syntax, morphology, semantics, and pragmatics that occur in language development during this period of development

◆ The major changes in children's cognitive skills that play a role in language development

◆ The multilinguistic differences when children from different language backgrounds are learning English, in addition to English dialect differences

◆ How to recognize signs of disorders in language and pragmatics

COGNITIVE DEVELOPMENT

Children between the ages of 2 and 6 are at the *preoperational stage* of Piaget's stages of cognitive development (Piaget, 1954). During the preschool stage, children's cognitive development emerges in the following areas (Segal, Bardige, Woika, & Leinfelder, 2006, p. 141):

Interested in learning new things

Intrigued by finding out how things work

Understand how things are alike and different

Able to count and sort objects into categories

Try out different ways of making objects work, move, or function

Learn from adults and imitate actions

Children's cognitive development in the preoperational stage includes an awareness of *time, space,* and *quantity* concepts. Time relations emerge (e.g., *first, next, before,* and *after*), as do spatial terms (e.g., *in* and *on*). More complex spatial terms emerge over time (e.g., *next to* and *between*). Quantity concepts also emerge in this stage (e.g., *less* and *more*).

Theory of Mind

One of the most important components of cognitive development at this stage is the acquisition of a **theory of mind (TOM)**, discussed in Chapter 1. TOM describes the ability to understand someone else's mental state (Miller, 2006). When children acquire a TOM, they have a better understanding of others' thoughts, beliefs, and feelings (Baron-Cohen, 1993, 1996), providing them with the ability to predict how someone will act and to explain why this person acted in a certain manner. These abilities support the understanding of certain *Wh-* questions, such as *why* (e.g., *Why is the boy crying?*). Children also are able to describe peoples' actions using **mental state verbs** (e.g., *think, know, believe*) and other terms that refer to the mind and human thought (de Villiers & de Villiers, 2003).

Growth in the use of mental state verbs (e.g., *think, know, feel,* and *believe*) occurs between the ages of 3 and 5 (Booth, Hall, Robison, & Kim, 1997). These verbs often develop through exposure to conversations about mental state concepts (Astington, 1990), such as discussions about someone's thoughts, beliefs, and actions.

Children with a TOM are able to express their own feelings and thoughts while also able to interpret those of others. This leads to improved interaction and conversation with others because children are better able to understand others' intentions or meaning during these events. TOM is also essential for understanding stories because children are able to then understand a character's actions (e.g., *why* the wolf dressed as Little Red Riding Hood's grandmother). Typically developing children lack a deep theory of mind before 3 years of age.

As noted in Chapter 1, toddlers, at 28 to 32 months, first begin to use (but do not truly understand) the mental state terms (e.g., *know, think, mean*). A deeper and true understanding of the mental state terms does not appear until around 31 months (Bartsch &Wellman, 1995). Tasks that ask children to "hide an object" from an adult show that younger children place the object on the adult's side of the screen (Gopnik & Meltzoff, 1994), not recognizing that the adult can actually see the object (even though the child cannot).

> After age 3, children develop an understanding of *what they can see* versus what the *other person can see* and place the object on their own side of the screen, hidden from the adult. This marks a major change in children's cognitive abilities and TOM.

Narrative or story knowledge helps children develop a TOM because stories often contain information about a character's feelings, beliefs, and thoughts, along with the language associated with these concepts (e.g., Little Red Riding Hood was *afraid* because she didn't *know* . . . the bears were *upset* because they *thought* . . .). Conversation also plays a role in developing a theory of mind, given that adults frequently converse about beliefs and mental states while using mental state terms, such as *think, know,* and *believe.*

Unlike typically developing children, children with a diagnosis of autism lack a theory of mind (Baron-Cohen, 1996). Differences between theory of mind in children with the diagnosis of autism and children with typical cognitive skills appear in the understanding of false beliefs (the belief that something is true when it is not), as shown in the example that follows (Wimmer & Perner, 1983), used to demonstrate the difference between typical and atypical children's cognitive skills.

A child puts a piece of candy in a kitchen *cabinet* and leaves the room to play. After he has left, his mother goes into the kitchen and moves the child's candy into a *drawer.* Note that the child has not witnessed the movement of the candy from the *cabinet* to the *drawer.*

Children were shown pictures of these events and asked, "Where will Maxi search for his candy: in the cabinet or the drawer?" When asked what Maxi would *think,* children with the diagnosis of autism answered that Maxi would search for the candy in the drawer (even though Maxi did not see his mother make the switch from *cabinet* to *drawer*).

Typically developing 4-year-olds answered that Maxi would look in the cabinet (the location where he originally placed the candy and *thought* it was located). Children who possess a theory of mind are able to understand what Maxi actually knew because they understand his beliefs. Because they possess a theory of mind, they are able to see things from his perspective.

Cognitive Factors That Develop During the Preschool Stage of Development

In addition to a theory of mind, there are additional cognitive factors that play a role in understanding false beliefs or what another person might think, feel, or believe. These cognitive factors consist of executive function and central coherence. Executive functions are mental processes that include planning, generating goal-directed behavior, organizing, maintaining attention, working memory (holds information in the mind to allow reasoning and processing), managing time and space, and problem solving. Without executive functions, responses are not internally controlled (Norman & Shallice, 1980) and strategic problem-solving skills are absent (Baddeley, 1991). Strategic problem-solving skills consist of the following (Zelazo, Carter, Reznick, & Frye, 1997):

Problem representation: Identify and analyze the problem and look beyond the obvious

Planning: Think of all possible solutions, evaluate the advantages or disadvantages of each solution, and consider the outcomes associated with similar problems (i.e., success or lack of success)

Execution: Solve the problem

Evaluation: Evaluate success in solving the problem

Central coherence involves interpreting the meaning of a context or situation by taking into account all aspects of a situation, along with any previous knowledge that relates to an event. Consequently, solving the false belief task that involves knowing what a child might think about the location of his candy could present problems. A child with autism would be unable to consider the entire sequence of events, such as where the candy was first placed, then moved without the child's knowledge, then searched for in the wrong location.

Children who lack central coherence favor parts and details over the whole (Happé, Briskman, & Frith, 2001). Thus, answers would focus only on one of the locations for the candy and ignore other factors, such as what the adult had done (moved the candy) and what the child might think (the candy was in the original location).

Another area of cognitive development during this stage of development is the loss of **egocentric** thought because children are no longer centered on their own thoughts and perspectives. By this stage of cognitive development, children have also achieved **decentration**. Decentration involves moving from a single perspective (the child's point of view) to viewing things from others' points of view (Piaget, 1962). Thus, there is a relationship between decentration and theory of mind because children are able to understand others' thoughts.

Cognitive development also includes **divergent thinking** (the ability to provide multiple solutions to a problem). Divergent thought is essential for creative thought and problem solving, allowing children to generate a number of solutions to a particular dilemma. This appears when another child wants to take a child's toy (a frequent occurrence in children's experiences). Divergent skills allow children to think of a more appropriate response than a physical tug-of-war over the toy.

Working Memory

Cognitive development also presents itself, partly, in **working memory**. Working memory is the system that allows us to retain information for processing and facilitates the temporary maintenance and manipulation of information. Working memory stores information in the mind for reasoning and comprehension and to make it available for further information processing in long-term memory. Consequently, children with intact working memory are able to retain lengthier directions and remember past events. Children use information related to past events to anticipate what might happen in the future, especially when there are similarities between current and prior experiences. *Anticipation* denotes the ability to predict the occurrence of an event, because it is preceded by a particular cause. An example is that a cup of juice may spill if pleased too close to the end of the table. Children are able to form models of current and prior events, allowing them to anticipate results (Klir, 1991). Consequently, children are now able to predict *what might happen next* in situations.

Magical Thinking

During this stage of development, we see that children engage in **magical thinking** (Subbotsky, 2010). Magical thinking occurs when a child assigns animacy to certain inanimate objects (e.g., *a talking rock* or *the belief that the Muppets live in the television set*). Learning to distinguish between fantasy (magic) and reality is an element of cognitive development. At age 3, children still practice magical thinking and may take adult comments literally (e.g., *Your nose is running*). Children begin to understand the difference between fantasy and reality as they move through the preschool period, but some fantasy continues to age 7 or 8, such as the belief in the existence of mythical figures (e.g., *Santa Claus*).

Expanded Symbolic Play Skills

Children's growing cognitive skills also appear in expanded symbolic play. Symbolic play appears when children use objects to represent other things (e.g., a box to represent a train) and use language to describe the activities associated with the play scheme (e.g., *Let's all get on the train*). Play skills expand at about 30 months, when children use a wider set of less frequently occurring activities, such as going to the store, school, or doctor.

Multischeme play sequences appear at about 3 years of age, when children expand single-scheme play (e.g., making a cake for a doll) to create a series of events (e.g., getting the ingredients to make a cake for the doll's birthday party, making the cake, serving the cake, cleaning up, and putting the doll to bed for the night). Another change occurs at around 3 to 3½, when children create a dialogue between themselves and their dolls or stuffed toys and talk for the toys.

Pretend play is related to the growth of cognitive development. Pretend play emerges from the observation of others in the environment, which involves decentering from the child's self and taking account of the actions of others (McCune-Nicolich, 1981). This is an important component of cognitive development because children with decentered play skills often possess better language skills (Fein, 1975). This is because pretend play requires the use of language to describe the context and behaviors associated with the play scheme. Pretend play may include playing house with imaginary food and furniture and imitation of adult behaviors (e.g., mopping the floor and feeding baby).

Tania and Marissa, at age 3, would play *house* in their room. Suddenly, we heard one of them crying. Running upstairs to see who had been hurt, we found that the twins were playing mother and baby, with one of the twins acting as the crying baby. The language used to create the pretend play scheme mirrored what they had observed in other contexts and in interactions between mothers and children.

Imagination develops further by 3½ to 4 years when children take on different roles in play. At this stage, they take on the roles of super hero, fire fighter, and other more familiar figures. Language develops in pretend play schemes because children must achieve the language skills to create and explain the play scheme to other children. By 3 to 5 years of age, children use their language skills to create and maintain a play scheme. There is less use of props because imagination has developed sufficiently so that children can create a more sophisticated play scheme.

PLAY AND LANGUAGE

Children establish play schemes based on making hypotheses about future events and solving problems. At around 4 years of age, they begin to produce **modal auxiliaries** (e.g., *can, could, would,* and *should*) and conjunctions (e.g., *and, but, if,* and *because*) that allow them to create more complex play schemes. Modal auxiliaries are verbs that are combined with other verbs to express obligation (*You **should** eat your dinner*), uncertainty (*I **could** go to the movies if my mother says okay*), ability (*I **can** lift this stone*), or permission (*You **can** use my bike*). Additional examples follow.

*We **can** make a house **because** my dad has big boxes in the garage*

*If we cut a hole in the box, we **could** make a window*

At age 5, when symbolic and pretend play skills involve coordinated sequences of events (e.g., shopping, cooking, and putting baby to bed), time relations appear, such as the temporal relations *first, next, before,* and *after*. Children acquire the distinction between the temporal relations *before* and *after* in the later stages of preschool development (Clark, 1971).

Children's cognitive and play skills develop during this stage. They have now achieved the language and cognitive skills that allow for the type of imaginative play that includes interaction with peers. Next we explore children's morphological development as they become aware of the smaller units in the meaning within words.

MORPHOLOGICAL DEVELOPMENT

As explained in Chapter 1, morphemes are the smallest units of meaning in a language. Note that the word *cat* /kæt/ cannot be reduced to one or two phonemes (e.g., /k/, /æ/, or /t/) without the loss of the meaning of this word. There are two categories of morphemes: free mor-

phemes (e.g., nouns, verbs, adjectives, adverbs, and prepositions) and bound morphemes (inflectional and derivational morphemes). An example of an inflectional morpheme is the plural -*s* (e.g., *cats*), and an example of a derivational morpheme is the use of -*er* to change the verb *farm* to a noun (i.e., *farmer*).

Around age 2, children begin to produce inflectional morphemes with derivational morphemes learned later. By age 5, children generally acquire derivational morphemes that act as noun suffixes, understanding and producing such words as *farmer* and *teacher* (*farm* + *er* and *teach* + *er*). The derivational -*ist* morpheme is acquired somewhat later (e.g., *pianist* and *cyclist*). There is a description of children's morphological development from ages 3 to 5 in Table 6–1.

Children acquire the regular form of adjectives between 3 and 5 years of age, producing the comparative -*er* and the superlative form -*est* suffixes (McLaughlin,

Table 6–1. *Grammatical Morpheme Development From Ages 3 to 5*

Age (years)	Morpheme	Example
3	Regular Plural -*s*	*My books are fun*
3	Possessive *'s*	*That is the cat's bowl*
3	Uncontractible Copula *be* (use of the *be* verb without contraction)	*He is (in response to "who is in the box?")*
3	Articles *a, the, an*	*We have a new doggie*
4–5	Regular Past Tense -*ed*	*He kicked me.*
4–5	Contractible Auxiliary *'s* (*am, is, are* contracted)	*Daddy's eating*

Source: From *Language Development: Understanding Language Diversity in the Classroom* (p. 144), by S. Levey & S. Polirstok (Eds.), 2011, Los Angeles, CA: Sage. Reprinted with permission.

1998). The following example describes the use of these morphemes with the word *big*.

Bigger   add the morpheme -*er* to the word *big*

Biggest   add the morpheme -*est* to the word *big*

There are irregular adjective forms that function as exceptions to the rule of adding the regular suffixes -*er* and -*est*. Examples are shown below for the words *good* and *bad*.

Comparative Form   *better, worse*

Superlative Form   *best, worst*

Morphophonemic rules refer to the changes that occur in a phoneme in certain environments because of the influence of the preceding sound. For example, the plural morpheme -*s* changes in certain environments, becoming voiced when following a voiced sound (e.g., /g/) and remaining unvoiced when following another unvoiced sound (e.g., /t/).

Dog + plural -s   /dɔg/ /dɔgz/

Cat + plural -s   /kæt/ /kæts/

Children's knowledge of plurals was examined with the novel word *wug* (Gleason, 1958). She presented children with an unfamiliar picture of a bird-like creature and told them this was a *wug*. Children were then presented with two pictures of the *wug* and asked to complete the sentence "*Now there are two* _____?" Preschool-age children, ages 4 to 5, were most successful, answering that there were two *wugs* /wʌgz/ (with a final /z/).

There are other changes that occur when certain words become plurals, shown in the following examples:

Horse + plural -s
   horse /hɔɚs/   horses /hɔɚsɪz/

Glass + plural -s
   glass /glæs/   glasses /glæsɪz/

Knife + -plural -s
   knife /knɑɪf/   knives /knɑɪvz/

Children were presented with another novel word, *tass*, chosen to elicit the plural form /ɪz/, as in *tasses* (similar to *glasses*). Difficulty with this plural form appeared for both preschool and first graders, who produced the plural form as *tass* (i.e., *Two tass*). Difficulty may be caused by the perception that the plural form already exists, because of the "s" ending on words, such as *glasses* and *horses*.

There are also changes to certain morphemes because of the effect of stress (discussed in Chapter 4). Certain syllables and morphemes do not receive stress or emphasis, as shown in the first and last syllables in the word *banana* and the auxiliary verb *is* (stressed syllables capitalized and bolded).

baNAna

HE* is *NICE

In these examples, the middle syllable in the word *banana* and the auxiliary verb *is* do not receive stress or emphasis, leading to children's perception difficulties for unstressed syllables and auxiliary verbs (Levey & Schwartz, 2002). Perceptual difficulties often result in the omission of certain syllables in young children's productions of words (Wexler, 1994), shown in the following examples. These perceptual difficulties occur because certain sounds in syllables are produced with less emphasis or stress than others. Note that parentheses indicate omission in the early stages of morphosyntactic development, although children acquire these unstressed forms by age 4 (Rice & Wexler, 1998).

> *Patsy walk(s) home*
> Third person *-s*

> *She (is) walking*
> Auxiliary verb *is* (auxiliary is used with another verb)

> *She (is) happy*
> Copula *is* (copula creates a link between the subject and attribute)

Early in the preschool period of development, children also have difficulty with the production of consonant clusters (two or three adjacent consonants at the beginning or end of a word). Words that contain consonant (C) clusters are shown in the following examples.

> *Cats* *-ts* **CVCC**
> Consonant cluster word final

> *Star* *st-* **CCVC**
> Consonant cluster word initial

> *Spring* *spr-* **CCCVC**
> Consonant cluster word initial

As noted, children may have difficulty with consonant clusters that occur in the final position in certain words (e.g., *cats* and *cuts*). Difficulty with these final clusters may also affect the production of inflectional morphemes, such as plural *-s* in *cats* (Bernhardt & Stemberger, 1998).

Production difficulties are also associated with words that end with certain phonemes (Johnson & Morris, 2007; Oetting & Horohov, 1997): Children may have difficulty producing the regular past tense inflectional morpheme *-ed* after stops, fricatives, and affricates:

> Stops /p, b, t, d, k, g/
> *capped, grabbed, batted, added, biked, bagged*

> Fricatives /f, v, ð, s, z,/
> *laughed, loved, bathed, passed, raised*

> Affricates /tʃ, dʒ/
> *pitched, judged*

Based on these examples, children may be better able to produce the *-ed* in the word *rolled* (i.e., /l/+ *-ed*) than the word *walked* (i.e., /k/ + *-ed*).

> Younger children are less likely to produce the past tense morpheme *-ed* in words that end in sounds made with the front portion of the tongue (e.g., /t, d, s, z, n/) (Berko, 1958; Marchman, Wulfeck, & Weismer, 1999). Consequently, children are less likely to produce the past tense morpheme in the word *wanted* than in the word *kicked*.

SYNTACTIC DEVELOPMENT

Children's syntax becomes adultlike by 4 years of age (Gopnik, 1997). At about 30 months, children begin sentence production with declarative sentences that take the form of subject + verb + object (e.g., *Daddy eat cookie*). At this age, they start to produce a greater variety of syntactic structures (e.g., questions and comments), expanded semantic content (e.g., different types of meanings), and expanded sentence lengths and complex structures. During the preschool stage, children begin to produce sentences that include auxiliary verbs (e.g., *is* and *am*) and morphological inflections, such as *-ing* (e.g., *Daddy is going*). By age 3½, children produce declarative sentences with double auxiliaries (e.g., *You will have to come*). Examples of the acquisition of children's sentence forms can be found in Table 6–2.

Table 6–2. The Acquisition of Sentence Forms*

Stage	Age in months	Declarative	Negative	Interrogative	Embedding	Conjoining
Early I (MLU: 1–1.5)	12–22	Agent + action; action + object	Single word -*no, all gone, gone*; *negative* + X	*Yes/no* asked with raising intonation on a single word; *what* and *where*		Serial naming without *and*
Late I (MLU: 1.5–2.0)	22–26	Subj. + verb + obj. appears	*No* and *not* used interchangeably	That + X; *what* + noun phrase + (*doing*)?	Prepositions *in* and *on* appear	*And* appears
Early II (MLU: 2.0–2.25)	27–28	Subj. + copula + complement appears		*Where* + noun phrase + (*going*)?		
Late II (MLU; 2.25–2.5)	28–30	Basic subject – verb – object used by most children	*No, not, don't,* and *can't* used interchangeably;	*What* or *where* + subj. + pred. Earliest inversion appears	*Gonna, wanna, gotta,* etc. appear	
Early III (MLU: 2.5–2.75)	31–32	Subj. + aux. + verb + obj. appears; auxiliary verb forms *can, do, have, will,* and *be* appear	Negative element placed between subject and predicate	Copula in *What/where* + copula + subj.		*But, so, or,* and *if* appear

162

continues

Stage	Age in months	Declarative	Negative	Interrogative	Embedding	Conjoining
Late III (MLU: 2.75 – 3.0)	33–34	Auxiliary verb appears with copula in subj. + aux. + copula + X	*Won't* appears	Auxiliary verbs *do, can,* and *will* begin to appear in questions; inversion of subject and auxiliary verb appears in yes/no questions		
Early IV (MLU: 3.0–3.5)	35–37		Negative appears with auxiliary verbs (subj. + aux. + neg. + verb)	Inversion of auxiliary verb and subject in *wh-* questions	Object noun – phrase complements appear with verbs such as *think, guess,* and *show;* embedded *wh-* questions	Causal conjoining with *and* appears (most children cannot produce this form until late stage V); *because* appears
Late IV (MLU: 3.5–3.75)	38–40	Double auxiliary verbs appear in subj. + aux. + aux. + verb + X	Adds *isn't, aren't, doesn't,* and *didn't*	Inversion of copula, and subject in yes/no questions; adds *do* to yes/no questions; adds *when* and *how*	Infinitive phrases appear at the ends of sentences	

Table 6–2. *continued*

Stage	Age in months	Declarative	Negative	Interrogative	Embedding	Conjoining
Stage V (MLU: 3.75–4.5)	41–46	Indirect object appears in subj. + aux. + verb + ind. obj. + obj.	Adds *wasn't, wouldn't, couldn't,* and *shouldn't*; negative appears with copula in subj. + copula + neg.	Adds modals; stabilizes inverted auxiliary; some adult-like tag questions appear	Relative clauses appear in object position; multiple embeddings appear by late stage V; infinitive phrases with same object as the main verb	Causal conjoining with *if* appears; three-clause declaratives appear
Post - V (MLU: 4.5 +)	47+		Adds indefinite forms *nobody, no one, none,* and *nothing*; has difficulty with double negatives	Questions other than one word *Why* questions appear; negative interrogative is beyond age 5	Gerunds appear; relative clauses attached to subject; embedding an conjoining appear within same sentence above and MLU of 5.0	Causal conjoining with *because* appears with *when, but,* and *so* beyond and MLU of 5.0; embedding and conjoining appear within the same sentence above a MLU of 5.0

*Based on approximately 50% of children using a structure.

Source: From *Language Development: An Introduction* (7th ed.), by R. E. Owens, 2008, Upper Saddle River, NJ: Pearson Education, Inc. Reprinted with permission.

As children's language develops, they begin to use a variety of sentence types.

Expanded noun phrases: *My **big red ball** is lost*

Expanded verb phrases: *He **ran fast and fell down***

Negative constructions: *I **don't** want peas*

Yes/no questions: ***Can** I have a cookie?*

Wh- questions: ***What** did you get for a present?*

Causal constructions: *He didn't get a cookie **because** he was bad*

Conditional constructions: ***If** I eat my peas, I'll get a cookie*

Temporal constructions: ***When** we get home, do I have to go to bed?*

Table 6–3 presents examples of pre-school-age children's morphosyntactic development as they acquire morphemes and syntax expands.

Interrogative sentences appear early. At around age 3, children are able to invert subjects and auxiliary verbs (e.g., *Is daddy coming, too?*). Earlier acquired *Wh-* words (i.e., *what* and *where*) show inversion (e.g., *What is that?*), whereas inversion will not appear in later acquired *Wh-* forms (e.g., ***Why** he is crying? **When** he go?* and ***How** he go?*).

Imperative sentences are produced by younger children using single words (e.g., *cookie!*). As pragmatic skills develop, children are able to express requests in a more polite manner by adding *please* and using modal auxiliaries at about 30 months (e.g., *can, could, should, would*) to produce sentences, such as *Can I have a cookie.*

Table 6–3. *Morphosyntactic Development From Ages 3 to 5*

Age	Morphosyntactic Characteristics	Examples
3	Declaratives	*I'm running*
	Interrogatives	*What is that?*
	Imperatives	*Throw the ball*
	Negative	*No more milk please*
	Use of quantities	*Can I have **two** cookies?*
	Use of adjectives	*He is a **big** doggie*
	Use of adverbs	*He runs **fast***
3½ to 4	Embedded phrases in sentences	*The boy **on the bike** is my friend*
	Subordinate clauses in sentences	*He's crying **because he fell***
4 to 5	Conjoined sentences using the conjunctions and, or, but, and because	*I ate the cookie **and** Seth drank the milk*

Source: From *Language Development: Understanding Language Diversity in the Classroom* (p. 144), by S. Levey & S. Polirstok (Eds.), 2011, Los Angeles, CA: Sage. Reprinted with permission.

Negative sentence forms begin with sentences, such as *I **not** crying* at about 27 months. Negative interrogatives generally do not emerge until age 5 (Owens, 2012). At that time, children produce the negative modal auxiliary verbs *can't, won't,* and *don't.*

Can't I have a cookie?

As noted in Chapter 5. it is important to understand that double negatives are a feature of some dialects of English with the production of such sentences as *Nobody don't like me.* These productions reflect *differences* that mark the rich variety of different forms of English and should not be viewed as signs of a language disorder.

Complex Sentence Development

When mean length of utterance (MLU) extends beyond 3.0, sentence complexity appears in children's language (Lahey, 1988; Paul, 1981, 2001). Thus, at about age 3, complex constructions appear (Diessel & Tomasello, 2001). Examples of complex constructions consist of sentences that contain a main clause, such as the phrase *I think* or *I see* and a subordinate clause beginning with a subordinate conjunction (e.g., *after, although, until, since, that, which, while,* and *if*). The subordinate clause is bolded in the example that follows.

After she sneezed, *she wiped her nose*

Three types of complex sentences are produced at this stage (Stefani, 2007), when children produce three-word utterances.

Coordination of clauses using the conjunction *and*: *Bread **and** butter*

Noun phrase (propositional) complements: *I think/know that **you did it***

Infinitives (with the same subject, i.e., *I*): *I want **to eat** a cookie*

Continued development appears in the production of embedded clauses when children begin to produce three- to four-word utterances:

Infinitives with different subjects (i.e., *I* and *you*): *I want you **to go home***

Relative clauses: *There's the dog **that ate my cookie***

Examples of children's complex sentences are shown in Table 6–4. It is expected that at least 20% of children's utterances will be complex by age 4 or 5.

Coordination

Sentence complexity increases in terms of sentential (sentence) and phrasal (phrase) coordination. In sentential coordination, two separate events are combined through use of the conjunction *and*. Note that the first event (*Daniel went to school*) and the second event (*He forgot his lunch*) can each stand alone as a complete sentence in the following example:

Daniel went to school

He forgot his lunch

These clauses or sentences can be combined through coordination.

*Daniel went to school **and** he forgot his lunch*

In phrasal coordination, the connective *and* is used and the redundant

Table 6–4. *Complex Sentence Descriptions and Examples*

Full propositional complement (Object noun phrase complement): Contains "cognitive" verb such as *think, guess, wish, know, hope, wonder, show, remember, pretend, mean, forget, say, tell*; may or may not contain *that*	I *hope* (that) we go to lunch soon. *Forget* that you did it.
Gerund: Contains an *-ing* form that functions as a noun (is not directly related to the auxiliary verb)	*Swimming* is fun.
Participle: Contains an *-ing* form that functions as an adjective (modifies a noun or pronoun) (is not related to the auxiliary verb)	I see the man *driving* down the street.
Simple infinitive: Contains *to* followed by a *verb*; subject is the same as the main sentence. This does not include early-developing catenatives such as *gonna, wanna, gotta, sposta, hafta, let's, lemme*	I need *to go.* They want *to sleep* in the tent.
Infinitive clause with different subject: Contains an infinitive (to + verb); the subject of the infinitive clause is different from the main sentence	I want *the baby to eat.* He needs *the dog to go away.*
Unmarked infinitive: Contains *make, help, watch,* or *let* without a *to* marker	*Watch* me run. *Let* me do it.
Simple *wh-* clause: Contains *who, what, where, when, why, how*; does not contain an infinitive *to* marker	See *how* fast I am. I remember *what* we do.
***Wh-* infinitive:** Contains a *wh-* word (*what, where, who, how, when*) and an infinitive	I don't know *what to wear.* You know *where to put it.*
Relative clause: Contains an embedded phrase that functions as an adjective; modifies an object or a subject noun phrase; may be marked by *who, which, that*	The man *who is running* is fast. That is the one *that I like.*
Simple conjoining: Contains two clauses that are joined by a conjunction	I ate fast *so* I could leave. I like cake *and* I like ice cream.
Embedded and conjoined: Contains both an embedded and conjoined clause; may include a catenative; will have 3 or more verbs	*Swimming* is fun because I like *to get* wet. I want *to stay* here, *but* my mommy says no.
Multiple embedding: Contains more than one embedded and conjoined clause; may include a catenative; will have 3 or more verbs	I *wanna start to run* now. I *know* that we have *to eat* soon.

Source: From "Identifying Embedded and Conjoined Complex: Making It Simple," by S. A. Steffani, 2007, *Contemporary Issues in Communication Science and Disorders, 34,* pp. 44–54. All rights reserved. Reprinted with permission.

element is deleted. In the example that follows, note that the pronoun *he* is deleted (**ellipsis**) because this pronoun is redundant (i.e., the listener knows that *he* refers to *Daniel*).

> *Daniel went to school **and** forgot his lunch*

The earliest forms of coordination consist of noun + noun phrases (Tager-Flusberg, de Villiers, & Hakuta, 1982), as shown in the following example:

> *He having carrots* (noun) ***and** peas* (noun)   26 months

In children's later language development, coordination first appears in frequently heard phrases (e.g., *bread and butter*) to respond to questions (e.g., *What do you want to eat?*).

Sentential and phrasal coordination appear at 2½ to 3 years of age (Bernstein & Levey, 2009) with sentential coordination for events at different times and places (e.g., *I ate my breakfast at home and took a nap in school*) and phrasal coordination for events at the same time and place (e.g., *I fell down and cried*). Bloom (1991) provided the following order of acquisition of *and* coordination.

Additives: the use of *and* to connect two propositions that go together
> *Mother is reading **and** Daddy is mowing the lawn*

Temporal: the use of *and* to designate a sequential ordering of events
> *Mommy will bake the cookies **and** let me put the sprinkles on top*

Causal: the use of *and* to indicate that one event led to another
> *She put a bandage on **and** it didn't hurt any more*

Adversative: the use of *and* or *but* to indicate a contrast relationship
> *I thought this was my book **but** it might be yours*

Noun Phrase or Propositional Complements

Children begin to use propositional complements following cognitive or mental state verbs. A propositional complement is introduced by a mental or cognitive verb, such as *think, guess, wish, know, hope, wonder, show, remember, pretend, mean, forget, say,* and *tell* (Stefani, 2007). The propositional complement may or may not contain *that*, shown in the example produced by Micah, at age 3½ (the complement is bolded).

> *I think **I want to wear this shirt today***

Examples of the production of propositional complements are shown next, which were produced by children aged 4 and 5, respectively (Lee & Rescorla, 2008, p. 33).

> *I thought **that the policeman was riding a motorcycle***

> *Let's pretend **that he knew somebody was coming over and he brought us a surprise***

Infinitives With the Same Subject

Infinitive phrases consist of *to* plus a verb (e.g., *to turn*). Children develop infinitive phrase embedding at ages 3 to 4 (Angel, 2009). Examples of the infinitive phrase include the following. Note that the second example consists of the embedded form.

> ***To run** is fun*

> *I like **to run** all day*

There are also more complex forms, such as *Wh-* infinitives.

*He did not say **when to open** my present*

The acquisition of the infinitive phrase begins at ages 2 and 3, when children use the infinitive forms of *wanna* and *gonna*. After acquiring *gonna, wanna, gotta, sposta, hafta,* and *lemme,* children produce a simple infinitive, with *to* followed by a verb (Stefani, 2007, p. 46). This occurs when children's MLU is between 4.0 and 5.0 (Paul, 2001). These early forms are gradually expanded as *I want to* and *I am going to.* For example, younger children may say *I wanna swim* at age 2 to 3, but will say *I want to swim* at age 3 to 4. In the example that follows, this utterance contains a single subject (i.e., *I*).

*I want **to go***

Around 3½, children produce the infinitive clause with at least two different subjects (i.e., *I* and *baby*).

*I want the baby **to eat***

Another level of development consists of the unmarked infinitive, produced with the verbs *make, help, watch,* or *let* without the use of the word *to* that marks the infinitive form (e.g., *I want you to watch me run*).

Watch me run

Relative Clause Development

A relative clause is a subordinate clause introduced by a relative pronoun (*that, which, whichever, who, whoever, whom, whomever, whose,* and *of which*). Relative clauses modify and follow nouns. They are dependent clauses that cannot stand alone. Relative clauses allow children to construct complex sentences and to qualify (offer further explanation) or restrict (limit) the meaning of a sentence, as shown in these examples:

*The boy **who is wearing a hat** is my friend*

*The books **that are on the red table** are free*

A relative clause can modify or describe the subject (subjective relative clause) or the object (objective relative clause) in a sentence. The following example shows the modification of an objective relative clause:

The story is about a little girl (object) ***who couldn't find her way home***

The following example shows the modification of a subjective relative clause:

The boy (subject) ***who is in the Kanga class** is my friend*

Children produce the modification of an objective relative clause after 5 years of age, but the modification of a subjective relative clause does not appear until at least age 7 (Bernstein & Levey, 2009).

> **Equative** clauses, containing a **copula** (a word used to connect the subject and predicate, such as *is*), and complement emerge last (Dever, 1978). A complement is a word, phrase, or clause that completes the meaning of an expression or assigns a property to a subject or object in the sentence, as shown in the following examples. In the first example, the predicate adjective

(*good*) is a subject complement. In the second example, the predicate adjective (*tired*) is an object complement.

*Jason is **good***

*Running made Jason **tired***

THE INTERACTION BETWEEN SYNTAX AND SEMANTICS

It is important to understand the connection between syntax (sentence structure) and semantics (meaning). This relationship can be described by **thematic roles** (the semantic relationships between verbs and noun phrases in sentences). Examples of thematic roles follow.

Agent: The one who performs an action
***Jane** threw the ball*

Patient: Something or somebody that undergoes a change specifically implied by the verb
*Jane threw the **ball***

Location: The place where action takes place
*The sun shines in **New York***

Goal: The place to which action is directed
*Put it on the **table***

Source: The place from which an action originates
*He ran from **home** to school*

Instrument: The means by which an action is performed
*She cut paper with **scissors***

Experiencer: One who perceives something
***He** heard her sing*

Causative: A natural force that causes a change
*The **wind** blew my hat away*

Possessor: One who owns or has something
***Baby's** rattle is on the floor*

Recipient: One who receives something
***Bob** got a cookie from Jane*

The correspondence between semantics and syntax is shown in how thematic roles (semantics) are linked to sentence structure (syntax). The sentence that follows demonstrates this correspondence.

Bob kissed Jane

The verb *kissed* involves the two individuals (i.e., *Bob* and *Jane*). The verb *kissed* describes the event, and the nouns *Bob* and *Jane* refer to the participants in the event. The verb is the **predicate** and the nouns are each an **argument**. The *argument* is an expression that helps to complete the meaning of a predicate. In the next example, *Bob* is the argument and *yawned* is the predicate.

Bob yawned

In the second example, *Jane* is the argument and *put* is the predicate with the two additional arguments *book* and *on the table*. For these arguments, thematic roles consist of *Jane* (agent), *book* (patient), and *on the table* (location).

Sentence	Thematic Role
Jane	Agent
put	
the book	Patient
on the table	Location

This set of relationships between *Bob* and *yawned* and between *book* and *Jane*) is called an argument structure.

The arguments in a sentence are determined by the meaning of the verb. As discussed in Chapter 5, certain verbs, such as *hit*, are two-argument verbs (expressing a relationship between two things) and require a transitive clause with a direct object (e.g., *Daddy hit the ball*). In contrast, the verb *cry* is a one-argument verb (e.g., *Mary cries*). As an intransitive verb, it does not require an object. There are differences in the number of nouns required for the verbs *laugh, cry,* and *frown* (i.e., one noun) and the verbs *hit, throw,* and *carry* (i.e., at least two). Thus, the meaning of the verb determines the argument structure. Syntactic development consists of a child's ability to associate predicates, such as "want," "more," and "go," with arguments (MacWhinney, 2003, p. 476).

Children learn to use the syntactic features of words to predict meaning. For example, the determiner "a" indicates a count noun (e.g., *a lamp* and *a cookie*), the inflectional morpheme *-ing* indicates a verb (e.g., *is running* and *is jumping*), and *some* indicates a mass noun (e.g., *some sugar* and *some sand*). In this way, children can capitalize on syntactic features to determine meaning. For example, children, aged 3 to 5 years of age, were presented with three pictures that depicted an action, a countable object, and a substance in a container. Children were then asked to identify the picture associated with the words *sibbing, the sib,* and *some sib* (Brown, 1957). Children identified *sibbing* as the action, *the sib* as the countable object, and *some sib* as the substance, showing that they were able to use the syntactic features of these novel words to predict the semantic properties (meaning) (Pinker, 1984). The article *the* cued the identity of a count noun, and the inflectional morpheme *-ing* indicated, in this case, a verb. In summary, children are aware of syntactic-semantic mappings that help them discover the meaning of words.

AN EXPLANATION OF SYNTACTIC DEVELOPMENT

It is also important to understand how syntactic development occurs. One theory of syntactic development is that children begin to learn adult forms of language by reproducing specific items of adult speech, such as words and phrases (Hodges, Krugler, & Law, 2004; Tomasello, 2000, 2003). This is termed the item-based theory of children's syntactic development. In this theory, verbs play an important role in their language development. In the early period, children's use of verbs is limited and item-based. This means that children use some verbs in certain syntactic structures (sentences) but not in others, as shown in the following examples of a child's productions (Tomasello, 1992b):

Cut: Used only for the action of cutting paper:
  Cut paper

Draw: Used for drawing, drawing on something, and drawing for someone:
  Draw, Draw on, Draw for

This example shows that children do not necessarily connect the use of words, given that some verbs may be used in only one type of sentence frame (e.g., *cut* for only paper), whereas other verbs may be used in complex frames and types (e.g., *draw, draw on, draw for*). This language behavior is explained by the verb island hypothesis, in which each verb has its own island of organization in the early period of learning language (Tomasello, 2000, p. 157). Verb island patterns appear when children begin to learn adult syntax (Tomasello, 1992b). Additional examples follow, showing that children learn verbs on a one-by-one basis with no connection between individual verbs and no generalization (use of a verb in different frames, such as *get + stick, find it + phone*, and *gone ball*).

Find + funny, bird, chess, bricks, ball, stick

Get + block, bottle, phone, towel, coffee, mama

Gone + Peter Pan, raisins, hammer, French fries

With verbs as the organizing element, children gradually construct adultlike syntactic constructions. At first, only certain verbs may be used to produce complex syntactic utterances (e.g., *I want to play* and *I want him to play*), even though other verbs exist in their vocabularies (e.g., *have, got, like, need*) (Hodges et al., 2004, p. 2). After age 3, children's language becomes more adultlike as they add other verbs to their complex sentence structures. In other words, their early verbs are no longer connected to specific syntactic patterns and constructional islands.

As syntax develops, children also begin to generalize and create schematic representations not found in adults' pro-

ductions (Bowerman, 1982). At this stage of syntactic development, the following productions show children's growth in the awareness of language structure with verb generalizations produced (e.g., *throwed/threw, eated/ate*, and *goed/went*). Note that these generalizations do not occur until children become aware of language and begin to form their own hypotheses about how language works.

Kendall *fall* that toy.	2;3
Who *deaded* my kitty cat?	2;6
They just *cough* me.	2;8
Don't *giggle* me.	3;0
I am gonna put the washrag in and *disappear* something under the washrag.	3;7

> These examples show that children's language becomes more complex at around 2 years of age. Their innate cognitive abilities provide them with the ability to learn the meaning of words that are similar (e.g., *pour/fill*) and to learn the meaning of words that are associated with specific linguistic contexts (e.g., *get, give, off*).

In summary, children's early language is organized in concrete, item-based linguistic schemas. This means that only certain verbs may be used to produce syntactic constructions, even though other verbs exist in their vocabularies. After age 3, children are able to analyze the patterns in adults' complex syntactic structures. Consequently, they now add verbs to a variety of other complex sentence structures.

There are other theories of syntactic development, referred to as *bootstrapping*. In these theories, there are cues in language that serve as bootstraps, which allow children to pull themselves up to higher language abilities. The syntactic **bootstrapping** hypothesis states that children learn language by analyzing syntactic structure and morphological markers associated with a novel or new word (Gleitman, 1990). These morphological markers that identify nouns consist of determiners (e.g., *a, the, an, some, any*) and adjectives (e.g., *big, dirty, dark*), whereas inflectional morphemes mark action words (e.g., *-ing*). These morphological markers allow children to point to the picture of an object when hearing the novel word *grop* and point to a picture that shows action when hearing the novel word *gropping* (Brown, 1957).

The semantic bootstrapping theory hypothesizes that children learn the meaning of verbs by observing their use in the environment. Children use semantic information to understand and learn syntax or sentence structures. For example, children link or associate the semantic roles of agent or patient to grammatical roles, such as subject and direct object. The following example shows this link:

Aaron	*is drinking*	*milk*
Agent	Action	Patient
Subject	Verb	Direct Object

In semantic bootstrapping, children bootstrap into syntactic structure by understanding that the agent links to the subject position and the patient to the object position. Children make errors in linking, even between 3 and 6 years of age (Bowerman, 1982), as shown in the following example:

*Can I **fill** some salt into the bear?*

In this case, the verb *fill* (associated with the patient *bear*) has been confused with the verb *pour* (associated with the agent *I*).

*Can I **pour** some salt into the bear?*

Bootstrapping allows children to understand that the focus of *fill* is associated with the direct object *bear*.

*Can I **fill the bear?***

In summary, children's syntax is adultlike by 4 years of age. They are able to take advantage of the language spoken in the environment, based on their cognitive conceptual skills.

SYNTACTIC DIFFERENCES

There are also differences among the syntactic structures (sentences) of different languages, along with differences associated with the structures of different English dialects. These variations lead to *differences* in the production of sentences in English. We begin with a presentation of language differences that may be observed among Asian speakers (Table 6–5) and that are consistent with learning English as a second language (Roseberry-McKibbin, 2008). Knowledge of these differences contributes to both evidence-based assessment and intervention (the provision of services based on knowledge

Table 6–5. *Language Differences Commonly Observed Among Asian Speakers*

Language Characteristics	Sample English Utterances
Omission of plurals	Here are 2 piece of toast. I got 5 finger on each hand.
Omission of copula	He going home now. They eating.
Omission of possessive	I have Phuong pencil. Mom food is cold.
Omission of past tense morpheme	We cook dinner yesterday. Last night she walk home.
Past tense double marking	He didn't went by himself.
Double negative	They don't have no books.
Subject-verb-object relationship	I messed up it.
Differences/omissions	He like.
Misordering of interrogatives	You are going now?
Misuse or omission of prepositions	She is in home. He goes to school 8:00.
Misuse of pronouns	She husband is coming. She said her wife is here.
Omission and/or overgeneralization of articles (overuse "the")	Boy is sick/I gave him the [a] cookie
Incorrect use of comparatives	This book is gooder than that book.
Omission of conjunctions	You _____ I going to the beach.
Omission, lack of inflection on auxiliary "do"	She _____ not take it. He do not have enough.
Omission, lack of inflection on	She have no money.
Forms of "have"	We _____ been the store.

Source: From *Multicultural Students with Special Language Needs: Practical Strategies for Assessment* (p. 129), by C. Roseberry-McKibbin, 2008, Oceanside, CA: Academic Communication Associates. Reprinted with permission.

of the differences and values of the people receiving services).

There are also language differences commonly observed among native Spanish speakers learning English (Table 6–6).

There are also examples of utterances produced by speakers of African American English (AAE), presented in Table 6–7. As noted in Chapter 5, these differences emerge from the influence on AAE of West African

Table 6–6. *Language Differences Commonly Observed Among Spanish Speakers*

Language Characteristics	Sample English Utterances
1. Adjective comes after noun.	The house green is big.
2. *'s* is omitted in plurals, possessives, and regular third person present tense	We have five plate here. The girl book is brown. The baby cry.
3. Past tense *-ed* is often omitted.	We walk yesterday.
4. Double negatives are used.	I don't have no more.
5. Negative imperatives may be used; *No* is used instead of *don't*.	No touch the hot stove.
6. *"No"* may be used before a verb to signify negation.	The kid no cross the street.
7. Superiority is demonstrated by using *more* before an adjective in a similar manner to the use of *mas* in Spanish	The cake is more big.
8. The adverb often follows the verb.	He drives very fast his motorcycle.
9. Post-noun modifiers are used.	This is the book of my sister.
10. Articles may be used with body parts.	I bruised the knee.
11. *"Have"* may be used in place of the copula when talking about age.	I *have* 12 years (Instead of I *am* 12 years old).
12. Articles are often omitted.	Papa is going to store.
13. When the subject has been identified in the previous sentence, it may be omitted in the next sentence.	Mama is sad. Lost her purse.
14. There may be noun-verb inversion in questions.	What this is? (Instead of *what is this?*)

Source: From *Multicultural Students with Special Language Needs: Practical Strategies for Assessment* (p. 104), by C. Roseberry-McKibbin, 2008, Oceanside, CA: Academic Communication Associates. Reprinted with permission.

Table 6–7. *Examples of Utterances by Speakers of African American Language*

Mainstream American English	African American Language
That boy looks like me.	That boy, he look like me.
If he kicks it, he'll be in trouble.	If he kick it, he be in trouble.
When the lights are off, it's dark.	When the lights be off, it dark.
It could be somebody's pet.	It could be somebody pet.
Her feet are too big.	Her feet is too big.
I'll get something to eat.	I will get me something to eat.
She is dancing and the music's on.	She be dancin' an' the music on.
What kind of cheese do you want?	What kind of cheese you want?
My brother's name is Joe.	My brother name is Joe.
I raked the leaves outside.	I raked the leaves outside.
After the recital, they shook my hand.	After the recital, they shaketed my hand.
They are standing around.	They is just standing around.
He is a basketball star.	He a basketball star.
They are in cages.	They be in cages.
It's not like a tree or anything.	It not like a tree or nothin'.
He does like to fish.	He do like to fish.
They are going to swim.	They gonna swim.
Mom already repaired the car.	Mom done repair the car.

Source: From *Multicultural Students with Special Language Needs: Practical Strategies for Assessment* (p. 81), by C. Roseberry-McKibbin, 2008, Oceanside, CA: Academic Communication Associates. Reprinted with permission.

languages, French, Native American languages, and English. Also note that knowledge of these differences is essential to distinguish differences from true disorders.

We next explore children's phonological processes, which we first reviewed in Chapter 5. At ages 3 to 5, certain processes disappear while others remain. However, children achieve most sounds in their native language by age 4.

PRESCHOOL CHILDREN'S PHONOLOGICAL PROCESSES

As children's language skills develop, they are better able to perceive sound contrasts (e.g., /p-b/) and establish more adultlike representations of sounds in words. Children's preference for a strong-weak stress pattern (e.g., *nana* for the target word *banana*) is lost by age 3, and they produce the unstressed syllables in words (e.g., *banana*) (Gerken, 1991). Phonological processes describe differences from an adult's production of target words. Children's phonological processes fall into two basic categories (Bernthal & Bankson, 2004): whole word processes (simplifications of words, syllables, or contrasts between sounds) and segment change processes (changes in sounds). Examples of these processes follow.

Whole Word Processes

Whole word processes include reduplication, final consonant deletion, cluster reduction, and unstressed syllable omission.

Reduplication: Daddy /dædi/ produced as *dada* [dædæ]

Final consonant deletion: Bus /bʌs/ produced as *buh* [bʌ]

Cluster reduction: Stop /stɑp/ produced as *top* [tɑp]

Unstressed syllable omission: Banana /bənænə/ produced as *nana* [bənænə]

Segment Change Processes

Segment changes are common in the speech of preschoolers, usually appearing when children produce longer sentences. There are increased demands on the sequencing of sounds in words when longer sentences are produced. Segment changes in children's productions are classified by place (where a sound is produced) or manner (how a sound is produced). Among these processes are fronting, backing, stopping, and gliding.

Fronting occurs when a sound that should be produced in a posterior place (e.g., /ʃ, ʒ, k, g/) is produced with an anterior sound (e.g., /s, z, t, d/. This process disappears by 2½ to 3 years of age.

key /ki/ produced as *tea* [ti]

Backing occurs when children replace anterior sounds with posterior sounds, such as the front sound /t/ with the back sound /k/.

tap /tæp/ produced as cap [kæp]

Stopping occurs when children replace a fricative (/f, v, θ, ð, s, z, ʃ, ʒ, h/) or an affricate (/tʃ, dʒ/) with a stop-plosive (/p, b, t, d, k, g/). Stopping disappears by 2½ to 3 years of age.

See /si/ produced as *tee* [ti]

Chop /tʃɑp/ produced as *top* [tɑp]

Gliding occurs when children substitute glides (i.e., /j, w/) for liquids (/l, r/) in their productions.

Red /rɛd/ produced as *wed* [wɛd]

Light /laɪt/ produced as *yight* [jaɪt]

Assimilation Processes

Assimilation appears when one sound is influenced by another. Two assimilation processes are consonant harmony and prevocalic voicing. *Consonant harmony* occurs when two consonant sounds in a word become more alike to one another in terms of their place or manner of articulation. Note that the target phoneme /d/ (a front voiced sound) becomes a back voiced sound when influenced by the final phoneme /k/.

Duck /dck/ produced as *guk* [gck]

Prevocalic voicing occurs when unvoiced consonants become voiced because of the influence of a following vowel in a word. In the following example, note that the unvoiced stop-plosive /t/ becomes its voiced cognate /d/.

Tea /ti/ is produced as *dee* [di]

> The phonological processes that should disappear by 3 years of age are unstressed syllable deletion (*banana* produced as *nana*), final consonant deletion (*bus* produced as *bu*), fronting (*key* produced as *tee*), consonant assimilation (*dog* produced as *gog*), reduplication (*daddy* produced as *dada*), and prevocalic voicing (*tea* produced as *key*).
>
> The phonological processes that may persist after 3 years of age are cluster reduction (*stop* produced as *top*), epenthesis (*cup* produced as *cupuh*), gliding (*red* produced as *wed*), vocalization (*car* produced as *cah*), stopping (*Sue* produced as *two*), depalatization (*chew* produced as *two*), and final devoicing (*dog* produced as *dok*).

Phonological Differences

Examples of word productions found in typically developing 3- to 4-year-old Spanish-speaking children of Puerto Rican descent when speaking English fol-low (Bernstein & Levey, 2009; Goldstein, 2000; Goldstein & Iglesias, 1996).

Word-final /s/ and /n/ may be deleted

The glide /j/ is produced as the voiced alveolar-palatal affricate /dʒ/

The labio-dental fricative /f/ becomes a bilabial fricative /ɸ/ in initial and medial positions in words

The intervocalic interdental fricative /θ/ is deleted

It is important to understand that these productions represent *differences*, as sounds in a speaker's native language may influence sounds in a second language. In addition, some of the sounds in the second language may be absent from the speaker's native language, such as the sound *th* (e.g., <u>th</u>row and ba<u>th</u>) that is absent from many languages in the world. In either case, the result is not indicative of a disorder. Table 6–8 presents the segmental/sound features that are characteristic of native Spanish-speaking children learning English as their second language.

The following examples describe the terminology used to describe the phonological features shown in Table 6–8.

♦ A dentalized sound is produced with lingual-dental (tongue-teeth) contact
♦ The phoneme /s/ → [ɛs] is classed as epenthesis (addition of a sound)
♦ A voiced sound produced as an unvoiced sound (e.g., /z/ →/s/) is classed as devoicing
♦ A fricative produced as an affricate (e.g., /ʃ/ → [tʃ] is classed as affrication
♦ A fricative produced as a stop (e.g., /θ/ and /ð/ to [t] and [d], respectively) is classed as stopping

Table 6–8. *Segmental Characteristics of Spanish-Influenced English*

Sound Class	Example[a]
Stops	
/t/ → [t̪u]	two /tu/ → [t̪u] (dentalized [t])
/d/ → [d̪]	do /du/ → [d̪u] (dentalized [d])
Nasals	
/n/ → [ŋ]	fan /fæn/ → fang [fæŋ]
Fricatives	
/s/ → [ɛs]	stamp /stæmp/ → estamp [ɛstæmp]
/s/ → [ø]	pace /pes/ → pa [pe]
/z/ → [s]	peas /piz/ → peace [pis]
/ʃ/ → [tʃ]	she /ʃɪ/ → chi [tʃɪ]
/z/ → [s]	his /hɪz/ → hiss [hɪs]
/v/ → [b]	vase /ves/ → base [bes]
/θ/ → [t]	thought /θɔt/ → taught [tɔt]
/ð/ → [d]	though /ðo/ → dough [do]
Affricates	
/dʒ/ → [tʃ]	gel /dʒɛl/ → chel [tʃɛl]
Liquids	
/ɹ/ → [ɹ]	road /rod/→ [ɹod] or [rod]
Glides	
/j/ → [dʒ]	yellow /jɛlo/ → jello [dʒɛlo]
Vowels	
Tense → lax	key /ki/ → kih [kɪ]
Lax → tense	kid /kɪd/ → keyed [kid]
Diphthongs → monophthongs	home /hoʊm/ → [hom]
Central to [ɑ]	away (uhway) /əwe/ → [ɑwe]
The phoneme /ɝ/ → [ɛɾ]	/kɝb/ curb → /kɛɾb/

[a] General American English → Spanish-influenced English.

Source: From "Transcription of Spanish and Spanish-Influenced English," by B. A. Goldstein, 2001, *Communication Disorders Quarterly, 23*(1), pp. 54–60. Reprinted with permission.

◆ The phoneme /ɹ/ can be produced as a trill [ɹ] or a flap [ɾ].

◆ The sound /ɾ/ represents the voiced alveolar flap because the articulation involves rapid movement of the tongue tip against the alveolar ridge (e.g., be**tt**er and ri**dd**le)

There are English sounds that are not found in Spanish (Goldstein, 2001), such as aspirated stops (e.g., /pʰ/ as in [pʰɛn] *pen*). Aspiration occurs when the vocal cords or folds remain open when a consonant is produced. There are also English vowel sounds that are absent in Spanish that consist of the lax front vowels (i.e., /æ/ *pan* and *hat*), the central vowels (i.e., /ə/ *above* and /ʌ/ *sun*), certain back vowels (i.e., /ʊ/ b**oo**k, /ɔ/ p**aw**, and /ɑ/ h**o**t), and the diphthongs (i.e., /ɑɪ/ p**ie**, /ɑʊ/ c**ow**, and /ɔɪ/ b**oy**). These differences may lead to the production of *heat* for *hit* when Spanish speakers attempt the vowel /ɪ/. This is because speakers tend to produce a vowel that exists in their native language (e.g., /i/ *heat*) when attempting a vowel absent in their native language (e.g., /ɪ/ *hit*).

Investigations also show that discrimination difficulties appear when native Spanish speakers are presented with vowel contrasts that are absent in Spanish (Levey & Cruz, 2004), such as discriminating differences between /ɪ/- /i/, /ɛ/-/e/, and /ʊ/-/u/. Note that the discrimination difficulties occur between vowels absent in Spanish (i.e., /ɪ/, /ɛ/, /ʊ/ and those present in Spanish and English (i.e., /i/, /e/, /u/).

AAE is a dialect of American English used by some, but not all, African American speakers. AAE is a regular, systematic dialect of English that contrasts with other English dialects in terms of grammar, pronunciation, and vocabulary. Examples of some of the phonological features of AAE are presented in Table 6–9 (Iglesias & Goldstein, 2004, p. 352).

There is often variation in language productions among speakers of different languages and dialects. For speakers of AAE, phonological acquisition is characterized by variation. For example, there is more use of these features by working-class than middle-class AAE speakers (Wolfram, 1986). These features also appear less often in more formal social settings. The sounds produced by some AAE speakers do not differ from those spoken by speakers of General American English (GAE) (Stockman, 1996) with one exception. This exception consists of the voiced interdental /ð/ (e.g., **th**ey, **th**ese, and **th**eir) produced as /d/ (e.g., **d**ey, **d**ese, and **d**eir).

One of the features of AAE is the simplification of word-final consonant clusters, shown in the production of the word *mist* /mɪst/ produced as *miss* [mɪs]. Although the words *mist* and *missed* have the same pronunciation and the same phonetic form (e.g., *mist* /mɪst/ and *missed* /mɪst/), their spelling (e.g., mist and missed) and meaning differ (e.g., *mist* means a haze or vapor and the word *missed* means forgetting to attend, an error, or ignoring something). The simplification of the final word cluster (e.g., -st) does not occur when the deletion of the consonant /t/ might affect word meaning (e.g., I **missed** the bus). In this case, the word *missed* is produced with the final consonant sound /t/ (e.g., [mɪst]). Thus, AAE speakers mark the difference between the production of *miss* and *mist*

Table 6–9. *Major Phonological Features Distinguishing African American English and General American English*

Word-final consonant cluster reduction	*test → tes*
Substitution of /r/	*sister → sistuh*
Deletion of /l/ in word-final adjacent consonants	*help → hep*
Substitution of /ɪ/ for /ɛ/ before nasals	*pin and pen → pin*
Realization of /r/ as a vowel	*throw → thow*
Substitution of /f/ for /θ/ in word-final position	*south → souf*
Substitution of /f/ for /θ/ and /v/ for /ð/ in intervocalic position	*nothing → nofing* *bathing → baving*
Stopping of word initial interdental consonants	*they → dey*
Metathesis	*ask → aks*

Source: From *Articulation and Phonological Disorders* (5th ed., p. 352), by J. D. Bernthal and N. W. Bankson, 2004, Upper Saddle River, NJ: Pearson Education, Inc. Reprinted with permission.

to distinguish the meaning of these words (Iglesias & Goldstein, 1998).

There are several languages in the world that use tone, or pitch, to distinguish word meaning. Mandarin Chinese has four tones (high, rising, fall-rising, and falling). Thus, the morpheme *ma* has different meanings based on different tones, as shown in the following examples:

High tone	*ma*	mother
Rising tone	*ma*	numb
Falling then rising tone	*ma*	horse
Falling tone	*ma*	scold

A native speaker from a language that uses tones to mark word meaning may have difficulty learning to speak a language that lacks tones (e.g., English).

There are also phoneme or sound differences in some languages that lead to differences in the productions of sounds when speaking English. For example, there is no phoneme /l/ in Japanese. In this case, a Japanese speaker learning English may pronounce the word *light* as *right*. There is also no phoneme /θ/ in Mandarin Chinese. In this case, the speaker may pronounce the word *thin* as *sin*.

Although it is difficult to generalize about Asian speakers' productions in English, there are commonly observed characteristics that have been described (Roseberry-McKibbin, 2008, p. 127). Table 6–10 presents examples of these productions.

Table 6–10. *Articulation Differences Observed Commonly Among Asian Speakers*

Articulation Characteristics	Sample English Utterances	
In many Asian language, words end in vowels only or in just a few consonants; speakers may delete many final consonants in English	ste/step	li/lid
	ro/robe	do/dog
Some languages are monosyllabic; speakers may truncate polysyllabic words or emphasize the wrong syllable	efunt/elephant	
	diversity/diversity (incorrect emphasis on first syllable)	
Possible devoicing of voiced cognates	beece/bees	pick/pig
	luff/love	crip/crib
r/l confusion	lize/rise	clown/crown
/r/ may be omitted entirely	gull/girl	tone/torn
Reduction of vowel length in word.	Words sound choppy to Americans.	
No voiced or voiceless "th"	dose/those	tin/thin
	zose/those	sin/thin
Epenthesis (addition of "uh" sound in blends, ends of words)	bulack/black	wooduh/wood
Confusion of "ch" and "sh"	sheep/cheap	beesh/beach
/ae/ does not exist in many Asian languages	block/black	shock/shack
b/v substitutions	base/vase	Beberly/Beverly
v/w substitutions	vork/work	vall/wall

Source: From Multicultural Students with Special Language Needs: Practical Strategies for Assessment (p. 130), by C. Roseberry-McKibbin, 2008, Oceanside, CA: Academic Communication Associates. Reprinted with permission.

It is important to understand that dialect differences do not indicate a disorder and that understanding and respect for multilinguistic and multicultural differences are essential in the field of speech-language pathology.

Phonological Awareness

Phonological awareness is defined as children's knowledge of the sound structure of words (Torgesen, 1999). Phonological awareness is an essential factor in reading development (MacDonald & Cornwall, 1995; Shankweiler et al., 1995; Torgesen, Wagner, & Rashotte, 1994; Troia, 2004) and a strong predictor of both preliteracy (Burgess & Lonigan, 1998) and later reading skills (Parrila, Kirby, & McQuarrie, 2004). One of the essential components of phonological awareness is the ability to discriminate the differences in sounds. Discrimination skills allow children to draw on the connection between sounds and letters for basic word recognition (Lonigan, Burgess, Anthony, & Barker, 1998), and to distinguish the visual differences between letters (Catts & Kahmi, 2005).

> The importance of phonological awareness is clear when children are confronted by unfamiliar words, given that decoding unfamiliar or novel words requires associating sounds with alphabetic orthography (Lyon & Moats, 1997). Children with reading disabilities have significant difficulty reading novel and pseudo words.

Children with limited literacy skills are unaware of sound differences (Durgunoğlu & Oney, 2002; Stanovich & Siegel, 1994). Thus, the ability to discriminate sounds, such as /p/ and /b/, is a basic factor in phonological awareness that supports early reading skills. The stages

of children's phonological awareness development can be found in Table 6–11.

Phonological awareness begins with the awareness of words (*banana*), followed by syllables (*ba - na - na*), and finally phonemic awareness, based on the recognition of segments in words (*c-a-t*). Phonological awareness includes the following abilities:

Segment syllables in words (banana): ba-na-na

Rhyme (What rhymes with cat?): bat, rat, sat

Blend sound segments (What word is d-o-g?): dog

Segment sounds in words (What are the sounds in cat?): "c " "a" "t"

Manipulate sounds (sound deletion: spot and stop): pot and top

Match words with initial phonemes (dog, dig, or house?): dog and dig

Produce alliteration: dirty dogs dig

Table 6–11. *The Development of Phonological Awareness From Ages 3 to 5*

Phonological Skill	Recognition Abilities	Example
Rhyming	Sameness or difference in sound contrasts	*bat-mat*
Alliteration	Words beginning with the same onset	*big bad bears* *eight apes ate*
Blending	Synthesize sounds, syllables, and words	*f - i -s -h = fish*
Segmentation	Breaking sounds into smaller units	*fish = f - i -s -h*
Manipulation	Adding sounds to form a word	*at + b = bat*
	Deleting sounds to form new words	*smile – s = mile*
	Substituting syllables or sounds	*bug → bun*

Source: From Language Development: Understanding Language Diversity in the Classroom (p. 43), by S. Levey & S. Polirstok (Eds.), 2011, Los Angeles, CA: Sage. Reprinted with permission.

Identify words with different final sounds (dog, dig, or toy?): dog and dig

and identify word(s) with the different initial sound: toy

Preschool-age children are able to segment syllables (e.g., understand that *banana* has three syllables) and recognize rhyme (e.g., *cat, rat, hat*). It is not until age 5 to 6 that children become aware of phoneme segments, signaling the presence of phonemic awareness: understanding (a) that words have symbols (alphabet letters) that correspond to sound segments, (b) that there is a correspondence between a letter and a sound, and (c) that unknown words can be recognized by "sounding out" the first letter, using context, and searching for words in the lexicon that have this sound (*The boy f_ _ _ _ money on the street*) (Torgesen, 1999). The most important factors that predict phoneme awareness are syllable and rhyme awareness (Carroll, Snowling, Hulme, & Stevenson (2003).

SEMANTIC DEVELOPMENT

Semantics is the component of language that describes meaning conveyed by words, sentences, conversation, and narratives. Children learn new concepts and how to code these concepts linguistically by forming sentences to convey their ideas and knowledge. The main concepts (discussed in Chapter 5) acquired between 2 and 5 years of age consist of spatial concepts (location), temporal concepts (time), quantity concepts (number), quality concepts (description), and social-emotional concepts (feelings), as shown in the following examples:

Spatial concepts: *in, on, over, between, across, along*

Temporal concepts: *before, after, later*

Quantity concepts: *more, less, empty, full*

Quality concepts : *rough, smooth, hard, soft*

Social-emotional concepts: *happy, sad*

Semantic development also appears in children's vocabulary development. The preschool years show growth in children's vocabulary skills, with a connection between children's vocabulary development and parental input. For example, children's use of cognitive state terms (e.g., *think* and *know*) is related to their mother's use of these terms (Bartsch & Wellman, 1995; Jenkins, Terrell, Kogushi, Lollis, & Ross, 2003).

Vocabulary increases rapidly, starting at age 2 (Golinkoff, Mervis, & Hirsh-Pasek, 1994) with 900 to 1,000 words at 3 years of age, 1,500 words at 4 years of age, and over 2,000 words acquired by 5 years of age (Owens, Metz, & Haas, 2000). Children also extend the meanings of words. Many animal names are first learned from books read to young children, and meaning may be extended when a child visits a zoo and is introduced to further meanings of words, such as *cat*. Children learn that the word *cat* can refer to *kitty cat, tiger*, and *lion*. Novel or new words are learned quickly following initial representations in both didactic (direct teaching) and informal contexts (Apel, Kahmi, & Dollaghan, 1985; Oetting, Rice, & Swank, 1995). The process of learning words in initial presentations is referred to as **fast mapping**.

During the late preschool period and into the early school years, children's word definitions are **concrete**. More abstract word definitions appear with the acquisition of synonymy (i.e., words with similar features, such as *sick* and *ill*), explanation (i.e., giving the reason for an action), and specifications of categorical relationships (i.e., placing entities in categories, such as *dog* and *bird* in the category *animal*) (Bernstein & Levey, 2009). Children learn that the word *block* can now apply to their neighborhood (*going around the block*) and to obstructions (*He's blocking me and I can't get through*).

Abstract lexical terms, such as words for time (*before, later, soon*), present difficulties for younger children because their meaning is not apparent (Gleitman, Cassidy, Nappa, Papafragou, & Trueswell, 2005). Abstract lexical terms do not label objects or observable actions. Thus, the former are termed *abstract terms* (e.g., words that label time) and the latter are termed *concrete terms* (e.g., words that label observable things and actions). Think of it this way: if you can point to it, it is concrete. Abstract terms in the lexical domains of color, quantity, and time duration can describe objects or events. For example, utterances, such as *in a minute*, may be difficult for a child to understand as an answer when they ask *When can I get a cookie?*

During the preschool period, children have an incomplete understanding of more abstract terms that refer to the actual duration of time (Shatz, Tare, Nguyen, & Young, 2010). For example, children were asked questions about *How long does it take to . . . ?* (e.g., *see a movie, eat breakfast*, and *puppies grow up to be dogs?*). They were given the option of answering *days, hours*, or *years*. Preschoolers' knowledge of these terms was found to be incomplete while these terms are still developing during the preschool years (Shatz et al.), whereas 6-year-olds performed above chance. Real understanding of these terms does not appear until the early school years.

Metalinguistic awareness also appears during the preschool years, allowing children to better understand the meaning of words. Metalinguistic awareness is defined as the ability to consciously reflect on the nature and properties of language (van Kleeck, 1982), such as the awareness that language consists of sounds, syllables, words, and phrases.

Metalinguistic awareness allows children to recognize syntactic, semantic, and phonological components that may contain errors, as shown in the following examples (Kahmi & Koenig, 1985, p. 209):

Semantic awareness: Jill "eats" cards versus Jill *plays* cards

Phonological awareness: He "locks" to school versus He *walks* to school

Syntactic awareness: He walk to school versus He *walks* to school

Typically developing children can identify and revise some errors by age 4, but metalinguistic skills do not generally develop until age 7 or 8. Metalinguistic skills require the development of intact language skills and differentiate typical from atypical language development. Metalinguistic awareness is also a factor in developing intact literacy skills for reading and writing abilities. For example, the metalinguistic skill of phonological awareness provides the ability to recognize rhymes (e.g., *cat, hat,* and *bat*) and to identify sounds in words (e.g., the word *cat* contains the three sounds "c," "a," and "t"). In summary, metalinguistic awareness is present when children are able to think about language itself (Yopp & Yopp, 2010), beyond the ability to express or understand spoken language.

There are vocabulary items that present younger preschool aged children with difficulty, such as certain determiners and quantifiers. The determiner *the* refers to a specific thing (*the book*) and *a* refers to a general set of things (*a book*). Children frequently make mistakes in article use until age 4 or older (Zdorenko & Paradis, 2011). The quantifiers *some* and *any* also present 3-year-olds with difficulty (Hurewitz, Papafragou, Gleitman, & Gelman, 2006). Some 3-year-olds interpret *some* to mean *at least some* and possibly *all*. The difference between the quantifiers *some* and *any* is acquired by 4 years of age.

When asked to provide opposites or to associate words, younger children often produce a word that belongs to a different grammatical class (Entwisle, 1966). The **syntagmatic-paradigmatic** process refers to responses that are from the same grammatical class as the word presented (paradigmatic) as opposed to responses that can be found in a syntactic sequence (syntagmatic). The following examples illustrate syntagmatic responses. Note that the child's response to the words *open* and *play* create a phrase or a sentence (e.g., *Open the door* and *Play with a ball*).

| Open | Open-door |
| Play | Play-ball |

The following examples illustrate a paradigmatic response (Woodward & Lowell, 1916), with responses indicating grammatical knowledge:

| Open | Open-close |
| Play | Play-work |

Older children provide a paradigmatic response that is in the same grammatical class as the stimulus word This shift from the syntagmatic to the paradigmatic response occurs at about ages 5 to 7.

Semantic Relations

Single words express meaning, such as the words *daddy* and *go*. When these words are combined to form a sentence (e.g., *daddy go*), a **semantic relation** exists (examples of semantic relations can be found in Table 6–12).

Semantic relations appear in preschool-age children's language productions (Bowerman, 1973; Brown, 1973; Fillmore, 1968). These examples show the progression of children's language skills (Leonard, Bolders, & Miller, 1976, p. 377).

Agent + Action: *He throw - He throw ball - He is throwing the ball*

Table 6–12. *Semantic Relations Expressed by Preschool-Age Children*

Semantic Relation	Example	Context
Agent + Action	Daddy throw	Daddy is throwing the ball
Action + Affected	Throw the ball	Throwing a ball
Possessor + Possession	Mommy's shoe	Pointing to his/her mother's shoe
Recurrence	More cookie	Asking for another cookie

Action + Object: *Eat cookie - I eating cookie - I am eating the cookie*

Demonstrative: *Ball - That ball - That's a ball*

Attribute + Entity: *Hot - Hot stove - The stove is hot*

Entity + Location: *Cookie pocket - Cookie in pocket - The cookie is in my pocket*

Possessor + Possession: *Mine - My doll - This is my doll*

Recurrence: *More - More juice (please) - Can I have more juice?*

Disappearance: *All gone - Allgone juice - The juice is gone*

Negation: *No bed - No go bed - I don't want to go to bed*

The same semantic relations appear in both 3- and 5-year-old children's productions, whereas older children's sentences may consist of longer utterances that combine the examples shown above (e.g., *I don't want to go to bed and I want more juice and a cookie*) (Leonard et al., 1976).

As noted in Appendix A, a 3- to 4-year-old may produce sentences that contain four or more words (e.g., *I want to watch another show*), whereas the 4- to 5-year-old's sentences may contain more details (e.g., *The orange bike is mine*).

Relational Terms

During the preschool years, children acquire relational terms that apply to temporal (time), spatial (location), and physical (place) concepts. Children also begin to acquire relational terms that apply to kinship relations. Examples of these relational terms include:

Temporal relational terms: *before/after*

Locational relational terms: *in/on*

Physical relational terms: *high/low*

Kinship terms: *mother/father*

Examples of the development of locational, physical, and kinship relational terms can be found in Table 6–13.

Table 6–13. *The Acquisition of Locational, Physical, and Kinship Terms*

Age (Years)	Locational Relationship	Physical Relationships	Kinship Term
3 to 4	Under	Big/Little	Mother/Father
		Hard/Soft	
		Heavy/Light	
4 to 4½	Next to	Tall/Short	Sister/Brother
	Behind	Long/Short	Grandfather/Grandmother
	In back of		
	In front of		
School age	Right/left	Deep/Shallow	Uncle/Aunt
		Thick/Thin	Cousin
		Wide/Narrow	Nephew/Niece

Source: From Language Development: Understanding Language Diversity in the Classroom (p. 147), by S. Levey & S. Polirstok (Eds.), 2011, Los Angeles, CA: Sage. Reprinted with permission.

Temporal Relations

Temporal relations include the terms *before, after, when, since,* and *while.* Children first acquire terms that refer to *sequencing (then, before, after),* followed by the acquisition of terms that refer to simultaneity *(while, at the same time).* Terms that refer to sequence and duration *(since, until)* are acquired by school-age children (Winskel, 2003).

Preschool-age children must achieve knowledge of syntactic structure to understand the terms *before* and *after* (Goodz, 1982) because younger children rely on the *order of mention* in sentences to understand these terms (Bever, 1970). For example, children interpret the event described in the main clause of a complex sentence as the *first event* that occurs, as shown in the following examples (Goodz, 1982, p. 822):

1. Put the boy [first mention] in the box *before* you put the cat in the box.
2. *Before* you put the boy [first mention] in the box, put the cat in the box.
3. *After* you put the boy [first mention] in the box, put the cat in the box.
4. Put the boy [first mention] in the box *after* you put the cat in the box.

Note that *order of mention* and *order of events* coincide in sentences 1 and 3 because *boy* and the direction *put the boy in the box* are mentioned first. However, in sentences 2 and 4, the word *boy* is **mentioned first**, despite the direction to **first** put *the cat in the box*. Children interpret the direction to mean that they should put the boy in the box first, given that *boy* is mentioned first. Children follow the order of mention during the preschool stages of language development and acquire an understanding of the terms *before* and *after* at about 5 years of age (Owens, 2012), when they have a better grasp of syntactic structure. At age 3½, Micah was given the following direction: *Before you walk across the living room, take off your shoes.* Micah walked across the living room and then took off his shoes, thinking he had followed the requested direction to first *walk* and then *take off his shoes.*

There is also a relationship between exposure to temporal relations, such as *yesterday* and *tomorrow,* based on caregivers' use of these terms (Hudson, 2006). By age 4, children are better able to conceptualize the time frame for events occurring in the past or future, which contributes to their understanding of the terms *yesterday* and *tomorrow.* Caregivers' use of these terms will allow a child to understand the connection between events and time.

Big/little

Tall/short and long/short

High/low

Thick/thin

Deep/shallow

Wide/narrow

> The polarity feature also plays a role in children's difficulty with the quantity concept terms *less* and *more.* Children have more difficulty with the term *less* in comparison with *more.* Given the direction to identify either term, children choose the larger amount of something or the larger object.

Physical Relations

Children acquire the physical relations *big/little* as young as 2 years of age (Sandhofer & Smith, 2001). Note that physical relations have a positive and a negative polarity with *big, up, tall,* and *high* on the positive pole and *little, down, short,* and *low* on the negative pole. These opposite poles are given the labels **marked** for negative pole terms and **unmarked** for positive pole terms. Children tend to acquire the unmarked member of an antonym (opposite) pair first (Clark, 1973). Brewer and Stone (1975) found that children make fewer errors for the unmarked member of opposites (e.g., *tall*) in the contrast *tall/short.* Examples of physical relation contrasts follow with positive polarity terms listed first in each pair.

Locational Terms

Children have a good grasp of the environment well before they learn the words associated with spatial concepts. Spatial terms begin with simple configurations, such as *in/on,* as children first understand support relations (e.g., something being either *in* or *on* a surface or object). Children begin by describing one target object (e.g., *a book*) in relation to a single landmark (e.g., *a table*).

Children understand support relations (*in/on*) before proximity relations (*by* and *next to*). Later learned configurations are *between, across,* and *along* (Weist, 2002). Consequently, children will have a better understanding of *the toy is in the bag* than *the toy is next to the bag* or *the book is between the bag and the box.* Before age 4, children use *in, on,* and *over* to label object location, whereas *up, down,* and *off* are used as locational prepositions and verb particles (e.g., *stand up* and *sit down*) (Owens, 2012).

We now explore children's narrative skill development. Note that there are also rules that apply to the structure of a narrative. Learning this aspect of semantics begins when young children are exposed to narratives in storybooks.

Narrative Development

Narrative is a form of discourse that differs from conversation because narratives do not require a listener's response. In contrast to conversational interaction, narratives consist of an extended monologue that incorporates the use of intonation, gesture, and prosody, along with the description of an event (Ukraninetz McFadden, 1991). Thus, rules that govern conversation, such as turn taking, do not apply.

Narrative involves a story structure that includes the setting (who, when, and where an event or events took place), the action being discussed, feelings associated with the action or event, and some sort of outcome. The elements of the narrative must be connected and the story expressed according to the actual sequence of events (i.e., what happened first, next, and last).

To produce a cohesive narrative, children must present all the information in an organized way. They must introduce and organize sequences so that events are related and lead to some conclusion. There are a number of different types of narratives. Narratives include sharing and recounting of personal events and experiences, self-generated stories, telling and retelling of familiar tales, and the retelling of stories from movies, books, and television shows.

Initially, children's narrative development lacks a cohesive order of events, as shown in Table 6–14 (Bernstein, 2011).

At 3 years of age, children produce *additive chains*, a set of events that relate to a central topic, with no particular temporal order. This level of narrative consists of sequences of events that can be arranged in any order with no effect on the meaning of the narrative. Apel and Masterson (1998, p. 5) provide an example of this level of narrative produced by a child aged 4 years and 5 months.

> *My mom went to outer space. And she saw a monster. And she ate moon cake. And she saw everything but nothing else. That was it.*

Temporal chains are produced between 3 and 5 years of age, when narrative is structured to include sequential information, expressed by temporal or timed sequences of events.

> *One day, I went to the park. A big boy pushed a little boy and he fell down. He cried. The end.*

At around 5 years of age, children produce simple causal chains that present an *episode* (a set of smaller scenes strung together to make a longer story). This level of narrative structure consists of *initiating event, attempt,* and *consequence*. The elements that are absent include *setting, internal response, internal plan, resolution,* and *ending*. In the causal chain, events are related by causal dependency because events cause other events. By 7 to 8 years

Table 6–14. *Narrative Production by Preschool-Age Children*

Age (years)	Narrative Type	Example
3	Primitive narrative	Central topic with no temporal order
4	Unfocused chains	Sequential information with no causal relations
5	Simple causal chains	Initiating event, attempt, and *consequence* (missing *setting, internal response,* and *internal plan*)
After 5	True narratives	*Setting, initiating event, internal response, internal plan, attempts, consequence, resolution/reaction,* and *ending*

Source: From *Language Development: Understanding Language Diversity in the Classroom* (p. 151), by S. Levey & S. Polirstok (Eds.), 2011, Los Angeles, CA: Sage. Reprinted with permission.

of age, children produce a complete episode, summarized next.

Setting: Introduction of characters, time, and place

Initiating Event: Problem

Internal Response: Characters' feelings about the initiating event

Internal Plan: Statement about fixing the problem

Attempt: Action to solve problem

Consequence: Event or events following the attempt

Resolution/Reaction: The final state following the attempt

Ending: A statement ending the story

With all elements present, the *Winnie the Pooh* story would include the following elements (bolded next) to provide a full narrative episode.

One day, Winnie the Pooh lost his honey pot. **He was sad. He decided to go out and find more honey.** *He met some bees. The bees told him to take some honey from the tree.* **He was happy because he got more honey. He lived happily ever after.**

Two types of narratives are produced by older preschool-age children: **personal narratives**, a description of "what happened," and **fictional narratives**, drawn from a child's imagination (Lahey, 1988). Children use personal narratives to describe their own experiences. Personal narratives can consist of **decontextualized narratives** that are descriptions of people, objects, and events absent from the immediate environment. Personal narratives can also consist of **contextualized narratives** that are descriptions of people and things present in the immediate environment. The use of decontextualized narratives characterizes more advanced cognitive skills.

The analysis of children's narratives can help us understand how a child conceptualizes an event and how well a child is able to organize information for a logical and connected narrative effort. The narrative skills of preschool children are also a good predictor of subsequent literacy achievement (Snow, Porche, Tabors, & Harris, 2007; Tabors, Snow, & Dickinson, 2001).

Cohesive devices are used to provide a well-organized narrative by creating a connection between elements of the story (McGregor, 2000, p. 57).

Additives: Conjunctions that link clauses through addition (e.g., *and*)

Temporal: Conjunctions that link clauses temporally (e.g., *then*, *next*)

Causal : Conjunctions that link clauses causally (e.g., *because, so*)

The order of acquisition of these, along with additional connective forms, is presented next (Bloom, Lahey, Hood, Lifter, & Fiess, 1980):

And then	temporal (time)
When	epistemic (knowledge of something)
Because	causal (cause)
So	causal
Then	temporal
If	epistemic
But	adversative (expressing opposition)
That	object specification

Narrative Differences

The traditional view of narrative is a topic-centered structure, whereas narrative styles and structures differ across languages and cultures (Bliss & McCabe, 2011). For example, African American English-speaking children may produce narratives using a topic-associating structure. Examples of these types of structures are presented next (de Villiers & Burns, 2003).

Topic-Centered Structure

Organized around a single topic or closely related topics

Main characters and temporal/locational grounding remain constant and lexically explicit

Clear thematic progression with beginning, middle, and end

Topic-Associating Structure

Organized around loosely linked topics

Does not adhere to a linear pattern of organization

Frequent shifts in key characters and temporal/locational grounding

Topic changes signaled by *shifts in pitch, contouring*, and *tempo*

Children from Spanish-speaking backgrounds produce narratives with broad topic maintenance. Essentially, their narrative skills have more of a conversational style and features, descriptive statements, focus on interpersonal relations, and possible disruptions in fluency when searching for a word in English (Silva & McCabe, 1996).

The narratives of Chinese and Korean children may express multiple experiences in a brief narrative style (Minami &

McCabe, 1991). Redundant elements are often omitted, such as the use of "*I*" in subsequent sentences (e.g., *I went to school . . . found a dollar . . . gave it to my mother . . .*). Thus, narrative styles differ among speakers of different dialects and languages.

PRAGMATIC DEVELOPMENT

Pragmatics involves three major communication skills: the use of language to greet, inform, and request (e.g., saying hello, giving information, and asking for something in an appropriate manner); changing and adapting language to different persons and situations to maximize their understanding (e.g., providing background information so the listener will understand the topic and simplifying language so younger listeners can understand) and following rules in conversation (e.g., such as turn taking, maintaining a topic, and staying on topic). Children first understand how to produce polite requests to achieve a better outcome when asking for something. This occurs when they begin to use the word *please* by age 3. Later, children produce **indirect speech acts** (e.g., *Can I go to the playground*) at about 3½ to 4 years of age (Bates, 1976).

Indirect Requests

In the preschool period, children begin to understand and use indirect requests, first produced at 3½ to 4 years of age (Bates, 1976; Wells, 1985). This occurs when they acquire modal auxiliaries (e.g., *can, could, would,* and *might*) and understand that the surface form (a question) is a more appropriate form to convey the underlying intention (e.g., *to get a cookie, to go to the playground,* or some other intent or

meaning). Examples of children's pragmatic development include adapting to a listener's needs, initiating a conversation, turn taking in a conversation, and forming polite requests (Westby, 1980).

More subtle forms of requests appear between 3 and 4 years of age when children are more aware of the benefits gained from more polite forms of requests (e.g., *Can I have a cookie?*). By age 3, children are able to use modal auxiliaries (*Can you . . . ?*) to produce indirect and more polite requests. Modal auxiliaries consist of the following: *can, could, shall, should, will, would, may, might,* and *must* and follow this order of development (Bliss, 1989; Wells, 1985).

can and *will:* 2 years and 6 months

should and *could:* 2 years 9 months to 3 years

may, might, and *must:* 3 years

Modals first appear with the production of *can* at about 30 months. Children produce indirect requests before they have acquired advanced syntactic skills and certain modal auxiliaries, as shown in these examples. The first example shows the omission of the later acquired modal *will* (Bliss, 1988) and the second example shows the absence of inversion (e.g., *Why can't I play?* versus *Why I can't play?*).

I show it to you tomorrow

Why I can't play

The negative forms of the earlier learned modal auxiliaries may appear as early as 30 months, that is, *can't, won't,* and *don't* (Owens, 2012). Inversion appears around age 3 for earlier acquired modal auxiliaries.

Why can't you come?

Conversational Development

At the preschool stage of development, conversation consists of four basic elements (Johnson, Johnston, & Weinrich, 1984, p. 2; Miller, 1978).

Performatives: A speaker's intent to produce a particular type of sentence (e.g., *question, declarative, imperative, request,* or *comment*)

Propositions: The truth or falsehood of a statement

Presuppositions: A speaker's assumptions or inferences about the context and the listener that has an effect on what a speaker says

Conversational postulates: A speaker's presuppositions that encode the nature of the dialogue

Performatives consist of a speaker's intention (meaning) when producing an utterance, such as expressing a *request* (e.g., *Can I have a cookie?*). **Propositions** can be true or false, given a particular context. For example, a child saying *I didn't break the vase* may be true or false, depending on who actually broke the vase.

Presuppositions consist of the assumption that the speaker and listener share knowledge regarding the topic at hand. For example, a conversation about something that happened the day before (*Johnny pushed me*) requires the presupposition that the listener is familiar with the event that took place on that day. By age 3, a child has acquired presuppositional skills and is able to determine the truth or falsehood of an utterance.

Conversational postulates describe the assumption that a speaker is telling the truth, is offering information that is new and relevant to the conversation, and is offering information that the listener genuinely wants to hear (Grice, 1975; Searle, 1965). For example, a child would not ask for a cookie (e.g., *Can I have a cookie*) unless these conditions were present: the listener actually had a cookie to give and the speaker genuinely wanted a cookie. See Table 6–15 for examples of children's communicative functions during the preschool stage.

Although children possess innate learning skills, language develops within a social context, gained through interaction with adults, peers, and children with more advanced language skills. In essence, communicative interaction with other language users is essential for language development. During the preschool stage of development, children's conversational skills develop as they become more aware of social settings and rules that lead to successful communicative interaction. Children learn more complex ways of using language socially. Their first attempts to initiate conversation may consist of saying *Hey* to gain someone's attention. This method gives way to more appropriate means to initiate this interaction (e.g., *Know what happened?*). Children's conversation also becomes more coherent (Berman & Slobin, 1994; Peterson & McCabe, 1983) as they express information in an organized manner. Children develop their conversational skills by participating in conversations; giving instructions; providing descriptions about objects, events, and people; and relating personal experiences and simple stories.

Table 6–15. *Communicative Functions During the Preschool Stage*

Communicative Function	Example
Requesting Information	*What's that?* *Can I have a cookie?* *Where are you going?* *Why can't I have it?*
Responding to requests	*It's in my pocket* *I didn't do it* *The doggy got it dirty*
Descriptions	*It's a big hole* *That's a really nice cookie* *That's my new bike*
Expressing facts and feelings	*I like you* *I don't like potatoes* *I know that*
Describing events and stories	*Little red riding hood got scared and ran all the way home*
Describing plans	*After I make the car, we can ride it down the hill*
Describing a past experience	*She pushed me so hard I fell down and hurt myself*
Complaint	*You always give the big one to him*
Criticisms	*Your picture is yucky*
Annoying	*I'll do it again and again and again and again*
Threatening	*Give it back or I will tell Mommy*

Source: From *Language Development: Understanding Language Diversity in the Classroom* (p. 149), by S. Levey & S. Polirstok (Eds.), 2011, Los Angeles, CA: Sage. Reprinted with permission.

Conversation is a communicative event that requires a speaker and a listener. Conversation involves a setting, a topic, rules for taking turns as speaker and listener, and common knowledge shared between the speaker and listener to ensure a successful interaction. Children's early conversation lacks these conventions that govern successful communication. Frequently, their conversation begins with the assumption of shared information. For example, a 2-year-old held up a toy to a telephone receiver and said *Mommy, look at my new toy*, based on the assumption that his mother shared his perspective. These early conversational attempts lack a TOM because children lack an understanding of what a listener sees or knows (that differs from the child's own perspective of the situation or context). Over time, children acquire the following principles that establish successful conversational interaction (Grice, 1975):

Quantity: *Provide sufficient but not an excessive amount of information*

Quality: *Be truthful*

Relation: *Your contribution should be relevant to the topic of the conversation*

Manner: *Messages must be organized, clear, and concise*

To summarize these principles, preschoolers learn not to interrupt or do all of the talking (the quantity principle); comments should be true (the quality rule); the speaker should maintain the topic being discussed and not interject irrelevant information (the relation rule); and the speaker should transmit information in a clear manner so that the message is understood (the manner rule). Children achieve the principles that govern conversation once they develop the language skills and rules for conversational interaction (Brinton & Fujiki, 1989), as shown in the following conversational rules that are acquired as children develop pragmatic skills:

Introduce topics with appropriate referents (background information)

Do not interrupt other speakers

Contribute to a topic

Understand the main point of the conversation

Make sure the topic is understood by others in the interaction

Children's early skills include the following inventory of conversational acts (Fey, 1986):

Assertive conversational acts

Questions: *What is that?*

Action requests: *Give me the ball*

Comments: *The ball is lost*

Statements: *I want that ball*

Responsive conversational acts

Answers: *A ball*

Action responses: *Take the ball*

Statement responses: *Okay, take it*

During the preschool stage, children's conversational development follows a certain order, based on the observation of 3-year-olds at play (Dore, 1974, 1975).

Requests actions and objects: *Gimme cookie*

Comments: *I like my new shoes*

Statements: *I ate all my vegetables*

Requesting information: *Where is daddy going?*

Responses to requests for information: *I don't know*

Preschool-age children learn to take turns in a conversation, to maintain the conversational topic, and to contribute new and relevant information. Children are able to maintain a topic established by a speaker by 3½ (McLaughlin, 1998).

Narratives are integrated in conversation when children relate stories about events (e.g., *You know what happened yesterday?* and *Let me tell you something*) (Umiker-Sebeok, 1977). There is considerable growth in the length, variety, and complexity of children's conversational narratives from 3 to 5 years of age. By age 4, children may produce three to nine sentences in narrative conversation, whereas

3-year-olds produce four. By age 5, the major change is providing greater information for the listener in terms of temporal orientation (*when*). The conversational topics of 4-year-olds consist of enacting scenarios, describing, and problem solving (Schober-Peterson & Johnson, 1989).

Cohesive relations also appear in children's conversation (Halliday & Hasan, 1976). *Reference* is the use of a pronoun to refer back to a subject, *substitution* is the use of a word to replace a word in a previous sentence, *ellipsis* is the omission of words that are redundant or implied by context, and *conjunction* is the connection of two sentences to show cause and effect. Cohesive relations are bolded in the following examples:

> Reference: **Seth** *got a new bike.* **He** *rode it to school*
>
> Substitution: *He got a new* **ball**. *He likes the old* **one** *better*
>
> Ellipsis: **Tania** *likes candy and* **Tania** *likes soda pop* → *Tania likes candy and soda pop*
>
> Conjunction: *Micah was tired* **so** *he went to bed*

Peterson and Dodsworth (1991) found that children were able to use these cohesive relations at age 3½ and reference, nominal ellipsis (omission of nouns), and substitution as MLU grew. The use of these cohesive relations is related to MLU with reference and nominal ellipsis appearing when MLU exceeded 2.5 and substitution when MLU exceeded 3.0.

Register

By age 4, children can adopt different roles in conversation by adjusting pitch and loudness (Anderson, 1992). For example, they use a deeper and louder voice when taking on a male role in play. By age 4, children are able to use **motherese** (child-directed speech) when interacting with younger children. This consists of a higher pitch and quieter voice. **Register** also includes the politeness forms developed when preschoolers learn that vocabulary and grammar play a role in communication, such as the use of indirect requests (e.g., *Can I have a cookie*). By age 5, they purposefully use polite forms.

Clarification and Conversational Repair

Conversational breakdowns can result from articulation difficulties, incomplete information, and lack of attention to the topic (Roth & Spekman, 1984). At age 2½, children are inconsistent in their understanding of the need to repair a breakdown when communication fails (Shatz & O'Reilly, 1990). At age 2, clarification requests consist of confused facial expressions.

Young preschool-age children request clarification by asking *Huh?* or *What?* (Ninio & Snow, 1996). At ages 3 to 5, children will attempt to repair a breakdown by repeating the previous word or utterance. It is not until the early school-age years that children are able to request specific clarification for better understanding of a speaker's message.

Topic Maintenance

Topic maintenance ensures **cohesion** (connection between elements) in a conversation. At age 2, only half of contributions to a conversation are on topic. By age 3½, children can sustain a topic of conversation about 75% of the time but will make more understandable contributions to a conversation when they are actively engaged in the topic at hand. Children have difficulty sustaining that topic beyond 1 or 2 turns at ages 2½ to 3, but 5-year-olds can sustain a conversation for about 12 turns (McLaughlin, 1998), based on stronger vocabulary and grammatical skills.

Decontextualized Language

Conversation frequently requires referring to entities or events that are absent from the context, defined as **decontextualized language**. During the preschool years, children learn to talk about objects absent from the immediate environment, events in the past and future, and personal experiences.

> Children are able to recall and discuss past events at 2 to 3 years of age, but reference to the actual time of past events may not occur until children achieve MLU of 3.5 (Peterson, 1990), or 35 to 40 months of age. Children frequently use *yesterday* as a term for any period in the past.

Deixis

Deictic terms are those that *point* to a particular reference in conversational discourse. Examples consist of the following terms (Roth & Spekman, 1984):

Personal pronouns: *I, you*

Demonstrative pronouns: *this, that*

Adverbs of location: *here, there*

Adverbs of time: *before, after*

Certain verbs: *come, go, bring, take*

Deixis is used in conversational discourse to direct a listener's attention to a point of reference. Without a particular reference, deictic terms lack meaning. Meaning is derived through context, such as a speaker, a listener, a place, and a topic. An example consists of a speaker telling a listener that he or she is going to bring a particular book to a particular place. In this utterance, the deictic terms are *I, bring, that,* and *here*.

I am going to bring that book here

The problem with the acquisition of certain deictic terms is that reference shifts, such as the changing roles of speaker and listener, which will affect the use of *I/you* and *me/you*.

Preschoolers begin to understand that the use of deictic terms can replace pointing to indicate something involved in the topic at hand. Deictic acquisition follows three stages (Owens, 2012, p. 242). In the first phase, children use terms, such as *here/there* and *this/that* interchangeably, with no meaningful distinction between these terms. In the second phase, children use the terms *this* and *here* correctly but also use these terms in place of *that* and *there*. In the final phase, children acquire the correct use of deictic terms, generally over the elementary school years (Roth & Spekman, 1984).

EMERGENT LITERACY

A comprehensive description of children's literacy development from birth through adolescence follows in Chapter 8. However, the preschool years provide the foundation for children's development of reading and writing abilities (Snow, Scarborough, & Burns, 1999). Children acquire knowledge about formal print before they begin to learn to read (Bryant, MacLean, & Bradley, 1990; Heath, 1996; Scarborough & Dobrich, 1990; Shaywitz, Fletcher, Holahan, & Shaywitz, 1992; Swanson, Mink, & Bocian, 1999; van Kleeck, 1995). The term for this period is **emergent literacy**. During this period of development, children learn the following skills (Bernstein & Levey, 2009):

Master print conventions: how to hold a book and understanding that English print is organized from left to right and top to bottom

Learn to write his or her name and produce scribbles to imitate writing

Begin to identify alphabet letters

Recognize that print represents words with meaning

Acquire the rudimentary skills of phonological awareness (syllable and rhyme awareness)

Children's literacy skills develop with infants' exposure to picture books because literacy skills and print awareness develop through book reading by parents (Justice & Ezell, 2000). Over time, children learn that books contain words that tell stories. Narratives and stories also promote the understanding of decontextualized language with descriptions of events outside the context of the here-and-now (Heath, 1996). Early exposure to print leads to better reading skills, as does the availability of print in the home (books, magazines, newspapers, postcards, nameplates). Nursery rhymes play a role in learning the rhythm and rhyme of spoken language. Children are prepared for academic contexts when adults label pictures and ask questions about characters and events in books (Heath, 1996), given that books are discussed on a daily basis in school.

There are culturally based differences in literacy events, parental guidance, and the preliteracy expectations of parents for preschool children (Nelson, 1993). In spite of these cultural differences, there is no effect on children's literacy abilities (Heath, 1996). In summary, children develop knowledge about print well before learning to read. In addition, there is no effect on children's development of literacy skills in spite of cultural differences that relate to literacy.

SUMMARY

Children's language skills develop during the preschool period and they achieve adultlike speech and language skills by 4 years of age with respect to their production of more complex and lengthy sentence structures, interaction communication, their production of sounds, vocabulary development, and their phonological awareness that supports literacy abilities.

◆ Cognitive development shows an interest in learning how things work and trying various methods of making things work.
◆ Cognitive development also shows an increased awareness of the concepts of time (e.g., when and how long), space (e.g., where), and quantity (e.g., how many and how much), and children acquire the relational terms that apply to these concepts (although a true

understanding of *time concepts* may not develop until about 6 years of age).

♦ Theory of mind develops and children are able to engage in more successful conversation and interaction because children can put themselves into the listener's shoes and understand his or her feelings, beliefs, and meanings.

♦ Syntactic development is characterized by the production of a greater range of sentence types, such as questions and comments, and expanded sentence length. Children now produce auxiliary verbs (e.g., *is, are*), morphological inflections (e.g., *-ing*), and double auxiliaries (e.g., *you will have to share*).

♦ Syntactic skills reflect greater sentence complexity at around age 3 with the production of sentences that include a main clause (e.g., *I think*) and a subordinate clause (e.g., *that*) to produce sentences such as *I think that I like that*.

♦ Pragmatic development reflects the use of more polite forms of request, such as the use of *please* by younger children, and indirect speech acts (e.g., *Can I* at about 3½ to 4 years of age).

♦ Children's word productions are closer to those of adults as their phonological skills develop when they have greater control of their production skills and better perception of sound contrasts that distinguish words (e.g., f/v, p/b/, t/d).

♦ Phonological awareness develops when children become more aware of sounds in words and the connection between spoken sounds and written letters.

♦ Semantic skills increase, during the ages of 3 to 5, when children develop a better understanding of language and acquire more abstract word meanings. For example, they now understand multiple word meanings (e.g., *toy block, don't block the doorway*, and *go around the block*).

♦ Semantic skills also develop as children produce stories with a central topic and temporal order (e.g., *This is a story about and first . . . then . . . next*).

♦ Multilinguistic differences also exist in children's language and speech productions because children come from different language and culture backgrounds. We understand that these differences do not indicate, in all cases, disorders.

♦ Children begin to gain knowledge about print, which further develops when they enter school.

Appendix B provides a guide to the identification of signs of disorders in language and pragmatics. To be competent to support children who may have disorders, it is essential that speech-language pathologists become aware of what constitutes a disorder (American Speech-Language-Hearing Association, 1988). As you review Appendix B, note that there are certain signs that a disorder may be present.

In Chapter 7, we examine children's language development from ages 6 through adolescence. There is a progression in language development from the early stages, which provides the foundation for later learning.

KEY WORDS

Argument

Bootstrapping

Cohesion

Cohesive devices

Concrete

Contextualized narratives

Conversational postulates

Copula

Decentration

Decontextualized language

Decontextualized narrative

Deictic terms

Deixis

Divergent thinking

Egocentric

Ellipsis

Emergent literacy

Equative

Fast mapping

Fictional narrative

Indirect speech acts

Magical thinking

Marked

Mental state verbs

Metalinguistic

Modal auxiliaries

Morphophonemic

Motherese

Paradigmatic

Performatives

Personal narrative

Phonological awareness

Predicate

Presuppositions

Propositions

Register

Semantic relation

Syntagmatic

Thematic roles

Theory of mind

Unmarked

Working memory

STUDY QUESTIONS

1. Describe the role of decentration in theory of mind and in children's play.

2. Describe the differences between early syntactic skills and complex language skills.

3. Describe the role of cohesive devices in narrative development.

4. Explain why derivational morphemes may develop later in children's language.

5. Consulting Appendix A, describe the language development of a typical 3-year-old child.

REFERENCES

American Speech-Language-Hearing Association. (1988). *Prevention of communication disorders* [Position statement]. Retrieved from http://www.asha.org/policy

American Speech-Language-Hearing Association. (2009). *How does your child hear can talk.* Retrieved from http://www.asha.org/public/speech/development/chart.htm

Anderson, E. (1992). *Speaking with style. The sociolinguistic skills of children.* London, England: Routledge.

Angel, C. A. (2009). *Language development and disorders: A case study approach.* Burlington, MA: Jones & Bartlett.

Apel, K., Kahmi, A., & Dollaghan, C. (1987, November). *Fast mapping skills in young children: Name that word.* Paper presented at the American Speech-Language-Hearing Association Convention, Washington, DC.

Apel, K., & Masterson, J. (1998). *Assessment and treatment of narrative skills: What's the story?* Rockville, MD: American Speech-Language-Hearing Association.

Astington, J. W. (1990). Narrative and the child's theory of mind. In B. K. Britton & A. D. Pellegrini (Eds.), *Narrative thought and narrative language* (pp. 151–171). Hillsdale, NJ: Erlbaum.

Baddeley, A. (1991). *Human memory: Theory and practice.* London, England: Lawrence Erlbaum.

Baron-Cohen, S. (1993). From attention-goal psychology to belief-desire psychology: The development of a theory of mind, and its dysfunction. In S. Baron-Cohen, H. Tager-Flusberg, & D. J. Cohen (Eds.), *Understanding other minds: Perspectives from autism* (pp. 59–82). New York, NY: Oxford University Press.

Baron-Cohen, S. (1996). *Mindblindness: An essay on autism and theory of mind.* Cambridge, MA: MIT Press.

Bartsch, K., & Wellman, H. (1995). *Children talk about the mind.* New York, NY: Oxford University Press.

Bates, E. (1976). *Language and context: The acquisition of pragmatics.* San Diego, CA: Academic Press.

Berko, J. (1958). The child's learning of English morphology. *Word, 14,* 150–177.

Berman, R. A., & Slobin, D. I. (1994). *Relating events in narrative: A crosslinguistic developmental study.* Hillsdale, NJ: Erlbaum.

Bernhardt, B. H., & Stemberger, J. P. (1998). *Handbook of phonological development: From the perspective of constraint-based nonlinear phonology.* San Diego, CA: Academic Press.

Bernstein, D. K. (2011). Language development from ages 3 to 5. In S. Levey & S. Polirstok (Eds.), *Language development: Understanding language diversity in the classroom* (pp. 139–160). Los Angeles, CA: Sage.

Bernstein, D. K., & Levey, S. (2009). Language development: A review. In D. K. Bernstein & E. Tiegerman-Farber (Eds.), *Language and communication disorders in children* (6th ed., pp. 28–100). Boston, MA: Allyn & Bacon.

Bernthal, J., & Bankson, N. (2004). *Articulation and phonological disorders* (4th ed.). Boston, MA: Allyn & Bacon.

Bever, T. G. (1970). The comprehension and memory of sentence with temporal relations. In W. J. M. Levelt & P. Flores d'Arcais (Eds.), *Advances in psycholinguistics* (pp. 312–316). Amsterdam, The Netherlands: North Holland.

Bliss, L. (1988). Modal usage by preschool children. *Journal of Applied Developmental Psychology, 9,* 253–261.

Bliss, L. (1989). Selected syntactic usage of language-impaired children. *Journal of Communication Disorders, 22,* 277–289.

Bliss, L., & McCabe, A. (2011). Educational implications of narrative discourse. In S. Levey & S. Polirstok (Eds.), *Language development: Understanding diversity in the classroom* (pp. 209–226). Los Angeles, CA: Sage.

Bloom, L. (1991). *Language development from two to three.* Cambridge, UK: Cambridge University Press.

Bloom, L., Lahey, M., Hood, L., Lifter, K., & Fiess, K. (1980). Complex sentences: Acquisition of syntactic connectives and the semantic relations they encode. *Journal of Child Language, 7,* 235–261.

Booth, J. R., Hall, W. S., Robison, G. C., & Kim, S. Y. (1997). Acquisition of the mental state verb know by 2- to 5-year old children. *Journal of Psycholinguistic Research, 26*(6), 581–603.

Bowerman, M. (1973). Structural relationships in children's utterances: Semantic or syntactic? In T. Moore (Ed.), *Cognitive development and the acquisition of language* (pp. 197–213). New York, NY: Academic Press.

Bowerman, M. (1982). Reorganisational processes in lexical and syntactic development. In E. Wanner & L. Gleitman (Eds.), *Language acquisition: The state of the art* (pp. 319–346). Cambridge, UK: Cambridge University Press.

Brewer, W. F., & Stone, J. B. (1975). Acquisition of spatial antonym pairs. *Journal of Experimental Child Psychology, 19,* 299–307.

Brinton, B., & Fujiki, M. (1989). *Conversational management with language impaired children.* Rockville, MD: Aspen.

Brown, R. (1957). Linguistic determinism and the part of speech. *Journal of Abnormal and Social Psychology, 55,* 1–5.

Brown, R. (1973). *A first language: The early stages.* Cambridge, MA: Harvard University Press.

Bryant, P., MacLean, M., & Bradley, L. (1990). Rhyme, language, and children's reading. *Applied Psycholinguistics, 11*(3), 237–252.

Burgess, S. R., & Lonigan, C. J. (1998). Bidirectional relations of phonological sensitivity and prereading abilities: evidence from a preschool sample. *Journal of Experimental Child Psychology, 70,* 117–141.

Carroll, J. M., Snowling, M. J., Hulme, C., & Stevenson, J. (2003). The development of phonological awareness in preschool children. *Developmental Psychology, 39*(5), 913–923.

Catts, H. W., & Kamhi, A. G. (Eds.). (2005). *Language and reading disabilities* (2nd ed.). Boston, MA: Allyn & Bacon.

Clark, E. V. (1971). On the acquisition of the meaning of *before* and *after. Journal of Verbal Learning and Verbal Behavior, 10*(3), 266–275.

Clark, E. V. (1973). What's in a word? On the child's acquisition of semantics in his first language. In T. E. Moore (Ed.), *Cognitive development and the acquisition of language.* New York, NY: Academic Press.

Dever, R. (1978). *TALK: Teaching the American language to kids.* Columbus, OH: Merrill/Macmillan.

De Villiers, P., & Burns, F. (2003, November). *Assessing narrative skills in children.* Paper presented at the annual meeting of the American Speech-Language-Hearing Association, Chicago, IL.

Diessel, H., & Tomasello, M. (2001). The acquisition of finite complement clauses in English: A corpus-based analysis. *Cognitive Linguistics, 12*(2), 97–141.

de Villiers, J. G., & de Villiers, P. A. (2003) Language for thought: Coming to understand false beliefs. In D. Gentner and S. Goldin-Meadow (Eds.), *Language in mind: Advances in the study of language and thought.* Cambridge, MA: MIT Press.

Dore, J. (1974). A pragmatic description of early language development. *Journal of Psycholinguistic Research, 4,* 343–350.

Dore, J. (1975). Holophrases, speech acts and language universals. *Journal of Child Language 2,* 20–40.

Durgunoğlu, A. Y., & Oney, B. (2002). Phonological awareness in literacy acquisition: It's not only for children. *Scientific Studies of Reading, 52,* 189–204.

Entwisle, D. R. (1966). *Word associations of young children.* Baltimore, MD: Johns Hopkins Press.

Fein, G. G. (1975). A transformational analysis of play. *Developmental Psychology, 11,* 291–296.

Fey, M. E. (1986). *Language intervention with young children.* Boston, MA: Allyn & Bacon.

Fillmore, C. J. (1968). The case for case. In E. Bach & R. T. Harms (Eds.), *Universals in linguistic theory* (pp. 1–88). New York, NY: Holt, Rinehart, and Winston.

Gerken, L. (1991). The metrical basis for children's subjectless sentences. *Journal of Memory and Language, 30,* 431–451.

Gleason, J. B. (1958). The child's learning of English morphology. *Word, 14,* 150–177.

Gleitman, L. (1990). The structural sources of verb meanings. *Language Acquisition, 1,* 3–5.

Gleitman, L. R., Cassidy, K., Nappa, R., Papafragou, A., & Trueswell, J. C. (2005). Hard words. *Language Learning and Development, 1*(1), 23–64.

Goldstein, B. (2000). *Cultural and linguistic diversity resource guide for speech-language pathologists.* San Diego, CA: Singular.

Goldstein, B. (2001). Transcription of Spanish and Spanish-influenced English. *Communication Disorders Quarterly, 23*(1), 54–60.

Goldstein, B., & Iglesias, A. (1996). Phonological patterns in normally developing Spanish-speaking 3- and 4-year-olds of Puerto Rican descent. *Journal of Communication Disorders, 29*(5), 367–387.

Golinkoff, R. M., Mervis, C. B., & Hirsh-Pasek, K. (1994). Early object labels: The case for a developmental principles framework. *Journal of Child Language, 21,* 125–155.

Goodz, N. S. (1982). Is before really easier to understand than after? *Child Development, 53*(3), 822–825.

Gopnik, M. (1997). Language deficits and genetic factors. *Trends in Cognitive Sciences, 1*(1), 5–9.

Gopnik, M., & Meltzoff, A. N. (1994). Minds, bodies and persons: Young children's understanding of the self and others as reflected in imitation and "theory of mind" research. In S. T. Parker, R. W. Mitchell, & M. L. Boccia (Eds.), *Self-awareness in animals and humans: Developmental Perspectives* (pp. 166–186). New York, NY: Cambridge University Press.

Grice, H. P. (1975). Logic and conversation. In P. Cole & J. L. Morgan (Eds.), *Speech acts* (pp. 41–58). New York, NY: Academic Press.

Halliday, M. A. K., & Hasan, R. (1976). *Cohesion in English.* London, England: Longman.

Happé, F., Briskman, J., & Frith, U. (2001). Exploring the cognitive phenotype of autism: Weak "central coherence" in parents and siblings of children with autism: I. experimental tests. *Journal of Child Psychology and Psychiatry, 42*(3), 299–307.

Heath, S. B. (1996). What no bedtime story means: Narrative skills at home and school. In D. Brenneis & R. K. S. Macaulay (Eds.), *The matrix of language* (pp. 12–38). Cumnor Hill, Oxford, UK: Westview Press.

Hodges, A., Krugler, V., & Law, D. (2004). A corpus study on the item-based nature of early grammar acquisition. *Colorado Research in Linguistics, 17*(1). Boulder: University of Colorado Press.

Hudson, J. A. (2006). The development of future time concepts through mother-child conversation. *Merrill-Palmer Quarterly, 52*(1), 70–95.

Hurewitz, F., Papafragou, A., Gleitman, L., & Gelman, R. (2006). Asymmetries in the acquisition in the acquisition of numbers and quantifiers. *Language Learning and Development, 2,* 77–96.

Iglesias, A., & Goldstein, B. (1998). Language and dialectal variations. In J. Bernthal & N. Bankson (Eds.), *Articulation and phonological disorders* (4th ed., pp. 148–171). Needham Heights, MA: Allyn & Bacon.

Iglesias, A., & Goldstein, B. (2004). Language and dialectal variations. In J. Bernthal & N. Bankson (Eds.), *Articulation and phonological disorders* (5th ed., pp. 348–375). Boston, MA: Allyn & Bacon.

Jenkins, J. M., Terrell, S. L., Kogushi, Y., Lollis, S., & Ross, H. S. (2003). A longitudinal investigation of the dynamics of mental state talk in families. *Child Development, 74,* 905–920.

Johnson, A. R., Johnston, E. B., & Weinrich, B. D. (1984). Assessing pragmatic skills in children's language. *Language, Speech, and Hearing Services in Schools, 15,* 2–9.

Johnson, B. W., & Morris, S. R. (2007). Clinical implications of the effects of lexical aspect and phonology on children's production of the regular past tense. *Child Language Teaching and Therapy, 23,* 287–306.

Justice, L. M., & Ezell, H. K. (2000). Enhancing children's print and word awareness through home-based parent intervention. *American Journal of Speech-Language Pathology, 9,* 257–269.

Kahmi, A. G., & Koenig, L. A. (1985). Metalinguistic awareness in normal and language-disordered children. *Language, Speech, and Hearing Services in Schools, 16,* 199–210.

Klir, George J. (1991). *Facets of systems science.* New York, NY: Plenum Press.

Lahey, M. (1988). 'What is language?' In *Language disorders and language development.* London, England: Collier Macmillan.

Lee, E. C., & Rescorla, L. (2008). The use of psychological state words by late talkers at ages 3, 4, and 5 years. *Applied Psycholinguistics, 28,* 21–39.

Leonard, L. B., Bolders, J. G., & Miller, J. A. (1976). An examination of the semantic relations reflected in the language usage of normal and disordered children. *Journal of Speech and Hearing Research, 19,* 371–392.

Levey, S., & Cruz, D. (2004). The discrimination of English vowels by bilingual Spanish/English and monolingual English speakers. *Contemporary Issues in Communication Science and Disorders, 31,* 162–172.

Levey, S., & Polirstok, S. (Eds.) (2011). *Language development: Understanding language diversity in the classroom.* Los Angeles, CA: Sage.

Levey, S., & Schwartz, R. G. (2002). Syllable omission by two-year-old children. *Communication Disorders Quarterly, 23*(4), 169–177.

Lonigan, C., Burgess, S. R., Anthony, J. L., & Barker, T. A. (1998). Development of phonological sensitivity in 2- to 5-year-old children. *Journal of Educational Psychology, 90,* 294–311.

Lyon, G. R., & Moats, L. C. (1997). Critical conceptual and methodological considerations in reading intervention research. *Journal of Learning Disabilities, 30,* 578–588.

MacDonald, G. W., & Cornwall, A. (1995). The relationship between phonological awareness and spelling achievement eleven years later. *Journal of Learning Disabilities, 28,* 523–527.

MacWhinney, B. (2003). The emergence of language from body, brain, and society. In *Chicago Linguistic Society.* Chicago, IL: University of Chicago Press.

Marchman, V. A., Wulfeck, B., & Weismer, S. E. (1999). Morphological productivity in children with normal language and SLI: A study of the English past tense. *Journal of Speech, Language, and Hearing Research, 42,* 206–219.

McCune-Nicolich, L. (1981). Toward symbolic functioning: Structure of early pretend games and potential parallels with language. *Child Development, 52,* 785–797.

McGregor, K. (2000). The development and enhancement of narrative skills in a preschool classroom. *American Journal of Speech-Language Pathology, 9,* 55–71.

McLaughlin, S. (1998). *Introduction to language development.* San Diego, CA: Singular.

Minami, M., & McCabe, A. (1991). Haiku as a discourse regulation device: A stanza analysis of Japanese children's personal narratives. *Language in Society, 20,* 577–600.

Miller, C. A. (2006). Developmental relationships between language and theory of mind. *American Journal of Speech-Language Pathology, 15,* 142–154.

Miller, L. (1978). Pragmaties and early childhood language disorders. *Journal of Speech and Hearing Disorders, 43,* 419–436.

Nelson, N. W. (1993). *Childhood language disorders in context: Infancy through adolescence.* New York, NY: Macmillan.

Ninio, A., & Snow, C. E. (1996). *Pragmatic development: Essays in developmental science.* Boulder, CO: Westview Press.

Norman, D., & Shallice, T. (1980). Attention to action: Willed and automatic control of behavior. In R. Davidon, G. Schwartz, & D. Shapiro (Eds.), *Consciousness and self-regulation* (Vol. 4, pp. 1–18). New York, NY: Plenum.

Oetting, J. B., & Horohov, J. E. (1997). Past-tense marking by children with and without specific language impairment. *Journal of Speech, Language, and Hearing Research, 40,* 62–74.

Oetting, J. B., Rice, M. L., & Swank, L. K. (1995). Quick incidental learning (QUIL) of words by school-age children with and without SLI. *Journal of Speech and Hearing Research, 38,* 434–445.

Owens, R. E., Jr. (2012). *Language development: An introduction* (8th ed.). Boston, MA: Allyn & Bacon.

Owens, R. E., Metz, D. E., & Haas, A. (2000). *Introduction to communication disorders: A life span perspective.* Boston, MA: Allyn & Bacon.

Parrila, R., Kirby, J. R., & McQuarrie, L. (2004). Articulation rate, naming speed, verbal short-term memory, and phonological awareness: Longitudinal predictors of early reading development? *Scientific Studies of Reading, 8*(1), 3–26.

Paul, R. (1981). Analyzing complex sentence development. In J. F. Miller (Ed.), *Assessing language production in children: An experimental procedure* (pp. 36–40). Needham Heights, MA: Allyn & Bacon.

Paul, R. (2001). *Language disorders from infancy through adolescence: Assessment and intervention.* St. Louis, MO: Mosby.

Peterson, C. (1990). The who, when and where of early narratives. *Journal of Child Language, 17*, 433–455.

Peterson, C., & Dodsworth, P. (1991). A longitudinal analysis of young children's cohesion and noun specification in narratives.

Peterson, C., & McCabe, A. (1983). *Developmental psycholinguistics: Three ways of looking at a child's narrative.* New York, NY: Plenum. *Journal of Child Language, 18*, 397–415.

Piaget, J. (1954). *The construction of reality in the child.* New York, NY: Basic Books.

Piaget, J. (1962). *Play, dreams, and imitation in childhood.* New York, NY: Norton.

Pinker, S. (1984). *Language learnability and language development.* Cambridge, MA: Harvard University Press.

Rice, M. L., & Wexler, K. (1998). Family histories of children with SLI who show extended optional infinities. *Journal of Speech, Language, and Hearing Research, 41*, 419–432.

Roseberry-McKibbin, C. (2008). *Multicultural students with special language needs: Practical strategies for assessment.* Oceanside, CA: Academic Communications Associates.

Roth, F. F., & Spekman, N. J. (1984). Assessing the pragmatic abilities of children: Part 1. Organizational framework and assessment parameters. *Journal of Speech and Hearing Disorders, 49*, 2–11.

Sandhofer, C. M., & Smith, L. B. (2001). Why children learn color and size words so differently: Evidence from adults' learning of artificial terms. *Journal of Experimental Psychology, 130*(4), 600–620.

Scarborough, H. S., & Dobrich, W. (1990). Development of children with early language delay. *Journal of Speech and Hearing Research, 33*, 70–83.

Schober-Peterson, D., & Johnson, C. J. (1989). Conversational topics of 4-year-olds. *Journal of Speech and Hearing Research, 32*, 857–870.

Searle, J. (1965). What is a speech act? In P. P. Giglioli (Ed.), *Language and social context* (pp. 136–154). Harmondsworth, England: Penguin Books.

Segal, M., Bardige, B., Woika, M. J., & Leinfelder, J. (2006). *All about child care and early education: A comprehensive resource for child care professionals.* Needham, MA: Allyn & Bacon.

Shankweiler, D., Crain, S., Katz, L., Fowler, A., Liberman, A., Brady, S., . . . Shaywitz, B. (1995). Cognitive profiles of reading-disabled children: Comparison of language skills in phonology, morphology, and syntax. *Psychological Science, 6*, 149–156.

Shatz, M., & O'Reilly, A. (1990). Conversational or communicative skill? A reassessment of two-year-olds' behavior in miscommunication episodes. *Journal of Child Language, 17*, 131–146.

Shatz, M., Tare, M., Nguyen, S. P., & Young, T. (2010). Acquiring non-object terms: The case for time words. *Journal of Cognitive Development, 1*(1): 16–36.

Shaywitz, B. A., Fletcher, J. M., Holahan, J. M., & Shaywitz, S. E. (1992). Discrepancy compared to low achievement definitions of reading disability: Results from the Connecticut longitudinal study. *Journal of Learning Disabilities, 25*(10), 639–648.

Silva, M. J., & McCabe, A. (1996). Vignettes of the continuous and family ties: Some Latino American traditions. In A. McCabe (Ed.), *Chameleon readers: Teaching children to appreciate all kinds of good stories* (pp. 116–136). New York, NY: McGraw-Hill.

Snow, C., Scarborough, H., & Burns, M. S. (1999). What SLPs need to know about early reading. *Topics in Language Disorders, 20*, 48–58.

Snow, C. E., Porche, M. V., Tabors, P. O., & Harris, S. R. (2007). *Is literacy enough? Pathways to academic success for adolescents.* Baltimore, MD: Paul Brookes.

Stanovich, K. E., & Siegel, L. S. (1994). The phenotypic performance profile of reading-disabled children: A regression-based test of the phonological-core variable difference model. *Journal of Education Psychology, 96*, 24–53.

Steffani, S. A. (2007). Identifying embedded and conjoined complex: Making it simple. *Contemporary Issues in Communication Science and Disorders, 34*, 44–54.

Stockman, I. J. (1996). The promises and pitfalls of language sample analysis as an assessment tool for linguistic minority children. *Language, Speech, and Hearing Services in Schools, 27*, 355–366.

Subbotsky, E. (2010). *Magic and the mind: Mechanisms, functions and the development of magical thinking and behavior.* Oxford, England: Oxford University Press.

Swanson, H. L., Mink, J., & Bocian, K. M. (1999). Cognitive processing deficits in poor readers with symptoms of reading disabilities and ADHD: More alike than different? *Journal of Educational Psychology, 91*(2), 321–333.

Tabors, P. O., Snow, C. E., & Dickinson, D. K. (2001). Homes and schools together: Supporting language and early literacy development. In D. K. Dickinson & P. O. Tabors (Eds.), *Beginning literacy with language.* Baltimore, MD: Paul Brookes.

Tager-Flusberg, H., de Villiers, J., & Hakuta, K. (1982). The development of sentence coordination. In S. A. Kuczaj (Ed.), *Language development. Volume 1: Syntax and semantics* (pp. 201–243). Hillsdale, NJ: Erlbaum.

Tomasello, M. (1992b). *First verbs.* Cambridge, UK: Cambridge University Press.

Tomasello, M. (2000). The item-based nature of children's early syntactic development. *Trends in Cognitive Sciences, 4*(4). Retrieved from http://www.sciencedirect.com/science/article/pii/S1364661300014625

Tomasello, M. (2003). *Constructing a language: A usage-based theory of language acquisition.* Cambridge, MA: Harvard University Press.

Torgesen, J. K. (1999). Assessment and instruction for phonemic awareness and word recognition skills. In H. W. Catts & A. G. Kamhi (Eds.), *Language and reading disabilities* (pp. 128–153). Boston, MA: Allyn & Bacon.

Torgesen, J. K., Wagner, R. K., & Rashotte, C. A. (1994). Longitudinal studies of phonological processing and reading. *Journal of Learning Disabilities, 27*, 276–286.

Troia, G. A. (2004). Building word recognition skills through empirically validated instructional practices: Collaborative efforts of speech-language pathologists and teachers. In E. R. Silliman & L. C. Wilkinson (Eds.), *Language and literacy learning in schools* (pp. 98–129). New York, NY: Guilford Press.

Ukraninetz McFadden, T. (1991). Narrative and expository language: A criterion-based assessment procedure for school-age children. *Journal of Speech Language Pathology and Audiology, 15*(3), 57–63.

Umiker-Seboek, D. (1977). Preschool children's interconversational narratives. *Journal of Child Language, 6*, 91–109.

Van Kleeck, A. (1982). The emergence of linguistic awareness: A cognitive framework. *Merrill-Palmer Quarterly, 28*(2), 237–265.

Van Kleeck, A. (1995). Learning about print before learning to read. In K. Butler (Ed.), *Best practices 11. The classroom as an interaction context* (pp. 3–23). Gaithersburg, MD: Aspen.

Weist, R. M. (2002). Temporal and spatial concepts in child language: Conventional and configurational. *Journal of Psycholinguistic Research, 31*(3), 195–210.

Wells, G. (1985). *Language development in the preschool years.* New York, NY: Cambridge University Press.

Westby, C. E. (1980). Assessment of cognitive and language abilities through play. *Language, Speech, and Hearing Services in Schools, 11*, 154–168.

Wexler, K. (1994). Optional infinitives. In D. Lightfoot & N. Hornsten (Eds.), *Verb movement* (pp. 305–350). New York, NY: Cambridge University Press.

Wimmer, H., & Perner, J. (1983). Beliefs about beliefs: Representation and constraining function of wrong beliefs in young children's understanding of perception. *Cognition, 13*, 103–128.

Winskel, H. (2003). The acquisition of temporal event sequencing: A cross-linguistic study using an elicited imitation task. *First Language 23*(1), 65–95.

Wolfram, W. (1986). Language variation in the United States. In O. L. Taylor (Ed.), *Nature of communication disorders in culturally and linguistically diverse populations* (pp. 73–116). San Diego, CA: College-Hill Press.

Woodward, H., & Lowell, F. (1916). Children's association frequency tables. *Psychological Monographs, 22*(5).

Yopp, H. K., & Yopp, R. H. (2010). *Purposeful play for early childhood phonological awareness.* Huntington Beach, CA: Shell Education.

Zdorenko, T., & Paradis, J. (2011). Articles in child L2 English: When L1 and L2 acquisition meet at the interface. *First Language,* 1–25.

Zelazo, P. D., Carter, A., Reznick, J. S., & Frye, D. (1997). Early development of executive function: A problem-solving framework. *Review of General Psychology, 1,* 198–226.

APPENDIX A
Developmental Milestones From Ages 3 to 5

Three to Four Years

Hearing and Understanding	Talking
◆ Hears you when you call from another room. ◆ Hears television or radio at the same loudness level as other family members. ◆ Answers simple "who?", "what?", "where?", and "why?" questions.	◆ Talks about activities at school or at friends' homes. ◆ People outside of the family usually understand child's speech. ◆ Uses a lot of sentences that have 4 or more words. ◆ Usually talks easily without repeating syllables or words.

Four to Five Years

Hearing and Understanding	Talking
◆ Pays attention to a short story and answers simple questions about it. ◆ Hears and understands most of what is said at home and in school.	◆ Uses sentences that give lots of details ("The biggest peach is mine"). ◆ Tells stories that stick to topic. ◆ Communicates easily with other children and adults. ◆ Says most sounds correctly except a few like *l, s, r, v, z, ch, sh, th.* ◆ Says rhyming words. ◆ Names some letters and numbers. ◆ Uses the same grammar as the rest of the family.

From *Language Development: Understanding Language Diversity in the Classroom* (pp. 53–54), by S. Levey & S. Polirstok (Eds.), 2011, Los Angeles, CA: Sage. Reprinted with permission.

APPENDIX B
Signs of Disorders in Children

Expressive Language

◆ Rarely initiates verbal interactions or activities with peers or family members.

◆ Does not respond verbally to questions or comments from peers or family members.

◆ Language observed to be lower than the level used by peers.

◆ Smaller vocabulary than expected for age, in first language or second (if second-language learner).

◆ Shorter, less complex sentences than expected for age.

◆ Difficulty communicating verbally with peers or family members.

◆ Relies heavily on gestures and non-verbal means to communicate.

◆ Peers rarely initiate verbal exchanges.

◆ Does not attempt to repair communication failures.

◆ Does not verbally request help or clarification when needed.

◆ Makes frequent use of empty, meaningless words: *it, thing, this,* or *that.*

◆ Peers have difficulty understanding the child's speech or language efforts.

Receptive Language

◆ Instructions need to be repeated.

◆ Slow in responding to questions or instructions.

◆ Does not learn new concepts or vocabulary.

◆ Forgets material assumed to be learned.

Pragmatics

◆ Does not take turns or maintain conversations with peers.

◆ Eye contact may be absent or inconsistent

◆ Does not engage peers in an appropriate manner (e.g., "Can I play with your truck please?")

From *Strategies to Identify Children with Communication Disorders* (Figure 3.2 on pages 53–54), by S. Levey, 2011, Los Angeles, CA: Sage. Reprinted by permission.

CHAPTER 7

Language Development in Middle and Late Childhood and Adolescence

Cheryl Smith Gabig

Samantha is an 8-year-old third grader who is a good student and enjoys reading and writing. Her parents are impressed with Samantha's ability to understand, write, and tell stories with complex sentences and advanced vocabulary. After reading this chapter, you will be able to understand the sources and aspects of language development that contribute to Samantha's skill in understanding and producing narratives.

Young children entering first grade are competent speech and language users. By kindergarten, most native English-speaking children, 5 to 6 years of age, have acquired the majority of the English phonemes, produce clear, intelligible speech, use grammatically correct sentences with varied vocabulary, and engage in conversation with their peers and adults. Despite the high degree of language competence seen in preschool and kindergarten children, research has revealed that language continues to develop past the preschool years into middle childhood (6–8 years), late childhood (9–12 years), and adolescence (13+ years) (Nippold, 1988, 2007; Scott & Stokes, 1995). Language development in school-age children and adolescents is subtle or less obvious than the language development seen in toddlers and preschool children.

The development of language beyond the *primary* language competence seen in kindergarten children is referred to as *secondary* language development (Smith Gabig, 2011). Secondary language development includes the use of more complex sentence forms; the acquisition of complex word structure containing derivational morphemes; the development of advanced semantic knowledge and vocabulary; the use of metaphoric language, idioms, and proverbs; advancements in broad metalinguistic knowledge; and social pragmatic functioning. These language changes can be observed in both spoken and written language domains. Language development during the school years and adolescence encompasses and integrates linguistic knowledge and processing across the domains of speaking, listening, reading, and writing.

CHAPTER OBJECTIVES

The purpose of this chapter is to identify the various sources of input and the psychosocial experiences that influence ongoing language learning in school-age children and adolescents. In addition, the goal is to describe changes in language processing and competence across the areas of form, content, and use in middle and late childhood and adolescence. After reading this chapter, you will be able to:

◆ Identify and discuss five sources that contribute to language development in school-age children and adolescents
◆ Define intrasentential growth and explain the syntactic mechanisms that contribute to lengthier and more complex sentences
◆ Discuss how different types of conjunctions convey aspects of meaning to the listener or reader
◆ Differentiate among the different types of morphemes and their relationship to morphological awareness in children and adolescents
◆ Explain the importance of vocabulary knowledge and development in school-age children and adolescents to support their reading skills
◆ Describe three different types of figurative language and explain why some forms are learned later and are more difficult for children to comprehend and use

◆ Discuss the continued development of narrative in school-age children in terms of narrative content and structure

SOURCES OF LANGUAGE DEVELOPMENT IN SCHOOL-AGE CHILDREN AND ADOLESCENTS

In order to learn language, an individual must have direct experience in processing all aspects of the language: its form (syntax or sentence structure), content (semantics or meaning conveyed in words and longer utterances), and ways of social-pragmatic functioning (the use of language in interaction). These direct experiences are referred to as input sources because they provide the necessary stimulation to the language learning system.

> During the primary language acquisition period, birth to approximately 5 years of age, the spoken language used by the caregiver or parents is the main source of input to a child. This input provides children with information on how language is structured, on vocabulary, and on the social conventions of the language (Gelman, 2009; Gelman, Coley, Rosengren, Hartman, & Pappas, 1998; Hoff-Ginsberg, 1990; Hoff-Ginsberg & Shatz, 1982).

Language is a method of communication, spoken, written, or gestural, consisting of the use of words as symbols in a structured, conventional way to communicate ideas. Language is a complex form of communication that can be encoded in both oral and written modes. Many factors contribute to the ongoing language development and refinement seen in children beyond the preschool years, including cognitive, psychosocial, and environmental factors. With this in mind, there are five sources of input that play a role in the continued language development of school-age children and adolescents (Figure 7–1):

◆ Academic discourse in the classroom
◆ Integration of spoken and written language
◆ Growth in social competence and social interaction
◆ Cognitive development
◆ Linguistic individualism

THE FIVE SOURCES THAT PLAY A ROLE IN LANGUAGE DEVELOPMENT

Academic Language and Classroom Discourse

A significant factor affecting children's ongoing language development and refinement is the academic language used in the educational setting. According to a report published by the University of Michigan Institute for Social Research (Hofferth & Sandberg, 2000), children ages 6 to 12 years in the United States attend school on the average of 32.5 hours a week. During the average 180-day school year, a child spends approximately 1,170 hours in the classroom or school setting. Within this social context, children and adolescents must learn to navigate the academic culture, acquire language discourse patterns, and learn performance expectations. This social context goes beyond the expectations and experiences in the home or playground. The academic context demands and allows for the development and integration of language across the modalities of listening, speaking, reading, and writing, along with various modes of communication.

Academic Language Discourse Pattern Within the Classroom

The academic language discourse pattern within the classroom possesses unique interactional rules. For example, the academic context includes the use of **decontextualized** language (Cazden, 2001) with the following examples of decontextualized language use:

Meaning conveyed through language, rather than use of contextual clues (e.g., describing things or events from outside of the present context)

The use of time referents (e.g., yesterday and tomorrow)

Sources of Language Development in Children and Adolescents

Academic discourse in the classroom	Integration of spoken and written language	Social cognition and social competence	Cognitive development	Linguistic individualism

Figure 7–1. *Sources contributing to the continued language development of school-age children and adolescents.*

Language used to convey new or novel information (e.g., information not known to the listener)

The use of cohesive devices to indicate a sequence of events (e.g., *and then . . . next*)

> Younger language users talk about the *here and now* (rather than past or future) and rely heavily on the context to convey meaning (e.g., pointing to or showing things to indicate meaning). Thus, the use of decontextualized language by school-age children and by teachers in classroom settings is a significant sign of more advanced language skills.

The classroom is a complex social system with many different purposes for talking (Cazden, 2001). Typically, classroom discourse is characterized by teacher-directed and teacher-mediated turns at talking because the teacher chooses the topics of talk and evaluates the content of the verbal turn by a child. This specific teacher-directed discourse pattern has been characterized as an "IRE" exchange, a three-part conversational structure in which the teacher *initiates*, the child *responds*, and the teacher *evaluates* (Cazden, 2001).

The Initiation, Response, and Evaluation (IRE) Context

In the IRE discourse context, communication expectations are unspoken and need to be inferred (surmised and understood) by the child in order to achieve both linguistic and social competence (Sturm & Nelson, 1997). In other words, children must be able to guess or deduce the teacher's expectations. There is evidence that children learn this unique discourse pattern and its accompanying linguistic demands early in the elementary years. Thus, children acquire a distinctive way of talking and engaging in social-communicative interaction within the complex social setting of the classroom.

> Academic discourse provides a linguistic milieu within which the school-age child and adolescent can acquire new vocabulary and concepts and a functional way of talking about content. Academic discourse is distinct from the language content and functional framework of language interaction seen in the home or in informal social settings.

Classroom Demands

Sturm and Nelson (1997) investigated changes in classroom communication demands in five classrooms at each of the first, third, and fifth grades. In terms of a teacher's use of language, the amount of linguistic quantity and complexity used in the classroom steadily grows from the first to the third grade and from the third to the fifth grade. For example, teacher talk becomes longer and more varied in vocabulary type by the fifth grade (Sturm & Nelson, 1997). However, children's linguistic quantity and complexity do not change significantly by grade, except for the use of longer utterances containing **mazes**, a type of utterance characterized by false starts, interruptions, or unattached fragments that do not contribute to the ongoing flow of meaning. For both teachers and students, the communicative functions used most frequently across the grades are the following:

- Conveying content (e.g., specific talk conveying information)
- Marking content (e.g., cueing listeners to important information to follow)

> Children begin to learn academic discourse function and interaction in the first grade at 6 years of age. Children steadily become more competent in engaging in academic discourse by grade five, evidenced by how and when they reply and convey information about curriculum content.

The Integration of Speaking, Listening, Reading, and Written Language

Perhaps the single most significant contributor to continued language development in school-age children and adolescents is the integration of oral and written language (i.e., print). **Linguistic awareness** of one's primary **aural/oral (hearing/speaking) language** system is critical to the reading process, a secondary or **visual language** system. Although reading and writing are learned later, learning to read and write is initially tied to the primary aural/oral language system.

> In one of the early studies of connection between oral/aural language and reading, Kavanagh & Mattingly (1972) stated that "Speaking and listening are primary linguistic activities; reading is a secondary and rather special sort of activity that relies critically upon the reader's awareness of these primary activities" (p. 133).

Oral language, although not sufficient on its own, provides an essential foundation for the development of reading and writing skills in children. Oral language also plays an important role in the literacy skills for children from other language backgrounds who are English-language learners (August & Shanahan, 2006). The connection between oral language and literacy skills is explained next (Moats, 2009, p. 7):

> Using words in communication requires and shows a deep level of word knowledge

> The ability to use a word in speaking and/or writing demonstrates true ownership of that word

The transfer of vocabulary knowledge from oral language to written language creates the ability to communicate without face-to-face interactions. Neurocognitive and reading research demonstrates that the intentional promotion of oral abilities (through storytelling, modeling vocabulary usage, and engaging in conversation) contributes to later success in reading, writing, and general academics (Moats, 2009; Sousa, 2005).

In summary, it is essential that the factors that lead to successful literacy skills (i.e., reading and writing) be present in early contexts: conversation, the use of rich language vocabulary, and storytelling.

The Aural/Oral Language System

Children initially learn to read and write an alphabetic script by relying on **phonological awareness** of the sound structure of words in their aural/oral language system (i.e., hearing/speaking). As a child gains skills and abilities in the written language system, the secondary language system begins to *inform* the primary, aural/oral language system. The relationship between oral and written language development becomes reciprocal and bi-directional, each system informing and reinforcing the other, as competence grows in the oral and written domains of language processing (Carlisle, 2000; Mahoney, Singson, & Mann, 2000; Nunes, Bryant, & Bindman, 2006). As noted by Nunes et al. (2006), "Learning to read and write transforms our knowledge of the structure of spoken language" (p. 767). Reading and writing skills and abilities inform the oral language system about the sublexical structure of words (i.e., the phonemes and morphemes that form the basic structure of words).

With this understanding of the symbiotic and reciprocal nature of the relation between the oral and written language systems, language development in school-age children and adolescents must be viewed within a more comprehensive, larger, language framework. As noted in Figure 7–2, a larger, more comprehensive language framework recognizes that expressive output and receptive input are integral parts of language processing for both auditory and visual language systems.

In the aural/oral language system, expressive output is accomplished by speech articulation, whereas receptive input is processed through the speech perceptual process. In the visual language system, expressive output of language is through writing, whereas receptive input is through reading. Language development in school-age children and adolescents entails interaction between the oral and visual language systems. This results in the expansion of language competence across both modalities of language processing.

The Role of Social Cognition and Social Competence in Language

A third source of input to the continuing development of language in the school-age child and adolescent is the development of **social competence that allows** successful interaction with their peers in specific settings (Cavell, 1990). Researchers in the area of social cognition and social competence in children conceptualize social competence as the ability to engage in social exchanges with others through successful social information processing (Dodge, Pettit, McClaskey, & Brown,

Larger General Language Framework

Medium		Expression Output	Product	Reception Input
Aural/Oral Language	→	Speech Articulation	Speech	Speech Perception
Visual Language	→	Writing	Script	Reading

Figure 7–2. *Products and processes of a larger general language framework.*

1986). According to Dodge et al. (1986) **social information processing** includes the ability to decode social cues; to access potential responses, either behavioral or verbal, or both; and to encode or produce the desired response.

> Of particular interest is the development of socially mediated language in school-age children during successful peer interactions. Peer interactions provide the opportunity for verbal exchanges, and the listener judges these verbal behaviors as socially acceptable or not.

As noted by Gallagher (1993), "Language is the primary means by which we make interpersonal contact, form relationships, socialize our children, regulate our interactions, and mediate concepts of ourselves and others as social beings" (p. 199).

Peer Relationships and Language Development

Gallagher (1993) noted two distinct types of peer relationships that may foster language development in children. One of the peer relationships is the close personal friendship that develops between co-equals. The other peer relationship is generalized acceptance by one's peers, or group popularity and inclusion.

During early elementary grades, children spend a great deal of time engaged in coordinated fantasy play with their peers and close friends. Fantasy play requires clear communication and negotiation of roles, props, and plot, necessitating considerable verbal interaction among children as members of the group. Successful

communication and social interaction during the fantasy play context provide the child with new and socially acceptable ways of talking, negotiating, and resolving conflicts while also allowing for the development of perspective taking (perceiving social or emotional situations from another person's point of view) and turn taking (being sender and receiver) in group discourse.

> Friendship and social competence are important to the young school-age child, and children with language impairments are at a disadvantage in learning these important language and communication skills, placing them at risk for ongoing difficulty in social-communicative interaction within the academic or social group (Brinton, Fujiki, & Powell, 1997; Conti-Ramsden & Botting, 2004).

Social Competence

The **pragmatic** aspect of language governs how individuals engage in social interaction. Social competence in school-age children and adolescents is critical because researchers have noticed a relationship between acceptance by peers and teachers and academic performance (Cavell, 1990; Wentzel, 1991). The older school-age child and adolescent's growth in social competence and subsequent language development is related to two sources. One source is the explicit understanding and use of pro-social skills and behaviors, and the other is the increasingly more individualized social experiences of the older child and adolescent (Cavell, 1990).

Pro-Social Behavior

Pro-social behavior is characterized by the willingness to engage in actions that benefit the other person or the group as a whole. Pro-social behavior includes the use of language that promotes social engagement, problem solving, and conflict resolution. One type of pro-social language functioning is the use of conflict resolution or interpersonal negotiation strategies to resolve differences between speakers in social settings (Cavell, 1990; Rydell, Hagekull, & Bohlin, 1997; Selman, Beardslee, Schultz, Krupa, & Podorefsky, 1986; Wentzel, 1991). The use of pro-social language functions by older children and adolescents allows for positive interactions with family members, classmates, and teachers (Cavell, 1990; Rydell et al., 1997; Selman et al., 1986). Successful conflict resolution involves specific communication skills associated with successful negotiation and conflict resolution.

There is a three-part hierarchy of communication for resolving conflicts (Selman et al., 1986):

◆ Defining the problem or conflict
◆ Proposing and justifying an action strategy to resolve the conflict
◆ Evaluating the impact of the action strategy on others' feelings

> Conflict resolution as a form of pragmatic language functioning is still developing in late childhood and is finally consolidated during late adolescence (Selman et al., 1986). Adolescents between 17 and 19 years of age are better at recognizing and defining the inherent problem and proposing and justifying an action or solution.

Cognitive Development

Cognitive development is a fourth contributing factor to language development in school-age children and adolescents. Children undergo significant changes in their cognitive development beginning in middle childhood and into adolescence.

The Preoperational Stage

Young children between 5 and 7 years of age are in the **preoperational stage** of cognitive development, a stage characterized by significant development in fantasy play and imagination as well as conceptual understanding of the relationships among the past, present, and future (Inhelder & Piaget, 1959). During this stage of cognitive development, children are also consolidating the linguistic marking of past/present/future tense, including the emergence of irregular past tense verbs, such as *wrote, blew, dug, swam*, and *fed* (Shipley, Maddox, & Driver, 1991). The focus on the child's cognitive development, seen in expanding imaginative play, contributes to the emergence of true narrative that includes all the components of story grammar (Botvin & Sutton-Smith, 1977; Klecan-Aker & Kelty, 1990).

The Concrete Operations Stage

Between 7 and 11 years, children enter the **concrete operations** stage of cognitive development, a stage characterized by the ability to reason logically about concrete events and to classify objects into sets (Piaget & Inhelder, 1969). Children in this stage of cognitive development can describe, in temporal order, the series of steps needed to complete a simple task or event and can engage in **reversibility**, the ability to think backward through the steps.

During this stage of cognitive development, children are able to explain how to play a game or how to make a sandwich. Classification is also important because cognitive development in this area contributes to the understanding of figurative language, such as the simple metaphor, a linguistic form wherein one referent is equated to a very different referent (e.g., *love is a blooming rose*). Cognitive development also contributes to the comprehension of comparative relationships and passive constructions, such as *Mary was pushed by Jan* (Wiig & Semel, 1973).

The Formal Operations Stage

Between 12 years of age and adulthood, children and adolescents are in the **formal operations** stage of cognitive development, characterized by logical operations and abstract thought. Children are able to understand and generate hypotheses (e.g., theories about how things work) in this stage of development. Adolescents in this stage are able to engage in deductive reasoning and to plan and execute problem solving. This stage of cognitive development has been linked to the comprehension of complex metaphors and idioms and the ability to engage in the abstract understanding of proverbs (Chan & Martinellie, 2008; Cometa & Eson, 1978; Douglas & Peel, 1979; Nippold & Fey, 1983).

Linguistic Individualism

The final source of language development for older children and adolescents is **linguistic individualism**, a concept that encompasses the language experiences of children and adolescents outside of the family or traditional academic setting (Nippold, 2007). Older children and adoles-cents experience increasingly more independence from the family and traditional academic settings as they mature, allowing for experiences in different social settings, extracurricular sports, or elective coursework. These experiences contain unique vocabulary or concepts, allowing the child or adolescent to acquire individualized, personal vocabulary or ways of talking.

> For example, an adolescent who volunteers in an assisted living facility through a church or scout group may acquire new vocabulary specific to the context or social conventions related to communication with residents, staff, or medical personnel. The language used in these experiences is beyond the language used in traditional social settings or academic coursework. Thus, these experiences contribute to the language knowledge of the child or adolescent.

Summary: Sources of Linguistic Input to School-Age Children and Adolescents

School-age children and adolescents have several sources of linguistic experience that shape and facilitate the growth of language knowledge and skills across all language components (e.g., syntax, semantics, and pragmatics). Children and adolescents spend a great deal of time in the classroom and academic settings. Learning to interact in the educational setting and to initiate and respond to academic discourse facilitates language processing. The integration of spoken language with written language is also critical to the child's and adolescent's awareness of language structure and to the ability to manipulate and use language. Finally, social development in middle and late childhood and into adolescence provides the individual with varied ways of talking to friends, acquaintances, and teachers.

DEVELOPMENTAL CHANGES IN LANGUAGE FORM: COMPLEX SYNTAX AND MORPHOLOGICAL KNOWLEDGE AND USE

Starting in early elementary through middle school and into high school, there are subtle yet significant changes in the child's understanding and use of **language form**, that is, the **structure** of the language system at the level of the word and sentence. **Form** refers to how words and sentences are constructed: words are constructed by combing phonemes and morphemes, whereas sentences are constructed by ordering words into phrases and combining the phrases into sentences.

The oral speech and phonological aspects of language are well developed by kindergarten, although some changes in the phonological system continue to appear in school-age children. These changes appear in phonological awareness (Troia, 2007), the acquisition of later developing phonemes (Vihman, 1988), phonological processing, the facilitation of internalized **phonological representations** of words in the mental lexicon (Troia, 2007), and the use of phonology in the development and consolidation of spelling ability (Nunes & Bryant, 2009).

Phonological awareness: Conscious awareness of the phonological structure of words including their syllables, individual sounds, and stress patterns

Phonological processing: Cognitive operations that use the phonological structure of words during their execution, including the cognitive operations of word recognition, language comprehension, storage, word retrieval, and production in both spoken and written language

Phonological representation: The phonological features of words coded and stored in the internal lexicon; phonological representations are accessed during cognitive operations, including word recognition, word comprehension, word retrieval, word production, and spelling

In addition to changes in phonological knowledge and use, two other aspects of language form also continue to develop: the use of complex sentence structures in spoken and written language and the acquisition of complex words containing **derivational morphemes** in the form of prefixes and suffixes (e.g., *happy – happiness – unhappiness*).

This section focuses on the structural language changes and refinements seen in the development and use of complex sentence types, conjunctions, noun and verb phrase expansions, and in the development of morphological knowledge about the structure of complex words.

Intrasentential Growth: Complex Sentence Structure

Whereas younger children's language development is chronicled using a mean length of utterance (MLU) measure, this type of measurement of language development is not appropriate for older school-age children and adolescents. The use of MLU to measure early language development is appropriate because increasing length of utterance is correlated with chronological age in young children (Miller & Chapman, 1981).

For older children, sentence complexity, rather than length, becomes the most important indicator of language development in the area of syntax. Language development in older children and adolescents is quantified by examining the number of clauses and words used in spoken or written language, which gives a measurement of average sentence length.

Researchers refer to the advances in syntactic knowledge and use seen in sentence length as **intra-sentential growth**, a term meant to capture syntactic changes within sentences. This means that children are able to link sentences by using grammatical devices. For example, greater sentence length is achieved by the use of **conjunction**s (e.g., *and, or, but)* to combine clauses into complex sentences and by expanding **noun phrases** and **verb phrases**, as shown in the following examples:

Noun phrase expansion: boy → the big boy → the big older boy

Verb phrase expansion: talks → talks loudly → talks loudly and rapidly

The Measurement of Average Sentence Length

There are two basic measurements used to determine average sentence length in the spoken or written language of school-age children and adolescents: the mean number of words in a *communication unit*

(**C- units**) and the mean number of words in a *terminable unit* (**T-units**) (Hunt, 1970; Klecan-Aker & Hedrick, 1985; Loban, 1976; Scott, 1988). Both C-units and T-units count each independent clause (e.g., **basic sentence**) plus any dependent clauses that modify the independent clause of the sentence (e.g., *I know **that she likes me***).

The difference between the use of C-units and T-units is that C-units include incomplete clauses or sentences if the utterance or phrase is a response to a question (e.g., Question: *"Where did you get your shirt?"* Response: *"At Target"*). T-units only include full, independent clauses (e.g., basic sentences) and any dependent clauses.

Sentence Types

English sentences fall into four types: *simple, compound, complex*, and *compound-complex*. Throughout the early and later grades of elementary school and into adolescence, children continue to modify and expand their knowledge and use of more complex syntax by elaborating and expanding the simple sentence to include other clauses, either dependent or independent. Table 7–1 shows the four sentence types: simple, compound, complex, and compound/complex. By the time typically developing children enter kindergarten or first grade (ages 5 to 6 years), they have acquired all four types of sentence and can elaborate and refine these sentence structures.

The Simple Sentence. A **simple sentence** is the basis for the construction of the other sentence types. It is made up of a clause containing a noun + a verb, such as *The cat is sleeping*. A **compound sentence** is two simple sentences with a conjunction (e.g., *and, but*), such as *"I ate my dinner and played video games"* or *"The girl ran quickly but she lost the race."*

Table 7–1. *Simple English Sentence Types*

Type	Definition	Example
Simple	At least one **independent clause** containing a subject noun + a verb An independent clause is a sentence that can stand alone	*The cat is sleeping.*
Compound	Two *independent clauses* joined by a <u>coordinating</u> conjunction Coordinating conjunctions include: *and, but, for, or, so, yet*	*The girl ran quickly but she lost the race!*
Complex	At least one **independent clause** and at least one **dependent clause** joined by a <u>subordinating</u> conjunction A **dependent clause** is group of words that contains a subject and a verb but cannot stand alone as a complete thought; it is attached to an independent clause Subordinating conjunctions include: *when, although, as, as if, before, than, unless, whether, because, in order, though, while, since, whenever, where*	*My mother picked me up before going to the grocery store.*
Compound-Complex	**Two independent clauses** and at least **one dependent clause**	*The girl will eat all the popcorn and drink the soda unless the pizza arrives soon.*

The Complex Sentence. **Complex sentences** are formed by the use of **subordinating conjunctions** (e.g., *when, although, as, as if, before, then, unless, whether, because, in order, though, while, since, whenever,* and *where*) to attach a dependent clause to a main clause. In the sentence, *"My mother picked me up before going to the grocery store,"* the dependent clause (*"before going to the grocery store"*) is conjoined to the main clause or simple sentence (*"My mother picked me up"*).

The Compound-Complex Sentence. A **compound-complex sentence** is a sentence with two or more independent clauses and at least one dependent clause. The complex-compound sentence type allows for the embedding of a number of different semantic **propositions** into a coherent sentence frame rather than simply linking parallel simple sentences with conjunctions. For example, the following sentence contains the dependent/subordinating clause *"who until now have not decided on which candidate to back in the upcoming presidential election"* and two independent clauses: (a) *Independent voters often make their decision based on shared beliefs with family members* and (b) *Independent voters can be persuaded by watching the televised presidential debates.*

> *"Independent voters, who until now have not decided on which candidate to back in the upcoming presidential election, often make their decision based on shared*

beliefs with family members, but can be persuaded by watching the televised presidential debates."

By embedding a subordinating clause, multiple semantic propositions can be linked within a sentence. In addition, the embedded clause (i.e., *who until now have not decided on which candidate to back in the upcoming presidential election*) adds additional meaning to the sentence but cannot stand alone as a complete thought.

> The use of embedded **subordination** is a more difficult syntactic form than using conjunctions (e.g., *and/but*) to conjoin two parallel simple sentences because children must have a good understanding of syntactic structures to know how to embed clauses.

The Growth in Sentence Type and Complexity

A C-unit is the number of words in an independent clause, plus its modifiers, including dependent clauses. The compound sentence, "*I walked around the village by myself and found a hammock on one of the verandas*" is one C-unit composed of two simple clauses and 16 words (e.g., "*I walked around the village by myself*" (and) "*I found a hammock on one of the verandas*"). The sentence *I wrote my memoir while living in France* is a simple sentence with a dependent clause (*while living in France*), consisting of one C-unit with eight words.

Table 7–2 contains a summary of the average number of words per C-unit in both spoken and written language reported for grades 1 to 12 (Loban, 1976). As noted in Table 7–2, there is steady growth in **sentence length** in both oral and written contexts throughout the grades.

Growth includes the use of conjunctions, dependent/subordinate clauses, and the expansion of noun phrases and verb phrases in sentences (Nippold, 2007; Scott, 1988; Scott & Stokes, 1995). Subordinating conjunctions do not appear in the speech and writing of younger school-age children but begin to appear at approximately 9 to 10 years in grade 5. Their usage peaks in grades 11 and 12 (Loban, 1976). Examples of these subordinating conjunctions are *after, although, if, now that, before, even if, until, since, before, unless, wherever,* and *while.* Note that the use of these subordinating conjunctions is essential in producing more complex sentences because a speaker is able to express greater meaning (e.g., I can skate → I can skate since my friend taught me how → I can skate since my friend taught me how, although I am not as good as he is).

The Continued Development of Conjunctions

In addition to acquiring knowledge and use of complex sentence structure, school-age children are also learning the role of the conjunction (e.g., *and, but*) in tying together two or more clauses, each with independent propositional meaning. The **communicative function** of the conjunction is to point the listener/reader to the logical relationship between the propositions (McClure & Steffensen, 1985). Conjunctions appear in the oral language of young children in Stage V of language development (Brown, 1973), especially the use of the early developing causal conjunction *because* and the additive conjunctions *and/but.* These conjunctions are not fully mastered by children until early to late elementary school, 6 to 9 years of age. Understanding of the semantic properties of the conjunction continues to develop,

Table 7–2. *Average Numbers of Words per Communication-Unit in Oral and Written Language by Grade*

Grade	Age/Years	Language Context	
		Oral	Written
1	6–7	6.88	(no measurement recorded)
2	7–8	7.56	(no measurement recorded)
3	8–9	7.62	7.60
4	9–10	9.00	8.02
5	10–11	8.80	8.70
6	11–12	9.82	9.04
7	12–13	9.80	8.90
8	13–14	10.71	10.37
9	14–15	10.96	10.05
10	15–16	10.68	11.79
11	16–17	11.20	10.70
12	17–18	11.70	13.27

Source: From *Language Development: Kindergarten Through Grade Twelve* (Research Report 18, p. 35), by W. Loban, 1976, Urbana, IL: National Council of Teachers of English. Reprinted by permission.

long after it appears in the oral language of younger children (Cain, Patson, & Andrews, 2005).

Conjunctions are connective terms that serve to conjoin or connect sentences and clauses. They also act to signal the listener/reader about how the sentences or clauses are related in meaning. Conjunctions are cohesive devices that indicate the semantic relations between different propositions and sentences and can signal an **additive** relation (*and*), a **temporal** relation (*then, when, before, after*), a **causal** relation (*because*), or an **adversative** relation (*but*).

Children's understanding of the semantic relations expressed by conjunctions is still developing in late childhood with semantic knowledge lagging behind the syntactic use of conjunctions in oral and written language. Children, 8, 9, and 10 years of age, were asked to read a sentence and replace a missing word to test their understanding of conjunctions (examples of the correct missing word are shown in parentheses) (Cain et al., 2005):

The boy (and) *girl went to school*

The boy cried (because) *he fell down*

He liked apples (but) *he liked candy better*

He ate (then) *he watched TV*

Children were better at correctly choosing the additive *and*, followed by the adversative conjunction *but*, with a greater number of errors on choosing the correct target conjunction indicating the temporal relationship *then* and the causal relationship *because*. Children's understanding of the semantic properties of conjunctions continues to develop into middle and late childhood, long after they appear in children's oral language productions.

Expansion of Noun Phrases and Verb Phrases

Sentences also become longer by expanding noun and verb phrases. For example, children learn to expand a noun phrase by adding appositives, prepositional phrases, infinitives, and gerunds (Scott & Stokes, 1988).

♦ An appositive is a noun or noun phrase that immediately follows and explains or defines another noun
  ♦ New York, **a busy city**, is great to visit

♦ A prepositional phrase begins with a preposition
  ♦ The book is **on** the table

♦ Infinitives begin with *to* plus a verb
  ♦ She likes **to read** books

♦ Gerunds are verbs that end in *-ing* and function as a nouns
  ♦ **Traveling** is interesting

Verb phrase expansion is accomplished using *modal auxiliary* verbs (e.g., *can, will, should, would*), *perfect aspect* (e.g., "He **had been** president for a year"), and the use of passive voice (e.g., "The ball *was smacked out of the ballpark by the relief pitcher*"). Table 7–3 contains examples of types of noun phrase and verb phrase expansion seen in school-age children.

In summary, there is a steady growth in the use of subordinating, dependent clauses in the oral and written language of older children and adolescents. Older

Table 7–3. *Types of Noun Phrase and Verb Phrase Expansions*

Noun Phrase Expansion	
• Appositives	*Mr. Kenney, **the principal of the school**, gave the commencement address.*
• Elaborated Subject Noun Phrases	*The **large, black and white** heifer gently nudged the fence.*
• Postmodification via Prepositional Phrases	*The mother gently rocked her baby in her arms **while humming a lullaby**.*
• Postmodification via a Verb	*The first climber **to reach the top of the mountain** planted the flag at the top.*
Verb Phrase Expansion	
• Use of Modal Auxiliary Verbs	*I **can** (e.g. **can/could; shall/should; will/would; may/might**) sweep out the garage.*
• Perfect Tense	*The city **has been** sweltering all week.*
• Passive Voice	*The horse was ridden **by the best jockey** in all of Kentucky.*

children and adolescents expand their knowledge and use of language by building on simple sentence structure through the use of dependent/subordinating clauses, conjunctions, noun and verb phrase expansions, and by acquiring modal auxiliary verbs. Table 7–4 summarizes highlights of language development for sentence structure and verb tenses for school-age children.

Knowledge and Awareness of Word Structure: Grammatical and Derivational Morphology

In addition to the expansive development of sentence structure in school-age children, there is also a development of morphological knowledge and growing awareness of the structure of words. Morphological awareness refers to the explicit,

Table 7–4. Summary of Syntax Development in School-Age Children

Age	Language Ability
Ages 5–6	Consolidate knowledge of pronouns and verb tenses, past and present. Complex sentences appear more frequently. Average number of words per C-Unit in oral communication is 6.8.
Ages 6–7	Progress in using complex sentences, especially adjectival clauses. Conditional dependent clauses beginning with *if* appear. Average number of words per C-Unit in oral communication is 7.5.
Ages 7–8	Use of relative pronouns as objects in subordinate adjectival clauses (e.g., I have a dog *that* I feed in the morning). Subordinate clauses beginning with *when*, *if* and *because* appear frequently. Average number of words per C-Unit in oral communication is 7. 6.
Ages 8, 9, 10	Begin to use conjunctions *meanwhile, unless, even if.* Fifty percent of children use subordinating conjunction *although* correctly. Average number of words per C-Unit in oral communication is 9.
Ages 10, 11, 12	Able to engage in hypotheses: use complex sentences with subordinate clauses which frame consequences, such as: *provided that*, *nevertheless, in spite of*, and *unless*. Modal auxiliary verbs *might, could,* and *should* appear. Difficulty with past perfect tense (He *had arrived* before I got there), present perfect tense (There *have been* snow storms in Tennessee), and future perfect (You *will have graduated* before you receive your diploma in the mail). Adverbial clauses more common in written language. Average number of words per C-Unit in oral communication is 9.5

Source: From *Language Development: Kindergarten Through Grade Twelve* (p. 75), by W. Loban, 1976, Champaign, IL: National Council of Teachers of English Research Report 18. Reprinted with permission.

conscious awareness of the morphological structure of words and the ability to reflect on and manipulate that structure (McCutchen, Green, & Abbott, 2008). English uses four types of morphemes to structure words: free lexical, free grammatical, inflectional, and derivational. Examples follow.

Lexical morphemes: Free lexical morphemes (nouns, verbs, adverbs, and adjectives

Derivational morphemes: Bound lexical morphemes (e.g., *un-*, *-less*)

Grammatical morphemes: Free grammatical morphemes (e.g., articles, prepositions, conjunctions, and pronouns)

Inflectional morphemes: Bound grammatical morphemes (e.g., plurals *-s*, possessive '*s*, third person present *-s*)

Lexical morphemes are considered free morphemes because they have meaning when standing alone. Free lexical and grammatical morphemes are vocabulary words or root words that provide meaning about everyday objects, events, and relations. The other two types of morphemes, inflectional and derivational, are bound morphemes because they cannot stand alone and must be affixed or attached to a free lexical morpheme to add meaning. Inflectional morphemes are endings placed on words to mark tense, number, and possession. Derivational morphemes are also bound morphemes but function differently in word structure in that they create new words (e.g., change a verb to a noun, such as *teach* to *teacher*).

Derivational morphemes are the prefixes and suffixes that are added to root lexical morphemes to create a new word. For example, by adding the suffix *-less* to the root word *home*, the word *homeless* is derived, meaning *without a home*. Similarly,

the prefix *-un* applied to the root word *cover* produces *uncover*, meaning *to reveal*.

Morphological Development

Children first develop explicit morphological awareness of the grammatical inflections marking tense (e.g., past, present, or future tense use), number (e.g. plural use), and possession (possessive morpheme use) in early elementary school, when they begin to read and spell words that contain these morphological endings (Rubin, 1988; Wolter, Wood, & D'Zatko, 2009).

> A critical area of language development for school-age children and adolescents is the knowledge of derivational morphemes and the ability to analyze complex words containing prefixes and suffixes to determine word meaning (Carlisle, 2000; Larsen & Nippold, 2007; Tyler & Nagy, 1989).

Children are exposed to, on average, 3,000 unfamiliar words each school year in academic reading material and as many as 80% of these words are morphologically complex (Nagy & Anderson, 1984; White, Power, & White, 1989). Children's knowledge of derivational morphology is significantly related to vocabulary development and reading comprehension (Anglin, 1993; Carlisle, 2000; Mahoney, Singson, & Mann, 2000). Consequently, it is essential to develop vocabulary skills for children to have successful reading comprehension.

The development of derivational morphology is a protracted process that begins in elementary school and extends into late adolescence with rapid growth between the fourth and eighth grades (Nagy, Diakidoy, & Anderson, 1993; Tyler

& Nagy, 1989). Children first develop relational knowledge that unfamiliar novel words share a familiar stem. For example, fourth graders are able to recognize that a novel complex word, such as *celebratory*, is related to the base root word *celebrate* (Tyler & Nagy, 1989). Later, children grasp the syntactic properties of derivational suffixes. For example, knowledge of the syntactic aspect of derivational morphemes would allow for the knowledge that the complex word *volition* is a noun because of the *-tion* suffix, even if the meaning of the vocabulary word is not grasped.

When children acquire the syntactic aspect of derivational suffixes, the ending of a complex word provides information about its syntactic category (e.g., noun vs. verb). By the fourth grade, children begin to identify the syntactic category of novel words with syntactic knowledge of suffix endings continuing to grow between the fourth and eighth grades (Tyler & Nagy, 1989). With increasing knowledge and awareness of the morphological structure of words, children and adolescents are able to decompose unfamiliar morphologically complex words, enabling them to gain access to a word's meaning, its pronunciation, and its grammatical category (e.g., noun or verb). This linguistic information is made available to the individual through the explicit analysis of prefixes, suffixes, and lexical roots (Berninger, Abbot, Nagy, & Carlisle, 2010; Carlisle & Fleming, 2003; Henry, 2003).

Morphological Transparency and Frequency of Occurrence

Two important factors that influence children's processing of morphologically complex words are (a) the transparency of words in the derived form and (b) the frequency of exposure to the complex word in speech and print (Carlisle, 1988; Carlisle

& Nomanbhoy, 1993; Carroll, Davies, & Richman, 1971; White, Sowell, & Yanagihara, 1989; Wolter, Wood, & Dzatko, 2009). Morphological transparency refers to the shifts in pronunciation, meaning, and spelling when a suffix is added to a root or base word. For example, the relationship between the words *harm/harmless* is considered to be transparent and easier to acquire for both meaning and pronunciation because the root word *harm* is clearly heard and seen in the derived form *harmless*. However, other related words are less transparent and, therefore, it is more difficult for children to grasp the relationship between the derived and base form, as is the case for the words *sign/signal* wherein the derived word undergoes a phonetic shift in pronunciation, i.e., /saɪn-sɪgnəl/.

Carlisle (1988) examined the transparency of derived words, based on their base pronunciation and spelling. Four possible types of changes (**transformations**) from the root word to the derived form were noted. These changes or transformational shifts included phonological changes (stress or sound changes), orthographic spelling changes, or a combination of both.

No change: good → goodness

Orthographic change:
  beauty → beautiful

Phonological change:
  magic → magician

Phonological and orthographic change:
  decide → decision

The most transparent type of derived word has no change in the pronunciation or spelling of a root word when a suffix is added (e.g., *good/goodness; teach/teacher*). The root word is clearly seen and pronounced within the derived form.

Next on the transparency continuum is the stable pronunciation of the root word, yet a change in the spelling of the root when adding the stem (e g. *beauty/beautiful*). The root word *beauty* is clearly pronounced when saying *beautiful*, yet there is a change in the root word spelling (e.g., *beauty → beauti*). A third type of transformation requires a phonetic shift or change in pronunciation from the base word to the derived form. These phonological shifts usually involve alterations in stress (e.g., **ma**gic/ma**gi**cian), and phonemes (e.g., /mædʒɪc/ → /mədʒɪʃən/) with the root word clearly seen within the derived form. However, the change in pronunciation may make it more difficult for children to grasp the relational meaning between these two words.

The least transparent and most complex of word transformations is seen when both the phonology and the orthography of the root word change as a result of adding a stem (e.g., *decide/decision*). In this example, the phonological shift is in the stress from the final to the second syllable (e.g., *decide/decision*) and the phonetic change is /dɪsaɪd/ → /dɪsɪʒən/, whereas the orthographic change is seen when the stem, *-sion*, is added onto the root morpheme, *decide*.

The morphological transparency of complex words plays an important role in the development of the knowledge and use of morphologically complex words. Children in the early elementary grades (first, second, and third) use, read, and spell words that require no change from base to derived form. Between the fourth and eighth grades, a gradual improvement is seen in children's recognition and spelling of complex words that are less transparent, such as words that involve several transformations of the root to the derived expression. Learning to pronounce and spell morphologically complex words with pho-

nologic changes, as well as complex words that involve both phonology and orthography, are not acquired until the eighth grade (Carlisle, 1988). Fourth-grade children tend to make more errors in the pronunciation and spelling of the least transparent words than children in the eighth grade.

Morphological Language Differences

Morphological awareness plays a significant role in the academic progress of both native English speakers and English-language learners (ELLs). Morphological awareness consists of the following abilities:

◆ The ability to understand the structure or morphemes of words (e.g., *un + believe + able*)
◆ The ability to extract the base or root form of a word (e.g., *believe*)
◆ The ability to recognize the connection between different forms of that word (e.g., *belief, believe, believable,* and *unbelievable*)

Spanish-speaking ELLS who are able to decompose words (the ability to identify morphemes that compose words) do better at English reading comprehension (Kieffer & Lesaux, 2008). Morphological awareness helps ELLs to understand texts that contain morphologically complex words and helps the learning of new vocabulary in a second language (L2). There are also differences that appear in Spanish-speaking ELLs' productions that are based on language differences between Spanish and English (Roseberry-McKibbin, 2008).

◆ The morpheme *'s* may be omitted in plurals (*Five book*), possessives (*The boy book is on the table*), and the regular third-person present tense (*The girl walk to school*)

- Past tense *-ed* is often omitted (*They walk to school yesterday*)
- Articles, such as *the*, are often omitted (*I am going to movies*) but used with body parts (*I hurt the knee*)

It should also be noted that some other ELLs, such as Japanese-speaking children, have similar language differences that are associated, in this case, with the differences between Japanese and English (Roseberry-McKibbin, 2008, p. 129).

- The morpheme *'s* may be omitted in plurals (*Five finger*), possessives (*Mom food cold*), and the regular third-person present tense (*He like it*)
- Past tense *-ed* is often omitted (*We cook dinner yesterday*)
- Articles, such as *the*, are often omitted (*Baby is sick*) or overgeneralized (*She went the home*)

There are also morphological and syntactic differences between mainstream American English (MAE) and African American English (AAE). As noted in Chapter 5, these differences derive from the large number of contributions to AAE from West African languages, Native American languages, French, and English. Note that the examples shown next for AAE speakers (Roseberry-McKibbin, 2008) mirror two of the morphological examples given for Spanish and Japanese speakers.

- The morpheme *'s* may be omitted in plurals (*Three box of crayons*), possessives (*That my brother bike*), and the regular third-person present tense (*She walk to school*)
- Past tense *-ed* may be omitted (*She live in New York*)

In summary, it is important to remember that there are differences in morphology across different languages.

Summary of Developmental Changes in Language Form

Significant changes in the school-age child's understanding of syntax and grammar are seen from early elementary school through high school with learning of more complex sentence structures and conjunctions and the expansion of noun phrases and verb phrases in spoken and written language. By the third grade, children appreciate the relational meaning between the transparent derived forms of words, such as *good/goodness*. Older school-age children and adolescents demonstrate linguistic refinement by acquiring structural knowledge about the syntactic function of suffixes. Children continue to learn the pronunciation and spelling of complex derived words that include changes in pronunciation and spelling of the root word.

> The refinement of knowledge about syntactic and morphological structure contributes significantly to reading comprehension, written language, and spelling in older school-age children and adolescents.

DEVELOPMENTAL CHANGES IN LANGUAGE CONTENT: VOCABULARY AND FIGURATIVE LANGUAGE

Most children from language-rich environments enter school at 6 years of age with a vast vocabulary, but vocabulary development is far from complete at this stage. The average 5- to 6-year-old has a vocabulary size between 2,500 and 5,000 words (Beck, Perfetti, & McKeown, 1982). By the 12th grade, estimates of students' vocabulary size range from 8,000 to 50,000 words (Stahl & Nagy, 2006).

It is estimated that school-age children learn approximately 3,000 words a year (Nagy & Herman, 1987) and that the majority of vocabulary expansion is through direct instruction, reading, and inferential processing (Beck, Perfetti, & McKeown, 1982; Biemiller, 2001; Biemiller & Slonim, 2001; Carlisle, 2007). Inferential processing requires that children draw a conclusion about the meaning of a word from some source of evidence. They may also use their cognitive skills to determine meaning, such as using their reasoning skills to draw a conclusion from a premise or idea.

What does it mean to know a vocabulary word? Word knowledge has been conceptualized in a number of ways, including continuum-based word knowledge, dimensional word knowledge, and contextualized and decontextualized word knowledge. Continuum-based word knowledge refers to the varying degrees of knowledge that an individual has about a word: no knowledge, a general sense of the meaning of a word, contextually based knowledge, and, finally, rich, decontextualized knowledge of the meaning of a word, including its relationship to others words and its metaphorical extension. For example, a rich, decontextualized understanding of the meaning of *hammering* would be necessary to grasp the metaphorical meaning of *hammering* in the phrase *"hammering away at the chores"* (Beck, McKeown, & Omanson, 1987).

Dimension of understanding is another way of conceptualizing word knowledge. There are three levels of depth of word knowledge in school-age children: *full concept* knowledge, *partial concept* knowledge,

and *verbal association* knowledge (Beck & McKeown, 1991). A child in grade 1 may know the word *hot* to mean *"having a high temperature,"* a verbal association level of knowledge of the meaning of this word. In contrast, the older student knows that the adjective *hot* can also be applied to express intense feeling (*hot temper*) and to express that something was stolen (*That's a hot Smartphone!*). The older student has a broader, full concept of word meaning and learns that the adjective *hot* is related morphologically to *hotbed* (dangerous context) and *hotheaded* (*impetuous, rash*).

The Developmental Order of Vocabulary Acquisition

School-age children acquire approximately two to four root words a day (Beck & McKeown, 1991). Biemiller and Slonim (2001) examined the development of root word vocabulary in 300 children in grades K through 6, representing three different groups: an English-first language group of children (EFL) from a wide range of socioeconomic status (SES) backgrounds, an advantaged upper-middle SES group, and a group of normative EFL children drawn from the same schools but given a different sample of words. Words consisted of common root words and uncommon root words that were not necessarily known by the children.

There was a significant gain in root word vocabulary between grades 1 and 2 for all groups of children. There was a steady growth in root word vocabulary between grade 2 and grade 6. In addition, root words appeared to be learned in roughly the same order by all of the children. Table 7–5 contains examples of root word vocabulary acquired by children by the end of grade 2 by level of difficulty.

Table 7–5. *Examples of Root Words Acquired and Ordered by Frequency and Difficulty for Living Word Vocabulary (LWV) Level 2*

Word	Meaning
fish	A water animal
flood	Unusual flow of water
throat	Passage from stomach to mouth
match	Thing to light fire
café	Eating place
spread	To distribute, buttering, painting
near	Close
voice	Sound from mouth
subtract	Take a number away
done	Finished
hope	To expect; to wish for
loop	A circled string
listen	To hear
drop	Fall
kept	Keeps
buckle	To fasten
boulder	A large rock
shadow	Dark spot cast by light
fresh	New, not spoiled

Source: From "Estimating Root Word Vocabulary Growth in Normative and Advantaged Populations: Evidence for a Common Sequence of Vocabulary Acquisition," by A. Biemiller and N. Slonim, 2001, *Journal of Educational Psychology*, *93*(3), p. 513. Adapted with permission.

Reading, Morphological Processing, and Vocabulary Growth

Both reading ability and time spent reading are important factors in the continued and expansive development of vocabulary in school-age children and adolescents. Reading abilities have a profound effect on vocabulary development and academic success with reading skills in younger grades having an influence on reading performance and greater engagement in reading activities in older elementary grades through high school (Cunningham & Stanovich, 1997). First graders are focused on recognizing words, and, by the third grade, children's reading becomes more automatic.

Reading skills continue to influence children's engagement in literacy activities both within and outside of school for older children and adolescents, while contributing to higher scores on measures of vocabulary and verbal intelligence (Cain & Oakhill, 2011). Word reading accuracy and reading fluency have a strong association with vocabulary development, which in turn facilitates reading comprehension (Beck, Perfetti, & McKeown, 1982; Cain & Oakhill, 2011) and academic success (Stanovich & Cunningham, 1992, 1993).

The importance of morphology and morphological processing to vocabulary development in school-age children cannot be ignored. In a seminal study of vocabulary development in school-age children, Anglin (1993) found that between the first and fifth grades, children added approximately 14,000 derived words to their lexicon. As noted in the previous section on morphology, complex derived words contain prefixes and suffixes that often change the part of speech or grammatical category of the root word and also add meaning. For example, the word *manager* is derived from the root word, *manage*, to mean *one who manages*. Researchers point to the presence of derived words in written texts, as well as reading accuracy and time spent reading, as contributing factors to the acquisition of complex vocabulary words in school-age children from grade 3 on (Nagy & Anderson, 1984; White, Power, & White, 1989).

High school students and adults continue to acquire and use more complex word structures with an added focus on words containing Latin and Greek roots and morphemes. Latin and Greek layers of language provide additional semantic meaning to the student (Henry, 2003). Science, social studies, and mathematics textbooks in the upper grades contain significant numbers of vocabulary words with Latin and Greek roots and morphology, such as *octagonal, polynomial, perpendicular, velocipede, duplication*, and so forth. Children and adolescents who are skilled and fluent readers are exposed to such derived words in content area texts, providing an opportunity to acquire specific vocabulary and to generalize morphological endings to similar words in order to identify their meaning.

Figurative Language

In addition to significant growth in vocabulary, school-age children and adolescents are also expanding their semantic knowledge by acquiring *figurative language,* a type of language that is meant to impart complex meaning different from the literal interpretation of the words. Figurative language encompasses the understanding and use of *metaphors, similes, proverbs,* and *idioms.* The development of each of these types of figurative language has its own trajectory with metaphors and similes being understood and used by children and adolescents before the full appreciation and use of idioms and proverbs (Nippold, 1991, 2007).

Metaphors and Similes

Metaphors and **similes** are figures of speech in which a term or phrase is applied to some other thing to suggest a comparison or resemblance. A *simile* makes a comparison between two referents by using the words *like* or *as* (e.g., *Busy as a bee* or *She acts like a queen*). The word *metaphor* is from the Greek word *metapherin*, meaning "transfer." There are two different types of metaphor: a *similarity metaphor* and a *proportional metaphor*. Both types of metaphor have a topic (first term) and vehicle (second term). An example of the similarity metaphor is *"That man is a snake,"* with the implication that the two terms have something in common. A proportional metaphor expresses an analogy in which the topic and vehicle refer to relations, not objects, and is missing one term. *The artist was an apple tree with no fruit* is an example of a proportional metaphor with the following construction: two vehicles (*apple tree* and *fruit*) and two topics (*artist* and the unverbalized topic *artwork*). The analogy follows:

> *Artist is to **artwork** as apple tree is to fruit* (with **artwork** missing)

The relationship expressed is one of proportion (apple tree : fruit) as (artist : X), where X is inferred to mean *artwork* (Nippold, 2007). Thus, the absent topic or vehicle must be inferred. Consequently, proportional metaphors are more complex and require a higher level of cognitive development in children in order for them to comprehend or use this type of figurative language.

Children acquire the similarity form and content first between 7 and 11 years of age when they are in the *concrete operational stage* of cognitive development. During this stage, children acquire the ability to group objects into hierarchies of classes and subclasses and to engage in reversibility, the ability to logically reverse operations (Piaget & Inhelder, 1969).

A *similarity metaphor* is a type of classificatory behavior in which children are able to comprehend the similar characteristics and features between a single referent and the reference, classifying them as the same, as in *"The girl is a slippery noodle."*

The more advanced *proportional metaphor* requires the comparison between two or more referents and two or more references, creating a proportional analogy that must be fully appreciated in order to be comprehended. This requires a more advanced level of cognitive development, the development of formal operations beginning after the age of 11 years (Billow, 1975). The ability to understand metaphor is not fully realized until later childhood and into adolescence, when cognitive development and metalinguistic abilities enable a child to make explicit comparisons between the literal use of terms and the secondary, implied meaning (Chan & Martinellie, 2008; Cometa & Eson, 1978; Douglas & Peel, 1979; Nippold & Fey, 1983; Winner, Rosensteil, & Garner, 1976).

Idioms and Proverbs

Idioms and **proverbs** are additional types of figurative language that are acquired later by school-age children. An *idiom* is a phrase used to express complex meaning in a concise way, as in *"John can't keep his head above water."* A *proverb* is a short saying or adage used within a specific linguistic culture to express a common truth or familiar experience, as in *"A leopard cannot change his spots"* or *"A penny saved is a penny earned."*

Idioms are frequently used in everyday language and in the classroom. For example, teachers have been found to frequently use figurative language when speaking to students in class (Lazar, Warr-Leeper, Nicholson, & Johnson, 1989), showing the need for comprehension of idiomatic phrases by children and adolescents. Lazar and colleagues (1989) investigated the amount of figurative language used by teachers in kindergarten through grade 8 and found that kindergarten teachers used idioms or multiple meaning expressions in 4.65% of their utterances. By the eighth grade, 20% of a teacher's utterances contained figurative language or idiomatic expressions, such as saying that some students will *"be in the doghouse"* or be in trouble if they do not behave (May, 1979). Nippold (1991) noted that idiomatic expressions are more likely to appear in printed materials beginning in the third grade. Thus, reading comprehension may be influenced by the presence of idioms in classroom texts (May, 1979).

Comprehension of idioms by children and adolescents is influenced by three factors (Nippold & Duthie, 2003):

Semantic transparency of the idiom

The role of **context** in assisting comprehension

The individual's past exposure to the expression

Semantic transparency refers to idiomatic expressions in which the figurative and literal meaning of the individual words is closely related, as when a speaker says, *"keep your fingers crossed."* If heard in context (e.g., when an individual is about to scratch a lottery ticket), an older child or adolescent may be able to discern the mental imagery and figurative meaning of the expression to mean, *Wish me good luck.*

Idioms that are not semantically transparent are called opaque. These idioms are more difficult to interpret because vocabulary does not assist in understanding the nonliteral interpretation. An example is, *"Talk until you are blue in the face,"* which has the literal meaning of continuing to talk until you run out of oxygen (and become blue in the face). The **meta-semantic hypothesis** states that individuals learn the figurative meaning of idioms by examining the vocabulary contained in the idiom (Nippold & Rudzinski, 1993). Therefore, transparent idioms are learned earlier than opaque idioms. Older school-age children, ages 11;7 to 12;9 (years; months) and adults, ages 19;3 to 55;6, report more relevant mental images for transparent idioms, also finding these idioms easier to comprehend than the opaque expressions (Nippold & Duthie, 2003).

Proverb understanding gradually improves in late childhood into adolescence and adulthood and follows a similar developmental process to idioms. Familiar, more easily transparent proverbs are understood earlier, before less familiar, more opaque, or abstract proverbs (Nippold & Haq, 1996). Younger children, prior to 12 years of age, often are quite literal in their interpretation of a proverb. For example, an 8-year-old interpreted the proverb, *"You can't teach an old dog new tricks"* to mean that "Well there's an old dog, and you're trying to get him to sit up or something and he won't sit up for you" (Nippold, 2007, p. 210). Proverbs

are more difficult for children to acquire because the understanding of proverbs is influenced by a shared cultural value or belief (Hirsch, Kett, & Trefil, 1988). Consequently, it is not easy for individuals from different cultures to understand each other's proverbs. Comprehension of proverbs may pose a significant difficulty for both typical and language-disordered children from different cultural or linguistic backgrounds (Roseberry-McKibbin, 2007).

Summary of Developmental Changes in Language Content

In summary, there is substantial growth in the semantic modality of language during middle and late childhood and into adolescence, especially in children's understanding of meaning in vocabulary and figurative language. The sources for expansion of the semantic system include direct instruction and participation in the academic classroom, specific vocabulary associated with content areas in the classroom, improved reading accuracy and fluency, and cognitive development because children are able to use reasoning to determine meanings.

PRAGMATIC LANGUAGE DEVELOPMENT: NARRATIVE AND EXPOSITORY LANGUAGE

The pragmatic aspect of language refers to both the linguistic (verbal) and nonlinguistic (nonverbal) behavior used by individuals when engaged in social-communicative interaction. We use language in social contexts in order to accomplish or obtain a desired functional outcome, such as requesting information or demanding an action. Previously, we discussed the role of social cognition and social competence in language development in school-age children and adolescents, especially in the acquisition of pro-social behaviors and the learning of pragmatic language strategies for conflict resolution. This section focuses on two types of functional language, **narrative** and **expository**, both complex types of discourse that continue to develop and expand in complexity in school-age children.

Narrative Language

A narrative is a story or an account of events or experiences, either real or imagined. Narrative discourse is a specific type of genre that focuses on people's actions and motivations and that unfolds in a temporal framework (Ravid, Dromi, & Kotler, 2010). Narrative is a form of decontextualized language that can take one of three forms: scripts, personal experiences, or fictional stories. Narrative language is common in classrooms and in written texts. Children and teachers use narrative discourse to share ideas, report a personal experience, or tell an imaginary story. Narrative language abilities are linked to literacy achievement and academic achievement (Boudreau, 2008; Catts, 1993; Nippold, 1988).

Narratives contain an underlying structure that children acquire and use when comprehending and producing fictional or personal narrative accounts (Stein & Glenn, 1979). The underlying structure of stories (e.g., fictional narratives) is a *Setting* and one or more *Episodes* with each episode made up of an initiating event (*a Problem*), a reaction of the character to the initiating event (*Character's Internal Response*), an attempt to deal with the initiating event *Goal*), an *Outcome* or con-

sequence, and an *Ending*. Researchers use the term **story grammar** when referring to the underlying componential structure of narratives because the component parts make up the syntactic structure of the narrative genre (Westby, 1984).

During the preschool years, children develop knowledge of the component parts of story grammar and their relationship to each other. Children produce primitive narratives by 4 to 5 years of age that contain characters, objects, and events. Events follow one another logically and contain explicit inferences about the internal thoughts of characters and about external events. Westby (1984) noted that the true narrative, containing all the subcomponent parts of the story grammar and characterized by the sequencing of events with well-developed plots, emerges by 5 to 6 years of age. At that point in time, children's cognitive development and their understanding of the temporal relationships between and among events facilitate the growth in narrative structure.

The Development of Narrative Discourse in Spoken Language

Although the basic macrostructure of story grammar is generally acquired by 5 to 6 years of age, narratives continue to develop in two ways during middle, late childhood, and adolescence. The first involves the number of propositions or idea units within the discourse (Clark & Clark, 1977; Kintsch, 1977). The use of semantic roles (e.g., *agent* or *actor*) and relationships to modify characters, objects, and events as well as the expression of characters' attitudes and intentions, are ways that children can add propositional content to narratives.

With increases in propositional content, narratives become longer in school-age children as a function of increased sentence length and number of words, the addition of multiple episodes within the narrative, and the appearance of subplotting or the use of subepisodes embedded within the dominant or main episodic structures (Botvin & Sutton-Smith, 1977; Liles, 1987, 1993; Nippold, 2007; Westby, 1984). For example, the narrative may begin with a story about a wood cutter who lives in the forest. Next, the narrative includes a story about some of the creatures that live in the forest. The narrative ends with a story about the wood cutter's relationship with the forest creatures. In this way, multiple episodes are embedded.

Cohesive Devices

Another way that narrative structure and content improve in school-age children is by using cohesive devices to express logical relationships across statements both within and across episodes (Liles, 1987). Cohesive devices are linguistic connectives, such as pronouns, to refer back to a stated person or object, and conjunctions that logically connect sentences, episodes, and subepisodes within the narrative. Subepisodes can consist of the report of an incident or event that is integrated within the main episode or story. For example, if a child is telling a story about a visit to the zoo, a subepisode might consist of recounting another and related event that occurred during this visit. Assessment of children's narrative productions is an effective way of measuring their cohesive abilities. Examples follow to show the development of cohesion (Bamberg, 1987).

Nominal strategy (used by younger children): the use of nouns

The bus is going to drive. The bus drives fast.

Thematic subject strategy (middle school-age children, ages 7, 8, and 9): the use of pronouns

The bus driver drives into a meadow. He sees a cow.

At the sentence level, the organization of specific sentences and their logical relationship to each other is the local level or the microlevel of narrative. Organization across episodes is broader and relates to how the episodes logically relate to each other, a macrolevel of narrative organization. The ability to organize multiple episodes in stories improves in children from 6 years of age to approximately 10 years of age (Liles, 1987).

Liles (1987) investigated the use of conjunctions as cohesive devices in the narrative retelling of a story by 20 language-disordered and 20 typically developing school-age children between 7 and 11 years of age. Conjunctions used by the children to conjoin sentences were categorized into four types: additive (e.g., *and*), temporal (e.g., *then, before, after*), causal (e.g., *because*), and adversative (e.g., *but*). The narratives were analyzed for the following components:

◆ The number of complete episodes
◆ The number of incomplete episodes
◆ The number of accurate conjunctions used to conjoin sentences across episodes
◆ The number of accurate conjunctions used to conjoin sentences within episodes

The number of episodes produced by children increased with age for both groups of children. Typically developing children were more accurate in their use of conjunctions than the language-disordered children, both within episodes and across episodes, and the correct use of conjunctions improved with age.

Expository Language

Expository discourse is the use of language to convey information (Nippold, Mansfield, Billow, & Tomblin, 2008). This is an important genre for assessing language skills in adolescents. This genre is required when an adolescent is asked to interpret a historical event (e.g., the cause of the Civil War), describe methods to solve a global problem (e.g., global warming), teach others to solve a problem (e.g., download an application on their iPhone), or explain how they will perform an academic task (e.g., an experiment in a science class).

> Expository discourse is a complex form of language that functions to provide or convey information in an organized and coherent manner. The expository genre is most often observed in written text, where new information is provided for the reader about a topic or concept, often with unfamiliar, abstract vocabulary and concepts. Expository discourse is a type of genre that focuses on ideas, concepts, and declarations of knowledge presented in an organized, causal context (Ravid, Dromi, & Kotler, 2010).

Typically, expository discourse is observed in academic settings, where children and adolescents are expected to analyze and summarize information about abstract concepts and content in academic areas, such as science or social studies (Nippold & Scott, 2010). Adoles-cents' ability to comprehend expository texts becomes increasingly more critical as they advance in academic settings. A significant proportion of the academic curriculum is presented in the expository form, including textbooks and classroom lectures, beginning in fourth grade, continuing through middle school, high school, and secondary education, and into the work setting (Snyder & Caccamise, 2010).

The Development of Expository Discourse in Spoken Language

Although the interest in expository language has been primarily in how children learn to negotiate and comprehend the expository genre within written text, expository discourse is also a factor in the spoken language of adolescents (Nippold, 2009; Nippold et al., 2008; Nippold, Mansfield, & Billow, 2007). Expository discourse differs from narrative discourse in that there is no internalized expository grammar, as found in the story grammar structure. Consequently, the focus of the development of expository discourse in the oral language of children and adolescents has been on the use of complex sentence structure to express complex information (Nippold, Hesketh, Duthie, & Mansfield, 2005).

Nippold and colleagues (2005) presented a Favorite Game or Sport (FGS) task to 120 children, adolescents, and adults ranging in age from 8 years to 44 years. This task provided the opportunity to talk about a topic that was familiar because it involved the explanation of how a game is played, the rules of the game, and how teams or members try to win. Each participant's FGS explanation was transcribed and analyzed for the average number of words per T-units, the average number of subordinate clauses, and a measure of clause density by examining the use of adverbial, nominal, and relative clause types. In other words, the measurement targeted complex sentence production.

There was an age-related increase in syntactic complexity that extended even into adulthood. Younger children used fewer words per T-unit and had a lower clause density than older children and adolescents. Two factors influence syntactic development and use of expository discourse genre: intellectual stimulation and cognitive advances (Nippold, 2010). Individuals experience intellectual stimulation during formal education, employment, and through life experiences, increasing a person's background knowledge and comprehension of events. This, in turn, prompts the need for individuals to use language that is more complex to communicate the expanded knowledge base in a well-organized manner.

Summary: Narrative and Expository Language

Two distinct discourse genres develop in the language of school-age children and adolescents: narrative discourse and expository discourse. Narrative discourse encompasses information about people, their actions, and their motivations. Narrative discourse unfolds in a temporal sequence in the form of stories, scripts, or personal accounts. The basic macrostructure of narrative language is observed in preschool children, but the content of narratives continues to develop in school-age children and adolescents to include complex propositions within phrases and sentences, the inclusion of multiple episodes, and the accurate use of conjunctions as cohesive devices that facilitate the organization of the story narrative.

Expository genre also develops throughout later elementary school, mid-

dle school, and through adolescence and into adulthood. Expository genre is most often affiliated with academic functioning in the classroom because this genre is concerned with expressing ideas and specific knowledge content within a logical causal context. The development of expository discourse in the oral language of school-age children and adolescents is best observed by the use of complex syntax characterized by longer T-units and by the use of subordination with various clausal types that include relative, nominal, and adverbial clauses. The development of oral expository narrative is associated with educational, word-related, and personal experiences that prompt the use of complex syntax to express complex knowledge.

SUMMARY OF LANGUAGE DEVELOPMENT IN MIDDLE AND LATE CHILDHOOD AND ADOLESCENTS

Children's language continues to develop during elementary, middle, and high school years when children are in middle childhood (6–8 years), late childhood (9–12 years), and into adolescence (12+ years). During these periods of development, children improve their language knowledge to include advances in the form, content, and use of language. Language expansion is facilitated in the child and adolescent through academic classroom experience, significant achievements in social cognition and interaction, integration of spoken and written language, cognitive/intellectual development, and individual language experiences. Specific language achievements of school-age children and adolescents include:

◆ Advances in syntax are characterized by significant intrasentential growth resulting, from the increased use of compound-complex sentence structure containing subordinating clauses and conjunctions, and the expansion of noun phrases and verb phrases

◆ Development of morphological awareness of complex words, including the use of lexical compounding and derivational morphemes

◆ Advances in morphological knowledge to include an understanding of the relational, syntactic, and distributional properties of morphemes

◆ Significant vocabulary expansion with a vocabulary size range of 8,000 to 50,000 words by 12th grade, which is an estimated growth of approximately 3,000 words per academic year

◆ Figurative language development, including the understanding and use of metaphors, similes, and proverbs

◆ Development of narrative discourse genre, including the addition of propositional content, episodic structure, and conjunctions used as cohesive ties within and across episodes

◆ Development of expository discourse genre facilitated by academic, work-related, and personal experiences and characterized by the use of complex syntax including longer T-units, the use of subordination, and clause density

It is also important that speech-language pathologists be aware of language differences that can be present when children are learning English as a second language, such as the difference in morphology and language structures across languages. It is important in assessment and intervention to understand that differences do not necessarily indicate disorders. To help prepare children and adolescents build successful academic skills, it is vital to learn the differences between their native language and English to aid them in learning the information required for communicating in English and acquiring successful literacy skills.

KEY WORDS

Additive

Adversative

Aural/oral (hearing/speaking) language

Basic sentences

Causal

Communicative function

Complex sentences

Compound sentences

Compound-complex sentence

Concrete operations

Conjunctions

Context

C-unit

Derivational morpheme

Expository

Form

Formal operations

Idioms

Intrasentential growth

Language form

Linguistic awareness

Linguistic individualism

Mazes

Metaphors

Meta-semantic hypothesis

Narrative

Noun phrases

Phonological awareness

Phonological representations

Pragmatic

Preoperational stage

Proposition

Proverbs

Reversibility

Semantic transparency

Sentence length

Similes

Simple sentence

Social competence

Social information processing

Story grammar

Structure

Subordinating conjunctions

Subordination

Temporal

Transformation

T-units

Verb phrase

Visual language

STUDY QUESTIONS

1. What are five sources of language input to school-age children and adolescents?

2. Describe two ways that syntax in sentence structure continues to develop in school-age children.

3. What are the three types of morphology, and how does morphological awareness of word structure contribute to vocabulary expansion in school-age children?

4. Contrast the differences among metaphors, idioms, and proverbs. What factors influence their comprehension and use?

5. Discuss how narrative language ability expands in school-age children.

REFERENCES

Anglin, J. M. (1993). Vocabulary development: A morphological analysis. *Monographs of the Society for Research in Child Development, 58*(Serial No. 238).

August, D., & Shanahan, T. (Eds.). (2006). *Developing literacy in second-language learners*. Mahwah, NJ: Erlbaum.

Bamberg, M. (1987). *The acquisition of narratives*. Berlin, Germany: Mouton de Gruyter.

Beck, I. L., & McKeown, M. G. (1991). Social studies texts are hard to understand: Mediating some of the difficulties. *Language Arts, 68*, 482–490.

Beck, I. L., McKeown, M. G., & Omanson, R. C. (1987). The effects and uses of diverse vocabulary instructional techniques. In M. McKeown & M. E. Curtis (Eds.), *The nature of vocabulary acquisition* (pp. 147–163). Hillsdale, NJ: Erlbaum.

Beck, I. L., Perfetti, C., & McKeown, M. G. (1982). Effects of long-term vocabulary instruction on lexical access and reading comprehension. *Journal of Educational Psychology, 74*, 506–521.

Biemiller, A. (2001). Teaching vocabulary: Early, direct, and sequential. *American Educator, 25*, 24–28.

Boudreau, D. (2008). Narrative abilities: Advances in research and implications for clinical practice. *Topics in Language Disorders, 28*, 99–114.

Beimiller, A., & Slonim, N. (2001). Estimating root word vocabulary growth in normative and advantaged populations: Evidence for a common sequence of vocabulary acquisition. *Journal of Educational Psychology, 93,* 498–520.

Berninger, V. W., Abbot, R. D., Nagy, W., & Carlisle, J. (2010). Growth in phonological, orthographic, and morphological awareness in grades 1-6. *Journal of Psycholinguistic Research, 39,* 141–163.

Billow, R. M. (1975). A cognitive developmental study of metaphor comprehension *Developmental Psychology, 11,* 415–423.

Botvin, G. J., & Sutton-Smith, B. (1977). The development of structural complexity in children's fantasy narratives. *Developmental Psychology, 13,* 377–388.

Brinton, B., Fujiki, M., & Powell, J. M. (1997). The ability of children with language impairment to manipulate topic in a structured task. *Language, Speech, and Hearing Services in School, 28,* 3–11.

Brown, R. (1973). *A first language: The early stages.* Cambridge, MA: Harvard University Press.

Cain, K., & Oakhill, J. (2011). Matthew effects in young readers reading comprehension and reading experience aid vocabulary development. *Journal of Learning Disabilities, 44,* 431–443.

Cain, K., Patson, N., & Andrews, L. (2005). Age- and ability-related differences in young readers' use of conjunctions. *Journal of Child Language,* 877–892.

Carlisle, J. F. (1988). Knowledge of derivational morphology and spelling ability in fourth, sixth, and eighth graders. *Applied Psycholinguistics, 9,* 247–266.

Carlisle, J. F. (2000). Awareness of the structure and meaning of morphologically complex words: Impact on reading. *Reading and Writing, An Interdisciplinary Journal, 12,* 169–200.

Carlisle, J. F. (2007). Fostering morphological processing, vocabulary development, and reading comprehension. In R. K. Wagner, A. E. Muse, & K. R. Tannenbaum (Eds.), *Vocabulary acquisition: Implications for reading comprehension* (pp. 78– 103). New York, NY: The Guilford Press.

Carlisle, J. F., & Fleming, J. (2003). Lexical processing of morphologically complex words in the elementary years. *Scientific Studies of Reading 7,* 239–253.

Carlisle, J. F., & Nomanbhoy, D. M. (1993). Phonological and morphological awareness in first graders. *Applied Psycholinguistics, 14*(2), 177–195.

Carroll, J. B., Davies, B., & Richman, B. (1971). *The American heritage word frequency book.* Boston, MA: Houghton-Mifflin.

Catts, H. W. (1993). The relationship between speech-language impairments and reading disabilities. *Journal of Speech and Hearing Research, 36,* 948–958.

Cavell, T. A. (1990). Social adjustment, social performance, and social skills: A tri- component model of social competence. *Journal of Clinical Child Psychology, 19,* 111–122.

Cazden, C. B. (2001). *Classroom discourse: The language of teaching and learning* (2nd ed.). Portsmouth, NH: Heinemann.

Chan, Y. L., & Martinellie, S. A. (2008). Definitions of idioms in preadolescents, adolescents, and adults. *Journal of Psycholinguistic Research, 37,* 1–20.

Clark, H. H., & Clark, E. V. (1977). *Psychology and language: An introduction to psycholinguistics.* San Diego, CA: Harcourt Brace Jovanovich.

Cometa, M. S., & Eson, M. E. (1978). Logical operations and metaphor interpretation: A Piagetian model. *Child Development, 49,* 649–659.

Conti-Ramsden, G., & Botting, N. (2004). Social difficulties and victimization in children with SLI at 11 years of age. *Journal of Speech-Language-Hearing Research, 47,* 145–161.

Cunningham, A. E., & Stanovich, 1997. Early reading acquisition and its relation to reading experience and ability 10 years later. *Developmental Psychology, 3,* 934– 945.

Dodge, K., Pettit, G., McClaskey, C., & Brown, M. (1986). Social competence in children. *Monographs of the Society for Research in Child Development, 51*(Serial No. 213).

Douglas, J. D., & Peel, B. (1979). The development of metaphor and proverb translation in children grades 1 through 7. *Journal of Educational Research, 73*, 116–119.

Gallagher, T. (1993). Language skill and the development of social competence in school-age children. *Language, Speech, and Hearing Services in Schools, 24*, 199–205.

Gelman, R. (2009). Learning in core and noncore domains. In L. Tommasi, M. A. Peterson, & L. Nadel (Eds.), *Cognitive biology: Evolutionary and development perspectives on mind, brain, and behavior* (Vol. 12, pp. 247–260). Cambridge, MA: MIT Press.

Gelman, S. A., Coley, J. D., Rosengren, K., Hartman, E., & Pappas, A. (1998). Beyond labeling: The role of maternal input in the acquisition of richly-structured categories. *Monographs of the Society for Research in Child Development, 63*(1) (Serial No. 253).

Henry, M. K. (2003). *Unlocking literacy: Effective decoding and spelling instruction*, Baltimore, MD: Paul H. Brookes.

Hirsch, E. D., Kett, J. F., & Trefil, J. (1988). *The dictionary of cultural literacy*. Boston, MA: Houghton Mifflin.

Hofferth, S. L., & Sandberg, J. F. (2000). How American children spend their time (Research Report No. 00-458). Institute for Social Research, University of Michigan. Retrieved from http://www.isr.umich.edu

Hoff-Ginsberg, E. (1990). Function and structure in maternal speech: Their relation to the child's development of syntax. *Developmental Psychology, 22*, 155–163.

Hoff-Ginsberg, E., & Shatz, M. (1982). Linguistic input and the child's acquisition of language. *Psychological Bulletin, 92*, 3–26.

Hunt, K. W. (1970). Syntactic maturity in school children and adults. *Monographs of the Society for Research in Child Development, 134*(1).

Inhelder, B., & Piaget, J. (1959). *The growth of logical thinking from childhood to adolescence*. New York, NY: Basic Books.

Kavanagh, J. F., & Mattingly, I. G. (1972). *Language by ear and by eye*. Cambridge, MA: MIT Press.

Kieffer, M. J., & Lesaux, N. K. (2008). The role of derivational morphology in the reading comprehension of Spanish-speaking English language learners. *Reading and Writing: An Interdisciplinary Journal, 21*, 783–804.

Kintsch, W. (1977). *Memory and cognition*. New York, NY: John Wiley & Sons.

Klecan-Aker, J. S., & Hedrick, D. L. (1985). A study of the syntactic language skills of normal school-age children. *Language, Speech, and Hearing Services in Schools, 16*, 187–198.

Klecan-Aker, J. S, & Kelty, K. R. (1990). An investigation of the oral narratives of normal and language-learning disabled children. *Communication Disorders Quarterly, 13*, 207–215.

Larsen, J. A., & Nippold, M. A. (2007). Morphological analysis in school-age children: Dynamic assessment of a word learning strategy. *Language, Speech, and Hearing Services in Schools, 38*, 201–212.

Lazar, R. T., Warr-Leeper, G. A., Nicholson, C. B., & Johnson, S. (1989). Elementary school teachers' use of multiple meaning expressions. *Language, Speech, and Hearing Services in Schools, 20*, 420–430.

Liles, B. Z. (1987). Episode organization and cohesive conjunctives in narratives of children with and without language disorder. *Journal of Speech-Language-Hearing Research, 30*, 185–196.

Liles, B. Z. (1993). Narrative discourse in children with language disorders and children with normal language: A critical review of the literature. *Journal of Speech-Language-Hearing Research, 36*, 868–882.

Loban, W. (1976). *Language development: Kindergarten through grade twelve*. (Research Report No. 18). Urbana, IL: National Council of Teachers of English.

Mahoney, D., Singson, M., & Mann, V. (2000). Reading ability and sensitivity to morphological relations. *Reading and Writing, An Interdisciplinary Journal, 12*, 191–218.

Mahoney, D., Singson, M., & Mann, V. (2000). The relation between reading ability and morphological skills: Evidence from derivational suffixes. *Reading and Writing: An Interdisciplinary Journal, 12*, 219–252.

May, A. B. (1979). All the angles of idiom instruction. *The Reading Teacher, 32,* 680–682.

McClure, E., & Steffensen, M. (1995). A study of the use of conjunctions across grades and ethnic groups. *Research in the Teaching of English, 19,* 217–236.

McCutchen, D., Green, L., & Abbott, R. D. (2008). Children's morphological knowledge: Links to literacy. *Reading Psychology, 29,* 289–314.

Miller, J. F., & Chapman, R. S. (1981). The relation between age and mean length of utterance in morphemes. *Journal of Speech and Hearing Research, 24,* 154–161.

Moats, L. C. (2009). Teachers with knowledge of language. *Journal of Learning Disabilities, 42*(5), 387–391.

Nagy, W., & Anderson, R. C. (1984). How many words are there in printed school English? *Reading Research Quarterly, 19,* 304–330.

Nagy, W., Diakidoy, I., & Anderson, R. (1993). The acquisition of morphology: Learning the contribution of suffixes to the meanings of derivatives. *Journal of Reading Behavior, 25,* 155–171.

Nagy, W. E., & Herman, P. A. (1987). Breadth and depth of vocabulary knowledge: Implications for acquisition and instruction. In M. McKeown & M. Curtis (Eds.), *The nature of vocabulary acquisition* (pp. 19–35). Hillsdale, NJ: Erlbaum.

Nippold, M. A. (1988). *Later language development: Ages nine through nineteen.* San Diego, CA: College-Hill.

Nippold, M. A. (1991). Evaluating and enhancing idiom comprehension in language-disordered students. *Language, Speech, and Hearing Services in Schools, 22,* 100–106.

Nippold, M. A. (2007). *Later language development: School-age children, adolescents, and young adults* (3rd ed.). Austin, TX: Pro-Ed.

Nippold, M. A. (2009). School-age children talk about chess: Does knowledge drive syntactic complexity? *Journal of Speech, Language, and Hearing Research, 52,* 856–871.

Nippold, M. A. (2010). Explaining complex matters: How knowledge of a domain drives language. In M. A. Nippold & C. M. Scott (Eds.), *Expository discourse in children,* adolescents, and adults (pp. 41–62). New York, NY: Psychology Press, Taylor & Francis.

Nippold, M. A., & Duthie, J. K. (2003). Mental imagery and idiom comprehension: A comparison of school-age children and adults. *Journal of Speech, Language, Hearing Research, 46,* 788–799.

Nippold, M. A., & Fey, S. H. (1983). Metaphoric understanding in preadolescents having a history of language acquisition difficulties. *Language, Speech, and Hearing Services in Schools, 14,* 171–180.

Nippold, M. A., & Haq, F. S. (1996). Proverb comprehension in youth: The role of concreteness and familiarity. *Journal of Speech and Hearing Research, 39,* 166– 176.

Nippold, M. A., Hesketh, L. J., Duthie, J. K., & Mansfield, T. C. (2005). Conversational versus expository discourse: A study of syntactic development in children, adolescents, and adults. *Journal of Speech, Language, and Hearing Research, 48,* 1048–1064.

Nippold, M. A., Mansfield, T. C., & Billow, J. L. (2007). Peer conflict explanations in children, adolescents, and adults: Examining the development of complex syntax. *American Journal of Speech-Language Pathology, 16,* 179–188.

Nippold, M. A., Mansfield, T. C., Billow, J. L., & Tomblin, J. B. (2008). Expository discourse in adolescents with language impairments: Examining syntactic development. *American Journal of Speech-Language Pathology, 17,* 356–366.

Nippold, M. A., & Rudzinski, M. (1993). Familiarity and transparency in idiom explanation: A developmental study of children and adolescents. *Journal of Speech and Hearing Research, 36,* 728–737.

Nippold, M., & Scott, C. M. (2010). Overview of expository discourse: Development and disorders. In M. A. Nippold & C. M. Scott (Eds.), *Expository discourse in children, adolescents, and adults* (pp. 1–11). New York, NY: Psychology Press, Taylor & Francis.

Nunes, T., & Bryant, P. (2009). *Children's reading and spelling: Beyond the first steps.* Hoboken, NJ: John Wiley & Sons.

Nunes, T., Bryant, P., & Bindman, M. (2006). The effects of learning to spell on children's awareness of morphology. *Reading and Writing*, 767–787.

Piaget, J., & Inhelder, B. (1969). *The psychology of the child*. New York, NY: Basic Books.

Ravid, D., Dromi, E., & Kotler, P. (2010). Linguistic complexity in school-age text production: Expository versus mathematical discourse. In M. A. Nippold & C. M. Scott (Eds.), *Expository discourse in children, adolescents, and adults* (pp. 123–153). New York, NY: Psychology Press, Taylor & Francis.

Roseberry-McKibbin, C. (2007). *Language disorders in children: A multicultural and case perspective*. Boston, MA: Pearson.

Roseberry-McKibbin, C. (2008). *Multicultural students with special language needs: Practical strategies for assessment and intervention* (3rd ed.). Oceanside, CA: Academic Communication Associates.

Rubin, H. (1988). Morphological knowledge and early writing ability. *Language and Speech, 31*, 337–354.

Rydell, A. M., Hagekull, B., & Bohlin, G. (1997). Measurement of two social competence aspects in middle childhood. *Developmental Psychology, 33*, 824–833.

Scott, C. M. (1988). Spoken and written syntax. In M. A. Nippold (Ed.), *Later language development: Ages nine through nineteen* (pp. 49–98). Boston, MA: College-Hill Press.

Scott, C. M., & Stokes, S. L. (1995). Measures of syntax in school-age children and adolescents. *Language, Speech, and Hearing Services in Schools, 26*, 309–319.

Selman, R. L., Beardslee, W., Schultz, L. H., Krupa, M., & Podorefsky, D. (1986). Assessing adolescent interpersonal negotiation strategies: Toward the integration of structural and functional models. *Developmental Psychology, 22*, 450–459.

Shipley, K. G., Maddox, M. A., & Driver, J. E. (1991). Children's development of irregular past tense verb forms. *Language, Speech, and Hearing Services in Schools, 22*, 115–122.

Smith Gabig, C. (2011). Language development from age 6 through adolescence. In S. Levey & S. Polirstok, (Eds.), *Language development: Understanding language diversity in the classroom* (pp. 161–184). Los Angeles, CA: Sage.

Snyder, L., & Caccamise, D. (2010). Comprehension processes for expository test: Building meaning and making sense. In M. A. Nippold & C. M. Scott (Eds.), *Expository discourse in children, adolescents, and adults* (pp. 13–39). New York, NY: Psychology Press, Taylor & Francis.

Sousa, D. A. (2005). *How the brain learns to read.* Thousand Oaks, CA: Corwin Press.

Stahl, S. A., & Nagy, W. E. (2006). *Teaching word meanings*. Mahwah, NJ: Erlbaum.

Stanovich, K. E., & Cunningham, A. E. (1992). Studying the consequences of literacy within a literate society: The cognitive correlates of print exposure. *Memory & Cognition, 20*, 51–68.

Stanovich, K. E., & Cunningham, A. E. (1993). Where does knowledge come from? Specific associations between print exposure and information acquisition. *Journal of Educational Psychology, 85*, 211–229.

Stein, N. L., & Glenn, C. G. (1979). An analysis of story comprehension in elementary school children. In R. O. Freedle (Ed.), *New directions in discourse processing* (Vol. 2, pp. 53–120). Norwood, NJ: Ablex.

Sturm, J. A., & Nelson, N. W. (1997). Formal classroom lesson: New perspective on a familiar discourse event. *Language, Speech, and Hearing Services in Schools, 28*, 255–273.

Troia, G. A. (2007). Phonological processing and its influence on literacy learning. In C. A. Stone, E. R. Silliman, B. J. Ehren, & K. Apel (Eds.), *Handbook of language and literacy* (pp. 271–301). New York, NY: The Guilford Press.

Tyler, A., & Nagy, W. (1989). The acquisition of English derivational morphology. *Journal of Memory and Language, 28*, 649–667.

Vihman, M. M. (1988). Later phonological development. In J. E. Bernthal & N. W. Bankson (Eds.), *Articulation and phonological disorders* (2nd ed., pp. 110–144). Englewood Cliffs, NJ: Prentice Hall.

Wentzel, K. (1991). Social competence at school: Relation between social responsibility and academic achievement. *Review of Educational Research, 61,* 1–24.

Westby, C. (1984). Development of narrative language abilities. In G. Wallach & K. Butler (Eds.), *Language learning disabilities in school-age children* (pp. 103–127). Baltimore, MD: Williams & Wilkins.

White, T. G., Power, M. A., & White, S. (1989). Morphological analysis: Implications for teaching and understanding vocabulary growth. *Reading Research Quarterly, 24,* 283–304.

White, T. G., Sowell, J., & Yanagihara, A. (1989). Teaching elementary students to use word part clues. *The Reading Teacher, 42,* 302–308.

Wiig, E. H., & Semel, E. M. (1973). Comprehension of linguistic concepts requiring logical operations by learning disabled children. *Journal of Speech and Hearing Research, 16,* 627–636.

Winner, E., Rosenteil, A. K., & Garner, H. (1976). The development of metaphoric understanding. *Developmental Psychology, 12,* 289–297.

Wolter, J. A., Wood, A., & Dzatko, K. W. (2009). The influence of morphological awareness in literacy development of first grade children. *Language, Speech, and Hearing Services in Schools, 40,* 286–298.

CHAPTER 8

The Development of Literacy Skills

Sylvia F. Diehl

A kindergartner is beginning to learn the relationship between sounds and written letters (i.e., the sound and symbol relationship). This child can now identify his own name and enjoys naming letters on signs and in books. After reading this chapter, you will understand why this ability is important in the development of literacy skills.

Literacy encompasses the ability to read, write, speak, listen, and think effectively (Meltzer, Smith, & Clark, 2001). Therefore, the development of literacy is indivisibly linked with the development of language (Nelson, 2010). The development of language is often seen as starting in infancy, whereas the development of literacy skills is seen as beginning during formal school instruction. Although it is true that the process of identifying letters and words is best when systematically taught, comprehension of the written word is a complex skill that includes a multitude of language and cognitive abilities (Kamhi, 2009). Therefore, the process of acquiring literacy cannot be seen as beginning with school instruction. Instead, the acquisi-

tion of literacy begins in infancy (Newman, Ratner, Juszcyk, & Juszcyk, 2006). Language and literacy skills foster one another and help each other to flourish. For example, oral language nourishes reading and writing development, while reading and writing development promotes growth in oral language. In short, literacy skills are a means for a child to learn and think about the world (Teale & Sulzby, 1986).

CHAPTER OBJECTIVES

The purpose of this chapter is to explore normal literacy development from infancy through adolescence. After reading this chapter, you should understand:

◆ The interdependence of language and literacy
◆ The importance of metalinguistics
◆ The developmental stages of literacy in the preschool through adolescent years
◆ Methods to support literacy development across all ages

This chapter begins with an examination of the relationship between language and literacy, followed by a review of the development of literacy for preschoolers, elementary school-age children, and adolescents. A brief discussion concerning methods to support literacy development follows each section.

THE DEVELOPMENT OF LITERACY

In infancy, when children are beginning to learn speech and language, abilities that form the framework for later literacy learning are also being developed. When a child's mother says, "Here comes your Daddy," the child learns to comprehend the word *Daddy* separately from the whole stream of words. This segmentation skill provides the foundation for formal segmentation tasks, such as "What is the first sound in *nap*?" Children also become aware of print well before school age when exposed to books, magazines, grocery lists, advertisements, television shows, and educational toys.

> Children learn that pictures or symbols stand for ideas. For example, young children easily identify the trademark symbol of their favorite fast food restaurant. These are just a few examples of the early foundational learning experiences that provide the underpinnings for conscious formal learning (Dickinson, Golinkoff, & Hirsch-Pasek, 2010).

EMERGENT LITERACY

Emergent literacy is typically associated with the preschool years (Storch & White-hurst, 2001; Whitehurst & Lonigan, 1998). From 3 to 5 years of age, children gather information about print and sounds. They make sense out of reading and writing in very elementary ways before they experience formal literacy instruction (Justice & Ezell, 2004). During this time, the child starts to learn to think about language in a more mindful way. This represents a transition from using language to communicate to conscious thought about the use of language. This ability is called **metalinguistic knowledge**, which means "thinking about language."

Metalinguistic skills are essential for learning to read and write (van Kleeck, 1994). As the child progresses through school, each area of language becomes the focus of metalinguistic examination (Justice, 2006). Early metalinguistic skills typically involve **print awareness** and **phonological awareness** (Justice, 2006; Justice & Ezell, 2004). Young children exhibit print awareness by realizing that the print underneath a picture gives additional information, as do the following examples of written language that are among their earliest introductions to literacy:

Menus listing food choices

Signs announcing a particular store or restaurant

The words in birthday cards that consist of letters

Covers of books showing the titles of the books

Labels showing different types of foods

Phonological awareness begins with an interest in the sounds in words and with enjoyment of rhymes, songs, and chants. Phonological awareness also involves a child's ability to understand how the sounds of language relate to one another to form the meaning of words. Examples of chidren's phonological awareness follow:

Being aware of the sound structure of words

Understanding that the word *dog* has one syllable and *banana* has three syllables

Understanding that the word *cat* consists of three alphabet letters

Having the ability to identify rhyming words and, later, to generate rhyme

Identifying the ending sound of the word *hat*

By 4 years of age, children become aware that print has certain conventions. For example, they learn that print is organized from left to right and that a grocery list is organized differently than a storybook. Children learn that print can represent distinct names, depending on the varied order of letters in words (Justice & Ezell, 2004). At this stage of development, children's phonological awareness becomes much more visible, graduating to the ability to segment sound units in words. Development goes from larger segments, such as parsing sentences into words, to smaller segments, such as dividing multisyllabic words into syllables (e.g., *ba-na-na* and *mon-key*) (Moats, 2009). They also begin to recognize when words rhyme (e.g., *hat-cat*).

As children grow, phonological awareness increases and more complex phonological awareness tasks are mastered. Earlier tasks typically involve matching letters (i.e., Can you find another "G?"), blending (i.e., What word does /b/- /i/- /n/ make?), and adding sounds to form new words (i.e., Add /s/ to the beginning of the word *top*). Later develop-

ing phonological tasks involve analysis, such as counting the number of segments in words (i.e., How many sounds are in the word *cough*?), segmenting (i.e., Say each sound in the word *sun)*, and deleting sounds (i.e., Say *spot* without the /s/) (Yopp & Yopp, 2009).

LITERACY DEVELOPMENT IN THE PRESCHOOL YEARS

The preschool years are an eventful time for building the foundation for literacy development (Chall, 1996; Justice, 2006; Moats, 2009; Shipley & McAfee, 2009; Tompkins, 2003; van Kleek, 2006; Wolfersberger, Reutzel, Sudweeks, & Fawson, 2004; Wood, 2007; Yopp & Yopp, 2009) (Table 8–1). By age 3, children are starting to think and communicate about their world in more complex ways. They are learning to communicate about people, objects, and events that are not actually present. This involves **decontextualized language**, or language used to refer to things not present in the immediate environment.

During the preschool years, children develop an understanding of simple **narratives** or stories. Vocabulary develops as children learn new words from books. This, in turn, feeds the growth of a larger and more varied vocabulary along with the ability to retell events.

Very early print awareness begins to appear when children develop an interest in print and realize that print carries meaning (Justice & Ezell, 2004). They first begin with an understanding of the letters in their own names and, in this way, learn that alphabet letters are "special" (Wood, 2007).

Table 8–1. Preschool Literacy Development and Literacy Activities

Print Concepts	Phonological Awareness	Spelling	Vocabulary	Narrative Development	Writing	Supporting Preschool Literacy Development
• Interest in print	• Enjoys playing with the sounds in words and songs	• Scribbling common	• Ever expanding vocabulary for words in their environment	• Retells stories that stay mostly on topic	• Starts out scribbling, which turns into writing that looks like letters and words	• A literacy-rich environment
• Groups of letters have meaning	• Can separate sentences into words and words into syllables	• May use letter symbols but no sound symbol correspondence	• Able to use subordinating and coordinating words to form more complex sentences	• Relates stories to personal experience	• Will interpret his or her writing and drawing for others to form a whole meaning	• Book sharing or dialogic reading
• Turns pages one at a time	• Knows words are made of sounds	• May be able to spell name		• By age 4, answers "wh" questions about read-aloud stories		• Pointing out details about print
• Looks from left to right and top to bottom	• Produces words that rhyme	• Direction of writing on page				• Songs, alliteration, finger-plays that play and manipulate words and sounds in words
		• Some letter sound matches by age 4				• Dramatic play
						• Varied writing experiences

250

By age 4, children's vocabulary and sentence forms continue to develop. They expand their ability to talk about the world around them. They are now able to tell stories that remain mostly on topic but do not have a typical story structure (Stadler & Ward, 2005). A description of children's narrative development is provided in Chapter 6, showing that children begin with simple recounts of events. This early knowledge of stories develops into an awareness of narrative **text structure** (Hedberg & Westby, 1993), which refers to the organization of written text. Examples of the features and organization of text structure for the story elements of fiction follow.

Characters: People involved in the story

Setting: Places where the action occurs

Problem: Challenges that the characters face

Solution: How the challenge is resolved

Plot: Events that make up a story

Examples of the features and organization of the text structure for nonfiction follow:

Cause and effect: A discussion of how one action can cause another action to occur

Sequence of events: The chronological order of actions or events

Description: A topic that is explained in terms of characteristics, features, and examples

Comparison and contrast: An explanation of how two or more events are alike and/or different

Knowledge of text structure supports children's comprehension of both fiction and nonfiction texts by providing them with a framework for the ideas presented in various types of texts, along with the relationship among these ideas. With knowledge of the framework of text structure, children are able to comprehend how words and sentences are arranged within varied types of texts, from a simple grocery list to the popular *Harry Potter* series. The process is this: children must organize their thinking to match the thought of the author of the text and arrive at an understanding of the sequence of events and the motivations of the characters (i.e., the reasons for their actions). Children who have difficulty with text comprehension approach reading without a basic framework or plan. Consequently, they may have difficulty understanding or remembering what they have read.

> Metalinguistic abilities are an integral part of language and literacy learning, because children must be aware of how to determine word meaning. In terms of word meaning (semantics), readers often consciously wonder about the meaning of an unfamiliar word. They may try to decipher the word in context (i.e., by determining the meaning via other words that surround it) or look it up in a dictionary.

SUPPORTING LITERACY DEVELOPMENT IN THE PRESCHOOL YEARS

Support for literacy skills in the preschool years is intended to ensure that a child has a variety of literacy experiences. During this stage of development, children are exposed to stories or narratives and are given the opportunity to engage in prewriting activities (e.g., scribbling and drawing). Four strategies are recommended to support literacy development in the preschool years: (1) providing a print-rich environment and prewriting activities; (2) book sharing; (3) phonological awareness activities; and (4) symbolic play (see Table 8–1).

> Children's early writing begins with a mix of drawing efforts with attempts to "write." Very young children begin their attempts to write with scribbling and move to drawing. There is a connection between these early writing attempts and children's oral language skills (Dyson, 2000), as the combination of writing, drawing, and language is integrated to form meaning.

Print-Rich Environment

Providing a print-rich environment at home is an important ingredient in this experiential effort to support children's literacy development (Guo, Justice, Kaderavek, & McGinty, 2012; Roskos & Neuman, 2001; Wolfersberger et al., 2004). There are a variety of reading materials that support different genres:

Stories

Poetry

Directions

Grocery lists and recipes

There is also an assortment of materials for writing that set the stage for purposeful encounters with reading and writing:

Construction paper, whiteboards, and easels

Chalk, crayons, and markers

Modeling writing and drawing with young children encourages their prewriting experience. Early drawing and writing attempts should be celebrated and proudly displayed in the classroom and on the refrigerator at home.

Book Sharing

Book sharing has been shown to provide an important experience for preschoolers (Pentimonti et al., 2012; van Kleeck, 2006; Zebenbergen & Whitehurst, 2003), allowing the novice reader to have a dialogue with a peer or an adult who is a more experienced reader (van Kleeck, 2006). Book sharing involves more than just reading books with a child. There are factors to consider before, during, and after reading.

Before reading, consider the choice of book being read. The content and length of the book and the complexity of the language should be a good match with the child's interest, attention span, and comprehension abilities. A child should be encouraged to make predictions about the book's content from its cover.

During reading, it is important that the adult make the experience a positive one by reading with expression and interest. With unfamiliar books, the adult should do more of the talking. As the child becomes more familiar with the book, the balance should shift to the child (Whitehurst et al., 1994).

After reading, it is important to talk about the story that has been read, discussing the elements of text structure that were discussed earlier in this chapter (e.g., characters, settings, problems, solutions, and the plot).

When the book is finished, the child and adult should talk about how the content relates to their lives and discuss the new words that they have encountered, along with what they would like to read the next time.

> Book sharing should be done frequently and routinely to help the child learn about the organization of books and the text structure found in them. New vocabulary words should be discussed as they appear in the text, along with periodic questions and comments about the story (Huebner, 2000; van Kleeck, 2008). Additionally, indicating aspects of print during reading, such as pointing to words while reading, has been shown to have a positive effect on reading acquisition (Pentimonti et al., 2012).

Phonological Awareness Activities

Playing with sounds helps build the phonological abilities needed when formal reading instruction begins (Phillips, Clancy-Menchetti, & Lonigan, 2008). Songs, poems, alliterative games, and rhyming books help provide early experiences with manipulating sound. For young children, these phonological awareness activities should not be seen as schoolwork but as an extension of play (Yopp & Yopp, 2009).

Symbolic Play Experiences

Symbolic play experiences are also foundational for successful literacy development (Vygotsky, 1967). In symbolic play, children use an object to represent something other than what it is (e.g., a box for a car or a block for a telephone). The ability to substitute or represent one thing for another is a rung on the ladder to realizing that letters grouped together can represent the spoken word. In other words, children realize that alphabet letters are symbols that represent spoken sounds and that these letters can be connected to represent words. Symbolic play also encourages the language growth needed in literacy attainment (Wilford, 2000). Through pretending, children practice using new vocabulary and learn how to take conversational roles tied to their play, as shown in the following example (Cowley, 1999):

> Children were observed in a preschool classroom acting out a book called *Mrs. Wishy Washy* that they had previously read as a class. This is a story about a farmwoman who washes her animals but they keep getting dirty. The teacher had put farm animals, a play bath tub, and a brown towel out in the reading center. The children loved getting the animals "dirty" by throwing them on the brown towel and repeating repetitive lines in the book like, "Oh, lovely mud!"

This play context helped cement the important language and literacy factors discussed, such as symbol development, character perspective, and expressive vocabulary.

LITERACY DEVELOPMENT IN THE ELEMENTARY SCHOOL YEARS

The elementary school years mark a time of enormous growth in literacy development (Blachman, 1997; Chall, 1996; Kaderavek & Justice, 2004; Shipley & McAfee, 2009; Tompkins, 2003; Wood, 2007) (see Tables 8–2 and 8–3). Children go from identifying sound and letter pairings in kindergarten to reading a variety of text genres (e.g., types of text) fluently by the fifth grade. Literacy development occurs across the critical literacy areas below:

◆ Phonological awareness
◆ Vocabulary
◆ Reading comprehension
◆ Spelling
◆ Reading fluency
◆ Writing

Phonological Awareness and Literacy Learning

Formal reading instruction begins in earnest when a child enters kindergarten. Phonological awareness is now a large part of formal literacy learning. Phonological awareness is a broad term that incorporates the size of a sound unit and how that sound unit is used in different contexts (Yopp & Yopp, 2009). There are levels of complexity for the sound units being learned:

Larger sound units—beginning with sentences then moving to words

Smaller sound units—beginning with syllables (e.g., ba – na – na) then moving to individual phonemes in words (e.g., /b/).

Children gradually develop awareness of the size of units, proceeding from the larger units of sentences and syllables in the preschool years to individual phonemes or sounds in the kindergarten years. The way in which sound units are manipulated (i.e., matching, blending, segmenting, substituting, and deleting) develops from kindergarten through grade 2 (Table 8–2).

In kindergarten, a child can identify the first sound of a spoken word and separate it from its rime. For example, the word *pin* begins with /p/, which is the onset, and the rime is "in."

> Monosyllabic words can be split into two parts—the onset and the rime. The onset is the initial consonant sound (*b-* in *bag* and *sw-* in *swim*) and the *rime* is the vowel and the rest of the syllable that follows (*-ag* in *bag* and *-im* in *swim*).

In grade 1, children continue to manipulate the sounds of words through compound word construction (e.g., *railroad*) and syllable deletion (e.g., omitting a syllable from a word). Examples consist of saying the word *railroad* without *road* and saying the word *fishing* without the *-ing*. By the end of the first grade and into second grade, children begin to work with even smaller sound segments. They can now count the number of phonemes or sound units in a word (e.g., *nut* has three sounds). They may be asked to delete the

Table 8–2. *Literacy Development From Kindergarten Through Grade 2*

Grade	Phonological Awareness	Spelling	Vocabulary	Fluency	Comprehension	Writing
K	• Segments onset and rime (m followed by -an) • Finds words that start with the same phoneme • Blends sounds together	• Knows the letters and their sounds • Identifies all upper-and lowercase letters • Can identify words in the same word family	• Can talk about things that are not physically present • Knows about 2,000 to 3,000 words	• Expands vocabulary using more words not in immediate environment	• Sight reads high-frequency words and some CVC words	• Predicts what is next in stories • Answers questions about read-aloud stories • Draws and writes
1	• Changes phonemes by adding, deleting, or substituting phonemes • Has more advanced abilities to blend sounds together	• Understands that words have a distinct spelling • Spells by sounding out • Spells CVC and sight words	• Understands the word relations of antonyms and synonyms	• Creates meaning while reading • Rereads to get words right	• Answers questions about text • Follows simple written instructions	• Begins with capital letters • Ends with period • Spacing irregular
2	• Reads longer words by sounding out using phonic abilities • Reads words with one and two syllables	• Traditional spelling increases • Consonant blends and digraphs are acquired • Some morphological structures are used	• Uses context of reading to help decode words • Begins to use root words, prefixes, and suffixes to decode words	• Reading speed increases	• Sequences events of story • Uses context clues to help comprehension	• Writes narrative and expository text with model • Variety of sentence forms • Writing has beginning, middle, and end • Legible writing • Regular spacing

initial or final phoneme of a word (e.g., Say *stop* without the /s/). In addition to deleting sounds, the first grader is able to blend sounds together to form words (Moats, 2009), such as blending "c-a-t" to form the word *cat*.

Some words are recognized by sight at this stage of development but many words are sounded out phoneme by phoneme. Additionally, during the second grade, word patterns are learned (i.e., the pattern of letters that form certain frequently encountered words, such as *the, is, are, these*, and other examples that occur frequently in written text). Word pattern recognition acts to speed up reading skills.

Vocabulary Development and Reading Comprehension

Vocabulary development is strongly tied to reading comprehension. In fact, vocabulary size in first grade is a predictor of reading comprehension in the 11th grade (Cunningham & Stanovich, 1997). Another factor in reading comprehension and vocabulary development is the amount of reading experience. For example, exposure to new words enhances children's memory for the pronunciation, spelling, and meaning of that word (Rosenthal & Ehri, 2008).

In kindergarten, the child's ability to read and discuss decontextualized ideas expands. Typically, topics discussed in the classroom are not physically present. For example, a preschool-age child may talk about a policeman when he sees a policeman on the street. In the kindergarten classroom, a discussion might be held about community helpers, such as policemen and firemen, but they need not be present for this discussion to occur. Ideas are discussed using oral language, pictures, and books. The kindergartner also expands his or her ability to tell stories or narratives that follow a sequential order of events (Stadler & Ward, 2005).

It is estimated that a first grader knows between 2,000 and 3,000 words and will learn about 3,000 words a year in the following years (Carlisle & Katz, 2005). By the third grade, children know between 4,000 and 6,000 words and are beginning to understand complex word relationships. Children enjoy nonliteral language, such as humor, idioms, and early **figurative language** (e.g., groups of words that change or exaggerate meaning because they are grouped together). The first grader uses this vocabulary to gather comprehension clues about pictures, titles, and headings within a book. He or she can make accurate predictions using this information.

In the second grade, language skills continue to expand and children are able to identify root words (*stand*), prefixes (*mis-*), and suffixes (*-ing*). This is an important step in helping the child move away from sound-by-sound reading into more fluent comprehension of text and words (i.e., *misunderstanding*). Second graders also have more fully developed narratives (Stadler & Ward, 2005). They can create a full episode including setting, plot, character, and resolution. Second graders start to comprehend written text without the aid of an adult (Wood, 2007). They become more independent in their reading and new word learning. They may use dictionaries and other resources to support comprehension. As they mature through elementary school, children are able to comprehend lengthier texts, such as books with chapters.

By the fourth grade, independent reading is well developed (Wood, 2007). By the fifth grade, children's vocabulary consists of between 5,000 and 8,000 words and they become more interested in exploring nonfiction reading and enjoy biographies.

Spelling

The development of spelling involves a blend of three types of linguistic knowledge (Bourassa & Treiman, 2001). It is the integration of these three types of linguistic knowledge that leads to spelling expertise:

The first type of linguistic knowledge is phonological knowledge, helping a child to form a link between sounds and letters.

The second type of linguistic knowledge is orthographic knowledge, allowing a child to understand that a sound can be represented in print in different ways (e.g., the *oo* sound in the word sh*oo*t can also be spelled as *oe* in the word sh*oe*).

The third type of linguistic knowledge is morphological knowledge, providing the knowledge of inflections such as *-er* or *-ing* (e.g., *bigger* and *running*).

Kindergartners and first graders primarily depend on their phonological knowledge (Ehri, 2000), using their understanding of the sound-symbol relationship to spell words. For example, children may spell the word *you* as "u" or the word *night* as "nit."

Next, children begin to spell words with short vowels in consonant-vowel-consonant form (i.e., *cat*, *rip*, *men*). They are able to spell words with two consonants together, such as the blends "sm" or "st." At this time, children are also able to spell words with **digraphs,** or words that have two consonants that make one sound (i.e., *th, sh, ch* used to spell *thumb*, *shoe*, and *chin*). Note that the phonetic representation of these sounds is a single phoneme: *th* /θ/, *sh* /ʃ/, and *ch* /tʃ/, as described in Chapters 1 and 3.

By the second grade, children begin to learn that words that "sound the same" may have different meanings and spellings (e.g., *two, too,* and *to*), and they are challenged by the different spellings of these words. When a child has to choose between alternative spellings (i.e., *for* versus *four*), words that the children have frequently seen in print provide orthographic guidance (Wright & Ehri, 2007). More exposure to reading provides children with the ability to recognize the meaning of these words, along with the ability to spell them.

In the second grade, children are now reading more frequently and independently and are exposed to more words in print. By the end of second grade, the use of inflections begins to appear with the use of past tense and plurals evident in children's productions (Carlisle, 1988; Walker & Hauerwas, 2006). Examples consist of the use of the past tense verb form *-ed* (e.g., *walked*) and the plural form *-s* (e.g., *cats*).

By the third grade, the use of morphological knowledge in spelling becomes commonplace and affixes are consistently used correctly (Tompkins, 2003). An affix is a word element, such as a prefix or suffix, that can only occur attached to a base, stem, or root, as demonstrated in the following examples:

Prefixes that occur before a root/stem:

un + kind	unkind
mis + lay	mislay
mis + understand	misunderstand

Suffixes that occur at the end of a root/stem:

care + full	careful
danger + ous	dangerous
happy + ness	happiness

Third graders are able to use meaningful chunks or segments of words in their spelling. More advanced inflectional endings are present, such as -*ness* or -*ship* (e.g., *happiness* and *ownership*). As children learn how to spell words, errors in adding prefixes, suffixes, inflectional endings, along with doubling errors, are common (e.g., "hamer" for *hammer*). Children are on their way to using the three types of linguistic knowledge in their spelling: phonological, morphological, and orthographic.

Reading Fluency

When children are first learning to read, their reading rate is quite slow because they are putting significant mental effort into the phonological process of sounding out the words sound by sound. In order to increase their rate, children must integrate their other linguistic abilities with spelling skills. These other linguistic abilities consist of orthographic skills (that allow children to quickly identify sight words) and morphologic skills (that allow children to identify prefixes and suffixes). They must also connect their orthographic skills with word meaning or semantic knowledge. When these abilities work in an integrative and automatic fashion, the child is said to read fluently and his or her reading rate typically increases.

The National Reading Panel (National Institute of Child Health and Human Development [NICHD], 2000) defines **fluency** as the ability to read a text quickly, accurately, and with proper expression. Fluent reading is connected with good reading comprehension and also requires good decoding. The correlation between the rate of oral reading and reading comprehension is strong during the elementary school years (Pinnell et al., 1995) but rapid reading skills do not always mean that the reader comprehends the text. Most readers, but not all, who can read text quickly are also good comprehenders. However, some children have the ability to read words quickly but do not understand what they are reading. The ability to read fluently is a complex skill that develops over time.

Reading fluency requires a cognitive process of analysis, in which children apply their knowledge of a wide number of unrelated facts about the world, along with an understanding of the relationship among various concepts (ideas about things) (Bialystok, 2001). Beginning and more advanced fluent reading (and writing) are based on different levels of cognitive processing and require different levels of language skills.

Consider the cognitive demands of conversation (low cognitive demands) versus giving a book report in class (high cognitive demands). In a similar manner, fluent reading depends on more advanced cognitive processes and language skills. Fluent reading also requires that the reader apply higher cognitive processes to comprehension, rather than the lower level processes assigned to recognizing individual words (Stanovich, Cunningham, & Freeman, 2009). The fluent reader holds sequences of words in short-term memory, the site of operation of comprehension processes on the words that have been read. This process leads to meaningful phrasing while reading and to the integration of words into a meaningful conceptual structure that can be stored in long-term memory.

Writing

As discussed earlier, children's earliest writings are combined with drawing. Their first written word is often their own name (Bloodgood, 1999). Children expand from that name knowledge and begin to pepper their drawings with letters (Harste, Woodward, & Burke, 1984). In kindergarten, children's early writing reflects their burgeoning phonological development and maturing motor skills.

> Most kindergartners can stay within the lines on big writing paper and their writing flows from left to right and top to bottom (Wood, 2007). There is inconsistency in their spacing but there are also attempts to group words separately.

In the beginning stages of writing, children typically prefer uppercase letters. Invented spelling is common (Moats, 2009), for example, *mommy* written as "MBXBC." By the first grade, writing is legible but still larger than typical writing.

It is not unusual to see a mix of upper- and lowercase letters. Although there is variability, basic writing conventions are followed, such as using capital letters when appropriate and ending with a period.

By the second grade, children still rely on lines to guide their placement of letters but writing has become more automatic. The diminished motor demands help children focus more on the content in their written efforts. By this stage of development, connected writing expands and children's written essays have a beginning, middle, and end (Wood, 2007). They develop more interest in writing **expository** text structure or informational assignments.

> The primary goal of expository text is to deliver information about a subject, common issue, a way to do something, or an idea. This represents the beginning of a journey into a variety of expository text structures, each of which has a different function (i.e., descriptive, sequence, comparison-contrast, cause-effect, and problem-solution) (Westby, 1999).

By the third grade, children are typically motorically fluent writers. They are ready to begin the draft and revision process for their writing efforts. Their plots include character development but may sometimes be fanciful and hard to believe. Fourth graders are ready to write at more length using information resources to develop the topic. Their budding ability to understand idioms and early figurative language appears in their attempts to include humor in their writing. They write in multiple genres including narratives and expositories, from letters to basic research papers.

Fifth graders continue to perfect the draft and revision process. Their plots become more complex and may include more than one episode (e.g., a story within another story). They continue to expand their enjoyment of different written genres through poetry writing, cartooning, and journaling (Wood, 2007). Their writing shows more awareness of who will read what they have written.

Because oral language and written language are so closely connected, children's oral language feeds the complexity of their written language. Their increasing language skills are especially important in the development of **cohesion** and **coherence** in their writing. Cohesion is how the ideas relate to each other. A paper with good cohesion is comprehensible and consistent. One thought naturally leads to another. Coherence can be conceived as the grammatical and lexical links that link one part of a text to another. This includes use of synonyms (words with the same meaning), lexical sets (a set of words with the same topic, function, or form), pronouns (words that replace nouns), verb tenses (verb forms that express the time an action took place), time references (words that indicate when an event occurs, occurred, or will occur), and grammatical forms (proper nouns, adjectives, prepositional phrases, and relative clauses), as shown in the following examples:

Synonyms: **Myths** often narrate historical beliefs. These **narratives** tell a story about what some people believe.

Lexical sets: We were looking for the lost **cat**. This **feline** was our pet

Pronouns: **Peter** was lost and **he** didn't know where **he** was

Verb tenses: He **went** *yesterday* and decided to **go** again tomorrow

Time references: **First**, he ate; **Next**, he took a nap; **and then**, he watched TV

Grammatical forms: The **little** girl ran **quickly around** the track

Adept use of cohesive ties helps writing grow in coherence and increases the clarity of the writing as the complexity increases (Dyson & Freedman, 1991). Both of these abilities grow throughout children's lives and well into adulthood.

SUPPORTING LITERACY DEVELOPMENT IN THE ELEMENTARY SCHOOL YEARS

A child's literacy program in the elementary school years should include five areas recommended by the National Reading Panel (NICHD, 2000): (1) phonemic awareness, (2) phonics, (3) fluency, (4) vocabulary, and (5) text comprehension. The child's reading program should be balanced, integrating all of these areas rather than a focused concentration on one or the other.

Phonemic Awareness

Phonemic awareness is an aspect of phonological awareness that deals with the phoneme. As stated in Chapters 1 and 3, a phoneme is the smallest sound unit of language. Whereas younger children deal with larger units like words and syllables, school-age children deal with phonemes. Phonemic awareness helps children realize that sounds can be put together to form words. Meaningful activities given to beginning readers provide practice with segmenting and blending individual sounds (Torgesen et al., 2001). Once children become aware of the individual sounds in words, they are able to understand *blending* and *segmenting* sounds in words. Segmenting involves breaking words into syllables (e.g., *ba-na-na*) or individual sounds (e.g., *cat = c-a-t*), whereas blending involves combining individual sounds to produce a word (e.g., *c-a-t = cat*).

Phonics

Whereas phonemic awareness deals with spoken language sounds, **phonics** describes the relationship between phonemes (sounds) and graphemes (written language). In other words, phonics teaches the child the connection between the sound that the phoneme makes and the letter representation. When presenting phonemic awareness activities, the connections to the grapheme(s) or the written letter or letters that correspond with sound should be made obvious to the child (NICHD, 2000; Torgesen et al., 2001). Phonics should be explicitly and systematically taught and children should be encouraged to use their phonic skills when reading or writing (NICHD, 2000).

Reading Fluency

Gaining fluency skills depends both on exposure to models of fluent reading and on experience with reading aloud. There are numerous ways of providing repeated experiences, such as student-adult reading, partner reading, choral reading, tape-assisted reading, and readers' theater. In student-adult reading and partner reading, the readers take turns reading aloud, whereas in choral reading, the whole class reads together at the same time. Tape-assisted reading allows the student to read along, while an experienced reader reads the book on an audiotape. As the child becomes more fluent, he or she could read in concert with the audiobook and then independently. Readers' theater allows students to rehearse a play that comes from their reading. The script is then performed for classmates with a minimum of preparation or props. Because it is in play form, it is a natural vehicle to increase fluent reading presentation.

Vocabulary

Vocabulary is learned both incidentally and by direct teaching (Nagy & Herman, 1985). Some word meanings are taught explicitly but it is impossible for teachers to directly teach all the word meanings needed. Therefore, students must be able to learn new words incidentally from oral language or by inferring meaning from context when reading. Teachers can support incidental word learning, however, by inspiring interest and inquisitiveness about learning new words. Modeling word-learning strategies and interest in word learning can help capitalize on incidental word learning while students are reading independently (NICHD, 2000).

Strategies That Support Reading Comprehension

Vocabulary knowledge is not all there is to reading comprehension. Understanding what is read takes more than just knowing the individual word meanings. Good readers think about meaning as they are reading, integrating the written text with what they already know.

There are many strategies that aid reading comprehension. These strategies include using graphic organizers, answering and asking questions about what was read, discussion of text structure, and summarizing texts (NICHD, 2000). One method incorporates four of these strategies (Palincsar & Brown, 1986). This method is called reciprocal teaching. In this method, the more experienced reader models and encourages asking questions about what is being read, clarifying unknown words, predicting what might happen next, and summarizing or using self-review.

LITERACY DEVELOPMENT IN ADOLESCENCE

By adolescence, children are fluent readers but this does not mean that their literacy development is complete (Table 8–3). In order to meet expectations in the content areas in the upper grades, it is imperative that their vocabulary, comprehension, fluency, and writing abilities continue to grow and expand. In this section, growth in these areas is highlighted along with methods to support adolescents' continued literacy growth.

Genre, Vocabulary, and Reading Comprehension

Throughout adolescence, children learn to enjoy, use, and comprehend a variety of genres or types of text, both fiction and nonfiction (Wood, 2007). In middle school, they begin reading newspapers, magazines, and biographies. These continue in high school along with song lyrics, poetry, drama, short stories, and novels. As noted earlier, familiarity with different types of text structure supports the comprehension of a text. This is especially helpful if the content of the text is unfamiliar to the reader (Wallach & Butler, 1994).

Knowing different kinds of text structure also helps support vocabulary development. When a student reads about the same subject in a variety of types of print, he or she comes into contact with related vocabulary more frequently. This helps the adolescent to learn a variety of high-frequency (more common) and low-frequency (less common) words related to the subject (Adams, 2011).

Along with varying text structure, comprehension in content areas depends on being able to master the oral and written language requirements presented in the varied subject areas found in different texts (Beck & Jeffrey, 2009). For example, each academic subject area has its own academic language register. An academic register is a specialized way of speaking or writing in accord with disciplinary requirements (Wilkinson & Silliman, 2008). Reading and understanding social studies is quite different from reading and understanding science.

As adolescents travel through middle school and high school, a significant percentage of their new vocabulary development is related to their subject study. Content area texts contain vocabulary that is challenging because it is often more scholarly and includes the specialized vocabulary of the discipline being studied (Silliman & Scott, 2009). For instance, let us consider this sample question taken from

Table 8–3. *Literacy Development From Grades 3 through 10*

Grade	Spelling	Vocabulary	Fluency	Comprehension	Writing
3	• Mostly adultlike spelling • Long vowel and r-control vowel (e.g., "er") spelling patterns • Complex consonant patterns	• Vocabulary continues to be enriched through reading • Knows between 4,000 and 6,000 words	• Reads at 114 words per minute • Word analysis skills when reading	• Monitors comprehension while reading • Clarifies when does not comprehend • Knows fact/opinion • Knows cause/effect	• Narratives, letters, simple expositories • Uses more cohesive devices
4–6	• Identifies misspellings by using orthographic knowledge • Applies inflectional endings • Uses syllabication	• Uses vocabulary effectively in writing • Knows between 5,000 and 8,000 words	• Fluent reading • Understands an increasing number of text structures	• Makes inferences from text • Can summarize and paraphrase	• Organizes writing into beginning, middle, and end • Main idea is evident • Develops characters and plots • Reviews and revises
7–10	• Uses phonological, orthographic, and morphologic knowledge to spell • Latin and Greek affixes and root words • Etymologies	• Attains vocabulary needed in content areas	• Reads fluently for learning and for entertainment	• Reads independently for new knowledge and research projects	• Complex sentences in writing • Coherent and cohesive writing • A variety of text structures are explored

a high school science state examination (NYSED, 2011):

> When the bacterium, Serratia marcescens, is grown on a sterile culture medium in a petri dish at 30°C, the bacterial colonies are cream colored. When this same bacterium is cultured under identical conditions, except at a temperature of 25°C, the colonies are brick red. This difference in color is most likely due to the effect of temperature on the expression of the gene for color.

The preceding passage contains advanced vocabulary, such as *sterile*, *medium*, and *expression*, along with specialized scientific vocabulary, such as *bacterium*, *culture*, and *gene*. This text also presents the adolescent reader with increased syntactic complexity: the second sentence contains a dependent clause and a phrase, in addition to the independent clause. These elements increase the length of the sentence and the density of ideas being communicated. Thus, the adolescent reader must possess good language skills when faced with this level of complexity.

Social literacy demands are also increasing during this period, given the variety of technologies that are available and widely used, such as texting, instant messaging, and other social networking media. There is greater motivation to fit in with peers. Consequently, the adolescent learns to meet the language demands found in humor and sarcasm. The closely related skills involved in the comprehension of figurative language (e.g., simile, metaphor, personification, hyperbole) are also increasing (Wood, 2007).

Reading Fluency

Adolescents vary significantly in reading fluency, as fluency is affected by the four following factors (Barth, Catts, & Anthony, 2009).

The first factor in reading fluency is word accuracy. Word accuracy is the ability to read or decode words using the phonological, orthographic, and morphological abilities described earlier in the chapter. The integration of phonological, orthographic, and morphological knowledge leads to more rapid recognition of a word.

The second factor in reading fluency is the ability to name the word quickly. It is thought that this quick naming retrieval plays a bigger part in fluency in younger than in older readers (Barth, Catts, & Anthony, 2009).

The third factor in reading fluency is working memory. This means that the reader can remember and manipulate information at the same time.

The fourth factor is language comprehension, which plays a large part in reading fluency for adolescents (Barth, Catts, & Anthony, 2009). This is the ability to create meaning from the text. This can be influenced by the students' familiarity with the text structure and content. Unfamiliar structure and content may need to be read more slowly than familiar structure and content.

Greater experience with reading helps makes these four factors work in concert more quickly. The beginning reader may have to focus almost entirely on the decoding process, reading one word at a time. Reading becomes more automatic to the more experienced adolescent readers and fluency continues to develop throughout the reader's lifetime.

Writing

Writing development in adolescence centers on improving the ability to revise written work, the ability to write in a variety of genres, and the ability to use multiple perspectives in writing. Writing in most classrooms consists of cycles of planning, writing, and reviewing (Graham & Sandmel, 2011). Beginning in early adolescence, the responsibility for the reviewing process shifts more formally from the teacher to the student. Students use dictionaries and thesaurus references independently while paying more attention to proper writing mechanics. Students are able to evaluate their own work with guidance from a checklist or a rubric and make successive revisions. They may also participate in critiquing their peers' work. As their ability to comprehend different text structure increases, so does their ability to write in different genres.

> Adolescents begin to take notes effectively and enjoy writing autobiographies, song lyrics, and poetry (Wood, 2007). They may enjoy formal collaborative writing in the form of the school newspaper or wikis. Throughout adolescence, the ability to look at a problem or life situation from different points of view continues to grow. Consequently, the ability to write persuasively matures.

SUPPORTING ADOLESCENT LITERACY DEVELOPMENT

Supporting adolescent literacy development successfully requires the use of many of the direct methods for comprehension support discussed for the elementary school-age child. These supports consist of explicit vocabulary instruction, awareness of text structure, self-monitoring, summarization, and activating schemas or prior knowledge (Biancarosa & Snow, 2004). For adolescents, there is an increased expectation of being able to interpret texts with more depth, rather than just obtaining basic information. For this reason, opportunities for extended discussion of the meaning and interpretation of text should be provided (Kamil et al., 2008).

With adolescents, motivation and engagement become especially important. Adolescents face self-esteem and identity challenges that can significantly influence their academic achievement (Wood, 2007). If an adolescent has had previous literacy experiences that were unsuccessful, this can translate into reduced motivation and effort (Ehren, Lenz, & Deshler, 2004). Therefore, it is important to provide a positive learning environment that provides relevant connections to the students' lives (Kamil et al., 2008).

SUMMARY

This chapter discussed the relationship of language and literacy and the development of literacy from preschool through adolescence. It also briefly reviewed supportive practices for teaching in literacy-related areas.

◆ Language and literacy development are interwoven and benefit each other. Good oral language makes learning to read easier and reading increases oral language abilities.
◆ Many underlying skills needed for literacy development are seen before formal literacy learning begins.

◆ Evidence-based practices for supporting literacy in preschool include providing a print-rich environment, shared book reading, phonological awareness play, and symbolic play.

◆ Literacy development in kindergarten is primarily focused on learning the sound-symbol relationship. In first and second grades, development targets use phonological awareness and phonics skills to blend and segment when reading and writing. Older elementary school students integrate phonological, orthographic, morphological, and semantic linguistic elements to become fluent in reading and writing.

◆ The National Reading Panel (NICHD, 2000) has designated a balanced reading program that includes phonemic awareness, phonics, fluency, vocabulary, and reading comprehension.

◆ Adolescent literacy development involves an expansion of fluency and knowledge of text structure along with an expansion of vocabulary needed for content area knowledge.

◆ Supports for reading comprehension should include knowledge of text structure, activating prior knowledge, questioning, self-monitoring, and summarization.

◆ Adolescent literacy instruction accounts for self-esteem and motivational issues along with the need to discuss texts on a more integrative level.

KEY WORDS

Coherence

Cohesion

Decontextualized language

Digraphs

Emergent literacy

Expository

Figurative language

Fluency

Metalinguistic knowledge

Narratives

Phonemic awareness

Phonics

Phonological awareness

Print awareness

Text structure

STUDY QUESTIONS

1. Discuss the connection between language and literacy development.

2. What is involved in the development of emergent literacy?

3. How do you support literacy in the preschool years?

4. After third grade, children become increasingly fluent readers. Discuss what abilities aid this process.

5. Consider the five areas of the reading program recommended by the National Reading Panel (NICHD, 2000) and illustrate how they should overlap to produce a balanced reading program.

6. What is the role of text structure in reading comprehension?

7. Identify and discuss five strategies that support adolescent literacy development.

REFERENCES

Adams, M. (2011). Advancing our students' language and literacy: The challenge of complex texts. *American Educator, Winter,* 3–11, 53.

Barth, A., Catts, H., & Anthony, J. (2009). The component skills underlying reading fluency in adolescent readers: A latent variable analysis. *Reading and Writing, 22,* 567–590.

Beck, S. W., & Jeffery, J. V. (2009). Genre and thinking in academic writing tasks. *Journal of Literacy Research, 41*(2), 228.

Bialystok, E. (2001). *Bilingual development: Language, literacy, and cognition.* Cambridge, UK: Cambridge University Press.

Biancarosa, G., & Snow, C. E. (2004). *Reading next: A vision for action and research in middle and high school literacy: A report to Carnegie Corporation of New York.* Washington, DC: Alliance for Excellent Education.

Blachman, B. A. (1997). Early intervention and phonological awareness: A cautionary tale. In B. A. Blachman (Ed.), *Foundations of reading acquisition and dyslexia* (pp. 409–430). Mahwah, NJ: Erlbaum.

Bloodgood, J. (1999). What's in a name? Children's name writing and literacy acquisition. *Reading Research Quarterly, 34,* 342–367.

Bourassa, D. C., & Treiman, R. (2001). Spelling development and disability: The importance of linguistic factors. *Language, Speech, and Hearing Services in Schools, 32,* 172–181.

Carlisle, J. F. (1988). Knowledge of derivational morphology and spelling ability in fourth, sixth, and eighth graders. *Applied Psycholinguistics, 9,* 247–266.

Carlisle, J. F., & Katz, L. A. (2005). Word learning and vocabulary instruction. In J. Birsch (Ed.), *Multisensory teaching of basic language skills* (2nd ed.). Baltimore, MD: Paul H. Brookes.

Chall, J. S. (1996). *Stages of reading development.* New York, NY: McGraw-Hill.

Cowley, J. (1999). *Mrs. Wishy-Washy.* New York, NY: The Wright Group.

Cunningham, A. E., & Stanovich, K. E. (1997). Early reading acquisition and its relation to reading experience and ability 10 years later. *Developmental Psychology, 33*(6), 934–945.

Dickinson, D., Golinkoff, R., & Hirsch-Pasek, K. (2010). Speaking out for language: Why language is central to reading development. *Educational Researcher, 39,* 305–310.

Dyson, A. (2000). Writing and the sea of voices: Oral language in, around, and about writing. In R. Indrisano & J. Squire (Eds.), *Perspectives on writing* (pp. 45–65). Newark, DE: International Reading Association.

Dyson, A. H., & Freedman, S. W. (2003). Writing. In J. Flood, D. Lapp, J. R. Squire, & J. M. Jensen (Eds.), *Handbook of research on teaching the English language arts* (2nd ed., pp. 967–992). Mahwah, NJ: Erlbaum.

Ehren, B., Lenz, B., & Deshler, D. (2004). Enhancing literacy proficiency with adolescents and young adults. In C. A. Stone, & E. R. Silliman (Eds.), *Handbook of language and literacy* (pp. 681–702). New York, NY: Guilford Press.

Ehri, L. (2000). Learning to read and learning to spell: Two sides of a coin. *Topics in Language Disorders, 20*(3), 19–49.

Graham, S., & Sandmel, K. (2011). The process writing approach: A meta-analysis. *The Journal of Educational Research, 104,* 396–407.

Guo, Y., Justice, L., Kaderavek, J., & McGinty, A. (2012). The literacy environment of preschool classrooms: Contributions to children's emergent literacy growth. *Journal of Research in Reading, 35,* 308–327.

Harste, J. C., Woodward, V. A., & Burke, C. L. (1984). *Language stories and literacy lessons.* Portsmouth, NH: Heinemann Educational Books.

Hedberg, N. L., & Westby, C. E. (1993). *Analyzing storytelling skills: Theory to practice.* Tucson, AZ: Communication Skill Builders.

Huebner, C. E. (2000). Promoting toddlers' language development through community-based intervention. *Journal of Applied Developmental Psychology, 21*(5), 513–535.

Justice, L. (2006). *Communication sciences and disorders: An introduction.* Upper Saddle River, NJ: Pearson Education.

Justice, L., & Ezell, H. (2004). Print-referencing: An emergent literacy enhancement technique and its clinical applications. *Language, Speech, and Hearing Services in Schools, 35,* 185–193.

Kaderavek, J., & Justice, L. (2004). Embedded-explicit emergent literacy: II. Goal selection and implementations in the early childhood classroom. *Language, Speech, and Hearing Services in Schools, 35,* 212–228.

Kamhi, A. (2009). Prologue: The case for the narrow view of reading. *Language, Speech, and Hearing Services in Schools.*

Kamil, M. L., Borman, G. D., Dole, J., Kral, C. C., Salinger, T., & Torgesen, J. (2008). *Improving adolescent literacy: Effective classroom and intervention practices: A practice guide* (NCEE #2008-4027). Washington, DC: National Center for Education Evaluation and Regional Assistance, Institute of Education Sciences, U.S. Department of Education. Retrieved from http://ies.ed.gov/ncee/wwc

Meltzer, J., Smith, N. C., & Clark, H. (2001). *Adolescent literacy resources: Linking research and practice.* Providence, RI: Brown University, Northeast and Islands Regional Educational Laboratory.

Moats, L. C. (2009). Knowledge foundations for teaching reading and spelling. *Reading and Writing: An Interdisciplinary Journal, 22,* 379–399.

Nagy, W. E., & Herman, P. A. (1985). Incidental vs. instructional approaches to increasing reading vocabulary. *Educational Perspectives, 23*(1), 16–21.

National Institute of Child Health and Human Development (NICHD). (2000). *Report of the National Reading Panel. Teaching children to read: An evidence-based assessment of the scientific research literature on reading and its implications for reading instruction* (NIH Publication No. 00-4769). Washington, DC: U.S. Government Printing Office.

Nelson, N. W. (2010). *Language and literacy disorders: Infancy through adolescence.* Boston, MA: Allyn & Bacon.

Newman, R., Ratner, N., Juszcyk, A., & Juszcyk, P. (2006). Infants' early ability to segment the conversational speech signal predicts later language development: A retrospective analysis. *Developmental Psychology, 42,* 643–655.

New York State Education Department (NYSED). (2011). *Living Environment Regents Examination Sampler.* Retrieved from http://www.p12.nysed.gov/ciai/mst/pub/livenvirsam1.pdf

Palincsar, A. S., & Brown, A. L. (1986). Interactive teaching to promote independent learning from text. *The Reading Teacher, 39,* 771–777.

Pentimonti, J., Zucker, T., Justice, L., Petscher, Y., Piasta, S., & Kaderavek, J. (2012). A standardized tool for assessing the quality of classroom-based reading: Systematic assessment of book reading. *Early Childhood Research Quarterly, 27,* 512–528.

Phillips, B. M., Clancy-Menchetti, J., & Lonigan, C. J. (2008). Successful phonological awareness instruction with preschool children: Lessons from the classroom. *Topics in Early Childhood Special Education, 28*(1), 3–17.

Pinnel, G., Pikulski, J., Wixson, K., Campbell, J., Gough, P., & Beatty, A. (1995). *Listening to children read aloud.* Washington, DC: Office of Educational Research and Improvement, United States Department of Education.

Rosenthal, J., & Ehri, L. C. (2008). The mnemonic value of orthography for vocabulary learning. *Journal of Educational Psychology, 100,* 175–191.

Roskos, K. A., & Neuman, S. B. (2001). Environment and its influences for early literacy teaching and learning. In S. B. Neuman and D. K. Dickinson (Eds.), *Handbook of early literacy research* (pp. 281–294). New York, NY: Guilford Press.

Shipley, K. G., & McAfee, J. G. (2009). *Assessment in speech-language pathology: A resource manual.* Florence, KY: Cengage.

Silliman, E. R., & Scott, C. M. (2009). Research-based oral language intervention routes to the academic language of literacy: Finding the right road. In S. Rosenfield, & V. W. Berninger (Eds.), *Implementing evidence-based academic interventions in school settings* (pp. 107–145). New York, NY: Oxford University Press.

Stadler, M. A., & Ward, G. C. (2005). Supporting the narrative development of young children. *Early Childhood Education Journal, 33*(2), 73–80.

Stanovich, K. E., Cunningham, A. E., & Freeman, D. J. (2009). Intelligence, cognitive skills, and early reading progress. *International Reading Association, 19*(3), 278–303.

Storch, S. A., & Whitehurst, G. J. (2001). The role of family and home in the literacy development of children from low-income backgrounds. *New Directions for Child and Adolescent Development, 92*, 53–71.

Teale, W., & Sulzby, E. (1986). *Emergent literacy: Writing and reading.* Norwood, NJ: Ablex.

Tompkins, G. (2003). *Literacy for the 21st century.* Upper Saddle River, NJ: Pearson Education.

Torgesen, J., Alexander, A., Wagner, R., Rashotte, C., Voeller, K., & Conway, T. (2001). Intensive remedial instruction for children with severe reading disabilities: Immediate and long-term outcomes from two instructional approaches. *Journal of Learning Disabilities, 34*, 33–58.

van Kleeck, A. (1994). Metalinguistic development. In G. Wallach and K. Butler (Eds.), *Language learning disabilities in school-age children and adolescents.* New York, NY: Merrill.

van Kleeck, A. (2006). Fostering inferential language during book sharing with pre-readers: A foundation for later text comprehension strategies. In A. van Kleeck (Ed.), *Sharing books and stories to promote language and literacy* (pp. 269–317). San Diego, CA: Plural.

Van Kleeck, A. (2008). Providing preschool foundations for later reading comprehension: The importance of and ideas for targeting inferencing in storybook-sharing interventions. *Psychology in the Schools, 45*(7), 627–643.

Vygotsky, L. S. (1967). Play and its role in the mental development of the child. *Soviet Psychology, 5*, 6–18.

Walker, J., & Hauerwas, L. B. (2006). Development of phonological, morphological, and orthographic knowledge in young spellers: The case of inflected verbs. *Reading and Writing, 19*, 819–843.

Wallach, G., & Butler, K. (1994). *Language learning disabilities in school-age children and adolescents.* New York, NY: Merrill.

Westby, C. (1999). Assessing and facilitating text comprehension problem. In H. W. Catts & A. G. Kamhi (Eds.), *Language and reading disabilities* (pp. 154–221). Boston, MA: Allyn & Bacon.

Whitehurst, G. J., Epstein, J. N., Angell, A. L., Payne, A. C., Crone, D. A., & Fischel, J. E. (1994). Outcomes of an emergent literacy intervention in Head Start. *Journal of Educational Psychology, 86*(4), 542–555.

Whitehurst, G. J., & Lonigan, C. J. (1998). Child development and emergent literacy. *Child Development, 69*(3), 848–872.

Wilford, S. (2000). *From play to literacy: Implications for the classroom* (Occasional paper no. 2). Bronxville, NY: Child Development Institute, Sarah Lawrence College.

Wilkinson, L. C., & Silliman, E. R. (2008). Academic language proficiency and literacy instruction in urban settings. In L. Wilkinson, L. Morrow, & V. Chou (Eds.), *Improving literacy achievement in urban schools: Critical elements in teacher preparation* (pp. 121–142). Newark, DE: International Reading Association.

Wolfersberger, M. E., Reutzel, D. R., Sudweeks, R., & Fawson, P. C. (2004). Developing and validating the classroom literacy environmental profile (CLEP): A tool for examining the "print richness" of early childhood and elementary classrooms. *Journal of Literacy Research, 36*(2), 211–272.

Wood, C. (2007). *Yardsticks: Children in the classroom ages 4–14.* Turner Falls, MA: Northeast Foundation for Children.

Wright, D., & Ehri, L. C. (2007). Beginners remember orthography when they learn to read words: The case of doubled letters. *Applied Psycholinguistics, 28*, 115–133.

Yopp, H. K., & Yopp, H. (2009). Phonological awareness is child's play! *Young Children, 64*(1), 12–18.

Zevenbergen, A. A., & Whitehurst, G. J. (2003). Dialogic reading: A shared picture book reading intervention for preschoolers. In A. van Kleeck, S. A. Stahl, & E. B. Bauer (Eds.), *On reading books to children: Parents and teachers.* Mahwah, NJ: Erlbaum.

CHAPTER 9

Factors Associated with Delivering Speech and Language Services to Bilinguals

Brian A. Goldstein

Yaitza is a 5-year-old native Spanish-English-speaking bilingual child who began to acquire English in preschool at age 4. After reading this chapter, you will understand how her language skills will develop. You will also learn basic information about how to assess her languages and treat her language problem should she be diagnosed with a language disorder.

There are over 5 million bilingual children in the schools in the United States who are learning English as a second language. Thus, it is essential that students majoring in speech-language pathology programs acquire knowledge of bilingual populations to provide them with evidence-based assessment and intervention when these services are required. The purpose of this chapter is to provide information on language development and disorders in bilingual children. Prior to reading this chapter, review the following statements

and think about and/or discuss whether you think they are myths or facts.

Myth or Fact?

◆ Bilingualism is defined as the ability to speak two languages fluently.
◆ We should try and determine in which language the bilingual child is dominant.
◆ Bilinguals who are typically developing acquire their languages more slowly than monolinguals.
◆ Language development for bilinguals proceeds at a steady pace over time.
◆ Bilingual children show the same language skills in each language.
◆ All bilingual children undergo a silent period.
◆ Children learn second languages quickly and easily, especially when learning a language at a young age.

- Being raised bilingually will confuse children. Therefore, each language should be spoken by different people.
- The frequency of transfer is high in bilingual children.
- Transfer is greatest if both parents "mix" languages.
- Language proficiency is control over grammar and speech sounds.

By the end of this chapter, you should know whether these statements are myths or facts. Your knowledge of these statements will provide insight and knowledge about how bilingual children acquire their languages and the characteristics of speech and language disorders in such children.

CHAPTER OBJECTIVES

After reading this chapter, you should understand and be able to:

- Describe socio-cultural factors related to bilingual language acquisition
- Summarize bilingual language development
- Apply best practice principles for assessment
- Describe cross-linguistic and bilingual approaches to intervention

The reader will learn and understand definitions of bilingualism and related terms, including:

- Dialect
- Code switching
- The stages of second-language learning
- Typical speech and language development in bilingual children
- Deceleration
- Acceleration

- Language proficiency
- Characteristics of bilingual children with speech and language disorders
- Appropriate assessment and intervention approaches
- Use of interpreters and translators

WHAT'S IN A NAME?

There are numerous terms for children who are acquiring more than one language. You will hear them commonly referred to as:

- Limited English proficient
- Non-English proficient
- Culturally and linguistically diverse
- English-language learners
- **Dual language learners**
- Bilingual
- **Multilingual**

Although these terms differ in meaning, they are often used interchangeably. Throughout this chapter, the term **bilingual** is used to refer to the children under discussion. This approach is taken to emphasize the fact that in bilingual speech and language development, *both* languages have an impact on acquisition. Terms like **limited English proficient**, **non-English proficient**, and **English-language learners** (ELL) tend to emphasize only one of the child's languages, and a term such as **culturally and linguistically diverse** denotes not only those who are acquiring more than one language but also those who might be using more than one **dialect** (i.e., a rule-governed variant of a language, such as Appalachian English).

Bilinguals then are those individuals who are acquiring more than one language, or as one of my students once said, "Bilinguals are those who are not monolingual" (DiMarzio, personal communication). Her definition was quite perceptive because we know that the speech and language development of bilinguals is not identical to that of monolingual children in either language. We will return to this issue later in the chapter.

As Baker (2006) has said, however, "[d]efining who is or is not bilingual is essentially elusive and ultimately impossible. Some categorization is often necessary and helpful to make sense of the world" (p. 13). It is in that spirit that the main types of bilinguals are presented. Bilinguals are often categorized as one of two main types: **simultaneous bilinguals** and **sequential bilinguals**.

> Simultaneous bilinguals are those who acquire both languages before the age of about 5 years. Simultaneous bilinguals who acquire both languages from birth are known to be undergoing **bilingual first-language acquisition** (de Houwer, 2009). That is, they are acquiring *two* first languages from birth.
>
> Sequential bilinguals are those who acquire a second language after a foundation in their first language.

The distinction between simultaneous bilinguals and sequential bilinguals is usually based on the age at which the second language is introduced.

> If the two languages are introduced before about age 5 (and often age 3), then the child is typically considered a simultaneous bilingual (McLaughlin, 1984; Meisel, 2004). If, however, the second language is introduced after age 5 (and often after age 3), then the child is typically considered a sequential bilingual (Paradis, Genesee, & Crago, 2011).

COMPLEXITY IN DEFINING *BILINGUAL*

Although the categories just described are the main labels used to group bilinguals, they are only one method used to classify bilinguals. Those two categories are based on one criterion—the age at which the second language was introduced. Bilingualism, however, is somewhat more complex than that because bilingualism "rather than being an absolute condition is a relative one. Bilingual individuals can be both *slightly* bilingual or *very* bilingual" (Valdés & Figueroa, 1994, p. 115, emphases original). What Valdés and Figueroa mean is that bilingual skills reside on a continuum. Being bilingual does *not* mean that one is equally skilled in both languages. That is, the speech and language skills that bilinguals have in one language are not simply mirrored in the other language. One can have superior skills in Language A over Language B. For example, a child acquiring Vietnamese and English might have superior speech and language skills in Vietnamese than in English. Over time, however, that balance might change. As the child becomes more embedded in the U.S. educational system, for example, her English skills might become stronger than her skills in Vietnamese.

Bilingual development is further complicated by the fact that a bilingual child's skills can vary by language domain (i.e., syntax, semantics, lexicon, phonology, and pragmatics). For example, a bilingual child theoretically could have greater skills in syntax in Language A but superior skills in phonology in Language B. Additionally, a bilingual child's speech and language skills are not equally distributed. Thus, the child might have knowledge in one language that he or she does not have in the other (Paradis et al., 2011). For example, a bilingual child might be able to label an object in one language but not in the other (Peña, Bedore, & Rappazzo, 2003).

When bilinguals are said to have skills in one language but not in the other, they are often referred to as having (language) *dominance* in one linguistic system over the other. **Language dominance**, however, is a term that is difficult to define and validly assess. Moreover, the term should be used with great caution because it is often misunderstood and misused (MacSwan & Rolstad, 2006). Language dominance most often connotes greater skill in one language over the other. As alluded to previously, bilingualism exists on a continuum, likely influenced by language domain. Thus, a bilingual will have some skills that are superior in Language A and other skills that are superior in Language B. For example, Peña and colleagues (2003) found such an effect in Spanish-English bilingual children. In their study, the children found receptive functions (e.g., show me what you do with a hammer) to be easier when asked in Spanish than when those same children were prompted about receptive functions in English. Results such as these call into question the validity of language dominance as it is most traditionally defined. Moreover, results from other studies are equivocal on the usefulness of such a construct.

In a group of Welsh-English bilingual children ages 2;6 to 5;0, Ball, Müller, and Munro (2001) found that Welsh-dominant children acquired the trill earlier than their peers who were English dominant.

In a group of 2-year-old French-English bilingual children, Paradis (2001) found that English-dominant

bilinguals preserved a higher frequency of second syllables in words (e.g., gi-RAFFE, *giraffe*) than did French-dominant bilinguals. However, French-dominant bilinguals preserved a higher frequency of third syllables (e.g., e-le-PHANT, *elephant*) than did English-dominant bilinguals.

In a group of Cantonese- and Putonghua-speaking bilingual children ages 2;6 to 4;11, Law and So (2006) found that both Cantonese-dominant and Putonghua-dominant children acquired Cantonese phonology first. That is, regardless of which language was considered the dominant one, the children learned Cantonese before Putonghua.

These equivocal results related to language dominance question its validity. What is necessary from a practical point of view is to determine the bilingual child's relative strengths and weaknesses in each of their languages across all domains of language. Attempting to determine dominance as an omnibus measure appears not to be warranted, especially as it relates to speech and language development.

BILINGUAL SPEECH AND LANGUAGE ACQUISITION

In discussing speech and language acquisition, it is helpful to embed it within a theoretical context. Speech and language acquisition in bilingual children is explained by a theoretical model of development. One such theory is the **Interactional Dual Systems Model** of bilingual language acquisition (Paradis, 2001). This model assumes that bilingual children develop distinct linguistic systems for each language. Those two systems, however, interact and are, thus, interdependent. That interdependence could serve to speed up (i.e., **acceleration**) and/or slow down (i.e., **deceleration**) speech and language development relative to that of monolinguals (Fabiano-Smith & Goldstein, 2010). There is evidence that both acceleration and deceleration occur in bilingual speech and language acquisition when the skills of bilinguals are compared to monolinguals. For example, Bialystock (2001) noted a cognitive advantage in terms of executive control functions, such as activation, selection, attention, inhibition, and organization of information (problem solving, planning), in bilinguals compared to monolinguals. By the way, this advantage in bilinguals increased commensurate with the amount of language the children heard in their environment and their levels of proficiency (i.e., how well they used each of their languages). Thus, the more of each language second language learners hear and the more skilled they are in speaking each one, the greater the cognitive advantage. This type of results seems to show support for acceleration of the language skills in bilinguals compared with monolinguals.

Although bilingual children might exhibit acceleration in their language skills in comparison to bilinguals, they might show deceleration as well. Deceleration indicates that development occurs more slowly in bilingual children than in monolingual children. Such a result has been shown for syntax, morphology, and phonology (Gildersleeve-Neumann, Kester, Davis, & Peña, 2008; Swain, 1972; Vihman, 1982). For example, in a group of Spanish-English bilingual 3-year-olds, Gildersleeve et al. (2008) found that overall consonant accuracy (i.e., how well children produce speech sounds) was lower in bilinguals than in monolinguals.

Despite the fact that the speech and language skills of bilinguals relative to monolinguals might be accelerated or decelerated, what is important to realize, however, is that "[d]espite the acquisition of two languages, bilingual children do *not* appear to be 'remarkably delayed nor remarkably advanced' relative to that of monolingual children" (Nicoladis & Genesee, 1996, p. 264, emphasis added). That is, the speech and language skills of bilinguals are similar, although not identical, to those of monolinguals in each constituent language (Goldstein, 2012). This result has been found across various domains of language such as syntax (e.g., Paradis & Genesee, 1996) and phonology (e.g., Goldstein, Fabiano, & Washington, 2005).

It is important to point out, however, that bilingual children do not proceed through the same linguistic stages at the same time in each language. Merino (1992) found that the order of acquisition of grammatical forms was different for monolinguals and bilinguals. For example, monolinguals first acquired the active tense (e.g., *ella come pan* [she eats bread]) followed by gender (gato rojo [*cat red*]), plural (gatos [cats]), regular past tense (*ella comió pan* [she ate bread]), and finally, irregular past (*ellos fueron a la casa* [they went home]). In contrast, bilingual children first acquired the active tense followed by gender, present progressive (*ella está comiendo* [she is eating]), plural, and finally, regular past. Findings such as these indicate that even though bilingual children might show overall commensurate language skills with monolinguals, there will be differences in those skills across each constituent language. It is likely that bilinguals will have skills that are greater in one language over the other. For example, bilinguals might exhibit more advanced syntactic skills in Language A vs. Language B (Paradis et al., 2011).

The speech and language trajectory of children who acquire a second language after some facility with a first language (i.e., sequential bilinguals) is somewhat different than that of monolingual children in either language. For example, Paradis (2007) found that after 21 months of exposure to English, 40% of the sequential bilinguals exhibited morphological skills within the normal range of monolinguals, 65% for receptive vocabulary, and 90% for story grammar. Additionally, after an average of 8 months of exposure to English, overall consonant accuracy for sequential bilinguals (ages 4;6 to 6;9) averaged 90% (Gilhool, Goldstein, Burrows, & Paradis, 2009). More specifically, consonant accuracy was less than 90% (average of 83%) for only 2 of 10 children. These data show that even children who acquire speech and language skills after experience in their first language approach monolingual norms after a relatively short time.

LANGUAGE DEVELOPMENT IN SECOND-LANGUAGE ACQUISITION

Children undergoing second-language acquisition go through five primary stages of speech and language development (Hearne, 2000). It should be noted that these stages are meant to be general in nature, given the known individual variation of speech and language development of second-language learners (and all children, in general).

Stage I: Preproduction. In this stage, children often undergo a silent period.

That is, they focus more on **receptive language** (i.e., language comprehension) than on **expressive language** (i.e., language production). The silent period is relatively short in duration—usually not more than 6 months (Tabors, 1997). It should be noted, however, that often during this phase, children use some expressive language (in the second language) with each other but less so with adults in the environment (Tabors, 1997). Also during this stage, children respond to simple commands and have a receptive vocabulary of about 500 words.

Stage II: Early Production. In this stage (approximately 3 to 6 months after introduction of the second language), the children are still focused more on receptive language than on expressive language. Specifically, they are comprehending yes/no and who/what/where questions. They typically use one- to three-word phrases and formulaic expressions (*gimme five*). Their receptive and expressive vocabulary consists of approximately 1,000 words.

Stage III: Speech Emergence. In this stage (approximately 6 months to 2 years after introduction of the second language), the children show increased comprehension, use simple sentences by expanding vocabulary, increase grammatical complexity but exhibit grammatical errors, and have a receptive and expressive vocabulary of around 3,000 words.

Stage IV: Intermediate Fluency. In this stage (approximately 3 years after introduction of the second language), the children show improved comprehension, a receptive and expressive vocabulary around 6,000 words, adequate face-to-face conversational skills, and more complex statements in which they express thoughts and opinions with few grammatical errors.

Stage V: Advanced Language Proficiency. In this stage (approximately 5 to 7 years after introduction of the second language), the children use specialized vocabulary related to content areas, use English grammar and vocabulary comparable to a native speaker, and are able to actively participate in grade level classroom activities.

TRANSFER AND CODE-MIXING

Bilingual children exhibit both acceleration and deceleration relative to monolingual development. They also show patterns of transfer. **Transfer** is defined as language-specific features found in productions of the other language (Paradis, 2001). This term is often used synonymously with **cross-linguistic effects**. Cross-linguistic effects usually connote that the features are bidirectional; that is, from Language A to Language B and vice versa.

Transfer is a hallmark of bilingual speech and language development. An example might be when a native Spanish speaker produces *red house* as *house red* because, in Spanish, nouns precede the adjectives that modify them. It should be noted that features of transfer are variable (Schnitzer & Krasinski, 1994, 1996), occur in both languages (Gildersleeve-Neumann et al., 2008), and are *not* equally represented in both languages (Goldstein, 2008). From a practical point of view, features of transfer are not true errors and thus would not be treated if the bilingual

child had a speech or language disorder and was receiving intervention.

Code-mixing is the "use of phonological, lexical, morphosyntactic, or pragmatic patterns from two languages in the same utterance or stretch of conversation" (Paradis et al., 2011, p. 89). According to Paradis et al. (2011), there are a number of types of code-mixing:

◆ Intra-utterance: *Alguien se murió en ese cuarto* [someone died in that room . . .] *that he sleeps in.*
◆ Inter-utterance: *Pa ¿me vas a comprar un jugo?* [are you going to buy me juice] *It cos' 25 cents.*
◆ Mixing words: *Estamos como marido y* [we are like man and] *woman.*
◆ Mixing clauses: *You know how to swim but no te tapa* [. . . it won't be over your head]

As is the case with transfer, code-mixing is a typical linguistic phenomenon in bilinguals. Code-mixing does *not* mean that the bilingual speaker lacks control or proficiency over the two languages. It is a natural occurrence in acquiring a second language. However, the more the bilingual child's parents code-mix, the more likely it is that he or she will code-mix (Lanza, 1992).

LANGUAGE LOSS/ LANGUAGE DISORDER

Another phenomenon typical in bilingual speakers is **language loss** (also termed *language attrition*) (Anderson, 2012). Language loss occurs when the speech and language features of the first language are no longer utilized by the speaker because he or she hears and uses less of the first language over time. Examples of language loss include the following:

◆ Deletion of grammatical markers (e.g., plural)
◆ Decreased number of different words (i.e., speakers will tend to use the same core group of words over and over rather than using a robust number of different words)
◆ Increased number of false starts, pauses, hesitation, and decreased organizational skills.

Unfortunately, these characteristics often are similar to those features that signal a true language disorder (i.e., not related to learning a second language). It is possible, however, to stave off language attrition with programs that support the first language (Restrepo & Gray, 2012).

Again, features of language attrition should *not* be confused with a true language disorder. That said, there is no doubt that bilingual speakers (be they simultaneous or sequential bilinguals) can exhibit a language disorder. What is interesting about language disorders in these children is that they show commensurate language skills to monolinguals with language impairments (Paradis, 2005), and they exhibit the same type and frequency of grammatical errors as monolinguals with language impairments (Paradis, Crago, Genesee, & Rice, 2003). Moreover, bilingual children with Down syndrome (DS) showed commensurate language skills to monolingual children with DS (Kay-Raining Bird et al., 2005), and bilingual children with language impairments exhibited (protracted) periods of plateaus or regressions in grammatical development, just as did monolinguals with language impairments (Kohnert, 2008).

Some speech-language pathologists (SLPs) and other practitioners are often wary of providing intervention to bilingual children in their non-English language. Their rationale is that bilingual children with language disorders will be even more "confused" by receiving services in the non-English language. The evidence presented previously seems to obviate that concern. Both languages of the bilingual benefit from input in the two languages. As Kohnert (2008, pp. 143–144) says, "[a] disorder in bilinguals is not caused by bilingualism or cured by monolingualism."

ASSESSMENT OF SPEECH AND LANGUAGE DISORDERS IN BILINGUAL CHILDREN

Identification of bilingual children for being at-risk for language disorders (specifically, semantics and syntax) is *not* predicted by being bilingual (Peña, Gillam, Bedore, & Bohman, 2011). Thus, although being bilingual does not "cause" or exacerbate a speech or language disorder, it does complicate diagnosing them differentially.

In assessing all children, it is necessary for the SLP to complete a case history in which he or she begins to determine the presenting problem and the possible medical, psychosocial, and environmental factors related to the speech or language disorder. When a child is acquiring more than one language (i.e., is not monolingual), the SLP must gather the following additional information, specific to bilingual children:

◆ The sociocultural characteristics of the community; it is important to understand the culture of the family and the community (e.g., Lynch & Hanson, 2011). The SLP might need a **cultural broker** to aid in understanding the community's culture.

A cultural broker is an individual, usually from the family's cultural background, who can provide an "insider's" information on that culture and aid in the interpretation of the family's linguistic and nonlinguistic characteristics.

◆ The structure of the non-English language: vocabulary, grammar, word meaning, speech sounds, and pragmatics.

◆ Age of acquisition: is the child a simultaneous or sequential bilingual? Also, at what age did the child begin to hear and use each language?

◆ **Language use**: how often and with whom each language is used.

◆ **Language proficiency**: how well each language is used.

Once the case history is completed, the SLP conducts testing to discern whether the child has a speech or language disorder and what the child's strengths and weaknesses are in each of the two languages.

Tests can be either formal or informal in nature. In speech-language pathology, formal tests are often standardized. A standardized test is used to measure a client's performance in one or more domains. That performance is then compared to a similar group on a measure that is not influenced by the person administering or interpreting the test (Tomblin, 2000). This standardized procedure allows us to assume that differences in performance are based on ability rather than on the testing procedure. The difficulty in utilizing such tests with bilingual children is that they rarely include bilingual children

in the normative data. In fact, they usually are specifically excluded. Even for non-English tests, bilingual children are rarely included. Finally, standardized tests that include bilingual children do not test the full range of bilingual skills (i.e., from a "little" bilingual to "a lot" bilingual"). Thus, there are few standardized tests available to use with bilingual children. To use standardized tests for bilingual children, it is important to determine if:

◆ The normative data include bilingual children.

◆ The bilingual children in the normative group are similar to the group with whom you will use the test.

◆ **Confidence intervals** (i.e., the score a child would receive if he or she theoretically took the test multiple times) are provided.

◆ The manual reports data on:
  ◆ **Sensitivity** (i.e., percentage of individuals correctly identified with a disorder)
  ◆ **Specificity** (i.e., percentage of individuals correctly identified as typically developing)

Informal Assessment Procedures

Because there are so few standardized tests available to use with bilingual children, informal means of assessment are implemented with bilingual children. SLPs often use standardized tests in an informal way. That is, they use the stimulus items from the tests but do not report the scores. Some examples of such informal procedures include:

◆ Giving more detailed explanations of tasks because not all children will have experience taking such tests

- Adding practice items, again because of the lack of experience taking tests
- Repeating stimuli and/or rewording the test
- Testing beyond the test's ceiling (i.e., above the point where administration of the test would stop if it were being scored according to the instructions in the test manual)
- Asking children to explain their answers in order to show if they comprehend the question
- Utilizing informal checklists (Roseberry-McKibbin, 2002) and parent questionnaires (Restrepo, 1998)
- Comparing data from the child being evaluated to published data on similar children
- Focusing more on process-based measures (rate and quality of "learning") rather than on static measures (Hwa-Froelich & Matsuo, 2005; Peña & Quinn, 1997)
- Analyzing narratives/conversational samples by measuring aspects, such as number of different words, number of clauses per utterance, and cohesion (Gutiérrez-Clellen, 2012)

Dynamic Assessment

One commonly used alternative assessment approach is **dynamic assessment** based on the work of Vygotsky (1978) and his concept of the zone of proximal development; that is, the "distance between the level of performance a child can reach unaided and the level of participation that can be accomplished when guided by a more knowledgeable participant" (Campione & Brown, 1987, p. 83). This zone can be interpreted as "potential." The goals of dynamic assessment are to profile learner's abilities, to observe learner's modifi-

ability, to induce an active, self-regulated learning, and to inform intervention. What dynamic assessment allows the assessor to do is to tap future skills, or the child's **modifiability** (i.e., change through mediation) (Peña, 1996). Modifiability involves three factors: child responsiveness (how the child responds to and uses new information); examiner effort (quantity and quality of effort needed to make a change); and transfer (generalization of new skills). All three factors are critical in determining if a child is not succeeding on a task because of experience or ability.

The format for dynamic assessment is test-teach-retest. In the test phase, the examiner determines the child's areas of weakness and the base level of functioning, without any aid or assistance. In the teach phase, the assessor models the target behaviors and strategies in meaningful contexts, makes the child aware of how the strategies are to be applied, allows the child to lead some of the time, and increases demands as the skills are mastered. In order to determine how the child has progressed after the teach phase she is retested, measuring examiner effort (i.e., how much aid is needed by individuals to maximize their performance), child responsiveness (i.e., how rapidly the child changes in response to teaching), and transfer (i.e., the generalization of the task to other tasks and other domains). Dynamic assessment has been used successfully to differentiate children's lack of experience from their lack of ability (Peña, Iglesias, & Lidz, 2001).

Do's and Don'ts

The process outlined previously indicates the type of assessment that should be completed with bilingual children.

Equally important is the kind of testing that should be avoided; that is, testing "don'ts." These include:

- Don't use norm-referenced tests only.
- Don't use only a language sample or multiple assessments to qualify someone for services.
- Don't use tests administered in English only.
- Don't assume that features of a second language are characteristics of a disorder (overdiagnosis).
- Don't assume that errors related to a true disorder are features of a second language (underdiagnosis).
- Don't use translated tests. Translated test should not be used for the following reasons:
  - There are differences in structure and content of each language.
  - It implies (mistakenly) that all children receive similar socialization, language input, and academic instruction in both languages.
  - Differences in the frequency of target words vary from language to language.
  - Grammatical forms may not be equivalent.
  - Such tests do not tap into a child's ability to acquire language.

Interpreters and Translators

In some sense, all SLPs are monolingual. That is, no SLP can possibly speak every language that their clients speak. It is estimated that only 4% of certified SLPs meet the definition of a bilingual service provider (ASHA, 2012). Thus, it is highly likely that monolingual SLPs will be providing services to bilinguals. The American Speech-Language-Hearing Associa-

tion (ASHA) (1985) has outlined a number of tasks that monolingual SLPs can perform with bilinguals. Those tasks include:

- Testing in English
- Performing an oral-peripheral exam
- Conducting hearing screenings
- Completing nonverbal assessments
- Conducting a family interview (with an interpreter or translator)
- Being an advocate for the client and family

It is likely, however, that at some point an SLP will need to utilize the services of an **interpreter** (conveys information from one language to another when the message is oral) or a **translator** (conveys information from one language to another when the message is written) to assess a bilingual child. Here we focus on interpreters; that is, the individual who serves as the bridge between the SLP and the family/child (Langdon & Cheng, 2002). It should be noted from the outset that the use of an interpreter does not negate the role of the SLP. It is the SLP's job to construct the assessment session (and the intervention) and to train the interpreter in how to work effectively. The training of an interpreter should include not only verbal interaction but also nonverbal cues, cultural effects, and contextual knowledge (i.e., how the environment of the assessment has shaped the interaction). Interpreters should be professionals who regularly serve in this role. It is not appropriate to have friends, neighbors, siblings, or relatives serve in this role because they do not have the objectivity needed to provide such services. Langdon and Cheng (2002) outline a three-step process for the session. The first phase is termed *briefing*. In this phase, the SLP plans the session, trains the interpreter, and reviews the critical questions and/or issues. The second phase is *interaction*. During this phase, the SLP and the interpreter interact with the client and her or his family. The role of the SLP during this phase is to make observations on the body language of the child and note if the interpreter uses too many words when instructing the child. The interpreter should record all responses and ask for clarification when questions arise. In the *debriefing* phase, the SLP and the interpreter review the outcomes. The SLP reviews the interpreter's impressions and the SLP and interpreter discuss any difficulties related to the process. All reports should state that an assessment was performed with the assistance of an interpreter. In the end, the SLP makes the final recommendations.

In summary, assessment for bilinguals is complex and multidimensional. It is far more important to describe in detail the child's skills in all domains in both languages rather than trying to determine, for example, in which language the child is "dominant." Moreover, rather than focusing on the *type* of bilingualism, *etiology* of the disorder, or *scores* on a standardized assessment, focus should be on behaviors, symptoms, and characteristics.

INTERVENTION

Although there have been a number of research studies focusing on the assessment of bilingual children, there are far fewer related to intervention for bilingual children with speech and language disorders. For example, since 1991, there have been only 103 papers published in the *American Journal of Speech-Language Pathology, Language, Speech and Hearing Services in Schools,* and *Journal of Speech-Language-Hearing Research* with *bilingual*

in the title and abstract (it should be noted that there are *many* other journals that include articles focusing on bilingual children but these are the three journals that practicing SLPs tend to read). This relative lack of studies has made it difficult to apply principles of **evidence-based practice** (EBP) to such children. EBP is an approach to clinical decision making in which valid, reliable evidence is given more validity than intuition, anecdote, and expert authority (Dollaghan, 2007; Justice & Fey, 2004). EBP includes not only the best available evidence but also clinical expertise and client values (Dollaghan, 2007). Thus, EBP requires the application of evidence in combination with the clinician's experience, or clinical craft, and understanding of the child's and family's unique demographic characteristics and sociocultural perspectives (Justice & Fey, 2004). As Kamhi (2011) has noted, however, " . . . the scientific method, with its emphasis on theoretical coherence, replicability, unbiased measurements, and logic, is diametrically opposed to flexible, dynamic, spontaneous, reactive, and creative clinical practice" (p. 61). It is such practice that must be provided to bilingual children with speech and language disorders given the paucity of research studies related to intervention.

Six-Step Process for Intervention

For bilingual children, the purpose of intervention is to systematically improve their communication skills *in both languages*, through intervention carried out by a culturally and linguistically competent professional. To do so, a six-step process for intervention is proposed here (see the Appendix for a complete description of these steps).

Step 1: Choose goals

Step 2: Choose targets

Step 3: Choose the goal attack strategy

Step 4: Choose the approach

Step 5: Choose the language of intervention

Step 6: Monitor Progress

MYTH OR FACT? REVISITED

Now that you have read this chapter, you should be able to answer myth or fact to the following statements. As before, read the statements and think about and/ or discuss whether you think they are myths or facts and indicate what evidence underlies your decision. As you read and discuss these statements, be aware that the answers are not likely to always be straightforward. Just like bilinguals themselves, the answers may be complex.

◆ Bilingualism is defined as the ability to speak two languages fluently.
◆ We should try and determine in which language the bilingual child is dominant.
◆ Bilinguals who are typically developing acquire their languages more slowly than monolinguals. Thus, language development for bilinguals is slower than that of monolinguals.
◆ Language development for bilinguals proceeds at a steady pace over time.
◆ Bilingual children show the same language skills in each language.
◆ All bilingual children undergo a silent period.
◆ Children, especially the young ones, learn second languages quickly and easily.

◆ Being raised bilingually will confuse children. Therefore, each language should be spoken by different people.
◆ The frequency of transfer is high in bilingual children.
◆ Transfer is greatest if both parents "mix" languages.
◆ Language proficiency is control over grammar and speech sounds.

SUMMARY

Acquiring more than one language is a complex, multilayered task that is neither quick nor easy. That said, bilingual language acquisition is similar, although not identical, to monolingual language acquisition. This holds true for bilingual children with speech and language disorders as well. That is, even children who have speech and language disorders are able to acquire two languages. Finally, there is significant interchild variation in the skills of bilingual children.

KEY WORDS

Acceleration

Bilingual

Bilingual first-language acquisition

Code-mixing

Confidence intervals

Cross-linguistic effects

Cultural broker

Culturally and linguistically diverse

Deceleration

Dialect

Dual language learners

Dynamic assessment

Effectiveness

Effects

Efficiency

English-language learners

Evidence-based practice

Expressive language

Interactional Dual Systems Model

Interpreter

Language dominance

Language loss

Language proficiency

Language use

Limited English proficient

Modifiability

Multilingual

Non-English proficient

Receptive language

Sensitivity

Sequential bilinguals

Simultaneous bilinguals

Specificity

Transfer

Translator

STUDY QUESTIONS

1. List three alternative methods to assessing bilingual children with speech and language disorders. Furthermore, indicate how these three ways are less biased than using standardized tests to assess these children.

2. In planning treatment for bilingual children, explain why the language of intervention is not the first decision to be made in this process.

3. How would you explain to a classroom teacher that using more than one language by bilingual children will not necessarily slow down their overall language development?.

4. Explain why characteristics of code-mixing are not features of a language problem in bilinguals.

REFERENCES

American Speech-Language-Hearing Association. (1985). *Clinical management of communicatively handicapped minority language populations* [Position statement]. Retrieved from http://www.asha.org/policy

American Speech-Language-Hearing Association. (2012). *Demographic profile of ASHA members providing bilingual services*. Retrieved from http://www.asha.org/uploadedFiles /Demographic-Profile-Bilingual-Spanish-Service-Members.pdf

Anderson, R. (2012). First language loss in Spanish-speaking children. In B. Goldstein (Ed.), *Bilingual language development and disorders in Spanish-English speakers* (2nd ed., pp. 193–212). Baltimore, MD: Brookes.

Baker, C. (2006). *Foundations of bilingual education and bilingualism*. Clevedon, UK: Multilingual Matters.

Ball, M. J., Müller, N. , & Munro, S. (2001). The acquisition of the rhotic consonants by Welsh-English bilingual children. *International Journal of Bilingualism, 5,* 71–86.

Bialystok, E. (2001). *Bilingualism in development: Language, literacy, and cognition*. New York: Cambridge University Press.

Campione, J., & Brown, A. (1987). Linking dynamic assessment with school achievement. In C. Lidz (Ed.), *Dynamic assessment: An interactional approach to evaluating learn-*

ing potential (pp. 82–115). New York, NY: Guilford Press.

de Houwer, A. (2009). *Bilingual first language acquisition*. Clevedon, UK: Multilingual Matters.

Dollaghan, C. (2007). *The handbook of evidence-based practice in communication disorders*. Baltimore, MD: Brookes.

Fabiano-Smith, L., & Goldstein, B. (2010). Early-, middle-, and late-developing sounds in monolingual and bilingual children: An exploratory investigation. *American Journal of Speech-Language Pathology, 19,* 66–77.

Fey, M. (1986). *Language intervention with young children*. San Diego, CA: College Hill Press.

Gildersleeve-Neumann, C., Kester, E., Davis, B., & Peña, E. (2008). English speech sound development in preschool-aged children from bilingual English-Spanish environments. *Language, Speech, & Hearing Services in Schools, 39,* 314–328.

Gilhool, A., Goldstein, B., Burrows, L., & Paradis, J. (2009). *English phonological skills of English language learners*. Seminar presented at the convention of the American Speech-Language-Hearing Association, New Orleans, LA.

Goldstein, B. (2008). Integration of evidence-based practice into the university clinic. *Topics in Language Disorders, 28,* 200–211.

Goldstein, B. (Ed.). (2012). *Bilingual language development and disorders in Spanish-English speakers* (2nd ed.). Baltimore, MD: Brookes.

Goldstein, B., Fabiano, L., & Washington, P. S. (2005). Phonological skills in predominantly English-speaking, predominantly Spanish-speaking, and Spanish-English bilingual children. *Language, Speech, and Hearing Services in Schools, 36,* 201–218.

Gutiérrez-Clellen, V. F. (1999). Language choice in intervention with bilingual children. *American Journal of Speech-Language Pathology, 8,* 291–302.

Gutierréz-Clellen, V. (2012). Narrative development and disorders in bilingual children. In B. Goldstein (Ed.), *Bilingual language development and disorders in Spanish-English speakers* (2nd ed., pp. 233–249). Baltimore, MD: Brookes.

Hearne, D. (2000). *Teaching 2nd language learners with learning disabilities*. Oceanside, CA: Academic Communication Associates.

Hwa-Froelich, D. A., & Matsuo, H. (2005). Vietnamese children and language-based processing tasks. *Language, Speech, & Hearing Services in Schools, 36,* 230–243.

Justice, L. M., & Fey, M. E. (2004, September 21). Evidence-based practice in schools: Integrating craft and theory with science and data. *The ASHA Leader,* 4–5, 30–32.

Kamhi, A. G. (2011). Balancing certainty and uncertainty in clinical practice. *Language, Speech, and Hearing Services in Schools, 42,* 59–64.

Kay-Raining Bird, E., Cleave, P., Trureau, N., Thordardottir, E., Sutton, A., & Thorpe, A. (2005). The language abilities of bilingual children with Down syndrome. *American Journal of Speech-Language Pathology, 14,* 187–199.

Kohnert, K. (2008). *Language disorders in bilingual children and adults*. San Diego, CA: Plural.

Kohnert, K., & Derr, A. (2012). Language intervention with bilingual children. In B. Goldstein (Ed.), *Bilingual language development and disorders in Spanish-English speakers* (2nd ed., pp. 337–356). Baltimore, MD: Brookes.

Langdon, H. W., & Cheng, L. L (2002). *Collaborating with interpreters and translators in the communication disorders field*. Eau Claire, WI: Thinking Publications.

Lanza, E. (1992). Can bilingual two-year-olds code-switch? *Journal of Child Language, 19,* 633–658.

Law, N. C. W., & So, L. K. H. (2006). The relationship of phonological development and language dominance in bilingual Cantonese-Putonghua children. *International Journal of Bilingualism, 10,* 405–428.

Lopez, L., & Greenfield, D. (2004). The cross-linguistic transfer of phonological skills of Hispanic Head Start children. *Bilingual Research Journal, 28,* 1–18.

Lynch, E., & Hanson, M. (Eds.). (2011). *Developing cross-cultural competence: A guide for working with children and their families* (4th ed.). Baltimore MD,: Brookes.

MacSwan, J., & Rolstad, K. (2006). How language proficiency tests mislead us about ability: Implications for English language learner placement in special education. *Teachers College Record, 108*(11), 2304–2328.

McLaughlin, B. (1984). *Second language acquisition in childhood: Volume 1. Preschool children* (2nd ed.). Hillsdale, NJ: Erlbaum.

Meisel, J. (2004). The bilingual child. In T. K. Bhatia & W. C. Ritchie (Eds.), *The handbook of bilingualism* (pp. 91–113). Malden, MA: Blackwell.

Merino, B. J. (1992). Acquisition of syntactic and phonological features in Spanish. In H. W. Langdon & L. L. Cheng (Eds.), *Hispanic children and adults with communication disorders* (pp. 57–98). Gaithersburg, MD: Aspen.

Nicoladis, E., & Genessee, F. (1996). A longitudinal study of pragmatic differentiation in young bilingual children. *Language Learning, 46,* 439–464.

Paradis, J. (2001). Do bilingual two-year-olds have separate phonological systems? *International Journal of Bilingualism, 5,* 19–39.

Paradis, J. (2005). Grammatical morphology in children learning English as a second language: Implications of similarities with specific language impairment. *Language, Speech & Hearing Services in Schools, 36,* 172–187.

Paradis, J. (2007). Second language acquisition in childhood. In E. Hoff & M. Shatz (Eds.), *Handbook of language development* (pp. 387–406). Oxford, England: Blackwell.

Paradis, J., Crago, M., Genesee, F., & Rice, M. (2003). Bilingual children with specific language impairment: How do they compare with their monolingual peers? *Journal of Speech, Language and Hearing Research, 46,* 1–15.

Paradis, J., & Genesee, F. (1996). Syntactic acquisition in bilingual children: Autonomous or interdependent? *Studies in Second Language Acquisition, 18,* 1–25.

Paradis, J., Genesee, F., & Crago, M. (2011). *Dual language development and disorders: A handbook on bilingualism and second language acquisition* (2nd ed.). Baltimore, MD: Brookes.

Peña, L. (1996). Dynamic assessment: The model and language applications. In K. Cole, P. Dale, & D. Thal (Eds.), *Assessment of communication and language* (pp. 281–307). Baltimore, MD: Paul H. Brookes.

Peña, E., Bedore, L. M., & Rappazzo, C. (2003). Comparison of Spanish, English, and bilingual children's performance across semantic tasks. *Language, Speech, & Hearing Services in Schools, 34,* 5–16.

Peña, E., Gillam, R., Bedore, L., & Bohman, T. (2011). Risk for poor performance on a language screening measure for bilingual preschoolers and kindergarteners. *American Journal of Speech-Language Pathology, 20,* 302–314.

Peña, E., Iglesias, A., & Lidz, C. (2001). Reducing test bias through dynamic assessment of children's word learning ability. *American Journal of Speech-Language Pathology, 10,* 138–154.

Peña, E., & Quinn, R. (1997). Task familiarity: Effects on the test performance of Puerto Rican and African American children. *Language, Speech, and Hearing Services in Schools, 28,* 323–332.

Restrepo, M. A. (1998). Identifiers of predominantly Spanish-speaking children with language impairment. *Journal of Speech, Language, and Hearing Research, 41,* 1398–1411.

Restrepo, M. A., & Gray, S. (2012). Professional development practices and content for professionals working with preschool dual language learners. In B. Goldstein (Ed.), *Bilingual language development and disorders in Spanish-English speakers* (2nd ed., pp. 365–378). Baltimore, MD: Brookes.

Roseberry-McKibbin, C. (2002). *Multicultural students with special needs* (2nd ed.). Oceanside, CA: Academic Communication Associates.

Schnitzer, M., & Krasinski, E. (1994). The development of segmental phonological production in a bilingual child. *Journal of Child Language, 21,* 585–622.

Schnitzer, M., & Krasinski, E. (1996). The development of segmental phonological production in a bilingual child: A contrasting second case. *Journal of Child Language, 23,* 547–571.

Swain, M. (1972). *Bilingualism as a first language* (Unpublished doctoral dissertation). University of California, Irvine.

Tabors, P. (1997). *One child, two languages: A guide for preschool educators of children learning English as a second language.* Baltimore, MD: Brookes.

Tomblin, B. (2000). Perspective on diagnosis. In B. Tomblin, H. Morris, & D. C., Spriestersbach (Eds.), *Diagnosis in speech-language pathology* (pp. 3–33). San Diego, CA: Singular.

Valdés, G., & Figueroa, R. A. (1994). *Bilingualism and testing: A special case of bias.* Norwood, NJ: Ablex.

Vihman, M. (1982). The acquisition of morphology by a bilingual child. *Journal of Child Language, 3,* 141–160.

Vygotsky, L. (1978). *Mind in society.* Cambridge, MA: Harvard University Press.

Williams, A. L. (2003). Target selection and treatment outcomes. *Perspectives on Language Learning and Education, 10(1),* 12–16.

APPENDIX 9–A
Intervention for Bilingual Children

Step 1: Choose Goals

In planning intervention for bilingual children, SLPs often mistakenly begin the process by attempting to determine in which language to provide intervention. Although that is an important step (and is discussed later), it is not the first step. As with anyone who requires services for a speech or language disorder, the first step is to choose the goals based on a comprehensive assessment, as described earlier in the chapter. Goals might be crafted that cut across two intersecting continua (Baker, 2006). The first continuum focuses on goals that are either context embedded or context reduced. That is, goals related to this continuum focus on the amount of contextual support available to the child. A context-embedded goal might be using one- to two-word responses related to an object in the environment. A context-reduced goal might be one where the child describes a television show.

The second continuum focuses on goals that are cognitively demanding or cognitively undemanding. Cognitively undemanding goals are those for which the child has relative mastery of the language skills needed to communicate easily. Cognitively demanding goals are those that are challenging due to the need for rapid processing of information. A cognitively undemanding goal might be one that focuses on the child talking about the weather. In contrast, a cognitively demanding goal is one in which the child has to explain and justify an opinion.

Step 2: Choose Targets

Once the goals are chosen, then the specific targets should be identified. For bilingual children, targets might be based on the child's language skills, error patterns, and errors in each of the two languages. For example, errors that are highly occurring in or common to *both* languages might be selected first. Such errors might be deletion of consonant clusters (e.g., /plen/ "plane" → [pen]), omission of the plural marker, and difficulties using the present progressive tense. Then targets that are highly occurring in only one language would be chosen. If the child were a Spanish-English bilingual speaker, the SLP might remediate final consonant deletion in English but flap and trill in Spanish.

Step 3: Choose the Goal Attack Strategy

Fey (1986) outlines three goal attack strategies. Those strategies are adapted here for bilingual speakers. First, utilize a vertical strategy in which one goal at a time is taught until the specified criterion is reached. The bilingual correlate would be to remediate an error that is common to both languages. The error would be remediated in only one language but monitored in the other language. For example, the SLP would target the use of plurals in Language A but monitor their use in Language B. Second, utilize a horizontal strategy in which more than one goal is addressed in a session. The bilingual correlate would be to target the same goal in Language A and in Language B. For example, the SLP would target plurals in Language A for a period, take a break, and then focus on plurals in Language B. Finally, utilize a cyclical strategy in which a number of goals are addressed over a set time period although only one goal is remediated within each session. The bilingual correlate would be to rotate not only specific targets but also languages. For example, at Time 1, focus on plural -*s* in Language A and present progressive in Language B. At Time 2, focus on present progressive in Language A and plural -*s* in Language B.

Step 4: Choose the Approach

Kohnert and Derr (2012) recommend two general approaches to intervention for bilinguals: the bilingual approach and the cross-linguistic approach. The bilingual approach emphasizes skills common to both languages by focusing on the cognitive principles common to all language learning (i.e., efficient processing and quickly attending to changes in form); training aspects of form, content, and use that are shared by both languages; and highlighting interactions between cognition and language or between Language A and Language B (e.g., contrastive analysis; translation). The cross-linguistic approach emphasizes skills that are unique to each constituent language. Such unique skills might relate to aspects such as word order variation, morphology, omission of subjects, word length, syllable types, and orthography, to name a few.

Step 5: Choose the Language of Intervention

It is likely that following the previous four steps provide insight about the language of intervention. That is, the goals, targets, strategies, and approaches dictate which language should be used for intervention. Initially, language of intervention will depend on a host of factors including, but not limited to:

◆ Language history (i.e., relative experience with each language)
◆ Use in each language (i.e., how frequently the child utilizes each of the languages)
◆ Proficiency in each language (i.e., how well the child understands and produces each language)
◆ Environment (i.e., where and with whom the child uses each language)
◆ Family considerations (i.e., the family's goals as part of EBP)
◆ The child's speech and language skills and errors/error patterns in each of the two languages

Regardless of the approach, it is almost certain that intervention will have to take place in *both* languages at some time during the course of treatment. Intervention in English only is unlikely to be an option. There is ample research evidence for providing intervention in both languages (see Gutiérrez-Clellen, 1999; Kohnert, 2008; and Kohnert & Derr, 2012, for reviews). Using a bilingual approach has shown to facilitate an increase in speech and language skills in both languages (Kohnert & Derr, 2012). For example, in a group of Spanish-English bilinguals, Lopez and Greenfield (2004) found that

English phonological awareness skills were predicted by (1) English oral proficiency, (2) Spanish oral proficiency, and (3) Spanish phonological awareness skills. That is, skills in Spanish predicted how well the children were performing in English. Research such as this indicates that if the goal of intervention is a bilingual child, then direct intervention in both languages is necessary; that children, even those with impaired language, are capable of acquiring more than one language; and that focusing on Language A will not impede acquisition in Language B, and in some cases, may facilitate it.

Step 6: Monitor Progress

It is imperative to monitor progress during the intervention process by determining **efficiency**, **effects**, and **effectiveness** (after Williams, 2003). Efficiency focuses on determining how long it took for the client to achieve the goals (e.g., number of treatment sessions), determining how much effort was needed to facilitate change by examining the child's response level (e.g., imitation vs. spontaneous production), and determining the hierarchy needed to produce change (e.g., incremental steps vs. a few gradual steps). Effects focuses on determining if the change was significant by charting outcomes throughout the intervention process. Finally, effectiveness measures whether the intervention provided to the child was the agent responsible for the change. To measure effectiveness, the SLP would take baseline data (e.g., measuring skill level before intervention begins), treatment data (e.g., collecting data on the goals and targets), and then withdrawal data (e.g., measuring skill level after intervention ceases). Ideally, follow-up data would be collected as well; that is, weeks or even months after working on a target.

CHAPTER 10

The Effect of
Hearing Loss on Language

Brian J. Fligor

You are a speech-language pathologist working in an early intervention program and a 2½-year-old boy on your caseload shows both receptive and expressive language delay. His attention seems limited and he is not easily redirected verbally. He often seems "out there" and not engaged easily on language tasks. He also has not made progress in acquiring new consonants. He is very frustrated with his inability to express his wants and needs. His eye contact is excellent and he seems extremely good at nonverbal problem-solving tasks. You do question if his hearing is normal, but he passed his newborn hearing screening. Could this little boy have a hearing loss? If so, is it medically treatable because it is caused by chronic ear infections? Or is it a permanent hearing loss, requiring audiological interventions?

AN OVERVIEW OF THE ROLE OF HEARING DEVELOPMENT

A child begins his or her interaction with the world with a fully functioning auditory system, tuned to the sound of a mother's voice. Language learning begins at the moment of birth, if not before, when children listen to their mothers' voices in utero. Children who have normal hearing abilities access the sounds of speech through an uncanny process. They dissect the pops, squeaks, and hums in the environment and perceive the differences between these non-speech sounds and spoken language. In response to interaction with language users, children begin producing their own approximations of the language that they are exposed to in their environment. Children who do not possess normal hearing need to be identified and provided with appropriate intervention to have the same language-learning opportunities as children with intact hearing abilities. When such identification and intervention are not provided, children lag behind in language learning, potentially lagging in the acquisition of literacy. These children also permanently require remediation for lost time and the opportunity to acquire language and achieve full academic or social potential. Results of a hearing assessment direct the audiologist and speech-language pathologist to maximize the communication development of a child with a hearing loss and to provide the child with the opportunity to become a socially, emotionally, and academically equipped adult.

CHAPTER OBJECTIVES

This chapter presents an overview of the impact of hearing loss on communication; a review of the methods for determining the type, degree, and configuration of a hearing loss; and audiological interventions for mitigating the negative impact of hearing loss. After reading this chapter, you should understand:

◆ The effect of hearing loss on speech and language skills
◆ The methods for assessment of a hearing loss
◆ Audiological interventions for a hearing loss
◆ Methods for the identification of a child with a possible hearing loss

AN EXPLANATION OF HEARING ABILITIES

Sound waves enter the outer ear and travel through the ear canal to the eardrum. In the ear canal, sound in the range of 2,500 to 3,500 hertz (Hz) resonates (i.e., is amplified), thereby increasing the energy transmitted in this **frequency** range to the eardrum. This sound energy from the incoming sound waves vibrates the eardrum and the energy is converted from sound energy to mechanical energy in the middle ear. Here, as a consequence of the size difference between the eardrum (entrance to the middle ear) and the oval window (exit from the middle ear into the inner ear) and the lever action of the bones (**ossicles**) in the middle ear (**malleus**, **incus**, and **stapes**), sound is further amplified. Those amplified vibrations enter the **cochlea** (inner ear), where the mechanical energy is converted to hydraulic pressure waves (Figure 10–1).

The cochlea is a fluid-filled organ with a membrane called the **basilar membrane**. **Sensory cells** (outer and inner hair cells) sit on top of the basilar membrane. The sound vibrations sent to the inner ear lead to a traveling wave along the basilar membrane as a result of the **electromotility** of the **outer hair cells** (the **motility** of the cochlear outer hair cells is an active process where the cell actually changes shape in response to the vibration across the bristly structures, the **stereocilia**, on top of the hair cell). This shape-change further amplifies the signal at the place on the basilar membrane that is best tuned to the frequency of the signal.

An overlying membrane (tectorial membrane) deflects as a result, which then interacts with the stereocilia on top of the **inner hair cells**. Deflection of the stereocilia on the inner hair cells causes them to depolarize and release neurotransmitters across the synapse between the inner hair cells and auditory nerve fibers. Here the sound waves are changed into electrical signals. These signals are carried by the auditory nerve to the brain. In the brain, the signal is translated into sound.

SOUND INTENSITY DEFINED

Sound intensity is measured in units of **decibels** (dB) that are calculated on a logarithmic scale. Sound intensity increases 10-fold for every additional 10 dB. In other words, each increase of 10 decibels represents a multiplication of the sound intensity by a factor of 10. Consequently, a

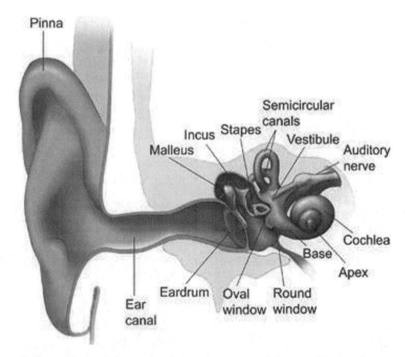

Figure 10–1. *Schematic of the structures of the ear. The outer ear comprises the pinna and ear canal and terminates at the eardrum; the middle ear comprises the eardrum, the ossicles (the malleus, incus, and stapes), and the air-filled space and terminates at the oval window; and the inner ear, which comprises the cochlea (from base to apex) as well as the vestibular system (vestibule and semicircular canals). Signals from the cochlea travel up the auditory nerve to the brain. From the National Institute on Deafness and Other Communication Disorders. Retrieved from http://www.nidcd.nih.gov/health/hearing/pages/noise.aspx. Reprinted with permission.*

change from 60 dB (the level of quiet conversation) to 90 dB (the level of heavy traffic) is equivalent to three 10-fold changes, and this change multiplies the intensity by a factor of $10 \times 10 \times 10$ (equal to a 1,000-fold intensity change).

> Examples of different intensity levels are jet aircraft takeoff (130 dB), snowmobiles (120 dB), rock concerts (110 dB), and gas-powered lawn mowers (95–100 dB), whereas conversational speech is lower (60 dB).

THE IMPACT OF A HEARING LOSS ON LANGUAGE DEVELOPMENT

Preliteracy skills (Burgess & Lonigan, 1998) and later reading skills (Parrila, Kirby, & McQuarrie, 2004) depend on **phonological awareness**. Phonological awareness consists of the ability to hear sounds and to associate these sounds with letters in words (e.g., the association of the speech sound /p/ with the written letter *p* in the word *pet*). The presence of any hearing loss places a child at risk for impaired phonological awareness, which may lead to an uncertain grasp of many of the grammatical aspects of spoken language.

Although seemingly of lesser significance, children with a "mild" degree of hearing loss possess word-reading and decoding skills that are lower than those with normal hearing sensitivity (Bess, Dodd-Murphy, & Parker, 1998). The early identification of children with hearing loss is essential to prevent difficulties in their learning and communication skills. The effects of a hearing loss on language include the following (Culbertson, 2007; Elfenbein, Hardin-Jones, & Davis, 1994; Tye-Murray, 2007):

◆ Difficulty with multiple meanings for words that sound alike but have different spellings
  ◆ Write/right
  ◆ Seen/scene
  ◆ Two/to/too
◆ Difficulty with morphemes
  ◆ Auxiliary verbs: *am, is, are, was, were, be, been, have, had*
  ◆ Inflectional morphemes: plurals (cat*s*); possessives (mommy*'s*); comparatives (bigg*er*); and superlatives (bigg*est*)
  ◆ Derivational morphemes, such as *-er*: farm*er*
  ◆ Present progressive *-ing*: go-*ing*
  ◆ Past tense *-ed*: wait-*ed*
  ◆ Determiners: *the, a, an*
◆ Speech errors
  ◆ Final consonant omission: *bus* produced as *bu*
  ◆ Voiced consonants (e.g., b, d, g) produced in place of voiceless (e.g., p, t, k)
  ◆ Difficulty with fricatives (e.g., s, z, f, v, h) and stops (i.e., p, b, t, d, k, g)

An examination of the audiological records of 54,000 school-age children in grades kindergarten through 12 revealed that 106 of these children had hearing loss in one ear (Oyler, Oyler, & Matkin, 1988). Findings were that 24% of these children repeated at least one grade and that 40% of them received special services, such as speech-language pathology intervention. Hearing loss was similar for male and female children, with the right ear two times more likely to be affected.

> Children with hearing loss have been found to have reduced vocabulary skills, shorter and simpler sentences, difficulty hearing sounds, lower reading and mathematical scores, and impaired social interaction (American Speech-Language-Hearing Association, 2009). These children also reported feeling isolated and without friends.

THE PERMANENCY OF HEARING LOSS

It is estimated that 3 to 4 of every 1,000 children are born with permanent hearing loss in the United States (Joint Committee on Infant Hearing [JCIH], 2007) with more children developing hearing loss between infancy and late adolescence. It is estimated that 19 of every 1,000 high school graduates have permanent hearing loss (Billings & Kenna, 1999).

Typically, permanent hearing loss is associated with a **sensorineural** hearing loss due to damage or dysfunction in the inner ear (the cochlea, shown in Figure 10–1), but it is possible that the middle-ear bones (the ossicles) or the external ear canal can be congenitally malformed. The latter two ear-related problems result in a **conductive** hearing loss of a permanent nature, which can be just as impairing to language development (or more so) than a sensorineural hearing loss.

The causes of sensorineural hearing loss vary widely and are mostly beyond the scope of this chapter. However, a congenital hearing loss is caused by birth complications roughly half the time (such as prematurity and resulting poor oxygenation provided by the immature lungs), and genetic causes are a factor in the other half (Billings & Kenna, 1999).

Although permanent hearing loss (either conductive or sensorineural) is typically considered most dire to normal language acquisition, it is not the most common cause of hearing impairment in children. On the contrary, conductive hearing loss secondary to **otitis media**

(an ear infection) is the most common cause of hearing loss. As many as 70% of all children under the age of 2 years have at least one bout of otitis media (Brooks, 1994) with half of those having multiple episodes. This conductive hearing loss is almost always temporary but hearing sensitivity fluctuates better to worse depending on the health status of the middle ear.

Ear infections are most common in children ages 6 months to 2 years and are caused by inflammation of the **eustachian tube** (Figure 10–2) and resultant eustachian tube dysfunction. Ear infections occur most often in children this age due to their lower immunity to upper respiratory tract infections (common colds), angle of the eustachian tube (it is more horizontal in children than in adults, thus it is more difficult to pop open), and length of the eustachian tube (shorter in children than

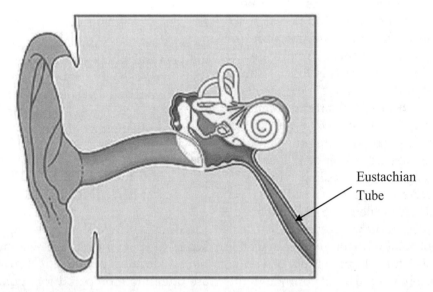

Figure 10–2. The Eustachian Tube. The eustachian tube connects the air-filled middle ear to the nasopharynx (top of the back of the throat). At rest the eustachian tube is closed but when yawning, chewing, or swallowing, or under voluntary control, it pops open, recycling air in the middle-ear space. From Getty Images Group. Reproduced with permission.

in adults), making it easier for bacteria in the nose and throat to migrate into the middle ear.

When the eustachian tube cannot open properly when one chews, swallows, or yawns, the air within the middle-ear pocket is not recycled. Consequently, the middle-ear mucosa (the tissue lining this air-filled pocket) absorbs the air, causing "negative pressure" or congestion. The body's immune system response is to excrete clear fluid to try to force open the eustachian tube. When this works, the eustachian tube is forced open and air pressure inside the middle ear returns to normal (i.e., the same pressure as atmospheric). If the eustachian tube remains closed, fluid inside the middle ear builds up and bacteria grow in the fluid, resulting in an ear infection.

Ear infections may result in fever, crankiness, and loss of appetite. However, sometimes this ear infection may not show overt symptoms. Regardless, the fluid sitting in the middle-ear space interferes with the transmission (or "conductance") of sound from the outer ear to the inner ear. This loss of sound energy through the middle ear results in decreased hearing sensitivity (Mencher, Gerber, & McCombe, 1997) for as long as the middle-ear fluid is present.

The degree of hearing loss from asymptomatic otitis media is typically 20 to 30 decibels hearing level (dB HL) (Fria, Cantekin, & Eichler, 1985). Note that "dB HL" represents hearing level (HL) in decibels (dB), relative to the average detection thresholds for a large sample of young, otologically normal adults. Although this degree of hearing loss is labeled "mild," it can contribute to delays in acquisition of spoken language. Although most common in children under the age of 2 years, conductive hearing loss secondary

to fluid in the middle ear is not uncommon in school-age children. This degree of hearing loss has been implicated in reduced academic achievement (Goldberg & McCormick Richburg, 2004).

SIGNS OF A HEARING LOSS

Cherry (2011, p. 68) provided a list of possible signs to help identify a child who may have a hearing loss. Children with a possible hearing loss may exhibit the following behaviors:

◆ Routinely ask for repetition
◆ Frequently misunderstand what is said
◆ Appear to be inattentive
◆ Have speech problems
◆ Watch others to see what they are doing
◆ Have fatigue at the end of the day
◆ Withdraw from situations that require careful listening

This list is not intended to be all-inclusive of the signs of hearing loss in toddlers and school-age children. In addition, this list should not be used to replace ongoing hearing screening, but if a child exhibited such signs, immediate audiological evaluation would be indicated.

AGE OF ONSET OF HEARING LOSS

Children with early, even brief, normal access to spoken language who adventitiously develop permanent hearing loss are often more prepared for spoken language acquisition than children with congenital onset of hearing loss (Northern & Downs, 2002). In other words, the more language that is acquired prior to the onset of hearing loss, the greater is the opportunity to lessen the negative impact of the hearing loss on language use.

Although it is a somewhat artificial distinction, **prelingual** onset requires greater **habilitative** efforts than does **postlingual** onset. *Habilitative* is the adjective of *to habilitate*, which means "to make able to do something." For example, language centers in the brain are stimulated from the earliest auditory experiences, and the greater the auditory experience the greater the stimulation (and, therefore, development) of the brain's language centers.

> Should hearing loss develop adventitiously or unexpectedly, these areas may become dormant or inactive. However, once identification of and intervention for the hearing loss occurs, these areas reawaken.

Typically developing children born with normal hearing who lose significant hearing between 18 and 30 months often "catch up" in their language to their normal hearing peers within 6 to 12 months (Martin & Clark, 1996). This is not to say that children with **congenital** (inborn) hearing loss do not catch up. On the contrary, they stand an excellent chance of having language on par with their normal-hearing peers. Other factors (specifically, age of identification and intervention) become the principal determinants in language outcome.

TYPE, DEGREE, AND CONFIGURATION OF HEARING LOSS

Hearing is neither "all or none," nor is degree of hearing loss clinically described as a "percent loss." Rather, the degree of hearing loss is described according to what has been historically understood to reflect the degree of impairment for accessing the **acoustic** or the sound cues of speech.

Hearing test results are thus plotted according to this goal: how much of the normal speech spectrum falls within the audible range for the child? For children with hearing loss, the **audiogram** describes the type, degree, and configuration of the hearing loss, thus indicating the "residual auditory area." The amount of the speech spectrum that falls within the residual auditory area determines which acoustic cues are accessible to the individual with hearing loss.

> Hearing loss may be **unilateral** (existing in one ear with normal hearing in the other ear) or **bilateral** (hearing loss in both ears). Further, if the hearing loss is bilateral, it may be **symmetrical** (similar degree of loss in both ears across frequencies) or **asymmetrical** (different degree of loss across frequencies between the two ears).

The pure tone audiogram is a fundamental component of the audiological evaluation. It is the graphical representation of an individual's detection threshold for frequency-specific stimuli in the conventional audiometric range (250–8,000 Hz). Considerable information is conveyed about the functional status of the conductive and sensorineural mechanisms of the ear on a graph spanning six octaves and roughly 130 dB.

The audiogram itself has a standard format with the distance between octaves on the abscissa (horizontal axis) equal to the distance between 20 dB on the ordinate (vertical axis). Such standardization allows the trained clinician quick visual recognition of type, degree, and configuration of a hearing loss regardless of the physical size of the audiogram on a report. As shown in Figure 10–3A, the octave stimulus frequencies in hertz are on the audiogram abscissa (horizontal), and the stimulus intensity, in decibels of hearing level, are on the audiogram ordinate (ver-

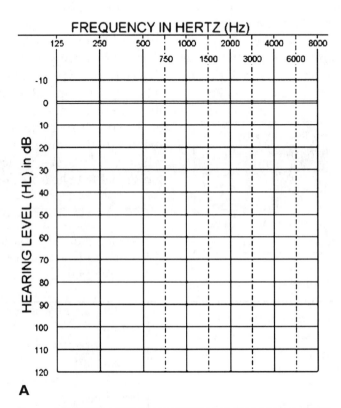

Figure 10–3. **A.** *The Audiogram. Stimulus frequencies, in hertz (Hz), are on the audiogram abscissa, and the stimulus intensity, in decibels in hearing level (dB HL), are on the ordinate.* **B.** *The Audiogram Legend. The symbol represents the threshold of hearing sensitivity at the frequency and intensity according to the method of sound presentation and whether or not contralateral masking was used in determining hearing threshold.*

tical). Interoctave frequencies (750, 1,500, 3,000, and 6,000 Hz) are typically represented with dashed or dotted lines.

The figure legend (Figure 10–3B) of the audiogram indicates the method of sound presentation (**air conduction** or **bone conduction**), whether the threshold was obtained using contralateral masking (**unmasked** or **masked**), if testing was completed via earphones or is not ear specific (e.g., sound field presentation or unmasked bone conduction), and if no response was obtained at the limits of the equipment (No Response; denoted as an arrow added to the lower portion of the appropriate symbol).

> Historically, bone conduction could not be performed at 8,000 Hz and so sensorineural thresholds would only be charted through 4,000 Hz. Newer instrumentation now allows for a limited intensity range of testing at 8,000 Hz.

Hearing Sensitivity

Normal hearing sensitivity (Figure 10–4A) in children is considered 15 dB HL or better (Northern & Downs, 2002) because hearing thresholds of 20 to 25 dB HL or poorer are considered of educational significance. On occasion, and particularly for the younger and developmentally delayed children, 20 dB HL may be considered the limit of normal hearing. However, it should be noted that this limit may overlook the presence of a slight conductive hearing loss in children with very good sensorineural hearing (bone-conduction thresholds of 0 dB HL or better). The degree of hearing loss is gener-

ally described according to air-conduction thresholds and is classified in the following list:

"Mild" when the loss is 21 to 40 dB HL

"Moderate" when the loss is 41 to 55 dB HL

"Moderately Severe" when the loss is 56 to 70 dB HL

"Severe" when the loss is 71 to 90 dB HL

"Profound" at 91 dB HL and greater

Conductive Hearing Loss

A conductive hearing loss is evidenced by air-conduction thresholds poorer than 20 dB HL and bone-conduction thresholds that are normal (better than 20 dB HL) and the **air-bone gap** (the difference between air-conduction and bone-conduction thresholds) is 10 dB or more. See Figure 10–4B for an example of bilateral mild conductive hearing loss. The exception to this general guideline is the child with air-conduction thresholds at 20 dB HL and bone-conduction thresholds of −10 to 5 dB HL; this child has at least a 15-dB air-bone gap and so would be considered to have a conductive impairment. The impact of conductive hearing loss is to reduce audibility of all sounds in a linear fashion; that is, the perceived loudness of a more intense sound is reduced by the same amount as a less intense sound.

Sensorineural Hearing Loss

When air-conduction and bone-conduction thresholds are poorer than 20 dB HL and within 10 dB HL of each other, the hearing loss is considered sensorineural (see

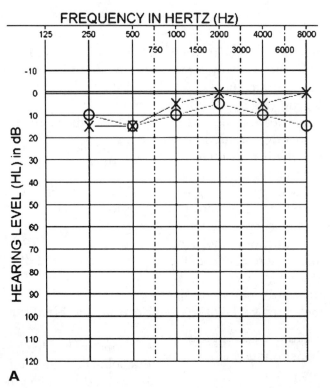

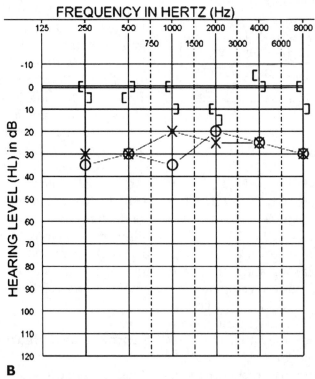

Figure 10–4. *Ear-Specific Pure Tone Audiograms.* (**A**) *Normal hearing bilaterally.* (**B**) *Mild conductive hearing loss.* (continues)

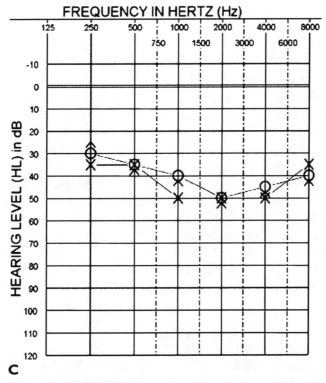

C

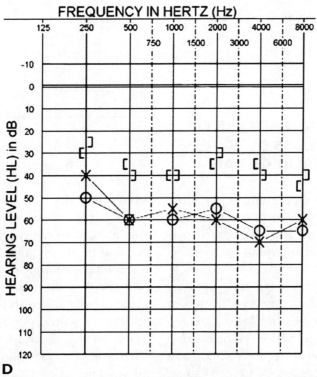

D

Figure 10–4. (continued) *(C) Moderate sensorineural hearing loss in both ears; unmasked bone conduction. (D) Mixed hearing loss showing masked bone conduction.*

Figure 10–4C). The impact of sensori-neural hearing loss (SNHL) is to reduce audibility of sounds in a nonlinear fashion: Sounds that fall below the threshold of audibility are not detected, whereas sounds that are above the threshold of audibility are audible, and typically as loud to the person with hearing loss as to a person with normal hearing, due to the phenomenon of loudness recruitment. When bone-conduction thresholds are poorer than 20 dB HL and air-conduction thresholds are elevated by another 10 dB or more (an air-bone gap is present), then a **mixed hearing loss** is present (see Figure 10–4D).

> The impact of a mixed hearing loss would be that of a nonlinear reduction in audibility (the sensorineural component) with an additional linear reduction in audibility (the conductive component).

CAVEATS TO THE TYPE OF HEARING LOSS DENOTED BY THE AUDIOGRAM

It is now evident that certain hearing loss etiologies result in "erroneous" results on the audiogram. For instance, in persons with an **auditory neuropathy spectrum disorder** (ANSD), also known as "auditory dys-synchrony," the pure tone audiogram can show any type, degree, or configuration of hearing loss, although not necessarily be indicative of hearing function (as is the audiogram when other hearing disorders are present) (Kumar & Jayaram, 2006). This hearing disorder, ANSD, is characterized by normal outer-,

middle-, and inner-ear function at least up to the level of the outer hair cells but with abnormal function of the inner hair cells or auditory nerve fibers (Berlin et al., 1998). The functional impact of this disorder is characterized by poor ability to understand speech, even if that speech is audible.

It should also be noted that the impact of hearing loss is not fully explained by the audiogram because two individuals with the same audiogram will have different levels of disability, owing in large part to age of onset and differences in environment in which the individual functions (Yoshinaga-Itano, Sedey, Coulter, & Mehl, 1998).

> Whether the hearing loss is bilateral and symmetrical or unilateral, conductive, or senso-rineural, the functional impact on the individual may require greater or lesser degrees of intervention to improve hearing function.

As noted previously, a "low fence" of a 15-dB HL limit for normal hearing sensitivity has been proposed for children, rather than the 25-dB HL limit for adults (Northern & Downs, 2002). This is due, in part, to the continued language-learning needs of children, as evidenced by children having poorer auditory closure than adults and requiring higher *signal-to-noise ratio* (SNR) than adults to achieve the same speech understanding. Consequently, hearing loss of 16 to 25 dB HL has been proposed to be classified as a minimal hearing impairment (MHI). This minimal loss places children at risk for academic difficulties (Goldberg & McCormick Richburg, 2004), along with effects on language and learning development.

Bess et al. (1998) examined the educational skills of 1,218 children in third, sixth, and ninth grades and found that 5.4% of children had an MHI. The third graders with MHI had difficulty with reading and language skills, along with difficulties with attention and communication. Across all three grades, children with MHI were significantly more likely to repeat a grade.

HEARING ASSESSMENT

Unless otherwise indicated by patient history, the audiologist's role in the audiological evaluation is to document hearing sensitivity for the sake of accessing spoken language. Normal hearing thresholds in at least one ear for octave frequencies 500 to 4,000 Hz essentially rules out a communicatively significant hearing loss for the child under the age of 3 years. Normal hearing thresholds in both ears for frequencies 500 to 4,000 Hz essentially rules out an educationally significant hearing loss for children age 3 years and up. However, the audiologist endeavors to document hearing sensitivity in both ears from 250 to 8,000 Hz, as long as responses are judged to be clear and replicable.

> There are also important but subtle speech cues outside the range of 500 to 4,000 Hz (Stelmachowicz, Pittman, Hoover, Lewis, & Moeller, 2004). When response reliability is questioned, testing typically is suspended so as to not call into question the reliability of all responses.

Categories of Assessment

Hearing assessment falls principally under two categories: behavioral audiometry and physiologic measures of the function of the auditory system. Behavioral methods of assessment include:

◆ Behavioral observation audiometry (BOA)
◆ Conventional audiometry
◆ Conditioned play audiometry (CPA)
◆ Visual reinforcement audiometry (VRA)

The three most commonly used physiologic measures in pediatric audiology include:

◆ Acoustic immittance (Tympanometry and middle ear muscle reflexes)
◆ Otoacoustic emissions (OAEs)
◆ Auditory brainstem response (ABR)

Such tests provide information regarding the functional integrity of the auditory system but do not directly assess the perceptual event that is called *hearing*. Regardless of the technique used, the examiner must interpret the behavioral or physiologic responses that are obtained and judge whether a given child's hearing is normal or if there is impairment in hearing function.

The reliability and validity of this judgment depends on the particular assessment technique that is used and the sophistication of the observer, based on skills and experience. For this reason, a judgment of normal or impaired hearing, based on a single evaluation or a single technique, should be regarded with caution.

A combination of several techniques and multiple evaluations over time is often necessary to arrive at a valid assessment of hearing in the very young child (Jerger & Hayes, 1976; Turner, 2003). The diagnosis of hearing loss is often a process, not an event.

Behavioral Audiometry

Behavioral audiometry requires that the child's responses be brought under the control of the stimulus. In other words, some response within the child's spontaneous or taught repertoire is structured in such a way that it occurs reliably when and only when the child hears the stimulus. To condition the child to participate in such a listening task and to judge whether a definitive behavioral response has occurred requires the skill of an audiologist experienced in testing children, particularly in the case of children younger than 4 or 5 years of age.

Conventional Audiometry (Ages 4 or 5 Years and Older)

The child is asked to raise the hand or push a button every time he or she hears a tone. The audiogram is obtained for separate ears through earphones and also using a bone-conduction oscillator at any frequency exhibiting hearing loss. Masking noise may be employed during air-conduction testing and/or bone-conduction testing, when indicated, to confirm that the test results reflect true hearing threshold rather than contribution from the opposite cochlea.

Conditioned Play Audiometry ([CPA]; Developmental Age 2 to 4 or 5 Years)

The child is shown, nonverbally, how to wait, listen, and perform a repetitive play task such as placing a peg in a pegboard every time he or she hears a tone. The audiogram usually is obtained through earphones and (if appropriate) a bone-conduction oscillator, but it may be necessary to use sound field audiometry for some 2-year-olds, who do not always accept earphones. When CPA is performed for a child wearing earphones, a single-audiologist test paradigm (with the audiologist operating the audiometer at a small table in the same room with the child) often succeeds. When this test is performed in the sound field, a trained tester-assist facilitates the testing and helps to keep the child on task. Thresholds obtained using CPA are as reliable as those obtained using conventional audiometry. If the child can be conditioned to ignore a masking noise (while still attending to the test signal), masking noise may be employed to determine true hearing threshold in the test ear without contribution from the nontest ear.

Visual Reinforcement Audiometry ([VRA]; Developmental Age 6 Months to 2 Years).

A trained tester-assist faces the child, who may be on a parent's lap or in a special positioning chair with a tray. Earphones, bone-conduction oscillator, or loudspeakers may be used to deliver stimuli. If the child looks up or to the side on hearing the stimulus, the child is rewarded by activation of a lighted, animated toy or short video cartoon clip. Although it is not always possible (nor necessary) to demonstrate hearing better than 20 dB HL for all frequencies in a normally hearing infant or toddler using VRA, response thresholds obtained by VRA for a normally developing child age 9 or 10 months and older with hearing loss typically match the true audiogram very closely but are likely to be suprathreshold for 6- to-8-month-old babies tested by VRA. The audiologist's impression of test reliability is helpful in judging whether the obtained response thresholds represent true thresholds of hearing sensitivity.

Behavioral Observation Audiometry ([BOA]; Developmental Age 0 to 5 Months).

BOA requires the same room arrangement as VRA. BOA may be employed for infants or developmentally delayed children who are not able to turn their head or eyes reliably toward the anticipated visual reinforcer during VRA. Any response on the part of the child, such as cessation of sucking on a pacifier, eye widening, or momentary breath-holding on presentation of a sound, may be accepted if repeatable and if it does not also occur randomly between stimuli. It should be noted that unlike the conditioned response obtained using convention, CPA, and VRA, the responses obtained from BOA are not conditioned but, rather, are reflexive.

An audiogram obtained by BOA is likely to be suprathreshold by an indeterminate amount and should serve as an adjunctive measure to physiologic (evoked potential and/or otoacoustic emissions) test results. The use of "normative" values for the decibel level at which a baby under 6 months of age is likely to show responses to sound can be dangerously misleading because a normally

hearing baby age 4 months may react to speech at 40 dB HL but a baby the same age with a 30 dB sensory hearing loss also may react to speech at 40 dB HL.

Speech Audiometry

Measures of a child's responses to speech stimuli not only corroborate the pure tone audiogram, but also may provide information about the clarity of sound received and perceived. Speech audiometric tests may be presented through earphones for separate ears, through a bone-conduction oscillator, or in a calibrated sound field. When speech audiometry is performed in the sound field, it may be for the purpose of assessing unaided function or the benefit of hearing aids or a cochlear implant speech processor.

Speech Awareness Threshold (SAT)

The **speech awareness threshold (SAT)** is the weakest intensity at which the child demonstrates awareness of the presence of sound, when a speech stimulus is presented through the audiometer using a developmentally appropriate test method (conventional audiometry, CPA, VRA, or BOA). The SAT may be obtained for separate ears, via bone conduction, or in the sound field. When the child is responding reliably, the SAT in decibels agrees closely with the best pure tone threshold in the range of 250 to 4000 Hz. The SAT can be estimated by presenting music through the audiometric transducer so that its average intensity level is calibrated.

Speech Recognition Threshold (SRT)

The **speech reception threshold (SRT)** is the weakest intensity at which the child can identify 50% of spondee words from a closed set of familiar items. A spondee word has two syllables with equal stress, such as "baseball" or "toothbrush." The child's response may be to repeat the words or to point to pictures representing the words. The SRT lies within 7 dB of the three-frequency pure tone average hearing level (the averaged pure tone thresholds at the frequencies 500, 1,000, and 2,000 Hz). In the case of a downward-sloping audiogram with a high-frequency loss, the SRT agrees with the averaged threshold at 500 and 1,000 Hz. It is possible to perform well on the SRT test by identifying only the vowels of the words and guessing at the words when a closed set such as "baseball," "toothbrush," "hotdog," "cowboy," "ice cream," or "pancake" is used. It is a common clinical observation that children can hear "ice cream" 5 dB weaker than other words. An SRT more than 10 dB better than the three-frequency pure tone average suggests that the pure tone audiogram may be wrong; the child either was not listening well for the audiogram or was malingering. Likewise, an SRT that is significantly poorer than the pure tone audiogram suggests that the audiologist may have been accepting some false-positive responses on the audiogram.

Word Recognition

Measures of **word recognition** estimate the child's ability to hear speech clearly when it is presented at a comfortable listening level, such as 30 to 50 dB above the SRT. Alternatively, word-recognition tests may be given at a level of 50 dB HL, even in the presence of partial hearing loss, to estimate the child's ability to perceive speech at a conversational intensity. The tests may be administered by calibrated live voice through the audiometer or using recorded materials presented through the audiometer. Word-recognition tests fall into various categories. "Closed-set" tests give the child a preset group of choices from which the stimulus items are chosen. Closed-set tests usually involve pointing to one of a set of pictures when the item is presented by the audiologist. "Open-set" tests give no range of choices so that any response is possible. The scoring of open-set tests can be complicated when the child's speech articulation ability is not normal. If the child repeats a word erroneously, he or she may have heard it correctly but may not have been able to reproduce all the sounds because of his or her developing speech patterns.

CENTRAL AUDITORY PROCESSING DISORDERS (CAPD)

Speech perception tests for the assessment of **central auditory processing disorders (CAPD)** are designed to test the abilities of school-age children who have normal pure tone audiograms but have difficulty perceiving speech that is degraded in any way by background noise, competing signals in the contralateral ear, rapid rate of presentation, or filtering. CAPD tests also address abilities, such as binaural integration, auditory memory, and retrieval of auditorily presented information. The child appropriate for CAPD evaluation may present with recurrent complaints from parents, siblings, peers, and classroom teachers of "not listening," although he or she passes school hearing screening tests. The child may be having difficulty following directions or reading.

Because many tests designed to test the ability of the central auditory nervous system to process complex speech require presentation of recorded materials at predetermined levels in a sound-treated suite, the evaluation of CAPD involves the audiologist; however, audiological CAPD testing must not be done in isolation (Baran, 1997; Musiek & Chermak, 2006a). One may discover central auditory processing abilities that are below age level and yet not be aware that those very abilities are the highest skills in that child's overall cognitive and perceptual profile.

CAPD testing requires a team approach including careful observation by the parent, speech-language pathologist, and classroom teacher. It usually includes language, reading, and cognitive evaluations as well to obtain a profile of the child's use of hearing for information gathering, storage, and retrieval. Without a team evaluation, CAPD may not be distinguishable from attention-deficit disorder, or it may be felt to be a single-modality deficit when a multimodal information processing deficit exists (Cacace & McFarland, 1998; Musiek & Chermak, 2006a). Children with sensorineural or conductive hearing loss may have central auditory processing deficits as well, but these deficits are more difficult to separate from the effects of early auditory-based language deprivation, and an accepted assessment protocol has yet to emerge.

Although detailed coverage of screening, diagnosis, and treatment of CAPD is beyond the scope of the current chapter, the interested reader is referred to two textbooks edited by Drs. Musiek and Chermak: *Handbook of (Central) Auditory Processing Disorders, Vol. 1: Auditory Neuroscience and Diagnosis* and *Handbook of (Central) Auditory Processing Disorders, Vol. 2: Comprehensive Intervention* (Musiek & Chermak, 2006a,b).

PHYSIOLOGIC MEASURES OF AUDITORY FUNCTION

Tympanometry

Tympanometry is conducted principally to assess middle-ear function (how well sound is conducted through the eardrum and ossicles), rather than as a test of hearing. A child with no hearing whatsoever will have normal tympanograms if the middle ears are clear. Conversely, a child with hearing in the range of normal sensitivity may have abnormal tympanograms if any middle-ear fluid is present.

Tympanometry is performed by placing a metal probe surrounded by a soft tip in the ear canal in such a way as to obtain an airtight seal. Varying amounts of positive and negative air pressure are introduced in the sealed ear canal while a calibrated tone is presented in the sealed ear canal. The measures of interest are the physical ear canal volume, peak pressure, peak compliance, and tympanic width (Nozza, Bluestone, Kardatzke, & Bachman, 1994). The presence versus absence of middle-ear fluid, eardrum perforation, or negative middle-ear pressure can be readily determined from these measures.

Otoacoustic Emissions

Otoacoustic emissions (OAEs) were described by Kemp (1978) as tiny sounds present in the ear canal that are generated by the outer hair cells of the cochlea. Evoked OAEs are measured using a probe in the ear canal when presenting sounds in the ear, recording tiny sounds that are thought to arise from the electromotility of the outer hair cells. Unlike tympanometry, the probe used for measuring OAEs does not have to be an airtight seal.

Evoked OAEs are absent in ears having greater than 30 to 50 dB of sensorineural hearing loss, and so the presence of normal OAEs suggests normal cochlear sensitivity (or no poorer than a mild-to-moderate sensorineural hearing loss) (Gorga et al., 1997). OAEs do not predict the ability of the child to perceive sound using the entire auditory system because the response is generated without contribution by the auditory nerve or higher neural pathways. Thus, OAEs cannot be used to predict degree of hearing loss: OAEs may be present even if there is a mild (and sometimes moderate) hearing loss and absent with greater degrees of loss. Nonetheless, OAEs are a popular method for conducting hearing screenings, particularly in well-baby nurseries.

Shown in Figure 10–5A are normal distortion product otoacoustic emissions (DPOAEs) obtained from an ear with normal hearing sensitivity. DPOAEs are frequency specific and can give some information regarding the configuration of a sensorineural hearing loss. In Figure 10–5B are the DPOAEs obtained from an ear with a moderate low-frequency sensorineural hearing loss with hearing thresholds rising to normal in the higher frequencies.

Auditory Brainstem Response

Several techniques exist for measuring the sound-evoked physiologic response of the auditory system. Of these, the measure most frequently used for testing infants and for children to confirm a diagnosis of permanent hearing loss is the **auditory brainstem response** (ABR). The ABR represents changes in electrical activity from the auditory nerve to midbrain level. These changes are recorded by three or four surface scalp electrodes and are time-locked to the onset of a repetitive sound such as a click or a tone burst. When the ABR is used to estimate the pure tone audiogram the patient must be sleeping with or without sedation. Typically, babies under 6 months of age can be tested in an unsedated sleep after a feeding. Children age 6 months and older usually are sedated for the ABR test.

Auditory stimuli for the ABR test may be delivered by air conduction, usually with insert earphones, or by bone conduction, with masking as needed. A broad-spectrum repetitive click signal is often used for screening purposes in newborn nurseries and is sensitive to hearing loss (conductive or sensorineural) of a mild degree or greater at 1,000 Hz and above. To estimate the configuration of a hearing loss, brief tone bursts with energy at different center frequencies are used in diagnostic testing. Shown in Figure 10–6 are the normal ABR waveforms elicited by different tone bursts in a 4-month-old infant. Additionally, ABR can be used to diagnose ANSD, which is a fairly rare hearing disorder. As noted briefly in the section on caveats to the type of hearing loss denoted on the audiogram, classically, a person with ANSD has normal outer-, middle-, and inner-ear function up to the level of the outer hair cells, but a problem exists with neural coding of timing cues. This problem with neural coding is evidenced on the ABR. Children with ANSD vary along a spectrum of function, from little impact to essentially no auditory function (Berlin et al., 1998). Furthermore, the pure tone audiogram often does not correlate with communication function (unlike conductive and sensorineural hearing losses).

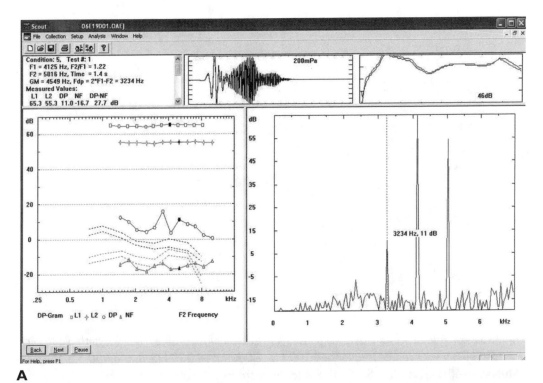

A

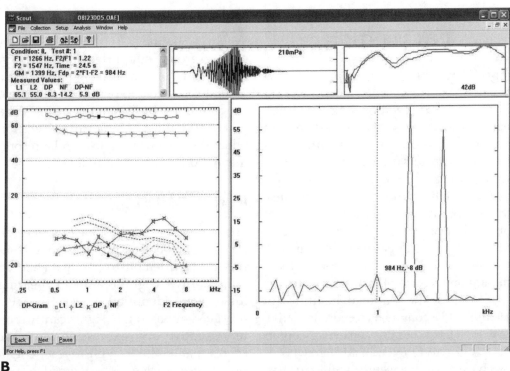

B

Figure 10–5. *Distortion Product Otoacoustic Emissions (DPOAE). (A) In the normal ear, interactions between the probe tones, f_1 and f_2, give rise to distortion. The distortion product radiates from the cochlea through the middle ear to the ear canal, where it can be detected by spectral analysis. (B) Reduced DPOAEs in the lower frequencies suggestive of lower frequency cochlear dysfunction.*

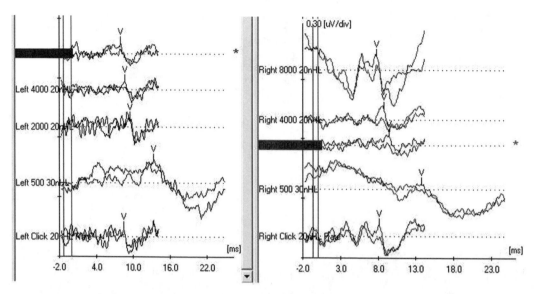

Figure 10–6. *Auditory Brainstem Response (ABR).Thresholds obtained in a 4-month-old to clicks and tone bursts with center frequencies 500 Hz, 2,000 Hz, 4,000 Hz, and 8,000 Hz.The peak of the wave of interest is marked with Roman numeral V.*

INTERVENTION

Age of Intervention

Prior to 1993, few hospitals provided newborn hearing screening tests except perhaps for those infants identified as having risk factors (indicators) for hearing loss. Such an approach identified at best 50% of infants with hearing loss because the others have no indicators apparent at birth. The average age of diagnosis of permanent hearing impairment at that time was felt to be 30 months, although documentation is lacking for this estimate.

In 1993, the National Institutes of Health held a consensus conference (NIH, 1993). The result of this consensus conference was to recommend that all newborns receive a hearing screening within the first 3 months of life with awareness that the practical means of accomplishing such universal screening in the United States would be to screen all babies prior to discharge from the newborn nursery.

In 1994, the JCIH (1994), a multiagency group, supported identification of all infants with hearing impairment by 3 months of age and onset of habilitative programming by 6 months of age. The JCIH added a list of indicators associated with late-onset hearing loss and a recommendation for monitoring them.

Newborn Screening

The seminal work of Yoshinaga-Itano et al. (1998) helped bolster the newborn screening effort by demonstrating that children with normal cognition whose hearing losses were identified before 6 months of age demonstrated significantly better receptive and expressive language scores than children with normal cognition whose hearing losses were identified after 6 months of age (regardless of the degree of hearing loss or several demographic variables). Since 1994, the JCIH has updated its recommendations, most recently in 2007 (JCIH, 2007).

Updates to previous position statements principally support that all newborns be screened within the first month of life, that permanent hearing loss be identified by 3 months of age, and that appropriate family-centered interventions be instituted by 6 months of age. In addition, JCIH (2007) reaffirmed the need for surveillance for adventitious onset of childhood hearing loss. The JCIH position statements are considered best practice for current clinical standards and also drive advocacy and public policy.

DEVICES USED FOR HEARING HABILITATION: FM SYSTEMS, HEARING AIDS, AND COCHLEAR IMPLANTS

FM Systems

Unilateral hearing loss typically does not cause delay in speech and language development but renders the child unable to localize the direction from which a sound is coming. The child with unilateral hearing loss has difficulty hearing a weak voice on the affected side and difficulty focusing on one voice in the presence of competing noises. The most significant effect of unilateral hearing loss is then on classroom performance; children with unilateral hearing loss are at significant risk for poor academic performance due to difficulty hearing in the typical (noisy) classroom environment. Even with preferential classroom seating near the teacher and acoustic treatment of the classroom to reduce reverberation of background noise, academic progress should be monitored closely and supports initiated if listening-related difficulties emerge. A hearing aid in the poorer hearing ear may be beneficial, but, typically, it does not improve the child's ability to hear in noise. However, in the classroom, **FM educational amplification systems** (either ear level or sound field) may be used to improve the amount by which the teacher's voice exceeds the background noise.

Children with bilateral hearing loss may experience significant psychosocial impact and educational needs, particularly in the case of late diagnosis and the resultant early language deprivation. As discussed previously, the audiogram describes the residual auditory area for a person with hearing loss. Typically, vowel sounds, which have lower frequency content and greater intensity, are audible in children with mild-to-moderate sensorineural hearing loss, whereas many consonant sounds (such as /k/, /p/, /f/, /s/, and /th/) are not audible.

Functionally, the child would be able to tell that someone is speaking (and so may alert appropriately) but not understand the content of the message. Understandably, this leads to speech-language delays and social-emotional and behavioral problems as a result of the frustration from the child's inability to communicate thoughts, needs, and desires.

Hearing Aids

As soon as a bilateral hearing loss has been documented and is not felt to be transient, there is no reason for delay in fitting **hearing aids**, even if the baby is only 1 or 2 months old. The process of obtaining funding for hearing aids and the necessity of earmold remakes to achieve an optimal fit tend to delay the process for a few weeks so prompt initiation of hearing aid fitting is advisable as soon as the family feels ready to proceed. With current hearing aid technology including advanced feedback management and miniaturization of microprocessor chips, even newborns with severe-to-profound hearing loss can be fitted successfully with behind-the-ear hearing aids.

Some young children use FM amplification even during infancy to provide better hearing of their parents at a distance. Some instruments have FM receivers built into their hearing aid cases or into boots that fit onto the bottom of the instruments, bringing the voice of the parent or teacher transmitted by FM radio waves to the children's ears. In-the-ear hearing aids are not feasible for young children because of the need for frequent remakes with growth, but they may be appropriate for some school-age children with mild-to-moderate hearing loss.

Newer devices, such as receiver-in-the-canal (RIC) behind-the-ear hearing aids, may be useful for older children as well because these are even more discreet than in-the-ear hearing aids. Noncustom earmolds, however, do not provide the excellent retention needed to keep the devices in or on the ear rather than in the mouth or lost on the playground; such devices should be recommended judiciously after the child has demonstrated that he or she can be adequately responsible for caring for the device.

The intent of fitting with hearing aids is to amplify speech sounds into the child's residual auditory area, thus giving the child access to speech sounds while still not uncomfortably loud. The explosion of technology in the area of digital hearing aids and directional microphones enables infants and young children to experience significant benefit from amplification. It is *imperative* that the output of the hearing aids be independently verified using real-ear probe microphone measurement equipment to ensure that the devices are providing an appropriate amount of amplification. Underfitting

of the devices will result in the child not receiving appropriate benefit and stalling speech and language development. Overfitting of the devices could result in noise-induced permanent threshold shift. Although the manufacturer software may appropriately follow prescriptive fitting guidelines for infants and young children, there is considerable variation between the ears of infants so independent verification is critical.

With appropriately fitted and verified hearing aids, it should be expected that children with up to a severe degree of hearing loss (less than 70 dB HL average across the speech frequencies) will have significantly better access to the sounds of speech than without using hearing aids.

> For a child with normal cognition and no other concomitant conditions, early diagnosis of hearing loss and fitting with hearing aids, coupled with speech-language therapy, ear-level FM system in the classroom, and educational and psychosocial support, speech and language outcomes should be within normal to near-normal abilities (Sininger, Grimes, & Christensen, 2010).

Cochlear Implants

Children with severe (71 to 90 dB HL) and profound (greater than 90 dB HL) bilateral hearing loss generally have delayed language development, unless language has been made accessible and habilitation has been well underway by 6 months of age. This includes use of hearing aids and/or eventually a **cochlear implant** if a sense of hearing and spoken language is a goal of the family. A cochlear implant is a device that includes a magnet and electrode array that is surgically implanted in the inner ear as well as an ear-level externally worn speech processor and microphone. Speech sounds picked up by the ear-level microphone are decoded by the speech processor and this decoded signal is transmitted wirelessly via a coil positioned over the magnet that rests just under the skin in a well drilled out in the temporal bone at the time of the implant surgery. The signal is then transmitted to select electrodes on the array to give the user a sense of "hearing." Historically, patients received only one cochlear implant, but more recently, a second implant is often sought to give patients better access to sound on both sides and perhaps to help hear better in noise.

Although a cochlear implant does not restore "normal" hearing, it does provide improved access to spoken language relative to the benefit obtained from hearing aids when the child's degree of hearing loss is severe to profound. If the child and family opt for a cochlear implant, these children may still vary in their ability to acquire spoken language and may benefit from the use of one of the several forms of visual communication (American Sign Language, total communication using both signed and spoken English, or Cued Speech).

> Each child and family presents an individual situation in terms of choice of communication modality and educational setting that ranges all the way from being mainstreamed in regular classes with support services to residential placement at a school for the deaf.

Regardless of choice of method and of educational placement, the audiologist, otolaryngologist, speech-language pathologist, teacher of the deaf, and parents work as a team to ensure that the child uses a language to which she has access, that the people in her environment use it effectively with her, that she is making demonstrable progress in that language sufficient to establish a basis for literacy, and that she is developing self-esteem as a successful communicator with her peers as well as with her family. The audiologist and speech-language pathologist have an opportunity to monitor the child's progress, support the parents, and cheer them on in their good work through routine monitoring of hearing and communication success.

SUMMARY

Good auditory access to the cues of speech is necessary to develop phonological awareness. Hearing loss, both transient and permanent, is not an uncommon disorder, but it can go undetected without universal newborn hearing screening and close surveillance for hearing loss through childhood. Scientifically valid measures of hearing, both behavioral as well as physiologic, exist to fully characterize residual hearing function and direct interventions. Interventions, when implemented in a timely, family-centered fashion, are effective at helping children with hearing loss develop language on par with their normal hearing peers as long as cognition is adequate to support such successes.

◆ Permanent hearing loss occurs in 3 to 4 per 1,000 newborns, and the number increases to 19 per 1,000 by high school graduation.

◆ Roughly 70% of all children have an ear infection by age 2 years with half of these having multiple episodes.

◆ Children with transient middle-ear fluid secondary to an ear infection (symptomatic or asymptomatic) have conductive hearing loss that could interfere with normal language development.

◆ A child with prelingual onset of permanent hearing loss typically requires greater habilitative efforts than a child with postlingual onset.

◆ The type, degree, and configuration of a hearing loss are plotted on an audiogram and this test result aids in determining the degree to which the hearing loss impairs access to spoken language.

◆ Behavioral audiometry techniques are employed to determine hearing status based on the child's developmental status when the child's developmental age is 6 to 8 months and older.

◆ These behavioral test methods are behavioral observation audiometry, visual reinforcement audiometry, conditioned play audiometry, and conventional audiometry as well as speech audiometry measures.

◆ Central auditory processing disorder evaluations require a team approach to determine whether a single-modality deficit or a multimodal information processing deficit exists.

◆ In children under the age of 6 months, and to confirm and complement behavioral audiometry test results, physiologic measures of the function of the auditory system are employed.

◆ The most commonly used physiologic measures are tympanometry, otoacoustic emissions, and auditory brainstem response.

◆ The current Joint Committee on Infant Hearing Position Statement (2007) proposes that all newborns have their hearing screened by age 1 month, that those who do not pass and have hearing loss are diagnosed by age 3 months, and that those with hearing loss receive appropriate interventions including fitting with hearing aids and enrollment in IDEA Part C Early Intervention.

◆ Children with unilateral hearing loss sometimes benefit from fitting a hearing aid on the poorer ear but more often benefit from improved signal-to-noise ratio (teacher's voice over background noise) provided by an FM educational amplification system (FM system).

◆ Children with confirmed permanent bilateral hearing loss should be fitted with hearing aids as soon as the family is ready to pursue this intervention, even if the baby is only 1 to 2 months old.

◆ The purpose of hearing aids is to amplify speech sounds into the child's residual auditory area. Underfitting (underamplifying) the hearing aids lessens the child's access to speech cues. Overfitting (overamplifying) risks a noise-induced hearing loss.

◆ For children with severe-to-profound hearing loss, cochlear implants are an option to provide access to spoken language should hearing aids provide limited benefit for supporting acquisition of spoken language.

◆ For children with severe-to-profound hearing loss, whether the family opts for cochlear implant or not, language acquisition supports in a visual mode are indicated.

◆ A team approach among the speech-language pathologist, audiologist, physicians, educators of the deaf, teachers, and family is vital to support the child's development of self-esteem and communication success.

KEY WORDS

Acoustic

Air-bone gap

Air conduction

Asymmetrical

Audiogram

Auditory brainstem response (ABR)

Auditory neuropathy spectrum disorder

Basilar membrane

Bilateral

Bone conduction

Central auditory processing disorder (CAPD)

Cochlea

Cochlear implant

Conductive

Congenital

Decibels

Electromotility

Eustachian tube

FM educational amplification systems

Frequency

Habilitative

Hearing aids

Incus

Inner hair cells

Malleus

Masked

Mixed hearing loss

Motility

Ossicles

Otitis media

Otoacoustic emissions (OAEs)

Outer hair cells

Phonological awareness

Postlingual

Prelingual

Sensory cells

Sensorineural

Speech awareness threshold (SAT)

Speech reception threshold (SRT)

Stapes

Stereocilia

Symmetrical

Tympanometry

Unilateral

Unmasked

Word recognition

STUDY QUESTIONS

1. What is the purpose of universal newborn hearing screening?

2. How could hearing be best assessed in a 4-year-old child with a speech-language delay?

3. A 2-year-old child with speech delay and recurrent ear infections might have what kind of hearing loss that has gone undetected but is contributing to the delays?

4. A 12-month-old child was tested via visual reinforcement audiometry and

is suspected of having a moderate sensorineural hearing loss. What physiologic test measures could be conducted to confirm this hearing loss?

5. A 7-year-old with a bilateral congenital moderate-to-severe sensorineural hearing loss has used hearing aids since he was 6 months old. He seems to continually miss the morphological marker for past tense /t/ (e.g., *walked* /wɑkt/). What limitation might he have with his current hearing aid output, and how could this be checked?

REFERENCES

American Speech-Language-Hearing Association. (2009). *Noisy toys, dangerous play.* Retrieved from http://www.asha.org/public/hearing/disorders/noisy_toys.htm/noise-center-home/children-and-noise/noisy-toys

Baran, J. A. (1997). Speech perception test materials for central auditory processing assessment. In L. L. Mendel & J. L. Danhauer (Eds.), *Audiologic evaluation and management and speech perception assessment* (pp. 149–168). San Diego, CA: Singular.

Berlin, C. I., Bordelon, J., St. John, P., Wilensky, D., Hurley, A., Kluka, E., & Hood, L. J. (1998). Reversing click polarity may uncover auditory neuropathy in infants. *Ear and Hearing, 19*(1), 37–47.

Bess, F. H., Dodd-Murphy, J., & Parker, R. A. (1998). Children with minimal sensorineural hearing loss: Prevalence, educational performance and functional status. *Ear and Hearing, 19*(5), 339–354.

Billings, K. R., & Kenna, M. A. (1999). Causes of pediatric sensorineural hearing loss. *Archives of Otolaryngology Head Neck Surgery, 125,* 517–521.

Brooks, A. C. (1994). Middle ear infections in children. *Science News, 146,* 332–333.

Burgess, S. R., & Lonigan, C. J. (1998). Bidirectional relations of phonological sensitivity and prereading abilities: Evidence from a preschool sample. *Journal of Experimental Child Psychology, 70,* 117–141.

Cacace, A. T., & McFarland, D. J. (1998). Central auditory processing disorder in school-aged children: A critical review. *Journal of Speech and Hearing Research, 41*(2), 355–373.

Cherry, R. (2011). Hearing and listening skills. In S. Levey & S. Polirstok (Eds.), *Language development: Understanding language diversity in the classroom* (pp. 59–78). Los Angeles, CA: Sage.

Culbertson, D. (2007). Language and speech for the deaf and hard of hearing. In R. L. Schow & M.A. Nerboone (Eds.), *Introduction to audiologic rehabilitation* (pp. 197–244). Boston, MA: Pearson Education.

Elfenbein, J. L., Hardin-Jones, M. A., & Davis, J. M. (1994). Oral communication skills of children who are hard of hearing. *Journal of Speech and Hearing Research, 37,* 216–226.

Fria, T. J., Cantekin, E. I., & Eichler, J. A. (1985). Hearing acuity of children with otitis media with effusion. *Archives of Otolaryngology, 111,* 10–16.

Goldberg, L. R., & McCormick Richburg, C. (2004). Minimal hearing impairment: Major myths with more than minimal implications. *Communication Disorders Quarterly, 25*(3), 152–160.

Gorga, M. P., Neely, S. T., Ohlrich, B., Hoover, B., Redner, J., & Peters, J. (1997). From laboratory to clinic: A large scale study of distortion product otoacoustic emissions in ears with normal hearing and ears with hearing loss. *Ear and Hearing, 18*(6), 440–455.

Jerger, J. F., & Hayes, D. (1976). The cross-check principle in pediatric audiology. *Archives of Otolaryngology, 102*(10), 614–620.

Joint Committee on Infant Hearing (JCIH). (1994). Position statement. *Pediatrics, 95,* 152–156.

Joint Committee on Infant Hearing. (JCIH). (2007). Year 2007 position statement: Principles and guidelines for early hearing detection and intervention programs. *Pediatrics, 120*(4), 898–914.

Kemp, D. T. (1978). Stimulated acoustic emissions from within the human auditory system. *Journal of the Acoustical Society of America, 64*, 1386–1391.

Kumar, U. A., & Jayaram, M. M. (2006). Prevalence and audiological characteristics in individuals with auditory neuropathy/auditory dyssynchrony. *International Journal of Audiology, 45*(6), 360–366.

Martin, F. N., & Clark, J. G. (1996). *Hearing care for children*. Boston, MA: Allyn & Bacon.

Mencher, G. T., Gerber, S. E., & McCombe, A. (1997). Audiology and auditory dysfunction. In G. T. Mencher, S. E. Gerber, & A. McCombe (Eds.), *Anatomy and physiology of the human ear* (pp. 105–232). Needham Heights, MA: Allyn & Bacon.

Musiek, F. E., & Chermak, G. D. (2006a). *Handbook of (central) auditory processing disorders, vol. 1: Auditory neuroscience and diagnosis*. San Diego, CA: Plural.

Musiek, F. E., & Chermak, G. D. (2006b). *Handbook of (central) auditory processing disorders, vol. 2: Comprehensive intervention*. San Diego, CA: Plural.

National Institutes of Health. (1993). *Early identification of hearing impairment in infants and young children consensus development conference statement*. Retrieved from http://consensus.nih.gov/1993/1993hearinginfants children092html.htm

Northern, J. L., & Downs, M. P. (2002). *Hearing in children* (5th ed.). Baltimore, MD: Lippincott Williams & Wilkins.

Nozza, R. J., Bluestone, C. D., Kardatzke, D., & Bachman, R. (1994). Identification of middle ear effusion by aural acoustic admittance and otoscopy. *Ear and Hearing, 15*, 310–323.

Oyler, R. F., Oyler, A. L., & Matkin, N. D. (1988). Unilateral hearing loss: Demographics and educational impact. *Language, Speech, and Hearing Services in Schools, 19*, 201–210.

Parrila, R., Kirby, J. R., & McQuarrie, L. (2004). Articulation rate, naming speed, verbal short-term memory, and phonological awareness: Longitudinal predictors of early reading development? *Scientific Studies of Reading, 8*(1), 3–26.

Sininger, Y. S., Grimes, A., & Christensen, E. (2010). Auditory development in early amplified children: Factors influencing auditory-based communication outcomes in children with hearing loss. *Ear and Hearing, 31*(2), 166–185.

Stelmachowicz, P. G., Pittman, A. L., Hoover, B. M., Lewis, D. E., & Moeller, M. P. (2004). The importance of high-frequency audibility in the speech and language development of children with hearing loss. *Archives of Otolaryngology Head and Neck Surgery, 130*(5), 556–562.

Turner, R. G. (2003). Double checking the cross-check principle. *Journal of the American Academy of Audiology, 14*(5), 269–277.

Tye-Murray, N. (2007). *Foundations of aural rehabilitation* (3rd ed.). Clifton Park, NY: Delmar Cengage Learning.

Yoshinaga-Itano, C., Sedey, A. L., Coulter, D. K., & Mehl, A. L. (1998). Language of early and later-identified children with hearing loss. *Pediatrics, 102*, 1161–1171.

Glossary

Abduct: Movement away from midline.

Abstract thought: Higher-level thinking processes that are characterized by organization and logic.

Acceleration hypothesis: At certain points in development, bilingual children might demonstrate a faster rate of acquisition than their monolingual peers.

Accommodation: If a new event does not fit into a cognitive schema that already exists (e.g., *penguin*) there is a change in the existing schema (e.g., *birds*) to accommodate the characteristics of this new information.

Acoustic resonance: The effect of different vocal tract configurations on the production of speech sounds. Alterations in the cross-sectional area of the vocal tract determine the frequencies at which sound energy will be minimally attenuated or diminished.

Acoustics: Relating to sound, the sense of hearing, or the science of the physics of sounds. Acoustics can also be defined as sound vibration propagating through air or the science of sound.

Adaptation: The tendency of an organism to change in response to the environment.

Additive: A type of conjunction used to unite one sentence or phrase with another, such as *and*, *as well as*, *also*.

Adduct: Movement toward midline.

Adversative: A type of conjunction used to compare or contrast words, phrases, or sentences. Examples consist of the conjunctions *but*, *although*, *yet*, and *however*. The use of an adversative conjunction qualifies or mitigates the meaning expressed in the first clause or sentence. For example, the use of the adversative conjunction *however* in the sentence: *The race was won by a nonresident of the town, however, the race committee is reviewing the residential requirements for participation*, the conjunction *however* provides information that qualifies or modulates the meaning of the first clause.

Afferent: Nerves that carry impulses from the body toward the brain or spinal cord, or blood vessels that carry blood to an organ.

Air-bone gap: The difference, in decibels, between air-conduction and bone-conduction thresholds.

Air conduction: A method of transmitting sound through the outer and middle ears to the inner ear through an earphone delivering sound to the outer ear.

Alveolar ridge: A bony prominence of the hard palate directly behind the upper incisors (teeth) that serves as an important place of articulation for certain speech sounds (e.g., /s/ and /t/).

Alveolar stop: A consonant sound created by bringing the tongue tip in contact with the alveolar ridge, forming a complete closure, then building up pressure behind the point of closure and suddenly releasing the occlusion (e.g., /t/, /d/).

Alveoli: Tiny air sacs within the lungs where the exchange of oxygen and carbon dioxide takes place.

Anaphora: Reference to a word or phrase used earlier by replacing it with a pronoun. An example is the clause *he did so* in the sentence *I told Paul to close the door and he did* so. The clause *he did so* makes use of anaphora.

Anaphoric term: A linguistic entity that indicates a referential tie to some other linguistic entity in the same text (e.g., *The monkey took the banana and ate it*). "It" is anaphoric because it refers to the banana.

Angular gyrus: A region of the inferior parietal lobe of the brain that is involved in the processing of auditory and visual input and in the comprehension of language.

Approximants: A class of speech sounds produced by bringing one articulator close to another without creating audible noise; the approximation of articulators is critical to the acoustic resonance of these sounds (i.e., /r/, /l/, /w/, /j/).

Apraxia: A neurological disorder that results in difficulty initiating, planning, and/or programming the production of speech sound sequences. Productions are inconsistent.

Arcuate fasciculus: A bundle of nerve fibers that connects Broca's and Wernicke's areas, connecting the speech and language areas in the brain.

Argument: Within grammar, a noun element in a clause that relates directly to the verb, such as the subject or object of the sentence. *An argument* is an expression that helps complete the meaning of a predicate (the verb). Subject and object phrases are examples of arguments, shown in the example of the sentence *John threw the ball. John* and *ball* are arguments: *John* is the subject argument and *ball* is the object argument.

Articulators: Structures in the vocal tract that are used to create speech sounds. There are dynamic (movable) articulators, such as the tongue and lips, and there are static (immovable) articulators, such as the alveolar ridge and teeth, to which the dynamic articulators approximate (make contact) in the production of speech sounds.

Assimilation: 1. In relation to cognition, this term applies to children's exposure to new information or an event. In this case, the new entity can be assimilated or incorporated into a schema that already exists when there is a good fit between the new information and the preexisting schema. 2. In relation to phonetics, this term describes the changing of a speech sound due to the influence of adjacent sounds.

Asymmetrical: A clinically significant difference in the degree of loss between the two ears; may be frequency specific.

Audiogram: A standard graph for representing hearing sensitivity, in decibels hearing level (dB HL), as a function of frequency.

Auditory brainstem response (ABR): The objective, physiologic measure most frequently used for testing infants and children to estimate hearing sensitivity and/or confirm a diagnosis of hearing loss. The ABR is an electroencephalographic (EEG) response that is recorded via three scalp electrodes and represents changes in electrical activity from the auditory nerve to midbrain level as a result of sound presented to the ear.

Auditory neuropathy spectrum disorder (ANSD): The hearing disorder characterized by normal outer-, middle-, and inner-ear function at least up to the level of the outer hair cells, but with abnormal function of the inner hair cells or auditory nerve fibers.

Aural/oral (hearing/speaking) language: *Aural* refers to hearing and *oral* refers to speaking.

Autism: A developmental disorder that appears by age 3 and that is diagnosed by the impaired ability to form normal social relationships, to communicate with others, and by stereotyped behavior patterns exhibited by a preoccupation with repetitive activities of restricted focus rather than with flexible and imaginative actions or patterns.

Autonomic nervous system (ANS): Innervates muscles and glands for involuntary actions (e.g., gland secretions). Responsible for the control of visceral functions (e.g., heart, digestion, and respiration).

Axon: A long fiber of a nerve cell (a neuron) that typically conducts electrical impulses away from the neuron's cell body.

Basal ganglia: Structure in the brain responsible for the control of muscle tone and posture, along with organization and guidance of complex motor functions.

Basic sentences: Sentences composed of Subject + Verb (e.g., *Susie ran*).

Basilar membrane: The membrane of the cochlea. This is a supporting membrane that aids in translating sound vibrations into electrical signals.

Bilabial stop: Sound produced by approximating the lips (e.g., /b/, /p/).

Bilateral: A bilateral hearing loss is a hearing impairment in both ears. When someone has a loss in only one ear, it is known as a unilateral hearing loss.

Bilingual: Describes an individual who has proficiency in two languages. It may also describe individuals who have varying degrees of proficiency in three, four, or even more languages.

Bilingual first-language acquisition: Acquiring two first languages from birth.

Bone conduction: A method of transmitting sound to the inner ear by mechanically vibrating the bones of the skull, thereby bypassing the outer and middle ears.

Bootstrapping: A process in which linguistic knowledge is acquired, enabling a child to analyze words or sentences well enough to acquire further knowledge of language. Figuratively, this early knowledge would serve as *bootstraps* by which the child pulls himself or herself up.

Brainstem: The lower part of the brain, adjoining and continuous with the spinal cord.

Broca's area: A region in the left frontal lobe of the brain associated with speech that controls movements of the tongue, lips, and vocal cords.

Bronchioles: Tiny air tubes within the lungs that are a continuation of the bronchus. The bronchioles connect to the alveoli (air sacs).

Bronchus: A large air tube that begins at the end of the trachea and branches into the lungs.

Causal: A set of conjunctions that represent the process of *cause*, shown by the conjunction *because*, used to explain *why* something happened.

Causality: The principle that everything that happens must have a cause.

Central auditory processing disorder (CAPD): A disorder in which school-age children have normal pure tone audiograms but have difficulty perceiving speech that is degraded in any way by background noise, reverberation, competing signals in the contralateral ear, rapid rate of presentation, or filtering.

Central nervous system (CNS): The part of the nervous system that consists of the brain and the spinal cord. The CNS controls motor activities (e.g., walking, sitting, and speech), and movements that are connected to essential body functions (e.g., breathing). The CNS is also responsible for thought processes that emerge from interaction with the environment.

Cerebellum: A region of the brain that plays an important role in motor control. The cerebellum contributes to coordination, precision, and accurate timing of motor skills.

Cerebrum: The largest and uppermost portion of the brain. The cerebrum consists of the right and left cerebral hemispheres and accounts for two-thirds of the total weight of the brain.

Chaining: A narrative form that appears at about 3 years of age, when children talk about events related to a central topic with no particular order of occurrence.

Cochlea: The end organ of hearing; the portion of the inner ear that contains the sensory cells for the auditory system. It is fluid filled and composed of two concentric labyrinths: the outer made of bone and the inner of membrane.

Cochlear: Reference to the spiral-shaped cavity of the inner ear that resembles a snail shell and contains the sensory cells and nerve endings essential for hearing.

Cochlear implant: A device that serves to give a sense of hearing to a person who otherwise does not have access to sound. It includes a magnet and electrode array that is surgically implanted in the inner ear as well as an externally worn ear-level speech processor and microphone.

Code-mixing: A code is a system of signals used for sending messages. Code-mixing or switching describes changes or mixes from one language or system to another. Speakers use code-switching to shift from a native language to a second language. Code-mixing can also be used to mark oneself as part of a particular ethnic group.

Cognition: The mental processes that consist of knowledge, along with the mechanisms to acquire knowledge. Cognitive skills consist of attention, working memory, reasoning, intuition, judgment, and perception.

Coherence: Involves interpreting the meaning of a context or situation by taking into account all aspects of a situation, along with any previous knowledge that relates to an event.

Cohesion: The use of transitional expressions and other devices to guide readers and show how the parts of a text (written or spoken) relate to one other.

Cohesive devices: Linking words and phrases to make an organized thought. In narrative, the use of words to connect the text (e.g., *and then . . .*).

Communication: 1. The exchange of information between people through speaking, writing, or using a common system of signs or behavior. 2. The vehicle for social interaction, consisting of both verbal (words, sentences, narratives, and conversations) and nonverbal acts (eye gaze, gesture, turn taking in conversation, and facial expressions).

Communicative competence: A person's knowledge of grammar, syntax, morphology, and phonology, along with an understanding of how and when to use this knowledge appropriately.

Communicative function: The purpose for communication, such as expressing needs, requests, or interacting with others to communicate information.

Communicative unit (C-unit): A method of separating spoken utterances or written sentences into distinct independent clauses

(simple sentence) and any dependent or subordinating clauses, often used to measure growth in language abilities.

Competition model: The model that views language processing as a series of competitions between lexical items, phonological forms, and syntactic patterns. The learning of language forms is based on the accurate recording of many exposures to words and patterns in different contexts.

Complex: When used to describe a sentence, complexity consists of the presence of an independent clause and at least one other independent or dependent clause. When used to describe language, complexity can consist of lengthy and complex utterances or reference to events not present in the current context.

Complex sentence: A sentence that contains an independent clause with one or more dependent clauses. A complex sentence always has a subordinator, such as *because, since, after, although,* or *when* or a relative pronoun, such as *that, who,* or *which.*

Compound-complex sentence: A sentence made up of more than one main clause and at least one subordinate clause. It is the combining of a compound sentence with a complex sentence.

Compound sentence: A sentence that contains two independent clauses joined by a coordinator, such as *for, and, nor, but, or, yet,* and *so.*

Concepts: Abstract ideas, thoughts, or notions that are formed by experiences or occurrences. Children's conceptual development is supplied by the environment and the cognitive ability to form concepts about spatial (location), temporal (time), quantitative (number), qualitative (description), or social-emotional (feelings) knowledge.

Concrete: Basic, non-complex, and easily understood.

Concrete operations stage: Stage of development that emerges at 6 years of age and continues until age 12. At this stage, children form ideas based on reasoning and are able to employ abstract thought.

Concrete (words): A concrete noun is one which can be experienced by our senses as we can touch it, or see it, or hear it (e.g., table, apple, and dogs). An abstract noun cannot be experienced by our senses because these nouns express a concept (e.g., truth).

Conductive hearing loss: A conductive hearing loss occurs when there is a loss of sound energy being transmitted through the outer ear or middle ear (tympanic membrane and/or ossicles). Conductive hearing loss decreases the sound energy reaching the cochlea for sounds of all intensity levels, thus making all sound perceived at levels more softly than would be perceived by a person with normal hearing sensitivity.

Confidence intervals: Give an estimated range of values, which is likely to include an unknown population parameter or the estimated range being calculated from a given set of sample data.

Congenital: Refers to a defect or condition in a fetus that is present at birth.

Conjunctions: Cohesive devices that indicate the semantic relations between different propositions and sentences and can signal an additive relation (*and*), a temporal relation (*then, when, before, after*), a causal relation (*because*), or an adversative relation (*but*).

Content: The meaning of an expression.

Context: A situation in which an event occurs. The word *context* frequently refers to the environment in which a child interacts with others or learns about the connection between meaning (words) and actions or things.

Contextualized language or narrative: Talk about the *here and now*, by referencing people, objects, and action present in the immediate context.

Continuity: The hypothesis that there is continuity between children's preverbal behaviors (e.g., gestures, eye contact, and prelinguistic vocalizations) and later language skills.

Conversational postulates: Conversation contains the conversational postulate or the assumption that a speaker is telling the truth, is offering information that is new and relevant to the conversation, and is offering information that the listener genuinely wants to hear.

Copula: In grammar, a linking verb that links the subject of a sentence with an adjective or noun phrase complement relating to it (e.g., *be* or *seem*).

Corpus callosum: A structure of the brain in the longitudinal fissure that connects the left and right cerebral hemispheres. This is the structure that facilitates communication between the two hemispheres.

Cross-linguistic effects: The bidirectional influence of one language on the other in bilingual speech and language production.

Cultural broker: An individual, usually sharing the family's cultural background, who can provide an insider's information on that culture and aid in the interpretation of the family's linguistic and nonlinguistic characteristics.

Culturally and linguistically diverse: Denotes not only those who are acquiring more than one language but also those who might be using more than one dialect (i.e., a rule-governed variant of a language, such as Appalachian English).

C-unit: See *Communicative unit.*

Deceleration: At certain points in development, bilingual children might demonstrate a slower rate of acquisition than their monolingual peers.

Decentration: Children are able to take into account multiple attributes of an object or situation (e.g., height and width of an object) and no longer rely on their own judgment of things or events.

Decibels (dB): A mathematically derived ratio of sound level based on the pressure exerted by a particular vibration relative to some reference pressure. Decibels hearing level (dB HL) refers to hearing sensitivity relative to normative data of sound pressure as a function of frequency.

Decode: 1. The ability to read something that has been written. 2. An individual is able to comprehend or understand information from another source.

Decontextualized language: Language that is understandable without contextual support (e.g., things that support the meaning of the utterance). Meaning is conveyed only via linguistic cues.

Decontextualized narrative: Refers to descriptions of people, objects, and events that are not present in the immediate environment.

Deep structure: In transformational grammar, the deep structure is an abstract representation of a sentence, whereas surface structure corresponds to the version of the sentence that can be spoken and heard. Surface structures are derived from deep structures by a series of transformations.

Deferred imitation: Imitation of an event after a period of delay, showing that the child understands an expression. The child's imitative response may change or expand the original utterance.

Deictic terms: The phenomenon wherein understanding the meaning of certain words and phrases in an utterance requires contextual information (e.g., *that one, over there, here, he,* and *she*). Words are deictic if their semantic meaning is fixed but their specific reference varies depending on time and/or place.

Deixis: An aspect of a communicative utterance whose full interpretation depends on knowledge of the context in which the communication occurs (e.g., the use of a word or expression such as *he, that, now,* or *here*).

Dendrites: Projections of the neuron that conduct stimulation received from other neurons to the cell body (soma) of a neuron.

Denial: Unwillingness to believe in something or admit that something exists.

Derivational morphemes: Prefixes and suffixes that are added to a root word to create additional meaning. This often changes the part of speech of the root word as in adding the suffix *-er* to the verb *teach* to create the noun *teacher*.

Dialect: A rule-governed variant of a language.

Digraphs: A pair of written letters that represent a single speech sound (e.g., *th, sh,* and *ch*).

Diphthongs: Vowel-like sounds that are produced with a gradually changing articulation (e.g., *how, boy,* and *sky*).

Discourse: The exchange of information or conversation between people consisting of the transmission of information, opinions, ideas, or feelings.

Disinhibited: Lacking the ability to restrain from impulsive actions.

Divergent thinking: The ability to explore and provide multiple solutions to a problem.

Dual language learners: Individuals acquiring two or more languages simultaneously while continuing to develop their first language.

Duration: The length of a syllable.

Dynamic assessment: An interactive approach to assessment that embeds intervention within the assessment process. This begins with a pretest, followed by intervention, and ending with a posttest. The goal is to determine the child's response to intervention.

Dysarthria: A motor speech disorder that affects the muscles of the mouth, face, pharynx, larynx, and respiratory system.

Effectiveness: A measure to determine whether intervention was responsible for the change.

Effects: Focuses on determining if change occurred as a result of intervention. Change can be measured by charting outcomes throughout the intervention process.

Efferent: Carrying information away from the central nervous system.

Efficiency: Determining how long it took the client to achieve the goals, how much effort was needed to facilitate change, and the hierarchy needed to produce a change.

Egocentric: Characterized by preoccupation with one's own internal world. The belief that you are the center of the universe and everything revolves around you.

Egocentric speech: Speech typically observed in young children that is not addressed to another person.

Egocentrism: Characterized by preoccupation with one's own internal world.

Electromotility: The motility resulting from change in shape of the cochlear outer hair cells in response to electrical changes within the outer hair cells.

Ellipsis: The omission of one or more words from a sentence, especially when the word that is omitted can be understood from the context. In the sentence, "I went but my wife didn't," the omission of "go" at the end of the sentence (e.g., "I went but my wife didn't **go**") is an example of ellipsis.

Embodied cognition: A theory that the body influences cognition through the motor system, the perceptual system, and the body's interaction with the environment. In this view, the motor system influences the body and the mind influences body actions. Children's cognitive skills develop through the relationship between the infant's mind and physical body.

Emergentism: The theory that language acquisition emerges from the interaction of biological forces and the environment. According to this theory, neither nature nor nurture alone is sufficient to prompt language learning and both of these influences must work in tandem to allow a child to acquire a language.

Emergent literacy: The period when preschoolers learn about print before they actually learn to read. The skills and knowledge about literacy that a child acquires before learning to read, such as knowing that the print on a page contains information about the story.

Encode: Encoding involves converting incoming information into meaning, such as spoken speech sounds into words. A sender transmits information (*encodes*) that a receiver comprehends or understands (*decodes*).

English-language learners (ELLS): Individuals who are learning the English language as another language.

Environment: The external factors influencing the life and activities of people, plants, and animals. Reference to the entities, things, and events that play a role in learning language.

Environmental: Relating to, or caused by, a person's interactions and surroundings.

Environmental theory: Environmental theories posit that the external environment provides the essential information to support language development.

Equilibrium: The process of fitting new information or input into an existing cognitive schema.

Equative: The term used to indicate that two entities are equated with each other. For example, the sentence *Mary is our teacher* equates two entities (*Mary* and *our teacher*).

Eustachian tube: A slender tube that connects the middle ear cavity with the nasal part of the pharynx and serves to equalize air pressure on either side of the eardrum.

Evidence-based practice: The integration of clinical expertise, expert opinion, external scientific evidence, and client/patient/caregiver perspectives to provide high-quality services reflecting the interests, values, needs, and choices of the individuals we serve.

Executive function: The cognitive processes of planning, problem solving, working memory, inhibition, and multitasking.

Expansions: An adult's more mature version of a child's utterance that preserves the word order of the child's utterance. (e.g., child says *doggie eat*, adult might say *The doggie is eating*).

Expository: A type of writing where the purpose is to describe, inform, explain, or define the author's subject to the reader.

Expressive language: The language an individual produces spontaneously. Expressive language skills consist of a variety of expressive skills, such as expressing words, ideas, and information.

Fast mapping: A hypothesized mental process whereby a new concept can be learned based only on a single exposure to a given unit of information. Fast mapping is thought by some researchers to be particularly important during language acquisition in young children.

Fictional narrative: A story drawn from a child's imagination and in which the content is invented.

Figurative language: Nonliteral phrases consisting of idioms, metaphors, similes, and proverbs.

Fissures: A series of valleys or depressions on the surface of the cerebrum.

Fluency: 1. The ability to read a text quickly, accurately, and with proper expression. This involves the ability to read with little effort and without conscious attention to the mechanics of reading. 2. The ability to speak, read, and/or write without difficulty.

FM educational amplification systems: Sound systems used in the classroom to improve the degree to which the teacher's voice exceeds the background noise at the location of the receiver, thereby improving signal-to-noise ratio.

Form: The structure of language (syntax) as opposed to meaning (content) or social use (pragmatics).

Formal operations: The formal operational stage begins at approximately age 12 and lasts into adulthood. During this time, children develop the ability to think about abstract concepts with the use of logical thought, deductive reasoning, and systematic planning.

Frequency: Sound is made up of changes in air pressure in the form of waves. Frequency is the property of sound that most determines pitch.

Generative grammar: A finite set of rules that can be applied to generate sentences that are grammatical in a given language. These rules are derived from a speaker's tacit grammatical knowledge of the system of that language.

Glides: Often referred to as semivowels, these are vowel-like sounds that do not make up the nucleus of a syllable (i.e., /j/ and /w/).

Glottis: The space between the vocal folds.

Grammar: The rules that govern the composition of sentences, phrases, and words in any given language.

Graphemes: Written symbols, letters, or combinations of letters that represent a single sound. For example, the phoneme /f/ can be represented as *f* in the word *fast,* as *ph-* in *phone,* and as *-gh* in *laugh.*

Guided distributional learning theory: The theory that is part of the emergentism theory, stating that language acquisition emerges from the interaction of biological forces and the environment. In this view, neither nature nor nurture alone is sufficient to prompt language learning.

Gyri: A series of elevations or ridges on the surface of the cerebral and cerebellar cortices.

Habilitative: Adjectival form of *habilitate,* meaning "to make able to do something."

Heaps: A stage in a child's prenarrative development. The child expresses an assortment of unrelated ideas rather than connected information. For example, a child might just label objects or actions with no connection among these pieces of information.

Hearing aids: An electroacoustic device that typically fits in or behind the user's ear and is designed to selectively amplify sound based on the user's hearing loss for the sake of giving improved access to speech sounds.

Heschl's gyrus: Gyri (prominent, rounded, elevated convolutions on the surfaces of the cerebral hemispheres) located on the upper surface of the temporal area of the cortex that are involved in the processing of auditory stimuli.

Homorganic: Having the same place of articulation in the vocal tract (e.g., /t/, /n/, and /d/).

Hypothalamus: A region of the brain located between the thalamus and the midbrain that controls the autonomic nervous system. For example, the hypothalamus regulates sleeping cycles, body temperature, and appetite.

Idioms: Expressions whose meanings cannot be predicted from the actual meaning of the constituents or words. An example is *kick the bucket.*

Incidental learning: The type of learning that occurs without direct teaching. Incidental learning describes children's learning of new words.

Incus: The middle bone of the ossicular chain in the middle ear. It articulates with the malleus at the top and has a projection that is joined to the stapes at the bottom.

Indirect speech acts: An utterance whose linguistic form does not directly refer to its communicative purpose (e.g., "I'm feeling cold" used to request the closing of a window).

Innate: Qualities or abilities that are inborn.

Innateness theory: Noam Chomsky's theory of language acquisition, which states that at least some linguistic knowledge exists in humans at birth.

Inner hair cells: Sensory cells that sit within the **Organ of Corti** that release neurotransmitters across the synapse between these cells and auditory nerve fibers. These signals are carried by the auditory nerve to the brain, where the signal is translated into sound.

Input: Sensory information that is processed from an outside influence and is then acted upon or integrated.

Instrumental: Playing a part in achieving a result or accomplishing a purpose.

Intention: The meaning conveyed by a speaker. A listener must understand the speaker's intent or intention to understand the meaning of an utterance.

Intentional: The use of communication to indicate specific wants, desires, or needs.

Intention reading: Occurs when the listener comprehends the speaker's intent or meaning.

Interaction: Communication or joint activity involving two or more people.

Interactional Dual Systems Model: A theory of bilingual language acquisition stating that bilingual children develop distinct linguistic systems for each language.

Interpreter: One who conveys information from one language to another.

Intonation: The rising or falling pitch of the voice when a word or syllable is produced.

Intrasentential growth: Refers to the advances in syntactic knowledge and use seen within the sentence. This is a term meant to capture more complex syntactic changes with phrases and clause structure rather than only focusing on sentence length.

Item-based: A usage-based model in which children imitatively learn concrete linguistic expressions from the language they hear around them. Children use their general cognitive and social-cognitive skills to combine these individually learned expressions and structures to develop language.

Jargon: 1. Sequences of variegated babbling that have the intonation shape of the child's native language. 2. The language and vocabulary associated with a particular discipline, often confusing to novices and persons not familiar with that discipline.

Joint action: The shared action of two individuals on a single object or a collective activity.

Joint attention: The process by which young children focus their attention on an object or event with a social partner through nonverbal communication. This may include joint gaze and pointing.

Labio-dental: Produced at a place of articulation involving the lower lip and upper teeth (e.g., /f/, /v/).

Language: A system of arbitrary symbols, which is rule based, dynamic, generative, and used as a social tool in communication.

Language acquisition device (LAD): The concept that infants have an instinctive mental capacity that enables them to acquire and produce language. This theory asserts that humans are born with the instinct or innate facility for acquiring language. It is believed that, without this innate knowledge of grammar, children would be unable to learn language as quickly as they do.

Language dominance: When bilinguals are said to have greater skills in one language than in the other.

Language form: The surface features of a language and how these are arranged according to the grammar of a language. As a means of connecting sound with meaning, language form incorporates morphology, syntax, and phonology.

Language loss: This process occurs over time when the speech and language features of the first language are no longer utilized by the speaker, possibly due to less hearing or use of the speaker's first language.

Language proficiency: How well each language is used.

Language use: How often and with whom each language is used.

Laryngeal system: The system within which the vocal folds are housed. The vocal folds are energized by air from the lungs and vibrate to produce phonation (sound produced by the vibration of the vocal folds).

Larynx: A set of structures that house the vocal folds.

Limbic system: A part of the brain that supports many functions, including emotions, long-term memory, self-preservation, and sensory processing (e.g., smells or scents).

Limited English proficient (LEP): The term used to describe a student who is limited in English proficiency and who has not yet mastered English in the four domains of reading, writing, listening, and speaking.

Lingua-alveolar: Sounds produced at a place of articulation in which the tongue completely or nearly closes against the alveolar ridge (e.g., /s/, /t/ and /d/).

Lingua-dental: Sounds produced at a place of articulation involving the tongue and teeth (e.g., /ð/, /θ/).

Lingua-palatal: Sounds produced when the tongue articulates with the hard palate (e.g., /ʃ/ and /ʒ/).

Lingua-velar: Sound produced at a place of articulation involving the tongue and velum or the soft palate (e.g., /k/ and /g/).

Linguistic awareness: Explicit knowledge about language, conscious perception, and sensitivity of learning language. A conscious understanding of the structure and function of a language, including its phonology, morphology, syntax, and pragmatic functions.

Linguistic individualism: The language experiences of children and adolescents outside of the family or traditional academic setting, consisting of unique vocabulary or concepts that allow a child or adolescent to acquire an individualized personal vocabulary or a different way of talking.

Liquids: A class of speech sounds also known as approximants (e.g., /l/ and /r/).

Magical thinking: Thinking that is most present in younger children, when children believe that their personal thought has a direct effect on the rest of the world.

Malleus: The largest of the ossicles. It is continuous with the eardrum and articulates with the incus, the next bone in the chain in the middle ear.

Mandible: The bone making up the lower jaw of the face.

Marked: Indicates a more complex set than the opposite *unmarked.*

Marked sounds: Less natural occurring sounds in most languages.

Masked: The use of a noise applied to the nontest ear while testing the hearing sensitivity of the other ear; used when hearing sensitivity of the nontest ear is possibly better than the test ear for the sake of determining true hearing sensitivity of the test ear.

Mazes: A series of words, initial parts of words, or unattached fragments that do not contribute meaning to the ongoing flow of language.

Means-end: A process in which the problem solver begins by envisioning the end, or ultimate goal, and then determines the best strategy for attaining the goal in his/her current situation.

Means-end behavior: Children's anticipation of an outcome allows them to achieve a goal.

Mean length of utterance (MLU): The average number of morphemes (basic units of meaning) a child produces. For example, *jump* is one morpheme, whereas *jumps* (*jump + s*) is two.

Mental lexicon: A mental dictionary that contains information regarding a word's meaning, pronunciation, and syntactic characteristics.

Mental state verbs: Verbs that refer to a person's mental state, for example, *frighten, like, disappoint, think, believe,* and *remember.* These verbs are sometimes called mental verbs.

Metacognition: Knowledge of one's own thoughts and the aspects that influence thinking. Metacognition involves self-reflection, self-responsibility, initiative, goal setting, and time management.

Metalinguistic: Metalinguistic awareness refers to the ability to objectify language as a process as well as a thing and to consciously reflect on the nature of language.

Metalinguistic knowledge: The ability to think about language in a conscious manner.

Metaphors: Figures of speech in which a word or phrase literally denotes one kind of object or idea in place of another to suggest a likeness or analogy between them. An example is the phrase *She is the light of my life.*

Meta-semantic hypothesis: The view that complex semantic units, such as proverbs, are learned through active analysis of the words they contain.

Mirror neurons: These are neurons in the brain that fire when we undertake an action or perceive the actions of others. They provide an inner simulation or mirror of the actions that we observe, allowing the viewer's brain to symbolize and understand the actions of others.

Mixed hearing loss: When bone-conduction thresholds are poorer than 20 dB HL and air-conduction thresholds are elevated by another 10 dB or more (an air-bone gap is present).

Modal auxiliaries: A verb that combines with another verb to express mood or tense (e.g., *can, could, would,* and *should*).

Models: Examples of more mature language that can be imitated by a child. These are consisted scaffolds that support language development.

Modifiability: Describes a child's responsiveness to intervention. This information consists of how the child responds to and

uses new information, the quantity and quality of effort needed to make a change, and transfer of goals or the generalization of new skills.

Morphemes: The minimal, meaningful, and distinctive components of grammar. Morphemes are commonly classified into free (morphemes that can occur as separate words) or bound forms (morphemes that cannot occur by themselves, such as affixes).

Morphology: The study of the system of rules for combining the smallest units of language into words.

Morphophonology: The study of the interaction between a language's morphemes and its phonological processes, focusing on the sound changes that occur when morphemes (minimal meaningful units) combine to form words.

Morphophonemic: Referring to the changes in pronunciation undergone by allomorphs of morphemes as they are modified by neighboring sounds, such as the change in the plural morpheme *-s* (i.e., /s/ to /z/) when following a voiced sound (e.g., cat**s** vs. dog**s**).

Morphosyntactic development: The addition of morphemes that expand a child's syntax or sentence length. Examples consist of the production of determiners (*the*) and inflectional morphemes (e.g., the present progressive morpheme *-ing* and the plural morpheme *-s*).

Motherese: A form of speech that differs from typical adult speech, usually delivered with a "cooing" pattern of intonation, slowed production, a higher pitch, and greater intonation changes.

Motility: Capable of or demonstrating movement.

Motor: Activities, such as walking, sitting, and speech that are controlled by the central nervous system.

Multilingual: Use of more than two languages.

Mutual exclusivity bias: Children's assumption that every object has only one label or name (e.g., *Mommy* cannot be called *Marissa*). This bias is often held until children learn that an entity or an object can have more than one name.

Myelin: A sheath that covers many axons in the central nervous system that is critical to neural transmission and normal muscle function by facilitating the rapid transmission of electrical impulses.

Nares: Nostrils.

Narrative: A verbal description of events that is longer than a single utterance. Narratives possess an internalized story structure that aids children's understanding of stories.

Nasal cavity: A cavity of the vocal tract that is important for the resonance of nasal sounds (i.e., /m/, /n/, and /ŋ/).

Nasals: Sounds produced by vocal fold vibration with the resonance of the nasal cavity added to the pharynx and oral cavity (e.g., /m/ *and* /n/).

National Institutes of Health: An agency of the U.S. Department of Health and Human Services that supports much of medical research.

Nerves: The fibers that form a network of pathways for conducting information throughout the body. Sensory (afferent) nerves carry information into the central nervous system about sensations (e.g., touch, temperature, and pain) and motor (efferent) nerves carry information away from the central nervous system for muscle control.

Nervous system: The system that consists of nerve tissues and structures of the central and peripheral nervous systems that are responsible for thought, muscle control, and sensory functions.

Neuroplasticity: The lifelong ability of the brain to reorganize neural pathways based on novel or new experiences, along with anatomical or physiological changes due to injury.

Neurotransmitters: Chemicals that facilitate the transmission of signals from one neuron to the next across synapses.

Non-English proficient: Having minimal or no English proficiency.

Nonexistence: Children at the one- and two-word utterance stage express nonexistence

to indicate disappearance (e.g., *Allgone cookie*).

Noun phrase: A part of a sentence that consists of a noun and its modifiers, including a noun clause, a word, or a pronoun, that can function as the subject or object of a verb.

Nucleus: The nucleus of a neuron contains genetic material (chromosomes) including information for cell development and synthesis of proteins necessary for cell maintenance and survival.

Object constancy: The understanding that objects remain the same even when viewed from a different perspective.

Object permanence: 1. The knowledge that objects have an existence in time and space, independent of whether or not they can be seen or touched. 2. The ability to remember that an object exists even when removed from sight.

Obligatory: An obligatory context is when a morpheme is required to make an equivalent grammatical sentence in adult speech, whether for linguistic or contextual reasons.

Olfaction (or olfactory): Perception of or the sense of smell.

Operant conditioning: Modification of voluntary behavior through reward/positive reinforcement (a consequence that increases the likelihood of a behavior) or through negative reinforcement (a consequence that decreases the likelihood of a behavior).

Oral cavity: An air-filled cavity of the vocal tract (the mouth) that contains the tongue, teeth, hard palate, and the velum.

Organ of Corti: A collection of cells within the scala media in the cochlea including **outer hair cells, inner hair cells,** supporting cells and the tectorial membrane.

Orthography: Written system of a language, such as letters that compose written words.

Ossicles: Small bones within the middle ear that consist of the malleus, incus, and stapes.

Otitis media: An inflammation or infection of the middle ear, with or without the presence of effusion (fluid), that occurs in the area between the eardrum (the end of the outer ear) and the inner ear, including the eustachian tube.

Otoacoustic emissions (OAEs): Tiny sounds present in the ear canal that are thought to be generated by the electromotility of the outer hair cells of the cochlea.

Outer hair cells: Sensory cells that sit within the **Organ of Corti** on top of the basilar membrane. Sound vibrations that arrive in the inner ear lead to a traveling wave along the basilar membrane as a result of the **electromotility** of the **outer hair cells.**

Overextension: The process in which a child applies a word's meaning to more exemplars than an adult would. A type of error in a child's early word usage that reflects overly inclusive definitions beyond acceptable adult usage. For example, a child may perceive similarities in the characteristics of entities and call them all the same name (e.g., all four-legged animals would be called *doggie*).

Overgeneralize: A process whereby children extend their use of grammatical features beyond the context of those in adult language, for example, use of *-ed, walk + ed* to signify past tense of all verbs (*eat + ed* as opposed to *ate*). The term *overgeneralization* refers to this typical developmental process.

Paradigmatic: A response in a word association task from the same class (e.g., *hot-cold*). This response appears around age 9 when children possess a more developed semantic system. See *syntagmatic*.

Paralinguistic: The nonverbal elements of communication that modify meanings and convey emotion, including the pitch, volume, and intonation of speech.

Parallel distributed processing: The theory that views the mind as composed of a great number of elementary units connected in a neural network. Mental processes are interactions between these units that excite and inhibit each other in parallel rather than sequential operations.

Parasympathetic: The parasympathetic nervous system plays a role in the processes of the body, such as digestion, control of the heart rate, and contraction of the pupils. In contrast, the sympathetic nervous system increases the heart rate and dilates the pupils.

Perception: The use of senses (e.g., visual and auditory perception) and one's own concepts to acquire information about the environment.

Perceptual: Relating to or involving sensory perception.

Performatives: Speech acts that constitute an act of some kind, such as promising, threatening, or requesting.

Peripheral nervous system (PNS): The PNS consists of two parts: the somatic nervous system and the autonomic nervous system.

Perseveration: The excessive repetition of a word, phrase, or longer utterance.

Personal function: When a child attempts to communicate to express his/her feelings or attitudes.

Personal narrative: A narrative that describes past events experienced by the narrator or someone familiar to the narrator.

Perspective taking: The perception of physical, social, or emotional situations from a point of view other than one's own.

Pharyngeal cavity: The cavity of the pharynx that consists of a part continuous anteriorly with the nasal cavity by way of the nasopharynx, a part opening into the oral cavity, and a part continuous posteriorly with the esophagus and opening into the larynx. Its anterior boundary is the root of the tongue and its posterior boundary is the pharyngeal wall.

Phonation: The process of setting the vocal folds into vibration to produce sound.

Phonemes: The smallest units of the sounds of a language that act to differentiate the meaning of words (e.g., /b/ in *bat* vs. /k/ in *cat*).

Phonemic awareness: A subset of phonological awareness that allows children to hear, identify, and manipulate phonemes.

Phonemic representations: Phonemic transcription is a system used for using letters or symbols to represent sounds in speech. The basis of phonetic and phonemic transcription is the phoneme, the smallest part of a word's sounds that can be clearly defined as a separate sound that affects meaning.

Phonetically consistent forms: Expression utilized to convey consistent meaning, such as *doggy* is used only to label dogs.

Phonetics: The study of the perception and production of speech sounds.

Phonics: Sound-letter or phoneme-grapheme correspondence.

Phonological awareness: An individual's awareness of the sound structure of words. This awareness consists of the ability to notice and manipulate the sounds of a language, separate from the meaning of the word.

Phonological processes: Children's simplification of words. These processes are predictable and consistent with typical development (e.g., "nana" produced in place of the word *banana*).

Phonological representations: Stored representations of a word's segments, syllable structure, and supersegmental features. Phonological representations undergo developmental changes as children and adolescents become more aware of a word's structure. These phonological features of words are coded and stored in the internal lexicon.

Phonology: Rules for the combination of sounds to form words in a language.

Phrase structure rules: Rules that describe a language's syntax and sentence structure.

Postlingual: After the development of speech and/or language.

Pragmatic: Relating to the rules for appropriate social interaction

Pragmatics: 1. The branch of linguistics that studies language use rather than language structure 2. The connection between language development and the environment or the context in which the communication occurs.

Predicate: The part of a sentence that provides information about the subject of the sentence, such as what the subject is doing

or how the subject is affected. A sentence contains a subject (what or whom the sentence is about) and a predicate (that tells us something about the subject).

Prelingual: The period between birth and 13 months of age when an infant uses sounds and gestures to communicate wants and needs before recognizable speech develops.

Preoperational stage: This stage begins at approximately 18 months and ends at 6 years of age. During this period of development, children form ideas based on their own perception of events. This derives from egocentrism, with children centered on themselves, their own experience, and their own desires.

Presuppositions: Beliefs that a particular state of affairs is true or false without the provision of evidence.

Print awareness: Knowledge that the printed word carries a message, including but not limited to the meaning and function of the printed word, recognition of words and letters, and terminology.

Private speech: This type of speech is often called egocentric speech with children's speech not adapted to a listener's understanding or needs.

Propositions: Statements claiming that something is true or false; in philosophy and logic, a proposition is the essential meaning expressed in a sentence.

Prosody: The suprasegmental aspects of speech, including, intonation, stress pattern, loudness, pausing, and rhythm.

Prospective mental development: What a child needs to learn with guidance from an adult or more experienced peer in relation to the child's *zone of proximal development*.

Proverbs: Statements of general truth. These are sayings that express commonly held ideas and beliefs. An example is the proverb *A stitch in time saves nine.*

Proximity: Closeness in time and/or space.

Recasts: An adult's correction or modifications of a child's utterances.

Receptive language: The language that people comprehend or understand.

Recurrence: A semantic relation produced by children to indicate the request of repetition (e.g., *More juice*).

Reduplicated babbling: Repeated sequences of consonant-vowel pairs (e.g., *bababababa*).

Referent absent: Reference to a person, thing, or event absent from the current environment.

Referent present: Reference to a person, thing, or event when these elements are present within the current environment to which a linguistic expression refers.

Reflexive: Without thought, such as an automatic or involuntary action.

Register: Modifications of language, influenced by the current situation (e.g., conversation with close friends as compared with conversation with professors).

Regulatory: Language used specifically to convey or to establish social dynamics between individuals. In child language, the attempt to regulate the behavior of another.

Rejection: The semantic relation used to reject (e.g., *no bed*).

Relational terms: The terms that express a syntactic relationship between elements in a phrase or a sentence (e.g., *less, more, longer, because,* and *between*). The understanding of relational terms develops as children develop the concepts that label these relationships.

Representational thought: The ability to picture something in your head.

Resonance: A phenomenon in which a body of air, having a naturally tendency to vibrate at a particular frequency or frequencies, is set into vibration by another structure vibrating at or near those frequencies.

Retrospective mental development: The current skills that a child has mastered in relation to the child's *zone of proximal development*.

Reversibility: The capacity to be reversed or undone.

Rhythm: The pattern formed by a sequence of stressed and unstressed syllables.

Scaffolds: Input from adults that provide children with cues and supports that allow them to acquire language.

Schema: 1. According to Piaget, the basic psychological structure for organizing information. 2. An organizational or conceptual pattern in the mind used to catagorize objects or ideas.

Scripts: A sequence of familiar comments, narratives, and events that have been routinized with familiarity to a situation or event.

Selection restrictions: Constraints on particular word meanings that govern potential word combinations.

Semantic features: The perceptual or functional aspects of meaning that characterize a word.

Semantic relations: The relationship between the concepts or meanings (e.g., agent + action = *Dogs bark*).

Semantic roles: A semantic role is the underlying relationship that a word has with the main verb in a clause, as shown in the relation of the semantic role of *agent* to the verb *left* in the sentence *The boy left yesterday.*

Semantics: 1. The study of *meaning* in a language as it is expressed in words, phrases, sentences, and longer spoken, written, or signed utterances. 2. The component of language that refers to meaning, and the rules that govern the assignment of meaning to entities (people, animals, and things) along with activities or events. 3. A subdivision of linguistics devoted to the study of meaning in language and how the meanings in language are formed by the use and interrelationships of words, phrases, and sentences.

Semantic transparency: Refers to the ease of extrapolating meaning from words or phrases. In idiomatic expressions, semantic transparency refers to how closely the figurative and literal meaning of the individual words are related, as when a speaker says, *"keep your fingers crossed,"* which has become known as a sign of wishing for a lucky outcome. In words containing derivational morphemes, semantic transparency refers to how easily the root word is seen or spelled within the derived word. For example, love/lovely is more transparent that sign/signal.

Sensitivity: 1. The ability to detect the presence of a signal; for example, hearing loss exists when there is diminished sensitivity to the sounds heard at intensity levels consistent with normal hearing. 2. The percentage of individuals correctly identified with a disorder.

Sensorineural hearing loss: Occurs when there is dysfunction in the cochlea, or the nerve pathways from the inner ear to the brain, resulting in loss of hearing sensitivity. This is the most common type of hearing loss and generally cannot be medically or surgically corrected.

Sensory cells: Outer and inner hair cells that sit on top of the basilar membrane.

Sensory information: Sensory acuity is the actual physical ability of the sensory organs to receive input, whereas sensory processing is the ability to interpret the information the brain has received. The processing of sensory information consists of tactile perception (touch), visual perception (vision), gustatory perception (taste), auditory perception (hearing), and olfactory perception (smell). Additional sensory information consists of the perception of pain, touch, temperature sense, and limb proprioception or limb position.

Sentence length: The number of clauses and words used in spoken or written language gives a measurement of average sentence length.

Sequential bilinguals: Those who acquire a second language after establishing a foundation in their first language.

Similes: Figures of speech in which two unlike things are compared. An example is *She is like a rose.*

Simple sentence: A sentence that contains only a subject and a verb (e.g., *dogs bark*).

Simultaneous bilinguals: Those who acquire at least two languages before about 5 years of age.

Social competence: Refers to the emotional and cognitive skills and behaviors that children need for successful social adaptation and social interaction.

Social information processing: The ways in which people think about themselves and the social world, including how they select, interpret, remember, and use social information.

Social interaction: Any action that is shared with others and contains a shared symbolic system.

Socio-interactional: Relating to social relations or social interaction as a factor in language development.

Soma: The main part of the neuron that contains the nucleus of the cell.

Somatic: Relating to the nerves that carry motor (movement) and sensory (e.g., hearing, touch, and sight) information to and from the central nervous system. These nerves are responsible for voluntary muscle movements and for processing sensory information.

Specificity: The percentage of individuals correctly identified as typically developing.

Speech: The neuromuscular process by which humans create a meaningful sound signal that is transmitted through the air (or another medium such as a telephone line) to a receiver.

Speech acts: A method of categorizing a speakers's intent or meaning (e.g., request, comment, or promise). These spoken utterances are called *acts* because many types are intended to result in action (e.g., *Can you pass the salt?*).

Speech awareness threshold (SAT): The weakest intensity at which the child demonstrates awareness of the presence of sound when a speech stimulus is presented through the audiometer using a developmentally appropriate test method.

Speech reception threshold (SRT): The weakest intensity at which the child can identify 50% of spondee words from a closed set of familiar items. A spondee word has two syllables with equal stress, such as *baseball* or *toothbrush*.

Stapes: The third and smallest of the ossicles in the middle ear.

Stereocilia: Small, hairlike projections situated on the top of the hair cells that are located in the inner ear.

Stop-plosive: A class of speech sounds produced by forming a complete closure in the oral cavity, building up pressure behind that closure, and suddenly releasing the closure to produce a brief noise burst.

Story grammar: The elements of a story that may include the title, setting, main characters, initiating event, internal response, attempt, consequence, reaction, and conclusion.

Structure: The sentence form. In transformational grammar, the outward form of a sentence. In contrast to deep structure (an abstract representation of a sentence), surface structure corresponds to the version of a sentence that can be spoken and heard. In transformational grammar, deep structures are generated by *phrase structure rules*, and surface structures are derived from deep structures by a series of transformations.

Subordinate dependent clause: Sometimes called a dependent clause, it is usually introduced by a subordinating element, such as a subordinating conjunction or relative pronoun. The subordinate dependent clause must always be attached to a main clause because it completes the meaning of this sentence (e.g., ***After Mary ate the sandwich***, *she cleaned the table*).

Subordinating conjunctions: Words that join a subordinate clause to a main clause, such as *after, although, because, until,* and *when.*

Subordination: This is a concept of syntactic formation with one clause subordinate to another. A dependent clause is called the subordinate clause and the independent clause is called the main clause. The subordinate clause is introduced with subordinate conjunctions, such as *after, because, before, while,* and *when* (e.g., ***Before we eat***, *we wash our hands*).

Sulci: A series of valleys or depressions on the surface of the cerebrum.

Supralaryngeal vocal tract: Consists of the oral, pharyngeal, and nasal cavities.

Surface structure: Structural characteristics of the actual spoken message. The surface structure derives from the deep structure through the utilization of phrase structure and transformational rules.

Symbolic functions: A word used to represent an entity or activity not present in the current context. Children's ability to think or label a person, thing, or event even when not present.

Symmetrical: Similar degree of hearing loss in both ears across frequencies.

Sympathetic: The part of the nervous system that plays an excitatory role, such as preparing the body for a fight-or-flight response.

Synapse: Connection between neurons through which signals flow from one neuron to another.

Syntagmatic: Relating to the function and behavior of a word or phrase within a syntactic unit. Within a word association task, a child's response that follows in a syntactic sequence (e.g., *big-ball*). By age 9, children respond with a word from the same class (a paradigmatic response).

Syntagmatic-paradigmatic shift: Refers to the change that occurs when children provide a response that is in the same grammatical class as the stimulus word (e.g., *table-chair*). Younger children provide a response that represents a syntactic form (e.g., *table-eat*).

Syntax: 1. Rules that govern the way words combine to form phrases, clauses, and sentences. 2. The order or arrangement of words in a sentence.

Tectorial membrane: The gelatinous structure that extends along the longitudinal length of the cochlea parallel to the basilar membrane. The tectorial membrane moves along with the pressure variations of the cochlear fluid with movement encoded into electrical digital signals to the brain through the cochlear nerve.

Temporal: Relating to time. Temporal expressions in language consist of the examples *then, when, before,* and *after.*

Text structure: The way written text is organized. Knowledge of text structure supports comprehension of the text.

Thalamus: A part of the brain associated with basic functions, such as sleep and attention.

The thalamus also relays information from eyes, ears, and spinal cord to the cerebral cortex.

Thematic roles: These terms (e.g., *agent, patient,* and *location*) label the semantic relationship between the verb and noun phrases of sentences (e.g., *agent + action = daddy go*).

Theory of mind (TOM): The ability to understand others' mental states, such as individuals' beliefs, intents, wishes, and knowledge.

Transfer: The generalization of new skills.

Transformation: The rules for transforming one type of sentence into another, such as the transformation of an active sentence (*John kicked the ball*) into a passive sentence (*The ball was kicked by John*).

Transformational rules: Rules that operate on strings of symbols, rearranging phrase structure elements to form an acceptable sentence for output.

Translator: Conveys information from one language to another.

T-units: A measurement used to determine average sentence length in the spoken or written language of school-age children and adolescents. T-units include only full, independent clauses (e.g., basic sentences) and any dependent clauses.

Tympanometry: A procedure conducted principally to assess middle-ear function (how well sound is conducted through the eardrum and ossicles), rather than a test of hearing.

Underextension: The use of a general word to mean one very specific thing, (e.g., "baba" may mean MY bottle and my bottle only).

Unilateral: Refers to a hearing loss in only one ear. A bilateral hearing loss is a hearing impairment in both ears.

Unmarked: A sound that appears to be naturally occurring and is acquired earlier. Unmarked sounds tend to occur more frequently across languages than marked sounds.

Unmasked: The unmasked threshold is the quietest level of a signal that can be perceived without a masking signal present when testing hearing sensitivity. The masked threshold is the quietest level of the signal perceived when combined with a specific masking noise.

Usage-based theory: A theory of language development in which children begin with a concrete understanding of language, beginning with imitation.

Use: A linguistic term that defines the pragmatics of language, or rules for using language in interaction.

Variegated babbling: A stage in babbling characterized by varied sequences of sounds in syllables. (e.g., *babigoogi*).

Velar stop: A sound produced when the dorsum of the tongue articulates against the velum (soft palate) (e.g., /k/, /g/).

Velopharyngeal closure: The closing of the nasal cavity from the oral and pharyngeal cavities.

Velum: A muscular extension of the hard palate also known as the soft palate. The velum is lowered during production of nasal sounds (e.g., /m/ and /n/) and is raised during production of all other English speech sounds.

Verb phrase: The predicate of a sentence that provides information about the subject (e.g., The car *was stolen*). The verb phrase (*was stolen*) consists of the information about the subject (*The car*).

Visual language: A part of the reading process that is considered a secondary system, based on the use of visual skills to successfully recognize words and gather meaning from the written text.

Vocables: Word-like productions that emerge at about 10 to 12 months. These words lack precise meaning but are perceived to sound like a real word.

Vocal folds: A pair of muscular tissues in the larynx that are separated during inhalation and achieve closure to be set into rapid vibration to produced sound (phonation). The vocal folds are also known as vocal cords.

Voiced fricatives: Produced by forming a significant constriction, building up pressure behind the constriction, and forcing air through the constriction. Voiced fricatives are produced while the vocal folds are set into vibration (e.g., /v/, /ð/, /z/, and /ʒ/).

Voiceless fricatives: Sounds produced by forming a significant constriction, building up pressure behind the constriction, and forcing air through the constriction. Voiceless fricatives are produced without vibration of the vocal folds (e.g., /f/, /θ/, /s/, /ʃ/, and /h/). All fricatives, with the exception of /h/, a glottal fricative, are created in the oral cavity.

Voiced stops: A class of speech sounds produced by forming a complete closure in the oral cavity, building up pressure behind that closure, and suddenly releasing the closure to produce a brief noise burst. Voiced stops are produced when the vocal folds are set into vibration (e.g., /b/, /d/, and /g/).

Voiceless stops: A class of speech sounds produced by forming a complete closure in the oral cavity, building up pressure behind that closure, and suddenly releasing the closure to produce a brief noise burst. Voiceless stops are produced without vibration of the vocal folds (e.g., /p/, /t/, and /k/).

Vowels: Speech sounds that are formed without a significant constriction of the oral and pharyngeal cavities and that serve as a syllable nucleus.

Wernicke's area: A region of the brain that is important in language development. Wernicke's area is located on the temporal lobe on the left side of the brain and is responsible for the comprehension of speech (Broca's area is related to the production of speech).

Word: A meaningful sound or combination of sounds that is a unit of language or its representation in a text.

Word recognition: How well the individual understands speech stimuli.

Working memory: A type of memory in which information is held while being processed. Working memory allows a child to understand and remember a series of directions.

Zone of proximal development: The distance between the actual developmental level, which is determined by autonomous problem solving, and to the level of potential development, determined through problem solving under adult guidance, or in collaboration with more proficient peers.

Index

Note: Page numbers in **bold** reference non-text material.